2012 Handbook for Preparing SEC Annual Reports and Proxy Statements

Lawrence D. Levin, Esq.

Adam R. Klein, Esq.

Katten Muchin Rosenman LLP

Wolters Kluwer

Law & Business

This publication is designed to provide accurate and authoritative information in regard to the subject matter covered. It is sold with the understanding that neither the author nor the publisher is engaged in rendering legal, accounting or other professional service. If legal advice or other expert assistance is required, the services of a competent professional person should be sought.

—From a *Declaration of Principles* jointly adopted by
a Committee of the American Bar Association and
a Committee of Publishers and Associations

ISBN: 978-0-8080-2818-5

Printed in the United States of America

SUSTAINABLE FORESTRY INITIATIVE

Certified Chain of Custody
Promoting Sustainable Forestry

www.sfiprogram.org
SFI-00756

About Wolters Kluwer Law & Business

Wolters Kluwer Law & Business is a leading global provider of intelligent information and digital solutions for legal and business professionals in key specialty areas, and respected educational resources for professors and law students. Wolters Kluwer Law & Business connects legal and business professionals as well as those in the education market with timely, specialized authoritative content and information-enabled solutions to support success through productivity, accuracy and mobility.

Serving customers worldwide, Wolters Kluwer Law & Business products include those under the Aspen Publishers, CCH, Kluwer Law International, Loislaw, Best Case, ftwilliam.com and MediRegs family of products.

CCH products have been a trusted resource since 1913, and are highly regarded resources for legal, securities, antitrust and trade regulation, government contracting, banking, pension, payroll, employment and labor, and healthcare reimbursement and compliance professionals.

Aspen Publishers products provide essential information to attorneys, business professionals and law students. Written by preeminent authorities, the product line offers analytical and practical information in a range of specialty practice areas from securities law and intellectual property to mergers and acquisitions and pension/benefits. Aspen's trusted legal education resources provide professors and students with high-quality, up-to-date and effective resources for successful instruction and study in all areas of the law.

Kluwer Law International products provide the global business community with reliable international legal information in English. Legal practitioners, corporate counsel and business executives around the world rely on Kluwer Law journals, looseleafs, books, and electronic products for comprehensive information in many areas of international legal practice.

Loislaw is a comprehensive online legal research product providing legal content to law firm practitioners of various specializations. Loislaw provides attorneys with the ability to quickly and efficiently find the necessary legal information they need, when and where they need it, by facilitating access to primary law as well as state-specific law, records, forms and treatises.

Best Case Solutions is the leading bankruptcy software product to the bankruptcy industry. It provides software and workflow tools to flawlessly streamline petition preparation and the electronic filing process, while timely incorporating ever-changing court requirements.

ftwilliam.com offers employee benefits professionals the highest quality plan documents (retirement, welfare and non-qualified) and government forms (5500/PBGC, 1099 and IRS) software at highly competitive prices.

MediRegs products provide integrated health care compliance content and software solutions for professionals in healthcare, higher education and life sciences, including professionals in accounting, law and consulting.

Wolters Kluwer Law & Business, a division of Wolters Kluwer, is headquartered in New York. Wolters Kluwer is a market-leading global information services company focused on professionals.

Important CCH Contact Information

To order any CCH title, go to http://onlinestore.cch.com, chat with us at http://support.cch.com/chat/booksupport, or call us at one of our direct lines:

- 800-449-6439 for Billing
- 800-344-3734 for Subscription Support
- 800-248-3248 for Book Sales & Support
- 800-835-0105 for Technical Support

About the Authors

Lawrence D. Levin is a Partner and a member of the Board of Directors of the law firm of Katten Muchin Rosenman LLP and is co-head of its National Securities Law Practice Group. Mr. Levin advises corporate clients and boards of directors on securities registration, regulation and compliance issues, as well as transactional and general corporate matters. Mr. Levin represents a wide range of clients, including privately held emerging growth companies, publicly traded companies and investment banks. He has represented issuers and investment banks in numerous public and private offerings of debt and equity securities and merger and acquisition transactions, and he counsels publicly held clients concerning corporate governance matters and SEC reporting and disclosure issues. Mr. Levin is a frequent speaker to professional and business groups on a variety of corporate and securities law issues affecting both public and private companies.

Mr. Levin is the former Chairman of the Chicago Bar Association's Securities Law Committee and of both its 1933 Act Registration and Reporting Subcommittee and its 1934 Act Reporting Subcommittee. Mr. Levin is also a member of the American Bar Association, where he is an active member of the Federal Regulation of Securities Committee of the Section of Business Law. Mr. Levin received his Juris Doctor degree from the University of Illinois College of Law and earned a Bachelor of Science degree, with Honors, from the University of Illinois. Prior to entering law school, Mr. Levin was employed as a Certified Public Accountant by an international public accounting firm in Chicago, Illinois.

Adam R. Klein is a Partner in the law firm of Katten Muchin Rosenman LLP. Mr. Klein is a member of the Corporate Department where he concentrates on representing issuers, investment banks and investors in public and private offerings of equity and debt securities. He also provides counseling to a number of public companies in connection with required public disclosure, corporate governance, mergers and acquisitions, tender offers, exchange offers, stockholder meetings, stock incentive plans, executive compensation and compliance with the federal securities laws and Nasdaq and NYSE rules. Mr. Klein is also chair of the firm's Sports Law Practice Group, which includes representing regional sports networks, sports investment banks and several professional sports teams in a variety of matters, as well as representing buyers and sellers of professional sports teams.

Mr. Klein earned a Bachelor of Science degree in Policy Analysis from Cornell University and received his Juris Doctor degree from Harvard Law School.

In memory of my father, Dr. Jacob Levin, whose genius, integrity and love of learning continues to guide me.
L.D.L.

In memory of my mother who taught me to never let my reach limit my grasp.
A.R.K.

Authors' Preface

This book is intended as a source book for all those who have responsibility for preparing and reviewing the following annual disclosure documents for public companies: the annual report on Form 10-K, the annual meeting proxy statement and the annual report to shareholders. In addition to a comprehensive analysis of the various rules and forms that apply to these documents, this book contains practical guidance based on our own experiences and those of our colleagues in representing various public companies over the years. Where appropriate, we have referenced informal SEC guidance from its Interpretive Releases and its Division of Corporation Finance's Compliance and Disclosure Interpretations. In addition, we have included various examples in the book to assist you in complying with the complicated federal securities laws and preparing proper disclosure. We have also highlighted where relevant the interplay among the SEC rules and those of the national securities exchanges and state corporate law. The focus of this book is on U.S. issuers that are subject to Regulation S-K and not smaller reporting companies under Rule 12b-2 under the Securities Exchange Act of 1934.

The *2012 SEC Handbook: Rules and Forms for Financial Statements and Related Disclosure*, 22nd Edition, an excellent compendium of various SEC rules, regulations and forms, is intended to be used as a companion to this volume. As has been done in the past, Chapters 2 and 3 of this book highlight new rules and SEC interpretations relevant to annual disclosure documents as well as those proposed rules that are likely to influence future filings.

The past three years have been among the most challenging in recent memory for the U.S. markets and economy. The turmoil in the markets brought forth significant proposals for regulatory reform, much of it focused on expanded reporting by public companies. Many of these earlier proposals for regulatory change led to the passage of major legislation and the adoption of final rules by the SEC during 2010 and 2011 (see Chapter 2).

Two actions taken during 2010 were expected to have a major impact on public company reporting in 2011 and 2012; the passage in July 2010 of the Dodd-Frank Wall Street Reform and Consumer Protection Act and the SEC's adoption in August 2010 of final rules intended to facilitate the ability of shareholders to nominate candidates for election as directors in opposition to the board's recommended nominees.

The Dodd-Frank Act, when fully implemented, will require significant new disclosures relating to corporate governance and executive compensation. As described in Chapters 3 and 7, certain of the corporate governance and disclosure requirements contained in the Dodd-Frank Act became effective on the date of the bill's enactment, and some, including those relating to shareholder votes on compensation of executive officers (say-on-pay), were finalized in 2011 and were effective for the 2011 proxy season. However, various provisions require additional rulemaking, including those relating to compensation committees and the use of compensation advisers, so-called "pay equity" disclosure and compensation clawbacks. The SEC has laid out a detailed timeline for this proposed rulemaking, with many of the final rules not expected to be issued until the first half of 2012 and thus not impacting public company disclosure until the 2013 proxy season.

Under the "proxy access" rules, shareholders who otherwise are provided the opportunity to nominate directors at a shareholder meeting under applicable state law would have been eligible to have their nominees included in the proxy materials of certain registrants if they owned at least three percent of the registrant's shares continuously for at least the prior three years. The proxy access rules, containing proposed amendments to Rule 14a-8 and a new Rule 14a-11, were scheduled to be effective on November 15, 2010. However, as described in Chapter 2, in response to a challenge to the validity of these rules, the U.S. Court of Appeals for the District of Columbia Circuit vacated new Rule 14a-11 and it did not become effective. Amendments to Rule 14a-8, which had been stayed by the SEC pending resolution of the challenge, became effective on September 20, 2011.

Other projects under way by the SEC could further impact annual SEC reporting for years to come. For example, in July 2010, the SEC issued a concept release seeking public comment on various aspects of the U.S. proxy system, including the mechanics of proxy distribution and collection. This comprehensive review of "proxy plumbing" could have a wide-ranging impact on future shareholder votes.

Several people must be singled out for special thanks in helping us prepare this book. First, we would like to thank Susan Urban and Lindy Thomas, our assistants who produced revision after revision of this book, and the many reference librarians, word processors and proofreaders at Katten Muchin Rosenman LLP's Chicago office who also assisted us. We would also like to thank our colleagues James Anderson, Douglas Gruener, Robert Kohl and Mark Wood for their editorial comments and our firm for its support. Most importantly, we would like to thank our families for supporting our effort even though it meant many evenings and weekends away from them.

Please keep in mind that the laws, rules and regulations applicable to public companies are complex and subject to frequent change. The views expressed in this book are those of the authors and do not necessarily reflect the views of Katten Muchin Rosenman LLP.

Lawrence D. Levin

Adam R. Klein

November 1, 2011

Chicago, Illinois

Summary Table of Contents

Table of Contents

Appendixes

CHAPTER 1

INTRODUCTION

A. Overview of the Securities Exchange Act of 1934.

The Securities Exchange Act of 1934, as amended (the "Exchange Act"), provides for a comprehensive system of reporting by public companies and their directors, officers and principal shareholders. With certain exceptions, the Exchange Act and its related rules require that public companies file with the Securities and Exchange Commission (the "SEC") extensive annual reports on Form 10-K, quarterly reports on Form 10-Q and, for certain events, current reports on Form 8-K. In addition, the rules promulgated under the Exchange Act require a proxy statement to be filed with the SEC and delivered to shareholders when management or others are soliciting proxies for proposals to be voted on at shareholder meetings. These rules also require delivery of an annual report to shareholders.

This book is intended to provide an in-depth analysis of public company disclosure, as well as a basic overview of the regulatory framework that governs the periodic reporting obligations of public companies, focusing on the preparation of the annual report on Form 10-K, the annual meeting proxy statement and the annual report to shareholders (hereinafter referred to as the "Annual Report").

B. Companies Required to File Periodic Reports.

Only companies that are "reporting companies" are required to file reports under the Exchange Act. Companies become reporting companies in one of two ways: registration of a public offering of securities under the Securities Act of 1933, as amended (the "Securities Act"), or registration of a class of equity securities under Section 12 of the Exchange Act.

1. Section 12. In general, Section 12 of the Exchange Act requires the following companies to register their securities with the SEC and thus become reporting companies:

(a) Any company with securities traded on a national securities exchange (e.g., the New York Stock Exchange ("NYSE"), the NASDAQ Stock Market ("NASDAQ"), or the NYSE Amex (Section 12(b)); or

(b) Any company that has, as of the last day of its fiscal year, total assets (as defined in Rule 12g5-2 of the Exchange Act) exceeding $10 million and a class of equity securities held of record (as defined in Rule 12g5-1 of the Exchange Act) by 500 or more persons, whether or not the equity securities are listed on a national securities exchange (Section 12(g)).[1]

2. Section 15(d). Section 15(d) of the Exchange Act requires any company that has filed a registration statement registering a public offering of securities under the Securities Act to, upon effectiveness of such registration statement, file substantially the same reports as are required to be filed by companies with securities registered under Section 12 of the Exchange Act (e.g., Forms 10-K, 10-Q and 8-K). However, such companies are not required to formally register such securities under the Exchange Act. As a result, such companies are not subject to the federal proxy rules (Section 14 of the Exchange Act), and thus do not have to distribute proxy statements or Annual Reports to their shareholders in connection with annual meetings. In addition, such companies are not subject to Section 16 of the Exchange Act, and therefore their directors, executive officers and greater than 10% shareholders need not file Form 3s, 4s or 5s with the SEC. However, by virtue of the requirements set forth in Sections 12(b) and 12(g), most companies to which Section 15(d) of the Exchange Act applies are also required to register their publicly offered securities under Section 12 of the Exchange Act at the time of their initial public offerings.

C. Registration Under the Exchange Act.

The forms that a U.S. issuer may use to register securities under the Exchange Act are Forms 8-A and 10.

1. Form 8-A is a short-form registration statement used for the registration of any class of equity or debt securities under Section 12(b), or equity securities under Section 12(g), of the Exchange Act. Form 8-A is primarily used by issuers at the same time that they are filing registration statements on Form S-1 under the Securities Act in connection with initial public offerings of securities. Form 8-A may also be used by issuers who are already required to file reports pursuant to Section 13 or 15(d) of the Exchange Act.

2. Form 10 is a long-form registration statement similar in breadth to Form S-1 that may be used to register a class of securities under Section 12(b) or (g) of the Exchange Act. Although a Form 10 would generally not be used when a Form 8-A could be substituted, there is no prohibition on doing so. Form 10 filings are typically made by issuers who, through private placements or employee stock

---

[1] Registration of the class of equity securities must occur within 120 days after the end of the fiscal year on the last day of which the issuer meets these thresholds (Section 12(g)(1)(B) of the Exchange Act). Section 12(g)(2) expressly exempts securities issued by investment companies, savings and loan associations, religious and charitable organizations and certain insurance companies.

plans, have accumulated a class of equity securities held by 500 or more security holders of record on the last day of their fiscal years along with total assets exceeding $10 million. These companies would be required to file a Form 10 pursuant to Section 12(g) of the Exchange Act, even though they have not filed a registration statement under the Securities Act. Form 10 filings are also made by companies whose securities are spun off from a former parent company.

D. Periodic Reports Required by the Exchange Act.

The principal periodic reports required to be filed with the SEC by reporting companies are:

1. The annual report on Form 10-K (required to be filed within 90 days[2] after the end of each fiscal year);

2. Quarterly reports on Form 10-Q (filed within 45 days[3] after the end of the first three fiscal quarters); and

3. Current reports on Form 8-K (usually required to be filed within four business days after occurrence of the event that the form requires to be reported).

The annual proxy statement and Annual Report, although not part of the periodic reporting requirements, also play key roles for substantially all reporting companies.

E. The SEC's Integrated Disclosure System.

The basic disclosure documents under the Securities Act and the Exchange Act generally call for a common core of information. Without the integration of the disclosure requirements under the Securities Act and the Exchange Act, there would be much duplication and overlap.

The SEC's integrated disclosure system was accomplished by setting forth substantially all of the financial statement requirements in Regulation S-X, and by making Regulation S-K the repository of virtually all other disclosure items

---

[2] Except with respect to "large accelerated filers" (as defined in Rule 12b-2 of the Exchange Act and described in Chapter 6) for which the number of days is 60, and "accelerated filers" that do not meet the definition of "large accelerated filers," for which the number of days is 75. The definition of "large accelerated filers" includes companies that have a public float of $700 million or more and meet the other conditions that apply to "accelerated filers." "Accelerated filers" whose public float has dropped below $50 million may exit accelerated filer status by filing a Form 10-K on a non-accelerated basis for the same fiscal year that the determination of public float is made. "Large accelerated filers" may exit large accelerated filer status once their public float has dropped below $500 million. See SEC Release No. 33-8644 (December 21, 2005).

[3] Except with respect to "large accelerated filers" and "accelerated filers" for which the number of days is 40 for quarterly reports. See SEC Release No. 33-8644 (December 21, 2005).

(including exhibits). Thus, the documents required to be filed with the SEC pursuant to the Securities Act and the Exchange Act (e.g., registration statements on Forms S-1 and S-3 and Forms 10-K and 10-Q) generally direct companies to Regulation S-K or S-X for the specific disclosure requirements of each item listed in the documents. In addition, some forms have unique disclosure requirements not found in Regulation S-K or S-X. On July 30, 1992, the SEC adopted a series of Small Business Initiatives that included a new and optional integrated registration, reporting and disclosure system based on Regulation S-B that could be used by all small business issuers. Regulation S-B items usually required less disclosure than their analogous Regulation S-K counterparts. Rules adopted by the SEC in December 2007 phased out use of Regulation S-B, moved the information required therefor to Regulations S-K and S-X, and replaced the concept of small business issuers with that of smaller reporting companies.[4] In general, the definition of a "smaller reporting company" is a company that has less than $75 million in public common equity float, regardless of annual revenues. Companies without a calculable public equity float will qualify for this scaled disclosure if their revenues were below $50 million in the previous year. Although the focus of this book is the integrated disclosure system for those registrants that are not smaller reporting companies, the disclosures required for smaller reporting companies are similar to, albeit less burdensome than, those required for other registrants.

1. Regulation S-K. Regulation S-K, adopted in 1977, standardized a number of disclosure items common to many of the SEC's disclosure documents. Regulation S-K currently has 13 "Subparts," each of which is divided into "Items." Subpart 1 generally explains the application of Regulation S-K and discusses the SEC's policy on projections. Subpart 800 includes a list of industry guides; Subpart 900 relates to Partnership Roll-up transactions; Subpart 1000 (Regulation M-A) relates to mergers and acquisitions; Subpart 1100 (Regulation AB) relates to asset-backed securities; and Subpart 1200 relates to disclosures by registrants engaged in oil and gas producing activities. The remaining seven subparts include substantive disclosure in the following areas:

> Subpart 100—Business (Items 101–103)
>
> Subpart 200—Securities of the Registrant (Items 201–202)
>
> Subpart 300—Financial Information (Items 301–308)
>
> Subpart 400—Management and Certain Security Holders (Items 401–407)
>
> Subpart 500—Registration Statement and Prospectus Provisions (Items 501–512)

---

[4] See Section J of Chapter 6 for a discussion of smaller reporting companies.

Subpart 600—Exhibits (Item 601)

Subpart 700—Miscellaneous (Items 701–703)

2. Regulation S-X. The rules included in Regulation S-X govern the form and content of, and requirements for, financial statements filed with the SEC. Regulation S-X includes uniform instructions governing the periods to be covered by financial statements included in most reporting forms filed with the SEC under the Securities Act and the Exchange Act and in Annual Reports. Regulation S-X generally requires audited balance sheets as of the end of each of the two most recent fiscal years and audited statements of income and changes in financial position for each of the three most recent fiscal years. These standardized financial statement requirements are different for smaller reporting companies.

CHAPTER 2

SYNOPSIS OF RECENT DEVELOPMENTS AFFECTING PREPARATION OF ANNUAL DISCLOSURE DOCUMENTS

A. Shareholder Approval of Executive Compensation and Golden Parachute Compensation.

On January 25, 2011, the SEC adopted amendments to its rules to implement the provisions of the Dodd-Frank Wall Street Reform and Consumer Protection Act (the "Dodd-Frank Act") relating to shareholder approval of executive compensation and "golden parachute" compensation arrangements (see SEC Release No. 33-9178). Section 951 of the Dodd-Frank Act amends the Exchange Act by adding Section 14A, which requires a company to conduct a separate shareholder advisory vote to approve the compensation of executives, as disclosed pursuant to Item 402 of Regulation S-K. Section 14A also requires a company to conduct a separate shareholder advisory vote to determine how often the company will conduct a shareholder advisory vote on executive compensation. In addition, Section 14A requires a company soliciting votes to approve merger or acquisition transactions to provide disclosure of certain "golden parachute" compensation arrangements and, in certain circumstances, to conduct a separate shareholder advisory vote to approve the golden parachute compensation arrangements.

For additional information regarding these amendments, see Section D of Chapter 7.

B. Facilitating Shareholder Director Nominations.

On August 25, 2010, the SEC adopted final rules containing changes to the federal proxy and other rules which were intended to facilitate the ability of the shareholders of a registrant to nominate candidates for election as directors in opposition to the board's recommended nominees (see SEC Release No. 33-9136, which is included in Appendix 2 hereto). These final rules contained amendments to Rule 14a-8 as well as a new Rule 14a-11. The rules were scheduled to be effective on November 15, 2010, but as a consequence of the litigation described below, the amendments to Rule 14a-8 did not become effective until September 20, 2011, and the new Rule 14a-11 did not become effective at all (see SEC Release No. 33-9259, which is included in Appendix 2 hereto). The amendments to Rule 14a-8 permit shareholders, under certain circumstances, to include in a registrant's proxy materials proposals to amend, or request the amendment of, the registrant's governing documents with respect to procedures for nominating directors.

The Business Roundtable and the U.S. Chamber of Commerce challenged the validity of new Rule 14a-11 in the U.S. Court of Appeals for the District of Columbia Circuit and filed a petition with the SEC seeking to stay the implementation of Rule 14a-11 pending resolution of the matter by the Court of Appeals. On October 4, 2010, the SEC granted the requested stay in the implementation of Rule 14a-11 and the effectiveness of amended Rule 14a-8. On July 22, 2011, the Court of Appeals vacated Rule 14a-11. The court held that the SEC was "arbitrary and capricious in promulgating Rule 14a-11" and thus violated the Administrative Procedure Act, and failed to adequately consider the rule's effect upon efficiency, competition and capital formation as required by Section 3(f) of the Securities Exchange Act of 1934 and Section 2(c) of the Investment Company Act of 1940. On September 6, 2011, the SEC confirmed that it was not seeking rehearing of the decision by the Court of Appeals vacating Rule 14a-11. The court's ruling did not address the related amendment to Rule 14a-8. The SEC had voluntarily stayed the effective date of the Rule 14a-8 amendments at the time it stayed the effective date of Rule 14a-11. On September 20, 2011, the stay on the effectiveness of the amendments to Rule 14a-8 was removed and the amendments became effective. As a result, shareholders may introduce proposals regarding proxy access standards in 2012 on a registrant-by-registrant basis.

New Rule 14a-11 would have required that registrants include director nominees of significant, long-term shareholders in their proxy materials alongside the nominees of management. Under these new "proxy access" rules, shareholders who otherwise are provided the opportunity to nominate directors at a shareholder meeting under applicable state or foreign law would have been eligible to have their nominees included in a registrant's proxy materials if they owned at least three percent of the registrant's shares continuously for at least the prior three years. By eliminating the cost to nominating shareholders of soliciting proxies for a partial opposition slate, these rules would have removed significant cost barriers to proxy contests.

For additional information regarding these new rules, see Section G of Chapter 7.

C. Dodd-Frank Act Corporate Governance and Disclosure Provisions.

On July 21, 2010, President Obama signed into law the Dodd-Frank Act. The Dodd-Frank Act is comprehensive in scope, providing for significant changes to the structure of federal financial regulation and new substantive requirements that apply to a broad range of market participants, including registrants that are not financial institutions. Among other measures, the Dodd-Frank Act includes corporate governance and executive compensation reforms applicable to publicly traded issuers. These reforms are generally contained in Subtitle E—Accountability and Executive Compensation Sections 951-957 of the Dodd-Frank Act. The Dodd-Frank Act also mandated significant changes to the authority of the SEC.

With the exception of the say-on-pay, say-on-golden parachute and broker discretionary voting requirements, the corporate governance and executive compensation provisions require further action by the SEC, the stock exchanges or other regulators before they are operative. Many of the regulatory actions were required to be taken within one year of the enactment of the Dodd-Frank Act; however, some of the provisions (such as the pay-for-performance, pay-parity, hedging disclosure and clawback requirements) do not have explicit deadlines for action by the applicable regulators. The SEC has published a schedule for proposing and adopting rules to implement the provisions of the Dodd-Frank Act. As noted, final rulemaking for many of the provisions is not expected before 2012. As a result, for registrants with calendar fiscal year-ends that hold their annual shareholder meetings in the spring of 2012, many of these provisions will not be effective until the 2013 proxy season.

The major corporate governance and executive compensation provisions of the Dodd-Frank Act are summarized below:

Final Rules Issued and Effective:

- **Say-on-Pay.** A registrant's first proxy statement or consent solicitation for a shareholders' meeting occurring after January 20, 2011 that includes compensation disclosure must include a separate non-binding shareholder vote to approve the compensation of executive officers. Such proxy statement must also include a proposal for a separate non-binding shareholder vote on whether the shareholders shall have a say-on-pay vote every one, two or three years. The say on pay proposal must be presented to shareholders no less frequently than once every three years, and the separate resolution on the frequency of the say-on-pay resolution must be presented to shareholders at least once every six years. As discussed above, the SEC published final rules on this matter on January 25, 2011.

- **Shareholder Approval of Golden Parachutes.** Any proxy statement or consent solicitation for a shareholder meeting occurring after January 20, 2011 relating to shareholder approval of an acquisition, merger, consolidation or proposed sale or disposition of all or substantially all the assets of a registrant must include a separate non-binding shareholder vote on any "golden parachute"-related compensation. The proxy statement must clearly disclose any agreements with named executive officers concerning any type of compensation (present, deferred or contingent) that is related to the transaction subject to shareholder approval. Disclosure must also include the aggregate total of all such compensation that may (and the conditions upon which it may) be paid to each such executive officer. As discussed above, the SEC published final rules on this matter on January 25, 2011.

● **Broker Voting.** Listed exchanges are required to mandate that their member brokers be prohibited from voting shares held in street name with respect to director elections, executive compensation or "any other significant matter" as determined under SEC rules, unless the beneficial owner provides the broker with specific voting instructions. This provision codifies and expands the scope of New York Stock Exchange Rule 452, which the NYSE enacted effective July 1, 2009. In September 2010, the SEC approved amendments to NYSE Rule 452, corresponding to Section 402.08 of the NYSE Listed Company Manual and NASDAQ Stock Market Rule 2251 to implement the Dodd-Frank Act's requirements. The SEC has not yet determined when it will issue rules defining "other significant matters."

Proposed Rules Issued:

● **Compensation Committee and Adviser Independence.** The SEC is required to adopt rules directing stock exchanges to prohibit the listing of any registrant that does not comply with additional independence requirements governing compensation committee members and consultants, legal counsel and other advisers to the compensation committee. The SEC rules will require that, for purposes of determining "independence," factors such as any consulting, advisory or other fees paid by the registrant to such director as well as the affiliations of the director with the registrant would need to be considered. The compensation committee would also be required to select compensation consultants, legal counsel or other advisers after determining the independence of such advisers under rules to be adopted by the SEC. The independence of such advisers would be based on factors such as the other services provided to the registrant, the amount of fees received as a percentage of the total revenues of the adviser, policies of the adviser that are designed to prevent conflicts of interest, any business or personal relationships of the adviser with the compensation committee, and any equity ownership of the registrant by the adviser. In addition, in any proxy solicitation materials for an annual meeting occurring after July 21, 2011, registrants would be required to disclose whether the compensation committee had retained a compensation consultant and whether the compensation consultant's services had raised any conflict of interest, and, if so, the nature of the conflict and how the conflict is being addressed. The compensation committee must have sole discretion to retain a compensation consultant and independent legal and other advisers and will be directly responsible for the selection, compensation and oversight of such advisers. The SEC may permit the exchanges to exempt a category of registrants from these requirements and is required to consider the impact on smaller reporting companies. The SEC published proposed rules on this matter on March 30, 2011 (see SEC Release No. 33-9199 and related discussion in Chapter 3). The SEC has indicated that it intends to adopt final rules on this matter in November or December 2011.

● **Financial Institutions' Executive Compensation.** Federal regulators are required to adopt regulations requiring "covered financial institutions" with assets greater than $1 billion to disclose incentive compensation to their appropriate federal regulator(s). Disclosure is required of all incentive-based compensation arrangements in sufficient detail for the regulator to determine whether the arrangement with the executive officer, employee, director or principal shareholder is excessive or could lead to a material financial loss. Within the same time frame, federal regulators are also required to prescribe regulations to prohibit any type of incentive-based compensation by "covered financial institutions" with assets greater than $1 billion that is excessive or could lead to material financial loss. Covered financial institutions include depository institutions, depository institution holding companies, credit unions, registered broker-dealers and registered investment advisers. The SEC published proposed rules on this matter on March 29, 2011 (see SEC Release No. 34-64140 and related discussion in Chapter 3). The SEC has indicated that it intends to adopt final rules on this matter between January and June 2012.

Proposed Rules Not Yet Issued:

● **Executive Compensation Clawbacks.** The SEC is required to adopt rules directing the stock exchanges to prohibit the listing of registrants that do not comply with rules to be adopted by the SEC requiring a registrant to implement policies (1) to disclose the policy for incentive-based compensation that is based on financial information required to be reported under the securities laws, and (2) to recover incentive-based compensation (including stock options awards) from any current or former executive in the event of an accounting restatement triggered by material noncompliance with any financial reporting requirement under the securities laws. There will be a three-year look-back period from the date of the restatement for compensation paid. The amount of the clawback would be any excess paid to the executive over the amount that the executive would have been paid giving effect to the accounting restatement. Note that these provisions are far broader than the Sarbanes-Oxley clawback provisions that (1) apply only to the compensation of the chief executive and chief financial officers, (2) apply only in the event of a restatement triggered by "material noncompliance of the registrant, as a result of misconduct . . ." and (3) provide for a look-back period of only twelve months. The SEC has indicated that it intends to propose rules on this matter in November or

December 2011 and adopt final rules on this matter between January and June 2012.

● **Pay for Performance and Pay Parity Disclosures.** The SEC is required to adopt rules requiring registrants to clearly disclose the relationship between executive compensation actually paid and the financial performance of the registrant, taking into account the change in the value of the shares of stock, dividends and any distributions. The SEC rules will also require disclosure of (1) the median of the annual total compensation of all employees other than the CEO; (2) the annual total compensation of the CEO; and (3) the ratio of the median total compensation of all employees to the total compensation of the CEO. Total compensation is calculated as in the proxy statement summary compensation table. The SEC has indicated that it intends to propose rules on this matter in November or December 2011 and adopt final rules on this matter between January and June 2012.

● **Hedging Disclosure.** The SEC is required to adopt rules requiring registrants to disclose in annual meeting proxy statements whether any director or employee (or his/her designee) is permitted to purchase financial instruments that are designed to hedge or offset any decrease in the market value of equity securities granted to employees or directors as compensation or otherwise directly or indirectly held. The SEC has indicated that it intends to propose rules on this matter in November or December 2011 and adopt final rules on this matter between January and June 2012.

● **Chairman and CEO Structures.** The SEC is required to adopt rules requiring registrants to disclose why they have separated or combined the positions of CEO and chairman of the board. Under current SEC rules, a registrant is now required to disclose its leadership structure and the reasons for adopting such a structure. No proposed rules have been published. The SEC has not indicated a timeline or whether current disclosures satisfy this requirement.

CHAPTER 3

SYNOPSIS OF PROPOSALS AFFECTING PREPARATION OF ANNUAL DISCLOSURE DOCUMENTS

A. Listing Standards for Compensation Committees.

On March 30, 2011, the SEC proposed amendments intended to implement the provisions of Section 952 of the Dodd-Frank Act that added Section 10C to the Exchange Act (see SEC Release No. 33-9199, which is included as Appendix 5 hereto). Section 10C requires the SEC to adopt rules directing the national securities exchanges and national securities associations to prohibit the listing of any equity security of a registrant that is not in compliance with Section 10C's compensation committee and compensation adviser requirements.

Proposed Rule 10C-1(b)(1)(i) under the Exchange Act would direct the exchanges to adopt listing standards that would require each member of a company's compensation committee, or any other committee that oversees executive compensation, to be a board member and independent. Proposed Rule 10C-1(b)(1)(ii) would require the exchanges to develop a definition of independence after considering relevant factors. Proposed Rule 10C-1(a)(3) would provide that the exchanges' listing standards may provide for a cure period if a member of a compensation committee ceases to be independent for reasons that are out of such person's control. Controlled companies, limited partnerships, companies in bankruptcy proceedings, open-ended management investment companies registered under the Investment Company Act of 1940 and any foreign private issuer that discloses in its annual report the reasons that it does not have an independent compensation committee would each be exempted from the compensation committee independence listing standards under proposed Rule 10C-1(b)(1)(iii). Proposed Rules 10C-1(b)(2) and 10C-1(b)(3) would direct the exchanges to adopt listing standards providing that compensation committees may obtain the advice of a compensation consultant, independent legal counsel or other adviser and be directly responsible for appointing, paying and overseeing their outside advisers. Listed registrants would also be required to provide funds for any such adviser. Proposed Rule 10C-1(b)(4) would require the exchanges to adopt a listing rule that provides that a compensation committee must consider specified factors when selecting a compensation adviser.

The proposed rules would also amend Item 407(e)(3)(iii) of Regulation S-K to require a registrant to disclose in its proxy statement whether its compensation committee has retained or obtained the advice of a compensation consultant or the work of a compensation consultant has raised any conflict of interest, and, if so, the nature of such conflict and how it is being addressed. The proposed amendments to Item 407(e)(3)(iii) would eliminate the current disclosure exception for services that are limited to consulting on any broad-based plans and the provision of information that is not customized for the registrant. However, the exception has been retained for purposes of fee disclosure requirements.

B. Incentive-Based Compensation Arrangements.

On March 29, 2011, the SEC, along with several other governmental agencies, proposed rules to implement Section 956 of the Dodd-Frank Act (see SEC Release No. 34-64140). The proposed rule would prohibit incentive-based compensation arrangements at a covered financial institution that encourage executive officers, employees, directors or principal shareholders ("covered persons") to expose the institution to inappropriate risks by providing the covered person excessive compensation. The proposed rule would prohibit a covered financial institution from establishing or maintaining any incentive-based compensation arrangements for covered persons that encourage inappropriate risks by the covered financial institution that could lead to material financial loss and require deferral of a portion of incentive-based compensation for executive officers of "larger covered financial institutions."

The proposal would also require that, at larger covered financial institutions, the board of directors or a committee of such a board identify those covered persons (other than executive officers) that have the ability to expose the institution to possible losses that are substantial in relation to the institution's size, capital or overall risk tolerance. The proposed rule would require that the board of directors, or a committee thereof, of the institution approve the incentive-based compensation arrangement for such individuals, and maintain documentation of such approval. In connection with these restrictions, the proposal would require covered financial institutions to maintain policies and procedures appropriate to their size, complexity and use of incentive-based compensation to help ensure compliance with these requirements and prohibitions.

C. Conflict Minerals.

On December 15, 2010, the SEC proposed amendments intended to implement Section 1502 of the Dodd-Frank Act (see SEC Release No. 34-63547).

Specifically, the proposed rules would require any registrant for which conflict minerals (minerals determined by the Secretary of State to be financing conflict in the Democratic Republic of Congo and adjoining countries) are "necessary to the functionality or production" of a product that the registrant manufactures or contracts to manufacture, to disclose in the body of its Form 10-K whether its conflict minerals originated in the Democratic Republic of the Congo or an adjoining country. If so, that registrant would be required to furnish a separate "Conflicts Minerals Report" as an exhibit to its Form 10-K that includes, among other matters, a description of the measures taken by the registrant to exercise due diligence on the source and chain of custody of its conflict minerals. These due diligence measures would include, but would not be limited to, an independent private sector audit of the registrant's report conducted in accordance with standards established by the Comptroller General of the United States. Further, any registrant furnishing such a report would be required, in that report, to certify that it obtained an independent private sector audit of its report, provide the audit report and make its reports available to the public on its website.

D. Short-Term Borrowings Disclosure.

On September 17, 2010, the SEC proposed amendments intended to enhance registrants' disclosure about short-term borrowing (see SEC Release No. 33-9143, which is included as Appendix 3 hereto). Specifically, the proposals would require a registrant to provide, in a separately captioned subsection of Management's Discussion and Analysis of Financial Condition and Results of Operations ("MD&A"), a comprehensive explanation of its short-term borrowings, including variations in borrowing levels during the reporting period. Registrants would be required to provide in MD&A quantitative information for each type of short term-borrowing they use and expanded qualitative information. The proposals include a designation of a new category of registrants that would be deemed "financial companies" and be subject to expanded disclosure requirements. The proposed amendments would apply to annual and quarterly reports, proxy or information statements that include financial statements and registration statements under both the Securities Act and the Exchange Act.

E. SEC Concept Release on the U.S. Proxy System (Proxy Plumbing).

On July 14, 2010, the SEC issued a concept release seeking public comment on various aspects of the U.S. proxy system, including the mechanics of proxy distribution and collection (see SEC Release No. 34-62495, which is included as Appendix 4 hereto). The release is intended to be a precursor to rule changes designed to promote greater efficiency and transparency in the system and to enhance the accuracy and integrity of the shareholder vote. The release solicits comment on a number of key issues in three main areas: (1) accuracy, transparency and efficiency of the proxy voting process; (2) communication and shareholder participation; and (3) the relationship between voting power and economic interest.

Within this framework, the release comprehensively analyzes a number of specific topics, including:

● **Over-voting and under-voting of shares.** Securities intermediaries sometimes cast more or fewer votes than they actually hold because of the way in which securities transactions are cleared and settled and the way in which intermediaries then "allocate" votes to investors. The SEC questions whether it should regulate this practice and whether intermediaries should disclose the procedures they use to allocate votes to investors on whose behalf they hold securities.

● **Vote confirmation.** Under the current system, investors have limited ability to confirm whether their shares have been voted according to their instructions. The release suggests the possibility of requiring a process for vote confirmation.

● **Proxy voting by institutional securities lenders.** The release evaluates the impact of institutional securities lenders on the proxy voting process. Shares on loan cannot be voted unless the lender "recalls" the shares. The SEC considers the possibility of advance notice of matters to be voted on, which would give lenders adequate time to recall their shares and vote on relevant issues. The release also questions whether there is a need for more transparent disclosure of votes cast by institutional holders of securities.

● **Proxy distribution fees.** The proxy distribution fee structure has consistently been an area of major concern for the SEC. The release addresses various options for revamping the structure and size of fees charged, including the revision or elimination of stock exchange maximum fee schedules.

● **Communication between registrants and beneficial owners of securities.** The practice of holding securities in street name and the rules enabling beneficial owners to conceal their identities from registrants have inhibited the ability of registrants to communicate with shareholders. The release seeks feedback on whether so-called "OBO" status should be revised or eliminated.

● **Means to facilitate retail investor participation.** Low retail investor participation rates have been an area of major concern for the SEC. The release suggests several initiatives to increase retail investor voting, including better investor education, enhanced brokers' Internet platforms, advance voting instructions, enhanced investor-to-investor communications and improved use of the Internet for the distribution of proxy materials.

● **Data-tagging proxy related materials.** The release examines the costs and benefits of data-tagging proxy statement disclosures and asks whether such organization of information would enhance investor participation in the proxy voting process.

● **Role and legal status of proxy advisory firms.** Institutional investors' increased reliance on proxy advisory firms has raised various concerns. The release examines the necessity of enhancing disclosure of potential conflicts of interest and improving regulatory supervision over the formation of advisory firms' voting recommendations.

● **Dual record dates.** Some new state laws (Delaware's, for example) permit dual record dates, thus changing the long-established procedure of using a single record date to determine which shareholders are entitled to notice of a meeting and which shareholders are entitled to vote at the meeting. If a registrant adopts dual record dates under such a new law, a shareholder who sells shares of the registrant after the notice record date, but before the voting record date, no longer holds the right to vote those shares. The release examines whether SEC rules should be revised to accommodate dual record dates.

● **Empty voting.** Investors have developed a variety of techniques to "decouple" voting rights from their economic interests in a registrant, resulting in the investors' having voting rights that exceed their economic interests in the registrant. The release examines whether such practice unduly influences voting results and asks whether disclosure of decoupling activities should be required.

CHAPTER 4

ELECTRONIC FILING UNDER EDGAR

A. EDGAR Background and Recent Developments.

The SEC's Electronic Data Gathering, Analysis, and Retrieval ("EDGAR") system mandates that specified persons file specified documents electronically with the SEC. The EDGAR system has been operational since 1992, with mandated electronic filings beginning in April 1993. Electronic filings are generally available in the "EDGAR Database" area of the SEC's website, www.sec.gov, on a real-time basis free of charge. EDGAR filings can also be found on several websites of third-party service providers on a subscription basis, including: www.knowledgemosaic.com, www.freeedgar.com, www.10kwizard.com and www.edgar-online.com.

On June 22, 1998, the SEC awarded to TRW, Inc. a contract for the modernization of the EDGAR system. The EDGAR architecture was expected to be converted to an Internet-based system using Hypertext Markup Language ("HTML") as the filing format, which supports the attachment of graphic files. The new system was expected to reduce the costs and efforts of preparing and submitting electronic filings, as well as permit more attractive and readable documents.

On June 28, 1999, the SEC began accepting live filings submitted in HTML, as well as documents submitted in American Standard Code for Information Interchange ("ASCII") format. Filers have the option of accompanying their required filings with unofficial copies in Portable Document Format ("PDF"). Filers also are encouraged to submit test filings that include documents in HTML and PDF formats. An unofficial PDF copy is not deemed "filed" for purposes of Section 18 of the Exchange Act, or otherwise subject to the liabilities of such section. An unofficial PDF copy is, however, subject to all other civil liability and anti-fraud provisions of the Exchange Act.[1]

On April 24, 2000, the SEC issued SEC Release No. 33-7855 adopting rule amendments in connection with the next stage of EDGAR modernization, which was implemented on May 30, 2000. The release addressed the following

---

[1] Rule 104(d) of Regulation S-T.

new features of the new system, hailed as "EDGAR II," and related rule changes:

- the ability to include graphic and image files in HTML documents;

- the expanded ability to use hyperlinks in HTML documents, including links between documents within a submission and to previously filed documents on the SEC's EDGAR database; and

- the addition of the Internet as an available means of transmitting filings to the EDGAR system.

On May 14, 2002, the SEC issued Release No. 33-8099 adopting rules requiring foreign issuers to make their SEC filings via EDGAR. The rules also eliminate the requirement that any first-time EDGAR filer, domestic or foreign, submit a paper copy of its electronic filing to the SEC. The rules became effective in 2002.

On May 7, 2003, the SEC issued Release No. 33-8230, which requires electronic filing of reports under Section 16 of the Exchange Act and also removed magnetic cartridges as a means of transmitting filings to the EDGAR system.

On February 3, 2005, the SEC issued Release No. 33-8529, which includes rule amendments to enable registrants to submit voluntarily supplemental tagged financial information using the eXtensible Business Reporting Language ("XBRL") format as exhibits to specified EDGAR filings.

On August 19, 2008, the SEC unveiled "IDEA," short for Interactive Data Electronic Applications, the proposed successor to EDGAR. IDEA is expected to give investors faster and easier access to key financial information about public companies and mutual funds. IDEA, based on a completely new architecture, will at first supplement and then eventually replace the EDGAR system. The EDGAR database will continue to be available as an archive of company filings for past years.

On January 30, 2009, the SEC issued a final rule release requiring certain companies to make financial disclosures using the XBRL format (see SEC Release Nos. 33-9002 and 33-9002A). Subject to a phase-in period, filers are required to include an exhibit containing interactive data with their registration statements, quarterly reports, annual reports, transition reports, and reports on Form 8-K that contain specified financial statements. Filers are also required to provide such interactive data on their websites. The required disclosures are "tagged" so that the information is machine readable (in a manner similar to bar codes) and include companies' financial statements, financial statement footnotes and financial statement schedules.

Filers must prepare electronic filings in accordance with the procedures and technical formatting requirements set forth in the EDGAR Filer Manual, which is updated periodically.[2] Copies of the EDGAR Filer Manual and the EDGAR-Link Software can be found at http://www.sec.gov/info/edgar/shtml.

B. Regulation S-T.

1. Regulation S-T. Regulation S-T is a separate regulation containing rules prescribing requirements for filing electronically and the procedures for making such filings. Regulation S-T supersedes a number of the outdated procedural requirements relating to paper filings set forth in the SEC's rules and forms, including requirements relating to paper size, binding and number of copies.

2. EDGAR Filer Questions. The SEC maintains a Filer Support Staff that can be reached each business day at (202) 551-8900 from 9:00 a.m. to 5:30 p.m. Eastern Time or via email at publicinfo@sec.gov to help answer questions regarding filing documents by EDGAR.

C. EDGAR Forms.

The SEC has created the following three forms specifically for use with the EDGAR system:

1. Form ID. This form is used to apply for the codes necessary for access to file on EDGAR. The Form ID also is used to provide identifying information on companies and individuals who are required to file with the SEC, as well as information on agents who are authorized to file on behalf of such persons. A filer also may submit an amended Form ID to change the codes received in response to the original Form ID application, in which case the filer should clearly mark the Form ID as an amendment. Each registrant, third-party filer, or agent must file the Form ID electronically. In addition, such persons must file with the SEC in paper by fax, within two business days before or after electronically filing the Form ID, a notarized document, manually signed by the applicant over the applicant's typed signature, that includes the information contained in the Form ID, confirms the authenticity of the Form ID and, if filed after electronically filing the Form ID, includes the accession number assigned to the electronically filed Form ID as a result of its filing. As an alternative to submitting the authenticating documents by fax, the filer may attach them to their online Form ID application in PDF format.[3]

2. Form SE. This form is required to be attached to any paper format exhibit filed by any electronic filer, including exhibits filed under a temporary or continuing hardship exemption.

3. Form TH. This form is required to accompany documents filed on paper under a temporary hardship exemption, as described below.

---

[2] Rule 301 of Regulation S-T.   [3] Rule 10(b) of Regulation S-T.

D. Entities and Persons Required to File Electronically.

The following persons or entities are subject to mandatory electronic filing:

1. Registrants and other entities whose filings are subject to review by the SEC's Division of Corporation Finance (e.g., reporting companies), including foreign private issuers and foreign governments;

2. Registrants whose filings are subject to review by the SEC's Division of Investment Management;

3. Persons or entities whose filings are subject to review by the SEC's Division of Market Regulation; and

4. Any party (including natural persons, foreign private issuers and foreign governments) that files a document jointly with, or as a third-party filer with respect to, a registrant that is subject to mandated electronic filing requirements.[4] For example, a foreign issuer named as a guarantor and co-registrant on a registration statement that pertains to a domestic issuer must currently file the registration statement and related documents on EDGAR.

E. Mandated Electronic Submissions.

Rule 101 of Regulation S-T lists those filings that are required to be submitted in electronic format. These mandated electronic submissions include:

1. Proxy Statements and Form 10-Ks. Statements, reports and schedules filed with the SEC pursuant to Section 13, 14 or 15(d) of the Exchange Act, and proxy materials required to be furnished for the information of the SEC in connection with Form 10-Ks filed pursuant to Section 15(d) of the Exchange Act.[5]

2. Correspondence and Supplemental Information. Any related correspondence and supplemental information is also generally required to be submitted in electronic format. Supplemental information submitted in electronic format is required to be stored in the nonpublic EDGAR data storage area as "correspondence." Supplemental information that is submitted in electronic format will not be returned by the SEC.[6]

3. Amendments to Filings. Amendments to filings by, or relating to, a registrant required to file electronically, including any amendment to a paper filing, are also required to be submitted in electronic format.[7]

F. Permitted Electronic Submissions.

Among the documents that may be submitted to the SEC in electronic format is the "glossy" Annual Report furnished for the information of the SEC pursuant

---

[4] Rule 100 of Regulation S-T.
[5] Rule 101(a)(1)(iii) of Regulation S-T.
[6] Rule 101(a)(3) of Regulation S-T.
[7] Rule 101(a)(2) of Regulation S-T.

to Rule 14a-3(c) or Rule 14c-3(b) under the Exchange Act, or pursuant to the requirements of a Form 10-K filed by a registrant pursuant to Section 15(d) of the Exchange Act.[8] Special treatment is provided to Annual Reports because they frequently contain extensive graphic information that is difficult to capture in electronic format. However, if any portion of the Annual Report is incorporated by reference into an electronic filing (e.g., Form 10-K), such portions of the Annual Report must be filed in an electronic format.[9]

G. Documents to Be Submitted in Paper Only.

Some documents should not be filed via EDGAR, and filers should exercise special care when submitting such documents.[10] Among the documents that should not be submitted in electronic format are:

1. Confidential treatment requests and the information with respect to which confidential treatment is requested;

2. Preliminary proxy materials and information statements with respect to a matter specified in Item 14 of Schedule 14A of the Exchange Act for which confidential treatment has been requested;

3. Supplemental information, if the submitter requests that the information be protected from public disclosure under the Freedom of Information Act[11] pursuant to a request for confidential treatment under Rule 83 of the SEC's FOIA Regulations or if the submitter requests that the information be returned after SEC staff review and the information is of the type typically returned by the staff pursuant to Rule 418(b) under the Securities Act or Rule 12b-4 under the Exchange Act; and

4. Shareholder proposals and all related correspondence submitted pursuant to Rule 14a-8 under the Exchange Act.

H. Signatures.

Required signatures to or within any electronic submission must be in typed form. Each signatory to an electronic filing is required to manually sign a signature page or other document authenticating, acknowledging or otherwise adopting his or her signature. Such document is required to be signed before or at the time the filing is made and retained by the filer for five years.[12]

I. Exhibits.

1. General. Exhibits to an electronic filing that have not previously been filed with the SEC are required to be filed in electronic format, absent a hardship

---

[8] Rule 101(b)(1) of Regulation S-T.
[9] Rule 303(b) of Regulation S-T.
[10] Rule 101(c) of Regulation S-T.
[11] 5 U.S.C. 552.
[12] Rule 302 of Regulation S-T.

exemption.[13] Previously filed exhibits, whether in paper or electronic format, may be incorporated by reference into an electronic filing to the extent permitted. However, exhibits to an SEC schedule filed pursuant to Section 13 or 14(d) of the Exchange Act may be filed in paper under cover of Form SE where such exhibits previously were filed in paper (prior to a registrant's becoming subject to mandated electronic filing or pursuant to a hardship exemption) and are required to be refiled pursuant to the schedule's general instructions.[14]

2. Amendments to Exhibits. Amendments to all exhibits are required to be filed in electronic format, absent a hardship exemption.[15]

3. Articles and Bylaws. An electronic filer must, upon amendment, restate in electronic format its entire articles of incorporation and bylaws, as so amended.[16]

4. Exhibits Filed Under a Hardship Exemption. Whenever an exhibit is filed in paper pursuant to a temporary or continuing hardship exemption, the letter "P" should be placed next to the listed exhibit in the exhibit index to reflect that the exhibit was filed in paper pursuant to such exemption. In addition, if the exhibit is filed in paper pursuant to Rule 311 of Regulation S-T, the filer must place the designation "Rule 311" next to the letter "P" in the exhibit index. If the exhibit is filed in paper pursuant to a temporary or continuing hardship exemption, the filer must place the letters "TH" or "CH," respectively, next to the letter "P" in the exhibit index. Whenever an electronic confirming copy of an exhibit is filed pursuant to a hardship exemption,[17] the exhibit index should specify where the confirming electronic copy can be located; in addition, the designation "CE" (confirming electronic) should be placed next to the listed exhibit in the exhibit index.[18]

J. Sanctions for Failing to File Electronically/Safe Harbor.

Failure to submit a required electronic filing, including any required confirming electronic copy of a paper filing made in reliance on a hardship exemption, will:

- result in ineligibility to use registration statements on Forms S-3, S-8, F-2 and F-3;[19]

- restrict incorporation by reference of the document submitted in paper;[20] and

- toll certain time periods associated with tender offers.[21]

---

[13] Rule 102(a) of Regulation S-T.
[14] Rule 311(b) of Regulation S-T.
[15] Rule 102(b) of Regulation S-T.
[16] Rule 102(c) of Regulation S-T.
[17] Rule 201 or 202(d) of Regulation S-T.
[18] Rule 102(d) of Regulation S-T.

[19] Rules 101, 201 and 202 of Regulation S-T.
[20] Rule 303 of Regulation S-T.
[21] Rule 13e-4(f)(12) and Rule 14e-1(e) under the Exchange Act.

However, Rule 103 of Regulation S-T provides a safe harbor against liability for errors in, or omissions from, documents filed electronically that result solely from electronic transmission beyond the control of the electronic filer. The safe harbor is available where the electronic filer takes corrective action as soon as reasonably practicable after becoming aware of the error or omission. This safe harbor also applies to interactive data filed in XBRL format (see Rule 406T(c) of Regulation S-T).

K. Hardship Exemptions.

Rules 201 and 202 of Regulation S-T provide for two hardship exemptions—a "temporary hardship exemption" and a "continuing hardship exemption." Both exemptions are available to permit a filing or other submission to be made in paper rather than electronic format.

1. Temporary Hardship Exemption. The temporary hardship exemption must be based on "unanticipated technical difficulties" in submitting an electronic document.[22] The exemption may be appropriate, for example, for a particular document that a filer is unable to file electronically because of computer problems. The exemption does not require an application, and no SEC staff involvement is required. However, the filer must make a paper filing under cover of Form TH (with a prescribed legend on the cover page identifying it as being submitted under Rule 201). An electronic copy must be filed within six business days of the paper filing.

Signatures to the paper document may be in typed form rather than manual format.[23] All other requirements relating to paper format filings must be satisfied. If the exemption pertains to a document filed pursuant to Section 13(a) or 15(d) of the Exchange Act (e.g., Form 10-K) and the paper format document is filed in the manner required, the filing will be deemed to have been filed by its required due date, and a Form 12b-25 notification of late filing need not be filed.

A temporary hardship exemption is also available for interactive data required to be filed in XBRL format (see Rule 201(c) of Regulation S-T). A filer using this exemption must file the interactive data within six business days after it was originally required.

2. Continuing Hardship Exemption. Unlike the temporary hardship exemption, the continuing hardship exemption requires a written application to the SEC staff. If the staff grants the exemption, the filer may make the submission in paper. An electronic filer may apply for a continuing hardship exemption if all or part of a filing or group of filings otherwise to be filed in electronic format cannot be filed without "undue burden or expense." The application must be made at least 10 business days prior to the required due

---

[22] Rule 201 of Regulation S-T.   [23] Rule 201(a)(3) of Regulation S-T.

date of the filing(s) or the proposed filing date. The written application must contain the information set forth in paragraph (b) of Rule 202 of Regulation S-T. This exemption is available to electronic filers under limited circumstances for exhibits or a filing or group of filings. For example, this exemption might be appropriate for exhibits involving voluminous material contracts of an acquired company that are not easily converted into electronic format without causing the acquirer undue hardship. If the exemption is granted, the paper filings submitted must be filed by the appropriate due date and include a legend on the cover page of the document identifying it as being submitted in paper under Rule 202 of Regulation S-T. If the filing is an exhibit only, then the filer must submit the document under cover of Form SE. A continuing hardship exemption is also available for interactive data required to be filed in XBRL format (see Rule 202(c) of Regulation S-T). Filers should direct inquiries concerning continuing hardship exemptions to the Office of Information Technology in the SEC's Division of Corporation Finance at (202) 551-3600.

3. Filing Date Adjustments. In addition to the two hardship exemptions, an electronic filer may request an adjustment of the filing date if it has in good faith attempted to submit a filing in a timely manner but encounters technical difficulties beyond its control that prevent electronic submission by the applicable due date.[24] There is no assurance that the SEC or its staff will grant such an adjustment.

L. Filing Hours/Filing Date.

The SEC accepts EDGAR filings by direct transmission, either through the Internet or by dial-up modem, from 6:00 a.m. until 10:00 p.m. Eastern Standard Time or Eastern Daylight Saving Time, whichever is in effect ("Eastern Time"), every day except for Saturdays, Sundays and Federal holidays.[25] Any direct transmission filing commencing before 5:30 p.m. Eastern Time, if accepted, will receive that day's filing date.

M. Payment of Filing Fees.

1. Lockbox Delivery. All electronic filers are required to pay fees to the SEC's U.S. Treasury lockbox depository maintained at the U.S. Bank in St. Louis, Missouri, not to the SEC's filing desk.[26] A filer may pay by wire transfer or by mailing or delivering a money order, certified check or cashier's check to the lockbox. Personal checks are not permitted. Rule 13(c) of Regulation S-T requires electronic filers to pay filing fees in accordance with these lockbox procedures even when physically filing paper documents at the SEC's filing

---

[24] Rule 13(b) of Regulation S-T.
[25] Rule 12(c) of Regulation S-T.

[26] Rule 13(c) of Regulation S-T and Rule 3a of the Rules Relating to Informal and Other Procedures.

desk. As discussed herein, SEC filing fees are not required in connection with Form 10-Ks, typical annual meeting proxy statements or for Annual Reports, which are only delivered to the SEC for informational purposes.

2. Payment Verification. EDGAR verifies fee payments made via wire transfer on a near real-time basis (every 15 minutes from 8:00 a.m. to 6:00 p.m. Eastern Time), while it verifies those made by other methods at 2:00 p.m. Eastern Time on each business day for payments received through 2:00 p.m. the previous business day. As a result, a payment made by a method other than wire transfer at 3:00 p.m. Eastern Time on Friday would not be verified until 2:00 p.m. Eastern Time on the following Tuesday! A filer should therefore pay fees for time-sensitive filings by wire transfer to expedite acceptance processing.

3. Payment Format. Rule 3a of the SEC's Rules Relating to Informal and Other Procedures sets forth the format that must be followed in making a filing fee wire transfer, including the requirement that the transferor's account (CIK) number be included. If the SEC staff cannot verify payment, EDGAR will place the filing in a suspense file for up to six business days, and the staff will so notify the filer. If the fee payment is confirmed within the six-day period, the filing will be considered filed on the business day on which verification occurs. If verification does not occur during the six-day period, the filing will be required to be resubmitted. Filers should direct questions concerning fee payment to SEC Filer Support at (202) 551-8900.

N. SEC Staff Suggestions for Avoiding Filing Errors.

The following is a list of SEC staff suggestions to help electronic filers avoid some of the more common errors associated with electronic filing. These suggestions were included in an article updated on October 3, 2006, *Electronic Filing and the EDGAR System: A Regulatory Overview*. The entire article can be found at: www.sec.gov/info/edgar/regoverview.htm.

● Registrants making EDGAR submissions "in-house" should not assign this responsibility to the least experienced person.

● Review documents in electronic format and error check using EDGARLink prior to transmitting documents for filing. For example, filers should check to make sure that they have specified the correct EDGAR form types (including a "/A" where it is needed to designate an amendment); included all documents within the submissions; and made certain that each document is complete.

● Use the correct CIK number. A submission under an incorrect CIK number is a submission for the wrong registrant. The filer will have to resubmit for the correct registrant. Some filings require additional steps. Do not assume that incorrect submissions will be deleted.

● Use the correct file numbers in submission headers, when required.

● Allow sufficient time to submit filings and confirm the status of filings. Filers should not wait until the last minute to make a time-sensitive filing. Adjustments to filing dates of "late" filings are granted only for the circumstances set forth in Rule 13(b) of Regulation S-T.

● Use the correct EDGAR submission type. The SEC staff, upon written request from the registrant, can correct some, but not all, erroneous submission types. Sometimes the registrant must formally withdraw and resubmit the filing. All requests for changes of submission types must be from the filer.

● Follow the procedures of Rule 3a of the SEC's Informal and Other Procedures in making fee payments. Filers should allow time for wire transfers prior to filing. EDGAR will not accept filings requiring fees until the fee payments are received. Include the correct CIK number when making check or wire payment.

● Make sure the submission contains the text of the correct document (and not an earlier draft or different document).

● Confirm the status of the filings after transmitting them to the SEC. The staff may grant filing date adjustments under Rule 13(b) of Regulation S-T as warranted for Exchange Act reports, but generally will not adjust a filing date over an extended period of time. It is not staff policy to grant filing date adjustments for Securities Act registration statements or other transactional filings since shareholder rights may be affected.

● Carefully read the message sent by EDGAR in response to each submission. If a filer uses an Internet address for notification, the filer should carefully read all filing acceptance and suspension notices. If a message does not include a FILING DATE, then an official filing has not been made.

● Do not file material intended for confidential treatment on EDGAR. All material submitted via EDGAR is made public, except that cover letters and correspondence are nonpublic to the extent described immediately below.

● Submit all correspondence related to an electronic filing via EDGAR, and include cover letters with submissions of public filings whenever appropriate. Cover letters submitted under document type "COVER" and correspondence submitted under document type "CORRESP" are treated initially as nonpublic and are not immediately disseminated. The SEC staff may release all or parts of these documents electronically if they relate to the staff's review process not less than 45 days after the staff completes a filing review. Include a typed letterhead on cover letters and correspondence, because printed letterheads on company or firm stationery will not appear in EDGAR documents.

● Label exhibits as indicated in Appendix C of the EDGAR Filer Manual.

● Make sure all co-registrants are listed in the header of the submission. Each co-registrant needs its own CIK and CCC numbers.

O. XBRL Interactive Data Disclosures.

eXtensible Business Reporting Language ("XBRL") is an Extensible Markup Language-based standard for use in business and financial reporting that was developed and is supported by XBRL International, a not-for-profit consortium of approximately 550 companies and agencies worldwide. XBRL is an open source standard developed to assist in the automatic processing of business and financial reporting data and to define and name such data and text through tags. XBRL tags give business and financial reporting data an identity and context, and organize it in a format that can be more easily read by software programs and analyzed across multiple companies and time periods. XBRL tags consist of:

● specific financial data, such as the line items presented in the financial statements; and

● words or labels, such as headers in the notes to the financial statements.

The SEC has expressed optimism that XBRL tagged data may enable registrants, as well as investors and regulators, to more easily examine the component parts of financial statement line items and view elements of the line items that are found in the notes to the financial statements. Moreover, XBRL tagged data may generally improve the ability to search for and locate particular data items by simply calling up the specified tags.

Taxonomies are the "dictionaries" used by XBRL, as they define the specific tags for individual items of data (such as "net profit"). Different taxonomies are required for different financial reporting purposes. XBRL International has established a Taxonomy Recognition Task Force to review and evaluate submitted taxonomies, and recognition of taxonomies by XBRL International is divided between those that are Approved (i.e., those that have to comply with the official XBRL guidelines for that type of taxonomy, as well as with the XBRL Specification) and those that are Acknowledged (i.e., those that just have to comply with the XBRL Specification). A list of the Approved and Acknowledged taxonomies can be found at http://www.xbrl.org/Taxonomies/, and a description of the process for taxonomy recognition can be found at http://www.xbrl.org/TaxonomyRecognition/. In 2006, the SEC contracted with XBRL U.S., XBRL International's U.S. jurisdiction representative, to develop the standard list of tags necessary for financial reporting in an interactive format consistent with U.S. generally accepted accounting principles ("GAAP") and SEC regulations.

The SEC has acknowledged that while the content of the standard taxonomies is based on generally accepted accounting principles and registrant disclosure practices, the taxonomies are not intended to be accounting standards or to require changes to current accounting standards or the content of reported information.

On February 3, 2005, the SEC adopted amendments to Regulation S-T that permitted voluntary submission of supplemental exhibits using XBRL for the purpose of allowing registrants, the SEC and others to test and evaluate tagging technology (see SEC Release No. 33-8529). In 2007, the SEC extended the program to enable mutual funds to voluntarily submit in interactive data format supplemental information contained in the risk/return summary section of their prospectuses.

Building on the voluntary filer program, on January 30, 2009, the SEC issued a final rule release requiring certain companies to make financial disclosures using the XBRL format (see SEC Release Nos. 33-9002 and 33-9002A). Subject filers are still required to file their financial statements using ASCII or HTML, but are also required to accompany these filings with an interactive data file in XBRL format (the "Interactive Data File"). In connection with its release, the SEC revised several rules contained in Regulation S-T and also added Rules 405 and 406T thereto. The phase-in schedule for meeting these requirements required domestic and foreign filers using U.S. GAAP (including smaller reporting companies), and all foreign private issuers that prepare their financial statements in accordance with International Financial Reporting Standards ("IFRS"), to comply with these requirements if the filing contains financial statements for fiscal periods ending on or after June 15, 2011. For new XBRL filers, the rules include two permissible grace periods. Under Rule 405(a)(2) of Regulation S-T, the initial XBRL exhibit will be required within 30 days after the earlier of the due date or filing date of the related report or registration statement. In year two, a filer will have a similar 30-day grace period for its first XBRL exhibit that includes detail-tagging of its footnotes and schedules. Assuming the exhibits are filed by amendment (e.g., a Form 10-K amendment), and assuming the sole purpose of such amendment is to include the Interactive Data File as Exhibit 101, the filer should include the cover page, an explanatory note, the signature page, an exhibit index, and Exhibit 101.[27]

A filer may not rely on Exchange Act Rule 12b-25 to extend the due date of an Interactive Data File.[28]

Rule 405 requires the Interactive Data File to consist of a complete set of information for all periods required to be presented in the corresponding filing (i.e., it is not permissible for the Interactive Data File to present only partial fact financial statements, such as by excluding comparative financial information

---

[27] See SEC's Division of Corporation Finance Compliance and Disclosure Interpretations–Interactive Data–Question 130.01 (May 29, 2009).

[28] See SEC's Division of Corporation Finance Compliance and Disclosure Interpretations–Interactive Data–Question 135.11 (May 29, 2009).

for prior periods).[29] The Interactive Data File will be identifiable as Exhibit 101 to the corresponding filing.[30] Financial statement footnotes and financial statement schedules initially will be tagged individually as a block of text, but after a year of such tagging, a filer will be required to tag the detailed quantitative disclosures within the footnotes and schedules and will be permitted, but not required, to tag each narrative disclosure.[31] Filers with corporate websites are required to provide the Interactive Data File on their websites no later than the end of the calendar day on the earlier of the date the Interactive Data File is submitted or is required to be submitted, and such data must remain posted on the website for at least 12 months.[32] Although the filer cannot comply with this requirement by providing a hyperlink on its website to the SEC's website, the filer may comply with this requirement by providing a hyperlink on its website directly to the Interactive Data File if the Interactive Data File is made available in the required time frame and access to the Interactive Data File is free of charge to the user.[33]

Rule 406T of Regulation S-T addresses liability for Interactive Data Files, and provides that they are subject to the same liability provisions as the corresponding filing, except for certain exceptions with respect to Interactive Data Files submitted to the SEC less than 24 months after the filer first was required to submit an Interactive Data File (but no later than October 31, 2014). During this time period, Interactive Data Files will be:

● deemed not filed or part of a registration statement or prospectus for purposes of Sections 11 or 12 of the Securities Act, deemed not filed for purposes of Section 18 of the Exchange Act or Section 34(b) of the Investment Company Act, and otherwise not subject to liability under these sections; and

● protected from liability for failure to comply with the tagging requirements if the Interactive Data File failed to meet those requirements despite the filer's good faith effort, and the filer corrected the failure promptly after becoming aware of it. "Promptly" is defined in Rule 11 of Regulation S-T as meaning "as soon as reasonably practicable under the facts and circumstances at the time. An amendment to the Interactive Data File made by the later of 24 hours or 9:30 a.m. Eastern Time, whichever is currently in effect, on the next business day after the electronic filer becomes aware of the need for such amendment shall be deemed to be 'promptly' made."

If a filer voluntarily submits an Interactive Data File before it "first was required to submit" such file for purposes of Rule 406T(d) of Regulation S-T,

---

[29] Rule 405(b) of Regulation S-T.
[30] Rule 601(b)(101) of Regulation S-K.
[31] Rule 405(f) of Regulation S-T.
[32] Rule 405(g) of Regulation S-T.

[33] See SEC's Division of Corporation Finance Compliance and Disclosure Interpretations–Interactive Data–Question 130.09 (September 14, 2009).

such voluntary submission does not start the rule's 24-month modified liability period.[34]

Interactive Data Files are excluded from the officer certification requirements under Rules 13a-14 and 15d-14 under the Exchange Act. However, in complying with (i) the requirement of Rules 13a-15 and 15d-15 under the Exchange Act that officers evaluate the effectiveness of the filer's disclosure controls and procedures, and (ii) the requirement of Item 307 of Regulation S-K that the filer disclose the officers' conclusions regarding the effectiveness of those disclosure controls and procedures, the officers must include consideration of the controls and procedures with respect to Interactive Data Files.[35]

On June 15, 2011 the staff of the SEC's Division of Risk, Strategy, and Financial Innovation published observations regarding filers' compliance with the SEC's rules concerning interactive data for financial reporting. The staff identified some of the most common and significant issues contained in interactive data submissions based on filings made in early 2011, which included 10-Ks from large accelerated filers, the largest of which provided detailed tagging of notes to the financial statements. The staff also reiterated its view that the rendered version of interactive data (XBRL) financial statements need not look exactly the same as HTML financial statements, emphasizing the primacy of quality, completeness and accuracy of tagging over the formatting and appearance of XBRL financial statements.

One of the most common errors filers make in interactive data submission, according to the staff's observations, is to incorrectly enter an amount with a negative value. The staff indicated that while a number may be presented as negative in HTML filings (such as a credit), numbers should almost always be tagged as positive numbers in XBRL submissions. The staff has provided examples of language in certain elements that can be entered as negative.

The staff's observations also included guidance regarding the propriety of extending elements in interactive data submissions versus using a GAAP element from the SEC's standard taxonomy. The staff also expressed concern that filers choose the most appropriate tag, ensuring that there is not a broader or narrower tag that would be more appropriate. The full text of the staff's observations from its review of interactive data financial statements can be found on the SEC's website.[36]

---

[34] See SEC's Division of Corporation Finance Compliance and Disclosure Interpretations–Interactive Data–Section 131. Rule 406T–Question 131.01 (September 17, 2010).

[35] See SEC's Division of Corporation Finance Compliance and Disclosure Interpretations—Exchange Act Rules— Questions and Answers of General Applicability—Section 162. Rule 13a-15 —Question 162.01 (May 29, 2009).

[36] See Staff Observations From Review of Interactive Data Financial Statements (June 15, 2011), available at http://www .sec.gov/spotlight/xbrl/staff-review-obser vations-061511.shtml.

CHAPTER 5

USING THE SAFE HARBOR FOR FORWARD-LOOKING STATEMENTS

A. Introduction.

On December 22, 1995, the Private Securities Litigation Reform Act of 1995 (the "PSLRA") was enacted.[1] The PSLRA created a new statutory safe harbor intended to reduce the risk of liability under the securities laws for issuers that voluntarily choose to make certain types of "forward-looking statements."[2] Provisions creating the new safe harbor were added as Section 27A to the Securities Act and as Section 21E to the Exchange Act. Registrants should take full advantage of the safe harbor when preparing Form 10-Ks and Annual Reports. For example, the Letter to Shareholders in an Annual Report often contains statements of management's goals, objectives and expectations. The safe harbor can help to protect these historically vulnerable forward-looking statements from securities fraud claims.

The statutory safe harbor was intended to provide significantly greater protection than the safe harbor available under Rule 175 under the Securities Act and Rule 3b-6 under the Exchange Act. As a result, public companies have significantly altered their disclosure policies and procedures, especially for "forward-looking statements," whether made in a public filing, press release or conversation with an analyst or institutional investor.

B. Description of the Safe Harbor.

The safe harbor provision of the PSLRA provides that a public company shall not be liable with respect to any forward-looking statement, whether written or oral, if and to the extent that the forward-looking statement (a) is "identified as a forward-looking statement, and is accompanied by meaningful cautionary statements identifying important factors that could cause actual results to differ materially from those in the forward-looking statement"; (b) is immaterial; or (c) is not proven by the plaintiff to have been made with actual knowledge that the statement

---

[1] Pub. L. No. 104-67, 109 Stat. 737 (1995).

[2] The federal safe harbor may not apply to state securities fraud lawsuits.

was false or misleading. Although these three independent tests for satisfying the safe harbor are included in the PSLRA, the second test relating to materiality is merely a codification of the prior common law.[3] The PSLRA specifically provides that the safe harbor provisions do not themselves impose a duty to update forward-looking statements. Notwithstanding this provision, many registrants include in their safe harbor statements an affirmative statement that, except as expressly required by federal securities laws, the registrants assume no obligation to publicly update or revise their forward-looking statements or the factors that could cause results to differ materially from those in the forward-looking statements.

C. Who Is Eligible for the Protection of the Safe Harbor?

Those eligible for protection under the PSLRA are: (i) a registrant that is an Exchange Act reporting company at the time that a forward-looking statement is made; (ii) a director, officer or employee of such a registrant; (iii) an outside reviewer retained by, and making a forward-looking statement on behalf of, such a registrant; and (iv) an underwriter making such a statement on the basis of information provided by such a registrant (or derived from information provided by such a registrant). The safe harbor is not available to certain securities laws violators and certain categories of issuers (e.g., "blank check" companies and "penny stock" issuers), most notably investment companies, partnerships and limited liability companies. In addition, the safe harbor does not provide protection to certain forward-looking statements, including those that are "included in a financial statement prepared in accordance with generally accepted accounting principles (GAAP)."[4]

D. What Is a Forward-Looking Statement?

The first element of the safe harbor requires the identification of forward-looking statements. A "forward-looking statement" is broadly defined to include statements addressing:

● projections of revenues, income (loss), earnings (loss) per share, capital expenditures, dividends, capital structure or other financial items;

---

[3] See *Slayton v. American Express*, 2010 WL 1960019 (2d Cir. May 18, 2010), where the court confirmed the disjunctive nature of the three tests. However, in *Lormand v. U.S. Unwired, Inc.*, 2009 WL 941505, at *14 (5th Cir. Apr. 9, 2009), the Fifth Circuit applied the safe harbor in the conjunctive, rejecting a safe harbor defense because plaintiff had adequately pled defendants' actual knowledge and noting that, even if the plaintiff had failed to plead actual knowledge, "the safe harbor provision still would not apply here, because the alleged misrepresentations are not accompanied by 'meaningful cautionary language.'"

[4] In *Slayton*, 2010 WL 1960019, the Second Circuit held that the safe harbor applied to forward-looking statements within MD&A based on both the text and legislative history of the PSLRA, which indicates that Congress understood financial statements and MD&A to be distinct, and based on the different treatment of financial statements and MD&A in SEC rules.

● plans and objectives of management for future operations, including plans or objectives related to the products or services of the registrant;

● future economic performance, including any such statement contained in a Management's Discussion and Analysis of Financial Condition and Results of Operations section;

● assumptions underlying or relating to any statement described in the items above;

● any report issued by an outside reviewer (e.g., accounting firm) retained by a registrant to the extent that such report assesses a forward-looking statement made by the registrant; and

● projections or estimates of such other items as the SEC may specify.

Statements that reflect a registrant's current expectations and projections about its future results, performance, prospects and opportunities are clearly forward-looking. In addition, it is fair to assume that any information that does not constitute historical or present facts may be regarded as forward-looking. Registrants usually state that they have tried to identify forward-looking statements by using words such as "will," "may," "expect," "anticipate," "believe," "intend," and similar expressions.

E. What Is a "Meaningful Cautionary Statement"?

Once it is established that there are forward-looking statements, the next requirement is that such statements have been accompanied by a "meaningful cautionary statement." On the one hand, the legislative history of the PSLRA notes that only "important factors" need to be identified, but not "all factors" or "the particular factor that ultimately causes the forward-looking statement not to come true." On the other hand, the legislative history is clear that boilerplate warnings do not qualify as "meaningful cautionary statements."[5] Rather, the

---

[5] See *Southland Sec. Corp. v. Inspire Ins. Solutions, Inc.,* 365 F.3d 353, 372 (5th Cir. 2004), where meaningful cautionary language was defined as "substantive company-specific warnings based on a realistic description of the risks applicable to the particular circumstances, not merely a boilerplate litany of generally applicable risk factors." See also *In re Nash Finch Co. Sec. Litig.,* 2007 WL 1266658 (D. Minn. May 1, 2007), where the court noted that the Eighth Circuit had not yet addressed the question of "whether allegations of actual knowledge defeat the safe harbor when cautionary language is present." In addition, see *Asher v. Baxter International Incorporated,* 377 F.3d 727 (7th Cir. No. 03-3189, July 29, 2004), where the Seventh Circuit denied the defendant corporation's motion to dismiss on the grounds that the defendant did not update its cautionary language even as its business risks changed and failed to mention in its cautionary language those sources of variance that (at the time of the projection) were the principal or important risks. See also *Employers Teamsters Local Nos. 175 and 505 Pension Trust Fund v. Clorox Co.,* 2004 WL 32963 (9th Cir. Jan. 7, 2004), where Clorox's Chief Financial Officer made statements to analysts that it would take approximately one year for Clorox to resolve problems arising from an acquired company's artificial inflation of

cautionary statements must convey "substantive information" about factors "relevant to the projections" that "realistically" could cause results to differ from those predicted. Therefore, registrants should (i) identify their forward-looking statements as specifically as possible, (ii) tailor their cautionary statements to particular forward-looking statements in order to make them "meaningful," and (iii) monitor and update their cautionary statements and risk factors to reflect new business developments, market conditions, and other risks associated with their businesses that could affect future results. Many registrants now include their cautionary statements in a separately identified section of the document. The headings for these sections include "Safe Harbor Statement Under the Private Securities Litigation Reform Act of 1995" and "Cautionary Note Regarding Forward-Looking Statements" and the disclosure usually cross-references the "Risk Factors" section in the Form 10-K. In tailoring the cautionary statements, management should attempt to qualify each forward-looking statement by identifying both the key assumptions on which it is based and the primary factors that are likely to impact the outcome of that prediction.

F. What Does "Accompanied by" Mean?

The requirement that the cautionary statement must "accompany" the forward-looking statement has received little attention by the courts. However, where cautionary language is adjacent or in close proximity to, or cross-references, the written forward-looking statement, such requirement should be met.[6] In an Annual Report, a registrant should consider placing a safe harbor legend at the end of the Letter to Shareholders or on the inside front cover of the Annual Report indicating that forward-looking statements have been included and cross-referencing to a discussion of cautionary factors later in the Annual Report.

(Footnote Continued)

short-term profits. The Ninth Circuit held that the Chief Financial Officer's disclaimer of certainty at the beginning of the analyst call, her reference to additional cautions in Clorox's Form 10-K and the indication that Clorox anticipated it would be losing money on a recent acquisition for several quarters were protected by the safe harbor because they were forward-looking statements accompanied by meaningful disclosures of caution identifying important factors that could lead to different results.

[6] Oral statements are treated differently and given more flexibility than written statements under the PSLRA. For oral statements, the speaker must identify the statement as forward-looking but need only refer to other "readily available" documents for the factors that could cause actual results to vary. For example, in quarterly conference calls to discuss earnings, many registrants will merely refer to risks and uncertainties included in their Exchange Act filings. Any document filed with the SEC is deemed to be "readily available."

G. Failure to Prove That the Forward-Looking Statement Was Made with Actual Knowledge of Its Falsity.

In the event that a forward-looking statement is not accompanied by cautionary statements or a court determines that the cautionary statements used do not qualify as "meaningful" under the PSLRA, the statutory safe harbor still provides protection if the plaintiff fails to prove (i) that the forward-looking statement was made with "actual knowledge" that it was "false and misleading," and (ii) if made by a business entity, that the forward-looking statement was made by, or with the approval of, an executive officer of the entity.

H. How Does the "Bespeaks Caution" Doctrine Relate to the PSLRA?

In crafting the safe harbor, Congress appears to have relied heavily on the judicially developed "bespeaks caution" doctrine, which has been adopted in recent years by a majority of the federal appellate courts. However, the PSLRA is not a codification or a substitute for the "bespeaks caution" doctrine. The "bespeaks caution" doctrine is premised on the assumption that, under certain circumstances, the qualifications surrounding a specific forward-looking statement sufficiently put an investor on notice of the risks of relying on the statement in making an investment decision such that any reliance on the unqualified truth of the statement would not be reasonable. Under such circumstances, the presence of cautionary statements renders the forward-looking statement immaterial as a matter of law. In applying the "bespeaks caution" doctrine, courts have generally required that the cautionary language be carefully tailored to the specific forward-looking statements at issue, sufficiently detailed to enable an investor to evaluate the risk that a forward-looking statement may not come true, and prominent enough to affect the "total mix" of the information available to the investor. To the extent that a prediction or estimate is based on particular assumptions, courts have generally required that those assumptions be disclosed. Until courts give more guidance on the meaning of such PSLRA phrases as "meaningful cautionary statements" and "important factors," prudence dictates that forward-looking statements be accompanied by cautionary language that would satisfy the still viable "bespeaks caution" doctrine.

I. What Are the Limits of Protection Under the Safe Harbor?

The PSLRA expressly provides that a person eligible to rely on the safe harbor provisions will not be liable in any private action brought under the Securities Act or the Exchange Act based on an allegation that a forward-looking statement that qualifies for protection under the safe harbor was false or misleading. However, only private actions are covered by the PSLRA. The statutory safe harbor does not affect either the ability of the SEC to proceed against a registrant in an injunctive or administrative proceeding on the basis of a forward-looking statement or the standards under which liability may be imposed in a proceeding brought by the SEC.

CHAPTER 6

THE FORM 10-K

A. Overview.

1. Purpose of the Form 10-K. The Form 10-K has become the central document in the SEC's integrated disclosure system. It provides a comprehensive annual update concerning the registrant's business and provides essential financial information. In addition, information contained in the Form 10-K is often incorporated by reference into, and therefore becomes a critical part of, registration statements on Forms S-3, S-4 and S-8 filed by registrants with the SEC to register the public offering of their securities under the Securities Act.

For many registrants, the Form 10-K has become the principal document through which to provide key information to their many constituencies. These constituencies include current and potential shareholders, employees, securities analysts, suppliers, customers, strategic partners and lenders. As a result of the general requirement that Form 10-Ks be filed electronically by EDGAR and the advancements in, and increased use of, Internet technology, each of these constituencies can obtain virtually immediate access to this information at no cost. For these reasons, registrants should consider the Form 10-K not merely as an annual obligation to provide the specific information required by Form 10-K, but also as an opportunity to provide their various constituencies with (1) a view of their achievements since the beginning of the last fiscal year, current strengths and goals for the future, and (2) an explanation of why certain undesirable events have occurred, or why certain expectations were not fulfilled, since the beginning of the last fiscal year.

The annual report to the SEC is filed on Form 10-K unless one of the following forms is prescribed: Form 11-K for employee benefits plans, Form 18-K for foreign governments and political subdivisions, Form 20-F for foreign private issuers or Form 40-F for certain Canadian issuers.

2. Summary of Contents of the Form 10-K. The Form 10-K is divided into four parts, plus a cover page and signature page. Part I of the Form 10-K requires a detailed overview of the registrant's business during the last fiscal year and is divided into six items:

● Item 1 requires a detailed description of the registrant's business;

● Item 1A requires a discussion of risk factors relating to the registrant's business;

● Item 1B requires disclosure of certain unresolved comments received from the SEC staff;

● Item 2 requires a description of the registrant's physical properties;

● Item 3 requires disclosure of certain material legal proceedings to which the registrant is a party or to which its property is subject; and

● Item 4 is reserved (it previously required information regarding matters submitted to a vote of the registrant's security holders during the fourth fiscal quarter).

Part II of the Form 10-K consists of eight items:

● Item 5 requires disclosure concerning the market price of the registrant's common equity securities, number of common equity holders and cash dividends declared on the registrant's common equity securities, as well as information concerning recent sales by the registrant of unregistered securities, the use of proceeds from the registrant's initial public offering and the registrant's repurchase of its equity securities;

● Item 6 requires disclosure in comparative columnar form of selected financial data for the registrant for certain fiscal years;

● Item 7 requires management's discussion and analysis of the registrant's financial condition and results of operations;

● Item 7A requires quantitative and qualitative disclosure about the registrant's market risk;

● Item 8 requires that financial statements of the registrant meeting the requirements of Regulation S-X be filed, along with certain supplementary financial information;

● Item 9 requires certain disclosures if the registrant's auditors have resigned or been dismissed during the two most recent fiscal years or any subsequent interim period;

● Item 9A requires disclosure of (i) the conclusions of the registrant's principal executive officer or officers and principal financial officer or officers, or persons performing similar functions, about the effectiveness of the registrant's disclosure controls and procedures based on their evaluation of these controls and procedures as of the end of the fiscal year covered by the report, (ii) any change in its internal control over financial reporting that occurred during the recently completed fourth fiscal quarter that has materially affected, or is reasonably likely to materially affect, the registrant's internal control over financial reporting, and (iii) management's annual report on internal control over financial reporting; and

● Item 9B requires disclosure of information that was required to be disclosed in a Form 8-K during the fourth quarter, but was not reported.

Part III of the Form 10-K, which many registrants incorporate by reference from their definitive annual meeting proxy statements, is divided into five items:

- Item 10 requires certain information concerning the registrant's directors, executive officers, significant employees and corporate governance practices and disclosure of delinquent filings under Section 16(a) of the Exchange Act (Forms 3, 4 and 5);

- Item 11 requires information concerning the registrant's compensation of certain of its executive officers and its directors, employment agreements with, and compensatory plans for, certain of its executive officers, and compensation committee interlocks and a report on executive compensation;

- Item 12 requires disclosure in tabular form of beneficial ownership of the registrant's equity securities by the registrant's directors, certain of the registrant's executive officers, beneficial owners of greater than 5% of any class of the registrant's voting securities and the registrant's directors and executive officers as a group, as well as a description of any arrangements that may result in a change in control of the registrant. The registrant must also include a table that discloses information about compensation plans that have been approved by security holders and compensation plans that have not been approved by security holders;

- Item 13 requires disclosure of certain relationships and transactions between the registrant and its directors, executive officers and certain other persons, as well as information regarding director independence; and

- Item 14 requires disclosure of fees paid to the principal auditor segregated into four categories (audit, audit-related, tax and all other fees), and disclosure of the audit committee's pre-approval policies and procedures.

Part IV of the Form 10-K consists solely of Item 15:

- Item 15 requires the listing and filing of all required financial statements, financial statement schedules and exhibits.

3. Timeliness and Scope of Disclosure. The information required to be disclosed in the Form 10-K, as summarized above, must be "given as of the latest practicable date," except where such information is required to be given for the fiscal year or as of a specified date.[1]

Example: A registrant's comparison of its results of operations for the past three fiscal years required by Item 7 of Form 10-K provides information for such fiscal years, while the registrant's identification of known trends, demands, commitments, events or uncertainties that will, or are reasonably likely to, materially affect its future financial condition or results of operations, which is also required by Item 7, is meant to address information known as of the time of filing the Form 10-K, even if not known as of the end of the last fiscal year.

---

[1] Form 10-K, General Instruction C(2).

In addition, the SEC cautions that in connection with the preparation of the Form 10-K, in addition to the information expressly required to be included in the Form 10-K, any additional material information necessary to make the required statements, in light of the circumstances under which they are made, not misleading should also be disclosed.[2]

Example: If a material event not expressly covered by any of the Form 10-K items has occurred since the beginning of the last fiscal year (e.g., the registrant's common stock is delisted from NASDAQ), the registrant should disclose that event in the Form 10-K.

B. Strategy on Completing the Form 10-K.

1. Prepare a Time and Responsibility Schedule. A detailed time and responsibility schedule is a key element of a registrant's required disclosure controls and procedures. The schedule is also critical to a smooth annual disclosure program because the timing of various events will have implications on the timing of other events. For example, the timing of the availability of the annual meeting proxy statement and Annual Report will have implications on the content of the Form 10-K and the timing of when to hold the annual meeting of shareholders. The timetable should provide a detailed list of obligations imposed by the SEC and pursuant to state corporate law. The timetable should:

- reflect all key dates relating to the annual meeting of shareholders, including record date, notice date and mailing date;

- show both target dates and deadlines for various SEC filings;

- allow for drafts of the Form 10-K to be circulated internally and to a registrant's independent auditors, audit committee, compensation committee and outside counsel enough time in advance of the targeted filing date to allow for meaningful review, comment and, if needed, revisions;

- allow for potential delays caused by shareholder proposals, SEC review, director and officer review and audit issues; and

- clearly assign responsibility for all tasks to the registrant's personnel, attorneys, accountants, transfer agent, etc.

Below is a sample timetable for a registrant that is a large accelerated filer incorporated in Delaware and listed on NASDAQ, with a December 31 fiscal year end:[3]

---

[2] Form 10-K, General Instruction C(3) and Rule 12b-20 under the Exchange Act.

[3] The sample timetable also assumes the registrant is using the full set delivery option to comply with the e-proxy rules. For those registrants that use the notice only option,

they will need to coordinate sending the notice of Internet availability to shareholders (and filing the notice with the SEC and posting proxy materials on a website) at least 40 calendar days prior to the Annual Meeting date (with intermediaries, such as brokers

TIMETABLE

DATE	ACTION REQUIRED	RESPONSIBLE PARTY
(2011) DECEMBER		
December 11	Deadline for receipt of shareholder proposals to be included in Annual Meeting Proxy Statement of XYZ Corporation ("XYZ") (120 days prior to the date corresponding to the date of XYZ's release of the prior year's proxy materials). *Rule 14a-8(e) under the Exchange Act.* Assumes 2011 proxy materials were sent out April 9, 2011.	XYZ
December 14– January 16	Review XYZ's disclosure controls and procedures and internal control over financial reporting. Nominating Committee to consider candidates to recommend for Board nomination.	XYZ
December 24	Confirm whether XYZ is an "accelerated filer" or a "large accelerated filer" based on XYZ's public float as of the last business day of the second calendar quarter of the preceding fiscal year.	XYZ
(2012) JANUARY		
January 4	XYZ's Disclosure Committee to begin assembling information for Annual Meeting Proxy Statement, including salary, bonus and perquisite data, equity incentive compensation data (stock options, etc.), beneficial ownership information and related transactions.	XYZ; Counsel
January 5	Provide Questionnaires to directors, nominees for director, executive officers and, if practical, greater than 5% shareholders (including, if applicable, biography from recent SEC filing to update).	XYZ; Counsel
January 6	Consult with Transfer Agent regarding solicitation procedures.	Counsel; Transfer Agent
January 12	Due diligence review of minute book and other corporate records.	XYZ; Counsel *continues*

(Footnote Continued)

and banks, being sent such notice enough time in advance so that they can turn around and provide the notice to shareholders within the 40-day deadline).

DATE	ACTION REQUIRED	RESPONSIBLE PARTY
January 20	Deadline for XYZ to file with the SEC an objection to the inclusion of a shareholder proposal in its proxy materials. Objection must be filed not later than 80 days prior to the date XYZ files definitive proxy materials with the SEC. XYZ must also inform proponent shareholder of intention to omit proposals. *Rule 14a-8(j)(1) under the Exchange Act.* Assumes definitive proxy materials are filed with the SEC on April 9, 2012.	XYZ; Counsel
January 23	2011 year-end audit complete.	Auditor
January 26	Board meeting and adoption of directors' resolutions regarding Annual Meeting items, including fixing meeting date and record date, determining meeting site, appointing inspectors, and approving proxy materials and management proposals such as nominees for directorships, amendments to equity plans, ratification of auditors, etc. Record date must be not less than 10 days (May 1) and not greater than 60 days (March 12) before the Annual Meeting. *Section 213 of Delaware General Corporation Law ("DGCL").* Assumes Annual Meeting date is May 11.	XYZ
	Schedule meetings for Board and committees to provide input regarding applicable portions of Form 10-K and proxy materials (e.g., CD&A and audited financial statements) and review charters, codes, policies, independence, performance, committee qualifications, etc.	XYZ
	Choose printer for Annual Report and begin layout, including selection of photos and graphics.	XYZ
January 27	Release 2011 year-end results by press release. At end of press release disclose date of Annual Meeting. Keep in mind that timing of disclosing Annual Meeting date can affect deadline for shareholder proposals and director nominations. *See XYZ's Bylaws.*	XYZ
	Furnish or file Form 8-K incorporating press release filed with SEC as an exhibit via EDGAR.	Counsel
January 30	Conference call with analysts to discuss 2011 year-end results (open up the call to the public and webcast the call). *Regulation FD.*	XYZ

continues

DATE	ACTION REQUIRED	RESPONSIBLE PARTY
FEBRUARY		
February 2	Notify Transfer Agent, NASDAQ, depositaries and brokers of record date, Annual Meeting date and matters to be voted upon. Request omnibus proxies from depositaries. Request listing of participants from depositaries, together with omnibus proxy. Send search cards to brokers, banks and nominees regarding quantities of materials. Search must be commenced at least 20 business days prior to record date (February 13 deadline, assuming a March 12 record date). *Rule 14a-13 under the Exchange Act.*	XYZ; Transfer Agent
February 3	Deadline for return of Questionnaires from directors, director nominees, executive officers and greater than 5% shareholders.	Counsel
	Fill out Broadridge fiscal year-end form. Obtain printing quotes for Annual Report and proxy materials.	XYZ
	Compile required information for Schedule 13G (to be filed by greater than 5% shareholders) and Form 5 (if any) filings for executive officers and directors. Draft Schedule 13G (make sure each filer has EDGAR codes) and Form 5 filings for executive officers and directors.	Counsel
February 7	Distribute first draft of Form 10-K to XYZ and Counsel for review.	XYZ; Counsel
February 9	Distribute Schedule 13Gs and Form 5s for signature.	Counsel
February 13	File Schedule 13Gs and Form 5s with SEC via EDGAR.	Counsel
	Revise Form 10-K per comments from XYZ and Counsel and distribute 2nd draft of Form 10-K to XYZ and auditors for review.	XYZ; Counsel
February 14	Deadline for applicable filers to file Schedule 13Gs and Form 5s.	Counsel
February 16	Finalize responses to shareholder proposals, if any. Finalize arrangements re meeting site.	XYZ; Counsel
February 17	Prepare first draft of Annual Report (without financials), including Letter to Shareholders; send to printer for first proof.	XYZ
	Revise Form 10-K per comments received from XYZ, Counsel and Auditors.	*continues*

DATE	ACTION REQUIRED	RESPONSIBLE PARTY
February 20	Distribute first draft of proxy materials and Annual Report, including notice of Internet availability of information; CD&A; Audit Committee report; and performance graph, to XYZ, Counsel and Auditors for review.	XYZ; Counsel
	Distribute 3rd draft of Form 10-K to XYZ, Counsel, Auditors and Board for review and signature.	
February 24	Revise proxy materials per comments received from XYZ, Counsel and Auditors.	XYZ; Counsel
February 27	Distribute 2nd draft of proxy materials and Annual Report to XYZ, Counsel and Board for review.	XYZ; Counsel
	File Form 10-K with SEC via EDGAR. Annual Report must be filed as an exhibit to Form 10-K if Form 10-K will incorporate by reference financial statements and other information included in the Annual Report.	XYZ; Counsel
February 29	Deadline to file Form 10-K with SEC via EDGAR.	XYZ
MARCH		
March 12	**RECORD DATE FOR MAY 11, 2012 ANNUAL MEETING.** Check with depositaries as to status of omnibus proxies (counsel to retain copies, send originals to Transfer Agent). Finalize count regarding necessary quantities of proxy materials and Annual Reports.	XYZ; Counsel
March 13	Deadline for submission of shareholder proposals, or nominations for Board of Directors, to be brought up at Annual Meeting. Proposals must be received not later than the later of (i) 60 days (March 12) prior to the Annual Meeting (May 11) or (ii) 10 days following public disclosure of the Annual Meeting date (disclosure scheduled for January 27). See XYZ's Bylaws.	XYZ; Counsel
March 16	File preliminary proxy materials with SEC via EDGAR if shareholders are voting on matter(s) other than election of directors, ratification of auditors and approval of stock incentive plans. Rule 14a-6(a) under the Exchange Act. A minimum of 10 days must be allowed between filing preliminary and definitive proxy materials during which period the SEC staff will decide whether to review the proxy materials. Keep in mind	XYZ; Counsel

continues

DATE	ACTION REQUIRED	RESPONSIBLE PARTY
	that the SEC could take a number of days after such 10-day period to review the preliminary proxy materials and issue comments to be addressed in an amended filing. Therefore, XYZ must leave enough time between filing preliminary proxy materials and deadline for filing definitive proxy materials if XYZ intends to incorporate by reference Part III information into Form 10-K.	
March 19	Prepare drafts of ballots, script (including discussion of contingencies), agenda, report of inspector of elections, affidavit of mailing of meeting notice and report of voting results. Plan presentation for Annual Meeting. Discuss with Transfer Agent, Auditor, Board, etc., respective roles at Annual Meeting.	XYZ; Counsel
March 23	Produce mailing labels for nominee list. Obtain certified listing of shareholders as of record date.	Transfer Agent; Broadridge
	Tabulate and verify nominee holder requests and check against reports from securities depositaries.	XYZ
	Provide Transfer Agent with necessary quantities of Annual Report and proxy materials for distribution commencing April 9. Transfer Agent must have materials at least one week in advance of mail date. Distribute proof of Annual Report to XYZ working group.	XYZ; Counsel
APRIL		
April 2	Send proxy materials to printer, including definitive proxy statement and proxy card.	XYZ; Counsel
April 6	Print proxy statement and imprint proxy cards.	Printer; Transfer Agent
	Annual Report available from printer. Send from printer to Transfer Agent, Broadridge and XYZ.	Printer; XYZ; Transfer Agent
April 9	Mail to shareholders proxy materials and Annual Report. *Rule 14a-3(b) under the Exchange Act.* Annual Reports may also be required to be delivered to other security holders, including option holders. Written notice, which will be part of the proxy materials, must be given to shareholders not less than 10 days (May 1) nor more than 60 days (March 12) prior to the Annual Meeting (May 11). *DGCL Section 222.*	Counsel; Transfer Agent

continues

DATE	ACTION REQUIRED	RESPONSIBLE PARTY
	Definitive proxy statement must be filed with the SEC via EDGAR not later than the time at which it is being sent to shareholders. *Rule 14a-6(b) under the Exchange Act.*	XYZ; Counsel
	Proxy materials and Annual Report must be posted on website at or prior to the time XYZ sends notice (within the proxy materials) to stockholders that the proxy materials and Annual Report are available on the Internet.	XYZ
	Seven (7) copies of the Annual Report must be delivered to SEC (solely for informational purposes) not later than the date on which Annual Report is sent to shareholders or on the date definitive proxy materials are filed with SEC, whichever is later. *Rule 14a-3(c) under the Exchange Act.* Three (3) copies of the Annual Report must be provided to NASDAQ.	XYZ; Counsel; Auditor
April 23	Release first quarter 2012 results by press release.	XYZ
	Furnish or file Form 8-K incorporating press release filed as an exhibit via EDGAR with SEC.	Counsel
April 24	Conference call with analysts to discuss first quarter 2012 results (open up the call to the public and webcast the call).	XYZ
April 30	Deadline to file definitive proxy statement with SEC via EDGAR (120 days after end of fiscal year) or to amend Form 10-K to include Part III information incorporated by reference to Form 10-K from proxy statement. *Form 10-K, General Instruction G(3).*	XYZ
MAY		
May 1	At least 10 days prior to meeting, a complete list of shareholders entitled to vote must be made available for examination at a place within the city where the meeting is to be held. Shareholder list must also be available for review by stockholders during the Annual Meeting. *DGCL Section 219(a).*	XYZ; Counsel; Transfer Agent
May 7-10	Review tabulation of votes and confirm execution of proxies by nominees.	XYZ; Transfer Agent; Broadridge
May 8	Finalize and rehearse script and preparation for meeting. Review questions that may be asked. Discuss information not to be disclosed. Review policy regarding financial projections/results. Finalize agenda, checklist and ballots. Consider opening up Annual Meeting attendance to public and/or allowing public to attend by conference call/webcast to avoid any Regulation FD violations.	XYZ

continues

DATE	ACTION REQUIRED	RESPONSIBLE PARTY
May 10	Deadline for filing Form 10-Q for quarter ended March 31, 2012, with SEC via EDGAR.	XYZ; Counsel
	Prepare to bring to Annual Meeting affidavit of mailing, certificate of inspector, oath of inspector of elections, extra ballots, shareholder list, binder for shareholder sign-in, name badges, take-home materials (proxy materials, Form 10-K, Annual Report).	XYZ
May 11	**ANNUAL MEETING DATE.** Set up audiovisual equipment, security, vote-tabulating area, check room and shareholder list. Review procedures with chairman, inspectors, accountants, lawyers, speakers, etc.	XYZ; Counsel; Auditor; Transfer Agent
	Board of Directors meeting before and after Annual Meeting.	
May 17	Deadline for filing Form 8-K with SEC via EDGAR to report the preliminary voting results of the Annual Meeting pursuant to Item 5.07 of Form 8-K.[4]	XYZ; Counsel
JUNE		
June 7	Final report with respect to tabulation of votes by inspectors.	Transfer Agent
June 13	Deadline for filing an amended Form 8-K with SEC via EDGAR to report the final voting results of the Annual Meeting pursuant to Item 5.07 of Form 8-K.	XYZ; Counsel

2. Review Any Changes Affecting Disclosure in the Form 10-K. Prior to preparing the Form 10-K, counsel should closely review any changes from the prior year to the Form 10-K disclosure requirements and SEC rules and regulations referenced therein (whether adopted or proposed), as well as concept releases, interpretive releases, policy statements and staff legal and accounting bulletins and Compliance and Disclosure Interpretations issued by the SEC during the prior year. Certain information required to be disclosed in prior years' Form 10-Ks may no longer be necessary or additional information may need to be disclosed in the current Form 10-K. Counsel should also review any recent or proposed changes to financial accounting standards that have affected or will in the future affect the registrant's financial statements.

---

[4] See also footnote 31 regarding amending such Form 8-K to report a registrant's decision on how often to hold say-on-pay votes.

Any relevant changes, releases and bulletins should be discussed with those persons responsible for the applicable disclosures.

3. Determine Whether Incorporation by Reference Will Be Used. A fundamental issue that must be decided by all registrants is whether and to what extent incorporation by reference will be used in completing the Form 10-K. As a result of the incorporation by reference rules, a registrant could provide substantially all of its Form 10-K disclosure in its Annual Report (Form 10-K, Items 1-9B) and annual meeting proxy statement (Form 10-K, Items 10-14).[5] This would allow the Form 10-K to consist merely of a facing page, any information required by Part IV of Form 10-K, a signature page and a cross-reference sheet setting forth the item numbers and captions in Parts I, II and III of Form 10-K and the page(s) in the referenced materials where the corresponding information appears.[6] It is common for registrants to incorporate by reference information for Part III of the Form 10-K from their annual meeting proxy statements because it allows more time for the registrants to collect such information (the proxy statements can be filed 30 days[7] after the deadline for filing the Form 10-K, as discussed below) and avoids the expense of printing the same information twice. In addition, registrants sometimes incorporate by reference information for portions of Part I and, to a lesser extent, Part II of the Form 10-K from their Annual Reports for similar reasons.

Registrants must describe on the cover page of the Form 10-K the document (e.g., Annual Report and/or proxy statement) from which information will be incorporated by reference and the Part of the Form 10-K into which such information will be incorporated.

Example: The following language would appear under the capitalized heading "Documents Incorporated by Reference":

Portions of the registrant's definitive proxy statement relating to the registrant's 2012 Annual Meeting of Shareholders to be filed hereafter are incorporated by reference into Part III of this Report on Form 10-K.

(a) When Is Incorporation by Reference into the Form 10-K Permitted? General Instruction G of the Form 10-K and Rule 12b-23 of the Exchange Act provide for the incorporation by reference of information in certain documents in answer or partial answer to required Items of the Form 10-K with the following limitations:

● Financial statements incorporated by reference must satisfy all the requirements called for by Form 10-K.

---

[5] Form 10-K, General Instructions G(2) and G(3).

[6] Form 10-K, General Instruction G(4).

[7] This period is longer for accelerated and large accelerated filers.

● Copies of any information or financial statement incorporated into the Form 10-K, or copies of the pertinent pages of the document containing such information, must be filed as an exhibit to the Form 10-K, except that portions of the proxy statement incorporated by reference in response to Part III of the Form 10-K need not be filed as exhibits.[8] However, if the definitive proxy statement will not be filed with the SEC within 120 days of the end of the registrant's fiscal year, the information required by Part III of the Form 10-K must be filed as part of the Form 10-K or, not later than the end of the 120-day period, as an amendment to the Form 10-K.[9]

● A registrant may not incorporate by reference from a document that incorporates information by reference from another document, or where such incorporation by reference would render the report incomplete, unclear or confusing.[10]

● Exhibits to the Form 10-K may be incorporated by reference from documents previously filed with the SEC, except that documents filed with the SEC under the Exchange Act more than five years prior may not be incorporated and must be refiled.[11] There is no time limit on the registrant's incorporation by reference of exhibits previously filed with a Securities Act registration statement and documents that the registrant specifically identifies by physical location by SEC file reference number, provided such materials have not been disposed of by the SEC pursuant to its Records Control Schedule.[12]

(b) Reasons Not to Incorporate by Reference. Registrants generally do not make full use of the incorporation by reference option for several reasons, including timing and liability considerations.

(1) Timing Considerations. Information contained in the Annual Report cannot be incorporated by reference into the Form 10-K unless the Annual Report has been completed. Because Annual Reports are often used by registrants as opportunities to market themselves to their shareholders and often contain photos, graphics and charts, they often are not completed prior to the deadline for filing the Form 10-K. In addition, those portions of an Annual Report that are incorporated by reference into the Form 10-K must be filed electronically by EDGAR as exhibits to the Form 10-K.[13] Where portions of the Annual Report are not incorporated by reference, the Annual Report need only be furnished to the SEC in paper form for informational purposes.[14]

---

[8] Form 10-K, General Instruction G(2), Note 2 and Rule 12b-23(b)(i) of the Exchange Act.

[9] Form 10-K, General Instruction G(3).

[10] Rule 12b-23(b) of the Exchange Act.

[11] Rule 411(c) of the Securities Act and Rules 24 and 80F of the SEC's Rules of Practice.

[12] See Rule 24 of the SEC's Rules of Practice and its Records Control Schedule.

[13] Item 601(b)(13) of Regulation S-K.

[14] Rules 14a-3 and 14c-3 of the Exchange Act.

Similarly, information with respect to Part III of the Form 10-K cannot be incorporated by reference from the definitive annual meeting proxy statement unless the proxy statement has been completed and filed with the SEC via EDGAR within 120 days of the end of the registrant's fiscal year.[15] If the registrant's annual meeting is being held far enough after the end of such 120-day period, then the registrant may not be able to mail the proxy materials at the time they are filed within such period because of the shareholder notice requirements for shareholder meetings under state corporate law.[16] If the proxy materials are mailed to shareholders a significant amount of time after they are filed with the SEC, the information may become outdated. Furthermore, a registrant may not be sure what proposals will be submitted to a shareholder vote in time to file definitive proxy materials with the SEC within the 120-day period. Also, if a registrant is required to file preliminary proxy materials with the SEC because a proposal other than the election of directors, ratification of auditors or adoption/amendment of a compensation plan is being voted on by shareholders, then the SEC review process may cause the registrant not to be in a position to file definitive proxy materials within the 120-day period. Lastly, if the registrant intends to file a registration statement on Form S-3 or S-4 after it files its Form 10-K for the prior fiscal year and incorporate by reference certain information from the Form 10-K, all of such information should either already be contained in the Form 10-K or if the Form 10-K incorporates by reference such information from the registrant's proxy statement, that proxy statement should be on file with the SEC prior to the applicable registration statement being declared effective by the SEC.

(2) Liability Considerations. To the extent that portions of an Annual Report are incorporated into a Form 10-K, it will be considered a "filed document" for purposes of Section 18 of the Exchange Act. Section 18 creates a private right of action for false or misleading documents filed with the SEC for a person who relies on such documents in connection with sales or purchases of securities. Thus, the disclosure in the Annual Report incorporated into the Form 10-K could be subject to liability under the Exchange Act. As mentioned above, because the Annual Report is often used as a marketing document, the registrant may describe its business in a more casual tone that could subject it to a greater risk of liability if such description is considered filed as part of the Form 10-K. Furthermore, the registrant's principal executive and financial officers must certify the Form 10-K and may be concerned about such certification covering future disclosure that is incorporated by reference.

In addition, incorporation by reference of the Annual Report into a Form 10-K may cause unintended liabilities under the Securities Act. For example, in

---

[15] Form 10-K, General Instruction G(3).

[16] For example, Delaware General Corporation Law ("DGCL") Section 222 does not allow written notice of shareholder meeting to be given to shareholders more than 60 days prior to the meeting.

many cases an S-3, S-4 or S-8 registration statement incorporates by reference information contained in a Form 10-K. If the Form 10-K in turn incorporates by reference information in the Annual Report, the Annual Report disclosure could be subject to liability under the Securities Act.

(c) Is Information Required to Be in Plain English? The risk factor, executive compensation, beneficial ownership, related party and corporate governance disclosure now required in a Form 10-K must comply with the plain English rules.[17]

4. Collection of Necessary Information. As part of a registrant's disclosure controls and procedures and to enable the chief executive officer and chief financial officer to provide the required certifications, the registrant and its chief executive officer and chief financial officer should assemble and examine information from a variety of sources in order to ensure that the disclosure contained in the registrant's Form 10-K is accurate, not misleading, relevant, complete, consistent and up to date. The following sources of information should be considered:

(a) Questionnaires. Questionnaires are a critical component of the annual disclosure process. For example, most registrants use "Directors' and Officers' Questionnaires" to solicit information from directors and executive officers (including former executive officers required to be included in the summary compensation tables in a registrant's Form 10-K and proxy statement). These questionnaires should also be given to nominees for director and, if practical, persons who are known to own of record or beneficially more than 5% of any class of the registrant's voting securities. The questionnaires serve as a critical source of information that is required to be disclosed by Items 10–13 of the Form 10-K or by the NYSE or NASDAQ (e.g., regarding independence). For example, Item 10 of the Form 10-K requires disclosure regarding compliance by the registrant's directors, executive officers and beneficial owners of more than 10% of the registrant's registered equity securities with Section 16(a) of the Exchange Act.[18] By obtaining a written representation from such persons in a questionnaire that no Form 5 is required, and by maintaining that representation for two years, the registrant need not identify those persons as having failed to file a Form 5.[19]

The form of questionnaire should be reviewed and updated annually to reflect any changes in disclosure required in the Form 10-K, proxy statement and Annual Report. For example, registrants should make sure that their Directors' and Officers' Questionnaires have been updated to address the recent disclosure requirements regarding directorships held by directors, nominees

---

[17] Rules 13a-20 and 15d-20 under the Exchange Act.

[18] Item 405 of Regulation S-K.

[19] Some registrants solicit this representation within the Directors' and Officers' Questionnaire, while others provide a separate Form 5 Questionnaire.

and executive officers, as well as legal proceedings to which such persons are subject, that are part of the proxy disclosure enhancements in SEC Release No. 33-9089 (December 16, 2009). The registrant should carefully review the completed questionnaires to ensure that all questions have been answered, and that such answers are consistent with facts known to the registrant. Many registrants will include with the questionnaire, where applicable, a copy of the recipient's most recent biography contained in an SEC filing of the registrant in order to allow the person completing the questionnaire to confirm the accuracy of such disclosure. This is because Item 10 of the Form 10-K requires disclosure of certain biographical information for the registrant's directors and executive officers.[20] A sample Directors' and Officers' Questionnaire is included as Appendix 6, a sample Supplement to Directors' and Executive Officers' Questionnaire for non-employee directors is included as Appendix 7, and a sample Form 5 Questionnaire is included as Appendix 8.

Questionnaires can also be used to make sure those providing the information for disclosure have thought about the key issues affecting their areas of responsibility. Questions should be asked regarding significant business developments, trends in the business, the impact of factors external to the business and critical accounting policies.

(b) Interviews with Management, Other Personnel and Outside Parties. Meetings with the registrant's officers, including heads of business units, and financial, accounting and human resources personnel should be conducted. These meetings provide good opportunities to question management and those in charge of, or significantly involved in, operations, financial reporting and executive compensation, to collect and verify information, and to seek clarification of items that are not understood. The Form 10-K should also be discussed with the registrant's audit committee, independent public accountant, outside legal counsel and compensation committee.

(c) Review of Registrant's Recent SEC Filings. The registrant's Form 10-Ks filed in recent years, as well as other recent Exchange Act filings by the registrant (e.g., Form 10-Qs, 8-Ks, etc.) and any registration statements filed by the registrant during the prior year under the Securities Act, should be examined to ensure consistent, complete disclosure and help identify changes from prior periods.

(d) Review of Competitor SEC Filings. A review of recent Exchange Act and Securities Act filings by competitors or companies in similar industries is useful in determining the scope of disclosure customary in the registrant's industry. For example, if a registrant's competitors are disclosing key statistics that are relevant to the business the companies are in, then the registrant should also consider disclosing that statistic for itself.

---

[20] Item 401 of Regulation S-K.

(e) Review of Recent Staff Comment Letters. Any comment letters received from the SEC staff in the last several years, along with related responses, should be reviewed to ensure that the disclosure in the Form 10-K addresses these comments and is consistent with any undertakings regarding future filings that the registrant has made to the SEC staff in its responses. The SEC publicly releases, free of charge, comment and response letters relating to disclosure filings made since August 1, 2004, that have been reviewed by the Division of Corporation Finance. The comment letters and response letters are released individually on a filing-by-filing basis through the EDGAR system at www.sec.gov. The SEC releases these letters no earlier than 45 days after the review of the disclosure filing is complete. See "How to Search for EDGAR Correspondence," available at http://www.sec.gov/answers/edgarletters.htm.

(f) Review of Minute Books and Other Corporate Records. Minutes of meetings of the board of directors, board committees and shareholders, as well as any board, committee or shareholder written consents and materials distributed with respect to such meetings and consents, should be reviewed. Litigation files, including all attorneys' responses to auditor requests for information concerning loss contingencies, and information provided to regulatory authorities (including FINRA, NYSE, NYSE Amex or NASDAQ) should be reviewed. Significant contracts should also be reviewed to make sure they are described correctly and for possible filing as exhibits to the Form 10-K.

(g) Review of Other Materials Concerning the Registrant. Other materials about the registrant issued, distributed or presented since the beginning of the last fiscal year that should be reviewed include press releases, earnings call transcripts, brochures, interim reports to shareholders, website information and materials presented to, and reports prepared by, securities analysts and rating agencies. This review will help ensure that a consistent story is being told by the registrant and that no material developments are omitted from the Form 10-K. Registrants should be particularly vigilant about ensuring that material information contained in press releases and earnings calls since the beginning of the last fiscal year is disclosed in the Form 10-K.[21] Reviewing analysts' reports also keeps the registrant informed about what information the market deems important.

Consistent with the SEC's recommendation in its August 29, 2002 Release, registrants should strongly consider establishing disclosure committees that prepare the Form 10-K, meet periodically to discuss the public disclosure of events, circumstances and conditions that have impacted, or are expected to impact, the registrant and help review and evaluate the registrants' disclosure controls and procedures and internal controls. This committee would report to

---

[21] See *In re Shared Medical Systems Corporation* (SEC Release No. 34-33632 (February 17, 1994)).

the chief executive officer and chief financial officer and could consist of the senior accounting officer who reports to the chief financial officer, the principal risk management officer, the general counsel, the chief investor relations officer and such other officers or employees as the registrant deems appropriate.

C. Preparing the Form 10-K.

1. The Cover Page. Information to be included on the cover page of the Form 10-K is prescribed by the Form. Areas on the cover page that require analysis and review are as follows:

(a) Well-Known Seasoned Issuer Status. The registrant must indicate by check mark whether it is a "well-known seasoned issuer" as defined in Rule 405 of the Securities Act. Well-known seasoned issuers are issuers who (i) are eligible to use Form S-3 or F-3 for a primary offering, (ii) as of a date within 60 days, have either $700 million of public common equity float or, with some exceptions, have issued $1 billion in registered non-convertible securities (other than common equity) in primary offerings for cash in the preceding three years and (iii) are current in their Exchange Act reports (other than certain items under Form 8-K) during the prior 12 months or such shorter period that the registrant has been a public filer.

(b) Voluntary Filer Status. The registrant must indicate by check mark whether it is not required to file reports pursuant to Section 13 or 15(d) of the Exchange Act. This lets investors know that a registrant is a voluntary filer (e.g., a company that completes a public offering under the Securities Act and continues to file Exchange Act reports even when no longer required under Section 15(d) and that may stop filing Exchange Act reports at any time, for any reason and without notice).

(c) Filing of Reports During Preceding 12 Months. The registrant must indicate by check mark whether (1) during the preceding 12 months it has complied with the filing requirements under Section 13 or 15(d) of the Exchange Act and (2) it has been subject to such filing requirements for the past 90 days. A "Yes" response will alert the registrant's shareholders that Rule 144 of the Securities Act is available to them as of the date of the Form 10-K for sales of the registrant's securities because as required, in some instances, by Rule 144, the registrant has been a reporting company for 90 days and is currently satisfying the public information requirements.[22] In

---

[22] Rule 144(c) under the Securities Act requires that the registrant has been subject to the reporting requirements of Section 13 of the Exchange Act for at least 90 days immediately preceding the sale of the securities and that the registrant has filed all required Exchange Act reports (other than Form 8-Ks) during the preceding 12 months (or for such shorter period that it has been a registrant). Non-affiliates need not comply with this requirement if at least one year has elapsed since the securities being sold were acquired from the registrant or an affiliate.

order to check "Yes," the registrant must confirm not only that all Form 10-Qs have been filed, but that all Form 8-Ks required to disclose certain events (e.g., changes of accountant, disclosure of certain acquisitions or dispositions, changes of control, etc.) have been filed. "Yes" can be checked even if filings were not timely filed. For example, if during the 12 months prior to a registrant's filing of a Form 10-K, the registrant filed a Form 8-K to disclose a significant acquisition six business days after the consummation of the acquisition (as opposed to within the four business days required by Item 2.01 of Form 8-K), the registrant could still check "Yes" on the cover of the Form 10-K. However, if as of the date of filing its Form 10-K, the registrant had still not filed its Form 8-K outside of the four business day period, then it would have to check "No" on the cover page (unless it is including the late Form 8-K information in Item 9B of Part II of the Form 10-K).[23]

A "No" response on the cover of the Form 10-K will also alert the SEC that the registrant cannot use a Form S-3 short-form registration statement.[24]

(d) Inclusion of XBRL Data. The registrant must indicate by check mark whether it has submitted electronically and posted on its corporate website, if any, every Interactive Data File required to be submitted and posted pursuant to Rule 405 of Regulation S-T during the preceding 12 months (or for such shorter period that the registrant was required to submit and post such files). Such file is financial disclosure included as an exhibit (often referred to as the XBRL exhibit) to the Form 10-K, Form 10-Q, certain Form 8-Ks and registration statements pursuant to Regulation S-K Item 601(101).[25]

(e) Disclosure of Delinquent Section 16 Filings. The registrant must indicate by check mark whether the Form 10-K contains (or, if applicable, the definitive proxy statement from which information incorporated by reference in Part III of the Form 10-K will contain) disclosure of delinquent filings under Section 16(a) of the Exchange Act. This disclosure of delinquent Form 3, 4 or 5 filings is specified pursuant to Item 405 of Regulation S-K and is included in Item 10 of the Form 10-K. The instruction to Item 10 makes it clear that such box is intended to facilitate Form 10-K processing and review and that failure to provide such indication will not create liability for violation of the federal securities laws. The space in the response should be checked only if (1) the registrant has completed its review of Section 16 filings made with respect to the past fiscal year and written representations regarding no Form 5s being required and (2) no Section 16 filing delinquencies are disclosed in the

---

[23] On the other hand, if this disclosure is meant to be consistent with Rule 144(c) under the Securities Act, such Rule excludes Form 8-Ks from the current reporting requirement and thus only looks at whether all Form 10-Qs and the Form 10-K have been filed within the past 12 months. See Note 1 to Rule 144(c).

[24] Form S-3, General Instruction I.A.

[25] The XBRL exhibit is now required for Form 10-Ks filed for fiscal years that end on or after June 15, 2011.

Form 10-K or no disclosure of such delinquencies will be incorporated by reference into the Form 10-K from the registrant's definitive proxy statement. If the registrant does not know at the time of filing its Form 10-K whether any delinquent filers will be identified in its proxy statement, the box should not be checked.

(f) **Large Accelerated, Accelerated or Non-Accelerated Filer or Smaller Reporting Company Status.** The registrant must indicate by check mark whether it is a "large accelerated filer," "accelerated filer," "non-accelerated filer" or "smaller reporting company" as defined in Rule 12b-2 of the Exchange Act.

(g) **Shell Company Status.** The registrant must indicate by check mark whether it is a shell company as defined in Rule 405 of the Securities Act and Rule 12b-2 of the Exchange Act. Shell companies are registrants that have (i) no or nominal operations and (ii) either (a) no or nominal assets, (b) assets consisting solely of cash and cash equivalents or (c) assets consisting of any amount of cash and cash equivalents and nominal other assets.

(h) **Disclosure of Market Value of Stock Held by Non-Affiliates of the Registrant.** The registrant must also state the aggregate market value of the voting and non-voting common equity held by non-affiliates of the registrant. The aggregate market value is based on the price at which the registrant's common equity was sold, or the average bid and ask prices of the registrant's common equity, as of the last business day of the registrant's most recently completed second fiscal quarter.

Rule 405 of the Securities Act defines an "affiliate" as a person that directly, or indirectly through one or more intermediaries, controls or is controlled by, or is under common control with, the person specified. A note to the cover page of the Form 10-K provides that if a determination as to whether a particular person or entity is an affiliate "cannot be made without involving unreasonable effort and expense, aggregate market value of the common stock held by nonaffiliates may be calculated on the basis of assumptions reasonable under the circumstances, provided that the assumptions are set forth in this Form."

Example: The following is an example of language regarding aggregate market value required to be disclosed on the cover of the Form 10-K:

> The aggregate market value of the registrant's voting stock held by non-affiliates of the registrant (assuming, for purposes of this calculation only, that the registrant's directors, executive officers and greater than 10% shareholders are affiliates of the registrant), based upon the closing sale price of the registrant's common stock on June 30, 2011, the last day of the registrant's most recently completed second fiscal quarter, was $792 million.

The aggregate market value calculation set forth on the cover of the Form 10-K will help alert the SEC as to whether the registrant (1) has become an accelerated filer and (2) is eligible to use a Form S-3 registration statement to register the issuance of securities by the registrant under the Securities Act without volume limitations. This is because becoming an accelerated filer and using the Form S-3 for primary offerings of securities without volume limitations are both contingent upon the aggregate market value of the voting and non-voting common equity held by non-affiliates of the registrant being at least $75 million.

2. Part I of the Form 10-K.

Item 1. Business. The registrant must furnish the information required by Item 101 of Regulation S-K, except that the discussion of the development of the registrant's business need only include developments since the beginning of the fiscal year for which the Form 10-K is being filed. Sections (a) through (d) of Item 101 require the following disclosures about the registrant's business:

(a) General Development of Business. This section requires disclosure of major changes in the operation of the registrant, including:

- any bankruptcy or similar proceedings with respect to the registrant or a significant subsidiary;

- any merger or consolidation involving the registrant or a significant subsidiary;

- the acquisition or disposition of material assets outside the ordinary course of business; and

- any material changes in the mode of conducting the business.

(b) Financial Information About Segments. This section requires that the registrant disclose and describe, for each of the registrant's last three fiscal years (or such shorter period that the registrant has been in business), certain financial information about the "segments" in which the registrant operates. If a registrant changes the structure of its internal organization in a manner that causes the composition of its reportable segments to change, the registrant must restate the corresponding information for earlier periods, including interim periods, unless it is impracticable to do so. Following a change in the composition of its reportable segments, a registrant must disclose whether it has restated the corresponding items of segment information for earlier periods. If it has not done so, it must disclose in the year in which the change occurs segment information for the current period under both the old basis and the new basis of segmentation, unless it is impracticable to do so. If the information provided conforms with generally accepted accounting principles ("GAAP"), the registrant may include in its financial statements a cross reference to this data instead of providing it in the financial statements. Conversely, the registrant may, and many do, cross-reference such segment information from the financial statements. Issues concerning segment presentation should be discussed with the registrant's auditors.[26]

(c) **Narrative Description of Business.** This section requires that the registrant describe the business done and intended to be done by it and its subsidiaries, focusing on the dominant segment or each reportable segment about which financial information is presented in the financial statements. To the extent that the following items are material to an understanding of the registrant's business taken as a whole, the description of each segment should include the principal products produced and services rendered by the registrant, the principal markets for, and methods of distribution of, the products and services and the status of a product or segment. The percentage of total revenue contributed by any class of similar products or services in each of the last three fiscal years is required to be disclosed if such products or services accounted for 10% or more of total revenues (15% if total revenues did not exceed $50 million annually in any of these three fiscal years). In addition, the registrant is required to disclose the name of each customer and its relationship with the registrant, if any, to whom sales accounted for 10% or more of the registrant's consolidated revenues if the loss of such customer would have a material adverse effect on the registrant and its subsidiaries taken as a whole.[27]

(d) **Financial Information About Geographic Areas.** This section requires that the registrant disclose and describe, for each of the registrant's last three fiscal years (or such shorter period that the registrant has been in business), certain financial information about geographic areas in which the registrant operates. For example, disclosure is required for revenues from external customers attributed to (1) the registrant's country of domicile, (2) all foreign countries, in total, from which the registrant derives revenues, and (3) any individual foreign country, if material. If providing the geographic information is impracticable, the registrant must disclose that fact. If the information provided conforms with GAAP, the registrant may include in its financial statements a cross reference to this data instead of providing it in the financial statements. Conversely, the registrant may, and many do, cross-reference such information from the financial statements.

(e) **Available Information.** This section requires a registrant to disclose the information required by paragraphs (e)(3) and (e)(4) of Item 101 of Regulation S-K if it is a large accelerated filer or an accelerated filer (as defined in Rule 12b-2 of the Exchange Act). Paragraph (e)(3) requires registrants that are large accelerated filers or accelerated filers to disclose their website address, if they have one, and other registrants are encouraged to disclose their website

---

[26] See Financial Accounting Standards Board ("FASB") Accounting Standards Codification ("ASC") Topic 280 and SEC Release No. 33-7620 (January 5, 1999).

[27] Item 101(c)(1)(vii) of Regulation S-K.

addresses, if available. To avoid incorporating by reference into the Form 10-K information on a registrant's website, the website address should be kept inactive in the Form 10-K filing so that a reader cannot directly hyperlink to such website by clicking on the address.

Paragraph (e)(4) requires registrants that are large accelerated filers or accelerated filers to disclose whether they make available free of charge on or through their websites (e.g., by a direct hyperlink), if they have them, their Form 10-K and other reports filed or furnished pursuant to Section 13(a) or 15(d) of the Exchange Act during the fiscal year covered by the Form 10-K, including exhibits thereto, as soon as reasonably practicable after they electronically file such material with, or furnish it to, the SEC (i.e., barring unforeseen circumstances, the same day as the filing). If the registrant does not make its filings available in this manner, it must also disclose:

● the reasons it does not do so (including, where applicable, that the registrant does not have a website); and

● whether the registrant will voluntarily provide electronic or paper copies of its filings free of charge upon request.

The SEC encourages registrants to provide ongoing, but at least 12 months', website access to their Form 10-Ks and other Exchange Act reports. The inclusion of a registrant's website address will not, by itself, include or incorporate by reference in the Form 10-K the information on the website, unless the registrant otherwise acts to incorporate such information by reference.[28]

Section 303A of the NYSE's listing standards also requires a registrant with securities listed on the NYSE to disclose in its Form 10-K (if it does not file an annual proxy statement) that its corporate governance guidelines, the charters of its most important committees (including at least the audit, compensation and nominating committees) and its code of business conduct and ethics are available on its website (and provide its website address).

Item 1A. Risk Factors. The registrant must set forth under the caption "Risk Factors," where appropriate, the risk factors described in Item 503(c) of Regulation S-K that are applicable to the registrant. The risk factor disclosure should describe the most significant factors that could adversely affect the registrant's business, operations, industry, financial position or future financial performance. This disclosure should be specific to the registrant (not boilerplate) and updated each year to account for new risks that are applicable to the registrant. In addition, the risk factor disclosure is required to be written in accordance with the same "plain English" standards as apply to prospectuses filed under the Securities Act.

---

[28] See SEC Release No. 33-8128 (September 5, 2002).

As described in Chapter 5, the Private Securities Litigation Reform Act of 1995 ("PSLRA") provides a safe harbor for forward-looking statements if they are identified as such and accompanied by meaningful cautionary statements identifying important factors that could cause actual results to differ materially from those in the forward-looking statements. As a result of the increased emphasis on forward-looking information and the protection afforded to such statements by the PSLRA, most registrants can now identify important factors that could cause actual results to differ materially from those in forward-looking statements in the Form 10-K by referencing the risk factor disclosure in their Form 10-Ks.

A registrant that files a Form S-3 registration statement (e.g., a shelf registration statement) should note that if its most recent Form 10-K contains up-to-date risk factors regarding the registrant and its industry, then it need not necessarily include such risk factors in such Form S-3 registration statement because it incorporates by reference such Form 10-K (instead it can focus on risk factors specific to the securities being registered and issued pursuant to the registration statement).

Item 1B. Unresolved Staff Comments. If the registrant is an accelerated filer or large accelerated filer as defined in Rule 12b-2 of the Exchange Act, or is a well-known seasoned issuer as defined in Rule 405 of the Securities Act, and has received written comments from the SEC staff regarding its Exchange Act reports, it must disclose the substance of any written comments that:

● the registrant believes are material;

● were issued more than 180 days before the end of the fiscal year to which the Form 10-K relates; and

● remain unresolved as of the date of the Form 10-K filing (comments that the registrant and SEC staff have agreed to address in future Exchange Act reports are considered to have been resolved).

This disclosure may provide other information, including the position of the registrant, with respect to any such comments.

Item 2. Properties. The registrant must furnish the information required by Item 102 of Regulation S-K. This Item requires a brief description of the location and general character of the principal plants, mines and other "materially important" physical properties of the registrant and its subsidiaries, including the segments that use the properties. For all properties that are not held in fee (e.g., leased), or that are held subject to a major encumbrance, a description of how the property is held is required. The description should include such information as reasonably will inform investors as to the suitability, adequacy, productive capacity and extent of utilization of the facilities by the registrant. This disclosure will vary considerably depending upon the importance of properties to the registrant's business. If a registrant has various facilities, the information can often be provided in tabular form. Detailed descriptions of the physical characteristics or legal descriptions of properties are not required. There are additional disclosure requirements for extractive enterprises, such as oil, gas or coal mining companies.

Item 3. Legal Proceedings. The registrant must furnish the information required by Item 103 of Regulation S-K. This Item requires a brief description of any material pending legal proceedings, other than ordinary routine litigation incidental to the registrant's business, to which the registrant or any of its subsidiaries is a party. Similar information is required for proceedings known to be contemplated by governmental authorities. As to any proceeding that was terminated during the fourth quarter of the fiscal year covered by the Form 10-K, information similar to that required by Item 103 of Regulation S-K, including the date of termination and a description of the disposition thereof with respect to the registrant and its subsidiaries, must be furnished.

Where disclosure is required, the following information must be provided:

- The name of the court or agency in which the proceedings are pending;

- The date instituted;

- The principal parties;

- A description of the factual basis alleged to underlie the proceedings; and

- The relief (e.g., amount of damages) sought.

The Instructions to Item 103 of Regulation S-K provide some specific guidance as to which proceedings are required to be described and those which may be excluded.

(a) Disclosure Not Required. The following proceedings are not required to be disclosed by this Item:

(1) Routine Business Litigation. If a business ordinarily results in actions for negligence or other claims, disclosure of such actions or claims is not required unless it departs from the normal kind of such actions.

(2) Immaterial Damages. Disclosure is not required for proceedings that involve primarily a claim for damages if the amount involved, exclusive of interest and costs, does not exceed 10% of the current assets of the registrant and its subsidiaries on a consolidated basis. However, if such proceeding presents in large degree the same legal and factual issues as other proceedings pending or known to be contemplated, the amount involved in such other proceedings must be included in computing the percentage.

(b) Disclosure Required. Notwithstanding the discussion above, the following proceedings are specifically required to be disclosed by this Item:

(1) Bankruptcy, Receivership, etc. Any material bankruptcy, receivership, or similar proceeding involving the registrant or any of its significant subsidiaries must be described.[29]

(2) Proceedings Between the Registrant and Specified Persons. Any material proceedings to which any director, officer or affiliate of the registrant or any beneficial holder of more than 5% of any class of the registrant's voting securities, or any associate of any such director, officer or affiliate, is a party which is adverse to the registrant or any of its subsidiaries must be disclosed. This could include a proceeding against an officer of the registrant that may require the registrant to indemnify the officer for damages if the exposure under the indemnification is material.

(3) Environmental Matters. Administrative or judicial proceedings arising under any federal, state or local provisions regulating the discharge of materials into the environment are specifically required to be disclosed if:

- Such proceeding is material to the registrant;

- Such proceeding involves primarily a claim for damages, or involves potential monetary sanctions, capital expenditures, deferred charges or charges to income and the amount involved, exclusive of interest or costs, exceeds 10% of the current assets of the registrant and its subsidiaries on a consolidated basis; or

- A governmental authority is a party to such proceeding, and it involves potential monetary sanctions, unless the registrant reasonably believes that such proceeding will result in no monetary sanctions, or in monetary sanctions, exclusive of interest or costs, of less than $100,000; provided, however, that such proceedings that are similar in nature may be grouped and described generically.

In preparing the legal proceedings disclosure, the following should also be considered:

- Proceedings in which the registrant or a subsidiary is a plaintiff or a defendant may be required to be disclosed.

- Where the plaintiff seeks damages in an amount that is material to the registrant and the registrant believes that the claim can be settled for a non-material amount, the registrant may describe the litigation with an indication of management's view of the claim.

- Any claim of indemnification, contribution or insurance coverage may be considered in determining materiality, but only if there are unlikely to be

---

[29] A "significant subsidiary" is defined in Rule 1-02(w) of Regulation S-X.

timing differences or questions regarding the ability to recover on the indemnification, contribution or insurance coverage.[30]

● Litigation threatened but not yet commenced by non-governmental (e.g., private) parties is not required to be disclosed under this Item but may be required to be disclosed in the MD&A as a known "contingency."

● Disclosure of any legal proceedings should be consistent with (i) any description of the related contingent liability contained in MD&A and financial statements and (ii) documents filed with any court or agency in which the proceeding is pending.

(c) IRS Penalties. The American Jobs Creation Act of 2004, through the creation of Section 6707A of the Internal Revenue Code, requires registrants to disclose penalties imposed on them by the IRS for failing to satisfy tax disclosure requirements regarding certain transactions that the IRS has identified as abusive.

Item 4. Reserved. This Item previously required disclosure of matters submitted to a vote of security holders through the solicitation of proxies or otherwise and whether at a meeting or by written consent during the fourth quarter of the registrant's fiscal year. Such disclosure is now required in Form 8-K.[31] The SEC has reserved this item number, however, in order to retain the overall current numbering so as to avoid confusion given references in professional literature to such current numbering.

3. Part II of the Form 10-K.

Item 5. Market Price for Registrant's Common Equity, Related Stockholder Matters and Issuer Purchases of Equity Securities. The information required to be disclosed under this Item is found in Items 201 and 701 of Regulation S-K.

(a) Market Price. Item 201(a) of Regulation S-K requires a registrant to disclose the following information:

● each principal U.S. securities exchange on which the registrant's common stock is traded (e.g., NASDAQ or the NYSE). Most registrants also indicate the trading symbols for their common stock on each such principal exchange and market. A registrant should disclose if it has dual

---

[30] See SEC Release No. 33-6835 (May 18, 1989) and Staff Accounting Bulletin No. 92 (June 8, 1993).

[31] Such disclosure in Form 8-K includes the number of votes cast for one, two and three years, as well as abstentions, for the say-on-frequency shareholders advisory vote (and within 150 days after the shareholders meeting, but no later than 60 days prior to the deadline for submissions of shareholder proposals under Rule 14a-8 under the Exchange Act, such Form 8-K must be amended to disclose the registrant's determination, in light of such vote, as to how frequently it will include a say-on-pay vote in its proxy materials).

class common stock and there is no established public trading market for one of the classes.

● for each quarter during the two most recent fiscal years (or such shorter period if the registrant became a public reporting company and listed on an exchange or quoted on a market within its past two fiscal years), the high and low sales or bid prices for the registrant's common stock on the principal exchange or market on which the common stock is traded. If a registrant has changed its principal exchange or market within the period for which it is required to disclose such market price range, the registrant should clarify which prices relate to each particular exchange/market. In addition, the registrant should adjust the high and low prices to give retroactive effect to any stock splits or reverse stock splits that have occurred during such time period so as to allow for comparability.

Example: The range of high and low sales or bid prices is often included in a table that looks like the following:

	High	Low
2011		
First Quarter	$	$
Second Quarter		
Third Quarter		
Fourth Quarter		
2010		
First Quarter		
Second Quarter		
Third Quarter		
Fourth Quarter		

(b) Holders. Item 201(b) of Regulation S-K requires the registrant to disclose the approximate number of holders of each class of the registrant's common stock as of the latest practicable date. As allowed by Instruction 3 to Item 201, most registrants base the approximate number of holders of their common stock on the number of record holders because this number can usually be easily and inexpensively obtained for the most recently completed trading day by making a phone call to their transfer agent. A registrant must clearly indicate when it is using this method of computation.

Example: As of March 12, 2012, there were approximately 2,850 holders of record of our common stock.

(c) Dividends. Item 201(c) of Regulation S-K requires the registrant to describe the following information:

● for the two most recent fiscal years, the frequency and amount of cash dividends declared by the registrant on each class of its common stock; and

● restrictions on the registrant's current and future ability to pay cash dividends on its common stock (e.g., covenants in a credit facility or senior equity securities). The registrant may provide this information by cross-referencing the discussion of these restrictions in MD&A or the financial statements.

In addition, registrants are encouraged, but not required, to disclose their present intention of paying cash dividends in the foreseeable future (i.e., if they have a history of paying or not paying cash dividends, do they intend to continue such practice (at a comparable rate/amount in the case of those that do pay dividends)). Many registrants that have not paid cash dividends on their common stock to date and do not intend to in the foreseeable future disclose that they intend to retain their earnings to finance operations and future growth and that any decision to pay cash dividends will be made by their boards of directors based on factors such as the registrants' results of operations and working capital requirements.

(d) Recent Sales of Unregistered Securities. For all equity securities sold by a registrant (including in exchange for services, property or other securities) during the fiscal year covered by the Form 10-K that were not registered under the Securities Act, Item 701(a)-(e) of Regulation S-K requires the registrant to disclose the following information to the extent it has not already publicly disclosed such information in a Form 10-Q or a Form 8-K (which now requires timely filing of such information):

● the date of the sale and the title and amount of securities sold;

● the names of any underwriters/placement agents and the names of the persons or the classes of persons to whom the securities were sold. Where many investors were involved in a private placement or an investor does not want to be publicized, the registrant can identify the classes of investors (e.g., individuals, trusts, partnerships, investment funds, etc.);

● the aggregate amount of consideration received by the registrant and the aggregate underwriting discounts or commissions;

● the section of the Securities Act or rule thereunder pursuant to which exemption from the registration was claimed (e.g., Section 4(2) and Regulation D of the Securities Act) and the facts relied upon to make the exemption available (e.g., the investors were accredited investors or sophisticated investors familiar with the registrant's business that represented that they were purchasing the securities for investment purposes without a view towards distribution). Registrants should note that to the extent their Form 10-K is reviewed by the SEC (e.g., pursuant to the review of a registration statement into which the Form 10-K is incorporated by reference), the SEC will often closely examine this disclosure to see if any recent sales of unregistered securities were made in violation of the registration requirements of Section 5 of the Securities Act; and

● if the unregistered securities are exercisable for, or convertible into, equity securities of the registrant (e.g., a warrant or option), the terms of conversion or exercise.

This disclosure regarding unregistered sales of securities is intended to make the registrant's shareholders aware of the potential dilution of such shares and the effects on the registrant that these unregistered sales may cause.[32]

(e) Use of Proceeds. As required by Rule 463 of the Securities Act and Item 701(f) of Regulation S-K, after a registrant's first registration statement filed under the Securities Act (e.g., its IPO Form S-1) is declared effective by the SEC, the registrant must disclose the effective date and SEC file number of the Securities Act registration statement and its use of proceeds from the registered offering in its subsequent Form 10-Qs and Form 10-Ks until the registrant has disclosed the use of all the offering proceeds or the termination of the offering, whichever is later.[33] In particular, the registrant must disclose:

● the amount of expenses incurred for underwriters' discounts and commissions, finders' fees and offering expenses and the resulting net proceeds the registrant received after deducting such total expenses.

● the amount of net offering proceeds used, from the effective date of the Securities Act registration statement to the end of the fiscal year covered by Form 10-K, for:

    ● construction of plants, buildings and facilities;

    ● purchase and installation of machinery and equipment;

    ● purchase of real estate;

    ● acquisition of other businesses;

    ● repayment of indebtedness;

    ● working capital;

    ● temporary investments (which must be specified); and

    ● any other purposes (which must be specified) for which at least the lesser of 5% of the registrant's total offering proceeds or $100,000 (whichever is less) has been used.

Because money is fungible and proceeds from an IPO are usually mixed with other funds, registrants often cannot know exactly whether cash used

---

[32] See SEC Release Nos. 33-7189 (June 27, 1995) and 34-37801 (October 10, 1996).

[33] This information was previously required to be disclosed on Form SR (which form was rescinded).

for a payment was from IPO proceeds as opposed to preexisting cash or cash from operations. Because the use of IPO proceeds must be reported until all the proceeds are accounted for, many registrants assume payments made with respect to the items enumerated above were from IPO proceeds when such use of proceeds is consistent with disclosure in the registrant's IPO prospectus.

● whether the amount of expenses incurred or net offering proceeds used is a reasonable estimate rather than an actual amount.

● whether the amount of expenses incurred or net offering proceeds used was direct or indirect payments to directors, officers or general partners of the registrant or their associates, persons owning 10% or more of any class of the registrant's equity securities, affiliates of the registrant, or others.

● any material change that the use of proceeds indicated in the Form 10-K represents from the use of proceeds indicated in the registrant's IPO prospectus. The registrant should note that any material changes in the use of proceeds will be especially scrutinized by the investment community if the registrant's stock price has declined since the IPO.

● the offering date, or if the offering has not commenced, an explanation of why.

● if the offering has terminated, whether it was terminated before all or any registered securities were sold.

● the names of any managing underwriters.

● the title of each class of security registered.

● for the registrant and for any selling security holders, the amount of each class of securities registered and sold and the aggregate offering price of the amount sold.

All of the above information required by Item 701(f) of Regulation S-K must be disclosed in the registrant's Form 10-K if it is the first periodic report filed by the registrant after the registrant's Securities Act registration statement is declared effective (i.e., the registrant has not filed a Form 10-Q yet). Afterwards, the above information need only be disclosed in a registrant's Form 10-K if the information has changed since its Form 10-Q was filed for the preceding third quarter. For example, if the first periodic report filed by the registrant after its IPO is its Form 10-K, all of the information described above must be included in the Form 10-K. If, however, the first periodic report filed by the registrant after its IPO is a Form 10-Q, the only information that usually changes, and thus must be discussed in the Form 10-K, is the use of the net offering proceeds through the end of the fiscal year.

(f) Issuer Repurchases. Item 703 of Regulation S-K requires a registrant to disclose the following information in the following tabular form for any repurchase by the registrant of its equity securities that are registered pursuant to Section 12 of the Exchange Act[34] that is made in a month within the fourth quarter of the fiscal year covered by the Form 10-K.[35] The disclosure is required for each issuer repurchase whether or not it satisfies the safe harbor from liability for manipulation provided by Rule 10b-18 under the Exchange Act.

Period	(a) Total Number of Shares (or Units) Purchased	(b) Average Price Paid per Share (or Unit)	(c) Total Number of Shares (or Units) Purchased as Part of Publicly Announced Plans or Programs	(d) Maximum Number (or Approximate Dollar Value) of Shares (or Units) That May Yet Be Purchased Under the Plans or Programs
Month #1 (identify beginning and ending dates)				
Month #2 (identify beginning and ending dates)				
Month #3 (identify beginning and ending dates)				
Total				

The registrant must also disclose in footnotes to the table for each publicly announced repurchase plan or program:

- the date of announcement;

- the dollar or share amount approved;

- the expiration date, if any, of such plan or program;

---

[34] As such, unless a registrant's stock options (as opposed to the underlying common stock) are registered under Section 12 of the Exchange Act, an option exchange or repurchase of options for cash by such registrant is not disclosable pursuant to Item 703 of Regulation S-K.

[35] See SEC Release No. 33-8335 (November 10, 2003).

● if true, that such plan or program has expired during the fourth quarter covered by the table; and

● if true, that the registrant has determined to terminate such plan or program prior to expiration or that the registrant does not intend to make further repurchases under such plan or program.

For purchases made other than pursuant to a publicly announced repurchase plan or program, the registrant must disclose in the footnotes to the table the nature of such transaction (e.g., open market and privately negotiated purchases, issuer tender offers and purchases pursuant to a person's exercise of a put right).

The SEC staff has informally indicated that the above-required disclosure applies not only to open market repurchases by a registrant, but also to certain private transactions that occur in connection with a registrant's equity compensation plans. For example, the disclosure is required when a holder delivers previously issued shares to pay a stock option's exercise price or withholding taxes in connection with the exercise of an option or vesting of restricted stock. On the other hand, the SEC staff has clarified that the disclosure is not required for net share settlements where the registrant withholds shares to pay an option's exercise price or withholding taxes (i.e., those shares are not being repurchased because they were never actually issued) or for shares forfeited when a holder of restricted stock fails to satisfy vesting conditions unless the registrant pays the holder for such forfeiture. Disclosure is required, however, if the registrant withholds shares to pay withholding taxes in connection with the vesting of restricted stock.

Item 6. Selected Financial Data. The information to be furnished under this Item is found in Item 301 of Regulation S-K.

(a) Income Statement and Balance Sheet Data. Registrants must compare the following information, subject to variation to conform to the nature of their businesses, in columns for the last five fiscal years (or the life of the registrant and its predecessors, if shorter) and any other fiscal years necessary to keep the information from being misleading:

● net sales or operating revenues;

● income (loss) from continuing operations;

● income (loss) from continuing operations per common share;

● total assets;

● long-term obligations and redeemable preferred stock; and

● cash dividends declared per common share.

The purpose of this information is to highlight significant trends in a registrant's financial condition and results of operations. In addition to these required line items from a registrant's income statement and balance sheet, the registrant may include additional items that it believes would enhance an understanding of, and highlight other trends in, its financial condition and results of operations. This additional information, however, is often instead discussed textually in MD&A.

(b) Comparability and Uncertainties. Registrants must also describe, or cross-reference to a discussion of, factors that materially affect the comparability of the selected financial data and any material uncertainties that might cause the data not to be indicative of future financial conditions or results of operations. Examples of these factors include accounting changes, business combinations and dispositions of operations. Registrants often satisfy this requirement by cross-referencing the disclosures in MD&A.

Item 7. Management's Discussion and Analysis of Financial Condition and Results of Operations. The registrant must furnish the information required by Item 303 of Regulation S-K. Item 303 requires disclosure of management's discussion and analysis of the registrant's financial condition and results of operations, commonly referred to as MD&A. Basically, MD&A requires the registrant to provide a textual description of its historical financial results and prospective financial information. In other words, registrants must describe the reasons for, and implications of, reported financial results and anticipated events. Item 303 specifically requires registrants to analyze three categories of financial information, most of which is contained in their audited financial statements included in their Form 10-Ks: results of operations, liquidity and capital resources. While this information must be provided on a consolidated basis, registrants that are required to report segment financial information under FASB ASC Topic 280 must also provide applicable information for each operating segment and major lines of products and services.[36] In addition, registrants should disclose any other information that they believe to be necessary (or of sufficient concern so as to affect a reader's ability) to understand their financial condition, changes in financial condition and results of operations. For example, registrants should disclose and discuss statistical data that, while not appearing in their financial statements, are key indicators of their business operations and financial performance. Increased focus has been put on the disclosure of such additional information since (i) the SEC's enactment of Regulation FD[37] and (ii) the SEC's interpretive guidance regarding MD&A published several years ago.[38] Because Regulation FD expressly prohibits selective disclosure of material, non-public information to certain parties (e.g., analysts and institutional investors) without a confidentiality agreement,

---

[36] See SEC Release No. 33-7620 (January 5, 1999).
[37] See SEC Release No. 33-7881 (August 15, 2000).
[38] See SEC Release No. 33-8350 (December 19, 2003), which is included as Appendix 9.

registrants cannot guide in preparing their models or pique the interests of institutional investor sing to them key metrics or developments that they have not disclosed blic. Therefore, if a registrant wants analysts and institutional invest w about certain information because it is an indicator of the registrant's current or future operating results or financial condition, it should publicly disclose such information in its MD&A. The SEC's interpretive MD&A guidance emphasizes the disclosure of key variables, including non-financial measures, used by management to manage and evaluate a registrant's business, including factors that are specific to the registrant, factors that are specific to the registrant's industry and macro-economic matters. Such disclosure should include a clear explanation of how such measures are calculated. Registrants are urged to review their public communications to see what material measures are being disclosed in order to avoid omitting such material information from MD&A such as to make their disclosure misleading and inadequate.

Example: The number of billable professionals employed, utilization rates and average monthly billable hours are important statistics in the consulting industry that let the public know how productive a consultant's workforce is by indicating whether a significant number of employees are working on client projects and generating revenue for the registrant or are being compensated by the registrant to sit around because business is slow. Therefore, registrants in the consulting industry should consider providing this information in their MD&A, especially if it has been used in the past to provide guidance to analysts.

Some helpful hints to drafting MD&A included in the SEC's interpretive guidance include:

● prominently present and clearly explain the most important information in an understandable fashion;

● consider using tables and headings to better organize MD&A and help readers understand key information;

● avoid unnecessary duplication of disclosure and detail that makes MD&A hard to read and distracts readers from material information;

● do not include immaterial and outdated information that does not help analyze a registrant's financial condition, changes in financial condition or results of operations; and

● present balanced MD&A disclosure—describe both company successes and failures and give readers a sense of whether past performance is likely to be indicative of future performance.

(a) Overview. Many registrants, as recommended by the SEC staff, begin their MD&A with a brief executive-level overview of key factors to their businesses that provides context for the remainder of MD&A, including how they generate revenues (e.g., product sales, consulting fees, software licenses), when revenue is recognized and on what they spend their cash (e.g., payroll, research and development, rent). A discussion is also often included about any customer concentration, including if any customer accounts for more than 10% of the registrant's consolidated total revenues for a reported fiscal year, as well as the breakdown of revenues that are generated from domestic and international operations. Furthermore, registrants should explain in the overview any material historical and prospective developments that have generally affected, or are expected to generally affect, their MD&A disclosures, such as material corporate transactions, relevant economic, industry-wide or company-specific factors and material opportunities, challenges and risks.

(b) Results of Operations. Results of operations provides a year-to-year explanation of material changes in line items of the registrant's income statement (e.g., revenues and expenses) over the past three fiscal years (or those fiscal years in which the registrant has been engaged in business, if shorter). For example, if a registrant is filing its Form 10-K for the fiscal year ended December 31, 2011, and has been in business for the past three fiscal years, it would compare its results of operations for 2011 versus 2010 and its results of operations for 2010 versus 2009. Some registrants first compare the two most recent fiscal years under one heading and then the second and third fiscal years under a separate heading. Others compare year 1 versus year 2 versus year 3 under one heading. This latter approach helps avoid repetition and seems to make the most sense when the explanations for why most of the line items have changed is generally the same over the three-year period. Within each two-year comparison, line items of the income statement are compared with material changes often being qualified in both absolute terms and as a percentage.

Example: Our total revenue increased $50 million, or 50%, to $150 million in 2011 from $100 million in 2010.

Keep in mind, however, that disclosing very large percentage increases that are due to early stage development generally does not provide useful information and may appear awkward.

In results of operations, the registrant then analyzes why a line item has changed from one year to the next, both the immediate reason and the reasons underlying such immediate reason. For example, why did revenues increase from $10 million to $20 million over the past two years or why did expenses decrease by $3.5 million over the past two years? If the immediate answer is because sales increased or decreased, as applicable, why did sales increase or decrease? Events and trends both internal and external to a registrant that have impacted the registrant's results must be described. Thus, a registrant must disclose economic factors (e.g., an economic recession has led to consumers purchasing less of a registrant's product), industry factors (e.g., an industry's product has become technologically obsolete) and specific company factors (e.g., a product defect or technology malfunction) that help readers understand why the registrant's net income or loss increased or decreased from the prior year. Registrants should be especially careful to make sure positive changes in results of operations that arise from changes in estimates, such as an accrual, are clearly explained so as not to mislead readers that such positive results are the product of operational improvements. Registrants are encouraged to drill down into the significant components of their revenues and expenses so that they can paint a clear picture of their results of operations. For example, if a registrant's operating expenses consist of marketing and advertising expenses, technology development expenses and selling, general and administrative expenses, the year-to-year change in each of these components should be described so that readers of the MD&A can better assess the registrant's results of operations. Important expense items are also often presented as a percentage of revenues to provide information regarding a registrant's operating margins. While it is important to identify the causes of changes in the registrant's operating results, offsetting developments that have caused a change not to be magnified should also be disclosed. To the extent material increases in a registrant's net sales or revenues are due to price increases, increases in the amount of goods or services sold or the introduction of new products or services, these factors should also be discussed.

The detailed analysis of the year-to-year changes of financial statement items, as opposed to just citing percentage changes and boilerplate explanations, is the cornerstone of effective MD&A disclosure.

(1) Unusual or Infrequent Events or Transactions. The registrant must describe any unusual or infrequent events or transactions or any significant economic changes that materially affected the amount of reported income from continuing operations, as well as the extent of such effect.

Example: Extraordinary gains and losses and non-recurring items (such as a one-time charge for an acquisition, a restructuring charge after laying off workers or income generated from the sale of significant property) that have materially impacted the registrant's results must be identified and quantified.

(2) Future Impact of Known Trends or Uncertainties; Critical Accounting Policies. Registrants must also describe any known trends or uncertainties that they reasonably expect will have material favorable or unfavorable impacts on net sales or revenues or income from continuing operations. The SEC has noted that "[o]f particular importance are factors which are expected to make reported historical results and trends either indicative or not indicative of future operating results and related financial condition."[39] Therefore, matters that (1) are reasonably expected to impact the registrant's future operations and have not impacted the registrant's past operations, (2) have had an impact on

---

[39] See SEC Release No. 33-6349 (September 28, 1981).

the registrant's reported operations and are not expected to impact the registrant's future operations, and (3) have had an impact on the registrant's reported operations and are expected to continue to impact the registrant's future operations should all be described qualitatively and, if possible, quantitatively.

Example: If a registrant has historically incurred significant marketing expenses to attract new customers and accelerate revenue growth, as reflected in its year-to-year comparison of increased expenses under results of operations, but at the time its Form 10-K is filed the registrant expects to materially decrease television and print advertising during the current year, the expected decline in marketing expenses (and reasonably expected effect on revenues, if material) should also be discussed in results of operations.

Registrants should note that the SEC does not apply Item 303 of Regulation S-K to impose a duty to disclose undisclosed preliminary merger negotiations as a known event that will materially affect results.[40] The need to disclose information is balanced against the risk of premature disclosure that jeopardizes consummation of a transaction. If negotiations have been disclosed or disclosure is otherwise required, however, there is no longer an interest in avoiding premature disclosure and the expected impact of such known event must be discussed. Other examples of known trends or uncertainties that could reasonably be expected to materially impact a registrant's results and thus would require disclosure include:

● a key customer or supply contract of the registrant is scheduled to expire later in the current fiscal year and may not be renewed or replaced;

● an event that adversely affects the registrant's industry or present and possibly future demand for the registrant's services or products (e.g., the material adverse effect of increased residential mortgage defaults on companies operating in the housing industry or of high-risk loans on financial lenders);

● the registrant has contracted to build or lease significant additional space for its operations;

● the registrant expects to launch a new product;

● the registrant acquired a business at the end of the past fiscal year;

● loss of competitive advantage due to technology changes or lack of intellectual property protection; or

● the registrant is ramping up commercial scale manufacturing or the sales and marketing of a key product.

In recent years, the SEC has focused its attention on ensuring that investors are made aware of the relationship between uncertainties and accounting

---

[40] See SEC Release No. 33-6835 (May 18, 1989).

measurements in a registrant's financial statements, including the susceptibility of reported results to change. In particular, since December 2001, the SEC has been encouraging registrants to include in their MD&A full, plain English explanations of their "critical accounting policies," the judgments and uncertainties affecting the application of these policies and the likelihood of materially different reported results if different assumptions or conditions were to prevail.[41] Examples of critical accounting policies involving judgments and uncertainties include revenue recognition, impairment of assets, impairment of inventory, loss reserves and impairment of accounts receivable. In May 2002, the SEC went a step further and proposed disclosure requirements for accounting estimates a registrant makes in applying its accounting policies and the initial adoption by a registrant of an accounting policy that has a material impact on its financial presentation.[42] While these proposed requirements have not been adopted as SEC rules, in December 2003, in its interpretive MD&A guidance, the SEC told registrants they should provide qualitative and quantitative disclosure about critical accounting estimates or assumption where (i) their nature is material because they are very subjective and relate to uncertain or changing methods and (ii) their impact on the registrant's financial condition or operating results is material. The disclosure of critical accounting policies in MD&A should not repeat the disclosure regarding such policies in the footnotes to the financial statements included in the Form 10-K. Rather, the MD&A disclosure should provide analysis regarding the uncertainties and judgments involved with such policies and the possible variety in results that could occur due to such uncertainty and judgments.

Registrants must also disclose any known events that will cause material changes in the relationship between costs and revenues, such as known future costs of labor or materials, price increases or inventory adjustments.

(3) Projections. Registrants are also encouraged, but not required,[43] to supply forward-looking information. The SEC has pointed out that the

---

[41] See SEC Release No. 33-8040 (December 12, 2001). Most registrants have been including such disclosure under the caption "Critical Accounting Policies" after their MD&A's overview section.

[42] See SEC Release No. 33-8098 (May 10, 2002), included as Appendix 10. Under the proposal, which suggests that most issuers would disclose three to five critical accounting policies, an accounting estimate would qualify as a critical accounting estimate requiring disclosure if both of the following questions are answered "yes": (1) Did the accounting estimate require the registrant to make assumptions about matters that were highly uncertain at the time the accounting estimate was made? and (2) Would different estimates that the registrant reasonably could have used in the current period, or changes in the accounting estimate that are reasonably likely to occur from period to period, have a material impact on the presentation of the registrant's financial condition, changes in financial condition or results of operations?

[43] The off-balance sheet and contractual obligations disclosure required in MD&A actually do require disclosure of forward-looking statements.

distinction between required prospective information and optional forward-looking information is based on the nature of the prediction:

● Required disclosure is based on currently known trends, events and uncertainties reasonably expected to have material effects; and

● Optional forward-looking disclosure involves anticipating a future trend, event or uncertainty or anticipating a less predictable impact of a known event, trend or uncertainty.[44]

Example: If a registrant anticipates expanding its operations into several foreign countries during the upcoming fiscal year to exploit new market opportunities, it could disclose such anticipation and that it expects an increase in revenues as products are sold overseas, partially offset by an expected increase in selling, general and administrative costs as salaries and other direct employment expenses attributable to establishing an administrative staff overseas are incurred.

These forward-looking statements are covered by the safe harbor provided by:

● Rule 175 of the Securities Act;

● Rule 3b-6 of the Exchange Act; and

● The Private Securities Litigation Reform Act of 1995 ("PSLRA").

In particular, the registrant should take advantage of the safe harbor afforded to forward-looking statements by the PSLRA by cross-referencing at the beginning of MD&A its forward-looking statement safe harbor language that appears elsewhere in the Form 10-K. See Chapter 5 for a more detailed discussion of the PSLRA.[45]

(4) Inflation. Registrants must discuss their views of any material effects that inflation and changes in prices have had on their net sales and revenues and on income from continuing operations for the past three fiscal years. Only a brief textual presentation is required by Item 303 of Regulation S-K; no specific financial data is required to be presented unless Rule 3-20(c) of Regulation S-X otherwise requires. The SEC encourages registrants to "focus on translating the potentially confusing situation concerning inflation into a meaningful discussion of the effects of changing prices on the registrant's business."[46] This

---

[44] See SEC Release No. 33-6835 (May 18, 1989).

[45] Item 303(c) of Regulation S-K codifies the application of the PSLRA safe harbor to the new off-balance sheet and contractual obligations disclosure required in MD&A.

[46] See SEC Release No. 33-6349 (September 28, 1981).

disclosure has not been relevant in recent years for most registrants because inflation has not had a material effect on their businesses.

(5) **Pro Forma (Non-GAAP) Financial Information.** To the extent that a registrant believes there is unaudited pro forma earnings information that is not in conformity with GAAP that presents a more accurate picture of what factors management looks at when analyzing the performance of the registrant's business (e.g., emphasizes the results of core operations or allows meaningful comparison to results for the same period of prior years), MD&A is the appropriate place to discuss this pro forma information. The SEC voiced concern in December 2001 that pro forma measures of operating performance can be used by registrants to selectively present a better picture of their businesses than GAAP would otherwise allow and may be materially misleading and confusing to shareholders that do not appreciate how such unstructured information differs from audited financial statements.[47] Reflecting the same concern, Section 401(b) of the Sarbanes-Oxley Act directed the SEC to adopt rules requiring that any public disclosure or release of a non-GAAP financial measure by a registrant be presented in a way that (1) does not contain an untrue statement of a material fact or omit to state a material fact necessary in order to make the non-GAAP financial measure, in light of the circumstances under which it is presented, not misleading; and (2) reconciles the non-GAAP financial measure presented with the financial condition and results of operations of the registrant under GAAP. As directed, the SEC adopted a new disclosure regulation, Regulation G, which applies to any public disclosure of material information by a public company that includes a non-GAAP financial measure, and amendments to Item 10 of Regulation S-K, which specifically applies to the use of non-GAAP financial measures in SEC filings and contains more detailed requirements than Regulation G.[48] These rules[49] require registrants that provide non-GAAP financial measures in an SEC filing (e.g., the Form 10-K) to also include:

● a presentation, with equal or greater prominence, of the most directly comparable financial measure calculated and presented in accordance with GAAP;

● a reconciliation (by schedule or other clearly understandable method), which is both quantitative for historic measures and quantitative, to the extent available without unreasonable efforts (but identifying unavailable

---

[47] See SEC Release No. 33-8039 (December 4, 2001). In addition, in January 2002, the SEC brought an enforcement action against Trump Hotels and Casino Resorts, Inc. for materially misleading use of pro forma financial data in an earnings release (see SEC Release No. 34-45287 (January 16, 2002)).

[48] See SEC Release No. 33-8176 (January 22, 2003).

[49] See also Question 8 of the Frequently Asked Questions Regarding the Use of Non-GAAP Financial Measures from the staff of the SEC's Division of Corporation Finance.

information and its probable significance), for prospective measures, of the differences between the non-GAAP financial measure presented and the most directly comparable financial measure or measures calculated and presented in accordance with GAAP;

● a statement disclosing the substantive reasons why the registrant's management believes that presentation of the non-GAAP financial measure provides useful information to investors regarding the registrant's financial condition and results of operations;[50]

● to the extent material, a statement disclosing the additional purposes, if any, for which the registrant's management uses the non-GAAP financial measure that are not disclosed;[51]

● disclosure of the limitations of the non-GAAP financial measure in evaluating the registrant's performance; and

● a statement that the non-GAAP financial measure is not prepared in accordance with GAAP and should not be considered an alternative to GAAP measures.

In addition, Item 10 of Regulation S-K prohibits (i) presenting non-GAAP financial measures on the face of a registrant's financial statements prepared in accordance with GAAP or the accompanying notes and (ii) using titles or descriptions of such measures that are confusingly similar to titles or descriptions of GAAP financial measures.

For purposes of Regulation G, a non-GAAP financial measure is a numerical measure of a registrant's historical or future financial performance, financial position or cash flows that:

● excludes amounts, or is subject to adjustments that have the effect of excluding amounts, that are included in the most directly comparable measure calculated and presented in accordance with GAAP in the statement of income, balance sheet or statement of cash flows (or equivalent statements) of the issuer; or

---

[50] These statements should be clear, understandable, not boilerplate and specific to the non-GAAP financial measure disclosed, the registrant, the nature of the registrant's business and industry and the manner in which the registrant assesses the non-GAAP financial measure and applies it to the management decisions. The SEC staff had been taking a tough stance in evaluating whether non-GAAP operating financial measures that go beyond traditional EBITDA or EBIT are truly useful (or more useful than the comparable GAAP measure) and were requiring removal of such non-GAAP measures from registrants' SEC filings (but allowing them in earnings releases not filed with the SEC). More recently, the SEC has loosened its stance regarding disclosure of such non-GAAP measures in SEC filings (including to try to maintain some consistency between public disclosure of such information in earnings releases and the Form 10-K).

[51] Id.

● includes amounts, or is subject to adjustments that have the effect of including amounts, that are excluded from the most directly comparable measure so calculated and presented.

An example of a non-GAAP financial measure would be a measure of operating income that excludes one or more expense or revenue items that are identified as "non-recurring."[52] Another example would be "EBITDA" (earnings before interest, taxes, depreciation and amortization) and variations thereof,[53] which could be calculated using elements derived from GAAP financial presentations but, in any event, is not presented in accordance with GAAP.

Non-GAAP financial measures do not include:

● operating and other statistical measures (such as unit sales, numbers of employees, numbers of subscribers, or numbers of advertisers);

● ratios or statistical measures that are calculated using exclusively one or both of: (i) financial measures calculated in accordance with GAAP (e.g., operating margin equal to operating income calculated in accordance with GAAP divided by revenue calculated in accordance with GAAP); and (ii) operating measures or other measures that are not non-GAAP financial measures;

● financial information that does not have the effect of providing numerical measures that are different from the comparable GAAP measures (e.g., expected indebtedness, planned repayments, estimated revenues or expenses of a new product line, so long as estimated in the same manner as would be computed under GAAP, measures of profit or loss and total assets for each segment required to be disclosed in accordance with GAAP); and

● financial measures required to be disclosed by GAAP, SEC rules or a system of regulation of a government, governmental authority or self-regulatory organization that is applicable to the registrant (e.g., measures of capital or reserves calculated for regulatory purposes).

---

[52] Adjusting a non-GAAP performance measure to eliminate or smooth items identified as non-recurring, infrequent or unusual is prohibited, however, when (i) the nature of the charge or gain is such that it is reasonably likely to recur within two years or (ii) there is a similar charge or gain within the prior two years. Registrants are also prohibited from excluding cash charges from a non-GAAP financial measure of liquidity (other than EBIT or EBITDA). See Item 10 of Regulation S-K.

[53] Registrants should note that the SEC staff frequently believes that if adjusted EBITDA is presented and excludes non-cash items, such as non-cash interest expense and non-cash compensation expense, then such information is a liquidity measure as opposed to a measure of operating performance and, therefore, net income is not the most comparable GAAP measure to which it should be reconciled (especially if one of the reasons it is presented is because it is used to monitor compliance with debt covenants).

(6) Non-Exchange Traded Contracts. In January 2002, the SEC asked for additional MD&A disclosures by registrants that are engaged, to a material extent, in trading activities involving commodity contracts (indexed to measures of weather, prices for energy storage, etc.) that are accounted for at fair value but where, due to a lack of market price quotations, fair value estimation techniques must be used. The SEC advised these registrants to provide comprehensive information about the trading activities, the contracts, modeling methodologies, assumptions and variables, and the different potential outcomes. Furthermore, the SEC proposed that registrants provide a schedule that "disaggregates realized and unrealized changes in fair market value; identifies changes in fair value attributable to changes in valuation techniques; disaggregates estimated fair values at the latest balance sheet date based on whether fair values are determined directly from quoted market prices or are estimated; and indicates maturities of contracts at the latest balance sheet date (e.g., within one year, within years one through three, within years four and five, and after five years)."[54]

(7) Related-Party Transactions. The SEC has advised registrants that their MD&A disclosure should contain detailed discussions of material related-party transactions to the extent needed to provide investors with an understanding of their current and prospective financial positions and operating results.[55] Going further, the SEC has asked registrants to consider including discussions regarding all material transactions with related persons or entities, as well as other parties with whom the registrants or the related parties have relationships that allow such other parties to negotiate transaction terms that may not be available from clearly independent parties on an arm's-length basis. The SEC recommended that registrants include in these discussions information regarding the nature, purpose and economic substance of, and risks associated with, the transactions. This MD&A disclosure is in addition to, and not in lieu of, the related-party transaction information that must be provided pursuant to Item 404 of Regulation S-K and in financial statement footnotes.

(c) Liquidity and Capital Resources. Liquidity is meant to disclose the registrant's ability to generate cash flow to meet its current and future cash needs. Capital resources is meant to describe what those cash needs are. As such, and as allowed by Item 303(a) of Regulation S-K, discussions of liquidity and capital resources are often combined. The discussion of liquidity and capital resources goes beyond a simple review of current assets and liabilities at a given date. For both the short-term (up to the next 12 months) and the long-term (beyond the next 12 months), the registrant should compare assured available resources to expected requirements and address any identified deficiencies, including the course the registrant intends to take to meet such deficiencies.[56]

---

[54] See SEC Release No. 33-8056 (January 22, 2002).

[55] Id.

[56] See SEC Release No. 33-6349 (September 28, 1981). The SEC has indicated that a registrant should not simply state

In September 2010, the SEC issued guidance regarding the presentation of liquidity and capital resources to help investors better understand a registrant's cash needs, cash sources and funding risks, especially as financing activities have become more complex and diverse (SEC Release No. 33-9144 (September 17, 2010), which is included as Appendix 1 hereto). The SEC also proposed requiring registrants to provide, in a separately captioned subsection of MD&A, a comprehensive quantitative and qualitative explanation of their short-term borrowings (SEC Release No. 33-9143 (September 17, 2010), which is included as Appendix 3 hereto).

(1) Source of Liquidity. The liquidity section provides an analysis and explanation of a registrant's statements of cash flow, including cash flow from operations, investing activities and financing activities. Registrants are required to identify and separately describe internal and external sources of liquidity, including material unused sources of liquidity. Examples of sources of liquidity include:

- cash balances;

- operating cash flows, including accounts receivable;

- assets readily convertible to cash;

- anticipated cash flows from expanded operations;

- external debt or equity financing, including bank lines of credit and proceeds from securities offerings;[57]

- off-balance sheet financing arrangements, such as transactions and other relationships with structured finance entities and other unconsolidated, limited-purpose entities;

- the sale of non-operating assets;

- tax refunds; and

- litigation settlements.

A registrant's liquidity requirements will depend on its capital expenditures, expanded working capital needs (to maintain operations, complete current projects and achieve plans), repurchase obligations and scheduled debt repayments. Liquidity has received a great amount of scrutiny for companies that have current

---

(Footnote Continued)

that it "has sufficient short-term funding to meet its liquidity needs for the next year." See SEC Release No. 33-8056 (January 22, 2002).

[57] Significant covenants contained in a debt or equity financing that could materially affect a registrant's operation of its business or ability to obtain additional financing (e.g., a covenant to maintain certain debt-to-equity ratios or not to make certain payments without the security holder's approval), and the registrant's ability to satisfy such covenants, should also be disclosed.

operating expenses (e.g., expenses for marketing, recruiting and hiring additional personnel and upgrading infrastructure) that significantly exceed their current revenues or that do not expect their near-term revenues to increase at a rate commensurate with the increased costs and expenditures they expect to continue incurring because these capital-intensive companies are extremely dependent upon external financing. Therefore, the availability and cost of anticipated sources of financing must be disclosed in such registrants' liquidity sections of MD&A.[58]

(2) Capital Resources. Registrants must describe their material commitments for capital expenditures as of the end of the prior fiscal year, including the general purposes of such commitments and the anticipated sources of funds needed to fulfill such commitments. Material commitments for capital expenditures can result from contractual commitments as well as known demands on a registrant's resources. For example, if a registrant intends to continue its recent growth, it should describe the related capital expenditures it will have to make. In analyzing the availability of funds for anticipated capital expenditures, a registrant should consider its ability to meet maturing obligations and to scale back plans if necessary.

(3) Known Trends, Demands, Commitments, Events or Uncertainties. Registrants must disclose any known trends, demands, commitments, events or uncertainties that will, or that are reasonably likely to, result in the registrants' liquidity materially increasing or decreasing. This requires a registrant to provide context for its working capital (current assets minus current liabilities), which can often misrepresent a registrant's liquidity because (i) there is uncertainty about the registrant's ability to convert current assets into cash (e.g., because of receivables that may not be paid or inventory that is not ready to be sold) or (ii) there is a future event that is likely to occur that will affect the registrant's cash flow or (iii) borrowings during the fiscal year may be materially different from the amount outstanding at the end of the fiscal year. The registrant's management must undertake a two-part analysis when a trend, demand, commitment, event or uncertainty is known:

● Is the known trend, demand, commitment, event or uncertainty reasonably likely to happen? If no, disclosure is not required; if yes, or it cannot be determined, then:

● The registrant must evaluate the consequences of the known trend, demand, commitment, event or uncertainty, assuming it will happen. Disclosure is required unless management determines that a material effect on the registrant's liquidity is not reasonably likely to occur.

---

[58] See SEC Release No. 33-8056 (January 22, 2002).

Example: A registrant must disclose when it knows that certain unused credit lines will no longer be available to it in the near future or expects that covenants in its debt agreements (e.g., maintenance of a certain debt-equity ratio), lowered credit ratings or changes in the debt markets will restrict its ability to obtain additional debt financing. Other examples of known or expected events that may require disclosure include acceleration of debt maturity, need for additional collateral support, problems in collecting accounts receivable, regulatory changes, liability exposure, litigation, restrictions on use of, or access to, cash or assets convertible into cash and industry uncertainties due to the economy.

Registrants should also disclose known trends or uncertainties relating to decisions regarding the use of cash resources (e.g., conservative cash management could lead to more cash on hand or less debt and related interest expense and lower expenses, but less growth in revenues) and risk management policies.

(4) Seeking Additional Capital. If a registrant has a deficiency in liquidity, it must disclose its remedy or that it has not chosen a remedy or cannot currently address the deficiency. As a related point, the registrant should describe any favorable or unfavorable material trends in its capital resources, including expected changes in the mix and relative cost of the registrant's capital resources (e.g., changes between equity, debt and any off-balance sheet financing arrangements).

Example: If cash generated from operations is insufficient to satisfy a registrant's current or anticipated liquidity requirements, its need to raise additional funds through public or private financings should be disclosed as well as when such funds will be needed and what the consequences of both receiving and not receiving the funds would be (e.g., may have to pay significant finders' fees to raise private funds and existing shareholders may suffer significant dilution if equity is issued; on the other hand, if funds are not obtained when needed, the registrant may need to significantly scale back its operations or delay its product development).

A registrant should give thought to disclosing any liquidity problems it can accurately foresee as early as possible so that it (i) has more time to effectively manage its raising of additional funds by minimizing the negative impact that such an announcement can have on customers, suppliers and lenders as well as financing negotiations and (ii) can avoid accusations from those with 20/20 hindsight that the registrant knew about and failed to disclose its liquidity problems.

(d) Off-Balance Sheet Arrangements. Section 401(a) of the Sarbanes-Oxley Act directed the SEC to adopt rules requiring disclosure in a Form 10-K of all material off-balance sheet transactions, arrangements, obligations and other relationships of a registrant with unconsolidated entities or persons that may have a material current or future effect on the registrant's financial condition, changes in financial condition, results of operations, liquidity, capital expenditures, capital resources or significant components of revenues or expenses. As directed, the SEC issued final rules in January 2003 that added to the disclosure required in the MD&A.[59] The rules adopted Item 303(a)(4) of Regulation S-K, which requires registrants to include in their MD&A a separately captioned section discussing the registrant's off-balance sheet arrangements (i.e., contractual arrangements to which an unconsolidated entity that is provided financial support by the registrant, through a financial guarantee, retained or contingent interest in transferred assets, derivative instrument, or material variable interest, is a party) that have or are reasonably likely to have a current or future effect on the registrant's financial condition, changes in financial condition, revenues or expenses, results of operations, liquidity, capital expenditures or capital resources that is material to investors.[60] The disclosure, which is meant to provide readers with the information necessary to understand and evaluate the off-balance sheet arrangement and its associated risks, is required to include:

● the nature and business purpose to the registrant of such off-balance sheet arrangements (e.g., to lease rather than acquire a facility or to finance inventory or research and development costs without recognizing a liability);

● the importance to the registrant of such off-balance sheet arrangements in respect of its liquidity, capital resources, market risk support, credit risk support or other benefits;

● the amounts of revenues, expenses and cash flows of the registrant arising from such arrangements; the nature and amounts of any interests retained, securities issued and other indebtedness incurred by the registrant in connection with such arrangements; and the nature and amounts of any other obligations or liabilities (including contingent obligations or liabilities) of the registrant arising from such arrangements that are or are reasonably likely to become material and the triggering events or circumstances that could cause them to arise;

● any known event, demand, commitment, trend or uncertainty that will result in or is reasonably likely to result in the termination, or material reduction in availability to the registrant, of its off-balance sheet arrangements that provide material benefits to it (e.g., a decline in the registrant's credit rating), and the course of action that the registrant has taken or proposes to take in response to any such circumstances; and

---

[59] See SEC Release No. 33-8182 (January 27, 2003).

[60] The analysis of what disclosure is required is similar to the two-part analysis described above when a trend, demand, commitment, event or certainty that could affect liquidity is known.

● such other information that the registrant believes is necessary for such an understanding of such arrangements.

The above-described disclosure covers the registrant's most recent fiscal year, but should also address changes from the previous year if necessary to understand the disclosure. To avoid repetition, off-balance sheet arrangements should be aggregated in groups or categories that provide information in an efficient and understandable manner. Registrants are also permitted to provide required information about off-balance sheet arrangements by clearly cross-referencing specific applicable information in the footnotes to their financial statements. Registrants with off-balance sheet arrangements are urged to review the Report and Recommendations Pursuant to Section 401(c) of the Sarbanes-Oxley Act of 2002 on Arrangements with Off-Balance Sheet Implications, Special Purpose Entities, and Transparency of Filings by Issuers released in June 2005 by the Office of the Chief Accountant, the Office of Economic Analysis and the Division of Corporation Finance. The report identifies several goals and recommendations for the improvement of financial reporting of transactions with off-balance sheet implications.

(e) Tabular Disclosure of Contractual Obligations. In January 2003, the SEC issued final rules that required additional disclosure in the MD&A concerning contractual obligations. The rules adopted Item 303(a)(5) of Regulation S-K, which requires a registrant, in order to provide readers with contextual information to assess the registrant's short-term and long-term liquidity and capital resources needs and demands, to include tabular disclosure as of the latest fiscal year end balance sheet date with respect to the registrant's known contractual obligations specified in the table below (i.e., cash requirements arising from contractual payment obligations). The registrant is required to provide amounts of payments due, aggregated by type of contractual obligation, for specified time periods. The registrant may disaggregate the specified categories of contractual obligations using other categories suitable to its business, but the presentation must include all of the obligations of the registrant that fall within the specified categories and must be clear, understandable and appropriately reflect the categories of obligations that are meaningful in light of the registrant's business and capital structure. The tabular presentation should be accompanied by footnotes that describe material provisions that create, increase or accelerate obligations, or other pertinent data to the extent necessary for an understanding of the timing and amount of the registrant's specified contractual obligations. Registrants may place the contractual obligations table wherever they deem appropriate within MD&A.

		Payment due by period			
Contractual Obligations	**Total**	**Less than 1 year**	**1–3 years**	**3–5 years**	**More than 5 years**
[Long-Term Debt Obligations][1]					
[Capital Lease Obligations][1]					
[Operating Lease Obligations][1]					
[Purchase Obligations][2]					
[Other Long-Term Liabilities Reflected on the Registrant's Balance Sheet under GAAP]					
[Total]					

[1] As defined by reference to the relevant GAAP accounting pronouncements (FASB ASC Topic 470 and FASB ASC Topic 840).
[2] Defined as agreements to purchase goods or services that are enforceable and legally binding on the registrant that specifies all significant terms, including quantities, price and approximate timing of the transaction.

(f) The Importance of MD&A.

(1) Environment. In light of the many high-profile cases of inadequate financial disclosure and business failure, the fluctuating economic climate and financial market conditions, and the Sarbanes-Oxley Act, registrants must place increased focus on the clarity and completeness of MD&A. The MD&A should be carefully crafted to provide financial disclosure transparency that enables investors to evaluate a registrant's performance, financial condition and prospects and see the registrant as it is seen by its own management.

(2) SEC Review. Form 10-K reviews by the SEC staff often occur when the SEC reviews a registration statement filed by a registrant under the Securities Act (e.g., a Form S-3 or S-4) that incorporates by reference the registrant's Form 10-K. In addition, pursuant to Section 408 of the Sarbanes-Oxley Act, which is discussed later in this chapter, the SEC is required "on a regular and systematic basis" and in no event "less frequently than once every 3 years" to review the Exchange Act filings (including financial statements) of certain registrants. In its review of the Form 10-K, the SEC staff often pays particular attention to MD&A. For example, if during the year following the year covered by the Form 10-K, a registrant reports negative operating results or experiences problems in liquidity, if the SEC staff is reviewing the Form 10-K, it (as well as plaintiffs' attorneys), with the benefit of 20/20 hindsight, will be focusing on whether the registrant disclosed any trends, conditions or events that contributed to such problems and were known by the registrant when it filed its Form 10-K. If the SEC staff finds a registrant's MD&A disclosure to be inadequate or inaccurate, depending on the severity of its findings, it may require the registrant to (i) file an amendment on Form 10-K/A to revise the disclosure or (ii) undertake to address the inadequacy in future Exchange Act filings. In responding to SEC comments, registrants should keep in mind that the SEC's comment letters and registrants' responses are proposed to become publicly available.

The SEC staff's review of a registrant's MD&A can also result in referral to the SEC enforcement division. A number of SEC enforcement actions have been brought against registrants for allegedly failing to provide adequate or accurate disclosure.[61] These actions help clarify what the SEC expects to be disclosed in MD&A and should be read by those who are involved in the preparation or review of MD&A disclosure. The SEC's 2000 Audit Risk Alert, which provided a list of economic and world developments that will most likely affect registrants' MD&A disclosures, the SEC's review of the Form 10-Ks filed by Fortune 500 companies in 2002 and the SEC's interpretive MD&A guidance issued at the end of 2003 indicate that MD&A has been a hot topic with the SEC for years.[62]

The SEC has been paying specific attention to the following areas of MD&A and financial statement disclosure:

● operating segments;

● credit risk exposures and provisions and allowances for loan losses;

● impact of economy on debt covenants, including satisfying financial tests, and cash management;

● subprime residential mortgage exposure;

● contingent liabilities, including estimates of possible losses or range of losses for litigation or regulatory actions (and consistency among risk factors, legal proceedings disclosure and disclosure of contingencies in MD&A and financial statements);

● off-balance sheet transactions;

● restructuring charges;

● impairment of assets (including long-lived assets, securities held for investment and goodwill and other intangible assets);

---

[61] *In the Matter of Caterpillar, Inc.* (SEC Release No. 34-30532 (March 31, 1992)); *In re Shared Medical Systems Corporation* (SEC Release No. 34-33632 (February 17, 1994)); *Salant Corporation and Martin F. Tynan* (SEC Release No. 34-34046 (May 12, 1994)); *In the Matter of Sony Corporation and Sumio Sano* (SEC Release No. 40305 (August 5, 1998)). See also *Bank of Boston* (SEC Release No. 34-36887 (February 26, 1996)) for the first fully litigated SEC decision based on allegations of deficient MD&A disclosure.

[62] Office of the Chief Accountant, "Letter: 2000 Audit Risk Alert to the American Institute of Certified Public Accountants" (October 13, 2000) and Division of Corporation Finance, "Summary by the Division of Corporation Finance of Significant Issues Addressed in the Review of the Periodic Reports of the Fortune 500 Companies" (February 27, 2003).

- descriptions of material intangible assets;

- critical accounting policies;

- hedge accounting;

- accounting for business combinations;

- non-GAAP financial information;

- pension income or expense;

- accounting treatment of equity-based compensation, such as option and restricted stock grants, under FASB ASC Topic 718;

- fair value disclosure regarding financial instruments;

- consistency between what is disclosed in MD&A and other sections of the Form 10-K, as well as in other SEC filings and earnings releases;

- environmental[63] and product liability disclosures; and

- revenue recognition.

(3) Preparation. In crafting an MD&A that satisfies Item 303 of Regulation S-K and provides a complete and accurate picture of the registrant's financial condition and results of operations, the following should be reviewed:

- Item 303 and SEC Release Nos. 33-6349 (September 28, 1981), 33-6835 (May 18, 1989), 33-8039 (December 4, 2001), 33-8040 (December 12, 2001), 33-8056 (January 22, 2002), 33-8182 (January 28, 2003), 33-8350 (December 19, 2003) and 33-9144 (September 17, 2010).

- SEC Staff Accounting Bulletin ("SAB") No. 99 regarding materiality (August 12, 1999), SAB No. 100 regarding restructuring and impairment charges (November 24, 1999) and SAB No. 101 regarding revenue recognition in financial statements (December 3, 1999).

- the Summary by the Division of Corporation Finance of Significant Issues Addressed in the Review of the Periodic Reports of the Fortune 500 Companies (February 27, 2003).

- the registrant's MD&A disclosure in each of the three Form 10-Qs for the past fiscal year as well as in the registrant's prior Form 10-K.

---

[63] See GAO-04-808, "Environmental Disclosure: SEC Should Explore Ways to Improve Tracking and Transparency of Information" (July 2004), at http://www.gao.gov/new.items/d04808.pdf in which the United States Government Accountability Office reported that the SEC "is taking steps to increase the tracking and transparency of key [environmental] information." See also SEC Release No. 33-9106 (February 2, 2010) for guidance regarding the SEC's existing disclosure requirements as they apply to climate change matters.

- the most recent MD&A disclosure for the registrant's competitors to see what information they deem important.

- the registrant's audited financial statements, including the footnotes, for the past fiscal year.

- internal reports and analyses (e.g., presentations to the board of directors and cash flow projections and operating budgets with related assumptions) to help identify material trends, events or conditions that are known or should be known by the registrant.

- the registrant's debt instruments.

- audit committee and board minutes.

- press releases, other corporate filings, news articles, analyst's reports, scripts or transcripts of earnings conference calls and investor presentations, and the letter to shareholders to be included in the Annual Report.

Item 7A. Quantitative and Qualitative Disclosures About Market Risks. The registrant must furnish the information required by Item 305 of Regulation S-K.

(a) Background. This Item was added in early 1997 as a result of increased use of "market risk sensitive instruments" (e.g., derivative financial and commodity instruments) as a means of managing market risk as well as significant, and sometimes unexpected, losses suffered by some registrants in utilizing such instruments.[64] These losses were often due to changes in interest rates, exchange rates and commodity prices, among other events. By requiring a registrant to provide this additional disclosure in this area, the SEC believes investors can better understand and evaluate the registrant's market risk exposures.

(b) Required Disclosure. Item 305 of Regulation S-K generally requires disclosure of quantitative information about risks arising from a registrant's ownership and use of market risk sensitive instruments. The information about these securities must be broken down into "instruments entered into for trading purposes and instruments entered into for other than trading purposes."[65] The registrant may present the information in any of three ways:

(1) a tabular presentation of information that identifies the "fair values" of the instruments, and sufficient information regarding contract terms to determine cash flows from those instruments;

(2) tabular information based on contract terms with sufficient detail to permit readers of the table to determine expected cash flows from the instruments for each of the next five years; or

---

[64] See SEC Release No. 33-7386 (January 1, 1997).

[65] See SEC Release No. 33-6349 (September 28, 1981).

(3) a grouping of instruments based on their "common characteristics," within each risk exposure category.[66]

Item 305 also includes extensive requirements concerning accounting disclosure of derivative financial and commodity instruments. Registrants should work closely with their accountants in putting together the disclosures required by Item 305.

Item 8. Financial Statements and Supplementary Data. The registrant must furnish consolidated financial statements meeting the requirements of Regulation S-X (except Rule 3-05 and Article 11 thereof) and the supplementary financial information required by Item 302 of Regulation S-K. Other financial statements and schedules required under Regulation S-X may be filed as "Financial Statement Schedules" pursuant to Item 15 in Part IV of the Form 10-K.

(a) Regulation S-X. Regulation S-X requires registrants to include the following financial statements in their Form 10-Ks:

● audited consolidated balance sheets as of the end of each of the two most recent fiscal years;[67]

● audited consolidated statements of income and cash flows and an analysis of changes in shareholders' equity for each of the three most recent fiscal years;[68] and

● business segment disclosure required by FASB ASC Topic 280 for each year a statement of income is presented.[69]

Many registrants satisfy the disclosure requirements of Item 8 of Form 10-K by filing their audited consolidated financial statements under Item 15 of Form 10-K and cross-referencing that Item.

(b) Supplementary Financial Information. Item 302 of Regulation S-K requires that all registrants disclose the following financial information for each full quarter within the two most recent fiscal years:

● net sales;

● gross profit (net sales less costs and expenses associated directly with, or allocated to, products sold or services rendered);

● income (loss) before extraordinary items and cumulative effect of a change in accounting (including on a per share basis); and

● net income (loss).

---

[66] Item 305(a)(1)(i)(A)(1)-(3) of Regulation S-K. Item 305 contains a suggested format for presenting this information.

[67] Rule 3-01(a) of Regulation S-X.

[68] Rules 3-02(a) and 3-04 of Regulation S-X.

[69] Rule 3-03(e) of Regulation S-X.

Registrants typically disclose this information in a table that contains eight columns (one for each quarter in the past two fiscal years). If the information in any quarter varies from the corresponding disclosure previously reported by the registrant in its Form 10-Q that relates to that quarter (e.g., when an error is corrected), the amounts must be reconciled and the reason for the difference must be described. Registrants must also describe any extraordinary, unusual or infrequently occurring items or business segment disposals that affected a quarter, as well as the aggregate effect and nature of adjustments (e.g., at year-end) that are material to the results of a quarter. In reviewing this quarterly data, the registrant's independent accountants must follow the guidelines set forth in Statement on Auditing Standards (SAS) No. 100.

Item 9. Changes in and Disagreements with Accountants on Accounting and Financial Disclosure. Pursuant to Item 304(b) of Regulation S-K, if during the fiscal year in which a registrant changes its principal independent accountants (i.e., accountants resigned, declined to stand for re-election or were dismissed) or during the subsequent fiscal year, there have been any transactions or events similar to those which involved a disagreement[70] or reportable event[71] that relates to the change in accountants and such transactions or events

---

[70] This exists where during the past two fiscal years and any subsequent interim period there were any disagreements (i.e., differences of opinion, not necessarily arguments) expressed orally or in writing with the former accountant at the decision-making level (i.e., between registrant personnel responsible for financial statement presentation and accounting firm personnel responsible for rendering the audit report) on any matter of accounting principles or practices, financial statement disclosure or auditing scope or procedure, which, if not resolved to the former accountant's satisfaction, would have caused it to refer to the disagreement in connection with its report. These disagreements are required to be disclosed on the Form 8-K required to be filed in connection with a change of accountants.

[71] This exists where the accountants have advised the registrant of any of the following reportable events (even if not previously disclosed as a disagreement) within the past two fiscal years or any subsequent interim period:

● the internal controls necessary for the registrant to develop reliable financial statements do not exist;

● information has come to the accountant's attention that has led it to no longer be able to rely on management's representations or has made it unwilling to be associated with the financial statements prepared by management;

● (i) the need to expand significantly the scope of its audit, or that information has come to the accountant's attention that if further investigated may (x) materially impact the fairness or reliability of either a previously issued audit report, the underlying financial statements or the financial statements issued or to be issued covering the fiscal period(s) subsequent to the date of the most recent financial statements covered by an audit report (including information that may prevent it from rendering an unqualified audit report on those financial statements), or (y) cause it to be unwilling to rely on management's representations or be associated with the registrant's financial statements, and (ii) due to the accountant's resignation (due to audit scope limitations or otherwise), dismissal or for any other reason, the accountant did not so expand the scope of its audit or conduct such further investigations; or

were material and were accounted for or disclosed in a manner different from that which the former accountants apparently would have concluded was required, the registrant must disclose the disagreement or reportable event and the effect on the financial statements if the method had been followed which the former accountants apparently would have concluded was required. This disclosure is required even if previously reported, but need not be made if the method asserted by the former accountants ceases to be generally accepted because of authoritative standards or interpretations subsequently issued.

Item 9A. Controls and Procedures. The information to be furnished under this Item is found in Items 307 and 308 of Regulation S-K.[72] Registrants should note that the SEC has required strict adherence to the precise information that is required to be disclosed.

(a) Evaluation of Disclosure Controls and Procedures. A registrant must disclose the conclusions of its principal executive officer or officers and principal financial officer or officers, or persons performing similar functions, about the effectiveness of the registrant's disclosure controls and procedures as of the end of the fiscal year covered by the Form 10-K based on their evaluation of these controls and procedures required by Rules 13a-15(b) and 15d-15(b) under the Exchange Act.

"Disclosure controls and procedures" is defined as controls and other procedures of a registrant that are designed to ensure that information required to be disclosed by the registrant in the reports filed or submitted by it under the Exchange Act is recorded, processed, summarized and reported within the time periods specified in the SEC's rules and forms.[73] These controls and procedures are designed to ensure that information required to be disclosed, including information regarding business developments and risks and executive compensation, is accumulated and communicated to the issuer's management, including its principal executive and financial officers, as appropriate to allow timely

---

(Footnote Continued)

● (ii) information has come to the accountant's attention that it has concluded materially impacts the fairness or reliability of either a previously issued audit report, the underlying financial statements or the financial statements issued or to be issued covering the fiscal periods(s) subsequent to the date of the most recent financial statements covered by an audit report (including information that, unless resolved to the accountant's satisfaction, would prevent it from rendering an unqualified audit report on those financial statements), and (ii) due to the accountant's resignation, dismissal or declination to stand for reelection or for any other reason, the issue has not been resolved to the accountant's satisfaction prior to its resignation, dismissal or declination to stand for reelection.

These reportable events are required to be disclosed on the Form 8-K required to be filed in connection with a change of accountants.

[72] See SEC Release No. 33-8238 (June 5, 2003), which was adopted in accordance with Section 404 of the Sarbanes-Oxley Act.

[73] Rules 13a-15(e) and 15d-15(e) under the Exchange Act.

decisions regarding required disclosure. The disclosure controls and procedures must be designed, maintained and evaluated to ensure full and timely disclosure not only in annual and quarterly reports, but also in current reports on Form 8-K and proxy statements. Many registrants have clarified that disclosure controls and procedures are designed only to provide reasonable assurance that the registrant's transactions are properly authorized, recorded and reported and they will meet their objectives or that there is no assurance that the disclosure controls and procedures will operate effectively under all circumstances. The SEC has accepted this language as long as the registrants state that the disclosure controls and procedures are designed to provide reasonable assurance of meeting their objectives and whether the principal executive and principal financial officers have concluded that the controls and procedures are actually effective at the reasonable assurance level.

(b) Changes in Internal Control over Financial Reporting. Registrants must also disclose any change (including improvements) in their internal control over financial reporting identified in connection with their evaluations of internal control over financial reporting (or disclosure controls and procedures when the management report described below is not yet required) that occurred during the registrant's fourth fiscal quarter that has materially affected, or is reasonably likely to materially affect, the registrant's internal control over financial reporting. "Internal control over financial reporting" is defined as a process designed by, or under the supervision of, the registrant's principal executive and principal financial officers, or persons performing similar functions, and effected by the registrant's board of directors, management and other personnel, to provide reasonable assurance regarding the reliability of financial reporting and the preparation of financial statements for external purposes in accordance with generally accepted accounting principles and includes those policies and procedures that:

● pertain to the maintenance of records that in reasonable detail accurately and fairly reflect the transactions and dispositions of the assets of the registrant;

● provide reasonable assurance that transactions are recorded as necessary to permit preparation of financial statements in accordance with generally accepted accounting principles, and that receipts and expenditures of the registrant are being made only in accordance with authorizations of management and directors of the registrant; and

● provide reasonable assurance regarding prevention or timely detection of unauthorized acquisition, use or disposition of the registrant's assets that could have a material effect on the financial statements.

There is substantial overlap between a registrant's disclosure controls and procedures and its internal control over financial reporting. However, there are some elements in each that are not necessarily part of the other. For example, a registrant's disclosure controls and procedures may not include the policies and procedures that relate to the safeguarding of assets that are part of its internal control over financial reporting (i.e., requirements regarding who must or can sign checks). While Item 308(c) of Regulation S-K does not explicitly require a registrant to disclose why its internal control over financial reporting changed in the fourth fiscal quarter, the registrant must evaluate whether such disclosure constitutes material information necessary to make the disclosure about the change not misleading.[74] Keep in mind that such changes can include both problems regarding a registrant's internal control over financial reporting (e.g., problems related to financial systems and procedures or personnel issues) and the remediation efforts taken by a registrant to improve its controls and address such problems.

(c) Management's Annual Report on Internal Control over Financial Reporting. A registrant must provide a report of management on the registrant's internal control over financial reporting (which is deemed furnished and not filed for purpose of Section 18 of the Exchange Act) that contains:

● a statement of management's responsibility for establishing and maintaining adequate internal control over financial reporting for the registrant;

● a statement identifying the framework used by management to evaluate the effectiveness of the registrant's internal control over financial reporting— such framework must be a suitable, recognized control framework that is established by a body or group that has followed due-process procedures, including the broad distribution of the framework for public comment;

● management's assessment of the effectiveness of the registrant's internal control over financial reporting as of the end of the registrant's most recent fiscal year, including a statement as to whether or not its internal control over financial reporting is effective. This discussion must include disclosure of any material weakness[75] in the registrant's internal control over financial reporting identified by management that exists as of the end of the fiscal year. Management is not permitted to conclude that the registrant's internal control over financial reporting is effective if there are one or more material weaknesses in the registrant's internal control over financial reporting that exist as of the end of the fiscal year. The registrant must maintain evidential matter, including documentation, to provide

---

[74] Rules 13a-15(f) and 15a-15(f).

[75] Rule 12b-2 under the Exchange Act and Item 1-02(p) of Regulation S-X define a "material weakness" as a deficiency, or a combination of deficiencies, in internal control over financial reporting, such that there is a reasonable possibility that a material misstatement of the registrant's annual or interim financial statements will not be prevented or detected on a timely basis. In determining whether a control deficiency constitutes a material weakness, management can consider other compensating controls that help reduce to an acceptable level the risk posed by the deficient control.

reasonable support for management's assessment of the effectiveness of the registrant's internal control over financial reporting; and

● a statement that the registered public accounting firm that audited the financial statements included in the Form 10-K has issued an attestation report on the registrant's internal control over financial reporting[76]—such attestation report must be included in the Form 10-K and the accounting firm must consent to the incorporation of such report into any Securities Act registration statement filing by a registrant. The SEC expects management's report and the auditors' attestation report to be placed near each other in the Form 10-K, either under MD&A or preceding the audited financial statements. Pursuant to the Dodd-Frank Act and recently adopted SEC rules, non-accelerated filers are not required to comply with the attestation requirement.[77]

A newly public company does not need to comply with the management report and attestation requirements until its second Form 10-K, but must state in its first Form 10-K that it does not include the management report or auditor attestation.[78]

After a number of the first Form 10-Ks to include the internal control over financial reporting disclosures had been filed by accelerated filers, the SEC hosted a roundtable discussion concerning the implementation of the internal control reporting provisions in April 2005. In the view of the SEC, the round-table meetings made clear that companies had realized improvements to their internal controls as a result of implementing the requirements. However, the feedback the SEC received also identified implementation areas that needed further attention or clarification. As a result, the SEC's Office of the Chief Accountant and Division of Corporation Finance provided guidance in May 2005 on a number of areas relevant to the internal control over financial reporting disclosure requirements, including the purpose of internal control over financial reporting, the concept of reasonable assurance, disclosures about material weaknesses and communications with auditors.[79] Significantly, after noting that a number of companies had reported material weaknesses in their internal control over financial reporting in the first year of implementation, the SEC staff suggested that companies consider including in their disclosures the following information to help investors understand the cause and effect of the control deficiencies that constitute a material weakness:

---

[76] SEC Release 33-8809 (June 20, 2007) revised Items 1-02(a)(2) and 2-02(f) of Regulation S-X and Item 308(a)(4) of Regulation S-K to clarify that the auditor is evaluating directly the registrant's internal control over financial reporting as opposed to evaluating management's evaluation thereof.

[77] SEC Release 33-9142 (September 10, 2010).

[78] See SEC Release No. 33-8760 (December 15, 2006).

[79] See Staff Statement on Management's Report on Internal Control Over Financial Reporting (May 16, 2005), available at http://www.sec.gov/info/accountants/stafficreporting.htm.

- the nature of any material weakness,
- its impact on financial reporting and the control environment, and
- management's current plans, if any, for remediating the weakness.

The SEC staff indicated that while disclosure of the existence of a material weakness is important, there is other information that also may be material and necessary to provide an overall picture that is not misleading. For example, while management is required to conclude and state in its report that internal control over financial reporting is ineffective when there is one or more material weakness, the SEC staff encouraged companies to provide disclosure that allows investors to assess the potential impact of each particular material weakness, including distinguishing those material weaknesses that may have a pervasive impact on internal control over financial reporting and those that do not.[80] In May 2006, the SEC and the Public Company Accounting Oversight Board (the "PCAOB") conducted a second roundtable to obtain feedback on accelerated filers' second year of compliance with the Section 404 requirements. Then, in June 2007, the SEC published interpretive guidance to help registrants focus on the internal controls that best protect against the risk of a material financial misstatement, while reducing unnecessary costs involved in identifying and reviewing controls that do not materially affect reported financial results.[81] The SEC also clarified in Rules 13a-15(c) and 15d-15(c) of the Exchange Act that following this interpretive guidance would satisfy the annual evaluation of internal control over financial reporting required by Rules 13a-15(b) and 15d-15(b) under the Exchange Act.[82]

Registrants should review the SEC's Management's Report on Internal Control Over Financial Reporting and Certification of Disclosure in Exchange Act Periodic Reports Frequently Asked Questions[83] and the PCAOB's Staff Questions and Answers: Auditing Internal Control Over Financial Reporting for further guidance concerning the preparation of management's report on internal control over financial reporting. Registrants that restate their financials should also review their prior disclosure with respect to their management reports

---

[80] The SEC also included the foregoing considerations regarding disclosure of material weaknesses in its interpretive guidance for compliance with Section 404 of the Sarbanes-Oxley Act described below (SEC Release No. 33-8810 (June 20, 2007)).

[81] See SEC Release No. 33-8810 (June 20, 2007). The guidance focuses on (i) clarifying risks that could result in a material misstatement of financial statements, (ii) identifying controls a registrant has in place and evaluating whether such controls, if operating effectively, can prevent or detect these risks and (iii) evaluating the operating effectiveness of the controls.

[82] See SEC Release No. 33-8809 (June 20, 2007).

[83] See Management's Report on Internal Control Over Financial Reporting and Certification of Disclosure in Exchange Act Periodic Reports Frequently Asked Questions (September 24, 2007), contained in Appendix 13.

regarding the effectiveness of their internal control over financial reporting (as well as disclosure regarding the effectiveness of their disclosure controls and procedures) to make sure they are not misleading.

Item 9B. Other Information. The registrant must disclose any information required to be disclosed in a Form 8-K during the fourth quarter of the fiscal year covered by a Form 10-K, but not so reported (even if the information is not otherwise required by Form 10-K).[84] Such disclosed information is not required to be repeated in a Form 8-K.

4. Part III of the Form 10-K.

General. In general, the information contained in Part III of the Form 10-K is also required to be disclosed in the registrant's annual meeting proxy statement. Therefore, this information is often incorporated by reference to the registrant's proxy statement, as described in Section B.3 of this Chapter. Except as described below, a detailed discussion of the information required to be disclosed pursuant to Items 10, 11, 12, 13 and 14 of Part III can be found in Chapter 7.[85]

Item 10. Directors, Executive Officers and Corporate Governance. Item 407(c)(3) of Regulation S-K requires a registrant to describe any material changes to its procedures by which security holders may recommend director nominees if those changes were implemented after the registrant's most recent proxy statement disclosure regarding such procedures. Such material changes include adopting such procedures after the registrant's most recent proxy statement disclosure stated that the registrant had no such procedures.[86]

Implementing the requirements of Section 407 of the Sarbanes-Oxley Act, Item 406 of Regulation S-K requires the registrant to disclose whether it has adopted a code of ethics that applies to the registrant's principal executive officer, principal financial officer, principal accounting officer or controller, or persons performing similar functions.[87] If the registrant has not adopted such a code of ethics, the registrant must explain why it has not done so.[88]

---

[84] See SEC Release No. 34-49424 (March 16, 2004).

[85] Registrants not incorporating by reference Part III information from their proxy statements should note that some of the corporate governance information required by Item 407 of Regulation S-K described below in Chapter 7 is not required to be included in the Form 10-K. For registrants that are incorporating by reference Part III information from their proxy statements, such corporate governance information is not deemed incorporated by reference into the Form 10-K.

[86] See SEC Releases 34-48825 (November 24, 2003) and 33-8732 (August 11, 2006) and Chapter 7.

[87] See SEC Release No. 33-8177 (January 23, 2003).

[88] A registrant may have separate codes of ethics for different types of officers. Furthermore, a code of ethics may be a portion of a broader document that addresses additional topics or that applies to more persons than those specified in this provision. A registrant need only file, post or provide the portions of a broader document that constitutes a code of ethics

Registrants should note that NASDAQ Listing Rules require NASDAQ-listed companies to adopt a publicly available code of conduct that has the same elements as the required code of ethics, but is applicable to a broader group of people—all employees and directors.

(a) Definition of a Code of Ethics. Item 406(b) provides that for purposes of Item 406 of Regulation S-K the term "code of ethics" means written standards that are reasonably designed to deter wrongdoing and to promote all of the following:

● Honest and ethical conduct, including the ethical handling of actual or apparent conflicts of interest between personal and professional relationships;

● Full, fair, accurate, timely and understandable disclosure in reports and documents that a registrant files with, or submits to, the SEC and in other public communications made by the registrant;

● Compliance with applicable governmental laws, rules and regulations;

● The prompt internal reporting of violations of the code to an appropriate person or persons identified in the code (such person(s) should not be involved in the matter giving rise to the violation and should be of sufficient status within the company); and

● Accountability for adherence to the code.

(b) Disclosure of the Code of Ethics. Pursuant to Item 406(c) of Regulation S-K, the registrant must either:

● File a copy of its code of ethics as an exhibit to its Form 10-K;

● Post the text of such code of ethics on its Internet website[89] and disclose, in its Form 10-K (or the proxy statement if the registrant is incorporating Item 10 of Form 10-K information from the proxy statement), its Internet address and the fact that it has posted such code of ethics on its Internet website; or

● Undertake in its Form 10-K (or the proxy statement if the registrant is incorporating Item 10 of Form 10-K information from the proxy statement), filed with the SEC to provide to any person without charge, upon

---

(Footnote Continued)

as defined in Item 406(b) of Regulation S-K and that apply to the persons specified in Item 406(a) of Regulation S-K.

[89] If a registrant elects to satisfy this requirement by posting its code of ethics on its website, the code of ethics must remain accessible on its website for as long as the registrant remains subject to the requirements of this Item and chooses to comply with this Item by posting its code on its website.

request, a copy of such code of ethics and explain the manner in which such request may be made.

(c) Amendments to and Waivers from the Code of Ethics. Item 5.05 of Form 8-K requires specified disclosure in the event of any amendment (other than technical, administrative or other non-substantive amendments) to or grant of a waiver from a provision of its code of ethics. However, paragraph (c) of Item 5.05 of Form 8-K provides that a registrant does not need to file a Form 8-K if it discloses the required information on its Internet website within four business days following the date of the amendment or waiver and the registrant has disclosed in its most recently filed annual report its Internet address and intention to provide disclosure in this manner. If the registrant elects to disclose the required information through its website, such information must remain available on the website for at least a 12-month period. Following the 12-month period, the registrant must retain the information for a period of not less than five years. Upon request, the registrant must furnish to the SEC or its staff a copy of any or all information retained pursuant to this requirement.

Item 12. Security Ownership of Certain Beneficial Owners and Management and Related Stockholder Matters. In December 2001, the SEC adopted amendments to Item 12 of Form 10-K and Item 201 of Regulation S-K to require registrants to disclose in their Form 10-K information about the securities that have been authorized for issuance under equity compensation plans[90] in effect[91] as of the end of the last completed fiscal year, whether or not the plans have been approved by security holders.[92] The disclosure is intended to address the SEC's concerns regarding (i) the absence of full disclosure to security holders about equity compensation plans; (ii) the potential dilutive effect of equity compensation plans; and (iii) the adoption of many plans without the approval of security holders.

(a) In specific, Item 201(d) of Regulation S-K requires tabular disclosure of the following information as of the most recently completed fiscal year[93] on an aggregated basis[94] for two categories of equity compensation plans—those

---

[90] Disclosure must be provided with respect to any compensation plan, including individual compensation arrangements and plans assumed in connection with acquisition transactions, but excluding qualified employee benefit plans (e.g., 401(k) plans), of the registrant or its parent, subsidiary or affiliate under which equity securities of the registrant are authorized for issuance to directors, employees, consultants, advisors, vendors, customers, suppliers and/or lenders as compensation for goods or services.

[91] A plan is deemed to be in effect if options, warrants or rights previously granted under the plan remain outstanding or securities remain authorized for issuance under the plan.

[92] See SEC Release No. 33-8048 (December 21, 2001).

[93] Registrants should consider also disclosing separately information regarding plans adopted or amended or securities issued under a plan after the most recently completed fiscal year to provide a current snapshot of its plans and the issuance of securities thereunder.

[94] Information is not required to be disclosed on a plan-by-plan basis.

previously approved by the registrant's security holders and those not previously approved by the registrant's security holders:[95]

(1) the number of securities to be issued upon the exercise of outstanding options, warrants or rights under such plan(s);

(2) the weighted average exercise price of such outstanding options, warrants and rights under such plan(s);[96] and

(3) other than securities to be issued upon the exercise of outstanding options, warrants or rights, the number of securities remaining available for future issuance under such plan(s).[97]

If a registrant has more than one class of equity security issued under its equity compensation plans, it should aggregate the plan information for each class of security. The required tabular format for this disclosure is as follows:

EQUITY COMPENSATION PLAN INFORMATION

Plan category	Number of securities to be issued upon exercise of outstanding options, warrants and rights	Weighted-average exercise price of outstanding options, warrants and rights	Number of securities remaining available for future issuance under equity compensation plans (excluding securities reflected in column (a))
	(a)	(b)	(c)
Equity compensation plans approved by security holders			
Equity compensation plans not approved by security holders			
Total			

In footnotes to the table, a registrant must disclose, to the extent applicable:

● on an aggregated basis, the number of securities to be issued under, and the weighted exercise price of, individual options, warrants and rights assumed in connection with a merger, consolidation or other acquisition transaction;

---

[95] Security holder approval of a plan assumed in an acquisition transaction refers to approval by the security holders of the acquiror (as opposed to the acquiree), such as separately in connection with the acquisition transaction.

[96] If there are securities outstanding for which a price cannot be determined, this should be explained in a footnote.

[97] Shares issuable under employee stock purchase plans should be a part of this number.

● separately for each plan that includes securities available for future issuance other than upon the exercise of an option, warrant or right (e.g., grants of restricted stock or performance shares), the number of securities and type of plan; and

● any formula used to calculate the number of securities available for issuance under a plan (e.g., an evergreen provision that automatically increases the number of securities available for issuance by a percentage of the number of outstanding securities of the registrant).

(b) A registrant must also describe briefly, in narrative form, the material features of each equity compensation plan adopted without the approval of its security holders (and file such plan as an exhibit pursuant to Item 601 of Regulation S-K). As an alternative, this information can be provided by cross-referencing such information in a registrant's financial statements and specifying the plan(s) that were not approved by security holders.[98] Registrants should consider also describing the material terms of their equity compensation plans that have been approved by security holders in order to provide a more balanced picture of their equity compensation.

(c) If security holders are acting on any compensation plan (equity or cash, such as a performance bonus plan, and including an amendment to a plan) at a meeting, the equity compensation plan disclosure must also be included in the registrant's proxy statement relating to the meeting at which security holders will be voting on the plan. As such, the information required to be disclosed in the Form 10-K can instead be incorporated by reference from a registrant's definitive proxy statement that involves the election of directors, if the definitive proxy statement is filed with the SEC not later than 120 days after the end of the fiscal year covered by the Form 10-K.

5. Part IV of the Form 10-K.

Item 15. Exhibits and Financial Statement Schedules. This Item requires the registrant to list the following documents filed as a part of the Form 10-K:

(a) All financial statements;

(b) Those financial statement schedules required to be filed by Item 8 of the Form 10-K, and the financial statement schedules required by Regulation S-X that are excluded from the Annual Report by Rule 14a-3(b) under the Exchange Act, including separate financial statements of subsidiaries not consolidated; and

(c) Exhibits required by Item 601 of Regulation S-K.

---

[98] This information would appear in the footnote disclosure required by FASB ASC Topic 718. If this FASB ASC Topic 718 footnote disclosure, however, does not disclose all of the material terms of a plan not approved by security holders, a registrant should not use such a cross reference to satisfy the disclosure requirements.

In preparing the list of exhibits to be included in the Form 10-K, Item 601 of Regulation S-K should be consulted. Item 601 provides an "Exhibit Table" identifying, in the last column, the exhibits that are required to be listed in the Form 10-K. The Exhibit Table assigns a number to each document type (e.g., articles of incorporation (3) and material contracts (10)). While preparing the list of exhibits, this numbering system should be used in identifying the exhibits. For example, if two "material contracts" are being filed as exhibits, they should be listed as Exhibits 10.1 and 10.2 or as 10(a) and 10(b). Exhibits that are typically filed either directly with the Form 10-K or through incorporation by reference into the Form 10-K, with their corresponding exhibit numbers, include: articles of incorporation and bylaws (3); instruments defining rights of security holders (4); material contracts (10); statement re: computation of per share earnings (11); statement re: computation of ratios (12); a code of ethics (14); a list of the registrant's subsidiaries (21); consent of auditors (23); Section 302 certifications (31); and Section 906 certification(s) (32).

Unlike the Form 10-Q, for which registrants need only file those exhibits that were entered into or became effective during the fiscal quarter covered by the Form 10-Q, the Form 10-K must include all exhibits that were entered into or became effective during the fiscal year covered by the Form 10-K and all previously filed exhibits that are still applicable to the registrant no matter when the filed document was entered into or became effective, even if the exhibits have been previously filed with the SEC. Therefore, to accurately put together a Form 10-K exhibit list, one should look at the exhibit list for the registrant's previously filed Form 10-K, delete any items that are no longer relevant and add any items filed as exhibits with the SEC during the year (e.g., with the Form 10-Q, a Form 8-K or a registration statement) and any other relevant items from the fourth quarter of the recently completed year.

In preparing the exhibit index, the following should also be considered:

● When a document has been previously filed with the SEC, the document may be incorporated into the Form 10-K by reference by noting in the exhibit index this fact and the location of the document (e.g., "Incorporated by reference to Exhibit 3.1 to the registrant's Quarterly Report on Form 10-Q for the period ended September 30, 2011").

● The registrant must identify in the exhibit list each management contract or compensatory plan or arrangement required to be filed as an exhibit to the Form 10-K (e.g., stock incentive plans in which the registrant's executive officers are eligible to participate, employment agreements with the registrant's executive officers and indemnification agreements with executive officers). This is often accomplished by using a separate footnote designation for these exhibits (e.g., "*Management contract or compensatory plan, contract or arrangement required to be filed as an exhibit to this annual report on Form 10-K").

● Counsel should discuss with the registrant whether any agreements entered into by the registrant that have not yet been filed with the SEC are material to the registrant.

● Except as discussed in Chapter 4, exhibits must be filed by EDGAR. Where documents to be filed as exhibits are not drafted by the registrant or its counsel (e.g., material agreements), upon completion of the document the registrant should request that a copy of the document be provided to the registrant or its counsel in electronic format (e.g., a computer disk, e-mail, etc.) to facilitate the EDGAR filing process.

● Material agreements include contracts made outside of the ordinary course of business that are material to the registrant and that are to be performed in whole or in part after the filing of the Form 10-K or were entered into not more than two years before the Form 10-K filing.

● All equity compensation plans in which any employee participates not approved by the registrant's security holders (unless immaterial in amount or significance and not involving any director or named executive officer as a participant) must be filed as material agreement exhibits.

● Material agreements and other documents filed as exhibits via EDGAR should contain conformed signatures in the place of the manual signature. For example:

/s/ JOHN DOE
John Doe

● Material amendments to previously filed exhibits are required to be filed unless such previously filed exhibit would not be currently required. In addition, registrants must restate their articles of incorporation or bylaws in their entirety if they are amended.[99]

● Previously filed documents that are no longer in effect or material contracts that are no longer "material" need not be listed or incorporated by reference.

● If two or more documents required to be filed as exhibits are substantially identical in all material respects except as to the parties thereto, the dates of execution or other details, the registrant can file one of such documents with a schedule identifying the other documents omitted and setting forth the material details in which such documents differ from the document filed.

---

[99] Item 601(b)(3) of Regulation S-K and Rule 102(c) of Regulation S-T.

● The SEC has recently become more vigilant in requiring that material contracts filed as exhibits include all attachments, schedules and exhibits thereto, especially if they contain material information.

6. Filing Confidential Treatment Requests. A registrant is often reluctant to file as exhibits certain required documents where it believes the public disclosure of such documents may adversely affect the company's business because of the competitive harm that could result from the disclosure. This issue frequently arises in connection with the requirement that a registrant file publicly all contracts material to its business other than those it enters into in the ordinary course of business pursuant to Item 601(b)(10) of Regulation S-K. Typical examples of information that raise this concern include pricing terms, technical specifications and milestone payments. To address the potential disclosure hardship, the SEC has a system allowing companies to request confidential treatment of information filed under the Securities Act and the Exchange Act. Rule 24b-2 under the Exchange Act sets forth the exclusive means for obtaining confidential treatment of information contained in a document filed under the Exchange Act that would be exempt from disclosure under the Freedom of Information Act ("FOIA"). FOIA requires all federal agencies to make specified information available to the public, including the information required to be filed publicly by SEC rules. FOIA contains, however, nine specific exemptions. The rules require that confidential treatment requests ("CTRs") contain an analysis of the applicable FOIA exemption. Most applicants rely on the exemption that covers "trade secrets and commercial or financial information obtained from a person and privileged or confidential" which is commonly referred to as "the (b)(4) exemption." For example, many registrants argue that redacted words or numbers constitute "commercial or financial information," the disclosure of which will result in "substantial competitive harm" to the registrant. Historically, the SEC staff reviewed and commented on all CTRs. Beginning in late 2001, as a consequence of the high volume of CTRs, some CTRs have received "no review" from the staff after skimming the applicable exhibit to ensure redactions are limited to certain types of information and only those words that are confidential.

In Staff Legal Bulletin No. 1 issued by the SEC's Division of Corporation Finance on February 28, 1997, and as amended in Staff Legal Bulletin No. 1A on July 11, 2001,[100] the staff summarized the requirements a registrant must satisfy when requesting confidential treatment of information. The staff provided both "substantive" and "procedural" guidelines.

---

[100] See Appendix 14 for Staff Legal Bulletin Nos. 1 and 1A.

(a) Substantive Guidelines.

(1) Confidential treatment cannot be granted if the information is publicly disclosed. The applicant must make every effort not to disclose any of the confidential information, including safeguarding copies of agreements and restricting access to only those who have a need to know the information or who are under a duty to keep the information confidential. The application must include an affirmative representation as to the confidentiality of the information it covers.

(2) Required and/or material information must be disclosed, even if confidential. Except in unusual circumstances, disclosure required by Regulation S-K or any other applicable disclosure requirement is not an appropriate subject for confidential treatment, regardless of the availability of an exemption under FOIA. The type of information specifically listed by the staff where a confidential treatment request would not be appropriate includes, for example:

- the identity of a 10% customer;
- the dollar amount of firm backlog orders;
- interest expense and other similar terms in a material credit agreement;
- the duration and effect of all patents, trademarks, licenses, franchises and concessions held;
- required disclosure in the MD&A section relating for instance to loan arrangements and installment payment obligations on debt; and
- disclosure about related party transactions.

(3) The application should not be overly broad. Applicants should be selective when identifying the information covered by their application. A CTR should cover only those numbers, words and phrases for which confidentiality is necessary and supported by FOIA and applicable SEC rules.

(4) Applicants must set forth their analyses of the exemption(s). The rules require that the application include a statement of the grounds of the objection referring to and analyzing the applicable exemption(s) from disclosure under the SEC's rule adopted under FOIA.[101] The application should avoid conclusory statements and must include a sufficient legal analysis, including case law references. Two seminal cases covering the definition of "confidential" information are *National Parks & Conservation Assn. v. Morton*, 498 F.2d 765 (D.C. Cir. 1974), and *National Parks & Conservation Assn. v. Kleppe*, 547 F.2d 673 (D.C. Cir. 1976). The application also should include a factual analysis of the basis for the exemption requested (for example, commercial harm to the filing party) with respect to the specific information that is the subject of the request.

---

[101] Rule 24b-2(b)(2)(ii) of the Exchange Act.

(5) Applicants must specify particular durations. The application must request a specific date (year, month and day) for the termination of confidential treatment of the subject information and an analysis that supports the period requested.[102]

(6) Applicants must identify clearly the information that is the subject of the application. To make sure there is a complete record as to which information has been granted confidential treatment, the application should describe each item or category of information omitted pursuant to the CTR.

(7) Applicants must consent to the release of the information for official purposes. The application must include a written consent to the furnishing of the confidential portion "to other government agencies, offices or bodies and to the Congress."[103]

(b) Procedural Guidelines.

(1) Applicants must file the applications with the Office of the Secretary. Applicants must send every application for confidential treatment to the Office of the Secretary of the SEC in envelopes marked "Confidential Treatment" which are separate from the envelope for any materials which are to be or have been filed publicly.[104]

(2) Applicants, including EDGAR filers, must file the applications in paper form. Applicants must file CTRs in paper form, not by EDGAR.

(3) Applicants should file applications at the same time they file the material from which they have omitted the confidential information. The confidential treatment process contemplates that issuers file CTRs at the same time that they file the publicly disclosed portions.[105]

(4) Applicants must omit from the public filings all of the information that is the subject of the application.

(5) Applicants must adequately mark the confidential portions of publicly filed documents. The applicant must "indicate at the appropriate place in the material filed that the confidential portion has been so omitted and filed separately with the SEC."[106] The staff recommends marking an asterisk or other mark in the precise place in the document where the applicant deletes information. The applicant should also mark the exhibit index to indicate that portions of the exhibit or exhibits have been omitted pursuant to a request for confidential treatment.

---

[102] *Id.*

[103] Rule 24b-2(b)(2)(iii) under the Exchange Act.

[104] Rule 24b-2(b)(3) under the Exchange Act.

[105] See Rule 24b-2(b) under the Exchange Act.

[106] *Id.*

(6) Applicants should show clearly which portions of the complete documents filed with the applications are the subjects of the CTRs. The application must include one complete copy of the document clearly marked to show those portions of the document covered by the CTR.

(7) Applicants should indicate to whom correspondence, orders and notices should be sent. Rule 406(b)(2)(v) under the Securities Act requires the application to include the name, address and telephone number of the person to whom all notices and orders issued under the rule should be directed.

(8) An applicant requesting the extension of a previously granted order for confidential treatment should submit the application before the expiration date of the earlier order. After the expiration date of an order, the subject information is publicly available upon request under FOIA.

7. Signature Requirements.

(a) Who Must Sign. The Form 10-K must be signed by the registrant, and on behalf of the registrant by its principal executive officer or officers (usually its chief executive officer), its principal financial officer (usually its chief financial officer), its controller or principal accounting officer (often the chief financial officer is also the principal accounting officer), and at least a majority of the directors currently serving on its board or persons performing similar functions (e.g., where the registrant does not have a principal executive officer or principal financial officer at the time of filing). Where the registrant is a limited partnership, the Form 10-K must be signed by the majority of the board of directors of any corporate general partner who signs the report. If there is more than one general partner, then a majority of the general partners must sign the Form 10-K. Any person who occupies more than one of the specified positions must indicate each capacity in which he or she signs the Form 10-K (e.g., if a person is both the registrant's principal executive officer and a director serving on the registrant's board). The name and office of each person who signs the Form 10-K must appear beneath his or her signature.

(b) Powers of Attorney. Signatures of officers and directors required for the Form 10-K, other than the Sections 302 and 906 certifications, may be provided by a power of attorney. Thus, an officer or director can grant a third party a power of attorney to sign the Form 10-K on his or her behalf. For example, this may be done if such person has reviewed the Form 10-K, but knows he or she will not be available to provide a signature for the Form 10-K. For practical purposes though, if someone has reviewed the Form 10-K (and all directors and officers signing the Form 10-K must), he or she should be able to sign the signature page of the Form 10-K just as easily as he or she can sign a power of attorney. After all, the power of attorney does not diminish the responsibility of the applicable officer or director to review the Form 10-K or any liability for disclosure deficiencies therein. Where a power of attorney is used, a copy of the power of attorney with a conformed signature must be filed as an exhibit to the Form 10-K.[107] In addition, where an officer signs on behalf of the registrant under a power of attorney, certified copies of the board resolution authorizing the use of the power of attorney must also be filed.[108]

(c) **Retention of Signature Pages.** For the EDGAR filing of the Form 10-K, a conformed signature should be used to indicate each person who has signed the Form 10-K. EDGAR filers must retain the manual signature pages for five years after the filing and provide them to the SEC upon request.[109] In addition, non-EDGAR filers (e.g., foreign private issuers and foreign governments) that make paper filings and elect to file a signature page containing facsimiles or copies of manual signatures must also retain such manual signature pages for five years.[110] The signature block of any board member who has not signed the Form 10-K should be left blank or the related signature block should be deleted.

8. Certifications.

(a) **Section 302 Certification.** Rules 13a-14 and 15d-14 under the Exchange Act, which were adopted by the SEC effective August 29, 2002, as directed by Section 302(a) of the Sarbanes-Oxley Act, require each principal executive officer and principal financial officer of a registrant, in addition to signing the Form 10-K on behalf of the registrant, to provide in an exhibit to the Form 10-K (including amendments and transition reports) a certification in the following form:

I, [identify the certifying individual], certify that:

1. I have reviewed this Form 10-K of [identify registrant];

2. Based on my knowledge, this report does not contain any untrue statement of a material fact or omit to state a material fact necessary to make the statements made, in light of the circumstances under which such statements were made, not misleading with respect to the period covered by this report;

3. Based on my knowledge, the financial statements, and other financial information included in this report, fairly present in all material respects the financial condition, results of operations and cash flows of the registrant as of, and for, the periods presented in this report;[111]

---

[107] Item 601(b)(24) of Regulation S-K.
[108] Form 10-K, General Instruction D(2).
[109] Rule 302(b) of Regulation S-T.
[110] Rule 12b-11(d) under the Exchange Act.
[111] The financial disclosure being certified includes footnotes to the financial statements, selected financial data and MD&A. The standard of a "fair presentation" is one of overall material accuracy and completeness that is broader than being in compliance with GAAP; according to the SEC, it includes "the selection of appropriate accounting policies, proper application of appropriate accounting policies, disclosure of financial information that is informative and reasonably reflects the underlying transactions and events and the inclusion of any additional disclosure necessary to provide investors with a materially accurate and complete picture." See SEC Release No. 33-8124 (August 29, 2002).

4. The registrant's other certifying officer(s) and I are responsible for establishing and maintaining disclosure controls and procedures (as defined in Exchange Act Rules 13a-15(e) and 15d-15(e)) and internal control over financial reporting (as defined in Exchange Act Rules 13a-15(f) and 15d-15(f)) for the registrant and have:

(a) Designed such disclosure controls and procedures, or caused such disclosure controls and procedures to be designed under our supervision, to ensure that material information relating to the registrant, including its consolidated subsidiaries, is made known to us by others within those entities, particularly during the period in which this report is being prepared;

(b) Designed such internal control over financial reporting, or caused such internal control over financial reporting to be designed under our supervision, to provide reasonable assurance regarding the reliability of financial reporting and the preparation of financial statements for external purposes in accordance with generally accepted accounting principles;

(c) Evaluated the effectiveness of the registrant's disclosure controls and procedures and presented in this report our conclusions about the effectiveness of the disclosure controls and procedures, as of the end of the period covered by this report based on such evaluation; and

(d) Disclosed in this report any change in the registrant's internal control over financial reporting that occurred during the registrant's fourth fiscal quarter that has materially affected, or is reasonably likely to materially affect, the registrant's internal control over financial reporting; and

5. The registrant's other certifying officer(s) and I have disclosed, based on our most recent evaluation of internal control over financial reporting, to the registrant's auditors and the audit committee of the registrant's board of directors:

(a) All significant deficiencies and material weaknesses in the design or operation of internal control over financial reporting which are reasonably likely to adversely affect the registrant's ability to record, process, summarize and report financial information; and

(b) Any fraud, whether or not material, that involves management or other employees who have a significant role in the registrant's internal control over financial reporting.[112]

---

[98] Prior to the first Form 10-K required to include management's internal control report pursuant to Item 308 of Regulation S-K for a company that has recently gone public (i.e., a newly public company's first Form 10-K), the Section 302 certification of principal executive and financial officers included in such Form 10-K need not include the following language:

● the introductory language in paragraph 4 need not certify that such officer and the other certifying officer(s) are also responsible for establishing and maintaining internal control over financial reporting for the registrant; and

The wording of the required certification as it appears in Form 10-K cannot be changed in any respect, even inconsequentially. The certifications of the principal executive and financial officers should be submitted separately as Exhibits 31.1 and 31.2 to the Form 10-K. A person required to provide the certification may not have the certification signed on his or her behalf pursuant to a power of attorney.[113]

Neither Section 302 of the Sarbanes-Oxley Act nor the rules promulgated by the SEC pursuant thereto contain any specific provisions regarding civil or criminal liability for making a false certification (in contrast to Section 906 of the Sarbanes-Oxley Act, which provides criminal liability for knowingly making a false certification under that Section). However, a violation of any of these provisions will constitute a violation of the Exchange Act and/or the rules and regulations thereunder. Specifically, an officer providing a false certification may potentially be subject to an SEC action for violating Section 13(a) or 15(d) of the Exchange Act (regarding filing of periodic and other reports) and to both SEC and private actions for violating Section 10(b) of the Exchange Act and Rule 10b-5 thereunder (the general anti-fraud provisions of the securities laws). In addition, a false certification made in a report that is incorporated by reference into a registration statement (e.g., a Form S-3) may result in liability under Sections 11 (regarding civil liabilities on account of a false or misleading statement in a registration statement) and 12(a)(2) (regarding civil liabilities on account of a false or misleading statement in a prospectus). Further, under Section 32(a) of the Exchange Act, as amended by the Sarbanes-Oxley Act, a willful violation of Section 302 and/or the SEC rules promulgated pursuant thereto could subject the violator to criminal liability, including a fine of up to $5 million and/or imprisonment for up to 20 years. Keep in mind also that, even without the certification, a registrant's chief executive and chief financial officers already are responsible as signatories for the registrant's disclosures under Exchange Act liability provisions and can be liable for material misstatements in, or omissions from, the certified reports under general antifraud standards and under the SEC's authority to seek redress against those who aid or abet securities law violations.

(b) Section 906 Certification. Each Form 10-K must also be accompanied by a written statement by the chief executive officer and chief financial officer of the issuer certifying that:

(Footnote Continued)

● certification (in paragraph 4(b)) that such officer and the other certifying officer(s) designed such internal control over financial reporting, or caused such internal control over financial reporting to be designed under their supervision, to provide reasonable assurance regarding the reliability of financial reporting and the preparation of financial statements for external purposes in accordance with generally accepted accounting principles.

[1] Rules 13a-14(d) and 15d-14(d) under the Exchange Act.

1. The Form 10-K fully complies with the requirements of Section 13(a) or 15(d) of the Exchange Act; and

2. That information contained in the Form 10-K fairly presents, in all material respects, the financial condition and results of operations of the registrant.

The information to be certified is not limited to that contained in the financial statements and necessarily includes the MD&A and other parts of the report.

The certification required to meet the requirement of Section 906 must be filed as Exhibit 32 to the Form 10-K. The principal executive and principal financial officer may either submit a single Section 906 certification that is signed by each of the certifying officers (which would be submitted as Exhibit 32) or they may submit separate Section 906 certifications (which would be submitted as Exhibits 32.1 and 32.2). A person required to provide the certification may not have the certification signed on his or her behalf pursuant to a power of attorney or other form of confirming authority.[114]

There has been no guidance from the SEC regarding the form or language of the certification (other than that in Section 906 itself). However, some counsel have advocated qualifying the certification by inserting language to the effect that the certification is to the officer's "knowledge" or "best knowledge and belief." Others have suggested including language to limit the purpose of the certification solely to fulfilling the requirements of Section 906. Qualification of the certification in any manner may raise questions as to whether those making the certifications have fulfilled their obligations under Section 906. It may also foster negative inferences in the minds of investors and the public as to the meaning of the certification; people may be suspicious of qualified certifications or view them less favorably than unqualified certifications. Further, submitting the certification in exactly the language contained in Section 906 is consistent with SEC guidance stating that the form of the certifications that were required of the CEOs and CFOs of 947 of the United States' largest public companies (pursuant to Order No. 4-460 issued on June 27, 2002) could not be modified if the certifications were to comply with the SEC's order. Note that, even without a knowledge qualifier, a signing executive can only be held criminally liable under Section 906 if he or she makes the certification with knowledge that it is untrue, as discussed below.

Section 906 requires that the certifications "accompany" the periodic report to which they relate. This is in contrast to Section 302, which requires the certifications to be included "in" the periodic report. In recognition of this difference, registrants may "furnish," rather than "file," the Section 906 certifications with the SEC. Thus, the certifications would not be subject to liability

---

[114] *Id.*

under Section 18 of the Exchange Act. Moreover, the certifications would not be subject to automatic incorporation by reference into a company's Securities Act registration statements, which are subject to liability under Section 11 of the Securities Act, unless the issuer takes steps to include the certifications in a registration statement.

Section 906 imposes criminal liability upon officers who certify (or "willfully" certify) any statement required by Section 906 "knowing" that the report accompanying the statement does not comport with the requirements of Section 906. The penalties for such violations can be severe—fines up to $1 million and/or imprisonment of up to 10 years for "knowing" violations and fines up to $5 million and/or imprisonment of up to 20 years for "willful" violations. Section 906 does not, however, specifically address the consequences of failure to file the required certification. Additionally, the potential exposure of officers to civil liability for making a false certification or for failure to file the certification is not yet clear. However, because Section 906 certifications are now exhibits filed under Item 601 of Regulation S-K, failure to furnish the certifications would violate Section 13(a) of the Exchange Act because the Form 10-K would be incomplete. An individual who willfully fails to submit the Section 906 certification may be subject to prosecution under Section 32 of the Exchange Act.

D. Filing with the SEC.

1. Timing of Filing. The Form 10-K must be filed by EDGAR with the SEC within 90 days after the end of the fiscal year covered by the report[115] with the following exceptions:[116]

(a) Accelerated Filers. If a registrant is an accelerated filer, its Form 10-K must be filed by EDGAR with the SEC within 75 days after the end of the fiscal year covered by the report:[117]

Pursuant to Rule 12b-2 under the Exchange Act, the term "accelerated filer" means a registrant after it first meets the following conditions as of the end of its fiscal year:[118]

(i) The aggregate worldwide market value of the voting and non-voting common equity held by non-affiliates of the registrant is $75 million or more, but less than $700 million;[119]

---

[115] Form 10-K, General Instruction A(2)(a)(i) and (b).

[116] A registrant should verify whether it is an accelerated filer or large accelerated filer before its fiscal year ends, given that will dictate whether its Form 10-K must be filed earlier with the SEC.

[117] Form 10-K, General Instruction A(2)(a)(ii) and (iii).

[118] These conditions for becoming an accelerated filer are based primarily on the requirements for a registrant to register a primary offering on a Form S-3 registration statement without volume limitations.

[119] The aggregate market value of the registrant's outstanding voting and non-voting common equity is computed using the last sales price, or the average of the

(ii) The registrant has been subject to the requirements of Section 13(a) or 15(d) of the Exchange Act for at least 12 calendar months;

(iii) The registrant has filed at least one Form 10-K pursuant to Section 13(a) or 15(d) of the Exchange Act; and

(iv) The registrant is not eligible to use the requirements for smaller reporting companies for its annual and quarterly reports.

Once a registrant becomes an accelerated filer as of the end of a fiscal year, it remains an accelerated filer with respect to the Form 10-K for that fiscal year and all subsequent fiscal years unless the registrant's public float falls below $50 million, in which case the accelerated filer may exit accelerated filer status by filing a Form 10-K on a non-accelerated basis for the same fiscal year that the determination of public float is made.[120] In that case, the registrant will not become an accelerated filer again unless it subsequently meets the conditions set forth in Rule 12b-2 under the Exchange Act.

(b) Large Accelerated Filers. If a registrant is a large accelerated filer, its Form 10-K must be filed by EDGAR with the SEC within 60 days after the end of the fiscal year covered by the report.

Pursuant to Rule 12b-2 under the Exchange Act, the term "large accelerated filer" means a registrant after it first meets the following conditions as of the end of its fiscal year:

(i) The aggregate worldwide market value of the voting and non-voting common equity held by non-affiliates of the registrant is $700 million or more;[121]

(Footnote Continued)

bid and ask prices, of such common equity, in the principal market for such common equity, as of the last business day of the registrant's most recently completed second fiscal quarter.

[120] Due to transition rules for accelerated filers, a company can be both an accelerated filer and a smaller reporting company at the same time. For example, if a company with a fiscal year-end of December 31 was an accelerated filer with respect to filings due in 2010 and had a public float of $60 million on the last business day of its second fiscal quarter of 2010, then for filings due in 2011 (i) the company would qualify as a smaller reporting company because it had less than $75 million in public float on the last business day of its second fiscal quarter in 2010, but (ii) the company would also still be an accelerated filer because it was required to have less than $50 million in public float on the last business day of its second fiscal quarter in 2010 to exit accelerated filer status in 2011. Such company may use the scaled disclosure requirements for smaller reporting companies in its Form 10-K, but the report is due 75 days after the end of its fiscal year. See SEC's Division of Corporation Finance Compliance and Disclosure Interpretations—Regulation   S-K—Questions and Answers of General Applicability— Section 102. Item 10—General—Question 102.01 (July 3, 2008).

[121] See footnote 119.

(ii) The registrant has been subject to the requirements of Section 13(a) or 15(d) of the Exchange Act for at least 12 calendar months;

(iii) The registrant has filed at least one Form 10-K pursuant to Section 13(a) or 15(d) of the Exchange Act; and

(iv) The registrant is not eligible to use the requirements for smaller reporting companies for its annual and quarterly reports.

Once a registrant becomes a large accelerated filer as of the end of the fiscal year, it remains a large accelerated filer with respect to the Form 10-K for that fiscal year and all subsequent fiscal years unless the registrant's public float falls below $500 million (but remains above $50 million), in which case the large accelerated filer becomes an accelerated filer. In that case, a registrant will not become a large accelerated filer again unless it subsequently meets the conditions set forth in Rule 12b-2 under the Exchange Act.[122]

(c) Saturdays, Sundays and Holidays. If the Form 10-K due date is on a Saturday, Sunday or holiday, the filing may be made on the first business day following the due date.[123]

(d) Part III Information. Information required to be included in Part III of the Form 10-K may be incorporated by reference from the registrant's proxy statement if it is (or is expected to be) filed by EDGAR with the SEC within 120 days after the end of the registrant's fiscal year.

Example: Registrants with a December 31 fiscal year-end will be required to file their definitive proxy statements for their 2012 annual meetings by May 2, 2012, in order to incorporate by reference from the proxy statement information required to be included in Part III of the registrants' Form 10-Ks for their 2011 fiscal year.

When the definitive proxy statement is filed on or before the 120th day, it is automatically incorporated by reference into the Form 10-K. If the proxy statement will not be filed within the 120-day period, the registrant must amend its Form 10-K prior to the end of the 120-day period to provide the information that was to be incorporated by reference.

(e) Financial Statement Schedules. The financial statement schedules required by Article 12 of Regulation S-X may be filed by amendment to the Form 10-K not later than 120 days after the fiscal year covered by the Form 10-K under cover of Form 10-K/A.

(f) The IPO Exception. For a registrant that has completed an initial public offering in the first quarter of its fiscal year, a Form 10-K may not be required to be filed for the fiscal year preceding the IPO. This will only be the

---

[122] See SEC Release No. 33-8644 (December 21, 2005).   [123] Rule 0-3 of the Exchange Act.

case where the final prospectus for such IPO contained certified financial statements for the prior fiscal year.[124] A registrant that has completed an IPO during the first fiscal quarter and has not included certified financial statements for the prior fiscal year in its final prospectus for such IPO will still be required to file the Form 10-K within 90 days of the end of its fiscal year.[125] In general,

---

[124] Rule 13a-1 of the Exchange Act requires that every issuer having securities registered pursuant to Section 12 of the Exchange Act (e.g., as a result of the issuer filing a Form 8-A registration statement for its common stock in connection with its IPO and listing of its common stock on NASDAQ) must file a Form 10-K for each fiscal year after the last full fiscal year for which financial statements were filed in its IPO S-1 registration statement. The rule also requires that such Form 10-K be filed within the period specified in Form 10-K. Thus, if a registrant's IPO Form S-1 registration statement is declared effective in the first quarter of a fiscal year and contained financial statements for the full prior fiscal year, no Form 10-K need be filed for such prior fiscal year. But, if such IPO registration statement did not contain financial statements for the full prior fiscal year, a Form 10-K must be filed for such fiscal year.

[125] Rule 15d-1 of the Exchange Act requires that every registrant under the Securities Act (which registrants that issued their common stock in an IPO will be as a result of filing a Form S-1 registration statement) must file a Form 10-K for the fiscal year in which the Form S-1 registration statement became effective and each fiscal year thereafter. The rule requires that such Form 10-K be filed within the period specified in Form 10-K. Rule 15d-2 of the Exchange Act requires that if the Form S-1 registration statement did not contain certified financial statements for the registrant's last full fiscal year preceding the year in which the registration statement became effective, then the registrant must file a special financial report on "the appropriate form for annual reports of the registrant" (e.g.,

Form 10-K) for such fiscal year within 90 days after the effective date of the registration statement. This "special financial report" would be filed under cover of the facing sheet of the appropriate annual report form (e.g., Form 10-K) and indicate on the facing sheet that it contains only financial statements for the fiscal year in question. However, the SEC's Division of Corporation Finance has clearly stated in its telephone interpretations manual that it is the SEC staff's position that a registrant is not permitted to file a special financial report pursuant to Rule 15d-2 under the Exchange Act in lieu of an annual report required by Rule 13a-1 of the Exchange Act. Therefore, the only companies that can actually take advantage of Rule 15d-2 under the Exchange Act and file a special financial report on Form 10-K until 90 days after effectiveness of their registration statement are companies that have filed a registration statement under the Securities Act, but do not have securities registered pursuant to Section 12 of the Exchange Act and, therefore, are only required to file annual reports under Section 15 of the Exchange Act and its related rules (and not under Section 13 of the Exchange Act and its related rules). An example of such a company would be one that files a Form S-1 registration statement to publicly offer debt securities, but does not file a Form 8-A because it is not listing such securities on a national securities exchange or market. Rule 15d-2 under the Exchange Act's special financial report is the only mention in the federal securities law of the ability of a registrant to extend the filing deadline for its Form 10-K to 90 days after the effective date of a registration statement, rather than 90 days after its fiscal year-end.

registrants that have recently gone public will not be able to extend the time period for filing of their Form 10-Ks.[126]

2. EDGAR Filing Requirements. Although General Instruction D(1) provides for the filing of paper copies with the SEC, such requirements do not apply to registrants subject to the EDGAR filing requirement. For discussion of these requirements, see Chapter 4.

3. Transmittal Letter. The instructions to the Form 10-K request that the transmittal letter that accompanies the Form 10-K indicate whether the financial statements in the Form 10-K reflect a change from the preceding year in any accounting principles or practices, or in the method of applying any such principles or practices.[127]

4. Filing Fees. No filing fee is required in connection with a Form 10-K.[128]

E. Other Required Distributions of the Form 10-K.

1. Filings with the Exchanges. The Form 10-K is required to be filed with each exchange on which any class of securities of the registrant is listed.[129] However, registrants listed on the NYSE, NYSE Amex or NASDAQ that file their Form 10-Ks by EDGAR do not have to file paper copies of the Form 10-Ks with the NYSE, NYSE Amex or NASDAQ, as applicable, because they are linked into the EDGAR system.[130]

2. Distribution to Shareholders. A registrant registered under the Exchange Act must also offer to send copies of the Form 10-K to shareholders upon request. The offer may be made in either the Annual Report or proxy statement, or, if proxies will not be solicited, in the information statement furnished in lieu of the proxy statement.[131] The registrant's proxy statement or Annual Report must contain an undertaking in boldface or otherwise reasonably prominent type to provide without charge to each person solicited, upon written request, a copy of the registrant's Form 10-K, and indicate the name and address (including title or department) of the person to whom such a written request is to be directed. The registrant need not undertake to furnish without charge copies of all exhibits to its Form 10-K provided that the copy of the

---

[126] With this in mind, registrants with a December 31 fiscal year-end that go public in the first fiscal quarter (e.g., January) and did not have the full prior fiscal year's financial statements in their IPO Form S-1 registration statement must remember that their Form 10-K, containing much of the same disclosure as the Form S-1, will soon after need to be filed with the SEC.

[127] Form 10-K, General Instruction D(3).

[128] See SEC Release No. 34-37692 (September 17, 1996) in which the SEC eliminated 'the $250 filing fee for Form 10-Ks.

[129] Section 13(a)(2) of, and Rule 12b-11 under, the Exchange Act.

[130] See SEC Release Nos. 34-39594 (January 28, 1998) and 34-40220 (July 16, 1998).

[131] Rules 14a-3(b)(10) and 14c-3(a)(1) under the Exchange Act.

Form 10-K furnished to requesting security holders is accompanied by a list briefly describing all the exhibits not contained in the Form 10-K, and the registrant indicates that it will furnish any exhibit upon the payment of a specified reasonable fee (the fee must be limited to the registrant's reasonable expenses in furnishing such exhibit). In addition, if the registrant's Annual Report complies with all of the disclosure requirements of Form 10-K and is filed with the SEC in satisfaction of its Form 10-K filing requirements, the registrant need not furnish a separate Form 10-K to security holders who receive a copy of such Annual Report.

3. Other Delivery Requirements. Registrants should also review agreements they have entered into regarding the incurrence of debt or issuance of equity (e.g., underwriting agreements, credit agreements and stock purchase agreements) because they commonly require timely delivery of periodic SEC filings, including the Form 10-K, to certain parties.

F. SEC Review.

Compared to certain registration statements filed under the Securities Act and some other Exchange Act filings (e.g., preliminary proxy materials and Schedule TOs), filings on Form 10-K have historically been reviewed less frequently by the SEC staff. However, Section 408 of the Sarbanes-Oxley Act[132] provides for enhanced review of periodic disclosures by the SEC. Pursuant to Section 408, the SEC is directed to review a registrant's periodic reports (including financial statements) filed under the Exchange Act on a regular and systematic basis, and in no event less frequently than once every three years. Based on the factors that Congress has directed the SEC to consider when scheduling reviews, certain registrants will be more likely to be the subject of frequent and thorough reviews, including registrants that:

- issued material restatements of financial results or have announced that their previously issued financials cannot be relied upon and must be restated;

- have experienced significant volatility in their stock price as compared to other companies;

- have large market capitalization;

- are emerging companies with disparities in price to earning ratios; or

- have operations that significantly affect any material sector of the economy.

In addition, an SEC review of a Form 10-K is likely to occur where the registrant's registration statement on Form S-3 or S-4, which incorporates by reference portions of the Form 10-K, is selected for review. A review may be

---

[132] Pub. L. No. 107-204, § 408, 116 Stat. 745 (2002).

limited to certain portions of the Form 10-K (e.g., MD&A) and may include other filings (e.g., Form 10-Qs and Form 8-Ks) filed since the Form 10-K.

G. Late Filings.

1. Consequences of Late Filing. The SEC has the authority to revoke registrations under Section 12(j) of the Exchange Act, including for registrants that are serial late filers or delinquent filers of periodic reports. There are also a number of adverse consequences that automatically befall the registrant that fails to file a Form 10-K on time, including:

● Being precluded from filing a "short form" registration statement on S-3,[133] F-2 or F-3 for the next 13 months without the SEC's prior consent. "Short form" registration statements allow the registrant to significantly reduce the amount of information directly contained in a registration statement filed under the Securities Act by incorporating by reference various information from the registrant's Exchange Act filings, including its Form 10-K, and in the case of "shelf registrations," allow for quick access to the debt and equity markets;

● Being precluded from incorporating by reference certain information into a Form S-4 or F-4 filing;

● Until the delinquent Form 10-K filing is made, the registrant cannot register the offer and sale of securities to employees under benefit plans on Form S-8;[134]

● Rule 144 of the Securities Act is unavailable, in some instances, for resales of restricted securities and resales by affiliates/control persons until the delinquent Form 10-K filing is made;

● The SEC may institute an administrative proceeding against any person for failure to file or for false statements or omissions of necessary statements. The SEC has authority to institute investigations, seek injunctions, or otherwise prosecute offenses for failure to file a Form 10-K or for false statements of omitted disclosure; and[135]

● NASDAQ, NYSE Amex and NYSE each have as a requirement for continued listing of a registrant's securities on such market or exchange that the registrant file its Form 10-K and other Exchange Act filings on a timely basis. Until the delinquent Form 10-K filing is made, the applicable securities exchange can suspend trading of the registrant's securities. Even after the delinquent Form 10-K filing is made, the exchange can continue such suspension or even delist the registrant's securities until satisfied that such delinquent filing will not happen again.

---

[133] Form S-3, General Instruction I.A.3.   [135] Section 21(a) of the Exchange Act.
[134] Form S-8, General Instruction A.1.

2. Notification of Late Filing; Extension of Time to File on Form 12b-25. If a registrant cannot file all or a part of the Form 10-K by the required deadline, Rule 12b-25 under the Exchange Act requires the registrant to file a Form 12b-25 with the SEC no later than one business day after the Form 10-K due date notifying the SEC of the registrant's inability to file the Form 10-K or part of the Form 10-K on time. The Form 12b-25, which provides a 15 calendar-day extension for filing of the Form 10-K, requires that the registrant state why the Form 10-K or portion thereof cannot be filed on time. The Form 12b-25 is required to be filed regardless of whether the registrant anticipates filing the Form 10-K within the 15-day extension period. It is critical to note that Rule 12b-25(b) specifically requires that portions of the Form 10-K that can be timely filed be filed on a timely basis. If the entire Form 10-K could not be timely filed because the registrant was "unable to do so without unreasonable effort or expense," the Form 10-K will be considered timely filed if the Form 12b-25 is properly filed and the Form 10-K is filed within the 15 calendar-day extension period. If the inability to timely file the Form 10-K is due to a third person's inability to furnish an opinion or other requisite information (e.g., the registrant's auditors cannot furnish their signed report), that person must furnish a statement to be attached to the Form 12b-25 as an exhibit that states the specific reasons why the opinion or information cannot be provided. There are no additional extensions of time beyond the 15 calendar days. The 15-day grace period does not apply to electronic filers who are late due to difficulties in filing electronically if they apply for and receive a hardship exemption[136] or an adjustment of the filing date.[137]

During the period between the due date of the Form 10-K and its actual filing, the registrant is not eligible to use (i.e., file) "short form" Securities Act registration statements predicated on timely filed Exchange Act reports.[138] However, during the extension period ongoing securities offerings utilizing a previously effective short form registration statement may continue. Use of the short form registration statement would be prevented though if the extension period terminates and the Form 10-K has not been filed. In addition, the registrant's security holders may continue to make resales under Rule 144 of the Securities Act during the extension period, but if the extension period has expired and the Form 10-K remains unfiled, the registrant will not be deemed to have satisfied the current public reporting requirement of Rule 144 during such extended period.

In the SEC Division of Corporation Finance's Current Issues and Rulemaking Projects Outline (November 14, 2000), the SEC staff indicated that it is concerned with the continued frequent use of Rule 12b-25, and in recent years has more closely monitored Form 12b-25 notices of late filing and taken appropriate action depending upon the registrant's reason for delay and whether the subject filing is subsequently filed during the extension period. Possible staff

---

[136] Rules 201 and 202 of Regulation S-T.
[137] Rule 13(b) of Regulation S-T.

[138] Rule 12b-25(d) under the Exchange Act.

action includes referral to the Division of Enforcement and prioritization of the subject report for staff review.

For example, the SEC has recently brought cases against registrants for omitting material facts that made statements in their Form 12b-25 regarding reasons for not filing their Form 10-Ks on time misleading. As such, registrants must remember that the Form 12b-25 should be treated like other SEC disclosure documents and avoid material misstatements and omissions. In addition to possible SEC action that may result from a Form 12b-25 filing, many members of the financial community consider the filing to be a potential "red flag" for financial or other issues that a registrant may be facing.

H. Amendments.

Amendments to a Form 10-K may be filed in order to revise disclosures previously provided or to provide previously omitted disclosures. Amendments are commonly filed in order to:

- Revise disclosures in response to SEC staff comments;

- Provide disclosures omitted pursuant to Form 12b-25 filings;

- Provide disclosures that were intended to be incorporated by reference from definitive proxy statements filed within 120 days of the registrant's fiscal year-end; or

- Restate materially incorrect financials.

Amendments to a Form 10-K are filed under cover of the Form 10-K with a "/A" added to designate the filing as an amendment (i.e., Form 10-K/A).[139] Because amendments must be numbered sequentially, many registrants place a parenthetical reference after the Form 10-K/A designation on the cover page (e.g., "Form 10-K/A (Amendment No. 1)"). When an amendment to a Form 10-K is requested by the SEC staff (e.g., in connection with an SEC staff review), registrants should consider requesting that the SEC staff review a draft of the amended filing before it is "filed." This may allow the registrant to avoid the often embarrassing need to file multiple amendments. To the extent that more than one Exchange Act report is being amended, a separate amendment must be filed for each such report.

Only those items being amended must be included in a Form 10-K amendment. Amendments to a Form 10-K, however, must set forth the complete text of each item amended.

Example: A change in the "Liquidity and Capital Resources" section of MD&A would require that the entire amended and restated Item 7,

---

[139] Rule 12b-15 under the Exchange Act.

Management's Discussion and Analysis of Financial Condition and Results of Operations, be included in a Form 10-K amendment. However, unless there were changes to any other items, the registrant could just include that item in the amendment and state at the bottom of the cover page of the Form 10-K/A that the amendment was being provided solely to amend and restate Item 7.

The Form 10-K amendment need only be signed by a duly authorized representative of the registrant. No signatures of the registrant's board members or specified officers are required on the Form 10-K/A. However, new certifications required by Rules 13a-14 and 15d-14 under the Exchange Act promulgated pursuant to Sections 302(a) and 906 of the Sarbanes-Oxley Act must also be included in any amendment filing (however, if no financial statements are included in the amendment, no paragraph 3 is required for Section 302 certifications and no Section 906 certification is required; if no disclosure regarding the information required by Item 307 or 308 of Regulation S-K is included in the amendment, paragraphs 4 and 5 may be omitted from the Section 302 certifications).[140]

I. Other Issues.

1. Liability Considerations. Section 18 of the Exchange Act provides civil remedies with regard to Form 10-K and other periodic filings under the Exchange Act. It provides these remedies for persons who:

- purchased or sold a security;
- in reliance on;
- false or misleading statements relating to a material fact;
- in a document "filed under the Exchange Act";
- if the price of the security was affected by such statement; and
- the person bringing the action did not know the statement was false or misleading.

This provision imposes liability on any person, including any director, who made the statement, or caused the statement to be made, although a defense is available by proving that the defendant acted in good faith and had no knowledge that such statement was false or misleading.[141] Persons held liable under Section 18 of the Exchange Act may recover contribution from a person who, if joined in the original suit, would have been liable to make this same payment.[142] The statute of limitations for these claims is one year after discovery and three years after the

---

[140] See Exchange Act Rule 12b-15, SEC's Division of Corporation Finance: Sarbanes-Oxley Act of 2002—Frequently Asked Questions—Section 302—Question 5 (November 14, 2002) and SEC's Division of Corporation Finance Compliance and Disclosure Interpretations—Exchange Act Rules—Questions and Answers of General Applicability—Section 161. Rule 13a-14—Question 161.01 (September 30, 2008).

[141] Section 18(a) of the Exchange Act.

[142] Section 18(b) of the Exchange Act.

action accrued.[143] An action accrues under Section 18 when a plaintiff purchases or sells a security that is complained of, as opposed to when the alleged false or misleading statements are filed with the SEC.

The Exchange Act also provides other provisions for actions based on the adverse effects of misleading statements, including Section 10(b), which prohibits use of manipulative or deceptive devices in contravention of SEC rules. "Reliance" on false statements or omissions is presumed in a Section 10(b) action once the materiality of the omission is established. Therefore, Section 10(b) is generally the more suitable remedy for actions based on the effects of misleading statements on market prices of stocks. However, in order to demonstrate a violation of Rule 10b-5, a plaintiff must generally prove the scienter of the defendant in making a material misrepresentation or omission. In addition, where the Form 10-K has been incorporated by reference into a registration statement under the Securities Act (e.g., Form S-3), the Form 10-K disclosure may be subject to the liability provisions of Sections 11, 12 and 17 of the Securities Act. These Securities Act provisions will often be relied upon by plaintiffs instead of Section 18 of the Exchange Act because they are generally more restrictive with respect to defenses.

2. Transition Reports. When a registrant changes its fiscal year, it is required to file a "Transition Report" on Form 10-K. The Transition Report covers the period following the end of the registrant's most recent fiscal year through the opening date of the registrant's new fiscal year. For example, if a registrant changes its fiscal year-end from April 30 to December 31, it will have to file a Form 10-K covering the eight-month transition period in the applicable year. The transition report cannot cover a period of longer than 12 months. Where the interim period is less than six months, a Form 10-Q may be filed instead.[144] If the interim period is one month or less, a Transition Report may not be required to be filed.[145] The Transition Report is required to be filed within 90[146] days of the later of:

- the end of the new fiscal year-end; or

---

[143] Section 18(c) of the Exchange Act. Section 804 of the Sarbanes-Oxley Act increased the statute of limitations for private rights of action commenced on or after July 30, 2002, involving claims of a fraud, deceit, manipulation, or contrivance in contravention of a regulatory requirement concerning the securities laws to not later than the earlier of two years after discovery or five years after the violation. The section amends 28 U.S.C. § 1658. Section 804 did not amend the Securities Act or the Exchange Act. Rather, it amended the Judicial Improvements Act of 1990, which provided a four-year statute of limitations for acts of Congress that do not otherwise have an explicit statute of limitations.

[144] Rule 13a-10(c) under the Exchange Act.

[145] Rule 13a-10(d) under the Exchange Act.

[146] Except with respect to "accelerated filers" (as defined in Rule 12b-2 under the Exchange Act) for which the number of days is 60.

● the date of the determination to change the year-end.

3. Suspension of Obligation to File. The obligation of a registrant to continue filing a Form 10-K and other periodic Exchange Act reports may be suspended if certain requirements are met, including:

● the number of record holders of its registered security falls below 300; or

● the number of record holders of its registered security falls below 500 and the registrant's total assets have not exceeded $10 million on the last day of each of its three most recent fiscal years.[147]

(a) A registrant with a security registered under Section 12(g) of the Exchange Act would file a Form 15 with the SEC pursuant to Rule 12g-4 under the Exchange Act to immediately terminate its obligation to file Exchange Act reports pursuant to Section 12(g). This would not, however, terminate registration under the Exchange Act until 90 days after the filing. This means that unless a request for acceleration is granted by the SEC, until the 90-day period lapses all reports required by Sections 13(d) and 16(a) are still required with respect to security holders of the issuer. A registrant registered under Section 12(b) of the Exchange Act (because it has securities listed on a national securities exchange) would notify the applicable exchange and file an application with the SEC for deregistration and delisting on Form 15 pursuant to Rule 12d2-2 under the Exchange Act. This filing will terminate the registrant's obligation to file Exchange Act reports upon the date stated in the filing, but not earlier than 10 days after the date of the filing, unless acceleration is requested.

(b) A registrant that has filed a Securities Act registration statement is also a Section 15(d) filer of Exchange Act reports and, therefore, must also file a Form 15 with the SEC pursuant to Rule 12h-3 to terminate its Exchange Act reporting obligations. The Form 15, however, in accordance with Rule 12h-3 of the Exchange Act, will only be applicable to classes of securities held of record by less than 300 persons. Further, the obligation to file Exchange Act reports under Section 15(d) will only terminate immediately upon filing the Form 15 if (i) the issuer has filed all such reports for the last three years and the stub period of the current year or, if shorter, since becoming subject to the reporting requirements of the Exchange Act and (ii) a Securities Act registration statement (including on Form S-8) has not become effective in the current fiscal year. If (i) or (ii) is not satisfied, the duty to file reports terminates at the end of the fiscal year.

4. Omission of Information by Certain Wholly-Owned Subsidiaries. Registrants whose equity securities are owned by a single person (e.g.,

---

[147] Rules 12g-4, 12h-3 and 15d-6 under the Exchange Act.

wholly-owned subsidiaries) are subject to more limited disclosure requirements when certain other requirements are met. These requirements include:

- being current with filings under Section 13, 14 or 15(d) of the Exchange Act; and

- having no material default on debt or payment of rentals under material long-term leases during the prior three years.[148]

Registrants meeting these conditions may omit significant disclosures from their Form 10-Ks, including the disclosures required by Items 4, 6, 10, 11, 12 and 13 of the form. In addition, the disclosures required by Items 1, 2 and 7 of the Form 10-K are significantly reduced.

J. Smaller Reporting Companies.

A simplified annual report form (Form 10-KSB) was historically available to a registrant that qualified as a "small business issuer" under the Exchange Act.

The Form 10-KSB was similar to a Form 10-K, but was tied to the provisions of Regulation S-B, rather than Regulation S-K. There were also a number of other differences in the disclosure requirements between the Form 10-K and Form 10-KSB. Regulation S-B items usually required less disclosure than their analogous Regulation S-K counterparts. Furthermore, some Regulation S-K items that require disclosure in Form 10-K did not have analogous counterparts in Regulation S-B. Thus, the Form 10-KSB had less disclosure than the Form 10-K. For example, one of the main differences between the Form 10-K and Form 10-KSB was that the Form 10-KSB only required an income statement for the past two years and a balance sheet for the past fiscal year.

At the end of 2007, the SEC adopted rules that:

- replaced the concept of small business issuers with "smaller reporting companies" that have a common stock public float of less than $75 million (or, if a company does not have a calculable public equity float, that have revenues of less than $50 million in the last fiscal year);

- eliminated the SB forms (including Form 10-KSB); and

- included simplified disclosure for smaller reporting companies in the forms (such as Form 10-K) used by other issuers by moving required information from Regulation S-B to Regulations S-K and S-X.[149]

---

[148] 10-K, General Instruction I.

[149] See SEC Release No. 33-8876 (December 9, 2007).

CHAPTER 7

THE PROXY STATEMENT

A. Introduction.

Most states have statutes that require corporations to hold annual meetings of shareholders at which directors are elected.[1] In addition, NASDAQ, the NYSE and NYSE Amex require all registrants that have securities listed on such exchanges to hold annual meetings of shareholders. Most states' corporate laws also allow shareholders to appoint proxies to vote their shares at annual meetings.[2] This use of proxies enables shareholders of public companies, who are usually geographically scattered, to vote at shareholder meetings without having to attend the meetings. Registrants solicit the proxies of their shareholders to pass various proposals at annual meetings that require shareholder approval. A "solicitation" includes any oral or written request for a proxy or to execute or not to execute, or to revoke, a proxy, as well as any communication that is reasonably calculated to result in the procurement, withholding or revocation of a proxy.[3] The term "solicitation" has been broadly construed by the SEC and the courts. The SEC's proxy rules, which are meant to protect shareholders from those that solicit the ability to vote their shares by proxy, derive from Section 14(a) of the Exchange Act. Section 14(a) prohibits a company that has securities registered under Section 12 of the Exchange Act from soliciting proxies other than under the rules set forth by the SEC. The SEC has promulgated extensive rules in Regulation 14A to govern proxy solicitations. These rules address, among other items, the information to be disclosed to security holders, to whom such information must be furnished, and when and how such information must be distributed.

---

[1] For example, see Sections 211(b) and (c) of the Delaware General Corporation Law (the "DGCL").

[2] For example, see Sections 212(b), (c) and (d) of the DGCL. In addition, the major national securities exchanges require listed registrants to solicit proxies for shareholder meetings.

[3] Rule 14a-1(1) under the Exchange Act.

B. Purpose of, and Information to be Included in, the Proxy Statement.

A proxy statement is intended to provide shareholders with the information necessary to make an informed voting decision on proposals for which proxies are solicited. The proxy rules therefore require standard disclosure items applicable to solicitations generally and also require additional disclosure of information relevant to the specific matter to be acted upon at the meeting. In particular, Rule 14a-3 of the Exchange Act prohibits solicitation of a shareholder's proxy unless the shareholder has been provided with a written proxy statement containing the information required by Schedule 14A.[4] Thus, the annual election of a registrant's directors that involves the solicitation of proxies to be voted at the registrant's annual meeting requires filing a proxy statement on Schedule 14A with the SEC and distributing the proxy statement to shareholders from whom proxies are being solicited.[5] As discussed below, Schedule 14A requires the annual meeting proxy statement to disclose certain information about the director nominees, the registrant's existing board of directors, executive officers and significant shareholders, executive compensation, any other matters being voted on, the meeting and how to vote. Although the SEC's plain English requirements do not apply to an annual meeting proxy statement,[6] many registrants put the required information about the meeting and voting procedures in a Q&A format in order to more easily explain what is often technical information and to not distract from specific disclosure regarding the registrant's management and the proposals being voted on at the meeting.

---

[4] However, Rule 14a-12 under the Exchange Act permits solicitations prior to furnishing shareholders a proxy statement and proxy card if certain disclosure is contained in the written communication and it is filed with the SEC under cover of Schedule 14A. Therefore, for example, a registration satisfying the requirements of Rule 14a-12 could place a notice in a major newspaper informing its shareholders of the persons it intends to nominate at an upcoming annual meeting before distributing proxy materials for the meeting.

[5] A registrant should keep in mind that when securities are offered pursuant to a Form S-8 registration statement, Rule 428(b)(5) under the Securities Act requires the proxy statement to be delivered to all employees participating in a stock option plan or plan fund that invests in the registrant's securities that are registered under the Form S-8 registration statement, unless an employee otherwise receives the proxy statement (e.g., as a shareholder). The registrant must deliver the proxy statement to such employees at the same time it delivers the proxy statement to its shareholders.

[6] However, because the executive compensation, beneficial ownership, related party and corporate governance disclosure required in a Form 10-K must comply with the plain English rules, such disclosure in the proxy statement must be in plain English if incorporated by reference into a registrant's Form 10-K.

C. Strategy on Completing the Proxy Statement.

1. Collection of Information. Because preparation of the proxy statement is often done in conjunction with the Form 10-K, much of what is discussed in Section B of Chapter 6 regarding the strategy on completing the Form 10-K also applies to the proxy statement. In addition, the timetable included in Section B of Chapter 6 contains dates and tasks for completing the proxy statement. As part of the process of preparing the proxy statement, the registrant will also need to coordinate with its compensation and audit committees for the drafting of their respective reports that are required in the proxy statement, as discussed below. While the registrant's board of directors is not required to sign the proxy statement, it is good practice to distribute a draft of the proxy statement to the board prior to filing it with the SEC and distributing it to the shareholders. After all, the registrant's proxy solicitation is being made on behalf of the board, much of the disclosure in the proxy statement is about the board and management and portions of the proxy statement are often incorporated by reference into a registrant's Form 10-K.

2. Notice of Annual Meeting. A registrant must remember to include with its proxy materials the notice of the annual meeting that is required by state corporate law and the registrant's certificate of incorporation or bylaws. For example, Section 222 of the DGCL requires a registrant to give shareholders 10 to 60 days' notice prior to the meeting. The applicable notice requirement affects the timing of when the proxy materials are eventually filed with the SEC and distributed to shareholders. Registrants should also consider the makeup of their shareholder base, whether a proposal is routine and how close a vote is expected to be when deciding how far in advance of the meeting to distribute proxy materials. After all, registrants will want to make sure that a quorum is present, that broker-dealers have enough time to forward the proxy materials to shareholders who beneficially own shares in street name and that enough time is given to solicit proxies. The registrant often includes the notice on the page following a cover letter from its chairman or CEO inviting shareholders to attend the meeting and urging shareholders to vote by proxy. The notice basically informs shareholders about when and where the meeting will be held, the proposals being voted on and the record date for the meeting.

3. Broker Searches. When preparing for an annual meeting, registrants must also remember to conduct broker searches in accordance with Rule 14a-13 under the Exchange Act. In particular, if a registrant knows that securities entitled to vote at the meeting for which it is soliciting proxies are held of record by a broker, dealer, voting trustee, bank, association or other entity that exercises fiduciary powers in nominee name or otherwise, the registrant must, at least 20 business days prior to the record date for the meeting, find out from such record holder the number of copies of the proxy materials and Annual Report that it will need to supply to the beneficial owners of the securities.

4. Preliminary Proxy Material Filing Requirements. Pursuant to Rule 14a-6(a) under the Exchange Act, a preliminary proxy statement must be filed with the SEC unless the only matters to be acted upon by shareholders at a meeting are:

- the election of directors;

- the election, approval or ratification of auditors;

- a shareholder proposal included pursuant to Rule 14a-8 under the Exchange Act;

- the approval or ratification of a plan as defined in Item 402(a)(6)(ii) of Regulation S-K or amendments to such a plan;[7] and/or

- a say-on-pay or say-on-frequency vote, including a vote to approve the compensation of executives of TARP recipients as required pursuant to Section 111(e)(1) of the Emergency Economic Stabilization Act of 2008.

When a preliminary proxy statement is required to be filed, it and the preliminary form of proxy, under a Schedule 14A cover sheet, must be filed by EDGAR with the SEC at least 10 days prior to the date on which the registrant intends to distribute definitive copies of its proxy materials to its shareholders. No filing fee is required for filing a proxy statement unless it involves an acquisition, merger, spinoff, consolidation or proposed sale or other disposition of substantially all of the assets of a registrant.[8] The SEC will generally advise the registrant within 10 calendar days of filing if it intends to review the preliminary proxy material. When the SEC advises the registrant that a review is being undertaken, the SEC staff tries to take no more than 30 days to complete its review and furnish comments. Therefore, if preliminary proxy materials are required to be filed, the possibility of an SEC review and the time needed to possibly respond to SEC comments should be taken into account when scheduling the date for filing the preliminary proxy materials, mailing definitive proxy materials (including the notice of the annual meeting) and holding the annual meeting. Preliminary proxy statements must be clearly marked "Preliminary Copies" and must disclose when definitive proxy materials are intended to be released to a registrant's shareholders. If the SEC reviews a preliminary proxy statement, the registrant can:

- wait for, respond to and clear all SEC comments;

- distribute the preliminary proxy statement while awaiting SEC comments, but without proxy cards. However, this is costly and potentially confusing to shareholders because a definitive proxy statement reflecting

---

[7] The exemption from filing preliminary proxy materials does not, however, extend to approval or ratification of awards made pursuant to such plans.

[8] Rule 14a-6(i) under the Exchange Act.

the registrant's responses to, and clearing of, SEC comments will also need to be sent to shareholders with the proxy card to vote; or

● distribute a definitive proxy statement with proxy cards without responding to and clearing all SEC comments. The risk, however, is that the SEC can bring an enforcement action if it believes the disclosure in the proxy statement is deficient.

5. Definitive Proxy Material Filing Requirements. Pursuant to Rule 14a-6(b) under the Exchange Act, a definitive copy of the proxy statement, form of proxy and all other soliciting material, in the same form in which such materials are being furnished to shareholders, must be filed by EDGAR under a Schedule 14A cover sheet with the SEC not later than the date such material is first sent or given to the shareholders. All definitive proxy statements must disclose the date on which copies were released, or if not yet released, the date on which they are intended to be released to shareholders.

D. Required Disclosure.

Schedule 14A specifies what information must be disclosed in a proxy statement. This Chapter focuses on disclosure that is required to be included in a proxy statement for an annual meeting at which the only matters to be voted on by shareholders are the election of directors, say-on-pay, say-on-frequency and approval of a compensation plan or an amendment to such a plan. Schedule 14A items that are not applicable to such matters are not discussed below and need not be mentioned in such a proxy statement. Pursuant to the Dodd-Frank Wall Street Reform and Consumer Protection Act (the "Dodd-Frank Act"), the SEC recently adopted Rule 14a-21(a) under the Exchange Act, which requires that the first proxy statement for an annual meeting, or other shareholders' meeting at which directors will be elected, that is held on or after January 21, 2011 must include a non-binding, advisory proposal that allows shareholders to approve executive compensation as disclosed pursuant to Item 402 of Regulation S-K (often referred to as the "say-on-pay vote").[9] Pursuant to Rule 14a-21(b) under the Exchange Act, at least once every six years thereafter, shareholders must also be given the separate opportunity to vote on whether the foregoing say-on-pay vote should be held every one, two or three years (this

---

[9] See SEC Release No. 33-9178 (January 25, 2011). The SEC also included the following example of such a say-on-pay proposal:

RESOLVED, that the compensation paid to the company's named executive officers as disclosed pursuant to the Item 402 of Regulation S-K, including the Compensation Discussion and Analysis, compensation tables and narrative discussion, is hereby APPROVED.

The reference to Item 402 of Regulation S-K in the foregoing resolutions can also be replaced with a plain English reference, such as "the compensation disclosure rules of the SEC."

vote, which is often referred to as the "say-on-frequency vote," is also non-binding and advisory).[10]

1. Item 1. Date, Time and Place Information. Item 1 of Schedule 14A requires the following disclosure:

(a) When and Where the Meeting Is Being Held. The proxy statement must state the date, time and place of the annual meeting and, unless otherwise disclosed in other materials (e.g., the Annual Report) furnished to shareholders with or before the proxy statement, the complete mailing address of the registrant's principal executive offices. Some registrants also provide their shareholders with directions and/or a map to where the meeting is to be held.

(b) When Proxy Materials Are Distributed. The first page of the proxy statement must state the approximate date on which the proxy statement and form of proxy are first sent or given to shareholders.

(c) Shareholder Proposal Information. Pursuant to Rule 14a-5 under the Exchange Act, the proxy statement must disclose the following dates under an appropriate caption:

(1) The registrant must disclose the date by which a shareholder proposal must be received in order to be included in the registrant's proxy statement and proxy for the registrant's next annual meeting. Question 5 of Rule 14a-8(e)(2) under the Exchange Act provides how to calculate the deadline for submitting a shareholder proposal for an annual meeting proxy statement. The proposal must be received at the registrant's principal executive offices not less than 120 calendar days before the date of the registrant's proxy statement released to shareholders in connection with the previous year's annual meeting. This means that when preparing a proxy statement for the current year, a registrant must disclose that a shareholder proposal must be received by the registrant on or prior to the one-year anniversary of the date 120 calendar days prior to the date of the current year's proxy statement in order to be included in the registrant's proxy statement for its next annual meeting.

Example: A registrant whose proxy statement for its 2011 annual meeting was dated May 4, 2011 should have disclosed that shareholder proposals must be received by January 4, 2012 in order to be included in the registrant's proxy materials for its 2012 annual meeting.

---

[10] Registrants can recommend a particular frequency for such vote, but must clarify that shareholders are not voting on such recommendation. Proxy cards that indicate neither a vote for one, two or three years nor an abstention can be voted by the registrants in accordance with their recommendation so long as language on the proxy card explains such voting of uninstructed shares in bold on the proxy card. See Part F below.

A registrant should keep in mind that if the date of its annual meeting changes by more than 30 days from the date of its annual meeting for the previous year, or if it did not hold an annual meeting the previous year, it must disclose in its earliest possible quarterly report on Form 10-Q under Item 5 the deadline for a shareholder proposal to be included in the registrant's proxy materials.[11] This deadline must be a reasonable time before the registrant begins to print and mail its proxy materials.

(2) The registrant must disclose the date by which a notice of a shareholder proposal must be received by the registrant in order for the proposal to be brought up at next year's annual meeting. This deadline is usually established by an advance notice provision in the registrant's bylaws. If, however, the registrant's bylaws do not contain an advance notice provision, the deadline is calculated in accordance with Rule 14a-4(c)(1) under the Exchange Act, which provides that the notice of a shareholder proposal must be received by a registrant at least 45 days before the date on which the registrant first mailed its proxy materials for its prior year's annual meeting.

Example: A registrant whose bylaws do not contain an advance notice provision that mailed its proxy statement for its 2011 annual meeting on May 4, 2011 should have disclosed that the registrant must receive a notice of a shareholder proposal by March 19, 2012 in order for the proposal to be brought up at the 2012 annual meeting.

A registrant should keep in mind that if the date of its annual meeting changes by more than 30 days from the date of its annual meeting for the previous year, or if it did not hold an annual meeting the previous year, it must also disclose in its earliest possible quarterly report on Form 10-Q under Item 5 the deadline for a shareholder proposal to be brought up at the annual meeting.[12] This deadline must be a reasonable time before the registrant mails its proxy materials.

2. Item 2. Revocability of Proxy. Item 2 of Schedule 14A requires a registrant to disclose whether or not a shareholder can revoke his or her proxy prior to its being exercised at the annual meeting and any limitations on, or procedures for, such revocation. In most instances, proxies solicited by registrants for voting on proposals at an annual meeting will not, under applicable state corporate law, be irrevocable because the proxies are not coupled with an interest in the underlying voting stock.[13] Typically, the disclosure required by Item 2 informs shareholders that they can revoke their previous proxy and change their vote at any time prior to the vote at the annual meeting by submitting to the

---

[11] Rule 14a-5(f) under the Exchange Act. If it is impracticable to disclose such new deadline in a Form 10-Q, the registrant may disclose it by any means reasonably calculated to inform shareholders.

[12] *Id.*

[13] For example, see Section 212(e) of the DGCL.

registrant a notice of revocation or a new, later dated proxy with a different vote or by attending the annual meeting and voting differently in person.

3. Item 4. Persons Making the Solicitation. Item 4 of Schedule 14A requires a clear statement that the proxy solicitation for the annual meeting is being made by the registrant. The registrant must also disclose the methods, other than the mailing of proxy materials, by which it will solicit proxies. For example, a registrant must disclose if its directors, officers and employees will solicit proxies in person, by telephone or by electronic communications and should also disclose if such persons will be paid any additional compensation for such solicitation activities. A registrant must also disclose the use of any proxy solicitation firm to assist it in distributing proxy materials soliciting proxies. In addition to identifying the firm, the registrant must also describe any material features of any contract or arrangement for such solicitation and the cost or anticipated cost of such solicitation. The registrant must state who is bearing the costs of soliciting proxies (presumably the registrant, though shareholders who access the proxy materials and/or vote over the Internet are responsible for Internet access charges they may incur). Most registrants also clarify that they reimburse brokerage firms and other custodians, nominees and fiduciaries for their reasonable out-of-pocket expenses for forwarding proxy materials to the beneficial owners of the shares for which they are record holders. Finally, Item 4 requires disclosure of both the name of any director of the registrant who has informed the registrant in writing that he or she intends to oppose an action intended to be taken by the registrant at an annual meeting and a description of the action.

4. Item 5. Interest of Certain Persons in Matters to Be Acted Upon. Item 5 of Schedule 14A requires a brief description of any direct or indirect substantial interest that each of the following persons has in any matter, other than elections to office, to be acted upon at an annual meeting:

- each person who has been a director or executive officer since the beginning of the last fiscal year;
- each nominee for election as a director; and
- each associate[14] of such persons.

This required disclosure includes interests that arise out of security holdings of the registrant, unless such ownership gives the holder no extra or special benefit not shared on a pro rata basis by all other holders of the same class of security. In a proxy statement that only relates to the election of directors and approval of a compensation plan, there usually is not anything to disclose pursuant to Item 5 other than the participation of directors and/or executive officers in the compensation

---

[14] See Rule 14a-2(a) under the Exchange Act for the definition of "associate."

plan. The disclosure required by Item 5 is meant to identify any conflicts of interest with respect to the matters for which proxies are being solicited.

5. Item 6. Voting Securities and Principal Holders Thereof. Item 6 of Schedule 14A requires disclosure of the following information:

(a) Shares Outstanding. The number of outstanding shares of each class of security entitled to be voted at the annual meeting. This number is given as of the record date described below and can be obtained from the registrant's transfer agent.

(b) Voting Power. The number of votes per share to which each class of security is entitled. For example, each share of common stock to be voted at a shareholder meeting is typically entitled to one vote. However, some companies have dual classes of common stock that provide one of the classes with super-voting power, such as five votes per share.

(c) Record Date. The record date for determining the shareholders and shares entitled to vote at the annual meeting. The registrant's bylaws in accordance with state corporate law, or if the bylaws are silent on the matter, state corporate law, will dictate what date the registrant can fix as the record date.[15]

(d) Cumulative Voting Rights. A description of any cumulative voting rights, including the conditions precedent to the exercise of such rights, held by the shareholders whose votes are being solicited. Under a straight voting system, each share of voting stock carries one vote (or multiple votes if super-voting power is granted) for each director position to be filled at the annual meeting. Cumulative voting enables a shareholder to allocate all of his or her votes to a single nominee or among several nominees.

Example: If several nominees have been nominated to fill three director positions and the registrant's common stock is entitled to one vote per share, a shareholder that holds one share of the registrant's common stock is entitled to cast one vote for each of the three positions under a straight voting system, but could cast all three votes for any single position or distribute the three votes among the positions in any manner desired if cumulative voting is allowed.

Cumulative voting gives minority shareholders the opportunity to potentially elect one or more directors.

(e) Security Ownership Information. The security ownership information required by Item 403 of Regulation S-K, to the extent known by the registrant,[16] for:

---

[15] For example, see Section 213 of the DGCL.

[16] The registrant should collect the required security ownership information for the applicable persons by reviewing its stock ownership records, directors' and officers' questionnaires, Section 16 forms filed by directors, executive officers and greater than 10% shareholders with the SEC and any Schedule 13D or 13G filed

● any person, including any group as defined in Section 13(d)(3) of the Exchange Act, who is known by the registrant to be the beneficial owner of more than 5% of any class of the registrant's voting securities;

● each director (even if the term of the director will not continue beyond the annual meeting) and director nominee;

● each "named executive officer" as defined in Item 402(a)(3) of Regulation S-K and discussed in Section 7 below; and

● all directors and executive officers as a group, without naming them.

For each person described above, the registrant must disclose the following information as of the most recent practicable date, in substantially the following tabular form:

Title of Class (1)	Name [and Address] of Beneficial Owner (2)	Amount and Nature of Beneficial Ownership (3)	Percent of Class (4)

(1) **Title of Class.** This column discloses the title of the class of security for which ownership information is being presented. Because most registrants have only one class of common stock as their voting securities, this column is often not presented in the beneficial ownership table. Rather, the lead-in to the table explains that information is being provided with respect to beneficial ownership of the registrants' common stock.

(2) **Name and Address of Beneficial Owner.** This column discloses the name of the beneficial owner and, in the case of greater than 5% shareholders, the business, mailing or residence address of the beneficial owner.

(3) **Amount and Nature of Beneficial Ownership.** This column discloses, for each greater than 5% shareholder, the total number of shares of any class of the registrant's voting securities beneficially owned by such person. For each director, each named executive officer and the directors and officers as a group, this column discloses the total number of shares of each class of equity

---

(Footnote Continued)

by greater than 5% shareholders with the SEC. In disclosing security ownership information for greater than 5% shareholders, a registrant is deemed to know the contents of any Schedule 13D or 13G filed with the SEC and can use such information unless it knows or has reason to know that such information is not complete or accurate or should have been amended. Registrants should not rely exclusively on Schedules 13D and 13G if they know of other greater than 5% shareholders who have not filed a Schedule 13D or 13G.

securities of the registrant or any of its parents or subsidiaries beneficially owned by such person or group. Whether or not a person is the "beneficial owner" of a security is determined in accordance with Rule 13d-3 under the Exchange Act. A person is the "beneficial owner" of a security if that person, directly or indirectly, through any contract, arrangement, understanding, relationship or otherwise, has or shares:

- the power to vote, or to direct the voting of, such security; and/or

- the power to dispose, or to direct the disposition, of such security.

A person is also the beneficial owner of a security if that person, directly or indirectly, creates or uses a trust, proxy, power of attorney, pooling arrangement or any other contract, arrangement or device with the purpose or effect of divesting that person of beneficial ownership of a security or preventing the vesting of such beneficial ownership. A person is also deemed to be the beneficial owner of a security if the person has the right to acquire beneficial ownership of such security at any time within 60 days, including, but not limited to, (i) through the exercise of any option, warrant or right, (ii) through the conversion of a security, (iii) pursuant to the power to revoke a trust, discretionary account or similar arrangement or (iv) pursuant to the automatic termination of a trust, discretionary account or similar arrangement. Registrants must keep in mind that even if a person is not the record holder of securities, that person might be the beneficial owner of securities held by others, including (i) a custodian, broker, nominee or pledgee; (ii) the person's spouse, children or other immediate family members that live in the person's household; (iii) an estate or trust in which the person has an interest as legatee or beneficiary or for which the person is the trustee; and (iv) a partnership of which the person is a partner.

This column also requires disclosure of the nature of the beneficial ownership of securities for which information is presented. This is usually done in a footnote to the table. For example, the registrant should disclose (i) whether the beneficial owner has sole or shared voting and/or investment power with respect to the shares, the nature of any indirect beneficial ownership (e.g., if a partnership is the record holder of shares and a director of the registrant, as the general partner of the partnership, is the beneficial owner of the shares because he has sole voting and investment power with respect to the shares), (ii) the number of shares acquirable within 60 days (e.g., upon exercise of options that are exercisable as of the date specified in the table or will be exercisable within 60 days thereof) and (iii) the number of shares pledged (including as part of a hedging arrangement or held in a brokerage margin account) as security by named executive officers, directors, director nominees and directors and executive officers as a group.[17] Registrants

---

[17] The Dodd-Frank Act requires the SEC to adopt rules requiring disclosure of whether directors or employees (or their designees) are permitted to purchase financial instruments (e.g., collars and swaps) that are designed to hedge or offset any decrease in

should note that the same security may be beneficially owned by more than one person. For example, several co-trustees or partners may share the power to vote or dispose of shares held by a trust or partnership. In such case, appropriate disclosure should be made to avoid confusion.

If a person disclaims beneficial ownership of any securities (e.g., because of the indirect nature of the beneficial ownership or the person's lack of direct pecuniary interest in the securities), such disclaimer, including the applicable number of securities, should be disclosed in a footnote to the table. It is also helpful to clarify in the footnote whether the amount of securities shown in the table for a person disclaiming beneficial ownership of shares includes or excludes such shares.

(4) Percent of Class. This column discloses the percentage of outstanding securities of the class beneficially owned by the applicable person or group. If the percentage of shares beneficially owned does not exceed 1%, the registrant can indicate that by footnote or asterisk rather than by furnishing the precise percentage. In such calculation, the denominator (shares outstanding) for each particular person should include any shares that though not outstanding are acquirable by such person within 60 days of the date being used for the security ownership table pursuant to options, warrants, rights or conversion privileges.[18] *Example*: If a person beneficially owns 4,000,000 shares of common stock, including 1,000,000 shares through the ownership of options that are exercisable within 60 days, and 9,000,000 shares are actually outstanding, the person beneficially owns 40% of the common stock (4,000,000 divided by (9,000,000 + 1,000,000)).

This column also requires disclosure of the nature of the beneficial ownership of securities for which information is presented. This is usually done in a footnote to the table. For example, the registrant should disclose whether the beneficial owner has sole or shared voting and/or investment power with respect to shares, the nature of any indirect beneficial ownership, and the number of shares acquirable within 60 days.

(5) Voting Agreements. The registrant must also disclose the amount of shares held by greater than 5% shareholders pursuant to any voting trust or similar agreement, the duration of the agreement, the names and addresses of the voting trustees and their voting rights and other powers under the trust or agreement.

(6) Change of Control Arrangement. The registrant must disclose any arrangement known to the registrant that may at a subsequent date result in a change of control of the registrant. This includes any pledge of securities by a

---

(Footnote Continued)

the market value of equity securities granted to directors or employees or otherwise directly or indirectly held by the director or employee.

[18] Rule 13d-3(d)(1)(i)(D) under the Exchange Act.

greater than 5% shareholder, but does not include ordinary default provisions contained in the charter, trust indenture or other governing instruments relating to securities of the registrant.

6. Item 7. Directors and Executive Officers. Item 7 of Schedule 14A requires disclosure of the following information, in tabular form to the extent practicable:

(a) Material Proceedings. Instruction 4 of Item 103 of Regulation S-K requires disclosure of any material proceeding in which any director or executive officer of the registrant, or any associate[19] of any such director or executive officer, is a party adverse to the registrant or has any material interest adverse to the registrant.

(b) Background Information. Item 401 of Regulation S-K requires the registrant to provide the following information for each director (unless such director's term of office will not continue after the annual meeting),[20] director nominee (unless such person has not consented to serve if elected), executive officer and person chosen to become an executive officer:[21]

● name and age.

● all positions and offices held with the registrant.

● the term of office as director or officer and the period which such person has served.

● a brief description of any arrangement between such person and any other third party (other than other directors or officers of the registrant acting solely in such capacities), which third party must be disclosed, pursuant to which such person was or is to be selected as a director, nominee or officer (e.g., the contractual right of the holders of certain securities to fill a board seat).

---

[19] See Rule 14a-1(a) under the Exchange Act for the definition of "associate."

[20] However, the SEC has recently clarified that biographical information is required even for a director whose term of office will not continue after the annual meeting if such information is disclosed directly in Part III of Form 10-K as opposed to incorporated by reference from the proxy statement.

[21] As an alternative, if the registrant is incorporating by reference information into its Form 10-K in reliance on General Instruction G thereto, it can provide the required background information for executive officers under a separate caption entitled "Executive Officers of the Regis-

trant" in Part I or III of its Form 10-K. Although the source of this alternative (Instruction 3 to Item 401(b) of Regulation S-K) does not state that the executive officers' business experience during the past five years, as required by Item 401(e) of Regulation S-K, can also be omitted from the proxy statement if it is included separately in the Form 10-K, the SEC has clarified that this is permissible. See SEC's Division of Corporation Finance Compliance and Disclosure Interpretations–Regulation S-K–Questions and Answers of General Applicability–Section 116. Item 401–Directors, Executive Officers, Promoters and Control Persons–Question 116.02 (July 3, 2008).

● the nature of any family relationship (by blood, marriage or adoption, not more remote than first cousin) between any such persons.

● a brief account of such person's business experience during the past five years (together with applicable dates), including principal occupations and employment during that period, the name and principal business of any corporation or other organization in which such occupations and employment were carried on, and whether such corporation or organization is a parent, subsidiary or other affiliate of the registrant. In addition, for each director (even those not up for election) and director nominee on an individual basis (i.e., not on a group basis), the registrant should briefly discuss the particular and specific experience, qualifications, attributes or skills (e.g., industry experience, technical skills, leadership qualities and experience with similarly situated companies) that led to the conclusion that the person should serve as a director for the registrant at the time that the disclosure is made, in light of the registrant's business and structure. If material, this disclosure should cover more than the past five years, including information about the person's particular areas of expertise or other relevant qualifications. If an executive officer has been employed by the registrant or a subsidiary of the registrant for less than five years, the registrant should include a brief explanation of the nature of such person's responsibilities in prior positions. What is required is information relating to the level of such person's professional competence, which may include, depending upon the circumstances, specific information such as the size of the operation supervised. Other biographical information (e.g., college and graduate school, and degrees earned, awards received, etc.) may also be included (and may be part of the person's background that led the board to conclude such particular person should serve as a director).

● all directorships held during the past five years by each director or nominee in publicly held companies or companies registered under the Investment Company Act of 1940, as amended.

● a description of any of the following events that occurred (based on when a final order, judgment or decree is entered or when any rights of appeal have lapsed or when an uncontested bankruptcy petition is filed or a contested petition becomes final) during the past ten years and that are material[22] to an evaluation of such person's integrity or ability (the registrant can also explain any mitigating circumstances relating to such events).[23]

---

[22] If any of such events is not disclosed because the registrant determines it is not material, the registrant may furnish to the SEC, as supplemental information, a description of the event and why the registrant omitted disclosure about the event.

[23] Most of the following events must also be described for (i) any "promoter" if the registrant has not been a public reporting company for the twelve months immediately prior to filing the proxy statement and had a promoter at any time

● a petition under the federal bankruptcy laws or any state insolvency law filed by or against, or a receiver, fiscal agent or similar officer appointed by a court for the business or property of, (i) such person, (ii) any partnership in which such person was a general partner at, or within two years before, the time of such event, or (iii) any corporation or business association of which such person was an executive officer at, or within two years before, the time of such event.

● being the subject of a conviction in a criminal proceeding or being named the subject of a pending criminal proceeding (excluding traffic violations and other minor offenses).

● any court order, judgment or decree, not subsequently reversed, suspended or vacated, of any court of competent jurisdiction, permanently or temporarily enjoining or otherwise limiting such person from any of the following activities:

> ● acting as a futures commission merchant, introducing broker, commodity trading advisor, commodity pool operator, floor broker, leverage transaction merchant, any other person regulated by the Commodity Futures Trading Commission, or an associated person of any of the foregoing, or as an investment advisor, underwriter, broker or dealer in securities, or as an affiliated person, director or employee of any investment company, bank, savings and loan association or insurance company, or engaging in or continuing any conduct or practice in connection with such activity;

> ● engaging in any type of business practice; or

> ● engaging in any activity in connection with the purchase or sale of any security or commodity or in connection with any violation of federal or state securities laws or federal commodities laws.

● being the subject of any order, judgment or decree, not subsequently reversed, suspended or vacated, of any federal or state authority barring, suspending or otherwise limiting for more than 60 days the right of such person to engage in any of the activities described above relating to investment banking or to be associated with persons engaged in any such activity.

(Footnote Continued)

during the past five fiscal years and (ii) any "control" person if the registrant has not been a public reporting company for the twelve months immediately prior to filing the proxy statement, if such events are material to a voting decision. The terms "promoter" and "control" are defined in Rule 405 under the Securities Act.

● being found by a court of competent jurisdiction in a civil action or by the SEC or the Commodity Futures Trading Commission to have violated any federal or state securities or commodities law where such judgment has not subsequently been reversed, suspended or vacated.

● except with respect to any settlement of a civil proceeding among private litigants, being the subject of, or a party to, any federal or state judicial or administrative order, judgment, decree or finding, not subsequently reversed, suspended or vacated, relating to an alleged violation of:

   ● any federal or state securities or commodities law or regulation;

   ● any law or regulation respecting financial institutions or insurance companies, including, but not limited to, a temporary or permanent injunction, order of disgorgement or restitution, civil money penalty or temporary or permanent cease-and-desist order, or removal or prohibition order; or

   ● any law or regulation prohibiting mail or wire fraud or fraud in connection with any business entity.

● being the subject of, or a party to, any sanction or order, not subsequently reversed, suspended or vacated, of any self-regulatory organization, any registered entity or any equivalent exchange, association, entity or organization that has disciplinary authority over its members or persons associated with a member.

As for determining which of the registrant's officers are executive officers, Rule 3b-7 under the Exchange Act defines an executive officer of a registrant as its president, any vice president in charge of a principal business unit, division or function (such as sales, administration or finance), any other officer who performs a policy-making function and any other person who performs similar policy-making functions.[24] Being designated an executive officer for the purposes of being listed as such in a registrant's proxy statement not only has disclosure ramifications, including disclosure of the person's compensation if he or she is a "named executive officer,"[25] but usually requires such person to also be deemed an executive officer who is subject to the short-swing profit rules of Section 16 of the Exchange Act and an affiliate who is subject to the stricter transfer restrictions under Rule 144 under the Securities Act. Thus, while some officers may feel slighted if they are not designated an "executive officer" of the registrant, they should balance this with the federal securities laws burdens that come with such classification. If the registrant employs persons who are not

---

[24] Executive officers of subsidiaries may also be deemed executive officers of the registrant if they perform policy-making functions for the registrant.

[25] See Section 7 below.

executive officers but who make or are expected to make significant contributions to the registrant's business (e.g., production managers, sales managers or research scientists), the registrant can still acknowledge such persons' importance by identifying them as key employees and disclosing their business experience as provided above. This disclosure, however, is not required.

In the proxy statement, a registrant will often provide basic biographical information in charts (e.g., name, age and current position with the registrant) that are followed by paragraphs describing each person's background and directorships, first for the director nominees, then for the other directors not up for election but remaining in office, then for executive officers and, if applicable, any key employees. In some cases, the registrant provides a picture of each such person.

(c) Certain Relationships and Related Transactions. Item 404(a) of Regulation S-K requires the registrant to describe certain transactions that are currently proposed or have occurred since its last fiscal year[26] to which it is to be or was a participant if:

- the amount involved exceeds $120,000—all periodic installments in the case of agreements providing for periodic payments or installments (e.g., a lease) must be included in this calculation; and

- any of the following persons, each a "related person," will have or had a direct or indirect (e.g., through his/her position or relationship with an entity that engages in a transaction with the registrant) material interest in the transaction:

  - a director, director nominee or executive officer of the registrant or a beneficial owner of greater than 5% of the registrant's voting securities;[27] and

  - any member of the immediate family of such persons[28] (including such persons' spouses, parents, stepparents' children, stepchildren,

---

[26] Because this disclosure is required for the period since the registrant's last fiscal year, if the transaction required to be disclosed occurred after the prior fiscal year but before the date of the registrant's proxy statement, the transaction would be disclosed in both that proxy statement and the following year's proxy statement.

[27] Disclosure is not required, however, if a transaction with any current 5% shareholder exceeded $120,000 but was concluded before the person became a 5% shareholder. Disclosure is required if the transaction (including receipt of payment) was continu-

ing when the person became a 5% shareholder or resulted in the person becoming a 5% shareholder. See SEC's Division of Corporation Finance Compliance and Disclosure Interpretations—Regulation S-K—Questions and Answers of General Applicability—Section 130. Item 404—Transactions with Related Persons, Promoters and Certain Control Persons—Question 130.03 (March 13, 2007).

[28] Therefore, registrants should keep in mind that amounts in excess of $120,000 that they pay to immediate family members of directors, director nominees,

siblings, and current mothers, fathers, sons, daughters, brothers and sisters-in-law, and any person (other than a tenant or employee) sharing the household of such persons).[29]

A "transaction" includes, but is not limited to, any financial transaction, arrangement or relationship (including purchasing, leasing or selling goods, services or property and incurring indebtedness or guaranteeing indebtedness) or any series of similar transactions, arrangements or relationships.

(1) Required Information. In addition to briefly describing such transactions, the registrant must provide the following information about such transactions:

● the name of the person with the material interest and the basis on which the person is a related person;

● the related person's interest in the transaction with the registrant, including such person's position(s) or relationship(s) with, or ownership in, a firm, corporation, or other entity that is a party to, or has an interest in, the transaction;

● the amount of such transaction (which for employment arrangements means all compensation, not just salary);

● the amount of the related person's interest in the transaction, without regard to the amount of profit or loss involved in the transaction;

● for any transaction involving indebtedness, the amount involved in the transaction must include the largest aggregate amount of principal outstanding during the period for which disclosure is provided, the amount outstanding as of the latest practicable date, the amount of principal paid during the period for which disclosure is provided, the amount of interest paid during the period for which disclosure is provided, and the rate or amount of interest payable on the indebtedness; and

---

(Footnote Continued)

executive officers or 5% shareholders as employees or otherwise will require disclosure under Item 404(a) of Regulation S-K unless such person's interest is not material or the transaction fits within one of the exemptions described herein.

[29] According to the SEC's Division of Corporation Finance Compliance and Disclosure Interpretations—Regulation S-K—Interpretive Responses Regarding Particular Situations—Section 230. Item 404—Transactions with Related Persons, Promoters and Certain Control Persons—Section 230.01 (March 13, 2007), (a) a person divorced from a director's daughter would no longer be a son-in-law whose transactions must be reported and (b) the husband of the sister of a director's spouse is not considered a brother-in-law, but the sister is considered a sister-in-law because only persons who are related by blood or step relationship to the reporting person or his/her spouse are deemed immediate family members.

● any other information regarding the transaction or the related person in the context of the transaction that is material to investors in light of the circumstances of the particular transaction.

(2) Materiality. As mentioned above, related-party transactions only need to be described if the related person's direct or indirect interest in the transaction is material. The materiality of any interest is determined on the basis of the significance of the information to investors in light of all the circumstances of the particular transaction, including:

● the importance of the interest to the person having the interest;

● the relationship of the parties to the transaction with each other; and

● the amount involved in the transaction.

Interests are not deemed material and, therefore, do not require disclosure under Item 404(a) of Regulation S-K if they arise solely from:

● the ownership by a related person individually, and by related persons in the aggregate, of less than 10% of the equity securities of another entity (other than a partnership) that is a party to the transaction;

● a related person's position as a director of the other entity that is a party to the transaction;

● a related person's position as a limited partner in a partnership in which all related persons have an interest of less than 10%; or

● a related person holding an equity interest (other than a general partnership interest) or a creditor interest in another person that is a party to a transaction that is not material to such other person.

(3) Disclosure Not Required. Furthermore, Item 404(a) of Regulation S-K does not require disclosure of related party transactions if:

● the rates/charges involved are determined by competitive bids involving formal procedures normally associated with competitive bidding situations (e.g., specifications for the property or services and indication of the basis upon which a bid will be accepted);

● the transaction involves the rendering of services as a common or contract carrier, or public utility, at rates/charges fixed in conformity with law or governmental authority;

● the transaction includes services as a bank depository of funds, transfer agent, registrar, trustee under a trust indenture or similar services;

● the interest of the person arises solely from ownership of a class of equity securities of the registrant and such person receives no extra or special benefit not shared on a pro rata basis;

- the transaction, including any compensation, is reported in response to Item 402 of Regulation S-K (e.g., salary paid to an executive officer that is disclosed in the Summary Compensation Table and fees paid to a director disclosed in the Director Compensation Table need not also be disclosed pursuant to Item 404(a)); or

- the executive officer is not an immediate family member and the compensation to such officer would have been reported under Item 402 of Regulation S-K if the officer was a named executive officer, and such compensation had been approved, or recommended to the board for approval, by the compensation committee (or group of independent directors performing a similar function) of the registrant.

In transactions involving indebtedness, certain items may be excluded from the calculation of the amount of indebtedness and need not be disclosed, including amounts due from the related person for purchases of goods and services subject to usual trade terms, for ordinary business travel and expense payments and for other transactions in the ordinary course of business. Also, in the case of transactions involving indebtedness, if the lender is a bank, savings and loan association, or broker-dealer extending credit under Federal Reserve Regulation T and the loans are not disclosed as nonaccrual, past due, restructured or potential problems, disclosure under Item 404(a) may consist of a statement, if correct, that the loans to such persons satisfied the following conditions:

- they were made in the ordinary course of business;

- they were made on substantially the same terms, including interest rates and collateral, as those prevailing at the time for comparable loans with persons not related to the lender (e.g., regular customers); and

- they did not involve more than the normal risk of collectibility or present other unfavorable features.

(4) Review, Approval or Ratification of Transactions with Related Persons. Item 404(b) of Regulation S-K requires a registrant to describe its policies and procedures for the review, approval or ratification of the types of transactions required to be reported under Item 404(a) (even when the registrant does not have any such transactions to report in the proxy statement). While the material features of such policies and procedures will vary, Item 404(b) suggests that such features may include, among other things:

- the types of transactions that are covered by such policies and procedures;

- the standards to be applied pursuant to such policies and procedures;

- the persons or groups of persons on the board or otherwise who are responsible for applying such policies and procedures; and

● a statement of whether such policies and procedures are in writing and, if not, how such policies and procedures are evidenced.

Furthermore, Item 404(b) requires the registrant to identify any transaction required to be reported under Item 404(a) since the beginning of the registrant's last fiscal year if such policies and procedures did not require review, approval or ratification or if such policies and procedures were not followed. Disclosure is not required under Item 404(b), however, if the transaction occurred at a time before the related person became a related person if such transaction did not continue after such person became a related person.

(d) Delinquent Section 16 Filings. Item 405 of Regulation S-K requires a registrant to provide the following information under the caption "Section 16(a) Beneficial Ownership Reporting Compliance":

● the identity of each person who, at any time during the last fiscal year, was a director, executive officer or beneficial owner of more than 10% of the registrant's equity securities registered pursuant to Section 12 of the Exchange Act and failed to file on a timely basis a Form 3, 4 or 5 required by Section 16(a) of the Exchange Act for the most recent fiscal year, or, if not yet disclosed, prior fiscal years; and

● for each such person, the number of late Form 3s, 4s and 5s, the number of transactions that were not reported on a timely basis and any known failure to file a required Form 3, 4 or 5 (e.g., a failure of a Section 16 reporting person to file a Form 3 or to file a Form 5 in the absence of a written representation that no Form 5 was required).

This disclosure can be based solely upon a registrant's review of (i) Form 3s and 4s furnished to the registrant pursuant to Rule 16a-3(e)[30] under the Exchange Act during its most recent fiscal year, (ii) Form 5s furnished to the registrant with respect to its most recent fiscal year; and (iii) a written representation from the Section 16 reporting person that no Form 5 is required (which must be maintained for two years and made available to the SEC upon request),[31] unless the registrant has actual knowledge that the representation is wrong. While this is the only required disclosure regarding delinquent Section 16 filings, many registrants also include brief explanations of the transactions that were not timely reported (e.g., an exercise of stock options or the acquisition of shares of common stock on the open market), including the reasons why the transactions were not timely reported (e.g., inadvertent failure to file a timely Form 4) and, if applicable, that the transactions were ultimately reported on late filings, or disclose that based on the review described above, all

---

[30] Rule 16a-3(e) under the Exchange Act requires Section 16 reporting persons to send the registrant copies of all Form 3s, 4s and 5s at the same time they are filed with the SEC.

[31] See Appendix 8 for an example of this Form 5 written representation.

required Section 16 reports were filed on a timely basis. The SEC does not impute constructive knowledge to a registrant that does not have actual knowledge of delinquent filings. Therefore, the registrant need not review records or contact other parties (other than reviewing Form 3s, 4s and 5s and contacting the parties preparing them) to identify or monitor reportable transactions.

   (e) Audit Committee. Item 407(d)(4) of Regulation S-K requires the registrant to disclose whether or not it has a standing audit committee of its board of directors or a committee performing similar functions. If the registrant has an audit committee, however designated, each committee member must be identified. If, however, the entire board is acting as the registrant's audit committee, the registrant must disclose that fact. For its audit committee, the registrant must disclose:[32]

● whether or not the registrant's board of directors has adopted a written charter for the audit committee and, if it does have a charter, whether a current copy of it is available on the registrant's website. If a current copy of the charter:

● is available on the registrant's website, the registrant should state its website address; or

● is not available on the registrant's website, a copy should be included as an appendix to the proxy statement at least once every three fiscal years, or as an appendix to the current proxy statement if the charter has been materially amended since the beginning of the registrant's last fiscal year (for years in which the charter is not so attached, the registrant should state the most recent prior fiscal year in which it did so attach a copy);

● if a listed registrant's board of directors determines, in accordance with the listing standards applicable to the registrant, to appoint a director to the audit committee who is not independent (apart from the requirements in Rule 10A-3 under the Exchange Act), including as a result of exceptional or limited or similar circumstances, the registrant must disclose the nature of the relationship that makes that individual not independent and the reasons for the board of directors' determination;

● a report by the audit committee (or in the absence of an audit committee, the board committee performing equivalent functions or the entire board of directors), which must state, above the name of each member, whether it:[33]

---

[32] See also SEC Release Nos. 34-42266 (effective January 31, 2000) and 34-47654 (effective April 25, 2003), which adopted required disclosure for audit committees.

[33] This information need only be provided one time during any fiscal year and is not deemed soliciting material, filed with the SEC, subject to Regulation 14A, subject to the liabilities of Section 18 under the Exchange Act or incorporated into another SEC filing, unless and to the extent the registrant specifically requests it

● reviewed and discussed the registrant's audited financial statements with management;

● discussed with the registrant's independent auditors the matters required to be discussed by Statement on Auditing Standards (SAS) No. 61, as amended;

● received the written disclosures and the letter from the registrant's auditor required by applicable requirements of the Public Company Accounting Oversight Board regarding the independent accountant's communications with the audit committee concerning independence, and has discussed with the accountants its independence; and

● based on the foregoing review, recommended to the board of directors that the audited financial statements be included in the registrant's Form 10-K.

(f) Audit Committee Financial Expert. Implementing the requirements of Section 407 of the Sarbanes-Oxley Act, Item 407(d)(5) of Regulation S-K requires the registrant to disclose[34] that the registrant's board of directors[35] has determined that the registrant either:

● has at least one audit committee financial expert serving on its audit committee; or

● does not have an audit committee financial expert serving on its audit committee.[36]

(1) Disclosure Concerning the Audit Committee Financial Expert(s). If the registrant discloses that it does have at least one audit committee financial expert serving on its audit committee, it must disclose the name of the audit committee financial expert and whether that person is independent, as that term is defined in the listing standards applicable to the registrant.[37] If the

---

(Footnote Continued)

to be treated as such or specifically incorporates it by reference. Many registrants also include disclaimer language in the audit committee report that states the limitations on the audit committee's responsibilities and upon what the committee has relied in carrying out such responsibilities.

[34] This disclosure is only required in a Form 10-K. Registrants need not provide the disclosure required by Item 407(d)(5) in a proxy statement unless that registrant is electing to incorporate this information by reference from the proxy statement into its Form 10-K pursuant to general instruction G(3) to Form 10-K.

[35] In the case of a foreign private issuer with a two-tier board of directors, for purposes of Item 401(h), the term "board of directors" means the supervisory or nonmanagement board.

[36] See SEC Release No. 33-8177 (January 23, 2003).

[37] See the listing standards of the NYSE, NYSE Amex and NASDAQ.

registrant's board of directors has determined that the registrant has more than one audit committee financial expert serving on its audit committee, the registrant may, but is not required to, disclose the names of those additional persons. A registrant choosing to identify such persons must indicate whether they are independent as described above.

(2) Disclosure of No Audit Committee Financial Expert. If the registrant discloses that it does not have at least one audit committee financial expert serving on its audit committee, it must explain why it does not have an audit committee financial expert.

(3) Definition of Audit Committee Financial Expert. An audit committee financial expert means a person who has all of the following attributes:

● An understanding of generally accepted accounting principles[38] and financial statements;

● The ability to assess the general application of such principles in connection with the accounting for estimates, accruals and reserves;

● Experience preparing, auditing, analyzing or evaluating financial statements that present a breadth and level of complexity of accounting issues that are generally comparable to the breadth and complexity of issues that can reasonably be expected to be raised by the registrant's financial statements, or experience actively supervising one or more persons engaged in such activities;

● An understanding of internal controls and procedures for financial reporting; and

● An understanding of audit committee functions.

A person must have acquired such attributes through any one or more of the following:

● Education and experience as a principal financial officer, principal accounting officer, controller, public accountant or auditor or experience in one or more positions that involve the performance of similar functions;

● Experience actively supervising a principal financial officer, principal accounting officer, controller, public accountant, auditor or person performing similar functions;

---

[38] In the case of a foreign private issuer, the term "generally accepted accounting principles" means the body of generally accepted accounting principles used by that issuer in its primary financial statements filed with the SEC.

● Experience overseeing or assessing the performance of companies or public accountants with respect to the preparation, auditing or evaluation of financial statements; or

● Other relevant experience.[39]

(4) Safe Harbor from Liability. Item 407(d)(5) of Regulation S-K provides a safe harbor from liability for designated financial experts, as follows:

(i) A person who is determined to be an audit committee financial expert will not be deemed an "expert" for any purpose, including, without limitation, for purposes of liability under Section 11 of the Securities Act, as a result of being designated or identified as an audit committee financial expert pursuant to Item 407(d)(5) of Regulation S-K.

(ii) The designation or identification of a person as an audit committee financial expert pursuant to Item 407 of Regulation S-K does not impose on such person any duties, obligations or liabilities that are greater than the duties, obligations and liabilities imposed on such person as a member of the audit committee and board of directors in the absence of such designation or identification.

(iii) The designation or identification of a person as an audit committee financial expert pursuant to Item 407 of Regulation S-K does not affect the duties, obligations or liabilities of any other member of the audit committee or board of directors.

(g) Director Independence. Item 407(a) of Regulation S-K provides that if the registrant has securities listed on a national securities exchange that has requirements that a majority of the board be independent, the registrant must identify each director and director nominee who is independent, as that term is defined in the listing standards applicable to the registrant. In addition, if such listing standards contain independent requirements for committees of the board, the registrant must identify each director that is a member of the compensation, nominating or audit committee that is not independent under such committee independence standards. If the registrant does not have a separately designated audit, nominating or compensation committee or committee performing similar functions, the registrant must provide the disclosure of directors that are not independent with respect to all members of the board applying such committee independence standards.

If the registrant is not a listed issuer, disclosure is required of those directors and director nominees that the registrant identifies as independent, and

---

[39] If a person qualifies as an audit committee financial expert by means of having "other relevant experience," the registrant must provide a brief listing of that person's relevant experience. Such disclosure may be made by reference to disclosures required under paragraph (e) of Item 401 of Regulation S-K.

committee members not identified as independent, using the definition of independence established by a national securities exchange specified by the registrant. Whatever definition the registrant chooses, it must use the same definition with respect to all directors and nominees for director as well as for purposes of determining the independence of members of the audit, nominating and compensation committees.

If a listed company is relying on an exemption from board or board committee requirements, the registrant must disclose the exemption relied upon and explain the basis for its conclusion that the exemption is applicable. Instruction 1 to Item 407(a) clarifies that this disclosure is also required for registrants that are not listed issuers but would qualify for an exemption under the listing standards selected.

Item 407(a) requires registrants using their own definitions of independence to disclose whether such definitions are available to security holders on the registrant's website and, if so, to provide the registrant's website address. If not, the registrant must include a copy of its independence policy in an appendix to the proxy statement that is provided to security holders at least once every three years or if the policies have been materially amended since the beginning of the registrant's last fiscal year.

In addition, for each director and nominee for director that is identified as independent, the registrant must describe, by specific category or type, any transactions, relationships or arrangements not disclosed pursuant to Item 404(a) of Regulation S-K that were considered by the board under the applicable independence definitions in determining that the director is independent. The description of the specific categories or types of transactions, relationships or arrangements must be provided in such detail as is necessary to fully describe the nature of the transactions, relationships or arrangements.

Independence disclosure is required for any person who served as a director during any part of the registrant's last completed fiscal year, even if the person no longer serves as a director at the time of filing the report or, if the information is in a proxy statement, if the director's term of office will not continue after the meeting. In this regard, the SEC believes that the independence status of a director is material while the person is serving as director, and not just as a matter of re-election.

(h) Nominating Committee. If a registrant does not have a nominating committee or committee performing similar functions, the registrant must disclose why its board of directors believes it is appropriate not to have such a committee and identify each director who participates in the consideration of director nominees.[40] Registrants must provide the following information regarding the director nomination process (in each case, the term nominating

---

[40] See SEC Release No. 33-8340 (November 24, 2003).

committee refers not only to nominating committees and committees performing similar functions, but also to groups of directors fulfilling the role of a nominating committee, including the entire board of directors):

- whether or not the nominating committee has a charter, and, if it does have a charter, whether a current copy of it is available on the registrant's website. If a current copy of the charter:

  - is available on the registrant's website, the registrant should state its website address; or

  - is not available on the registrant's website, a copy should be included as either an appendix to the proxy statement at least once every three fiscal years or as an appendix to the current proxy statement if the charter has been materially amended since the beginning of the registrant's last fiscal year (for years in which the charter is not so attached, the registrant should state the most recent prior fiscal year in which it did so attach a copy).

- whether or not the nominating committee has a policy regarding the consideration of director candidates recommended by security holders.

  - if it does have such a policy, the registrant must disclose the material elements of such policy, including whether it will consider such director candidates; or

  - if it does not have such a policy, the registrant must disclose why its board of directors believes it is appropriate not to have such a policy.

- if the nominating committee considers director candidates recommended by security holders, the procedures security holders should follow to submit such recommended director candidates.

- a description of (i) any specific, minimum qualifications that the nominating committee believes must be met by a director nominee nominated by the committee and (ii) any specific qualities or skills that the nominating committee believes are necessary for one or more directors to possess (these are often found in the committee's charter and/or the registrant's corporate governance guidelines and may include qualifications, qualities and skills such as business background, industry and leadership experience, sufficient time, ability to contribute to board diversity, etc.).

- the nominating committee's process for identifying and evaluating director nominees, including those recommended by security holders and any differences in the manner of evaluating nominees recommended by security holders, and whether, and if so how, the nominating committee considers diversity (which is broadly interpreted to include different skills, business experiences, educational backgrounds and viewpoints, as well as race, nationality and gender) in identifying nominees for director. If the nominating committee has a policy with regard to the consideration of diversity in identifying director nominees, the registrant should describe how this policy is implemented and how its effectiveness is assessed.

● which of the following categories of persons recommended each director nominee (other than executive officers or directors standing for re-election) approved by the nominating committee for inclusion on the registrant's proxy card: security holder, non-management directors, chief executive officer, other executive officer, third-party search firm or other specified source.

● the function performed by each third party to whom the registrant pays a fee to identify or evaluate, or help identify or evaluate, potential director nominees.

● if the registrant's nominating committee received a recommended nominee from a security holder or group of security holders that beneficially owns, in the aggregate, more than 5% of the registrant's voting common stock for at least one year as of the date of such recommendation[41] and such recommendation was received by a date no later than the 120th calendar day before the anniversary of the registrant's proxy statement for the previous year's annual meeting,[42] the registrant must disclose:

 ● the identity of the candidate and the recommending security holder(s);[43] and

 ● whether the nominating committee chose to nominate the candidate.

(i) **Compensation Committee.** If a registrant does not have a compensation committee or committee performing similar functions, the registrant must

---

[41] This determination of percentage ownership may be made using information set forth in the registrant's most recent Exchange Act report, unless the party relying on the report knows or has reason to know such information is not correct. If the recommending security holder is a registered holder of securities, the percentage ownership and holding period may be determined by the registrant. If the recommending security holder is not the registered holder of the securities (e.g., held by a broker or bank), he or she can submit the following evidence: (i) a written statement by the record holder verifying that the recommending security holder held the required securities for one year or (ii) a copy of the recommending security holder's Schedule 13D, Schedule 13G, Form 3, Form 4 and/or Form 5 that reflect ownership of the required securities and a written statement that the securities were held for at least one year.

[42] If the date of the annual meeting has been changed by more than 30 days from the date of the previous year's annual meeting, the disclosure is instead required if the recommendation is received a reasonable time before the registrant begins to print and mail its proxy materials.

[43] The disclosure is only required if the written consent of the nominee and the recommending security holder(s) to be identified and proof of required ownership percentage and holding period is received by the registrant.

disclose why its board of directors believes it is appropriate not to have such a committee and identify each director who participates in the consideration of executive officer and director compensation. For registrants that do have a compensation committee, registrants must provide the following information:

- whether or not the compensation committee has a charter and if it does have a charter, whether a current copy of it is available on the registrant's website. If a current copy of the charter:

    - is available on a registrant's website, the registrant should state its website address; or

    - is not available on the registrant's website, a copy should be included as either an appendix to the proxy statement at least once every three fiscal years or an appendix to the current proxy statement if the charter has been materially amended since the beginning of the registrant's last fiscal year (for years in which the charter is not so attached, the registrant should state the most recent prior fiscal year in which it did so attach a copy).

- provide a narrative description of the registrant's processes and procedures for the consideration and determination of executive and director compensation, including:

    (i) the scope of authority of the compensation committee (or persons performing similar functions), and the extent to which the compensation committee (or persons performing the similar functions) may delegate any such authority to other persons, specifying what authority may be so delegated and to whom;

    (ii) any role of executive officers in determining or recommending the amount or form of executive and director compensation; and

    (iii) any role of compensation consultants in determining or recommending the amount or form of executive and director compensation (other than any role limited to (x) consulting on any broad-based plan that does not discriminate in scope, terms or operation in favor of executive officers or directors of the registrant, and that is available generally to all salaried employees (e.g., a 401(k) plan); or (y) providing information that either is not customized for a particular registrant or is customized based on parameters that are not developed by the compensation consultant, and about which the compensation consultant does not provide advice) during the registrant's last completed fiscal year, identifying such consultants, stating whether such consultants were engaged directly by the compensation committee (or persons performing the equivalent functions) or any other person, describing the nature and scope of their assignment, the material elements of the instructions or directions given to the consultants with respect to the performance of their duties under the engagement and the following information regarding fees paid to the compensation consultants and their affiliates:

- if such compensation consultant was engaged by the compensation committee (or persons performing the equivalent functions) to provide advice or recommendations on the amount or form of executive and director compensation and the compensation consultant or its affiliates also provided additional services (e.g., other consulting services, brokerage services, actuarial services or executive search services) to the registrant or its affiliates in an amount in excess of $120,000 during the registrant's last completed fiscal year, then the registrant must disclose the aggregate fees for executive and director compensation services, the aggregate fees for such other additional services, whether the decision to engage the compensation consultant or its affiliates for these other services was made or recommended by management, and whether the compensation committee or the board approved such other additional services of the compensation consultant or its affiliates; or

- if the compensation committee (or persons performing the equivalent functions) has not engaged a compensation consultant, but management has engaged a compensation consultant to provide advice or recommendations on the amount or form of executive and director compensation and such compensation consultant or its affiliates has provided additional services to the registrant in an amount in excess of $120,000 during the registrant's last completed fiscal year, then the registrant must disclose the aggregate fees for executive and director compensation services and the aggregate fees for such other additional services provided by the compensation consultant or its affiliates.[44]

(j) Other Committee Disclosure. Though not required, registrants often also provide disclosure regarding members, number of meetings and functions for other standing committees (e.g., executive, corporate governance[45] and finance committees).

---

[44] Pursuant to the Dodd-Frank Act, the SEC has proposed rules to require stock exchange listing standards to require registrants' compensation committees to comply with certain independence requirements and select advisors, including compensation consultants and legal advisors, only after considering certain factors regarding the advisors' independence. Registrants would also be required to disclose whether a compensation consultant has been engaged by, or provided advice to, a registrant's compensation committee and, if so, the nature of any conflicts of interest arising from such work and how they are being addressed. See SEC Release No. 33-9199 (March 30, 2011).

[45] Furthermore, many registrants are disclosing their various corporate governance practices under one caption in the proxy statement so as to make it easier for readers, including corporate governance ratings services, to determine what those practices are. Many registrants have their nominating committee also serve as their corporate governance committee.

(k) Number of Board Meetings. The registrant must state the total number of meetings of its board of directors that were held during the last full fiscal year. This number should include regularly scheduled and special meetings, whether in person, or by phone or by videoconference, but should not include actions taken by written consent. The registrant must also identify each current director who, during the last full fiscal year, attended less than 75% of the aggregate of (i) the total number of meetings of the board of directors (held during the period for which such person was a director) and (ii) the total number of meetings held by all committees of the board on which such director served (during the period that such director so served).

The registrant is also required to (i) describe any policy it has with regard to board members' attendance at annual meetings and (ii) state the number of board members that attended the prior year's annual meeting. The information regarding board members' attendance at annual meetings and a registrant's process for security holders to send communications to the board can be replaced with a reference to the registrant's website address if the required information appears on such website.

(l) Communication with the Board. A registrant must disclose whether or not its board of directors provides a process for security holders to send communications to the board and if it does not have such a process, explain why its board believes it is appropriate not to have such a process.[46] If the registrant does have such a process, it must describe:

● the manner in which security holders can send communications to the board and, if applicable, specific individual directors (e.g., providing an address for written communications, an e-mail address for electronic communications or a telephone hotline number for oral communications); and

● the process for determining which communications are sent to board members if security holder communications are not sent directly to board members (though the process for collecting and organizing security holder communications and similar or related activities is not required to be disclosed if the process is approved by a majority of the independent directors). For example, the corporate secretary may review communications first to screen and exclude individual customer complaints or commercial solicitations and/or to summarize such communications for the directors.

(m) Board Leadership Structure and Role in Risk Oversight. A registrant must briefly describe the leadership structure of the registrant's board, such as whether and why the same person serves as both principal executive officer and chairman of the board, or whether and why two individuals serve in

---

[46] See SEC Release No. 34-48825 (November 24, 2003). "Security holder communications" do not include (i) shareholders' proposals made pursuant to Rule 14a-8 under the Exchange Act, (ii) communications from a registrant's officers or directors or (iii) communications from a registrant's employees or agents, unless made in their capacities as security holders.

those positions. If one person serves as both principal executive officer and chairman of the board, the registrant must also disclose whether the registrant has a lead independent director and what specific role the lead independent director plays in the leadership of the board. This disclosure should indicate why the registrant has determined that its leadership structure is the most appropriate at the time the disclosure is made, given the specific characteristics or circumstances of the registrant (e.g., a particular person may serve as both CEO and chairman because such person (i) has specific knowledge, skills and experience that allow such person to effectively manage operations and establish and communicate strategy, (ii) is subject to effective corporate governance guidelines and (iii) works with a strong, independent lead director). In addition, the registrant must disclose the extent of the board's role in the risk oversight of the registrant (e.g., operational, financial, strategic and compliance risks), such as how the board administers its oversight function, and the effect that this has on the board's leadership structure. This disclosure should include general risk oversight processes, general controls and procedures and roles played by specific committees, such as the audit committee's role in risk management and the compensation committee's focus on not encouraging risky behavior that is reasonably likely to materially adversely affect the registrant.

(n) **Disclosure Required by the NYSE and NASDAQ.** For registrants that have securities listed on the NYSE, such registrants are required by Section 303A of the NYSE's listing standards to disclose the information required by Item 407(a) of Regulation S-K regarding independent directors discussed above, as well as the following information:[47]

- the identity of the director chosen to preside over regular executive sessions of non-management directors or the procedure by which a presiding director is selected for each executive session;

- a method by which interested parties can communicate concerns directly to the presiding director or the non-management directors as a group;

- if a registrant does not limit the number of audit committees on which its audit committee members may serve, the registrant's determination that the service of an audit committee member on the audit committees of more than three public companies, if applicable, does not impair such member's ability to serve on the registrant's audit committee;

- any charitable contributions made by the registrant to a charitable organization in which an independent director serves as an executive officer if, within the past three years, contributions in any single fiscal year

---

[47] Section 303A of the NYSE's listing standards permits most of this information to instead be disclosed on or through the registrant's website so long as the registrant discloses in its annual proxy statement that such information is posted on or through its website and provides the website address.

exceeded the greater of $1 million and 2% ⸻ h charitable organization's consolidated gross revenues;

● if applicable, that the registrant is a c ⸻ l company (i.e., more than 50% of its voting power is held by a pers⸻ p or another company) that takes advantage of exemptions from the ⸻ s requirements regarding a majority of independent directors, nominating/corporate governance committee and/or compensation committees and its basis for such determination; and

● that the registrant's (i) corporate governance guidelines, (ii) code of business conduct and ethics and (iii) charters for its audit committee, compensation committee and nominating/corporate governance committee are available on its website and provide its website address.

For registrants that have securities listed on NASDAQ, such registrants are required by Section 5605 of the NASDAQ Listing Rules to disclose information required by Items 407(a) (including Instruction 1 thereto) and, if applicable, 407(d)(2) of Regulation S-K discussed above. They are also required by Section 5615 of the NASDAQ Listing Rules to disclose, if applicable, the determination by the board that membership of a director who does not meet NASDAQ's independence requirements on the compensation or nominating committee is in the best interests of the registrant and its shareholders and the relationship that causes such director not to be independent.[48]

7. Item 8. Compensation of Directors and Executive Officers. Item 8 of Schedule 14A requires disclosure of the detailed information regarding director and executive compensation required by Item 402 of Regulation S-K in annual meeting proxy statements so that shareholders can consider the compensation decisions of a registrant's board when voting for the election of directors (e.g., whether the interests of executives have been aligned with those of shareholders). Before preparing the compensation disclosure required by Item 402 of Regulation S-K, registrants should review SEC Release No. 33-8732A (August 11, 2006), No. 33-8765 (December 22, 2006) and No. 33-9089 (December 16, 2009), which provide guidance as to the detailed tabular and textual compensation disclosure that is now required by the complex, updated rules of Item 402.[49] The updated compensation rules are meant to give shareholders a clear and complete understanding of all elements of compensation paid to executives. In addition to the new disclosure rules, enforcement activity by the SEC has emphasized the focus on the adequacy of executive compensation

---

[48] This disclosure requirement can instead be satisfied by disclosing such information on or through the registrant's website.

[49] As clarified in the Executive Compensation and Related Person Disclosure Transition Questions and Answers from the staff of the SEC's Division of Corporation Finance, registrants will not be required to restate previously reported compensation disclosure under the new rules for fiscal years in which the registrant was required to apply the old rules.

disclosure. In April 2005, the SEC settled an enforcement proceeding against Tyson Foods, Inc. for failing to fully and accurately disclose perquisites received by its former senior chairman and his family and friends;[50] in December 2004, the SEC entered a cease and desist order against Walt Disney Company for failing to fully and accurately disclose benefits and services provided to its directors and their family members;[51] and in September 2004, the SEC settled enforcement proceedings against General Electric Company for failing to fully and accurately disclose retirement benefits that its former chairman and CEO was entitled to receive.[52] The compensation disclosure is required to be written in accordance with the same "plain English" standards that apply to prospectuses filed under the Securities Act.

(a) **Compensation Tables.** Item 402 of Regulation S-K requires the clear, concise and understandable tabular presentation of all compensation paid or awarded to, or earned by, certain executive officers and directors of the registrant for all services such person rendered to the registrant and its subsidiaries during specified fiscal years, even if awarded or paid by a third party. The tables must follow specific formats, and very few changes in the highly formatted tables, including adding or omitting columns, altering column headings or combining tables, are allowed. In general, a table or column may be omitted only if it is not applicable because there has been no compensation awarded or paid to, or earned by, any of the executive officers required to be reported in that table or column in any fiscal year covered by the table. Each table that requires disclosure as of or for a completed fiscal year should contain the applicable fiscal year in the title for such table.

Registrants should note that required disclosure of compensation earned by certain executive officers can be a very sensitive issue because it results in those outside, as well as inside, the company knowing what these individuals were compensated for their employment. Amounts paid to a third party in a transaction covered by Item 404 of Regulation S-K, when a purpose of the transaction was to compensate a named executive officer, should be reported pursuant to Item 402.

(b) **Executive Officers Included in Compensation Tables.** The executive officers of the registrant for whom compensation must be disclosed, known as "named executive officers," are the following:

● anyone who served as principal executive officer ("PEO") during the last fiscal year, regardless of that person's compensation and regardless of whether that person is still PEO. Therefore, if two people served as PEO during the last fiscal year, whether as co-PEOs or at separate points in time, compensation disclosure is required for each of them;

---

[50] See SEC Litigation Release No. 19208 (April 28, 2005).

[51] See SEC Litigation Release No. 50882 (December 20, 2004).

[52] See SEC Litigation Release No. 50426 (September 23, 2004).

● anyone who served as principal financial officer ("PFO") during the last fiscal year, regardless of that person's compensation and regardless of whether that person is still PFO. Therefore, if two people served as PFO during the last fiscal year, whether as co-PFOs or at separate points in time, compensation disclosure is required for each of them;

● the three executive officers, other than the PEO and PFO, who had the highest total compensation[53] in excess of $100,000[54] for, and who were serving as executive officers at the end of, the last completed fiscal year[55] (even if the person left the employ of the registrant or was demoted to non-executive employee after the end of the last completed fiscal year[56]). Keep in mind that the group of current executive officers, from which at least some of these named executive officers will likely come, is disclosed either elsewhere in the proxy statement or in the Form 10-K pursuant to Item 401 of Regulation S-K;[57] and

● up to two additional individuals who would have been among the three most highly compensated executive officers but for the fact that the individual was not serving as an executive officer at the end of the last completed fiscal year. This is meant to cover up to two persons who (a) were executive officers during the last fiscal year, (b) received total compensation in excess of $100,000 during the fiscal year and (c) would have been one of the three most highly compensated executive officers at the end of the fiscal year, but for the fact that the person was fired, quit or was demoted to non-executive employee prior to the end of the fiscal year.

(c) **Compensation Discussion and Analysis ("CD&A").** The registrant must discuss all material elements of the compensation of its named executive

---

[53] Total compensation for purposes of determining the most highly compensated executive officers is determined as described below for the "Total" column in the Summary Compensation Table, but without including amounts that would be disclosed in the "Change in Pension Value and Non-qualified Deferred Compensation Earnings" column in the Summary Compensation Table. The SEC has clarified that when a registrant recovers (or "claws back") a portion of an executive officer's bonus, the portion of the bonus that is clawed back should not be deducted from total compensation for purposes of determining whether the executive is a named executive officer. See SEC's Division of Corporation Finance Compliance and Disclosure Interpretations–Regulation S-K–Questions and Answers of General Applicability–Section 117. Item

402(a)–Executive Compensation; General–Question 117.03 (August 14, 2009).

[54] Including, if applicable, any compensation the executive officer earned during the last fiscal year while he or she was a non-executive employee prior to becoming an executive officer.

[55] If fewer than three executive officers earned total compensation in excess of $100,000, then such executive officers are named executive officers for whom compensation disclosure is required.

[56] Registrants typically add a footnote to the compensation tables that discloses if a named executive officer is no longer employed by, or is no longer employed as an executive officer of, the registrant.

[57] See Section 6 above, which also includes a description of who constitutes an executive officer.

officers so that investors can understand the registrant's compensation policies and decisions (i.e., why named executive officers were compensated the way they were for the most recently completed fiscal year (as reflected in the compensation tables and the accompanying textual disclosure) and why—to the extent they affect a fair understanding of executive compensation for such fiscal year—any actions regarding executive compensation (such as adoption or implementation of new or amended programs or policies) were taken after such fiscal year's end).[58] The CD&A must explain the following:[59]

- The objectives of the registrant's compensation programs;

- What the compensation program is designed to reward;

- Each element of (current and post-employment) compensation;

- Why the registrant chooses to pay each element;

- How the registrant determines the amount (and, if applicable, the formula) for each element to pay;

- How each compensation element and the registrant's decisions regarding that element fit into the registrant's overall compensation objectives and affect decisions regarding other elements; and

- Whether and, if so, how the registrant has considered the results of the most recent say-on-pay shareholder advisory vote in determining compensation policies and decisions and, if so, how that consideration has affected the registrant's executive compensation decisions and policies.[60]

While the material information to be disclosed under the CD&A will vary depending upon, and must be tailored to, a registrant's particular facts and circumstances, examples of such information may include, among other things, the following:

---

[58] The CD&A requirement is modeled after MD&A, and registrants are cautioned not to use boilerplate disclosure. Like MD&A, the principal executive officer and principal financial officer should keep in mind that their Section 302 and 906 certifications for the Form 10-K described in Chapter 6 cover the CD&A disclosure.

[59] As discussed below, registrants must also disclose, when material, the relationship between their compensation policies and the incentives such policies may create for executive officers and non-executive officers to take risks that could harm the registrants in order to meet compensation targets.

[60] Investors will be interested in how registrants react to say-on-pay proposals that are rejected by shareholders or receive a significant number of votes against. Investors may, for example, withhold their authority to vote for compensation committee members when they are nominated again to the board of a registrant that has ignored the most recent say-on-pay vote in determining compensation policies and decisions. Some shareholders have even brought say-on-pay shareholder derivative actions alleging breach of directors' fiduciary duties of care and loyalty in connection with shareholders rejecting a registrant's recommended approval of what they deem to be excessive executive compensation. For example, see *Haberland v. Dex One Corp.* (U.S. District Court of Eastern District of North Carolina).

● The policies for allocating between long-term and currently paid out compensation;

● The policies for allocating between cash and non-cash compensation, and among different forms of non-cash compensation, including the extent to which amounts awarded/paid under one element of compensation impacts the amount awarded/paid under other elements of compensation (e.g., if tally sheets are used, disclosing what they contain and how they were used to impact compensation decisions);

● For long-term compensation, the basis for allocating compensation to each different form of award (such as relationship of the award to the achievement of the registrant's long-term goals, management's exposure to downside equity performance risk and the correlation between cost to the registrant and expected benefits to the registrant);

● How the determination is made as to when awards are granted, including awards of equity-based compensation such as options (which includes disclosure of any program, plan or practice to (i) select option grant dates for executives in coordination with the release of material, non-public information or (ii) award options with an exercise price based on the stock's price on a date other than the actual grant date);[61]

● What specific items of corporate performance (e.g., corporate performance targets such as EBITDA, earnings per share, growth in market share and operational or strategic goals) are taken into account in setting compensation policies and making compensation decisions and how such items are calculated;[62]

---

[61] This has become a hot topic with the recent focus on option backdating and option grant timing, such as timing option grants to precede the release of good news or follow the release of bad news.

[62] The SEC expects registrants to quantify all performance targets that must be achieved in order for named executive officers to earn their incentive compensation. However, according to Instruction 4 to Item 402(b), registrants are not required to disclose target levels with respect to specific quantitative or qualitative performance-related factors considered by the compensation committee or the board of directors, or any other factors or criteria involving confidential trade secrets or confidential commercial or financial information that has not been disclosed publicly, the disclosure of which would result in substantial competitive harm for the registrant. The standard to use when determining whether disclosure would cause substantial competitive harm for the registrant is the same standard that would apply when a registrant requests confidential treatment of confidential trade secrets or confidential commercial or financial information pursuant to Rule 24b-2 under the Exchange Act. A registrant is not required to seek confidential treatment under the procedures in Rule 24b-2 if it determines that the disclosure would cause competitive harm in reliance on this instruction (though if the SEC reviews a registrant's CD&A, the registrant may be required to supplementally demonstrate that a nondisclosed target meets the confidential treatment standard, but the SEC is not likely to consider this standard satisfied if target

● How specific forms of compensation are structured and implemented to reflect these items of the registrant's performance, including whether discretion can be or has been exercised (either to award compensation absent attainment of the relevant performance goal(s) or to reduce or increase the size of any award or payout), identifying any particular exercise of discretion, and stating whether it applied to one or more specified named executive officers or to all compensation subject to the relevant performance goal(s);

● How specific forms of compensation are structured and implemented to reflect the named executive officer's individual performance and/or individual contribution to these items of the registrant's performance, describing the elements of individual performance and/or contribution that are taken into account (e.g., specifically identifying material differences in compensation policies and decisions for individual named executive officers);

● Registrant policies and decisions regarding the adjustment or recovery of awards or payments if the relevant registrant performance measures upon which they are based are restated or otherwise adjusted in a manner that would reduce the size of an award or payment;

● The factors considered in decisions to increase or decrease compensation materially;

● How compensation or amounts realizable from prior compensation are considered in setting other elements of compensation (e.g., how gains from prior option or stock awards are considered in setting retirement benefits);

● With respect to any contract, agreement, plan or arrangement, whether written or unwritten, that provides for payment(s) at, following, or in

---

(Footnote Continued)

levels for the most recently completed fiscal year were based on the registrant achieving certain levels of performance with respect to financial metrics that it publicly discloses (such as earnings per share or EBITDA)). To the extent a registrant has an appropriate basis for omitting specific targets, the registrant must discuss how difficult it will be for the executive or how likely it will be for the registrant to achieve the undisclosed target levels or other factors (e.g., how challenging performance goals are so as to justify executives being rewarded for performance that satisfies such goals). In addition, disclosure of target levels that are non-GAAP financial measures will not be subject to Regulation G and Item 10(e) of Regulation S-K, but disclosure must be provided as to how the number is calculated from the registrant's audited financial statements. However, non-GAAP financial measures presented in CD&A for any other purpose (e.g., to explain the relationship between pay and performance) are subject to Regulation G and Item 10(e) (though the required information can be provided by prominent cross-reference to an annex to the proxy statement or to the pages in the registrant's Form 10-K that contain such disclosure). See SEC's Division of Corporation Finance Compliance and Disclosure Interpretations - Regulation S-K - Questions and Answers of General Applicability - Section 118. Item 402(b)-Executive Compensation; Compensation Discussion and Analysis - Question 118.08 (July 8, 2011).

connection with any termination or change-in-control, the basis for selecting particular events as triggering payment (e.g., the rationale for providing a single trigger for payment in the event of a change-in-control);

● The impact of the accounting and tax treatments of the particular form of compensation;

● The registrant's equity or other security ownership requirements or guidelines (specifying applicable amounts and forms of ownership), and any registrant policies regarding hedging the economic risk of such ownership;

● Whether the registrant engaged in any benchmarking of total compensation, or any material element of compensation, identifying the benchmark, its components (including component companies), why such benchmark was chosen and how data collected from the benchmark is being utilized by the registrant to set compensation (e.g., the degree to which the benchmark companies are considered comparable to the registrant and whether total compensation fell within the targeted percentile range and if not, why); and

● The role of executive officers and consultants in determining or recommending the amount or form of executive compensation.

The SEC's Division of Corporation Finance completed its initial review of executive compensation disclosure of 350 public companies under the new rules related thereto and published its observations in October 2007.[63] The two general comments offered by the SEC are that registrants must focus more on (1) specific analysis in CD&A (how and why registrants arrived at executive compensation decisions and policies, including consideration of individual performance, as opposed to compensation program mechanics) and (2) presenting information in a clear, concise and organized fashion, including through the use of plain English and tables. A number of registrants have begun to place an executive summary using charts and tables at the beginning of their CD&A in order to highlight how performance related to targets and different components of compensation, such as incentives. It should also be noted that financial institutions participating in the Troubled Asset Relief Program established by the Emergency Economic Stabilization Act of 2008 are required to certify in their CD&A that they have complied with Treasury regulations implementing the executive compensation provisions of the Act.

(d) Summary Compensation Table. The registrant must disclose the following compensation information in the following table for each named executive officer:

---

[63] The report, entitled "Staff Observations in the Review of Executive Compensation Disclosure," is available online at www.sec.gov/divisions/corpfin/guidance/execcompdisclosure.htm.

SUMMARY COMPENSATION TABLE

Name and Principal Position	Year	Salary ($)	Bonus ($)	Stock Awards ($)	Option Awards ($)	Non-Equity Incentive Plan Compensation ($)	Change in Pension Value and Nonqualified Deferred Compensation Earnings ($)	All Other Compensation ($)	Total ($)
	(1)	(2)	(2)	(3)	(3)	(4)	(5)	(6)	(7)
PEO									
PFO									
A									
B									
C									

(1) Year. The required compensation information must be presented for each of the last three completed fiscal years. However, the compensation disclosure is not required for any fiscal year prior to the last completed fiscal year in which the registrant was not a public reporting company at any time during that year, unless the compensation information for such prior fiscal year was required to be provided in response to an SEC filing requirement.

Example: If a registrant with a fiscal year that ends December 31 priced its IPO during 2011, it would only have to disclose in its 2012 proxy statement the required compensation information for each named executive officer for 2010 (because though the registrant was not a public reporting company in 2010, this information would have been required to be disclosed in its IPO S-1 registration statement) and 2011.

The clear and uniform presentation of the various pieces of compensation for a three-year period enables shareholders to evaluate trends in the registrant's compensation of senior executives and compare such compensation with that of other registrants. If a registrant changes its fiscal year, required compensation information must be reported for the stub period (without being annualized or restated) and the last three completed fiscal years, except for any fiscal year prior to the last completed fiscal year in which the registrant was not a public reporting company at any time during that year, unless the compensation information for such prior fiscal year was required to be provided in response to an SEC filing requirement. This disclosure would be provided for four periods (three full fiscal years and the stub period) until there is disclosure for three full fiscal years after the stub period.[64]

---

[64] For example, if a registrant changed its fiscal year-end from June 30 to December 31 in the second half of 2011, the summary compensation table for its 2012 proxy statement would provide compensation disclosure for:

- July 1, 2011 to December 31, 2011;
- July 1, 2010 to June 30, 2011;

Compensation information (i) for a PEO or PFO is not required for any fiscal year in which the person did not serve at any time as PEO or PFO and (ii) for any of the most highly compensated executive officers is not required for any fiscal year in which the person was not at any time an executive officer. When compensation information is disclosable for a named executive officer in a given fiscal year, all compensation earned by, or paid or awarded to, such person in such year should be disclosed, even if earned, paid or awarded prior to such person being PEO, PFO or an executive officer.

(2) Salary and Bonus. This column consists of the dollar value of cash and non-cash[65] base salary or bonus, as applicable, earned by the named executive officer during the applicable fiscal year, including amounts deferred and any amount of salary or bonus, as applicable, forgone at the named executive officer's election pursuant to a program of the registrant under which stock, equity-based or other forms of non-cash compensation may be received by such named executive officer in lieu of a portion of annual compensation.[66] The registrant must disclose in a footnote if the amount of salary or bonus, as applicable, for the last fiscal year cannot be calculated through the latest practicable date (e.g., because bonuses have not been finalized for the previous fiscal year), including when that amount is expected to be determined. That amount should then be disclosed in a Current Report on Form 8-K under Section 5.02(f) and in the Summary Compensation table for the next fiscal year in the applicable column for the fiscal year earned. A discretionary cash bonus not based on any performance criteria under a plan is disclosed in this column as opposed to a bonus pursuant to a plan intended to serve as incentive for performance to occur over a specified time period, which is disclosed in the "Non-Equity Incentive Compensation Plan" column.

Disclosing salary and bonus in separate columns allows shareholders to separately evaluate an executive's fixed compensation, which is usually tied to the executive's position, responsibilities or work experience, and discretionary compensation, which is often tied to performance or targets.

(Footnote Continued)

● July 1, 2009 to June 30, 2010; and
● July 1, 2008 to June 30, 2009.
See SEC's Division of Corporation Finance Compliance and Disclosure Interpretations —Regulation S-K—Interpretive Responses Regarding Particular Situations—Section 217. Item 402(a). Executive Compensation; General—Section 217.05 (January 24, 2007).

[65] The dollar value of non-cash compensation is its fair market value at the time it is awarded or earned.

[66] The receipt of any such non-cash compensation instead of salary or bonus, however, must be disclosed in a footnote to the "Salary" or "Bonus" column, as applicable, that, when applicable, cross-references the Grants of Plan-Based Awards Table when the stock option or non-equity incentive plan award elected by the named executive officer is reported.

(3) Stock and Option Awards. This column consists of the aggregate grant date fair value computed in accordance with FASB ASC Topic 718 for stock awards or option awards, as applicable, granted to the named executive officer in previous fiscal years and during the applicable fiscal year. "Stock" means instruments such as common stock, restricted stock, restricted stock units, phantom stock, phantom stock units, common stock equivalent units or any similar instruments that do not have option-like features, and the term "option" means instruments such as stock options, stock appreciation rights ("SARs") and similar instruments with option-like features. The registrant must include a footnote disclosing all assumptions made in the valuation by reference to a discussion of those assumptions in the registrant's financial statements, footnotes to the financial statements, or discussion in MD&A.

If at any time during the last completed fiscal year, the registrant has adjusted or amended the exercise price of options or SARs previously awarded to a named executive officer, whether through amendment, cancellation or replacement grants, or any other means, or otherwise has materially modified such awards, the registrant must include, as awards required to be reported in the column applicable to option awards, the incremental fair value, computed as of the repricing or modification date in accordance with FASB ASC Topic 718, with respect to those repriced or modified awards.

For any awards that are subject to performance conditions, the registrant should report the value at the grant date based upon the probable outcome of such conditions (even if the actual outcome of such conditions is known as of the date of the proxy statement). This amount should be consistent with the estimate of aggregate compensation cost to be recognized over the service period determined as of the grant date under FASB ASC Topic 718, excluding the effect of estimated forfeitures. In a footnote to the table, the registrant must disclose the value of the award at the grant date assuming that the highest level of performance conditions will be achieved if an amount less than the maximum was included in the table.

(4) Non-Equity Incentive Plan Compensation. This column consists of the dollar value of all earnings for services performed during the fiscal year pursuant to awards under non-equity incentive plans and all earnings on any outstanding awards. The term "incentive plan" means any plan providing compensation intended to serve as incentive for performance to occur over a specified period, whether such performance is measured by reference to financial performance of the registrant or an affiliate, the registrant's stock price or any other performance measure. An "equity incentive plan" is an incentive plan or portion thereof under which awards are granted that fall within the scope of FASB ASC Topic 718.[67] A "non-equity incentive plan" is an incentive plan

---

[67] This includes plans that have a performance or market condition that determine the fair value of an award (e.g., by affecting vesting, exercisability or exercise price).

or portion thereof that is not an equity incentive plan. If the relevant performance measure is satisfied during the fiscal year (including for a single year in a
plan with a multi-year performance measure), the earnings are reportable for
that fiscal year, even if not payable until a later date, and are not reportable
again in the fiscal year when amounts are paid to the named executive officer.
All earnings on non-equity incentive plan compensation must be identified and
quantified in a footnote to this column, whether the earnings were paid during
the fiscal year, payable during the period but deferred at the election of the
named executive officer or payable by their terms at a later date.

(5) **Change in Pension Value and Nonqualified Deferred Compensation
Earnings.** This column consists of the sum of:

(A) The aggregate change in the actuarial present value of the named executive officer's accumulated benefit under all defined benefit and actuarial pension
plans (including supplemental plans) from the pension plan measurement date
used for financial statement reporting purposes with respect to the registrant's
audited financial statements for the prior completed fiscal year to the pension
plan measurement date used for financial statement reporting purposes with
respect to the registrant's audited financial statements for the covered fiscal
year. This applies to each plan that provides for the payment of retirement benefits,
or benefits that will be paid primarily following retirement, including, but not
limited to, tax-qualified defined benefit plans and supplemental executive retirement plans, but excluding tax-qualified defined contribution plans and nonqualified defined contribution plans. For purposes of this disclosure, the registrant
should use the same amounts required to be disclosed for the covered fiscal year
and the amounts that were or would have been required to be reported for the
executive officer in the Pension Benefits table described below for the prior completed fiscal year; and

(B) Above-market or preferential earnings on compensation that is deferred
on a basis that is not tax-qualified, including such earnings on nonqualified defined
contribution plans. Interest on deferred compensation is above-market only if the
rate of interest exceeds 120% of the applicable federal long-term rate, with compounding (as prescribed under section 1274(d) of the Internal Revenue Code) at
the rate that corresponds most closely to the rate under the registrant's plan at the
time the interest rate or formula is set. In the event of a discretionary reset of the
interest rate, the requisite calculation must be made on the basis of the interest rate
at the time of such reset, rather than when originally established. Only the above-
market portion of the interest must be included. If the applicable interest rates vary
depending upon conditions such as a minimum period of continued service, the
reported amount should be calculated assuming satisfaction of all conditions to
receiving interest at the highest rate. Dividends (and dividend equivalents) on
deferred compensation denominated in the registrant's stock are preferential
only if earned at a rate higher than dividends on the registrant's common stock.
Only the preferential portion of the dividends or equivalents must be included.

Footnote or narrative disclosure may be provided explaining the registrant's criteria for determining any portion considered to be above-market.

The registrant must identify and quantify by footnote the separate amounts attributable to each of the change in pension value and nonqualified deferred compensation earnings. If the change in pension value is negative, it should be disclosed by footnote, but it should not be reflected in the sum reported in this column.

(6) All Other Compensation. This column consists of all other compensation received or earned by the named executive officer for the applicable fiscal year that cannot be properly reported in any other column of the Summary Compensation table, including, without limitation:

a. Perquisites and other personal benefits or property (valued at the aggregate incremental cost to the registrant and its subsidiaries), unless the aggregate amount of such compensation is less than $10,000. Each perquisite or other personal benefit for the last fiscal year must be identified by type, and each perquisite and personal benefit that exceeds the greater of $25,000 and 10% of the total amount of perquisites and personal benefits for a named executive officer must be quantified (and the methodology for computing the registrant's aggregate incremental cost must be described) in a footnote or a paragraph accompanying the table so that shareholders can fully understand what the person is receiving. An item is not a perquisite or personal benefit if it confers a benefit directly related to the performance of the executive's duties (i.e., is needed by an executive to do his or her job, such as business travel, business entertainment or a laptop computer or handheld device that allows an executive to communicate with clients and fellow employees and to work on documents while outside of the office). An item is a perquisite or personal benefit if it confers a direct or indirect personal benefit that has a personal aspect, even if provided for some business reason or for convenience to the registrant and even if determined to be an ordinary or necessary business expense for tax or other reasons, unless generally available on a non-discriminatory basis to all employees. Examples of perquisites and other personal benefits include education assistance programs, personal financial, legal or tax advice, the registrant's paying for the personal use (i.e., unrelated to, and not exclusively for the purpose of facilitating the conduct of, the registrant's business) of a car, housing or a country club membership, the personal use of company property, such as a car, apartment or plane, security provided at a personal residence or during personal travel and discounts on the registrant's products or services not generally available to employees on a non-discriminatory basis. If a named executive officer uses company property or property paid for by the registrant for both personal and business purposes, the incremental cost to the registrant should be allocated between the two uses (e.g., based on the amount of time the property is used for each purpose) and need only be disclosed for the personal use.[68] Information

---

[68] See SEC Release No. 33-5904 (February 6, 1978), which, though it predates the new executive compensation rules, also has a good discussion in Q&A format of perquisites.

regarding group life, health, hospitalization or medical reimbursement plans are disclosable as perquisites only if they discriminate in scope, terms or operation in favor of executive officers or directors or are not available generally to all salaried employees. Registrants should review the disclosure under this column carefully because the SEC has focused in recent years on the adequacy of disclosure of perquisites and other personal benefits received by named executive officers, including the use of company assets to which a disingenuous incremental cost of nonbusiness use is assigned in order to avoid or minimize disclosure and lucrative retirement benefits that are not explained in sufficient detail.

b. All "gross-ups" or other amounts reimbursed during the fiscal year for the payment of taxes (including with respect to taxes owed for perquisites or other personal benefits).[69]

c. The compensation cost, if any, computed in accordance with FASB ASC Topic 718 for discounts on securities of the registrant or its subsidiaries purchased from the registrant or its subsidiaries, unless the discounts are available generally to all security holders or all salaried employees of the registrant.

d. Amounts paid or accrued (e.g., because completion of performance is necessary to earn an amount to be paid) pursuant to a plan or arrangement in connection with (i) the termination of the named executive officer's employment with the registrant (including through retirement, resignation and constructive termination) or (ii) a change in control of the registrant.

e. Annual contributions or other allocations by the registrant to vested and unvested defined contribution plans (e.g., contributions to a 401(k) plan).

f. The dollar value of any insurance premiums paid by, or on behalf of, the registrant during the applicable fiscal year with respect to term life insurance for the benefit of the named executive officer.

g. The dollar value of any dividends or other earnings paid on stock or option awards, when those amounts were not factored into the grant date fair value required to be reported under the "Grant Date Fair Value of Stock and Option Awards" column in the Grants of Plan-Based Awards Table.

Any compensation reported under this column for the last completed fiscal year that is not a perquisite or personal benefit and the value of which exceeds

---

[69] When a tax gross-up payment is provided in the current year, that gross-up payment must be reported in the Summary Compensation Table for the current year, even if it is not payable by the registrant until next year. See SEC's Division of Corporate Finance Compliance and Disclosure Interpretations–Regulation S-K–Questions and Answers of General Applicability–Section 119. Item 402(c)–Executive Compensation; Summary Compensation Table–Question 119.19 (May 29, 2009).

$10,000 should be identified and quantified in a footnote. Registrants do not need to report under this column benefits paid pursuant to defined benefit or actuarial plans, which are instead disclosed in the "Change in Pension Value and Nonqualified Deferred Compensation Earnings" column described above, unless accelerated pursuant to a change in control.

(7) Total Compensation. This column discloses the sum of all amounts reported in the other columns of this table for each named executive officer.

(e) Grants of Plan-Based Awards Table. The registrant must disclose the following information in the following table for awards granted to each named executive officer in the last completed fiscal year (each grant of an award to a named executive officer should be on a separate line and if awards are made under multiple plans, the specific plan should be identified for each grant):

GRANTS OF PLAN-BASED AWARDS

Name	Grant Date	Estimated Future Payouts Under Non-Equity Incentive Plan Awards			Estimated Future Payouts Under Equity Incentive Plan Awards			All Other Stock Awards: Number of Shares of Stock or Units (#)	All Other Option Awards: Number of Securities Underlying Options (#)	Exercise or Base Price of Option Awards ($/Sh)	Grant Date Fair Value of Stock and Option Awards
		Threshold ($)	Target ($)	Maximum ($)	Threshold (#)	Target (#)	Maximum (#)				
	(1)	(2)	(2)	(2)	(3)	(3)	(3)	(4)	(5)	(6)	(7)
PEO											
PFO											
A											
B											
C											

(1) Grant Date. This column discloses the grant date for equity-based awards reported in the table. If such grant date is different than the date on which the compensation (or functionally equivalent) committee or full board takes action or is deemed to take action to grant such awards, a separate, adjoining column shall be added showing such date.

(2) Estimated Future Payouts (Non-Equity). This column discloses the dollar value of the estimated future payout upon satisfaction of the conditions in question under non-equity incentive plan awards granted in the fiscal year, or the applicable range of estimated payouts denominated in dollars (threshold (minimum amount payable for a certain level of performance), target (amount payable if specified performance target(s) are reached) and maximum (maximum payout possible) amount.[70] If non-equity incentive plan awards

---

[70] If the award provides only for a single estimated payout, that amount must be reported as the target in the columns described in clauses (2) and (3). In the columns described in clauses (2) and (3), a registrant must provide a representative amount based on the

are denominated in units or other rights, a separate, adjoining column should be added quantifying the units or other rights awarded.

(3) Estimated Future Payouts (Equity). This column consists of the number of shares of stock, or the number of shares underlying options, to be paid out or vested upon satisfaction of the conditions in question under equity incentive plan awards granted in the fiscal year, or the applicable range of estimated payouts denominated in the number of shares of stock, or the number of shares underlying options under the award (threshold (minimum amount payable for a certain level of performance), target (amount payable if specified performance target(s) are reached) and maximum (maximum payout possible) amount). If awards are denominated in dollars, the dollar values of the awards should instead be disclosed with a footnote describing that the payout will consist of a number of securities having such dollar values.

(4) All Other Stock Awards. This column consists of the number of shares of stock granted in the fiscal year that are not required to be disclosed in the column described in clause (3). If awards are denominated in dollars, the dollar values of the awards should instead be disclosed with a footnote describing that the payout will consist of a number of securities having such dollar values.

(5) All Other Option Awards. This column consists of the number of securities underlying options granted in the fiscal year that are not required to be disclosed in the column described in clause (3). If awards are denominated in dollars, the dollar values of the awards should instead be disclosed with a footnote describing that the payout will consist of a number of securities having such dollar values.

(6) Exercise or Base Price. This column consists of the per-share exercise or base price of the options granted in the fiscal year. If such exercise or base price is less than the closing market price of the underlying security on the date of the grant, a separate, adjoining column showing the closing market price on the date of the grant should be added. "Closing market price" is the price at which the registrant's security was last sold in the principal U.S. market for such security as of the date for which the closing market price is determined. If no market exists, the registrant may use any other formula prescribed for the security. Whenever the reported exercise or base price reported is not the closing market price, the registrant must describe the methodology for determining the exercise or base price either by a footnote or accompanying textual narrative.

(7) Grant Date Fair Value. This column consists of the aggregate grant date fair value of each stock award or option award, computed in accordance

---

(Footnote Continued)

previous fiscal year's performance if the target amount is not determinable.

with FASB ASC Topic 718. If at any time during the last completed fiscal year, the registrant has adjusted or amended the exercise price of options or SARs previously awarded to a named executive officer, whether through amendment, cancellation or replacement grants, or any other means ("repriced"), or otherwise has materially modified such awards, the registrant must include, as awards required to be reported in this column, the incremental fair value, computed as of the repricing or modification date in accordance with FASB ASC Topic 718, with respect to that repriced or modified award.[71] For any awards that are subject to performance conditions, the registrant should report the value at the grant date based upon the probable outcome of such conditions. This amount should be consistent with the estimate of aggregate compensation cost to be recognized over the service period determined as of the grant date under FASB ASC Topic 718, excluding the effect of estimated forfeitures.

A tandem grant of two instruments, only one of which is granted under an incentive plan, such as an option granted in tandem with a performance share, need be reported only in the column described in clause (4) or (5), as applicable. For example, an option granted in tandem with a performance share would be reported only as an option grant in the column described in clause (5), with the tandem feature noted either by a footnote or accompanying textual narrative. The dollar amount of consideration, if any, paid by the executive officer for an award should be disclosed in a footnote to the appropriate column.

(f) Narrative Disclosure to Summary Compensation Table and Grants of Plan-Based Awards Table. The registrant must provide a narrative description of any material factors necessary to an understanding of the information disclosed in the Summary Compensation and Grants of Plan-Based Awards Tables. Examples of such factors may include, among other things:

● The material terms of each named executive officer's employment agreement or arrangement, whether written or unwritten;

● If at any time during the last fiscal year, any outstanding option or other equity-based award was repriced or otherwise materially modified (such as by extension of exercise periods, the change of vesting or forfeiture conditions, the change or elimination of applicable performance criteria or the change of the bases upon which returns are determined), a description of each such repricing or other material modification (this does not apply to any repricing that occurs through a pre-existing formula or mechanism in the plan or award that results in the periodic adjustment of the option or SAR exercise or base price, an antidilution provision in a plan or award, or

---

[71] This disclosure requirement does not apply to any repricing that results from a preexisting formula or mechanism in the applicable plan or award agreement that periodically adjusts the exercise or base price, an antidilution provision in a plan or award agreement or a recapitalization that equally affects all holders of securities underlying the options or SARs.

a recapitalization or similar transaction equally affecting all holders of the class of securities underlying the options or SARs);

● The material terms of any reported award, including a general description of the formula or criteria to be applied in determining the amounts payable, and the vesting schedule. For example, the registrant should (i) state, if applicable, that dividends will be paid on stock, and if so, the applicable dividend rate and whether that rate is preferential and (ii) describe any performance-based conditions, and any other material conditions, that are applicable to the award (performance-based conditions include both performance conditions and market conditions, as those terms are defined in FASB ASC Topic 718);

● The forfeiture of amounts previously reported in a table for a prior fiscal year (e.g., due to subsequent company performance or discontinued service by the named executive officer); and

● An explanation of the amount of salary and bonus in proportion to total compensation.

(g) Outstanding Equity Awards at Fiscal Year-End Table. The registrant must disclose for each named executive officer the following information in the following table for unexercised options, stock that has not vested and equity incentive plan awards outstanding as of the end of the registrant's last completed fiscal year.

OUTSTANDING EQUITY AWARDS AT FISCAL YEAR-END

Name	Option Awards					Stock Awards			
	Number of Securities Underlying Unexercised Options (#) Exercisable	Number of Securities Underlying Unexercised Options (#) Unexercisable	Equity Incentive Plan Awards: Number of Securities Underlying Unexercised Unearned Options (#)	Option Exercise Price ($)	Option Expiration Date	Number of Shares or Units of Stock That Have Not Vested (#)	Market Value of Shares or Units of Stock That Have Not Vested ($)	Equity Incentive Plan Awards: Number of Unearned Shares, Units or Other Rights That Have Not Vested (#)	Equity Incentive Plan Awards: Market or Payout Value of Unearned Shares, Units or Other Rights That Have Not Vested ($)
	(1)	(1)	(2)	(3)	(3)	(4)	(4)	(5)	(5)
PEO									
PFO									
A									
B									
C									

(1) Securities Underlying Unexercised Options. This columns consists of, on an award-by-award basis, the number of securities underlying unexercised options, including awards that have been transferred other than for value (which transfer should be disclosed in a footnote), that are exercisable or unexercisable, as applicable, and that are not reported as unearned in the column described in clause (2) (i.e., performance condition not yet satisfied).

(2) Securities Underlying Unexercised Unearned Options. This column consists of, on an award-by-award basis, the total number of shares underlying unexercised options awarded under any equity incentive plan that have not been earned.

(3) Exercise Price and Expiration Date. This column consists of the exercise or base price or expiration date, as applicable, for each option. Multiple awards may be aggregated where the expiration date and the exercise and/or base price of the instruments is identical. A single award consisting of a combination of options, SARs and/or similar option-like instruments should be reported as separate awards with respect to each tranche with a different exercise and/or base price or expiration date.

(4) Number and Market Value of Unvested Shares. This column consists of the total number, or the aggregate market value, as applicable, of shares of stock that have not vested and that are not reported as unearned in the column described in clause (5).

(5) Number and Market Value of Unvested Unearned Shares. This column consists of the total number and aggregate market or payout value, as applicable, of shares of stock, units or other rights awarded under any equity incentive plan that have not vested and that have not been earned and, if applicable, the number of shares underlying any such unit or right.

The vesting dates of options, shares of stock and equity incentive plan awards held at fiscal-year end must be disclosed by footnote to the applicable column where the outstanding award is reported. The market value of stock and equity incentive plan awards of stock is computed by multiplying the closing market price of the registrant's stock at the end of the last completed fiscal year by the number of shares or units of stock or the amount of equity incentive plan awards, respectively. The number of unearned shares or units, and the payout value, is based on achieving threshold performance goals, except that if the previous fiscal year's performance has exceeded the threshold, the disclosure should be based on the next higher performance measure (target or maximum) that exceeds the previous fiscal year's performance. If the award provides only for a single estimated payout, that amount should be reported. If the target amount is not determinable, a registrant must provide a representative amount based on the previous fiscal year's performance.

(h) Option Exercises and Stock Vested Table. The registrant must disclose the following information in the following table for exercised options and vesting of stock during the last completed fiscal year for each named executive officer on an aggregate basis:

OPTION EXERCISES AND STOCK VESTED

Name	Option Awards		Stock Awards	
	Number of Shares Acquired on Exercise (#)	Value Realized on Exercise ($)	Number of Shares Acquired on Vesting (#)	Value Realized on Vesting ($)
	(1)	(2)	(3)	(4)
PEO				
PFO				
A				
B				
C				

(1) Shares Acquired on Exercise. This column consists of the aggregate number of shares with respect to which options were exercised by the named executive officer during the last completed fiscal year.[72] If no options were exercised by the named executive officers during the last completed fiscal year, the registrant can state this and omit this column.

(2) Value Realized. This column consists of the aggregate dollar value realized upon exercise of options (equal to the fair market price of the underlying shares upon exercise minus the exercise or base price of the grant), or the transfer of an award for value, by the named executive officer during the last completed fiscal year, not including the value of any related payment or other consideration provided or to be provided by the registrant to, or on behalf of, any named executive officer (e.g., in payment of the exercise price or related taxes[73]). If no option grants were exercised by the named executive officers during the last completed fiscal year, the registrant can state this and omit this column.

(3) Number of Shares Acquired on Vesting. This column consists of the total number of shares that have vested as of the end of the last completed fiscal year.

(4) Value Realized on Vesting. This column consists of the aggregate dollar value realized upon the vesting of stock or upon the transfer of an award for value. This amount is computed by multiplying the number of shares by the market value of the shares on the vesting date (with any amounts realized upon exercise or vesting that are deferred being quantified and described in a footnote).

(i) Pension Benefits Table. The registrant must disclose the following information in the following table for each plan (other than tax-qualified and

---

[72] This includes any shares surrendered as payment in connection with a cashless exercise. Therefore, this column can be changed to "Number of Securities Underlying Options Exercised."

[73] Keep in mind that reimbursement of tax obligations by the registrant should be disclosed under the "All Other Compensation" column in the Summary Compensation Table.

nonqualified defined contribution plans) that provides benefits at, following or in connection with retirement (a separate row should be provided for each such plan in which a named executive officer participates).

PENSION BENEFITS

Name	Plan Name	Number of Years Credited Service (#) (1)	Present Value of Accumulated Benefit ($) (2)	Payments During Last Fiscal Year ($) (3)
PEO				
PFO				
A				
B				
C				

(1) Years of Credited Service. This column consists of the number of years of service credited to the named executive officer under the plan, computed as of the same pension plan measurement date used for financial statement reporting purposes with respect to the registrant's audited financial statements for the last completed fiscal year. If a named executive officer's number of years of credited service with respect to any plan is different from the named executive officer's number of actual years of service with the registrant, the amount of the difference and any resulting benefit augmentation should be disclosed in a footnote.

(2) Present Value of Benefit. This column consists of the actuarial present value of the named executive officer's accumulated benefit under the plan, computed as of the same pension plan measurement date used for financial statement reporting purposes with respect to the registrant's audited financial statements for the last completed fiscal year. The registrant must use the same assumptions used for financial reporting purposes under generally accepted accounting principles, except that retirement age should be assumed to be the normal retirement age as defined in the plan, or if not so defined, the earliest time at which a participant may retire under the plan without any benefit reduction due to age. The registrant must disclose in the accompanying textual narrative the valuation method and all material assumptions applied in quantifying the present value of the current accrued benefit. A registrant may satisfy all or part of this disclosure by reference to a discussion of those assumptions in the registrant's financial statements, footnotes to the financial statements, or discussion in MD&A. For purposes of allocating the current accrued benefit between tax-qualified defined benefit plans and related supplemental plans, a registrant should apply the limitations applicable to tax-qualified defined benefit plans established by the Internal Revenue Code and the regulations thereunder that applied as of the pension plan measurement date.

(3) Payments. This column consists of the dollar amount of any payments and benefits paid to the named executive officer during the registrant's last completed fiscal year.

Under the table, the registrant should provide a succinct narrative description of any material factors necessary to an understanding of each plan covered by the table, which may include, among other things:

● The material terms and conditions of payments and benefits available under the plan, including the plan's normal retirement payment and benefit formula and eligibility standards, and the effect of the form of benefit elected on the amount of annual benefits. For this purpose, normal retirement means retirement at the normal retirement age as defined in the plan, or if not so defined, the earliest time at which a participant may retire under the plan without any benefit reduction due to age;

● If any named executive officer is currently eligible for early retirement under any plan, the identity of that named executive officer and the plan, and a description of the plan's early retirement payment and benefit formula and eligibility standards. For this purpose, early retirement means retirement at the early retirement age as defined in the plan, or otherwise available to the executive under the plan;

● The specific elements of compensation (e.g., salary, bonus, etc.) included in applying the payment and benefit formula, identifying each such element;

● With respect to named executive officers' participation in multiple plans, the different purposes of each plan; and

● Registrant policies with regard to such matters as granting extra years of credited service.

(j) Nonqualified Defined Contribution and Other Nonqualified Deferred Compensation Plans. The registrant must disclose the following information for each named executive officer with respect to each defined contribution or other plan that provides for the deferral of compensation on a basis that is not tax-qualified in the following table:

NONQUALIFIED DEFERRED COMPENSATION

Name	Executive Contributions in Last FY ($)	Registrant Contributions in Last FY ($)	Aggregate Earnings in Last FY ($)	Aggregate Withdrawals/ Distributions ($)	Aggregate Balance at Last FYE ($)
PEO					
PFO					
A					
B					
C					

The registrant should provide (1) a footnote quantifying the extent to which amounts reported in the contributions and earnings columns are reported as compensation in the last completed fiscal year in the registrant's Summary Compensation Table and amounts reported in the aggregate balance at last fiscal year-end previously were reported as compensation to the named executive officer in the registrant's Summary Compensation Table for previous years and (2) a succinct narrative description of any material factors necessary to an understanding of each plan covered by tabular disclosure required by this paragraph, which may include, among other things:

● The type(s) of compensation permitted to be deferred, and any limitations (by percentage of compensation or otherwise) on the extent to which deferral is permitted;

● The measures for calculating interest or other plan earnings (including whether such measure(s) are selected by the executive or the registrant and the frequency and manner in which selections may be changed), quantifying interest rates and other earnings measures applicable during the registrant's last fiscal year; and

● Material terms with respect to payouts, withdrawals and other distributions.

(k) Potential Payments upon Termination or Change-in-Control. Regarding each contract, agreement, plan or arrangement, whether written or unwritten, that provides for payment(s) to a named executive officer at, following or in connection with any termination, including, without limitation, resignation, severance, retirement or a constructive termination of a named executive officer, or a change in control of the registrant or a change in the named executive officer's responsibilities,[74] for each named executive officer the registrant must describe, explain and quantify the following information:

● The specific circumstances that would trigger payment(s) or the provision of other benefits, including perquisites and health-care benefits;

● The estimated payments and benefits that would be provided in each covered circumstance, whether they would or could be lump sum, or annual, disclosing the duration, and by whom they would be provided. Perquisites and other personal benefits or property may be excluded only if the aggregate amount of such compensation will be less than $10,000. Individual perquisites and personal benefits shall be identified and quantified as required under the "All Other Compensation" column in the Summary Compensation Table. For purposes of quantifying health care benefits, the

---

[74] The registrant need not provide information with respect to contracts, agreements, plans or arrangements to the extent they (1) do not discriminate in scope, terms or operation in favor of executive officers of the registrant and (2) are available generally to all salaried employees.

registrant must use the assumptions utilized for financial reporting purposes under generally accepted accounting principles;

● How the appropriate payment and benefit levels are determined under the various circumstances that trigger payments or provision of benefits;

● Any material conditions or obligations applicable to the receipt of payments or benefits, including, but not limited to, non-compete, non-solicitation, non-disparagement or confidentiality agreements, including the duration of such agreements and provisions regarding waiver of breach of such agreements; and

● Any other material factors regarding each such contract, agreement, plan or arrangement.

The quantitative disclosure should assume that the triggering event took place on the last business day of the registrant's last completed fiscal year and the price per share of the registrant's securities is the closing market price as of that date. For purposes of valuing accelerated options, the registrant should use the difference between the market price as of fiscal year-end and the exercise price. In the event that uncertainties exist as to the provision of payments and benefits or the amounts involved, the registrant is required to make, based on forward-looking information, a reasonable estimate (or a reasonable estimated range of amounts) applicable to the payment or benefit and disclose material assumptions underlying such estimates or estimated ranges in its disclosure. To the extent that the form and amount of any payment or benefit that would be provided in connection with any triggering event is fully disclosed pursuant to the Pension Benefits or Nonqualified Deferred Compensation Table, reference may be made to that disclosure. However, to the extent that the form or amount of any such payment or benefit would be enhanced or its vesting or other provisions accelerated in connection with any triggering event, such enhancement or acceleration must be disclosed in this section.

Where a triggering event has actually occurred for a named executive officer and that individual was not serving as a named executive officer of the registrant at the end of the last completed fiscal year, the disclosure required for that named executive officer shall apply only to that triggering event.

Many registrants use a table to clearly identify specific categories of potential payments (e.g., continued payment of salary, potential or earned bonuses, accelerated vesting of options or restricted stock, etc.) in different change-in-control or termination scenarios (e.g., for cause, without cause, for good reason, etc.). When using such a table, registrants should remember to have a column that shows the total amount that would be payable.

(l) Compensation of Directors. The registrant must provide the following information, concerning the compensation of the directors for the registrant's last completed fiscal year, in the following table:[75]

DIRECTOR COMPENSATION

Name	Fees Earned or Paid in Cash ($)	Stock Awards ($)	Option Awards ($)	Non-Equity Incentive Plan Compensation ($)	Change in Pension Value and Nonqualified Deferred Compensation Earnings	All Other Compensation ($)	Total ($)
	(1)	(2)	(2)	(3)	(4)	(5)	(6)
A							
B							
C							
D							
E							

(1) Fees. This column consists of the aggregate dollar amount of all fees earned or paid in cash for services as a director, including annual retainer fees, committee and/or chairmanship fees and meeting fees and including deferred amounts and any fee foregone at the director's election pursuant to a program of the registrant under which non-cash compensation may be received by such director in lieu of a portion of fees.[76] The registrant must disclose in a footnote if the amount of any fees for the last fiscal year cannot be calculated through the latest practicable date, including when that amount is expected to be determined. That amount should then be disclosed as having been earned in the previous year but paid in the last completed fiscal year in a footnote to the Director Compensation Table for the following fiscal year.

(2) Stock and Option Awards. These columns consist of the aggregate grant date fair value with respect to the fiscal year computed in accordance with FASB ASC Topic 718. The registrant must include a footnote disclosing all assumptions made in the valuation by reference to a discussion of those assumptions in the registrant's financial statements, footnotes to the financial statements

---

[75] A director need not be included in the table if he or she is also a named executive officer and his or her compensation for service as a director is fully reflected in the Summary Compensation Table and otherwise as required in the other tables described above required by Item 402 of Regulation S-K. Two or more directors may be grouped in a single row in the table if all elements of their compensation are identical. The names of the directors for whom disclosure is presented on a group basis, however, should be clear from the table. Disclosure should be provided for each person who served as a director at any time during the applicable fiscal year even if the person was not serving as a director at the end of such fiscal year.

[76] This non-cash compensation, however, must be disclosed in a footnote to this column.

or discussion in MD&A. If at any time during the last completed fiscal year the registrant has adjusted or amended the exercise price of options or SARs previously awarded to a director, whether through amendment, cancellation or replacement grants or any other means, or otherwise has materially modified such awards, the registrant must include in a footnote the incremental fair value, computed as of the repricing or modification date in accordance with FASB ASC Topic 718, with respect to that repriced or modified award. For each director, the registrant should disclose by footnote to the appropriate column the aggregate number of stock awards and the aggregate number of option awards outstanding at fiscal year-end.

(3) Non-Equity Incentive Compensation. This column consists of the dollar value of all earnings for services performed during the fiscal year pursuant to non-equity incentive plans and all earnings on any outstanding awards. If the relevant performance measure is satisfied during the fiscal year (including for a single year in a plan with a multi-year performance measure), the earnings are reportable for that fiscal year, even if not payable until a later date, and are not reportable again in the fiscal year when amounts are paid to the director. All earnings on non-equity incentive plan compensation must be identified and quantified in a footnote to this column, whether the earnings were paid during the fiscal year, payable during the period but deferred at the election of the director, or payable by their terms at a later date.

(4) Change in Pension Value and Nonqualified Deferred Compensation Earnings. This column consists of the sum of the following amounts:

(A) The aggregate change in the actuarial present value of the director's accumulated benefit under all defined benefit and actuarial pension plans (including supplemental plans) from the pension plan measurement date used for financial statement reporting purposes with respect to the registrant's audited financial statements for the prior completed fiscal year to the pension plan measurement date used for financial statement reporting purposes with respect to the registrant's audited financial statements for the covered fiscal year. This applies to each plan that provides for the payment of retirement benefits, or benefits that will be paid primarily following retirement, including but not limited to tax-qualified defined benefit plans and supplemental executive retirement plans, but excluding tax-qualified defined contribution plans and nonqualified defined contribution plans; and

(B) Above-market or preferential earnings on compensation that is deferred on a basis that is not tax-qualified, including such earnings on nonqualified defined contribution plans. Interest on deferred compensation is above-market only if the rate of interest exceeds 120% of the applicable federal long-term rate, with compounding (as prescribed under section 1274(d) of the Internal Revenue Code) at the rate that corresponds most closely to the rate under the registrant's plan at the time the interest rate or formula is set. In the event of a discretionary reset of the interest rate, the requisite calculation must be made on the basis of the interest rate at the time of such reset, rather than when originally established. Only the above-market portion of the interest must be included. If the applicable interest rates vary depending upon conditions such as a minimum period of continued service, the reported amount should be calculated assuming satisfaction of all conditions to receiving interest at the highest rate. Dividends (and dividend equivalents) on deferred compensation denominated in the registrant's stock are preferential only if earned at a rate higher than dividends on the registrant's common stock. Only the preferential portion of the dividends or equivalents must be included. Footnote or narrative disclosure may be provided explaining the registrant's criteria for determining any portion considered to be above-market.

The registrant must identify and quantify by footnote the separate amounts attributable to each of the change in pension value and nonqualified deferred compensation earnings. If the change in pension value is negative, it should be disclosed by footnote but should not be reflected in the sum reported in this column.

(5) All Other Compensation. This column consists of all other compensation for the covered fiscal year that the registrant could not properly report in any other column of the Director Compensation Table. Each compensation item that is not properly reportable in the other columns, regardless of the amount of the compensation item, must be included in this column. Such compensation must include, but is not limited to:

● Perquisites and other personal benefits or property (valued on the basis of the aggregate incremental cost to the registrant), unless the aggregate amount of such compensation is less than $10,000. If the total value of all perquisites and personal benefits is $10,000 or more for any director, then each perquisite or personal benefit, regardless of its amount, must be identified by type. If perquisites and personal benefits are required to be reported for a director pursuant to this rule, then each perquisite or personal benefit that exceeds the greater of $25,000 or 10% of the total amount of perquisites and personal benefits for that director must be quantified and disclosed in a footnote;

● All "gross-ups" or other amounts reimbursed during the fiscal year for the payment of taxes (including for taxes owed with respect to perquisites and other personal benefits);

● For any security of the registrant or its subsidiaries purchased from the registrant or its subsidiaries (through deferral of salary or bonus, or otherwise) at a discount from the market price of such security at the date of purchase, unless that discount is available generally, either to all security holders or to all salaried employees of the registrant, the compensation cost, if any, computed in accordance with FASB ASC Topic 718;

● The amount paid or accrued to any director pursuant to a plan or arrangement in connection with (1) the resignation, retirement or any other termination of such director; or (2) a change in control of the registrant;

● Registrant contributions or other allocations to vested and unvested defined contribution plans;

● Consulting fees earned from, or paid or payable by the registrant and/or its subsidiaries (including joint ventures);

● The annual costs of payments and promises of payments pursuant to director legacy programs and similar charitable award programs. A program in which a registrant agrees to make donations to one or more charitable institutions in a director's name, payable by the registrant currently or upon a designated event, such as the retirement or death of the director, is considered a charitable awards program. The registrant should provide footnote disclosure of the total dollar amount payable under the program and other material terms of each such program for which disclosure is provided under this column;

● The dollar value of any insurance premiums paid by, or on behalf of, the registrant during the covered fiscal year with respect to life insurance for the benefit of a director; and

● The dollar value of any dividends or other earnings paid on stock or option awards, when those amounts were not factored into the grant date fair value required to be reported for the stock or option award in the "Stock Awards" or "Option Awards" column:

Any item reported for a director that is not a perquisite or personal benefit and whose value exceeds $10,000 must be identified and quantified in a footnote to the column.

(6) Total Compensation. This column consists of the dollar value of total compensation for the covered fiscal year, which equals the sum of all amounts reported in the other columns.

The registrant should provide a narrative description of any material factors necessary to an understanding of the director compensation disclosed in the table. While material factors will vary depending upon the facts, examples of such factors may include, among other things:

● A description of standard compensation arrangements (such as fees for retainer, committee service, service as chairman of the board or a committee and meeting attendance); and

● Whether any director has a different compensation arrangement, identifying that director and describing the terms of that arrangement.

(m) **Compensation Committee Interlocks and Insider Participation.** Item 407(e)(4) of Regulation S-K requires the registrant, under the caption "Compensation Committee Interlocks and Insider Participation,"[77] to (i) disclose each person who served as a member of the compensation (or equivalent) committee of the registrant's board of directors during the last completed fiscal year and (ii) indicate each committee member who:

● was during the fiscal year an officer or employee of the registrant;

● was formerly an officer of the registrant; or

● had any relationship requiring disclosure by the registrant under Item 404 of Regulation S-K, including making the disclosure required by Item 404 (even if also disclosed elsewhere in response to Item 404).[78]

If there was no such committee, the registrant must identify each officer and employee of the registrant and any former officer of the registrant who, during the last completed fiscal year, participated in deliberations of the registrant's board concerning executive officer compensation.

The registrant must also disclose the following relationships that existed during the last completed fiscal year, as well as the disclosure required by Item 404 of Regulation S-K for the applicable person (even if also disclosed elsewhere in response to Item 404):[79]

● an executive officer of the registrant served on the compensation (or equivalent) committee, or the entire board if there was no such committee, of another entity[80] that had an executive officer serve on the compensation (or equivalent) committee, or the entire board if there was no such committee, of the registrant or as a director of the registrant; and

● an executive officer of the registrant served as a director of another entity that had an executive officer serve on the compensation (or equivalent) committee, or the entire board if there was no such committee, of the registrant.

This compensation committee interlock and insider participation disclosure enables shareholders to evaluate the independence of those making executive compensation decisions when voting for the election of directors.

---

[77] The caption can be omitted if the identity of committee members is the only required disclosure that would be applicable.

[78] Because this Item 404 disclosure must be provided under the "Compensation Committee Interlocks and Insider Participation" caption, registrants will often cross-reference this disclosure when providing other Item 404 disclosure instead of repeating the information.

[79] Id.

[80] This does not include a 501(c)(3) tax-exempt entity.

(n) Compensation Committee Report. Item 407(e)(5) of Regulation S-K requires the compensation (or equivalent) committee, or the entire board if there was no such committee, to state the following information (i) under the caption "Compensation Committee Report" and (ii) over the name of each member of such committee or board:

● the committee or board has reviewed and discussed the CD&A; and

● based on such review and discussions, the committee recommended to the board of directors (or the board recommended, if applicable) that the CD&A be included in the registrant's Form 10-K or proxy statement.

The compensation committee report is not deemed soliciting material or filed for liability purposes of Section 18 of the Exchange Act, except to the extent that the registrant specifically requests that the information be treated as soliciting material or specifically incorporates it by reference into a document filed under the Securities Act or the Exchange Act.[81]

(o) Narrative Disclosure of Compensation Policies and Practices Relating to Risk Management. A registrant must discuss risks related to its compensation policies and practices for its employees, not just executive officers, to the extent such risks are reasonably likely to have a material adverse effect on the registrant. The situations requiring disclosure will vary depending on the particular registrant and compensation policies and practices, but situations that may trigger disclosure include, among others, compensation policies and practices:

● at a business unit of the registrant that carries a significant portion of the registrant's risk profile;

● at a business unit with compensation structured significantly differently than other units within the registrant;

● at a business unit that is significantly more profitable than others within the registrant;

● at a business unit where compensation expense is a significant percentage of the unit's revenues; and

● that vary significantly from the overall risk and reward structure of the registrant, such as when bonuses are awarded or incentive compensation vests (especially in a lump sum or pursuant to cliff vesting) upon accomplishment of a task or achievement of short-term targets, while the income

---

[81] If the registrant elects to incorporate this information by reference from the proxy statement into its Form 10-K, the compensation committee report will be deemed furnished in the Form 10-K and will not be deemed incorporated by reference into any filing under the Securities Act or the Exchange Act as a result of furnishing the disclosure in this manner.

and risk to the registrant from the task or the target extend over a significantly longer period of time.

The purpose of this disclosure is to provide investors material information concerning how the way in which registrant compensates and incentivizes its employees may create risks that are reasonably likely to have a material adverse effect on the registrant. While the information to be disclosed pursuant to this disclosure will vary depending upon the nature of the registrant's business and the compensation approach, the following are examples of the issues that the registrant may need to address for the business units or employees discussed:

● the general design philosophy of the registrant's compensation policies and practices for employees whose behavior would be most affected by the incentives established by the policies and practices, as such policies and practices relate to or affect risk taking by employees on behalf of the registrant, and the manner of their implementation;

● the registrant's risk assessment or incentive considerations, if any, in structuring its compensation policies and practices or in awarding and paying compensation;

● how the registrant's compensation policies and practices relate to the realization of risks resulting from the actions of employees in both the short term and the long term, as well as policies that are intended to mitigate risks, such as policies requiring clawbacks,[82] holding periods or stock ownership;

● the registrant's policies regarding adjustments to its compensation policies and practices to address changes in its risk profile;

● material adjustments the registrant has made to its compensation policies and practices as a result of changes in its risk profile; and

● the extent to which the registrant monitors its compensation policies and practices to determine whether its risk management objectives are being met with respect to incentivizing its employees.

Registrants will presumably need to coordinate an evaluation of risk management and risk-taking incentives related to their compensation policies and practices with their human resources, legal and risk management departments, as well as their compensation and audit committees.

---

[82] The Dodd-Frank Act requires the SEC to adopt rules that require stock exchange listing standards to require registrants to establish, maintain and disclose clawback policies that allow for the recovery of excess incentive-based compensation (including options) from any current or former executive if the registrant has an accounting restatement due to material noncompliance with financial reporting requirements under securities laws.

(p) Additional Disclosure that Will Be Required by the Dodd-Frank Act. The Dodd-Frank Act requires the SEC to adopt rules that require each registrant to clearly disclose:

- the relationship between its executive compensation actually paid and the financial performance of such registrant (including change in the stock price of, and dividends or distributions by, the registrant);

- the median annual total compensation (as calculated in accordance with the Summary Compensation Table) of all employees other than the CEO;

- the annual total compensation of the CEO; and

- the ratio of the median annual total compensation of all employees other than the CEO to the annual total compensation of the CEO.

8. Item 9. Independent Public Accountants. Item 9 of Schedule 14A requires the registrant to provide the following information about its independent public accountant in its annual meeting proxy statement:

- the name of the principal accountant for the current fiscal year (if no accountant has been selected, the registrant should state this and describe why).

- whether or not representatives of the principal accountant for the current year and the most recent fiscal year:

    - are expected to be present at the annual meeting;

    - will have the opportunity to make statements if they desire to do so; and

    - are expected to be available to respond to appropriate questions.[83]

- if during the registrant's two most recent fiscal years or any subsequent interim period either (i) an independent accountant previously engaged as the principal accountant to audit the registrant's financial statements (or on whom the principal accountant expressed reliance in its report regarding a significant subsidiary) has resigned or indicated it will decline to stand for re-election after completion of the current audit or (ii) a new independent accountant has been engaged as the principal accountant to audit the registrant's financial statements (or on whom the principal accountant expressed reliance in its report regarding a significant subsidiary), then the detailed information described in Item 304(a) of Regulation S-K must be provided, even if previously disclosed.[84]

---

[83] Note that it is common practice to have representatives of the accounting firm for the current fiscal year present at the annual meeting and available to answer appropriate questions.

[84] However, instead of filing an accountant's letter as an exhibit as described in S-K Item 304(a), the former and/or new accountant(s) may present their views in a brief statement, ordinarily expected not to exceed 200 words, to be included in the

- the fees paid to the principal auditor for each of the two most recent fiscal years segregated into four categories ("audit," "audit-related," "tax" and "all other"):

    - under the caption "Audit Fees," the aggregate fees billed or expected to be billed by the registrant's independent auditors for the audit of annual financial statements and the review of the financial statements included in the registrant's Form 10-Qs or for services that are normally provided by the accountant in connection with statutory and regulatory filings or engagements (e.g., comfort letters, consents, statutory audits).

    - under the caption "Audit-Related Fees," the aggregate fees billed for assurance and related services (e.g., due diligence services) by the registrant's principal accountant that are reasonably related to the performance of the audit or review of the registrant's financial statements and are not reported under the prior paragraph.[85] Registrants must describe the nature of the services comprising the fees disclosed under this category.

    - under the caption "Tax Fees," the aggregate fees billed for professional services rendered by the registrant's principal accountant for tax compliance, tax advice and tax planning. Registrants must describe the nature of the services comprising the fees disclosed under this category.

    - under the caption "All Other Fees," the aggregate fees billed for products and services provided by the principal accountant, other than the above-reported services. There is no requirement to break down these other fees in detail, but registrants must describe the nature of the services comprising these other fees.

- if greater than 50%, the percentage of hours expended on the principal accountant's engagement to audit the registrant's financial statements for the most recent fiscal year that were attributed to work performed by

---

(Footnote Continued)

proxy statement. In addition, the written views of the newly engaged accountants described in S-K Item 304(a) should be filed as an exhibit to a concurrently filed Form 8-K if those views have not been previously filed with the SEC.

[85] More specifically, these services would include, among others, employee benefit plan audits, due diligence related to mergers and acquisitions, accounting consultations and audits in connection with acquisitions, internal control reviews, attest services related to financial reporting that are not required by statute or regulation and consultation concerning financial accounting and reporting standards. Fees paid for operational audits would not be considered "Audit-Related Fees" but rather should be included in the "All Other Fees" category. See Questions 30 and 31 of "Office of the Chief Accountant: Application of the January 2003 Rules on Auditor Independence Frequently Asked Questions" issued August 13, 2003.

persons other than the principal accountant's full-time, permanent employees. This disclosure is required in response to recent transactions in which accounting firms have sold their non-audit practices to financial services companies. In these types of transactions, employees of the accounting firm became employees of the financial services company and are then leased back to the accounting firm when necessary. The SEC believes that investors should be informed when participants in the audit are not directly employed by the accounting firm and may therefore not be subject to the auditor's independence requirements.

● the audit committee's pre-approval policies and procedures described in paragraph (c)(7)(i) of Rule 2-01 of Regulation S-X. Under this provision, the registrant's auditors may not render audit or non-audit services to the registrant or its subsidiaries unless either (a) the engagement receives advance approval from the registrant's audit committee; or (b) the engagement is entered into pursuant to pre-approval policies and procedures established by the audit committee which are detailed as to the particular service, the audit committee is informed of each service and such policies and procedures do not include delegation of the audit committee's responsibilities to management.[86] With respect to the provision of services other than audit, review or attest services, the pre-approval requirement is waived if:

● the aggregate amount of all such services provided constitutes no more than 5% of the total amount of revenues paid by the audit client to its accountant during the fiscal year in which the services are provided;

● such services were not recognized by the issuer at the time of the engagement to be non-audit services; and

---

[86] Use of broad, categorical approvals would not meet the requirement that the policies must be detailed as to the particular services to be provided. Likewise, the establishment of monetary limits would not, alone, constitute policies that are detailed as to the particular services to be provided and would not, alone, ensure that the audit committee would be informed about each service. The determination of the appropriate level of detail for the preapproval policies will differ depending upon the facts and circumstances of the issuer. However, a key requirement is that the policies cannot result in a delegation of the audit committee's responsibility to management. As such, if a member of management is called upon to make a judgment as to whether a proposed service fits within the preapproved services, then the preapproval policy would not be sufficiently detailed as to the particular services to be provided. Similarly, preapproval policies must be designed to ensure that the audit committee knows precisely what services it is being asked to preapprove so that it can make a well-reasoned assessment of the impact of the service on the auditor's independence. For example, if the audit committee is presented with a schedule or cover sheet describing services to be preapproved, that schedule or cover sheet must be accompanied by detailed backup documentation regarding the specific services to be provided. See Questions 22-24 of "Office of the Chief Accountant: Application of the January 2003 Rules on Auditor Independence Frequently Asked Questions" issued August 13, 2003.

● such services are promptly brought to the attention of the audit committee and approved prior to the completion of the audit by the audit committee or by one or more members of the audit committee who are members of the board of directors to whom authority to grant such approvals has been delegated by the audit committee.

● the percentage of services described under the captions "Audit-Related Fees," "Tax Fees" and "All Other Fees" (Items 9(e)(2) through 9(e)(4) of Schedule 14A) that were approved by the audit committee pursuant to paragraph (c)(7)(i)(C) of Rule 2-01 of Regulation S-X which, as described above, provides for the waiver of the pre-approval requirement for services other than audit, review and attest services if specified requirements are met.

9. Item 10. Compensation Plans. A registrant may submit the adoption of a compensation plan (e.g., a stock incentive plan) or an amendment to such a plan for shareholder approval for several reasons, including the following:

● The registrant may have contractually agreed to obtain shareholder approval of a compensation plan or awards pursuant to the plan.

● The rules of the securities exchange on which the registrant's securities are listed may require shareholder approval of a particular compensation plan or an amendment to such a plan.[87]

---

[87] The NYSE's Listed Company Manual and Nasdaq's Listing Rules require shareholder approval of all equity compensation plans and material revisions to such plans, subject to limited exemptions. "Equity compensation plan" is defined broadly and includes a compensatory grant of options or other equity securities that is not made under a plan. Certain types of grants are exempted from shareholder approval, including: (1) inducement awards to a person upon first becoming an employee of the issuer or any of its subsidiaries or being rehired following a bona fide period of interruption of employment; (2) mergers and acquisitions, when conversions, replacements or adjustments of outstanding options or other equity compensation awards are necessary to reflect the transaction, and when shares available under certain plans acquired in corporate acquisitions and mergers may be used for certain post-transaction grants without further shareholder approval; and (3) plans intended to meet the requirements of Section 401(a) of the Internal Revenue Code (e.g., ESOPs), plans intended to meet the requirements of Section 423 of the Internal Revenue Code, and parallel excess plans. In circumstances in which equity compensation plans and amendments to plans are not subject to shareholder approval, the plans and amendments still are generally subject to the approval of the company's compensation committee or a majority of the company's independent directors. The NYSE and NASDAQ provide a non-exclusive list of "material revisions" to a plan that would require shareholder approval (e.g., materially increasing the number of shares available, materially extending the duration of the plan, and expanding the types of options or awards available under the plan, materially expanding the class of eligible participants, etc.). The rules also clarify when plans containing an "evergreen formula" and when the "repricings" of op-tions in plans would require shareholder approval. The NYSE also amended NYSE Rule 452 to prohibit member organizations from voting on equity compensation plans unless the

● Section 162(m) of the Internal Revenue Code generally prohibits a public company from deducting compensation in excess of $1 million paid during a taxable year to a "covered employee." Section 162(m) may dictate obtaining shareholder approval of a compensation plan or an amendment to such plan. For example, under Section 162(m), compensation includes gains on the exercise of stock options, which may in certain years be the largest component of executive compensation. The covered employees of a registrant are its PEO and any other employee whose compensation is required to be reported to shareholders under the Exchange Act because such employee is one of the three highest compensated executive officers of the registrant (other than the PEO and the PFO).[88] The limitation on deductibility imposed by Section 162(m) does not apply, however, to gains on the exercise of stock options if, among other things, the registrant's shareholders approve the plan pursuant to which such options are granted.

● Incentive stock options (ISOs) offer significant tax advantages to a registrant's employees, but certain disadvantages to registrants issuing such options. ISOs, to the extent they are issued, must be granted pursuant to a plan that is approved by the shareholders of the granting corporation within 12 months of the plan's adoption.[89]

● Section 16(b) of the Exchange Act provides for the disgorgement of "short-swing profits" (generally, profits from purchases and sales of a registrant's securities within a six-month period by an executive officer, director or holder of more than 10% of the registrant's common stock). Rule 16b-3 under the Exchange Act exempts from Section 16(b) certain grants, awards and other transactions by a registrant to, or with, its executive officers and directors. The exemption provided by Rule 16b-3 can be obtained by having the registrant's shareholders approve specific awards or the plan or agreement under which they are made. However, the exemption can also be obtained by having awards under a plan approved by either the registrant's entire board of directors or the compensation committee (as long as it is comprised solely of two or more "non-employee directors") of the registrant's board of directors.

● Some registrants obtain shareholder approval of plans because they believe it is good corporate governance practice.

(Footnote Continued)

beneficial owner of the shares has given voting instructions.

[88] See IRS Notice 2007-49. Thus, the term covered employees does not match with the term named executive officers because it does not include those individuals for whom disclosure is required under the Exchange Act on account of being the PFO.

[89] However, if shareholder approval of a plan is received within 12 months of the plan's adoption but after ISOs have been granted, there may be adverse accounting consequences to the registrant.

(a) Required Textual Disclosure. If a registrant seeks shareholder approval of the adoption or amendment of a plan[90] pursuant to which cash or noncash compensation may be paid or distributed, Item 10 of Schedule 14A requires the registrant to provide the following information:

- a description of the material features of the plan (e.g., what awards can be granted under the plan; how the exercise price, vesting period, transfer restrictions and other terms of an award will be determined; what happens to an award upon termination of the recipient's association with the registrant or upon a change-in-control of the registrant; and the federal income tax consequences of awards granted under the plan).

- identification of each class of persons eligible to participate in the plan, the approximate number of people in such class and the basis of such participation.

A copy of any written plan to be acted upon must be filed with the SEC along with the proxy statement, but only needs to be provided to shareholders if it is a part of the proxy statement. Many registrants include a copy of the plan as an appendix to the proxy statement so that shareholders voting on the plan or an amendment to the plan can review the complete plan. A registrant must supplementally disclose to the SEC when it first files the proxy statement when the options, warrants or rights and the underlying shares will be registered under the Securities Act, or if such registration is not contemplated, the section of the Securities Act or rule of the SEC under which exemption from such registration is claimed and the facts relied upon to make the exemption available.

(b) New Plan Benefits Table. The registrant must also disclose in the table provided below the benefits or amounts that will be received by, or allocated to, each of the following persons under a plan being voted on if such amounts or benefits are determinable or, if such amounts are not determinable, the benefits or amounts that would have been received by, or allocated to, the following persons for the last completed fiscal year if the plan had been in effect, if such amounts or benefits can be determined:

- each named executive officer as described in Section 7 (stating his or her name and position);

- all current executive officers as a group;

- all current directors who are not executive officers as a group; and

---

[90] As defined in Item 402(a)(6)(ii) of Regulation S-K, the term "plan" includes, but is not limited to, any of the following: any plan, contract, authorization or arrangement, whether or not set forth in any formal documents and even if applicable to only one person, pursuant to which cash, securities, similar instruments or any other property may be received.

● all employees, including all current officers who are not executive officers, as a group.

NEW PLAN BENEFITS[91]

Plan Name[1]

Name and Position	Dollar Value ($)	Number of Units[2]
CEO		
A		
B		
C		
D		
E		
F		
Executive Group		
Non-Executive Director Group		
Non-Executive Officer Employee Group		

[1] Additional columns should be added to the table for each plan for which information is required.

[2] For option plans, the number of underlying option shares should be provided in the "Number of Units" column, and the "Dollar Value" column should be left blank.

This tabular information regarding benefits or amounts that will be received is typically only applicable if (1) the plan is one with set benefits or amounts (e.g., a directors' option plan with specified automatic grants) or (2) awards have been made under the plan subject to shareholder approval (e.g., if awards have been made and shareholder approval is sought to increase shares eligible for issuance under the plan to cover such awards). The tabular information regarding benefits or amounts that would have been received if the plan had been in effect is typically for an existing plan being amended to alter a formula or other objective criteria that can be applied to the variables of the prior year to determine benefits. In each case, the tabular information regarding benefits or amounts that will or would have been received is not applicable to plans under which all awards are discretionary because the amounts or benefits are not determinable for such plans.

   (c) Pension or Retirement Plan. Item 10 of Schedule 14A also requires the following additional information to be disclosed regarding any pension or retirement plan submitted for shareholder approval:

---

[91] If the table is required, all individuals and groups for whom information is required should be listed, even if the amount reported is zero for such individual or group.

● the approximate total amount necessary to fund the plan with respect to past services, the period over which such amount is to be paid and estimated annual payments necessary to pay such amount over such period; and

● the estimated annual payment to be made with respect to current services, which may be furnished in the format specified for the Pensions Benefit Table required by Item 402(h) of Regulation S-K.

(d) Amendments. If shareholder approval of a material amendment to a plan is being sought (including to increase the number of shares reserved for issuance under a plan), then all of the required disclosure must be provided with respect to the plan as proposed to be amended and must also indicate any material differences from the existing plan.

(e) Equity Compensation Plan Disclosure. Pursuant to the equity compensation plan disclosure rules, Item 10 of Schedule 14A provides that if security holders are acting on any compensation plan (equity or cash, such as a performance bonus plan, and including an amendment to a plan) at the annual meeting, the equity compensation plan disclosure required by Item 201(d) of Regulation S-K must be included in the registrant's related proxy statement. This required disclosure is described in Chapter 6, Section C.4. Registrants should note, however, that securities under an equity compensation plan (or an amendment to an equity compensation plan) that is being submitted for shareholder approval and thus the subject of a proposal in the proxy statement should not be included in the disclosure required by Item 201(d) of Regulation S-K.

10. Item 21. Voting Procedures. Item 21 of Schedule 14A requires the registrant to disclose the vote required for approval of each matter submitted to the vote of its shareholders (other than approval of auditors) or election of directors and how votes will be counted, including the treatment and effect of abstentions and broker non-votes[92] under applicable state law and the registrant's charter and bylaws. Although not required by Item 21 of Schedule 14A, most registrants also disclose the quorum needed for valid shareholder action to be taken at the annual meeting, as well as the effect of abstentions and broker non-votes on determining the presence of a quorum.

---

[92] A broker non-vote occurs with respect to a matter when (a) the beneficial owner of shares that are held in "street name" by a broker does not provide the broker, who is the shareholder of record and thus the person entitled to vote the shares, with directions as to how to vote its shares and (b) the broker does not have discretionary authority to vote on such matters according to the rules of the applicable securities exchange or market (e.g., nonroutine matters, such as a merger, a contested proposal, or pursuant to the NYSE's rules regarding equity compensation plans found in Section 303A.08 of the NYSE's listing standards; registrants should also note that (i) the NYSE has eliminated broker discretionary voting for all director elections and (ii) the Dodd-Frank Act requires securities exchanges to not allow broker discretionary authority to vote on director elections, executive compensation (including say-on-pay proposals) or any other significant matters as determined by SEC rules).

(a) Quorum. A combination of state corporate law and the registrant's certificate of incorporation and bylaws will prescribe the number of shares and/or amount of voting power of the registrant that needs to be present at the meeting in order for valid action to be taken at the annual meeting. For example, Section 216 of the Delaware General Corporation Law ("DGCL") states that, unless otherwise required by the corporate statute, a registrant's certificate of incorporation or bylaws can specify the number of shares and/or the amount of voting power that must be present or represented by proxy at the annual meeting to constitute a quorum. However, pursuant to Section 216 of the DGCL:

- a quorum cannot consist of less than one-third of (1) the shares entitled to vote at the meeting or (2) when a separate vote of a class(es) or series is required, such class(es) or series; and

- if the registrant's certificate of incorporation and bylaws do not specify what constitutes a quorum, then (1) a majority of the shares entitled to vote, present in person or by proxy, will constitute a quorum and (2) when a separate vote of a class(es) or series is required, a majority of the outstanding shares of such class(es) or series, present in person or by proxy, will constitute a quorum.

Registrants should also be aware that the securities exchange(s) on which their securities are listed may also have rules regarding what constitutes a quorum. For example, Rule 5620(f) of the NASDAQ Listing Rules provides that a registrant whose securities are listed on NASDAQ cannot have a quorum for a meeting of holders of common stock that is less than one-third of the registrant's outstanding shares of common voting stock.

How a quorum is counted under state corporate law and a registrant's certificate of incorporation and bylaws will also determine the effect of broker non-votes and abstentions on determining if a quorum exists. In accordance with Delaware corporate law, abstentions and broker non-votes, whether represented by a shareholder who actually attends the annual meeting or who returns a properly executed proxy, are counted as present at the meeting in determining the presence of a quorum (even though not voted on a particular matter(s)).

(b) Required Vote. A combination of state corporate law and the registrant's certificate of incorporation and bylaws will also prescribe the vote required to approve a proposal at the annual meeting. For example, Section 216 of the DGCL also allows, unless otherwise required under the corporate statute,[93] a registrant's certificate of incorporation or bylaws to specify the vote

---

[93] For example, (i) Section 242 of the DGCL requires the affirmative vote of a majority of the outstanding stock entitled to vote and a majority of the outstanding stock of each class entitled to vote as a class to amend a registrant's certificate of incorporation and (ii) Section 251 of the DGCL requires the affirmative vote of a majority of the outstanding stock entitled to vote to approve a merger involving a registrant.

necessary for the transaction of business. Pursuant to Section 216 of the DGCL, if the registrant's certificate of incorporation and bylaws do not specify the vote required for a specified action:

- directors are elected by a plurality of the votes of the shares present in person or represented by proxy at the meeting and entitled to vote on the election of directors;[94]

- for all other matters, the affirmative vote of the majority of shares present in person or represented by proxy at the meeting and entitled to vote on the matter is the act of the shareholders; and

- when a separate vote of a class(es) or series is required, the affirmative vote of the majority of shares of such class(es) or series present in person or represented by proxy at the meeting is the act of such class(es) or series.

A registrant should also be aware that regulatory authorities governing a registrant's activities or the securities exchanges on which its securities are listed may also have rules regarding the required vote for specific proposals that may be voted on at an annual meeting. For example, Rule 5635 of the NASDAQ Listing Rules (a) requires NASDAQ companies to obtain shareholder approval of certain issuances of securities and (b) states that the minimum vote that will constitute shareholder approval will be a majority of the votes cast on the proposal in person or by proxy.

What vote is required to approve a proposal under state corporate law and a registrant's certificate of incorporation and bylaws will also determine the effect of broker non-votes and objections on the vote. Assuming the vote of a plurality of the shares voted in person or by proxy is required to elect directors, broker non-votes[95] and abstentions have no effect on the vote for directors because when a plurality vote is required, it does not matter how many total votes are received by a nominee as long as the nominee receives more votes than other candidates. Under Delaware corporate law, broker non-votes are not considered present and entitled to vote because they do not empower the record holder to vote on a particular proposal, while abstentions are considered present and entitled to vote because a person cannot abstain unless he or she is present and entitled to vote. Therefore, on matters requiring the affirmative vote of a percentage (e.g., a majority) of shares present in person or represented by proxy at the meeting and entitled to vote:

- broker non-votes have no effect on a proposal because they do not count in the numerator as affirmative votes or in the denominator as present and

---

[94] A "plurality" means with respect to the specified number of director seats being voted on, such number of nominees who receive the highest number of "FOR" votes will be elected.

[95] There presumably will not be any broker non-votes if an unopposed slate of persons are nominated for election as directors because that will constitute a routine matter for which brokers have discretionary authority to vote.

entitled to vote when calculating whether the required vote has been obtained; and

- abstentions will have the same effect as votes against these matters because they do not count in the numerator as an affirmative vote, but are counted in the denominator as present and entitled to vote when calculating whether the required vote has been obtained.[96]

On the other hand, on matters requiring the affirmative vote of a percentage (e.g., a majority) of the shares outstanding and entitled to vote:

- broker non-votes will have the same effect as votes against the matters because under Delaware corporate law, those extraordinary actions (e.g., merger and certificate of incorporation amendment) for which the DGCL requires approval by at least a majority of the outstanding shares entitled to vote, the reference is to voting rights of the shares as opposed to voting power of the holder. Therefore, broker non-votes do not count in the numerator as affirmative votes, but they do count in the denominator as outstanding shares entitled to vote when calculating whether the required vote has been obtained; and

- abstentions will also have the same effect as votes against the matters because they do not count in the numerator as affirmative votes, but they do count in the denominator as outstanding shares entitled to vote when calculating whether the required vote has been obtained.

See Section C of Chapter 6 for a discussion of when the actual results of the shareholder vote must be disclosed in an Exchange Act filing.

11. Item 23. Delivery of Documents to Shareholders Sharing an Address. Effective December 4, 2000, the SEC amended the proxy rules to permit registrants to satisfy the delivery requirements for proxy and information statements with respect to two or more security holders sharing the same address.[97] This method of delivery is often referred to as "householding." A registrant will be considered to have delivered a proxy statement or an Annual Report to all security holders of record who share an address if it meets the following requirements of Exchange Act Rule 14a-3(e):

(a) The registrant delivers one proxy statement or Annual Report, as applicable, to the shared address;

---

[96] See *Berlin v. Emerald Partners*, 552 A.2d 482 (1989) wherein the court upheld distinction between shares present for quorum purposes and voting power present for voting purposes.

[97] SEC Release No. 33-7912 (October 27, 2000). This conformed the provisions regarding the householding of proxy statements to the provisions that permit householding of Annual Reports contained in SEC Release No. 33-7766 (November 4, 1999).

(b) the registrant addresses the proxy statement or Annual Report, as applicable, to:

● the security holders as a group (e.g., "ABC Fund [or Corporation] Security Holders," "Jane Doe and Household," or "The Smith Family");

● each of the security holders individually (e.g., "John Doe and Jane Doe"); or

● the security holders in a form to which each of the security holders has consented in writing;

(c) The security holders consent, in accordance with Rule 14a-3(e)(1)(ii) under the Exchange Act, to delivery of one proxy statement or Annual Report, as applicable;

(d) With respect to delivery of the proxy statement, the registrant delivers, together with or subsequent to delivery of the proxy statement, a separate proxy card for each security holder at the shared address; and

(e) The registrant must furnish the following information in the proxy statement:

● a statement that only one proxy statement or Annual Report, as applicable, is being delivered to multiple security holders sharing an address unless the registrant has received contrary instructions from one or more of the security holders;

● an undertaking to deliver promptly upon written or oral request a separate copy of the proxy statement or Annual Report, as applicable, to a security holder at a shared address to which a single copy of the documents was delivered and instructions as to how a security holder can notify the registrant that the security holder wishes to receive a separate copy of a proxy statement or Annual Report, as applicable;

● the phone number and mailing address to which a security holder can direct a notification to the registrant that the security holder wishes to receive a separate proxy statement or Annual Report; and

● instructions about how security holders sharing an address can request delivery of a single copy of a proxy statement or an Annual Report if they are receiving multiple copies of proxy statements or Annual Reports.

If a security holder, orally or in writing, revokes consent to householding delivery of a proxy statement or Annual Report to a shared address, the registrant must begin sending individual copies to that security holder within 30 days after the registrant receives revocation of the security holder's consent. Registrants can "household" the notice of Internet availability described in Section I of this Chapter by sending a single copy of the notice to the shareholders living at the same address, but must provide the ability of each shareholder to execute a separate proxy (e.g., each shareholder must be provided his, her or its own control or identification number).

12. Item 24. Shareholder Approval of Executive Compensation. Registrants required to provide a say-on-pay or say-on-frequency vote must:

- disclose they are providing such vote pursuant to Section 14 of the Exchange Act;

- briefly explain the general effect of each vote (such as whether the vote is non-binding); and

- when applicable, disclose the current frequency of say-on-pay votes and when the next such vote will occur.

E. Presentation of Information in Proxy Statement.

Rule 14a-5 under the Exchange Act governs the presentation of information in the proxy statement and requires the following:

- clear presentation of information in the proxy statement, including grouping information according to subject matter under appropriate headings and putting information in tables where practical and appropriate;

- with respect to the information required by the various items and sub-items of Schedule 14A:

  - the order of the items and sub-items in Schedule 14A does not need to be followed when disclosing the information required by such items and sub-items;

  - if more than one item requires disclosure of the same information, that information need not be repeated; and

  - if the information required by an item or sub-item is inapplicable, nothing needs to be said with respect to such item or sub-item.

- all printed proxy statements must be in roman type at least as large and as legible as ten-point modern type, except to the extent necessary for convenient presentation, financial statements and other tabular data (which type must still be at least two points and for which the footnotes may be in roman type at least as large and as legible as eight-point modern type).[98]

Rule 14a-5 under the Exchange Act allows:

- required information that must be determined in the future to be stated in terms of present knowledge and intention; and

- information contained in other proxy materials that have been furnished to the shareholders being solicited in connection with the same meeting or

---

[98] Rule 14a-5(d)(2) under the Exchange Act explains that for proxy statements delivered electronically, registrants may satisfy type size and font requirements by presenting all required information in formats readily communicated to investors.

subject matter to be omitted from the proxy statement if a clear reference to the particular document containing the information is made.

F. Form of Proxy.

Rule 14a-4 under the Exchange Act prescribes the requirements for proxy cards used by a registrant to solicit proxy votes for proposals being voted on at an annual meeting. A proxy card cannot be delivered to a shareholder unless such shareholder also receives at the same time, or has already received, the related definitive proxy statement filed with the SEC. The form of proxy card must be filed as an appendix at the end of the proxy statement.

1. Required Language. Rule 14a-4 under the Exchange Act requires that a proxy card:

● indicate in boldfaced type that the proxy is solicited on behalf of the registrant's board of directors;

● provide a specifically designated blank space for dating the proxy card. This enables the proxy holder to determine which is the latest proxy if multiple proxies are submitted by a shareholder, and thus the one in effect;

● identify clearly and impartially each separate matter intended to be acted upon, whether or not related to or conditioned upon the approval of other matters, and whether proposed by the registrant or by security holders,[99] including:

　● for each matter other than the election of directors, shareholders must be able to specify in boxes their approval or disapproval of, or abstention with respect to, such matters (other than a vote on the frequency of say-on-pay votes, for which shareholders must be given the choice of one, two or three years (or can be worded every year, every other year or every three years) or the ability to abstain);[100] and

　● for the election of directors, the name of each nominee and in boldfaced type a statement that if authority to vote for a nominee is not withheld then

---

[99] For matters as to which discretionary authority is conferred pursuant Rule 14a-4(c) under the Exchange Act, as discussed below, reference need not be made to such matters.

[100] The proxy card or the proxy statement should also provide that, subject to reasonable specified conditions, the shares represented by the proxy will be voted, and where a choice is given with respect to the matter being voted on, the shares will be voted in accordance with the specifications made. This helps make sure that a regis-trant cannot avoid the quorum requirements by not actually voting proxies when the registrant knows it does not have enough votes to carry a proposal. If a signed proxy card is returned without indicating how the shares represented thereby are to be voted on a matter, the proxy may confer discretionary authority with respect to the matter as long as the proxy card states in boldface type how such shares are intended to be voted (e.g., in favor of the registrant's proposals).

the shareholder is deemed to grant authority to vote for the election of such nominee. Shareholders must be given the ability to withhold authority to vote for each nominee by one of the following means:[101]

● a box opposite the name of each nominee that can be marked to indicate that authority to vote for such nominee is being withheld;

● an instruction in boldfaced type that indicates that the authority to vote for a nominee may be withheld by lining through or striking out the name of such nominee;

● designated blank spaces in which the names of nominees for whom the authority to vote is withheld can be entered; or

● any other similar means as long as clear instructions are furnished indicating how to withhold authority to vote for any nominee.

If a proxy card grants authority to vote for nominees as a group it must also provide similar means for withholding authority to vote for such group of nominees.

2. Unauthorized Proxies. Rule 14a-4(d) under the Exchange Act prohibits proxy cards from conferring authority to:

● vote for the election of any person to any office for which a bona fide nominee is not named in the proxy statement. If the registrant fails to nominate enough people to fill all vacancies on its board of directors, it should disclose the following information in the proxy statement:

● why a vacancy is not being filled;

● that the proxy cannot be used by the proxyholder to vote for an unnamed substitute to fill any vacancies; and

● what will happen with respect to any vacancies, including if the registrant currently intends to fill a vacancy with a specific person, in which case it would be good practice for the registrant to disclose the information required by Item 7 of Schedule 14A (as described in Section 6) with respect to such person.

● vote at any annual meeting other than the next annual meeting, or any adjournment thereof, to be held after the date on which the proxy statement and proxy are first sent to shareholders;

● vote with respect to more than one meeting, and any adjournment thereof; and

---

[101] However, if applicable state law gives legal effect to votes cast against a nominee, then in lieu of, or in addition to, providing a means by which the authority to vote for each nominee can be withheld, the registrant should also provide a similar means to vote against each nominee.

- authorize or consent to any action other than the action proposed to be taken in the proxy statement or for which discretionary authority to vote may be conferred, as discussed below.

3. Discretionary Authority. Pursuant to Rule 14a-4(c) under the Exchange Act, a proxy can confer discretionary authority to vote on any of the following matters:

- a matter for which the registrant did not receive at least 45 days' notice before the date on which the registrant first mailed its proxy materials for the prior year's annual meeting (however, if a date is specified by an advance notice provision in the registrant's bylaws, that date should be used instead even if the provision does not specifically reference the use of discretionary authority) as long as a specific statement to that effect is made in the proxy card or proxy statement;[102]

- a matter for which the registrant receives timely notice in accordance with the previous bullet point as long as the registrant includes in the proxy statement advice on the nature of the matter and how the registrant intends to exercise its discretion to vote on the matter,[103] unless the proponent of the proposal:

  - provides the registrant with a written statement, within the time frame described in the bullet point above, that the proponent intends to deliver a proxy statement and form of proxy to shareholders holding enough shares to pass the proposal;

  - includes the written statement in its proxy materials filed with the SEC; and

  - immediately after soliciting shareholders holding at least enough shares to pass the proposal, provides the registrant with a statement from any solicitor or other person with knowledge that the necessary steps were taken to deliver the proxy statement and form of proxy to shareholders holding at least enough shares to pass the proposal.[104]

- the election of any person to any office for which a bona fide nominee is named in the proxy statement and such nominee is unable to serve or for good cause will not serve;

---

[102] If, however, the registrant did not hold an annual meeting in, or the date of the meeting has changed more than 30 days from, the prior year, then notice must not have been received at a reasonable time, based on the facts and circumstances, before the registrant mails its proxy materials for the current year.

[103] A registrant should keep in mind that additional disclosure may also be neces-

sary to satisfy its obligations under Rule 14a-9 under the Exchange Act.

[104] If the registrant wants to vote its proxies on the matter at the annual meeting, it must include the matter on its proxy card and provide the necessary disclosure in the proxy statement, including how and why it intends to vote on the matter.

- any proposal omitted from the proxy statement and proxy card pursuant to Rule 14a-8 or 14a-9 under the Exchange Act; and

- matters incident to conduct of the meeting.[105]

For those matters for which discretionary authority is conferred, shares can be voted on the matters in accordance with the judgment of the proxyholders without obtaining the explicit approval of shareholders to do so (i.e., shareholders need not be given the opportunity to vote for or against the ability of the proxyholder to exercise such discretionary authority) and without discussing the matters in the proxy statement.

G. Shareholder Proposals.

With respect to an annual meeting, in addition to management's proposals (e.g., election of directors, approval of a compensation plan and ratification of auditors), shareholders will sometimes seek to have their own proposals recommending or requiring that the registrant or its board of directors take or refrain from taking action submitted to a vote of the shareholders (e.g., currently popular proposals include eliminating shareholder protection measures, such as poison pills, supermajority provisions and staggered boards, executive compensation issues, including pay for performance and ratification of executive pay, and majority voting in director elections). Rule 14a-8 under the Exchange Act, which is in a Q&A format, governs when a registrant is required to include a shareholder's proposal in its form of proxy when the registrant holds an annual or special meeting of shareholders. Those registrants that receive shareholder proposals that they are asked to include in their proxy statements and proxy cards should read the SEC's Division of Corporation Finance Staff Legal Bulletin Nos. 14 (July 13, 2001), 14A (July 12, 2002), 14B (September 15, 2004), 14C (June 28, 2005), 14D (November 7, 2008), 14E (October 27, 2009) and 14F (October 18, 2011), included as Appendix 11 hereto, which provide guidance regarding issues that often arise under Rule 14a-8.

In general, Rule 14a-8 requires a registrant to include a shareholder proposal in its proxy materials if the submitting shareholder has complied with certain eligibility and procedural requirements,[106] unless the proposal fits into one of the following substantive categories:

---

[105] If the registrant believes there is a strong possibility that it may need to adjourn a meeting in order to have more time to solicit the vote needed to approve an item being voted on, it should consider putting a box on the proxy card to allow shareholders to vote on whether to allow such an adjournment by proxyholders so as to avoid disgruntled shareholders objecting to such an adjournment at the time of the meeting.

[106] In particular, a shareholder can only submit one proposal per meeting and must (a) have continuously held at least $2,000 in market value, or 1%, of the registrant's securities entitled to be voted on the proposal at the meeting for at least one year by the date of submitting the proposal and (b) continue to

- the proposal is not a proper subject for action by shareholders under the laws of the jurisdiction of the registrant's organization (which is why shareholders often phrase proposals as recommendations for the board as opposed to requiring action);

- the proposal would, if implemented, cause the registrant to violate any state, federal or foreign law to which it is subject;

- the proposal or supporting statement is contrary to any of the SEC's proxy rules, including Rule 14a-9, which prohibits materially false or misleading statements in proxy soliciting materials, such as in the following circumstances (merely objecting to assertions because they are not supported, may be disputed or countered, may be interpreted by shareholders in a manner unfavorable to the registrant or because they represent opinions that are not specifically identified as such will not be good enough to exclude a proposal —such objections should be put in a registrant's statement of objection):

  - statements that directly or indirectly impugn character, integrity or personal reputation, or directly or indirectly make charges concerning improper, illegal or immoral conduct or association, without factual foundation;

  - the registrant demonstrates objectively that a factual statement is materially false or misleading;

  - the resolution contained in the proposal is so inherently vague or indefinite that neither the shareholders voting on the proposal, nor the registrant implementing the proposal (if adopted), would be able to determine with any reasonable certainty exactly what actions or measures the proposal requires—this objection also may be appropriate where the proposal and the supporting statement, when read together, have the same result; and

  - substantial portions of the supporting statements are irrelevant to a consideration of the subject matter of the proposal, such that there is a strong likelihood that a reasonable shareholder would be uncertain as to the matter on which he or she is being asked to vote.

- the proposal relates to the redress of a personal claim or grievance against the registrant or any other person, or is designed to result in a benefit to the shareholder, or to further a personal interest, which is not shared by the other shareholders at large;

(Footnote Continued)

hold those securities through the date of the meeting. In addition, the proposal, which along with any accompanying supporting statement cannot exceed 500 words, must be received at the registrant's principal executive offices by the date explained in Section D(1)(c) above.

● the proposal relates to operations that account for less than 5% of the registrant's total assets at the end of its most recent fiscal year, and for less than 5% of its net earnings and gross sales for its most recent fiscal year, and is not otherwise significantly related to the registrant's business;

● the registrant would lack the power or authority to implement the proposal. Staff Legal Bulletin No. 14C (June 28, 2005) (i) classifies how the staff applies the "no power" basis for exclusion to proposals calling for independent directors (i.e., depends on whether the proposal requires continued independence at all times, which a registrant does not have the power to ensure) and (ii) clarifies how the staff applies the "ordinary business operations" basis for exclusion to proposals referencing environmental or public health issues (i.e., depends on whether the proposal requires minimizing/eliminating operations as opposed to internally assessing the risks or liabilities of operations);

● the proposal deals with a matter relating to the registrant's ordinary business operations (this is one of the most frequently relied upon exclusions and often depends upon whether the proposal involves significant policy that goes beyond ordinary business);[107]

● the proposal (i) would disqualify a nominee standing for election, (ii) would remove a director before the expiration of his or her term, (iii) questions the competence, business judgment or character of one or more nominees or directors, (iv) seeks to include a specific individual in the registrant's proxy materials for election of directors or (v) otherwise could affect the outcome of the upcoming election of directors;[108]

---

[107] *Id.*

[108] The SEC amended Rule 14a-8(i)(8) under the Exchange Act to codify its interpretation of that rule that proposals relating to the election or nomination of directors, including the procedure therefor, may be excluded by registrants. The amendment was in direct response to, and specifically intended to reverse the holding of, the decision by the U.S. Court of Appeals for the Second Circuit in *American Federation of State, County & Municipal Employees, Employees Pension Plan v. American International Group, Inc.*, 462 F.3d 121 (2d Cir. 2006). In that decision, the Second Circuit held that AIG could not rely on Rule 14a-8(i)(8) to exclude a shareholder proposal seeking to amend a registrant's bylaws to establish a procedure under which a company would be required, in specified circumstances, to include shareholder nominees for director in the company's proxy materials. The SEC believed that such decision resulted in uncertainty and confusion and did not believe that the election exclusion should be limited in that way. See SEC Release No. 34-56914 (December 6, 2007). The SEC also amended Rule 14a-8(i)(8) to allow shareholders, under certain circumstances, to require registrants to include in their proxy materials proposals that would amend, or that request an amendment of, the registrant's governing documents regarding nomination procedures or disclosures related to shareholder nominations. See SEC Release No. 33-9136 (August 5, 2010). However, Business Roundtable and the U.S. Chamber of Commerce challenged the validity of proposed new Rule 14a-11 under the Exchange Act, which would have required registrants to include shareholders' directors nominees in registrants' proxy materials in

- the proposal directly conflicts with one of the registrant's own proposals to be submitted to shareholders at the same meeting;

- the registrant has already substantially implemented the proposal;[109]

- the proposal substantially duplicates another proposal previously submitted to the registrant by another shareholder that will be included in the registrant's proxy materials for the same meeting;

- the proposal deals with substantially the same subject matter as another proposal or proposals that previously has or have been included in the registrant's proxy materials within a specified time frame and did not receive a specified percentage of the vote; or

- the proposal relates to specific amounts of cash or stock dividends.

If a registrant receives a shareholder proposal on a timely basis, it can take one of the following courses of action:

- include the proposal in its proxy materials and not comment on such proposal;

- include the proposal in its proxy materials along with a statement in opposition that explains the registrant's reasons as to why its shareholders should vote against the proposal. The registrant must send a copy of the statement in opposition to the proposing shareholder within 30 calendar days before the registrant files its definitive proxy materials with the SEC;

- seek to exclude the proposal from its proxy materials because the shareholder has not complied with an eligibility or procedural requirement by notifying the shareholder of the defect(s) within 14 calendar days of

---

(Footnote Continued)

certain circumstances, in the U.S. Court of Appeals for the District of Columbia Circuit and filed a petition with the SEC seeking to stay the implementation of Rule 14a-11 pending resolution of the matter by the Court of Appeals. On October 4, 2010, the SEC granted the requested stay in the implementation of Rule 14a-11 and the effectiveness of amended Rule 14a-8. On July 22, 2011, the Court held that the SEC was arbitrary and capricious in promulgating Rule 14a-11 and vacated the rule. The Court did not address the amendments to Rule 14a-8. The SEC's stay on amended Rule 14a-8 expired without further SEC action when the Court's decision was finalized on September 20, 2011. Amended Rule 14a-8 allows shareholder proposals regarding shareholder proxy access standards on a registrant-by-registrant basis.

[109] Shareholder proposals regarding shareholder advisory say-on-pay or say-on-frequency votes can be excluded if in the most recent shareholder advisory vote on say-on-frequency a single year (i.e., one, two or three) received an approval of the majority of votes cast on the matter and the registrant adopted a policy regarding the frequency of say-on-pay votes consistent with such majority vote.

receiving the proposal. The shareholder then has 14 calendar days after receiving the notification to respond;[110] or

● seek to exclude the proposal from its proxy materials because the shareholder has failed to cure the eligibility or procedural defect in a timely manner or because the registrant does not believe the proposal fits into one of the substantive categories described above, in either case by submitting a no-action request to the SEC that explains its reasons for being able to exclude the proposal, including reference to any recent applicable authority (e.g., SEC no-action letters or case law), a supporting opinion of counsel if the proposed exclusion is based on matters of state or foreign law (which may be contested by the shareholder proponent submitting its own supporting opinion of counsel) and copies of relevant contracts if the proposed exclusion is based on causing the registrant to breach such contracts, as well as all relevant correspondence exchanged with the shareholder. The registrant must send a no-action request simultaneously to the SEC and proposing shareholder within 80 calendar days before it files its definitive proxy materials with the SEC, unless the registrant can demonstrate good cause for missing the deadline (e.g., the proposal was not received by the registrant until after the 80-day deadline had passed). Because the date for receipt of a response from the SEC is often very close to the mailing date for the proxy statement and past the date for submitting the opposition statement to the proposing shareholder, registrants should consider submitting their no-action requests as soon as possible.

The registrant has the burden of proving that it is entitled to exclude a proposal. The SEC, in determining whether it agrees with the registrant's determination to exclude a proposal, will consider how the basis for exclusion described by the registrant and any arguments made by the proposing shareholder apply to the specifically worded proposal. After reaching a decision, the SEC will send to the registrant and the shareholder an indication as to whether or not it agrees with the registrant's view that it may exclude the proposal.[111] This indication may take the form of requiring the shareholder to revise the

---

[110] The SEC urges registrants to (i) provide adequate detail in the notice about what must be done to remedy the defects, (ii) include a copy of Rule 14a-8 with the notice, (iii) explicably state in the notice that the shareholder proponent has 14 calendar days to respond and (iv) send the notice by a means that allows the registrant to determine when the notice is received by the proponent shareholder. No notice of defect(s) is necessary if the defect cannot be remedied (e.g., if the shareholder failed to submit a proposal to the registrant by the required deadline); however, in situations in which a registrant's records indicate that the proposal proponent does not satisfy the ownership eligibility requirements in Rule 14a-8(b) and the registrant intends to exclude the proposal based on such failure, the registrant must inform the proponent that the proponent must provide proof of ownership that satisfies the requirements of Rule 14a-8(b).

[111] While providing comfort to a registrant as to whether the SEC agrees with its position to exclude a shareholder proposal, a letter from the SEC indicating it will not take any action if the registrant excludes such proposal is not binding on a court.

proposal in order to allow its inclusion in the proxy statement.[112] If a share-holder proposal is included in a registrant's proxy statement, the registrant must either disclose the proposing shareholder's name and address or indicate that it will provide the information to shareholders upon request.

H. False or Misleading Statements.

Schedule 14A and the federal proxy rules are aimed at ensuring that adequate disclosure of relevant facts is made to enable shareholders to make informed voting decisions on matters for which their proxies are solicited. Rule 14a-9 under the Exchange Act prohibits proxy solicitations by means of any proxy materials or other oral or written communications containing any statement that, at the time and in the light of the circumstances in which it was made, is false or misleading with respect to any material fact or that omits to state any material fact necessary in order to make the statements therein not false or necessary to correct any statement in an earlier communication with respect to the solicitation for the same meeting or subject matter that has become false or misleading.[113] As stated in the notes to Rule 14a-9, examples of statements that may be misleading, depending on the facts and circumstances, include the following:

- predictions as to future market values;

- material that impugns character, integrity or personal reputation, or makes charges concerning improper, illegal or immoral conduct or associations, without factual foundation;

- failure to distinguish proxy materials from soliciting materials of another person for the same meeting or subject matter; and

- claims made prior to a meeting regarding the results of a solicitation.

Violations of Rule 14a-9 under the Exchange Act can result in a private lawsuit, as well as an SEC enforcement action, which can result in costly payouts by the registrant and damage to the registrant's public reputation. Even if these actions are successfully defended, they can be expensive to defend, time consuming and divert the attention and resources of the registrant. If information from the proxy statement is incorporated by reference into a Form 10-K, which may in turn be incorporated by reference into a registration statement filed under the Securities Act, additional liability for false or misleading statements may be incurred under Section 10(b) or 18 of the Exchange Act or Section 11, 12 or 17 of the Securities Act.

---

[112] In which case, the registrant must provide the shareholder with a copy of its statement in opposition within five calendar days before it files its definitive proxy materials.

[113] As disclosed in Rule 14a-9(b) under the Exchange Act, filing proxy materials with the SEC or review of such materials by the SEC (a) is not deemed a finding by the SEC that such materials are accurate and complete or not false or misleading and (b) does not mean the SEC has approved or determined the merits of any statement or proposal contained in such materials.

I. Electronic Delivery of Annual Meeting Materials, Electronic Voting and Electronic Shareholder Forums.

As technology has evolved and more people have access to, and communicate via, the Internet, many registrants have taken advantage of the Internet to deliver proxy materials and Annual Reports and to receive proxy votes. This use of technology to fulfill obligations under the federal securities laws has been especially appealing to registrants whose businesses are centered around the Internet, telecommunications products or services or cutting-edge technologies —it is an opportunity to directly show their shareholders that they are up to speed with using current technology. Historically, three SEC Releases outlined the guidelines for electronic delivery of securities-related documents: SEC Release Nos. 33-7233 (October 13, 1995), 33-7288 (May 15, 1996) and 33-7856 (April 28, 2000). In these releases, the SEC basically focused on three areas of compliance: shareholder consent to such electronic delivery, shareholder access to information that is substantially equivalent to the information provided to shareholders that receive the materials in paper form (e.g., substantially the same text and graphics) and notice when the materials are available electronically and shareholders being able to keep permanent records if they so desire (e.g., by printing or downloading the proxy materials). In 2007, the SEC adopted amendments to the proxy rules, commonly referred to as the e-proxy rules, that specifically require all registrants to electronically deliver proxy materials (i.e., the proxy statement with notice of the annual meeting, a proxy card and the Annual Report) to their shareholders by posting such materials on an Internet website and sending shareholders a notice that such materials are available on the Internet (also known as the notice and access delivery method).[114]

1. Electronic Delivery. Registrants have two options to choose from in complying with the new e-proxy rules, neither of which is exclusive (i.e., a registrant can use one option for some shareholders and the other option for the rest of its shareholders, depending on their voting habits):

(a) the notice only option—under this option, the registrant must:

---

[114] See SEC Release No. 34-55146 (January 22, 2007) and SEC Release No. 34-55146A (March 17, 2008) included as Appendix 12 hereto, which initially adopted a voluntary model, and SEC Release No. 34-56135 (July 26, 2007) included as Appendix 15 hereto, which adopted the mandatory model. See also SEC Release No. 33-9108 (February 22, 2010) included as Appendix 12 hereto, which provided additional flexibility to the e-proxy rules. The rules, which also apply to non-registrant soliciting parties, do not apply to proxy solicitations for mergers, acquisitions or other business combinations. A paper copy of the required notice of Internet availability of proxy materials can be sent by mail or can be sent electronically to shareholders who have affirmatively consented to such electronic delivery.

● post its proxy materials on a publicly accessible website (other than the SEC's EDGAR website) no later than the date the notice is sent to shareholders (other than additional soliciting materials sent after the notice is sent to shareholders, which must be posted on the website no later than the date such materials are first sent to shareholders). In addition:

   ● the proxy materials must remain accessible on the website free of charge[115] until the conclusion of the annual meeting;

   ● the proxy materials must be posted in a format or formats that make them convenient to read and print and must be substantially identical to the paper copies (e.g., HTML for viewing and PDF for printing);

   ● the website address to which shareholders are directed must take the shareholders directly to the proxy materials and not to a home page that requires the shareholders to search for the proxy materials; and

   ● the anonymity of shareholders accessing the proxy materials on the website must be maintained (e.g., no tracking the identities of such shareholders or requiring them to install cookies to collect personal information);

● send a notice of Internet availability of proxy materials to its shareholders at least 40 calendar days before the annual meeting date.[116] The notice must:

   ● be in plain English;

   ● contain a prominent legend in boldfaced type that states: "Important Notice Regarding the Availability of Proxy Materials for the Shareholder Meeting to Be Held on [insert date]";

   ● include an indication that the communication is not a form of voting and presents only an overview of the more complete proxy materials, which contain important information and are available on the Internet or by mail, and encourage shareholders to access and review the proxy materials before voting;

   ● include the date, time and location of the meeting;

---

[115] If software is needed to view the materials, the registrant must provide a link that enables the shareholders to obtain such software free of charge.

[116] Given that shareholders often hold their shares in street name through brokers, banks and other intermediaries, registrants that require intermediaries to use the notice only approach must send the intermediaries the necessary information in sufficient time (probably at least 5 business days) for the intermediary to send its own notice to such shareholders at least 40 calendar days before the annual meeting. Such notice is substantially similar to that of the registrant, with revisions as are necessary to reflect the difference between registered holders and beneficial owners.

● include instructions on how a shareholder may request a paper or e-mail copy of the proxy materials, at no charge, including the date by which a shareholder should make the request to facilitate timely delivery, and an indication that the shareholder will not otherwise receive a paper or e-mail copy;

● include a clear and impartial identification of each separate matter intended to be acted upon and the registrant's recommendation, if any, regarding those matters (but no supporting statements)—this does not, however, have to mirror the proxy card;

● list the materials that are being made available at the specified website;

● provide a toll-free number, e-mail address and website address where the shareholder may request a copy of the proxy materials;

● include any control or identification number that the shareholder needs to access the shareholder's proxy card and instructions on how to access the proxy card (but such instructions cannot enable the shareholder to execute a proxy without having access to the proxy statement and Annual Report—the notice cannot provide telephone numbers or website addresses that allow the shareholder to vote or be accompanied by a proxy card); and

● inform shareholders about how to attend the meeting and vote in person.

The notice cannot contain or be accompanied by any other information other than a pre-addressed, postage paid reply card allowing the shareholder to request a paper or e-mail copy of the proxy materials, any information required by state law and an explanation for the registrant's use of the notice and access model and the process for receiving and reviewing the proxy materials and voting. The notice is considered additional proxy soliciting materials and must be filed with the SEC on Schedule 14A no later than the date it is first sent to shareholders; and

● provide shareholders a method for executing proxies at the time the notice (and thus access to the proxy materials) is first sent to shareholders; thus while the notice itself cannot contain the means by which to execute a proxy, the website on which the proxy materials are posted and to which shareholders are directed should provide for electronic voting, a toll-free telephone number for voting and/or printing of a proxy card.

If a registrant wants to further solicit shareholders, it can send a proxy card to shareholders (i) within 10 calendar days after sending the notice if it is accompanied by a copy of the proxy statement and Annual Report in the same medium (i.e., e-mail or paper copy) and (ii) 10 calendar days or more after sending the notice if the notice is included with the proxy card (thus reminding shareholders to access the proxy materials); and

● provide a paper or e-mail copy of the proxy materials, free of charge, to any requesting shareholder within three business days after receiving the request by first-class mail or any other reasonably prompt means of delivery[117] and allow shareholders to permanently elect to receive paper or e-mail copies of the proxy materials (and maintain records of such elections).

(b) the full set delivery option—under this option, the registrant uses the traditional method of mailing the shareholders paper copies of the proxy materials, but also must:

● send a notice of Internet availability of proxy materials to its shareholders that either accompanies, or is incorporated into, the full set of proxy materials (including the proxy card); the information required to be set forth in the notice is the same as described above for the notice only option, except that given a full set of paper proxy materials (including a proxy card) is being delivered to shareholders, the notice does not need to include language regarding the nature of the communication, the means by which to request a paper or e-mail copy of the proxy materials or instructions on how to access the proxy card or additional methods by which to execute a proxy; and

● post the proxy materials on a website (in the same manner as described above for the notice only option) no later than the date on which the notice is first sent to shareholders.

The other most significant difference between the notice only and full set delivery options is that under the full set delivery option, the notice need not be provided 40 days prior to the annual meeting. In addition, further solicitation of shareholders through additional proxy cards may be sent by the registrant at any time without having to also send the notice.

Electronic delivery of proxy materials through the notice only option can enable registrants to save significant expense by eliminating the need for printing and mailing paper copies of these materials, though notices of Internet availability will still need to be printed and mailed. The amount of savings, however, will be largely dependent on how many shareholders request paper copies. In addition, a registrant will need to determine whether the benefit of potential cost savings outweighs the need to have proxy materials finalized at least 40 days in advance of the annual meeting and the possibility that there will be a decrease in shareholder voting because some shareholders expect to receive a proxy card as opposed to printing out a card from the website or voting via the Internet or telephone. A

---

[117] Such a request can be made after, but prior to the one year anniversary of, the annual meeting but in such event the registrant need not send the proxy materials by first-class mail within three business days.

registrant interested in delivering proxy materials by the notice only option should make sure that the corporate law of its state of incorporation allows it to electronically distribute to its shareholders notice of an annual meeting.

2. Electronic Voting. Electronic voting, whether by Internet or through touch-tone telephone, also provides a number of advantages to registrants, including:

- convenient for shareholders—shareholders just enter some basic information to register and point and click or push the appropriate telephone buttons, as applicable, to vote;

- the ability to obtain votes in a short period of time—registrants do not need to wait for the return of proxy cards by mail; and

- easier to solicit proxies from individuals that beneficially hold stock in "street name"—allows these shareholders to conveniently give voting instructions to broker-dealer record holders.

A registrant looking to allow Internet or touch-tone telephone voting must first make sure that its certificate of incorporation and bylaws and the law of its state of incorporation permit electronic proxy voting for registered shareholders.[118] Keep in mind that even if electronic proxy voting is not permitted, beneficial street name holders can still vote over the Internet or by touch-tone telephone if their brokers provide such a service because certificates of incorporation, bylaws and state corporate law typically only address proxy voting (as opposed to providing voting instructions to the record holder who will then vote by proxy or in person at the annual meeting). Registrants that allow shareholders to vote electronically should describe the electronic voting procedures in the proxy statements and provide instructions on the attached proxy cards. Usually, the proxy card will direct shareholders (1) to a dedicated website where they can vote by proxy by filling out electronic ballots after typing in control numbers that appear on the proxy cards sent to them and/or (2) to a toll-free telephone number where they can vote by proxy by pushing the appropriate buttons in response to automated voice instructions after typing in control numbers that appear on the proxy cards. Registrants should keep in mind that while allowing electronic voting may increase voter participation for the reasons discussed above, it may also increase the unpredictability of votes because shareholders can literally wait until immediately before the stated deadline to electronically submit their proxies and announcements or proxy solicitations that occur close in time to the annual meeting may actually have effects on the outcome of particular votes. Registrants will not necessarily save costs by allowing Internet

---

[118] For example, Section 212(c) of the DGCL allows a shareholder to authorize another person to act as its proxy by sending an electronic transmission to the proxyholder. According to the SEC Telephone Interpretations Manual, the validity under applicable state law of proxies granted pursuant to the electronic transmission should be disclosed in the proxy statement (Section IV. Proxy Rules and Schedule 14A - No. 45).

or touch-tone telephone voting unless they couple such electronic voting with notice only electronic delivery of proxy materials, thus eliminating the need to send consenting shareholders physical proxy cards and prepaid postage return envelopes.

3. Electronic Shareholder Forums. In January 2008, the SEC issued new Rule 14a-17, and an amendment to Rule 14a-2, under the Exchange Act to facilitate the use of electronic shareholder forums by registrants and their shareholders (SEC Release No. 34-57172). The amendments are designed to address the concern under the former proxy rules that statements made by participants in an electronic shareholder forum will be construed as "solicitations" subject to the proxy rules and the concern that someone who establishes, maintains, or operates an electronic shareholder forum will be liable under the federal securities laws for statements made by forum participants.

Rule 14a-2(b)(6) clarifies that a communication on an electronic shareholder forum that could potentially constitute a proxy solicitation in connection with an annual or special meeting of shareholders that would be subject to SEC regulations is exempt from most of the proxy rules. This could include, for example, a registrant-sponsored online forum used to provide a means for management to communicate with shareholders on matters of shareholder interest. Any communication on an electronic shareholder forum must meet the following conditions to qualify for the exemption:

● The electronic shareholder forum communication must occur more than 60 days before the date announced by a registrant for the annual or special meeting of shareholders or, if the registrant announces the shareholder meeting less than 60 days before the meeting date, the communication cannot occur more than two days after the registrant's announcement; and

● The person posting the communication (or on whose behalf the communication is posted) on an electronic shareholder forum must not be seeking the power to act as a proxy for a shareholder.

A person who participates in an electronic shareholder forum in reliance on Rule 14a-2(b)(6) can later solicit proxies after the date that the exemption is no longer available, or is no longer being relied upon, if the later solicitation complies with the SEC's proxy rules.

Rule 14a-17 clarifies that a shareholder, registrant or third party acting on behalf of a shareholder or registrant who establishes, maintains or operates an electronic shareholder forum will not be liable under the federal securities laws for any statements made by another person participating in the forum, if the forum is conducted in compliance with the federal securities laws, applicable state law and the registrant's charter and bylaws.

Persons providing information to, or making statements on, an electronic shareholder forum, however, will remain liable for the content of those communications under traditional liability provisions of the federal securities laws, such as Rules 10b-5 and 14a-9 under the Exchange Act.

CHAPTER 8

THE ANNUAL REPORT TO SHAREHOLDERS

A. Introduction.

1. Purpose of the Annual Report.

The Annual Report has become the primary means by which many registrants communicate with their shareholders. Annual Reports are also read by several other key constituencies, including securities analysts, the media, regulators, prospective investors, and current or prospective employees, customers and suppliers. The document carries the image of the registrant to this large and diverse audience and gives the registrant the opportunity to promote itself and highlight its successes. For these reasons, the Annual Report often contains more information than is required by SEC rules.

2. Requirement to Prepare and Distribute the Annual Report.

Rules 14a-3 and 14c-3 under the Exchange Act provide that proxy solicitations relating to an annual or special meeting of shareholders at which directors are to be elected, or a written consent in lieu of such a meeting, must be accompanied or preceded by an Annual Report.[1] To comply with this requirement and to reduce postage costs, most registrants mail their Annual Reports in the same envelopes as their proxy statements and proxy cards. As described below, registrants may send their Form 10-Ks to shareholders instead of Annual Reports. Also, as described in Section B.3 of Chapter 6, registrants may "incorporate by reference" portions of their Annual Reports into their Form 10-Ks. Registrants are also required to post their annual reports and other proxy materials on their company websites.

---

[1] Foreign private issuers are exempt from the Annual Report requirement. Rule 3a12-3 under the Exchange Act.

3. Summary of Required Contents of the Annual Report.

Rule 14a-3(b) under the Exchange Act specifies financial and other disclosure required to be included in the Annual Report. The following is a brief summary of these requirements.

(a) Summary of Required Financial Information.

● audited consolidated balance sheets as of the end of the two most recent fiscal years;

● audited consolidated statements of income and cash flows for each of the three most recent fiscal years;

● unaudited consolidated quarterly financial data for the two most recent fiscal years, except in the case of foreign private issuers;

● selected financial data described in Item 301 of Regulation S-K; and

● information relating to the registrant's industry segments, classes of similar products or services, foreign and domestic operations and export sales.

(b) Summary of Other Required Information.

In addition, the Annual Report must contain:

● a brief description of the business of the registrant and its subsidiaries;

● management's discussion and analysis of financial condition and results of operations ("MD&A") required by Item 303 of Regulation S-K;

● quantitative and qualitative disclosures about market risk required by Item 305 of Regulation S-K;

● information concerning changes in, and disagreements with, accountants required by Item 304 of Regulation S-K;

● the market price of, and dividends on, the registrant's common equity securities and related security holder matters as required by Item 201 of Regulation S-K;

● the performance graph required by Item 201(e) of Regulation S-K; and

● certain information concerning each of the registrant's directors and executive officers.

4. Summary of Other Typical Disclosure Contained in the Annual Report.

Provided an Annual Report meets the requirements of the SEC's rules, it may be "in any form deemed suitable by management."[2] As is described in

---

[2] Rule 14a-3(b)(11) under the Exchange Act.

detail below, most Annual Reports contain a "Letter to Shareholders" from the registrant's chairman and/or president and other narrative disclosure that highlights the registrant's performance during the preceding year and discusses plans for the future. In addition, as discussed in Chapter 5, with the passage of the PSLRA, many registrants provide safe harbor statements regarding forward-looking statements in their Annual Reports.

B. Role of Participants.

1. Attorney.

Although the Annual Report is thought by many to be one of the primary information documents used by investors, it has historically been reviewed less closely by counsel than Form 10-Ks, proxy statements and other documents that are formally "filed" with the SEC. In part because of the informality often associated with the disclosure contained in the Annual Report, counsel needs to exercise a high degree of diligence to confirm that procedures are in place to ensure that all disclosure is accurate and complete. For specific procedures to be followed in connection with the MD&A, see Chapter 6. In reviewing the Annual Report, counsel should ensure that:

● all required disclosure is present;

● statistics and other information have been verified; and

● the disclosure is consistent with the registrant's internal analyses (e.g., those contained in board presentations) and other public disclosure (e.g., SEC filings, websites, press releases, brochures, etc.).

2. Management.

Management, often with the assistance of consultants (public relations and advertising), develops the theme for the Annual Report and usually drafts the narrative disclosure highlighting the registrant's performance during the preceding year and discussing future plans. The registrant's chairman or president, as applicable, drafts the Letter to Shareholders. Management should review the entire Annual Report closely to ensure it is accurate and conveys the appropriate tone.

3. Board of Directors.

Because the directors are not signatories to the Annual Report, their input and comments are often not solicited. However, even though as described in Section H of this Chapter, the Annual Report is not deemed "filed" with the SEC, the Annual Report may be a liability document. As a result, it is good practice to provide the Board a near final copy of the Annual Report for review, especially if information is incorporated by reference from the Annual Report into the Form 10-K.

C. Preparing the Annual Report/Format.

SEC rules do not prescribe how the information required to be included in an Annual Report is to be presented. As a consequence, registrants are given wide latitude in presenting such information. Based on recent survey data described in Section G of this Chapter, a majority of companies follow the practice of utilizing the Form 10-K (usually without those portions that are incorporated by reference in the proxy statement) wrapped by a Letter to Shareholders and a glossy cover as their Annual Reports. Such Annual Reports are generally referred to as a "10-K Wrap" or "Wrap 10-K." Many other companies prepare a traditional "glossy" covered Annual Report containing various non-required information in the front portion, with the required financial and other information generally placed in the back.

1. Cover Page.

The cover page of the "glossy" Annual Report is generally designed to attract the reader's attention and in many cases set the tone for the report. Some registrants provide very plain cover pages in years where their performance has been poor and bright cover pages in good years. At a minimum, the cover of an Annual Report usually provides the registrant's name, logo and the year to which the Annual Report relates.

2. Inside Front Cover/Operating Highlights.

Many registrants will use the inside front cover of the Annual Report for a table of contents or a table comparing the past year's financial and operating highlights to that of prior years.

● *Example*: The inside front cover of Intel Corporation's 2010 Annual Report contains a 5-year comparison in several different areas, including diluted earnings per share, research and development expense, and dividends per share paid.

3. Letter to Shareholders.

A Letter to Shareholders from the registrant's chairman and/or president has become commonplace.[3] In fact, the release of the annual Letters to Shareholders by prominent executives of large registrants (e.g., Berkshire Hathaway's Warren Buffet) has become a much anticipated event. These letters generally detail a registrant's recent accomplishments, current activities and plans for the

---

[3] Section 616 of the NYSE Amex Company Guide provides: "Most annual reports contain a letter to shareholders from the President or other officer of the company. The Exchange expects that such letter, as well as all other releases and statements by the company, will be factual and that judgment and restraint will be used in not publicizing information which may be construed as over-optimistic, slanted or promotional."

future. In addition, some letters have been used for other purposes, including urging shareholders to fight particular regulation or legislation, or to report major management changes. The letters are typically a few pages in length, although Mr. Buffet's February 2011 letter was 25 pages!

4. Text.

Following the Letter to Shareholders, registrants generally provide additional information regarding their accomplishments during the year, often tied to a particular theme. Key customers or suppliers are often highlighted in the context of case studies. This text is often surrounded by photographs and a variety of data presented in various graphic designs.

5. Financial Statements and Information.

(a) Required Financial Statements.

● audited consolidated balance sheets as of the end of the two most recent fiscal years;

● audited consolidated statements of income and cash flows for each of the three most recent fiscal years; and

● unaudited consolidated quarterly financial data for the two most recent fiscal years, except in the case of foreign private issuers, and other supplementary financial information required by Item 302(a) of Regulation S-K.

(b) Other Required Financial Information.

● selected financial data described in Item 301 of Regulation S-K; and

● information relating to the registrant's industry segments, classes of similar products or services, foreign and domestic operations and export sales required by Items 101(b), (c)(1)(i) and (d) of Regulation S-K.

(c) Inclusion of Management's Report on Internal Control Over Financial Reporting and the Auditor's Report on Management's Assessment of Internal Control Over Financial Reporting. Exchange Act Rules 14a-3 and 14c-3 do not specifically require that the Annual Report include management's report on internal control over financial reporting and the auditor's report on management's assessment of internal control over financial reporting. However, the staffs of the Office of the Chief Accountant and the Division of Corporation Finance have indicated that they believe that the intent of Section 404 of the Sarbanes-Oxley Act and the SEC's rules is that such reports be included and that they intend to recommend to the SEC that amendments be made to Rules 14a-3 and 14c-3(a) and Item 13 of Schedule 14A to include such a requirement.[4] Such staffs have further indicated that "[i]f

---

[4] See Question 10 of Management's Report on Internal Control Over Financial Reporting and Certification of Disclosure in Exchange Act Periodic Reports-

management states in their report that internal control over financial reporting is ineffective or the auditor's report takes any form other than an unqualified opinion and these reports are not included in the annual report to shareholders, our view is that an issuer would have to consider whether the annual report to shareholders contained a material omission that made the disclosures in the annual report misleading."

(d) **Form of Presentation.** Registrants are encouraged to utilize tables, schedules, charts and graphic illustrations to present financial information in an understandable manner.[5] Any presentation of financial information must be consistent with the data in the financial statements contained in the Annual Report and, if appropriate, should refer to relevant portions of the financial statements and notes thereto.

(e) **Type Size Requirements.** Financial statements and notes thereto must be presented in roman type at least as large and as legible as ten-point modern type. If necessary for convenient presentation, the financial statements may be in roman type as large and as legible as eight-point modern type. All type must be leaded at least two points.

6. Management's Discussion and Analysis.

The MD&A disclosure required to be contained in an Annual Report is identical to that required in the Form 10-K. For a discussion of the required MD&A disclosure, see Chapter 6.

7. Other Required Information.

(a) **Description of the Business.** The Annual Report must contain a brief description of the business done by the registrant and its subsidiaries during the most recent fiscal year which will, in the opinion of management, indicate the general nature and scope of the business of the registrant and its subsidiaries.[6] This disclosure often appears within the textual information preceding the financial statements.

(b) **Market Risk Disclosures.** The Annual Report must contain the information concerning quantitative and qualitative disclosures about market risk required by Item 305 of Regulation S-K. For a discussion of the required market risk disclosure, see Chapter 6.

(Footnote Continued)

Frequently Asked Questions (9/24/07), which is included as Appendix 13. It is important to note, however, that the answers to such frequently asked questions represent the views of the staffs of the Office of the Chief Accountant and the Division of Corporation Finance. They are not rules, regulations or statements of the SEC. Further, the SEC has neither approved nor disapproved them.

[5] Rule 14a-3(b)(11) under the Exchange Act.

[6] Rule 14a-3(b)(6) under the Exchange Act.

(c) Information Concerning Changes in and Disagreements with Accountants. The Annual Report must contain the information concerning changes in, and disagreements with, accountants on accounting and financial disclosure required by Item 304 of Regulation S-K. For a discussion of the required Item 304 disclosure, see Chapter 6.

(d) Information Concerning Directors and Executive Officers. The Annual Report must identify each of the registrant's directors and executive officers, and indicate the principal occupation or employment of each such person and the name and principal business of any organization by which such person is employed.[7] This information can be presented in any form and is often included in a listing at the end of the Annual Report under the headings "Board of Directors" and "Executive Officers." Often individual or group photographs of such persons are also included in the Annual Report.

(e) Stock Price and Dividend History. The Annual Report must contain information relating to the market price of, and dividends on, the registrant's common equity securities and related security holder matters required by Items 201(a), (b) and (c) of Regulation S-K.[8] Item 201(a) of Regulation S-K specifies the requirements for market information, Item 201(b) for information concerning the number of record holders and Item 201(c) for dividend information. Disclosure of securities authorized for issuance under equity compensation plans, required by Item 201(d) of Regulation S-K, is not required to be included in the Annual Report. For a detailed discussion of the required Item 201 disclosure, see Chapter 6. Registrants will often include the quarterly stock price information in a table that also includes quarterly financial information. The number of record holders and dividend information is often included as a footnote to or following the table containing quarterly financial information.

(f) Performance Graph. Rule 14a-3(b)(9) under the Exchange Act requires that if the Annual Report precedes or accompanies a proxy statement relating to an annual meeting of security holders at which directors are to be elected (or special meeting or written consents in lieu of such meeting), the registrant must furnish the performance graph required by Item 201(e) of Regulation S-K. Such information will not be deemed to be incorporated by reference into any filing under the Securities Act or the Exchange Act, except to the extent that the registrant specifically incorporates it by reference. The performance graph may also be included in the Form 10-K and/or proxy statement, but such inclusion will not obviate the requirement to include the performance

---

[7] Rule 14a-3(b)(8) under the Exchange Act.

[8] Rule 14a-3(b)(9) under the Exchange Act.

graph in the Annual Report unless the registrant includes the performance graph in the "Form 10-K Wrap" to satisfy the Annual Report delivery requirements.[9] Smaller reporting companies are not required to include the performance graph in the Annual Report.

Item 201(e) of Regulation S-K requires the registrant to present a line graph comparing the yearly[10] percentage change in its cumulative total shareholder return on its common stock[11] during the "measurement period" with:

- the cumulative total return of a broad equity market index, assuming reinvestment of dividends, that includes companies whose equity securities are listed on the same exchange or NASDAQ market or are of comparable market capitalization as the registrant[12]; and

- the cumulative total return, assuming dividend reinvestment, of one of the following:

  - a published industry or line-of-business index prepared by a party other than the registrant or an affiliate[13] (unless it is widely recognized and used) that is accessible to the registrant's shareholders;

  - peer issuer(s) selected in good faith, including disclosure of the basis for selection if the peer issuer(s) are not selected on an industry or line-of-business basis and the identity of the peer issuer(s).[14] If the registrant has disclosed specific public reporting companies as

---

[9] See SEC's Division of Corporation Finance Compliance and Disclosure Interpretations—Regulation S-K—Questions and Answers of General Applicability—Section 106. Item 201—Market Price of and Dividends on the Registrant's Common Equity and Related Stockholder Matters—Questions 106.11 and 106.12 (March 13, 2007).

[10] Monthly or quarterly returns can also be plotted for the entire performance graph as long as each return is plotted at the same interval and the annual changes are reflected clearly. See SEC's Division of Corporation Finance Compliance and Disclosure Interpretations—Regulation S-K—Questions and Answers of General Applicability—Section 106. Item 201—Market Price of and Dividends on the Registrant's Common Equity and Related Stockholder Matters—Question 106.06 (March 13, 2007).

[11] This is calculated by dividing (i) the sum of (x) the cumulative amount of dividends for the measurement period, assuming dividend reinvestment, and (y) the difference

between the registrant's share price at the end and the beginning of the measurement period, by (ii) the share price at the beginning of the measurement period.

[12] If the registrant is a member of the S&P 500 Stock Index, it must use that index to satisfy this requirement.

[13] An index prepared by a trade group is treated the same as an index prepared by an affiliate of the registrant. SEC Release No. 33-7009 (August 3, 1993) at Section V.B.2.

[14] Each component issuer must be weighted according to the issuer's stock market capitalization at the beginning of each period for which a return is indicated. See SEC's Division of Corporation Finance Compliance and Disclosure Interpretations—Regulation S-K—Questions and Answers of General Applicability—Section 106. Item 201—Market Price of and Dividends on the Registrant's Common Equity and Related Stockholder Matters—Question 106.07 (March 13, 2007).

competitors in its most recent Form 10-K or registration statement, the peer issuers will presumably consist of, or be selected from, that group of companies; or

● issuer(s) with similar market capitalization if the registrant does not use a published industry or line-of-business index and does not believe it can reasonably identify a peer group, including disclosure of a statement of the reasons for this selection and the identity of the issuer(s).

The "measurement period" consists of the period beginning at the measurement point established by the market close on the last trading day before the beginning of the registrant's fifth preceding fiscal year (with the closing price at this measurement point being converted into a fixed investment, stated in dollars (for ease of use, most registrants use $100), in the stock of the registrant, index or group, as applicable) through and including the end of the registrant's last completed fiscal year, or such shorter period time as the registrant has been a public reporting company.[15] The graph can cover a longer period of time, but the measurement point is still established by the market close on the last trading day before the beginning of the registrant's fifth preceding fiscal year. Each fiscal year should be plotted with points showing the cumulative return as of that year. This is measured as the change from the fixed investment, stated in dollars, in the stock of the registrant, index or group, as applicable, at the measurement point described above. The value of each investment as of each plot point on a given return line is the number of shares held at that point multiplied by the then-prevailing share price.

Example: To calculate a registrant's cumulative return for each year in the five-year period ending 12/31/11, starting with 2007, add the registrant's closing stock price on 12/31/07 to cash dividends in 2007 and subtract the registrant's closing stock price on 12/31/06. Then divide that number by the closing stock price on 12/31/06. For 2008, the closing stock price on 12/31/08 would be added to the cumulative cash dividends from 12/31/06 through 12/31/08 and the closing stock price on 12/31/06 would then be subtracted. Then divide that number by the closing stock price on 12/31/06. This would continue through and including 2011. For purposes of plotting the performance graph, assuming $100 is invested in the registrant's stock, $100 would be the plot point for

---

[15] If a registrant's IPO was within its past five fiscal years, the measurement point will be the closing price of the registrant's shares on the first day that they were publicly traded (as opposed to the IPO price or the opening price on the first day of public trading). However, no performance graph is required for a registrant in the fiscal year following its IPO if it was a public reporting company for 30 days or less in the prior fiscal year. See SEC's Division of Corporation Finance Compliance and Disclosure Interpretations— Regulation S-K—Questions and Answers of General Applicability—Section 106. Item 201—Market Price of and Dividends on the Registrant's Common Equity and Related Stockholder Matters—Question 106.09 (March 13, 2007).

12/31/06. If the registrant's closing stock price on 12/31/06 was $20 per share, then the $100 investment would equal 5 shares. If no dividends were paid by the registrant during 2007 and the registrant's closing stock price on 12/31/07 was $25 per share, then the 5 shares have an investment value equal to $125 on 12/31/07 and $125 would be the plot point for 12/31/07. If no dividends were paid by the registrant during 2008 and the registrant's closing stock price on 12/31/08 was $30 per share, then the 5 shares would have an investment value equal to $150 on 12/31/08 and $150 would be the plot point for 12/31/08. This would continue through and including 12/31/10.

If the registrant selects a different index, peer group or market capitalization group from that which was used for the immediately preceding fiscal year, it must explain the reasons for the change and also compare its total return to both the new and old index, peer group or market capitalization group, as applicable. A registrant should keep in mind that just because its total return currently compares favorably to a particular index, peer group or market capitalization group does not mean this will always be the case in the future, and a change in the index, peer group or market capitalization group will require this added disclosure. However, if entities comprising a peer group or market capitalization group change (i) because an entity is no longer in the line of business or industry, was acquired or is no longer a public reporting company or (ii) as a result of the application of pre-established objective criteria, the registrant's total return need not be compared to the "old" peer group or market capitalization group. However, the reason for the change in the peer group or market capitalization group and the name of any deleted issuer must still be disclosed. In addition to total return, a registrant can also graphically compare other performance measures (e.g., return on average common shareholders' equity).

(g) **Undertaking to Deliver Form 10-K.** Finally, the Annual Report or the proxy statement must contain an undertaking in boldface or other reasonably prominent type that the registrant will provide, without charge to any shareholder, a copy of the Form 10-K, including the financial statements and financial statement schedules. The registrant need not undertake to furnish, without charge, the exhibits to the Form 10-K. If the exhibits are not to be included, (i) the Form 10-K must contain a list briefly describing all the exhibits not included and (ii) the Annual Report must also contain a statement that the exhibits to the Form 10-K will be furnished upon request upon payment of a specified reasonable fee, which fee shall be limited to the registrant's reasonable expenses in furnishing such exhibits. The undertaking is not required where the Annual Report contains all the information that would be required in the Form 10-K (e.g., where the Annual Report is filed as the Form 10-K or is wrapped around or attaches a copy of the registrant's Form 10-K).[16]

---

[16] Rule 14a-3(b)(10) under the Exchange Act.

8. Additional Information Commonly Provided.

Other information commonly contained in the Annual Report includes:

● the date, time and location of the registrant's upcoming annual meeting;

● the registrant's web address(es), including contact information for investor relations personnel;

● the name of the registrant's independent auditors;

● contact information for the registrant's transfer agent and registrar; and

● a safe harbor statement for forward-looking statements.

D. Alternative Formats.

1. Integrated Annual Report and Form 10-K ("Wrap 10-K").

General Instruction H to the Form 10-K specifically provides that the Annual Report may be combined with the Form 10-K. Because the Form 10-K encompasses substantially all of the disclosure required in the Annual Report, most registrants, as a cost and time saving measure, follow the practice of utilizing the Form 10-K (usually without those portions that are incorporated by reference in the proxy statement) wrapped by a Letter to Shareholders and a glossy cover as their Annual Report.[17] The reduced costs and production time associated with using the Form 10-K as the Annual Report should be balanced against the increased paper and mailing costs associated with including the full Form 10-K in the Annual Report.

2. Summary Annual Reports.

For many years the SEC has considered proposals to pare down the disclosure included in the Annual Report. For example, as part of the SEC's efforts to improve the effectiveness and efficiency of its disclosure system, the SEC proposed "streamlined Annual Reports."[18] Proponents of Annual Report simplification believe that streamlined Annual Reports would allow registrants to communicate more effectively with shareholders in their Annual Reports by being able to highlight key financial items and to reduce the costs of preparing and delivering the Annual Report. Various approaches have been suggested to accomplish the streamlining. One, which was proposed by the SEC, would have permitted an eligible registrant to use financial statements with significantly abbreviated notes in Annual Reports. In addition, "Summary Annual Reports," which would not include the full MD&A or the full stock price and dividend information and business description currently mandated by Rule 14a-3 under the Exchange Act, were proposed. Under the Summary Annual Report approach,

---

[17] For example, see the 2010 Annual Report of Myers Industries.

[18] SEC Release No. 33-7183 (September 17, 1995).

registrants would still be required to deliver financial information to shareholders. Under no-action letters issued to General Motors Corporation[19] and McKesson Corporation,[20] the SEC has permitted issuers to exclude audited financial statements and MD&A from the Annual Report under certain circumstances. Many companies, like Duke Energy in its 2010 Annual Report, have taken advantage of this opportunity to provide a briefer Annual Report.

E. Delivery to the SEC.

Seven copies of the Annual Report must be mailed to the SEC, "solely for its information," not later than the date on which such report is provided to security holders.[21] Because the Annual Report is typically mailed along with the proxy statement, which contains the formal notice of the annual meeting, the mailing date of the Annual Report is generally tied to the date when notice must be provided to shareholders.[22]

F. Other Required Distributions of Annual Report.

1. Filing with the Exchanges.

(a) New York Stock Exchange.

(1) Timing of Delivery. NYSE listed U.S. companies must simultaneously make their Annual Reports available to shareholders on or through the company's website. Companies must also post to their website a prominent undertaking to provide all holders (including preferred stockholders and bondholders) the ability, upon request, to receive a hard copy of their complete audited financial statements free of charge. In addition, simultaneously with this posting, the company must issue a press release stating that its Annual Report has been filed with the SEC. This press release must also specify the company's website address and indicate that shareholders have the ability to receive a hard copy of the company's complete audited financial statements free of charge upon request. A listed company that is subject to the U.S. proxy rules is not required to issue the press release or post the undertaking required above.[23]

(2) Number of Copies. The NYSE requires the filing of six copies of proxy materials.[24]

---

[19] See *General Motors Corporation* (available January 20, 1987).

[20] See *McKesson Corporation* (available May 15, 1987).

[21] Rule 14a-3(c) under the Exchange Act.

[22] For example, Section 222 of the DGCL provides that shareholders must receive notice of the annual meeting 10 to 60 days prior to the meeting.

[23] NYSE Listed Company Manual Section 203.01.

[24] NYSE Listed Company Manual Section 402.01.

(b) NYSE Amex.

(1) Timing of Delivery. NYSE Amex listed U.S. companies must simultaneously make their Annual Reports available to shareholders on or through their websites. Companies must also post to their websites a prominent undertaking to provide all holders (including preferred stockholders and bondholders) the ability, upon request, to receive a hard copy of their complete audited financial statements free of charge. In addition, simultaneously with this posting, the company must issue a press release stating that its Annual Report has been filed with the SEC. This press release must also specify the company's website address and indicate that shareholders have the ability to receive a hard copy of the company's complete audited financial statements free of charge upon request. A listed company that is subject to the U.S. proxy rules is not required to issue the press release or post the undertaking required above.[25]

(2) Number of Copies. The NYSE Amex requires three copies.[26]

(c) NASDAQ.

(1) Timing of Delivery. NASDAQ Rule 5250(d)(1) requires NASDAQ listed companies to make available to shareholders Annual Reports containing audited financial statements within a "reasonable period of time" following filing with the SEC.

(2) Number of Copies. A registrant listed on NASDAQ is not required to deliver to NASDAQ any copies of its Annual Report if it is filed with the SEC via EDGAR. If it is not filed via EDGAR, the registrant must deliver two copies to NASDAQ or mail an electronic version of the report to NASDAQ at continuedlisting@nasdaq.com.[27]

2. Distribution to Shareholders.

(a) Delivery to Shareholders. Rule 14a-3 under the Exchange Act provides that proxy solicitations relating to an annual or special meeting of shareholders at which directors are to be elected must be accompanied or preceded by an Annual Report. However, the delivery requirements of Rule 14a-3(b)(13) under the Exchange Act do not apply to solicitations made on behalf of the registrant before the financial statements are available if a solicitation is being made at the same time in opposition to the registrant, and if the registrant's proxy statement includes an undertaking in boldface type to furnish such Annual Report to all persons being solicited at least 20 calendar days before the date of the meeting; or, if the solicitation refers to a written consent or

---

[25] NYSE AMEX Company Guide Section 610.

[26] NYSE AMEX Company Guide Section 701.

[27] NASDAQ Rule 5250(c)(1).

authorization in lieu of a meeting, at least 20 calendar days prior to the earliest date on which it may be used to effect corporate action.

(b) Delivery to Households and Electronic Delivery. See Chapter 7 for a discussion of the householding and electronic delivery of the Annual Report.

(c) Termination of Obligation to Deliver an Annual Report. Unless state law requires otherwise, a registrant is not required to send an Annual Report, proxy statement or Notice of Internet Availability of Proxy Materials to a security holder if either: (i) an Annual Report, a proxy statement or Notice of Internet Availability of Proxy Materials for two consecutive annual meetings; or (ii) all, and at least two, payments (if sent by first class mail) of dividends or interest on securities, or dividend reinvestment confirmations, during a 12-month period, have been mailed to such security holder's address and have been returned as undeliverable. If any such security holder delivers or causes to be delivered to the registrant written notice setting forth his or her then current address for security holder communications purposes, the registrant's obligation to deliver an Annual Report, a proxy statement or Notice of Internet Availability of Proxy Materials is reinstated.[28]

G. Trends and Practices in the Annual Report Process.

In recent years, many registrants have supplemented their paper Annual Reports with those in a variety of other media, including: (i) electronic format (e-mail); (ii) audio cassette version; (iii) Braille; and (iv) CD ROM or floppy disk. In addition, paper copies have often been provided in a style other than a typical 8½ × 11 inch format, including magazine and newspaper formats. Some have included free samples, discount coupons, etc.

In October 2008, the National Investor Relations Institute ("NIRI") published the results of a survey of Annual Report practices and trends (the "NIRI Survey"). The NIRI Survey participants, a national sample of 182 NIRI members, completed questionnaires on key aspects of Annual Report design, production and distribution. Highlights of the results of the NIRI Survey are as follows:

1. Online Version. 45% of online versions were formatted as an interactive HTML document and 17% contained downloadable financial data for use in spreadsheets.

2. Archiving. Number of years Annual Reports were archived:

- 4%—one year or less
- 6%—two years
- 25%—three years
- 3%—four years

---

[28] Rule 14a-3(e)(2) under the Exchange Act.

- 27%—five years

- 35%—six or more years

3. Content. Percentages of companies including various content in the Annual Report:

- 14% included a letter from the Chairman of the Board;

- 96% included a letter from the CEO;

- 67% included a five-year financial history and 11% included a ten-year financial history; and

- 24% included corporate and social responsibility information.

4. Alternative Formats. 52% of respondents disseminated a Wrap 10-K. Of the remainder:

- 34% used a traditional Annual Report; and

- 13% used a Summary Annual Report;

5. Page Length. 62% of Annual Reports were under 100 pages and 14% were over 150 pages.

6. Print Runs. Print runs for the Annual Report:

- 70% printed under 30,000 copies;

- 18% printed between 30,000 and 100,000 copies; and

- 12% printed over 100,000 copies.

H. Liability Considerations.

In the past, because the Annual Report was not deemed "filed" with the SEC for purposes of liability and is not deemed "soliciting material" under the proxy rules, registrants and their counsel did not review the disclosure with the same level of scrutiny as documents "filed" with the SEC. However, with the expansion of securities law liability and the practice of incorporating by reference portions of the Annual Report into other filings, the Annual Report should be given greater scrutiny and considered as a "liability" document. In addition to the broad enforcement powers of the SEC (e.g., to bring injunctive or administrative proceedings), actions relating to the Annual Report may be brought under various theories under the Exchange Act and the Securities Act.

1. Exchange Act.

(a) Section 18. Section 18(a) of the Exchange Act creates a private remedy for false or misleading statements of material facts contained in documents "filed" with the SEC in favor of a person who relies on such documents in connection with the purchase or sale of securities. Although the Annual Report must be "mailed" to the SEC, it is not deemed to be "soliciting material" or to have been "filed" with the SEC for purposes of liability under Section 18 of the Exchange Act,[29] except to the extent that the registrant specifically requests that the Annual Report be treated as a part of the proxy soliciting material or incorporates it by reference into the Form 10-K. As a result, if information from the Annual Report is incorporated into a Form 10-K, the information in the Annual Report that responds to required items in the Form 10-K will be subject to Section 18 liability. When the Annual Report is filed as the Form 10-K, responses to the items of the Form 10-K are subject to Section 18 of the Exchange Act notwithstanding Rule 14a-3(c) under the Exchange Act.[30]

(b) Rule 10b-5. The general anti-fraud prohibitions against use of manipulative or deceptive practices contained in Section 10(b) of, and Rule 10b-5 under, the Exchange Act may also serve as a basis for liability for the Annual Report. For example, very optimistic or speculative statements contained in the Letter to Shareholders may constitute a "material misstatement" subjecting the registrant to fraud claims under Rule 10b-5.

(c) Section 14(a). Section 14(a) of the Exchange Act makes it unlawful for any person to solicit any proxy or consent in contravention of SEC rules. As a result, any violation of the disclosure rules contained in Rule 14a-3 (e.g., a material misstatement or omission in the Annual Report) could constitute a violation of Section 14(a), which could subject the registrant and others to liability under Section 14(a).

(d) Section 20. Controlling persons (e.g., directors, officers and significant shareholders) of the registrant could also be held jointly and severally liable with persons that they control under Section 20 of the Exchange Act. This might occur with respect to an Annual Report for violations of Rule 14a-3 by the registrant. As a consequence, such controlling persons will want to ensure that they can show they acted in good faith and conducted a due diligence review of the Annual Report.

2. Securities Act.

Disclosure contained in the Annual Report may be incorporated by reference into the Form 10-K, which in turn may be incorporated by reference into a registration statement filed under the Securities Act. As a result, registrants may incur liability under Sections 11, 12 and 17 of the Securities Act for such Annual Report disclosures.

---

[29] Rule 14a-3(c) under the Exchange Act.

[30] Rule 14a-3(d) under the Exchange Act.

Appendixes

APPENDIX 1

Commission Guidance on Presentation of Liquidity and Capital Resources Disclosures in Management's Discussion and Analysis

SECURITIES AND EXCHANGE COMMISSION

17 CFR PARTS 211, 231 and 241

Release Nos. 33-9144; 34-62934; FR-83

Commission Guidance on Presentation of Liquidity and Capital Resources Disclosures in Management's Discussion and Analysis

AGENCY: Securities and Exchange Commission.

ACTION: Interpretation.

SUMMARY: We are providing interpretive guidance that is intended to improve discussion of liquidity and capital resources in Management's Discussion and Analysis of Financial Condition and Results of Operations in order to facilitate understanding by investors of the liquidity and funding risks facing the registrant.

EFFECTIVE DATE: September 28, 2010.

FOR FURTHER INFORMATION CONTACT: Questions about specific filings should be directed to staff members responsible for reviewing the documents the registrant files with the Commission. For general questions about this release, contact Christina L. Padden, Attorney Fellow in the Office of Rulemaking, at (202) 551-3430 or Stephanie L. Hunsaker, Associate Chief Accountant, at (202) 551-3400, in the Division of Corporation Finance; or Wesley R. Bricker, Professional Accounting Fellow, Office of the Chief Accountant at (202) 551-5300; U.S. Securities and Exchange Commission, 100 F Street, NE, Washington, DC 20549.

SUPPLEMENTARY INFORMATION:

I. BACKGROUND

Over the past several years, we have provided guidance and have engaged in rulemaking initiatives to improve the presentation of information about funding and liquidity risk.[1] In a companion release, we are proposing amendments to enhance the disclosure that registrants present about short-term borrowings.[2] The proposals in that release would require a registrant to provide, in a separately captioned subsection of Management's Discussion and Analysis of Financial Condition and Results of Operations ("MD&A"), a comprehensive explanation of its short-term borrowings, including both quantitative and qualitative information. The proposed amendments to MD&A would be applicable to annual and quarterly reports, proxy or information statements that include financial statements, registration statements under the Securities Exchange

---

[1] *See, e.g.*, Commission Statement About Management's Discussion and Analysis of Financial Condition and Results of Operations, Release No. 33-8056 (Jan. 22, 2002) [67 FR 3746]; Disclosure in Management's Discussion and Analysis About Off Balance Sheet Arrangements, Contractual Obligations and Contingent Liabilities and Commitments, Release No. 33-8144 (Nov. 4, 2002) [67 FR 68054]; Disclosure in Management's Discussion and Analysis About Off Balance Sheet Arrangements, Contractual Obligations and Contingent Liabilities and Commitments, Release No. 33-8182 (Jan. 28, 2003) [68 FR 5982] (adopting rules for disclosure in MD&A of off-balance sheet arrangements and aggregate contractual obligations); and Commission Guidance Regarding Management's Discussion and Analysis of Financial Condition and Results of Operations, Release No. 33-8350 (Dec. 19, 2003) [68 FR 75056] (providing interpretive guidance on disclosure in MD&A, including liquidity and capital resources).

[2] *See* Short-Term Borrowings Disclosure, Release No. 33-9143 (the "Proposing Release").

Act of 1934, and registration statements under the Securities Act of 1933. We are also proposing conforming amendments to Form 8-K so that the Form would use the terminology contained in the proposed short-term borrowings disclosure requirement. To further improve the discussion of liquidity and capital resources in MD&A in order to facilitate understanding by investors of the liquidity and funding risks facing the registrant, we are also providing the following guidance with respect to existing MD&A requirements.

II. GUIDANCE ON PRESENTATION OF LIQUIDITY AND CAPITAL RESOURCES DISCLOSURES IN MANAGEMENT'S DISCUSSION AND ANALYSIS

A. Liquidity Disclosure

As discussed in the Proposing Release, companies have expanded the types of funding methods and cash management tools they use. We remind registrants that Item 303(a)(1) of Regulation S-K requires them to "identify and separately describe internal and external sources of liquidity, and briefly discuss any material unused sources of liquidity." Accordingly, as the financing activities undertaken by registrants become more diverse and complex, it is increasingly important that the discussion and analysis of liquidity and capital resources provided by registrants meet the objectives of MD&A disclosure.

In 2003, the Commission issued interpretive guidance relating to MD&A disclosures of liquidity and capital resources, as well as MD&A generally.[3] We encourage registrants to review that guidance when preparing their MD&A, as it covers topics relating to the discussion of cash requirements, cash management, sources and uses of cash, as well as a registrant's debt instruments, guarantees and related covenants, that continue to be relevant to investors.

As we have stated in the past, MD&A requires companies to provide investors with disclosure that facilitates an appreciation of the known trends and uncertainties that have impacted historical results or are reasonably likely to shape future periods.[4] This disclosure should both discuss and analyze the company's business from the perspective of management.[5] In the context of liquidity, Item 303(a)(1) of Regulation S-K requires disclosure of known trends or any known demands, commitments, events or uncertainties that will result in, or that are reasonably likely to result in, the registrant's liquidity increasing or decreasing in any material way.[6] In past guidance, the Commission has highlighted a number of issues for management to consider when identifying trends, demands, commitments, events and uncertainties that require disclosure in MD&A.[7] Some additional important trends and uncertainties relating to liquidity might include, for example, difficulties accessing the debt markets, reliance on commercial paper or

---

[3] See Commission Guidance Regarding Management's Discussion and Analysis of Financial Condition and Results of Operations, Release No. 33-8350 (Dec. 19, 2003) [68 FR 75056] (the "2003 Interpretive Release").

[4] See Disclosure in Management's Discussion and Analysis About Off Balance Sheet Arrangements, Contractual Obligations and Contingent Liabilities and Commitments, Release No. 33-8182 (Jan. 28, 2003) [68 FR 5982] (the "OBS Adopting Release"), at 5982 ("MD&A also provides a unique opportunity for management to provide investors with an understanding of its view of the financial performance and condition of the company, an appreciation of what the financial statements show and do not show, as well as important trends and risks that have shaped the past and are reasonably likely to shape the future.").

[5] "MD&A should be a discussion and analysis of a company's business as seen through the eyes of those

who manage that business. Management has a unique perspective on its business that only it can present. As such, MD&A should not be a recitation of financial statements in narrative form, or an otherwise uninformative series of technical responses to MD&A requirements, neither of which provides this important management perspective." See 2003 Interpretive Release, supra note 3, at 75056.

[6] "The scope of the discussion should thus address liquidity in the broadest sense, encompassing internal as well as external sources, current conditions as well as future commitments and known trends, changes in circumstances and uncertainties." See Commission Statement About Management's Discussion and Analysis of Financial Condition and Results of Operations, Release No. 33-8056 (Jan. 22, 2002) [67 FR 3746] (the "2002 Interpretive Release"), at 3748 n.11.

[7] See 2002 Interpretive Release, supra note 5, at 3748.

other short-term financing arrangements, maturity mismatches between borrowing sources and the assets funded by those sources, changes in terms requested by counterparties, changes in the valuation of collateral, and counterparty risk.

In addition, in the context of liquidity and capital resources, if the registrant's financial statements do not adequately convey the registrant's financing arrangements during the period, or the impact of those arrangements on liquidity, because of a known trend, demand, commitment, event or uncertainty, additional narrative disclosure should be considered and may be required to enable an understanding of the amounts depicted in the financial statements. For example, depending on the registrant's circumstances, if borrowings during the reporting period are materially different than the period-end amounts recorded in the financial statements, disclosure about the intra-period variations is required under current rules to facilitate investor understanding of the registrant's liquidity position.

Moreover, the Commission's staff has noted that there may be confusion on the part of registrants about how to address disclosure of certain repurchase agreements that are accounted for as sales, as well as other types of short-term financings that are not otherwise fully captured in period-end balance sheets.[8] Again, disclosure is required in MD&A where a known commitment, event or uncertainty will result in (or is reasonably likely to result in) the registrant's liquidity increasing or decreasing in a material way.[9] The absence of specific references in existing disclosure requirements for off-balance sheet arrangements or contractual obligations to repurchase transactions that are accounted for as sales, or to any other transfers of financial assets that are accounted for as sales, does not relieve registrants from the disclosure requirements of Item 303(a)(1).[10] Further, as stated in the 2002 Interpretive Release, legal opinions regarding "true sale" issues do not obviate the need for registrants to consider whether disclosure is required.[11] In evaluating whether disclosure in MD&A may be required in connection with a repurchase transaction, securities lending transaction, or any other transaction involving the transfer of financial assets with an obligation to repurchase financial assets, that has been accounted for as a sale under applicable accounting standards, the registrant should consider whether the transaction is reasonably likely to result in the use of a material amount of cash or other liquid assets. Disclosure may be required in the discussion of liquidity and capital resources, particularly where the registrant does not otherwise include such information in its off-balance sheet arrangements or its contractual obligations table. A registrant may determine where in its MD&A this information would be most informative based on the type of obligation and potential exposure involved, with an emphasis on providing disclosure that is clear and not misleading.

---

[8] In its 2005 OBS Report, the Commission's staff identified transfers of assets with continuing involvement as one of the principal areas in need of improvement in disclosure of off-balance sheet arrangements. *See* Staff of the U.S. Securities and Exchange Commission, Report and Recommendations Pursuant to Section 401(c) of the Sarbanes-Oxley Act of 2002 On Arrangements with Off-Balance Sheet Implications, Special Purpose Entities and Transparency of Filings by Issuers (June 2005), *available at* http://www.sec.gov/news/studies/soxoffbalancerpt.pdf. *See also*, the Division of Corporation Finance, Sample Letter Sent to Public Companies Asking for Information Related to Repurchase Agreements, Securities Lending Transactions, or Other Transactions Involving the Transfer of Financial Assets (Mar. 2010), *available at* http://www.sec.gov/divisions/corpfin/guidance/cforepurchase0310.htm., and the Division of Corporation Finance, Sample Letter Sent to Public Companies That Have Identified Investments in Structured Investment Vehicles, Conduits or Collateralized Debt Obligations (Off-balance Sheet Entities) (Dec. 2007)

available at http://www.sec.gov/divisions/corpfin/guidance/cfoffbalanceltr1207.htm.
[9] *See* Item 303(a)(1) [17 CFR 229.303(a)(1)].
[10] We also note that, in 1986, the Commission adopted changes to Rule 4-08 of Regulation S-X to require financial statement footnote disclosure of the nature and extent of a registrant's repurchase and reverse repurchase transactions and the degree of risk involved. *See* Disclosure Amendments to Regulation S-X Regarding Repurchase and Reverse Repurchase Agreements, Release No. 33-6621 (Jan. 22, 1986) [51 FR 3765]. These requirements focus on disclosure of risk of loss due to counter-party default. *See* Rule 4-08(m) of Regulation S-X [17 CFR §210.4-08m]. However, the adopting release indicates that the requirements do not affect obligations under MD&A requirements to discuss "any material impact on liquidity or operations and risk resulting from involvement with repurchase and reverse repurchase agreements."
[11] *See* 2002 Interpretive Release, *supra* note 5, at 3749.

To provide context for the exposures identified in MD&A, companies should also consider describing cash management and risk management policies that are relevant to an assessment of their financial condition. Banks, in particular, should consider discussing their policies and practices in meeting applicable banking agency guidance on funding and liquidity risk management, or any policies and practices that differ from applicable agency guidance. In addition, a company that maintains or has access to a portfolio of cash and other investments that is a material source of liquidity should consider providing information about the nature and composition of that portfolio, including a description of the assets held and any related market risk, settlement risk or other risk exposure. This could include information about the nature of any limits or restrictions and their effect on the company's ability to use or to access those assets to fund its business operations.

Transparent financial reporting that conveys a complete and understandable picture of a company's financial position reduces uncertainty in our markets. Surprises to investors can be reduced or avoided when a company provides clear and understandable information about known trends, events, demands, commitments and uncertainties, particularly where they are reasonably likely to have a current or future material impact on that company. The economic environment is not static. Circumstances and risks change and, as a result, disclosure about those circumstances and risks must also evolve. As we stated in the 2003 Interpretive Release, if prior disclosure "does not adequately foreshadow subsequent events, or if new information that impacts known trends and uncertainties becomes apparent . . . additional disclosure should be considered and may be required."[12] This principle is equally applicable in the context of liquidity and capital resources disclosure.

B. Leverage Ratio Disclosures

Where a registrant includes capital or leverage ratio disclosure in its filings with the Commission, and there are no regulatory requirements prescribing the calculation of that ratio, or where a registrant includes capital or leverage ratios that are calculated using a methodology that is modified from its prescribed form, we remind registrants of our long-standing approach to disclosure of financial measures and non-financial measures in MD&A. First, the registrant should determine whether the measure is a financial measure. If the measure is not a financial measure, registrants should refer to the guidance we provided in 2003 for disclosures relating to non-financial measures, such as industry metrics or value metrics.[13] If the measure is a financial measure, the registrant should next determine whether the measure falls within the scope of our requirements for non-GAAP financial measures, and if it is, the registrant would need to follow our rules and guidance governing the inclusion of non-GAAP financial measures in filings with the Commission.[14]

In any event, any ratio or measure included in a filing should be accompanied by a clear explanation of the calculation methodology. The explanation would need to clearly articulate the treatment of any inputs that are unusual, infrequent or non-recurring, or that are otherwise adjusted so that the ratio is calculated differently from directly comparable

---

[12] See 2003 Interpretive Release, *supra* note 3, at 75061, and Management's Discussion and Analysis of Financial Condition and Results of Operations; Certain Investment Company Disclosures, Release No. 33-6835 (May 18, 1989) [54 FR 22427] (the "1989 Interpretive Release"). The 1989 Interpretive Release clarifies that material changes to items disclosed in MD&A in annual reports should be discussed in the quarter in which they occur. The 2003 Interpretive Release states that "there may also be circumstances where an item may not be material in the context of a discussion of annual results of operations but is material in the context of interim results."

[13] See 2003 Interpretive Release, *supra* note 3, at 75060.

[14] See Conditions for Use of Non-GAAP Financial Measures, Release No. 33-8176 (Jan. 22, 2003) [68 FR 4820] and Item 10(e) of Regulation S-K [17 CFR 229.10(e)(5)]. We note that existing rules and guidance governing the inclusion of non-GAAP financial measures in filings with the Commission do not apply to financial measures that are "required to be disclosed by GAAP, Commission rules, or a system of regulation of a government or governmental authority or self-regulatory organization that is applicable to the registrant.

measures. Similar to our guidance for the disclosure of non-financial measures, if the financial measure presented differs from other measures commonly used in the registrant's industry, the registrant would need to consider whether a discussion of those differences or presentation of those measures would be necessary to make the disclosures not misleading. Finally, a registrant would need to consider its reasons for presenting the particular financial measure, and should include disclosure clearly stating why the measure is useful to understanding its financial condition. Where the ratio is being presented in connection with disclosure on debt instruments and related covenants, registrants should also consult our past guidance on disclosure of debt instruments, guarantees and related covenants.[15]

C. Contractual Obligations Table Disclosures

As an aid to understanding other liquidity and capital resources disclosures in MD&A, the contractual obligations tabular disclosure should be prepared with the goal of presenting a meaningful snapshot of cash requirements arising from contractual payment obligations. The Commission's staff has observed that divergent practices have developed in connection with the contractual obligations table disclosure, with registrants drawing different conclusions about the information to be included and the manner of presentation. The requirement itself permits flexibility so that the presentation can reflect company-specific information in a way that is suitable to a registrant's business. Accordingly, registrants are encouraged to develop a presentation method that is clear, understandable and appropriately reflects the categories of obligations that are meaningful in light of its capital structure and business. Registrants should highlight any changes in presentation that are made, so that investors are able to use the information to make comparisons from period to period.

Since the adoption of Item 303(a)(5), registrants and industry groups have raised questions to our staff about how to treat a number of items under the contractual obligations requirement, including: interest payments, repurchase agreements, tax liabilities, synthetic leases, and obligations that arise under off-balance sheet arrangements. In addition, a variety of questions has been raised with our staff in the context of purchase obligations. Because the questions that arise tend to be fact-specific and closely related to a registrant's particular business and circumstances, we have not issued general guidance as to how to treat these items or other questions regarding the presentation of the contractual obligations table. The purpose of the contractual obligations table is to provide aggregated information about contractual obligations and contingent liabilities and commitments in a single location so as to improve transparency of a registrant's short-term and long-term liquidity and capital resources needs and to provide context for investors to assess the relative role of off-balance sheet arrangements;[16] registrants should prepare the disclosure consistent with that objective. Uncertainties about what to include or how to allocate amounts over the periods required in the table should be resolved consistent with the purpose of the disclosure. To that end, footnotes should be used to provide information necessary for an understanding of the timing and amount of the specified contractual obligations, as indicated in the instructions contained in Item 303(a)(5)(i), or, where necessary to promote understanding of the tabular data, additional narrative discussion outside of the table should be considered. Registrants should determine how best to present the information that is relevant to their own business in a manner that is clear, consistent with the purpose of the disclosure and not misleading, and should provide additional disclosure where necessary to explain what the tabular data includes and does not include.[17]

---

[15] *See* 2003 Interpretive Release, *supra* note 3, at 75064.

[16] *See* OBS Adopting Release, *supra* note 4, at 5990.

[17] As an example, if useful to a clear understanding of the information presented, a registrant might consider separating amounts in the table into those that are reflected on the balance sheet and those arising from off-balance sheet arrangements, particularly where such a distinction helps to tie the information to financial statement disclosure and other MD&A discussion.

III. CODIFICATION UPDATE

The "Codification of Financial Reporting Policies" announced in Financial Reporting Release 1 (April 15, 1982) [47 FR 21028] is updated by adding new Section 501.03.a.i, captioned "Additional Guidance on Presentation of Liquidity and Capital Resources Disclosures" to the Financial Reporting Codification and under that caption including the text in Section II of this release.

The Codification is a separate publication of the Commission. It will not be published in the Federal Register/Code of Federal Regulations.

List of Subjects

17 CFR Part 211, 231 and 241

Securities.

Amendments to the Code of Federal Regulations.

For the reasons set forth above, the Commission is amending title 17, chapter II of the Code of Federal Regulations as set forth below:

PART 211 — INTERPRETATIONS RELATING TO FINANCIAL REPORTING MATTERS

1. Part 211, Subpart A, is amended by adding Release No. FR-83 and the release date of September 17, 2010 to the list of interpretive releases.

PART 231 — INTERPRETATIVE RELEASES RELATING TO THE SECURITIES ACT OF 1933 AND GENERAL RULES AND REGULATIONS THEREUNDER

2. Part 231 is amended by adding Release No. 33-9144 and the release date of September 17, 2010 to the list of interpretive releases.

PART 241 — INTERPRETATIVE RELEASES RELATING TO THE SECURITIES EXCHANGE ACT OF 1934 AND GENERAL RULES AND REGULATIONS THEREUNDER

3. Part 241 is amended by adding Release No. 34-62934 and the release date of September 17, 2010 to the list of interpretive releases.

By the Commission.

Elizabeth M. Murphy
Secretary

Dated: September 17, 2010

APPENDIX 2

Facilitating Shareholder Director Nominations

[Corrected to Conform to Federal Register Version]

SECURITIES AND EXCHANGE COMMISSION

17 CFR PARTS 200, 232, 240 and 249

[Release Nos. 33-9259; 34-65343; IC-29788; File No. S7-10-09]

RIN 3235-AK27

FACILITATING SHAREHOLDER DIRECTOR NOMINATIONS

AGENCY: Securities and Exchange Commission.

ACTION: Final rule; notice of effective date.

SUMMARY: This release provides notice of the effective date of the amendment to Exchange Act Rule 14a-8, the shareholder proposal rule, which will require companies to include in their proxy materials, under certain circumstances, shareholder proposals that seek to establish a procedure in the company's governing documents for the inclusion of one or more shareholder director nominees in the company's proxy materials. This release also provides notice of the effective date of related rule changes adopted concurrently with the amendment to Rule 14a-8.

DATES: The effective date of the additions of § 200.82a, § 240.14a-18, § 240.14n-1 through § 240.14n-3, and § 240.14n-101, and the amendments to § 232.13, § 240.13a-11, § 240.13d-1, § 240.14a-2, § 240.14a-4, § 240.14a-5, § 240.14a-6, § 240.14a-8, § 240.14a-9, § 240.14a-12, § 240.15d-11, § 240.13d-102, § 240.14a-101, and § 249.308, published on September 16, 2010 (75 FR 56668), is September 20, 2011. Section 240.14a-11 was vacated by the United States Court of Appeals for the District of Columbia Circuit (No. 10-1305, July 22, 2011) and therefore is not effective.

FOR FURTHER INFORMATION CONTACT: Tamara Brightwell, Lillian Brown, or Ted Yu, Division of Corporation Finance, at (202) 551-3200, U.S. Securities and Exchange Commission, 100 F Street, NE, Washington DC 20549.

SUPPLEMENTARY INFORMATION: By order dated October 4, 2010 (Release No. 33-9149, 34-63031, IC-29456), the Securities and Exchange Commission stayed from November 15, 2010 until the resolution of the petition for review of Exchange Act Rule 14a-11 in *Business Roundtable et al. v. Securities and Exchange Commission*, No. 10-1305 (D.C. Cir., filed Sept. 29, 2010), the effective and compliance dates of amendments to the federal proxy and related rules that the Commission adopted to facilitate the effective exercise of shareholders' traditional state law rights to nominate and elect directors to company boards of directors. On October 20, 2010, a notice of the stay was published in the Federal Register (75 FR 64641). That announcement stated that a notice of the effective and compliance dates of the final rules would be published in the Federal Register following the resolution of the petition for review. On July 22, 2011, the United States Court of Appeals for the District of Columbia Circuit issued an order vacating Rule 14a-11 and on September 14, 2011, the Court issued its mandate. Because the mandate concludes the litigation in the Court of Appeals, the stay expired by its terms. The Court's order did not affect the amendment to Rule 14a-8, which was not challenged in the litigation, or the related rules and amendments adopted concurrently with Rule 14a-11 and the amendment to Rule 14a-8. Accordingly, those rules and amendments are effective upon publication of this notice in the Federal Register.

As discussed in the preamble above, the final rules noted in the DATES section of this document and published on September 16, 2010 (75 FR 56668) amending Title 17, Chapter II of the Code of Federal Regulations, are effective September 20, 2011, with the exception, as noted, of Rule 14a-11 (17 CFR 240.14a-11).

Elizabeth M. Murphy
Secretary

September 15, 2011

Facilitating Shareholder Director Nominations

[Corrected—conforming to non-substantive changes in Federal Register version]

SECURITIES AND EXCHANGE COMMISSION

17 CFR PARTS 200, 232, 240 and 249

[Release Nos. 33-9136; 34-62764; IC-29384; File No. S7-10-09] RIN 3235-AK27

FACILITATING SHAREHOLDER DIRECTOR NOMINATIONS

AGENCY: Securities and Exchange Commission.

ACTION: Final rule.

SUMMARY: We are adopting changes to the federal proxy rules to facilitate the effective exercise of shareholders' traditional state law rights to nominate and elect directors to company boards of directors. The new rules will require, under certain circumstances, a company's proxy materials to provide shareholders with information about, and the ability to vote for, a shareholder's, or group of shareholders', nominees for director. We believe that these rules will benefit shareholders by improving corporate suffrage, the disclosure provided in connection with corporate proxy solicitations, and communication between shareholders in the proxy process. The new rules apply only where, among other things, relevant state or foreign law does not prohibit shareholders from nominating directors. The new rules will require that specified disclosures be made concerning nominating shareholders or groups and their nominees. In addition, the new rules provide that companies must include in their proxy materials, under certain circumstances, shareholder proposals that seek to establish a procedure in the company's governing documents for the inclusion of one or more shareholder director nominees in the company's proxy materials. We also are adopting related changes to certain of our other rules and regulations, including the existing solicitation exemptions from our proxy rules and the beneficial ownership reporting requirements.

DATES: Effective Date: November 15, 2010

Compliance Dates: November 15, 2010, except that companies that qualify as "smaller reporting companies" (as defined in § 17 CFR 240.12b-2) as of the effective date of the rule amendments will not be subject to Rule 14a-11 until three years after the effective date.

FOR FURTHER INFORMATION CONTACT: Lillian Brown, Tamara Brightwell, or Ted Yu, Division of Corporation Finance, at (202) 551-3200, or, with regard to investment companies, Kieran G. Brown, Division of Investment Management, at (202) 551-6784, U.S. Securities and Exchange Commission, 100 F Street, NE, Washington, DC 20549.

SUPPLEMENTARY INFORMATION: We are adding new Rule 82a of Part 200 Subpart D—Information and Requests,[1] and new Rules 14a-11,[2] and 14a-18,[3] and new Regulation 14N[4] and Schedule 14N,[5] and amending Rule 13[6] of Regulation S-T,[7] Rules 13a-11,[8]

---

[1] 17 CFR 200.82a.
[2] 17 CFR 240.14a-11.
[3] 17 CFR 240.14a-18.
[4] 17 CFR 240.14n *et seq.*

[5] 17 CFR 240.14n-101.
[6] 17 CFR 232.13.
[7] 17 CFR 232.10 *et seq.*
[8] 17 CFR 240.13a-11.

13d-1,[9] 14a-2,[10] 14a-4,[11] 14a-5,[12] 14a-6,[13] 14a-8,[14] 14a-9,[15] 14a-12,[16] and 15d-11,[17] Schedule 13G,[18] Schedule 14A,[19] and Form 8-K,[20] under the Securities Exchange Act of 1934.[21] Although we are not amending Schedule 14C[22] under the Exchange Act, the amendments will affect the disclosure provided in Schedule 14C, as Schedule 14C requires disclosure of some items contained in Schedule 14A.

Table of Contents

---

[9] 17 CFR 240.13d-1.
[10] 17 CFR 240.14a-2.
[11] 17 CFR 240.14a-4.
[12] 17 CFR 240.14a-5.
[13] 17 CFR 240.14a-6.
[14] 17 CFR 240.14a-8.
[15] 17 CFR 240.14a-9.
[16] 17 CFR 240.14a-12.
[17] 17 CFR 240.15d-11.

[18] 17 CFR 240.13d-102.
[19] 17 CFR 240.14a-101.
[20] 17 CFR 249.308.
[21] 15 U.S.C. 78a *et seq.* (the "Exchange Act"). Part 200 Subpart D—Information and Requests and Regulation S-T are also promulgated under the Securities Act of 1933 [15 U.S.C. 77a *et seq.*] (the "Securities Act").
[22] 17 CFR 240.14c-101.

I. BACKGROUND AND OVERVIEW OF AMENDMENTS

A. Background

On June 10, 2009, we proposed a number of changes to the federal proxy rules designed to facilitate shareholders' traditional state law rights to nominate and elect directors. Our proposals sought to accomplish this goal in two ways: (1) by facilitating the ability of shareholders with a significant, long-term stake in a company to exercise their rights to nominate and elect directors by establishing a minimum standard for including disclosure concerning, and enabling shareholders to vote for, shareholder director nominees in company proxy materials; and (2) by narrowing the scope of the Commission rule that permitted companies to exclude shareholder proposals that sought to establish a procedure for the inclusion of shareholder nominees in company proxy materials.[23] We recognized at that time that the financial crisis that the nation and

---

[23] *See Facilitating Shareholder Director Nominations*, Release No. 33-9046, 34-60089 (June 10, 2009) [74 FR 29024] ("Proposal" or "Proposing Release"). The Proposing Release was published for comment in the Federal Register on June 18, 2009, and the initial comment period closed on August 17, 2009. The Commission re-opened the comment period as of December 18, 2009 for thirty days to provide interested persons the opportunity to comment on additional data and related analyses that were included in the public comment file at or following the close of the original comment period. In total, the Commission received approximately 600 comment letters on the proposal. The public comments we received are available on our website *at* http://www.sec.gov/comments/s7-10-09/ s71009.shtml. Comments also are available for website viewing and copying in the Commission's Public Reference Room, 100 F Street, NE, Washington, DC 20549, on official business days between the hours of 10:00 a.m. and 3:00 p.m.

markets had experienced heightened the serious concerns of many shareholders about the accountability and responsiveness of some companies and boards of directors to shareholder interests, and that these concerns had resulted in a loss of investor confidence. These concerns also led to questions about whether boards were exercising appropriate oversight of management, whether boards were appropriately focused on shareholder interests, and whether boards need to be more accountable for their decisions regarding issues such as compensation structures and risk management.

A principal way that shareholders can hold boards accountable and influence matters of corporate policy is through the nomination and election of directors. The ability of shareholders to effectively use their power to nominate and elect directors is significantly affected by our proxy regulations because, as has long been recognized, a federally-regulated corporate proxy solicitation is the primary way for public company shareholders to learn about the matters to be decided by the shareholders and to make their views known to company management.[24] As discussed in detail below, in light of these concerns, we reviewed our proxy regulations to determine whether they should be revised to facilitate shareholders' ability to nominate and elect directors. We have taken into consideration the comments received on the proposed amendments as well as subsequent congressional action[25] and are adopting final rules that will, for the first time, require company proxy materials, under certain circumstances, to provide shareholders with information about, and the ability to vote for a shareholder's, or group of shareholders', nominees for director. We also are amending our proxy rules to provide shareholders the ability to include in company proxy materials, under certain circumstances, shareholder proposals that seek to establish a procedure in the company's governing documents for the inclusion of one or more shareholder director nominees in the company's proxy materials.

Regulation of the proxy process was one of the original responsibilities that Congress assigned to the Commission as part of its core functions in 1934. The Commission has actively monitored the proxy process since receiving this authority and has considered changes when it appeared that the process was not functioning in a manner that adequately protected the interests of investors.[26] One of the key tenets of the federal proxy

---

[24] *See, e.g.,* Securit[ies] and Exchange Commission Proxy Rules: Hearings on H.R. 1493, H.R. 1821, and H.R. 2019 Before the House Comm. on Interstate and Foreign Commerce, 78th Cong., 1st Sess., at 17-19 (1943) (Statement of the Honorable Ganson Purcell, Chairman, Securities and Exchange Commission) (explaining the initial Commission rules requiring the inclusion of shareholder proposals in company proxy materials: "We give [a stockholder] the right in the rules to put his proposal before all of his fellow stockholders along with all other proposals . . . so that they can see then what they are and vote accordingly. . . . The rights that we are endeavoring to assure to the stockholders are those rights that he has traditionally had under State law, to appear at the meeting; to make a proposal; to speak on that proposal at appropriate length; and to have his proposal voted on. But those rights have been rendered largely meaningless through the process of dispersion of security ownership through[out] the country. . . . [T] he assurance of these fundamental rights under State laws which have been, as I say, completely ineffective . . . because of the very dispersion of the stockholders' interests throughout the country[;] whereas formerly . . . a stockholder might appear at the meeting and address his fellow stockholders[, t]oday he can only address the assembled proxies which are lying at the head of the table. The only opportunity that the stockholder has today of expressing his judgment

comes at the time he considers the execution of his proxy form, and we believe . . . that this is the time when he should have the full information before him and ability to take action as he sees fit."); *see also* S. Rep. 792, 73d Cong., 2d Sess., 12 (1934) ("[I]t is essential that [the stockholder] be enlightened not only as to the financial condition of the corporation, but also as to the major questions of policy, which are decided at stockholders' meetings.").

[25] Dodd-Frank Wall Street Reform and Consumer Protection Act, Pub. L. No. 111-203, §971, 124 Stat. 1376 (2010) ("Dodd-Frank Act").

[26] For example, the Commission has considered changes to the proxy rules related to the election of directors in recent years. *See Security Holder Director Nominations,* Release No. 34-48626 (October 14, 2003) [68 FR 60784] ("2003 Proposal"); *Shareholder Proposals,* Release No. 34-56160 (July 27, 2007) [72 FR 43466] ("Shareholder Proposals Proposing Release"); *Shareholder Proposals Relating to the Election of Directors,* Release No. 34-56161 (July 27, 2007) [72 FR 43488] ("Election of Directors Proposing Release"); and *Shareholder Proposals Relating to the Election of Directors,* Release No. 34-56914 (December 6, 2007) [72 FR 70450] ("Election of Directors Adopting Release"). When we refer to the "2007 Proposals" and the comments received in 2007, we are referring to the Shareholder Proposals Proposing Release and the Election of Directors Proposing

rules on which the Commission has consistently focused is whether the proxy process functions, as nearly as possible, as a replacement for an actual in-person meeting of shareholders.[27] This is important because the proxy process represents shareholders' principal means of participating effectively at an annual or special meeting of shareholders.[28] In our Proposal we noted our concern that the federal proxy rules may not be facilitating the exercise of shareholders' state law rights to nominate and elect directors. Without the ability to effectively utilize the proxy process, shareholder nominees do not have a realistic prospect of being elected because most, if not all, shareholders return their proxy cards in advance of the shareholder meeting and thus, in essence, cast their votes before the meeting at which they may nominate directors. Recognizing that this failure of the proxy process to facilitate shareholder nomination rights has a practical effect on the right to elect directors, the new rules will enable the proxy process to more closely approximate the conditions of the shareholder meeting. In addition, because companies will be required to include shareholder-nominated candidates for director in company proxy materials, shareholders will receive additional information upon which to base their voting decisions. Finally, we believe these changes will significantly enhance the confidence of shareholders who link the recent financial crisis to a lack of responsiveness of some boards to shareholder interests.[29]

The Commission has, on a number of prior occasions, considered whether its proxy rules needed to be amended to facilitate shareholders' ability to nominate directors by having their nominees included in company proxy materials.[30] Most recently, in June 2009, we proposed amendments to the proxy rules that included both a new proxy rule, Exchange Act Rule 14a-11, that would require a company's proxy materials to provide shareholders with information about, and the ability to vote for, candidates for director nominated by long-term shareholders or groups of long-term shareholders with significant holdings, and amendments to Rule 14a-8(i)(8) to prohibit exclusion of certain shareholder proposals seeking to establish a procedure in the company's governing documents for the inclusion of one or more shareholder director nominees in the company's proxy materials. We received significant comment on the proposed amendments. Overall, commenters were sharply divided on the necessity for, and the workability of, the proposed amendments. Supporters of the amendments generally believed that, if adopted, they would facilitate shareholders' ability to exercise their state law right to nominate directors and provide meaningful opportunities to effect changes in the

---

(Footnote Continued)

Release and the comments received on those proposals, unless otherwise specified.

[27] Professor Karmel has described the Commission's proxy rules as having the purpose "to make the proxy device the closest practicable substitute for attendance at the [shareholder] meeting." Roberta S. Karmel, *The New Shareholder and Corporate Governance: Voting Power Without Responsibility or Risk: How Should Proxy Reform Address the De-Coupling of Economic and Voting Rights?*, 55 Vill. L. Rev. 93, 104 (2010).

[28] Historically, a shareholder's voting rights generally were exercised at a shareholder meeting. As discussed in the Proposing Release, in passing the Exchange Act, Congress understood that the securities of many companies were held through dispersed ownership, at least in part facilitated by stock exchange listing of shares. Although voting rights in public companies technically continued to be exercised at a meeting, the votes cast at the meeting were by proxy and the voting decision was made during the proxy solicitation process. This structure continues to this day.

[29] *See* letters from American Federation of Labor and Congress of Industrial Organizations ("AFL-CIO");

California Public Employees' Retirement System ("CalPERS"); Council of Institutional Investors ("CII"); Lynne L. Dallas ("L. Dallas"); Los Angeles County Employees Retirement Association ("LACERA"); Laborers' International Union of North America ("LIUNA"); The Nathan Cummings Foundation ("Nathan Cummings Foundation"); Pax World Management Corp. ("Pax World"); Pershing Square Capital Management, L.P. ("Pershing Square"); Relational Investors, LLC ("Relational"); RiskMetrics Group, Inc. ("RiskMetrics"); Shareowner Education Network and Shareowners.org ("Shareowners.org"); Social Investment Forum ("Social Investment Forum"); State of Wisconsin Investment Board ("SWIB"); International Brotherhood of Teamsters ("Teamsters"); Trillium Asset Management Corporation ("Trillium"); Universities Superannuation Scheme—UK ("Universities Superannuation"); Washington State Investment Board ("WSIB").

[30] For a discussion of the Commission's previous actions in this area, *see* the Proposing Release and the 2003 Proposal.

composition of the board.[31] These commenters predicted that the amendments would lead to more accountable, responsive, and effective boards.[32] Many commenters saw a link between the recent economic crisis and shareholders' inability to have nominees included in a company's proxy materials.[33]

Commenters opposed to our Proposal believed that recent corporate governance developments, including increased use of a majority voting standard for the election of directors and certain state law changes, already provide shareholders with meaningful opportunities to participate in director elections.[34] These commenters viewed the amendments as inappropriately intruding into matters traditionally governed by state law or imposing a "one size fits all" rule for all companies and expressed concerns about "special interest" directors, forcing companies to focus on the short-term rather than the creation of long-term shareholder value, and other perceived negative effects of the amendments, if adopted, on boards and companies.[35]

---

[31] *See* letters from CII; Colorado Public Employees' Retirement Association ("COPERA"); CtW Investment Group ("CtW Investment Group"); L. Dallas; Thomas P. DiNapoli ("T. DiNapoli"); Florida State Board of Administration ("Florida State Board of Administration"); International Corporate Governance Network ("ICGN"); Denise L. Nappier ("D. Nappier"); Ohio Public Employees Retirement System ("OPERS"); Pax World; Teamsters.

[32] *Id.*

[33] *See* letters from AFL-CIO; CalPERS; California State Teachers' Retirement System ("CalSTRS"); CII; L. Dallas; LACERA; LIUNA; Nathan Cummings Foundation; Pax World; Pershing Square; Relational; RiskMetrics; Shareowners.org; Social Investment Forum; SWIB; Teamsters; Trillium; Universities Superannuation; WSIB.

[34] *See* letters from Group of 26 Corporate Secretaries and Governance Professionals ("26 Corporate Secretaries"); 3M Company ("3M"); Advance Auto Parts, Inc. ("Advance Auto Parts"); The Allstate Group, Inc. ("Allstate"); Avis Budget Group, Inc. ("Avis Budget"); American Express Company ("American Express"); Anadarko Petroleum Corporation ("Anadarko"); Association of Corporate Counsel ("Association of Corporate Counsel"); AT&T Inc. ("AT&T"); Lawrence Behr ("L. Behr"); Best Buy Co., Inc. ("Best Buy"); The Boeing Company ("Boeing"); Business Roundtable ("BRT"); Robert N. Burt ("R.Burt"); State Bar of California, Corporations Committee of Business Law Section ("California Bar"); Sean F. Campbell ("S. Campbell"); Carlson ("Carlson"); Caterpillar Inc. ("Caterpillar"); U.S. Chamber of Commerce Center for Capital Markets Competitiveness ("Chamber of Commerce/CMCC"); Chevron Corporation ("Chevron"); CIGNA Corporation ("CIGNA"); W. Don Cornwell ("W. Cornwell"); CSX Corporation ("CSX"); Cummins Inc. ("Cummins"); Davis Polk & Wardwell LLP ("Davis Polk"); Dewey & LeBoeuf ("Dewey"); E.I. du Pont de Nemours and Company ("DuPont"); Eaton Corporation ("Eaton"); Michael Eng ("M. Eng"); FedEx Corporation ("FedEx"); FMC Corporation ("FMC Corp."); FPL Group, Inc. ("FPL Group"); Frontier Communications Corporation ("Frontier"); General Electric Company ("GE"); General Mills, Inc. ("General Mills"); Charles O. Holliday, Jr. ("C. Holliday"); Honeywell International Inc. ("Honeywell"); Constance J. Horner ("C. Horner"); International

Business Machines Corporation ("IBM"); Jones Day ("Jones Day"); Keating Muething & Klekamp PLL ("Keating Muething"); James M. Kilts ("J. Kilts"); Reatha Clark King, Ph.D. ("R. Clark King"); Ned C. Lautenbach ("N. Lautenbach"); MeadWestvaco Corporation ("MeadWestvaco"); MetLife, Inc. ("MetLife"); Motorola, Inc. ("Motorola"); O'Melveny & Myers LLP ("O'Melveny & Myers"); Office Depot, Inc. ("Office Depot"); Pfizer Inc. ("Pfizer"); Protective Life Corporation ("Protective"); Sullivan & Cromwell LLP ("S&C"); Safeway Inc. ("Safeway"); Sara Lee Corporation ("Sara Lee"); Shearman & Sterling LLP ("Shearman & Sterling"); The Sherwin-Williams Company ("Sherwin-Williams"); Sidley Austin LLP ("Sidley Austin"); Simpson Thacher & Bartlett LLP ("Simpson Thacher"); Tesoro Corporation ("Tesoro"); Textron Inc. ("Textron"); Texas Instruments Corporation ("TI"); Gary L. Tooker ("G. Tooker"); UnitedHealth Group Incorporated ("UnitedHealth"); Unitrin, Inc. ("Unitrin"); U.S. Bancorp ("U.S. Bancorp"); Wachtell, Lipton, Rosen & Katz ("Wachtell"); Wells Fargo & Company ("Wells Fargo"); West Chicago Chamber of Commerce & Industry ("West Chicago Chamber"); Weyerhaeuser Company ("Weyerhaeuser"); Xerox Corporation ("Xerox"); Yahoo! ("Yahoo").

[35] *See* letters from 26 Corporate Secretaries; American Bar Association ("ABA"); ACE Limited ("ACE"); Advance Auto Parts; AGL Resources ("AGL"); Aetna Inc. ("Aetna"); Allstate; Alston & Bird LLP ("Alston & Bird"); American Bankers Association ("American Bankers Association"); The American Business Conference ("American Business Conference"); American Electric Power Company, Inc. ("American Electric Power"); Anadarko; Applied Materials, Inc. ("Applied Materials"); Artistic Land Designs LLC ("Artistic Land Designs"); Association of Corporate Counsel; Avis Budget; Atlantic Bingo Supply, Inc. ("Atlantic Bingo"); L. Behr; Best Buy; Biogen Idec Inc. ("Biogen"); James H. Blanchard ("J. Blanchard"); Boeing; Tammy Bonkowski ("T. Bonkowski"); BorgWarner Inc. ("BorgWarner"); Boston Scientific Corporation ("Boston Scientific"); The Brink's Company ("Brink's"); BRT; Burlington Northern Santa Fe Corporation ("Burlington Northern"); R. Burt; California Bar; Callaway Golf Company ("Callaway"); S. Campbell; Carlson; Carolina Mills ("Carolina Mills"); Caterpillar; Chamber of Commerce/CMCC; Chevron; Rebecca Chicko ("R.

Finally, commenters worried about the impact of the proposed amendments on small businesses.[36]

After considering the comments and weighing the competing interests of facilitating shareholders' ability to exercise their state law rights to nominate and elect directors against potential disruption and cost to companies, we are convinced that adopting the proposed amendments to the proxy rules serves our purpose to regulate the proxy process

---

(Footnote Continued)

Chicko"); CIGNA; Comcast Corporation ("Comcast"); Competitive Enterprise Institute's Center for Investors and Entrepreneurs ("Competitive Enterprise Institute"); W. Cornwell; CSX; Edwin Culwell ("E. Culwell"); Cummins; Darden Restaurants, Inc. ("Darden Restaurants"); Daniels Manufacturing Corporation ("Daniels Manufacturing"); Davis Polk; Delaware State Bar Association ("Delaware Bar"); Tom Dermody ("T. Dermody"); Devon Energy Corporation ("Devon"); DTE Energy Company ("DTE Energy"); Eaton; The Edison Electric Institute ("Edison Electric Institute"); Eli Lilly and Company ("Eli Lilly"); Emerson Electric Co. ("Emerson Electric"); M. Eng; Erickson Retirement Communities, LLC ("Erickson"); ExxonMobil Corporation ("ExxonMobil"); FedEx; Financial Services Roundtable ("Financial Services Roundtable"); Flutterby Kissed Unique Treasures ("Flutterby"); FPL Group; Frontier; GE; Allen C. Goolsby ("A. Goolsby"); C.Holliday; IBM; Investment Company Institute ("ICI"); Intelect Corporation ("Intelect"); JPMorgan Chase & Co. ("JPMorgan Chase"); Jones Day; R. Clark King; Leggett & Platt Incorporated ("Leggett"); Teresa Liddell ("T. Liddell"); Little Diversified Architectural Consulting ("Little"); McDonald's Corporation ("McDonald's"); MeadWestvaco; MedFaxx, Inc. ("MedFaxx"); Medical Insurance Services ("Medical Insurance"); MetLife; Mary S. Metz ("M. Metz"); Microsoft Corporation ("Microsoft"); John R. Miller ("J. Miller"); Marcelo Moretti ("M. Moretti"); Motorola; National Association of Corporate Directors ("NACD"); National Association of Manufacturers ("NAM"); National Investor Relations Institute ("NIRI"); O'Melveny & Myers; Office Depot; Omaha Door & Window ("Omaha Door"); The Procter & Gamble Company ("P&G"); PepsiCo, Inc. ("PepsiCo"); Pfizer; Realogy Corporation ("Realogy"); Jared Robert ("J. Robert"); Marissa Robert ("M. Robert"); RPM International Inc. ("RPM"); Ryder System, Inc. ("Ryder"); Safeway; Ralph S. Saul ("R. Saul"); Shearman & Sterling; Sherwin-Williams; Raymond F. Simoneau ("R. Simoneau"); Society of Corporate Secretaries and Governance Professionals, Inc. ("Society of Corporate Secretaries"); The Southern Company ("Southern Company"); Southland Properties, Inc. ("Southland"); The Steele Group ("Steele Group"); Style Crest Enterprises, Inc. ("Style Crest"); Tesoro; Textron; Theragenics Corporation ("Theragenics"); TI; Richard Trummel ("R. Trummel"); Terry Trummel ("T. Trummel"); Viola Trummel ("V. Trummel"); tw telecom inc. ("tw telecom"); Laura D'Andrea Tyson ("L. Tyson"); United Brotherhood of Carpenters and Joiners of America ("United Brotherhood of Carpenters"); UnitedHealth; U.S. Bancorp; VCG Holding Corporation ("VCG");

Wachtell; The Way to Wellness ("Wellness"); Wells Fargo; Whirlpool Corporation ("Whirlpool"); Xerox; Yahoo; Jeff Young ("J. Young").

[36] See letters from ABA; American Mailing Service ("American Mailing"); All Cast, Inc. ("All Cast"); Always N Bloom ("Always N Bloom"); American Carpets ("American Carpets"); John Arquilla ("J. Arquilla"); Beth Armburst ("B. Armburst"); Artistic Land Designs; Charles Atkins ("C. Atkins"); Book Celler ("Book Celler"); Kathleen G. Bostwick ("K. Bostwick"); Brighter Day Painting ("Brighter Day Painting"); Colletti and Associates ("Colletti"); Commercial Concepts ("Commercial Concepts"); Complete Home Inspection ("Complete Home Inspection"); Debbie Courtney ("D. Courtney"); Sue Crawford ("S. Crawford"); Crespin's Cleaning, Inc. ("Crespin"); Don's Tractor Repair ("Don's"); Theresa Ebreo ("T. Ebreo"); M. Eng; eWareness, Inc. ("eWareness"); Evans Real Estate Investments, LLC ("Evans"); Fluharty Antiques ("Fluharty"); Flutterby; Fortuna Italian Restaurant & Pizza ("Fortuna Italian Restaurant"); Future Form Inc. ("Future Form Inc."); Glaspell Goals ("Glaspell"); Cheryl Gregory ("C. Gregory"); Healthcare Practice Management, Inc. (Healthcare Practice"); Brian Henderson ("B. Henderson"); Sheri Henning ("S. Henning"); Jaynee Herren ("J. Herren"); Ami Iriarte ("A. Iriarte"); Jeremy J. Jones ("J. Jones"); Juz Kidz Nursery and Preschool ("Juz Kidz"); Kernan Chiropractic Center ("Kernan"); LMS Wine Creators ("LMS Wine"); Tabitha Luna ("T. Luna"); Mansfield Children's Center, Inc. ("Mansfield Children's Center"); Denise McDonald ("D. McDonald"); Meister's Landscaping ("Meister"); Merchants Terminal Corporation ("Merchants Terminal"); Middendorf Bros. Auctioneers and Real Estate ("Middendorf"); Mingo Custom Woods ("Mingo"); Moore Brothers Auto Truck Repair ("Moore Brothers"); Mouton's Salon ("Mouton"); Doug Mozack ("D. Mozack"); Ms. Dee's Lil Darlins Daycare ("Ms. Dee"); Gavin Napolitano ("G. Napolitano"); NK Enterprises ("NK"); Hugh S. Olson ("H. Olson"); Parts and Equipment Supply Co. ("PESC"); Pioneer Heating & Air Conditioning ("Pioneer Heating & Air Conditioning"); RC Furniture Restoration ("RC"); RTW Enterprises Inc. ("RTW"); Debbie Sapp ("D. Sapp"); Southwest Business Brokers ("SBB"); Security Guard IT&T Alarms, Inc. ("SGIA"); Peggy Sicilia ("P. Sicilia"); Slycers Sandwich Shop ("Slycers"); Southern Services ("Southern Services"); Steele Group; Sylvron Travels ("Sylvron"); Theragenics; Erin White Tremaine ("E. Tremaine"); Wagner Health Center ("Wagner"); Wagner Industries ("Wagner Industries"); Wellness; West End Auto Paint & Body ("West End"); Y.M. Inc. ("Y.M."); J. Young.

in the public interest and on behalf of investors. We are not persuaded by the arguments of some commenters that the provisions of Rule 14a-11 are unnecessary.[37] Those commenters argued that changes in corporate governance over the past six years have obviated the need for a federal rule to allow shareholders to place their nominees in company proxy materials and that shareholders should be left to determine whether, on a company-by-company basis, such a rule is necessary at any particular company.

While we recognize that some states, such as Delaware,[38] have amended their state corporate law to enable companies to adopt procedures for the inclusion of shareholder director nominees in company proxy materials,[39] as was highlighted by a number of commenters, other states have not.[40] These commenters noted that, as a result, companies not incorporated in Delaware could frustrate shareholder efforts to establish procedures for shareholders to place board nominees in the company's proxy materials by litigating the validity of a shareholder proposal establishing such procedures, or possibly repealing shareholder-adopted bylaws establishing such procedures. In addition, due to the difficulty that shareholders could have in establishing such procedures, we believe that it would be inappropriate to rely solely on an enabling approach to facilitate shareholders' ability to exercise their state law rights to nominate and elect directors. Even if bylaw amendments to permit shareholders to include nominees in company proxy materials were permissible in every state, shareholder proposals to so amend company bylaws could face significant obstacles.

We also considered whether the move by many companies away from plurality voting to a general policy of majority voting in uncontested director elections should lead to a conclusion that our actions are unnecessary or whether we should premise our actions on the failure of a company to adopt majority voting.[41] We agree with

---

[37] See, e.g., letters from 26 Corporate Secretaries; 3M; Advance Auto Parts; Allstate; Avis Budget; American Express; Anadarko; Association of Corporate Counsel; AT&T; L. Behr; Best Buy; Boeing; BRT; R. Burt; California Bar; S. Campbell; Carlson; Caterpillar; Chamber of Commerce/CMCC; Chevron; CIGNA; W. Cornwell; CSX; Cummins; Davis Polk; Dewey; DuPont; Eaton; M. Eng; FedEx; FMC Corp.; FPL Group; Frontier; GE; General Mills; Joseph A. Grundfest, Stanford Law School (July 24, 2009) ("Grundfest"); C. Holliday; Honeywell; C. Horner; IBM; Jones Day; Keating Muething; J. Kilts; R. Clark King; N. Lautenbach; MeadWestvaco; Metlife; Motorola; O'Melveny & Myers; Office Depot; Pfizer; Protective; S&C; Safeway; Sara Lee; Shearman & Sterling; Sherwin-Williams; Sidley Austin; Simpson Thacher; Tesoro; Textron; TI; G. Tooker; UnitedHealth; Unitrin; U.S. Bancorp; Wachtell; Wells Fargo; West Chicago Chamber; Weyerhaeuser; Xerox; Yahoo.

[38] We refer to Delaware law frequently because of the large percentage of public companies incorporated under that law. The Delaware Division of Corporations reports that over 50% of U.S. public companies are incorporated in Delaware. See http://www.corp.delaware.gov.

[39] Del. Code Ann. tit. 8, § 112. In December 2009, the Committee on Corporate Laws of the American Bar Association Section of Business Law Committee adopted amendments to the Model Act that explicitly authorize bylaws that prescribe shareholder access to company proxy materials or reimbursement of proxy solicitation expenses. See ABA Press Release, "Corporate Laws Committee Adopts New Model Business Corporation Act Amendments to Provide For Proxy

Access And Expense Reimbursement," December 17, 2009, available at http://www.abanet.org/abanet/media/release/news_release.cfm?releaseid=848.

In addition, in 2007, North Dakota amended its corporate code to permit 5% shareholders to provide a company notice of intent to nominate directors and require the company to include each such shareholder nominee in its proxy statement and form of proxy. N.D. Cent. Code § 10-35-08 (2009); see North Dakota Publicly Traded Corporations Act, N.D. Cent. Code §10-35 et al. (2007).

[40] See letters from American Federation of State, County and Municipal Employees ("AFSCME"); AllianceBernstein L.P. ("AllianceBernstein"); Amalgamated Bank LongView Funds ("Amalgamated Bank"); Association of British Insurers ("British Insurers"); CalPERS; CII; The Corporate Library ("Corporate Library"); L. Dallas; Florida State Board of Administration; ICGN; LIUNA; D. Nappier; Paul M. Neuhauser ("P. Neuhauser"); Comment Letter of Nine Securities and Governance Law Firms ("Nine Law Firms"); Pax World; Pershing Square; the RacetotheBottom.org ("RacetotheBottom"); RiskMetrics; Schulte Roth & Zabel LLP ("Schulte Roth & Zabel"); Sodali ("Sodali"); Teachers Insurance and Annuity Association of America and College Retirement Equities Fund ("TIAA-CREF"); United States Proxy Exchange ("USPE"); ValueAct Capital, LLC ("ValueAct Capital").

[41] Despite the rate of adoption of a majority voting standard for director elections by companies in the S&P 500, only a small minority of firms in the Russell 3000 index have adopted them. See discussion in footnote 69 in the Proposing Release.

commenters[42] who argued that a majority voting standard in director elections does not address the need for a rule to facilitate the inclusion of shareholder nominees for director in company proxy materials. While majority voting impacts shareholders' ability to elect candidates put forth by management, it does not affect shareholders' ability to exercise their right to nominate candidates for director.

We also do not believe that the recent amendments to New York Stock Exchange (NYSE) Rule 452, which eliminated brokers' discretionary voting authority in director elections, negate the need for the rule. Certain commenters specifically noted their concurrence with us on this point.[43] The amendments to NYSE Rule 452 address who exercises the right to vote rather than shareholders' ability to have their nominees put forth for a vote. While these and other changes have been important events, they bolster shareholders' ability to elect directors who are already on the company's proxy card, not their ability to affect who appears on that card. We therefore are convinced that the federal proxy rules should be amended to better facilitate the exercise of shareholders' rights under state law to nominate directors.

We also considered whether we should amend Rule 14a-8 to narrow the "election exclusion," without also adopting Rule 14a-11. We note that a significant number of commenters supported the proposed amendments to Rule 14a-8(i)(8).[44] We concluded, however, as certain commenters pointed out, that adopting only the proposed amendments to Rule 14a-8(i)(8), without Rule 14a-11, would not achieve the Commission's stated objectives.[45] We believe that the amendments to Rule 14a-8(i)(8) will provide shareholders with an important mechanism for including in company proxy materials proposals that would address the inclusion of shareholder director nominees in the company's proxy materials in ways that supplement Rule 14a-11, such as with a lower ownership threshold, a shorter holding period, or to allow for a greater number of nominees if shareholders of a company support such standards.

We recognize that many commenters advocated that shareholders' ability to include nominees in company proxy materials should be determined *exclusively* by what individual companies or their shareholders affirmatively choose to provide, or that companies or their shareholders should be able to opt out of Rule 14a-11 or otherwise alter its terms for individual companies (the "private ordering" arguments).[46] After careful consideration of the numerous comments advocating this perspective,[47] we believe that the arguments in favor of this perspective are flawed for several reasons.

---

[42] See letters from AFSCME; AllianceBernstein; CalPERS; CII; L. Dallas; D. Nappier; P. Neuhauser; RiskMetrics; TIAA-CREF. One commenter characterized a majority voting standard as a mechanism for "registering negative sentiment" about an incumbent board nominee, not a mechanism to ensure board accountability. See letter from AFSCME.

[43] See letters from CII; Sodali; USPE.

[44] For a list of these commenters, see footnotes 677, 678, and 679 below.

[45] See letters from CII; USPE.

[46] See letters from 26 Corporate Secretaries; ABA; ACE; Advance Auto Parts; AGL; Aetna; Allstate; Alston & Bird; American Bankers Association; American Business Conference; American Electric Power; Anadarko; Applied Materials; Artistic Land Designs; Association of Corporate Counsel; Avis Budget; Atlantic Bingo; L. Behr; Best Buy; Biogen; J. Blanchard; Boeing; T. Bonkowski; BorgWarner; Boston Scientific; Brink's; BRT; Burlington Northern; R. Burt; California Bar; Callaway; S. Campbell; Carlson; Carolina Mills; Caterpillar; Chamber of Commerce/ CMCC; Chevron; R. Chicko; CIGNA; Comcast; Competitive Enterprise Institute; W. Cornwell; CSX; E. Culwell; Cummins; Darden Restaurants; Daniels Manufacturing; Davis Polk; Delaware Bar; T. Dermody; Devon; DTE Energy; Eaton; Edison Electric Institute; Eli Lilly; Emerson Electric; M. Eng; Erickson; ExxonMobil; FedEx; Financial Services Roundtable; Flutterby; FPL Group; Frontier; GE; A. Goolsby; Grundfest; C. Holliday; IBM; ICI; Intelect; JPMorgan Chase; Jones Day; R. Clark King; Leggett; T. Liddell; Little; McDonald's; MeadWestvaco; MedFaxx; Medical Insurance; Metlife; M. Metz; Microsoft; J. Miller; M. Moretti; Motorola; NACD; NAM; NIRI; O'Melveny & Myers; Office Depot; Omaha Door; P&G; PepsiCo; Pfizer; Realogy; J. Robert; M. Robert; RPM; Ryder; Safeway; R. Saul; Shearman & Sterling; Sherwin-Williams; R. Simoneau; Society of Corporate Secretaries; Southern Company; Southland; Steele Group; Style Crest; Tesoro; Textron; Theragenics; TI; R. Trummel; T. Trummel; V. Trummel; tw telecom; L. Tyson; United Brotherhood of Carpenters; UnitedHealth; U.S. Bancorp; VCG; Wachtell; Wellness; Wells Fargo; Whirlpool; Xerox; Yahoo; J. Young.

[47] See id.

First, corporate governance is not merely a matter of private ordering. Rights, including shareholder rights, are artifacts of law, and in the realm of corporate governance some rights cannot be bargained away but rather are imposed by statute. There is nothing novel about mandated limitations on private ordering in corporate governance.[48]

Second, the argument that there is an inconsistency between mandating inclusion of shareholder nominees in company proxy materials and our concern for the rights of shareholders under the federal securities laws[49] mistakenly assumes that basic protections of, and rights of, particular shareholders provided under the federal proxy rules should be able to be abrogated by "the shareholders" of a particular corporation, acting in the aggregate. The rules we adopt today provide individual shareholders the ability to have director nominees included in the corporate proxy materials if state law[50] and governing corporate documents permit a shareholder to nominate directors at the shareholder meeting and the requirements of Rule 14a-11 are satisfied. Those rules similarly facilitate the right of individual shareholders to vote for those nominated, whether by management or another shareholder, if the shareholder has voting rights under state law and the company's governing documents. The rules we adopt today reflect our judgment that the proxy rules should better facilitate shareholders' effective exercise of their traditional state law rights to nominate directors and cast their votes for nominees. When the federal securities laws establish protections or create rights for security holders, they do so individually, not in some aggregated capacity. No provision of the federal securities laws can be waived by referendum. A rule that would permit some shareholders (even a majority) to restrict the federal securities law rights of other shareholders would be without precedent and, we believe, a fundamental misreading of basic premises of the federal securities laws. In addition, allowing some shareholders to impair the ability of other shareholders to have their director nominees included in company proxy materials cannot be reconciled with the purpose of the rules we are adopting today. In our view, it would be no more appropriate to subject a federal proxy rule that provides the ability to include nominees in the company proxy statement to a shareholder vote than it would be to subject any other aspect of the proxy rules—including the other required disclosures—to abrogation by shareholder vote.

Third, the net effect of our rules will be to expand shareholder choice, not limit it. Our rules will result in a greater number of nominees appearing on a proxy card. Shareholders will continue to have the opportunity to vote solely for management candidates, but our rules will also give shareholders the opportunity to vote for director candidates who otherwise might not have been included in company proxy materials.

---

[48] For example, quite a few aspects of Delaware corporation law are mandatory (*i.e.*, not capable of modification by agreement or provision in the certificate of incorporation or bylaws), including: (i) the requirement to hold an annual election of directors (Del. Code Ann., tit. 8, §211(b); *Jones Apparel Group v. Maxwell Shoe Co.*, 883 A.2d 837, 848-849 (Del. Ch. 2004) *citing Rohe v. Reliance Training Network, Inc.*, 2000 Del. Ch. LEXIS 108 at *10-*11 (Del. Ch. July 21, 2000)); (ii) the limitation against dividing the board of directors into more than three classes (Del. Code Ann., tit. 8, §141(d); *see also Jones Apparel*); (iii) the entitlement of stockholders to inspect the list of stockholders and other corporate books and records (Del. Code Ann., tit. 8, §§219(a) and 220(b); *Loew's Theatres, Inc. v. Commercial Credit Co.*, 243 A.2d 78, 81 (Del. Ch. 1968)); (iv) the right of stockholders to vote as a class on certain amendments to the certificate of incorporation (Del. Code Ann., tit. 8, §242(b)(2)); (v) appraisal rights (Del. Code Ann., tit. 8, §262(b)); and (vi) fiduciary duties of corporate directors (*Siegman v.*

Tri-Star Pictures, Inc., C.A. No. 9477 (Del. Ch. May 5, 1989, *revised* May 30, 1989), reported at 15 Del. J. Corp. L. 218, 236 (1990); *cf.* Del. Code Ann., tit. 8, § 102(b)(7), permitting elimination of director liability for monetary damages for breach of the duty of care). *See also* Edward P. Welch and Robert S. Saunders, *What We Can Learn From Other Statutory Schemes: Freedom And Its Limits In The Delaware General Corporation Law*, 33 Del. J. Corp. L. 845, 857-859 (2008); Jeffrey N. Gordon, *Contractual Freedom In Corporate Law: Articles & Comments; The Mandatory Structure Of Corporate Law*, 89 Colum. L. Rev. 1549, 1554 n.16 (1989) (identifying several of these and other mandatory aspects of Delaware corporation law).

[49] *See* letters from Grundfest; Form Letter Type A. *Cf.* letter from Nine Law Firms.

[50] In the case of a non-U.S. domiciled issuer that does not qualify as a foreign private issuer (as defined in Exchange Act Rule 3b-4), we will look to the underlying law of the jurisdiction of organization. See Rule 14a-11(a).

In addition to these basic conclusions, we note that there are other significant concerns raised by a private ordering approach. A company-by-company shareholder vote on the applicability of Rule 14a-11 would involve substantial direct and indirect, market-wide costs, and it is possible that boards of directors, or shareholders acting with their explicit or implicit encouragement, might seek such shareholder votes, perhaps repeatedly, at no financial cost to themselves but at considerable cost to the company and its shareholders. Another concern relates to the nature of the shareholder vote on whether to opt out of Rule 14a-11: specifically, in that context management can draw on the full resources of the corporation to promote the adoption of an opt-out, while disaggregated shareholders have no similarly effective platform from which to advocate against an opt-out.

In addition, the path to shareholder adoption of a procedure to include nominees in company proxy materials is by no means free of obstructions. While shareholders may ordinarily have the state law right to adopt bylaws providing for inclusion of shareholder nominees in company proxy materials even in the absence of an explicit authorizing statute like Delaware's, the existence of that right in the absence of such a statute may be challenged. Moreover, we understand that under Delaware law, the board of directors is ordinarily free, subject to its fiduciary duties, to amend or repeal any shareholder-adopted bylaw.[51] In addition, not all state statutes confer upon shareholders the power to adopt and amend bylaws, and even where shareholders have that power it is frequently limited by requirements in the company's governing documents that bylaw amendments be approved by a supermajority shareholder vote.[52]

After careful consideration of the options that commenters have suggested, we have determined that the most effective way to facilitate shareholders' exercise of their traditional state law rights to nominate and elect directors would be through Rule 14a-11 and the related amendments to the proxy rules that we proposed in June 2009. We have concluded that the ability to include shareholder nominees in company proxy materials pursuant to Rule 14a-11[53] must be available to shareholders who are entitled under state law to nominate and elect directors, regardless of any provision of state law or a company's governing documents that purports to waive or prohibit the use of Rule 14a-11. In this regard, we note that although the rules we are adopting do not permit a company or its shareholders to opt out of or alter the application of Rule 14a-11, the amendments do contemplate that any additional ability to include shareholder nominees in the company's proxy materials that may be established in a company's governing documents will be permissible under our rules. Moreover, our amendments to Rule 14a-8 will facilitate the presentation of proposals by shareholders to adopt company-specific procedures for including shareholder nominees for director in company proxy materials, and our adoption of new Exchange Act Rule 14a-18 (which requires disclosure concerning the nominating shareholder or group and the nominee or nominees that generally is consistent with that currently required in an election contest) will help assure that investors are adequately informed about shareholder nominations made through such procedures.

In contrast, if state law[54] or a provision of the company's governing documents were ever to prohibit a shareholder from making a nomination (as opposed to including a

---

[51] It has been argued to us, as a basis for excluding a shareholder proposal under Rule 14a-8, that Delaware law does not permit a bylaw to deprive the board of directors of the power to amend or repeal it, where the corporation's certificate of incorporation confers upon the board the power to adopt, amend and repeal bylaws. *See, e.g., CVS Caremark Corp.*, No-Action Letter (March 9, 2010). *See also* Del. Code Ann., tit. 8, § 109(b) and *Centaur Partners, IV v. National Intergroup, Inc.*, 582 A.2d 923, 929 (Del. 1990).

[52] *See* Beth Young, The Corporate Library, "The Limits of Private Ordering: Restrictions on Shareholders' Ability to Initiate Governance Change and

Distortions of the Shareholder Voting Process" (November 2009), *available at* http://www.sec.gov/comments/s7-10-09/s71009-568.pdf. *See, e.g.,* Ind. Code §23-139-1; Okla. Stat., tit. 18, §18-1013.

[53] Throughout this release, when we refer to "a nomination pursuant to Rule 14a-11," a "Rule 14a-11 nomination," or other similar statement, we are referring to a nomination submitted for inclusion in a company's proxy materials pursuant to Rule 14a-11.

[54] In the case of a non-U.S. domiciled issuer that does not qualify as a foreign private issuer, we will look to the underlying law of the jurisdiction of organization. *See* footnote 50 above.

validly nominated individual in the company's proxy materials), Rule 14a-11 would not require the company to include in its proxy materials information about, and the ability to vote for, any such nominee. The rule defers entirely to state law as to whether shareholders have the right to nominate directors and what voting rights shareholders have in the election of directors.

While we have concluded that we should provide shareholders the means to have nominees included in proxy materials in certain circumstances, we also are mindful that to accomplish this goal the regulatory structure must arrive at a solution that ultimately is workable.Accordingly, we are adopting a number of significant changes to the rules we proposed in order to address the many thoughtful and constructive comments we received on the specifics of our proposed amendments. The changes that we are making to the amendments are described in detail throughout this release. There also were a number of suggested changes that we considered and decided not to adopt, as detailed below.

B. Our Role in the Proxy Process

Several commenters challenged our authority to adopt Rule 14a-11.[55] We considered those comments carefully but continue to believe that we have the authority to adopt Rule 14a-11 under Section 14(a) as originally enacted.[56] In any event, Congress confirmed our authority in this area and removed any doubt that we have authority to adopt a rule such as Rule 14a-11.[57] As described more fully below, Rule 14a-11 is necessary and appropriate in the public interest and for the protection of investors.[58] Additionally, as explained below, the terms and conditions of Rule 14a-11 are also in the interests of shareholders and for the protection of investors.[59] Therefore, this challenge is now moot.

Although our statutory authority to adopt Rule 14a-11 is no longer at issue, the constitutionality of Rule 14a-11 also has been challenged by commenters. We disagree with their arguments.[60] Proxy regulations do not infringe on corporate First Amendment rights both because "management has no interest in corporate property except such interest as derives from the shareholders," and because such regulations "govern speech by a corporation *to itself*" and therefore "do not limit the range of information that the corporation may contribute to the public debate."[61] Even if statements in proxy materials are viewed as more than merely internal communications, this communication is of a commercial—not political—nature, and regulation of such statements through Rule 14a-11 is consistent with applicable First Amendment standards.[62]

---

[55] *See* letters from Ameriprise; AT&T; L. Behr; BRT; Burlington Northern; CMCC; Dewey; M. Eng; FedEx; Grundfest; Keating Muething; OPLP; Sidley Austin.

[56] When it adopted Section 14(a) of the Exchange Act, Congress determined that the exercise of shareholder voting rights via the corporate proxy is a matter of federal concern, and the statute's grant of authority is not limited to regulating disclosure. *Roosevelt v. E.I. DuPont de Nemours & Co.*, 958 F.2d 416, 421-422 (D.C. Cir. 1992) (Congress "did not narrowly train [S]ection 14(a) on the interest of stockholders in *receiving information* necessary to the intelligent exercise of their" state law rights; Section 14(a) also "shelters use of the proxy solicitation process as a means by which stockholders . . . may *communicate with each other*."); *see also, e.g., TSC Indus., Inc. v. Northway, Inc.*, 426 U.S. 438, 449 n.10 (1976) (Section 14(a) is a grant of "broad statutory authority"). The adoption of Rule 14a-11 reflects our continuing purpose to ensure that proxies are used as a means to

enhance the ability of shareholders to make informed choices, especially on the critical subject of who sits on the board of directors.

[57] Dodd-Frank Act § 971(a) and (b). These provisions expressly provide that the Commission may issue rules permitting shareholders to use an issuer's proxy solicitation materials for the purpose of nominating individuals to membership on the board of directors of the issuer.

[58] Exchange Act § 14(a) and Investment Company Act § 20(a).

[59] Dodd-Frank Act § 971(b).

[60] *See* letter from BRT.

[61] *Pacific Gas and Electric Company v. Public Utilities Comm'n of California*, 475 U.S. 1, 14 n.10 (1986) (emphasis in original).

[62] Nor does Rule 14a-11 violate the Fifth Amendment, as it does not constitute a regulatory taking. *See, e.g., Lingle v. Chevron U.S.A.*, 544 U.S. 528, 546-47 (2005); *Penn Central Transp. Co. v. City of New York*, 438 U.S. 104 (1978).

C. Summary of the Final Rules

As noted above, we carefully considered the comments and have decided to adopt new Exchange Act Rule 14a-11 with significant modifications in response to the comments. We believe that the new rule will benefit shareholders and protects investors by improving corporate suffrage, the disclosure provided in connection with corporate proxy solicitations, and communication between shareholders in the proxy process. Consistent with the Proposal, Rule 14a-11 will apply only when applicable state law or a company's governing documents do not prohibit shareholders from nominating a candidate for election as a director. In addition, as adopted, the rule will apply to a foreign issuer that is otherwise subject to our proxy rules only when applicable foreign law does not prohibit shareholders from making such nominations. Also consistent with the Proposal, companies may not "opt out" of the rule—either in favor of a different framework for inclusion of shareholder director nominees in company proxy materials or no framework. In addition, as was proposed, the rule will apply regardless of whether any specified event has occurred to trigger the rule and will apply regardless of whether the company is subject to a concurrent proxy contest.[63] Also as proposed, the final rule will apply to companies that are subject to the Exchange Act proxy rules, including investment companies and controlled companies, but will not apply to "debt-only" companies. The rule will apply to smaller reporting companies, but we have decided to delay the rule's application to these companies for three years. We believe that a delayed effective date for smaller reporting companies should allow those companies to observe how the rule operates for other companies and should allow them to better prepare for implementation of the rules. Delayed implementation for these companies also will allow us to evaluate the implementation of Rule 14a-11 by larger companies and provide us with the additional opportunity to consider whether adjustments to the rule would be appropriate for smaller reporting companies before the rule becomes applicable to them. To use Rule 14a-11, a nominating shareholder or group will be required to satisfy an ownership threshold of at least 3% of the voting power of the company's securities entitled to be voted at the meeting. Shareholders will be able to aggregate their shares to meet the threshold. The required ownership threshold has been modified from the Proposal, which would have required that a nominating shareholder or group hold 1%, 3%, or 5% of the company's securities entitled to be voted on the election of directors, depending on accelerated filer status or, in the case of registered investment companies, depending on the net assets of the company. The final rule requires that a nominating shareholder or group must hold both investment and voting power, either directly or through any person acting on their behalf, of the securities. In calculating the ownership percentage held, under certain conditions, a nominating shareholder or member of the nominating shareholder group would be able to include securities loaned to a third party in the calculation of ownership. In determining the total voting power held by the nominating shareholder or any member of the nominating shareholder group, securities sold short (as well as securities borrowed that are not otherwise excludable) must be deducted from the amount of securities that may be counted towards the required ownership threshold. In addition, a nominating shareholder (or in the case of a group, each member of the group) will be required to have held the qualifying amount of securities continuously for at least three years as of the date the nominating shareholder or group submits notice of its intent to use Rule 14a-11 (on a filed Schedule 14N), rather than for one year, as was proposed. Consistent with the proposed amendments, we are adopting a requirement that the nominating shareholder or members of the group must continue to own the qualifying amount of securities through the date of the meeting at which directors are elected and provide disclosure concerning their intent with regard to continued ownership of the securities after the election of directors. In addition, the nominating shareholder (or where there is a nominating shareholder group, any member of the nominating shareholder group) may not be holding the company's securities with the

---

[63] Throughout this release, the terms "proxy contest," "election contest," and "contested election" refer to any election of directors in which another party commences a solicitation in opposition subject to Exchange Act Rule 14a-12(c).

purpose, or with the effect, of changing control of the company or to gain a number of seats on the board of directors that exceeds the maximum number of nominees that the company could be required to include under Rule 14a-11, and may not have a direct or indirect agreement with the company regarding the nomination of the nominee or nominees prior to filing the Schedule 14N.

The nominating shareholder or group must provide notice to the company of its intent to use Rule 14a-11 no earlier than 150 days prior to the anniversary of the mailing of the prior year's proxy statement and no later than 120 days prior to this date. The final rule differs from the Proposal, which would have required the nominating shareholder or group to provide notice to the company no later than 120 days prior to the anniversary of the mailing of the prior year's proxy statement or in accordance with the company's advance notice provision, if applicable. As was proposed, under the final rule the nominating shareholder or group will be required to file on EDGAR and transmit to the company its notice on Schedule 14N on the same date.

The rule also includes certain requirements applicable to the shareholder nominee. Consistent with the Proposal, the final rule provides that the company will not be required to include any nominee whose candidacy or, if elected, board membership would violate controlling state or federal law, or the applicable standards of a national securities exchange or national securities association, except with regard to director independence requirements that rely on a subjective determination by the board, and such violation could not be cured during the provided time period.[64] In addition, the rule we are adopting provides that a company will not be required to include any nominee whose candidacy or, if elected, board membership would violate controlling foreign law. As we proposed, the rule does not include any restrictions on the relationships between the nominee and the nominating shareholder or group.

As was proposed, under Rule 14a-11, a company will not be required to include more than one shareholder nominee, or a number of nominees that represents up to 25% of the company's board of directors, whichever is greater. Where there are multiple eligible nominating shareholders, the nominating shareholder or group with the highest percentage of the company's voting power would have its nominees included in the company's proxy materials, rather than the nominating shareholder or group that is first to submit a notice on Schedule 14N, as we had proposed. We also have clarified in the final rule that when a company has a classified (staggered) board, the 25% calculation would still be based on the total number of board seats. In addition, in response to public comment, we have added a provision to the rule designed to prevent the potential unintended consequences of discouraging dialogue and negotiation between company management and nominating shareholders. Under this provision, shareholder nominees of an eligible nominating shareholder or group with the highest qualifying voting power percentage that a company agrees to include as company nominees after the filing of the Schedule 14N would count toward the 25%.

The notice on Schedule 14N will be required to include:

- Disclosure concerning:
  - ○ The amount and percentage of voting power of the company's securities entitled to be voted by the nominating shareholder or group and the length of ownership of those securities;
  - ○ Biographical and other information about the nominating shareholder or group and the shareholder nominee or nominees, similar to the disclosure currently required in a contested election;

---

[64] In the case of an investment company, the nominee may not be an "interested person" of the company as defined in Section 2(a)(19) of the Investment Company Act of 1940 (15 U.S.C. 80a-2(a)(19)). *See* Section II.B.3.b. for a more detailed discussion of the applicability of Rule 14a-11 to registered investment companies.

- o Whether or not the nominee or nominees satisfy the company's director qualifications, if any (as provided in the company's governing documents);
- Certifications that, after reasonable inquiry and based on the nominating shareholder's or group's knowledge, the:
  - o Nominating shareholder (or where there is a nominating shareholder group, each member of the nominating shareholder group) is not holding any of the company's securities with the purpose, or with the effect, of changing control of the company or to gain a number of seats on the board of directors that exceeds the maximum number of nominees that the company could be required to include under Rule 14a-11;
  - o Nominating shareholder or group otherwise satisfies the requirements of Rule 14a-11, as applicable; and
  - o Nominee or nominees satisfy the requirements of Rule 14a-11, as applicable;
- A statement that the nominating shareholder or group members will continue to hold the qualifying amount of securities through the date of the meeting and a statement with regard to the nominating shareholder's or group member's intended ownership of the securities following the election of directors (which may be contingent on the results of the election of directors); and
- A statement in support of each shareholder nominee, not to exceed 500 words per nominee (the statement would be at the option of the nominating shareholder or group).

These requirements for Schedule 14N are largely consistent with the Proposal, with some modifications made in response to comments. Among the modifications is the new disclosure requirement concerning whether, to the best of the nominating shareholder's or group's knowledge, the nominee or nominees satisfy the company's director qualifications, if any (as provided in the company's governing documents). We also have revised the certifications to require certification not only with regard to control intent, but also with regard to the other nominating shareholder and nominee eligibility requirements.

A company that receives a notice on Schedule 14N from an eligible nominating shareholder or group will be required to include in its proxy statement disclosure concerning the nominating shareholder or group and the shareholder nominee or nominees, and include on its proxy card the names of the shareholder nominees. The nominating shareholder or group will be liable for any statement in the notice on Schedule 14N which, at the time and in light of the circumstances under which it is made, is false or misleading with respect to any material fact or that omits to state any material fact necessary to make the statements therein not false or misleading, including when that information is subsequently included in the company's proxy statement. The company will not be responsible for this information. These liability provisions are included in the final rules largely as proposed, but with two changes in response to comments. Final Rule 14a-9(c) makes clear that the nominating shareholder or group will be liable for any statement in the Schedule 14N or any other related communication that is false or misleading with respect to any material fact, or that omits to state any material fact necessary to make the statements therein not false or misleading, regardless of whether that information is ultimately included in the company's proxy statement. In addition, consistent with the existing approach in Rule 14a-8, under Rule 14a-11 as adopted, a company will not be responsible for any information provided by the nominating shareholder or group and included in the company's proxy statement. Under the Proposal, a company would not have been responsible for any information provided by the nominating shareholder or group except where the company knows or has reason to know that the information is false or misleading.

A company will not be required to include a nominee or nominees if the nominating shareholder or group or the nominee fails to satisfy the eligibility requirements of Rule 14a-11. A company that determines it may exclude a nominee or nominees must provide a notice to the Commission regarding its intent to exclude the nominee or nominees. The company also may submit a request for the staff's informal view with respect to the company's determination that it may exclude the nominee or nominees (commonly referred to as "no-action" requests). In addition, a company could exclude a nominating shareholder's or group's statement of support if the statement exceeds 500 words per nominee and could seek a no-action letter from the staff with regard to this determination if it so desired. In the event that a nominating shareholder or group or nominee withdraws or is disqualified prior to the time the company commences printing the proxy materials, under certain circumstances companies will be required to include a substitute nominee if there are other eligible nominees. Therefore, companies seeking a no-action letter from the staff with respect to their decision to exclude any Rule 14a-11 nominee or nominees would need to seek a no-action letter on all nominees that they believe they can exclude at the outset.

We also have adopted two new exemptions, slightly modified from the Proposal, to the proxy rules for solicitations in connection with a Rule 14a-11 nomination. The first exemption applies to written and oral solicitations by shareholders who are seeking to form a nominating shareholder group. Reliance on this new exemption will require:

- that the shareholder not be holding the company's securities with the purpose, or with the effect, of changing control of the company or to gain a number of seats on the board of directors that exceeds the maximum number of nominees that the registrant could be required to include under Rule 14a-11;

- limiting the content of written communications to certain information specified in the rule;

- filing all written soliciting materials sent to shareholders in reliance on the exemption with the Commission or, in the case of oral communications, a filing under cover of Schedule 14N with the appropriate box checked before or at the same time as the first solicitation in reliance on the new exemption; and

- no solicitations in connection with the subject election of directors other than pursuant to the provisions of Rule 14a-11 and the new exemption described below.

Shareholders that do not want to rely on this new exemption could opt to rely on other exemptions from the proxy rules (*e.g.*, Rule 14a-2(b)(2), which is limited to solicitations of not more than 10 persons).

The second new exemption applies to written and oral solicitations by or on behalf of a nominating shareholder or group whose nominee or nominees are or will be included in the company's proxy materials pursuant to Rule 14a-11 in favor of shareholder nominees or for or against company nominees. Reliance on this new exemption will require:

- that the nominating shareholder or group does not seek the power to act as a proxy for another shareholder;

- disclosing certain information (including the identity of the nominating shareholder or group, and a prominent legend about availability of the proxy materials) in all written communications;

- filing all written soliciting materials sent to shareholders in reliance on the exemption with the Commission under cover of Schedule 14N with the appropriate box checked; and

- no solicitations in connection with the subject election of directors other than pursuant to the provisions of Rule 14a-11 and this new exemption.

Consistent with the Proposal, we also are amending our beneficial ownership reporting rules so that shareholders relying on Rule 14a-11 would not become ineligible to file a Schedule 13G, in lieu of filing a Schedule 13D, solely as a result of activities in connection with inclusion of a nominee under Rule 14a-11. Also consistent with the proposed amendments, we are not adopting an exclusion from Exchange Act Section 16 for activities in connection with a nomination under Rule 14a-11 that may trigger a filing requirement by nominating shareholders. In addition, after considering the comments, we are not adopting a specific exclusion from the definition of affiliate for nominating shareholders.

Finally, consistent with the Proposal, we are narrowing the scope of the exclusion in Rule 14a-8(i)(8) relating to the election of directors. The revised rule will provide that companies must include in their proxy materials, under certain circumstances, shareholder proposals that seek to establish a procedure in the company's governing documents for the inclusion of one or more shareholder director nominees in a company's proxy materials.

As we proposed, the final rules provide that a nominating shareholder that is relying on a procedure under state law or a company's governing documents to include a nominee in a company's proxy materials would be required to provide disclosure concerning the nominating shareholder and nominee or nominees to the company on Schedule 14N and file the Schedule 14N on EDGAR. In response to comment, we have clarified that the disclosure also would be required for nominations made pursuant to foreign law.[65] The disclosure requirements on Schedule 14N for nominations made pursuant to a procedure under state or foreign law, or a company's governing documents largely mirror those for a Rule 14a-11 nomination. As with Rule 14a-11 nominees, a company would include in its proxy materials disclosure concerning the nominating shareholder or group and shareholder nominee similar to the disclosure currently required in a contested election. The nominating shareholder or group would have liability for any statement in the notice on Schedule 14N or in information otherwise provided to the company and included in the company's proxy materials which, at the time and in light of the circumstances under which it is made, is false or misleading with respect to any material fact or that omits to state any material fact necessary to make the statements therein not false or misleading. The company would not be responsible for the information provided to the company and required to be included in the company proxy statement.

II. CHANGES TO THE PROXY RULES

A. Introduction

After careful consideration of the comments received on the Proposal, we are adopting amendments to the proxy rules to facilitate the effective exercise of shareholders' traditional state law rights to nominate and elect directors to company boards of directors. Under the new rules, shareholders meeting certain requirements will have two ways to more fully exercise their right to nominate directors. First, we are adopting a new proxy rule, Rule 14a-11, which will, under certain circumstances, require companies to provide shareholders with information about, and the ability to vote for, a shareholder's, or group of shareholders', nominees for director in the companies' proxy materials. This requirement will apply unless state law, foreign law,[66] or a company's governing documents[67] prohibits shareholders from nominating directors.[68] In addition to the standards provided in new Rule 14a-11, provisions under state law, foreign law, or a company's governing documents[69] could provide an additional avenue for shareholders to submit nominees for inclusion in company proxy materials, but would not act as a substitute for Rule 14a-11. Thus, Rule 14a-11 will continue to be available to shareholders regardless of whether they also can avail themselves of a provision under state law, foreign law, or a company's governing documents.

---

[65] *See* Section II.C.5. below.

[66] *See* discussion in footnote 50 above.

[67] Under state law, a company's governing documents may have various names. When we refer to governing documents throughout the release and rule text, we generally are referring to a company's charter, articles of incorporation, certificate of incorporation, declaration of trust, and/or bylaws, as applicable.

[68] We are not aware of any law in any state or in the District of Columbia or in any country that currently prohibits shareholders from nominating directors. Nonetheless, should any such law be enacted in the future, Rule 14a-11 will not apply.

[69] *See* discussion in Section II. C. 5. below.

Second, we are amending Rule 14a-8(i)(8) to preclude companies from relying on Rule 14a-8(i)(8) to exclude from their proxy materials shareholder proposals by qualifying shareholders that seek to establish a procedure under a company's governing documents for the inclusion of one or more shareholder director nominees in the company's proxy materials. A company must include such a shareholder proposal under the final rules as long as the procedural requirements of Rule 14a-8 are met and the proposal is not subject to exclusion under one of the other substantive bases. In this regard, a shareholder proposal seeking to limit or remove the availability of Rule 14a-11 would be subject to exclusion under Rule 14a-8.[70]

As described throughout this release, we have made many changes to the final rules in response to comments received. We believe the final rules reflect a careful balancing of the policy, workability, and other comments we received on the Proposal.

B. Exchange Act Rule 14a-11

1. Overview

Based on the comments received in response to our solicitation of public input on the Proposal and on prior releases and in roundtables,[71] we understand that shareholders face significant obstacles to effectively exercising their rights to nominate and elect directors to corporate boards. We have received significant public comment supporting the view that including shareholder nominees for director in company proxy materials would be the most direct and effective method of facilitating shareholders' rights in connection with the nomination and election of directors.[72]

On the other hand, many commenters have expressed concern that mandating shareholder access to company proxy materials would lead to more proxy contests or "politicized elections,"[73] which would be distracting, expensive, time-consuming, and inefficient for companies, boards, and management.[74] Commenters also opined that the increased likelihood of a contested election could discourage experienced and capable individuals from serving on boards, making it more difficult for companies to recruit qualified directors or create boards with the proper mix of experience, skills, and char-

---

[70] As would currently be the case if a state law permitted a company to prohibit shareholders from nominating candidates for director, a shareholder proposal seeking to prohibit shareholder nominations for director generally or, conversely, to allow shareholder nominations for director, would not be excludable pursuant to Rule 14a-8(i)(8).

[71] See the Proposing Release; the 2003 Proposal; the Election of Directors Proposing Release; and the Shareholder Proposals Proposing Release. See also the Roundtable on the Federal Proxy Rules and State Corporation Law and the Roundtable on Proposals of Shareholders available at http://www.sec.gov/spotlight/proxyprocess.htm.

[72] See letters from CII; COPERA; CtW Investment Group; L. Dallas; T. DiNapoli; Florida State Board of Administration; ICGN; D. Nappier; OPERS; Pax World; Teamsters.

[73] See letters from ABA; Advance Auto Parts; Atlas Industries, Inc. ("Atlas"); J. Blanchard; Samuel W. Bodman ("S. Bodman"); Boeing; Brink's; BRT; Burlington Northern; Callaway; Cargill ("Cargill"); Carlson; Carolina Mills; Chamber of Commerce/CMCC; Jaime Chico ("J. Chico"); Consolidated Edison, Inc. ("Con Edison"); Anthony Conte ("A. Conte"); W. Cornwell; Crown Battery Manufacturing Co. ("Crown Battery"); CSX; Darden Restaurants; Eaton; FedEx; FPL Group; Frontier; Hickory Furniture Mart ("Hick-

ory Furniture"); IBM; Keating Muething; Little; Louisiana Agencies LLC ("Louisiana Agencies"); Massey Services, Inc. ("Massey Services"); John B. McCoy ("J. McCoy"); D. McDonald; MedFaxx; Metlife; M. Metz; Norfolk Southern Corporation ("Norfolk Southern"); O3 Strategies, Inc. ("O3 Strategies"); Office Depot; Victor Pelson ("V. Pelson"); PepsiCo; Pfizer; Ryder; Sidley Austin; Southland; Style Crest; Tenet Healthcare Corporation ("Tenet"); TI; tw telecom; L. Tyson; United Brotherhood of Carpenters; T. White.

[74] See letters from ABA; Anonymous letter dated June 26, 2009 ("Anonymous #2"); Atlas; AT&T; Book Celler; Carlson; Carolina Mills; Chamber of Commerce/CMCC; Chevron; Crespin; M. Eng; Erickson; ExxonMobil; Fenwick & West LLP ("Fenwick"); GE; General Mills; Glass, Lewis & Co., LLC ("Glass Lewis"); Glaspell Goals ("Glaspell"); Intelect; R. Clark King; Koppers Inc. ("Koppers"); MCO Transport, Inc. ("MCO"); MeadWestvaco; MedFaxx; Medical Insurance; Merchants Terminal; Dana Merilatt ("D. Merilatt"); NAM; NIRI; NK; O3 Strategies; Roppe Holding Company ("Roppe"); Rosen Hotels and Resorts ("Rosen"); Safeway; Sara Lee; Schneider National, Inc. ("Schneider"); Southland; Style Crest; Tenet; TI; tw telecom; Rick VanEngelenhoven ("R. VanEngelenhoven"); Wachtell; Wells Fargo; Weyerhaeuser; Yahoo.

acteristics.[75] The current filing and other requirements applicable to shareholders who wish to propose an alternate slate are, in the view of these commenters, more appropriate than including shareholder nominees for director in company proxy materials.[76]

As we also noted in the Proposing Release, we recognize that there are long-held and deeply felt views on every side of these issues. To the extent shareholders have the right to nominate directors at meetings of shareholders, the federal proxy rules should facilitate the exercise of this right. We believe the rules we are adopting today will better accomplish this goal and will further our mission of investor protection.

New Rule 14a-11 will require companies to include information about shareholder nominees for director in company proxy statements, and the names of the nominee or nominees as choices on company proxy cards, under specified conditions.[77] The rule will permit companies to exclude a nominee or nominees from the company's proxy materials under certain circumstances, such as when a nominating shareholder or group fails to satisfy the eligibility requirements of the rule. In the following sections we describe, in detail, the final rules, comments received on the Proposal, and changes made in response to the comments.

2. When Rule 14a-11 Will Apply

In this section, we address the rule's application, including when there are conflicting or overlapping provisions under state or foreign law or a company's governing documents, during concurrent proxy contests, and in the absence of any specific triggering events. We also address the reasons why neither an opt-in nor opt-out provision is necessary or appropriate.

a. Interaction with state or foreign law

While we are not aware of any law in any state or in the District of Columbia that prohibits shareholders from nominating directors, consistent with the Proposal, a company to which the rule would otherwise apply will not be subject to Rule 14a-11 if applicable state law or the company's governing documents prohibit shareholders from nominating candidates for the board of directors. The final rule also clarifies that, in the case of a non-U.S. domiciled issuer that does not meet the definition of foreign private issuer under the federal securities laws, the rule will not apply if applicable foreign law prohibits shareholders from nominating a candidate for election as a director.[78] If a company's governing documents prohibit shareholder nominations, shareholders could seek to amend the provision by submitting a shareholder proposal under Rule 14a-8.[79]

Consistent with the Proposal, Rule 14a-11 will apply regardless of whether state or foreign law or a company's governing documents prohibit inclusion of shareholder director nominees in company proxy materials or set share ownership or other terms that are more restrictive than Rule 14a-11 under which shareholder director nominees will be included in company proxy materials. For example, if applicable state or foreign law or a company's governing documents were to require that shareholder nominees be included in company proxy materials only if submitted by a 10% shareholder of the company, a shareholder who does not meet the 10% threshold but does meet the requirements of Rule 14a-11, including the 3% ownership threshold described below, would be

---

[75] *See* letters from 3M; ABA; American Electric Power; Atlantic Bingo; AT&T; Avis Budget; Biogen; Boeing; BRT; Burlington Northern; Callaway; Carlson; Chamber of Commerce/CMCC; CIGNA; Columbine Health Plan ("Columbine"); Cummins; CSX; John T. Dillon ("J. Dillon"); Emerson Electric; Erickson; ExxonMobil; FedEx; Headwaters Incorporated ("Headwaters"); C. Holliday; IBM; Intelect; R. Clark King; Lange Transport ("Lange"); Louisiana Agencies; MetLife; NIRI; O3 Strategies; V. Pelson; PepsiCo; Pfizer; Roppe; Rosen; Ryder; Sara Lee; Sidley Austin; tw telecom; Wachtell; Wells Fargo; Weyerhaeuser; Yahoo.

[76] *See* letters from Ameriprise; Anonymous #2; Artistic Land Designs; Chamber of Commerce/CMCC; Crown Battery; Evelyn Y. Davis ("E. Davis"); Kernan; Medical Insurance; Mouton; Unitrin; R. VanEngelenhoven; Wells Fargo.

[77] *See* new Exchange Act Rule 14a-11.

[78] *See* letters from S&C; Curtis, Mallet-Prevost, Colt & Mosle LLP ("Curtis").

[79] *See* footnote 70 above.

able to submit their nominee or nominees for inclusion in the company's proxy materials pursuant to Rule 14a-11. If, on the other hand, applicable state or foreign law or a company's governing documents sets the ownership threshold lower than the 3% ownership threshold required under Rule 14a-11, then Rule 14a-11 would not be available to holders with ownership below the Rule 14a-11 threshold. Those shareholders meeting the lower ownership threshold would have the ability to have their nominees included in the company's proxy materials to whatever extent is provided under applicable state or foreign law or the company's governing documents. In this instance, new Exchange Act Rule 14a-18, discussed in Section II.C.5. below, would require specified disclosures concerning the nominating shareholder or group and the shareholder nominee or nominees.

There also may be situations where applicable state or foreign law or a company's governing documents are more permissive in certain respects, and more restrictive in other respects, than Rule 14a-11. For example, applicable state or foreign law or a company's governing documents could require 10% ownership to have a nominee or nominees included in a company's proxy materials, but allow a shareholder that owns 10% to have nominees up to the full number of board seats included in a company's proxy materials or to otherwise have a change in control intent. While Rule 14a-11 would continue to be available in that case for a shareholder that is eligible to use it, a shareholder could choose to proceed under the alternate procedure and standards. In this instance, a shareholder would be required to clearly evidence its intent to rely either on Rule 14a-11 or on the applicable state or foreign law or company's governing documents, and then meet all of the requirements of whichever procedure it selects.[80] A shareholder could not "pick and choose" different aspects of different procedures. If a shareholder chooses to rely on a provision under applicable state or foreign law or a company's governing documents to include a nominee in a company's proxy materials, it would be required to satisfy the disclosure requirements of new Rule 14a-18.

b. Opt-in not required

In the Proposing Release, we requested comment on whether Rule 14a-11 should apply only if shareholders of a company elect to have it apply at their company. While commenters did not specifically address the possibility of shareholders opting into Rule 14a-11, many commenters opposed the Commission's Proposal on the basis that it would create a "one size fits all" federal rule that intrudes into matters that traditionally have been the province of state or local law.[81] Those commenters asked the Commission to permit private ordering so that companies and shareholders could devise, if they chose to, a process for the inclusion of shareholder director nominees in company proxy materials that best suits their particular circumstances. Commenters also

---

[80] New Schedule 14N, which is described further in Section II.B.8. below, includes check boxes where a nominating shareholder or group must specify whether it is seeking to include the nominee or nominees in the company's proxy materials under Rule 14a-11 or pursuant to a provision in state law, foreign law, or a company's governing documents.

[81] *See* letters from 26 Corporate Secretaries; ABA; ACE; Advance Auto Parts; AGL; Aetna; Allstate; Alston & Bird; American Bankers Association; American Business Conference; American Electric Power; Anadarko; Applied Materials; Artistic Land Designs; Association of Corporate Counsel; Avis Budget; Atlantic Bingo; L. Behr; Best Buy; Biogen; J. Blanchard; Boeing; T. Bonkowski; BorgWarner; Boston Scientific; Brink's; BRT; Burlington Northern; R. Burt; California Bar; Callaway; S. Campbell; Carlson; Carolina Mills; Caterpillar; Chamber of Commerce/CMCC; Chevron; R. Chicko; CIGNA; Comcast; Competitive Enterprise Institute; W. Cornwell; CSX; E. Culwell; Cummins; Darden Restaurants; Daniels Manufacturing; Davis Polk; Delaware Bar; T. Dermody; Devon; DTE Energy; Eaton; Edison Electric Institute; Eli Lilly; Emerson Electric; M. Eng; Erickson; ExxonMobil; FedEx; Financial Services Roundtable; Flutterby; FPL Group; Frontier; GE; A. Goolsby; Grundfest; C. Holliday; IBM; ICI; Intelect; JPMorgan Chase; Jones Day; R. Clark King; Leggett; T. Liddell; Little; McDonald's; MeadWestvaco; MedFaxx; Medical Insurance; MetLife; M. Metz; Microsoft; J. Miller; M. Moretti; Motorola; NACD; NAM; NIRI; O'Melveny & Myers; Office Depot; Omaha Door; P&G; PepsiCo; Pfizer; Realogy; J. Robert; M. Robert; RPM; Ryder; Safeway; R. Saul; Shearman & Sterling; Sherwin-Williams; R. Simoneau; Society of Corporate Secretaries; Southern Company; Southland; Steele Group; Style Crest; Tesoro; Textron; Theragenics; TI;. R. Trummel; T. Trummel; V. Trummel; tw telecom; L. Tyson; United Brotherhood of Carpenters; UnitedHealth; U.S. Bancorp; VCG; Wachtell; Wellness; Wells Fargo; Whirlpool; Xerox; Yahoo; J. Young.

expressed fears that the Commission's Proposal, if adopted, would stifle future innovations relating to inclusion of shareholder director nominees in company proxy materials and corporate governance in general.[82] On the other hand, some commenters expressed general support for uniform applicability of proposed Rule 14a-11, unless state law or the company's governing documents prohibit shareholders from nominating candidates to the board.[83]

Though we considered commenters' views concerning a private ordering approach, as discussed in Section I.A. above, we have concluded that our rules should provide shareholders the ability to include director nominees in company proxy materials without the need for shareholders to bear the burdens of overcoming the substantial obstacles to creating that ability on a company-by-company basis. Rule 14a-11 is designed to facilitate the effective exercise of shareholder director nomination and election rights. Requiring shareholders to persuade other shareholders to opt into a system that better facilitates such state law rights would frustrate the benefits that our new rule seeks to promote.

c. No opt-out

In the Proposing Release, we sought comment on whether Rule 14a-11 should be inapplicable where a company has or adopts a provision in its governing documents that provides for, or prohibits, the inclusion of shareholder director nominees in the company's proxy materials. We also sought comment on whether Rule 14a-11 should apply in various circumstances, such as where shareholders approve provisions in the governing documents that are more or less restrictive than Rule 14a-11.

Commenters were divided on whether companies and shareholders should be permitted to adopt alternative requirements for shareholder director nominations, or to completely opt out of Rule 14a-11. Many commenters generally supported a provision that would permit companies and shareholders to adopt alternative requirements for shareholder director nominations that could be either more restrictive or less restrictive than those of Rule 14a-11.[84] Among these commenters, some argued that creating a "one-size-fits-all" rule that cannot be altered by companies and shareholders conflicts with the traditional enabling approach of state corporation laws and denies shareholder choice.[85] Some commenters advocated allowing companies to opt out of Rule 14a-11 through a shareholder-approved bylaw (including through a Rule 14a-8 shareholder proposal), with some suggesting that Rule 14a-11 apply initially only to companies that have not opted out through a shareholder-approved process by the time of the first annual meeting held after the adoption of the proposed rules.[86]

On the other hand, several commenters expressed support for the uniform applicability of Rule 14a-11.[87] These commenters expressed general support for the Commission's

---

[82] *See* letters from ABA; BRT; Davis Polk; Delaware Bar; Frontier; IBM; Protective.

[83] *See* letters from 13D Monitor ("13D Monitor"); AFL-CIO; CalPERS; CFA Institute Centre for Market Integrity ("CFA Institute"); CII; Florida State Board of Administration; ICGN; LIUNA; D. Nappier; P.Neuhauser; OPERS; Pax World; RiskMetrics; SWIB; Teamsters; USPE.

[84] *See* letters from ABA; Advance Auto Parts; Aetna; American Bankers Association; American Electric Power; American Express; Applied Materials; Association of Corporate Counsel; Best Buy; BRT; California Bar; Carlson; J. Chico; Cleary Gottlieb Steen & Hamilton LLP ("Cleary"); Comcast; Con Edison; CSX; Cummins; L. Dallas; Davis Polk; Devon; Dupont; ExxonMobil; Financial Services Roundtable; FPL Group; IBM; JPMorgan Chase; Keating Muething; Koppers; Alexander Krakovsky ("A. Krakovsky"); Group of 10 Harvard Business School and

Harvard Law School Professors ("Lorsch et al."); Brett H. McDonnell ("B. McDonnell"); Motorola; O'Melveny & Myers; P&G; Pfizer; S&C; Sara Lee; Group of Seven Law Firms ("Seven Law Firms"); Shearman & Sterling; Securities Industry and Financial Markets Association ("SIFMA"); Society of Corporate Secretaries; Southern Company; U.S. Bancorp; Wachtell.

[85] *See* letters from ABA; BRT; Delaware Bar.

[86] *See* letters from DTE Energy (endorsing the opt-out approach described in the letter submitted by the Society of Corporate Secretaries); JPMorgan Chase; P&G; Seven Law Firms; Society of Corporate Secretaries; U.S. Bancorp.

[87] *See* letters from 13D Monitor; AFL-CIO; CalPERS; CFA Institute; CII; Florida State Board of Administration; ICGN; LIUNA; D. Nappier; P. Neuhauser; Pax World; OPERS; RiskMetrics; SWIB; Teamsters; USPE.

Proposal that Rule 14a-11 apply to all companies subject to the federal proxy rules unless state law or the company's governing documents prohibit shareholders from nominating candidates to the board.[88] Several commenters stated they oppose a provision that would permit companies to opt out of Rule 14a-11.[89] Some commenters expressed a general concern that if companies are allowed to opt out of the rule, boards would adopt provisions in a company's governing documents that are so restrictive that it would be impossible for shareholders to have their candidates included in company proxy materials,[90] with one commenter noting that the laws of most states would allow a board to adopt such provisions in a company's bylaws without a shareholder vote.[91] Further, a commenter warned that boards would use corporate funds to defeat shareholders' attempts to change such board-adopted provisions through shareholder proposals.[92] One commenter argued that the "idea that individual corporations should be given the right to 'opt out' of the proposed regulations through bylaws or otherwise is contrary to the Commission's entire regulatory scheme" and referred to Section 14 of the Securities Act,[93] which voids "[a]ny condition, stipulation, or provision binding any person acquiring any security to waive compliance with any provision of this title or of the rules and regulations of the Commission. . . ."[94]

After carefully considering the comments, we have determined that Rule 14a-11 should not provide an exemption for companies that have or adopt a provision in their governing documents that provides for or prohibits the inclusion of shareholder director nominees in the company's proxy materials. Thus, regardless of whether a company has a provision for the inclusion of shareholder nominees in its proxy materials, Rule 14a-11 will apply. As noted, the only exception is if state or foreign law or a company's governing documents prohibits shareholders from making director nominations.

We believe the rights to nominate and elect directors are traditional state law rights of all shareholders and we believe the current proxy rules could better facilitate the effective exercise of these state law rights. We do not believe that it is appropriate for our rules to permit a company's board or a majority of shareholders to elect to opt out of Rule 14a-11 and thus deprive other shareholders of an effective means to exercise their state law right to nominate directors and to freely exercise their franchise rights. Thus, allowing a vote to opt out of the rule would contravene a fundamental rationale of Rule 14a-11—improving the degree to which shareholders participating through the proxy process are able "to control the corporation as effectively as they might have by attending a shareholder meeting."[95]

When shareholders have the right to nominate candidates for director at a shareholder meeting, we believe shareholder choice is enhanced if our rules facilitate the ability of shareholders to nominate candidates for director through the proxy process. Allowing a company or a majority of its shareholders to opt out of the rule would diminish the rights of shareholders who participate by proxy by preventing shareholder nominees from being included in company proxy materials, thus reducing shareholder choice in the critical area of director elections. Similarly, allowing a company or a majority of its shareholders to opt out of the rule would diminish the ability of shareholders to vote for nominees put forth by other shareholders.

---

[88] *See* letters from 13D Monitor; AFL-CIO; Cal-PERS; CFA Institute; CII; Florida State Board of Administration; ICGN; LIUNA; D. Nappier; P. Neuhauser; Pax World; OPERS; RiskMetrics; SWIB; Teamsters; USPE.

[89] *See* letters from AFL-CIO; Amalgamated Bank; William Baker ("W. Baker"); Florida State Board of Administration; International Association of Machinists and Aerospace Workers ("IAM"); The Marco Consulting Group ("Marco Consulting"); P. Neuhauser; Nine Law Firms; Norges Bank Investment Management ("Norges Bank"); Relational; Shamrock Capital Advisors, Inc. ("Shamrock"); TIAA-CREF; USPE; ValueAct Capital.

[90] *See* letters from Florida State Board of Administration; P. Neuhauser; Shamrock.

[91] *See* letter from Shamrock.

[92] *See* letter from P. Neuhauser.

[93] Letter from Nine Law Firms.

[94] 15 U.S.C. 77n.

[95] *Business Roundtable v. SEC*, 905 F.2d 406, 410 (D.C. Cir. 1990).

In addition, companies and their shareholders do not have the option to elect to opt out of other federal proxy rules and we do not believe they should have the ability to do so with this rule. In our view, shareholders' electoral rights through the proxy process should not be impaired by a unilateral act of the board of directors, or even by a shareholder vote supported by management. Further, as we describe above, allowing some portion of shareholders to alter the application of Rule 14a-11 would effectively reduce choices for shareholders who do not favor that decision.[96]

Finally, we considered the objections of some commenters to a "one-size-fits-all" rule and concerns that for some companies with various capital structures the rule may raise more complex issues.[97] As we have noted, no federal proxy rule allows shareholders or boards to alter how the rules apply to companies. The concept that our rules are not subject to company-by-company variation is entirely consistent with our mandate to protect all investors. In this regard, we are not persuaded that we should allow our rules to be altered by shareholders or boards to the potential detriment of other shareholders. We believe that having a uniform standard that applies to all companies subject to the rule will simplify use of the rule for shareholders and allowing different procedures and requirements to be adopted by each company could add significant complexity and cost for shareholders and undermine the purposes of our new rule. While other procedures and standards could be adopted by companies or shareholders to supplement Rule 14a-11, shareholders would benefit from the predictability of the uniform application of Rule 14a-11 at all companies.

It is important to note that while Rule 14a-11 facilitates the existing rights of shareholders and we do not believe the rule should be altered, it is not the exclusive way by which a candidate other than a management nominee may be put to a shareholder vote. Shareholders may continue to choose to conduct traditional proxy contests. Regardless of whether a shareholder uses Rule 14a-11 or conducts a traditional proxy contest to nominate a candidate for director, a company concerned about how such a shareholder nominee fits into its particular capital structure or other unique fact patterns presumably would address that concern in its proxy materials.

---

[96] Our view in this regard has been sharply criticized. *E.g.*, Joseph A. Grundfest, *The SEC's Proposed Proxy Access Rules: Politics, Economics, and the Law*, 65 BUS. LAW. 361, 370 (2010) (this article also was included as an attachment to the January 18, 2010 letter from Joseph A. Grundfest ("Grundfest II")) ("there is no intellectually credible argument that shareholders are . . . competent to elect directors but incompetent to determine the rules governing the election of directors. There is also no support for the proposition that shareholders can be trusted to relax the mandatory minimum standards established by the Commission, but not to strengthen them."). In our view, these assertions are flawed. This is not an issue of shareholder competence. It is, instead, a recognition that permitting a company or a group of shareholders to prevent shareholders from effectively participating in governing the corporation through participation in the proxy process is fundamentally inconsistent with the goal of federal proxy regulation. See *Business Roundtable*, 905 F.2d at 410.

[97] *See* letters from 26 Corporate Secretaries; ABA; ACE; Advance Auto Parts; AGL; Aetna; Allstate; Alston & Bird; American Bankers Association; American Business Conference; American Electric Power; Anadarko; Applied Materials; Artistic Land Designs; Association of Corporate Counsel; Avis Budget; Atlantic Bingo; L. Behr; Best Buy; Biogen; J. Blanchard; Boeing; T. Bonkowski; BorgWarner; Boston Scientific; Brink's; BRT; Burlington Northern; R. Burt; California Bar; Callaway; S. Campbell; Carlson; Carolina Mills; Caterpillar; Chamber of Commerce/CMCC; Chevron; R. Chicko; CIGNA; Comcast; Competitive Enterprise Institute; W. Cornwell; CSX; E. Culwell; Cummins; Darden Restaurants; Daniels Manufacturing; Davis Polk; Delaware Bar; T. Dermody; Devon; DTE Energy; Eaton; Edison Electric Institute; Eli Lilly; Emerson Electric; M. Eng; Erickson; ExxonMobil; FedEx; Financial Services Roundtable; Flutterby; FPL Group; Frontier; GE; A. Goolsby; C. Holliday; IBM; ICI; Intelect; JPMorgan Chase; Jones Day; R. Clark King; Leggett; T. Liddell; Little; McDonald's; MeadWestvaco; MedFaxx; Medical Insurance; Metlife; M. Metz; Microsoft; J. Miller; M. Moretti; Motorola; NACD; NAM; NIRI; O'Melveny & Myers; Office Depot; Omaha Door; P&G; PepsiCo; Pfizer; Realogy; J. Robert; M. Robert; RPM; Ryder; Safeway; R. Saul; Shearman & Sterling; Sherwin-Williams; R. Simoneau; Society of Corporate Secretaries; Southern Company; Southland; Steele Group; Style Crest; Tesoro; Textron; Theragenics; TI;. R. Trummel; T. Trummel; V. Trummel; tw telecom; L. Tyson; United Brotherhood of Carpenters; UnitedHealth; U.S. Bancorp; VCG; Wachtell; Wellness; Wells Fargo; Whirlpool; Xerox; Yahoo; J. Young.

d. No triggering events

Under the Commission's 2003 Proposal, a company would have been subject to the shareholder director nomination requirements after the occurrence of one or both of two possible triggering events. The first triggering event was that at least one of the company's nominees for the board of directors for whom the company solicited proxies received withhold votes from more than 35% of the votes cast at an annual meeting of shareholders at which directors were elected.[98] The second triggering event was that a shareholder proposal submitted under Rule 14a-8 providing that a company become subject to the proposed shareholder nomination procedure was submitted for a vote of shareholders at an annual meeting by a shareholder or group of shareholders that held more than 1% of the company's securities entitled to vote on the proposal and the shareholder or group of shareholders held those securities for one year as of the date the proposal was submitted, and the proposal received more than 50% of the votes cast on that proposal at the meeting.[99] In 2003, these triggering events were included because they were believed to be indications that a company had a demonstrated corporate governance issue, such that shareholders should have the opportunity to include director nominees in the company's proxy materials.

Unlike the 2003 Proposal, our current proposal did not include a triggering event requirement in Rule 14a-11. As noted in the Proposing Release, we did not include such a requirement because we were concerned that the federal proxy rules may be impeding the exercise of shareholders' ability under state law to nominate and elect directors at all companies, not just those with demonstrated governance issues. In addition, we noted our concern, and the concern expressed by commenters on the 2003 Proposal, that the inclusion of triggering events would result in unnecessary complexity and would delay the operation of the rule. However, we solicited comment about whether triggers for the application of Rule 14a-11 would be appropriate.

Many commenters opposed the inclusion of a triggering event requirement,[100] with some commenters expressing concern that triggering events would cause significant delays and introduce undue complexity into the rule.[101] On the other hand, other commenters supported the inclusion of a triggering event requirement, believing that such a requirement would serve as a useful indicator of the companies with demonstrated governance issues (*e.g.*, companies that do not act within a certain time period on a shareholder proposal that received majority support).[102]

We remain concerned that the federal proxy rules may not be facilitating the exercise of shareholders' ability under state law to nominate and elect directors and this concern is not limited to shareholders' ability to nominate directors at companies with demonstrated governance issues. Indeed, allowing shareholders to include nominees in company proxy materials before there are demonstrated governance failures could have the benefit of increasing director responsiveness and avoiding future governance failures. In addition, we share the concerns of some commenters that inclusion of triggering events

---

[98] This triggering event could not occur in a contested election to which Rule 14a-12(c) would apply or an election to which the proposed shareholder nomination procedure would have applied.

[99] Only votes for and against a proposal would have been included in the calculation of the shareholder vote.

[100] *See* letters from AFSCME; CalSTRS; CFA Institute; CII; COPERA; T. DiNapoli; Florida State Board of Administration; ICGN; N. Lautenbach; LIUNA; D. Nappier; Nathan Cummings Foundation; OPERS; Pax World; Relational; Sodali; SWIB; TIAA-CREF; G. Tooker; USPE; ValueAct Capital.

[101] *See* letters from AFSCME; CFA Institute; CII; T. DiNapoli; LIUNA.

[102] *See* letters from Automatic Data Processing, Inc. ("ADP"); Alaska Air Group, Inc. ("Alaska Air"); Allstate; American Electric Power; Anadarko; AT&T; Avis Budget; Barclays Global Investors ("Barclays"); Biogen; Boeing; BRT; Burlington Northern; R. Burt; Callaway; Chevron; CIGNA; CNH Global N.V. ("CNH Global"); Comcast; Cummins; Deere & Company ("Deere"); Eaton; ExxonMobil; FedEx; FMC Corp.; FPL Group; Frontier; General Mills; C. Holliday; IBM; ITT Corporation ("ITT"); J. Kilts; Ellen J. Kullman ("E.J. Kullman"); N. Lautenbach; McDonald's; J. Miller; Motorola; Office Depot; O'Melveny & Myers; P&G; PepsiCo; Pfizer; Protective; Ryder; Sara Lee; Sherwin-Williams; Theragenics; TI; tw telecom; G. Tooker; UnitedHealth; Xerox.

would introduce undue complexity to the rule. Therefore, we are adopting the rule as proposed, without a triggering event requirement.

e. Concurrent proxy contests

As proposed, Rule 14a-11 would apply regardless of whether a company is engaged in, or anticipates being engaged in, a concurrent proxy contest; however, we requested comment on whether a company should be exempted from complying with Rule 14a-11 if another party commences or evidences its intent to commence a solicitation in opposition subject to Rule 14a-12(c). Of the commenters that responded, a few stated that shareholders of a company that is the subject of a traditional proxy contest should be allowed to use Rule 14a-11 to have nominees included in the company's proxy materials,[103] and others stated that shareholders of a company engaged in a traditional proxy contest should not be allowed to use Rule 14a-11 to have nominees included in the company's proxy materials.[104]

In support of enabling shareholders to use Rule 14a-11 during a traditional proxy contest, one commenter argued that exempting companies subject to a traditional proxy contest from Rule 14a-11 would be inconsistent with the Commission's objective of changing the proxy process to better reflect the rights shareholders would have at a shareholder meeting, and that dissatisfied shareholders who are not seeking a change in control and who otherwise meet the eligibility criteria under Rule 14a-11 would be disenfranchised.[105] The commenter stated that dissatisfied shareholders should not be forced to make a choice between a change in control or "business as usual." Another commenter stated that contested elections have been conducted successfully with more than two slates.[106]

On the other hand, commenters that sought a limitation on use of Rule 14a-11 during a traditional proxy contest were concerned that Rule 14a-11 could have the effect of facilitating a change in control of the company.[107] Commenters noted that under certain staff positions,[108] as well as the Commission's discussion of Rule 14a-4(d)(4), as set forth in the *Proxy Disclosure and Solicitation Enhancements* proposing release,[109] a dissident shareholder could "round out" its short-slate proxy card by seeking authority to vote for Rule 14a-11 shareholder nominees, thereby facilitating a change in control.[110] Further, commenters believed that under the Proposal shareholders that submit nominees in reliance on Rule 14a-11 would not be barred from actively soliciting for the nominees of a shareholder using a traditional proxy contest and, conversely, a shareholder using a traditional proxy contest could actively engage in soliciting activities for Rule 14a-11 shareholder nominees.[111] Commenters also worried that multiple groups of shareholders who simultaneously propose different directors for different purposes could lead to substantial confusion for other shareholders.[112] Commenters warned that shareholder confusion would increase if there are two or more proxy cards with more than twice the number of nominees than available slots.[113] According to these commenters, further confusion would result from any assumption by shareholders that the Rule 14a-11 slate is allied with the insurgent slate, despite the Rule 14a-11 representation regarding the lack

---

[103] *See* letters from CII; Florida State Board of Administration; Sodali; USPE.

[104] *See* letters from ABA; American Express; Biogen; BorgWarner; BRT; Davis Polk; Dewey; Eli Lilly; Fenwick; Honeywell; JPMorgan Chase; Leggett; PepsiCo; Seven Law Firms; Society of Corporate Secretaries; Tenet; U.S. Bancorp; Verizon; Wachtell.

[105] *See* letter from CII.

[106] *See* letter from Florida State Board of Administration.

[107] *See* letters from ABA; BRT; Davis Polk; Eli Lilly; Seven Law Firms; Society of Corporate Secretaries.

[108] *See Eastbourne Capital LLC* No-Action Letter (March 30, 2009) and *Icahn Associates Corp.* No-Action Letter (March 30, 2009).

[109] Release No. 33-9052, 34-60280 (July 10, 2009) [74 FR 35076].

[110] *See* letters from ABA; Eli Lilly; JPMorgan Chase; Society of Corporate Secretaries.

[111] *See* letters from ABA; Society of Corporate Secretaries.

[112] *See* letters from ABA; BRT; Davis Polk; Eli Lilly; PepsiCo; Seven Law Firms; Society of Corporate Secretaries.

[113] *See* letters from ABA; Davis Polk.

of control intent.[114] One commenter also argued that, despite the Rule 14a-11 representation regarding the lack of control intent, it is "easy to imagine that in some contested elections, a [R]ule 14a-11 nominee would be the swing vote, tipping the majority of the board and thus control of the company."[115] Citing these same concerns, another commenter recommended that when a company's board receives notice of a traditional proxy contest, the company should be permitted to exclude Rule 14a-11 nominees from the company's proxy materials (and, if the proxy materials have already been distributed, to issue supplemental proxy materials eliminating these nominees from the company's materials).[116]

Finally, some commenters argued that Rule 14a-11 is unnecessary when a company is engaged in a traditional proxy contest because the company's shareholders are already effectively exercising their rights under state law to nominate and elect directors.[117] One commenter stated that if the Commission decides not to prohibit a concurrent vote on Rule 14a-11 nominees and nominees presented through a traditional proxy contest, it should at least provide that the nominees presented through the traditional proxy contest be counted against the number of permissible Rule 14a-11 nominees to reduce the likelihood of a change in control.[118] The commenter stated that if Rule 14a-11 could be used concurrently with a traditional proxy contest, the nominating shareholder should not be allowed to be a "participant" (as defined under Schedule 14A) in the traditional proxy contest or to engage in any soliciting activity for a nominee of another shareholder. The commenter also suggested that dissidents in a traditional proxy contest be precluded from including Rule 14a-11 nominees on their proxy card. Acknowledging the possibility of collusion, shareholder confusion, and change in control, one commenter expressed support for reasonable limitations on a Rule 14a-11 nomination if there is a simultaneous proxy contest.[119]

While we appreciate commenters' concerns, we do not believe that our efforts to facilitate the exercise of shareholders' state law right to nominate directors should be limited by the activities of other persons engaged in a traditional proxy contest. We also believe that, as described below, Rule 14a-11 and the related rule amendments, together with our staff review process, can adequately address concerns about investor confusion and potential abuse of the process by those seeking a change in control. Therefore, we are adopting the rule as proposed, without an exception for companies that are subject to or anticipate being subject to a concurrent proxy contest. In this regard, we agree with those commenters that opposed including a limitation because to do so would be inconsistent with the goals of our rulemaking, which are not limited by the nomination activities of other persons. In addition, we note that there is no current limitation in the federal proxy rules on the number of proxy contests that can take place simultaneously and we do not believe that there is sufficient reason to provide such a limitation in this circumstance. Companies and shareholders have been able, to date, to successfully navigate multiple slates on those occasions when more than one person undertakes a proxy contest. In addition, we believe that a company can address commenters' concerns through disclosure in its proxy materials. For example, the company may disclose in its proxy statement potential effects of electing non-management nominees (whether those nominees are included in the company's materials or in other soliciting persons' materials), such as the potential to cause the company to violate law or the independence requirements of the exchange listing standards, and allow shareholders to consider that information when making their voting decisions. Similarly, we believe that appropriate disclosure in the company's proxy materials, as well as the dissident's proxy materials, could serve to potentially avoid shareholder confusion about how many nominees a shareholder may vote for and how to mark the card.

---

[114] *See* Section II.B.4. below for a further discussion of change in control intent and the certifications required by the new rules.

[115] Letter from Davis Polk.

[116] *See* letter from Society of Corporate Secretaries.

[117] *See* letters from BRT; Verizon.

[118] *See* letter from ABA.

[119] *See* letter from P. Neuhauser.

We also have not revised Rule 14a-11, as suggested by commenters, to count nominees put forth by persons outside of Rule 14a-11 for purposes of the calculation of the maximum number of nominees required to be included in the company's proxy materials pursuant to Rule 14a-11. We believe that to do so would, like an outright exception, be inconsistent with the goal of our rulemaking—to change the proxy process to better reflect the rights shareholders would have at a shareholder meeting, which are not limited by the nomination activities of other persons.

While we are not adopting an exception from the rule for companies that are, or anticipate being, subject to a concurrent proxy contest, we do understand concerns about the possibility of confusion and abuse in this area absent clear guidance.[120] Accordingly, we have made clear in our discussion, in Section II.B. 10. below, that a nominating shareholder or group relying on new Rule 14a-2(b)(7) or (8) to engage in an exempt solicitation to form a nominating shareholder group or in connection with a nomination included in the company's proxy materials pursuant to Rule 14a-11 would lose the exemption if they engage in a non-Rule 14a-11 solicitation for directors or another person's solicitation with regard to the election of directors. In addition, we are adopting an instruction to Rule 14a-11[121] to make clear that, in order to rely on Rule 14a-11 to have a nominee or nominees included in a company's proxy materials, a nominating shareholder or group or any member of the nominating shareholder or group may not be a member of any other group with persons engaged in solicitations or other nominating activities in connection with the subject election of directors; may not separately conduct a solicitation in connection with the subject election of directors other than a Rule 14a-2(b)(8) exempt solicitation in relation to those nominees it has nominated pursuant to Rule 14a-11 or for or against the company's nominees; and may not act as a participant in another person's solicitation in connection with the subject election of directors.

3. Which Companies Are Subject to Rule 14a-11

a. General

In this section, we discuss which companies will be subject to new Rule 14a-11, including the rule's application to investment companies, controlled companies, "debt-only" companies, voluntary registrants, and smaller reporting companies.

New Rule 14a-11 will apply to companies that are subject to the Exchange Act proxy rules, including investment companies registered under Section 8 of the Investment Company Act of 1940.[122] The rule also will apply to controlled companies and those companies that choose to voluntarily register a class of securities under Section 12(g). Smaller reporting companies will be subject to the rule, but on a delayed basis. Consistent with the Proposal, we have excepted from the rule's application companies that are subject to the proxy rules solely because they have a class of debt registered under Section 12 of the Exchange Act. In addition, foreign private issuers are exempt from the Commission's proxy rules with respect to solicitations of their shareholders, so the rule will not apply to these issuers.[123]

b. Investment companies

Under the Proposal, Rule 14a-11 would apply to registered investment companies. We sought comment on whether Rule 14a-11 should apply to these companies.[124]

---

[120] *See, e.g.,* letters from ABA; Seven Law Firms.

[121] *See* Instruction to Rule 14a-11(b).

[122] 15 U.S.C. 80a *et seq.* Registered investment companies currently are required to comply with the proxy rules under the Exchange Act when soliciting proxies, including proxies relating to the election of directors. *See* Investment Company Act Rule 20a-1 [17 CFR 270.20a-1] (requiring registered investment companies to comply with regulations adopted pursuant to Section 14(a) of the Exchange Act that would be applicable to a proxy solicitation if it were made in respect of a security registered pursuant to Section 12 of the Exchange Act).

[123] Exchange Act Rule 3a12-3 [17 CFR 240.3a12-3] exempts securities of certain foreign private issuers from Section 14(a) of the Exchange Act.

[124] The Commission has considered the impact of this issue on investment companies on prior occasions. *See, e.g.,* 2003 Proposal.

Several commenters supported including registered investment companies in the rule.[125] Commenters noted that investment company boards, like other boards, must be responsive and accountable to their shareholders;[126] that some investment company boards are "too cozy" with the company's investment adviser;[127] and that the proposed rule will add competition to the board nomination process, which may create some traction in board negotiations with the company's investment adviser.[128] A number of commenters did not believe that the rule would result in unreasonable cost or an excessive number of contested elections.[129] One commenter suggested that investment company shareholders would use the rule infrequently and then only if the investment company is experiencing a real governance or other failure.[130]

On the other hand, a number of commenters, largely from the investment company industry, opposed the inclusion of registered investment companies in the rule.[131] Commenters asserted that the Commission had not presented any empirical evidence of governance problems with respect to investment companies that would support extending the rule to them and that the trend for investment company boards is to have strong governance practices.[132] Commenters also argued that investment companies are subject to a unique regulatory regime under the Investment Company Act that provides additional protection to investors, such as the requirement to obtain shareholder approval to engage in certain transactions or activities,[133] and that investment companies and their boards have very different functions from non-investment companies and their boards.[134] One commenter noted that the Proposal would be inappropriate and not particularly useful for most open-end management investment companies, because open-end management investment company shares are held on a short-term basis and open-end management investment companies are not typically required to hold annual meetings under state law.[135]

---

[125] *See, e.g.*, letters from AFSCME; CalPERS; CII; Mutual Fund Directors Forum ("MFDF"); Julian Reid ("J. Reid"); Jennifer S. Taub ("J. Taub"); TIAA-CREF.

[126] *See* letter from MFDF.

[127] Letter from J. Reid.

[128] *See* letter from J. Taub.

[129] *See, e.g.*, letters from AFSCME; J. Taub.

[130] *See* letter from J. Taub.

[131] *See, e.g.*, letters from ABA; American Bar Association (September 18, 2009) ("ABA II"); Barclays; ICI; Investment Company Institute and Independent Directors Counsel ("ICI/IDC"); Independent Directors Council ("IDC"); S&C; T. Rowe Price Associates, Inc. ("T. Rowe Price"); The Vanguard Group, Inc. ("Vanguard"). One commenter opposed the inclusion of business development companies in the rule for the same reasons that it opposed including registered investment companies in the rule. *See* letter from ICI. Business development companies are a category of closed-end investment companies that are not registered under the Investment Company Act, but are subject to certain provisions of that Act. *See* Sections 2(a)(48) and 54-65 of the Investment Company Act [15 U.S.C. 80a-2(a)(48) and 80a-53-64]. We are including business development companies in the rule for the same reasons provided below with respect to registered investment companies.

[132] *See* letters from ICI; ICI/IDC; IDC; T. Rowe Price; S&C. Among other things, commenters noted that 90% of fund complexes have boards that are 75% or more comprised of independent directors and the vast majority of fund boards have an independent director serving as chairman or as lead independent director. *See* letters from ICI/IDC; IDC. Two letters also cited a 1992 report by Commission staff that observed that the governance model embodied by the Investment Company Act is sound and should be retained with limited modifications. *See* letters from ICI; ICI/IDC.

[133] One joint comment letter noted that the Investment Company Act requires investment companies to obtain shareholder approval of contracts with the company's investment adviser and distributor and to change from an open-end, closed-end, or diversified company; to borrow money; to issue senior securities; to underwrite securities issued by other persons; to purchase or sell real estate or commodities; to make loans to other persons, except in accordance with policy in the company's registration statement; to change the nature of its business so as to cease to be an investment company; or to deviate from a stated policy with respect to concentration of investments in an industry or industries, from any investment policy which is changeable only by shareholder vote, or from any stated fundamental policy. The commenters also noted that investment company shareholders have the right to bring an action against the company's investment adviser for breach of fiduciary duty with respect to receipt of compensation. *See* letter from ICI/IDC.

[134] *See* letters from ABA; Barclays; ICI; ICI/IDC; IDC; T. Rowe Price; S&C; Vanguard. However, we note that, in response to the 2003 Proposal, ABA and ICI indicated that there were no reasons to treat investment companies differently from non-investment companies. *See* letter from Investment Company Institute (December 22, 2003) on File No. S7-19-03; letter from American Bar Association (January 7, 2004) on File No. S7-19-03.

[135] *See* letter from ABA. *See also* letter from S&C (urging that at a minimum Rule 14a-11 should not apply to open-end investment companies, "which do

Commenters also were concerned about the costs of the Proposal, particularly for fund complexes that utilize a "unitary" board consisting of one group of individuals who serve on the board of every fund in the complex, or "cluster" boards consisting of two or more groups of individuals that each oversee a different set of funds in the complex.[136] Commenters noted that if a shareholder-nominated director were to be elected to a unitary or cluster board, the investment companies in the fund complex would incur significant additional administrative costs and burdens (*e.g.,* the shareholder-nominated director would have to leave during discussions that pertain to the other investment companies in the complex, board materials would have to be customized for the director, and the fund complex would face challenges in preserving the status of privileged information) and the benefits of the unitary or cluster board that result in the increased effectiveness of such boards would be lost.[137] One commenter also stated that if a shareholder nomination causes an election to be "contested" under rules of the New York Stock Exchange, brokers would not be able to vote client shares on a discretionary basis, making it difficult and more expensive for investment companies to achieve a quorum for a meeting.[138]

After considering these comments, we agree with the commenters who believe that Rule 14a-11 should apply to registered investment companies, as was proposed. The purpose of Rule 14a-11 is to facilitate the exercise of shareholders' traditional state law rights to nominate and elect directors to boards of directors and thereby enable shareholders to participate more meaningfully in the nomination and election of directors at the companies in which they invest. These state law rights apply to the shareholders of investment companies, including each investment company in a fund complex, regardless of whether or not the fund complex utilizes a unitary or cluster board.[139] Moreover, although investment companies and their boards may have different functions from non-investment companies and their boards, investment company boards, like the boards of

---

(Footnote Continued)

not generally hold regular meetings and for which compliance would be particularly burdensome"). An open-end management investment company is an investment company, other than a unit investment trust or face-amount certificate company, that offers for sale or has outstanding any redeemable security of which it is the issuer. *See* Sections 4 and 5(a)(1) of the Investment Company Act [15 U.S.C. 80a-4 and 80a-5(a)(1)].

[136] *See* letters from ABA; ICI; ICI/IDC; IDC; MFDF; S&C; T. Rowe Price; Vanguard. Commenters noted that a recent survey of fund complexes representing 93% of the industry's total net assets indicated that 83% of fund complexes had a unitary board structure and 17% of fund complexes had a cluster board structure. *See* letters from ICI/IDC; IDC. However, one comment letter included materials noting that, while the average number of registered investment companies per fund complex is five, the median number of registered investment companies per fund complex is one. *See* letter from ICI/IDC. In cases where the fund complex consists of only one company, commenters' concerns about the loss of the unitary board would not be present.

Commenters also noted that among fund complexes that use unitary or cluster boards there are other aspects of board organization that vary from complex to complex. *See* letter from ICI/IDC. For example, one board may oversee all of the open-end funds in the complex and all but three of its closed-end funds, while a second board oversees the other closed-end funds. Alternatively, one board may oversee the open-end and

closed-end fixed income funds advised by one particular adviser, while a second board oversees the open-end and closed-end equity and international funds advised by a second adviser, etc. However, the commenters did not note any specific issues that would be raised by the use of different structures among fund complexes using unitary or cluster boards if the Proposal were to be adopted.

[137] Commenters noted that unitary and cluster boards can result in enhanced board efficiency and greater board knowledge of the many aspects of fund operations that are complex-wide in nature. *See, e.g.,* letters from ABA; ICI; ICI/IDC; IDC; MFDF; S&C; T. Rowe Price; Vanguard. For instance, commenters noted that many of the same regulatory, valuation, compliance, disclosure, accounting, and business issues may arise for all of the funds that the unitary or cluster board oversees and that consistency among funds in the complex greatly enhances both board efficiency and shareholder protection. *See, e.g.,* letter from ICI/IDC. One joint comment letter also suggested that "[b]ecause they are negotiating on behalf of multiple funds, unitary and cluster boards have a greater ability than single fund boards to negotiate with management over matters such as fund expenses; the level of resources devoted to technology; and compliance and audit functions." *See id.*

[138] *See* letter from S&C.

[139] We note that "unitary" or "cluster" boards are not required by state law.

other companies, have significant responsibilities in protecting shareholder interests, such as the approval of advisory contracts and fees.[140] Therefore, we are not persuaded that exempting registered investment companies would be consistent with our goals. We also do not believe that the regulatory protections offered by the Investment Company Act (including requirements to obtain shareholder approval to engage in certain transactions and activities), the trend asserted by commenters for investment companies to have good governance practices, or the fact that open-end management investment companies are not required by state law to hold annual meetings serves to decrease the importance of the rights that are granted to shareholders under state law.[141] In fact, the separate regulatory regime to which investment companies are subject emphasizes the importance of investment company directors in dealing with the conflicts of interest created by the external management structure of most investment companies.[142] We also note that some commenters have raised governance concerns regarding the relationship between boards and investment advisers.[143]

We are cognizant of the fact that the rule will impose some costs on investment companies. We believe, however, that policy goals and the benefits of the rule justify these costs. As discussed above, we believe that facilitating the exercise of traditional state law rights to nominate and elect directors is as much of a concern for investment company shareholders as it is for shareholders of non-investment companies. We continue to believe that parts of the proxy process may frustrate the exercise of shareholders' rights to nominate and elect directors arising under state law, and thereby fail to provide fair corporate suffrage. The new rules seek to facilitate shareholders' effective exercise of their rights under state law to both nominate and elect directors. In this regard, we note that commenters have stated that interest in mutual fund governance has increased in recent years.[144]

We recognize that it may be more costly for investment companies to achieve a quorum at shareholder meetings if a shareholder director nomination causes an election to be "contested" under rules of the New York Stock Exchange and brokers cannot vote customer shares on a discretionary basis. Furthermore, for fund complexes that utilize unitary or cluster boards, the election of a shareholder director nominee may, in some circumstances, increase costs and potentially decrease the efficiency of the boards.

---

[140] *See Jones v. Harris Assocs.*, 130 S.Ct. 1418, 1423, 176 L. Ed. 2d 265, 273-274 (2010). *See also* S. Rep. No. 91-184; 91st Congress 1st Session; S. 2224 (1969) ("This section is not intended to authorize a court to substitute its business judgment for that of the mutual fund's board of directors in the area of management fees. . . . The directors of a mutual fund, like directors of any other corporation will continue to have . . . overall fiduciary duties as directors for the supervision of all of the affairs of the fund."); letter from ICI/IDC ("The Investment Company Act of 1940 and the rules under it impose significant responsibilities on fund directors in addition to the duties of loyalty and care to which directors are typically bound under state law.").

[141] In the 1992 report cited by two comment letters in footnote 132 above, the Commission staff also observed that the Investment Company Act "establishes a comprehensive regulatory framework predicated upon principles of corporate democracy" and was intended to provide an additional safeguard for investors by according "voting powers to investment company shareholders *beyond those required by state corporate law.*" Division of Investment Management, U.S. Securities and Exchange Commission, *Protecting Investors: A Half Century of Investment Company Regulation*, at pp. 251-52, 260 (May 1992) (emphasis added).

[142] *See, e.g.,* Commission Guidance Regarding the Duties and Responsibilities of Investment Company Boards of Directors with Respect to Investment Adviser Portfolio Trading Practices, Release No. IC-28345 (July 30, 2008) [73 FR 45646, 45649 (August 6, 2008)] ("In addition to statutory and common law obligations, fund directors are also subject to specific fiduciary obligations relating to the special nature of funds under the Investment Company Act. . . . A fund board has the responsibility, among other duties, to monitor the conflicts of interest facing the fund's investment adviser and determine how the conflicts should be managed to help ensure that the fund is being operated in the best interest of the fund's shareholders.") (footnotes omitted); Interpretive Matters Concerning Independent Directors of Investment Companies, Release No. IC-24083 (October 14, 1999) [64 FR 59877, 59877-78 (November 3, 1999)] (listing various duties and responsibilities of the independent directors of an investment company and noting that "Each of these duties and responsibilities is vital to the proper functioning of fund operations and, ultimately, the protection of fund shareholders.").

[143] *See* letters from J. Reid; J. Taub.

[144] *See* letters from AFSCME; J. Taub.

We note, however, that these costs are associated with the state law right to nominate and elect directors, and are not costs incurred for including shareholder nominees in the company's proxy statement. With respect to fund complexes utilizing unitary or cluster boards, we note that any increased costs and decreased efficiency of an investment company's board as a result of the fund complex no longer having a unitary or cluster board would occur, if at all, only in the event that investment company shareholders elect the shareholder nominee. Investment companies may include information in the proxy materials making investors aware of the company's views on the perceived benefits of a unitary or cluster board and the potential for increased costs and decreased efficiency if the shareholder nominees are elected. Moreover, we note that a fund complex can take steps to minimize the cost and burden of a shareholder-nominated director by, for example, entering into a confidentiality agreement in order to preserve the status of confidential information regarding the fund complex.[145]

We believe that the costs imposed on investment companies will be less significant than the costs imposed on other companies for three reasons. First, to the extent investment companies do not hold annual meetings as permitted by state law, investment company shareholders will have less opportunity to use the rule.[146] Second, even when investment company shareholders do have the opportunity to use the rule, the disproportionately large and generally passive retail shareholder base of investment companies will probably mean that the rule will be used less frequently than will be the case with non-investment companies.[147] Third, because we have sought to limit the cost and burden on all companies, including investment companies, by limiting use of Rule 14a-11 to shareholders who have maintained significant continuous holdings in the company for at least three years, and because many funds, such as money market funds, are held by shareholders on a short-term basis,[148] we believe that the situations where shareholders will meet the eligibility requirements will be limited.

Although commenters argued that the election of a shareholder-nominated director to a unitary or cluster board will necessarily result in decreased effectiveness of the board, we disagree. In this regard, one commenter argued that competition in the board nomination process may improve efficiency by providing additional leverage for boards in negotiations with the investment adviser.[149] In any event, we believe that investment company shareholders should have a more meaningful opportunity to exercise their traditional state law rights to elect a non-unitary or non-cluster board if they so choose.

c. Controlled companies

As proposed, Rule 14a-11 would allow eligible shareholders to submit director nominees at all companies subject to the Exchange Act proxy rules other than companies that are subject to the proxy rules solely because they have a class of debt registered under Section 12 of the Exchange Act. We sought comment on whether Rule 14a-11 also should provide an exception for controlled companies.

In response to our request for comment, one commenter argued that controlled companies should not be excluded from Rule 14a-11,[150] acknowledging that while there may be no mathematical possibility of a shareholder nominee submitted pursuant to Rule 14a-11 being elected at a controlled company, in a controlled company there could be an even greater need for non-controlling shareholders to express their concerns. The

---

[145] Two commenters argued in a joint comment letter that there are a number of practical and legal issues that prevent confidentiality agreements from being sufficient to address the issues that arise when a shareholder-nominated director is elected to the board of an investment company in a fund complex using a unitary or cluster board. *See* letter from ICI/IDC. We emphasize that entering into a confidentiality agreement is only one method of preserving the confidentiality of information revealed in board meetings attended by the shareholder-nominated director. The fund complex can have separate meetings and board materials for the board with the shareholder-nominated director, especially if particularly sensitive legal or other matters will be discussed or to protect attorney-client privilege. For a further discussion of this comment, *see* Section IV.E.1.

[146] *See* letters from ABA; MFDF.

[147] *See* letter from J. Taub.

[148] *See* letter from ABA.

[149] *See* letter from J. Taub.

[150] *See* letter from P. Neuhauser.

commenter noted that a large—even if not a majority—vote by non-controlling share-holders could send an important message to the board. Other commenters noted that con-trolled companies are commonly structured with dual classes of stock, which allows shareholders of the non-controlling class of stock to elect a set number of directors that is less than the full board.[151] Another commenter noted that dual-class companies with supervoting stock often can benefit the most from having the interests of non-controlling shareholders better represented in the boardroom.[152] This commenter encouraged the Com-mission to include some means by which minority shareholders of dual-class and parent-controlled companies could meaningfully avail themselves of the rule, even if a different set of eligibility or disclosure requirements is determined to be more appropriate in these cases.

On the other hand, several commenters argued that controlled companies should be excluded from Rule 14a-11.[153] According to these commenters, providing shareholders the ability to include nominees in company proxy materials in this context would be ineffective and needlessly disruptive and costly because there is no prospect that a shareholder nominee would be elected.[154] Two of these commenters also noted that subjecting these companies to Rule 14a-11 would possibly cause investor confusion.[155] These commenters remarked that shareholders would continue to have other avenues to express their views to the company, such as through the Rule 14a-8 process. Commenters who supported an exclusion for controlled companies suggested that for purposes of the exclusion the definition of "controlled company" should be similar to the definition used by the national securities exchanges in connection with director independence require-ments.[156] Some commenters suggested that if Rule 14a-11 excluded controlled compa-nies using the same definition as the national securities exchanges in connection with director independence requirements, then the rule should contain an instruction provid-ing that whether more than 50% of the voting power of a company is held by an individual, group, or other company would be determined by any schedules filed under Section 13(d) of the Exchange Act.[157]

After considering the issue further, we are persuaded that Rule 14a-11 should apply to controlled companies, as we proposed. As commenters noted, it is common for compa-nies structured with dual classes of stock to allow shareholders of the non-controlling class to elect a set number of directors that is less than the full board. In that situation, it may be useful for non-controlling shareholders to be able to include shareholder nomi-nations in company proxy materials with respect to the directors the non-controlling class is entitled to elect. In addition, though applying Rule 14a-11 to controlled compa-nies would be unlikely to result in the election of shareholder-nominated directors in cases in which these are not directors elected exclusively by the non-controlling share-holders, we appreciate that shareholders at controlled companies may have other reasons for nominating candidates for director.[158]

d. "Debt only" companies

As proposed, Rule 14a-11 would allow eligible shareholders to submit director nominees at all companies subject to the Exchange Act proxy rules other than companies that are subject to the proxy rules solely because they have a class of debt securities

---

[151] *See* letters from ABA; Duane Morris; Media General, Inc. ("Media General"); The New York Times Company ("New York Times").

[152] *See* letter from T. Rowe Price.

[153] *See* letters from ABA; AllianceBernstein; Cleary; Seven Law Firms; Duane Morris LLP ("Duane Mor-ris"); Sidley Austin.

[154] *See* letters from ABA; AllianceBernstein; Cleary; Seven Law Firms; Duane Morris; Sidley Austin.

[155] *See* letters from ABA; Seven Law Firms.

[156] *See* letters from ABA; AllianceBernstein; Cleary; Seven Law Firms; Duane Morris; Sidley Austin. *See, e.g.,* New York Stock Exchange Rule 303A.00 and NASDAQ Stock Market LLC Rule 5615(c) (defining

"controlled companies" as a company of which more than 50% of the voting power for the election of directors is held by an individual, group or another company).

[157] *See* letters from AllianceBernstein; Duane Morris.

[158] We note that controlled companies are not excluded from Rule 14a-8 despite the same improb-ability that a shareholder proposal will receive the approval of the majority of the votes cast at a con-trolled company. Shareholders may use Rule 14a-8 to submit a proposal to the board even though controlling shareholders may vote against the proposal and prevent it from being approved.

registered under Section 12 of the Exchange Act. We sought comment on whether this exclusion from Rule 14a-11 was appropriate.

Commenters that specifically addressed this question agreed with our approach and stated generally that Rule 14a-11 should not apply to companies subject to the federal proxy rules solely because they have a class of debt securities registered under Exchange Act Section 12.[159] Most of these commenters stated that the ability to submit nominees for inclusion in a company's proxy materials should be limited to holders of equity securities registered under the Exchange Act.[160] One commenter warned that subjecting companies with a registered class of debt securities to Rule 14a-11 would deter private companies from accessing the public debt market and, in any case, private companies typically have shareholder agreements and other arrangements in place that address the election of directors.[161]

We are adopting this exclusion as proposed. We note that this approach was supported by investor and corporate commenters. We believe that Rule 14a-11 should not apply to companies that are subject to the federal proxy rules solely because they have a class of debt securities registered under Section 12 of the Exchange Act.

e. Application of Exchange Act Rule 14a-11 to companies that voluntarily register a class of securities under Exchange Act Section 12(g)

In the Proposing Release, we noted that Rule 14a-11 would apply to companies that have voluntarily registered a class of equity securities pursuant to Exchange Act Section 12(g); however, we solicited comment on whether Rule 14a-11 should apply to these companies.[162] We also asked whether nominating shareholders of these companies should be subject to the same ownership eligibility thresholds as those shareholders of companies that were required to register a class of equity securities pursuant to Section 12, or whether we should adjust any other aspects of Rule 14a-11 for these companies.

Three commenters stated that Rule 14a-11 should apply to companies that voluntarily register a class of equity securities under Exchange Act Section 12(g).[163] One explained that investors in securities registered under Section 12 should be provided some assurance that the company is subject to various rules safeguarding their interests, such as the proposed rule, and expressed concern that less than uniform application could lead to investor confusion.[164] One commenter stated that nominating shareholders of voluntarily-registered companies should be subject to the same ownership thresholds as shareholders of companies that were required to register a class of securities under Exchange Act Section 12.[165]

We agree with the commenters that Rule 14a-11 generally should apply to those companies that choose to avail themselves of the obligations and benefits of Section 12(g) registration. As Section 12 registrants, these companies are subject to the full panoply of the Exchange Act, including Section 14(a), and their shareholders receive proxy materials

---

[159] *See* letters from ABA; CII; Cleary; S&C.

[160] *See* letters from ABA; Cleary; S&C.

[161] *See* letter from S&C. This commenter also stated that Rule 14a-11 should not apply to those reporting companies who voluntarily continue to file Exchange Act reports while they are not required to do so under Exchange Act Section 13(a) or Section 15(d). It argued that these voluntary filers should be treated the same as companies with Exchange Act reporting obligations relating solely to debt securities. We note that Rule 14a-11 will not apply to a company filing Exchange Act reports when neither Exchange Act Section 13(a) nor Section 15(d) requires that it do so (for example, to comply with a covenant contained in an indenture relating to outstanding debt securities).

[162] A company must register a class of equity securities under Section 12(g) if, on the last day of its fiscal year, the class of equity securities is held by 500 or more record holders and the company has total assets of more than $10 million. An issuer may, however, register any class of equity securities under Section 12(g) even if these thresholds have not been met. Reporting after this form of voluntary registration is distinguished from a company that continues to file Exchange Act reports when neither Exchange Act Section 13(a) nor Section 15(d) requires that it do so. *See* footnote 161 above.

[163] *See* letters from ABA; CII; USPE.

[164] *See* letter from USPE.

[165] *See* letter from ABA.

in connection with annual and special meetings of shareholders in accordance with the proxy rules. We believe disparate treatment among these Section 12 registrants is unwarranted and shareholders of these companies should enjoy the same protections generally available to shareholders of other companies with a class of equity securities registered pursuant to Section 12. Accordingly, Rule 14a-11 will apply to companies that have voluntarily registered a class of equity securities pursuant to Exchange Act Section 12(g), with the same ownership eligibility thresholds as those of companies that were required to register a class of equity securities pursuant to Section 12.

f. Smaller reporting companies

Under the Proposal, Rule 14a-11 would apply to all companies subject to the proxy rules, other than companies that are subject to the proxy rules solely because they have a class of debt registered under Exchange Act Section 12. Thus, Rule 14a-11, as proposed, would apply to smaller reporting companies. We sought comment in the Proposal on what effect, if any, the application of Rule 14a-11 would have on any particular group of companies, and in particular, smaller reporting companies.[166]

A number of commenters stated generally that Rule 14a-11 should not apply to small businesses.[167] One commenter argued that Rule 14a-11 should be limited to accelerated filers and that there should possibly be a transition period where the rule was only applicable to large accelerated filers.[168] That commenter believed that smaller companies would have trouble recruiting directors because the pool of qualified directors is already small for smaller companies, and directors would not want to risk the exposure to a proxy contest. Another commenter argued that we should implement Rule 14a-11 on a pilot basis for large accelerated filers for two years and then revisit whether application of the rule would be appropriate for smaller companies.[169]

Other commenters stated that smaller reporting companies should not be excluded from the application of Rule 14a-11.[170] One commenter agreed with the Commission that exempting small entities would be inconsistent with the stated goals of the Proposal and the costs and burden for such entities would be minimal.[171] Other commenters believed that small companies are "just as likely" to have poorly functioning boards

---

[166] The Commission has considered this issue on prior occasions. *See, e.g.,* 2003 Proposal; Division of Corporation Finance, Briefing Paper for Roundtable Discussion on the Proposed Security Holder Director Nominations Rules, February 25, 2004, *available at* http://www.sec.gov/spotlight/dir-nominations/dir-nom-briefing.htm.

[167] *See* letters from ABA; American Mailing; All Cast; Always N Bloom; American Carpets; J. Arquilla; B. Armburst; Artistic Land Designs; C. Atkins; Book Celler; K. Bostwick; Brighter Day Painting; Colletti; Commercial Concepts; Complete Home Inspection; D. Courtney; S. Crawford; Crespin; Don's; T. Ebreo; M. Eng; eWareness; Evans; Fluharty; Flutterby; Fortuna Italian Restaurant; Future Form; Glaspell; C. Gregory; Healthcare Practice; B. Henderson; S. Henning; J. Herren; A. Iriarte; J. Jones; Juz Kidz; Kernan; LMS Wine; T. Luna; Mansfield Children's Center; D. McDonald; Meister; Merchants Terminal; Middendorf; Mingo; Moore Brothers; Mouton; D. Mozack; Ms. Dee; G. Napolitano; NK; H. Olson; PESC; Pioneer Heating & Air Conditioning; RC; RTW; D. Sapp; SBB; SGIA; P. Sicilia; Slycers Sandwich Shop; Southern Services; Steele Group; Sylvron; Theragenics; E. Tremaine; Wagner; Wagner Industries; Wellness; West End; Y.M.; J. Young.

[168] *See* letter from ABA. A large accelerated filer is an issuer that, as of the end of its fiscal year, had an aggregate worldwide market value of voting and non-voting common equity held by its non-affiliates of $700 million or more, as of the last business day of the issuer's most recently completed second fiscal quarter; has been subject to the reporting requirements of Section 13(a) or 15(d) of the Exchange Act for at least 12 calendar months; has filed at least one annual report pursuant to Section 13(a) or 15(d) of the Act; and is not eligible to use the requirements for smaller reporting companies for its annual and quarterly reports. *See* Exchange Act Rule 12b-2(2).

[169] *See* letter from Theragenics. *See also* letter from Alston & Bird, recommending that we consider adopting a phase-in approach, whereby companies would be permitted to follow a phase-in schedule for mandatory compliance based on their size, similar to the Commission's rules regarding internal controls reporting and XBRL. *See Management's Report on Internal Control Over Financial Reporting and Certification of Disclosure in Exchange Act Periodic Reports,* Release No. 33-8238; 34-47968 [69 FR 9722] (June 5, 2003) and *Interactive Data to Improve Financial Reporting,* Release No. 33-9002; 34-59324 [74 FR 6776] (Jan. 30, 2009).

[170] *See* letters from AFSCME; CII; D. Nappier.

[171] *See* letter from CII.

as their larger counterparts.[172] Another commenter argued that Rule 14a-11 would not impose a material burden on any company subject to the proxy rules because companies already have to distribute proxy cards and it would not be an imposition if they were required to add additional nominees to those cards.[173]

In the recently enacted Dodd-Frank Act, Congress confirmed our authority to require inclusion of shareholder nominees for director in company proxy materials.[174] In addition, in Section 971(c) of the Dodd-Frank Act Congress specifically provided the Commission with the authority to exempt an issuer or class of issuers from requirements adopted for the inclusion of shareholder director nominations in company proxy materials. In doing so, this provision instructs the Commission to take into account whether such requirement for the inclusion of shareholder nominees for director in company proxy materials disproportionately burdens small issuers.[175]

After considering the comments, amended Section 14(a), and Section 971(c) of the Dodd-Frank Act, we continue to believe that Rule 14a-11 should apply regardless of company size, as was proposed. As noted above, the purpose of Rule 14a-11 is to facilitate the exercise of shareholders' traditional state law rights to nominate and elect directors to company boards of directors and thereby enable shareholders to participate more meaningfully in the nomination and election of directors at the companies in which they invest. We are not persuaded that exempting smaller reporting companies would be consistent with these goals. As stated above, we expect the rule changes will further investor protection by facilitating shareholder rights to nominate and elect directors and providing shareholders a greater voice in the governance of the companies in which they invest. We believe shareholders of smaller reporting companies should be afforded these same protections.

Nonetheless, we recognize that smaller reporting companies may have had less experience with existing forms of shareholder involvement in the proxy process (*e.g.*, Rule 14a-8 proposals), and thus may have less developed infrastructures for managing these matters. We believe that a delayed effective date for smaller reporting companies should allow those companies to observe how the rule operates for other companies and should allow them to better prepare for implementation of the rules. We also believe that delayed implementation for these companies will allow us to evaluate the implementation of Rule 14a-11 by larger companies and provide us with the additional opportunity to consider whether adjustments to the rule would be appropriate for smaller reporting companies before the rule becomes applicable to them. Therefore, we are delaying implementation for companies that meet the definition of smaller reporting company in Exchange Act Rule 12b-2.[176] New Rule 14a-11 will become effective for these

---

[172] *See* letters from AFSCME; D. Nappier.

[173] *See* letter from USPE.

[174] Dodd-Frank Act §§ 971(a) and (b).

[175] Dodd-Frank Act § 971(c). A comment letter on July 28, 2010 from the Society of Corporate Secretaries & Governance Professionals invoked this new legislation in support of a request to re-open the period for comment on the Proposal as it relates to small companies. As noted, we did specifically request comment in the Proposal on the rule's effect on smaller reporting companies, and we received and have considered numerous comments on this topic. Accordingly, we believe we have substantially achieved the objective stated in that letter, namely to identify and evaluate any "unique and significant challenges that access to the proxy will create for small and mid-sized companies." Moreover, our determination to delay implementation of Rule 14a-11 in respect of smaller companies will further allow us to evaluate the implementation of Rule 14a-11 by larger companies and provide us with the additional opportunity to consider whether adjustments

to the rule would be appropriate for smaller reporting companies.

[176] *See* Exchange Act Rule 12b-2. A smaller reporting company is defined as "an issuer that is not an investment company, an asset-backed issuer, or a majority-owned subsidiary of a parent that is not a smaller reporting company and that: had a public float of less than $75 million as of the last business day of its most recently completed second fiscal quarter, computed by multiplying the aggregate worldwide number of shares of its voting and non-voting common equity held by non-affiliates by the price at which the common equity was last sold, or the average of the bid and asked prices of common equity, in the principal market for the common equity; or in the case of an initial registration statement under the Securities Act or Exchange Act for shares of its common equity, had a public float of less than $75 million as of a date within 30 days of the date of the filing of the registration statement, computed by multiplying the aggregate worldwide number of such shares held by non-affiliates

companies three years after the date that the rules become effective for companies other than smaller reporting companies. In addition, as discussed below, in an effort to limit the cost and burden on all companies subject to the rule, including smaller reporting companies, we have limited use of Rule 14a-11 to nominations by shareholders who have maintained significant continuous holdings in the company for an extended period of time. As discussed further below, we have extended the required holding period to at least three years at the time the notice of nomination is filed with the Commission and transmitted to the company. In addition, we have made modifications to the ownership threshold that, in combination with the three-year holding period, we believe should facilitate shareholders' ability to exercise their state law rights to nominate and elect directors without unduly burdening companies, including smaller reporting companies. We proposed a tiered ownership threshold that included a 5% ownership threshold for non-accelerated filers; however, we are adopting a 3% ownership threshold for all companies subject to the rule. In adopting the uniform 3% ownership threshold, we carefully considered, among other factors, the potential that the rule would have a disproportionate impact on small issuers. Despite identifying that concern in the Proposal, however, the comments we received did not substantiate that concern, and comments from companies overwhelmingly supported uniform ownership thresholds for all public companies. Moreover, the data we examined did not indicate any substantial difference in share ownership concentrations between large accelerated filers and non-accelerated filers. Thus, we expect that the eligibility requirements will help achieve the stated objectives of the rule without disproportionately burdening any particular group of companies.

4. Who Can Use Exchange Act Rule 14a-11

a. General

In an effort to facilitate fair corporate suffrage, we could have proposed and adopted a rule pursuant to which the ability to use Rule 14a-11 would be conditioned solely on whether the shareholder lawfully could nominate a director, and not include any ownership thresholds or holding period. However, we believe it is appropriate to take a measured approach that balances competing interests and seeks to ensure investor protection. Accordingly, Rule 14a-11 will be available to shareholders that hold a significant, long-term interest in the company, have provided timely notice of their intent to include a nominee in the company's proxy materials, and provide specified disclosure concerning themselves and their nominees. More specifically, as described in detail in this section, a company will be required to include a shareholder nominee or nominees if the nominating shareholder or group:[177]

- Holds, as of the date of the shareholder notice on Schedule 14N,[178] either individually or in the aggregate,[179] at least 3% of the voting power (calculated as

---

(Footnote Continued)

before the registration plus, in the case of a Securities Act registration statement, the number of such shares included in the registration statement by the estimated public offering price of the shares; or in the case of an issuer whose public float as calculated under paragraph (1) or (2) of this definition was zero, had annual revenues of less than $50 million during the most recently completed fiscal year for which audited financial statements are available." Whether or not an issuer is a smaller reporting company is determined on an annual basis.

[177] In some circumstances, the requirements of Rule 14a-11 applicable to a nominating shareholder group must be satisfied by each member of the group individually (*e.g.*, no member of the group may be holding the company's securities with the purpose of, or with

the effect, of changing control of the company or to gain more than the maximum number of nominees that the registrant would be required to include under the rule). *See also* Section II.B.4.

[178] Throughout this release, when we say "as of the date of the notice on Schedule 14N" we mean the date the nominating shareholder or group files the Schedule 14N with the Commission and transmits the notice to the company. *See* Section II.B.8.c.ii. below for a further discussion of the timing requirements for filing a Schedule 14N.

[179] The manner in which a nominating shareholder or group would establish its eligibility to use new Rule 14a-11 is discussed further in Section II.B.4.b.iv. below.

required under the rule)[180] of the company's securities that are entitled to be voted on the election of directors at the annual meeting of shareholders (or, in lieu of such an annual meeting, a special meeting of shareholders) or on a written consent in lieu of a meeting;[181]

- Has held the qualifying amount of securities used to satisfy the minimum ownership threshold continuously for at least three years as of the date of the shareholder notice on Schedule 14N (in the case of a shareholder group, each member of the group must have held the amount of securities that are used to satisfy the ownership threshold continuously for at least three years as of the date of the shareholder notice on Schedule 14N);[182]

- Continues to hold the required amount of securities used to satisfy the ownership threshold through the date of the shareholder meeting;[183]

- Is not holding any of the company's securities with the purpose, or with the effect, of changing control of the company or to gain a number of seats on the board of directors that exceeds the maximum number of nominees that the company could be required to include under Rule 14a-11;[184]

- Does not have an agreement with the company regarding the nomination;[185]

- Provides a notice to the company on Schedule 14N, and files the notice with the Commission,[186] of the nominating shareholder's or group's intent to require that the company include that nominating shareholder's or group's nominee in the company's proxy materials no earlier than 150 calendar days, and no later than 120 calendar days, before the anniversary of the date that the company mailed its proxy materials for the prior year's annual meeting;[187] and

- Includes the certifications required in the shareholder notice on Schedule 14N.[188]

b. Ownership threshold

As proposed, a nominating shareholder or group would have been required to beneficially own 1%, 3%, or 5% of the company's securities entitled to be voted on the election of directors at the shareholder meeting, depending on the company's accelerated filer status or, in the case of registered investment companies, depending on the net assets of the company. We received significant comment on this topic, which we discuss further

---

[180] See Instruction 3 to new Rule 14a-11(b)(1).

[181] See new Rule 14a-11(b)(1).

[182] See new Rule 14a-11(b)(2). The three-year holding period requirement applies only to the amount of securities that are used for purposes of determining the ownership threshold.

[183] See new Rule 14a-11(b)(2).

[184] See new Rule 14a-11(b)(6).

[185] See new Rule 14a-11(b)(7).

[186] See Section II.B.8. for a discussion of new Schedule 14N and the disclosures required to be filed. The Schedule 14N may be filed by an individual shareholder that meets the ownership threshold, an individual shareholder that is a member of a nominating shareholder group that is aggregating the individual members' securities to meet the ownership threshold but is choosing to file the notice on Schedule 14N individually, or a nominating shareholder group through their authorized representative, as provided for in Rule 14n-1(b)(1).

[187] The dates would be calculated by determining the release date disclosed in the previous year's proxy statement, increasing the year by one, and counting back 150 calendar days and 120 calendar days for the

beginning and end of the window period, respectively. In this regard, we note that the deadline could fall on a Saturday, Sunday or holiday. In such cases, the deadline should be treated as the first business day following the Saturday, Sunday or holiday, similar to the treatment filing deadlines receive under Exchange Act Rule 0-3. See Instruction 1 to Rule 14a-11(b)(10). If the company did not hold an annual meeting during the prior year, or if the date of the meeting has changed by more than 30 days from the prior year, then the nominating shareholder or group must provide notice pursuant to new Item 5.08 a reasonable time before the company mails its proxy materials, as specified by the company in a Form 8-K filed within four business days after the company determines the anticipated meeting date. See new Rule 14a-11(b)(10) and Instruction 2 to that paragraph. See further discussion in Section II.B.8.c.ii.

[188] See new Rule 14a-11(b)(11) and Item 8 of new Schedule 14N. Pursuant to new Schedule 14N, the nominating shareholder or group would be required to include in its notice to the company a certification that the nominating shareholder or group satisfies the requirements in Rule 14a-11.

below, and have made alterations to the final rule to reflect the concerns expressed by commenters.

As adopted, to rely on Rule 14a-11, a nominating shareholder or group will be required to hold, as of the date of the shareholder notice on Schedule 14N, either individually or in the aggregate, at least 3% of the voting power of the company's securities that are entitled to be voted on the election of directors at the annual (or a special meeting in lieu of the annual) meeting of shareholders or on a written consent in lieu of a meeting. The nominating shareholder or group or member of a nominating shareholder group will be required to hold both the power to dispose of and the power to vote the securities, as discussed below. The nominating shareholder or member of a nominating shareholder group also will be required to have held the qualifying amount of securities for at least three years as of the date of the notice on Schedule 14N, and to hold that amount through the date of the election of directors. Each aspect of the ownership requirement is discussed further below.

i. Percentage of securities

We proposed tiered ownership thresholds for large accelerated, accelerated, and non-accelerated filers in an effort to address the possibility that certain companies could be affected disproportionately based on their size.[189] Many commenters criticized the proposed ownership thresholds or recommended generally higher thresholds.[190] Of these, most commenters criticized the tiered ownership thresholds and recommended a uniform ownership threshold generally higher than the proposed thresholds.[191] Many of these commenters questioned whether the data on shareholdings discussed in the Proposal in relation to the proposed thresholds took into account the fact that shareholders could aggregate their holdings in order to use Rule 14a-11.[192] One of these commenters

---

[189] Similarly, we proposed tiered ownership thresholds for registered investment companies with the tiers based on net assets.

[190] *See* letters from 26 Corporate Secretaries; ABA; Australian Council of Superannuation Investors ("ACSI"); ADP; Advance Auto Parts; Aetna; Alaska Air; Alcoa Inc. ("Alcoa"); Allstate; American Express; Anadarko; Applied Materials; Association of Corporate Counsel; AT&T; Avis Budget; Barclays; Best Buy; J. Blanchard; Boeing; BorgWarner; BRT; Burlington Northern; R. Burt; Calvert Group, Ltd. ("Calvert"); Caterpillar; CFA Institute; Chevron; J. Chico; Committee on Investment of Employee Benefit Assets ("CIEBA"); CIGNA; Peter Clapman ("P. Clapman"); Cleary; CNH Global; Comcast; Con Edison; Capital Research and Management Company ("CRMC"); CSX; Cummins; Darden Restaurants; Davis Polk; Deere; Dewey; W. Brinkley Dickerson, Jr. ("W. B. Dickerson"); J. Dillon; DTE Energy; DuPont; Craig Dwight ("C. Dwight"); Eaton; Edison Electric Institute; Eli Lilly; Emerson Electric; eWareness; ExxonMobil; FedEx; Financial Services Roundtable; FMC Corp.; FPL Group; GE; General Mills; A. Goolsby; Home Depot; Honeywell; IBM; ICI; Intel; ITT; JPMorgan Chase; J. Kilts; Koppers; E.J. Kullman; N. Lautenbach; Leggett; Lionbridge Technologies, Inc. ("Lionbridge Technologies"); Lorsch et al.; M. Metz; McDonald's; MeadWestvaco; J. Miller; Motorola; Norfolk Southern; Northrop Grumman Corporation ("Northrop"); Office Depot; PepsiCo; Pfizer; P&G; Praxair, Inc. ("Praxair"); Protective; Stephen Lange Ranzini ("S. Ranzini"); Rosen; Ryder; Sara Lee; S&C; Seven Law Firms; Shearman & Sterling; Sherwin-Williams; SIFMA; Society of Corporate Secretaries; Southern Company; Tenet; Tesoro; Textron; TI; TIAA-CREF; Tidewater Inc. ("Tidewater"); Tompkins Financial Corporation ("Tompkins"); G. Tooker; T. Rowe Price; tw telecom; L. Tyson; UnitedHealth; U.S. Bancorp; ValueAct Capital; Vanguard; Verizon Communications Inc. ("Verizon"); Bruno de la Villarmois ("B. Villarmois"); Wachtell; Wells Fargo; Weyerhaeuser; Xerox.

[191] *See* letters from ACSI; ADP; Advance Auto Parts; Allstate; American Express; Applied Materials; Association of Corporate Counsel; AT&T; Avis Budget; Barclays; Best Buy; J. Blanchard; Boeing; BRT; Burlington Northern; R. Burt; Calvert; Caterpillar; CFA Institute; J. Chico; CIGNA; CNH Global; Comcast; Con Edison; CSX; Darden Restaurants; Davis Polk; Deere; Dewey; W. B. Dickerson; J. Dillon; DTE Energy; DuPont; Eaton; Edison Electric Institute; Eli Lilly; Emerson Electric; ExxonMobil; FedEx; Financial Services Roundtable; FMC Corp.; FPL Group; General Mills; Home Depot; IBM; Intel; ITT; JPMorgan Chase; J. Kilts; E.J. Kullman; Lorsch et al.; McDonald's; M. Metz; Motorola; N. Lautenbach; Office Depot; PepsiCo; Praxair; Protective; S. Ranzini; Sara Lee; S&C; Seven Law Firms; Shearman & Sterling; Sherwin-Williams; Society of Corporate Secretaries; Southern Company; Tesoro; Textron; TI; TIAA-CREF; Tompkins; G. Tooker; T. Rowe Price; tw telecom; L. Tyson; UnitedHealth; U.S. Bancorp; ValueAct Capital; Vanguard; Verizon; Weyerhaeuser; Xerox.

[192] *See* letters from ABA; ABA II; BRT; Business Roundtable (January 19, 2010) ("BRT II"); Cleary; Davis Polk; Honeywell; SIFMA.

described formation of a nominating group as "the most likely scenario" to qualify for use of Rule 14a-11,[193] and another commenter submitted that with a significant ownership threshold an "inability to aggregate shareholders to reach the ownership threshold is unreasonable."[194]

A few commenters criticized generally the proposed thresholds as too high and recommended lower thresholds.[195] One commenter opposed the tiered ownership thresholds because a number of companies regularly move from one category of filer to another as the aggregate worldwide market value of their voting and non-voting common equity changes from fiscal year to fiscal year, which the commenter believed would lead to uncertainty under the Commission's tiered approach.[196] Commenters from the investment company industry noted that the proposed eligibility thresholds were based on data for non-investment companies and were not supported by empirical data analysis for investment companies.[197]

On the other hand, we also received comment generally supporting the proposed tiered ownership thresholds.[198] One commenter expressed general support for the proposed thresholds and stated that the proposed thresholds would achieve the Commission's and commenter's shared objective of facilitating the exercise of shareholders' nomination rights.[199] Another commenter explained that the thresholds would "ensure[] that only those long-term shareholders who are seriously concerned about the governance of portfolio companies will have a seat at the table."[200]

With regard to an appropriate uniform ownership threshold, commenters recommended a number of different possibilities, including:

- at least 1% of the company's outstanding shares for an individual shareholder and 5% for a group of shareholders;[201]
- at least 2% of a company's voting securities;[202]
- 3% of a company's shares;[203]
- 5% of the company's voting securities for an individual shareholder and 10% for a group of shareholders;[204]
- 5% of a company's outstanding shares;[205]

---

[193] Letter from BRT II.
[194] Letter from California State Teachers' Retirement System (Nov. 18, 2009) ("CalSTRS II").
[195] See letters from Committee of Concerned Shareholders ("Concerned Shareholders"); L. Dallas; USPE.
[196] See letter from Shearman & Sterling.
[197] See, e.g., letters from ICI; S&C; T. Rowe Price.
[198] See letters from AFL-CIO; AFSCME; British Insurers; CalPERS; CalSTRS; COPERA; CRMC; Florida State Board of Administration; Glass Lewis; IAM; ICGN; LACERA; Marco Consulting; D. Nappier; Nathan Cummings Foundation; P. Neuhauser; Norges Bank; OPERS; Pax World; RiskMetrics; David E. Romine ("D. Romine"); Shamrock; Sodali; Teamsters; WSIB.
[199] See letter from CII.
[200] Letter from AFL-CIO.
[201] See letter from Deere.
[202] See letter from ADP.
[203] See letters from CSI; Calvert; CFA Institute; Labour Union Co-operative Retirement Fund ("LUCRF"); S. Ranzini.

[204] See letters from Advance Auto Parts; Alaska Air; American Express; Association of Corporate Counsel; Avis Budget; Best Buy; J. Blanchard; Boeing; BRT; Burlington Northern; Callaway; CIGNA; CNH Global; Comcast; Con Edison; Darden Restaurants; Dewey; J. Dillon; DTE Energy; DuPont; Eaton; Edison Electric Institute; Eli Lilly; Emerson Electric; ExxonMobil; FedEx; FMC Corp.; FPL Group; General Mills; Home Depot; Intel Corporation ("Intel"); JPMorgan Chase; E.J. Kullman; McDonald's; N. Lautenbach; PepsiCo; Praxair; Protective (recommending this threshold if its proposed 35% withhold vote triggering event is not included; if included, it recommended a 3% threshold); Sara Lee; Seven Law Firms; Sherwin-Williams; Society of Corporate Secretaries; Textron; Tompkins; G. Tooker; Weyerhaeuser; Xerox.
[205] See letters from Applied Materials; R. Burt; CSX; Financial Services Roundtable; IBM (recommending 5% as one of the two acceptable thresholds); ITT; J. Kilts; Shearman & Sterling; Southern Company; Tesoro; TIAA-CREF; T. Rowe Price; tw telecom; UnitedHealth; U.S. Bancorp; Verizon.

- 5% of a company's outstanding shares for an individual shareholder and a higher but unspecified threshold for a group of shareholders;[206]
- with regard to investment companies, a 5% threshold;[207]
- from 5% to 10% of a company's shares;[208]
- 10% of the company's shares;[209]
- 10% of the company's outstanding shares for an individual shareholder and 15% of the outstanding shares for a group of shareholders;[210]
- 5% to 15% of the company's outstanding shares;[211]
- 15% of the company's shares;[212] and
- 20% of a company's shares.[213]

Two of the commenters that criticized the proposed threshold as too high recommended that Rule 14a-11 have the same ownership threshold as Rule 14a-8,[214] with one of these commenters expressing the belief that the proposal, with its ownership thresholds, would enable only institutional shareholders to access the corporate ballot.[215] Another of the commenters opposing the proposed thresholds asserted that the threshold for non-accelerated filers is too high and cited figures indicating that a significant number of such filers do not have any shareholders that would satisfy the proposed threshold.[216] This commenter suggested that for an individual shareholder or a group of shareholders, the threshold should be based on the dollar value of the shares held (*e.g.*, $250,000) or a lower percentage of shares (*e.g.*, 0.25%).

After considering the comments, we believe that it is appropriate to apply a uniform 3% ownership threshold to all companies subject to the rule, regardless of whether they are classified as large accelerated, accelerated, or non-accelerated filers under the federal securities laws. As an initial matter, as we did at the time we issued the Proposing Release, we considered whether and why Rule 14a-11 should include any ownership threshold. Because the Commission's proxy rules seek to enable the corporate proxy process to function, as nearly as possible, as a replacement for in-person participation at a meeting of shareholders, some may argue that once a shareholder has satisfied any procedural requirements to a director nomination that a company is allowed to impose under state law, then that nomination should be included in the company's proxy materials. Each time we consider and adopt amendments to our rules, however, we balance competing interests.

Based on our consideration of these competing interests, including balancing and facilitating shareholders' ability to participate more fully in the nomination and election process against the potential cost and disruption of the amendments, we have determined that requiring a significant ownership threshold is appropriate to use Rule 14a-11. Indeed, we believe that the 3% ownership threshold—combined with the other requirements of the rule—properly addresses the potential practical difficulties of requiring inclusion of shareholder director nominations in a company's proxy materials, and some concerns that both company management and other shareholders may have about the application of Rule 14a-11. Providing this balanced, practical, and measured limitation in Rule 14a-11 is consistent with the approach we have taken in many of our other proxy rules[217] and reflects our desire to proceed cautiously with these new amendments to our rules.

---

[206] *See* letters from Applied Materials; U.S. Bancorp.

[207] *See* letters from S&C; TIAA-CREF.

[208] *See* letters from Davis Polk; Lorsch et al.

[209] *See* letters from Allstate; Caterpillar; J. Chico; W. B. Dickerson; IBM (recommending 10% as one of the two acceptable thresholds); ICI; M. Metz; Office Depot; L. Tyson; ValueAct Capital; Vanguard.

[210] *See* letter from Motorola.

[211] *See* letter from Barclays.

[212] *See* letter from TI.

[213] *See* letter from AT&T.

[214] *See* letters from Concerned Shareholders; USPE.

[215] *See* letter from Concerned Shareholders.

[216] *See* letter from L. Dallas.

[217] *See, e.g.*, Exchange Act Rule 14a-8(b) (requiring shareholders to have "continuously held at least $2,000 in market value, or 1%, of the company's securities entitled to be voted on the proposal at the meeting for

We also considered whether the ownership threshold we adopt for Rule 14a-11 should be tiered based on the size and related filing status (or net assets) of the company, or uniform for all companies, and what percentage of ownership would be most appropriate. We have decided to adopt a uniform standard for all companies for several reasons. First, we determined that a uniform standard would reduce the complexities of Rule 14a-11. As noted by one commenter,[218] the potential for the filing status of a company to change would result in uncertainty about the availability of the provisions of Rule 14a-11 as a result of market fluctuations in share prices, acquisitions, or divestitures. A uniform standard avoids that uncertainty and the resulting potential for the costs and burdens of disputes over the selection of the appropriate tier. Elimination of that uncertainty, moreover, would make the availability of Rule 14a-11 more predictable and therefore more useful for shareholders in planning nominations in reliance on the rule. A uniform standard also will avoid any ability on the part of management to structure corporate actions to modify the impact of Rule 14a-11 by placing the company in a different tier. The concern we expressed in the Proposal—that companies could be disproportionately affected by adoption of the rule based on their size—was not supported by comments of potentially affected companies; to the contrary, comments from companies overwhelmingly supported uniform ownership thresholds.[219] In addition, as discussed below, we are deferring implementation of Rule 14a-11 for smaller reporting companies.[220]

A comparison of the share ownership concentrations in large accelerated filers and non-accelerated filers produced relatively minor observable difference. The results, adjusted to give effect to a three-year holding period requirement, are summarized in the table below:[221]

(Footnote Continued)

at least one year by the date" they submit a shareholder proposal); Exchange Act Rule 14a-6(g) (requiring a soliciting person that "owns beneficially securities of the class which is the subject of the solicitation with a market value of over $5 million" to file a notice with the Commission); Regulation S-K, Item 404(a) (requiring disclosure of transactions with related parties that exceed $120,000).

[218] *See* letter from Shearman & Sterling.

[219] *See* letters from General Mills; Tesoro; T. Rowe Price; ValueAct Capital; Verizon (explicitly opposing variation in percentage ownership requirement based on issuer size); and letters identified in footnotes 199-211 above (commenters supporting various uniform ownership thresholds).

[220] As noted in Section II.B.3.f., we have adopted a three-year delay in implementation for smaller reporting companies.

[221] The percentages in the table are derived from the data set described in the Proposing Release involving companies that have held meetings between January 1, 2008 and April 15, 2009 (the "Proposing Release data"). *See* Section III.B.3. of the Proposing Release. The percentages have been adjusted, however, because the Proposing Release data did not give effect to any holding period requirement, and we have attempted to estimate what those percentages would have been had they given effect to the three-year holding period we are adopting. By the calculation described below, we have estimated a reasonable adjustment to the reported percentages in the Proposing Release data by using the

data presented in a November 24, 2009 memorandum based on the analysis of Schedule 13F filings, data which did give effect to holding period requirements. *See* Memorandum from the Division of Risk, Strategy, and Financial Innovation regarding the Share Ownership and Holding Period Patterns in 13F data (November 24, 2009), *available at* http://www.sec.gov/comments/s7-10-09/s71009-576.pdf (the "November 2009 Memorandum"). The two data sets have overlapping statistics that can be used for comparison and adjustment: both sets report percentages of a broad sample of public companies and identify percentages of companies having (i) at least one shareholder with holdings of 3% of more, (ii) at least two shareholders with holdings of 3% or more, (iii) at least one shareholder with holdings of 1% or more, and (iv) at least two shareholders with holdings of 1% or more. Comparing the percentages reflected in the November 2009 Memorandum (giving effect to a three-year holding period requirement) with the percentages in the Proposing Release data (not reflecting any holding period requirement), we observe that the percentages in the Proposing Release data exceed the percentages reported in the November 2009 memorandum by amounts ranging from 56% to 69%. In order to derive the approximate percentages in the table, we adjusted downward by 62.5% the percentages reported in the Proposing Release data, to account at least approximately for the application of the three-year holding period requirement.

	Non-Accelerated Filers (approximate percentages)	Large Accelerated Filers (approximate percentages)
Companies with at least one 1% shareholder	37%	37%
Companies with at least one 3% shareholder	33%	32%
Companies with at least one 5% shareholder	22%	16%
Companies with at least two 1% shareholders	36%	37%
Companies with at least two 1.5% shareholders	33%	33%
Companies with at least two 2.5% shareholders	27%	25%

Our further review of relevant data has persuaded us that applying different ownership thresholds to large accelerated filers and non-accelerated filers is not justified.[222]

As noted above, we have decided to adopt a uniform ownership threshold for all categories of public companies. We determined that a 3% ownership threshold is an appropriate standard for all such companies—not just accelerated filers. We believe that the 3% threshold, while higher for many companies and lower for others than the thresholds advanced in the Proposal, properly balances our belief that Rule 14a-11 should facilitate shareholders' traditional state law rights to nominate and elect directors with the potential costs and impact of the amendments on companies. The ownership threshold we are establishing should not expose issuers to excessively frequent and costly election contests conducted through use of Rule 14a-11, but it is also not so high as to make use of the rule unduly inaccessible as a practical matter.

We selected the uniform 3% threshold based upon comments received, our analysis of the data available to us, and the fact that the rule allows for shareholders to form groups to aggregate their holdings to meet the threshold. We also considered that our amendments to Rule 14a-8 remove barriers to the ability of shareholders to have proposals included in company proxy materials to establish a procedure under a company's governing documents for the inclusion of one or more nominees in the company's proxy materials. Because of these amendments, shareholders who believe the 3% threshold is too high can take steps to seek to establish a lower ownership threshold.[223]

We note that we considered a lower threshold, such as 1%, and a higher threshold, such as 5%, both of which were thresholds in the proposed tiers. Quite a few commenters, including a number who generally supported the adoption of Rule 14a-11, advocated for an ownership threshold higher than the 1% level we proposed for large accelerated filers.[224] One large institutional investor, for example, "strongly urg[ed] the adoption of proposed Rule 14a-11" and argued that "existing reforms are incomplete as long as

---

[222] *See* letter from P. Neuhauser (suggesting only two ownership eligibility tiers because data show "almost no difference in ownership characteristics between smaller accelerated filers and non-accelerated filers.").

[223] As noted in Section II.C., we are adopting an amendment to Rule 14a-8(i)(8) to preclude companies from relying on that basis to exclude from their proxy materials shareholder proposals that seek to establish a procedure under a company's governing documents for the inclusion of one or more shareholder director nominees in the company's proxy materials. Such a shareholder proposal would, of course, have to satisfy the other requirements of the rule, like other Rule 14a-8 shareholder proposals.

[224] *See* letters from ACSI (advocating a uniform 3% threshold); Calvert (same); LUCRF (same); S. Ranzini (same); TIAA-CREF (advocating a uniform 5% threshold); T. Rowe Price (same).

boards retain the exclusive control of the proxy card and sole discretion over the mechanisms that govern their own elections," but also stated the belief that "in order to use company resources to nominate a director, a significant amount of capital must be represented and 5% is an acceptable threshold."[225] Similarly, the manager of a large family of investment companies stated its "support [for] the Commission's intent to facilitate shareholders' rights to participate in the governance process," yet commented that "a 1% threshold is too low, in our opinion, to maintain the critical balance between serving the interests of eligible nominating shareholders and serving the interests of a company's shareholder base at large."[226] That commenter recommended a "flat 5% threshold for all companies" because it "represents significant economic stake." Other commenters recommended a uniform 3% ownership threshold in the interest of avoiding "frivolous or vexatious nominations,"[227] or because it "is not so small that it would allow a board nomination for only a de minimis investment in [a non-accelerated filer]," but "would not be so large as to prevent all but the largest institutional share-owners to submit nominees for [large accelerated filers]."[228]

In light of such comments we have determined not to adopt the 1% threshold we had proposed with respect to large accelerated filers. We also have determined not to adopt, as the uniform standard, the 5% threshold we had proposed for non-accelerated filers. Several commenters from the investor community explicitly opposed a 5% uniform threshold, maintaining that it would as a practical matter exclude all but the largest institutional investors.[229] On the other hand, although some companies supported a uniform 5% threshold,[230] most other companies urged the adoption of a substantially higher threshold, either for individual shareholders or for shareholder groups, or both. For example, companies and their counsel generally believed a higher threshold should apply to group nominations and overwhelmingly recommended a 10% minimum own-ership requirement for nominations by shareholder groups.[231] We note, however, that at a 10% threshold for groups, the likelihood of forming a group sufficient to meet the minimum ownership requirement would likely be significantly reduced compared to a 3% threshold. Given a three-year holding period, the data in the November 2009 Mem-orandum identify combinations totaling 10% or more but involving five or fewer share-holders as achievable in as little as 7% of public companies, compared to at least 21% of public companies at a 5% threshold and at least 31% of public companies at a 3% threshold. In addition, the data suggest that it would be even more unlikely that a company would have an individual shareholder that would meet a 10% ownership threshold.[232] While some commenters suggested a 5% threshold was appropriate because that amount is consistent with other filing requirements such as Schedule 13D and 13G,[233] we ultimately were not persuaded because the underlying principles of such filing requirements[234] are quite different from those underlying the ownership condition

---

[225] Letter from TIAA-CREF.

[226] Letter from T. Rowe Price.

[227] Letters from SCSI and LUCRF.

[228] Letter from CFA Institute.

[229] See letters from CFA Institute; P. Neuhauser; RiskMetrics.

[230] See letters from CSX; ITT; Southern Company; Tesoro; tw telecom; UnitedHealth; Verizon.

[231] See letters from Advance Auto Parts; Alaska Air; American Express; Association of Corporate Counsel; Avis Budget; Best Buy; J. Blanchard; Boeing; BRT; Burlington Northern; Callaway; CIGNA; CNH Global; Comcast; Con Edison; Darden Restaurants; Dewey; J. Dillon; DTE Energy; DuPont; Eaton; Edison Electric Institute; Eli Lilly; Emerson Electric; ExxonMobil; FedEx; FMC Corp.; FPL Group; General Mills; Home Depot; Intel; JPMorgan Chase; E.J. Kullman; McDo-nald's; N. Lautenbach; PepsiCo; Praxair; Protective (recommending this threshold if its proposed 35% withhold vote triggering event is not included; if

included, it recommended a 3% threshold); Sara Lee; Seven Law Firms; Sherwin-Williams; Society of Cor-porate Secretaries; Textron; Tompkins; G. Tooker; Weyerhaeuser; Xerox.

[232] The data in the November 2009 Memorandum suggest that just 4% of companies would have at least one shareholder with 10%.

[233] See, e.g., letters from CSX; ITT; Shearman & Sterling; Tesoro; T. Rowe Price; tw telecom.

[234] See, e.g., Release No. 34-26598, Reporting of Beneficial Ownership in Publicly-Held Companies (March 6, 1989) ("The beneficial ownership reporting requirements embodied in Sections 13(d) and 13(g) of the [Exchange Act] and the regulations adopted thereunder are intended to provide to investors and to the subject issuer information about accumulations of securities that may have the ability to change or influence control of the issuer."). See also Release No. 34-50699 (proposing to require disclosure of persons holding 5% of an ownership interest in a securities

to Rule 14a-11. After considering the comments and available data, we have decided that a 3% ownership threshold—including where shareholders form groups to satisfy the threshold—is an appropriate and workable approach for the rule.

In adopting a uniform 3% threshold for all companies, as opposed to a lower ownership threshold for all companies, we are mindful that the rule will allow shareholders to form a group by aggregating their holdings to meet the ownership threshold.[235] Indeed, as we assumed in the Proposing Release and as some commenters told us, in many cases shareholders will need to form groups to meet the ownership threshold for the purpose of submitting director nominations pursuant to Rule 14a-11.[236] Commenters also pointed to instances of coordinated shareholder activity in recent "vote no" campaigns as support for the ability of shareholders to form groups.[237] We have adopted a number of amendments to our rules that will facilitate the formation of groups for this purpose.[238] We understand the result of our ownership threshold determination may be that shareholders will need to convince other shareholders to support their attempt to use Rule 14a-11. We believe this outcome reduces the potential for excessive costs to be incurred by companies and their shareholders.

The data available to us also suggest that reaching the 3% ownership threshold we are adopting is possible for a significant number of shareholders either individually or by a number of shareholders aggregating their holdings in order to satisfy the ownership requirement. In particular, the data presented in the November 2009 Memorandum indicate that a sizeable percentage (33%) of public companies have at least one institutional investor owning at least 3% of their securities for at least three years, and thus potentially qualified to meet the Rule 14a-11 ownership threshold individually. As noted, however, the data are based on Form 13F filings, which include holders that are custodians and may not be likely users of the rule. The data in the November 2009 Memorandum also suggest that forming nominating shareholder groups with holdings aggregating 3% is achievable at many companies by a relatively small number of shareholders. Even factoring in the requirement of continuous ownership for three years, 31% of public companies have three or more holders with at least 1% share ownership each; and 29% have two or more holders with at least 2% share ownership each.[239] Moreover, neither of these categories includes companies with one holder of 2% and another holder of at least 1%, and none of these percentages includes companies having a relatively small number (*e.g.,* four to ten) of holders whose aggregate holdings exceed 3% but whose individual holdings do not bring the company within any of the categories identified in the data.

We are concerned, however, that use of Rule 14a-11 may not be consistently and realistically viable, even by shareholder groups, if the uniform ownership threshold were set at 5% or higher. At the 5% minimum ownership requirement for individuals as advocated by many of those same commenters, only 20% of public companies had

---

(Footnote Continued)

exchange because the principles underlying such disclosure were similar to those underlying other filing requirements: "The 5% reporting threshold and the information proposed to be required to be disclosed about such ownership is modeled on the beneficial ownership reporting requirements of the Williams Act, embodied in Sections 13(d) and 13(g) of the Exchange Act and the rules and regulations thereunder. These Exchange Act provisions are intended to provide information to the issuer and the marketplace about accumulations of securities that may have the potential to change or influence control of an issuer." (footnotes omitted)).

[235] Some commenters suggested that the data on share ownership dispersion referred to in the Proposing Release were insufficient because we did not focus on

the possibility that shareholders could form groups to satisfy the minimum ownership requirement. *See* letters from American Bar Association (January 19, 2010) ("ABA III"); BRT II.

[236] *See* letters from AFL-CIO ("[I]t will be necessary to permit aggregation of holdings to prevent the Proposed Access Rule from being usable only by hedge funds."); Florida Board of Administration ("Public funds would need to form a nominating group in order to meet the hurdle in nearly all cases.").

[237] *See* letter from BRT II.

[238] *See, e.g.,* Rule 14a-2(b)(7).

[239] We note that it is unlikely that the ownership test used in calculating the data tracks the definition that we are adopting for Rule 14a-11. As a result, the percentages in the data may be over-or under-inclusive.

even one shareholder satisfying that requirement. Finally, even applying a 5% threshold for shareholder groups, the data identify combinations involving five or fewer shareholders that add up to 5% or more as theoretically achievable in as few as 21% of public companies—at least 25% fewer than with a 3% threshold.[240]

All of these data thus suggest that a uniform 5% ownership requirement would be substantially more difficult to satisfy than the 3% requirement we are adopting. Moreover, our resulting concern about the viability of a 5% ownership threshold is exacerbated by several limitations on the data reported in the November 2009 Memorandum. While those data do account for the application of a three-year holding period requirement, they may overstate in several ways the potential to meet the ownership threshold. First, they may include controlling shareholders that may be unlikely to rely on Rule 14a-11. Second, the data are based on filings on Form 13F, in which ownership is defined differently than under Rule 14a-11, and thus may yield a higher number of larger shareholdings. Finally, the data include large shareholdings by institutions which report aggregated holdings of securities held for multiple beneficial owners.[241]

Nevertheless, and principally because they give effect to holding period requirements, we considered the data in the November 2009 Memorandum to be the most pertinent to our selection of a uniform minimum ownership percentage. We received additional data relating to large companies, however, that offer some additional indication about the number of shareholders potentially available to form a group to meet the 3% ownership threshold. One study indicated that in the top 50 companies by market capitalization as of March 31, 2009, the five largest institutional investors held from 9.1% to 33.5% of the shares, and an average of 18.4% of the shares.[242] That same study found that among a sample of 50 large accelerated filers, the median number of shareholders holding at least 1% of the shares for at least one year was 10.5, with 45 of the 50 companies in the sample having at least seven such shareholders.[243] Another study that was reported to us[244] similarly suggests relatively high concentration of share ownership. According to that analysis of S&P 500 companies, 14 institutional investors could satisfy a 1% threshold at more than 100 companies, eight could meet that threshold at over 200 companies, five could meet it at over 300 companies, and three could meet it at 499 of the 500. Information from specific large issuers likewise suggests the achievability of shareholder groups aggregating 3%.[245]

---

[240] At the 10% threshold for groups urged by many commenters, for example, the likelihood of forming a group sufficient to meet the minimum ownership requirement would be more sharply constrained: the data in the November 2009 Memorandum identify combinations totaling 10% or more but involving five or fewer shareholders as theoretically achievable in as little as 7% of public companies.

[241] On the other hand, the data in the November 2009 Memorandum may understate the number of large shareholdings, because the data may exclude smaller holdings in multiple institutions that are subject to common voting control, and in any event, do not include holdings of less than 1% at all, even though such holdings could contribute to the formation of a group eligible to use Rule 14a-11. Likewise, those data do not include securities held by institutions holding less than $100 million in securities because Exchange Act Section 13(f) does not require such institutions to report their holdings. See letters from ABA III; BRT II.

[242] See "Report on Effects of Proposed SEC Rule 14a-11 on Efficiency, Competitiveness and Capital Formation, in Support of Comments by Business

Roundtable" by NERA Economic Consulting ("NERA Report"), Appendix Table 1, submitted with the letter from BRT.

[243] Id. at 13-14, Figure 2.

[244] See letter from JPMorgan Chase.

[245] See letters from AT&T (eight shareholders owning 1% or more, although holding periods not identified); AGL Resources (same); CIGNA (20 1%+ shareholders, although holding periods not identified); Cummins (36 1+% shareholders, although holding periods not identified); General Mills (one 5%+ shareholder holding for at least 6 years, over 12 1%+ shareholders, and over 25 0.5%+ shareholders, although holding periods not identified); ITT (14 1%+ shareholders, although holding periods not identified); McDonald's (10 holders owning 1% or more, one shareholder owning 5%, although holding periods not identified); UnitedHealth (four 3%+ shareholders, six 2%+ shareholders, nine 1%+ shareholders, 20 0.5%+ shareholders, 32 0.25% shareholders, applying a 2-year holding period); Weyerhaeuser (three 5%+ shareholders, 20 1%+ shareholders, although holding periods not identified).

We realize these data likely overstate the number of eligible shareholders or shareholders whose holdings could be grouped to meet the ownership threshold, as these data generally do not appear to reflect any continuous holding requirement.

In any event, our assessment of the percentage of companies with various share ownership concentrations cannot be taken as an assurance that shareholder nominating groups will or will not be formed at any particular combination of percentage ownership and holding period requirements or of the likelihood that persons with large securities holdings would be inclined or disinclined to use Rule 14a-11.[246] Taking all of this information into account, overall we believe that our selection of a 3% ownership threshold strikes an appropriate balance between the benefits of facilitating shareholder participation in the process of electing directors of public companies and the costs and disruption associated with contested elections of directors conducted pursuant to new Rule 14a-11. We also believe, and as noted, many commenters supported, that a threshold tied to a significant commitment to the company is an important feature of our amendments. Of course, to the extent that shareholders believe the 3% threshold is too high our amendments to Rule 14a-8 will facilitate their ability to adopt a lower ownership percentage.[247]

We proposed to apply the same thresholds for registered investment companies and business development companies as for non-investment companies, except that the applicability of the particular thresholds for registered investment companies would have depended on the net assets of the company, rather than the company's accelerated filer status. No commenters recommended a higher threshold for investment companies than for non-investment companies. While some commenters noted the absence of data specifically relating to the impact of various ownership thresholds on investment companies,[248] no commenter supplied any data suggesting the need for an ownership threshold for investment companies different from that applicable to non-investment companies.[249] Although two commenters suggested a 5% ownership threshold for investment companies, both of these commenters also suggested a 5% threshold for non-investment companies.[250]

We believe that it is appropriate to apply to registered investment companies and business development companies the same 3% ownership threshold that we are applying to other companies. We also believe that, similar to non-investment companies, our selection of a 3% ownership threshold strikes an appropriate balance between the benefits of facilitating shareholder participation in the process of electing directors of

---

[246] *See* letter from Council of Institutional Investors (January 14, 2010) ("CII II"). This comment refers to research indicating that in a small sample of accelerated and non-accelerated filers, the holdings of the ten largest public pension funds, if aggregated, would not exceed 5% and would also be unlikely to meet a 3% threshold, while a 1% threshold could be met. Apart from the sample size, however, this research itself appears limited in that it apparently does not include other types of shareholders and is not adjusted for any holding period.

[247] *See* footnote 223 above.

[248] *See, e.g.,* letters from ICI; S&C; T. Rowe Price.

[249] One joint comment letter provided data regarding the net assets of investment companies and the dollar value of the shares that would be necessary to meet the proposed 1%, 3%, or 5% thresholds. *See* letter from ICI/IDC. The data provided by the commenters suggest that there are a limited number of small investment companies with net assets ranging from $50,000 to $351,000, where the 3% threshold could be met by an investment ranging from $1,500 to $10,530. However, the data also indicate that the vast majority of funds are significantly larger, and would therefore require a

significantly larger investment to meet the 3% threshold (e.g., 90% of long-term mutual funds, money market funds, and closed-end funds have total net assets greater than $19 million, $100 million, and $57 million, respectively; the median long-term mutual fund, money market fund, and closed-end fund have total net assets of $216 million, $844 million, and $216 million, respectively).

[250] *See* letters from S&C (recommending "with respect to the ownership thresholds applicable to shareholders of [registered investment companies], a minimum percentage of no less than the 5% threshold recommended in the Seven Law Firm Letter" (to which Sullivan & Cromwell was a party and which recommended that ownership thresholds of non-investment companies be adjusted upwards to 5% for individual shareholders and higher for groups of shareholders)); TIAA-CREF (recommending "that the Commission adopt a 5% ownership requirement across the board regardless of the company's size" and "[w]ith respect to investment companies, . . . that the 5% requirement be applied at the fund complex level rather than at the individual fund level").

investment companies and the costs and disruption associated with contested elections of directors conducted pursuant to Rule 14a-11.

We are not adopting the suggestion of commenters that the eligibility thresholds for investment companies be based on the holdings for the fund complex in the case of unitary boards or the cluster in the case of cluster boards.[251] We believe that eligibility should be based on holdings for the investment company, not the entire fund complex or cluster, because under state law, shareholder voting is determined based on the holdings in the investment company. Fund complexes have flexibility to organize their funds into one or more investment companies. Thereafter, state law governs which shareholders vote as a group for directors. Because Rule 14a-11 is intended to facilitate the exercise of traditional state law rights to nominate and elect directors, we believe that the rule should follow state law.

ii. Voting power

We proposed that the ownership threshold be determined as a percentage of the securities entitled to be voted on the election of directors. Some commenters sought clarification of how the ownership threshold would be calculated where companies have multiple classes of stock with varying voting rights.[252] These commenters observed that the proposed rule did not adequately address voting regimes where the voting rights have been separated from the economic rights of ownership.[253] One commenter explained that in situations where ownership of securities does not correlate with voting power,[254] shares will have voting rights disproportionate to the number of shares held, and that creates a disparity between the two classes in terms of the economic value of a single vote.[255] One commenter advised that further clarification was needed for companies with two or more outstanding classes of voting securities with disparate voting rights, including those companies with classes of voting securities and nonvoting securities, so that those companies would be treated in a manner consistent with companies that have one class of voting securities.[256]

In proposing that the ownership threshold be determined as a percentage of securities entitled to be voted on the election of directors, our goal was to have the requirement tie to the percentage of votes that could be cast for the director nominees. In response to these commenters, we have revised the rule text to clarify that the ownership threshold will be determined as a percentage of *voting power* of the securities entitled to be voted on the election of directors at the meeting, rather than as a percentage of *securities* entitled to be voted on the election of directors, as was proposed. Accordingly, where a company has multiple classes of stock with unequal voting rights and the classes vote together on the election of directors, then voting power would be calculated based on the collective voting power.[257] If a company has multiple classes of stock that do not vote together in the election of all directors (where, for example, each class elects a subset of directors), then voting power would be determined only on the basis of the voting power of the class or classes of stock that would be voting together on the election of the person or persons sought to be nominated by the nominating shareholder or group, rather than the voting power of all classes of stock.[258] We believe this approach properly bases the availability of Rule 14a-11 on the right to vote for the nominees that may be included in the company's proxy materials, which is both consistent with the intent of the provisions of a company's governing documents and in accord with the principle that class directors are elected by the votes of the holders of the class.

---

[251] *See* letters from Barclays; T. Rowe Price; TIAA-CREF.

[252] *See* letters from ABA; Duane Morris; Media General; P. Neuhauser; New York Times. These letters illustrated a scenario where one publicly-issued class of stock is entitled to one vote per share, while the privately-held controlling class of stock is entitled to 10 votes per share and both classes vote together on the election of directors.

[253] *See* letters from ABA; P. Neuhauser; Duane Morris; Media General.

[254] *See, e.g.,* discussion in footnote 252 of common ten-to-one voting provisions of a structure with Class A and Class B securities.

[255] *See* letter from ABA.

[256] *See* letter from Duane Morris.

[257] *See* Rule 14a-11(b)(1) and Instruction 3 and the discussion below.

[258] *See* Instruction 3 to Rule 14a-11(b)(1).

iii. Ownership position

In the Proposing Release, we solicited comment about whether beneficial ownership is the appropriate standard of ownership to use for purposes of the minimum ownership threshold in the rule or whether another standard would be more appropriate. In this regard, we requested comment about whether a net long requirement should be used and, if so, what other modifications would be required. We received a number of comments addressing the appropriate standard of ownership and supporting the inclusion of a net long requirement.[259] Commenters suggested that we adopt an "ultimate" beneficial owner definition that included, among other things, a requirement that the nominating shareholder or group hold the entire bundle of voting and economic rights to any securities used to determine eligibility under the rule.[260] At least one of these commenters thought the ownership definition should be adopted this way in order to remove the possibility that multiple parties may count the same securities toward their individual securities ownership totals.[261] Moreover, many commenters were concerned that without requiring net long ownership, shareholders could engage in hedging strategies to obtain the requisite amount of ownership while eliminating or reducing their economic exposure.[262] Some commenters expressed the view that shares loaned to a third party should be taken into account when determining whether the nominating shareholder or group satisfies the relevant ownership threshold.[263] Commenters explained that institutional investors who hold shares for the long-term may lend their shares to others periodically while retaining the right to recall those shares to cast votes.[264] Commenters suggested several conditions for counting these shares: the shareholder has a legal right to recall the shares and cast votes;[265] the shareholder discloses in the Schedule 14N an intention to vote the shares;[266] the shareholder holds the shares through the date of the meeting;[267] and the shares are held past the date of the election.[268]

After considering the comments, we have modified in several respects the ownership requirement of Rule 14a-11 so that it is consistent with our intent to limit use of Rule 14a-11 to long-term shareholders with significant ownership interests. First, in order to satisfy the ownership requirement, the nominating shareholder or member of the nominating shareholder group must hold a class of securities subject to the proxy solicitation rules.[269] Limiting Rule 14a-11 nominations to holders of securities that are subject to the proxy rules appropriately excludes from the calculation private classes of voting securities held by persons that would have no expectation that our proxy rules would be available to facilitate their state law nomination rights. Further, if we included securities not covered by the proxy rules in the calculation, those securities could dilute the relative holdings of shareholders holding securities that our rules are designed to protect. Second, the nominating shareholder or member of the nominating shareholder group must hold both investment and voting power, either directly or through any person acting on their behalf, of the securities. By requiring that a nominating shareholder or member of a nominating shareholder group

---

[259] See letters from 26 Corporate Secretaries; Advance Auto Parts; Aetna; Alaska Air; Alcoa; Alston & Bird;American Express; BorgWarner; BRT; Burlington Northern; CSX; L. Dallas; Dewey; DuPont; FPL Group;Florida State Board of Administration; GE; Honeywell; ICI; JPMorgan Chase; Kirkland & Ellis LLP ("Kirkland & Ellis"); Leggett; P. Neuhauser; PepsiCo; Protective; Seven Law Firms; SIFMA; Society of Corporate Secretaries; T. Rowe Price; tw telecom; UnitedHealth; ValueAct Capital; Xerox.

[260] See letters from BRT; Devon; IBM; P. Neuhauser; Society of Corporate Secretaries.

[261] See letter from ABA.

[262] See letters from 26 Corporate Secretaries; ABA; Advance Auto Parts; Alaska Air; Allstate; Applied Materials; Association of Corporate Counsel; AT&T; J. Blanchard; Biogen; BRT; CIEBA; Cleary; Devon; Dewey; Headwaters; IBM; JPMorgan Chase; PepsiCo;

Sara Lee; Seven Law Firms; Shearman & Sterling; Sidley Austin; Society of Corporate Secretaries; Verizon.

[263] See letters from AFL-CIO; CalPERS; CII; COPERA; IAM, LIUNA; Marco Consulting; P. Neuhauser; D. Nappier; Sheet Metal Workers National Pension Fund ("Sheet Metal Workers"); SWIB.

[264] See letters from AFL-CIO; Marco Consulting; Sheet Metal Workers; SWIB.

[265] See letters from CalPERS; CII; COPERA; IAM; LIUNA; D. Nappier.

[266] See letters from AFL-CIO; CalPERS; CII; IAM; D. Nappier.

[267] See letters from CalPERS; CII; IAM; D. Nappier.

[268] See letters from COPERA.

[269] This would include securities registered pursuant to Section 12 of the Exchange Act or subject to Investment Company Act Rule 20a-1.

hold investment and voting power of the securities that are used for purposes of determining whether the ownership requirement has been met, we are addressing the concerns raised by certain commenters that the provisions of Rule 14a-11 should only be available to shareholders that possess ultimate ownership rights over the shares.

Similar to the provisions in Exchange Act Rule 13d-3,[270] the definition of voting power for purposes of Rule 14a-11 includes the power to vote, or to direct the voting of, such securities and investment power for purposes of Rule 14a-11 includes the power to dispose, or to direct the disposition of, such securities.[271] Unlike the provisions in Rule 13d-3, however, the ownership requirement of Rule 14a-11 includes both voting and investment power—as opposed to just one or the other—and voting and investment power for purposes of Rule 14a-11 does not exist over securities that a nominating shareholder or member of a nominating shareholder group merely has the right to acquire. For example, a nominating shareholder or member of a nominating shareholder group will not be able to count securities that could be acquired, such as securities underlying options that are currently exercisable but have not yet been exercised.

For purposes of meeting the ownership threshold in Rule 14a-11, a nominating shareholder or group will include investment and voting power of the company's securities that is held "either directly or through any person acting on their behalf." We are adopting the ownership provisions with this language to account for the common situation when financial intermediaries, such as banks or brokers, hold securities on behalf of their clients.[272] This additional language also covers relationships, such as parent and subsidiary, when for organizational or tax reasons, among others, investment and voting power is held by an entity that is controlled by another entity. This provision, however, would not include securities that are held in a pooled investment vehicle in which the nominating shareholder or member of a nominating shareholder group does not have voting and investment power over the securities held in the pooled investment vehicle.

Third, we have adopted a provision in the ownership requirement in Rule 14a-11 that, subject to specific conditions, allows for securities that have been loaned to a third party by or on behalf of the nominating shareholder or member of a nominating shareholder group to be considered in the calculation. We recognize that share lending is a common practice, and we believe that loaning securities to a third party is not inconsistent with a long-term investment in a company.[273] To capture only securities where voting power can ultimately be exercised by the nominating shareholder or member of a nominating shareholder group in the election of directors, however, securities that have been loaned by or on behalf of the nominating shareholder or any member of the nominating shareholder group to another person may be counted toward the ownership requirement only if the nominating shareholder or member of the nominating shareholder group:

- has the right to recall the loaned securities; and
- will recall the loaned securities upon being notified that any of the nominees will be included in the company's proxy materials.

Absent satisfaction of these conditions—in addition to holding the requisite investment power over the loaned securities—we believe it is appropriate to exclude securities that have been loaned to another person from the calculation of voting power because, generally, the person to whom the securities have been loaned has the ability to vote those securities.[274] If the rule were to allow loaned securities that either will not or

---

[270] 17 CFR § 240.13d-3. Like the approach under Rule 13d-3, we are including and excluding certain securities from the determination of who has voting power for policy reasons. Those inclusions and exceptions and the policy reasons underlying them are discussed throughout this section.

[271] *See* Instruction 3.c. to Rule 14a-11(b)(1).

[272] The rule also clarifies that financial intermediaries, such as banks or brokers, that may hold securities on behalf of their clients could not use the provisions of Rule 14a-11. *See* Instruction 3.c. to Rule 14a-11(b)(1).

[273] *See* letters from AFL-CIO; CalPERS; CII; COPERA; IAM; LIUNA; Marco Consulting; P. Neuhauser; D. Nappier; Sheet Metal Workers; SWIB.

[274] *See* letter from P. Neuhauser.

cannot be recalled to be included for purposes of the ownership calculation, then the voting power of a nominating shareholder or member of a nominating shareholder group may potentially be inflated because the calculation could include votes that the nominating shareholder or member of a nominating shareholder group cannot actually cast.

In determining the total voting power of the company's securities held by or on behalf of the nominating shareholder or any member of the nominating shareholder group, the voting power would be reduced by the voting power of any of the company's securities that the nominating shareholder or any member of a nominating shareholder group has sold in a short sale during the relevant periods.[275] In addition, the rule text explicitly excludes borrowed shares because the rule is intended to be used by holders with a significant long-term commitment to the company, and including shares that are merely borrowed is inconsistent with that purpose. The instruction makes clear that to the extent borrowed securities are not already excluded through the subtraction of securities sold short, borrowed securities would be subtracted in computing the relevant amount. We recognize that by requiring the voting power of securities sold short or borrowed for purposes other than a short sale to be subtracted from the ownership calculation, we are potentially reducing the eligibility of certain shareholders to rely on Rule 14a-11.[276] Nevertheless, as noted above, we believe that eligibility for Rule 14a-11 should be limited to those shareholders that have a significant interest in the company.[277] We agree with commenters who suggested that selling a company's securities short may divest that shareholder of the economic risks of ownership.[278]

For purposes of determining whether the nominating shareholder or any member of a nominating shareholder group has sold a company's securities short, the term "short sale" will have the meaning provided in Exchange Act Rule 200(a).[279] Under that rule, a

---

[275] *See* Instruction 3.b.3 to Rule 14a-11(b)(1). We note that in a typical short sale the person selling the securities short would not have the power to vote the securities subject to the short sale. Nevertheless, the provisions of Rule 14a-11 require that the voting power of the securities subject to the short sale be deducted from the voting power held directly or on behalf of the nominating shareholder or member of the nominating shareholder group to address our concerns about limiting the application of Rule 14a-11 to shareholders that retain significant ownership interests in a company. Likewise, a person whose ownership of shares arises solely from borrowing them for purposes of short sale would be deemed to have no share ownership for purposes of the ownership requirement of Rule 14a-11(b)(1).

[276] The ownership provisions related to short sales do not apply to securities that have been sold in a short sale where the nominating shareholder or member of the nominating shareholder group had no control over such transactions. *See* Instruction 3.b.3. to Rule 14a-11(b)(1) (covering short sales by "the nominating shareholder or any member of the nominating shareholder group, as the case may be, or any person acting on their behalf . . . "). For example, a nominating shareholder would not be required to exclude securities that have been sold short by a pooled investment vehicle in which the nominating shareholder or member of a nominating shareholder group has invested as long as the shareholder does not have the ability to direct the investments held in the pooled investment vehicle. Similarly, securities held by the pooled investment vehicle with respect to which the shareholder does not have the ability to direct the investments held in the pooled investment vehicle would not be included in the amount of holdings of the shareholder.

[277] We recognize that selling a company's securities short is only one of a number of ways that a shareholder can hedge the economic risk of its investment. Indeed, a number of commenters suggested that we adopt a beneficial ownership definition for purposes of Rule 14a-11 that netted all hedging arrangements (derivatives, swaps, *etc.*). We believe, however, that it is appropriate at this time to adopt the ownership threshold for Rule 14a-11 with the provision only relating to short sales as it contributes significantly towards the goal of excluding votes from the ownership calculation securities where the voting and economic interests are separated and does not unduly complicate the rule. Further, by excluding securities that the holder merely has the right to acquire (such as securities underlying options) and securities that have been loaned and cannot be recalled, we have further narrowed the application of the rule to address concerns about separating economic interest and voting power.

[278] *See* letters from 26 Corporate Secretaries; ABA; Advance Auto Parts; Alaska Air; Allstate; Applied Materials; Association of Corporate Counsel; AT&T; J. Blanchard; Biogen; BRT; CIEBA; Cleary; Devon; Dewey; Headwaters; IBM; JPMorgan Chase; PepsiCo; Sara Lee; Seven Law Firms; Shearman & Sterling; Sidley Austin; Society of Corporate Secretaries; Verizon.

[279] 17 CFR § 242.200(a). We note that certain of the provisions in Exchange Act Rule 200, including when a "person shall be deemed to own a security" as defined in Rule 200(b), differ from the provisions we have adopted for purposes of Rule 14a-11. For instance, Rule 200(b) extends ownership of a security to options that have been exercised. As noted above, however, we have not extended ownership for purposes of Rule 14a-11 to options. We believe that these different, but not

short sale is "any sale of a security which the seller does not own or any sale which is consummated by the delivery of a security borrowed by, or for the account of, the seller."

In calculating the voting power required to satisfy the 3% voting power eligibility requirement described above, nominating shareholders or members of a nominating shareholder group must first determine the total number of votes that can be derived from their holdings of securities that are subject to the proxy rules. This determination is made as of the date the Schedule 14N is filed. The total number of votes can be increased by the number of votes attributable to securities which have been loaned (subject to the conditions previously noted) and must be reduced by the number of votes attributable to any securities that have been sold in a short sale that is not closed out as of that date or borrowed for purposes other than a short sale. This adjusted number of votes is the qualifying number of votes eligible to be used as the numerator in calculating the percentage held of the company's total voting power. The number of securities to which these qualifying votes are attributable is the amount of securities that must be used for evaluating compliance with the continuous holding period requirements specified in Rule 14a-11(b)(2), and discussed below.

In determining the total voting power of the company's securities, nominating shareholders and members of a nominating shareholder group will be entitled to rely on the most recent quarterly, annual or current report filed by the company unless the nominating shareholder or member of a nominating shareholder group knows or has reason to know that the information in the reports is inaccurate.[280] We believe that a nominating shareholder or member of a nominating shareholder group should be able to rely on the filings made by the company in making the calculation of voting power for purposes of Rule 14a-11 even if the number of securities outstanding has changed since the last report so that a nominating shareholder or member of a nominating shareholder group can easily make a determination about the percentage of voting power that they hold.

iv. Demonstrating ownership

Under the Proposal, a nominating shareholder or member of a nominating shareholder group would be able to demonstrate ownership in several ways.[281] If the nominating shareholder or member of the nominating shareholder group is the registered holder of the shares, he or she could state as much. In this instance, the company would have the ability to independently verify the shareholder's ownership. Where the nominating shareholder or member of the nominating shareholder group is not the registered holder of the securities, the nominating shareholder or member of the nominating shareholder group would be required to demonstrate ownership by attaching to the Schedule 14N a written statement from the "record" holder of the nominating shareholder's shares (usually a broker or bank) verifying that, at the time of submitting the shareholder notice to the company on Schedule 14N, the nominating shareholder or member of the nominating shareholder group continuously held the securities being used to satisfy the applicable ownership threshold for a period of at least one year.[282] In the alternative, if the nominating shareholder or member of the nominating shareholder group has filed a Schedule 13D, Schedule 13G, Form 3, Form 4, and/or Form 5, or amendments to those

---

(Footnote Continued)

conflicting, approaches are appropriate and reflect the policy objectives for adopting each rule.

[280] *See* Instruction 1 to Rule 14a-11(b)(1). In the case of a registered investment company, in determining the total voting power of the securities that are entitled to be voted on the election of directors for purposes of establishing whether the 3% voting power threshold has been met, the nominating shareholder or group may rely on information set forth in the following documents, unless the nominating shareholder or group knows or has reason to know that the information

contained therein is inaccurate: (1) in the case of a series company, a Form 8-K that will be required to be filed in connection with the meeting where directors are to be elected; or (2) in the case of other registered investment companies, the company's most recent annual or semi-annual report filed with the Commission on Form N-CSR. *See* Instruction 2 to Rule 14a-11(b)(1).

[281] *See* Item 5 of proposed Schedule 14N.

[282] *See* the discussion below regarding the holding period we are adopting.

documents, the shareholder or group member may so state and attach a copy or incorporate that filing or amendment by reference.

Commenters generally did not object to the proposed methods of demonstrating ownership; however, they did suggest some revisions to the rule. Two commenters believed that the nominating shareholder or group, if requested by the company, should be required to provide evidence from its broker-dealer or custodian certifying that its ownership position meets the requisite threshold through a date that is within five days of the shareholders' meeting.[283] Another commenter recommended a revision to the proposed rule to allow the written statement to be dated no more than seven days prior to the date of submission of the nomination to the company.[284] The commenter explained that it may be difficult for a group of nominating shareholders to obtain letters from the "record" holders on the exact same date they submit the nomination to the company and file a Schedule 14N and cited similar problems in the context of the Rule 14a-8 process as an example. Another commenter recommended more generally that the written statement be dated a short period before the filing of the Schedule 14N.[285] Other commenters submitted various suggestions as to who should provide the required written statement.[286]

While we are adopting the requirements to demonstrate ownership as proposed, we agree with the commenters that additional clarity is needed with regard to how far in advance of the notice date the statement of the broker or bank may be dated, as well as what type of bank or broker may provide the written statement on behalf of the shareholder. We believe the date should be as close as practicable to the notice date, and believe that seven calendar days should provide a workable time frame that is still close in time to the notice date. Accordingly, we have revised the rule to clarify that the statement from the registered holder, broker, or bank may be dated within seven calendar days prior to the date the nominating shareholder or group submits the notice on Schedule 14N.[287]

Also, to provide additional clarity about these requirements, the final rule includes an example of a form of written statement verifying share ownership that may be used if the nominating shareholder or any member of the nominating shareholder group (i) is not the registered holder of the shares, (ii) is not proving ownership by providing previously filed Schedules 13D or 13G or Forms 3, 4, or 5, and (iii) holds the shares in an account with a broker or bank that is a participant in the Depository Trust Company ("DTC") or a similar clearing agency acting as a securities depository.[288] An instruction to Schedule

---

[283] See letters from BorgWarner; Society of Corporate Secretaries.

[284] See letter from CII.

[285] See letter from P. Neuhauser.

[286] See letters from ABA; CII; ICI; P. Neuhauser; Schulte Roth & Zabel; Seven Law Firms; S&C. Litigation subsequent to the Proposal has underscored the utility of clarifying the source of verification of ownership by shareholders who are not themselves registered owners of the shares. See Apache Corp. v. Chevedden, 696 F. Supp. 2d 723 (S.D.Tex. Mar. 10, 2010) (interpreting the proof of ownership requirement in Rule 14a-8(b)(2)).

[287] We note that a nominating shareholder may have changed brokers or banks during the time period in which it has held the shares it is using to meet the ownership threshold. In such cases, the nominating shareholder would need to obtain a written statement from each broker or bank with respect to the shares held and specify the time period in which the shares were held.

[288] This form of written statement from a bank or broker is a modification to the Proposal, and is provided

as a non-exclusive example of an acceptable method of satisfying the requirement in Rule 14a-11(b)(3). See Instruction to Item 4 of new Schedule 14N. We note that the written statements would not reflect all aspects of the ownership requirement, such as the percentage of voting power held, and thus, would not be dispositive with regard to whether the nominating shareholder or group satisfied the ownership threshold. For purposes of complying with Rule 14a-11(b)(3), loaned securities may be included in the amount of securities set forth in the written statements. Consistent with the Proposal, a nominating shareholder or group proving ownership by using a previously filed Schedule 13D or 13G or Form 3, 4, or 5 could attach a copy of the filing to the Schedule 14N or incorporate it by reference into the Schedule. We note that the calculation of voting power of a company's securities for purposes of Rule 14a-11 differs from the determination of beneficial ownership for purposes of those schedules and forms. In addition, as adopted, we are clarifying that the schedules or forms used to provide proof of ownership must reflect ownership of the securities as of or before the date on which the three-year eligibility period begins.

14N describes more fully what information should be provided if a nominating share-holder or any member of the nominating shareholder group holds the securities through a broker or bank (*e.g.*, in an omnibus account) that is not a participant in DTC or a similar clearing agency.[289]

We note that satisfying the requirement in Rule 14a-11(b)(3) to demonstrate owner-ship is different from satisfying the requirement in Rules 14a-11(b)(1) and 14a-11(b)(2) that a shareholder or shareholder group hold the requisite amount of the company's securities that are entitled to be voted on the election of directors for three years, as calculated pursuant to the Instruction to paragraph (b)(2). It is possible for a shareholder to be able to demonstrate ownership pursuant to Rule 14a-11(b)(3), and yet not satisfy the total voting power and holding period requirements in Rules 14a-11(b)(1) and (b)(2).

c. Holding period

With respect to duration of ownership, we proposed a one-year holding requirement for each nominating shareholder or member of a nominating shareholder group. Al-though many commenters supported the proposed one-year holding period,[290] the ma-jority of commenters suggested a holding period longer than the proposed one-year period, with many recommending alternative holding periods ranging from 18 months to four years.[291] Some commenters, for example, expressed a belief that increasing the duration of the minimum holding period would ensure that use of Rule 14a-11 is limited to holders of a significant, long-term interest and would dissuade shareholders from using the rule to nominate and elect directors to make short-term gains at the expense of long-term shareholders.[292] A small number of commenters believed that Rule 14a-11 should not include a holding period requirement.[293] One commenter believed that all holders of the same securities should have the same rights under Rule 14a-11 regardless of how long the securities have been held.[294] Another commenter stated that a short-term shareholder has the same risk as long-term shareholders; thus their rights under Rule 14a-11 should be equal.[295]

After considering the comments, we have decided to adopt a three-year holding requirement, rather than the proposed one-year requirement. This decision is based on our belief that holding securities for at least a three-year period better demonstrates a

---

[289] *See* the Instruction to Item 4 of new Schedule 14N.

[290] *See* letters from ADP; AFSCME; Callaway; CalPERS; CalSTRS; Calvert; CFA Institute; J. Chico; CII; Corporate Library; Dominican Sisters of Hope ("Dominican Sisters of Hope"); GovernanceMetrics International ("GovernanceMetrics"); ICGN; Lorsch et al.; LUCRF; Mercy Investment Program ("Mercy Investment Program"); Motorola; D. Nappier; Nathan Cummings Foundation; P. Neuhauser; Norges Bank; Pax World; RiskMetrics; Shamrock; Shearman & Sterling; Sisters of Mercy Regional Community of Detroit Charitable Trust ("Sisters of Mercy"); Social Investment Forum; Sodali; Tri-State Coalition for Responsible Investment ("Tri-State Coalition"); Trillium; T. Rowe Price; Ursuline Sisters of Tildonk ("Ursuline Sisters of Tildonk"); USPE; ValueAct Capital; Walden Asset Management ("Walden").

[291] *See* letters from 26 Corporate Secretaries; ABA; Advance Auto Parts; Aetna; AFL-CIO; Alaska Air; Alcoa; Allstate; Alston & Bird; Amalgamated Bank; American Express; Anadarko; Applied Materials; Association of Corporate Counsel; AT&T; Avis Budget; Biogen; J. Blanchard; Boeing; BorgWarner; BRT; Burlington Northern; Caterpillar; Chevron; CIEBA; CIGNA; CNH Global; P. Clapman; Comcast; Con Edison; CSX; CtW Investment Group; Cummins; L.

Dallas; Darden Restaurants; E. Davis; Deere; Devon; Dewey; DTE Energy; DuPont; Eaton; Eli Lilly; ExxonMobil; FedEx; Fenwick; FMC Corp.; FPL Group; General Mills; Headwaters; Home Depot; Honeywell; IAM; IBM; ICI; Intel; ITT; JPMorgan Chase; Lionbridge Technologies; LIUNA; Marco Consulting; McDonald's; M. Metz; J. Miller; NACD; D. Nappier (expressing a willingness to accept a two-year holding period instead of the proposed one-year holding period); Northrop; Office Depot; OPERS; Pfizer; P&G; Praxair; Protective; RiskMetrics (accepting a two-year holding period as alternative to the proposed one-year holding period); Sara Lee; S&C; Sheet Metal Workers; Sidley Austin; SIFMA; Society of Corporate Secretaries; Southern Company; Teamsters; Tesoro; Textron; Theragenics; TI; TIAA-CREF; Tidewater; Time Warner Cable Inc. ("Time Warner Cable"); tw telecom; L. Tyson; UnitedHealth; U.S. Bancorp; Wells Fargo; Weyerhaeuser; Xerox; Vanguard; Verizon; B. Villiarmois.

[292] *See* letters from BRT; CIEBA; IBM; McDonald's; Society of Corporate Secretaries.

[293] *See* letters from 13D Monitor; ACSI; British Insurers; Ironfire Capital LLC ("Ironfire"); LUCRF.

[294] *See* letter from British Insurers.

[295] *See* letter from 13D Monitor.

shareholder's long-term commitment and interest in the company.[296] We also based our decision to have a holding period longer than one year on the strong support of a variety of commenters. For instance, we received comments that advised that we should "adopt a more reasonable holding period of at least two years,"[297] and "a minimum holding period of at least two years is appropriate" because a "shorter holding period would allow shareholders with a short-term focus to nominate directors who, if elected, would be responsible for dealing with a company's long-term issues."[298] Another commenter stated that "three years would be a more reasonable test with respect to longevity of stock ownership."[299] Although two commenters suggested even longer holding periods,[300] we believe that a three year holding period reflects our goal of limiting use of the rule to significant, long-term holders and appropriately responds to commenters' suggestions regarding the length of the holding period. In this regard, as noted previously, some commenters suggested a two year holding period, but others stated it should be "at least" two years. Given the support expressed for a significant holding period, we believe a three year holding period, rather than one or two years, strikes the appropriate balance in providing shareholders with a significant, long-term interest with the ability to have their nominees included in a company's proxy materials while limiting the possibility of shareholders attempting to use Rule 14a-11 inappropriately, as discussed further below.

We also factored our desire to limit the use of Rule 14a-11 to shareholders who do not possess a change in control intent with regard to the company into our decision to extend the holding period. Although we have, as noted below, adopted specific requirements in Rule 14a-11 to address the control issue, we believe that a longer holding period is another safeguard against shareholders that may attempt to inappropriately use Rule 14a-11 as a means to quickly gain control of a company. Finally, we note that if shareholders believe that the three-year period should be shorter, the amendment that we decided to adopt to Rule 14a-8 will remove barriers to proposals that seek to establish a different procedure with a lesser (or no) holding period condition.

The requirement we are adopting is that shareholders seeking to use Rule 14a-11 to have a nominee or nominees included in a company's proxy materials must have held the minimum amount of securities used to satisfy the 3% ownership threshold continuously for at least three years.[301] Similar to the calculation of voting power discussed above, in order to satisfy the three-year holding requirement, the nominating shareholder or member of the nominating shareholder group must have investment and voting power over the amount of securities, and the amount of securities held during the period will have to be reduced by the amount of securities of the same class that are the subject of short positions or are borrowed for purposes other than a short sale during the period.[302] The

---

[296] One commenter pointed to the Aspen Principles, *available at* http://www.aspeninstitute.org/sites/default/files/content/docs/pubs/Aspen_Principles_with_signers_April_09.pdf, suggesting that companies that are often forced to react to short-term investors are constrained from creating valuable goods and services, investing in innovations, and creating jobs. *See also* letter from AFL-CIO.

[297] Letter from Teamsters.

[298] Letter from BRT.

[299] Letter from Tesoro.

[300] *See* letters from E. Davis; Fenwick.

[301] As proposed, a nominating shareholder or group would have been required to hold "the securities that are used for purposes of determining the applicable ownership threshold" and intend to continue to hold "those securities" through the date of the meeting. *See* proposed Rule 14a-11(b)(2). The Proposal also would have required the nominating shareholder or group to provide a statement that the nominating shareholder or group intends to continue to own the "requisite shares"

through the date of the meeting. *See* proposed Rule 14a-18(f). As adopted, we are modifying Rule 14a-11 to require the nominating shareholder or each member of the nominating shareholder group to have held the "amount of securities" that are used for satisfying the ownership requirement and to continue to hold that amount of securities through the date of the meeting, rather than referring to the "requisite securities." In addition, even though the ownership requirement is based on the percentage of voting power held, the requirement refers to "amount" rather than "percentage" so that satisfaction of the ownership requirement can be accurately determined. We believe it would be unduly burdensome to require that a nominating shareholder or group determine whether its holdings exceeded 3% of the company's voting power continuously for a three-year period prior to the filing of the Schedule 14N.

[302] *See* the Instruction to Rule 14a-11(b)(2). For purposes of this calculation, the amount of the short position or borrowed securities at any point in time

rule also allows securities loaned to a third party to be considered held during the period, provided that the nominating shareholder or group has the right to recall the loaned securities during the period.[303] As discussed above, we do not believe that the common practice of lending securities is inconsistent with a long-term investment. While we believe it is important to include both of the recall provisions for purposes of allowing loaned securities to be used in the 3% ownership threshold calculation in Rule 14a-11(b)(1), we believe it is only necessary for the nominating shareholder or member of a nominating shareholder group to have the right to recall the loaned securities to satisfy the three-year holding period requirement.[304] Finally, the rule requires the amount of securities to be adjusted for stock splits, reclassifications or other similar adjustments made by the company during the period.[305]

A commenter suggested that we clarify that a nominating shareholder or each member of the group must have continuously held only the minimum number of shares used to satisfy the ownership requirement.[306] We agree that a nominating shareholder or member of a nominating shareholder group is not required to have continuously held shares in excess of the amount used to attain eligibility for purposes of Rule 14a-11. For example, under Rule 14a-11(b)(2), which requires continuous holding of "the amount of securities that are used for purposes of satisfying the *minimum* ownership required of paragraph (b)(1) . . . ," if a nominating shareholder owns 400,000 shares and those shares comprise 4% of the issuer's voting power as of the date of filing of the Schedule 14N, that shareholder is not required to have held 400,000 shares continuously during the preceding three years and through the date of election of directors. Rather, the nominating shareholder would be required to continuously hold the minimum amount of shares required to satisfy the 3% ownership threshold in paragraph (b)(1), assuming no adjustments (in this example, at least 300,000 shares).

We also believe that it is important that any shareholder or member of a nominating shareholder group that intends to submit a nominee to a company for inclusion in the company's proxy materials continue to maintain the qualified minimum amount of securities in the company needed to satisfy the ownership provisions in the rule through the date of the meeting at which the shareholder's or group's nominee is presented to a vote of shareholders. To meet the eligibility criteria in proposed Rule 14a-11(b)(2), a nominating shareholder or member of a nominating shareholder group would have been required to "intend to continue to hold" the securities used to meet the ownership threshold through the date of the meeting. Commenters on the Proposing Release generally supported a holding requirement through the date of the meeting,[307] and one commenter suggested that we clarify that shareholders would be required to hold the securities used for determining ownership through the election of directors.[308] We agree with the suggestion and are modifying the language in Rule 14a-11(b)(2) to clarify that a nominating shareholder or member of a nominating shareholder group "must continue to hold" the requisite amount of securities through the date of the meeting.[309]

(Footnote Continued)

during the three year holding period would be deducted from the amount of securities otherwise held at that point in time.

[303] *Id.*

[304] *Id.* The recall provisions are discussed in Section II.B.4.b.iii. above. We note that at the time the nominating shareholder or group calculates its ownership and submits a nominee or nominees, it may not be certain that its nominee or nominees will be included in the company's proxy materials. We do not believe it is necessary to require a nominating shareholder or group to recall loaned shares that it has the right to recall and vote prior to the time that the nominating shareholder or group is notified that its nominee or nominees will be included in the company's proxy materials.

[305] *See* the Instruction to Rule 14a-11(b)(2).

[306] *See* letter from AFSCME.

[307] *See* letters from ABA; Advance Auto Parts; Alston & Bird; American Express; Association of Corporate Counsel; J. Blanchard; BorgWarner; CalPERS; CII; Cleary; Comcast; CSX; Dewey; W. B. Dickerson; Florida State Board of Administration; General Mills; Headwaters; JPMorgan Chase; Nathan Cummings Foundation; Protective; Schulte Roth & Zabel; Seven Law Firms; Shearman & Sterling; Society of Corporate Secretaries; tw telecom; ValueAct Capital.

[308] *See* letter from ABA.

[309] For purposes of determining whether the requirement to hold the specified amount of securities from the date of the filing of the Schedule 14N through the date of the election of directors is satisfied, a

If a nominating shareholder or member of a nominating shareholder group fails to continue to hold the requisite amount of securities as required by the rule, a company could exclude the nominee or nominees submitted by the nominating shareholder or group.[310]

We also are adopting, as proposed, the requirement that a nominating shareholder or member of a nominating shareholder group provide a statement as to the nominating shareholder's or group member's intent to continue to hold the qualifying minimum amount of securities through the date of the meeting.[311] In addition, we proposed that nominating shareholders or members of a nominating shareholder group disclose their intent with regard to continued ownership of their shares after the election (which may be contingent on the election's outcome). As noted above, commenters generally supported the requirement for the nominating shareholder or group to hold the requisite amount of securities through the date of the meeting, although some commenters expressed opposition to the proposed disclosure requirement or any requirement for the nominating shareholder or group to disclose their intent to hold the company's shares after the date of the election.[312] One commenter explained that the nominating shareholder or group may not know its intent at the time the Schedule 14N is filed and, depending on the outcome of the director election, the nominating shareholder or group may, in fact, purchase more stock or sell some stock.[313] Another commenter observed that it is impractical for shareholders to represent that they would hold their position beyond the election and instead favored disclosure in an amended Schedule 14N of any change in the ownership of more than 1% of the voting shares or net economic position during a period after the election (*e.g.*, 60 days).[314] Other commenters supported the proposed disclosure requirement regarding the nominating shareholder's or group's intent to hold shares after the meeting, or recommended that the Commission require instead that the nominating shareholder or group hold the requisite amount of shares for a specific period after the date of the meeting.[315]

We believe that a requirement to hold the securities through the date of the election of directors is appropriate to demonstrate the nominating shareholder's or group member's commitment to the director nominee and the election process. In addition, we are adopting the disclosure requirement, as proposed, concerning the nominating shareholder's or group member's intent with respect to continued ownership of their shares after the

---

(Footnote Continued)

nominating shareholder or group must hold (as determined pursuant to the instruction to the rule) the qualifying minimum amount of securities, which can include securities that are loaned to a third party if the nominating shareholder or group has the right to recall the securities, and will recall them upon being notified that any of the nominees will be included in the company's proxy materials. Of course, between the date of the filing of the Schedule 14N and the date of the election of directors previously loaned securities may be returned. Likewise, the amount of securities held during the period from the filing of the Schedule 14N through the date of the election of directors must be reduced by the amount of securities of the same class that are sold in a short sale.

[310] *See* new Rule 14a-11(b)(2) and Rule 14a-11(g). The company would be required to provide notice to the staff in accordance with Rule 14a-11(g) and could seek a no-action letter from the staff with regard to the determination to exclude the nominee at that time if the company so wished. In the event that the nominating shareholder's or group's failure to continue to hold the securities comes to light after the company has printed its proxy materials, the company would be permitted to

exclude the nominee or nominees and send a revised proxy card to its shareholders. For additional information about a company's obligations in the event a nominee withdraws or is disqualified, *see* Section II.B.7.b. below.

[311] *See* new Rule 14a-11(b)(4) and proposed Rule 14a-18(f).

[312] *See* letters from Alston & Bird; Amalgamated Bank; Calvert; CII; Florida State Board of Administration; P. Neuhauser; Norges Bank; Schulte Roth & Zabel; TIAA-CREF; USPE; ValueAct Capital.

[313] *See* letter from CII.

[314] *See* letter from Cleary.

[315] *See* letters from 26 Corporate Secretaries; ABA; Aetna; AGL; Alaska Air; Alcoa; Anadarko; Applied Materials; Association of Corporate Counsel; Avis Budget; BRT; Burlington Northern; Callaway; Caterpillar; Comcast; L. Dallas; Darden Restaurants; Devon; W. B. Dickerson; Dupont; Eli Lilly; FPL Group; General Mills; Home Depot; Honeywell; Intel; Lionbridge Technologies; Lorsch et al.; Keating Muething; Office Depot; PepsiCo; Pfizer; Protective; Sara Lee; SIFMA; Tesoro; Textron; TI; UnitedHealth; U.S. Bancorp; Verizon; Xerox.

election.[316] We are not, however, adopting a requirement for a nominating shareholder or member of a nominating shareholder group to continue to hold their shares for a certain period of time after the date of the election. We believe that disclosure of a nominating shareholder's or group member's intent with respect to continued ownership in a Schedule 14N or amended Schedule 14N will provide investors with the information they need for this purpose.

d. No change in control intent

Under the Proposal, to rely on Rule 14a-11, a nominating shareholder or member of a nominating shareholder group would have been required to provide a certification in the filed Schedule 14N that it did not hold the securities with the purpose, or with the effect, of changing the control of the company or gaining more than a limited number of seats on the board.[317] We noted that this certification, along with the other required disclosures, would assist shareholders in making an informed decision with regard to any nominee or nominees put forth by the nominating shareholder or group, in that the information would enable shareholders to gauge the nominating shareholder's or group's interest in the company, longevity of ownership, and intent with regard to continued ownership in the company.

Most commenters on this aspect of the Proposal agreed generally that Rule 14a-11 should not be available to shareholders seeking to effect a change in control of a company (or to obtain more than a specified number of board seats) and supported a certification requirement regarding the lack of change in control intent.[318] Some commenters, however, expressed concern about the lack of a remedy when a certification regarding control intent proves to be false or when a nominating shareholder or group changes its intent.[319] Suggested remedies included excluding the nominee of any nominating shareholder or group that changes intent and barring the nominating shareholder or group from using the rule for the following two annual meetings,[320] requiring disclosure of a change of intent and resignation of the Rule 14a-11 director,[321] and imposing liability under Rule 14a-9.[322]

We are adopting this requirement with some modifications from the Proposal. To rely on Rule 14a-11, the nominating shareholder (or where there is a nominating shareholder group, any member of the nominating shareholder group) must not be holding any of the company's securities with the purpose, or with the effect, of changing control of the company[323] or to gain a number of seats on the board of directors that exceeds the maximum number of nominees that the registrant could be required to include under Rule 14a-11 and must provide a certification to this effect in its filed Schedule 14N.[324]

The final requirement differs from the Proposal in three respects. First, in addition to requiring the certification to address the absence of change in control intent or intent to gain more than the maximum number of seats provided under the rule, we also have

---

[316] *See* new Rule 14a-11(b)(5) and new Item 4(b) of Schedule 14N.

[317] *See* Item 8 of proposed Schedule 14N.

[318] *See* letters from ABA; Advance Auto Parts; American Bankers Association; American Express; Americans for Financial Reform ("Americans for Financial Reform"); BRT; CalSTRS; CII; Cleary; COPERA; Corporate Library; Dewey; Dominican Sisters of Hope; Eli Lilly; Emerson Electric; Florida State Board of Administration; A. Goolsby; GovernanceMetrics; ICI; JPMorgan Chase; Sen. Carl Levin ("C. Levin"); Mercy Investment Program; Metlife; Nathan Cummings Foundation; P. Neuhauser; Protective; RiskMetrics; Seven Law Firms; SIFMA; Sisters of Mercy; Social Investment Forum; Society of Corporate Secretaries; Sodali; SWIB; TIAA-CREF; Trillium; Tri-State Coalition; T. Rowe Price; tw telecom; Ursuline Sisters of Tildonk; Wachtell; Walden; B. Villiarmois.

[319] *See* letters from American Bankers Association; Dewey; Emerson Electric; A. Goolsby; Metlife; Protective; Seven Law Firms; SIFMA.

[320] *See* letter from Seven Law Firms.

[321] *See* letter from Protective.

[322] *See* letter from P. Neuhauser.

[323] Although Rule 14a-11 does not contain a requirement that the shareholder nominee or nominees do not have an intent to change the control of the company, a nominating shareholder's or group's ability to meet the requirement and certify that it does not have such an intent will be impacted by the intentions and actions of its nominee or nominees. For example, a nominating shareholder would not be able to certify that it does not hold the company's securities for the purpose, or with the effect, of changing the control of the company if its nominee is engaged in its own proxy contest or tender offer while the Rule 14a-11 nomination is pending.

[324] *See* certifications in Item 8 of new Schedule 14N.

added this condition as an explicit requirement to the rule.[325] We believe that this more directly achieves our intent—that the rule not be used by shareholders that have an intent to change the control of the company or gain more than the maximum number of seats specified in the rule.

Second, we have clarified the language of the requirements so that it provides that the rule is available only if the nominating shareholder or group members do not have an intent to change control of the company[326] or gain more seats on the board than the maximum provided for under Rule 14a-11. We slightly revised the language of the requirement to clarify our intended meaning. The Proposal used the language "gain more than a limited number of seats on the board," which was intended to refer to the limitations within the rule on the maximum number of nominees required to be included in the company's proxy materials. The final rule states this more explicitly.

Finally, we have added an instruction to clarify that in order to rely on Rule 14a-11 to include a nominee or nominees in a company's proxy materials, a nominating shareholder or a member of a nominating shareholder group may not be a member of any other group with persons engaged in solicitations or other nominating activities in connection with the subject election of directors; may not separately conduct a solicitation in connection with the subject election of directors other than a Rule 14a-2(b)(8) exempt solicitation in relation to those nominees it has nominated pursuant to Rule 14a-11 or for or against the company's nominees; and may not act as a participant in another person's solicitation in connection with the subject election of directors.[327]

We understand that companies have concerns that shareholders using Rule 14a-11 may inaccurately assert that they do not have a change in control intent, and that this can be a difficult factual issue. If a company determines that it can exclude a nominee based on this eligibility condition, it will be required to notify the nominating shareholder, members of the nominating shareholder group, or, where applicable, the nominating shareholder group's authorized representative, of a deficiency in its notice on Schedule 14N and provide the nominating shareholder or group the opportunity to respond. The company also would be required to submit a notice to the Commission stating its intent to exclude a nominee from its proxy materials (which would be required to include a description of the company's basis for exclusion) and, if it wished to, it could seek the staff's informal view with regard to its determination to exclude the nominee (commonly referred to as a "no-action" request).[328] In addition, a nominating shareholder and each member of a nominating shareholder group will have liability under Rule 14a-9 for a materially false or misleading certification in the Schedule 14N. Questions concerning the nomination also may be resolved by the parties outside the staff process provided in Rule 14a-11(g), including through private litigation where necessary, similar to the way they resolve issues arising in traditional proxy contests.[329] Finally, we note that the Commission also could take enforcement action with respect to companies that inappropriately exclude nominees under Rule 14a-11 or shareholders that provide false certifications in their Schedule 14N. We believe these measures should provide sufficient means to address situations in which a nominating shareholder or member of a nominating shareholder group provides a false certification regarding change in control intent.

e. Agreements with the company

In the Proposing Release, we noted that a shareholder nomination process that includes limits on the number of nominees that a company is required to include in its proxy materials presents the potential risk of nominating shareholders or groups acting merely as a surrogate for the company or its management in order to block usage of the

---

[325] *See* Rule 14a-11(b)(6).

[326] A change in control includes, but is not limited to, an extraordinary corporate action, such as a merger or tender offer.

[327] *See* new Instruction to Rule 14a-11(b).

[328] *See* Section II.B.9.b. below for further discussion of determinations to exclude a nominee or nominees.

[329] *See* Sections II.B.8. and II.B.9. for an explanation of the disclosure requirements applicable to a nomination made pursuant to Rule 14a-11 and the process for excluding a nominee.

rule by another nominating shareholder or group. We proposed to address this concern by providing that a nominating shareholder or group using Rule 14a-11 would be required to represent that no agreement between the nominating shareholder or group and the company and its management exists.[330] To avoid any uncertainty about the breadth of this requirement, the Proposal included an instruction noting that prohibited agreements would not include unsuccessful negotiations with the company to have the nominee included in the company's proxy materials as a management nominee, or negotiations that are limited to whether the company is required to include the shareholder nominee in the company's proxy materials under Rule 14a-11.

Commenters generally supported the proposed requirement, including the clarifying instruction regarding certain negotiations with the company.[331] One commenter specifically supported the portion of the proposed rule providing that unsuccessful negotiations or negotiations that were limited to whether the company is required to include a shareholder nominee under Rule 14a-11 would not be deemed to be a direct or indirect agreement.[332] One commenter was concerned about possible manipulation by companies and supported a prohibition on agreements.[333] According to that commenter, negotiations that resulted in a nomination being included in the proxy statement should be treated as a company nominee and not a shareholder nominee under Rule 14a-11.

Some commenters encouraged us to allow negotiations that resulted in inclusion of shareholder nominees as management nominees and cautioned that the proposal could discourage constructive dialogue between companies and shareholders.[334] Three commenters opposed limits on some or all relationships between the company and the nominating shareholder, group, or shareholder nominee.[335] These commenters believed that the Commission should not prohibit agreements between a company and a nominating shareholder or group. They warned that restricting the ability of companies to reach agreements with a nominating shareholder or group would limit the dialogue between companies and investors. One commenter suggested that proposed Rule 14a-18(d) be revised to permit a company to agree not to contest the eligibility of a shareholder nominee.[336] The commenter also suggested that if a company settled a threatened election contest by placing a shareholder nominee on the board, additional shareholder nominees should not be permitted for a specified period of time.

After careful review of the comments, we continue to believe that it is appropriate to provide that a nominating shareholder or group will not be eligible to have a nominee or nominees included in a company's proxy materials under Rule 14a-11 if the nominating shareholder, group, or any member of the nominating shareholder group, has any agreement with the company with respect to the nomination. We have revised the rule to make it clearer that this is an eligibility condition by listing it as a condition in the rule, rather than only a representation required in Schedule 14N.[337] We have incorporated, as proposed, the instruction with respect to unsuccessful negotiations (*i.e.* negotiations that do not result in an agreement) regarding whether a company is required to include a nominee in order to make clear that those negotiations would not be disqualifying.

As described above, a nominating shareholder or group will not be eligible to use Rule 14a-11 if there is an agreement with the company regarding the nomination of the nominee.[338] When a nominating shareholder or group files its Schedule 14N, this

---

[330] In this regard, we also proposed to require a nominating shareholder or group to represent that no relationships or agreements between the nominee and the company and its management exist. This aspect of the rule is discussed in Section II.B.5.c. below.

[331] *See* letters from ADP; BRT; Calvert; CFA Institute; CII; Seven Law Firms; TIAA-CREF; USPE.

[332] *See* letter from CII.

[333] *See* letter from USPE.

[334] *See* letters from BRT; Seven Law Firms; Society of Corporate Secretaries.

[335] *See* letters from ABA; Steve Quinlivan ("S. Quinlivan"); Verizon.

[336] *See* letter from S. Quinlivan.

[337] We note that a nominating shareholder or members of a nominating shareholder group will be required to provide a certification in the Schedule 14N that the requirements of Rule 14a-11 are satisfied, which will include the "no agreements" requirement. A nominating shareholder or member of a nominating shareholder group will be liable, pursuant to Rule 14a-9(c), for a false or misleading certification provided in Schedule 14N.

[338] *See* Rule 14a-11(b)(7). *See also* Rule 14a-11(d)(7) which clarifies that if a nominee, nominating shareholder or any member of a nominating group has

requirement will apply, and the certification required by Schedule 14N will have the effect of confirming that there are no agreements. We believe this is an important safeguard to prevent actions that could undermine the purpose of the rule. If, after the Schedule 14N is filed, a nominating shareholder or group reached an agreement with the company for the nominee to be included in the company's proxy materials as a management nominee, the nominating shareholder or group would no longer be proceeding under Rule 14a-11. Consequently, there is no need to revise the "no agreements" requirement in Rule 14a-11 to address that fact pattern.

Although we are adopting the "no agreements" requirement largely as proposed, we are persuaded by commenters that we should revise our final rules so that they do not unnecessarily discourage constructive dialogue between shareholders and companies. However, we believe this concern is more appropriately addressed in the method of calculation of the maximum number of permissible nominees, and the question of whether that number should include management nominees that were originally put forward as shareholder nominees under Rule 14a-11. Our revisions to that provision are discussed in Section II.B.6. below.

f. No requirement to attend the annual or special meeting

Under Rule 14a-11 as proposed, a nominating shareholder or group would have no obligation to attend the annual or special meeting at which its nominee or nominees is being presented to shareholders for a vote. We received comment on the Proposal, however, suggesting that we require a nominating shareholder or group, or a qualified representative of the nominating shareholder or group, to attend the company's shareholder meeting and nominate its director candidate(s) in person.[339] One commenter explained that this requirement would be consistent with state law requirements for nominations and many companies' advance notice bylaws.[340] Another commenter suggested that, as required under Rule 14a-8(h)(3) for shareholder proposals, if the nominating shareholder or group (or its qualified representative) fails, without good cause, to appear and nominate the candidate, the company should be permitted to exclude from its proxy materials for the following two years all nominees submitted by that nominating shareholder or members of the nominating group.[341]

We have decided not to include a requirement that the nominating shareholder or qualified representative appear at the meeting and present the nominee because we believe that shareholders will have sufficient incentive to take steps to assure that their nominees are voted on at the meeting, whether through attending the meeting or sending a qualified representative, or through other arrangements with the company, and we do not want to add unnecessary complexities and burdens to the rule. We note that state law will control what happens if a candidate is not nominated at the meeting because the person supporting the candidate does not attend the meeting or make other arrangements.[342]

(Footnote Continued)

an agreement with the company or an affiliate of the company regarding the nomination of a candidate for election, other than as specified in Rule 14a-11(d)(5) or (6), any nominee or nominees from such shareholder or group shall not be counted in calculating the number of shareholder nominees for purposes of Rule 14a-11(d).

[339] *See* letters from ABA; BRT.

[340] *See* letter from ABA.

[341] *See* letter from BRT.

[342] While state statutes are largely silent on the subject of presentation of nominations, motions or other business at meetings of shareholders, the chair-

man of the meeting typically has broad discretionary authority over its conduct (*see, e.g.*, Model Business Corporation Act § 7.08(b)). As we understand, it is prevailing practice for the chairman to invite nominations of directors from the meeting floor. *See* David A. Drexler, et al., Delaware Corporation Law and Practice, ¶ 24.05[3] (2009 supp.); Carroll R. Wetzel, *Conduct of a Stockholders' Meeting*, 22 Bus. Law. 303, 313-314 (1967); American Bar Association Corporate Laws Committee and Corporate Governance Committee, Business Law Section, Handbook for the Conduct of Shareholders' Meetings (2d ed. 2010) at 151.

g. No limit on resubmission

Under the Proposal, a nominating shareholder's or group's ability to use Rule 14a-11 would not be impacted by prior unsuccessful use of the rule. In response to our request for comment, a number of commenters supported a provision that would render a nominating shareholder or group ineligible to use Rule 14a-11 for a period of time (*e.g.*, one, two, or three years) if the nominating shareholder or group presented a nominee who failed to receive significant shareholder support in a previous election (*e.g.*, 10%, 15%, 25%, or 30%).[343] One commenter indicated that this resubmission threshold would have a dual purpose: (i) when the nominee failed to garner significant support from shareholders, it would be inappropriate to require the company to expend resources repeatedly to include the unsuccessful nominee;[344] and (ii) other shareholders would have an opportunity to submit their own nominations.[345] On the other hand, some commenters opposed a provision that would render a nominating shareholder or group ineligible to use Rule 14a-11 for a period of time if the nominating shareholder or group presented a nominee who failed to receive a specified percentage of shareholder votes at a previous election.[346] One commenter pointed out that management nominees are not subject to similar limits.[347] After consideration of the comments we do not believe it is necessary or appropriate to include a limitation on use of Rule 14a-11 by nominating shareholders or groups that have previously used the rule. We continue to believe that such a limitation would not facilitate shareholders' traditional state law rights and would add unnecessary complexity to the rule's operation.

5. Nominee Eligibility under Exchange Act Rule 14a-11

a. Consistent with applicable law and regulation

Under the Proposal, a company would have been able to exclude a nominee where the nominee's candidacy or, if elected, board membership would violate controlling state law, federal law, or rules of a national securities exchange or national securities association (other than rules of a national securities exchange or national securities association that set forth requirements regarding the independence of directors, which the rule addresses separately) and such violation could not be cured.[348]

Commenters generally supported this requirement.[349] These commenters suggested that the rule require the nominating shareholder or group to provide any information necessary to ensure compliance with these laws or regulations. Some of these commenters noted that there are various federal and state laws that govern or affect the ability of a person to serve as a director, such as the Federal Power Act and related FERC regulations, federal maritime laws and regulations, Department of Defense security clearance requirements, Department of State export licensing requirements, bank holding company laws, FCC licensing requirements, state gaming licensing requirements, Federal Reserve regulations, FDIC regulations, U.S. government procurement regulations,

---

[343] *See* letters from 26 Corporate Secretaries; ABA; ADP; Advance Auto Parts; Aetna; Alcoa; AllianceBernstein; Anadarko; Applied Materials; Avis Budget; Boeing; BorgWarner; BRT; Burlington Northern; Caterpillar; Chevron; CIGNA; Cleary; Comcast; CSX; Darden Restaurants; Deere; Dewey; DTE Energy; Dupont; Eaton; FedEx; Florida State Board of Administration; FMC Corp.; FPL Group; General Mills; Headwaters; Intel; ITT; JPMorgan Chase; Kirkland & Ellis; E.J. Kullman; Leggett; P. Neuhauser; Northrop; PepsiCo; Pfizer; Protective; RiskMetrics; Sara Lee; Seven Law Firms; SIFMA; Society of Corporate Secretaries; Southern Company; T. Rowe Price; tw telecom; U.S. Bancorp; Wells Fargo; Weyerhaeuser; Whirlpool; Xerox.

[344] *See* discussion in Section II.B.5.e. below with regard to resubmission of unsuccessful shareholder nominees.

[345] *See* letter from Society of Corporate Secretaries.

[346] *See* letters from CII; Norges Bank; Solutions; USPE; Walden.

[347] *See* letter from CII.

[348] In the Proposing Release, we described an exception from the provision if the violation could be cured. We inadvertently did not include language for this provision in the proposed regulatory text.

[349] *See* letters from 26 Corporate Secretaries; American Bankers Association; Association of Corporate Counsel; BRT; Dewey; Emerson Electric; Financial Services Roundtable; GE; Intel; JPMorgan Chase; O'Melveny & Myers; Protective; Sidley Austin; Tenet; Xerox.

Section 8 of the Clayton Act, Section 1 of the Sherman Act, and Section 5 of the Federal Trade Commission Act.[350] One commenter, for example, explained that banking laws and regulations impose their own eligibility standards for directors.[351] One commenter stated more generally that it does not oppose the proposed requirement that a company would not have to include a shareholder nominee in its proxy materials if the nominee's candidacy or election would violate federal law or state law and such violation could not be cured.[352] It noted, however, that "there is not a lot of law" that disqualifies a person from serving as a director and described concerns about state law barriers as a "red herring."

On the other hand, one commenter stated that a company should not be allowed to exclude a shareholder nominee from its proxy materials because the election of the nominee would result in the violation of state law or federal law.[353] The commenter explained that allowing such exclusion "would make it prohibitively expensive for most shareowners to submit nominations under the proposed rule. It would lead to many shareowner nominees being disqualified based on technicalities or invented legal theories."

After considering the comments, we continue to believe that Rule 14a-11 should address federal law, state law, and applicable exchange requirements (other than the requirements related to objective independence standards, which are addressed separately under the rule). Requiring compliance with basic legal requirements regarding nominees should encourage nominating shareholders to bring forward candidates that may be more likely to be able to be elected and serve as directors, and should reduce disruption and expense for companies of opposing a candidate who could not serve on the board if elected because their service would violate law.[354] Thus, under Rule 14a-11, a nominee will not be eligible to be included in a company's proxy materials if the nominee's candidacy, or if elected, board membership will violate federal law, state law, or applicable exchange requirements, if any,[355] other than those related to independence standards, and such violation could not be cured during the time period provided in the rule.[356]

b. Independence requirements and other director qualifications

Under the Proposal, the nominating shareholder or each member of the nominating shareholder group would have been required to provide a representation that the shareholder nominee meets the *objective criteria* for "independence" of the national securities exchange or national securities association rules applicable to the company, if any, or, in the case of a registrant that is an investment company, a representation that the nominee is not an "interested person" of the registrant, as defined in Section 2(a)(19) of the Investment Company Act.[357] For registrants other than investment companies, the representation would not have been required in instances where a company is not subject to the requirements of a national securities exchange or a national securities association. We also noted that exchange rules regarding director independence generally include some standards that depend on an objective determination of facts and other standards that depend on subjective determinations.[358] Under our Proposal, the representation

---

[350] *See* letters from American Bankers Association; BRT; Emerson Electric; GE; O'Melveny & Myers; Sidley Austin; Tenet.

[351] *See* letter from American Bankers Association.

[352] *See* letter from CII.

[353] *See* letter from USPE.

[354] We note that this condition would not disqualify a nominee unless the violation could not be cured during the time period in which a nominating shareholder or group has to respond to a company's notice of deficiency.

[355] We are not aware of other exchange requirements related to director qualifications, but should an exchange adopt new requirements, this provision would apply.

[356] As discussed in Section II.B.9.b., a company that intends to exclude a shareholder nominee or nominees

will be required to notify the nominating shareholder or group of the basis on which the company plans to exclude the nominee or nominees and the nominating shareholder or group will have 14 calendar days to cure the deficiency (where curable).

[357] Pursuant to proposed Rule 14a-18(c), a nominating shareholder or group would include a representation in its notice to the company that the nominee satisfies the existing independence or "interested person" standards.

[358] *See* proposed Rule 14a-18(c) and the Instruction to paragraph (c). For example, the NYSE listing standards include both subjective and objective components in defining an "independent director." As an example of a subjective determination, Section 303A.02(a) of the NYSE Listed Company Manual

would not cover subjective determinations. Also, the representation would not cover additional independence or director qualification requirements imposed by a board on its independent members, although we requested comment on whether it should.

Commenters generally supported the requirement regarding the objective independence standards.[359] Institutional and other investors agreed that nominating shareholders should not be required to represent that nominees satisfy the subjective independence standards of the relevant exchange or national securities association, and also agreed that they should not be subject to any director independence or qualification standards set by the board or the nominating committee.[360] One of these commenters expressed agreement with the Proposal that where a company is not subject to the independence standards of an exchange or national securities association, the nominating shareholder or group should not be required to provide disclosure concerning whether nominees would be independent.[361] To the extent that a company has independence standards that are more stringent than those of an exchange, then the commenter would not oppose the application of those standards to the shareholder nominee as long as the standards are objective. Two commenters expressed the view that the Section 2(a)(19) test is more appropriate for investment company directors than the independence standard applied to non-investment company directors,[362] with one noting that the Section 2(a)(19) test is tailored to the types of conflicts of interest faced by investment company directors and that the Section 2(a)(19) provision is critical given that investment companies must have a specified percentage of independent directors to be able to comply with certain statutory and regulatory requirements.[363]

A significant number of commenters from the corporate community stated generally that shareholder nominees should satisfy not just the objective director independence standards of the relevant exchange or national securities associations, but all of the company's director qualifications and independence standards (including, if applicable, more stringent objective independence standards imposed by the board, subjective director independence standards, director qualification standards, board service guidelines,

---

(Footnote Continued)

provides that no director will qualify as "independent" unless the board of directors "affirmatively determines that the director has no material relationship with the listed company (either directly or as a partner, shareholder or officer of an organization that has a relationship with the company)." On the other hand, Section 303A.02(b) provides that a director is not independent if he or she has any of several specified relationships with the company that can be determined by a "bright-line" objective test. For example, a director is not independent if "the director has received, or has an immediate family member who has received, during any twelve-month period within the last three years, more than $120,000 in direct compensation from the listed company, other than director and committee fees and pension or other forms of deferred compensation for prior service (provided such compensation is not contingent in any way on continued service)." Similar to the NYSE rules, the NASDAQ Listing Rules require a company's board to make an affirmative determination that individuals serving as independent directors do not have a relationship with the company that would impair their independence. The NASDAQ rules include certain objective criteria, similar to those provided in NYSE Section 303A.02(b), for making such a determination. See NASDAQ Rule 5605(a)(2) and IM-5605.

[359] See letters from ABA; ACSI; Advance Auto Parts; Aetna; Alaska Air; Alcoa; Anadarko; Avis

Budget; Biogen; The Board Institute ("Board Institute"); BorgWarner; BRT; Burlington Northern; Callaway; CalSTRS; Caterpillar; CIGNA; Cleary; Comcast; Con Edison; CII; COPERA; CSX; Cummins; Darden Restaurants; Deere; Dewey; DTE Energy; Eaton; Edison Electric Institute; Einstein Noah Restaurant Group, Inc. ("Einstein Noah"); Emerson Electric; ExxonMobil; FedEx; FMC Corp.; FPL Group; General Mills; A. Goolsby; Headwaters; Home Depot; Honeywell; Horizon Lines, Inc. ("Horizon"); C. Horner; IBM; Intel; JPMorgan Chase; Keating Muething; E.J. Kullman; LUCRF; McDonald's; Merchants Terminal; Metlife; P. Neuhauser; Norfolk Southern; Northrop; Office Depot; O'Melveny & Myers; P&G; PepsiCo; Pfizer; Protective; S&C; Seven Law Firms; Sidley Austin; SIFMA; Society of Corporate Secretaries; Southern Company; Tenet; Tesoro; Theragenics; TI; TIAA-CREF; Tompkins; tw telecom; UnitedHealth; U.S. Bancorp; ValueAct Capital; Verizon; Wells Fargo; Weyerhaeuser.

[360] See letters from ACSI; CalSTRS; CII; COPERA; LUCRF; P. Neuhauser; TIAA-CREF; ValueAct Capital.

[361] See letter from CII.

[362] See letters from ABA II; ICI.

[363] See letter from ICI. One commenter stated that the application of the "interested person" standard of Section 2(a)(19) is unnecessary. See letter from Norges Bank.

and code of conduct in the company's governance principles and committee charters) applicable to all directors and director nominees.[364] Many commenters warned that exempting shareholder nominees from a company's director independence and qualification standards could cause the company to be exposed to legal issues, lower the quality and diversity of the board, and create difficulties in recruiting qualified directors.[365] Other commenters also believed that exempting shareholder nominees from the subjective director independence standards of the relevant exchange or national securities association would put companies at risk of noncompliance with the exchange's or association's rules regarding independent directors, burden the remaining independent directors with additional duties by forcing them to serve on more board committees, make it more difficult for companies to recruit the independent directors needed for the board committees, and force companies to increase the size of the board and conduct additional searches for directors qualifying as independent.[366]

After carefully considering the comments, we are adopting the requirement largely as proposed. We believe that the Rule 14a-11 process should be limited to nominations of board candidates who meet any objective independence standards of the relevant securities exchange. While we understand the concerns expressed by many commenters from the corporate community, particularly with respect to the risk of noncompliance with listing standards, we continue to believe that the rule should not extend to subjective independence standards. We note that Rule 14a-11 only addresses when a company must include a nominee in its proxy materials—it does not preclude a nominee from ultimately being subject to any subjective determination of independence for board committee positions. We believe the concerns regarding independent directors being forced to take on additional duties, companies needing to increase the size of the board or conducting additional searches for independent directors are best addressed through disclosure. A company could include disclosure in its proxy materials advising shareholders that the shareholder nominee would not meet the company's subjective criteria, as appropriate. This would provide shareholders with the opportunity to make an informed choice with regard to the candidates for director.

We believe that it is in both the company's and shareholders' interest for the company to continue to meet any applicable listing standards, and requiring that Rule 14a-11 nominees meet the objective independence standards will further that interest. It also should help reduce disruption and expense for companies opposing a candidate it believes would cause it to violate applicable listing standards. To clarify that this is an affirmative requirement for Rule 14a-11 nominees, we have revised the rule to include this provision as an eligibility requirement rather than a representation.[367]

A nominating shareholder or group also will be required to provide a statement in Schedule 14N that the nominee or nominees meets the objective independence standards of the applicable exchange rules.[368] For this purpose, the nominee would be required to meet the definition of "independent" that is applicable to directors of the company generally and not any particular definition of independence applicable to members of the audit committee of the company's board of directors.[369] To the extent a rule imposes a standard regarding independence that requires a subjective determination by the board

---

[364] *See* letters from ABA; Advance Auto Parts; Aetna; Alaska Air; Alcoa; Anadarko; Avis Budget; Biogen; Board Institute; BorgWarner; BRT; Burlington Northern; Callaway; Caterpillar; CIGNA; Cleary; Comcast; Con Edison; CSX; Cummins; Darden Restaurants; Deere; Dewey; DTE Energy; Eaton; Edison Electric Institute; Einstein Noah; Emerson Electric; ExxonMobil; FedEx; FMC Corp.; FPL Group; General Mills; A. Goolsby; Headwaters; Home Depot; Honeywell; Horizon; C. Horner; IBM; Intel; JPMorgan Chase; Keating Muething; E.J. Kullman; McDonald's; Merchants Terminal; Metlife; Norfolk Southern; Northrop; Office Depot; O'Melveny & Myers; P&G;

PepsiCo; Pfizer; Protective; S&C; Seven Law Firms; Sidley Austin; SIFMA; Society of Corporate Secretaries; Southern Company; Tenet; Tesoro; Theragenics; TI; Tompkins; tw telecom; UnitedHealth; U.S. Bancorp; Verizon; Wells Fargo; Weyerhaeuser.

[365] *See* letters from Board Institute; BRT; Con Edison; C. Horner; TI; Verizon.

[366] *See* letters from Metlife; O'Melveny & Myers; Seven Law Firms; Wells Fargo.

[367] *See* Rule 14a-11(b)(9).

[368] *See* Item 5(f) of new Schedule 14N.

[369] *See* new instruction to paragraph (b)(9) in Rule 14a-11.

or a group or committee of the board (for example, requiring that the board of directors or any group or committee of the board of directors make a determination that the nominee has no material relationship with the listed company), this element of an independence standard would not have to be satisfied.[370] Where a company (other than an investment company) is not subject to the standards of a national securities exchange or national securities association, the requirement would not apply.

While we acknowledge commenters' concerns about nominees not being subject to subjective independence requirements, we believe that including such requirements would create undue uncertainty for shareholders seeking to nominate directors and make it difficult to evaluate the board's conclusion regarding independence. In addition, if a board believes a nominee would not be considered independent under its subjective independence evaluation, it could describe its reasons for that view in its proxy statement. In this regard, we note that in a traditional proxy contest an insurgent's nominee or nominees do not have to comply with any requirements, including the independence requirements applicable to the company.[371] We also agree with the commenter who noted that the "interested person" test under Section 2(a)(19) is tailored to the types of conflicts of interest faced by investment company directors and that the Section 2(a)(19) provision is critical given that investment companies must have a specified percentage of independent directors to be able to comply with certain statutory and regulatory requirements.[372] Accordingly, under the final rule, a company will be required to include a shareholder nominee in its proxy materials if the shareholder nominee meets the objective criteria for "independence" of the national securities exchange or national securities association rules applicable to the company, if any, or, in the case of a company that is an investment company, the nominee is not an "interested person" of the registrant, as defined in Section 2(a)(19) of the Investment Company Act.[373]

As noted above, we did not propose to require a shareholder nominee submitted pursuant to Rule 14a-11 to be subject to the company's director qualification standards. With regard to these standards, we believe that a nominee's compliance with a company's director qualifications is best addressed through disclosure. Under state law, shareholders generally are free to nominate and elect any person to the board of directors, regardless of whether the candidate satisfies a company's qualification requirement at the time of nomination and election.[374] Many commenters recommended a requirement that the shareholder nominee complete the company's standard director questionnaire or otherwise provide information required of other nominees.[375] While we do not believe nominees submitted pursuant to Rule 14a-11 should be required to complete a

---

[370] The rule addresses only the requirements under Rule 14a-11 to be included in a company's proxy materials—it would not preclude a nominee from ultimately being subject to the subjective determination test of independence for board committee positions. A company could include disclosure in its proxy materials advising shareholders that the shareholder nominee for director would not meet the company's subjective criteria, as appropriate. If a shareholder nominee is elected and the board determines that the nominee is not independent, the board member presumably would be included in the group of non-independent directors for purposes of applicable listing standards.

[371] If a shareholder nominee did not meet the independence requirements of a listed market, that listed market may provide for a cure period during which time the company may resolve this deficiency. See, e.g., NASDAQ Rule 5810(c)(3)(E) ("If a Company fails to meet the majority board independence requirement in Rule 5605(b)(1) due to one vacancy, or because one director ceases to be independent for reasons beyond his/her reasonable control, the Listing Qualifications Department will promptly notify the

Company and inform it has until the earlier of its next annual shareholders meeting or one year from the event that caused the deficiency to cure the deficiency.").

[372] See letter from ICI.

[373] See new Rule 14a-11(b)(9).

[374] See, e.g., Triplex Shoe Co. v. Rice & Hutchins, Inc., 152 A. 342, 375 (Del. 1930). See also 1-13 David A. Drexler et al., Delaware Corporation Law and Practice §13.01 n. 42 (citing Triplex for the proposition that "a bylaw requiring a director to be a stockholder required a director to own stock prior to entering into the office of director, not prior to election").

[375] See letters from 26 Corporate Secretaries; Advance Auto Parts; Alaska Air; Anadarko; Aetna; American Express; Association of Corporate Counsel; BorgWarner; BRT; Callaway; Caterpillar; Dewey; DTE Energy; Dupont; Emerson Electric; eWareness; ExxonMobil; Financial Services Roundtable; IBM; ICI; McDonald's; O'Melveny & Myers; PepsiCo; Praxair; Seven Law Firms; Society of Corporate Secretaries; Theragenics; UnitedHealth; U.S. Bancorp; Xerox.

company's director questionnaire, we are persuaded that information should be provided regarding whether the nominee meets the company's director qualifications, if any. Accordingly, although we have not revised the rule to allow exclusion of nominees who do not meet any director qualification requirements, we have adopted a requirement that a nominating shareholder or group disclose under Item 5 of Schedule 14N whether, to the best of their knowledge, the nominating shareholder's or group's nominee meets the company's director qualifications, if any, as set forth in the company's governing documents.[376] The company also may choose to provide disclosure in its proxy statement about whether it believes a nominee satisfies the company's director qualifications, as is currently done in a traditional proxy contest. Where a company's governing documents establish certain qualifications for director nominees that, consistent with state law, would preclude the company from seating a director who does not meet these qualifications, we believe this would be important disclosure for shareholders.

c. Agreements with the company

As discussed above with regard to the eligibility requirements for a nominating shareholder or group, we recognize that certain limitations of the rule create the potential risk of nominating shareholders or groups acting merely as a surrogate for the company or its management in order to block usage of the rule by another nominating shareholder or group.[377] Under the Proposal as it relates to nominee eligibility, a nominating shareholder or group would have been required to represent that no agreements between the nominee and the company and its management exist regarding the nomination of the nominee.[378] The Proposal included an instruction clarifying that negotiations between a nominating shareholder or group, nominee, and nominating committee or board of a company to have the nominee included in the company's proxy materials, where the negotiations were unsuccessful or were limited to whether the company was required to include the nominee in accordance with Rule 14a-11, would not represent a direct or indirect agreement with the company.[379]

Commenters generally supported this proposed requirement.[380] Most of the comments addressed negotiations or agreements between the nominating shareholder or group and the company rather than the relationship or agreements between a nominee and the company.[381]

Consistent with our approach to agreements with nominating shareholders, we are adopting the requirement that there not be any agreements between the nominee and the company and its management regarding the nomination of the nominee largely as proposed. In this regard, we believe it would undermine the purpose of the rule to allow nominees under Rule 14a-11 to have such agreements with the company because of the potential risk of a nominating shareholder or group acting merely as a surrogate for a company. In order to clarify that this is an affirmative requirement of Rule 14a-11, we have revised the rule to make clear that this is an eligibility condition by listing it as a condition in the rule, rather than only in a representation required in Schedule 14N.

d. Relationship between the nominating shareholder or group and the nominee

We did not propose a requirement that the nominee must be independent or unaffiliated with the nominating shareholder or group, but we requested comment on whether

---

[376] See Item 5(e) of new Schedule 14N.

[377] See the discussion in Section II.B.4.e. above regarding relationships or agreements between the nominating shareholder or group and the company and its management.

[378] In this regard, we also proposed to require a nominating shareholder or group to represent that no relationships or agreements between the nominee and

the company and its management exist. This aspect of the rule is discussed in Section II.B.5.d. below.

[379] See instruction to proposed Rule 14a-18(d).

[380] See letters from ADP; BRT; Calvert; CFA Institute; CII; Seven Law Firms; TIAA-CREF; USPE.

[381] See Section II.B.4.e. above for a further discussion of the comments.

we should include such a requirement.[382] A large number of commenters supported generally an independence requirement that would limit some or all relationships between the nominating shareholder or group and its nominee.[383] Commenters explained that an independence requirement would reduce the risk that a successful shareholder nominee would represent only the nominating shareholder or group, avoid potential disruptions and divisiveness from having "special interest" directors, ameliorate the issue of preserving confidentiality within the boardroom and avoiding misuse of material non-public information, and lessen the likelihood that Rule 14a-11 would be used for change in control attempts.[384]

With regard to the degree of independence needed and types of relationships that should be prohibited, numerous commenters recommended a prohibition on any affiliation between the nominating shareholder or group and the shareholder nominee.[385] Some commenters recommended that Rule 14a-11 prohibit a shareholder nominee from being (1) a nominating shareholder, (2) a member of the immediate family of any nominating shareholder, or (3) a partner, officer, director or employee of a nominating shareholder or any of its affiliates.[386] They noted that a similar limitation was included in the 2003 Proposal. Two commenters recommended that the Commission impose the same restrictions and disclosure requirements that were included in the 2003 Proposal.[387]

One commenter noted the Commission's assertion in the Proposing Release that "such limitations may not be appropriate or necessary" because, if elected, a director would be subject to state law fiduciary duties owed to the company.[388] The commenter, however, expressed skepticism that fiduciary obligations would adequately resolve the issue of "special interest" directors. One commenter would not require independence between the nominating shareholder or group and the nominee if the nominating shareholder or group could use Rule 14a-11 to nominate only one candidate; however, if the nominating shareholder or group is allowed to nominate more than one candidate using Rule 14a-11, then the commenter believed independence between the nominating shareholder or group and the nominees is needed.[389] The commenter asserted that a lack of an independence requirement between multiple nominees and the nominating shareholder could give rise to control issues because the nominees, if elected, could be beholden to a single nominating shareholder or group. In addition, the commenter claimed that a lack of independence could give rise to "single issue" or "special interest" directors, thereby causing balkanization of boards. According to this commenter, if independence is not required, then Schedule 14N should require detailed disclosure about the nature of relationships between the nominating shareholder or group and the nominees.[390]

---

[382] The 2003 Proposal included such a requirement. For a discussion of this aspect of the 2003 Proposal and the comments received, *see* the Proposing Release.

[383] *See* letters from ABA; Advance Auto Parts; Aetna; Alaska Air; Association of Corporate Counsel; Avis Budget; Biogen; Boeing; BorgWarner; Brink's; BRT; Callaway; Caterpillar; CIGNA; Comcast; Cummins; Darden Restaurants; Deere; Dewey; Dupont; Eaton; Eli Lilly; ExxonMobil; FedEx; Financial Services Roundtable; FMC Corp.; FPL Group; General Mills; Headwaters; Honeywell; JPMorgan Chase; E.J. Kullman; Leggett; Norfolk Southern; Office Depot; O'Melveny & Myers; Pax World; Protective; Sara Lee; Seven Law Firms; SIFMA; Society of Corporate Secretaries; Southern Company; Tenet; U.S. Bancorp; Vinson & Elkins LLP ("Vinson & Elkins"); Wells Fargo; Weyerhaeuser.

[384] *See* letters from ABA; Alaska Air; Eli Lilly; Leggett.

[385] *See* letters from Advance Auto Parts; Aetna; Association of Corporate Counsel; Avis Budget; Boe-

ing; Brink's; CIGNA; Cummins; Deere; Eaton; FedEx; FMC Corp.; FPL Group; General Mills; E.J. Kullman; Pax World; Protective; Sara Lee.

[386] *See* letters from Alaska Air; BorgWarner; Caterpillar; JPMorgan Chase; O'Melveny & Myers; Society of Corporate Secretaries.

[387] *See* letters from BRT; Intel.

[388] Letter from BRT.

[389] *See* letter from Seven Law Firms.

[390] *Id.* The recommended disclosures included: familial relationships with a nominating shareholder or group member; ownership interests (or other participation) in a nominating shareholder, group member, or affiliates; employment history with a nominating shareholder, group member, or affiliates; prior advisory, consulting or other compensatory relationships with a nominating shareholder, group member, or affiliates; and agreements with a nominating shareholder, group member, or affiliates (other than relating to the nomination).

A few commenters recommended requiring disclosure in the Schedule 14N of any direct or indirect relationships between the nominating shareholder or group and the nominee, including family or employment relationships, ownership interests, commercial relationships and any other arrangements or agreements.[391] One commenter recommended that a nominating shareholder or group provide "[d]isclosure about any agreements or relationships with the Rule 14a-11 nominee other than those relating to the nomination of the nominee."[392]

Other commenters opposed generally any requirement that the nominating shareholder or group be independent from the shareholder nominee.[393] Of these, some commenters recommended the Commission require full disclosure of any affiliations and business relationships instead of an outright prohibition.[394] One commenter noted that no such restriction or prohibition applies to current director candidates, some of whom have various personal and professional links to the company and its executives.[395] Another commenter noted that the NYSE recognized the issue of share ownership when crafting its director independence rules and determined that even significant share ownership should not be dispositive as to a determination of a director's independence.[396] Two commenters opposed a prohibition on any affiliation between the nominating shareholder and its nominee because they believed that fears regarding the election of "special interest" directors are unfounded or exaggerated, as any nominee would have to gain the support of a broad array of shareholders to be elected.[397] One commenter asserted that existing fiduciary duties are an adequate safeguard against "special interest" directors.[398]

We continue to believe that such limitations are not appropriate or necessary. Rather, we believe that Rule 14a-11 should facilitate the exercise of shareholders' traditional state law rights and afford a shareholder or group meeting the requirements of the rule the ability to propose a nominee for director that, in the nominating shareholder's view, better represents the interests of shareholders than those put forward by the nominating committee or board. We note that once a nominee is elected to the board of directors, that director will be subject to state law fiduciary duties and owe the same duty to the corporation as any other director on the board.[399] To the extent a company board is concerned that a director nominee will not represent the views of shareholders, the board could address those points in the company's proxy materials opposing the candidate's election. In addition, we believe the disclosure requirements about the relationships between a nominating shareholder or group and the nominee that we are adopting, combined with the fact that any nominee elected will be subject to fiduciary duties, should help address any "special interest" concerns.

e. No limit on resubmission of shareholder director nominees

Under the Proposal, an individual would not be limited in their ability to stand as a nominee under the rule based on prior unsuccessful nominations under the rule. A number of commenters supported a provision under which a shareholder nominee who failed to receive a specified threshold (*e.g.*, 10%, 15%, 25%, or 30%) of support at a previous election would be ineligible to be nominated again pursuant to Rule 14a-11 for a specified period (*e.g.*, one, two, or three years).[400] One commenter reasoned that

---

[391] *See* letters from O'Melveny & Myers; SIFMA; UnitedHealth. *See also* letter from CII.

[392] Letter from IBM.

[393] *See* letters from Amalgamated Bank; CalSTRS; CFA Institute; CII; COPERA; Nathan Cummings Foundation; P. Neuhauser; Norges Bank; Pershing Square; Relational; RiskMetrics; Solutions by Design ("Solutions"); TIAA-CREF; USPE; B. Villiarmois.

[394] *See* letters from CFA Institute; CII; COPERA; P. Neuhauser; Pershing Square; Relational; USPE; B. Villiarmois.

[395] *See* letter from CII.

[396] *See* letter from Relational.

[397] *See* letters from CII; Nathan Cummings Foundation.

[398] *See* letter from TIAA-CREF.

[399] *See* E. Norman Veasey & Christine T. DiGuglielmo, *How Many Masters Can a Director Serve? A Look at the Tensions Facing Constituency Directors*, 63 BUS. LAW. 761 (2008).

[400] *See* letters from 26 Corporate Secretaries; ABA; Aetna; Anadarko; BorgWarner; BRT; Burlington Northern; Caterpillar; Cummins; Dewey; Headwaters; JPMorgan Chase; Kirkland & Ellis; Leggett; P. Neuhauser; Northrop; PepsiCo; Pfizer; Protective; Sara Lee; SIFMA; Society of Corporate Secretaries; TIAA-CREF; T. Rowe Price; Xerox.

"[t]his would allow more shareholders to participate in the process and would motivate them to propose high quality candidates."[401] On the other hand, other commenters opposed a provision under which a shareholder nominee who failed to receive significant support at a previous election would be ineligible to be nominated again pursuant to Rule 14a-11 for a specified period.[402] One commenter reasoned that "[s]imilar resubmission requirements aren't applicable to management's candidates, so they shouldn't apply to candidates suggested by shareowners."[403] We agree with those commenters who opposed a provision that would limit the ability of a shareholder nominee to be nominated based on the level of support received in a prior election. We do not believe that such a limitation would facilitate shareholders' traditional state law rights and would add undue complexity to the rule's operation.

6. Maximum Number of Shareholder Nominees to Be Included in Company Proxy Materials

a. General

Under the Proposal, a company would be required to include no more than one shareholder nominee or the number of nominees that represents 25% of the company's board of directors, whichever is greater.[404] Where the term of a director that was nominated pursuant to Rule 14a-11 continues past the meeting date, that director would continue to count for purposes of the 25% maximum.

As noted in the Proposing Release, we do not intend for Rule 14a-11 to be available for any shareholder or group that is seeking to change the control of the company or to gain more than a limited number of seats on the board.[405] The existing procedures regarding contested elections of directors are intended to continue to fulfill that purpose.[406] We also noted that by allowing shareholder nominees to be included in a company's proxy materials, part of the cost of the solicitation is essentially shifted from the individual shareholder or group to the company and thus, all of the shareholders.[407] We do not believe that we should require that an election contest conducted by a shareholder to change the control of the company or to gain a number of seats on the board of directors that exceeds the maximum number of nominees that the registrant could be required to include under Rule 14a-11 be funded out of corporate assets.

Some commenters supported generally the proposed limit on the number of shareholder nominees.[408] While agreeing that the Commission's proposed limit on the number of shareholder nominees is needed to ensure a more measured approach towards inclusion of shareholder nominees in company proxy materials, one commenter supported the general principle that shareholders should be entitled to nominate as many directors as necessary to focus the board's attention on optimizing company performance, profitability and sustainable returns.[409] On the other hand, many commenters disagreed with the

---

[401] Letter from Northrop.

[402] *See* letters from CII; Corporate Library; Dominican Sisters of Hope; First Affirmative Financial Network LLC ("First Affirmative"); Mercy Investment Program; Sisters of Mercy; Social Investment Forum; Tri- State Coalition; Trillium; Ursuline Sisters of Tildonk; USPE.

[403] Letter from CII.

[404] *See* proposed Rule 14a-11(d)(1). According to information from RiskMetrics, based on a sample of 1,431 public companies, in 2007, the median board size was 9, with boards ranging in size from 4 to 23 members. Approximately 40% of the boards in the sample had 8 or fewer directors, approximately 60% had between 9 and 19 directors, and less than 1% had 20 or more directors.

[405] The final rule clarifies the second part of this requirement by specifying that a nominating shareholder or group may not be seeking to gain a number of seats on the board of directors that exceeds the maximum number of nominees that the registrant could be required to include under Rule 14a-11.

[406] *See, e.g.,* Exchange Act Rule 14a-12(c).

[407] In this regard, we anticipate that shareholders seeking election of nominees included in the company's proxy materials may need to engage in solicitation efforts for which they will incur expenses.

[408] *See* letters from CalPERS; CalSTRS; CFA Institute; ICGN; Nathan Cummings Foundation; P. Neuhauser; Norges Bank; Protective; RiskMetrics; TIAA-CREF; T. Rowe Price; WSIB.

[409] *See* letter from CalPERS.

proposed limit or recommended different limits.[410] Some commenters expressed a general concern that the proposed limit would affect a significant portion of the board, disrupt the board, facilitate a change in control of the company, and possibly require companies to integrate numerous new directors into their boards each year.[411] Other commenters wanted more shareholder nominees to be allowed because they feared that a single shareholder-nominated director would be ineffective due to the lack of a second for motions at board meetings, hostile board members, possible exclusion from key committees, and being effectively cut out of key discussions.[412] Commenters' suggestions as to the appropriate limitation on the number of shareholder nominees ranged from a limit of one shareholder nominee, regardless of the size of the board,[413] to at least two nominees, but less than a majority of the board.[414] Other commenters recommended various limits ranging from 10% to 15% of the board.[415]

We carefully considered commenters' concerns regarding the limitation on the number of Rule 14a-11 nominees; however, we are adopting the limitation largely as proposed. We believe the rule we are adopting strikes the appropriate balance in allowing shareholders to more effectively exercise their rights to nominate and elect directors, but does not provide nominating shareholders or groups using the rule with the ability to change control of the company. The limitation on the number of Rule 14a-11 nominees that a company is required to include should also limit costs and disruption as compared to a rule without such a limit. We also believe that a lower threshold, such as 10% or 15%, may result in only one shareholder-nominated director at many companies. In addition, we note that our rule only addresses the inclusion of nominees in the company's proxy materials. After reviewing all of the disclosures provided by the company and the nominating shareholder or group, shareholders will be able to make an informed decision as to whether to vote for and elect a shareholder nominee. We believe that the modifications we are making to the rule, as described below, help to alleviate concerns that the election of shareholder nominees would unduly disrupt the board. As to concerns about the possibility that a single shareholder-nominated director would be ineffective due to actions of other members of the board, the rule is not intended to address the interactions of board members after the election of directors. In this respect, we note that any shareholder-nominated directors and board-nominated directors would be subject to fiduciary duties under state law.

---

[410] *See* letters from 13D Monitor; ABA; ACSI; Advance Auto Parts; Aetna; Alcoa; Allstate; American Express; Americans for Financial Reform; Association of Corporate Counsel; Avis Budget; Best Buy; J. Blanchard; Boeing; BorgWarner; BRT; Burlington Northern; R. Burt; Callaway; CalPERS; Caterpillar; CIGNA; CII; Cleary; CNH Global; Comcast; Concerned Shareholders; COPERA; Cummins; L. Dallas; Darden Restaurants; Deere; Dupont; Eaton; Eli Lilly; Dale C. Eshelman ("D. Eshelman"); ExxonMobil; FedEx; FMC Corp.; FPL Group; Frontier; GE; General Mills; Headwaters; C. Holliday; Honeywell; IBM; ICI; ITT; JPMorgan Chase; J. Kilts; E. J. Kullman; N. Lautenbach; Leggett; C. Levin; Lionbridge Technologies; LUCRF; McDonald's; Motorola; Office Depot; O'Melveny & Myers; OPERS; P&G; Nathan Cummings Foundation; Northrop; Pax World; PepsiCo; Sara Lee; S&C; Schulte Roth & Zabel; Sherwin-Williams; Sidley Austin; SIFMA; Society of Corporate Secretaries; Solutions; SWIB; Teamsters; TI; G. Tooker; tw telecom; Universities Superannuation; U.S. Bancorp; Verizon; USPE; B. Villiarmois; Wachtell; Wells Fargo; Weyerhaeuser; WSIB.

[411] *See* letters from BRT (citing a July 2009 survey showing many companies would have to integrate multiple new directors); CII; Eaton; N. Lautenbach; McDonald's; Sherwin-Williams; Sidley Austin; Society of Corporate Secretaries; G. Tooker; WSIB.

[412] *See* letters from CII; L. Dallas; C. Levin; Nathan Cummings Foundation; Universities Superannuation.

[413] *See* letters from Advance Auto Parts; Avis Budget; BRT; Caterpillar; CIGNA; CNH Global; Comcast; Cummins; Darden Restaurants; Deere; Eaton; Eli Lilly; FedEx; FMC Corp.; FPL Group; Frontier; General Mills; ICI; ITT; E. J. Kullman; N. Lautenbach; Leggett; McDonald's; Office Depot; O'Melveny & Myers; PepsiCo; Sherwin-Williams; TI; G. Tooker; tw telecom; Verizon; Wachtell; Weyerhaeuser.

[414] *See* letters from ACSI; Americans for Financial Reform; CalPERS; CII (stating that while it supports the Commission's proposed limit, shareholders should be allowed to nominate two candidates in all cases); COPERA; C. Levin; LUCRF; Nathan Cummings Foundation; SWIB; Teamsters.

[415] *See, e.g.,* Aetna; Association of Corporate Counsel; Barclays; J. Blanchard; BorgWarner; Dewey; ExxonMobil; Headwaters; Honeywell; Lionbridge Technologies; Northrop; Sidley Austin; Society of Corporate Secretaries; U.S. Bancorp.

As adopted, Rule 14a-11(d) will not require a company to include more than one shareholder nominee or the number of nominees that represents 25% of the company's board of directors, whichever is greater.[416] Consistent with the Proposal, where a company has a director (or directors) currently serving on its board of directors who was elected as a shareholder nominee pursuant to Rule 14a-11, and the term of that director extends past the date of the meeting of shareholders for which the company is soliciting proxies for the election of directors, the company will not be required to include in its proxy materials more shareholder nominees than could result in the total number of directors serving on the board that were elected as shareholder nominees being greater than one shareholder nominee or 25% of the company's board of directors, whichever is greater.[417] We believe this limitation is appropriate to reduce the possibility of a nominating shareholder or group using Rule 14a-11 as a means to gain a number of seats on the board of directors that exceeds the maximum number of nominees that the company could be required to include under Rule 14a-11 or to effect a change in control of the company by repeatedly nominating additional candidates for director. One commenter requested that we explain how Rule 14a-11 would apply to different board structures, and in particular, classified boards.[418] In the case of a staggered board, the rule provides that the 25% limit will be calculated based on the total number of board seats,[419] not the lesser number that are being voted on because it is the size of the full board, not the number up for election, that would be relevant for considering the effect on control.

We note that in the 2003 Proposal, the Commission proposed to require companies to include a set number of nominees, rather than a percentage of the board.[420] We believe that using a percentage in the rule will promote ease of use and alleviate any concerns that a company may increase its board size in an effort to reduce the effect of a shareholder nominee elected to the board.

We understand the concerns addressed by some commenters that this limitation could result in shareholder-nominated directors being less influential,[421] as well as the concerns of other commenters that the possibility of 25% of the board changing through the Rule 14a-11 process could present significant changes to the board.[422] For the reasons discussed above, we believe the limitation as adopted strikes an appropriate balance and is an appropriate safeguard to assure that the Rule 14a-11 process is not used as a means to effect a change in control.

Though we are adopting this requirement largely as proposed, we have added certain clarifications, which are described below, to address situations at companies where shareholders are able to elect only a subset of the board, revised the standard for determining which nominating shareholder or group will have their nominee or nominees included in the company's proxy materials where there is more than one eligible nominating shareholder or group, and made other modifications designed to facilitate negotiations between companies and nominating shareholders.

b. Different voting rights with regard to election of directors

Several commenters responded to the Commission's request for comment about how to calculate the maximum number of candidates a nominating shareholder or group could

---

[416] *See* new Rule 14a-11(d)(1).

[417] *See* new Rule 14a-11(d)(2). This requirement is adopted as it was proposed in Rule 14a-11(d)(2). Depending on board size, 25% of the board may not result in a whole number. In those instances, the maximum number of shareholder nominees for director that a registrant will be required to include in its proxy materials will be the closest whole number below 25%. *See* the Instruction to paragraph (d)(1).

[418] *See* letter from ABA.

[419] *See* Rule 14a-11(d)(2).

[420] Comments on the 2003 Proposal provided a range of views regarding the appropriate number of share-

holder nominees. Commenters that supported the use of a percentage, or combination of a set number and a percentage, to determine the number of shareholder nominees suggested percentages ranging from 20% to 35%. *See* Comment File No. S7-19-03, *available at* http://www.sec.gov/rules/proposed/s71903.shtml.

[421] *See* letters from CII; L. Dallas; C. Levin; Nathan Cummins Foundation; Universities Superannuation.

[422] *See* letters from BRT (citing a July 2009 survey showing many companies would have to integrate multiple new directors); CII; Eaton; N. Lautenbach; McDonald's; Sherwin-Williams; Sidley Austin; Society of Corporate Secretaries; G. Tooker; WSIB.

nominate under Rule 14a-11 when certain directors are not elected by all shareholders. Some commenters noted that controlled companies are commonly structured with dual classes of stock which allow shareholders of the non-controlling class of stock to elect a set number of directors that is less than the full board.[423]

In the context of a company where shareholders are only entitled to elect a subset of the total number of directors, the rule as proposed potentially would have allowed shareholders to nominate more candidates than may be elected by the nominating shareholders. Two commenters argued that Rule 14a-11 should be modified so that the maximum number of shareholder nominees is based on the number of directors that may be elected by the class of securities held by the shareholders making the nomination, as opposed to the number of total directors.[424] Another commenter urged us to revise Rule 14a-11 so that it would be limited to a percentage of the number of directors that are elected by the public shareholders (rather than a percentage of all directors) and would not apply to directors that are elected by shareholders of a class of stock having a right to nominate and elect a specified number or percentage of directors, or preferred shareholders having such right as a result of the company's failure to pay dividends.[425] Another commenter argued that, as proposed, Rule 14a-11 would not allow companies with multiple classes of voting shares the ability to make choices about how to best implement access to the company's proxy to fit their capital structure.[426] One commenter suggested that Rule 14a-11 address how it would apply to companies with multiple classes of stock to prevent shareholders from using the rule to change control of the class of directors those shareholders have the right to elect.[427] Other commenters, by contrast, believed that the maximum number of nominees that companies should be required to include should be based on the total number of director seats, regardless of whether a class of shares only gets to elect a subset of the board.[428]

We also sought comment on how to calculate the maximum number of nominees where the company is contractually obligated to permit a certain shareholder or group to elect a set number of directors to the board. Commenters' views differed on how to calculate the maximum number of nominees a shareholder or shareholder group may nominate in that case. Some commenters believed that the maximum number of nominees should be based on the total board size, regardless of whether a company has granted rights to nominate.[429] One such commenter noted that if Rule 14a-11 contained an exception for board seats subject to contractual rights, companies would have an incentive to enter into contractual agreements in order to evade its application.[430] Other commenters, however, asserted that the maximum number of nominees that shareholders should be permitted to nominate under Rule 14a-11 should be limited to 25% of the "free" seats on the board—that is, only those board seats that are not subject to a contractual nomination right that existed as of the date of the submission and filing of a Schedule 14N.[431] These commenters suggested taking board seats subject to contractual nomination rights "off the table" and basing the 25% calculation on the number of nominees that the nominating committee is free to name. One such commenter remarked that unless board seats subject to contractual nomination rights are excluded, companies may be limited in their ability to offer contractual nominating rights to shareholders without running a heightened risk of change of control, which could result in increased costs of capital and a decrease in the number of strategic alternatives.[432]

We believe that the maximum number of candidates a shareholder can nominate using Rule 14a-11 at companies with multiple classes of stock should be based on the total board size, as is the case at other companies. Thus, we are adopting this requirement as

---

[423] *See* letters from ABA; Duane Morris; Media General; New York Times.

[424] *See* letters from Media General; New York Times.

[425] *See* letter from Sidley Austin.

[426] *See* letter from BRT.

[427] *See* letter from Media General.

[428] *See* letters from CII; P. Neuhauser.

[429] *Id.*

[430] *See* letter from P. Neuhauser.

[431] *See* letters from Seven Law Firms; Sidley Austin; ValueAct Capital.

[432] *See* letter from Seven Law Firms.

proposed. We believe the changes we are adopting with regard to calculating ownership and voting power, as discussed above, should address concerns about the possibility that the rule could be used to change control of the company or to affect the rights of shareholders as established by a particular company's capital structure.[433] Where shareholders have the right to elect a subset of the full board, however, we believe it is appropriate to provide that the maximum number of nominees a company may be required to include under Rule 14a-11 may not exceed the number of director seats the class of shares held by the nominating shareholder is entitled to elect.[434] We believe the right to nominate is an integral part of the right to elect, therefore we are linking the ability under Rule 14a-11 for a shareholder to nominate directors to instances in which the shareholder can elect directors. Limiting the number of nominations to the number of director seats the class of shares held by the nominating shareholder is entitled to elect presumably would allow to be fully expressed the views of the shareholder about who should sit in the director seats in respect of which the shareholder has nomination rights.

The shareholder nomination provisions in Rule 14a-11 are available only for holders of classes of securities that are subject to the Exchange Act proxy rules, provided that a company is otherwise subject to the rule. If a company subject to Rule 14a-11 has multiple classes of eligible securities, however, the maximum number of candidates a shareholder can nominate will be determined based on the number of director seats the class of shares held by the nominating shareholder is entitled to elect.[435]

c. Inclusion of shareholder nominees in company proxy materials as company nominees

As discussed in Section II.B.4.e. above, commenters expressed concern that the rule, as proposed, might discourage constructive dialogue between shareholders and companies.[436] These commenters noted that companies would be discouraged from discussing potential board candidates with shareholders planning to use Rule 14a-11 and including them as management nominees because such nominees would not reduce the maximum number of shareholder nominees that the company would be required to include under Rule 14a-11. Subject to certain safeguards, we believe our rule should not discourage dialogue between nominating shareholders and companies and agree that the rule, as proposed, could have the effect of discouraging constructive dialogue if shareholder nominees nominated by a company as a result of that dialogue do not count toward the maximum number of shareholder nominees a company is required to include in its proxy materials. Consequently, under our final rule, where a company negotiates with the nominating shareholder or group that has filed a Schedule 14N before beginning any discussion with the company about the nomination and that otherwise would be eligible to have its nominees included in the company's proxy materials, and the company agrees to include the nominating shareholder's or group's nominees on the company's proxy card as company nominees, those nominees will count toward the 25% maximum set forth in the rule.[437] As noted, this would only apply where the nominating shareholder or group has filed its notice on Schedule 14N before beginning discussions with the company. Although this limitation may reduce somewhat the utility of this provision, we believe limiting the treatment to situations in which the nominating shareholder or group has filed a Schedule 14N will reduce the possibility that this exception is used by a company to avoid having to include shareholder director nominees submitted by shareholders or groups of shareholders that are not affiliated with or not working on behalf of the company.

---

[433] *See* Section II.B.4.b. above.

[434] *See* new Rule 14a-11(d)(3).

[435] *See* new Rule 14a-11(d)(3).

[436] *See* letters from BRT; Seven Law Firms; Society of Corporate Secretaries.

[437] *See* new Rule 14a-11(d)(4). In this regard, we note that we would view such an agreement as a ter-

mination of a Rule 14a-11 nomination. Thus, the nominating shareholder or group would be required to file an amendment to Schedule 14N to disclose the termination of the nomination as a result of the agreement with the company regarding the inclusion of the nominee or nominees. *See* Item 7 of Schedule 14N and Rule 14n-2.

In the Proposing Release, we requested comment as to whether it would be appropriate for the rule to take into account incumbent directors who were nominated pursuant to Rule 14a-11 for purposes of determining the maximum number of shareholder nominees, or whether there should be a different means to account for such incumbent directors. One commenter argued that incumbent Rule 14a-11 directors should not count towards the 25% limit.[438] It reasoned that, once elected, the Rule 14a-11 director represents all shareholders and that future use of Rule 14a-11 by other shareholders should not be restricted. A number of commenters stated that incumbent Rule 14a-11 directors should count towards the maximum number of shareholder nominees allowed under the rule,[439] with some suggesting that this should be the case in limited circumstances, such as when a Rule 14a-11 director is re-nominated by the board or as long as the director continues on the board.[440] Commenters expressed concerns that the method of calculating the maximum number of directors subject to Rule 14a-11 nominations—which as proposed would not include directors previously elected following a Rule 14a-11 nomination unless they are nominated again by a shareholder using Rule 14a-11—would not encourage boards to integrate these directors.[441] Some commenters asserted that failing to count such a director toward the 25% limit would cause boards to be disinclined to include these directors as company nominees in future elections.[442] They viewed this as counterproductive to efficient board integration and functioning.

While we appreciate commenters' views, we are not persuaded that it is appropriate to provide an exception to the general method of calculating the maximum number of Rule 14a-11 nominees in the case of a shareholder-nominated incumbent director that is re-nominated by the company. As noted previously, by adopting Rule 14a-11 we are seeking to facilitate shareholders' ability under state law to nominate and elect directors, not necessarily to enhance shareholder representation on the board. We do not believe that a Commission rule is needed to facilitate the working relationship between the shareholder-nominated director and the company-nominated directors, or to provide an incentive for the board to integrate the shareholder-nominated director into its activities. To the extent that a shareholder nominee is elected to the board, the company-nominated directors and the shareholder-nominated director will have a fiduciary duty to act in the best interests of the company and its shareholders.

7. Priority of nominations received by a company

a. Priority when multiple shareholders submit nominees

Proposed Rule 14a-11(d)(3) addressed situations where more than one shareholder or group would be eligible to have its nominees included in the company's form of proxy and disclosed in its proxy statement pursuant to the proposed rule. In those situations, the company would have been required to include in its proxy materials the nominee or nominees of the first nominating shareholder or group from which it receives timely notice of intent to nominate a director pursuant to the rule, up to and including the total number of shareholder nominees required to be included by the company. We proposed this standard because we believed that there would be a benefit to enabling companies to begin preparing their proxy materials and coordinating with the nominating shareholder or group immediately upon receiving an eligible nomination rather than requiring companies to wait to see whether another nomination from a larger nominating shareholder or group was submitted before the notice deadline.

Commenters were almost uniformly opposed to the proposed "first-in" standard. A large number of commenters expressed general opposition to the proposed first-in

---

[438] *See* letter from Florida State Board of Administration.

[439] *See* letters from ABA; Aetna; American Express; BorgWarner; BRT; Chevron; Cleary; Davis Polk; DTE Energy; Dupont; Edison Electric Institute; Eli Lilly; ExxonMobil; FPL Group; Home Depot; ICI; JPMorgan Chase; Metlife; P. Neuhauser; Pfizer; Protective; RiskMetrics; S&C; Seven Law Firms; Sidley Austin; SIFMA; Society of Corporate Secretaries; Verizon; Vinson & Elkins; Wells Fargo.

[440] *See* letters from P. Neuhauser; RiskMetrics.

[441] *See* letters from ABA; BRT; Seven Law Firms.

[442] *See* letters from Davis Polk; Society of Corporate Secretaries.

approach, with many presenting their own recommendations.[443] Commenters expressed concern that the first-in approach would rush shareholders to submit nominations.[444] One commenter worried that even if the Commission included a window period for submission of shareholder nominees in the final rule, the first-in approach would encourage a race to file, discourage constructive dialogue between shareholders and management, and encourage a "gamesmanship" attitude among possible nominating shareholders or groups.[445] Another commenter argued that the first-in approach would undercut the Commission's stated objectives in proposing Rule 14a-11.[446] One commenter worried that the "first in" approach would favor large shareholders, who have greater resources to prepare their submission materials, over small shareholders who must aggregate to reach the ownership threshold and need to pool resources to prepare their submission materials.[447]

Some commenters expressed general concern about how companies should handle multiple nominations received on the same date.[448] Two commenters worried that it would be difficult for companies to determine which nomination was received first because nominations could be submitted by various methods (*e.g.*, fax transmission, mail, hand delivery) or arrive on the same date.[449] Another commenter feared that a company that receives several nominations on the same date could choose the nomination submitted by shareholders friendly to management.[450]

Many commenters that opposed the first-in approach suggested alternatives. Of these, the majority preferred to give priority to the largest shareholder or group that submits a nomination.[451] Noting that the 2003 Proposal included this standard and that it received

---

[443] *See* letters from 13D Monitor; 26 Corporate Secretaries; ABA; ACSI; Advance Auto Parts; Aetna; AFLCIO; AFSCME; Allstate; Alston & Bird; Amalgamated Bank; American Bankers Association; Anadarko; Applied Materials; Avis Budget; Blue Collar Investment Advisors ("BCIA"); Best Buy; Boeing; BorgWarner; Brink's; BRT; Burlington Northern; CalPERS; CalSTRS; Caterpillar; CFA Institute; Chevron; CIGNA; CII; Cleary; Con Edison; COPERA; Corporate Library; CSX; Cummins; Darden Restaurants; Deere; Devon; Dewey; T. DiNapoli; Dominican Sisters of Hope; DuPont; Eaton; Emerson Electric; ExxonMobil; FedEx; Financial Services Roundtable; First Affirmative; Florida State Board of Administration; FMC Corp.; FPL Group; Frontier; General Mills; A. Goolsby; Honeywell; IAM; IBM; ICI; Intel; JPMorgan Chase; Kirkland & Ellis; C. Levin; Leggett; LIUNA; LUCRF; Marco Consulting; J. McCoy; McDonald's; Joel M. McTague ("J. McTague"); MeadWestvaco; Mercy Investment Program; Metlife; Motorola; D. Nappier; Nathan Cummings Foundation; P. Neuhauser; Norfolk Southern; Norges Bank; Office Depot; OPERS; PACCAR Inc. ("PACCAR"); Pershing Square; PepsiCo; Pfizer; S. Quinlivan; Racetothe-Bottom; RiskMetrics; Ryder; Sara Lee; Social Investment Forum; Seven Law Firms; Shearman & Sterling; Sheet Metal Workers; Sidley Austin; SIFMA; Sisters of Mercy; Society of Corporate Secretaries; Sodali; Southern Company; SWIB; Teamsters; Tenet; TI; TIAA-CREF; Tri-State Coalition; Trillium; T. Rowe Price; Textron; tw telecom; Universities Superannuation; Ursuline Sisters of Tildonk; U.S. Bancorp; USPE; ValueAct Capital; Verizon; Wachtell; Walden; Wells Fargo; Weyerhaeuser; Whirlpool; WSIB; Xerox.

[444] *See* letters from ABA; BRT; Con Edison; First Affirmative; C. Levin; Verizon.

[445] Letter from ABA.

[446] *See* letter from BRT.

[447] *See* letter from Con Edison.

[448] *See* letters from IBM; S. Quinlivan; USPE; Verizon; Xerox.

[449] *See* letters from IBM; Verizon.

[450] See letter from USPE.

[451] *See* letters from 13D Monitor; 26 Corporate Secretaries; ABA (recommending this approach as one of several recommendations); ACSI; Advance Auto Parts; Aetna; AFL-CIO; AFSCME; Allstate; Amalgamated Bank; Anadarko; Applied Materials; Avis Budget; BCIA; Best Buy; Boeing; BorgWarner; Burlington Northern; CalPERS; CalSTRS; Caterpillar; CFA Institute; Chevron; CIGNA (recommending this approach as an alternative to another recommendation that the shareholder that held the shares the longest be given priority); CII; Cleary; Con Edison; COPERA; Corporate Library; Cummins; Darden Restaurants; Deere; Devon; Dominican Sisters of Hope; DuPont; Eaton; Emerson Electric; ExxonMobil; FedEx; Financial Services Roundtable; First Affirmative; Florida State Board of Administration (supporting this approach as an alternative to the first-in approach); FMC Corp.; Frontier; A. Goolsby; IAM; ICI; JPMorgan Chase; Kirkland & Ellis; C. Levin; Leggett; LIUNA; LUCRF; Marco Consulting; J. McCoy; McDonald's; J. McTague; Mercy Investment Program; Metlife; D. Nappier; Nathan Cummings Foundation; P. Neuhauser; Norfolk Southern; Office Depot; PACCAR; Pershing Square; PepsiCo; Pfizer; RiskMetrics; Ryder; Sara Lee; Shamrock; Social Investment Forum; Sodali; Seven Law Firms; Shearman & Sterling; Sheet Metal Workers; Sidley Austin; SIFMA; Sisters of Mercy; Society of Corporate Secretaries; Southern Company; SWIB; Teamsters; Tenet; TI; TIAA-CREF; Tri-State Coalition; Trillium; T. Rowe Price; Textron; tw telecom; Universities Superannuation; Ursuline Sisters of Tildonk; U.S. Bancorp; Verizon; Wachtell; Walden; Wells Fargo; Whirlpool; WSIB.

the most support, one commenter argued that what matters most is not who is the fastest to nominate but which shareholder or group has the "greatest stake in the director election and, ultimately, the long-term performance of the company" (with the added benefits of avoiding "gamesmanship" and "administrative challenges").[452] Further, commenters believed that an approach based on the largest holdings would provide sufficient certainty because the number of shares of the largest shareholder or group could be determined from the Schedule 14N filing.[453]

Commenters presented a wide range of views or recommendations for determining priority. Some commenters suggested that when the largest shareholder or group nominates fewer than the maximum number of nominees allowed under Rule 14a-11, then the second largest shareholder or group should have the right to have its nominees included (up to the maximum number allowable), and so on.[454] Commenters also suggested that a nominating shareholder or group be required to "rank" their nominees in the order of preference to facilitate any necessary "cutbacks."[455]

A few commenters stated that in the case of competing nominations submitted by shareholders with equally-sized holdings, the shareholder that held the shares for the longest period of time should be allowed to include its nominees.[456] Two commenters recommended that when determining the order of priority, an individual shareholder should have priority over a nominating group.[457]

One commenter recommended that nominees be ordered in accordance with the largest qualifying shareholdings, but subject to the qualification that the Commission impose a cap on either the permitted number of members in a nominating group or on the aggregate holdings of a nominating group and limit each nominating shareholder or group to only one Rule 14a-11 nomination at an annual meeting.[458] If shareholders are not limited to one nomination, then companies should be allowed to order the nominees based on the largest holdings. Alternatively, the commenter recommended awarding Rule 14a-11 nomination slots first to the nominating shareholder or group with the largest holdings, next to the nominating shareholder or group with the longest holding period, then to the next largest holder, and so on.

One commenter stated that priority should be given to the largest nominating shareholder or group based on the number of voting securities over which such shareholder or group has voting control (as opposed to beneficial ownership).[459] Another commenter stated that in the case of nominating groups, the determination of the largest holder should be based on the largest shareholder within the nominating group.[460]

Other commenters recommended that the shareholder or group holding a company's shares for the longest period be permitted to submit nominees under Rule 14a-11.[461] These commenters argued that this approach would be more consistent with the Commission's stated goal of making Rule 14a-11 available to shareholders with a long-term interest.

Some commenters preferred to give priority based on a combination of factors, such as length of ownership and size of ownership stake.[462] Several commenters preferred to let companies (*e.g.*, the nominating committee) choose either the shareholder nominees or

---

[452] Letter from CII.

[453] *See* letters from CII; Society of Corporate Secretaries.

[454] *See* letters from Amalgamated Bank; CII; COPERA; P. Neuhauser; Protective; T. Rowe Price.

[455] *See* letters from Amalgamated Bank; CFA Institute; CII; COPERA; P. Neuhauser; Protective; T. Rowe Price.

[456] *See* letters from Allstate; Boeing; Pfizer.

[457] *See* letters from Honeywell; Sara Lee.

[458] *See* letter from ABA.

[459] *See* letter from Kirkland & Ellis.

[460] *See* letter from Seven Law Firms.

[461] *See* letters from BRT; CIGNA (recommending this approach as an alternative to its recommendation that the largest shareholder be given priority); Cummins; Darden Restaurants; FPL Group; General Mills; IBM (recommending this approach as an alternative to its recommendation that the largest shareholder be given priority); Motorola; TIAA-CREF; Xerox.

[462] *See* letters from L. Dallas; T. DiNapoli; Nathan Cummings Foundation; OPERS; Southern Company.

the method for deciding which shareholder nominees are included in the proxy materials when there are multiple nominations.[463] Under this approach, companies would disclose the method in the previous year's proxy statement or in a Form 8-K.

A small number of commenters supported the proposed first-in approach.[464] While understanding the concern about "a rush to the courthouse," one commenter indicated that this concern may not necessarily be justified because the "'first' proponent may have sufficiently prepared beforehand for the nomination process."[465] Further, the commenter believed that "[a]llowing the largest shareholder group to essentially trump the first smaller, but no less committed or relevant, shareholder submission is not good governance." Another commenter believed that the first-in approach would best give effect to the proposed rule.[466] If the standard was based on the amount of securities held instead, the commenter would be concerned that long-term owners of companies with index-tracking portfolios might be frozen out of the process. One commenter believed the first-in approach would provide certainty, but companies should be required to set the dates in calendar form and announce the dates in Form 8-K filings at least 30 days prior to the date of effectiveness.[467]

After considering the comments, we have revised the manner in which the rule addresses multiple qualifying nominations. Rather than a first-in standard, as was proposed, a company will be required to include in its proxy materials the nominee or nominees of the nominating shareholder or group with the highest qualifying voting power percentage.[468] In this regard, in light of the comments received, we are concerned that a first-in standard would result in shareholders rushing to submit nominations, discourage constructive dialogue between shareholders and management, and encourage gamesmanship among possible nominating shareholders or groups. When there are multiple qualifying nominations, giving priority to the shareholder or group with the highest voting power percentage is consistent with our overall approach to facilitate director nominations by shareholders with significant commitments to companies. Finally, we seek to avoid the confusion that could result if multiple nominating shareholders or groups submitted their notices on the same day.

We believe that the standard we are adopting, under which the nominating shareholder or group with the highest qualifying voting power percentage will have its nominees included in the company's proxy materials, up to the maximum of 25% of the board, addresses these concerns. We are persuaded that this standard is more consistent with the other limitations of Rule 14a-11 that seek to balance facilitating shareholder rights to nominate directors with practical considerations.

As adopted, Rule 14a-11 addresses situations where more than one shareholder or group would be eligible to have its nominees included on the company's proxy card and disclosed in its proxy statement pursuant to the rule. Given that we are adopting a highest qualifying voting power percentage standard rather than a first-in standard, the company will determine which shareholders' nominees it must include in its proxy statement and on its proxy card by considering which eligible nominating shareholder or group has the highest qualifying voting power percentage, as opposed to which eligible nominating shareholder or group submitted a timely notice first. A company will be required to include in its proxy statement and on its proxy card the nominee or nominees of the nominating shareholder or group with the highest qualifying voting power percentage in the company's securities as of the date of filing the Schedule 14N, up to and including

---

[463] *See* letters from Alston & Bird; CSX; Textron.

[464] *See* letters from Calvert; Florida State Board of Administration; Hermes Equity Ownership Services Ltd. ("Hermes"); Protective.

[465] Letter from Calvert.

[466] *See* letter from Hermes.

[467] *See* letter from Florida State Board of Administration.

[468] *See* Rule 14a-11(e). Rule 14a-11(e)(4) prescribes a limited variation on this principle where the company has more than one class of voting shares subject to the proxy rules and eligible nominating shareholders or shareholder groups from more than one of those classes submit nominations that exceed the 25% maximum. In this circumstance, priority of nominations will be determined by reference to the relative voting power of the classes in question.

the total number of shareholder nominees required to be included by the company.[469] Where the nominating shareholder or group with highest qualifying voting power percentage that is otherwise eligible to use the rule and that filed a timely notice does not nominate the maximum number of directors allowed under the rule, the nominee or nominees of the nominating shareholder or group with the next highest qualifying voting power percentage that is otherwise eligible to use the rule and that filed a timely notice of intent to nominate a director pursuant to the rule would be included in the company's proxy materials, up to and including the total number of shareholder nominees required to be included by the company. This process would continue until the company included the maximum number of nominees it is required to include in its proxy statement and on its proxy card or the company exhausts the list of eligible nominees. If the number of eligible nominees exceeds the maximum number required under Rule 14a-11 and the shareholder or group with the next highest qualifying voting power percentage submitted more nominees than there are remaining available director slots, the nominating shareholder would have the option to specify which of its nominees are to be included in the company's proxy materials.[470]

b. Priority when a nominating shareholder or group or a nominee withdraws or is disqualified

Under the Proposal, we did not address what would be expected of a company if a nominating shareholder or group or nominee withdraws or is disqualified after the company has provided notice to the nominating shareholder or group of its intent to include the nominee in the company's proxy materials. One commenter asked for guidance on how to handle such situations.[471] Another commenter stated that it opposed allowing a nominating shareholder group to change its composition to correct an identified deficiency, such as a failure of the group to meet the requisite ownership threshold.[472] Two commenters believed that if any member of a nominating shareholder group becomes ineligible due to a failure to own the requisite number of shares, then the entire group and its nominee also should be ineligible to use Rule 14a-11.[473] On the other hand, one commenter recommended that a nominating shareholder group should be allowed to change its composition to correct an identified deficiency, such as the failure of the group to meet the requisite threshold.[474] The commenter also addressed a situation in which a nominating shareholder group qualifies to use Rule 14a-11, provides the necessary notice, submits its nominees, but then becomes disqualified before the meeting at which its nominees would have been put to a shareholder vote. The commenter stated that while it "generally believe[s] that the nominating shareowner should have a short window within which to add a shareowner who would meet all eligibility requirements, a lapse that cannot be cured in that fashion should be remedied by going to the 'second' candidate(s)."

Consistent with the Proposal, under our final rules, neither the composition of the nominating shareholder group nor the shareholder nominee may be changed as a means to correct a deficiency identified in the company's notice to the nominating shareholder or nominating shareholder group—those matters must remain as they were described in the notice to the company.[475] We believe that to allow otherwise could serve to undermine the purpose of the notice deadline provided for in the rule. Thus, a nominating shareholder or group should be sure that it and its nominees meet the requirements of the rule—including the ownership and holding period requirements—before it files its Schedule 14N, as a nominating shareholder or group will not be permitted to add or substitute another shareholder or nominee in order to satisfy the requirements.[476]

---

[469] *See* new Rule 14a-11(e) and proposed Rule 14a-11(d)(3).

[470] *See* Instruction 2 to new Rule 14a-11(e).

[471] *See* letter from Best Buy.

[472] *See* letter from ABA.

[473] *See* letters from CFA Institute; Verizon.

[474] *See* letter from CII.

[475] *See* Instruction 2 to Rule 14a-11(g) and proposed Rule 14a-11(f)(6).

[476] In this regard, we note that if a member of a nominating shareholder group withdraws, the nominating shareholder group and its nominee or nominees would continue to be eligible so long as the group continues to meet the requirements of the rule. If the withdrawal of a member of the nominating shareholder group would result in the group failing to meet the ownership threshold, a company would no longer be required to include any nominees submitted by the

In the Proposing Release, we solicited comment on how we should address situations where a nomination is submitted and the nominating shareholder subsequently becomes ineligible under the rule. We also sought comment as to the circumstances under which a second shareholder or group should be able to have its nominees included in a company's proxy materials. Some commenters stated that if a nominating shareholder or group does not remain eligible, the company should be allowed to withdraw the nominating shareholder's or group's candidate from its proxy materials.[477] Some commenters believed that a company should not be required to include a substitute shareholder nominee if the original shareholder nominee is excluded by a company after receiving a no-action letter from the Commission staff regarding the nomination, is withdrawn by the nominating shareholder or group, or otherwise becomes ineligible.[478] These commenters generally argued that a company would not have enough time to seek the exclusion of such a substitute nominee. Still other commenters argued that a nominating shareholder or group should be allowed to submit a new nominee if its original nominee is determined to be ineligible,[479] especially if the company sought and obtained a no-action letter from the staff concerning the company's determination to exclude the nominee.[480] One commenter worried that a prohibition on substitute shareholder nominees would encourage an unduly adversarial approach by both sides.[481] Another commenter recommended that if the first nominating shareholder or group becomes ineligible, then the nominating shareholder or group with the second-largest holdings should be allowed to submit their own nominees.[482]

Our final rule provides that if a nominating shareholder or group withdraws or is disqualified (*e.g.*, because the nominating shareholder or a member of the group[483] failed to continue to hold the qualifying amount of securities) after the company provides notice to the nominating shareholder or group of the company's intent to include the nominee or nominees in its proxy materials, the company will be required to include in its proxy statement and form of proxy the nominee or nominees of the nominating shareholder or group with the next highest voting power percentage that is otherwise eligible to use the rule and that filed a timely notice in accordance with the rule, if any.[484] This process would continue until the company included the maximum number of nominees it is required to include in its proxy materials or the company exhausts the list of eligible nominees.

If a nominee withdraws or is disqualified after the company provides notice to the nominating shareholder or group of the company's intent to include the nominee in its proxy materials, the company will be required to include in its proxy materials any other eligible nominee submitted by that nominating shareholder or group.[485] If that nominating shareholder or group did not include any other nominees in its notice filed on Schedule 14N, then the company will be required to include the nominee or nominees of the nominating shareholder or group with the next highest voting power percentage that is otherwise eligible to use the rule and that filed a timely notice in accordance with the rule, if any, until the maximum number of nominees is included in the company's proxy materials or the list of eligible nominees is exhausted.

(Footnote Continued)

nominating shareholder group. As another example, if after a nominating shareholder or group submits one nominee for inclusion in a company's proxy materials and the nominee subsequently withdraws or is disqualified, a company will not be required to include a substitute nominee from that nominating shareholder or group.

[477] *See* letters from BorgWarner; Society of Corporate Secretaries.

[478] *See* letters from 26 Corporate Secretaries; ABA; Allstate; American Express; BorgWarner; DTE Energy; Dupont; FPL Group; Honeywell; IBM; Pfizer;

RiskMetrics; Seven Law Firms; Society of Corporate Secretaries; Xerox.

[479] *See* letters from AFL-CIO; P. Neuhauser; USPE.

[480] *See* letter from P. Neuhauser.

[481] *See* letter from Universities Superannuation.

[482] *See* letter from CFA Institute.

[483] If one member of a group becomes ineligible to use the rule but the group continues to qualify to use the rule without that member, the group would remain eligible overall.

[484] *See* new Rule 14a-11(e)(2).

[485] *See* new Rule 14a-11(e)(3).

We believe that these requirements are appropriate in order to give effect to the intent of our rule—to facilitate shareholders' ability to nominate and elect directors. If the nominating shareholder or group with the highest voting power percentage used all available Rule 14a-11 nominations in a company's proxy materials and the nominating shareholder or group with the second highest voting power percentage had its nominees excluded even after one or more nominees from the nominating shareholder or group with the highest voting power percentage withdrew or was disqualified, we believe the purpose of our rule would be undermined. However, in order to address practical considerations, Rule 14a-11(e)(2) provides that once a company has commenced printing its proxy materials it will not be required to include a substitute nominee or nominees. We believe that at that point in the process it would be too difficult and costly for a company to change course to include a new nominee or nominees. If a nominating shareholder or group or nominee withdraws or is disqualified after the company has commenced printing its proxy materials, the company may determine whether it wishes to print (and furnish) additional materials and a proxy card, delete the disqualified or withdrawn nominee, or instead provide disclosure through additional soliciting materials informing shareholders about the change.[486]

8. Notice on Schedule 14N

a. Proposed notice requirements

As proposed, in order to submit a nominee for inclusion in the company's proxy statement and form of proxy, Rule 14a-11 would require that the nominating shareholder or group provide a notice on Schedule 14N to the company of its intent to require that the company include that shareholder's or group's nominee or nominees in the company's proxy materials.[487] The shareholder notice on Schedule 14N also would be required to be filed with the Commission on the date it is first sent to the company.

We proposed to require the notice to be provided to the company and filed with the Commission by the date specified in the company's advance notice bylaw provision, or where no such provision is in place, no later than 120 calendar days before the date the company mailed its proxy materials for the prior year's annual meeting. If the company did not hold an annual meeting during the prior year, or if the date of the meeting changes by more than 30 calendar days from the prior year, the nominating shareholder must provide notice a reasonable time before the company mails its proxy materials. The company would be required to disclose the date by which the shareholder must submit the required notice in a Form 8-K filed pursuant to proposed Item 5.07 within four business days after the company determines the anticipated meeting date.[488]

As proposed, the notice on Schedule 14N would include disclosures relating to the nominating shareholder's or group's interest in the company, length of ownership, and eligibility to use Rule 14a-11. The notice on Schedule 14N also would include disclosure required by proposed Rule 14a-18 about the nominating shareholder or group and the nominee for director, as well as disclosure regarding the nature and extent of relationships between the nominating shareholder or group and nominee or nominees and the company. The disclosure provided by the nominating shareholder or group would be similar to the disclosure currently required in a contested election and would be included by the company in its proxy materials.

In addition, as proposed, the notice on Schedule 14N also would include the following representations by the nominating shareholder or group:

---

[486] We note that pursuant to Exchange Act Rule 14a-4(c)(5) a completed proxy card containing a disqualified or withdrawn nominee or nominees could, under certain circumstances, confer discretionary authority to vote on the election of a substitute director or directors.

[487] *See* proposed Rule 14a-11(c), Rule 14a-18 and Rule 14n-1.

[488] *See* proposed Instruction 2 to Rule 14a-11(a) and proposed Rule 14a-18.

- the nominee's candidacy or, if elected, board membership, would not violate controlling state or federal law, or rules of a national securities exchange or national securities association other than rules relating to director independence;[489]

- the nominating shareholder or group satisfies the eligibility conditions in Rule 14a-11;[490]

- in the case of a company other than an investment company, the nominee meets the objective criteria for "independence" of the national securities exchange or national securities association rules applicable to the company, if any, or, in the case of a company that is an investment company, the nominee is not an "interested person" of the company as defined in Section 2(a)(19) of the Investment Company Act of 1940;[491] and

- neither the nominee nor the nominating shareholder (or any member of a nominating shareholder group) has an agreement with the company regarding the nomination of the nominee.[492]

Proposed Item 8 of Schedule 14N would have required a certification from the nominating shareholder or each member of the nominating shareholder group that the securities used for purposes of meeting the ownership threshold in Rule 14a-11 are not held for the purpose, or with the effect, of changing control of the company or to gain more than a limited number of seats on the board.

b. Comments on the proposed notice requirements

Commenters generally supported the proposed content requirements of Schedule 14N on the general principle that the Commission should impose disclosure requirements on nominating shareholders and their nominees.[493] Two of these commenters also stated that additional disclosures or representations are not needed.[494] In addition, some commenters recommended that all nominees be subject to any new disclosure rules adopted by the Commission as part of its proxy disclosure and solicitation enhancements rulemaking.[495] Four commenters asked that companies be allowed to require additional disclosure from a nominating shareholder or group through, for example, the advance notice bylaws, as long as such requirements are consistent with state law.[496] One commenter argued that the nominating shareholder, group, or nominee should provide any disclosure required under a company's governing documents as long as such disclosure is required of all nominees.[497] One commenter asked that all content requirements be set forth in Schedule 14N itself, as it found the structure of the Schedule and the references to disclosure requirements to be unnecessarily complicated.[498] The commenter recommended that we include a requirement that the nominating shareholder or group disclose information about the nature and extent of the relationships between the nominating shareholder, group and the nominee and the company or its affiliates.[499] Another

---

[489] See proposed Rule 14a-18(a). Proposed Rule 14a-11 also included this provision as a direct requirement. Thus, a company would not be required to include a shareholder nominee in its proxy materials if the nominee's candidacy or, if elected, board membership would violate controlling state law, federal law, or rules of a national securities exchange or national securities association (other than rules of a national securities exchange or national securities association that set forth requirements regarding the independence of directors).

[490] See proposed Rule 14a-18(b) (which referred to the requirements in proposed Rule 14a-11(b)).

[491] See proposed Rule 14a-18(c).

[492] See proposed Rule 14a-18(d).

[493] See letters from ABA; Alston & Bird; Americans for Financial Reform; CalSTRS; CFA Institute; CII;

Corporate Library; Dominican Sisters of Hope; Florida State Board of Administration; GovernanceMetrics; ICI; Mercy Investment Program; Protective; Risk-Metrics; Sisters of Mercy; Tri-State Coalition; Ursuline Sisters of Tildonk; USPE; Walden.

[494] See letters from CII; USPE.

[495] See letters from ABA; Alaska Air; Robert A. Bassett ("R. Bassett"); BorgWarner; Eli Lilly; NACD; O'Melveny & Myers; Pfizer; Society of Corporate Secretaries; UnitedHealth.

[496] See letters from ABA; Chevron; Sidley Austin; SIFMA.

[497] See letter from Cleary.

[498] See letter from ABA.

[499] Id.

commenter recommended the rules include a representation that the nominee is not controlled by the nominating shareholder or group.[500]

We also sought comment on the proposed representations to be provided by the nominating shareholder or group in Schedule 14N. One commenter stated that the proposed representations are appropriate and no additional representations are needed.[501] This commenter opposed a requirement for a shareholder nominee to make any representation either in addition to, or instead of, those made by the nominating shareholder or group. One commenter stated simply that none of the proposed representations in Schedule 14N should be eliminated.[502] It also observed generally that the shareholder nominee should be required to make the representations (*e.g.*, regarding independence) because he or she would know the facts relating to the representations and therefore should accept responsibility. One commenter opposed the requirement for a representation that a shareholder nomination (or election of the shareholder nominee) would not violate state law, federal law, or listing standards.[503] The commenter also believed it would be inappropriate to require a representation that the nomination complies with any independence requirement under federal law, state law, or listing standards.

c. Adopted notice requirements

We are adopting the notice requirements substantially as proposed, with differences noted below. In addition, we agree that the rules as proposed could be streamlined to reduce complexity. As adopted, Schedule 14N will contain the disclosure items that were included in the Schedule as proposed, as well as the disclosures proposed in Rule 14a-11, Rule 14a-18 and Rule 14a-19. We believe that the disclosure requirements we are adopting will provide transparency and facilitate shareholders' ability to make an informed voting decision on a shareholder director nominee or nominees without being unnecessarily burdensome on nominating shareholders or groups.

i. Disclosure

Schedule 14N will require a nominating shareholder or group to provide the following information about the nominating shareholder or group and the nominee:[504]

- The name and address of the nominating shareholder or each member of the nominating shareholder group;

- Information regarding the amount and percentage of securities held and entitled to vote on the election of directors at the meeting and the voting power derived from securities that have been loaned or sold in a short sale that remains open, as specified in Instruction 3 to Rule 14a-11(b)(1);[505]

- A written statement from the registered holder of the shares held by the nominating shareholder or each member of the nominating shareholder group, or the brokers or banks through which such shares are held, verifying that, within seven calendar days prior to submitting the notice on Schedule 14N to the company, the shareholder continuously held the qualifying amount of securities for at least three years;[506]

- A written statement of the nominating shareholder's or group's intent to continue to hold the qualifying amount of securities through the shareholder meeting at which directors are elected. Additionally, the nominating shareholder or group

---

[500] *See* letter from IBM.

[501] *See* letter from CII.

[502] *See* letter from ABA.

[503] *See* letter from USPE.

[504] The disclosure requirements proposed in Rule 14a-18(e)–(*l*) are now contained in new Item 4(b) and new Item 5 of Schedule 14N.

[505] *See* Item 3 of new Schedule 14N.

[506] *See* Item 4(a) of new Schedule 14N. A nominating shareholder would not be required to provide this statement if the nominating shareholder is the registered holder of the shares or is attaching or incorporating by reference a previously filed Schedule 13D, Schedule 13G, Form 3, Form 4, and/or Form 5, or amendments to those documents to prove ownership.

would provide a written statement regarding the nominating shareholder's or group's intent with respect to continued ownership after the election;[507]

- A statement that the nominee consents to be named in the company's proxy statement and form of proxy and, if elected, to serve on the board of directors;[508]

- Disclosure about the nominee as would be provided in response to the disclosure requirements of Items 4(b), 5(b), 7(a), (b), and (c) and, for investment companies, Item 22(b) of Schedule 14A, as applicable;[509]

- Disclosure about the nominating shareholder or each member of a nominating shareholder group as would be required in response to the disclosure requirements of Items 4(b) and 5(b) of Schedule 14A, as applicable;[510]

- Disclosure about whether the nominating shareholder or any member of a nominating shareholder group has been involved in any legal proceeding during the past ten years, as specified in Item 401(f) of Regulation S-K;[511]

- Disclosure about whether, to the best of the nominating shareholder's or group's knowledge, the nominee meets the director qualifications set forth in the company's governing documents, if any;[512]

- A statement that, to the best of the nominating shareholder's or group's knowledge, in the case of a company other than an investment company, the nominee meets the objective criteria for "independence" of the national securities exchange or national securities association rules applicable to the company, if any, or, in the case of a company that is an investment company, the nominee is not an "interested person" of the company as defined in Section 2(a)(19) of the Investment Company Act of 1940;[513]

- Disclosure about the nature and extent of the relationships between the nominating shareholder or group, the nominee, and/or the company or any affiliate of the company,[514] such as:

  o Any direct or indirect material interest in any contract or agreement between the nominating shareholder or any member of the nominating shareholder group, the nominee, and/or the company or any affiliate of the company (including any employment agreement, collective bargaining agreement, or consulting agreement);

  o Any material pending or threatened litigation in which the nominating shareholder or any member of the nominating shareholder group and/or the nominee is a party or a material participant, and that involves the company, any of its officers or directors, or any affiliate of the company; and

---

[507] *See* Item 4(b) of new Schedule 14N. These requirements were proposed in Rule 14a-18(f) and Item 5(b) of Schedule 14N.

[508] *See* Item 5(a) of new Schedule 14N and proposed Rule 14a-18(e).

[509] *See* Item 5(b) of new Schedule 14N and proposed Rule 14a-18(g).

[510] *See* Item 5(c) of new Schedule 14N and proposed Rule 14a-18(h). If a nominating shareholder is organized in a form other than a corporation or partnership, comparable disclosure with respect to persons in similar capacities would be required.

[511] *See* Item 5(d) of new Schedule 14N and proposed Rule 14a-18(i). As proposed, the rule would have required disclosure regarding a nominating shareholder's involvement in any legal proceedings during the past five years. Recently, the Commission amended

Item 401(f) of Regulation S-K to require disclosure regarding involvement in legal proceedings for the prior ten years. *See Proxy Disclosure Enhancements,* Release No. 33-9089; 34-61175 (Dec. 16, 2009) [74 FR 68334] ("Proxy Disclosure Enhancements Adopting Release"). Accordingly, as adopted, Item 5(d) will require disclosure about a nominating shareholder's involvement in legal proceedings during the past ten years.

[512] *See* Item 5(e) of new Schedule 14N.

[513] *See* Item 5(f) of new Schedule 14N.

[514] We note that this disclosure requirement would apply to relationships between the nominating shareholder or group and the nominee, as well as the relationships between the nominating shareholder or group or the nominee and the company or its affiliates. *See* Item 5(g) of new Schedule 14N.

- ○ Any other material relationship between the nominating shareholder or any member of the nominating shareholder group, the nominee, and/or the company or any affiliate of the company not otherwise disclosed;[515]
- • Disclosure of any Web site address on which the nominating shareholder or group may publish soliciting materials;[516] and
- • If desired to be included in the company's proxy statement, a statement in support of the shareholder nominee or nominees, which may not exceed 500 words per nominee.[517]

The disclosure provided by the nominating shareholder or group in Item 5 of Schedule 14N would be included by the company in its proxy materials,[518] along with the company's disclosure in response to Items 4(b) and 5(b) of Schedule 14A.[519]

In a traditional proxy contest, shareholders receive the disclosure required by Items 4(b), 5(b), 7, and 22, as applicable, of Schedule 14A from both the company and the insurgent when the contest relates to an annual election of directors. The new Schedule 14N disclosure requirements are somewhat more expansive in that they also include the disclosures concerning ownership amount, length of ownership, intent to continue to hold the shares through the date of the meeting and with respect to continued ownership after the meeting, and disclosure regarding the nature and extent of the relationships between the nominating shareholder or group and nominee and the company or any affiliate of the company. We believe that these disclosures will assist shareholders in making an informed voting decision with regard to any nominee or nominees put forth by the nominating shareholder or group using Rule 14a-11, in that the disclosures will enable shareholders to gauge the nominating shareholder's or group's interest in the company, longevity of ownership, and intent with regard to continued ownership in the company. These disclosures also will be important to the company in determining whether the nominating shareholder or group is eligible to rely on Rule 14a-11 to require the company to include a nominee or nominees in the company's proxy materials.

In some cases, the requirements in new Schedule 14N are slightly different than we proposed. We have clarified that the nominating shareholder or group will be required to include disclosure in the Schedule 14N concerning specified relationships between the nominating shareholder or group and the nominee or nominees. As discussed in Section II.B.5.d. above, we received comment suggesting that, in the absence of a limitation on relationships between the nominating shareholder or group and their nominee or nominees, we should adopt a disclosure requirement concerning relationships between the

---

[515] *See* Item 5(g) of new Schedule 14N and proposed Rule 14a-18(j).

[516] *See* Item 5(h) of new Schedule 14N and proposed Rule 14a-18(k).

[517] *See* Item 5(i) of new Schedule 14N and proposed Rule 14a-18(*l*). This requirement is discussed in more detail in this section. If a nominating shareholder or group submits a statement in support that exceeds 500 words per nominee, a company will be required to include the nominee or nominees, provided that the eligibility requirements are met, but may exclude the statement in support from its proxy materials pursuant to Rule 14a-11(g). In this instance, the company would provide notice to the staff and could, if desired, seek a no-action letter from the staff. *See* new Rule 14a-11(c) and Rule 14a-11(g). The 500 words would be counted in the same manner as words are counted under Rule 14a-8. Any statements that are, in effect, arguments in support of the nomination would constitute part of the supporting statement. Accordingly, any "title" or "heading" that meets this test would be counted toward the 500-word limitation. Inclusion of a Web site

address in the supporting statement would not violate the 500-word limitation; rather, the Web site address would be counted as one word for purposes of the 500-word limitation.

[518] *See* Item 7(e) of Schedule 14A. Similarly, if a company receives a nominee for inclusion in its proxy materials pursuant to a procedure set forth under applicable state or foreign law, or the company's governing documents providing for the inclusion of shareholder director nominees in the company's proxy materials, the disclosure provided by the nominating shareholder or group in response to Item 6 of Schedule 14N would be included in the company's proxy materials. *See* Item 7(f) of Schedule 14A.

[519] Instruction 3 to Rule 14a-12(c) clarifies that though inclusion of a nominee pursuant to Rule 14a-11 or solicitations by a nominating shareholder or nominating shareholder group that are made in connection with that nomination would constitute solicitations in opposition subject to Rule 14a-12(c), they would not be treated as such for purposes of Exchange Act Rule 14a-6(a).

parties.[520] Similarly, and as discussed in Section II.B.5.b., we have added a requirement that a nominating shareholder or group disclose whether, to the best of their knowledge, the nominating shareholder's or group's nominee meets the company's director qualifications, if any, as set forth in the company's governing documents.[521] We added this requirement because we believe that this information will be useful to shareholders in making a voting decision by enabling them to consider whether shareholder nominees would meet a company's director qualifications. Shareholders will provide this disclosure "to the best of their knowledge" to address the fact that the standards will be company standards and thus could be subject to interpretation.

We also have added an instruction to Item 4 of Schedule 14N to provide a form of written statement that may be used for verifying the amount of securities held by the nominating shareholder, and that the qualifying amount of securities has been held continuously for at least three years.[522] A statement will be required from a nominating shareholder that is not the registered holder of the securities and is not proving ownership by providing previously filed Schedules 13D or 13G, or Forms 3, 4, or 5. We believe that providing a form of written statement will make it easier for nominating shareholders and the persons through which they hold their securities to comply with the requirement and reduce complexity for shareholders and companies in determining whether satisfactory proof of ownership has been provided.[523] In addition, as noted above, Item 5(d) will require disclosure about each nominating shareholder's involvement in legal proceedings during the past ten years rather than the past five years as proposed, consistent with the changes recently adopted by the Commission for board nominees in general.

In connection with our revisions to the rule concerning calculation of ownership, we also have added new Items 3(c) and (d) to the Schedule 14N to require disclosure of the voting power attributable to securities that have been loaned or sold in a short sale that is not closed out, or that have been borrowed for purposes other than a short sale, as specified in Instruction 3 to Rule 14a-11(b)(1).

Finally, as proposed, a nominating shareholder or group could provide a statement in support of a shareholder nominee or nominees, which could not exceed 500 words if the nominating shareholder or group elects to have such a statement included in the company's proxy materials. Two commenters stated that a limit of 500 words would be appropriate,[524] five commenters recommended that a nominating shareholder or group be permitted to include a supporting statement of more than 500 words,[525] and four commenters proposed a limit of either 750 or 1000 words.[526] We believe it is appropriate to allow a nominating shareholder or group to provide a statement in support of the shareholder nominee or nominees which may not exceed 500 words for each nominee, rather than 500 words for all nominees in total,[527] if the nominating shareholder or group elects to have such a statement included in the company's proxy materials. We believe that a limitation of 500 words per nominee is sufficient for a nominating shareholder or group to express their support for a nominee. In this regard, we note that shareholders and companies are familiar with the 500 word limitation, as it is the limit on the number of words that may be used to support a shareholder proposal submitted under Rule 14a-8. While we believe it is appropriate to limit the length of the supporting statement that the company is required to include, we note that if a nominating shareholder or group wishes to provide additional information, it is free to do so in supplemental materials, provided

---

[520] *See* letters from CII; IBM; O'Melveny & Myers; SIFMA; UnitedHealth.

[521] *See* Item 5(e) of new Schedule 14N.

[522] *See* the Instruction to Item 4 of new Schedule 14N.

[523] In this regard, we note that providing proper proof of ownership has proved to be an area of confusion for some shareholder proponents using Rule 14a-8 who must obtain a written statement from the "record" holder of the proponent's securities. Thus, we believe that providing a form of written statement that

may be used to provide proof of ownership for purposes of Rule 14a-11(b)(3) will alleviate any potential confusion that could arise in this context.

[524] *See* letters from CII; Florida State Board of Administration.

[525] *See* letters from ACSI; AFSCME; Hermes; Pax World; USPE.

[526] *See* letters from AFSCME; L. Dallas; P. Neuhauser; USPE.

[527] We are adopting this modification in Item 5(i) of Schedule 14N.

it complies with the requirements of Rule 14a-2(b)(8). If a nominating shareholder or group submits a statement in support that exceeds 500 words per nominee, a company will be required to include the nominee or nominees, provided that the eligibility requirements are met, but the company may exclude the statement in support from its proxy materials provided it provides notice to the staff of its intent to do so.[528]

As noted above, we proposed to require certain representations to be provided in the Schedule 14N, either in the form of representations or as certifications. As adopted, we are including the proposed representations and certifications as direct requirements in Rule 14a-11.[529] Consequently, we have simplified the requirements so that under the final rules a nominating shareholder or group will be required to certify, in its notice on Schedule 14N filed with the Commission, that it does not have a change in control intent or an intent to gain more than the maximum number of board seats provided for under Rule 14a-11 and that the nominating shareholder and the nominee satisfies the applicable requirements of Rule 14a-11.[530] We have retained the certification with regard to no change in control intent or intent to gain more than the maximum number of board seats provided for under Rule 14a-11, even though this is also a direct requirement in Rule 14a-11 as adopted, because we believe it is important to highlight this requirement for nominating shareholders or groups signing the certification. As was proposed, the nominating shareholder or each member of the nominating shareholder group (or authorized representative) will be required to certify when signing the Schedule 14N that, "after reasonable inquiry and to the best of my knowledge and belief," the information in the statement is "true, complete and correct." Though all disclosure in the Schedule 14N would be covered by this representation, we have specifically included it in the certifications concerning compliance with the requirements of Rule 14a-11 as well.

We have revised the rule to delete the provision that had the effect of allowing exclusion of a nominee if any required representation or certification was materially false or misleading.[531] Rather than allowing companies to exclude Rule 14a-11 nominees on that basis, we believe companies should address any concerns regarding false or misleading disclosures through their own disclosures, as in traditional proxy contests. This change will limit the bases on which a company may exclude a nominee,[532] but we emphasize that the nominating shareholder or group will have Rule 14a-9 liability for any statement included in the Schedule 14N or which it causes to be included in a company's proxy materials which, at the time and in light of the circumstances under which it is made, is false or misleading with respect to any material fact or that omits to state any material fact necessary to make the statements therein not false or misleading. In addition, as discussed in Section II.E. below, we have provided in the final rules that the company is not responsible for the information provided by the nominating shareholder or group in its Schedule 14N and included by the company in its proxy materials.

ii. Schedule 14N filing requirements

We proposed to require the notice to be provided to the company and filed with the Commission by the date specified in the company's advance notice bylaw provision, or where no such provision is in place, no later than 120 calendar days before the date the

---

[528] *See* new Rule 14a-11(c) and Rule 14a-11(g).

[529] *See also* Section II.B.4. and Section II.B.5. above, regarding nominating shareholder and nominee eligibility.

[530] *See* new Rule 14a-11(b)(11) and Item 8(a) of new Schedule 14N. We note that in some cases, an authorized representative may file a Schedule 14N for each member of a nominating shareholder group and would provide the required disclosures and certifications. In such cases, each member of the nominating shareholder group represented by the authorized representative will be deemed to have provided the certifications.

[531] *See* proposed Rule 14a-11(a)(5).

[532] *See* Section II.B.9. below for a discussion of the requirements for a company receiving a nomination submitted pursuant to Rule 14a-11 and the process for seeking a staff no-action letter with respect to a company's decision to exclude a nominee. As noted below, assertions that a certification or disclosure provided by a nominating shareholder or group is false or misleading will not be a basis for excluding a nominee or nominees. A company seeking a no-action letter from the staff with regard to a determination to exclude a nominee or nominees would need to assert that a requirement of the rule has not been met.

company mailed its proxy materials for the prior year's annual meeting. A significant number of commenters suggested using a uniform deadline for all companies, as is the case in Rule 14a-8.[533] Many of these commenters believed that the proposed timing requirement would create difficulties for companies with advance notice bylaws providing a later deadline and, thus, would preclude those companies from engaging in the proposed staff process.[534] Some commenters supported the proposed default 120 calendar day deadline,[535] while others argued that the 120 calendar day deadline would provide too little time for companies.[536] Some commenters worried that the proposed deadline would not give sufficient time for companies to resolve any eligibility issues presented by potential nominees, including resolution through the Rule 14a-11 no-action process, Commission appeals, and litigation.[537]

We are adopting a uniform deadline of no later than 120 calendar days before the anniversary of the date that the company mailed its proxy materials for the prior year's annual meeting for all companies subject to the rule.[538] We believe that a uniform deadline will benefit shareholders by providing them with one standard to comply with at all companies and should address concerns of companies that an advance notice bylaw deadline would provide too little time. We also believe that a deadline of 120 calendar days will provide adequate time for companies to take the steps necessary to include or, where appropriate, to exclude a shareholder nominee for director that is submitted pursuant to Rule 14a-11.[539]

In the Proposing Release, we solicited comment as to whether a window period should be provided for the submission of the notice on Schedule 14N and the appropriate time period for the window. A number of commenters recommended a window period during which a nominating shareholder or group could submit its Rule 14a-11 nomination.[540] These commenters believed that including such a requirement would prevent a race to file among shareholders that could discourage dialogue with the board and force the board to address nominations throughout the year.[541] We agree and are adopting a

---

[533] See letters from 26 Corporate Secretaries; ABA; Alaska Air; American Express; Anadarko; Boeing; BorgWarner; BRT; Caterpillar; CIGNA; CII; Dewey; Florida State Board of Administration; FPL Group; Honeywell; JPMorgan Chase; Keating Muething; P. Neuhauser; PepsiCo; Pfizer; Praxair; Schulte Roth & Zabel; Seven Law Firms; Shearman & Sterling; Sidley Austin; Society of Corporate Securities; Thompson Hine LLP ("Thompson Hine"); TI; USPE; Wells Fargo; Xerox.

[534] See letters from ABA; Alaska Air; BRT; Caterpillar; CIGNA; Dewey; Honeywell; JPMorgan Chase; Keating Muething; PepsiCo; Sidley Austin; Society of Corporate Securities; Thompson Hine; TI; Wells Fargo.

[535] See letters from Alaska Air; Boeing; Borg-Warner; CII; Dewey; JPMorgan Chase; P. Neuhauser; O'Melveny & Myers; PepsiCo; Praxair; Seven Law Firms; Shearman & Sterling; Society of Corporate Secretaries; Thompson Hine; USPE.

[536] See letters from 26 Corporate Secretaries; ABA; Alcoa; Allstate; American Express; Boeing; BRT; Con Edison; Davis Polk; FPL Group; JPMorgan Chase; McDonald's; P. Neuhauser; Pfizer; Protective; Risk-Metrics; Seven Law Firms; TI; Xerox.

[537] See letters from ABA; BRT; Con Edison; TI.

[538] See new Rule 14a-11(b)(10). The Schedule 14N would, of course, have to contain all required disclosure as of the date of filing.

[539] We note that as with Rule 14a-8, Rule 14a-11 requires a company to provide notice to the Commission if it intends to exclude a nominee. Also as with

Rule 14a-8, if a company determines that it may exclude a nominee, the rule does not require the company to seek a no-action letter from the staff with regard to the determination to exclude the nominee. In this regard, we note that the 120-day deadline in Rule 14a-8 appears to provide companies with sufficient time in which to consider complex matters. For example, companies routinely consider whether a proposal submitted pursuant to Rule 14a-8 would cause the company to violate federal or state law and submit requests for no-action letters, along with detailed legal opinions, with respect to those proposals. We believe that a company will consider nominees submitted pursuant to Rule 14a-11 in a similar manner. Thus, we believe a deadline of 120 calendar days before the date that the company mailed it proxy materials the prior year is sufficient.

[540] See letters from 26 Corporate Secretaries; Aetna; Allstate; Boeing; BorgWarner; L. Dallas; DuPont; Florida State Board of Administration; FPL Group; Kirkland & Ellis; Leggett; P. Neuhauser; PepsiCo; Pfizer; S. Quinlivan; RiskMetrics; Schulte Roth & Zabel; Shearman & Sterling; SIFMA; Society of Corporate Secretaries; Southern Company; TI; USPE; Wells Fargo; Xerox.

[541] The commenters generally mentioned various 30 day ranges that we requested comment on (e.g., no earlier than 180 days and no later than 150 days before the date that the company mailed its proxy materials for the prior year's annual meeting; no earlier than 150 calendar days and no later than 120 calendar days before the date that the company mailed its proxy

window period for the submission of the notice to the company. Limiting the time period during which Rule 14a-11 nominations could be made should help reduce disruptions that might occur when a company receives shareholder nominations for director submitted pursuant to Rule 14a-11. In this regard, as noted above, commenters generally supported a 30-day window period. We believe that a window of 30 days is sufficient for the submission of the notice on Schedule 14N because it provides shareholders with an opportunity to submit a nomination, as well as the opportunity to consider any nominations that have been submitted and whether the shareholder would like to submit a nomination, either individually or as a group. Therefore, we are adopting a requirement that the notice on Schedule 14N be transmitted to the company and filed with the Commission no earlier than 150 calendar days, and no later than 120 calendar days, before the anniversary of the date that the company mailed its proxy materials for the prior year's annual meeting. As proposed, we are adopting a requirement that if the company did not hold an annual meeting during the prior year, or if the date of the meeting has changed by more than 30 calendar days from the prior year, then the nominating shareholder must provide notice a reasonable time before the company mails its proxy materials.[542] In that case, the company will be required to disclose the date by which the shareholder must submit the required notice in a Form 8-K filed pursuant to new Item 5.08 within four business days after the company determines the anticipated meeting date.[543]

As noted, the notice on Schedule 14N must be transmitted to the company[544] and filed with the Commission on the same day.[545] Consistent with the Proposal, the Schedule 14N must be filed with the Commission on EDGAR. To file the Schedule 14N on EDGAR, a nominating shareholder or group and any nominee will need to have or obtain EDGAR filing codes and user identification numbers, which may be obtained by filing electronically a Form ID in advance of filing the Schedule 14N.[546] We encourage

---

(Footnote Continued)

materials for the prior year's annual meeting; no earlier than 120 calendar days and no later than 90 calendar days prior to the anniversary of the company's last annual meeting). One commenter suggested that the Commission limit the nomination process to a 45-day window period commencing four months after the company's annual shareholder meeting. *See* letter from Aetna. Another commenter suggested that nominations be submitted within a 30-day period commencing five months after the company's annual meeting. *See* letter from SIFMA. We believe that starting the period for nominations earlier than 150 calendar days before the anniversary of the date the company mailed its proxy materials for the prior year's annual meeting would not provide the current board with sufficient opportunity to perform its duties and demonstrate its performance, nor would it provide shareholders with enough time to evaluate the board's performance, to make an informed decision with respect to a potential nomination.

[542] In addition, if a company is holding a special meeting in lieu of an annual meeting, the nominating shareholder must provide notice a reasonable time before the company mails its proxy materials.

[543] *See* new Rule 14a-11(b)(10). *See also* proposed Instruction 2 to Rule 14a-11(a) and Rule 14a-18. This would be similar to the requirement currently included in Rule 14a-5(f), which specifies that, where the date of the next annual meeting is advanced or delayed by more than 30 calendar days from the date of the annual meeting to which the proxy statement relates, the company must disclose the new meeting date in the company's earliest possible quarterly report on Form 10-Q. Although registered investment companies gen-

erally are not required to file Form 8-K, we are requiring them to file a Form 8-K disclosing the date by which the shareholder notice must be provided if the company did not hold an annual meeting during the prior year, or if the date of the meeting has changed by more than 30 calendar days from the prior year. For a further discussion of the Form 8-K filing requirement for registered investment companies, *see* Section II.D.1.

[544] Rule 14n-3 specifies that the Schedule 14N must be transmitted to the company at its principal executive office.

[545] *See* new Rule 14n-1. In this regard, we are adopting an amendment to Rule 13(a)(4) of Regulation S-T, as proposed, to provide that a Schedule 14N will be deemed to be filed on the same business day if it is filed on or before 10 p.m. Eastern Standard Time or Eastern Daylight Saving Time, whichever is currently in effect. This will allow nominating shareholders additional time to file the notice on Schedule 14N and transmit the notice to the company.

[546] To file the Schedule 14N on EDGAR, a nominating shareholder or group and any nominee that does not already have EDGAR filing codes, and to which the Commission has not previously assigned a user identification number, which we call a "Central Index Key" (CIK) code, will need to obtain the codes by filing electronically a Form ID (17 CFR 293.63; 249.446; and 274.402) *at* https://www.filermanagement.edgarfiling.sec.gov. The applicant also will be required to submit a notarized authenticating document. If the authenticating document is prepared before the applicant makes the Form ID filing, the authenticating document may be

nominating shareholders and groups to take the steps necessary to obtain an EDGAR filing code and CIK code well in advance of the deadline for filing a notice on Schedule 14N.

The Schedule 14N will:

- Include a cover page in the form set forth in Schedule 14N with the appropriate box on the cover page marked to specify that the filing relates to a Rule 14a-11 nomination;[547]

- Be made under the subject company's Exchange Act file number (or in the case of a registered investment company, under the subject company's Investment Company Act file number); and

- Be made on the date the notice is first transmitted to the company.

We are adopting, as proposed, a requirement that the Schedule 14N be amended promptly for any material change to the disclosure and certifications provided in the originally-filed Schedule 14N.[548] In this regard, we would view withdrawal of a nominating shareholder or group (or any member of the group), or of a director nominee, and the reasons for any such withdrawal, as a material change. For example, such a withdrawal could be material because it may result in a group no longer meeting the required ownership threshold under Rule 14a-11. We also would view as material entering into an agreement between the company and the nominating shareholder or group for the company to include a nominee in the company's proxy materials as a company nominee.[549] The nominating shareholder or group also will be required, as proposed, to file a final amendment to the Schedule 14N disclosing within 10 days of the final results of the election being announced by the company the nominating shareholder's or group's intention with regard to continued ownership of its shares.[550] As discussed above, the nominating shareholder or group would be required to disclose its intent with regard to continued ownership of the company's securities in its original notice on Schedule 14N.[551] Filing an amendment to the Schedule 14N within 10 days after the announcement of the final results of the election will provide shareholders with information as to whether the outcome of the election may have altered the intent of the nominating shareholder or group and what further plans the nominating shareholder or group may have with regard to the company.

As was proposed,[552] the Schedule 14N may be signed either by each person on whose behalf the statement is filed or his or her authorized representative. We assume that in many cases group members will choose to appoint an authorized representative from among the group. If the statement is signed on behalf of a person by his authorized representative other than an executive officer or general partner of the filing person, evidence of the representative's authority to sign on behalf of such person must be filed

---

(Footnote Continued)

uploaded as a Portable Document Format (PDF) attachment to the electronic filing. An applicant also may submit the authenticating document by faxing it to the Commission within two business days before or after electronically filing the Form ID. The authenticating document would need to be manually signed by the applicant over the applicant's typed signature, include the information contained in the Form ID, and confirm the authenticity of the Form ID. If the authenticating document is filed after electronically filing the Form ID, it would need to include the accession number assigned to the electronically filed Form ID as a result of its filing. *See* 17 CFR 232.10(b)(2).

[547] The Schedule 14N also would be used for disclosure concerning the inclusion of shareholder nominees in company proxy materials when made pursuant

to an applicable state or foreign law provision or a company's governing documents. *See* new Rule 14a-18 and proposed Rule 14a-19, as discussed in Section II. C.5. below.

[548] *See* new Rule 14n-2(a).

[549] We note that if this occurs, the nominee would no longer be a Rule 14a-11 nominee. *See* Section II.B.6.c. for a discussion of how this would affect the calculation of the maximum number of Rule 14a-11 nominees.

[550] *See* new Rule 14n-2(b).

[551] *See* Item 4(b) of new Schedule 14N.

[552] While the proposed Schedule 14N included the instruction regarding the signing of the Schedule by an authorized representative, we did not discuss this aspect of the proposed rule text in the narrative portion of the release.

with the statement, provided, however, that a power of attorney for this purpose which is already on file with the Commission may be incorporated by reference.

The Schedule 14N, as filed with the Commission, as well as any amendments to the Schedule 14N, will be subject to the liability provisions of Exchange Act Rule 14a-9 pursuant to new paragraph (c) to the rule.[553]

9. Requirements for a Company That Receives a Notice from a Nominating Shareholder or Group

a. Procedure if company plans to include Rule 14a-11 nominee

In the Proposing Release, we proposed a process for a company to follow once it received a nomination submitted pursuant to Rule 14a-11. Upon receipt of a shareholder's or group's notice of its intent to require the company to include in its proxy materials a shareholder nominee or nominees pursuant to Rule 14a-11, the company would determine whether it would include the nominee or whether it believed it would be desirable to, and that the company had a basis upon which it could rely to, exclude a nominee. If a company determined it would include the nominee, the company would notify in writing the nominating shareholder or group no later than 30 calendar days before the company files its definitive proxy statement and form of proxy with the Commission that it will include the nominee or nominees.[554] The company would be required to provide this notice in a manner that provides evidence of timely receipt by the nominating shareholder or group.

We are adopting this requirement as proposed, with a clarification regarding the timing of the company's transmission of the notice and receipt by the nominating shareholder or group.[555] As adopted, if a company will include a shareholder nominee, a company will be required to notify the nominating shareholder or group (or their authorized representative). Rather than including the proposed requirement that the company must provide the notice in a manner that evidences timely receipt by the shareholder, we are adopting a requirement that the notification must be postmarked or transmitted electronically no later than 30 calendar days before it files its definitive proxy materials with the Commission.[556] We believe this will provide for ease of use and administration because it should be clear when the notice was transmitted. We also note that it is consistent with the transmission standard we are adopting for submitting a notice of intent with respect to a nomination pursuant to Rule 14a-11(b)(10). We note that while we are not adopting a requirement regarding the evidence of timely receipt by the nominating shareholder or group, we believe it is in a company's interest to send the notice to the nominating shareholder or group in a manner that will allow the company to demonstrate that the nominating shareholder or group received the notice, as doing so may avoid potential disputes.

b. Procedure if company plans to exclude Rule 14a-11 nominee

The Proposal also included a process for a company to follow if it determined that it could exclude a nominee submitted pursuant to Rule 14a-11.[557] As proposed, a company could determine that it is not required under Rule 14a-11 to include a nominee from a nominating shareholder or group in its proxy materials if:

- Proposed Rule 14a-11 is not applicable to the company;
- The nominating shareholder or group has not complied with the requirements of Rule 14a-11;

---

[553] For further discussion, *see* Section II.E.

[554] *See* proposed Rule 14a-11(f)(2).

[555] *See* new Rule 14a-11(g)(1) and Instruction 1 to Rule 14a-11(g).

[556] This 30-day deadline for this notice should provide a nominating shareholder or group with sufficient time to engage in soliciting activities with respect to its

nominee or nominees, if it has not done so already, or pursue any legal remedies that may be available if the company determines it will exclude the nominating shareholder's or group's nominee or nominees.

[557] The process was modeled after the staff no-action process used in connection with shareholder proposals under Rule 14a-8.

- The nominee does not meet the requirements of Rule 14a-11;
- Any representation required to be included in the notice to the company is false or misleading in any material respect; or
- The company has received more nominees than it is required to include by proposed Rule 14a-11 and the nominating shareholder or group is not entitled to have its nominee included under the criteria proposed in Rule 14a-11(d)(3).[558]

Under the Proposal, the nominating shareholder or group would need to be notified of the company's determination not to include the shareholder nominee in sufficient time to consider the validity of any determination to exclude the nominee and respond to such a notice.[559] In this regard, we noted the time-sensitive nature of Rule 14a-11 and the interpretive issues that may arise in applying the new rule. After the company provided such a notice to a nominating shareholder or group and afforded the nominating shareholder or group the opportunity to respond, the company would be required to provide a notice to the Commission regarding its intent not to include a shareholder nominee in its proxy materials. The company could seek a no-action letter from the staff with respect to its decision to exclude the nominee.[560]

The proposed process would have afforded a nominating shareholder or group the opportunity to remedy certain eligibility or procedural deficiencies in a nomination.[561] The various time deadlines set out in the proposed process were determined by considering the appropriate balance between companies' needs in meeting printing and filing deadlines for their shareholder meetings with shareholders' need for adequate time to satisfy the requirements of the rule.[562] Specifically, as proposed, a company determining that the nominating shareholder or group or nominee or nominees has not satisfied the eligibility requirements could exclude the shareholder nominee or nominees, subject to the following requirements:

- The company would notify in writing the nominating shareholder or group of its determination. The notice would be required to be postmarked or transmitted electronically no later than 14 calendar days after the company receives the shareholder notice of intent to nominate. The company would have to provide the notice in a manner that provides evidence of receipt by the nominating shareholder or group;[563]
- The company's notice to the nominating shareholder or group that it determined that the company may exclude a shareholder nominee or nominees would be required to include an explanation of the company's basis for determining that it may exclude the nominee or nominees;[564]
- The nominating shareholder or group would have 14 calendar days after receipt of the written notice of deficiency to respond to the notice and correct any eligibility or procedural deficiencies identified in the notice. The nominating shareholder or group would have to provide the response in a manner that provides evidence of its receipt by the company;[565]

---

[558] *See* proposed Rule 14a-11(a). More specifically, under the proposal a company would not be required to include a nominee where (1) applicable state law or the company's governing documents prohibit the company's shareholders from nominating a candidate for director; (2) the nominee's candidacy, or if elected, board membership, would violate controlling state law, federal law or rules of a national securities exchange or national securities association; (3) the nominating shareholder or group does not meet the rule's eligibility requirements; (4) the nominating shareholder's or group's notice is deficient; (5) any representation in the nominating shareholder's or group's notice is false in any material respect, or (6) the nominee is not required to be included in the company's proxy materials due to

the proposed limitation on the number of nominees required to be included.

[559] *See* proposed Rule 14a-11(f).

[560] *See* proposed Rule 14a-11(f)(7)–(14).

[561] *See* proposed Rule 14a-11(f)(3)–(6).

[562] We considered the timing requirements and deadlines in Rule 14a-8 when crafting the proposed requirements and deadlines for Rule 14a-11; however, due to the potential complexity of the nomination process, we determined in the proposal that it would be appropriate to provide additional time for the process.

[563] *See* proposed Rule 14a-11(f)(3).

[564] *See* proposed Rule 14a-11(f)(4).

[565] *See* proposed Rule 14a-11(f)(5).

- If, upon review of the nominating shareholder's or group's response, the company determines that the company still may exclude the shareholder nominee or nominees, after providing the requisite notice of and time for the nominating shareholder or group to remedy any eligibility or procedural deficiencies in the nomination, the company would be required to provide notice of the basis for its determination to the Commission no later than 80 calendar days before it files its definitive proxy statement and form of proxy with the Commission. The Commission staff could permit the company to make its submission later than 80 calendar days before the company files its definitive proxy statement and form of proxy if the company demonstrates good cause for missing the deadline;[566]

- The company's notice to the Commission would be required to include:

  ○ Identification of the nominating shareholder or each member of the nominating shareholder group, as applicable;

  ○ The name of the nominee or nominees;

  ○ An explanation of the company's basis for determining that it may exclude the nominee or nominees; and

  ○ A supporting opinion of counsel when the company's basis for excluding a nominee or nominees relies on a matter of state law;[567]

- The company would be required to file its notice of intent to exclude with the Commission and simultaneously provide a copy to the nominating shareholder or each member of the nominating shareholder or group;[568]

- The nominating shareholder or group could submit a response to the company's notice to the Commission. The response would be required to be postmarked or transmitted electronically no later than 14 calendar days after the nominating shareholder's or group's receipt of the company's notice to the Commission. The nominating shareholder or group would be required to provide a copy of its response to the Commission simultaneously to the company;[569]

- If requested by the company, the Commission staff would, at its discretion, provide an informal statement of its views (commonly known as a no-action letter) to the company and the nominating shareholder or group;[570]

- The company would provide the nominating shareholder or group with notice, no later than 30 calendar days before it files its definitive proxy statement and form of proxy with the Commission, of whether it will include or exclude the shareholder nominee or nominees.[571]

Some commenters supported the proposed staff review process for handling disputes regarding a company's determination to exclude a shareholder nominee.[572] Other commenters expressed concerns about the staff's expertise and ability to handle disputes in a timely manner.[573] With respect to the timing requirements in the proposed process, two commenters supported the proposed 14-day time period for the company to respond to a nominating shareholder's or group's notice.[574] A number of commenters criticized the proposed 14-day time period as too short or requested a longer time period for the company to respond.[575] Commenters explained that boards would need time to consider various issues, such as if the election of a shareholder nominee would trigger issues under the laws and regulations relevant to the company's business (*e.g.*, antitrust laws, government procurement, security clearances and export control) as well as under listing

---

[566] *See* proposed Rule 14a-11(f)(7).
[567] *See* proposed Rule 14a-11(f)(8).
[568] *See* proposed Rule 14a-11(f)(10).
[569] *See* proposed Rule 14a-11(f)(11).
[570] *See* proposed Rule 14a-11(f)(12).
[571] *See* proposed Rule 14a-11(f)(13).
[572] *See* letters from CFA Institute; CII; P. Neuhauser; Schulte Roth & Zabel; Universities Superannuation.

[573] *See* letters from ABA; Anadarko; BRT; Cleary; Davis Polk; Delaware Bar; ExxonMobil; E.J. Kullman; Protective; S. Quinlivan; Seven Law Firms; Weyerhaeuser.
[574] *See* letters from CFA Institute; CII.
[575] *See* letters from 26 Corporate Secretaries; Boeing; Con Edison; Honeywell; Kirkland & Ellis; Pfizer; Protective; UnitedHealth; USPE; Wells Fargo; Whirlpool.

standards and state law.[576] Two commenters supported the proposed 14-day time period for a nominating shareholder or group to respond to a company's notice of deficiency.[577] Two commenters worried the 14-day time period would give too little time for a response and recommended instead a 21-day time period.[578] One commenter warned that the Commission is underestimating the number of boards that would challenge shareholder nominees and the level of intensity of these challenges.[579] This commenter suggested that such challenges and possible litigation would demand significant time and resources from the Commission's staff.[580] Commenters also argued that challenges to Rule 14a-11 nominations likely would raise highly complex issues that fall outside the scope of the staff's expertise (e.g., whether a candidacy would violate state law).[581] One commenter pointed to difficulties arising from the "dueling" legal opinions situation in the Rule 14a-8 no-action process.[582] A couple commenters believed that courts, rather than the staff, would be better able to resolve disputes regarding shareholder director nominations.[583]

After considering the comments, we believe that it is in shareholders' and companies' interest to have a process available for seeking to resolve certain disputes regarding nominations submitted pursuant to Rule 14a-11.[584] Therefore, the rules we are adopting set out the process by which a company would determine whether to include a shareholder nominee and notify the nominating shareholder or group (or their authorized representative) of its determination.[585] The rules also include a process by which a company would notify a nominating shareholder or group (or their authorized representative) of a deficiency in its notice on Schedule 14N, the nominating shareholder or group would have the opportunity to respond, and the company would send a notice to the Commission if the company intends to exclude a shareholder nominee from its proxy materials. Consistent with the Proposal, a company making the determination to exclude a shareholder nominee will be required to submit a notice to the Commission regarding its determination, and it may also choose to avail itself of the process to seek a no-action letter from the staff with respect to its decision.[586] While we understand the concerns raised by commenters regarding the rule's timing requirements, we believe the requirements are appropriate in light of the need to facilitate the process between a company and its shareholders in time for an annual meeting.[587] In addition, the staff is committed to timely addressing these matters.

We are changing and clarifying the requirements related to the timing of sending and receiving notifications. As proposed, if a company determined that it could exclude a shareholder nominee, it would be required to notify the nominating shareholder or group and the notification would be required to be postmarked or transmitted electronically no later than 14 calendar days after the company received the notice on Schedule 14N. The

---

[576] See letters from Boeing; Honeywell.

[577] See letters from CFA Institute; CII.

[578] See letters from Protective; USPE.

[579] See letter from BRT.

[580] Id.

[581] See letters from ABA; BRT.

[582] See letter from ABA.

[583] See letters from ABA; Delaware Bar.

[584] In this regard, we note that the staff process for aiding in the resolution of disputes related to nominations made pursuant to Rule 14a-11 is non-exclusive. As discussed throughout this release, a company can seek the staff's view with regard to its determination to exclude a nominee from its proxy materials, but it is not required to do so. A company could engage in negotiations with a nominating shareholder or group and ultimately reach a resolution outside of the staff process, or the parties could avail themselves of other alternatives, such as litigation.

[585] Other than the modifications to the standards relating to transmission and receipt of notices and responses, which are described below, we are adopting the process as proposed.

[586] We encourage companies and shareholders to attempt to resolve disputes independently. To the extent that a company and nominating shareholder or group are able to resolve an issue at any point during the staff process, the company should withdraw its request for a no-action letter from the staff.

[587] The final rule does not include the proposed 30-calendar day notice requirement when a company determines to exclude a nominee. We believe this requirement is rendered unnecessary by the requirement in paragraph (g)(3) of Rule 14a-11 that the company provide notice to the Commission staff and nominating shareholder or group no later than 80 calendar days before the company files its definitive proxy statement and form of proxy. In addition, if a company seeks the staff's informal view with respect to the company's determination to exclude a nominee, promptly following receipt of the staff's response a company would be required to provide a notice to the nominating shareholder or group stating whether it will include or exclude the nominee.

proposed rule stated that the company would be responsible for providing the notice in a manner that evidences timely receipt by the nominating shareholder or group. The proposed rule also included similar requirements for a response to the notice by the nominating shareholder or group. As adopted, the rules will keep the deadlines as they were proposed but will use a transmission standard in determining the deadlines, similar to the standard discussed above for new Rule 14a-11(g)(1). We believe using such a uniform standard for all notification aspects of the rule will provide clarity and ease of use. Under the final rule, a company's notification must be postmarked or transmitted electronically no later than 14 calendar days after the close of the window period for submission of nominations pursuant to Rule 14a-11. We believe this change from the Proposal is appropriate because it will allow shareholders to submit their nominations, and companies to receive all the nominations, before requiring a company to send a notice to the nominating shareholder or group (or their authorized representative) as to whether it will include or exclude a nominee. Thus, a company will be able to make an informed decision with respect to individual nominations because it will be able to evaluate and respond to all the nominations it has received at one time, rather than evaluating and responding to the nominations as they are received. This approach should help reduce the possibility of any confusion that could result from requiring a company to respond to each nomination no later than 14 days after it is transmitted.[588] A nominating shareholder's or group's response to the company's notice must be postmarked or transmitted electronically no later than 14 calendar days after receipt of the company's notification. We note that a timely transmission standard applies in both instances; however, we urge companies to send the notification, and nominating shareholders or groups to send a response, in a manner that will allow them to demonstrate when the communication is received, as doing so may avoid potential disputes.

Under new Rule 14a-11(g), a company may exclude a shareholder nominee because:

- Rule 14a-11 is not applicable to the company;

- the nominating shareholder or group or nominee failed to satisfy the eligibility requirements in Rule 14a-11(b);[589] or

- including the nominee or nominees would result in the company exceeding the maximum number of nominees it is required to include in its proxy statement and form of proxy.[590]

In addition, a company would be permitted to exclude a statement in support of a nominee or nominees if the statement in support exceeds 500 words for each nominee.[591] In such cases, a company would be required to include the nominee or nominees, provided the eligibility requirements were satisfied, but would be permitted to exclude

---

[588] For example, suppose a company decided it did not have a reason to exclude a nominee submitted by a nominating shareholder during the first week of the window period. If we were to require that a company must respond to a nomination no later than 14 days after it was transmitted, the company would be required to respond to the nominating shareholder or group before the window period closed, and the company would inform the nominating shareholder that it intends to include the nominee. If, subsequent to the company sending a notice to the nominating shareholder of its intent to include the nominee, a nominating shareholder with a higher qualifying ownership percentage submits a nomination for the maximum number of nominees the company would be required to include under the rule, the company would be required to include those nominees assuming that the company determined that it did not have a reason to exclude the nominees. In that situation, confusion could result because, under the rule, the company would no longer

be required to include the nominee submitted by the nominating shareholder during the first week of the window period, even though the company had informed the nominating shareholder it would include its nominee.

[589] Specifically, the final rule provides that a company could exclude a shareholder nominee because the nominating shareholder or group, or the nominee, fails to satisfy the applicable eligibility requirements in Rule 14a-11(b). In this regard, we note that the nominating shareholder or each member of the nominating shareholder group (or authorized representative) would be required to certify that, after reasonable inquiry and to the best of its knowledge and belief, the nominating shareholder or member of the nominating shareholder or group and the nominee satisfied the applicable requirements of Rule 14a-11(b).

[590] *See* new Rule 14a-11(d).

[591] *See* new Rule 14a-11(c).

the statement in support. Although we did not propose to allow for exclusion of a supporting statement that exceeds the length specified in the rule, we believe that it is appropriate to provide the ability to do so in the final rule.[592]

We note that, in a change from the Proposal, under the final rule a company may not exclude a nominee or a statement in support on the basis that, in the company's view, the Schedule 14N (which will include the statement in support) contains materially false or misleading statements. Nominating shareholders and groups will have liability for any materially false or misleading information or for making a false or misleading certification in the notice filed on Schedule 14N, and companies will not be responsible for this information.[593] We believe that such disputes concerning whether information is false or misleading should be handled through disclosure, and if necessary, through private litigation, rather than through exclusion of the nominee under our rule. A company and the nominating shareholder or group will be in possession of the facts and circumstances regarding any disputes that arise about the truthfulness or accuracy of information or representations made by a nominating shareholder or group; thus, they will be in a better position than the staff to resolve those disputes. In addition, we note that in traditional proxy contests, companies and insurgents regularly use disclosure to communicate with a company's shareholders about an insurgent's nominee(s) and provide related information, including disclosure disputing the information provided by the other party. We believe that it is appropriate for companies and nominating shareholders engaged in the Rule 14a-11 nomination process to work together to resolve these types of issues. While we encourage private parties to resolve disputes under this provision, the Commission could, of course, bring enforcement actions in appropriate instances. All filings associated with a nomination included in the company's proxy materials pursuant to Rule 14a-11, including the Schedule 14N, the company's proxy statement and any additional soliciting materials provided by the company or the nominating shareholder, will be subject to the staff's proxy contest review procedures and, as noted, will be subject to the Rule 14a-9 prohibition against materially false or misleading statements.

In the Proposing Release, we noted that:

- Unless otherwise provided in Rule 14a-11 (*e.g.*, the nominating shareholder's or group's obligation to demonstrate that it responded to a company's notice of deficiency, where applicable, within 14 calendar days after receipt of the notice of deficiency), the burden would be on the company to demonstrate that it may exclude a nominee or nominees; and

- All materials submitted to the Commission in relation to proposed Rule 14a-11(g) would be publicly available upon submission.

We are adopting these aspects of the rules as proposed. We did not receive significant comment on these aspects of the proposed rules, although two commenters requested that companies bear the burden of proof when objecting to a nominee.[594] The rule, as adopted and proposed, specifies that the burden is on the company to demonstrate that it may exclude a nominee or statement of support, unless otherwise specified.[595] In addition, as we discussed in the Proposing Release, the staff's responses to the submissions made pursuant to new Rule 14a-11(g) would reflect only informal views. The staff determinations reached in these responses would not, and cannot, adjudicate the merits of a company's position with respect to exclusion of a shareholder nominee under Rule 14a-11. Accordingly, a discretionary staff determination would not preclude an interested person from pursuing a judicial determination regarding the application of Rule 14a-11.

---

[592] In this regard, we note that this is consistent with Rule 14a-8, which specifies that a company may exclude a proposal if the proposal, including any accompanying supporting statement, exceeds 500 words.

[593] *See* new Rule 14a-9(c) and Rule 14a-11(f).

[594] *See* letters from CII; Universities Superannuation.

[595] In the Proposal, we noted that the exclusion of a nominee or nominees where the exclusion was not permissible would result in a violation of the rule. We are adopting that provision as proposed.

As noted above, if a nominee withdraws or is disqualified, a company will be required to include an otherwise eligible nominee submitted by the shareholder or group with the next highest qualifying ownership percentage, if any. The company would be required to continue replacing withdrawn or disqualified nominees until it included the maximum number of nominees it is required to include in its proxy materials or the list of shareholder nominees is exhausted. As described above, a company will be required to give notice that it plans to exclude a nominee for any nominee that it intends to exclude, and the notice must include the reasons for the exclusion. If a company anticipates that it would seek a no-action letter from the staff with respect to its decision to exclude any Rule 14a-11 nominee or nominees, it should seek a no-action letter with regard to all nominees that it wishes to exclude at the outset and should assert all available bases for exclusion at that time. For example, if a company receives more nominees than it is required to include, its reasons for exclusion would note that basis. In addition, if the company believes it has other bases to exclude the nominee, it should note those other bases in its notice and include the other bases in its request for a no-action letter.

c. Timing of Process

The process generally would operate as follows:

Due Date	Action Required
No earlier than 150 calendar days, and no later than 120 calendar days, before the anniversary of the date that the company mailed its proxy materials for the prior year's annual meeting	Nominating shareholder or group must provide notice on Schedule 14N to the company and file the Schedule 14N with the Commission
No later than 14 calendar days after the close of the window period for submission of nominations	Company must notify the nominating shareholder or group (or its authorized representative) of any determination not to include the nominee or nominees
No later than 14 calendar days after the nominating shareholder's or group's receipt of the company's deficiency notice	Nominating shareholder or group must respond to the company's deficiency notice and, where applicable, cure any defects in the nomination
No later than 80 calendar days before the company files its definitive proxy statement and form of proxy with the Commission	Company must provide notice of its intent to exclude the nominating shareholder's or group's nominee or nominees and the basis for its determination to the Commission and, if desired, seek a no-action letter from the staff with regard to its determination
No later than 14 calendar days after the nominating shareholder's or group's receipt of the company's notice to the Commission	Nominating shareholder or group may submit a response to the company's notice to the Commission staff
As soon as practicable	If requested by the company, Commission staff would, at its discretion, provide an informal statement of its views to the company and the nominating shareholder or group
Promptly following receipt of the staff's informal statement of its views	Company must provide notice to the nominating shareholder or group stating whether it will include or exclude the nominee

d. Information required in company proxy materials

i. Proxy statement

As discussed in Section II.B.8. above, we proposed and are adopting a requirement that a company that is including a shareholder director nominee in its proxy statement and form of proxy pursuant to Rule 14a-11 include certain disclosure about the nominating shareholder or group and the nominee in the company proxy statement. This disclosure will be provided by the nominating shareholder or group in its notice on Schedule 14N in response to Item 5 of that Schedule and will be included in the company's proxy statement pursuant to Item 7(e) (and, in the case of investment companies, Item 22(b)(18)) of Schedule 14A.[596] As we proposed, the company will not be responsible for the disclosure; rather, the nominating shareholder or group will have liability for any materially false or misleading statements.[597]

As discussed in Section II.B.8., the disclosures to be included in the company's proxy statement include:

- A statement that the nominee consents to be named in the company's proxy statement and form of proxy and, if elected, to serve on the company's board of directors;

- Disclosure about the nominee as would be provided in response to the disclosure requirements of Items 4(b), 5(b), 7(a), (b) and (c) and, for investment companies, Item 22(b) of Schedule 14A, as applicable;

- Disclosure about the nominating shareholder or each member of a nominating shareholder group as would be required of a participant in response to the disclosure requirements of Items 4(b) and 5(b) of Schedule 14A, as applicable;

- Disclosure about whether the nominating shareholder or any member of a nominating shareholder group has been involved in any legal proceeding during the past ten years, as specified in Item 401(f) of Regulation S-K;

- Disclosure about whether, to the best of the nominating shareholder's or group's knowledge, the nominee meets the director qualifications set forth in the company's governing documents, if any;

- A statement that, to the best of the nominating shareholder's or group's knowledge, in the case of a registrant other than an investment company, the nominee meets the objective criteria for "independence" of the national securities exchange or national securities association rules applicable to the company, if any, or, in the case of a registrant that is an investment company, the nominee is not an "interested person" of the registrant as defined in Section 2(a)(19) of the Investment Company Act of 1940;

- The following information regarding the nature and extent of the relationships between the nominating shareholder or group, the nominee, and/or the company or any affiliate of the company:

    o Any direct or indirect material interest in any contract or agreement between the nominating shareholder or any member of the nominating shareholder group, the nominee, and/or the company or any affiliate of the company (including any employment agreement, collective bargaining agreement, or consulting agreement);

    o Any material pending or threatened litigation in which the nominating shareholder or any member of the nominating shareholder group and/or the nominee is a party or a material participant, and that involves the company, any of its officers or directors, or any affiliate of the company;

    o Any other material relationship between the nominating shareholder or any member of the nominating shareholder group, the nominee, and/or the company or any affiliate of the company not otherwise disclosed; and

    o The Web site address on which the nominating shareholder or nominating shareholder group may publish soliciting materials, if any.

---

[596] Refer to Section II.B.8. for a discussion of comments received on the proposed disclosure and changes made in response to these comments. We did not receive comment specifically on new Items 7(e) or 22(b)(18) of Schedule 14A.

[597] See new Rule 14a-11(f).

The disclosures set out in Items 4(b) and 5(b) of Schedule 14A are specifically tailored to contested elections and currently are provided by both companies and insurgents in traditional proxy contests. The disclosures required pursuant to Item 4(b) include:

- Who is making the solicitation and the methods of solicitation;
- If employees of the soliciting party are engaged in the solicitation, what types of employees are engaged in the solicitation and the manner and nature of their employment;
- If specially engaged employees are engaged in the solicitation, the material features of the engagement, the cost, and the number of employees;
- The total amount estimated to be spent and the total expenditures to date for the solicitation;
- Who will bear the cost of the solicitation; and
- The terms of any settlement between the company and the soliciting parties, including the cost to the company.

The disclosures included pursuant to Item 5(b) include:

- Any substantial interest of the soliciting party in the matter to be voted on;
- Certain biographical information about the soliciting party, such as name and business address, principal occupation, and any criminal convictions in the past 10 years;
- The amount of company securities beneficially owned and owned of record;
- Dates and amounts of any securities purchased or sold within the past two years and the amount of funds borrowed and owed to purchase the securities;
- Whether the soliciting person is or was within the past year a party to any contracts, arrangements or understandings with respect to the company's securities and the terms of the contract, arrangement or understanding;
- Beneficial ownership of company securities by any associate of the soliciting person;
- Beneficial ownership by the soliciting person of any parent or subsidiary of the company;
- Disclosure responsive to Item 404(a) of Regulation S-K with regard to the soliciting person and any associate;
- Disclosure of any arrangements concerning future employment or transactions with the company; and
- Any substantial interest in the vote, either by security holdings or otherwise, held by a party to an arrangement or understanding related to a director nominee.

The company also will include in its proxy statement disclosure about the management nominees responsive to Items 4(b), 5(b), 7(a), (b) and (c) and, for investment companies, Item 22(b) of Schedule 14A, as applicable, as well as disclosure concerning the persons making the solicitation for the management nominees responsive to Items 4(b) and 5(b) of Schedule 14A, as applicable. We did not amend the disclosure requirements in this regard, as companies are already required to make these disclosures in the context of a "solicitation in opposition," under Rule 14a-12(c).[598]

---

[598] We have clarified in new Instruction 3 to Rule 14a-12 that inclusion of a shareholder director nominee pursuant to Rule 14a-11, an applicable state or foreign law provision, or a company's governing documents as they relate to the inclusion of shareholder director nominees in the company's proxy materials, or solici- tations that are made in connection with that nomina- tion, constitute solicitations subject to Rule 14a-12(c), except for purposes of the requirement for the company to file their proxy statement in preliminary form pur- suant to Rule 14a-6(a).

In addition, as discussed in Section II.B.8., we proposed and adopted a requirement that the company include in its proxy statement the nominating shareholder's or group's statement in support of the shareholder nominee or nominees, if the nominating shareholder or group elects to have such statement included in the company's proxy materials. As discussed in Section II.B.8., we had proposed that this statement not exceed 500 words total, but in response to commenters' concerns, we have revised this provision in the final rule to enable a nominating shareholder or group to include up to 500 words for each nominee. The company also would have the option to include a statement of support for the management nominees.[599]

ii. Form of proxy

Under the Proposal, a company that is required to include a shareholder nominee or nominees on its form of proxy could identify the shareholder nominees as such and recommend whether shareholders should vote for, against, or withhold votes on those nominees and management nominees on the form of proxy.[600] In addition, the company could determine the order in which its nominees and any shareholder nominees are listed in the form of proxy. The company would otherwise be required to present the nominees in an impartial manner in accordance with Rule 14a-4.

Under the current rules, a company may provide shareholders with the option to vote for or withhold authority to vote for the company's nominees as a group, provided that shareholders also are given a means to withhold authority for specific nominees in the group. In our view, as we stated in the Proposal, this option would not be appropriate where the company's form of proxy includes shareholder nominees, as grouping the company's nominees may make it easier to vote for all of the company's nominees than to vote for the shareholder nominees in addition to some of the company nominees. Accordingly, when a shareholder nominee is included (either pursuant to Rule 14a-11, an applicable state law provision, or a company's governing documents), we proposed an amendment to Rule 14a-4 to provide that a company may not give shareholders the option of voting for or withholding authority to vote for the company nominees as a group, but instead must require that shareholders vote on each nominee separately.

Commenters were mixed on the appropriate presentation of nominees on the form of proxy. Several commenters supported the proposed amendments to Rule 14a-4 to prohibit the option of voting for management's slate as a whole,[601] with one of these commenters characterizing the current option of "elect all directors" as "a convenience in uncontested director elections" but warning that providing that option in contested elections "tilts the scales unduly in favor of management."[602] The commenter believed that shareholders would not have any difficulty in identifying the management nominees and disagreed with the argument that a form of proxy listing all nominees would be confusing. As a possible solution, the commenter suggested a legend such as "There are six candidates. Vote for no more than five." Another commenter argued that the advantage of voting for each individual nominee is the de facto plurality voting standard that would result.[603] Numerous commenters opposed the proposed amendments to

---

[599] In the Proxy Disclosure Enhancements Adopting Release, we amended our rules to require disclosure about directors that will provide investors with more meaningful disclosure to enable them to determine whether and why a director or nominee is an appropriate choice for a particular company. The information is required in the company's proxy statement for each director nominee and each director who will continue to serve after the shareholder meeting. Under revised Item 401 of Regulation S-K, a nominating shareholder or group will be required to discuss the particular experience, qualifications, attributes or skills of the nominee or nominees that led the nominating share-

holder or group to conclude that the person should be put forward as a candidate for director on the company's board of directors.

[600] This would be similar to the current practice with regard to shareholder proposals submitted pursuant to Rule 14a-8 where companies identify the shareholder proposals and provide a recommendation to shareholders as to how they should vote on each of those proposals.

[601] See letters from CII; COPERA; P. Neuhauser; RiskMetrics; USPE.

[602] Letter from CII.

[603] See letter from RiskMetrics.

Rule 14a-4 and argued that the form of proxy should allow shareholders to vote for the entire slate of management nominees.[604] Many of these commenters believed that such an option is needed to minimize shareholder confusion,[605] with several commenters justifying such an option on the basis that boards expend considerable efforts in selecting the complete slate of management nominees (*e.g.*, considering issues as the independence of the board as whole).[606] One commenter stated that individual shareholders (unlike large institutional investors who have outsourced the actual proxy voting process for their portfolio) would be discouraged from voting if the proxy voting process becomes overly tedious as a result of the inability to vote for (or withhold votes for) a group of nominees.[607] The commenter analogized to the shareholders' voting options for shareholder proposals, where shareholders are allowed to vote on all matters as recommended by management through the exercise of discretionary voting authority. It noted that, under the existing proxy rules, companies often allow shareholders to vote "For All, except" and then allow them to identify the specific nominees for whom the proxy is not authorized to vote. The commenter recommended that companies be permitted to have this same option when there are shareholder nominees included in the proxy materials (with a clear statement in the form of proxy that the shareholder should indicate a vote for the shareholder nominee in the space provided for that nominee). One commenter argued that the ability to vote on the entire slate is essential in the event that the proposed rules are applied to investment companies, as such entities have a far higher proportion of retail shareholders than most operating companies and consequently have more difficulty in achieving a quorum.[608]

We are adopting this aspect of the Proposal largely as proposed,[609] because we continue to believe that grouping the company's nominees and permitting them to be voted on as a group would make it easier to vote for all of the company's nominees than to vote for the shareholder nominees in addition to some of the company nominees. This would result in an advantage to the management nominees and would be inconsistent with an impartial approach and the goals of Rule 14a-11. The final rule clarifies that the change would apply not only when a nominee is included pursuant to Rule 14a-11, applicable state law, or a company's governing documents, but also where a nominee is included pursuant to a provision in foreign law.

We believe that potential confusion that may result from not providing the option to vote for the company's slate can be mitigated to the extent that companies provide clear voting instructions, particularly with respect to the number of candidates for which a shareholder can vote. In addition, we do not believe that requiring shareholders to vote for candidates individually, rather than as a group, creates a burden that will result in discouraging shareholders from voting at all in director elections. In this regard, we note that a company could clearly designate the nominees on its form of proxy as company nominees or shareholder nominees.

e. No preliminary proxy statement

Under the Proposal, inclusion of a shareholder nominee in the company's proxy materials would not require the company to file a preliminary proxy statement provided that the company was otherwise qualified to file directly in definitive form. In this regard, the Proposal made clear that inclusion of a shareholder nominee would not be

---

[604] *See* letters from 26 Corporate Secretaries; ABA; Aetna; Alcoa; American Express; Anadarko; Boeing; BorgWarner; BRT; ExxonMobil; Fenwick; Honeywell; ICI; Intel; JPMorgan Chase; Pfizer; Seven Law Firms; Society of Corporate Secretaries; Tenet; U.S. Bancorp.

[605] *See* letters from Aetna; American Express; Boeing; BorgWarner; JPMorgan Chase; Seven Law Firms; Society of Corporate Secretaries; U.S. Bancorp.

[606] *See* letters from BorgWarner; Pfizer; Society of Corporate Secretaries; Tenet.

[607] *See* letter from ABA.

[608] *See* letter from ICI.

[609] *See* new Rule 14a-4(b)(2)(iv). We anticipate that companies would continue to be able to solicit discretionary authority to vote a shareholder's shares for the company nominees, as well as to cumulate votes for the company nominees in accordance with applicable state law, where such state law or the company's governing documents provide for cumulative voting.

deemed a solicitation in opposition.[610] We did not receive a significant amount of comment on this aspect of the rule, although two commenters agreed that inclusion of a Rule 14a-11 shareholder nominee should not require the company to file preliminary proxy materials.[611] We are adopting this provision largely as proposed. As adopted, a company would not be required to file a preliminary proxy statement in connection with a nomination made pursuant to Rule 14a-11, an applicable state or foreign law provision, or a company's governing documents.[612]

10. Application of the Other Proxy Rules to Solicitations by the Nominating Shareholder or Group

a. Rule 14a-2(b)(7)

As noted in the Proposing Release, we anticipate that shareholders may engage in communications with other shareholders in an effort to form a nominating shareholder group to aggregate their holdings to meet the applicable minimum ownership threshold to nominate a director. While consistent with the purpose of Rule 14a-11, such communications would be deemed solicitations under the proxy rules. Accordingly, we proposed an exemption from the proxy rules for written communications made in connection with using proposed Rule 14a-11[613] that are limited in content and filed with the Commission.[614] As noted in the Proposal, we believed this limited exemption would facilitate shareholders' use of proposed Rule 14a-11 and remove concerns shareholders seeking to use the rule may have regarding certain communications with other shareholders regarding their intent to submit a nomination pursuant to the rule.

Some commenters supported the proposed exemption for soliciting activities by shareholders seeking to form a group for purposes of Rule 14a-11.[615] One of these commenters stated that because "many institutional investors lack incentives to invest actively in seeking governance benefits that would be shared by their fellow shareholders," the rule should avoid imposing unnecessary hurdles or costs on shareholders organizing or joining a nominating group.[616] Another supporter of the exemption stated that soliciting activities to form a group for the purpose of submitting nominations under Rule 14a-11, state law, or a company's governing documents generally should be exempt, with no filing requirement prior to giving the company notice and filing a Schedule 14N.[617] Another commenter also recommended that any exemption also cover solicitations for nominations submitted under state law or a company's governing documents.[618] Finally, one commenter expressed support for the proposed exemption so shareholders could communicate with other investors to explain their nominee's qualifications and the rationale for submitting their nominations as long as they file all materials with the Commission and do not solicit proxies on behalf of their nominees.[619]

On the other hand, several commenters opposed the creation of a new exemption for soliciting activities to form a nominating group.[620] Two of these commenters stated that the proposed exemption in Rule 14a-2(b)(7) is unnecessary, given the existing exemptions available to nominating shareholders (e.g., Rule 14a-2(b)(2) exemption for communications with up to 10 shareholders and Rule 14a-2(b)(6) for communications in an electronic shareholder forum).[621] One commenter indicated that a solicitation to form a "control" group could have significant implications affecting control of a company if there are no limits on the number of shareholders or aggregated holdings of a nominating

---

[610] See proposed revisions to Rule 14a-6(a)(4) and Note 3 to that rule.

[611] See letters from ABA; CII.

[612] See also discussion in footnote 598 above.

[613] Under the Proposal, the exemption would not apply to solicitations made when seeking to have a nominee included in a company's proxy materials pursuant to a procedure specified in the company's governing documents or pursuant to applicable state law (as opposed to pursuant to Rule 14a-11).

[614] See proposed Rule 14a-2(b)(7)(i).

[615] See letters from Group of 80 Professors of Law, Business, Economics and Finance ("Bebchuk, et al."); CalSTRS; CII; P. Neuhauser; RiskMetrics; Schulte Roth & Zabel; USPE.

[616] Letter from Bebchuk, et al.

[617] See letter from CII.

[618] See letter from P. Neuhauser.

[619] See letter from RiskMetrics.

[620] See letters from ABA; Anadarko; BRT; Seven Law Firms.

[621] See letters from ABA; Seven Law Firms.

group.[622] The commenter asserted that, absent these limits, a shareholder could build a nominating group with hundreds of shareholders owning far in excess of the ownership threshold needed to use Rule 14a-11. The commenter warned that the proposed exemption could facilitate avoidance of the proposed requirements of Rule 14a-11 because the exempt solicitations could be the first stage of a campaign against incumbent directors and in favor of shareholder nominees. This commenter also believed that the exemption should not apply to solicitations undertaken by shareholders to form a nominating shareholder group in order to submit nominees pursuant to state law or a company's governing documents.[623]

Commenters also suggested the following changes to the proposed exemption:

- The exemption should not be available if the shareholder or any member of the nominating group uses another available exemption for a nomination to be presented at the same shareholder meeting;[624]

- The exemption should not be available for a "data gathering strategy" in which a shareholder is "testing the waters" for other purposes, such as for a traditional proxy contest;[625]

- The shareholder should certify that it has a bona fide intent to present a Rule 14a-11 nomination and the shareholder should be prohibited from nominating directors at the same meeting through means other than Rule 14a-11;[626] and

- The exemption should not be available if the company or another shareholder has publicly announced that the company would be facing a traditional proxy contest.[627]

One commenter stated generally that allowing the "permitted activity among shareholders wishing to nominate a director" would "increase the need for the Commission to police group activity that may be undertaken with an undisclosed control intent."[628]

Two commenters agreed with the Commission that the Rule 14a-2(b)(7) exemption should not be available for solicitations conducted through oral communications.[629] These commenters warned that there would be no way to ensure that orally-communicated information is being provided to shareholders in a consistent manner and in accordance with the rule's requirements. One commenter recommended specific changes to the rule to clarify that the exemption is not available for oral communications.[630] On the other hand, several commenters believed that oral communications should be exempt.[631] Some commenters pointed out that such communications are exempt in other contexts and are difficult to monitor in any case.[632] To mitigate the risk of inappropriate communications, one commenter suggested that the Commission require that oral communications made in reliance on the exemption not be inconsistent with any communications previously filed by the shareholder in connection with the nomination.[633]

Two commenters expressed general support for the proposal requiring that a nominating shareholder or group file any soliciting materials published, sent or given to shareholders pursuant to the exemption no later than the date that the material is first published, sent, or given.[634] One commenter argued that if the Commission retains the requirement that solicitations be in writing, then it should relax the "date of first use" filing deadline (with a three business day deadline being its preference).[635] One commenter supported the filing requirement of Rule 14a-2(b)(7)(ii) for soliciting materials published, sent or given to shareholders solicited to become part of a nominating

---

[622] *See* letter from ABA.
[623] *Id.*
[624] *See* letters from ABA; Seven Law Firms.
[625] *Id.*
[626] *See* letter from ABA.
[627] *See* letters from ABA; Seven Law Firms.
[628] Letter from Biogen.
[629] *See* letters from ABA; Seven Law Firms.

[630] *See* letter from Seven Law Firms.
[631] *See* letters from CII; Cleary; P. Neuhauser; Schulte Roth & Zabel; USPE.
[632] *See* letters from CII; USPE.
[633] *See* letter from Cleary.
[634] *See* letters from ABA; CII.
[635] *See* letter from Schulte Roth & Zabel.

group,[636] while three commenters opposed the filing requirement.[637] Of those opposing the requirement, one commenter noted that under the Williams Act, persons contemplating an actual change in control are not required to publicly disclose their activities until a group owning 5% of the company's shares has been formed.[638] One commenter stated that it is possible that a group of shareholders ultimately may decide not to submit a shareholder nominee.[639] Therefore, this commenter believed, any requirement for filings before the group submits a nominee would place an unfair disadvantage on the process of first determining if a nomination is the right course of action, and if so, who the nominee should be. Another commenter suggested that the filing requirement be triggered on the date the shareholder proposes a nominee, not on the date of solicitation.[640] The commenter believed that a shareholder should not be burdened with the filing requirement at the initial stages of determining the feasibility of forming a group.

Three commenters recommended that communications made for the purpose of forming a nominating shareholder group should be permitted to identify possible or proposed nominees,[641] with one commenter adding the condition that the nominee first agree to being named.[642] Two commenters recommended the following additional disclosure in any written soliciting materials used in reliance on the Rule 14a-2(b)(7) exemption:

- the period that the soliciting shareholder held the specified number of shares;

- a description of any short positions or other hedging arrangements through which the soliciting shareholder reduced or otherwise altered its economic stake in the company;

- a description of any contracts, arrangements, understandings or relationships between the soliciting shareholder and any other person with respect to any securities of the company; and

- a description of any plans or proposals of the shareholder or group with respect to the organization, business or operations of the company.[643]

One commenter added that the required disclosure should be consistent with that required by Items 4 and 6 of Schedule 13D,[644] while another commenter stated that shareholders should be permitted to include a brief statement of the reasons for the formation of the nominating group.[645]

After considering the comments, we are adopting the proposed exemption with certain modifications, including modifications to enable shareholders to communicate orally, to require the filing of a cover page in the form set forth in Schedule 14N (with the appropriate box on the cover page marked) no later than when the solicitation commences, and to clarify the circumstances under which the exemption will be available.[646] We believe that this limited exemption will facilitate shareholders' use of Rule 14a-11 and remove concerns shareholders seeking to use the rule may have regarding certain communications with other shareholders regarding their intent to submit a nomination pursuant to the rule.

---

[636] *See* letter from ABA.

[637] *See* letters from CalSTRS; COPERA; P. Neuhauser.

[638] *See* letter from P. Neuhauser.

[639] *See* letter from COPERA.

[640] *See* letter from CalSTRS.

[641] *See* letters from ABA; CII; USPE.

[642] *See* letter from ABA.

[643] *See* letters from ABA; Seven Law Firms.

[644] *See* letter from ABA.

[645] *See* letter from Schulte Roth & Zabel.

[646] Shareholders also would have the option to structure their solicitations in connection with the formation of a nominating shareholder group, whether written or oral, to comply with an existing exemption from the proxy rules, including the exemption for solicitations of no more than 10 shareholders (Exchange Act Rule 14a-2(b)(2)) and the exemption for certain communications that take place in an electronic shareholder forum (Exchange Act Rule 14a-2(b)(6)). For example, a shareholder could rely on Rule 14a-2(b)(2) to solicit no more than 10 shareholders in an effort to form a nominating shareholder group. If the shareholder's efforts did not result in the formation of a group large enough to meet the ownership thresholds, the shareholder could then rely on Rule 14a-2(b)(7) to continue its efforts to form a nominating shareholder group for the purpose of submitting a nomination pursuant to Rule 14a-11.

New Rule 14a-2(b)(7) provides an exemption from the generally applicable disclosure, filing, and other requirements of the proxy rules for solicitations by or on behalf of any shareholder in connection with the formation of a nominating shareholder group, provided that the shareholder is not holding the company's securities with the purpose, or with the effect, of changing control of the company or to gain a number of seats on the board of directors that exceeds the maximum number of nominees that the registrant could be required to include under Rule 14a-11(d). In addition, any written communication may include no more than:

- A statement of the shareholder's intent to form a nominating shareholder group in order to nominate a director under Rule 14a-11;

- Identification of, and a brief statement regarding, the potential nominee or nominees or, where no nominee or nominees have been identified, the characteristics of the nominee or nominees that the shareholder intends to nominate, if any;

- The percentage of voting power of the company's securities that are entitled to be voted on the election of directors that each soliciting shareholder holds or the aggregate percentage held by any group to which the shareholder belongs; and

- The means by which shareholders may contact the soliciting party.

Any written soliciting material published, sent or given to shareholders in accordance with the terms of this provision must be filed with the Commission by the nominating shareholder or group, under the company's Exchange Act file number (or in the case of a registered investment company, under the company's Investment Company Act file number), no later than the date the material is first published, sent or given to shareholders. The soliciting material would be required to be filed with a cover page in the form set forth in Schedule 14N, with the appropriate box on the cover page marked to identify the filing as soliciting material pursuant to Rule 14a-2(b)(7).[647] This requirement is largely consistent with the Proposal; however, under the final rule, the solicitation will be filed on Schedule 14N rather than as definitive additional soliciting materials on Schedule 14A, as was proposed. We have made this change to avoid confusion between soliciting materials filed in connection with the formation of a nominating shareholder group under Rule 14a-11 (or in connection with a Rule 14a-11 nomination), as discussed further below, and other proxy materials that may be filed by companies or by participants in a traditional proxy contest.

We also have expanded the exemption to cover oral solicitations. As noted in the Proposal, we originally proposed to limit the exclusion to written communications to address our concern that oral communications could not easily satisfy the filing requirement (which would make it more difficult to monitor use of the exemption). However, after further consideration, we agree with commenters that oral communications should be included within the exemption because it is likely that shareholders will need to speak to each other in order to effectively form a nominating shareholder group. Oral communications will not be limited in content in the way that written communications are limited. In an effort to better monitor and avoid abuse under the exemption, however, a shareholder seeking to form a nominating shareholder group in reliance on the exemption in Rule 14a-2(b)(7) will be required to file a Schedule 14N notice of commencement of the oral solicitation. Because there are no limits on the number of holders that can be solicited in reliance on the new rule, or the contents of the oral communications, we believe it is important for our staff and the markets to be aware of the commencement of these activities.

The Schedule 14N filing for oral solicitations will consist of a cover page in the form set forth in Schedule 14N, with the appropriate box on the cover page marked to identify the filing as a notice of solicitation pursuant to Rule 14a-2(b)(7). This filing would be

---

[647] Materials filed in connection with the new solicitation exemptions will be filed under a cover page of Schedule 14N and will appear as a Schedule 14N-S on EDGAR. *See* new Rule 14a-2(b)(7)(ii). We note that written communications include electronic communications, such as e-mails and Web site postings, and scripts used in connection with oral solicitations.

made under the company's Exchange Act file number (or in the case of a registered investment company, under the company's Investment Company Act file number), no later than the date of the first communication made in reliance on the rule.

As noted above, some commenters were opposed to the filing requirement for solicitations for various reasons. We have decided to adopt the filing requirement because we believe it is important to provide companies and shareholders with information about potential nominations under Rule 14a-11 when the new solicitation exemption is used to pursue such a nomination. We do not believe that the filing requirement is burdensome, particularly in light of the fact that we are providing shareholders with the opportunity to engage in activities for which they would otherwise need to file a proxy statement or have another exemption available.

More generally, we understand commenters' concerns regarding the solicitation exemptions, including the exemption for oral communications when seeking to form a group, being used as a means to engage in a contest for control, but we believe that requiring a nominating shareholder or group to file a Schedule 14N to provide notice of such communications, along with the other limitations in the rule we are adopting, should mitigate these concerns. In response to commenters' concerns, we have clarified in the rule that a shareholder or group that chooses to rely on new Rule 14a-2(b)(7) would lose that exemption if they subsequently engaged in a non-Rule 14a-11 nomination or solicitation in connection with the subject election of directors other than solicitations exempt under Rule 14a-2(b)(8), or if they become a member of a group, as determined under Section 13(d)(3) of the Exchange Act and Rule 13d-5(b)(1), or otherwise, with persons engaged in soliciting or other nominating activities in connection with the subject election of directors.[648] This could result in the shareholder or group being deemed to have engaged in a non-exempt solicitation in violation of the proxy rules. In addition, we have clarified that, consistent with Rule 14a-11, the exemption is available only where the shareholder is not holding the company's securities with the purpose, or with the effect, of changing control of the company or to gain a number of seats on the board of directors that exceeds the maximum number of nominees that the registrant could be required to include under Rule 14a-11(d). Thus, we do not believe that it is likely that a shareholder or group will use the exemption as a means to engage in a contest for control.

Consistent with the Proposal, neither this exemption nor the exemption set forth in Rule 14a-2(b)(8) (discussed below) will apply to solicitations made when seeking to have a nominee included in a company's proxy materials pursuant to a procedure specified in the company's governing documents (as opposed to pursuant to Rule 14a-11). As we noted in the Proposal, in this instance, companies and/or shareholders would have determined the parameters of the shareholder's or group's access to the company's proxy materials. Given the range of possible criteria companies and/or shareholders could establish for nominations, we continue to believe it would not be appropriate to extend the exemption to those circumstances. Also consistent with the Proposal, we have not extended the exemption to nominations made pursuant to applicable state law provisions,[649] again because state law could establish any number of possible criteria for nominations. A shareholder would need to determine whether one of the existing exemptions applies to their solicitation conducted in connection with a nomination made pursuant to a company's governing documents or state law.

b. Rule 14a-2(b)(8)

Both the nominating shareholder or group and the company may wish to solicit in favor of their nominees for director by various means, including orally, by U.S. mail, electronic mail, and Web site postings. While the company ultimately would file a proxy statement and therefore could rely on the existing proxy rules to solicit outside the proxy

---

[648] *See* new Instruction to Rule 14a-2(b)(7).

[649] Similarly, the exemption would not be available for solicitations in connection with nominations made pursuant to foreign law provisions.

statement,[650] shareholders could be limited in their soliciting activities under the current proxy rules. Accordingly, our Proposal included a new exemption to the proxy rules for solicitations by or on behalf of a nominating shareholder or group in support of its nominee who is included in the company's proxy statement and form of proxy.

As proposed, the exemption would be available only where the shareholder is not seeking proxy authority. In addition, any written communications would be required to include specified disclosures, including:

- the identity of the nominating shareholder or group;

- a description of his or her direct or indirect interests, by security holdings or otherwise; and

- a legend advising shareholders that a shareholder nominee is or will be included in the company's proxy statement and that they should read the company's proxy statement when available and that the proxy statement, other soliciting material, and any other relevant documents are or will be available at no charge on the Commission's Web site.

Under the Proposal, written soliciting materials also would be required to be filed with the Commission under the company's Exchange Act file number no later than the date the material is first published, sent or given to shareholders.[651] The soliciting material would be required to include a cover page in the form set forth in Schedule 14A, with the appropriate box on the cover page marked.[652]

Three commenters supported the proposed Rule 14a-2(b)(8) exemption for soliciting activities by or on behalf of a nominating shareholder or group in support of the shareholder nominees included in a company's proxy materials, with soliciting materials filed no later than the date that the materials are first used.[653] Two of these commenters explained that because management would solicit votes against the shareholder nominees and for their own nominees, the nominating shareholder, group, and shareholder nominees should have the same ability to solicit, so long as they do not request proxy authority.[654] Another commenter stated that the exemption should apply to solicitations for nominations made pursuant to Rule 14a-11, state law, or a company's governing documents.[655] The commenter opposed any limitations on the soliciting activities by a nominating shareholder or group and viewed such soliciting activities as the same as a company's disclosure opposing a shareholder proposal. One commenter supported the Rule 14a-2(b)(8) exemption for solicitations by a nominating shareholder or group in favor of a shareholder nominee who is included in a company's proxy materials (or against a management nominee), but recommended that the rule specify that the exemption only applies to solicitations in favor of a shareholder nominee (or against a board nominee) that occur after the distribution of the company's proxy materials—this would help avoid confusion and misunderstandings about whether solicitation may occur before the company's proxy materials are available.[656] This commenter also recommended that the exemption not be available if the company or another shareholder has publicly announced that the company would be facing a traditional proxy contest, even from an unrelated shareholder. The commenter also believed that the exemption should be available for any written solicitation by or on behalf of a nominating shareholder or group in support of a nominee included in a company's proxy materials pursuant to state law or the company's governing documents, as long as the nominating shareholder or group does not use a form of proxy that differs from that of the company, does not furnish or otherwise request a form of revocation, abstention, consent or authorization, and files its solicitation material for its nominees (or against the management nominees) with the Commission on the date of first use.

---

[650] *See* Exchange Act Rule 14a-12.

[651] For a registered investment company, the filing would be made under the company's Investment Company Act file number.

[652] *See* proposed Rule 14a-2(b)(8)(iii).

[653] *See* letters from CII; COPERA; P. Neuhauser.

[654] *See* letters from COPERA; P. Neuhauser.

[655] *See* letter from CII.

[656] *See* letter from ABA.

To the extent that it is not included in either the company's proxy materials or Schedule 14N, the commenter also recommended that additional disclosure be required to be included in solicitations made pursuant to Rule 14a-2(b)(8).[657] Another commenter also stated that Rule 14a-2(b)(8) should apply only to solicitations in favor of a share-holder nominee that occur after the mailing of a company's proxy materials.[658] Further, the commenter explained that solicitations should not occur at a time when shareholders do not have access to the more complete and balanced disclosure about all of the nominees in a company's proxy materials.

As adopted, Rule 14a-2(b)(8) provides an exemption from the generally applicable disclosure, filing, and other requirements of the proxy rules for solicitations by or on behalf of a nominating shareholder or group, provided that:

- The soliciting party does not, at any time during such solicitation, seek directly or indirectly, either on its own or another's behalf, the power to act as proxy for a shareholder and does not furnish or otherwise request, or act on behalf of a person who furnishes or requests, a form of revocation, abstention, consent or authorization;[659]

- Each written communication includes:[660]

   ○ The identity of the nominating shareholder or group and a description of his or her direct or indirect interests, by security holdings or otherwise;

   ○ A prominent legend in clear, plain language advising shareholders that a shareholder nominee is or will be included in the company's proxy statement and that they should read the company's proxy statement when available because it includes important information. The legend also must explain to shareholders that they can find the proxy statement, other soliciting material, and any other relevant documents at no charge on the Commission's Web site; and

- Any soliciting material published, sent or given to shareholders in accordance with this exemption must be filed by the nominating shareholder or group with the Commission on Schedule 14N, under the company's Exchange Act file number or, in the case of an investment company registered under the Investment Company Act of 1940, under the company's Investment Company Act file number, no later than the date the material is first published, sent or given to shareholders. Three copies of the material would at the same time be filed with, or mailed for filing to, each national securities exchange upon which any class of securities of the company is listed and registered. The soliciting material would be required to include a cover page in the form set forth in Schedule 14N, with the appropriate box on the cover page marked.[661]

We are adopting certain modifications to Rule 14a-2(b)(8) from the Proposal to clarify when a party may begin to rely on the exemption and to require that all soliciting

---

[657] The recommended disclosures included: the period that the soliciting shareholder held the specified number of shares; a description of any short positions or other hedging arrangements through which the soliciting shareholder reduced or otherwise altered its economic stake in the company; a description of any contracts, arrangements, understandings or relationships between the soliciting shareholder and any other person with respect to any securities of the company; and a description of any plans or proposals of the shareholder or group with respect to the organization, business or operations of the company.

[658] See letter from Seven Law Firms.

[659] See new Rule 14a-2(b)(8)(i). The language in this provision generally follows the language in Rule 14a-2(b)(1) and, therefore, we interpret both provisions in the same manner. In this regard, we note the discussion in the *Proxy Disclosure and Solicitation Enhancements* proposing release of our view of the scope of the term "form of revocation" within the meaning of Rule 14a-2(b)(1) and the proposed amendment to that rule to clarify that the term does not include an unmarked copy of the company's proxy card that is requested to be returned directly to management. See Securities Act Release No. 33-9052; 34-60280 (July 10, 2009) [74 FR 35076]. If we act on the proposed amendments to Rule 14a-2(b)(1), we would expect to make conforming changes to Rule 14a-2(b)(8).

[660] See new Rule 14a-2(b)(8)(ii).

[661] See new Rule 14a-2(b)(8)(iii).

material be filed on new Schedule 14N.[662] The exemption is otherwise consistent with the Proposal.

We have added a new instruction to the exemption clarifying that a nominating shareholder or group may rely on the exemption provided in Rule 14a-2(b)(8) after receiving notice from the company in accordance with Rule 14a-11(g)(1) or (g)(3)(iv) that the company will include the nominating shareholder's or group's nominee or nominees.[663] As proposed, a nominating shareholder or group would not have been able to rely on the exemption until their nominee or nominees are actually included in the company's proxy materials. We received little comment on the appropriate timing for commencement of soliciting activities under the proposed exemption, with one commenter suggesting that Rule 14a-2(b)(8) apply only to solicitations that occur after the mailing of a company's proxy materials,[664] and another suggesting generally that there should be no limitations on soliciting activities by nominating shareholders or groups.[665]

After further consideration, we have determined that a nominating shareholder or group should be able to begin soliciting once there is certainty as to whether their nominees will be included in the company's proxy materials rather than being required to wait for the company to furnish its proxy materials. In this regard, we note that the exemption is consistent with the treatment of insurgent soliciting materials in a traditional proxy contest, as an insurgent may rely on Rule 14a-12(a) to engage in soliciting activities before furnishing shareholders with a proxy statement provided that the soliciting party provides certain disclosure and files a definitive proxy statement before or at the same time as the forms of proxy, consent or authorization are furnished to or requested from shareholders.[666] We have included the requirement that the nominating shareholder or group have received notice that their nominee or nominees will be included in the company's proxy materials before commencing solicitations to avoid confusion and potential abuse of the exemption.

We also have modified the filing requirements for written soliciting materials. Similar to the filing requirements for relying on Rule 14a-2(b)(7), any written soliciting material published, sent or given to shareholders in accordance with the terms of Rule 14a-2(b)(8) must be filed with the Commission on a Schedule 14N, under the company's Exchange Act file number (or in the case of a registered investment company, under the company's Investment Company Act file number), no later than the date the material is first published, sent or given to shareholders. The soliciting material would be required to be filed with a cover page in the form set forth in Schedule 14N, with the appropriate box on the cover page marked to identify the filing as soliciting material pursuant to Rule 14a-2(b)(8). This requirement is largely consistent with the Proposal, however, under the final rule, the solicitation will be filed on Schedule 14N rather than as definitive additional soliciting materials on Schedule 14A, as was proposed. As noted above, we received comment supporting the filing of soliciting materials,[667] however, the commenters did not specifically address whether the filing should be made under cover of Schedule 14N or Schedule 14A. As discussed above with respect to filings made pursuant to Rule 14a-2(b)(7), we have made the change to Schedule 14N to avoid confusion between soliciting materials filed in connection with the formation of a nominating shareholder group under Rule 14a-11 (or in connection with a Rule 14a-11 nomination) and other proxy materials that may be filed by companies or by participants in a traditional proxy contest.

As described in Section II.B.2.e. above, the rules we are adopting today will not prohibit shareholders from submitting Rule 14a-11 nominations for inclusion in company proxy materials when a proxy contest is being conducted by another person concurrently. We are, however, adding a clarification to new Rule 14a-2(b)(8), similar to Rule 14a-2(b)(7), in response to commenters' concern that the exemptions could be used as the first stage of a contest for control. As adopted, the exemption will be lost if a

---

[662] As noted above, the soliciting material will be filed under cover of Schedule 14N and will appear as Schedule 14N-S on EDGAR.

[663] *See* Instruction 1 to Rule 14a-2(b)(8).

[664] *See* letter from ABA.

[665] *See* letter from CII.

[666] *See* Exchange Act Rule 14a-12(a).

[667] *See* letters from CII; COPERA; P. Neuhauser.

shareholder or group subsequently engages in a non-Rule 14a-11 nomination or solicitation in connection with the subject election of directors or if they become a member of a group, as determined under Section 13(d)(3) of the Exchange Act and Rule 13d-5(b)(1), or otherwise, with persons engaged in soliciting or other nominating activities in connection with the subject election of directors. The risk of losing the Rule 14a-2(b)(8) exemption and potential liability for engaging in non-exempt solicitations should prevent nominating shareholders or groups from soliciting in relation to any other person's nominees.[668] Further, as discussed in Sections II.B.2.e. and II.B.10.a. above, under Rule 14a-11 a company will not be required to include a nominee or nominees if the nominating shareholder or group is a member of any other group with persons engaged in solicitations in connection with the subject election of directors or other nominating activities; separately conducts a solicitation in connection with the subject election of directors other than a Rule 14a-2(b)(8) exempt solicitation in relation to those nominees it has nominated pursuant to Rule 14a-11 or for or against the company's nominees; or is acting as a participant in another person's solicitation in connection with the subject election of directors. All of these restrictions are designed to address commenters' concerns about collusion and potential abuse of the process. We also believe these restrictions are consistent with the desire to limit Rule 14a-11 to those shareholders or groups that do not have an intent to change the control of the company or to gain a number of seats on the board of directors that exceeds the maximum number of nominees that the registrant could be required to include under Rule 14a-11. Finally, we have clarified in an instruction to Rule 14a-2(b)(8)[669] that Rule 14a-2(b)(8) is the only exemption upon which Rule 14a-11 nominating shareholders or groups may rely for their soliciting activities in support of nominees that are or will be included in the company's proxy materials or for or against company nominees. This will help ensure that these persons will not seek proxy authority and will file written communications in connection with their soliciting efforts and, we believe, will help to address some of commenters' concerns with regard to confusion and potential abuse of the exemption.

Consistent with the Proposal and as discussed above with regard to Rule 14a-2(b)(7), the exemption will not apply to solicitations made when seeking to have a nominee included in a company's proxy materials pursuant to a procedure specified in the company's governing documents (as opposed to pursuant to Rule 14a-11). As we noted in the Proposal, in this instance, companies and/or shareholders would have determined the parameters of the shareholder's or group's access to the company's proxy materials. Given the range of possible criteria that companies and/or shareholders could establish for nominations, we continue to believe it would not be appropriate to extend the exemption to those circumstances. Also consistent with the Proposal, we have not extended the exemption to nominations made pursuant to applicable state law provisions, again because state law could establish any number of possible criteria for nominations.[670] A shareholder would need to determine whether one of the existing exemptions applies to their solicitation conducted in connection with a nomination made pursuant to a company's governing documents or state law.

11. 2011 Proxy Season Transition Issues

Rule 14a-11 contains a window period for submission of shareholder nominees for inclusion in company proxy materials of no earlier than 150 calendar days, and no later than 120 calendar days, before the anniversary of the date that the company mailed its proxy materials for the prior year's annual meeting.[671] Shareholders seeking to use new Rule 14a-11 would be able to do so if the window period for submitting nominees for a particular company is open after the effective date of the rules. For some companies, the window period may open and close before the effective date of the new rules. In those cases, shareholders would not be permitted to submit nominees pursuant to Rule 14a-11

---

[668] *See* Instruction 3 to Rule 14a-2(b)(8).

[669] *See* Instruction 2 to Rule 14a-2(b)(8).

[670] Similarly, the exemption would not be available for solicitations in connection with nominations made pursuant to foreign law provisions.

[671] *See* Rule 14a-11(b)(10) and discussion in Section II.B.8.c.ii. above.

for inclusion in the company's proxy materials for the 2011 proxy season. For other companies, the window period may open before the effective date of the rules, but close after the effective date. In those cases, shareholders would be able to submit a nominee between the effective date and the close of the window period.

C. Exchange Act Rule 14a-8(i)(8)

1. Background

Currently, Rule 14a-8(i)(8) allows a company to exclude from its proxy statement a shareholder proposal that relates to a nomination or an election for membership on the company's board of directors or a procedure for such nomination or election. This provision currently permits the exclusion of a proposal that would result in an immediate election contest or would set up a process for shareholders to conduct an election contest in the future by requiring the company to include shareholders' director nominees in the company's proxy materials for subsequent meetings.

When the Commission adopted the current language of Rule 14a-8(i)(8) in December 2007,[672] it noted that many disclosures are required for election contests that are not provided for in Rule 14a-8.[673] In this regard, several Commission rules, including Exchange Act Rule 14a-12, regulate contested proxy solicitations to assure that investors receive disclosure to enable them to make informed voting decisions in elections. The requirements to provide these disclosures to shareholders from whom proxy authority is sought are grounded in Rule 14a-3, which requires that any party conducting a proxy solicitation file with the Commission, and furnish to each person solicited, a proxy statement containing the information in Schedule 14A. Items 4(b) and 5(b) of Schedule 14A require numerous specified disclosures if the solicitation is subject to Rule 14a-12(c), and Item 7 of Schedule 14A also requires important specified disclosures for any director nominee. Finally, all of these disclosures are covered by the prohibition on making a solicitation containing materially false or misleading statements or omissions that is found in Rule 14a-9.

2. Proposed Amendment

In the Proposal, we proposed an amendment to Rule 14a-8(i)(8), the election exclusion, to enable shareholders, under certain circumstances, to require companies to include in their proxy materials shareholder proposals that would amend, or that request an amendment to, a company's governing documents regarding nomination procedures or disclosures related to shareholder nominations, provided the proposal does not conflict with proposed Rule 14a-11.[674] The purpose of the proposed amendment was to further facilitate shareholders' rights to nominate directors and promote fair corporate suffrage, while still providing appropriate disclosure and liability protections.

Under the proposed amendment, the shareholder proposal would have to meet the procedural requirements of Rule 14a-8 (*e.g.*, the proposal could be excluded if the shareholder proponent did not meet the ownership threshold under Rule 14a-8) and not be subject to one of the other substantive bases for exclusion in the rule.[675] The

---

[672] *See* Election of Directors Adopting Release.

[673] *See* Election of Directors Adopting Release.

[674] Under the Proposal, Rule 14a-8(i)(8) would allow shareholders to propose additional means, other than Rule 14a-11, for inclusion of shareholder nominees in company proxy materials. Therefore, under the Proposal, a shareholder proposal that sought to provide an additional means for including shareholder nominees in the company's proxy materials pursuant to the company's governing documents would not be deemed to conflict with Rule 14a-11 simply because it would establish different eligibility thresholds or require more extensive disclosures about a nominee or nominating shareholder than would be required under Rule 14a-11.

A shareholder proposal would conflict with proposed Rule 14a-11, however, to the extent that the proposal would purport to prevent a shareholder or shareholder group that met the requirements of proposed Rule 14a-11 from having their nominee for director included in the company's proxy materials.

[675] Currently, Rule 14a-8 requires that a shareholder proponent have continuously held at least $2,000 in market value, or 1%, of the company's securities entitled to be voted on the proposal at the meeting for a period of at least one year by the date the proponent submits the proposal. *See* Rule 14a-8(b). These requirements would remain the same.

proposed revision of Rule 14a-8(i)(8) would not restrict the types of amendments that a shareholder could propose to a company's governing documents to address the company's provisions regarding nomination procedures or disclosures related to shareholder nominations, although any such proposals that conflict with proposed Rule 14a-11 or state law could be excluded.[676]

In the Proposal, we stated that we continued to believe that, under certain circumstances, companies should have the right to exclude proposals related to particular elections and nominations for director from company proxy materials where those proposals could result in an election contest between company and shareholder nominees without the important protections provided for in the proxy rules. Therefore, while proposing the revision to Rule 14a-8(i)(8) as discussed above, we also proposed to codify certain prior staff interpretations with respect to the types of proposals that would continue to be excludable pursuant to Rule 14a-8(i)(8). As proposed, a company would be permitted to exclude a proposal under Rule 14a-8(i)(8) if it:

- Would disqualify a nominee who is standing for election;

- Would remove a director from office before his or her term expired;

- Questions the competence, business judgment, or character of one or more nominees or directors;

- Nominates a specific individual for election to the board of directors, other than pursuant to Rule 14a-11, an applicable state law provision, or a company's governing documents; or

- Otherwise could affect the outcome of the upcoming election of directors.

The proposed codification was not intended to change the staff's prior interpretations or limit the application of the exclusion; it was intended to provide more clarity to companies and shareholders regarding the application of the exclusion.

3. Comments on the Proposal

The proposal to amend Rule 14a-8 to revise the election exclusion received widespread support. Numerous commenters expressed general support for the proposed amendments to Rule 14a-8(i)(8), with many of the commenters supporting the Commission's proposal as a whole[677] and other commenters supporting the amendments while

---

[676] In this regard, the proposed revision to Rule 14a-8(i)(8) would not make a distinction between binding and non-binding proposals.

[677] See letters from 13D Monitor; ACSI; AFL-CIO; AFSCME; Joseph Ahearn ("J. Ahearn"); Rahim Ali ("R. Ali"); AllianceBernstein; Amalgamated Bank; Americans for Financial Reform; Australian Reward Investment Alliance ("ARIA"); AUST(Q) Superannuation ("AUST(Q)"); W. Baker; Barclays; BCIA; Bebchuk, et al.; R. Blake; William B. Bledsoe ("W. Bledsoe"); Brigham and Associates, LLC ("Brigham"); British Insurers; Ethan S. Burger ("E. Burger"); J. Burke; CalPERS; CalSTRS; Calvert; Cbus ("Cbus"); CFA Institute; John P. Chaney ("J. Chaney"); The Christopher Reynolds Foundation of New York ("Christopher Reynolds Foundation"); CII; COPERA; Corporate Library; Central Pension Fund of the International Union of Operating Engineers ("CPF"); CRMC; L. Dallas; Mike G. Dill ("M. Dill"); T. DiNapoli; Dominican Sisters of Hope; Andrew H. Dral ("A. Dral"); D. Eshelman; First Affirmative; Florida State Board of Administration; Martin Fox ("M. Fox"); Raymond E. Frechette ("R. Frechette"); Glass Lewis; James J. Givens ("J. Givens"); Govern-

ance for Owners ("Governance for Owners"); GovernanceMetrics; Michael D. Grabowski ("M. Grabowski"); Greenlining Institute ("Greenlining"); Hermes; HESTA Super Fund ("HESTA"); Sheryl Hogan ("S. Hogan"); David G. Hood ("D. Hood"); IAM; ICGN; Frank Coleman Inman ("F. Inman"); Ironfire; Melinda Katz ("M. Katz"); Michael E. Kelley ("M. Kelley"); Peter C. Kelly ("P. Kelly"); Key Equity Investors, Inc. ("Key Equity Investors"); Victor Kimball ("V. Kimball"); Jeffery Kondracki ("J. Kondracki"); A. Krakovsky; Paul E. Kritzer ("P. Kritzer"); LACERA; C. Levin; Lanny D. Levin ("L. Levin"); LIUNA; LUCRF; Marco Consulting; Maine Securities Corporation ("Maine Securities"); B. McDonnell; James McRitchie ("J. McRitchie"); Mercy Investment Program; M. Metz; David B. Moore ("D. Moore"); Karen L. Morris ("K. Morris"); Robert Moulton-Ely ("R. Moulton-Ely"); Motor Trades Association of Australia Superannuation Fund Pty Limited ("MTAA"); Murray & Murray & Co., LPA ("Murray & Murray"); William J. Nassif ("W. Nassif"); Tom Nappi ("T. Nappi"); D. Nappier; Nathan Cummings Foundation; P. Neuhauser; Nine Law Firms; New Jersey State Investment Council opposing Rule 14a-11.[678] Some commenters expressly supported the adoption of both Rule 14a-11 and amendments to Rule 14a-8(i)(8).[679] Some commenters indicated that the adoption of only the proposed amendments to Rule 14a-8(i)(8), without Rule 14a-11, would not address current shortcomings in corporate governance and achieve the Commission's stated objectives.[680] Of the commenters that supported the Rule 14a-8 amendments but opposed Rule 14a-11, many believed the amendments to Rule 14a-8 would allow procedures for the inclusion of shareholder nominees in company proxy materials to evolve and private ordering under state law to continue, unfettered by the complexities of a federal standard that would apply uniformly to differently situated companies operating under diverse state law regimes.[681]

While supporting the amendments to Rule 14a-8(i)(8), some commenters expressed concerns about certain aspects of the amendments or recommended certain changes.[682] Two commenters expressed concerns about the codification of staff policies and interpretations under the current version of Rule 14a-8(i)(8).[683] One commenter expressed concerns that the proposed amendments to Rule 14a-8(i)(8) are broader than necessary to allow proposals seeking to establish access to a company's proxy materials and have the potential of significantly changing the administration of Rule 14a-8(i)(8) with respect to other types of proposals.[684] The commenter also noted that the fact that only four types of proposals have been addressed by the staff in the Rule 14a-8 process could be attributed to the fact that the current standard under Rule 14a-8(i)(8) operated to avoid other impermissible proposals from being presented in the first place. If the current standard is repealed, this commenter worried that the staff would have no basis upon which to assess proposals that attempt to circumvent or supplement the Commission's proxy solicitation rules. The commenter believed that eliminating the current standard would go beyond what is needed to permit shareholders to submit proposals seeking to amend, or request an amendment to, a company's governing documents to establish a procedure for including shareholder-nominated candidates for director in a company's proxy materials. The commenter suggested retaining the current standard in Rule 14a-8(i)(8) and amending the language only to specifically authorize proposals seeking

---

(Footnote Continued)

("NJSIC"); Norges Bank; Non-Government School Superannuation Fund ("Non-Government"); Ontario Teachers' Pension Plan Board ("Ontario Teachers"); OPERS; Thomas Paine ("T. Paine"); Pax World; Pershing Square; Karl Putnam ("K. Putnam"); S. Ranzini; RacetotheBottom; Joan Reekie ("J. Reekie"); Relational; RiskMetrics; D. Roberts; D. Romine; Joseph Rozbicki ("J. Rozbicki"); Schulte Roth & Zabel; Shamrock; Shareowners.org; Sheet Metal Workers; Sisters of Mercy; Social Investment Forum; Sodali; Solutions; Laszlo Sterbinszky (L. Sterbinszky"); Stringer Photography ("Stringer"); SWIB; J. Taub; Teamsters; Aleta Thielmeyer ("A. Thielmeyer"); TIAA-CREF; Trillium; TriState Coalition; T. Rowe Price; L. Tyson; Ursuline Sisters of Tildonk; Universities Supernnuation; USPE; ValueAct Capital; The Value Alliance and Corporate Governance Alliance ("Value Alliance"); R.VanEngelenhoven; Walden; B. Wilson; Leslie Wolfe ("L. Wolfe"); Steve Wolfe ("S. Wolfe"); Neil Wollman ("N. Wollman"); WSIB; Marcelo Zinn ("M. Zinn").

[678] See letters from 26 Corporate Secretaries; 3M; ABA; Advance Auto Parts; Aetna; AGL; Alcoa; Allstate; Alston & Bird; Ameriprise; American Bankers Association; American Express; Anadarko; Applied Materials; Association of Corporate Counsel; Avis Budget; Best Buy; Boeing; Boston Scientific; Brink's; BRT; Burlington Northern; California Bar; Callaway; Caterpillar; Chevron; P. Clapman; Comcast; CSX;

Cummins; Davis Polk; Deere; Devon; DTE Energy; DuPont; Eaton; Einstein Noah; Eli Lilly; ExxonMobil; FedEx; Financial Services Roundtable; FMC Corp.; FPL Group; Frontier; GE; General Mills; A. Goolsby; C. Holliday; Home Depot; Honeywell; IBM; ICI; Intel; JPMorgan Chase; E. J. Kullman; N. Lautenbach; MetLife; Microsoft; J. Miller; Motorola; NACD; NIRI; O'Melveny & Myers; Office Depot; P&G; PepsiCo; Pfizer; Piedmont; Praxair; Protective; Ryder; S&C; Safeway; Seven Law Firms; Shearman & Sterling; Sherwin-Williams; SIFMA; Simpson Thacher; Society of Corporate Secretaries; Southern Company; Tenet; Tesoro; Textron; Theragenics; Tidewater; Tompkins; G. Tooker; tw telecom; United Brotherhood of Carpenters; U.S. Bancorp; The Valspar Corporation ("Valspar"); Wachtell; Wells Fargo; Xerox.

[679] See letters from AFL-CIO; CFA Institute; CII; Governance for Owners; C. Levin; Marco Consulting; SWIB.

[680] See letters from CII; USPE.

[681] See letters from American Express; Brink's; BRT; CSX; Davis Polk; DuPont; C. Holliday; GE; General Mills; MetLife; Safeway; Tenet; Verizon.

[682] See letters from ABA; BorgWarner; CII; J. McRitchie; P. Neuhauser; O'Melveny & Myers; Seven Law Firms.

[683] See letters from ABA; Seven Law Firms.

[684] See letter from ABA.

to establish access to a company's proxy materials and require the disclosure provided in proposed Rule 14a-19.

4. Final Rule Amendment

As noted above in Section I.A., we do not believe that adopting changes to Rule 14a-8(i)(8) alone, without adopting Rule 14a-11, will achieve our goal of facilitating shareholders' ability to exercise their traditional state law rights to nominate directors. We believe that revising Rule 14a-8 will provide an additional avenue for shareholders to indirectly exercise those rights; therefore, the final rules include a revision to Rule 14a-8(i)(8). As adopted, companies will no longer be able to rely on Rule 14a-8(i)(8) to exclude a proposal seeking to establish a procedure in a company's governing documents for the inclusion of one or more shareholder nominees for director in the company's proxy materials.[685]

In addition, we are adopting the proposed amendment to codify the prior staff interpretations largely as proposed. As adopted, companies will be permitted to exclude a shareholder proposal pursuant to Rule 14a-8(i)(8) if it:

- Would disqualify a nominee who is standing for election;
- Would remove a director from office before his or her term expired;
- Questions the competence, business judgment, or character of one or more nominees or directors;
- Seeks to include a specific individual in the company's proxy materials for election to the board of directors; or
- Otherwise could affect the outcome of the upcoming election of directors.[686]

We believe that shareholders and companies will benefit from the enhanced clarity that the amended rule will provide concerning the application of the rule. We do not believe that the amendments will result in confusion with regard to the rule's application because the amendments do not change the manner in which Rule 14a-8(i)(8) has been, and will continue to be, interpreted by the staff with respect to other types of proposals.

The amendments to Rule 14a-8(i)(8) could result in shareholders proposing amendments to a company's governing documents that would establish procedures under a company's governing documents for the inclusion of one or more shareholder nominees for director in company proxy materials. These proposals could seek to include a number of provisions relating to nominating directors for inclusion in company proxy materials, and disclosures related to such nominations, that require a different ownership threshold, holding period, or other qualifications or representations than those contained in Rule 14a-11. To the extent that shareholders are successful in adopting amendments to a company's governing documents to establish procedures for the inclusion of one or more shareholder nominees for director in the company's proxy materials, we note that the provision would be an additional avenue for shareholders to submit nominees for inclusion in company proxy materials, not a substitute for, or restriction on, Rule

---

[685] As we stated in the Proposing Release, a proposal would continue to be subject to exclusion under other provisions of Rule 14a-8. For example, a proposal would be excludable under Rule 14a-8(i)(2) if its implementation would cause the company to violate any state, federal, or foreign law to which it is subject, or under Rule 14a-8(i)(3), if the proposal or supporting statement was contrary to any of the Commission's proxy rules.

[686] We note that the rule text adopted differs slightly from the proposed rule text as a result of technical modifications we made to better reflect our intent with respect to the rule. We are adopting amended Rule 14a-8(i)(8) with the language "seeks to include a specific individual in the company's proxy materials for election to the board of directors" rather than "nominates a specific individual for election to the board of directors, other than pursuant to Rule 14a-11, an applicable state law provision, or a company's governing documents." The change in the language from "nominates" to "seeks to include" more accurately reflects the fact that Rule 14a-8 cannot be used as a means to nominate a candidate for election to the board of directors. We also deleted the language regarding Rule 14a-11, an applicable state law provision, or a company's governing documents because we believe it is unnecessary.

14a-11. While such amendments proposed by shareholders through Rule 14a-8 would not be excludable under Rule 14a-8(i)(8) as amended, a company may seek to exclude such a proposal on another basis. For example, to the extent a proposal sought to limit the application of Rule 14a-11, a company could seek to exclude the proposal pursuant to Rule 14a-8(i)(3) on the basis that it is contrary to the proxy rules. We considered whether permitting proposals to allow additional means for shareholder director nominees to be included in company proxy materials would create confusion or lack of certainty for companies and their shareholders in light of the final provisions of Rule 14a-11. In the end, however, we have concluded that this possibility of confusion can be addressed through disclosure and is more than offset by the benefits of facilitating shareholders' ability to determine that their companies should have additional provisions allowing for inclusion of shareholder nominees in company proxy materials.

One commenter opposed the application of proposed Rule 14a-8(i)(8) to investment companies for the same reasons that it opposed the application of proposed Rule 14a-11 to investment companies.[687] We have decided to make amended Rule 14a-8(i)(8) applicable to investment companies for the same reasons that we are making Rule 14a-11 applicable to investment companies. Rule 14a-8(i)(8) is intended to further facilitate shareholders' traditional state law rights to nominate directors, which apply to the shareholders of investment companies. As discussed above, we do not believe that the regulatory protections offered by the Investment Company Act or the fact that open-end management investment companies are not required by state law to hold annual meetings serves to decrease the importance of the rights that are granted to shareholders under state law. For further discussion of our reasons for applying the rule to investment companies, see Section II.B.3.b.

5. Disclosure Requirements

We did not propose any new disclosure requirements for a shareholder that submits a proposal that would amend, or that requests an amendment to, a company's governing documents to address the company's nomination procedures for inclusion of shareholder nominees in company proxy materials or disclosures related to those shareholder provisions.[688] We solicited comment on whether additional disclosure from a shareholder submitting such a proposal would be appropriate. Three commenters opposed requiring disclosure from shareholders who submit such a proposal pursuant to Rule 14a-8 that differs from disclosure required of shareholders who submit other types of Rule 14a-8 proposals.[689] Three commenters recommended generally that a shareholder who submits a Rule 14a-8 proposal regarding a procedure to include shareholder nominees for director in a company's proxy materials should be required to provide additional disclosure (*e.g.*, disclosure about its long-term interest in the company and intentions regarding the shareholder proposal) so that other shareholders could make a fully-informed voting decision.[690] They argued that disclosure at the time of a nomination pursuant to such a procedure would relate only to the election of specific nominees; it would not provide shareholders with enough information to make a voting decision on the proposed procedure and its effect.

As we stated in the Proposing Release, it is our view that disclosure at the time a nominee is submitted and an actual vote is taken on a shareholder nominee is sufficient. Therefore, we are not adopting any new disclosure requirements for a shareholder simply submitting such a proposal because we believe that a shareholder may simply want to amend the company's procedures for including shareholder nominees in company proxy materials, but may not intend to nominate any particular individual.[691]

---

[687] *See* letter from ICI.

[688] Shareholders submitting a proposal that seeks to establish a procedure under a company's governing documents for the inclusion of one or more shareholder director nominees in the company's proxy materials would be subject to Rule 14a-8's current requirements. *See* footnote 685 above.

[689] *See* letters from CII; Florida State Board of Administration; United Brotherhood of Carpenters.

[690] *See* letters from ICI; Keating Muething; O'Melveny & Myers.

[691] This approach is different from the disclosure requirements the Commission proposed in the Shareholder Proposals Release in 2007; however, it is con-

In proposing amendments to Rule 14a-8(i)(8), we noted that the amendments could result in shareholder proposals that would establish procedures for nominating directors and disclosures related to such nominations that require a different ownership threshold, holding period, or other qualifications or representations than those proposed in Rule 14a-11. In addition, a state could set forth in its corporate code,[692] or a company may choose to amend its governing documents, to establish nomination or disclosure provisions in addition to those provided pursuant to Rule 14a-11 (*e.g.*, a company could choose to allow shareholders to have their nominees included in the company's proxy materials regardless of ownership—in that instance, the company's provision would apply for certain shareholders who otherwise could not have their nominees included in the company's proxy materials pursuant to Rule 14a-11). Accordingly, we proposed amendments to our proxy rules to address the disclosure requirements when a nomination is made pursuant to such a provision.[693]

As proposed, Rule 14a-19 would apply to a shareholder nomination for director for inclusion in the company's proxy materials made pursuant to procedures established pursuant to state law or by a company's governing documents. The proposed rule would require a nominating shareholder or group to include in its shareholder notice on Schedule 14N (which, under the Proposal, also would be filed with the Commission on the date provided to the company) disclosures about the nominating shareholder or group and their nominee that are similar to what would be required in an election contest.[694]

Specifically, the notice on Schedule 14N, as proposed, would be required to include:

- A statement that the nominee consents to be named in the company's proxy statement and to serve on the board if elected, for inclusion in the company's proxy statement;[695]

- Disclosure about the nominee complying with the requirements of Item 4(b), Item 5(b), and Items 7(a), (b) and (c) and, for investment companies, Item 22(b) of Exchange Act Schedule 14A, as applicable, for inclusion in the company's proxy statement;[696]

- Disclosure about the nominating shareholder or members of a nominating shareholder group consistent with the disclosure currently required pursuant to Item 4(b) and Item 5(b) of Schedule 14A;[697]

(Footnote Continued)

sistent with the overall requirements relating to the submission of shareholder proposals—generally, shareholder proponents are not required to provide any specific type of disclosure along with their proposal.

[692] *See* North Dakota Publicly Traded Corporations Act, N.D. Cent. Code § 10-35-08 (2009). In 2007, North Dakota amended its corporate code to permit five percent shareholders to provide a company notice of intent to nominate directors and require the company to include each such shareholder nominee in its proxy statement and form of proxy. *See* N.D. Cent. Code § 10-35 *et al* (2007).

[693] *See* proposed Rule 14a-19.

[694] *See* proposed Rule 14a-19.

[695] *See* proposed Rule 14a-19(a).

[696] *See* proposed Rule 14a-19(b). This information would identify the nominee, describe certain legal proceedings, if any, related to the nominee, and describe certain of the nominee's transactions and relationships with the company. *See* Items 7(a), (b), and (c) of Schedule 14A. This information also would

include biographical information and information concerning interests of the nominee. *See* Item 5(b) of Schedule 14A. With respect to a nominee for director of an investment company, the disclosure would include certain basic information about the nominee and any arrangement or understanding between the nominee and any other person pursuant to which he was selected as a nominee; information about the positions, interests, and transactions and relationships of the nominee and his immediate family members with the company and persons related to the company; information about the amount of equity securities of funds in a fund complex owned by the nominee; and information describing certain legal proceedings related to the nominee, including legal proceedings in which the nominee is a party adverse to, or has a material interest adverse to, the company or any of its affiliated persons. *See* paragraph (b) of Item 22 of Schedule 14A.

[697] *See* proposed Rule 14a-19(c).

- Disclosure about whether the nominating shareholder or any member of a nominating shareholder group has been involved in any legal proceeding during the past five years, as specified in Item 401(f) of Regulation S-K. Disclosure pursuant to this section need not be provided if provided in response to Items 4(b) and 5(b) of Schedule 14A;[698]

- The following disclosure regarding the nature and extent of the relationships between the nominating shareholder or group and nominee and the company or any affiliate of the company:

  ○ Any direct or indirect material interest in any contract or agreement between the nominating shareholder or group or the nominee and the company or any affiliate of the company (including any employment agreement, collective bargaining agreement, or consulting agreement);

  ○ Any material pending or threatened litigation in which the nominating shareholder or group or nominee is a party or a material participant, and that involves the company, any of its officers or directors, or any affiliate of the company; and

  ○ Any other material relationship between the nominating shareholder or group or the nominee and the company or any affiliate of the company not otherwise disclosed;[699] and

- Disclosure of any Web site address on which the nominating shareholder or group may publish soliciting materials.[700]

These disclosures would be included in the company's proxy materials pursuant to proposed new Item 7(f) of Schedule 14A, or in the case of investment companies, proposed Item 22(b)(19) of Schedule 14A.

In addition, under the Proposal, the nominating shareholder or group would be required to identify the shareholder or group making the nomination and the amount of their ownership in the company on Schedule 14N. The filing would be required to include, among other disclosures:

- The name and address of the nominating shareholder or each member of the nominating shareholder group; and

- Information regarding the aggregate number and percentage of the securities entitled to be voted, including the amount beneficially owned and the number of shares over which the nominating shareholder or each member of the nominating shareholder group has or shares voting or disposition power.

We did not receive a significant amount of comment specifically addressing proposed Rule 14a-19. One commenter believed that the disclosure requirements of Rules 14a-18 and 14a-19 should be virtually identical.[701] The commenter highlighted certain discrepancies, such as the intent to retain the requisite shares through, and subsequent to, the date of election. Another commenter saw no need for a separate rule to deal with nominations submitted under state law or a company's governing documents and therefore urged the Commission not to adopt Rule 14a-19.[702] The commenter believed there are no policy grounds to justify disparate treatment of nominations submitted under state law or a company's governing documents. It warned that a separate rule would only create confusion. Another commenter suggested that we extend the disclosure requirement to nominations submitted pursuant to a provision under foreign law.[703]

As we stated in the Proposing Release, we believe the proposed additional disclosure requirements are necessary to provide shareholders with full and fair disclosure of information that is material when a choice among directors to be elected is presented;

---

[698] *See* proposed Rule 14a-19(d).
[699] *See* proposed Rule 14a-19(e).
[700] *See* proposed Rule 14a-19(f).

[701] *See* letter from P. Neuhauser.
[702] *See* letter from Cleary.
[703] *See* letter from Curtis.

thus, we are adopting the disclosure requirement largely as proposed.[704] As noted above, one commenter suggested that the disclosure standard should apply to nominations made pursuant to foreign law. We agree that the disclosure is necessary regardless of the source of the ability to nominate candidates for director. We therefore have clarified that the disclosure requirement extends not only to nominations made pursuant to state law or a company's governing documents, but also pursuant to foreign law (in the case of a non-U.S. domiciled company that does not qualify as a foreign private issuer). We continue to believe that these disclosures will assist shareholders in making an informed voting decision with regard to any nominee or nominees put forth by the nominating shareholder or group, in that the disclosures would enable shareholders to gauge the nominating shareholder's or group's interest in the company. We understand the concern that a separate disclosure rule for nominations made pursuant to state or foreign law provisions, or a company's governing documents could create confusion. We note, however, that certain disclosure provisions or certifications applicable to Rule 14a-11 nominations may not be applicable to nominations made pursuant to other provisions. For example, state or foreign law provisions, or the company's governing documents may require different ownership thresholds or holding periods. Therefore, we believe it is necessary to have separate disclosure requirements for nominations made pursuant to state or foreign law, or a company's governing documents. As with disclosures made in connection with a Rule 14a-11 nomination, the nominating shareholder or group would be liable for any materially false or misleading statements in these disclosures pursuant to new paragraph (c) of Rule 14a-9.[705]

As noted above, we have restructured Rule 14a-11, Rule 14a-18, and Schedule 14N. Similarly, while we are adopting the disclosure requirements largely as proposed in Rule 14a-19,[706] they are now included in Item 6 of Schedule 14N. In addition, because we moved the disclosure requirements for Rule 14a-11 from proposed Rule 14a-18 into Schedule 14N, the requirements for shareholders submitting nominations pursuant to a provision in state law or a company's governing documents are being adopted as new Rule 14a-18.

Under the Proposal, a shareholder submitting a nomination pursuant to a state law provision or a provision in a company's governing documents would be required to file a Schedule 14N (with the disclosures required by that Schedule) by the date specified in the advance notice provision, or where no such provision is in place, no later than 120 calendar days before the date the company mailed its proxy materials for the prior year's annual meeting.[707] We are adopting this requirement as proposed. We note that it is likely that a state or foreign law provision or a provision in a company's governing documents will provide a deadline for submission of nominations made pursuant to those provisions. While we believe that shareholders submitting nominations pursuant to those provisions should provide the disclosure required by Schedule 14N, we believe it is appropriate to defer to the deadline, if any, set forth in those provisions. In this regard, we note that timing concerns present in the Rule 14a-11 nomination context (*e.g.*, timing requirements for engaging in the staff no-action process) are not present in this context.

---

[704] As noted in footnote 511 above, the applicable disclosure requirement in Item 401(f) of Regulation S-K was amended in the Proxy Disclosure Enhancements Adopting Release to require disclosure regarding legal proceedings for the past 10 years as opposed to past five years. Thus, disclosure would be required about a nominee's or nominating shareholder's participation in legal proceedings during the past 10 years. We also are making clarifying changes to the disclosure required regarding the nature and extent of relationships between the nominating shareholder or group and/or nominee and/or the company or its affiliates. *See* footnote 514 and accompanying text in Section II.B.8.c.i. above.

[705] *See* proposed Rule 14a-9(c).

[706] As adopted, Item 6(d) of Schedule 14N will require disclosure about a nominating shareholder's involvement in legal proceedings during the past ten years, rather than five years as was proposed. This is due to the Commission's recent amendment of Item 401(f) of Regulation S-K. *See* footnotes 511 and 704 above.

[707] If a company did not hold an annual meeting during the prior year, or if the date of the meeting has changed by more than 30 calendar days from the prior year, then the nominating shareholder or group must provide notice a reasonable time before the registrant mails its proxy materials.

D. Other Rule Changes

1. Disclosure of Dates and Voting Information

As proposed, if a company did not hold an annual meeting during the prior year, or if the date of the meeting has changed by more than 30 days from the prior year, within four business days of determining the anticipated meeting date a company would be required to file a Form 8-K to disclose the date by which a nominating shareholder or group must submit notice to include a nominee in the company's proxy materials pursuant to Rule 14a-11.[708] The date disclosed as the deadline for such shareholder nominations for director would be required to be a reasonable time before the company mails its proxy materials for the meeting. We also proposed to require a registered investment company that is a series company to file a Form 8-K disclosing the company's net assets as of June 30 of the calendar year immediately preceding the calendar year of the meeting and the total number of the company's shares that are outstanding and entitled to vote for the election of directors (or if votes are to be cast on a basis other than one vote per share, then the total number of votes entitled to be voted and the basis for allocating votes) at the annual meeting of shareholders (or, in lieu of such an annual meeting, a special meeting of shareholders) as of the end of the most recent calendar quarter.

We did not receive much comment on this aspect of the rule. One commenter urged the Commission not to require the Form 8-K filing for investment companies, which generally are not required to file Form 8-K.[709] The commenter favored instead a requirement for investment companies to inform shareholders through another method (or combination of methods) of disclosure reasonably designed to provide notice of the date, including via a press release or posting information on the company's Web site. One commenter supported the proposed instruction to Item 5.07 of Form 8-K.[710]

We are adopting this requirement substantially as proposed, although the requirement will be in new Item 5.08 of Form 8-K. A company will be required to file a Form 8-K, within four business days of determining the anticipated date of the meeting, disclosing the date by which a nominating shareholder or group must submit notice to include a nominee in the company's proxy materials pursuant to Rule 14a-11, which date shall be a reasonable time before the registrant mails its proxy materials for the meeting.[711] We also have clarified that where a company is required to include shareholder director nominees in the company's proxy materials pursuant to an applicable state or foreign law provision, or a provision in the company's governing documents then the company is required to disclose the date by which a nominating shareholder or nominating shareholder group must submit the Schedule 14N required pursuant to Rule 14a-18.

A registered investment company that is a series company also must disclose the total number of the company's shares that are outstanding and entitled to vote for the election of directors (or if votes are to be cast on a basis other than one vote per share, then the total number of votes entitled to be voted and the basis for allocating such votes) at the shareholder meeting as of the end of the most recent calendar quarter.[712] We believe it is important to provide shareholders with information regarding the deadline for submitting such nominations in the event that the date of the meeting at which the election of directors will take place changes significantly. Moreover, we have decided to require registered investment companies to make the disclosures on Form 8-K, as proposed,

---

[708] *See* proposed Item 5.07 to Form 8-K.

[709] *See* letter from ICI.

[710] *See* letter from ABA.

[711] *See* new Item 5.08 of Form 8-K and new General Instruction B.1. to Form 8-K. A late filing of such form would result in the registrant not being current or timely for purposes of rules and regulations related to form eligibility and the resale of securities. The company would be deemed current once the Form 8-K is filed.

[712] *See* General Instruction B.1 and Item 5.08(b) of Form 8-K; Rules 13a-11(b)(3) and 15d-11(b)(3); and Instruction 2 to Rule 14a-11(b)(1). In the case of registered investment companies, nominating shareholders may rely on the information contained in the Form 8-K filed in connection with the meeting, unless the nominating shareholder or group knows or has reason to know that the information contained therein is inaccurate. *See* discussion in footnote 280.

rather than through another method or combination of methods because we believe that the information that we are requiring is important information that should be filed with the Commission and accessible on EDGAR rather than merely disclosed on a Web site or in a press release.[713]

Exchange Act Rule 14a-5 requires registrants to disclose in a proxy statement the deadlines for submitting shareholder proposals and matters submitted pursuant to advance notice bylaws. We are amending Rule 14a-5 to also require companies to disclose the deadline for submitting nominees for inclusion in the company's proxy materials for the company's next annual meeting of shareholders. This provision will apply with respect to inclusion of nominations in a company's proxy materials pursuant to Rule 14a-11, an applicable state or foreign law provision, or a company's governing documents.[714] We believe that it is necessary to conform the existing requirements in Rule 14a-5, consistent with the proposal to give adequate notice to shareholders about their ability to submit a nominee or nominees for inclusion in a company's proxy materials pursuant to Rule 14a-11. The change should help to avoid any potential confusion regarding the date by which shareholders seeking to have a nominee included in a company's proxy materials would need to submit a Schedule 14N pursuant to Rule 14a-11 or Rule 14a-18.

2. Beneficial Ownership Reporting Requirements

As adopted, Rule 14a-11 requires that a nominating shareholder or group hold at least 3% of the voting power of the company's securities entitled to be voted on the election of directors. Although unnecessary to be able to use the rule, it is possible that in aggregating shares to meet the ownership requirement, a nominating shareholder or group will trigger the reporting requirements of Regulation 13D-G, which requires that a shareholder or group that beneficially owns more than 5% of a voting class of any equity security registered pursuant to Section 12 file beneficial ownership reports.[715] Therefore, nominating shareholders will need to consider whether they have formed a group under Exchange Act Section 13(d)(3) and Rule 13d-5(b)(1) that is required to file beneficial ownership reports. Any person (which includes a group as defined in Rule 13d-5(b)(1)) who is directly or indirectly the beneficial owner of more than 5% of a class of equity securities registered under Exchange Act Section 12 must report that ownership by filing an Exchange Act Schedule 13D with the Commission.[716] There are exceptions to this requirement, however, that permit such a person to report that ownership on Schedule 13G rather than Schedule 13D. One exception permits filings on Schedule 13G for a specified list of qualified institutional investors who have acquired the securities in the ordinary course of their business and with neither the purpose nor the effect of changing or influencing control of the company.[717] A second exception applies to persons who beneficially own more than 5% of a subject class of securities if they acquired the securities with neither the purpose nor the effect of changing or influencing control of the company and they are not directly or indirectly the beneficial owner of 20% or more of the subject class of securities.[718]

Central to Schedule 13G eligibility under the exceptions discussed above is that the shareholder be a passive investor that has acquired the securities without the purpose, or the effect, of changing or influencing control of the company. In addition, shareholders

---

[713] We are not adopting the proposed requirement that a registered investment company that is a series company file a Form 8-K disclosing the company's net assets as of June 30 of the calendar year immediately preceding the calendar year of the meeting. We proposed this requirement in connection with our proposal to use tiered thresholds based on net assets to determine eligibility under Rule 14a-11. Since the rule we are adopting does not use tiered thresholds, the proposed requirement is no longer necessary.

[714] *See* new Rule 14a-5(e)(3).

[715] The term equity security also includes any equity security of any insurance company which would have been required to be registered pursuant to Section 12 of the Exchange Act except for the exemption contained in Section 12(g)(2)(G) of the Act or any equity security issued by a closed-end investment company registered under the Investment Company Act of 1940. *See* Exchange Act Rule 13d-1(i).

[716] *See* Exchange Act Rule 13d-1.

[717] *See* Exchange Act Rule 13d-1(b).

[718] *See* Exchange Act Rule 13d-1(c).

who are filing as qualified institutional investors must have acquired the securities in the ordinary course of their business. Typically, persons who seek to nominate candidates for a company's board of directors would be unable to meet these eligibility requirements to file on Schedule 13G. As we stated in the Proposing Release, however, we believe that the formation of a shareholder group solely for the purpose of nominating one or more directors pursuant to proposed Rule 14a-11, the nomination of one or more directors pursuant to proposed Rule 14a-11, or soliciting activities in connection with such a nomination (including soliciting in opposition to a company's nominees) should not result in a nominating shareholder or nominating shareholder group losing its eligibility to file on Schedule 13G. As a result, we proposed to revise the requirement that the first and second categories of persons who may report their ownership on Schedule 13G must have acquired the securities without the purpose or effect of changing or influencing control of the company and, in the case of Rule 13d-1(b), in the ordinary course of business, to provide an exception for activities solely in connection with a nomination under Rule 14a-11.

Comments on the proposal were mixed. Some commenters generally supported the proposed exceptions from the Schedule 13D filing obligation for a nominating shareholder or group conducting activities solely in connection with a Rule 14a-11 nomination so that it would be eligible to report on Schedule 13G rather than Schedule 13D.[719] One such commenter added that the exceptions also should be available to a nominating shareholder or group submitting nominees pursuant to state law or a company's governing documents.[720] One commenter predicted the amendment would encourage use of Rule 14a-11 by large shareholders who are knowledgeable about the company but may be reluctant to take action that may jeopardize their Schedule 13G filer status.[721] One commenter observed more generally that a Schedule 13D filing is unnecessary if the filing requirement of Rule 14a-2(b)(7) is retained because such filings would provide sufficient notice to the market.[722] Even if such filing requirement is not retained, the commenter believed that a Schedule 13D is unnecessary because the underlying assumption of Rule 14a-11 is that there is no control intent.

On the other hand, other commenters opposed generally the proposed exceptions from the Schedule 13D filing obligation.[723] Some of these commenters expressed reservations about creating a broad exemption or carve-out from Exchange Act Section 13(d) "control" concepts.[724] One commenter noted that Rules 13d-1(b), (c) and (e) track the use of the phrase "changing or influencing control of the issuer" from Exchange Act Section 13(d)(5).[725] This commenter did not believe there is a persuasive basis for the Commission to provide that, under all circumstances, a shareholder or group seeking to nominate a director, in opposition to the election of incumbent directors, is not seeking to "influence" control of the company. One commenter stated that most election contests would fall within the concept of "influencing the control of the issuer" because they focus on the governance, strategic direction and policy initiatives of the company.[726] Another commenter noted that the Schedule 14N certifications require only that a nominating shareholder has no intention of "changing control" of the company, but does not require the nominating shareholder to certify that it has no intention of "influencing control."[727]

---

[719] *See* letters from CalSTRS; CFA Institute; CII; Florida State Board of Administration; ICI; Schulte Roth & Zabel. Another commenter, ICGN, did not expressly address the proposed amendment but asked the Commission to clarify the definition of "group" so that shareholders would not be dissuaded from acting collectively to use Rule 14a-11 out of concern that a Schedule 13D filing obligation would arise.

[720] *See* letter from CII. In contrast, two commenters stated that the proposed exceptions should not be extended outside the context of Rule 14a-11, and agreed that it would not be possible to address the eligibility standards in provisions of state law or a company's governing documents or ensure that there is no change in control attempt. *See* letters from ABA; Alston & Bird.

[721] *See* letter from Schulte Roth & Zabel.

[722] *See* letter from P. Neuhauser.

[723] *See* letters from ABA; Alston & Bird; BRT; Cleary; Microsoft; Seven Law Firms; Shearman & Sterling; Society of Corporate Secretaries; Vinson & Elkins.

[724] *See* letters from ABA; Cleary; Microsoft; Seven Law Firm; Shearman & Sterling.

[725] *See* letter from ABA.

[726] *See* letter from Seven Law Firms.

[727] *See* letter from ABA.

Several commenters expressed concerns about inadequate disclosures that would result from the proposed exceptions or pointed to the useful disclosure required by Schedule 13D.[728] One commenter observed that if a nominating shareholder or group has no plans regarding significant changes in the company or relationships with other parties regarding securities of the company, a Schedule 13D filing would not require significant information from a nominating shareholder or group beyond that required by Schedule 14N.[729] This commenter noted that if a nominating shareholder or group, however, has more complicated relationships or intentions relating to the company or its securities, the Schedule 13D filing would provide additional information that shareholders would find useful.[730]

We continue to believe that it is appropriate to provide an exception for activities solely in connection with a nomination pursuant to Rule 14a-11 to allow a nominating shareholder or group to report on Schedule 13G. Accordingly, we are adopting, as proposed, the exception from the requirement to file a Schedule 13D (and therefore permitting filing on Schedule 13G) for activities undertaken solely in connection with a nomination under Rule 14a-11. In addition, we are adopting a change to the certifications in Schedule 13G to reflect this exception.[731]

It is important to note that any activity other than those provided for under Rule 14a-11 would make the exception inapplicable. For example, approaching a company's board and urging them to consider strategic alternatives (*e.g.*, sale of non-core assets or a leveraged recapitalization) would constitute activities outside of the Rule 14a-11 nomination, and any nominating shareholder or group engaging in such activities most likely would be ineligible to file on Schedule 13G. The rule changes will not apply to nominating shareholders or groups that submit a nomination pursuant to an applicable state or foreign law provision, or a company's governing documents because in those instances the applicable provisions may not limit the number of board seats for which a shareholder or group could nominate candidates or include a requirement that the nominating shareholder or group lack intent to change the control of the issuer or to gain a number of seats on the board of directors that exceeds the maximum number of nominees that the registrant could be required to include under Rule 14a-11 (as is the case under Rule 14a-11). Accordingly, we do not believe it would be appropriate to make a general determination by rule as to whether a nominating shareholder or group under an applicable state or foreign law provision, or a company's governing documents would be eligible to file on Schedule 13G. Instead, this would be a fact-specific inquiry.

We believe that the disclosures about the nominating shareholder or group required by Rule 14a-11 and Schedule 14N are adequate to allow shareholders to make an informed decision and to keep the market apprised of developments regarding board nomination activities, and do not believe that requiring the additional disclosures in Schedule 13D is necessary for activities solely in connection with a nomination under Rule 14a-11. Because this exception is only available for purposes of the nomination, a nominating shareholder or group would need to reassess its eligibility to continue to report on Schedule 13G as a passive or qualified institutional investor after the election. For example, if a nominating shareholder is also the nominee and is successfully elected to the board, then the shareholder would likely be ineligible to continue filing on Schedule 13G due to its ability as a director to directly or indirectly influence the management and policies of the company. We believe the limited scope of the exemption addresses commenters' concerns about nominating shareholders or groups influencing control of the issuer while reporting on Schedule 13G.

---

[728] *See* letters from ABA; Alston & Bird; BRT; Seven Law Firms; Society of Corporate Secretaries; Vinson & Elkins.

[729] *See* letter from ABA.

[730] *Id.*

[731] We did not propose the change to the certifications in Schedule 13G; however, we believe this conforming change is necessary to reflect the intent of the exception.

3. Exchange Act Section 16

Section 16[732] applies to every person who is the beneficial owner of more than 10% of any class of equity security registered under Exchange Act Section 12 ("10% owners"), and each officer and director (collectively with 10% owners, "insiders") of the issuer of such security. We did not propose an exemption from Section 16 for groups formed solely for the purpose of nominating a director pursuant to Rule 14a-11.[733] In the Proposal, we explained that we believed the existing analysis of whether a group has formed[734] and whether Section 16 applies[735] should continue to apply. We also explained that because the proposed ownership thresholds for Rule 14a-11 were significantly lower than 10%, we did not believe that the lack of an exclusion would have a deterrent effect on the formation of groups, and therefore did not believe it was necessary to propose an exclusion from Section 16.

We also noted in the Proposal that some shareholders, particularly institutions and other entities, may be concerned that successful use of Rule 14a-11 to include a director nominee in company proxy materials may result in the nominating person also being deemed a director under the "deputization" theory developed by courts in Section 16(b) short-swing profit recovery cases.[736] Under this theory it is possible for a person to be deemed a director subject to Section 16, even though the issuer has not formally elected or otherwise named that person a director. We did not propose standards for establishing the independence of the nominee from the nominating shareholder, or members of the nominating shareholder group.

Although we did not propose an exemption from Section 16, we requested comment on, among other things, whether a nominating shareholder group should be excluded from Section 16 and whether subjecting such groups to Section 16 would be a disincentive to using Rule 14a-11. A few commenters recommended that the Commission create an exemption from Section 16 for a group of shareholders that aggregated their holdings in order to submit a nominee pursuant to Rule 14a-11.[737] Commenters reasoned that members of a nominating group that owns more than 10% of the shares could not reasonably be considered company "insiders."[738] These commenters noted that the group would exist for the sole purpose of nominating a candidate and, absent special facts, would have no access to inside information about the company. Thus, these commenters argued that the statutory purpose of Section 16—the prevention of insider trading—would not be relevant to such groups. Other commenters did not support an exemption from Section 16.[739] Some of these commenters further agreed that no standard should be adopted regarding application of the judicial doctrine concerning "deputized directors."[740]

After considering the comments, we continue to believe that an exclusion from Section 16 is not appropriate for groups formed solely for the purpose of nominating a director pursuant to Rule 14a-11, soliciting in connection with the election of that

---

[732] 15 U.S.C. 78p.

[733] As discussed in the Proposing Release, the Commission had previously proposed, in 2003, that a group formed solely for the purpose of nominating a director pursuant to Rule 14a-11, soliciting in connection the election of that nominee, or having that nominee elected as a director be exempted from Exchange Act Section 16 reporting.

[734] See Exchange Act Rule 13d-5(b) [17 CFR 240.13d-5(b)].

[735] See Exchange Act Rule 16a-1(a)(1) [17 CFR 240.16a-1(a)(1)].

[736] See Feder v. Martin Marietta Corp., 406 F.2d 260 (2d Cir. 1969), cert. denied, 396 U.S. 1036 (1970); Blau v. Lehman, 368 U.S. 403 (1962); and Rattner v. Lehman, 193 F.2d 564 (2d Cir. 1952). The judicial decisions in which this theory was applied do not

establish precise standards for determining when "deputization" may exist. However, the express purpose of Section 16(b) is to prevent the unfair use of information by insiders through their relationships to the issuer. Accordingly, one factor that courts may consider in determining if Section 16(b) liability applies is whether, by virtue of the "deputization" relationship, the "deputizing" entity's transactions in issuer securities may benefit from the deputized director's access to inside information.

[737] See letters from ICI; Schulte Roth & Zabel; ValueAct Capital.

[738] See letters from ICI; Schulte Roth & Zabel.

[739] See letters from ABA; Alston & Bird; CII; Seven Law Firms.

[740] See letters from ABA; CII; Seven Law Firms.

nominee, or having that nominee elected as director. We also believe that it is not necessary to change the existing analysis of whether a group has formed and whether Section 16 applies. Because the ownership threshold we are adopting for Rule 14a-11 eligibility is significantly less than 10%, shareholders will be able to form groups with holdings sufficient to meet the Rule 14a-11 threshold without reaching the 10% threshold in Section 16. Thus, we do not believe that Section 16 commonly will be a deterrent to use of Rule 14a-11. As such, we believe that shareholders forming a group to submit a nominee for director pursuant to Rule 14a-11 should be analyzed in the same way as any other group for purposes of determining whether group members are 10% owners subject to Section 16. Similarly, we are not adopting standards regarding application of the "deputized director" doctrine, which will be left to existing case law and courts.

4. Nominating Shareholder or Group Status as Affiliates of the Company

We proposed that Rule 14a-11(a) contain a safe harbor providing that a nominating shareholder would not be deemed an "affiliate" of the company under the Securities Act or the Exchange Act solely as a result of using Rule 14a-11.[741] Under the Proposal, this safe harbor would apply not only to the nomination of a candidate, but also where that candidate is elected, provided that the nominating shareholder or group does not have an agreement or relationship with that director otherwise than relating to the nomination. We were concerned that, without such a safe harbor, some nominating shareholders may be deterred from using Rule 14a-11.

We solicited comment on the appropriateness of the proposed safe harbor and posed some specific questions concerning its application. We also asked whether we should include a similar safe harbor provision for nominating shareholders that submit a nominee for inclusion in a company's proxy materials pursuant to an applicable state law provision or a company's governing documents rather than using the proposed rule.

Three commenters provided statements of general support for the proposed safe harbor.[742] One commenter believed that a safe harbor also would be warranted for shareholders submitting nominees pursuant to state law or a company's governing documents.[743] Another commenter believed the safe harbor should not be available once the shareholder nominee is elected.[744] One commenter recommended that Instruction 1 to Rule 14a-11(a) clarify that the presence of agreements, other than those relating only to the nomination, between a nominating shareholder and a candidate or director would not necessarily confer affiliate status on the nominating shareholder, and that Rule 14a-11 is not intended to change the current law regarding affiliate status.[745]

Two commenters opposed the safe harbor.[746] One commenter believed that we should not adopt such a safe harbor without addressing the issue of affiliate status more broadly.[747] It argued that as long as the Commission follows the historical, facts-and-circumstances analysis for the determination of affiliate status in other contexts, it also should follow this practice in the context of Rule 14a-11. Both commenters opposing the safe harbor also did not believe that proposed Instruction 1 to Rule 14a-11(a) would significantly reduce the interpretive analysis needed to determine whether a nominating shareholder is an "affiliate."[748] They argued that it rarely would be clear whether a

---

[741] This safe harbor was set forth in Instruction 1 to proposed Rule 14a-11(a). The safe harbor was intended to operate such that the determination of whether a shareholder or group is an "affiliate" of the company would continue to be made based upon all of the facts and circumstances regarding the relationship of the shareholder or group to the company, but a shareholder or group would not be deemed an affiliate "solely" by virtue of having nominated that director.

[742] *See* letters from CII; Protective; Schulte Roth & Zabel.

[743] *See* letter from CII.

[744] *See* letter from Protective.

[745] *See* letter from Schulte Roth & Zabel. The commenter explained that nominees often request agreements, such as indemnification agreements, that clearly relate only to their nomination. In other situations, however, nominees and nominating shareholders enter into other agreements, including compensation agreements, which may not relate exclusively to the nomination.

[746] *See* letters from ABA; Seven Law Firms.

[747] *See* letter from ABA.

[748] *See* letters from ABA; Seven Law Firms.

nominating shareholder's relationship with the company would consist "solely" of its nominating and soliciting activities, no matter how a safe harbor may be worded. They also expressed concern that the safe harbor would discourage nominating shareholders from participating in potentially fruitful discussions with the company, for fear that such participation would go beyond "solely" nominating and soliciting for a director candidate.

After considering the comments, we do not believe that the proposed safe harbor would provide a level of certainty to nominating shareholders concerning their potential "affiliate" status sufficient to warrant a departure from the current application of the term. We believe it is more appropriate to conduct a facts-and-circumstances analysis in this regard, as would currently be the case in other situations. We agree with commenters' views on the limited utility of the safe harbor's application in practice, acknowledging that a nominating shareholder would be obligated to conduct a facts-and-circumstance analysis to determine affiliate status even if we were to adopt the safe harbor as proposed. We also recognize that some nominating shareholders or members of nominating shareholder groups may be reluctant to engage in certain activities that would further the general purpose of Rule 14a-11 due to concerns that such activities would jeopardize their ability to use the safe harbor.

In this light, it does not appear that the proposed safe harbor would meaningfully facilitate use of Rule 14a-11, if at all, and may, in fact, deter it because some nominating shareholders or members of nominating shareholder groups may limit their activities out of concern that their activities would jeopardize reliance on the safe harbor. Accordingly, we have decided neither to adopt a safe harbor under the rule nor to adopt a similar safe harbor for shareholders submitting nominees pursuant to state law or a company's governing instruments. Instead, as is currently the case in other contests, those who use the rule will need to analyze affiliate status on a case-by-case basis, taking into consideration all relevant facts and circumstances, including the circumstances surrounding a nomination and election of a shareholder nominee.

E. Application of the Liability Provisions in the Federal Securities Laws to Statements Made By a Nominating Shareholder or Nominating Shareholder Group

It is our intent that a nominating shareholder or group relying on Rule 14a-11, an applicable state or foreign law provision, or a company's governing documents to include a nominee in company proxy materials be liable for any statement included in the Schedule 14N or other related communications, or which it causes to be included in a company's proxy materials, which, at the time and in light of the circumstances under which it is made, is false or misleading with respect to any material fact or omits to state any material fact necessary to make the statements therein not false or misleading. To this end, we proposed to add a new paragraph (c) to Rule 14a-9 to specifically address a nominating shareholder's or group's liability when providing information on a Schedule 14N to be included in a company's proxy materials pursuant to Rule 14a-11.

As proposed, new paragraph (c) stated that "no nominee, nominating shareholder or nominating shareholder group, or any member thereof, shall cause to be included in a registrant's proxy materials, either pursuant to the federal proxy rules, an applicable state law provision, or a registrant's governing documents as they relate to including shareholder nominees for director in registrant proxy materials, any statement which, at the time and in the light of the circumstances under which it is made, is false or misleading with respect to any material fact, or which omits to state any material fact necessary in order to make the statements therein not false or misleading or necessary to correct any statement in any earlier communication with respect to a solicitation for the same meeting or subject matter which has become false or misleading."

Commenters generally supported the proposal to impose Rule 14a-9 liability on nominating shareholders or groups that caused false or misleading statements to be included in a company's proxy materials. One commenter supported the use of Rule 14a-9 as the standard for assigning liability, as the standards under that rule are well known and therefore would promote uniformity.[749] The commenter further stated that Rule 14a-9(c) makes sufficiently clear that a nominating shareholder or group would be liable for statements included in its Schedule 14N or notice to the company that is included in the company's proxy materials. As for the consequences of providing materially false information or representations in a Schedule 14N, the commenter stated that such a situation should be handled in the same way as materially false statements or omissions in a Schedule 14A or other soliciting material filed in connection with a proxy contest. Another commenter suggested that the disclosure provided to the company by the nominating shareholder or group and included in the company's proxy materials be treated as the shareholder's or group's soliciting materials.[750] The commenter did not believe that Rule 14a-9(c) makes clear that the nominating shareholder or group would be liable for any information included in its Schedule 14N or notice to the company that is included in the company's proxy materials. One commenter stated that members of a nominating group should be jointly and severally liable to the company for material misstatements or omissions provided to the company about the group or its members.[751] Another commenter, noting investors' concerns about exposure to joint liability from participating with other investors to nominate a candidate, requested that the Commission add additional commentary about the limits of joint liability for unapproved statements of other members of a nominating group.[752] One commenter suggested that a nominating shareholder or group should be required to indemnify the company for any costs incurred in connection with any misstatements or omissions in the information provided to the company for inclusion in the company's proxy materials.[753]

We are adopting Rule 14a-9(c) largely as proposed, but with specific references to statements made in the Schedule 14N and other related communications and a clarification that the rule would apply where a nominee is submitted pursuant to a foreign law provision in addition to a state law provision or the company's governing documents. New Rule 14a-9(c) provides that "no nominee, nominating shareholder or nominating shareholder group, or any member thereof, shall cause to be included in a registrant's proxy materials, either pursuant to the federal proxy rules, an applicable state or foreign law provision, or a registrant's governing documents as they relate to including shareholder nominees for director in registrant proxy materials, include in a notice on Schedule 14N, or include in any other related communication, any statement which, at the time and in the light of the circumstances under which it is made, is false or misleading with respect to any material fact, or which omits to state any material fact necessary in order to make the statements therein not false or misleading or necessary to correct any statement in any earlier communication with respect to a solicitation for the same meeting or subject matter which has become false or misleading." The changes to the rule text are intended to clarify that a nominating shareholder or group would be liable for statements it makes regarding the nomination, regardless of whether those statements ultimately appear in the company's proxy statement, as we consider any statements that are made in the Schedule 14N or in other communications to be part of the solicitation by the nominating shareholder or group. Consistent with this view, the Schedule 14N filing (as well as any other related communications) would be considering soliciting materials for purposes of Section 14(a) liability.

Under the Proposal, the rule also included express language providing that the company would not be responsible for information that is provided by the nominating shareholder or group under Rule 14a-11 and then repeated by the company in its proxy statement, except where the company knows or has reason to know that the information is false or misleading.[754] A similar provision was proposed in Rule 14a-19 with regard to information provided by the nominating shareholder or group in connection with a nomination made pursuant to an applicable state law provision or a company's governing documents.[755]

---

[749] *See* letter from CII.
[750] *See* letter from Protective.
[751] *See* letter from Verizon.
[752] *See* letter from Universities Superannuation.

[753] *See* letter from Verizon.
[754] *See* proposed Rule 14a-11(e).
[755] *See* Note to proposed Rule 14a-19.

A number of commenters opposed the "knows or has reason to know" standard.[756] Many commenters argued generally that because the Commission's Proposal would eliminate the board's involvement in selecting the shareholder nominees and prevent a company from excluding any information from its proxy materials, the company should not be liable for information provided by the nominating shareholder, group, or nominee.[757] Commenters further noted that companies would not have adequate time or sufficient means to investigate the statements made by the nominating shareholder, group, or nominee.[758] Therefore, these commenters argued that it would be inappropriate to shift onto companies any liability for statements made by a nominating shareholder, group, or nominee or impose a duty to investigate or otherwise confirm the accuracy of the information provided by a nominating shareholder, group, or nominee.[759] One commenter predicted that if a company is liable for information provided by a nominating shareholder or group and included in a company's proxy materials pursuant to Rule 14a-11, an applicable state law provision, or a provision in a company's governing documents, it would challenge in court any information provided by a nominating shareholder, group, or nominee that it suspects is materially false or misleading.[760] The commenter asserted that this type of expensive and time-consuming litigation likely would undermine the Commission's goals for the rule. Some commenters believed that the appropriate standard would be the standard in Rule 14a-8(l)(2) and Rule 14a-7(a)(2)(i): "the company is not responsible for the contents of [the shareholder proponent's] proposal or supporting statement."[761] Other commenters recommended generally that the Commission allow companies to provide certain disclaimers in their proxy materials regarding the statements provided by the nominating shareholder or group,[762] with one commenter suggesting that companies also should be able to set the nominating shareholder's or group's statements apart from their own statements by using different fonts, colors, graphics or other visual devices.[763]

Two commenters addressed the issue of a company's liability for disclosure provided by a nominating shareholder or group that is determined to be materially false or misleading after the proxy materials have been sent.[764] One commenter stated that companies should not have liability for failing to correct or recirculate proxy materials if, after the company mails its proxy materials, it is notified (or learns) that the information provided by a nominating shareholder or group is (or has become) materially false or misleading.[765] The commenter noted that the burden of updating and correcting information provided by a nominating shareholder or group should be solely the obligation of that shareholder or group. Another commenter provided similar views, noting that "[i]n situations where the registrant's changes have not been permitted, and certainly after the proxy materials have been published, we think the burden [of correcting or recirculating proxy materials] should be on the nominating shareholder and that the exception imposing liability on the registrant should not apply."[766] One commenter recommended that if Rule 14a-11 is adopted, the rule should state that liability is only attached when "the company knows or is grossly negligent in not knowing that the information is false or misleading."[767] Another commenter asked that the company be liable for false and

---

[756] *See* letters from ABA; Alaska Air; American Bankers Association; Ameriprise; BorgWarner; BRT; Caterpillar; Cleary; DTE Energy; ExxonMobil; Honeywell; ICI; Protective; S. Quinlivan; Seven Law Firms; Sidley Austin; Society of Corporate Secretaries; Southern Company; UnitedHealth; Verizon.

[757] *See* letters from American Bankers Association; Ameriprise; BorgWarner; BRT; Caterpillar; ExxonMobil; Honeywell; S. Quinlivan; UnitedHealth; Verizon.

[758] *See* letters from Alaska Air; BorgWarner; BRT; DTE Energy; Protective; Seven Law Firms; Society of Corporate Secretaries.

[759] *See* letters from Alaska Air; BorgWarner; BRT; DTE Energy; Protective; Seven Law Firms; Sidley

Austin; Society of Corporate Secretaries; Southern Company; United Health; Verizon.

[760] *See* letter from ABA.

[761] *See* letters from ABA; BorgWarner; BRT; Caterpillar; Society of Corporate Secretaries; Southern Company.

[762] *See* letters from Alaska Air; BorgWarner; BRT; ICI; Protective.

[763] *See* letter from BRT.

[764] *See* letters from ABA; Sidley Austin.

[765] *See* letter from ABA.

[766] Letter from Sidley Austin.

[767] *See* letter from Ameriprise.

misleading information provided by a nominating shareholder or group only if it knew the information was false or misleading.[768]

After considering the comments, we are adopting the proposed provision stating that companies will not be responsible for information that is provided by the nominating shareholder or group under Rule 14a-11 and then repeated by the company in its proxy statement. This is the same standard used in Rule 14a-8. We modified the proposed provision in response to commenters to remove the reference to information that the company knows or has reason to know is false or misleading. We believe that the standard that currently is used in Rule 14a-8 is well understood and that it would add unnecessary confusion and create significant uncertainty for companies to alter the standard in the context of Rule 14a-11. Using the Rule 14a-8 standard also is consistent with our revision to Rule 14a-11 to remove as a basis for exclusion of a nominee that information in the Schedule 14N is false or misleading. Accordingly, the final rule contains express language providing that the company will not be responsible for information that is provided by the nominating shareholder or group under Rule 14a-11 and then reproduced by the company in its proxy statement.[769] A similar provision is included in an instruction to new Rule 14a-18 with regard to information that is provided by the nominating shareholder or group in connection with a nomination made pursuant to an applicable state or foreign law provision, or the company's governing documents.[770]

As noted above, commenters raised concerns about correcting or recirculating proxy materials and potential liability for failing to correct or recirculate proxy materials after learning that material a nominating shareholder or group provided is false or misleading. As discussed above, under the rules as adopted, a company will not be responsible for any information that is provided by the nominating shareholder or group under Rule 14a-11 and then reproduced by the company in its proxy statement—the nominating shareholder or group will have liability for that information. Accordingly, a company will not be required to recirculate or correct proxy materials if it learns that the materials provided to shareholders included false or misleading information from the nominating shareholder or group.

Under the Proposal, any information provided to the company in the notice from the nominating shareholder or group under Rule 14a-11 (and, as required, filed with the Commission by the nominating shareholder or group) and then included in the company's proxy materials would not be incorporated by reference into any filing under the Securities Act, the Exchange Act, or the Investment Company Act unless the company determines to incorporate that information by reference specifically into that filing.[771] A similar provision was proposed regarding information provided by the nominating shareholder or group in connection with a nomination made pursuant to an applicable state law provision or a company's governing documents.[772]

Those commenting on this provision stated that information provided by a nominating shareholder, group, or nominee should not be deemed to be incorporated by reference into Securities Act, Exchange Act or Investment Company Act filings,[773] but if it is, it should be treated as the responsibility of the nominating shareholder, group, or nominee rather than the company.[774]

We are adopting this provision as proposed.[775] To the extent the company does specifically incorporate the information by reference or otherwise adopt the information

---

[768] *See* letter from ICI.

[769] *See* Rule 14a-11(f).

[770] *See* Instruction to new Rule 14a-18. *See also* Note to proposed Rule 14a-19.

[771] *See* the Instruction to proposed Item 7(e) of Schedule 14A; Instruction to proposed Item 22(b)(18) of Schedule 14A.

[772] *See* the Instruction to proposed Item 7(f) of Schedule 14A; Instruction to proposed Item 22(b)(19) of Schedule 14A.

[773] *See* letters from ABA; CII; Protective.

[774] *See* letters from ABA; Protective.

[775] *See* the Instruction to Item 7(e) of Schedule 14A and Instruction to Item 22(b)(18) of Schedule 14A with regard to information provided in connection with a Rule 14a-11 nomination. *See* the Instruction to Item

as its own, however, we will consider the company's disclosure of that information as the company's own statements for purposes of the anti-fraud and civil liability provisions of the Securities Act, the Exchange Act, or the Investment Company Act, as applicable.

III. PAPERWORK REDUCTION ACT

A. Background

Certain provisions of the final rules contain "collection of information" requirements within the meaning of the Paperwork Reduction Act of 1995.[776] We published a notice requesting comment on the collection of information requirements in the Proposing Release for the rules, and we submitted these requirements to the Office of Management and Budget for review in accordance with the PRA.[777] The titles for the collections of information are:

(1) "Proxy Statements—Regulation 14A and Schedule 14A" (OMB Control No. 3235-0059);

(2) "Information Statements—Regulation 14C and Schedule 14C" (OMB Control No. 3235-0057);

(3) "Form ID" (OMB Control No. 3235-0328);

(4) "Schedule 14N";

(5) "Securities Ownership—Regulation 13D and 13G (Commission Rules 13d-1 through 13d-7 and Schedules 13D and 13G)" (OMB Control No. 3235-0145);

(6) "Form 8-K" (OMB Control No. 3235-0060); and

(7) "Rule 20a-1 under the Investment Company Act of 1940, Solicitations of Proxies, Consents, and Authorizations" (OMB Control No. 3235-0158).

These regulations, rules and forms were adopted pursuant to the Exchange Act and the Investment Company Act, among other statutes, and set forth the disclosure requirements for securities ownership reports filed by investors, proxy and information statements,[778] and current reports filed by companies to provide investors with the information they need to make informed voting or investing decisions. The hours and costs associated with preparing, filing, and sending these schedules and forms constitute reporting and cost burdens imposed by each collection of information. An agency may not conduct or sponsor, and a person is not required to respond to, a collection of information unless it displays a currently valid OMB control number. Compliance with the rules is mandatory. Responses to the information collection will not be kept confidential and there is no mandatory retention period for the information disclosed.

B. Summary of the Final Rules and Amendments

As discussed above in more detail, the final rules provide shareholders with two ways to more fully exercise their traditional state law rights to nominate and elect directors.

(Footnote Continued)

7(f) of Schedule 14A and Instruction to Item 22(b)(19) of Schedule 14A with regard to information provided in connection with a nomination made pursuant to applicable state law or a company's governing documents.

[776] 44 U.S.C. 3501 *et seq.*

[777] 44 U.S.C. 3507(d) and 5 CFR 1320.11.

[778] The proxy rules apply only to domestic companies with securities registered under Section 12 of the Exchange Act and to investment companies registered under the Investment Company Act. The number of annual reports by reporting companies may differ from the number of proxy and information statements filed with the Commission in any given year. This is because some companies are subject to reporting requirements by virtue of Section 15(d) of the Exchange Act, and therefore are not covered by the proxy rules. Also, some companies are subject to the proxy rules only because they have a class of debt registered under Section 12. These companies generally are not required to hold annual meetings for the election of directors. In addition, companies that are not listed on a national securities exchange or national securities association may not hold annual meetings and therefore would not be required to file a proxy or information statement.

First, new Exchange Act Rule 14a-11 will, under certain circumstances, require companies to include in their proxy materials shareholder nominees for director submitted by long-term shareholders or groups of shareholders with significant holdings. Rule 14a-11 will apply to all reporting companies subject to the Exchange Act proxy rules, with a few exceptions. Rule 14a-11 will apply only when applicable state or foreign law or a company's governing documents do not prohibit shareholders from nominating a candidate for election as a director. Further, Rule 14a-11 will not apply to companies subject to the proxy rules solely because they have a class of debt securities registered under Section 12 of the Exchange Act. Rule 14a-11 will apply to smaller reporting companies, but on a delayed basis. Consistent with the Proposal, companies are not able to "opt out" of the rule in favor of a different framework for including shareholder director nominees in company proxy materials. In addition, as was proposed, the rule will apply regardless of whether any specified event has occurred to trigger the rule and regardless of whether the company is subject to a concurrent proxy contest.

A nominating shareholder or group seeking to use Rule 14a-11 to require a company to include a nominee or nominees in the company's proxy materials will be required to meet certain conditions, including an ownership threshold and holding period and filing a Schedule 14N to provide required disclosures and certifications. Under the rule, a company will not be required to include a shareholder nominee or nominees for director in the company's proxy materials where the nominating shareholder or group holds the securities with the purpose, or with the effect, of changing control of the company or to gain a number of seats on the board of directors that exceeds the maximum number of nominees that the company could be required to include under Rule 14a-11. A company also will not be required to include a nominee submitted pursuant to Rule 14a-11 who does not meet the requirements of the rule. For example, a company would not be required to include a nominee if that nominee's candidacy, or if elected, board membership, would violate applicable federal law, state law, foreign law, or the rules of a national securities exchange or a national securities association (other than the rules related to director independence) and such violation could not be cured during the time period provided in the rule.[779]

Second, the new amendment to Exchange Act Rule 14a-8(i)(8)[780] will preclude a company from relying on Rule 14a-8(i)(8) to exclude from its proxy materials shareholder proposals by qualifying shareholders seeking to establish procedures under a company's governing documents for the inclusion of one or more shareholder nominees in a company's proxy materials including, for example, proposals to allow lower ownership thresholds or higher numbers of shareholder director nominees.[781]

In connection with Rule 14a-11 and the amendment to Rule 14a-8(i)(8), we also are adopting new rules that will require a notice to be filed with the Commission on new Schedule 14N, and transmitted to the company, when a shareholder seeks to submit a nomination to a company pursuant to Rule 14a-11 or pursuant to applicable state or foreign law provision or the company's governing documents.[782] The Schedule 14N will require a nominating shareholder or group to provide disclosure similar to the disclosure currently required in a contested election. The company will be required to include the disclosure provided by the nominating shareholder or group in its proxy materials. Thus, the new rules will require a company to provide additional disclosure on Schedules 14A

---

[779] For an additional discussion of the Rule 14a-11 eligibility requirements, *see* Section II.B.4 above.

[780] Exchange Act Rule 14a-8 requires a company to include a shareholder proposal in its Schedule 14A unless the shareholder has not complied with the procedural requirements in Rule 14a-8 or the proposal falls within one of the 13 substantive bases for exclusion in Rule 14a-8, including Rule 14a-8(i)(8).

[781] In this regard, we note that to the extent that a shareholder proposal seeks to establish a procedure for the inclusion of shareholder nominees for director in a

company's proxy materials, generally any such proposal adopted by shareholders would not affect the availability of Rule 14a-11. To the extent that a proposal seeks to restrict shareholder reliance on Rule 14a-11, the proposal would be subject to exclusion pursuant to Rule 14a-8(i)(2) because it would cause the company to violate federal law or pursuant to Rule 14a-8(i)(3) because the proposal would be contrary to the proxy rules.

[782] *See* Sections II.B.8 and II.C.5 above.

and 14C,[783] as well as Form 8-K, and a nominating shareholder or group to provide disclosure on new Schedule 14N.

When filed in connection with Rule 14a-11, Schedule 14N requires disclosure about the amount and percentage of securities entitled to be voted on the election of directors by the nominating shareholder or group and the length of ownership of such securities. Schedule 14N also requires disclosure similar to the disclosure currently required for a contested election and disclosure of whether the nominee satisfies the company's director qualifications.[784] Schedule 14N also requires a certification that the nominating shareholder or group is not holding any of the company's securities with the purpose, or with the effect, of changing control of the company or to gain a number of seats on the board of directors that exceeds the maximum number of nominees that the company could be required to include under Rule 14a-11. A nominating shareholder or group also will be required to certify that the nominating shareholder or group and the nominee satisfy the applicable requirements of Rule 14a-11.

When a Schedule 14N is filed in connection with a nomination pursuant to an applicable state or foreign law provision or a company's governing documents providing for the inclusion of one or more shareholder director nominees in company proxy materials, the Schedule 14N requires similar, but more limited, disclosures than a Schedule 14N filed in connection with a nomination pursuant to Rule 14a-11.[785] In addition, a nominating shareholder or group filing a Schedule 14N in connection with a nomination submitted for inclusion in a company's proxy materials pursuant to applicable state or foreign law or a company's governing documents will be required to provide a more limited certification than is required for a nomination pursuant to Rule 14a-11.[786]

We also are adopting two new exemptions from the proxy rules for solicitations by a shareholder or group in connection with a nomination pursuant to Rule 14a-11.[787] The first exemption addresses written and oral solicitations by shareholders that are seeking to form a nominating shareholder group, provided that certain requirements are met.[788] The second new exemption will apply to written and oral solicitations by or on behalf of a nominating shareholder or group that has met the requirements of Rule 14a-11 in favor of shareholder nominees or for or against company nominees.[789] Each of these new exemptions requires the shareholder or group soliciting in connection with a nomination pursuant to Rule 14a-11 to file under cover of Schedule 14N any written materials published, sent or given to shareholders no later than the date such materials are first published, sent or given to shareholders. In addition, persons relying on Rule 14a-2(b)(7) to commence oral solicitations must file a notice of such solicitation under cover of Schedule 14N.

C. Summary of Comment Letters and Revisions to Proposal

We requested comment on the PRA analysis in the Proposing Release. Three commenters addressed our estimate of 30 burden hours for a company that is associated with including a nominee in its proxy materials.[790] According to a survey that BRT

---

[783] Schedule 14A prescribes the information that a company with a class of securities registered under Exchange Act Section 12, or a person soliciting shareholders of such a company, must include in its proxy statement to provide shareholders with material information relating to voting decisions.

Schedule 14C prescribes the information that a company with a class of securities registered under Exchange Act Section 12 must include in its information statement in advance of a shareholders' meeting when it is not soliciting proxies from its shareholders, including when it takes corporate action by written authorization or consent of shareholders.

Investment Company Act Rule 20a-1 requires registered investment companies to comply with Exchange Act Regulation 14A or 14C, as applicable.

The annual responses to Investment Company Act Rule 20a-1 reflect the number of proxy and information statements that are filed by registered investment companies.

[784] See Item 5 of Schedule 14N.

[785] See Item 6 of Schedule 14N.

[786] See Item 8(b) of Schedule 14N.

[787] For further discussion of these exemptions, see Section II.B.10 above.

[788] See new Rule 14a-2(b)(7).

[789] See new Rule 14a-2(b)(8).

[790] See letters from BRT; S&C; Society of Corporate Secretaries. In response to these comments, we have increased some of our burden estimates. See footnotes 815 and 817 below.

conducted, two commenters noted that if a company determines that it will include a shareholder nominee, the costs of preparing a written notice to the nominating shareholder or group, as well as including in the company's proxy materials the name of, and other disclosures concerning, the nominee, and preparing the company's own statement regarding the shareholder nominee would require a total of an average of 99 hours of company personnel time and outside costs of $1,159,073 per company for each shareholder nominee.[791] One commenter asserted that we underestimated the burden associated with these three actions because our estimate did not account for the fact that a company or its corporate governance committee is likely to undertake a lengthy process before determining whether to support the candidate.[792] This commenter asserted that our estimate began only once a company has already determined to include the nominee, and did not account for the amount of time necessary for a company to fully and completely evaluate shareholder nominees. This would include, for example, determinations about the nominee's eligibility, investigation and verification of information provided by the nominee, research into the nominee's background, analysis of the relative merits of the shareholder nominee as compared to management's own nominees, multiple meetings of the relevant board committees, and analysis of whether a nomination would conflict with any federal law, state law or director qualification standards.

The commenter asserted that our burden estimate of 65 hours for a company that determines not to include a nominee in its proxy materials does not account for "significant" costs and the "enormous" amount of time that management and the board will likely spend on the proxy contest itself.[793] The commenter also indicated that our estimates did not account for the burdens on registered investment companies as a result of their unique circumstances. The commenter noted that subjecting registered investment companies to Rule 14a-11 will result in significant administrative burdens on open-end funds and fund complexes, and increased costs. This commenter, however, did not provide alternative cost estimates. Another commenter questioned our assumption that the cost of submitting a no-action request pursuant to Rule 14a-11 is comparable to that of a no-action request submitted pursuant to Rule 14a-8.[794] This commenter argued that due to the fundamental issues at stake, boards will likely expend significantly more resources to challenge shareholder nominees and elect their own nominees than they will to oppose a shareholder proposal submitted pursuant to Rule 14a-8.

One commenter submitted the results of a survey it conducted in which the participants predicted that, on average, 15% of companies listed on U.S. exchanges could expect to face a shareholder director nomination under Rule 14a-11 in 2011.[795] As explained in greater detail below, we believe the actual number of shareholders or groups of shareholders that will seek to use Rule 14a-11 may be much smaller. While we note that there are inherent uncertainties involved in providing this estimate, we estimate for purposes of the PRA requirements, based on available data on the number of contested elections, that 45 companies other than registered investment companies and six registered investment companies with shareholders eligible to submit nominees pursuant to Rule 14a-11 will receive such a nomination each year.

D. Revisions to PRA Reporting and Cost Burden Estimates

As discussed above, the rules we are adopting include several substantive modifications to the Proposal; however, the Schedule 14N disclosure requirements we are adopting are substantially similar to the proposed disclosure requirements. In addition to the disclosure we proposed to be included in Schedule 14N, the schedule also will require disclosure of whether the shareholder nominee satisfies the company's director qualifications.[796] As discussed more fully below, we are revising our estimates in response to

---

[791] *See* letters from BRT; Society of Corporate Secretaries.

[792] *See* letter from S&C.

[793] *Id.*

[794] *See* letter from BRT.

[795] *See* letter from Altman. The survey had 47 participants that were primarily issuers. The median forecast of this survey was 10%. The survey was based on the eligibility criteria contained in the Proposing Release.

[796] *See* Item 5(e) of Schedule 14N.

commenters' suggestions and the modifications to the Proposal that we are adopting in the final rules. The burden estimates discussed below relate to the hours and costs associated with preparing, filing and sending the above schedules and forms, and constitute estimates of reporting and cost burdens imposed by each collection of information.

For purposes of the PRA, we estimate the total annual incremental paperwork burden resulting from new Rule 14a-11 and the related rule changes for reporting companies (other than registered investment companies) and registered investment companies to be approximately 4,113 hours of internal company or management time and a cost of approximately $548,200 for the services of outside professionals.[797] For purposes of the PRA, we estimate the total annual incremental paperwork burden to nominating shareholders and groups from Schedule 14N to be approximately 7,870 hours of shareholder personnel time, and $1,049,300 for services of outside professionals. As discussed further below, these total costs include all additional disclosure burdens associated with the final rules, including burdens related to the notice and disclosure requirements. The total costs described above also include the burden hours resulting from the new exemptions for solicitations by nominating shareholders or groups in connection with a nomination pursuant to Rule 14a-11.[798] As noted above, smaller reporting companies will not be subject to Rule 14a-11 until three years after the effective date of the rule. For purposes of the PRA, we have calculated the burden estimates as if the rule has been fully phased in for all companies.

As amended, Rule 14a-8(i)(8) will no longer permit companies to exclude, under that basis, shareholder proposals that seek to establish a procedure under a company's governing documents for the inclusion of one or more shareholder director nominees in the company's proxy materials. For purposes of the PRA, we estimate the total annual incremental paperwork burden resulting from the amendment to Rule 14a-8(i)(8) and the related rule changes for reporting companies (other than registered investment companies), registered investment companies, and shareholders to be approximately 17,994 hours of internal company or shareholder time and a cost of approximately $2,399,200 for the services of outside professionals.[799]

1. Rule 14a-11

New Rule 14a-11 will require any company subject to the rule to include disclosure about a nominating shareholder's or group's nominee or nominees for election as director in the company's proxy statement, and the name of the nominee or nominees on the company's proxy card, when the conditions of the rule are met. The rule will not apply if the company is subject to the proxy rules solely as a result of having a class of debt registered under Section 12 of the Exchange Act or if state law, foreign law or a company's governing documents prohibit shareholders from nominating a candidate or candidates for election as director. A nominating shareholder or group will be required to file Schedule 14N to disclose information about the nominating shareholder or group and the nominee or nominees, and the company will be required to include certain information regarding the nominating shareholder or group and nominee or nominees in the company's proxy statement unless the company determines that it is not required to include the nominee or nominees in its proxy materials.[800] A nominating shareholder or group also will be afforded the opportunity to include in the company's proxy statement a statement of support for its nominee or nominees not to exceed 500 words per nominee.

---

[797] For convenience, the estimated PRA hour burdens have been rounded to the nearest whole number. We estimate an hourly cost of $400 for the service of outside professionals based on our consultations with several registrants and law firms and other persons who regularly assist registrants in preparing and filing proxy statements and related disclosures with the Commission.

[798] See new Rules 14a-2(b)(7) and 14a-2(b)(8).

[799] This corresponds to 6,510 hours of shareholder time and $868,000 for the shareholders' use of outside professionals and 11,484 hours of company time and $1,531,200 for the company's use of outside professionals.

[800] The burdens associated with Schedule 14N are discussed below.

The nominee or nominees also will be included on the company's form of proxy in accordance with Exchange Act Rule 14a-4.

Under the final rule, shareholders or groups owning at least 3% of the voting power of a company's securities entitled to be voted on the election of directors for at least three years as of the date of filing their notice on Schedule 14N with the Commission, and transmitting the notice to the company, will be eligible to submit a nominee for election as director to be included in the company's proxy materials,[801] provided certain other eligibility requirements are met[802] and subject to certain limitations on the overall number of shareholder nominees for director.

In the Proposing Release, we estimated that 208 companies with eligible shareholders would receive nominations pursuant to Rule 14a-11. That number was based in part on data, which we used to estimate that approximately 4,163 reporting companies (other than registered investment companies) would have at least one shareholder who met the eligibility criteria set forth in the Proposing Release. We then estimated that 5% of those companies would receive a nomination from an eligible shareholder or group of shareholders, resulting in 208 companies receiving nominations pursuant to Rule 14a-11 annually.[803] In the Proposing Release, we also estimated that 61, or 5%, of 1,225 registered investment companies responding to Rule 20a-1 each year would receive shareholder nominations for inclusion in their proxy materials. After further consideration, we believe that a better indicator of how many shareholders might submit a nomination is the number of contested elections and board-related shareholder proposals that have been submitted to companies.[804] We believe starting with this number is better because it indicates shareholders or groups of shareholders who have shown an interest in using currently available means under our rules to influence governance matters. The number of contested elections and board-related shareholder proposals, however, does not reflect the additional eligibility requirements that are being adopted in new Rule 14a-11. For example, Rule 14a-11 requires that a shareholder or group of shareholders satisfy an ownership threshold of at least 3% of the company's voting power; that amount of securities must have been held continuously for at least three years as of the date the nominating shareholder or group submits notice of its intent to use Rule 14a-11; and the nominating shareholder or group must execute a certification that it is not holding the securities with the purpose, or with the effect, of changing control of the company or to gain a number of board seats that exceeds the maximum number of nominees that the company could be required to include under Rule 14a-11. As a result of the additional eligibility requirements and certifications required by Rule 14a-11, we believe it is reasonable to significantly reduce the number of contested elections and board-related shareholder proposals for purposes of estimating the number of shareholders or groups of

---

[801] *See* Section II.B.4.b. above for a discussion of how voting power is determined.

[802] The eligibility requirements are provided in Rule 14a-11(b). As discussed in more detail in Section II.B.4., a nominating shareholder or group must not be holding the securities used to meet the ownership threshold with the purpose, or with the effect, of changing the control of the company or to gain a number of seats on the board of directors that exceeds the maximum number of nominees that the company could be required to include under Rule 14a-11. A nominating shareholder or group also must provide certain statements and disclosure regarding its ownership and the nominee or nominees must meet the applicable eligibility requirements.

[803] If we used the same data for estimating the number of nominees that would be submitted pursuant to the final rules as adopted, there would be approximately 2,117 companies with at least one shareholder eligible to submit a nomination. If we were to assume that 5% of those companies with at least one share-

holder eligible to submit a nomination would receive a nomination, then we would estimate that 106 companies would receive a nomination each year.

[804] In this regard, we note that it is estimated that there were 57 contested solicitations in 2009. *See* Georgeson, 2009 Annual Corporate Governance Review Executive Summary (*available at* http://www.georgeson.com/usa/acgr09.php) and footnote 828 below. In addition, approximately 118 Rule 14a-8 shareholder proposals related to board issues were submitted to shareholders for a vote in the 2008-2009 proxy season. Board related proposals include proposals to have an independent chairman of the board, proposals to allow for cumulative voting and proposals to require a majority vote to elect directors. *See* Risk-Metrics 2009 Proxy Season Scorecard, May 15, 2009. We believe these actions related to contested solicitations or board issues, 175 in total, provide useful information about the degree of interest in using Rule 14a-11.

shareholders who may submit a nomination pursuant to Rule 14a-11. For purposes of this analysis, we estimate that 45 companies other than registered investment companies will receive nominees from shareholders[805] for inclusion in their proxy materials.[806] We further estimate that six registered investment companies will receive nominees from shareholders pursuant to Rule 14a-11 annually.[807]

We estimate for PRA purposes that each company that receives nominees pursuant to Rule 14a-11 will receive two nominees from one shareholder or group. The median board size based on a 2007 sample of public companies was nine.[808] Approximately 60% of the boards sampled had between nine and 19 directors. In the case of registered investment companies, we estimate that the median board size is eight.[809] Thus, although some shareholders or groups could seek to include fewer than two nominees and others would be permitted to include more than two nominees, depending on the size of the board, we assume for purposes of the PRA that each shareholder or group would submit two nominees. As a result, for reporting companies, we estimate up to 211 total company burden hours per company (which is the sum of the bullets below doubled where appropriate to reflect two nominees) which corresponds to 158 hours (211 x 0.75) of company time, and a cost of approximately $21,100 (211 x 0.25 x $400) for the services of outside professionals. In each case, this estimate includes:

- if the company determines that it will include a shareholder nominee, the company's preparation of a written notice to the nominating shareholder or group (five burden hours per notice);

- the company's inclusion in its proxy statement and form of proxy of the name of, and other related disclosures concerning, a person or persons nominated by a shareholder or shareholder group (five burden hours per nominee);[810]

- the company's preparation of its own statement regarding the shareholder nominee or nominees (40 burden hours per nominee); and

---

[805] We further estimate that 75% of the 45 submissions, or 34, will be made by groups of shareholders, and the remaining 11 will be made by individuals. *See* the discussion below regarding the estimated increase in Schedule 13G filings.

[806] For the reasons noted above, we discounted the 175 contested elections and board-related shareholder proposals by approximately 75% to reflect the much more stringent eligibility requirements under new Rule 14a-11 as compared to Rule 14a-8. The 45 filings that we estimate for purposes of the PRA are equal to 2.1% of the 2,117 companies we estimate to have at least one eligible shareholder meeting the ownership requirements of the rule.

[807] In this regard, we estimate that there were 11 contested elections in 2009, based on the number of EDGAR filings on form-type PREC14A with respect to unique investment companies in 2009. In addition, the average number of no-action letters issued by the staff regarding proposals seeking to amend a registered investment company's bylaws to provide for shareholder director nominations received in calendar years 2007, 2008 and 2009, rounded to the nearest whole number greater than zero, is one. We estimate that investment companies currently receive as many proposals regarding nomination procedures or disclosures as there are contested elections and no-action letters issued by the staff, resulting in a total of 24 contested elections and board-related shareholder proposals per year. For reasons similar to those articulated above for non-investment companies, we believe these actions related to contested solicitation or board issues, 24 in

total, provide useful information about the degree of interest in using Rule 14a-11. However, as discussed above, Rule 14a-11 contains different eligibility requirements than our current rules that will likely result in fewer companies receiving nominations submitted pursuant to the rule. Similar to non-investment companies, we believe it is reasonable to discount the 24 contested elections and board-related shareholder proposals by approximately 75%, resulting in six investment companies receiving nominations pursuant to Rule 14a-11. We further estimate that 75% of the submissions, or five, will be made by groups of shareholders and the remaining one will be made by an individual. *See* the discussion below regarding the estimated increase in Schedule 13G filings.

[808] According to information from RiskMetrics, based on a sample of 1,431 public companies the median board size in 2007 was 9, with boards ranging in size from 4 to 23 members. Approximately 40% of the boards in the sample had 8 or fewer directors, approximately 60% had between 9 and 19 directors, and less than 1% had 20 or more directors.

[809] *See* Investment Company Institute and Independent Directors Council, *Overview of Fund Governance Practices 1994-2006*, at 6-7 (November 2007), *available at* http://www.ici.org/pdf/rpt_07_fund_gov_practices.pdf (noting that the median number of independent directors per fund complex in 2006 was six and that independent directors held 75% or more of board seats in 88% of fund complexes).

[810] The requirement is in amended Rule 14a-4.

- if a company determines that it may exclude a shareholder nominee submitted pursuant to the new rule, the company's preparation of a written notice to the nominating shareholder or group followed by written notice of the basis for its determination to exclude the nominee to the Commission staff (116 burden hours per notice).[811]

For purposes of this PRA analysis, we assume that approximately 41 (or 90% of 45) reporting companies (other than registered investment companies) and 5 (or 90% of 6) registered investment companies that receive a shareholder nominee for director will be required to include the nominee in their proxy materials. In the other 10% of cases, we assume that the company will be able to exclude the shareholder nominee (after providing notice of its reasons to the Commission). If a company determines to include a shareholder nominee, it must provide written notice to the nominating shareholder or group. We estimate the burden associated with preparing this notice to be five hours. For reporting companies (other than registered investment companies), this will result in 205 aggregate burden hours (41 companies x 5 hours/company), which corresponds to 154 burden hours of company time (41 companies x 5 hours/company x 0.75) and $20,500 in services of outside professionals (41 companies x 5 hours/company x 0.25 x $400). For registered investment companies, this will result in 25 aggregate burden hours (5 companies x 5 hours/company), which corresponds to 19 burden hours of company time (5 companies x 5 hours/company x 0.75), and $2,500 for services of outside professionals (5 companies x 5 hours/company x 0.25 x $400).

We estimate the annual disclosure burden for companies to include nominees and related disclosure in their proxy statements and on their form of proxy to be 5 burden hours per nominee, for a total of 410 aggregate burden hours (41 responses x 5 hours/response x 2 nominees) for reporting companies (other than registered investment companies), and 50 aggregate burden hours (5 responses x 5 hours/response x 2 nominees) for registered investment companies. For reporting companies (other than registered investment companies), this corresponds to 308 burden hours of company time, and $41,000 for services of outside professionals.[812] For registered investment companies, this corresponds to 38 hours of company time, and $5,000 for services of outside professionals.[813]

We estimate that 41 reporting companies (other than registered investment companies) and 5 registered investment companies will include a statement with regard to the shareholder nominees.[814] We anticipate that the burden to include a statement will include time spent to research the nominee's background, determinations about the nominee's eligibility, investigation and verification of information provided by the nominee, analysis of the relative merits of the shareholder nominee as compared to management's own nominees, multiple meetings of the relevant board committees, analysis of whether a nomination will conflict with any federal law, state law or director qualification standards, preparation of the statement, and company time for review of the statement by, among others, the nominating committee and legal counsel. In the Proposing Release we estimated that this burden will be approximately 20 hours per nominee. Based on comments received, however, we believe it is appropriate to increase this estimate to 40 hours per nominee.[815] For reporting companies (other than registered

---

[811] As discussed below, for companies that exclude a nominee but do not request no-action relief, we estimate this burden to be 100 hours.

[812] The calculations for these numbers are: 410 burden hours x 0.75 = 308 burden hours of company time and 410 burden hours x 0.25 x $400 = $41,000 for services of outside professionals.

[813] The calculations for these numbers are: 50 burden hours x 0.75 = 38 hours of company time and 50 burden hours x 0.25 x $400 = $5,000 for services of outside professionals.

[814] We assume that each company that includes a shareholder nominee in its proxy materials would include such a statement.

[815] In its comment letter and based on its survey of its members, BRT estimated that the preparation of a notice to the nominating shareholder, inclusion of related disclosure in the company's proxy materials, and preparation of its own statement regarding the shareholder nominee will require an average of 99 hours of personnel time. In the Proposing Release, we estimated the burden for these three actions to be 30 hours. We note that the survey conducted by the BRT provides useful information regarding the amount of

investment companies), this will result in 3,280 aggregate burden hours (41 statements x 40 hours/statement x 2 nominees). This corresponds to 2,460 hours of company time (41 statements x 40 hours/statement x 2 nominees x 0.75) and $328,000 for services of outside professionals (41 statements x 40 hours/statement x 2 nominees x 0.25 x $400) for reporting companies (other than registered investment companies). For registered investment companies, this will result in 400 aggregate burden hours (5 statements x 40 hours/statement x 2 nominees). This corresponds to 300 hours of company time (5 statements x 40 hours/statement x 2 nominees x 0.75) and $40,000 for services of outside professionals (5 statements x 40 hours/statement x 2 nominees x 0.25 x $400).

Further, for purposes of this analysis, we assume that approximately 9 (or 20% of 45) reporting companies (other than registered investment companies) and 1 (or 20% of 6) registered investment companies that receive a shareholder nominee for director for inclusion in their proxy materials will make a determination that they are not required to include a nominee in their proxy materials because the requirements of Rule 14a-11 are not met and will file a notice of intent to exclude that nominee.[816] We further estimate that 3 (or 33% of 9) of those reporting companies (other than registered investment companies) will not seek no-action relief from the Commission and will only provide the required notice to the nominating shareholder or group and the Commission. We estimate that the remaining 6 reporting companies other than registered investment companies and the one registered investment company that makes a determination that it is not required to include a nominee in its proxy materials will seek no-action relief in order to exclude the nomination. We estimate that the burden hours associated with preparing and submitting the company's notice to the nominating shareholder or group and the Commission regarding its intent to exclude a shareholder nominee that includes a request for no-action relief would be 116 hours per notice.[817] We estimate that the burden hours associated with preparing and submitting the company's notice to the nominating shareholder or group and the Commission regarding its intent to exclude a

---

(Footnote Continued)

personnel time that a company will spend responding to a Rule 14a-11 nomination, however, the survey represents a limited number of companies. While we are persuaded that the burden to companies of preparing a statement with regard to the shareholder nominee may require more than the 20 hours we estimated in the Proposing Release, we believe that 99 hours may represent the high end of the range. In light of this information, we believe it is appropriate to increase our estimate and we believe it is adequate to double our estimate of this component from 20 to 40 hours to reflect the average burden across all companies. Thus, we estimate that the internal burden associated with these three actions would be 50 hours.

[816] With respect to companies other than registered investment companies, we assume that 6 of these submissions ultimately would be excludable under the rule.

[817] This estimate is based on data provided by the BRT in its comment letter dated August 17, 2009. In its letter, the BRT provided data from a survey of its own members indicating that the average burden associated with preparing and submitting a single no-action request to the Commission staff in connection with a shareholder proposal is approximately 47 hours and associated costs of $47,784. Although the letter did not specify as much, assuming these costs correspond to legal fees, which we estimate at an hourly cost of $400, we estimate that this cost is equivalent to approximately 120 hours ($47,784/$400). We note that this estimate is higher than the 65 hours we estimated in the Proposing

Release, where we relied on 2003 data provided by the American Society of Corporate Secretaries indicating 30 hours and associated costs of $13,896, or 35 hours ($13,896/$400). The BRT survey also indicated that if a company opposes a shareholder nominee, it would incur an additional average of 302 hours of company time. This would be in addition to its estimate of 99 hours for the actions described above. As noted above, the survey conducted by the BRT provides useful estimates for us to consider, but the survey represents a limited number of companies. In addition, it is unclear whether the 302 hours is inclusive of the no-action process. We believe this estimate is high and believe the revised number discussed below is a better estimate because it attempts to reflect the burden across all companies. For purposes of the PRA, we assume that submitting the notice and reasons for excluding a shareholder nominee to the staff will be comparable to preparing a no-action request to exclude a proposal under Rule 14a-8. While it appears, based on commenters' estimates, that associated costs may have increased since 2003, based on estimates provided by other commenters on the costs of preparing and submitting a no-action request (*see, e.g.*, letter from S&C), we believe an average of the two estimates provides a more representative estimate of the spectrum of reporting companies, as opposed to those who participated in the BRT survey. Thus, we estimate that the burden to submit the notice and reasons for excluding a shareholder nominee and request no-action relief would be approximately 116 hours ([167 hrs + 65 hrs]/2).

shareholder nominee and its reasons for doing so would be 100 hours.[818] One commenter questioned our assumption that submitting a request to the staff to exclude a shareholder nominee will be comparable to preparing a no-action request to exclude a proposal under Rule 14a-8.[819] This commenter argued that due to the fundamental issues at stake, boards are likely to expend significant resources to challenge shareholder nominees and elect their own nominees. We recognize the possibility that companies might expend greater resources in opposing a shareholder nominee than a shareholder proposal. We believe, however, that some of the resources to oppose a shareholder nominee will be allocated to the use of other means outside of the required disclosure in the proxy statement (*e.g.,* "fight letters") so we have not factored that into our collection of information estimate. We believe that a portion of the burden associated with this will be reflected in the company's preparation of its own statement regarding the shareholder nominee, rather than in the preparation of a no-action request, and accordingly, as discussed above, we have increased our estimate of the associated burden from 20 to 40 hours. Although we have increased the burden to the company associated with preparing its own statement, we are not persuaded that also increasing the burden associated with preparing a request to exclude the nominee will be an accurate estimate. We are, however, as discussed above, increasing to 116 hours our estimate for preparing a notice of intent to exclude the nominee and request no-action relief based on 2009 data received from commenters.[820]

In the case of reporting companies (other than registered investment companies) that have determined they may exclude a nominee and seek no-action relief from the staff, we estimate that this will result in an aggregate burden of 696 hours (6 notices x 116 hours/ notice), corresponding to 522 hours of company time (6 notices x 116 hours/notice x 0.75) and $69,600 for the services of outside professionals (6 notices x 116 hours/notice x 0.25 x $400). In the case of registered investment companies that have determined they may exclude a nominee and seeking no-action relief from the staff, we estimate that this will result in 116 aggregate burden hours (1 notice x 116 hours/notice), which will correspond to 87 hours of company time (1 notice x 116 hours/notice x 0.75) and $11,600 for the services of outside professionals (1 notice x 116 hours/notice x 0.25 x $400). For companies (other than registered investment companies) that have determined they may exclude a nomination but not to seek no-action relief from the staff, we estimate that this will result in an aggregate burden of 300 hours (3 notices x 100 hours/notice), corresponding to 225 hours of company time (3 notices x 100 hours/notice x 0.75) and $30,000 for the services of outside professionals (3 notices x 100 hours/ notice x 0.25 x $400).[821] These burdens would be added to the PRA burdens of Schedules 14A and 14C or, in the case of registered investment companies, Rule 20a-1.

We also estimate that the annual burden for the nominating shareholder's or group's participation in the no-action process[822] available pursuant to Rule 14a-11 would average 60 hours per nomination.[823] For nominating shareholders or groups of reporting companies (other than registered investment companies), this will result in 360 total

[818] We believe that even if a company is not seeking no-action relief the company will still spend significant time preparing its notice to exclude the nominee. Because the notice will be required to include the reasons that the nominee is being excluded, we believe that the burden will be similar to, though not quite as extensive as, preparing a request for no-action relief.

[819] *See* letter from BRT.

[820] Our prior estimate of 65 hours in the Proposing Release was based on 2003 data.

[821] As discussed above, we estimate that only one registered investment company will make a determination that it is not required to include a nominee in its proxy material and that this company will seek no-action relief.

[822] There is no corresponding burden for shareholders or groups whose nomination is excluded by the company, and the company does not seek no-action relief. If the shareholder objects to the exclusion, there is no requirement that the shareholder seek redress from the staff or the Commission. As a result, we have not provided an estimated burden.

[823] As noted in footnote 817, we estimate that the average burden to a company associated with preparing and submitting a no-action request to the staff is approximately 116 burden hours. We believe that the average burden for a shareholder proponent to respond to a company's no-action request is likely to be less than a company's burden to prepare the request; therefore, we estimate it will take approximately half the time (or 60 burden hours) for a nominating shareholder or group to respond to a company's notice to the Commission of its intent to exclude.

burden hours (6 responses x 60 hours/response). This will correspond to 270 hours of shareholder time (6 responses x 60 hours/response x 0.75) and $36,000 for services of outside professionals (6 responses x 60 hours/response x 0.25 x $400). For nominating shareholders or groups of registered investment companies, this will result in 60 total burden hours (1 response x 60 hours/response). This will correspond to 45 hours of shareholder time (1 response x 60 hours/response x 0.75) and $6,000 for services of outside professionals (1 response x 60 hours/response x 0.25 x $400). This burden would be added to the PRA burden of Schedule 14N.

We also are adopting two new exemptions from the proxy rules for solicitations by shareholders or groups in connection with a nomination pursuant to Rule 14a-11. The first exemption addresses written and oral solicitations by shareholders that are seeking to form a nominating shareholder group, provided that certain requirements are met.[824] Solicitations made in reliance on this exemption would be required to be filed under cover of Schedule 14N with the appropriate box marked on the cover page. As discussed above, we estimate that 34 of the submissions made to companies (other than registered investment companies) pursuant to Rule 14a-11 will be by groups of shareholders formed for purposes of satisfying the eligibility requirements of the rule. We estimate that 31 (90% of 34) of these groups will avail themselves of Rule 14a-2(b)(7). In the case of reporting companies (other than registered investment companies), this will result in an aggregate burden of 31 hours (31 solicitations x 1 hour/solicitation), which corresponds to 23 hours of shareholder time (31 solicitations x 1 hour/solicitation x 0.75) and $3,100 for the services of outside professionals (31 solicitations x 1 hour/solicitation x 0.25 x $400). In the case of registered investment companies, we estimate that five of the submissions made pursuant to Rule 14a-11 will be by groups of shareholders formed for purposes of satisfying the eligibility requirements of the rule. We estimate that all of these groups will avail themselves of Rule 14a-2(b)(7) (90% of 5 rounds up to 5). This will result in an aggregate burden of 5 hours (5 solicitations x 1 hour/solicitation), which corresponds to 4 hours of shareholder time (5 solicitations x 1 hour/solicitation x 0.75) and $500 for the services of outside professionals (5 solicitations x 1 hour/solicitation x 0.25 x $400). These burden hours would be added to the PRA burden of Schedule 14N.

The second new exemption will apply to written and oral solicitations by or on behalf of a nominating shareholder or group that has met the requirements of Rule 14a-11 in favor of shareholder nominees or for or against company nominees.[825] Although nominating shareholders or groups will not be required to engage in written solicitations, if the nominating shareholder or group does so, the exemption will require inclusion in any written soliciting materials filed under cover of Schedule 14N of a legend advising shareholders to look at the company's proxy statement when available and advising shareholders how to find the company's proxy statement. For purposes of this analysis, we assume that 50% of nominating shareholders or groups ultimately included in a company's proxy statement will solicit in favor of their nominee or nominees outside the company's proxy statement. In the case of reporting companies (other than registered investment companies), this will result in an aggregate burden of 20 hours (20 solicitations x 1 hour/solicitation), which corresponds to 15 hours of shareholder time (20 solicitations x 1 hour/solicitation x 0.75) and $2,000 for services of outside professionals (20 solicitations x 1 hour/solicitation x 0.25 x $400). These burden hours would be added to the PRA burden of Schedule 14N. In the case of registered investment companies, this will result in an aggregate burden of 3 hours (3 solicitations x 1 hour/solicitation), which corresponds to 2 hours of shareholder time (3 solicitations x 1 hour/solicitation x 0.75) and $300 for services of outside professionals (3 solicitations x 1 hour/solicitation x 0.25 x $400). These burden hours would be added to the PRA burden of Schedule 14N.

2. Amendment to Rule 14a-8(i)(8)

Under our amendment to Rule 14a-8(i)(8), the election exclusion, a company will no longer be able to rely on this basis to exclude a shareholder proposal that seeks to

---

[824] *See* new Rule 14a-2(b)(7).   [825] *See* new Rule 14a-2(b)(8).

establish a procedure under a company's governing documents for the inclusion of one or more shareholder director nominees in the company's proxy materials. The shareholder proposal will have to meet the procedural requirements of Rule 14a-8 and not be subject to one of the substantive exclusions other than the election exclusion (*e.g.*, the proposal could be excluded if the shareholder proponent did not meet the ownership threshold under Rule 14a-8).

Historically, shareholders have made relatively few proposals relating to shareholder access to a company's proxy materials. The staff received 368 no-action requests from companies seeking to exclude shareholder proposals during the 2006-2007 fiscal year. Of these requests, only three (or approximately one percent) related to proposals for bylaw amendments providing for shareholder nominees to appear in the company's proxy materials. During the 2007-2008 fiscal year, the staff received 423 no-action requests to exclude shareholder proposals pursuant to Rule 14a-8. Of these no-action requests, six (or approximately two percent) related to proposals for bylaw amendments providing for shareholder nominees to appear in the company's proxy materials. During the 2008-2009 fiscal year, the staff received 365 no-action requests to exclude shareholder proposals pursuant to Rule 14a-8. Of these requests, seven related to shareholders' ability to have their nominee included in a company's proxy materials. One such request sought to exclude a proposal to directly amend a company's governing documents to permit shareholder director nominations; the remaining six no-action requests related to proposals requesting that the company reincorporate in North Dakota where the relevant state corporate law gives qualified shareholders the right to submit director nominees for inclusion in the company's proxy materials.[826] Although these reincorporation proposals did not seek to amend the companies' bylaws, by seeking reincorporation into North Dakota it appears they sought the ability for shareholders to have nominees included in a company's proxy materials. As of July 23, 2010, during the 2009-2010 fiscal year, the staff has received 353 no-action requests to exclude shareholder proposals pursuant to Rule 14a-8, none of which related to shareholders' ability to have their nominee included in a company's proxy materials. While we believe that these proposals are helpful in gauging the level of shareholder interest in nominating directors, because our amendment to Rule 14a-8(i)(8) narrows the scope of the exclusion and no longer permits companies to exclude certain proposals that are excludable under current Rule 14a-8(i)(8), and Rule 14a-11 as adopted includes meaningful eligibility standards, we believe there may be an increase in the number of shareholder proposals seeking to establish procedures under a company's governing documents for the inclusion of one or more shareholder nominees in a company's proxy materials to allow, for example, lower ownership thresholds or higher numbers of shareholder director nominees.

While the number of no-action requests the staff has received in the past is a useful starting point for the PRA analysis, other data also is helpful to gauge shareholder interest in nominating directors and to predict the anticipated impact on the number of proposals submitted pursuant to Rule 14a-8 that seek to establish procedures under a company's governing documents for the inclusion of one or more shareholder nominees in a company's proxy materials that otherwise would be excludable under current Rule 14a-8(i)(8). For example, based on publicly available information, from 2001 to 2005, there were, on average, 14 contested elections per year.[827] It is estimated that in 2009 there were at least 57 contested elections,[828] and in 2008 it is estimated that there were at

---

[826] *See* North Dakota Publicly Traded Corporations Act, N.D. Cent. Code § 10-35-08 (2009).

[827] *See* Lucian A. Bebchuk, *The Myth of the Shareholder Franchise*, 93 VA. L. REV. 675, 683 (2007) ("Bebchuk (2007)")(citing data from proxy solicitation firm Georgeson Shareholder). *See* footnote 314 in the Proposing Release.

[828] *See* Georgeson, 2009 Annual Corporate Governance Review (stating that as of the end of September

2009 it had tracked 57 formal proxy contests); *see also* RiskMetrics Group, 2009 Postseason Report Summary, A New Voice in Governance: Global Policymakers Shape the Road to Reform, October 2009, *available at* http://www.riskmetrics.com/docs/2009-postseason-report (noting that during the 2009 proxy season there were at least 39 proxy contests, and 36 negotiated settlements prior to a shareholder vote).

least 50 contested elections.[829] For purposes of the PRA, we believe that as a result of the amendment to Rule 14a-8(i)(8), shareholders may submit at least as many shareholder proposals to establish procedures under a company's governing documents for the inclusion of shareholder nominees for director in company proxy materials as there are contested elections. We believe that if shareholders are willing under the current proxy rules to put forth the expense and effort to wage a contest to put forth their own nominees in 57 instances, there may be a similar number of proposals submitted to companies pursuant to Rule 14a-8, as amended, because companies will no longer be permitted to exclude some proposals that currently are excludable under Rule 14a-8(i)(8). We also believe that some shareholders that have submitted proposals in the past with regard to other board issues will submit proposals seeking to establish procedures under a company's governing documents for the inclusion of shareholder nominees for director in company proxy materials. As noted in the Proposing Release, according to information from RiskMetrics, approximately 118 Rule 14a-8 shareholder proposals regarding board issues were submitted to shareholders for a vote in the 2008-2009 proxy season.[830] For purposes of the PRA, we estimate that approximately half of these shareholders may submit a proposal regarding procedures for the inclusion of shareholder nominees for director in company proxy materials, resulting in up to 59 proposals in lieu of proposals related to other board issues.[831]

In the case of reporting companies (other than registered investment companies), we believe that the amendment to Rule 14a-8(i)(8) may result in an increase of up to 64 (57 + 7 2009 shareholder proposals) proposals annually from 2009, and a total of 123 proposals (59 proposals + 57 + 7) to companies per year regarding procedures for the inclusion of shareholder nominees for director in company proxy materials.[832] We estimate the annual incremental burden for the shareholder to prepare the proposal to be 10 burden hours per proposal, for a total of 640 burden hours (64 proposals x 10 hours/proposal). This will correspond to 480 hours of shareholder time (64 proposals x 10 hours/proposal x 0.75) and $64,000 for the services of outside professionals (64 proposals x 10 hours/proposal x 0.25 x $400).[833]

We recognize that a company that receives a shareholder proposal has no obligation to submit a no-action request to the staff under Rule 14a-8. We anticipate that because the proposals that would be submitted pursuant to amended Rule 14a-8 could affect the composition of the company's board of directors, nearly all companies receiving such proposals would submit a written statement of its reasons for excluding the proposal to the staff. We estimate that there will be a total of 123 proposals per year regarding procedures for the inclusion of shareholder nominees in the company's proxy statement. This number includes the 64 (57 + 7) new proposals plus the 59 proposals submitted in lieu of other proposals. Thus, we estimate that 90% of the estimated 123 companies

---

[829] *See* letter from BRT (citing data from Georgeson, "2008 Annual Corporate Governance Review"). *See also* RiskMetrics Group, 2008 Postseason Report Summary, Weathering the Storm: Investors Respond to the Global Credit Crisis, October 2008, *available at* http://www.riskmetrics.com/docs/2008postseason_review_summary.

[830] *See* footnote 804 above.

[831] We note that we used this estimate in the Proposing Release and did not receive comment on it. *See* Section IV.C.2. of the Proposing Release. We acknowledge the possibility that the number of Rule 14a-8 proposals relating to director nomination procedures may decrease with shareholders' ability to submit a nominee for inclusion in company proxy materials pursuant to Rule 14a-11, but we believe that any decrease may be countered by an increase in shareholder proposals to establish company-specific requirements that are different than Rule 14a-11.

[832] The increase is calculated by adding the number of proxy contests in 2009 (57) plus the number of no-action requests received in 2009 regarding proposals seeking to amend a company's bylaws to provide for shareholder director nominations (seven). We have not included an estimated 59 proposals in this increase because we believe they will be submitted in lieu of other types of proposals (a shareholder is limited to submitting one shareholder proposal to each company).

[833] We note that this calculation is for incremental, not total, costs. One commenter estimated that the average approximate total cost for shareholders to include a Rule 14a-8 proposal was $30,000. *See* letter from CalPERS. Assuming these costs correspond to legal fees, which we estimate at an hourly cost of $400, we estimate that this cost will be equivalent to approximately 75 hours.

receiving proposals seeking to establish procedures under a company's governing documents for the inclusion of one or more shareholder nominees in a company's proxy materials will submit a written statement of their reasons for excluding the proposal to the staff and would seek no-action relief.

We estimate that companies would determine that they could exclude, and would seek staff concurrence through the no-action letter process for, 110 proposals (123 proposals x 90%) per proxy season. We estimate that the annual burden for the company's submission of a notice of its intent to exclude the proposal and its reasons for doing so would average 116 hours per proposal, for a total of 12,760 burden hours (110 proposals x 116 hours/proposal) for reporting companies (other than registered investment companies). This will correspond to 9,570 hours of company time (110 proposals x 116 hours/ proposal x 0.75) and $1,276,000 for the services of outside professionals (110 proposals x 116 hours/proposal x 0.25 x $400).

We also estimate that the annual burden for the proponent's participation in the Rule 14a-8 no-action process would average 60 hours per proposal, for a total of 6,600 burden hours (110 proposals x 60 hours/proposal).[834] This will correspond to 4,950 hours of shareholder time (110 proposals x 60 hours/proposal x 0.75) and $660,000 for services of outside professionals (110 proposals x 60 hours/proposal x 0.25 x $400). These burdens would be added to the PRA burden of Schedules 14A and 14C.

In the case of registered investment companies, we anticipate that the amendment to Rule 14a-8(i)(8) will result in an increase of 12 proposals annually, and a total of 24 proposals regarding procedures for the inclusion of shareholder nominees for director in company proxy materials to companies per year.[835] We estimate the annual incremental burden for the shareholder proponent to prepare the proposal to be 10 hours per proposal, for a total of 120 burden hours (12 proposals x 10 hours/proposal). This would correspond to 90 hours of shareholder time (12 proposals x 10 hours/proposal x 0.75) and $12,000 for the services of outside professionals (12 proposals x 10 hours/proposal x 0.25 x $400).

Similar to reporting companies other than investment companies, we assume that 90% of registered investment companies that receive a shareholder proposal seeking to establish procedures under a company's governing documents for the inclusion of one or more shareholder nominees in a company's proxy materials will determine that they may exclude the proposal from their proxy materials and request concurrence through the no-action letter process (so registered investment companies will seek to exclude 22 such proposals per proxy season). Also similar to reporting companies other than registered investment companies, we assume that the annual burden for the company's submission of a notice of its intent to exclude the proposal and its reasons for doing so would average 116 hours per proposal, for a total of 2,552 burden hours for registered investment companies (22 proposals x 116 hours/proposal). This corresponds to 1,914 hours of

---

[834] As noted in footnote 817 above, we estimate that the average burden to a company associated with preparing and submitting a no-action request to the staff was approximately 116 burden hours. As noted above in footnote 823, we estimate 60 burden hours for a shareholder proponent to respond to a company's notice of intent to exclude and request for no-action relief to the Commission. In this regard, we also estimate that the average incremental burden for a shareholder proponent to submit a shareholder proposal would be 10 hours. We note that one commenter estimated that the average approximate cost to shareholders of submitting a proposal is $30,000. See letter from CalPERS. We note that this commenter's estimate corresponds to the burden to shareholders of submitting a proposal, whereas our estimate of 60

burden hours corresponds to the burden to shareholders in responding to a company's no-action request.

[835] The increase is estimated based on the number of registered investment company proxy contests in calendar year 2009 (11) plus the average number of no-action letters issued by the staff regarding proposals seeking to amend a registered investment company's bylaws to provide for shareholder director nominations received in calendar years 2007, 2008, and 2009 rounded to the nearest whole number greater than zero (1). In addition, we estimate that investment companies currently receive as many proposals regarding nomination procedures or disclosures as there are contested elections and no-action letters issued by the staff, resulting in a total of an estimated 24 proposals regarding nomination procedures or disclosures related to director nominations to companies per year.

company time (22 proposals x 116 hours/proposal x 0.75) and $255,200 for the services of outside professionals (22 proposals x 116 hours/proposal x 0.25 x $400). We also estimate that the annual burden for the proponent's participation in the Rule 14a-8 no-action process would average 60 hours per proposal, for a total of 1,320 burden hours (22 proposals x 60 hours/proposal). This corresponds to 990 hours of shareholder time (22 proposals x 60 hours/proposal x 0.75) and $132,000 for the services of outside professionals (22 proposals x 60 hours/proposal x 0.25 x $400). These burdens would be added to the PRA burden of Rule 20a-1.

3. Schedule 14N and Exchange Act Rule 14a-18

Rule 14n-1 establishes a new filing requirement for the nominating shareholder or group, under which the nominating shareholder or group will be required to file notice of its intent to include a shareholder nominee or nominees for director pursuant to Rule 14a-11, applicable state law provisions, or a company's governing documents, as well as disclosure about the nominating shareholder or group and nominee or nominees on new Schedule 14N. New Schedule 14N was modeled after Schedule 13G, but with more extensive disclosure requirements than Schedule 13G. Schedule 14N will require, among other items, disclosure about the amount and percentage of securities owned by the nominating shareholder or group, the length of ownership of such amount, and a written statement that the nominating shareholder or group will continue to hold the securities through the date of the meeting.

In addition, Schedule 14N will contain the disclosure required to be included in the nominating shareholder's or group's notice to the company of its intent to require that the company include the shareholder's or group's nominee in the company's proxy materials pursuant to Rule 14a-11 or pursuant to applicable state or foreign law provisions or a company's governing documents. With regard to the latter, we are seeking to assure that nominating shareholders or groups that submit a shareholder nomination for inclusion in a company's proxy materials pursuant to applicable state or foreign law provisions or the company's governing documents also provide disclosure similar to the disclosure required in a contested election to give shareholders the information needed to make an informed voting decision.

Schedule 14N will require disclosures regarding the nature and extent of the relationships between the nominating shareholder or group, the nominee and the company or any affiliate of the company. Pursuant to Items 7(e)-(f) of Schedule 14A and, in the case of an investment company, Items 22(b)(18)-(19) of Schedule 14A, the company will be required to include certain information set forth in the shareholder's notice on Schedule 14N in its proxy materials. A nominating shareholder or group filing a Schedule 14N to provide disclosure when submitting a nominee for inclusion in a company's proxy materials pursuant to applicable state or foreign law provisions or the company's governing documents will not be required to provide certain statements and certifications required for nominating shareholders or groups using Rule 14a-11.

We estimate that compliance with the Schedule 14N requirements will result in a burden greater than Schedule 13G[836] but less than a Schedule 14A.[837] Therefore, we estimate that compliance with Schedule 14N will result in 47 hours per response per nominee submitted pursuant to Rule 14a-11.[838] We also note that the burden associated

---

[836] We currently estimate the burden per response for preparing a Schedule 13G filing to be 12.4 hours.

[837] We currently estimate the burden per response for preparing a Schedule 14A filing to be 101.5 hours and a Schedule 14C to be 102.62 hours.

[838] We estimate that the burden of preparing the information in Schedule 14N for a nominating shareholder or group would be 1/3 of the disclosures typically required by a Schedule 14A filing, which results in approximately 34 burden hours. For purposes of this analysis, we estimate that the 34 burden hours will be added to the 12.4 hours associated with filing a Schedule 13G, resulting in a total of approximately 47 burden hours. We estimate that 75% of the burden of preparation of Schedule 14N will be borne internally by the nominating shareholder or group, and that 25% will be carried by outside professionals. We believe the nominating shareholder or group will work with their nominee to prepare the disclosure and then have it reviewed by outside professionals.

with filing a Schedule 14N in connection with a nomination made pursuant to an applicable state or foreign law provision or the company's governing documents may be slightly less than a nomination made pursuant to Rule 14a-11 because certain disclosures, statements, and certifications will not be required (including a statement that the nominating shareholder will continue to own the amount of securities through the date of the meeting, disclosure about the nominating shareholder's or group's intent with respect to continued ownership of the securities after the election, the certifications that will be required to use Rule 14a-11 (such as the certification concerning lack of intent to change control or to gain a number of seats on the board that exceeds the maximum number of nominees that the company could be required to include under Rule 14a-11, or the certifications that the nominating shareholder or group and the nominee satisfy the requirements of Rule 14a-11), and a supporting statement from the nominating shareholder or group. Therefore, we estimate that compliance with Schedule 14N when a shareholder or group submits a nominee or nominees to a company pursuant to an applicable state or foreign law provision or the company's governing documents will result in 40 hours per response per nominee.

For purposes of the PRA, we estimate the total annual incremental burden for nominating shareholders or groups to prepare the disclosure that will be required under this portion of the final rules to be approximately 7,870 hours of shareholder time, and $1,049,300 for the services of outside professionals.[839] This estimate includes the nominating shareholder's or group's preparation and filing of the notice and required disclosure and, as applicable, certifications on Schedule 14N and filings related to new Rules 14a-2(b)(7) and 14a-2(b)(8).

We do not expect that every shareholder that meets the eligibility threshold to submit a nominee for inclusion in a company's proxy materials pursuant to Rule 14a-11, an applicable state or foreign law provision, or a company's governing documents will do so. As discussed above, we estimate that 45 reporting companies (other than registered investment companies) and 6 registered investment companies will receive notices of intent to submit nominees pursuant to Rule 14a-11. We anticipate that some companies will receive nominees from more than one shareholder or group, though, as discussed above, for purposes of PRA estimates, we assume companies with an eligible shareholder would receive two nominees from only one shareholder or group.

We estimate that compliance with the requirements of Schedule 14N submitted pursuant to Rule 14a-11 will require 4,230 burden hours (45 notices x 47 hours/notice x 2 nominees/shareholder) in aggregate each year for nominating shareholders or groups of reporting companies (other than registered investment companies), which corresponds to 3,173 hours of shareholder time (45 notices x 47 hours/notice x 2 nominees/shareholder x 0.75) and costs of $423,000 (45 notices x 47 hours/notice x 2 nominees/shareholder x 0.25 x $400) for the services of outside professionals. In the case of registered investment companies, we estimate that a nominating shareholder's or group's compliance with the requirements of Schedule 14N will require 564 burden hours (6 responses x 47 hours/response x 2 nominees) in aggregate each year, which corresponds to 423 hours of shareholder time (6 responses x 47 hours/response x 2 nominees x 0.75) and costs of $56,400 for the services of outside professionals (6 responses x 47 hours/response x 2 nominees x 0.25 x $400). Therefore, we estimate a total of 4,794 burden hours for all reporting companies, including investment companies, broken down into 3,596 hours of shareholder time and $479,400 for services of outside professionals.

We assume that all nominating shareholders or groups will prepare a statement of support for the nominee or nominees, and we estimate the disclosure burden for the nominating shareholder or group to prepare a statement of support for its nominee or nominees to be approximately 10 burden hours per nominee. In the case of companies

---

[839] This figure represents the aggregate burden hours attributed to Schedule 14N and is the sum of the burden associated with Schedules 14N submitted pursuant to Rule 14a-11, applicable state or foreign law provisions, and a company's governing documents.

other than registered investment companies, this results in an aggregate burden of 900 (45 statements x 10 hours/statement x 2 nominees/shareholder), which corresponds to 675 hours of shareholder time (45 statements x 10 hours/statement x 2 nominees/shareholder x 0.75) and $90,000 for services of outside professionals (45 statements x 10 hours/statement x 2 nominees/shareholder x 0.25 x $400) for shareholders of reporting companies (other than registered investment companies). For registered investment companies, this will result in an aggregate burden of 120 (6 statements x 10 hours/statement x 2 nominees/shareholder), which corresponds to 90 hours of shareholder time (6 statements x 10 hours/statement x 2 nominees/shareholder x 0.75) and $12,000 for services of outside professionals (6 statements x 10 hours/statement x 2 nominees/shareholder x 0.25 x $400). Therefore, we estimate a total of 1,020 burden hours for all reporting companies, including investment companies, broken down into 765 hours of shareholder time and $102,000 for services of outside professionals.

When a nominating shareholder or group submits a nominee or nominees to a company pursuant to an applicable state or foreign law provision or the company's governing documents, the nominating shareholder or group will be required to file a Schedule 14N to provide disclosure about the nominating shareholder or group and the nominee or nominees. As discussed, a company will be required to include certain disclosures about the nominating shareholder or group and the nominee or nominees in its proxy statement. As noted above, we estimate that the burden associated with filing a Schedule 14N in connection with a nomination made pursuant to an applicable state or foreign law provision or a company's governing documents is 40 hours per nominee. We also estimate that approximately 30 nominating shareholders or groups of reporting companies (other than registered investment companies) will submit a nomination pursuant to an applicable state or foreign law provision or a company's governing documents.[840] Thus, we estimate compliance with the requirements of Schedule 14N for nominating shareholders or groups submitting nominations pursuant to an applicable state or foreign law provision or the company's governing documents would result in 2,400 aggregate burden hours (30 notices x 40 hours/notice x 2 nominees/shareholder) each year for nominating shareholders or groups of reporting companies (other than registered investment companies), broken down into 1,800 hours of shareholder time (30 notices x 40 hours/notice x 2 nominees/shareholder x 0.75) and costs of $240,000 for the services of outside professionals (30 notices x 40 hours/notice x 2 nominees/shareholder x 0.25 x $400). In the case of registered investment companies, we estimate that approximately 12 nominating shareholders or groups will submit a nomination pursuant to an applicable state or foreign law provision or a company's governing documents.[841] We estimate that a nominating shareholder's or group's compliance with the requirements of Schedule 14N would result in 960 aggregate burden hours (12 notices x 40 hours/notice x 2 nominees/shareholder) each year, which corresponds to 720 hours of shareholder time (12 notices x 40 hours/notice x 2 nominees/shareholder x 0.75) and costs of $96,000 for the services of outside professionals (12 notices x 40 hours/notice x 2 nominees/shareholder x 0.25 x $400). Therefore, we estimate that the total burden hours would be 3,360

---

[840] As discussed above, according to information from RiskMetrics, approximately 118 Rule 14a-8 shareholder proposals regarding board issues were submitted to shareholders for a vote in the 2008-2009 proxy season. *See* footnote 804. We believe this data is a useful starting point for estimating the number of shareholders who may avail themselves of our new rules, including the use of Schedule 14N. Also as discussed above, we estimate that approximately half of these shareholders may submit a proposal pursuant to Rule 14a-8 regarding procedures for the inclusion of shareholder nominees for director in company proxy materials, resulting in 59 proposals. We believe the number of shareholders submitting nominees pursuant to a state or foreign law provision will be lower than the number of shareholders submitting proposals pur-

suant to Rule 14a-8. As a result, we estimate that approximately 30 shareholder proponents will submit nominations pursuant to applicable state or foreign law provisions or a company's governing documents.

[841] We estimate that approximately half of the 24 shareholders submitting proposals to registered investment companies regarding the inclusion of one or more shareholder nominees for director in company proxy materials will make submissions pursuant to applicable state or foreign law provisions or a company's governing documents. As a result, we estimate that approximately 12 shareholder proponents will submit to registered investment companies nominations pursuant to applicable state or foreign law provisions or a company's governing documents.

for all reporting companies, including investment companies, broken down into 2,520 hours of shareholder time and $336,000 for services of outside professionals.

We assume that all nominating shareholders or groups that submit a nominee or nominees pursuant to an applicable state or foreign law provision or a company's governing documents will prepare a statement of support for the nominee or nominees,[842] and we estimate the disclosure burden for the nominating shareholder or group to prepare a statement of support for its nominee or nominees to be approximately 10 burden hours per nominee. This results in an aggregate burden of 600 hours (30 statements x 10 hours/statement x 2 nominees/shareholder) for shareholders of reporting companies (other than registered investment companies), which corresponds to 450 hours of shareholder time (30 statements x 10 hours/statement x 2 nominees/shareholder x 0.75) and $60,000 for services of outside professionals (30 statements x 10 hours/statement x 2 nominees/shareholder x 0.25 x $400). For registered investment companies, this results in an aggregate burden of 240 hours (12 statements x 10 hours/statement x 2 nominees/shareholder), which corresponds to 180 hours of shareholder time (12 statements x 10 hours/statement x 2 nominees/shareholder x 0.75) and $24,000 for services of outside professionals (12 statements x 10 hours/statement x 2 nominees/shareholder x 0.25 x $400). This results in a total of 840 burden hours, broken down into 630 hours of shareholder time and $84,000 for the services of outside professionals.

4. Amendments to Exchange Act Form 8-K

Under Rule 14a-11, a nominating shareholder or group will be required to file with the Commission, and transmit to the company, a notice on Schedule 14N of its intent to require the company to include the nominating shareholder's or group's nominee in the company's proxy materials. The nominating shareholder or group must file and transmit the notice on Schedule 14N no earlier than 150, and no later than 120, calendar days before the anniversary of the date that the company mailed its proxy materials for the prior year's annual meeting. If the company did not hold an annual meeting during the prior year, or if the date of the meeting has changed more than 30 days from the prior year, then the nominating shareholder or group will be required to provide notice a reasonable time before the company mails its proxy materials, as specified by the company in a Form 8-K filed pursuant to new Item 5.08 of Form 8-K. The final rules also require a registered investment company that is a series company to file a Form 8-K disclosing the total number of the company's shares that are entitled to vote for the election of directors at the annual meeting of shareholders (or, in lieu of such an annual meeting, a special meeting of shareholders) as of the end of the most recent calendar quarter.[843]

For purposes of the PRA, we estimate that approximately 4% of reporting companies (other than registered investment companies) will be required to file a Form 8-K because the company did not hold an annual meeting during the prior year, or the date of the meeting has changed by more than 30 days from the prior year.[844] Based on our estimate that there are approximately 11,000 reporting companies (other than registered investment companies), this corresponds to 440 companies that will be required to file a Form 8-K. In accordance with our current estimate of the burden of preparing a Form 8-K, we estimate 5 burden hours to prepare, review and file the Form 8-K, for a total burden of 2,200 hours (440 filings x 5 hours/filing). This total burden corresponds to 1,650 hours of

---

[842] We are assuming for PRA purposes that any applicable state or foreign law provision or company's governing documents will allow for inclusion of such a statement by the nominating shareholder or group.

[843] The amendment to Rule 14a-8(i)(8) is not expected to impact Form 8-K, so the burden estimates solely reflect the burden changes resulting from new Item 5.08, including when a nomination is submitted pursuant to a company's governing documents or pursuant to applicable state law.

[844] Based on information obtained in 2003 from the Investor Responsibility Research Center, 3.75% of companies (other than registered investment companies) did not hold an annual meeting during the prior year or the date of the meeting changed by more than 30 days from the prior year. *See also* footnote 195 in the 2003 Proposal.

company time (440 filings x 5 hours/filing x 0.75) and $220,000 for services of outside professionals (440 filings x 5 hours/filing x 0.25 x $400).

In the case of registered investment companies, we estimate that, similar to reporting companies other than registered investment companies, 4% of registered closed-end management investment companies subject to Rule 14a-11 that are traded on an exchange would be required to file a Form 8-K because the company did not hold an annual meeting during the prior year or the date of the meeting has changed by more than 30 days from the prior year.[845] We estimate that approximately 625 of the 1,225 registered investment companies responding to Investment Company Act Rule 20a-1 are closed-end funds that are traded on an exchange, resulting in 25 closed-end funds that will be required to file Form 8-K for these purposes (625 registered closed end management investment companies x 0.04).[846] However, we estimate that few, if any, registered open-end management investment companies regularly hold annual meetings. Therefore, we estimate that 600 registered investment companies are not closed-end investment companies and will be required to file Form 8-K. This results in a total of 625 registered investment companies required to file Form 8-K (25 closed-end management investment companies + 600 other registered investment companies) and 3,125 burden hours (625 filings x 5 hours/filing). This total burden corresponds to 2,344 hours of company time (625 filings x 5 hours/filing x 0.75) and $312,500 for services of outside professionals (625 filings x 5 hours/filing x 0.25 x $400).[847] Adding the totals for reporting companies (other than registered investment companies) and registered investment companies results in a total burden of 5,325, which corresponds to 3,994 hours of company time and $532,500 for services of outside professionals. This includes the requirement for a registered investment company that is a series company to file a Form 8-K disclosing the total number of the company's shares that are entitled to vote for the election of directors at the annual meeting of shareholders (or, in lieu of such an annual meeting, a special meeting of shareholders) as of the end of the most recent calendar quarter.

5. Schedule 13G Filings

Shareholders will be permitted to aggregate holdings for purposes of meeting the eligibility threshold in Rule 14a-11 and therefore we anticipate that some groups of shareholders may beneficially own in the aggregate more than 5% of a voting class of an equity security registered pursuant to Section 12. In these circumstances, nominating shareholders will need to consider whether they have formed a group under Exchange Act Section 13(d)(3) and Rule 13d-5(b)(1) that is required to file beneficial ownership reports.[848] To the extent nominating shareholder groups exceed the 5% threshold and file a Schedule 13G, this will result in an increased number of Schedule 13G filings. With respect to reporting companies other than registered investment companies, we estimate that 25% (11) of the nominees submitted pursuant to Rule 14a-11 will be from shareholders who individually meet the eligibility thresholds (25% of 45), and 75% (34) will be from shareholder groups (75% of 45). We estimate that 75% of the 34 groups formed will exceed the 5% threshold and will file a Schedule 13G. As a result, we estimate that an additional 26 Schedule 13G filings will be made annually. The total burden associated with this increase in the number of filings is 322 burden hours (26 additional Schedule

---

[845] We believe that the percentage for registered closed-end investment companies will be similar to other reporting companies because such investment companies are traded on an exchange and are required to hold annual meetings of shareholders.

[846] We estimate that 1,225 registered investment companies hold annual meetings each year based on the number of responses to Rule 20a-1. Based on data provided by Lipper, the Commission estimates that approximately 625 registered closed-end management investment companies are traded on an exchange.

[847] Consistent with the current estimates for Form 8-K, we estimate that that 75% of the burden of prep-

aration of Form 8-K is carried by the company and that 25% of the burden of preparation of Form 8-K is carried by outside professionals at an average cost of $400 per hour. The burden includes disclosure of the date by which a nominating shareholder or group must submit the notice required by Rule 14a-11(c) as well as disclosure of net assets, outstanding shares, and voting.

[848] We recognize that each shareholder group will need to analyze its own facts and circumstances in order to determine whether it is required to file a Schedule 13G; however, we expect that most groups will file a Schedule 13G.

13Gs x 12.4 hours/schedule). This burden corresponds to 81 hours of shareholder time (26 additional Schedule 13Gs x 12.4 hours/Schedule x 0.25) and $96,720 for services of outside professionals (26 additional Schedule 13Gs x 12.4 hours/Schedule x 0.75 x $400).

With respect to registered investment companies, we estimate that approximately 3 (50% of 6) of the shareholder nominees will be submitted by shareholders of closed-end funds whose shareholders are required to file beneficial ownership reports under the Exchange Act.[849] We estimate that 25% (1) of the nominees for director of closed-end funds submitted pursuant to Rule 14a-11 will be from shareholders who individually meet the eligibility thresholds (25% of 3), and 75% (2) will be from shareholder groups (75% of 3). We estimate that 75% of the two groups formed to nominate directors of closed-end funds will exceed the 5% threshold and file a Schedule 13G. As a result, we estimate that an additional 2 Schedule 13G filings will be made annually (75% of two groups rounds up to two). The total burden associated with this increase in the number of filings is approximately 25 burden hours (2 additional Schedule 13Gs x 12.4 hours/ schedule). This burden corresponds to 6 hours of shareholder time (2 additional Schedule 13Gs x 12.4 hours/schedule x 0.25) and $7,440 for services of outside professionals (2 additional Schedule 13Gs x 12.4 hours/schedule x 0.75 x $400).

Adding the totals for reporting companies (other than registered investment companies) and registered investment companies results in a total burden of 347 hours, which corresponds to 87 hours of shareholder time and $104,160 for services of outside professionals.

6. Form ID Filings

Under Rule 14n-1 and Rule 14a-11, a shareholder who submits a nominee or nominees for inclusion in the company's proxy statement must provide notice on Schedule 14N to the company of its intent to require that the company include the nominee or nominees in the company's proxy materials. The notice on Schedule 14N must be filed with the Commission on the date the notice is transmitted to the company. We anticipate that some shareholders who submit a nominee or nominees for inclusion in a company's proxy materials will not previously have filed an electronic submission with the Commission and will file a Form ID. Form ID is the application form for access codes to permit filing on EDGAR. The final rules are not changing the form itself, but we anticipate that the number of Form ID filings may increase due to shareholders filing Schedule 14N when submitting a nominee or nominees for inclusion in its proxy materials pursuant to Rule 14a-11, applicable state or foreign law provisions, or a company's governing documents. We estimate that 90% of the shareholders who submit a nominee or nominees for inclusion in a company's proxy materials will not have filed previously an electronic submission with the Commission and will be required to file a Form ID. As noted above, we estimate that approximately 45 reporting companies (other than registered investment companies) and 6 registered investment companies will receive shareholder nominations submitted pursuant to Rule 14a-11. This corresponds to 46 additional Form ID filings (90% of 51). In addition, as noted above, we estimate that approximately 30 reporting companies (other than registered investment companies) and 12 registered investment companies will receive shareholder nominations submitted pursuant to an applicable state or foreign law provision or a company's governing documents. This corresponds to an additional 38 Form ID filings (90% of 42). As a result, the additional annual burden would be 13 hours (84 filings x 0.15 hours/filing).[850]

---

[849] Under Section 13(d) of the Exchange Act, only holders of equity securities of closed-end funds are required to file beneficial ownership reports with the Commission. Holders of open-end funds are not subject to this requirement. Previously, we estimated that approximately 625 (or slightly over 50%) of the 1,225 registered investment companies responding to Investment Company Act Rule 20a-1 are closed-end funds that are traded on an exchange. We estimate that the percentage of the shareholder nominees that will be submitted by shareholders of closed-end funds will be approximately equal to the percentage of closed-end funds that are traded on an exchange.

[850] We currently estimate the burden associated with Form ID is 0.15 hours per response.

For purposes of the PRA, we estimate that the additional burden cost resulting from the new rules will be zero because we estimate that 100% of the burden will be borne internally by the nominating shareholder or group.

E. Revisions to PRA Reporting and Cost Burden Estimates

Table 1 below illustrates the incremental annual compliance burden of the collection of information in hours and in cost for securities ownership reports filed by investors, proxy and information statements, and current reports under the Exchange Act. The burden was calculated by multiplying the estimated number of responses by the estimated average number of hours each entity spends completing the form. We estimate that 75% of the burden of preparation of the proxy and information statement and current reports is carried by the company internally, while 25% of the burden of preparation is carried by outside professionals at an average cost of $400 per hour. We estimate that 75% of the burden of preparation of Schedule 14N, any soliciting materials with regard to formation of a nominating shareholder group, and any soliciting materials regarding the nomination will be carried by the nominating shareholder or group internally and that 25% of the burden of preparation will be carried by outside professionals retained by the nominating shareholder or group. We estimate that 25% of the burden of preparation of Schedule 13G (for nominating shareholder groups that beneficially own more than 5% of a voting class of any equity security registered pursuant to Section 12) will be carried by the nominating shareholder or group internally and that 75% of the burden of preparation will be carried by outside professionals retained by the nominating shareholder or group. The portion of the burden carried by outside professionals is reflected as a cost, while the portion of the burden carried internally by the company and nominating shareholder or group is reflected in hours.

Table 1: Calculation of Incremental PRA Burden Estimates[*]

	Current Annual Responses (A)	Proposed Annual Responses (B)	Current Burden Hours (C)	Increase in Burden Hours (D)	Proposed Burden Hours (E)=C+D	Current Professional Costs (F)	Increase in Professional Costs (G)	Proposed Professional Costs =F+G
Sch 14A	7,300	7,300	671,970	16,370	688,340	$79,214,887	$2,182,590	$81,397,477
Sch 14C	680	680	631,152	1,819	632,971	$7,393,639	$242,510	$7,636,149
Sch 14N	0	162	0	7,870	7,870	$0	$1,049,300	$1,049,300
Form 8-K	115,795	116,860	493,436	3,994	497,430	$65,791,500	$532,500	$66,324,000
Form ID	65,700	65,784	9,855	13	9,868	$0	$0	$0
Sch 13G	12,500	12,528	35,577	87	35,664	$42,694,200	$104,160	$42,798,360
Rule 20a-1	1,225	1,225	142,958	3,438	146,396	$20,090,000	$458,300	$20,548,300
Total				33,591			$4,569,360	

*The incremental burden estimate for Rule 20a-1 includes the disclosure that would be required on Schedule 14A and 14C, discussed above, with respect to funds.

IV. COST-BENEFIT ANALYSIS

A. Background

The Commission is adopting new rules that, under certain circumstances, will require companies to include in their proxy materials shareholder nominees for director, as well as other disclosure regarding those nominees and the nominating shareholder or group. In addition, the new rules will require companies, under certain circumstances, to include in their proxy materials a shareholder proposal that seeks to establish a procedure in the company's governing documents for the inclusion of shareholder director nominees in the company's proxy materials. As a result, a company's proxy materials may be required, under certain circumstances, to provide shareholders with information about, and the ability to vote for, a shareholder nominee for director. The new rules will therefore facilitate shareholders' ability to exercise their traditional state law rights to nominate and elect directors by improving the disclosure provided in connection with corporate proxy solicitations and communication between shareholders in the proxy process.

We requested comment on all aspects of the cost-benefit analysis contained in the Proposing Release, including identification of any additional costs and benefits. We have considered these comments carefully and made responsive changes to the rules in order to minimize the potential costs. Below we consider the benefits and costs of the economic effects of the new rules and discuss the comments we received, as applicable.

B. Summary of Rules

Rule 14a-11 will require companies to include shareholder nominations for director and disclosure about the nominating shareholder or group and the nominee in a company's proxy materials if, among other things, the nominating shareholder or group held, as of the date of the shareholder notice on Schedule 14N, either individually or in the aggregate, at least 3% of the voting power of the company's securities that are entitled to be voted on the election of directors at the annual meeting of shareholders (or, in lieu of such an annual meeting, a special meeting of shareholders) or on a written consent in lieu of such meeting and has held the qualifying amount of securities used to satisfy the ownership threshold continuously for at least three years as of the date of the shareholder notice on Schedule 14N (in the case of a shareholder group, each member of the group must have held the amount of securities that are used to satisfy the ownership threshold for at least three years as of the date of the shareholder notice on Schedule 14N). The nominating shareholder or group also will be required to hold the shares through the date of the meeting. A nominating shareholder or group that includes a nominee or nominees in a company's proxy materials pursuant to Rule 14a-11 will be required to provide in its notice on Schedule 14N filed with the Commission and transmitted to the company disclosures similar to the disclosures required in a traditional contested election. Pursuant to Item 7(e) of Schedule 14A (and, in the case of registered investment companies and business development companies, Item 22(b)(18) of Schedule 14A), the company will be required to include in its proxy materials certain disclosure provided by the nominating shareholder or group in its notice on Schedule 14N. In addition, the new rules will enable shareholders to engage in limited solicitations to form nominating shareholder groups and engage in solicitations in support of their nominee or nominees without disseminating a proxy statement.[851]

The Commission also is adopting an amendment to Rule 14a-8 to narrow the exclusion in paragraph (i)(8) of the rule, which addresses director elections. Under the amendment, a company will not be permitted to rely on Rule 14a-8(i)(8) to omit from its proxy materials a shareholder proposal that seeks to establish a procedure in the company's governing documents for the inclusion of shareholder nominees for director in the company's proxy materials. The current procedural requirements for submitting a shareholder proposal pursuant to Rule 14a-8 will remain the same. No additional disclosures will be required from any shareholder that submits such a proposal; however, a nominating shareholder or group that includes a nominee or nominees in a company's proxy materials pursuant to an applicable state or foreign law provision or the company's governing documents will be required to file with the Commission and transmit to the company, in its notice on Schedule 14N, disclosures similar to the disclosures required in a traditional contested election. Pursuant to Item 7(f) of Schedule 14A (and, in the case of registered investment companies and business development companies, Item 22(b)(19) of Schedule 14A), the company will be required to include in its proxy

---

[851] *See* Rules 14a-2(b)(7) and 14a-2(b)(8).

materials certain disclosures provided by the nominating shareholder or group in its notice on Schedule 14N.

C. Factors Affecting Scope of the New Rules

Our discussion of the economic effects of the new rules takes into account various factors, such as the incentives and actions of certain parties, that will affect the rules' scope and influence.

Any future actions of the states and their legislatures could affect the applicability of the new rules. Rule 14a-11, for instance, will not apply to companies incorporated in states or other jurisdictions that prohibit nominations of directors by shareholders or permit companies to prohibit such nominations and where the company's governing documents do so.[852] Under Rule 14a-8, shareholder proposals must be proper subjects for action by shareholders under the laws of the jurisdiction of the company's organization. To the extent that states or other jurisdictions change their laws, for example, to prohibit the nomination of directors by shareholders, Rule 14a-11 and Rule 14a-8 would apply less broadly.

Future actions of boards may affect the applicability of the new rules. In the case of Rule 14a-11, we believe that the applicability of the rule is not likely to be affected by future actions of a board because companies generally may not prohibit shareholders from nominating directors under existing state law.[853] In addition, a company will not be permitted to exclude pursuant to amended Rule 14a-8(i)(8) a shareholder proposal that would establish a procedure under a company's governing documents for the inclusion of one or more shareholder nominees for director in the company's proxy materials. It is reasonable to expect that some shareholders will submit this type of proposal, particularly shareholders who perceive that the current board does not represent, or possibly may come to not represent, their interests and are not otherwise able to use Rule 14a-11 (such as if the shareholder does not qualify to submit a nominee or if larger shareholders have exhausted the nomination slots available pursuant to Rule 14a-11). Finally, boards seeking to limit the effect of shareholder-nominated candidates submitted pursuant to Rule 14a-11 and elected as directors may, in some instances, choose to expand the board size to dilute, to an extent, the influence of those directors.[854]

The actions and intentions of shareholders also may affect the applicability of the new rules. To rely on Rule 14a-11, the nominating shareholder (or where there is a nominating shareholder group, each member of the nominating shareholder group) must not be holding any of the company's securities with the purpose, or with the effect, of changing control of the company[855] or to gain a number of seats on the board of directors that exceeds the maximum number of nominees that the company could be required to include under Rule 14a-11 and must provide a certification to this effect in its filed Schedule 14N.[856] The effect of the rule also is affected by the limitation on the number

---

[852] As noted above, we are not aware of any states that currently prohibit shareholder nominations for director.

[853] Several commenters also stated that they were unaware of any law in any state or in the District of Columbia that prohibits shareholders from nominating directors. *See* letters from ABA; BRT; CII; Eaton.

[854] As an example, a board of eight directors, with two new shareholder-nominated directors, may expand to up to 11 directors. Such an expansion would dilute the influence of the shareholder-nominated directors without increasing the number of director slots for shareholder nominees for director in the proxy materials because Rule 14a-11 includes a provision allowing companies to round down the number of nominees that must be included when calculating the 25% maximum.

[855] Although Rule 14a-11 does not contain a requirement that the shareholder nominee or nominees do not have an intent to change the control of the company, a nominating shareholder's or group's ability to meet the requirement and certify that it does not have such an intent will be impacted by the intentions and actions of its nominee or nominees. For example, a nominating shareholder will not be able to certify that it does not hold the company's securities for the purpose, or with the effect, of changing the control of company if its nominee launches its own proxy contest or tender offer. For further discussion, *see* Section II.B.4.d. above.

[856] *See* certifications in Item 8 of new Schedule 14N.

of shareholder director nominees that a company is required to include in its proxy materials. Under Rule 14a-11, a company will not be required to include shareholder nominations for more than a maximum of one director or 25% of the existing board, whichever is greater. If one shareholder or group that is eligible to use Rule 14a-11 nominates the maximum allowable number of candidates, a company will be permitted to exclude any other shareholder's or group's nominees from the company's proxy materials.[857] Further, if the maximum allowable number of existing shareholder director nominees is currently in place on the board, additional shareholder director nominees are not required to be disclosed in the proxy materials pursuant to the rule.[858]

Shareholders seeking to establish a procedure in a company's governing documents and submit nominees for director using such a provision will need to initiate a two-step process to have their nominees included in a company's proxy materials.[859] Unlike the use of Rule 14a-11, this two-step process depends on both the likelihood that a shareholder will initiate such a process and on its success at each step of the process (*e.g.*, the successful inclusion of the shareholder proposal in the company's proxy materials and adoption of the proposal by the appropriate shareholder vote). The likelihood that a shareholder will initiate the two-step process could be limited by the costs arising from the time needed to complete the process (*e.g.*, including opportunity costs of holding securities where the shareholder may consider the company's board composition to be sub-optimal) and the added risk of failure due to the need to complete two separate steps to include its director nominees in the proxy materials. The likelihood that a shareholder will initiate this process is also affected by the existence of Rule 14a-11, which some eligible shareholders may seek to use instead.

Lastly, the scope of the effects of Rule 14a-11, including the expected benefits and costs described below, is affected by the size of the eligible population of shareholder groups and companies. Consequently, the scope of the direct effects of Rule 14a-11 will narrow to the extent that the rule's eligibility criteria reduce the number of shareholders eligible to take advantage of the rule. According to the data from Form 13F filings, 33% of the 6,416 public issuers included in the sample would have one or more shareholders that, on its own, satisfies the 3% ownership threshold and three-year holding period requirement of Rule 14a-11.[860] Our extension of the holding period from a one-year period, as proposed, to the three-year period in the final rule, as well as the increase in the ownership threshold from that proposed for large accelerated filers, limit the number of shareholders eligible to use the rule and the number of companies directly affected by the rule. For non-accelerated filers, the uniform 3% ownership threshold is lower than the 5% ownership threshold that we proposed for that class of filers. This may result in an increase in the number of shareholders eligible to use Rule 14a-11 and the number of companies directly affected by the rule as compared to those shareholders and companies affected under the proposed one year and 5% minimum standards; however, we believe that the extension of the holding period from one to three years may limit any increase in

---

[857] Prior to the time a company has commenced printing its proxy statement and a form of proxy, if a nominating shareholder or group withdraws its shareholder director nominee or the nominee becomes disqualified, the company will be required to include in its proxy materials the director nominee or nominees of the nominating shareholder or group with the next highest voting power percentage that is otherwise eligible to use the rule and that filed a timely notice in accordance with the rule, if any. This process will continue until the company includes the maximum number of nominees that it is required to include in its proxy materials or the company exhausts the list of eligible nominees. For further discussion, *see* Section II.B.7.b above.

[858] This could be the case when shareholder-nominated candidates for director are elected at a company

with a classified board or when a company decides to nominate previously-elected shareholder-nominated directors after their first term in office.

[859] The first step of this two-step process would be the submission of a shareholder proposal pursuant to Rule 14a-8 seeking to establish a procedure in a company's governing documents for the inclusion of shareholder nominees for director in the company's proxy materials and shareholder approval of the proposal. The second step would be the submission and inclusion of shareholder director nominees in the company's proxy materials pursuant to the nomination procedures adopted by shareholders.

[860] November 2009 Memorandum. *See* Section II.B.4.b. above for a discussion of the data, including its limitations.

the number of shareholders eligible to use the rule at smaller reporting companies. The comments we received on the Proposal did not substantiate the concern that the rule would have a disproportionate impact on small issuers, and comments from companies overwhelmingly supported uniform ownership thresholds for all public companies.

D. Benefits

We believe that Rule 14a-11 and the amendment to Rule 14a-8(i)(8), where applicable, will (1) facilitate shareholders' ability to exercise their traditional state law rights to nominate and elect directors; (2) establish a minimum uniform procedure pursuant to which shareholders will be able to include their director nominees in a company's proxy materials and enhance shareholders' ability to propose alternative procedures that further shareholders' rights to nominate and elect directors; (3) potentially improve overall board and company performance; and (4) result in more informed voting decisions in director elections due to improved disclosure of shareholder director nominations and enhanced communications between shareholders regarding director nominations.

1. Facilitating Shareholders' Ability to Exercise Their State Law Rights to Nominate and Elect Directors

Facilitating shareholders' ability to exercise their traditional state law rights to nominate and elect directors is a direct benefit of the new rules for shareholders. The new rules do so by requiring the company proxy materials to include shareholder nominees under certain conditions and, as a result, providing alternative means for shareholders to nominate and elect director candidates other than through a traditional proxy contest. Some eligible shareholders may view the new rules as more advantageous than traditional proxy contests and, hence, the new rules may influence their behavior. In addition, eligible shareholders who would have considered launching a proxy contest for purposes other than to change control of the company may prefer to use the new rules instead. The availability of the new rules also may encourage shareholders who would not have previously considered conducting a proxy contest to take a greater role in the governance of their company by using the new rules to have their nominees for director included in a company's proxy materials.

The precise level of the direct benefits to shareholders will depend on a number of other factors. The benefits may be enhanced to the extent that companies' governing documents are modified to require inclusion of shareholder nominees for director in the company's proxy materials from a broader spectrum of shareholders (for example, by lowering the ownership threshold required to have a nominee included in the company's proxy materials or shortening the holding period).[861] The instances of such changes to provisions in governing documents may increase as a result of the amendment to Rule 14a-8(i)(8).[862] We also recognize the possibility that certain quantifiable benefits for shareholders, such as a nominating shareholder's or group's savings in the direct costs of printing and mailing proxy materials, may be less than the quantifiable costs for a company subject to the new rules. We note, however, that the benefits of the new rules are not limited to those that are quantifiable (such as the direct savings in printing and mailing costs) and instead include benefits that are not as easily quantifiable (such as the possibility of greater shareholder participation and communication in the director nomination process), as discussed below. We believe that these benefits, collectively, justify the costs of the new rules.

---

[861] As adopted, Rule 14a-11 requires the nominating shareholder individually, or the nominating group in the aggregate, to hold at least 3% of the total voting power of the company's securities that are entitled to be voted on the election of directors at the annual (or a special meeting in lieu of the annual) meeting of shareholders, or on a written consent in lieu of such meeting, on the date the nominating shareholder or nominating group provides notice to the company on Schedule 14N.

[862] As amended, companies will no longer be able to rely on Rule 14a-8(i)(8) to exclude a shareholder proposal that seeks to establish a procedure in the company's governing documents for the inclusion of shareholder nominees for director in the company's proxy materials.

We discuss below the ways in which the new rules will facilitate shareholders' exercise of their traditional state law rights and the benefits for shareholders (particularly as compared to a traditional proxy contest). We discuss specific monetary cost savings, both direct and indirect, as well as other changes and the resulting benefits for shareholders.

Shareholders generally have the right under state law to nominate and elect their own director candidates—a right that many shareholders believe they should be able to exercise.[863] Currently, however, a shareholder or group that wishes to present its director nominations for a shareholder vote must generally conduct a proxy contest, which is a costly endeavor. The nominating shareholder or group would have to incur costs involved with preparing proxy materials with the required disclosures regarding the director nominations and mailing the proxy materials to each shareholder solicited.[864] Several commenters stated that the costs of traditional proxy contests have made them prohibitively expensive for shareholders wishing to exercise their traditional state law rights to nominate and elect directors.[865]

Further, the concern about the costs of conducting a traditional proxy contest is not limited to the fact that the nominating shareholder or group must incur these costs directly. A collective action problem also exists. The time and effort spent by a shareholder in nominating and advocating for new directors are not shared by other shareholders. This unequal cost sharing may serve to discourage any one shareholder from assuming the costs of running a traditional proxy contest on its own, even though a successful contest could result in a greater aggregate benefit for all shareholders.[866] As a result, there is the added economic cost of foregone opportunities where a qualified director candidate fails to be nominated because no one shareholder or group wishes to bear alone the costs of an election contest for the benefit of all shareholders.

We believe Rule 14a-11 will further our stated goal of facilitating shareholders' ability to nominate and elect their own director candidates by allowing shareholders to avoid certain direct costs of conducting a traditional proxy contest and reducing the overall costs to shareholders for nominating and electing directors—a belief shared by several commenters.[867] The new rules also will mitigate collective action and free-rider concerns

---

[863] *See* letters from AFSCME; Sodali; Universities Superannuation (citing a June 2009 survey conducted by *ShareOwners.org* showing that 82% of the respondents believed that shareholders should be able to "nominate and elect directors of their own choosing to the boards of the companies they own," while 16% of the respondents stated that "shareholders should not be able to propose directors to sit on the boards of the companies they own.").

[864] Proxy contests waged in connection with efforts to obtain control may involve costs related to not only preparing proxy materials and engaging in solicitation efforts, but to the purchase or lock-up of a significant amount of the voting securities of the target company. Such costs could be high.

[865] *See* letters from Americans for Financial Reform; CalPERS; CII; Florida State Board of Administration; M. Katz; J. McRitchie; S. Ranzini; Teamsters.

[866] *See, e.g.,* letters from Bebchuk, et al. ("In evaluating eligibility and procedural requirements, the SEC should also keep in mind that many institutional investors lack incentives to invest actively in seeking governance benefits that would be shared by their fellow shareholders."); Lucian A. Bebchuk and Scott Hirst ("Bebchuk/Hirst") (submitting the article by Lucian A. Bebchuk and Scott Hirst, *Private Ordering and the Proxy Access Debate*, 65 Bus. Law. 329 (2010) ("Bebchuk and Hirst (2010)"), in which the authors

state: "Thus, challengers who might be able to improve the management of the company may be discouraged from running because they will bear all of the costs but capture only a fraction of the benefits from any improvement in governance." *See also* Lynn A. Stout, *The Mythical Benefit of Shareholder Control*, 93 VA. L. REV. 789, 789 (2007) ("Stout (2007)") ("In a public company with widely dispersed share ownership, it is difficult and expensive for shareholders to overcome obstacles to collective action and wage a proxy battle to oust an incumbent board.") (cited in the Proposing Release, Section V.B.1.).

[867] *See* letters from CII; Key Equity Investors; Pershing Square. The benefit of a reduction in the cost of a proxy solicitation exists only to the extent that the nominating shareholder or group views Rule 14a-11 as a substitute for a traditional proxy contest. Even with the adoption of Rule 14a-11, some shareholders may prefer to conduct a traditional proxy contest due to the various restrictions on the use of the rule. For example, the rule restricts the number of shareholder director nominees that a company will be required to include in its proxy materials. The rule also will be available only to shareholders that do not hold the securities in the company with the purpose, or with the effect, of changing control of the company. These elements of Rule 14a-11 impose restrictions that are not present in a traditional proxy contest. Some shareholders also may

that may have otherwise deterred many shareholders from exercising their rights under state law to nominate directors.

Direct cost savings, particularly as compared to the cost of a traditional proxy contest, come from two sources. First, a nominating shareholder or group may see direct cost savings due to reduced printing and postage costs. Based on the information available,[868] we calculate that a shareholder using Rule 14a-11 to submit a director nominee or nominees to be included in a company's proxy materials will save at least $18,000 on average in printing and postage costs.

Second, and significantly, a nominating shareholder or group may see direct cost savings related to reduced expenditures for advertising and promotion of its candidates as a result of its ability to use the company's proxy materials to directly solicit other shareholders. To the extent that the nominating shareholder or group decides to reduce its public relations and advertising expenditures to promote its candidates, or to engage proxy solicitors, the cost savings will be greater. These reductions in costs may remove a disincentive for shareholders to submit their own director nominations, mitigate the collective action concern, and serve the goal of facilitating shareholders' ability to exercise their traditional state law rights to nominate and elect directors.

We received significant comment questioning the need for the new rules to reduce the costs described above or the degree to which the reduction in costs will actually facilitate shareholder director nominations.[869] One commenter characterized the direct printing and mailing cost savings as the sole benefit of the new rules for shareholders and one that is not justified by the costs and disruption that would result from the rules.[870] The commenter observed that the average of $18,000 in estimated savings identified in the Proposing Release represented less than 5% of the cost of a traditional proxy contest and did not include costs that would be incurred by a shareholder actively seeking the election of its nominee, such as costs related to legal counsel, proxy solicitors, public relations advisers and advertising.

We recognize that the adoption of the new rules may not relieve a nominating shareholder or group of all expenditures that could be incurred for an active campaign that may be more successful to support the election of its candidate to the company's board of directors. The new rules, however, are not intended to serve that purpose. Instead, the new rules' goal is to facilitate shareholders' ability to present their own director nominees for a vote at a shareholder meeting by eliminating or reducing barriers in the proxy solicitation process—one of which is the direct cost of printing and mailing proxy materials—that have contributed to frustrating shareholder director nominations.[871]

(Footnote Continued)

prefer a traditional proxy contest over Rule 14a-11 for reasons related to their strategy for the conduct of the election contest, such as having greater control over the mailing schedule and contents of their proxy materials. *See, e.g.,* letter from Carl T. Hagberg ("C. Hagberg") (stating that "most truly serious nominators of director candidates will surely produce their own proxy materials, and take control of their own 'electioneering' with materials and proxy cards of their own, if they want to stand a reasonable chance to win."). Therefore, while Rule 14a-11 may encourage some shareholders seeking to nominate and elect their candidates to use the rule instead of conducting a traditional proxy contest, other shareholders may continue to prefer a traditional contest. For such shareholders, the expected reduction in a shareholder's proxy solicitation costs will not materialize.

[868] According to a study of proxy contests conducted during 2003, 2004, and 2005, the average cost of a proxy contest to a soliciting shareholder was $368,000.

See letter from Automatic Data Processing, Inc. (April 20, 2006) regarding *Internet Availability of Proxy Materials,* Exchange Act Release No. 34-52926 (December 8, 2005) (File No. S7-10-05). The costs included those associated with proxy advisors and solicitors, processing fees, legal fees, public relations, advertising, and printing and mailing of proxy materials. Approximately 95% of the costs were unrelated to printing and postage. The cost of printing and postage averaged approximately $18,000.

[869] *See* letters from 26 Corporate Secretaries; 3M; Ameriprise; Association of Corporate Counsel; BRT; Cummins; DuPont; ExxonMobil; FMC Corp.; Frontier; GE; General Mills; Honeywell; IBM; Keating Muething; Motorola; Schneider; Sidley Austin; Simpson Thacher; Time Warner Cable; Wachtell; Wells Fargo; Xerox.

[870] *See* letter from BRT.

[871] We recognize that other factors may have similarly frustrated the effective exercise of this state law

We also recognize that the direct printing and mailing cost savings of $18,000, on their own, may not be viewed by some to be significant enough to drive the behavior of large shareholders of public companies. The comments that we received regarding the likely increase in the number of election contests resulting from the new rules, however, seem to undercut this view and suggest instead that shareholders' behavior may indeed be influenced by the rules.[872] The extent to which election contests are predicted to increase as a result of shareholders nominating their own director candidates for inclusion in the company's proxy materials strongly indicates that the benefits of the new rules cannot be fairly characterized as a "mere $18,000 in estimated savings"[873]—a characterization that we believe obfuscates the significance of this benefit of our new rules.

We received comment that while certain shareholders may be relieved of certain costs to run a traditional proxy contest as a result of the new rules, the rules may simply shift those costs onto the company and, indirectly, all shareholders.[874] Therefore, while the rules may reduce the direct costs of solicitation by a particular shareholder for its director nominees, it may result in an increase in the overall cost of a company's proxy solicitation for a director election (*e.g.*, additional printing and mailing costs arising from the disclosure of the shareholder director nominations) and indirectly the cost to all shareholders, particularly if the new rules lead to an increase in the number of shareholder director nominations. We have some reason to believe, however, that the increased costs for the company may not be as much as would otherwise result if that shareholder engaged in a traditional proxy contest.[875] We also note that, to the extent that the new rules help to address the collective action concern, it could remove disincentives that previously deterred shareholders from submitting director nominations that may have ultimately benefited all shareholders.

Other commenters observed that savings in printing and mailing costs could be obtained through our notice and access model for electronic delivery of proxy materials[876] or stated that the notice and access model has already reduced the costs for shareholders to effect changes in the membership of a board.[877] We note that this observation applies only to the direct printing and mailing costs, rather than all of the other monetary cost savings discussed throughout this section. We agree that the notice

---

(Footnote Continued)

right. We discuss below these factors and how the new rules will reduce or eliminate these factors.

[872] *See, e.g.*, letters from Altman (stating that participants in its survey predicted that, on average, 15% of companies listed on U.S. exchanges could expect to face a shareholder director nomination submitted under Rule 14a-11 in 2011, based on the eligibility criteria of the Proposal); BRT (stating that the new rules "will increase the frequency of contested elections . . ."); Chamber of Commerce/CCMC (noting that if the new rules are adopted, "it is likely that proxy contests (in which the company is required to solicit proxies on behalf of shareholders) will increase greatly and may become customary.").

[873] *See* letter from BRT.

[874] *See* letter from ABA. We recognized this possibility in the Proposing Release as well, noting that the rule "may result in a decrease in costs to shareholders that would have to conduct proxy contests in the absence of [proposed] Rule 14a-11, but may increase the costs for companies." *See* Proposing Release, Section V.C.3.

[875] One commenter on the 2003 Proposal estimated that a Rule 14a-11 contest would cost a company approximately one-third what a full proxy contest costs. *See* letter from Stephen M. Bainbridge submitted in connection with the 2003 Proposal (File No. S7-19-

03) ("Bainbridge 2003 Letter"). Based on this assumption and relying on data from a late 1980s survey, this commenter estimated that the costs of such a contest to a public company would be $500,000. This commenter also cited data estimating companies' annual expenditures on Rule 14a-8 shareholder proposals to be $90 million. While this commenter noted the belief that it is unlikely that there will be as many Rule 14a-11 election contests as Rule 14a-8 shareholder proposals, the commenter asserted that incumbent boards are likely to spend considerably more on opposing each Rule 14a-11 contest than on opposing a Rule 14a-8 shareholder proposal. This commenter estimated that $100 million may be an appropriate estimate for the lower boundary of the range within which Rule 14a-11's direct costs will fall. Commenters did not provide any data during the comment period for the Proposal that compared these costs for a company.

[876] *See, e.g.*, letters from 26 Corporate Secretaries; Ameriprise; BRT.

[877] *See* letters from 26 Corporate Secretaries; 3M; Ameriprise; Association of Corporate Counsel; BRT; Cummins; DuPont; ExxonMobil; FMC Corp.; Frontier; GE; General Mills; Honeywell; IBM; Keating Muething; Motorola; Schneider; Sidley Austin; Simpson Thacher; Time Warner Cable; Wachtell; Wells Fargo; Xerox.

and access model may decrease significantly the printing and mailing costs associated with a proxy solicitation. To the extent that a shareholder chooses to nominate and elect its director candidates through a traditional proxy contest using the notice and access model, the expected benefit of a reduction in printing and mailing costs will be somewhat lower. The notice and access model, however, may not necessarily provide a soliciting shareholder with the same cost savings possible under Rule 14a-11. Under the model, a soliciting shareholder will still incur the costs of printing and mailing notices of availability of proxy materials to shareholders from whom the person is soliciting proxy authority.[878] Further, as we recognized at the time we created the notice and access model, additional printing and mailing costs will be incurred to the extent that a solicited shareholder requests paper copies of the proxy materials.[879] A soliciting shareholder also may prefer using the new rules over a traditional proxy contest conducted through the notice and access model for reasons related to its strategy for the conduct of the election contest, such as avoiding the need and cost to use Exchange Act Rule 14a-7 to obtain a shareholder list from the company (or have the company send proxy materials on its behalf)[880] as well as the requirement to file preliminary proxy materials at least ten calendar days before definitive materials are first sent to shareholders.[881]

The new rules will do more than reduce the direct monetary costs described above. We recognize that shareholders today are widely dispersed and the corporate proxy is the principal means through which state law voting rights are exercised. The dispersed nature of ownership creates certain intangible disincentives to the effective exercise of shareholders' ability to nominate and elect their own director candidates, as discussed below. As we stated in the Proposing Release, the proxy process provides the only practical means for shareholders to solicit votes from other shareholders in favor of the election of their nominees. The current inability of many shareholders to utilize the proxy process for this purpose means that shareholder director nominees do not have a realistic prospect of being elected because most, if not all, shareholders would have cast their votes well in advance of the shareholder meeting. Shareholders are deprived of not only the ability to exercise a traditional state law right, but the

---

[878] Exchange Act Rule 14a-16(*l*)(2). A soliciting person other than the company could limit the cost of a solicitation by soliciting proxies only from a select group of shareholders, such as those with large holdings, without furnishing other shareholders with any information. This flexibility would allow a soliciting person other than the company to reduce even further its printing and mailing costs by soliciting only those persons who have not previously requested paper copies of the proxy materials. Certain practical reasons, however, may deter a soliciting person other than the company from taking full advantage of this flexibility, such as the fact that institutional investors may prefer receiving paper copies of proxy materials. *See* Jeffrey N. Gordon, *Proxy Contests in an Era of Increasing Shareholder Power: Forget Issuer Proxy Access and Focus on E-Proxy*, 61 VAND. L. REV. 476, 488 (2008) (noting that institutional investors "generally may request paper delivery to minimize their own printing costs.") (cited in the letters from BRT and Simpson Thacher).

[879] *See Internet Availability of Proxy Materials*, Release No. 34-55146 (January 22, 2007) ("Internet Proxy Availability Release") (noting that "to the extent that some shareholders request paper copies of the proxy materials, the benefits of the amendments in terms of savings in printing and mailing costs will be reduced.").

[880] Exchange Act Rule 14a-7 sets forth the obligation of companies either to provide a shareholder list to a

requesting shareholder or to send the shareholder's proxy materials on the shareholder's behalf. The rule provides that the company has the option to provide the list or send the shareholder's materials, except when the company is soliciting proxies in connection with a going-private transaction or a roll-up transaction. Under Rule 14a-7(e), the shareholder must reimburse the company for "reasonable expenses" incurred by the company in providing the shareholder list or sending the shareholder's proxy materials.

[881] Exchange Act Rule 14a-6 requires that preliminary copies of the proxy statement and form of proxy be filed with the Commission at least ten calendar days prior to the date that definitive copies of such materials are first sent or given to security holders, except if the solicitation relates to certain matters to be acted upon at the meeting of security holders. Accordingly, the proxy statement and form of proxy for a traditional proxy contest must be filed in preliminary form. By contrast, under the amendments to Rule 14a-6 that we are adopting today, the inclusion of a shareholder director nominee in the company's proxy materials will not require the company to file preliminary proxy materials, provided that the company is otherwise qualified to file directly in definitive form. In this regard, the inclusion of a shareholder director nominee will not be deemed a solicitation in opposition for purposes of the exclusion from filing preliminary proxy materials.

opportunity to assess and vote on qualified candidates who could have been presented for a vote if the proxy process functioned as intended. As with the direct monetary costs, reducing the costs arising from the dispersed nature of ownership discussed below will help address any related collective action concerns.

Some commenters observed that a shareholder seeking to nominate and elect its own director candidates through a traditional proxy contest is disadvantaged by the fact that its candidates are presented to shareholders through a separate set of proxy materials.[882] A nominating shareholder or group may encounter difficulties in having its nominees evaluated in the same manner as those of management by shareholders who are used to receiving only the company's proxy materials and who may react differently, and perhaps negatively, to the shareholder's nominees simply because the nominees are presented in a separate, unfamiliar set of proxy materials.

As we stated throughout this release, the federal proxy rules should not frustrate the exercise of a shareholder's traditional state law right to present its own director candidates for a shareholder vote. To the extent that the exercise of this right is hindered simply because of a nominating shareholder's or group's need to deliver a separate set of proxy materials and potentially negative reaction by shareholders to the appearance of this set of materials, we believe that our new rules will help address that concern. With the new rules, a shareholder will have the ability to include its director nominees in the company's proxy materials, provided that the rules' requirements are met. The fact that a nominating shareholder or group could have its director nominees included in a company's proxy materials—as opposed to being included in its own proxy materials—pursuant to the new rules may be viewed by the shareholder or group as a significant improvement in its ability to have its nominees evaluated by shareholders in the same manner as they evaluate management's nominees. Shareholders who are interested in effecting a change in the company's leadership or direction may be less likely to be deterred by the prospect that their director nominees will not be assessed on their merit. Nominating shareholders also may see less need for additional soliciting efforts, such as the hiring of proxy solicitors, public relations advisors, or advertising, if their director nominees are presented alongside those of management in a set of company proxy materials with which the company's shareholders are familiar.[883]

Shareholders also may be hindered in making their voting decisions in a traditional proxy contest due to the fact that they have to evaluate more than one set of proxy materials—one sent by a company and another sent by an insurgent shareholder—when evaluating whether and how to grant authority to vote their shares by proxy.[884]

---

[882] *See* letters from Bebchuk/Hirst (submitting the Bebchuk and Hirst (2010) study, which noted the ability of shareholders to include their nominees in the company's proxy materials would "avoid intangible disadvantages that may result from being on a separate card."); Pershing Square (stating that "the absence of universal ballots, on which shareholders can vote from among all nominees regardless of who proposed them, is glaring and clearly anti-choice" and that "[o]ur hope is that, outside the control context, selection of the best nominees in a contest will be based more on character, competency, and relevancy of their experience rather than the identity of the person nominating the candidate.").

At the October 7, 2009 "Proxy Access Roundtable" held by the Harvard Law School Program on Corporate Governance (the transcript of which was submitted as part of a comment letter from S. Hirst), Roy Katzovicz, the Chief Legal Officer of Pershing Square Capital Management, L.P. explained:

As a cultural matter, there are two sub-points. First and foremost, having the decision of choosing two people, one next to the other, invites, we think, a more intelligent analysis on the part of shareholders generally. In particular, we think that if the basis for election for a nominee is their merit as an individual, a fund or an investor of any type that can identify the deadweight on the board, and in place of that deadweight find ideal candidates from a skills perspective to round out the board, they're going to have an easier time getting shareholder support for their nominee. Their ability to vote among all the nominees and from all proponents, I think, facilitates that kind of person-by-person analysis, versus slate-by-slate analysis.

[883] As discussed in Section II.B.9.d.ii. above, we have adopted the proposed amendments to Exchange Act Rule 14a-4 out of a similar desire to avoid giving management's director nominees an advantage over those of a nominating shareholder or group and to create an impartial presentation of the nominees for whom a shareholder may vote.

[884] One commenter stated that if enabling shareholders to evaluate a board more efficiently and make more informed voting decisions is the goal of the

Presenting the competing director nominees on one proxy card, with the related disclosure contained in one proxy statement, may simplify the shareholder's decision-making process and reduce the potential for any confusion on the part of shareholders.[885] The result may be a greater degree of participation by shareholders through the proxy process in the governance of their companies.

2. Minimum Uniform Procedure for Inclusion of Shareholder Director Nominations and Enhanced Ability for Shareholders to Adopt Director Nomination Procedures

Rule 14a-11, as adopted, will provide shareholders of companies subject to the federal proxy rules the ability to include their director nominees in the company's proxy materials, provided that the rule's requirements are met.[886] Further, with our adoption of the amendment to Rule 14a-8(i)(8), shareholders will be able to present in the company's proxy materials a proposal that would seek to establish a procedure in the company's governing documents for the inclusion of shareholder nominees for director in the company's proxy materials.[887] Shareholders will have a greater ability to present for a shareholder vote a director nomination procedure with requirements, such as the requisite ownership threshold or holding period, that differ from those of Rule 14a-11.[888]

We received significant comment regarding the uniform applicability of Rule 14a-11 and the amendment to Rule 14a-8(i)(8).[889] While there was widespread support for the amendment to Rule 14a-8(i)(8), commenters were divided on the extent to which companies and shareholders should be permitted to use Rule 14a-8 to propose alternative requirements for shareholder director nominations and on the related issue of whether shareholders and companies should be able to opt out of Rule 14a-11 entirely. Some commenters believed that the amendment to Rule 14a-8(i)(8) should facilitate private ordering under state law by enabling shareholders to include in the company's proxy materials a Rule 14a-8 proposal that would impose more restrictive eligibility criteria than those of Rule 14a-11.[890] A number of commenters also believed that shareholders

---

(Footnote Continued)

Proposal, then enhancing proxy disclosure, rather than facilitating proxy contests, will better achieve that goal. *See* letter from Davis Polk. We recognize the importance of enhancing the disclosure provided in connection with proxy solicitations and recently adopted new rules to better enable shareholders to evaluate the leadership of public companies. *See* Proxy Disclosure Enhancements Adopting Release. These rules, however, do not dispense with the need for Rule 14a-11 and the amendment to Rule 14a-8(i)(8). The new rules we are adopting will complement the recently-adopted proxy disclosure enhancement rules by enabling shareholders to submit their own director nominees if, after evaluating a company's public disclosures and performance, they are displeased with that company's current leadership or direction.

[885] As discussed in Section IV.D.4. below, the new disclosure requirements that we are adopting for shareholder director nominations submitted pursuant to Rule 14a-11, a state or foreign law provision, or a provision in the company's governing documents also will facilitate more informed voting decisions by providing shareholders with important disclosures and enhancing their ability to communicate with each other regarding director nominations.

[886] For a discussion of the companies that are subject to Rule 14a-11, *see* Section II.B.3. above. As discussed in that section, foreign private issuers and companies

that are subject to the federal proxy rules solely because they have a class of debt securities registered under Exchange Act Section 12 will not be subject to Rule 14a-11. For smaller reporting companies, Rule 14a-11 will become effective three years after the date that the rule becomes effective for all other companies.

[887] As previously discussed, a shareholder proposal seeking to establish such a procedure will continue to be subject to exclusion under other provisions of Rule 14a-8.

[888] As discussed in Section II.C. above, a provision in a company's governing documents establishing a procedure for the inclusion of shareholder director nominees in a company's proxy materials will not affect the operation of Rule 14a-11, regardless of whether the company's shareholders have approved the provision.

[889] For further discussion of the comments regarding the uniform applicability of Rule 14a-11 and the amendment to Rule 14a-8(i)(8), *see* Sections II.B.2. and II.C. above.

[890] *See* letters from American Express; BorgWarner; Brink's; BRT; CIGNA; P. Clapman; Con Edison; CSX; Davis Polk; DTE Energy; DuPont; GE; General Mills; C. Holliday; JPMorgan Chase; Metlife; P&G; Pfizer; Safeway; Seven Law Firms; Society of Corporate Secretaries; Southern Company; Tenet; U.S. Bancorp; Verizon.

should be able to elect to have their companies opt out of Rule 14a-11, including through the submission of a Rule 14a-8 proposal.[891] To facilitate private ordering, a significant number of commenters supported the adoption of the amendment to Rule 14a-8(i)(8) while opposing adoption of Rule 14a-11.[892]

By contrast, other commenters supported an amendment enabling shareholders to include in a company's proxy materials a Rule 14a-8 proposal that establishes a shareholder director nomination procedure but only if the procedure would provide shareholders with a greater ability to include their director nominees in the company's proxy materials.[893] A number of commenters also opposed any provision that would permit companies to opt out of Rule 14a-11[894] and preferred the uniform applicability of Rule 14a-11 to all companies.[895]

We considered these comments carefully. As discussed above, and noted in the Proposal, the purpose of the rules is to facilitate shareholders' traditional state law rights to nominate and elect their own director candidates. As such, we believe that a uniform application of Rule 14a-11 to companies subject to the federal proxy rules is the best way to enable shareholders of these companies to do so without having to incur the types of costs and other disadvantages that shareholders traditionally have encountered. A single, uniform rule will provide shareholders of any company subject to the rule with the ability to meaningfully exercise their traditional state law rights to present their own director candidates for a vote at a shareholder meeting may be invoked through the proxy process. With the adoption of the amendment to Rule 14a-8(i)(8), shareholders will be able to establish procedures that can further facilitate this ability, if they wish.

By contrast, we believe that exclusive reliance on private ordering under state law would not be as effective and efficient in facilitating the exercise of these rights. Commenters identified procedural and legal difficulties that they believe would hinder the establishment of a shareholder director nomination procedure under private ordering, including: a supermajority voting standard for approval of the proposal;[896] the constraints imposed by the 500-word limit for a Rule 14a-8 proposal;[897] the significant percentage of companies that restrict shareholders' ability to amend or propose bylaws;[898] and the potential ability of a board to repeal or amend a shareholder-adopted bylaw procedure.[899] Some commenters also expressed a general concern that under private ordering, the provisions in a company's governing documents regarding

---

[891] See letters from DTE Energy; JPMorgan Chase; P&G; Seven Law Firms; Society of Corporate Secretaries; U.S. Bancorp.

[892] See, e.g., letters from ABA; BRT; Society of Corporate Secretaries.

[893] See letters from CII; Governance for Owners; D. Nappier.

[894] See letters from AFL-CIO; Amalgamated Bank; W. Baker; Florida State Board of Administration; IAM; Marco Consulting; P. Neuhauser; Nine Law Firms; Norges Bank; Relational; Shamrock; TIAA-CREF; USPE; ValueAct Capital.

[895] See letters from AFSCME; CalPERS; CalSTRS; CII; COPERA; Florida State Board of Administration; John C. Liu ("J. Liu"); D. Nappier; Nathan Cummings Foundation; Phil Nicholas ("P. Nicholas"); OPERS; State Universities Retirement System of Illinois ("SURSI"); SWIB; WSIB.

[896] See B. Young, footnote 52, above ("Data on bylaw amendment limitations show that at between 38 and 43% of companies, depending on the index, shareholders are either unable to amend the bylaws or face significant challenges in the form of supermajority vote requirements."); see also letters from AFSCME; Bebchuk/Hirst; Florida State Board of Administration; J. Liu.

[897] See letters from Bebchuk/Hirst; CII; Florida State Board of Administration.

[898] See letters from AFSCME; Florida State Board of Administration; Nathan Cummings Foundation; SWIB.

[899] See letters from AFSCME; Corporate Library; Sodali. See also Michael E. Murphy, *The Nominating Process for Corporate Boards of Directors: A Decision-Making Analysis*, 5 Berkeley Bus. L.J. 131, 144 (2008) (discussing how a company's management defeated a shareholder proposal regarding shareholder director nominations through the use of a bylaw requiring a super-majority shareholder vote in favor of such a shareholder proposal and noting that "[t]he super-majority requirement was one of several potential defenses that management might have employed; it might also have imposed inconvenient notice requirements, stringent shareholder qualification rules, or restrictions mirroring the conditions of SEC rule 14a-8. If these barriers proved insufficient, management might have considered counter-initiatives; it is an open question in Delaware and certain other states whether the board of directors has the power to repeal a shareholder-initiated bylaw by adopting a superseding bylaw amendment.")

shareholder director nominations may be so restrictive that it would be impossible for shareholders to have candidates included in company proxy materials.[900] Other commenters, however, disagreed that these difficulties would actually interfere with the establishment of a procedure under a private ordering approach.[901]

As previously discussed, we believe that our rules should provide shareholders with the ability to include director nominees in a company's proxy materials without the need for shareholders to bear the burdens of overcoming substantial obstacles to creating that ability on a company-by-company basis.[902] Private ordering based on an opt-in approach would require shareholders to incur significant costs, regardless of the presence of the difficulties described above. Shareholders would need to expend both time and funds to draft and submit a proposal, such as a Rule 14a-8 proposal, establishing a shareholder director nomination procedure on a company-by-company basis.[903] These costs may be higher if the company opposes and solicits against adoption of the proposal—a possibility that is very likely at companies where disagreements between incumbent directors and a nominating shareholder or group already exist.[904] Further, shareholders may be disinclined to undergo a two-step process to submit their own nominees—first, to establish a nomination procedure through a Rule 14a-8 shareholder proposal and, second, to submit their director candidates for inclusion in the company's proxy materials—given the length of time that they will have to hold the requisite amount of securities and, perhaps more importantly, the risk of failure at each step of the process.

Different but equally significant issues would arise under an opt-out approach. Shareholders who wish to retain their ability to include their director nominees in the company's proxy materials pursuant to Rule 14a-11 may find it difficult to successfully oppose an opt-out proposal due to management's ability to draw on the company's resources to promote the adoption of the proposal.[905] We also believe that if we were to allow an opt-out approach, even one in which only shareholders could approve an opt out, there is a high likelihood that the effort to procure such approval could be supported by management and funded by company assets, while opposing views could not be advanced effectively. Shareholders of these companies would find themselves, once again, left without an effective or efficient ability to nominate and elect their own director candidates. Further, as some commenters observed, both the opt-in and opt-out approaches may impose unnecessary complexity and administrative burdens for shareholders with diversified holdings in numerous companies and may hinder their exercise of a traditional state law right.[906]

---

[900] *See* letters from Florida State Board of Administration; P. Neuhauser; Shamrock.

[901] *See* letters from AT&T; ABA; BRT; J. Grundfest; Keller Group; Lemonjuice.biz ("Lemonjuice"); Seven Law Firms.

[902] *See* Section II.B.2. above, for additional discussion of our consideration of a private ordering approach.

[903] *See* letters from CalPERS; Florida State Board of Administration; D. Nappier; P. Neuhauser. One of these commenters estimated that the approximate cost for shareholders of "running a proposal" is $30,000. *See* letter from CalPERS. The commenter estimated that it would cost $351,000,000 to attempt to establish the right of shareholders of Russell 3000 companies to include their director nominees in a company's proxy materials.

[904] The reluctance of companies to support the establishment of a shareholder director nomination procedure was noted in an article submitted by a commenter. *See* letter from Bebchuk/Hirst (referring to Bebchuk and Hirst (2010)). In their article, the authors observed that while the establishment of such a procedure is permissible under the existing laws of some

states, including Delaware, only three companies have in fact established a shareholder director nomination procedure.

[905] In this regard, we note that a survey that one commenter conducted showed that, if available, a large majority of its member companies—approximately two-thirds—would seek to implement an opt-out from Rule 14a-11. *See* letter from Society of Corporate Secretaries. This survey suggests that shareholders of many companies may, once again, be limited in their ability to have their director candidates included in companies' proxy materials.

[906] *See* letters from CFA Institute; CII; COPERA; D. Nappier; OPERS. One commenter countered that most long-term institutional shareholders are unlikely to submit director candidates at a large number of companies simultaneously and predicted that private ordering will lead to "some degree of standardization" in the types of shareholder director nomination procedures. *See* letter from Society of Corporate Secretaries. While we appreciate these points, we believe that adoption of Rule 14a-11, in fact, provides such "standardization." The amendment to Rule 14a-8(i)(8) complements Rule 14a-11 by enabling shareholders to

3. Potential Improved Board Performance and Company Performance

As discussed throughout this release, we are adopting the new rules with the goal of facilitating shareholders' ability under state law to nominate and elect directors for election to the board. Because state law provides shareholders with the right to nominate and elect directors to ensure that boards remain accountable to shareholders and to mitigate the agency problems associated with the separation of ownership from control, facilitating shareholders' exercise of these rights may have the potential of improving board accountability and efficiency and increasing shareholder value. In the Proposing Release, we requested comment on the assertion that the Proposal could improve board performance and, hence, company performance—both for boards that include shareholder-nominated directors elected pursuant to the new rules and for boards that may be more attentive and responsive to shareholder concerns to avoid the submission of shareholder director nominations pursuant to the new rules.[907]

We received significant comment regarding this assertion. Many commenters agreed that the new rules may result in the benefit of more accountable, more responsive, and generally better-performing boards.[908] Other commenters, however, questioned whether the new rules would in fact promote board accountability,[909] warned of the costs of distracting and expensive election contests,[910] and disputed the conclusions of a study regarding the benefits enjoyed by companies with "hybrid boards" that was cited in the Proposing Release.[911] Commenters also challenged the basis for any suggestions in the

---

(Footnote Continued)

consider and vote on proposals that provide shareholders with an even greater ability to present their own director candidates for a shareholder vote. Lastly, we recognize that the amendment to Rule 14a-8(i)(8) could result in some complexity as well, in that shareholders could establish director nomination procedures that require, for example, a different ownership threshold or holding period than those contained in Rule 14a-11. We believe, however, that such complexity is justified because it furthers our goal of facilitating, as much as possible, the effective exercise of shareholders' traditional state law right of shareholders to nominate their own director candidates for a vote at a shareholder meeting.

[907] *See* Proposing Release, Section V.B.3.

[908] *See* letters from AFSCME; Bebchuk, et al.; Brigham; CalPERS; CII; L. Dallas; T. DiNapoli; A. Dral; GovernanceMetrics; Governance for Owners; Hermes; M. Katz; LUCRF; J. McRitchie; R. Moulton-Ely; D. Nappier; P. Neuhauser; NJSIC; OPERS; Pax World; Pershing Square; Relational; RiskMetrics; D. Romine; Shareowners.org; Social Investment Forum; Teamsters; TIAA-CREF; Universities Superannuation; USPE; Walden. One commenter added that the benefits of the right to include shareholder director nominees in the company's proxy materials, including enhanced shareholder value from hybrid boards and directors becoming "more alert to their duties," are "less easy to quantify." *See* letter from P. Neuhauser.

[909] *See, e.g.,* letters from Alaska Air; Ameriprise; Brink's; Comcast; CSX; General Mills; Piedmont; Praxair; William H. Steinbrink ("W. Steinbrink"); Time Warner Cable; United Brotherhood of Carpenters.

[910] *See* letters from ABA; Atlas; AT&T; Book Celler; Carlson; Carolina Mills; Chamber of Commerce/CCMC; Chevron; Crespin; M. Eng; Erickson; ExxonMobil; Fenwick; GE; General Mills; Glass Lewis; Glaspell; Intelect; R. Clark King; Koppers; MCO;

MeadWestvaco; MedFaxx; Medical Insurance; Merchants Terminal; D. Merilatt; NAM; NIRI; NK; O3 Strategies; Roppe; Rosen; Safeway; Sara Lee; Schneider; Southland; Style Crest; Tenet; TI; tw telecom; R. VanEngelenhoven; Wachtell; Wells Fargo; Weyerhaeuser; Yahoo.

[911] *See, e.g.,* letters from IBM; Simpson Thacher. These commenters questioned the conclusions of the study by Chris Cernich, et al., "Effectiveness of Hybrid Boards," IRRC Institute for Corporate Responsibility (May 2009) ("Cernich (2009)"), *available at* http://www.irrcinstitute.org/pdf/IRRC_05_09_EffectiveHybridBoards.pdf (cited in the Proposing Release, Section V.B.3.). For example, one of these commenters stated that the study "demonstrates that the objectives of successful dissidents were often short-term in nature" and "suggests that companies with dissidents on their board perform better than their peers over a one-year period, but that they perform worse over a three-year period." *See* letter from Simpson Thacher. The other commenter stated that "the only conclusion that could fairly be drawn from the data is that some companies perform better, and many perform worse, under such circumstances" and "of the companies with dissident directors studied for three years after the contest period, share performance averaged just 0.7%, which is 6.6% less than peer companies."

We recognize the limitations of the Cernich (2009) study as well. While it provides useful documentation of patterns of behavior of activist investors, its long-term findings on shareholder value creation are difficult to interpret. Return estimates are presented without standard errors. For long-term returns in particular, this shortcoming makes it difficult to infer whether results arise because returns are different than peers in expectation, or because of random chance. Other studies cited in this release do use standard statistical

Proposing Release that the recent economic crisis was somehow linked to the inability of shareholders to include their director nominees in the company's proxy materials, pointing out that we have contemplated similar regulatory efforts several times before the recent crisis occurred.[912]

The comments reflect the sharp divide on the question of whether facilitating shareholders' ability to exercise their rights to nominate and elect directors would lead to the benefit of improved board and company performance. We have considered these comments carefully and appreciate both the fact that the empirical evidence may appear mixed and the potential for negative effects due to management distraction and discord on the board that some commenters identified. After assessing the costs and benefits identified by commenters, and for reasons discussed below, we believe that the totality of the evidence and economic theory supports the view that facilitating shareholders' ability to include their director nominees in a company's proxy materials has the potential of creating the benefit of improved board performance and enhanced shareholder value—both in companies with the actual election of shareholder-nominated directors and in companies that react to shareholders' concerns because of the possibility of such directors being elected. Thus, as discussed below, it is our conclusion that the potential benefits of improved board and company performance and shareholder value justify the potential costs.

By facilitating shareholders' exercise of their traditional state law rights to nominate and elect directors, we believe that eligible shareholders may prefer to use the new rules over a costly traditional proxy contest, making election contests a more plausible avenue for shareholders to participate in the governance of their company. This may have two beneficial effects on the governance of a company. First, the board and management of a company may be increasingly responsive to shareholders' concerns, even when contested elections do not occur, because of shareholders' ability to present their director nominees more easily. Second, new shareholder-nominated directors may be more inclined to exercise judgment independent of the company's incumbent directors and management.

The new rules will remove or reduce some of the current disincentives to shareholders' exercise of their traditional state law rights to nominate director candidates. Once the rules become effective, boards' responsiveness to concerns expressed by shareholders may increase because shareholders could more easily nominate their own directors to run against incumbent directors.[913] In response to the Proposal, commenters submitted studies regarding the effects of reducing incumbent directors' insulation from

---

(Footnote Continued)

inference techniques to approach similar questions. *See, e.g.*, J. Harold Mulherin and Annette B. Poulsen, *Proxy Contests and Corporate Change: Implications For Shareholder Wealth*, J. Fin. Econ. (March 1998) ("Mulherin and Poulsen (1998)") (cited in the NERA Report submitted as part of the letter from BRT).

[912] *See* letters from 3M; ACE; Ameriprise; American Bankers Association; BRT; Devon; Dewey; GE; A. Goolsby; C. Holliday; Honeywell; IBM; Jones Day; Norfolk Southern; Pfizer; Sidley Austin; Simpson Thacher; TI; tw telecom; Unitrin; Wachtell. *See also* letters from BRT (submitting the study by Andrea Beltratti and René M. Stulz, *Why Did Some Banks Perform Better During the Credit Crisis? A Cross-Country Study of the Impact of Governance and Regulation* (July 2009) ("Beltratti and Stulz (2009)"), in which the authors found "no consistent evidence that better governance led to better performance during the crisis" but found "strong evidence that banks with more shareholder-friendly boards performed worse."); Chamber of Commerce/CCMC (submitting an article by Brian R. Cheffins, *Did Corporate Governance*

"Fail" During the 2008 Stock Market Meltdown? The Case of the S&P 500 ("Cheffins (2010)"), which stated that because "corporate governance functioned tolerably well in companies removed from the S&P 500 and that a combination of regulation and market forces will likely prompt financial firms to scale back the free-wheeling business activities that arguably helped to precipitate the stock market meltdown, the case is not yet made for fundamental reform of current corporate governance arrangements.").

[913] The Supreme Court's recent opinion in *Citizens United v. FEC*, 130 S. Ct. 876 (2010) underscores the importance of board responsiveness to shareholder concerns. In *Citizens United*, the government asserted an interest in limiting independent expenditures by corporations in political campaigns in order to prevent dissenting shareholders from being compelled to fund corporate political speech with which they disagreed. *Citizens United*, 130 S. Ct. at 911. The Court, however, stated that any such coercion could be addressed "through the procedures of corporate democracy." *Id.*, quotation omitted.

removal, which showed measures that make incumbent directors more vulnerable to replacement by shareholder action have salutary deterrent effects against board complacency and improve corporate governance and shareholder value.[914] Further, by creating a new threat of removal, the new rules could lead to greater accountability on the part of incumbent directors to the extent they see a close link between their performance and the prospect of removal.[915] In response to the Proposal, one commenter also submitted studies that showed that anti-takeover provisions protecting incumbent management are associated with economically significant reductions in firm valuation, returns and performance, and share prices increase when activists prompt elimination of provisions such as staggered boards.[916] Conversely, the creation of a staggered board structure was found to be associated with a reduction in firm value.[917] Because our new rules may make director elections more competitive by facilitating shareholders' ability to nominate and elect their own director candidates and, hence, also make some incumbent directors less secure in their positions, we believe that the rules may have analogous salutary effects.

As we noted in the Proposing Release, the presence of directors nominated by shareholders may have an effect on company performance and shareholder value.[918] We also

---

[914] *See* letter from L. Bebchuk (noting the article by Lucian A. Bebchuk and Alma Cohen, *The Costs of Entrenched Boards*, J. Fin. Econ. (November 2005) ("Bebchuk and Cohen (2005)"), in which the authors stated: "Staggered boards are associated with an economically meaningful reduction in firm value . . . [w]e also provide suggestive evidence that staggered boards bring about, and not merely reflect, an economically significant reduction in firm value . . . [f]inally, the correlation with reduced firm value is stronger for staggered boards that are established in the corporate charter (which shareholders cannot amend) than for staggered boards established in the company's bylaws (which shareholders can amend).").

Commenters also submitted empirical studies indicating that facilitating shareholders' rights and voice may result in better company performance. *See* letters from L. Bebchuk; CalSTRS; Nathan Cummings Foundation (noting the study by Paul Gompers, Joy Ishii and Andrew Metrick, *Corporate Governance and Equity Prices*, 118 Q.J. Econ. 107 (2003), in which the authors found that "firms with stronger shareholder rights had higher firm value, higher profits, higher sales growth, lower capital expenditures, and made fewer corporate acquisitions."); letters from CalSTRS; Nathan Cummings Foundation (noting the study by B. Lawrence Brown and Marcus Caylor, *The Correlation Between Corporate Governance and Company Performance*, Research Commissioned Institutional Shareholder Services (2004), in which the authors found that "firms with weaker governance perform more poorly, are less profitable, more risky, and have lower dividends than firms with better governance."). *See also* letter from T. Yang (noting the study by Bonnie Buchanan, Jeffry M. Netter, and Tina Yang, *Proxy Rules and Proxy Practice: An Empirical Study of US and UK Shareholder Proposals* (September 2009) ("Buchanan, Netter, and Yang (2009)"), in which the authors found that "after receiving a shareholder proposal, [U.S.] firms exhibit higher stock returns and the improvement is greater [ ] when the proposal is likely to be wealth maximizing or sponsored by a shareholder owning a relatively large equity stake in the target firm.").

[915] As we noted in the Proposing Release, economists have put forth theory and evidence on the link between incentives that are associated with account-

ability and performance. *See, e.g.*, Benjamin E. Hermalin and Michael S. Weisbach, *Endogenously Chosen Board of Directors and Their Monitoring of the Board*, 88 Am. Econ. Rev. 96 (1998) (cited in the Proposing Release, Section V.B.3); Milton Harris and Artur Raviv, *Control of Corporate Decisions: Shareholders vs. Management* (May 29, 2008), *available at* http://papers.ssrn.com/sol3/papers.cfm?abstract_id=965559 (cited in the Proposing Release, Section V.B.3.).

[916] *See* Bebchuk and Hirst (2010) (noting the "substantial empirical evidence indicating that director insulation from removal is associated with lower firm value and worse performance"). *See also* letter from L. Bebchuk (noting the following articles: Lucian A. Bebchuk, Alma Cohen and Allen Ferrell, *What Matters in Corporate Governance?*, 22 Rev. Fin. Stud. 783 (2009) ("Bebchuk, Cohen, and Ferrell (2009)") ("We put forward an entrenchment index based on six provisions: staggered boards, limits to shareholder bylaw amendments, poison pills, golden parachutes, and supermajority requirements for mergers and charter amendments . . . [w]e find that increases in the index level are monotonically associated with economically significant reductions in firm valuation as well as large negative abnormal returns during the 1990-2003 period."); Re-Jin Guo, Timothy A. Kruse and Tom Nohel, *Undoing the Powerful Anti-Takeover Force of Staggered Boards*, J. Corp. Fin. (June 2008) ("Guo, Kruse and Nohel (2008)") ("We find that de-staggering the board creates wealth and that shareholder activism is an important catalyst for pushing through this change."); Olubunmi Faleye, *Classified Boards, Firm Value, and Managerial Entrenchment*, J. Fin. Econ. (February 2007) ("Faleye (2007)") (noting that "classified boards significantly insulate management from market discipline, thus suggesting that the observed reduction in value is due to managerial entrenchment and diminished board accountability.")).

[917] *See* Bebchuk and Hirst (2010); Bebchuk and Cohen (2005).

[918] *See* Proposing Release, Section V.B.3. (citing Cernich (2009)). Moreover, as we noted in the same section of the Proposing Release, empirical evidence has indicated that the ability of significant shareholders to hold corporate managers accountable for activity that does not benefit investors may reduce agency costs

noted in the Proposing Release that academic literature indicates the benefit to shareholders of having an independent, active and committed board of directors.[919] Directors are charged under state law to act as disinterested fiduciaries on behalf of all shareholders, but it has been recognized that the difficult agency problem created by the separation in public companies of ownership from control creates conflicts not completely addressed by state law. We received comment expressing concern regarding the close relationships between directors and a company's management and the degree to which the nomination process is dominated by management.[920] Directors nominated by shareholders pursuant to the new rules will owe their presence on the board to their nomination by one or more significant shareholders and therefore may be independent in a way that is fundamentally different from directors nominated by the incumbent directors. We found to be relevant the empirical evidence cited in our Proposing Release and by commenters regarding the effect on shareholder value of so-called "hybrid boards" (*i.e.*, boards composed of a majority of incumbent directors and a minority of dissident directors).[921] Such boards are a close, but not perfect, analog to the results from an election in which shareholder nominees submitted pursuant to the new rules are elected and typically result when the shareholder's nominees join the board through an actual or threatened proxy contest, but without a change of control. In the study cited in the Proposing Release, ongoing businesses with a minority of dissident directors posted increases in shareholder value of 9.1%, relative to peers, during the contest period, indicating that the market viewed the contest as having a positive effect on shareholder value.[922] Other commenters adduce evidence that boards with a minority of dissident directors produce positive changes in corporate governance structures and strategy and result in increased shareholder value measured in both absolute returns and relative to peers.[923] Amending our proxy rules to facilitate the operation of state laws permitting shareholder nominations of directors may allow shareholders to elect directors who, without obtaining control, can exercise similar influence over decisions critical to shareholder value.

We recognize the existence of studies that reached conclusions contrary to those discussed above.[924] Other commenters warn that the new rules will lead to election

---

(Footnote Continued)

and increase shareholder value. *See, e.g.,* Brad M. Barber, "Monitoring the Monitor: Evaluating CalPERS' Activism" (November 2006), *available at* http://papers.ssrn.com/sol3/papers.cfm?abstract_id=890321 (cited in the Proposing Release, Section V.B.3.). *See also* Deutsche Bank, Global Equity Research, "Beyond the Numbers: Corporate Governance in Europe," (March 5, 2005) (cited in the Proposing Release, Section V.B.3).

[919] *See* Proposing Release, Section V.B.3. (citing Fitch Ratings, "Evaluating Corporate Governance" (December 12, 2007), *available at* http://www.fitchratings.com/corporate/reports/report_frame.cfm?rpt_id=363502).

[920] *See, e.g.,* letters from CII (noting that "some boards are dominated by the chief executive officer, who often plays the key role in selecting and nominating directors" and quoting a view expressed by a prominent investor that "[t]hese people [chief executive officers] aren't looking for Dobermans . . . . They're looking for cocker spaniels."); J. McRitchie ("It is well known that until recently the vast majority of board vacancies were filled via recommendations from CEOs who also are typically chairmen of the boards . . . Recent requirements for an 'independent' nominating committee provide little assurance against continued management domination. These 'independent' board members serve at the pleasure of the CEOs and the other board members; they have no independent base of power.").

[921] Cernich (2009). *See also* letters from D. Romine; GovernanceMetrics; P. Neuhauser; Social Investment Forum; TIAA-CREF; Universities Superannuation.

As we previously noted, the Cernich (2009) study cites long-term return results, relative to peers, which are positive over the subsequent year but negative over the subsequent three years. However, these results are not reported with standard errors, making it difficult to determine whether the expected returns following contests are different from peers, or whether the realized long-term returns during the sample period are merely the result of random chance. Other research, such as Mulherin and Poulsen (1998), is consistent with these findings, but investigates the impact of proxy contests generally, rather than hybrid boards.

[922] Cernich (2009).

[923] *See* letters from D. Romine; GovernanceMetrics; P. Neuhauser; Social Investment Forum; TIAA-CREF; Universities Superannuation. *See also* Mulherin and Poulsen (1998); James F. Cotter, Anil Shivdasani, and Marc Zenner, *Do Independent Directors Enhance Target Shareholder Wealth During Tender Offers?*, J. Fin. Econ. (February 1997) (finding, after examining a sample of 169 tender offers conducted from 1989 through 1992, that target shareholder gains from tender offers were approximately 20% greater when the board was independent).

[924] *See* letter from BRT (referring to the "Report on Effects of Proposed SEC Rule 14a-11 on Efficiency, Competitiveness and Capital Formation, in Support of

contests that will be distracting, time-consuming, and inefficient for companies, boards, and management.[925]

We have reviewed these studies and have reason to question some of their conclusions either because of questions raised by subsequent studies,[926] limitations acknowledged by the studies' authors,[927] or our own concerns about the studies' methodology or scope.[928]

(Footnote Continued)

Comments by Business Roundtable" by NERA Economic Consulting ("NERA Report")); David Ikenberry and Joself Lakonishok, *Corporate Governance Through the Proxy Contest: Evidence and Implications*, 66 J. Bus. 420 (1993) ("Ikenberry and Lakonishok (1993)") (claiming that "companies with dissident board members substantially underperform compared to their peers."") (cited in the NERA Report); Lisa Borstadt and Thomas Zwirlein, *The Efficient Monitoring Role of Proxy Contests: An Empirical Analysis of Post-Contest Control Changes and Firm Performance*, Fin. Mgm't (1992) ("Borstadt and Zwirlein (1992)") (asserting that, in the long run, proxy contests destroy shareholder value) (cited in NERA Report); Beltratti and Stulz (2009) (submitted as part of the letter from BRT and cited in letters from AT&T, BRT, and Seven Law Firms); Cheffins (2010) (examining thirty-seven companies removed from the S&P 500 index during 2008 and concluding that corporate governance functioned "tolerably well" in these companies to negate the need for fundamental reform of the current corporate governance arrangements) (submitted as part of the letter from Chamber of Commerce/CCMC); Ali C. Akyol, Wei Fen Lim and Patrick Verwijmeren, *Shareholders in the Boardroom: Wealth Effects of the SEC's Rule to Facilitate Director Nominations* (December 14, 2009) ("Akyol, Lim, and Verwijmeren (2009)") (documenting negative stock price reactions to the announcements of regulatory activities related to shareholders' right to include director nominees in the company's proxy materials, including the Proposal) (submitted as part of the letter from J. Grundfest); David F. Larcker, Gaizka Ormazabal and Daniel J. Taylor, *The Regulation of Corporate Governance* (January 16, 2010)) ("Larcker, Ormazabal, and Taylor (2010)") (submitted as part of the letter from David F. Larcker ("D. Larcker")).

[925] *See* letters from ABA; Atlas; AT&T; Book Celler; Carlson; Carolina Mills; Chamber of Commerce/CCMC; Chevron; Crespin; M. Eng; Erickson; ExxonMobil; Fenwick; GE; General Mills; Glass Lewis; Glaspell; Intelect; R. Clark King; Koppers; MCO; MeadWestvaco; MedFaxx; Medical Insurance; Merchants Terminal; D. Merilatt; NAM; NIRI; NK; O3 Strategies; Roppe; Rosen; Safeway; Sara Lee; Schneider; Southland; Style Crest; Tenet; TI; tw telecom; R. VanEngelenhoven; Wachtell; Wells Fargo; Weyerhaeuser; Yahoo.

[926] For example, we note that a study highlighted a methodological flaw in the Ikenberry and Lakonishok (1993) study. Mulherin and Poulsen (1998) noted that this study had required that companies exist as the same entity in the COMPUSTAT database subsequent to the contest, eliminating some of the most favorable outcomes of proxy contests from consideration and biasing the estimate of long-term returns downward.

After making corrections for this statistical bias and examining a sample of 270 proxy contests for board seats conducted from 1979 to 1994, the authors found that the market had a favorable response to the initiation of the proxy contest with an average abnormal return of 8.04% in the initiation period, followed by long-run returns statistically indistinguishable from those of comparable stocks. Their analysis showed that the wealth gains during proxy contests stemmed mainly from firms that were acquired. Overall, the authors concluded that proxy contests generally create value, and for companies that were not acquired, "the occurrence of management turnover [had] a significant, positive effect on shareholder wealth relative to the firms that do not replace senior management." In the Borstadt and Zwirlein (1992) study, the finding of a negative risk-adjusted return, conditional on dissidents winning, was based on a sample of 32 firms. Borstadt and Zwirlein note that, overall, "dissident activity leads to gains for shareholders and is often followed by corporate reforms . . . such that the realized gains over the contest period appear to be permanent." A survey article on corporate governance confirmed that this is the current academic consensus, stating that "[t]he latest evidence suggests that proxy fights provide a degree of managerial disciplining and enhance shareholder value." *See* Marco Becht, Patrick Bolton and Ailsa Roell, *Corporate Governance and Control*, Handbook of the Economics of Finance (2003) ("Becht, Bolton and Roell (2003)").

[927] For example, we believe that attempts to draw sharp inferences from the Beltratti and Stulz (2009) study may not be warranted because, as the authors themselves noted, the evidence leaves much to interpretation. The authors concluded that negative conclusions about board effectiveness may be unwarranted because it is unfair to evaluate ex-ante decisions using hind-sight. In particular, they explained that:

> Such a result does not mean that good governance is bad. Rather it is consistent with the view that banks that were pushed by their boards to maximize shareholder wealth before the crisis took risks that were understood to create shareholder wealth, but were costly ex post because of outcomes that were not expected when the risks were taken.

Beltratti and Stulz (2009) at 3.

[928] For example, the relatively short timeframe and small number of companies examined in Cheffins (2010) study alone justify some caution in attempting to draw any sharp inferences from the study. As for the Akyol, Lim, and Verwijmeren (2009) and Larcker, Ormazabal, and Taylor (2010) studies, we note that, even if facilitating shareholders' ability to include their nominees in a company's proxy materials enhances

While we recognize that there are strongly-held views on every side of this debate, we believe that, as discussed throughout this release and supported by commenters' views and empirical data, we have a reasonable basis for expecting the benefits described above.

We are aware, of course, that the new rules are additive to many existing means of monitoring and "disciplining" a company's board and management,[929] which include: hostile takeovers; stockholders "voting with their feet" by selling their shares; board members being replaced by other means when the company's stock performance is poor; and management turnover following poor performance or wrongdoing.[930]

We acknowledge these alternatives, but believe that, for the reasons noted above, directors nominated pursuant to the new rules will have a degree of independence that is not present in the existing means of "disciplining" a company's board and management. Moreover, the ability of shareholders to "vote with their feet" or submit to a takeover bid may be unattractive from a shareholder's perspective if those transactions occur after a period of weak management that has depressed the company's share price. Further, shareholders who invest in indices may not be readily able to sell securities of a particular company that is part of the index, making it difficult for them to "vote with their feet." The high costs involved with other existing mechanisms for "management discipline," such as a traditional proxy contest, often mean that the prospect of replacing incumbent directors is remote unless the company's performance falls below a very low threshold. By that time, a significant amount of shareholder value will have, by hypothesis, already been lost and will require additional time to recoup. We believe that the new rules will help shareholders exert "management discipline" by reducing the cost of, and otherwise making more plausible, shareholder nominations.

We also acknowledge concerns expressed by commenters that the Proposal would encourage boards to make decisions to improve results in the short-term at the expense of long-term shareholder value creation.[931] For the reasons described above, we believe the new rules have the potential to lead to improved company performance and enhanced shareholder value for both short-term and long-term shareholders. Evidence suggests that, historically, proxy contests have created value in both the short-run and long-run for shareholders.[932] The possible inclusion and potential election of shareholder director nominees in company proxy materials would not negate the board's fiduciary obligations, which are to all shareholders. Finally, shareholder director nominees are subject to election by both long-term and short-term shareholders, who will express their interest through their vote. In sum, we do not expect that the prospect that such holders would nominate directors should lead boards to take short-term actions that would detract from long-term value in order to avoid nominations.

A number of commenters expressed special concerns with respect to the Proposal's effect on investment companies, asserting that the election of a shareholder director nominee may, in some circumstances, increase costs and potentially decrease

---

(Footnote Continued)

shareholder value, it may be possible to observe negative stock price reactions for a particular set of public announcement dates. The problem lies in ascertaining the first time investors learned about the regulatory efforts to facilitate this shareholder right. On that initial date, investors may have adjusted share prices for both the capitalized value of the benefits (or costs) associated with the regulatory effort and the probability of the effort's success. Subsequent public announcements may simply cause investors to update these initial assessments of the valuation impact and the probability of success. Consequently, it is difficult to infer whether the price reactions are independent of past announcements or simply a revision of the inves-

tors' prior expectations. It is important, therefore, to disentangle investor expectations about the probability of the success of the regulatory effort from the associated valuation implications. It appears that the Akyol, Lim, and Verwijmeren (2009) and Larcker, Ormazabal, and Taylor (2010) studies did not focus on this distinction.

[929] *See* NERA Report.
[930] *Id.*
[931] *See, e.g.*, letters from BRT; GE; General Mills; IBM; Metlife; Office Depot; Safeway; Wachtell.
[932] *See* Mulherin and Poulsen (1998) and discussion in footnote 926 above.

the effectiveness and efficiency of a unitary or cluster board utilized by a fund complex.[933] Some of these commenters noted their belief that investment company governance presents a special case, arguing that the rules should not be extended to them absent empirical evidence specifically related to boards in this industry.[934] Commenters also argued that investment companies are subject to a unique regulatory regime under the Investment Company Act that provides additional protection to investors, such as the requirement to obtain shareholder approval to engage in certain transactions or activities, and that investment companies and their boards have very different functions from non-investment companies and their boards.[935] We understand these concerns, but we also note that some commenters have raised governance concerns regarding the relationship between boards and investment advisers.[936] Moreover, although investment companies and their boards may have different functions from non-investment companies and their boards, investment company boards, like the boards of other companies, have significant responsibilities in protecting shareholder interests, such as the approval of advisory contracts and fees.[937] We also do not believe that the regulatory protections offered by the Investment Company Act (including requirements to obtain shareholder approval to engage in certain transactions and activities) serve to decrease the importance of the rights that are granted to shareholders under state law. In fact, the separate regulatory regime to which investment companies are subject emphasizes the importance of investment company directors in dealing with the conflicts of interest created by the external management structure of most investment companies.[938]

Lastly, improved board performance may result from the possible increase in the pool of qualified director candidates. When a company does not include shareholder nominees for director in its proxy materials, it loses the opportunity to increase the pool of qualified nominees. Further, it deprives shareholders of the opportunity to consider and assess all qualified candidates if asked to make an informed voting decision in director elections. As we stated in the Proposing Release, facilitating shareholders' ability to include director nominations in a company's proxy materials may result in a larger pool of qualified director nominees from which to choose.[939] By allowing shareholders to submit their own director nominees for inclusion in the company's proxy materials, the demand for qualified individuals who may be willing to serve as shareholder-nominated directors also may increase. This increased demand may, in turn, encourage more individuals to present themselves as potential shareholder director nominees, resulting in a large pool of potential candidates. We recognize, however, this benefit may be offset by the possibility that some qualified individuals may be less willing to be nominated to serve on a board if faced with a contested election.[940]

4. More Informed Voting Decisions in Director Elections Due to Improved Disclosure of Shareholder Director Nominations and Enhanced Shareholder Communications

There was widespread support among commenters for the principle that the Commission should require disclosures regarding nominating shareholders and their nominees.[941] The new requirements in Rule 14a-11, Rule 14n-1, and Schedule 14N will

---

[933] See, e.g., letters from ABA; ICI; ICI/IDC; IDC; MFDF; S&C; T. Rowe Price; Vanguard.

[934] See letters from ICI; ICI/IDC; S&C; T. Rowe Price.

[935] See letters from ABA; Barclays; ICI; ICI/IDC; IDC; T. Rowe Price; S&C; Vanguard.

[936] See letters from J. Reid; J. Taub.

[937] See Jones v. Harris Assocs., 130 S. Ct. 1418, 1423, 176 L. Ed. 2d 265, 273-274 (2010). See also S. Rep. No. 91-184; 91st Congress 1st Session; S. 2224 (1969) ("This section is not intended to authorize a court to substitute its business judgment for that of the mutual fund's board of directors in the area of management fees. . . . The directors of a mutual fund, like

directors of any other corporation will continue to have . . . overall fiduciary duties as directors for the supervision of all of the affairs of the fund.").

[938] See footnote 142 above.

[939] See Proposing Release, Section V.B.3.

[940] For a more detailed discussion, see Section IV.E.1. below.

[941] See letters from ABA; Alston & Bird; Americans for Financial Reform; CalSTRS; CFA Institute; CII; Corporate Library; Dominican Sisters of Hope; Florida State Board of Administration; GovernanceMetrics; ICI; Mercy Investment Program; Protective; RiskMetrics; Sisters of Mercy; Tri-State Coalition; Ursuline Sisters of Tildonk; USPE; Walden.

require certain disclosures and certifications to be provided on Schedule 14N by share-holders who submit a nominee under Rule 14a-11. A nominating shareholder or group will be required to provide disclosure of the information similar to that currently required in a proxy contest regarding the nominating shareholder and nominee[942] as well as certain certifications required for use of Rule 14a-11.[943] Rule 14a-18, Rule 14n-1 and Schedule 14N will require similar disclosures when a shareholder or group uses an applicable state or foreign law provision or company's governing documents to include shareholder nominees for director in the company's proxy materials. The information provided by the disclosures and certifications will help provide transparency to share-holders when voting on shareholder nominees for director and therefore may lead to better informed voting decisions.

With respect to Rule 14a-8(i)(8), companies previously have been permitted to ex-clude shareholder proposals to establish procedures for including shareholder director nominees in the company's proxy materials. This exclusion arose out of the concern that allowing such proposals would result in the occurrence of contested elections without the disclosure that otherwise would be required in a traditional proxy contest.[944] The new disclosure requirements applicable to nominations made pursuant to state or foreign law or a company's governing documents address that concern by mandating disclosure that is similar to that required in a traditional proxy contest.[945]

In addition to improved disclosure, our new rules will enhance shareholders' ability to communicate with each other regarding director nominations and elections through the proxy process. Shareholders eligible to use Rule 14a-11 will be able to utilize the company's proxy materials to present their own director nominees for a vote by other shareholders. They will be able to include in the company's proxy materials a statement supporting their director nominees.[946] Shareholders who are dissatisfied with the com-pany's existing board or the company's director nominees will be able to communicate this view and their preference for alternative candidates through the votes they cast under the proxy process.

The new solicitation exemptions also will facilitate communications between share-holders.[947] Shareholders interested in forming a nominating group to use Rule 14a-11 can contact other shareholders—through both oral and written communications—for that purpose without fear that their communications would be viewed as solicitations under the proxy rules, as long as the exemption's conditions are satisfied.[948] If its director nominees are included in the company's proxy materials pursuant to Rule 14a-11, the nominating shareholder or group can solicit other shareholders to vote in favor of its nominees, or against the company's own nominees, as long as the exemption's condi-tions are satisfied.[949]

---

[942] Among the information included in Schedule 14N is the disclosure required by Items 4(b), 5(b), 7 and, for investment companies, Item 22(b) of Schedule 14A. This disclosure is the same disclosure required for a solicitation subject to Exchange Act Rule 14a-12(c).

[943] Item 8 of Schedule 14N. These certifications include: a certification that the nominating shareholder (or where there is a nominating shareholder group, each member of the nominating shareholder group) is not holding any of the company's securities with the purpose, or with the effect, of changing control of the company or to gain a number of seats on the board that exceeds the maximum number of nominees that the company could be required to include under Rule 14a-11; a certification that the nominating shareholder or group satisfies the applicable eligibility requirements of Rule 14a-11; a certification that the shareholder director nominee satisfies the applicable eligibility requirements of Rule 14a-11; and a certification that the information set forth in the notice on Schedule 14N is true, complete, and correct.

[944] See Shareholder Proposal Proposing Release (proposing amendments to Rule 14a-8 to "make clear that director nominations made pursuant to [bylaw amendments concerning shareholder nominations of directors] would be subject to the disclosure require-ments currently applicable to proxy contests" and noting that such disclosure is of "great importance" to an informed voting decision by shareholders).

[945] See Rule 14a-18, Rule 14n-1, and Schedule 14N.

[946] See Item 7(e) of Schedule 14A and Item 5(i) of Schedule 14N.

[947] See Rules 14a-2(b)(7) and 14a-2(b)(8).

[948] See Rule 14a-2(b)(7).

[949] See Rule 14a-2(b)(8).

With the new amendment to Rule 14a-8(i)(8), shareholders will benefit from a greater ability to present a proposal to establish an alternative procedure under a company's governing documents for the inclusion of one or more shareholder director nominees in the company's proxy materials. Thus, shareholders will be able to present for consideration by other shareholders a director nomination procedure that they believe is appropriate for their company. Through their votes on the proposal, shareholders will then have an opportunity to communicate their views on this proposal to other shareholders and the company's management.

E. Costs

We anticipate that the new rules, where applicable, may result in costs related to (1) potential adverse effects on company and board performance; (2) additional complexity in the proxy process; and (3) preparing the required disclosures, printing and mailing, and costs of additional solicitations.

1. Costs Related to Potential Adverse Effects on Company and Board Performance

Rule 14a-11 and the amendment to Rule 14a-8(i)(8) may result in potential adverse effects on the performance of a company and its board of directors.

First, we received significant comment stating that election contests are distracting and time-consuming for companies, boards, and management.[950] Further, to the extent that a more competitive nomination and election process motivates incumbent directors to be more responsive to shareholders' concerns, the board may incur costs in attempting to institute policies and procedures it believes will address shareholder concerns. It is possible that the time a board spends on shareholder relations could reduce the time that it otherwise would spend on strategic and long-term thinking and overseeing management, which, in turn, may negatively affect shareholder value.[951]

We considered these comments and appreciate commenters' concerns regarding these costs. We believe it is important to note that these costs are associated with the traditional state law right to nominate and elect directors, and are not costs incurred for including shareholder nominees for director in the company's proxy materials. Further, the ownership threshold and holding period that we adopted in response to commenters' concerns should limit the use of Rule 14a-11 to only holders who demonstrate a long-term, significant commitment to the company. To encourage constructive dialogue between a company and a nominating shareholder or group regarding the director nominees to be presented to shareholders for a vote, we revised the rule so that if a company

---

[950] *See* letters from ABA; Atlas; AT&T; Book Celler; BRT; Carlson; Carolina Mills; Chamber of Commerce/CCMC; Chevron; Crespin; M. Eng; Erickson; ExxonMobil; Fenwick; GE; General Mills; Glass Lewis; Glaspell; Intelect; R. Clark King; Koppers; MCO; MeadWestvaco; MedFaxx; Medical Insurance; Merchants Terminal; D. Merilatt; NAM; NIRI; NK; O3 Strategies; Roppe; Rosen; Safeway; Sara Lee; Schneider; Southland; Style Crest; Tenet; TI; tw telecom; R. VanEngelenhoven; Wachtell; Wells Fargo; Weyerhaeuser; Yahoo.

[951] *See, e.g.,* Akyol, Lim, and Verwijmeren (2009) (finding that, based on the market response of a sample of 1,315 firms, "the proposed rule is perceived as costly by shareholders," "that increasing shareholder rights, specifically by facilitating director nominations by shareholders, may actually be detrimental to shareholder wealth," and that "empowering shareholders is not necessarily perceived as a good thing by most shareholders."); Stout (2007) ("Perhaps the most obvious [economic function of board governance] is

promoting more efficient and informed business decisionmaking. It is difficult and expensive to arrange for thousands of dispersed shareholders to express their often-differing views on the best way to run the firm."); *see generally* Stephen M. Bainbridge, *Response to Increasing Shareholder Power: Director Primacy and Shareholder Disempowerment,* 119 Harv. L. Rev. 1735 (2006) (discussing how concern for accountability may undermine decision-making discretion and authority) (cited in the Proposing Release, Section V.C.1.). *But see* Lucian Arye Bebchuk, *The Case for Increasing Shareholder Power,* 118 Harv. L. Rev. 833, 883 (2005) ("[M]ere recognition that back-seat driving might sometimes be counter-productive is hardly sufficient to mandate general deference to management. Such mandated deference would follow only if one assumes that shareholders are so irrational or undisciplined that they cannot be trusted to decide for themselves whether deference would best serve their interests.") (cited in the Proposing Release, Section V.C.1.).

negotiates with the nominating shareholder or group that otherwise would be eligible to have its nominees included in the company's proxy materials after the nominating shareholder or group has submitted its nomination on Schedule 14N, and the company agrees to include the nominating shareholder's or group's nominees on the company's proxy card as company nominees, those nominees will count toward the 25% maximum set forth in the rule.[952] We believe that the cost described above may be offset by other factors as well. The additional communication between a board and the company's shareholders may lead to enhanced transparency into the board's decision-making process, more effective monitoring of this process by shareholders, and, ultimately, a better decision-making process by the board. The cost also may be offset to the extent that shareholders understand that the board's time and other resources are in scarce supply and will take these considerations into account in deciding to nominate directors, recognizing that the cost of a distracted board may not justify pursuing their own specific concerns.

Second, the new rules may lead some companies to re-examine their current procedures for shareholders to submit their own director nominees for consideration by either the company's board or nominating committee, especially if the company is subject to, or thinks it likely will be subject to, shareholder-nominated director candidates submitted pursuant to Rule 14a-11. These companies may incur costs associated with such a re-examination and any resulting adjustments to their procedures.[953] These costs may be limited, however, to the extent that the new rules improve the overall efficiency of the director nomination process and lead to improvements in the existing procedures for director nominations.

Third, the new rules could, in some cases, result in lower quality boards.[954] The quality of a company's board may decrease if, as some commenters predicted, unqualified individuals are elected to the board.[955] Commenters worried, in particular, that a shareholder director nominee will be elected without undergoing the same extensive vetting process or having to comply with the same independence or director qualification standards applicable to other director nominees.[956] The presence of directors who lack the proper qualifications may result in a lower quality board and represent a cost to companies and shareholders. It is important to recognize that Rule 14a-11 provides for only the inclusion of a shareholder director nominee in the company's proxy materials, not the election of that nominee. Further, the new disclosure requirements contained in the Proposal will provide shareholders with information for them to assess whether a shareholder nominee possesses the necessary qualifications and experience to serve as a director.[957] Accordingly, as other commenters have noted, an unqualified individual, even if nominated, will still need to receive the support of a significant number of

---

[952] *See* new Rule 14a-11(d)(5). For a discussion of this modification, *see* Section II.B.6.c. above.

[953] *See, e.g.,* letters from Biogen; GE.

[954] *See* letters from 3M; ABA; American Electric Power; Atlantic Bingo; AT&T; Avis Budget; Biogen; Boeing; BRT; Burlington Northern; Callaway; Carlson; Chamber of Commerce/CCMC; CIGNA; Columbine; Cummins; CSX; J. Dillon; Emerson Electric; Erickson; ExxonMobil; FedEx; Headwaters; C. Holliday; IBM; Intelect; R. Clark King; Lange; Louisiana Agencies; Metlife; NIRI; O3 Strategies; V. Pelson; PepsiCo; Pfizer; Roppe; Rosen; Ryder; Sara Lee; Sidley Austin; tw telecom; Wachtell; Wells Fargo; Weyerhaeuser; Yahoo. *See also* Stephen M. Bainbridge, *A Comment on the SEC Shareholder Access Proposal* (November 14, 2003) at 17, *available at* http://ssrn.com/abstract=470121 ("The likely effects of electing a shareholder representative therefore will not be better governance. It will be an increase in affectional conflict . . . . It will be a reduction in the trust-

based relationships that causes horizontal monitoring within the board to provide effective constraints on agency costs.") (cited in the Proposing Release, Section V.C.1.).

[955] *See* letters from AGL; Air Tite, Inc. ("Air Tite"); All Cast; John C. Astle ("J. Astle"); Astrum Solar ("Astrum"); Atlantic Bingo; Burlington Northern; Glen Burton ("G. Burton"); R. Chicko; Columbine; Darden Restaurants; Erickson; Fluharty; Horizon; Lange; Mama's; Massey Services; NIRI; O3 Strategies; P&G; PepsiCo; W. Steinbrink; Stringer; Theragenics; VCG; Wachtell; and Wells Fargo.

[956] *See* letters from AGL; Astrum; Boeing; R. Burt; G. Burton; S. Campbell; Carolina Mills; Columbine; W. Cornwell; Erickson; Fenwick; FPL Group; Intelect; Little; McDonald's; MedFaxx; Norfolk Southern; P&G; Rosen; UnitedHealth; VCG; Wells Fargo; Xerox; Yahoo.

[957] *See* Rules 14a-11, 14a-18 and 14n-1, and Schedule 14N.

shareholders in order to be elected to the board.[958] Therefore, the cost arising from unqualified directors may be limited to the extent that shareholders understand that experience and competence are important director qualifications and cast their votes for the most-qualified candidates. Moreover, as adopted, the rule will require a company to include in its proxy materials no more than one shareholder director nominee or a number of nominees that represent 25% of the company's board, whichever is greater.[959] We believe that this provision will limit the effect of any potential decrease in the overall quality of a board. Lastly, to the extent that there is a risk of unqualified individuals being elected as directors, it is a risk that arises because shareholders are given the right under state or foreign law to determine who sits on the board of directors.

The quality of a board also may decrease if, as some commenters warned, the increased likelihood of a contested election discourages experienced and capable individuals from serving on boards, making it more difficult for companies to recruit qualified directors or create a board with the proper mix of experience, skills, and characteristics.[960] Some commenters noted that it is already difficult to recruit qualified independent directors.[961] Other commenters, however, did not believe that Rule 14a-11 will discourage experienced, capable directors from serving,[962] with one commenter stating that it encountered no difficulty in finding executives willing to serve on a shareholder-nominated slate.[963] To the extent that the prospect of a contested election deters an otherwise qualified individual from considering a board seat, this will represent a cost to both the company and its shareholders. This cost may be mitigated, however, by the ability of other individuals—those who would not have been considered or nominated by the incumbent directors—to be nominated and presented for a shareholder vote pursuant to Rule 14a-11 or a procedure in the company's governing documents established through Rule 14a-8. The cost may be further mitigated to the extent that the new rules lead to the election of individuals who will present a greater diversity of views for the board's consideration, thereby leading to a better decision-making process, and, ultimately, greater shareholder value.[964] Lastly, as we stated in the Proposing Release,[965] the possibility of qualified candidates being discouraged from running for a board seat may be limited by shareholders' understanding that board dynamics can be important, and that changing them may not always be beneficial.

Fourth, potential disruptions in boardroom deliberations represent another possible cost to shareholders and companies. If a shareholder director nominee is elected and disruptions or polarization in boardroom dynamics occur as a result, the disruptions may delay or impair the board's decision-making process. Such boardroom disruption may occur when one or more directors seek to promote an agenda that conflicts with that of the rest of the board. We received significant comment that the presence of shareholder-nominated directors could disrupt the collegiality and efficiency of boards.[966] We

---

[958] *See* letters from BCI; Bebchuk, et al.; CII; T. DiNapoli; Florida State Board of Administration; Governance for Owners; A. Krakovsky; P. Neuhauser; NJSIC; Relational; Shamrock; Social Investment Forum.

[959] *See* Rule 14a-11(d)(1).

[960] *See* letters from 3M; ABA; American Electric Power; Atlantic Bingo; AT&T; Avis Budget; Biogen; Boeing; BRT; Burlington Northern; Callaway; Carlson; Chamber of Commerce/CCMC; CIGNA;Columbine; Cummins; CSX; J. Dillon; Emerson Electric; Erickson; ExxonMobil; FedEx; Headwaters; C. Holliday; IBM; Intelect; R. Clark King; Lange; Louisiana Agencies; Metlife; NIRI; O3 Strategies; V.Pelson; PepsiCo; Pfizer; Roppe; Rosen; Ryder; Sara Lee; Sidley Austin; tw telecom; Wachtell; Wells Fargo; Weyerhaeuser; Yahoo.

[961] *See, e.g.,* letters from Ameriprise; BRT; Chamber of Commerce/CCMC.

[962] *See* letters from Florida State Board of Administration; Pershing Square.

[963] *See* letter from Pershing Square.

[964] *See* letters from L. Dallas (citing Jerry Goodstein et al., *The Effects of Board Size and Diversity on Strategic Change,* 15 STRATEGIC MGMT. J. 241 (1994) and Lynne L. Dallas, *The New Managerialism and Diversity on Corporate Boards of Directors,* 76 TULANE L. REV. 1363 (2002)); LIUNA; RiskMetrics (noting that it tracked over a four-year period the returns of a portfolio of companies where activists gained board seats in 2005, found that the portfolio outperformed the S&P 500 index even during the recent market turmoil, and saw no indication that the presence of dissident directors on boards had a detrimental impact on shareholder value); Teamsters.

[965] *See* Proposing Release, Section V.C.1.

[966] *See, e.g.,* letters from Association of Corporate Counsel; BRT; Chamber of Commerce/CCMC; GE; IBM; McDonald's; O'Melveny & Myers; P&G; PepsiCo; Seven Law Firms; Society of Corporate Secretaries (also presenting data that the average hedge fund

recognize the view that for companies whose boards are already well-functioning, such disruption could be counterproductive and could delay the board's decision-making process and a delay or impairment in the decision-making process could constitute an indirect economic cost to shareholder value. For the reasons discussed above, however, we believe that boards with directors who were not nominated by the incumbent directors would, on balance, improve company performance and increase shareholder value.[967]

In addition, it may be possible for an investor to submit director nominees through the new rules with the intention of having the nominees, if elected, advocate for board decisions that maximize the investor's private gains but at the expense of other shareholders.[968] In the case of Rule 14a-11, the cost may be limited to the extent that the ownership threshold and holding requirement allow the use of the rule by only holders who demonstrated a significant, long-term commitment to the company. This cost may be limited to the extent that a director nominee with narrow interests must still gain the support of a significant number of shareholders to be elected.[969] The disclosure requirements that we are adopting also may alert shareholders to the narrow interests of the nominating shareholder or group in advance of the election so that they can cast their votes in favor of the candidate who will best serve the interests of all shareholders.[970] The cost may be further limited to the extent that a shareholder director nominee, once elected to the board, will be subject to the same fiduciary duties applicable to all other directors.[971] The possibility of a director seeking to promote private gain at the expense of shareholders generally—and the related costs to the board's overall performance and dynamics—should be limited to the extent that such a director recognizes these duties and strives to fulfill these legal obligations. The cost also may be limited to the extent that shareholders recognize the potential harm from misuse of the board's decision-making process and therefore do not vote for the nominee if they view the cost as sufficiently high.

Fifth, to the extent that the need to comply with the new rules makes the U.S. public equity markets less attractive,[972] discourages private companies from conducting public offerings in the U.S.,[973] or encourages U.S. reporting companies to become non-reporting companies, this would be a cost of the new rules because investors' investment opportunities could be limited. This cost may be mitigated to the extent that the new rules help improve board accountability and corporate governance, generate stronger company performance, and increase shareholder value. Investors may be more willing to invest or continue to invest in companies in which they have the ability to present their

---

(Footnote Continued)

ownership is 7.15%, the number of S&P 500 companies with hedge fund ownership at or above 5% is 273, and the number of S&P 500 companies with hedge fund ownership at or above 10% is 104); Vinson & Elkins; Wachtell; Xerox; Yahoo. *See also* Larcker, Ormazabal, and Taylor (2010)(stating that "the evidence suggests shareholders react negatively to regulation of proxy access, and that the reaction is decreasing in the number of large blockholders and increasing in the number of small institutional investors," and that "the market perceives that shareholders of firms with many large blockholders are harmed by proxy access and is consistent with critics' claims that large blockholders will use the privileges afforded them by proxy access regulation to manipulate the governance process to make themselves better off at the expense of other shareholders.").

[967] *See* Section IV.D.3. above.

[968] *See, e.g.*, letters from BRT; Eaton; IBM; McDonald's; Seven Law Firms; Society of Corporate Secretaries; UnitedHealth. *See also* Stout (2007) at 794

("[B]y making it easier for large shareholders in public firms to threaten directors, a more effective shareholder franchise might increase the risk of intershareholder 'rent-seeking' in public companies.").

[969] *See* letters from BCIA; Bebchuk, et al.; CII; T. DiNapoli; Florida State Board of Administration;Governance for Owners; A. Krakovsky; P. Neuhauser; NJSIC; Relational; Shamrock; Social Investment Forum.

[970] *See* Rule 14a-11, Rule 14a-18, Rule 14n-1, and Schedule 14N.

[971] *See* letter from CII. *See also* Veasey & DiGuglielmo, above.

[972] *See* letter from BRT.

[973] *See* letters from Altman (stating that its survey of 36 public companies showed that 80.85% of respondents believe the new rules "will deter some U.S. private companies from going public and some foreign companies from listing on U.S. exchanges."); BRT; Richard Tullo ("R. Tullo").

own shareholder director nominees in the company's proxy materials if they are displeased with the company's performance. We also note that shareholders in many foreign countries already have the ability to include their director nominees in the company's proxy materials.[974] We therefore believe that the new rules may bring the U.S. capital markets closer in line with international practice by giving shareholders of U.S. companies an ability that may already be enjoyed by shareholders of many non-U.S. companies.

Lastly, with respect to investment companies, a number of commenters expressed concern that the election of a shareholder director nominee may, in some circumstances, increase costs and burdens (e.g., the shareholder-nominated director would have to leave during discussions that pertain to the other investment companies in the complex, board materials would have to be customized for the director, and the fund complex would face challenges in preserving the status of privileged information) and potentially decrease the efficiency of a unitary or cluster board utilized by a fund complex.[975] We recognize that for fund complexes that utilize unitary or cluster boards, the election of a shareholder director nominee may, in some circumstances, increase costs and potentially decrease the efficiency of the boards.[976] We note, however, that these costs are associated with the traditional state law right to nominate and elect directors, and are not costs incurred for including shareholder nominees in the company's proxy materials. We also note that any increased costs and decreased efficiency of an investment company's board as a result of the fund complex no longer having a unitary or cluster board would occur, if at all, only in the event that the investment company shareholders elect the shareholder nominee. Investment companies may include information in the proxy materials making investors aware of the company's views on the perceived benefits of a unitary or cluster board and the potential for increased costs and decreased efficiency if the shareholder nominees are elected. Moreover, we note that a fund complex can take steps to minimize the cost and burden of a shareholder-nominated director who is elected by, for example, entering into a confidentiality agreement in order to preserve the status of confidential information regarding the fund complex.

Two commenters in a joint comment letter argued that there are a number of practical and legal issues that prevent confidentiality agreements from being sufficient to protect the interests of fund shareholders, and included a memorandum from a law firm discussing concerns about Regulation FD, enforceability of confidentiality agreements, whether shareholder-nominated directors would sign confidentiality agreements, compliance, and loss of attorney-client privilege.[977] We considered the issues raised by the joint comment letter. To the extent that material non-public information is discussed by boards in a fund complex, we emphasize that entering into a confidentiality agreement is only one method of preserving the confidentiality of information revealed in board meetings attended by the shareholder-nominated director. The fund complex can have separate meetings and board materials for the board with the shareholder-nominated director, especially if particularly sensitive legal or other matters will be discussed or to protect attorney-client privilege. Finally, we believe the concerns expressed in the memorandum about confidentiality agreements were either not compelling or speculative in nature.

Although commenters argued that the election of a shareholder-nominated director to a unitary or cluster board will necessarily result in decreased effectiveness of the board, we disagree. In this regard, one commenter argued that competition in the board nomination process may improve efficiency by providing additional leverage for boards in negotiations with the investment adviser.[978] In any event, we believe that investment

---

[974] See letters from ACSI; CalPERS; ICGN; LUCRF; Pax World; RiskMetrics; Social Investment Forum; SWIB.

[975] See, e.g., letters from ABA; ICI; ICI/IDC; IDC; MFDF; S&C; T. Rowe Price; Vanguard.

[976] See, e.g., letters from ICI; ICI/IDC; IDC; MFDF; Vanguard.

[977] See letter from ICI/IDC (including attached legal memorandum).

[978] See letter from J. Taub.

company shareholders should have the opportunity to exercise their traditional state law rights to elect a non-unitary or non-cluster board if they so choose.

2. Costs Related to Additional Complexity of Proxy Process

The new rules that we are adopting will, for the first time, require that company proxy materials include information about, and the ability to vote for, director nominees submitted by shareholders. The rules will facilitate shareholders' ability to exercise their traditional state law rights to nominate and elect their own director candidates. One of the costs of this newly-enhanced ability, however, is the additional complexity in the proxy process as both companies and shareholders may have to consider and address the issue of shareholder director nominations more frequently than in the past.

Several commenters expressed concern that the inability of companies and shareholders to opt out of Rule 14a-11, or establish a shareholder director nomination procedure with criteria different than those of Rule 14a-11, may create workability and implementation issues for companies, as they struggle to comply with a rule that does not fit their specific capital and governance structures.[979] One commenter, for example, identified several of these issues, such as: the operation of the rule in a company with multiple classes of stock, a cumulative voting standard, or a majority voting standard; the treatment of derivatives and other synthetic ownership under the rule; the need for adequate protection against use of the rule for change of control attempts; and the consequences of false certifications by a nominating shareholder or group.[980] We recognize the possibility that attempting to comply with a highly-complex rule without the necessary flexibility to adapt the rule to a company's specific situation may create certain costs for companies, such as the cost of legal advice and possible litigation if uncertainties must be resolved in courts. We also recognize the possibility that shareholders may have to incur similar costs if they attempt to use a highly-complex and unclear rule.

The requirements of Rule 14a-11, such as the eligibility criteria, may add a certain degree of complexity in the proxy process. For example, the process of determining which shareholder director nominee will be in the company's proxy materials and the limitations on the number of shareholder nominees for director that a company is required to include in its proxy materials may add complexity. If several shareholders or groups desire (and qualify) to nominate the maximum number of directors they are allowed to place in the company's proxy materials, only the shareholder or group holding the largest qualifying ownership interest will succeed. Another potential source of complexity under Rule 14a-11 is the number of shareholder director nominees that a nominating shareholder or group may submit to a company during a particular proxy season. For example, if the maximum allowable number of shareholder director nominees currently serves on the board, a company will not be required to include additional shareholder director nominees in the company's proxy materials. These sources of complexity and any uncertainty that may arise in implementing the new rules could result in costs to companies, shareholders seeking to have their nominees included in the companies' proxy materials, and shareholder director nominees. For example, both companies and shareholders could incur costs to seek legal advice in connection with shareholder nominations submitted pursuant to Rule 14a-11, the inclusion of shareholder director nominees in a company's proxy materials, submission of a notice of intent to exclude a nominee or nominees, and the process set forth in the rule for seeking an informal statement of the staff's views with respect to the company's determination to exclude a shareholder director nominee. Companies and shareholders also could incur costs to

---

[979] *See, e.g.,* letters from ABA ("Workability requires that the rule or bylaw be easily understandable, be able to be readily administered, address all relevant issues, operate in a time frame that permits proper conduct of shareholder meetings and action by a fully informed shareholder body, recognize the role and fiduciary responsibility of the board of directors, comply with the requirements of the Commission's rules and other applicable law and allow the company and its shareholders sufficient flexibility to respond to changed circumstances in a timely manner."); Keller Group; Wachtell.

[980] *See* letter from Wachtell.

seek legal advice in connection with shareholder proposals submitted pursuant to Rule 14a-8 and the process for submission of a no-action request to exclude the proposal. To the extent disputes on whether to include particular nominees or proposals are not resolved between the company and shareholders, companies and/or shareholders may seek recourse in courts, which will increase costs.

As discussed throughout the release, the rules we are adopting include modifications to the proposed rules. We believe that the modifications will help minimize the complexity of the new rules and clarify uncertainties as much as possible. For example, our decision to adopt a uniform ownership threshold instead of the proposed tiered approach simplifies this particular eligibility requirement and should reduce some of the uncertainties identified by a commenter.[981] We also clarified the availability of Rule 14a-11 when there is a concurrent proxy contest,[982] provided standards for the order of priority of shareholder director nominees upon the withdrawal or disqualification of another shareholder director nominee,[983] addressed issues regarding the application of Rule 14a-11 to certain corporate structures (such as staggered boards and different classes of voting securities),[984] and adopted a uniform deadline for the submission of shareholder director nominations pursuant to Rule 14a-11 that is generally applicable to companies subject to the rule.[985] The costs arising from any complexity or uncertainty arising from the new rules may be mitigated to the extent that companies and shareholders gain greater familiarity with the new rules over time,[986] additional guidance is provided by the Commission or its staff,[987] and, if necessary, uncertain legal issues are resolved by courts.

Lastly, as discussed above, we believe the overall proxy solicitation process for contested director elections may be less confusing for shareholders as a result of our new rules.[988] Presenting the competing director nominees on one proxy card, with the related disclosure contained in one proxy statement, may simplify the shareholder's decision-making process, reduce the potential for any confusion on the part of shareholders, and address any reluctance on the part of shareholders to consider an insurgent shareholder's nominee solely because the nominee was not presented in the company's proxy materials.

3. Costs Related to Preparing Disclosure, Printing and Mailing and Costs of Additional Solicitations and Shareholder Proposals

The new rules will impose additional direct costs on companies and shareholders related to the preparation of required disclosure, printing and mailing costs, and costs of additional solicitations that may be undertaken as a result of including one or more shareholder nominees for director in the company's proxy materials pursuant to Rule 14a-11, a company's governing documents, or an applicable state or foreign law provision.[989]

First, the new rules will impose direct costs onto companies and shareholders due to the rules' disclosure and procedural requirements. For example, companies that determine that they may exclude a shareholder director nominee pursuant to Rule 14a-11 will be required to provide a notice to the nominating shareholder or group regarding any eligibility or procedural deficiencies in the nomination and provide to the Commission notice of the basis for its determination.[990] Companies also may incur costs in preparing any statements regarding the shareholder director nominees that they wish to include in

---

[981] *See* letter from Shearman & Sterling (opposing the tiered ownership thresholds because a number of companies regularly move from one category of filer to another as the aggregate worldwide market value of their voting and non-voting common equity changes from fiscal year to fiscal year, which it believed would lead to uncertainty).

[982] *See* Section II.B.2.e. above.

[983] *See* Section II.B.7.b. above.

[984] *See* Sections II.B.4.b. and II.B.6.a. above.

[985] *See* Section II.B.8.c.ii. above.

[986] *See* letter from CII.

[987] For example, we are adopting, as proposed, a procedure by which companies could send a notice to the Commission where the company intends not to include a shareholder director nominee in its proxy materials and could seek informal staff views—through a no-action request—with respect to that determination.

[988] *See* Section IV.D.1. above.

[989] We note that these increased costs may be less for companies using the notice and access model. *See* Internet Proxy Availability Release.

[990] For purposes of the PRA analysis, we estimate these disclosure requirements would result in 225

their proxy materials. Nominating shareholders or groups and the nominees also will be required to disclose information about themselves, which may be costly.[991] Most of this disclosure will be provided by the nominating shareholder or group in the notice to the company, which would be filed on new Schedule 14N. The Schedule 14N also will include information regarding the length of ownership, certifications, and other information. Companies could incur additional costs to investigate or verify the information regarding shareholder director nominees provided by nominating shareholders or groups, determine whether nominations will conflict with any laws, and analyze the relative merits of the shareholder director nominees and the companies' own director nominees.[992] For purposes of the PRA analysis, we estimate that the disclosure burden of Rule 14a-11 on reporting companies (other than registered investment companies) and registered investment companies is 4,113 hours of personnel time and $548,200 for the services of outside professionals. We also estimate for purposes of the PRA analysis that the disclosure burden to shareholders of Schedule 14N will be 7,870 hours of shareholder time and $1,049,300 for the services of outside professionals. We also received estimates from commenters regarding the costs described above.[993] These estimates are described in the PRA analysis above.[994]

Companies also could incur costs due to the potential increase in the number of shareholder proposals submitted to companies as a result of the expansion in the types of proposals permitted under Rule 14a-8. Under the amendment to Rule 14a-8(i)(8), companies will no longer be able to rely on this basis to exclude from their proxy materials shareholder proposals that seek to establish a procedure in the company's governing documents for the inclusion of shareholder nominees for director in the company's proxy materials. This will likely result in increased costs to companies related to reviewing and processing such proposals to determine matters such as shareholder eligibility and whether there is another basis for excluding these proposals under Rule 14a-8. If a company decides to exclude the shareholder proposal, it will have to incur the costs, such as legal fees, needed to prepare and submit a notice to the Commission regarding its basis for excluding the proposal. In this regard, we received several estimates from commenters regarding the costs related to a Rule 14a-8 shareholder proposal. Based on its July 2009 survey of its member companies, one commenter stated that companies spend an estimated 47 hours and associated costs of $47,784 to prepare and submit a notice of intent to exclude a shareholder proposal.[995] An investment company estimated that its costs for including a shareholder proposal in its complex-wide proxy materials exceeded $3 million in "tabulation expenses."[996] One commenter, however, described the costs to companies resulting from the amendment to Rule 14a-8(i)(8) as "negligible" (with such costs confined to any additional costs of printing and distributing the proposal in the company's proxy materials).[997] For purposes of the PRA analysis, we estimate that shareholders will submit a total of 147 proposals regarding procedures for the inclusion of shareholder nominees in company proxy materials per year to reporting companies, including registered investment companies. Assuming that 90% of reporting companies (including registered investment companies), or 132 companies, prepare and submit a notice of intent to exclude these proposals, the resulting costs to companies will result in approximately 11,484 hours and $1,531,200 for the

---

(Footnote Continued)

burden hours of company time, and $30,000 for the services of outside professionals.

[991] For purposes of the PRA analysis, we estimate the total burden for Schedule 14N for shareholders submitting nominees pursuant to Rule 14a-11 would result in a total of 7,870 hours of shareholder time and $1,049,300 for the services of outside professionals.

[992] See, e.g., letter from S&C.

[993] See letters from BRT; Society of Corporate Secretaries.

[994] See Section III.C. above, for discussion of the estimates included in the letters from BRT and Society of Corporate Secretaries.

[995] See letter from BRT.

[996] See letter from Vanguard. The commenter did not elaborate on the nature of these "tabulation expenses." It also noted that this figure does not include "incremental printing and mailing costs because the proposal was included in the proxy statement and did not require a separate mailing."

[997] See letter from CII.

services of outside professionals.[998] These costs could decrease to the extent that the Rule 14a-8 no-action process provides guidance from the staff on which types of proposals are excludable. Further, because a company that receives a shareholder proposal has no obligation to make a submission under Rule 14a-8 unless it intends to exclude the proposal from its proxy materials, these costs also may decrease to the extent that the company does not seek to exclude the proposal. Lastly, the costs may be limited to the extent that shareholders do not submit proposals related to director nomination procedures due to the uniform applicability of Rule 14a-11 to all companies subject to the rule and availability of the rule for eligible shareholders.[999]

Second, the new rules may increase the incremental costs of printing and mailing a company's proxy materials due to the need to include additional names and background information of shareholder director nominees in the proxy materials and the increased weight of these materials. These costs may increase as the number of shareholder director nominees to be included in the company's proxy materials increases. Thus, this may result in a decrease in the costs to shareholders that would have had to conduct traditional proxy contests in the absence of Rule 14a-11, but may increase the costs for companies.[1000]

Companies also will incur additional printing and mailing costs with respect to the inclusion of a shareholder proposal related to changes to a company's governing documents regarding inclusion of shareholder director nominees in the company's proxy materials. We have two sources of information estimating such costs. Based on its July 2009 survey of its member companies, one commenter stated that companies spend an estimated 20 hours and associated costs of $18,982 to print and mail one shareholder proposal.[1001] The responses to a questionnaire that the Commission made available in 1997 relating to 1998 amendments to Rule 14a-8 suggest such costs to the responding companies averaged $50,000.[1002] As noted above, for purposes of the PRA, we estimate that the amendment to Rule 14a-8(i)(8) could result in the annual submission of 147 shareholder proposals regarding procedures for the inclusion of shareholder director nominees in company proxy materials. Based on this information, for purposes of our analysis, we assume printing and mailing costs of one shareholder proposal in a company's proxy materials could be in the range of approximately $18,000 to $50,000. Assuming each of these proposals were included in company proxy materials, it could result in a total cost of approximately $2,646,00 to $7,350,00 for the affected companies.

Finally, the new rules may lead to an increase in soliciting activities by both companies and shareholders. Companies may increase solicitations to vote for their slate of

---

[998] This estimate is based on the assumption that shareholders of reporting companies (other than registered investment companies) will submit approximately 123 proposals per year regarding procedures for inclusion of shareholder nominees for director in company's proxy materials, and that 90% of companies that receive such a shareholder proposal will seek to exclude the proposal from their proxy materials. Thus, we estimate that companies will seek to exclude 110 such proposals (123 proposals x 90%) per proxy season. We estimate that the annual burden for the company's submission of a notice of its intent to exclude the proposal and its reasons for doing so would average 116 hours per proposal, for a total of 12,760 burden hours (110 proposals x 116 hours/proposal) for reporting companies (other than registered investment companies). This will correspond to 9,570 hours of company time (110 proposals x 116 hours/proposal x 0.75) and $1,276,000 for the services of outside professionals (110 proposals x 116 hours/proposal x 0.25 x $400). For registered investment companies, we estimate for purposes of the PRA that the total burden

hours will be 2,552 hours, which corresponds to 1,914 hours of company time and $255,200 for the services of outside professionals. See Section III.D.2. above.

[999] As discussed in Section II.B.3. above, Rule 14a-11 will not apply to certain types of companies.

[1000] However, as explained in footnote 875 above, the increased costs for the company may not be as much as would otherwise result if the shareholders engaged in a traditional proxy contest.

[1001] See letter from BRT. This cost is in addition to the estimated 47 hours and associated costs of $47,784 that companies spend to prepare and submit a notice of intent to exclude a shareholder proposal.

[1002] In the adopting release for the amendments to Rule 14a-8 in 1998, we noted that responses to a questionnaire we made available in February 1997 suggested the average cost spent on printing costs (plus any directly related costs, such as additional postage and tabulation expenses) to include shareholder proposals in company proxy materials was approximately $50,000. The responses received may have accounted for the printing of more than one proposal.

directors, to vote against shareholder director nominees, or to vote against shareholder proposals. Shareholders may increase solicitations to vote for shareholder proposals, to withhold votes for a company's nominees for director, or to vote for the shareholder director nominees. This increase in soliciting activities by both companies and shareholders will result in an increase in costs as well. These solicitation costs are not, however, required under our rules.

We received a significant amount of comment regarding the extent to which companies will solicit against the election of a shareholder director nominee. One commenter predicted that boards will take "extraordinary efforts" to campaign against the shareholder director nominees, including significant media and public relations efforts, advertising in a number of forums, mass mailings, and other communication efforts, as well as the hiring of outside advisors and the expenditure of significant time and effort by the company's employees.[1003] As examples of these costs, the commenter pointed to the costs of recent proxy contests, which ranged from $14 million to $4 million, as well as the costs of contests at smaller companies, which ranged from $3 million to $800,000. Another commenter conducted a survey of its member companies and indicated that an average total of 302 hours of company personnel and director time will be needed if a company opposes a shareholder director nominee.[1004] One commenter estimated its own annual costs for defending against a shareholder director nominee to be approximately $330,000 and 275 hours of management's time.[1005] Another commenter noted that it had direct costs of approximately $11 million in 2008 and more than $9 million in 2009—in addition to the substantial indirect costs in management time and attention—as a result of the proxy contests that it faced.[1006]

We understand that company boards may be motivated by the issues at stake to expend significant resources to challenge shareholder director nominees, elect their own nominees, or solicit votes against a shareholder proposal. We therefore recognize that, as a practical matter, it can reasonably be expected that the boards of some companies likely would oppose the election of shareholder director nominees. If the incumbent board members incur large expenditures to defeat shareholder director nominees, those expenditures will represent a cost to the company and, indirectly, all shareholders. It is also possible that some shareholders may perceive the use of corporate funds to oppose the election of nominees submitted by shareholders as having a negative effect on the value of their investments.

These costs, however, may be limited by two factors. They may be limited to the extent that the directors' fiduciary duties prevent them from using corporate funds to resist shareholder director nominations for no good-faith corporate purpose.[1007] Some commenters, in fact, characterized the costs incurred by incumbent directors to defeat shareholder director nominees as discretionary because Rule 14a-11 itself does not require such efforts.[1008] Other commenters disagreed with this characterization, asserting that the directors' fiduciary duties may compel them to expend company resources to oppose a shareholder director nominee.[1009] We recognize that, under certain circumstances, company directors likely would oppose a particular shareholder director nominee and expend company resources in that effort, which would increase the costs to the company resulting from Rule 14a-11.[1010] However, the costs for companies may be less to the extent that directors determine not to expend such resources to oppose the election

---

[1003] *See* letter from Chamber of Commerce/CCMC.
[1004] *See* letter from BRT.
[1005] *See* letter from Ryder.
[1006] *See* letter from Biogen.
[1007] *See Hall v. Trans-Lux Daylight Picture Screen Corp.*, 171 A. 226, 228 (Del. Ch. 1934) ("where reasonable expenditures are in the interest of an intelligent exercise of judgment on the part of the stockholders upon policies to be pursued, the expenditures are proper; but where the expenditures are solely in the personal interest of the directors to maintain themselves in office, expenditures made in their campaign for proxies are not proper.").
[1008] *See* letters from CalSTRS; CII; Florida State Board of Administration.
[1009] *See* letters from ABA; BRT.
[1010] The Commission is not expressing a view as to the scope of directors' state law fiduciary duties in responding to shareholder director nominations or expressing a view as to what conduct would be consistent with these duties.

of the shareholder director nominees and simply include the shareholder director nominees and the related disclosure in the company's proxy materials.[1011] The requisite ownership threshold and holding period of Rule 14a-11 may also limit the number of shareholder director nominations that a board may receive, consider, and possibly contest.

4. Other Costs

The new rules may result in additional costs, as described below.

With respect to investment companies, one commenter stated that if a shareholder nomination causes an election to be "contested" under rules of the New York Stock Exchange, brokers would not be able to vote client shares on a discretionary basis, making it difficult and more expensive for investment companies to achieve a quorum for a meeting.[1012] We recognize that it may be more costly for investment companies to achieve a quorum at shareholder meetings if a shareholder director nomination causes an election to be "contested" under the rules of the New York Stock Exchange and brokers cannot vote shares on a discretionary basis. We believe, however, that the costs imposed on investment companies will be limited for three reasons. First, to the extent investment companies do not hold annual meetings as permitted by state law, investment company shareholders will have less opportunity to take advantage of the new rules.[1013] Second, even when investment company shareholders do have the opportunity to take advantage of the new rules, the disproportionately large and generally passive retail shareholder base of investment companies suggests that the new rules will be used less frequently than will be the case with non-investment companies.[1014] Third, because we have sought to limit the cost and burden on all companies, including investment companies, by limiting Rule 14a-11 to nominations by shareholders who have maintained significant continuous holdings in the company for at least three years, and because, as suggested by one commenter, many funds, such as money market funds, are held by shareholders on a short-term basis,[1015] we believe that the situations where shareholders will meet the eligibility requirements will be limited.

Our decision to adopt, as proposed, the revisions to Rule 14a-6(a)(4) and Note 3 to the rule[1016] means that the inclusion of a shareholder director nominee in the company's proxy materials will not require the company to file preliminary proxy materials, provided that the company was otherwise qualified to file directly in definitive form. Because the proxy materials will not be filed in preliminary form, the Commission staff may not have the opportunity to review these proxy materials before companies make definitive copies available to shareholders. Staff review of preliminary materials can benefit shareholders by helping to assure that companies comply with the federal proxy rules and provide appropriate disclosure to shareholders. We believe, however, that any cost related to the staff's inability to review preliminary proxy materials is mitigated by the staff's ability to review the disclosure contained in the Schedule 14N as well as in any additional soliciting materials filed by either the company or the nominating shareholder or group. Further, as we recently stated, the staff retains the right to comment on proxy materials filed in definitive form if the staff deems that to be appropriate under the circumstances.[1017]

[1011] For example, the costs that are incurred only if the incumbent directors choose to challenge or solicit against a shareholder director nominee (e.g., the legal fees arising from the company's efforts to exclude the nominee from its proxy materials) are distinguishable from the costs that must be incurred irrespective of whether the directors oppose the shareholder director nomination (e.g., the increased printing costs caused by the inclusion of the shareholder director nominees and related disclosures in the company's proxy materials).

[1012] See letter from S&C. NYSE Rule 452 provides that, with respect to registered investment companies,

brokers may not vote uninstructed shares in contested elections.

[1013] See letters from ABA; MFDF.

[1014] See letter from J. Taub.

[1015] See letter from ABA.

[1016] The revisions make clear that inclusion of a shareholder director nominee would not be deemed a solicitation in opposition for purposes of the exclusion from filing preliminary proxy materials.

[1017] See *Shareholder Approval of Executive Compensation of TARP Recipients*, Exchange Act Release No. 34-61335 (Jan. 12, 2010) (adopting an amendment

V. CONSIDERATION OF BURDEN ON COMPETITION AND PROMOTION OF EFFICIENCY, COMPETITION AND CAPITAL FORMATION

Section 23(a)(2) of the Exchange Act[1018] requires us, when adopting rules under the Exchange Act, to consider the impact that any new rule would have on competition. In addition, Section 23(a)(2) prohibits us from adopting any rule that would impose a burden on competition not necessary or appropriate in furtherance of the purposes of the Exchange Act. Section 3(f) of the Exchange Act[1019] and Section 2(c) of the Investment Company Act[1020] require us, when engaging in rulemaking that requires us to consider or determine whether an action is necessary or appropriate in the public interest, to consider, in addition to the protection of investors, whether the action will promote efficiency, competition and capital formation.

We are adopting new rules that will, under certain circumstances, require that company proxy materials include information about, and the ability to vote for, director nominees submitted by shareholders. The rules will facilitate the exercise of shareholders' rights to nominate and elect directors and provide shareholders with information about a nominating shareholder or group and its nominees for director. Rule 14a-11 will provide for the inclusion of shareholder nominees for director in the company's proxy materials under certain circumstances and disclosure regarding the nominating shareholder or group and nominees submitted pursuant to the rule. The amendment to Rule 14a-8(i)(8) will provide an avenue for shareholders to submit proposals that would seek to establish a procedure under a company's governing documents for the inclusion of one or more shareholder director nominees in the company's proxy materials. No longer permitting companies to exclude these types of proposals pursuant to Rule 14a-8(i)(8) should enable shareholders to better reflect their preferences for director nomination procedures that would further facilitate their ability to nominate and elect their own director candidates. In addition, the new rules require disclosure of information regarding nominating shareholders or groups and any nominees submitted pursuant to an applicable state or foreign law provision or a company's governing documents, which provides shareholders a more informed basis for deciding how to vote for nominees for election to the board of directors.

We requested comment on whether the new rules will promote efficiency, competition and capital formation or have an impact or burden on competition. We received a number of comments that addressed this section. The comments we received, and our consideration of those comments, are discussed below.

The analysis below is based on our understanding that while no state currently prohibits shareholders from nominating candidates for the board of directors,[1021] shareholders generally do not have a right under existing state law to require a company to include their director nominees in the company's proxy materials.[1022]

We expect that the new rules will promote efficiency in the capital markets in a number of ways. First, we have already considered extensively the expected costs and benefits of the new rules in the Cost-Benefit Analysis and throughout the release. As we believe the benefits (including the possible benefit of improved board accountability and

---

(Footnote Continued)

to Exchange Act Rule 14a-6(a) to add the shareholder advisory vote on executive compensation required for participants in the Troubled Asset Relief Program ("TARP") to the list of items that do not trigger a preliminary filing requirement).

[1018] 15 U.S.C. 78w(a)(2).

[1019] 15 U.S.C. 78c(f).

[1020] 15 U.S.C. 80a-2(c).

[1021] We are not aware of any law in any state or in the District of Columbia that prohibits shareholders from nominating directors. For further discussion, see Section II.B.2.a. above.

[1022] One notable exception exists under the North Dakota Publicly Traded Corporations Act, which permits holders of at least five percent of the outstanding shares of a company subject to the statute to submit a notice of intent to nominate directors and requires the company to include each such shareholder nominee in its proxy statement and form of proxy. See North Dakota Publicly Traded Corporations Act, N.D. Cent. Code §10-35-08 (2009).

company performance) justify the costs, we expect the new rules to promote efficiency of the economy on the whole.

We believe the new rules will promote efficiency by reducing several different types of costs that previously discouraged potentially beneficial actions. The new rules will reduce the cost of shareholders' exercise of their rights to nominate and elect directors.[1023] To the extent that facilitating shareholders' ability to nominate and elect directors of their own choosing is expected to produce the economic benefits for investors described elsewhere in this release, the new rules will bring about these benefits at a reduced cost and thereby promote efficiency. Some commenters asserted that although the new rules may relieve certain shareholders of costs that they are unwilling to incur to run a traditional short-slate election contest, those costs will simply be shifted onto the company and indirectly borne by all shareholders.[1024] This burden may be justified, however, because these costs may not be as much as would otherwise result if that shareholder engaged in a traditional proxy contest,[1025] resulting in a reduction in the overall cost of changing a limited percentage of a board's membership. The burden may be further justified because the new rules may mitigate any collective action concerns.[1026]

The new rules also will promote efficiency by reducing the cost of administering informed shareholder voting—to the extent that a shareholder director nominee is submitted for inclusion in a company's proxy materials pursuant to Rule 14a-11, a company's governing documents, or a state or foreign law provision—by providing for director nominees to be included on one proxy card with clear disclosure[1027] for shareholders to evaluate when deciding whether and how to grant authority to vote their shares by proxy, as opposed to having to evaluate more than one set of proxy materials sent by a company and an insurgent shareholder.[1028] Presenting the competing director nominees on one proxy card, with the related disclosure contained in one proxy statement, may simplify the shareholder's decision-making process, reduce the potential for any confusion on the part of shareholders, and address any reluctance on the part of shareholders to consider an insurgent shareholder's nominee solely because the nominee was not presented in the company's proxy materials.[1029]

The new rules could promote efficiency by reducing the cost of effective communication between shareholders and directors, potentially resulting in enhanced board responsiveness and accountability as described elsewhere in the release.[1030] Such communications may, in some cases, address the concerns that prompted the shareholders to

---

[1023] Many commenters noted the general ineffectiveness or prohibitive cost of the existing means to effect a change in the membership of a board, such as a traditional proxy contest, Rule 14a-8 shareholder proposals, and communications with a company's nominating committee or board. *See* letters from Americans for Financial Reform; Brigham; CalPERS; CII; Florida State Board of Administration; Ironfire; M. Katz; J. McRitchie; Nathan Cummings Foundation; P. Neuhauser; Pax World; S. Ranzini; Teamsters; TIAA-CREF; USPE. Moreover, only a traditional proxy contest was viewed by some commenters to be a realistic method of effecting change in the board's membership. *See* letters from Americans for Financial Reform; CalPERS; CII; Florida State Board of Administration; M. Katz; J. McRitchie; S. Ranzini; Teamsters. Yet, according to these commenters, the high costs of such a proxy contest hinder shareholders' ability to nominate and elect directors. For further discussion of these costs, *see* Section IV.C.1. above.

[1024] *See* letter from ABA.

[1025] *See* Bainbridge 2003 Letter.

[1026] *See* Section IV.D.1. above.

[1027] It is assumed here that the private cost of making the required disclosure and the cost to the company for including the disclosure in the company's proxy materials is lower than the total information cost for voting shareholders.

[1028] As discussed in footnote 884 above, we do not believe that our recent adoption of rules enhancing proxy solicitation disclosure dispenses with the need for Rule 14a-11 and the amendment to Rule 14a-8(i)(8).

[1029] *See* Section IV.D.1. above.

[1030] *See* letters from AFSCME; Bebchuk, et al.; Brigham; CalPERS; CII; L. Dallas; T. DiNapoli; A. Dral; GovernanceMetrics; Governance for Owners; Hermes; M. Katz; LUCRF; J. McRitchie; R. Moulton-Ely; D. Nappier; P. Neuhauser; NJSIC; OPERS; Pax World; Pershing Square; Relational; RiskMetrics; D. Romine; *Shareowners.org*; Social Investment Forum; Teamsters; TIAA-CREF; Universities Superannuation; USPE; Walden. According to these commenters, the prospect of an election contest may create greater incentives for incumbent directors to communicate with shareholders, address their concerns, and consider

submit their own director nominations and help avert any distracting election contests.[1031] Enhanced communication with shareholders also may result in better decision-making by the board as shareholders may provide the board with new ideas or information that the board has not considered.

We considered potential negative effects of the new rules on the efficiency of U.S. public companies, as discussed below.

As discussed elsewhere in the release, if the number of election contests increases as a result of the new rules, boards may end up devoting less time to overseeing their companies' business operations. Election contests have been described by many commenters as distracting, time-consuming, and inefficient for companies, boards, and management.[1032] To the extent that a board's attention is drawn away by the demands of election contests or shareholders, the new rules may impair companies' ability to compete efficiently. To limit the use of Rule 14a-11 to only holders who demonstrate a significant, long-term commitment to the company, we adopted a uniform 3% ownership threshold and three-year holding period. We also continue to believe that this concern may be mitigated to the extent that shareholders, while voicing their concerns and seeking the board's attention, understand the board's time may be in scarce supply and take this factor into consideration when deciding to nominate director candidates.[1033]

The efficiency of U.S. public companies could be negatively affected if shareholders use the new rules to promote their narrow interests at the expense of other shareholders.[1034] If the new rules facilitate the ability of shareholders with narrow interests to place directors on the board, the new rules may impair efficiency by increasing the cost of board deliberations and resulting in companies taking actions that benefit only a few shareholders. This negative effect, however, could be limited to the extent that the disclosure requirements related to Rule 14a-11 alert shareholders to the narrow interests

---

(Footnote Continued)

shareholders' preferences regarding nominations for director.

[1031] We have changed certain provisions of Rule 14a-11 from their proposed form to further encourage communication between boards and shareholders. *See,* *e.g.,* Rule 14a-11(d)(5).

[1032] *See, e.g.,* letters from ABA; Atlas; AT&T; Book Celler; Carlson; Carolina Mills; Chamber of Commerce/CCMC; Chevron; Crespin; M. Eng; Erickson; ExxonMobil; Fenwick; GE; General Mills; Glass Lewis; Glaspell; Intelect; R. Clark King; Koppers; MCO; MeadWestvaco; MedFaxx; Medical Insurance; Merchants Terminal; D. Merilatt; NAM; NIRI; NK; O3 Strategies; Roppe; Rosen; Safeway; Sara Lee; Schneider; Southland; Style Crest; Tenet; TI; tw telecom; R. VanEngelenhoven; Wachtell; Wells Fargo; Weyerhaeuser; Yahoo.

[1033] *See* Proposing Release, Section V.C.1.

[1034] *See, e.g.,* letters from 3M; ACE; AGL; Alaska Air; Alcoa; Allstate; American Bankers Association; American Business Conference; American Express; Ameriprise; Artistic Land Designs; Association of Corporate Counsel; J. Astle; Astrum; Atlantic Bingo; Avis Budget; J. Blanchard; Board Institute; Boeing; Boston Scientific; Brink's; BRT; Burlington Northern; Callaway; S. Campbell; Cargill; Carpet and Tile ("Carpet and Tile"); Caterpillar; Chamber of Commerce/CCMC; Kevin F. Clune ("K. Clune"); P. Clapman; Chevron; J. Chico; CIGNA; CNH Global; Columbine; Competitive Enterprise Institute; A. Conte; W. Cornwell; Crown Battery; Cummins; Darden Res-

taurants; Data Forms, Inc. ("Data Forms"); Deere; T. Dermody; Dewey; A. Dickerson; W. B. Dickerson; J. Dillon; Eaton; Emerson Electric; A. England; Engledow; Mike Emis ("M. Emis"); FedEx; FMC Corp.; FPL Group; Frontier; GE; General Mills; Healthcare Practice; Home Depot; Honeywell; Horizon; Karen L. Hubbard ("K. Hubbard"); IBM; ICI; Instrument Piping Tech; Theodore S. Jablonski ("T. Jablonski"); Keating Muething; Koppers; C. Leadbetter; Leggett; Little; Louisiana Agencies; ITT; Leggett; Brittany D. Lunceford ("B. Lunceford"); Melvin Maltz ("M. Maltz"); Massey Services; J. McCoy; McDonald's; D. McDonald; MCO; McTague; MeadWestvaco; MedFaxx; D. Merilatt; Metlife; M. Metz; J. Miller; E. Mitchell; Moore Brothers; Motorola; MT Glass; NAM; NIRI; Norfolk Southern; O'Melveny & Myers; Office Depot; Omaha Door; P&G; V. Pelson; PepsiCo; Pinch a Penny ("Pinch a Penny"); Protective; Realogy; J. Rosen; RTW; Ryder; S&C; Safeway; Sara Lee; R. Saul; Schneider; Seven Law Firms; Sidley Austin; Southern Company; Southern Services; M. Sposato; Ralph Strangis ("R. Strangis"); Tenet; Tesoro; E. Tremaine; tw telecom; L. Tyson; UnitedHealth; U.S. Bancorp; VCG; Vinson & Elkins; Wachtell; Wagner Industries; Wells Fargo; Weyerhaeuser; Xerox; Yahoo. One commenter added that many recent election contests were directed towards achieving short-term financial objectives, including proposals to sell the company or effect a buyback or special dividend. *See* letter from Simpson Thacher.

of the nominating shareholder or group in advance of the election so that they can cast their votes in favor of the candidate who will best serve the interests of all shareholders.[1035] Directors with potentially narrow interests also will be subject to the same fiduciary duties as directors nominated by the company.[1036]

The increased likelihood of a contested election may discourage some qualified candidates from running for a board seat, making it more difficult for companies to recruit qualified directors and negatively affecting the efficiency of U.S. public companies.[1037] Nevertheless, as discussed elsewhere in the release, a countervailing effect that the new rules may have is the impact on the labor market for director candidates and potential increase in the demand for individuals who can serve as shareholder director nominees.[1038]

Finally, compliance with the new rules may impose additional financial costs on companies, such as for legal services, printing and mailing of proxy materials, and additional proxy solicitation efforts.[1039] The workability and implementation issues identified by commenters, in particular, may force companies to incur significant time and funds to resolve.[1040] Increased litigation costs also represent a possible negative effect of the new rules, as companies and nominating shareholders or groups expend resources to resolve legal disputes in federal and state courts. Incurring such costs could negatively affect the efficiency of the capital markets. As discussed throughout the release, we have modified several aspects of the rules we proposed to clarify any uncertainties identified by commenters and to address workability issues. We also have taken steps to address commenters' concerns regarding a company's liability for misrepresentations or omissions in the nominating shareholder's or group's information that is repeated in the company's proxy materials.[1041] As described above, we have made modifications to clarify that a company will not be liable for materially false or misleading information provided by the nominating shareholder or group.[1042] Finally, additional guidance from the Commission, its staff, or courts should further resolve any uncertainties regarding the new rules' implementation and may reduce the need for parties to resort to litigation.

With respect to investment companies, a number of commenters expressed concern that the election of a shareholder director nominee may, in some circumstances, decrease the effectiveness and efficiency of a unitary or cluster board utilized by a fund complex.[1043] In addition, one commenter noted that small investment companies are likely to be particularly affected by the Proposal and its attendant costs, including the loss of the benefits of a cluster or unitary board.[1044] According to the commenter, "the expected

---

[1035] *See* Rule 14a-11, Rule 14a-18, Rule 14n-1, and Schedule 14N.

[1036] Veasey & DiGuglielmo, at 774 ("Directors will generally be responsible for protecting the best interests of the corporation and all its stockholders, despite the directors' designation by some particular constituency, because fiduciary duties generally will trump contractual expectations in the corporate context."). *See also* letters from ACSI; LUCRF (indicating that they are unaware of any breaches of fiduciary or statutory duties, including Regulation FD, by shareholder-nominated directors in jurisdictions that allow shareholder director nominations in the company's proxy materials).

[1037] *See* letters from 3M; ABA; American Electric Power; Atlantic Bingo; AT&T; Avis Budget; Biogen; Boeing; BRT; Burlington Northern; Callaway; Carlson; Chamber of Commerce/CCMC; CIGNA; Columbine; Cummins; CSX; J. Dillon; Emerson Electric; Erickson; ExxonMobil; FedEx; Headwaters; C. Holliday; IBM; Intelect; R. Clark King; Lange; Louisiana Agencies; Metlife; NIRI; O3 Strategies; V. Pelson; PepsiCo; Pfizer; Roppe; Rosen; Ryder; Sara Lee; Sidley Austin; tw telecom; Wachtell; Wells Fargo; Weyerhaeuser; Yahoo.

[1038] *See* Section IV.D.3. above.

[1039] For a discussion of these costs, *see* Section IV. E.3. above.

[1040] *See, e.g.,* letters from ABA; Wachtell.

[1041] *See* letters from ABA; Alaska Air; American Bankers Association; Ameriprise; BorgWarner; BRT; Caterpillar; Cleary; DTE Energy; ExxonMobil; Honeywell; ICI; Protective; S. Quinlivan; Seven Law Firms; Sidley Austin; Society of Corporate Secretaries; Southern Company; UnitedHealth; Verizon.

As originally proposed, under Rule 14a-11(e) and Note to Rule 14a-19, a company would not be responsible for information that is provided by the nominating shareholder or group under Rule 14a-11, an applicable state law provision, or the company's governing documents and then repeated by the company in its proxy statement, except where the company "knows or has reason to know that the information is false or misleading."

[1042] For further discussion, *see* Section II.E. above.

[1043] *See, e.g.,* letters from ABA; ICI; ICI/IDC; IDC; MFDF; S&C; T. Rowe Price; Vanguard.

[1044] *See* letter from ICI.

smaller rate of return on capital may dissuade some entrepreneurs from entering the investment company industry, and force the exit of some fund advisers with thin profit margins," negatively affecting both efficiency and competition.

We recognize that for fund complexes that utilize unitary or cluster boards, the election of a shareholder director nominee may, in some circumstances, increase costs and potentially decrease the efficiency of the boards.[1045] We note, however, that any decrease in efficiency and competition is associated with the state law right to nominate and elect directors, and not from including shareholder nominees in the company's proxy materials. We also note that any decreased efficiency of an investment company's board, or any decrease in competition, as a result of the fund complex no longer having a unitary or cluster board would occur, if at all, only in the event that investment company shareholders elect the shareholder nominee. Investment companies may include information in the proxy materials making investors aware of the company's views on the perceived benefits of a unitary or cluster board and the potential for increased costs and decreased efficiency if the shareholder nominees are elected. Furthermore, we believe that exempting small investment companies from the new rules would not be appropriate because doing so would interfere with achieving the goal of facilitating shareholders' ability to participate more meaningfully in the nomination and election of directors and to promote the exercise of shareholders' traditional state law rights to nominate and elect directors.[1046] Although commenters argued that the election of a shareholder-nominated director to a unitary or cluster board will necessarily result in decreased effectiveness of the board, we disagree. In this regard, one commenter argued that competition in the board nomination process may improve efficiency by providing additional leverage for boards in negotiations with the investment adviser.[1047] In any event, we believe that investment company shareholders should have the opportunity to exercise their traditional state law rights to elect a non-unitary or non-cluster board if they so choose.

We considered the possible effects that the new rules may have on competition, as discussed below.

With the possible effect of improved board accountability and corporate governance, the new rules may ultimately increase shareholder value, generate stronger company performance, and increase competition. Investors also may be more willing to invest in companies in which they have the ability to present their own shareholder director nominees in the company's proxy materials if they become displeased with the company's performance. Nevertheless, it is possible that some companies may be more reluctant to conduct public offerings in the U.S. or may wish to avoid being a reporting company due to the need to comply with new rules, making the U.S. public equity markets less attractive.[1048] Companies may instead attempt to raise capital through private placements or in foreign equity markets instead of through public offerings in the U.S. equity markets. We note that shareholders in many foreign countries already have the ability to include their director nominees in the company's proxy materials.[1049] We therefore believe that the new rules may bring the U.S. capital markets closer in line with international practice by giving shareholders of U.S. companies an ability that may already be enjoyed by shareholders of many non-U.S. companies. Lastly, we note that the new rules will not apply to foreign private issuers because they are exempt from the Commission's proxy rules.[1050] Therefore, we do not believe that the new rules will affect the willingness of such issuers to raise capital in the U.S. capital markets.

[1045] *See, e.g.,* letters from ICI; ICI/IDC; IDC; MFDF; Vanguard.

[1046] For a specific discussion of the impact of the rule on small companies and the alternatives we considered in lieu of applying the rule to such entities, *see* Section VI. below.

[1047] *See* letter from J. Taub.

[1048] *See* letters from Altman (stating that its survey of 36 public companies showed that 80.85% of respondents believe the new rules "will deter some

U.S. private companies from going public and some foreign companies from listing on U.S. exchanges."); BRT; R. Tullo.

[1049] *See* letters from ACSI; CalPERS; ICGN; LUCRF; Pax World; RiskMetrics; Social Investment Forum; SWIB.

[1050] Exchange Act Rule 3a12-3 exempts securities of certain foreign issuers from Section 14(a) of the Exchange Act.

We also believe that directors nominated by shareholders pursuant to the new rules and elected to the board may be more inclined to exercise independent judgment in the boardroom due to the fact that they were nominated by shareholders, not the incumbent directors. The impact of these shareholder-nominated directors may lead to greater competition when the board considers strategic alternatives, including in the market for corporate control. Board members play a key role in evaluating corporate control transactions and, while the new rules are not intended to facilitate a change in control, shareholder-nominated directors may not share the same bias as incumbent directors regarding a transaction that may be contrary to their interests but beneficial for shareholders. The presence of these directors, therefore, may lead to increased competition in the market for corporate control. We recognize that since the number of shareholder director nominees that a company is required to include in its proxy materials pursuant to Rule 14a-11 is limited, the potential effect on competition for corporate control may also be limited.

Lastly, the requirement that a nominating shareholder or member of the nominating shareholder group using Rule 14a-11 provide proof of ownership in the form of written statements with respect to securities held on deposit with a clearing agency acting as a securities depository may affect the competitive position of brokers or banks that are not securities depository participants.[1051] Due to the need for a nominating shareholder or member of a nominating shareholder group to obtain a separate written statement from a broker or bank that is not a clearing agency participant (*e.g.*, when a broker or bank of the nominating shareholder or member of the nominating shareholder group holds shares of the shareholder or member in an omnibus account at another broker or bank), it is possible that some shareholders may prefer to hold their securities directly through a clearing agency participant to avoid having to obtain more than one written statement to prove their ownership of the requisite amount of securities. If so, the competitive positions of clearing agency participants and clearing agencies themselves in the marketplace may be enhanced. Their competitive position also may be enhanced if a nominating shareholder is reluctant to change its broker or bank because it would need to obtain a written statement from each broker or bank with respect to the shares that it is using to meet the ownership threshold and specify the time period during which the shares were held.

We considered the possible effects that the new rules may have on capital formation, as discussed below.

We expect that potential investors may be more willing to invest in a company if they have greater confidence in the abilities of the company's board members. The new rules allow for a more competitive election process—one in which shareholders will have the opportunity to evaluate qualified alternatives to the board's own nominees and select the person that they feel is most qualified. To the extent that the overall quality of a company's board increases as a result of a more competitive election, the company's ability to attract the necessary capital in the marketplace may be enhanced as well.

Further, potential investors may be more willing to invest in a company if they know that they have a meaningful way to nominate directors for election. The new rules will facilitate investors' ability to nominate and elect director candidates, and may thereby have the effect of holding boards more accountable. Investors may also be attracted to the potential increase in shareholder value that may result from an increased ability to replace directors and enhancement of shareholders' rights.[1052] Lastly, potential investors could prefer to invest in companies with boards that they feel are more open and responsive to their views.

By enabling greater board accountability to shareholders, the new rules also may contribute to restoring investor confidence in the U.S. markets and address any reluctance to invest in U.S. companies.[1053] Companies attempting to raise capital in the U.S.

[1051] *See* Instruction 4 to new Schedule 14N.
[1052] *See* Section IV.D.3. above.

[1053] *See, e.g.*, letters from AFSCME and Sodali (noting a June 2009 survey of investors conducted by

markets may therefore encounter greater willingness on the part of potential investors to participate in their securities offerings.[1054]

As part of our rulemaking process, we considered possible alternatives to the new rules that may serve the same function—and to the same degree—of promoting efficiency, competition, and capital formation. In this regard, we received significant comment that the rules are unnecessary in light of recent corporate governance reforms that already increased the accountability of boards to shareholders.[1055] While each of these reforms may enhance to some degree the boards' accountability and responsiveness to shareholders or shareholders' ability to effect change in the board's membership, we believe they may not be as efficient, effective, or optimal as the new rules. Our consideration of recent corporate governance reforms and suggested alternatives are discussed throughout the release.

We recognize the passage of recent amendments to state corporation laws to enable companies to provide in their governing documents an ability for shareholders to include their director nominees in the company's proxy materials, and that private ordering is an alternative to our new rules.[1056] However, as discussed throughout the release, we have reason to believe that reliance on private ordering under state law would be insufficient to meet our goal of facilitating the exercise of shareholders' traditional state law rights to nominate and elect directors.[1057] For example, companies, particularly those that have performed poorly or have activist shareholders, may be reluctant to amend their governing documents to provide for an ability of shareholders to include director nominees in the company's proxy materials, even if permitted by state corporation law.[1058] In that regard, one commenter observed that most of the companies currently able to provide such an ability in their governing documents under state law have, in fact, not done so.[1059] Further, as previously discussed, establishing such an ability on a company-by-

---

(Footnote Continued)

ShareOwners.org that indicated 57% of the respondents feel strong federal action would "restore their lost confidence in the fairness of the markets" and 81% of the respondents identified "overpaid CEOs and/or unresponsive management and boards" as the top reason for the loss of investor confidence in the markets); letter from Universities Superannuation (noting that "Governance Metrics International now ranks the United States behind Britain, Australia, Canada, and Ireland in corporate governance quality" and that "the CFA Institute 2009 Financial Market Integrity Index survey of investment professionals found a marked decline over the past year in global sentiment of investment professionals toward the United States, with only 43 percent of non-U.S. respondents reporting they would recommend investing in the United States (based solely on ethical behavior and regulation of capital market systems), down from 67 percent a year earlier.").

[1054] *See* letter from Universities Superannuation.

[1055] *See* letters from 26 Corporate Secretaries; 3M; Advance Auto Parts; Allstate; Avis Budget; American Express; Anadarko; Association of Corporate Counsel; AT&T; L. Behr; Best Buy; Boeing; BRT; R. Burt; California Bar; S. Campbell; Carlson; Caterpillar; Chamber of Commerce/CCMC; Chevron; CIGNA; W. Cornwell; CSX; Cummins; Davis Polk; Dewey; DuPont; Eaton; M. Eng; FedEx; FMC Corp.; FPL Group; Frontier; GE; General Mills; C. Holliday; Honeywell; C. Horner; IBM; Jones Day; Keating Muething; J. Kilts; R. Clark King; N. Lautenbach; MeadWestvaco; Metlife; Motorola; O'Melveny & Myers; Office Depot; Pfizer; Protective; S&C; Safe-

way; Sara Lee; Shearman & Sterling; Sherwin-Williams; Sidley Austin; Simpson Thacher; Tesoro; Textron; TI; G. Tooker; UnitedHealth; Unitrin; U.S. Bancorp; Wachtell; Wells Fargo; West Chicago Chamber; Weyerhaeuser; Xerox; Yahoo.

[1056] For example, Delaware recently amended the Delaware General Corporation Law to add new Section 112 clarifying that the bylaws of a Delaware corporation may provide that, if the corporation solicits proxies with respect to an election of directors, the corporation may be required to include in its solicitation materials one or more individuals nominated by a shareholder in addition to the individuals nominated by the board of directors. The obligation of the corporation to include such shareholder nominees will be subject to the procedures and conditions set forth in the bylaw adopted under Section 112. In addition, the American Bar Association's Committee on Corporate Laws has adopted similar changes to the Model Business Corporation Act. *See* American Bar Association, Section of Business Law, Committee on Corporate Laws Amendments to The Model Business Corporation Act Approved on Third Reading at the Committee's Meeting on December 12, 2009 (*available at* http://www.abanet.org/media/docs/Amendments_to_MCBA_121709.pdf).

[1057] *See* Sections II.B.2. and IV.D.2. above.

[1058] *See* letters from CalPERS; D. Nappier; P. Neuhauser; Pershing Square; Schulte Roth & Zabel.

[1059] *See* letter from TIAA-CREF. Further, based on its survey of its member companies, one commenter stated that a large majority—approximately two-thirds—would seek to opt out of Rule 14a-11, if possible. *See* letter from Society of Corporate Secretaries.

company basis may be more costly and inefficient than under our new rules.[1060] For shareholders with a diverse portfolio of securities, the administrative burden of tracking each company's requirements for including a director nominee in the company's proxy materials may add another degree of inefficiency.[1061] Some commenters also expressed concerns about the ability of shareholders to adopt a provision in a company's governing documents for the inclusion of shareholder director nominees through the Rule 14a-8 process due to the rule's requirements (such as the 500-word limit on shareholder proposals)[1062] or procedural requirements for shareholder-proposed bylaw amendments, such as a super-majority voting requirement for adoption of amendments.[1063]

We considered the recent amendments to state corporation laws to enable a company to include in its governing documents a provision for reimbursement of a shareholder's proxy solicitation costs.[1064] We note, however, that poorly-performing companies may be reluctant to include such a provision, forcing shareholders to undergo the potentially costly and time-consuming process of establishing such a provision themselves (for example, through a Rule 14a-8 shareholder proposal). Even if reimbursement arrangements were to exist at all public companies, we believe that the ability of shareholders to be reimbursed for their proxy solicitation costs may be less efficient in facilitating changes in the board or increasing board accountability or responsiveness because shareholders would still need funds to maintain an election contest.[1065] This may create a disparity among shareholders as shareholders with greater resources are able to take advantage of the right and conduct a proxy contest (with the knowledge they will be reimbursed) while those who lack such resources are unable to do so.

We also considered the trend towards adopting a majority voting standard in director elections, which gives shareholders a greater voice in director elections and the company's corporate governance. It is important to note, however, that a majority voting standard in director elections, while increasingly common, is not yet used by all companies.[1066] Further, commenters pointed out that even with a majority voting standard, some boards have disregarded the outcome of the elections by, for example, refusing to accept the resignations of directors who failed to receive a majority vote.[1067] Further, while a majority voting standard facilitates shareholders' ability to elect candidates put forth by a company's management, it does not facilitate shareholders' ability to exercise their right to nominate candidates for director.

We considered the growing effectiveness of "withhold" or "vote no" campaigns in director elections, particularly at companies with a majority voting standard for director elections. "Withhold" or "vote no" campaigns have long been available but appear only

---

[1060] *See* letters from CalPERS; D. Nappier; P. Neuhauser.

[1061] *See* letter from CII.

[1062] *Id.*

[1063] *See* letter from CII (stating that, based on a November 2009 white paper commissioned by the CII and ShareOwners.org, many companies have super-majority voting requirements to amend the bylaws, thereby "making shareholder-proposed bylaw amendments nearly impossible to implement").

[1064] Delaware also added new Section 113 of the Delaware General Corporation Law, which allows a Delaware corporation's bylaws to include a provision that the corporation, under certain circumstances, will reimburse a shareholder for the expenses incurred in soliciting proxies in connection with an election of directors.

[1065] *See* letter from Florida State Board of Administration.

[1066] *See* letters from CalPERS (noting that the standard has "only been adopted by 294 companies in the S&P 500 and just 734 companies out of the 3,369 companies according to the Corporate Library Board Analyst database."); TIAA-CREF (noting that "[o]nly about half of S&P 500 companies and a small minority of Russell 3000 companies have adopted this reform.").

[1067] *See* letters from CalPERS; RiskMetrics; TIAA-CREF (noting that "[t]here are currently over 40 directors at U.S. companies who continue to serve without having received majority support."). *See also City of Westland Police & Fire Ret. Sys. v. Axcelis Technologies, Inc.*, 2009 Del. Ch. LEXIS 173 (September 28, 2009), aff'd, 2010 Del. LEXIS 382 (Del., August 11, 2010) (finding "no credible basis" to infer wrongdoing by directors who refused to accept resignations by other directors who failed to achieve the majority vote required by board policy).

occasionally to have resulted in a change in composition of the board or senior manage-ment.[1068] By definition, however, such campaigns lack what Rule 14a-11 facilitates, namely a direct means to include shareholder-nominated candidates for election as directors, rather than merely express disapproval of incumbent directors.[1069]

We considered the effect of adoption of our notice and access model for electronic delivery of proxy materials, which reduces the printing and mailing costs for share-holders' proxy solicitations. As discussed above, the notice and access model, while reducing the printing and mailing costs, does not necessarily provide the same cost savings as Rule 14a-11.[1070] Further, a shareholder may find the use of the model to be unattractive for the reasons related to its strategy for the conduct of the election contest.[1071]

Lastly, one commenter pointed out that the market already provides multiple means of "management discipline."[1072] Shareholders could express their displeasure with current management by selling their securities in the company, board members could be replaced, and managers could be removed for wrongdoing. In addition, the commenter stated that the threat of takeover attempts that management faces and higher levels of board independence suggest the success of existing means of "management discipline."

While we are aware of these means of "management discipline," we believe the relevant issue is whether investors will benefit from our new rules. Shareholders' ability to express their displeasure with current management through the sale of securities may be limited if the market for the securities is illiquid or the shareholder is constrained by its policies to invest in all companies within a given index. Replacing board members or removing managers under the current regulatory scheme is expensive and often requires considerable time during which significant shareholder value may be lost. By providing a more efficient means for shareholders with a significant, long-term stake to nominate directors, the new rules will promote competition and enable shareholders to nominate and elect directors.

Commenters also argued that it was not necessary to make investment companies subject to the new rules because they are subject to a unique regulatory regime under the Investment Company Act that provides additional protection to investors, such as the requirement to obtain shareholder approval to engage in certain transactions or activi-ties.[1073] However, we do not believe that the regulatory protections offered by the Investment Company Act (including requirements to obtain shareholder approval to engage in certain transactions and activities) serve to decrease the importance of the rights that are granted to shareholders under state law. In fact, the separate regulatory regime to which investment companies are subject emphasizes the importance of invest-ment company directors in dealing with the conflicts of interest created by the external management structure of most investment companies.[1074]

VI. FINAL REGULATORY FLEXIBILITY ANALYSIS

This Final Regulatory Flexibility Analysis ("FRFA") has been prepared in accordance with the Regulatory Flexibility Act.[1075] It relates to amendments to the rules and forms under the Exchange Act and the Investment Company Act that would, under certain limited circumstances, require companies to include in their proxy materials shareholder nominees for election as director. It also relates to the amendments to the rules that will prohibit companies from excluding shareholder proposals pursuant to Rule 14a-8(i)(8) that seek to establish a procedure under a company's governing documents for the

---

[1068] *See* J.W. Verret, *Pandora's Ballot Box, Or a Proxy with Moxie? Majority Voting, Corporate Ballot Access, and the Legend of Martin Lipton Re-Examined,* 62 BUS. LAW. 1007, 1014 (2007) (reporting on one replacement of a board chairman following a withhold campaign resulting in a 43% withhold vote).

[1069] *See* letter from AFSCME.

[1070] *See* Section IV.D.1. above.

[1071] *Id.*

[1072] *See* letter from BRT (referring to the NERA Report).

[1073] ABA; Barclays; ICI; IDC; T. Rowe Price; S&C; Vanguard.

[1074] *See* footnote 142 above.

[1075] 5 U.S.C. 601.

inclusion of one or more shareholder director nominees in the company's proxy materials. The amendments will require, under certain circumstances, a company's proxy materials to provide shareholders with information about, and the ability to vote for, a shareholder's, or group of shareholders', nominees for director. The amendments will facilitate the exercise of shareholders' traditional state law rights to nominate and elect directors to boards of directors and thereby enable shareholders to participate more meaningfully in the nomination and election of directors at the companies in which they invest.

A. Need for the Amendments

As described in this release and the Proposing Release, the final rules include features from the proposals on this topic in 2003 and 2007, and reflect much of what we learned through the public comment that the Commission has received concerning this topic over the past seven years. The final rules are intended to facilitate shareholders' ability to participate more meaningfully in the nomination and election of directors, to promote the exercise of shareholders' traditional state law rights to nominate and elect directors, to open up communication between a company and its shareholders, and to provide shareholders with more information to make an informed voting decision by requiring disclosure about a nominating shareholder or group and its nominee or nominees. In particular, the final rules will enable long-term shareholders, or groups of long-term shareholders, with significant holdings to have their nominees for director included in company proxy materials. In addition, the amendment to Rule 14a-8(i)(8) will narrow the exclusion and will not permit companies to exclude, under Rule 14a-8(i)(8), shareholder proposals that seek to establish a procedure under a company's governing documents for the inclusion of one or more shareholder director nominees in the company's proxy materials.

The final rules are intended to achieve the stated objectives without unduly burdening companies. We sought to limit the cost and burden on companies by limiting Rule 14a-11 to nominations by shareholders who have maintained a significant continuous ownership interest in the company for at least three years at the time the notice of nomination is submitted, and by limiting the number of nominees a company is required to include in its proxy materials under Rule 14a-11. These aspects of the final rules will limit the number of nominees a company will be required to consider for inclusion in its proxy materials and thus will lower the cost to companies while facilitating the exercise of shareholders' traditional state law rights to nominate and elect directors to boards of directors, thereby enabling shareholders to participate more meaningfully in the nomination and election of directors at the companies in which they invest. We believe the new rules will benefit shareholders by improving corporate suffrage, the disclosure provided in connection with proxy solicitations, and communication between shareholders through the proxy process.

The final rules include a phase-in period that delays the compliance date for Rule 14a-11 for smaller reporting companies, which include most small entities, for three years from the effective date of the rule for other companies.[1076] We believe the delayed compliance date will allow those companies to observe how the rule operates for other companies and may allow them to better prepare for the implementation of the rules. We also believe that delayed implementation for these companies will provide us with the opportunity to evaluate the implementation of Rule 14a-11 by larger companies and to consider whether adjustments to the rule would be appropriate for smaller reporting companies before the rule becomes applicable to them.[1077] In addition, in an effort to

---

[1076] For purposes of this FRFA, we are required to consider the impact of our rules on small entities, including "small business." See footnote 1088 and the related discussion. The new rules will have a delayed effective date for smaller reporting companies as defined in Exchange Act Rule 12b-2. Whether a company is a small business is determined based on a company's assets while the determination of whether a company is a smaller reporting company is generally based on a company's public float. We expect that most small businesses that would be subject to the new rules also would qualify as smaller reporting companies.

[1077] As discussed in Section II.B.3. above, the recent Dodd-Frank Wall Street Reform and Consumer Protection Act provided the Commission with exemptive

limit the cost and burden on all companies subject to the rule, including smaller reporting companies, we have limited use of Rule 14a-11 to nominations by shareholders who have maintained significant continuous holdings in the company, and we have extended the required holding period to at least three years at the time the notice of nomination is filed with the Commission and transmitted to the company. We expect that these eligibility requirements will help achieve the stated objective without unduly burdening any particular group of companies.

B. Significant Issues Raised by Public Comments

In the Proposing Release, we requested comment on any aspect of the Initial Regulatory Flexibility Act Analysis ("IRFA"), including the number of small entities that would be affected by the proposed rules, the nature of the impact, how to quantify the number of small entities that would be affected, and how to quantify the impact of the proposed rules. We also considered, and sought comment on, excluding from operation of the rule smaller reporting companies either permanently or on a temporary basis through staggered compliance dates based on company size. We did not receive comments specifically addressing the IRFA. Several commenters, however, addressed aspects of the proposed rules that could potentially affect small entities.

In particular, many commenters stated generally that Rule 14a-11 should not apply to small businesses.[1078] Some commenters argued that the Proposal, if adopted, would hurt their larger corporate suppliers which would, in turn, increase their own costs of doing business.[1079] Two commenters recommended that Rule 14a-11 exclude companies that are not at least accelerated filers and be limited, at least initially, to large accelerated filers.[1080] These commenters expressed concern about the burden Rule 14a-11 would place on smaller companies, including difficulty in recruiting qualified directors and costs of conducting due diligence on shareholder nominees.[1081] One commenter noted that small investment companies, which may operate with thin profit margins, would be particularly affected by the Proposal and its attendant costs, including the loss of the benefits of a cluster or unitary board.[1082] By contrast, some commenters stated that Rule 14a-11 should apply to small businesses.[1083] At least one commenter argued that Rule 14a-11 would not impose a material burden on any company subject to the proxy rules

---

(Footnote Continued)

authority with respect to rules permitting the inclusion of shareholder director nominations in company proxy materials. In doing so, Congress noted that the Commission shall take into account whether any such requirement to permit inclusion of shareholder nominees for director in company proxy materials would disproportionately burden small issuers.

[1078] *See* letters from ABA; American Mailing; All Cast; Always N Bloom; American Carpets; J. Arquilla; B. Armburst; Artistic Land Designs; C. Atkins; Book Celler; K. Bostwick; Brighter Day Painting; Colletti; Commercial Concepts; Complete Home Inspection; D. Courtney; S. Crawford; Crespin; Don's; T. Ebreo; M. Eng; eWareness; Evans; Fluharty; Flutterby; Fortuna Italian Restaurant; Future Form; Glaspell; C. Gregory; Healthcare Practice; B. Henderson; S. Henning; J. Herren; A. Iriarte; J. Jones; Juz Kidz; Kernan; LMS Wine; T. Luna; Mansfield Children's Center; D. McDonald; Meister; Merchants Terminal; Middendorf; Mingo; Moore Brothers; Mouton; D. Mozack; Ms. Dee; G. Napolitano; NK; H. Olson; PESC; Pioneer Heating & Air Conditioning; RC; RTW; D. Sapp; SBB; SGIA; P. Sicilia; Slycers Sandwich Shop; Southern Services; Steele Group; Sylvron; Theragenics; E. Tremaine; Wagner; Wagner Industries; Wellness; West End; Y.M.; J. Young.

[1079] *See* letters from Always N Bloom; Brighter Day Painting; Caswells; Complete Home Inspection; Darrell's Automotive; Data Forms; Fluharty; E. Garcia; S. Henning; T. Luna; Magnolia; American Mailing; H. Olson; T. Roper; Solar Systems; E. Sprenkle; Steele Group; R. Trummel; T. Trummel; V. Trummel; Wagner; T. White.

[1080] *See* letters from ABA; Theragenics.

[1081] In this regard, one commenter suggested that our estimate of the burden to companies of evaluating a shareholder nominee's background to determine eligibility, investigation and verification of information provided by the nominee, research into the nominee's background, analysis of the relative merits of the shareholder nominee as compared to management's own nominee, meetings of the relevant board committees, and analysis of whether a nomination would conflict with any federal or state law, or director qualification standards was too low. This commenter estimated that the burden hours associated with the above actions would be 99 hours of company personnel time. *See* letter from S&C (citing results of a survey conducted by BRT). For a discussion of burden estimates, *see* Section III. above.

[1082] *See* letter from ICI.

[1083] *See* letters from AFSCME; CII; D. Nappier.

because companies already have to distribute proxy cards and it would not be an imposition if they were required to add additional nominees to those cards.[1084] Another commenter argued that exempting small entities would be inconsistent with the stated goals of the Proposal and the costs and burden to such entities would be minimal.[1085]

We believe that exempting small companies, including small investment companies, from the new rules would not be appropriate because doing so would interfere with achieving the goal of facilitating shareholders' ability to participate more meaningfully in the nomination and election of directors, to promote the exercise of shareholders' rights to nominate and elect directors, to open up communication between a company and its shareholders and to provide shareholders with better information from which to make an informed voting decision. Some commenters noted that small companies are "just as likely" to have dysfunctional boards as their larger counterparts.[1086] Also, one commenter agreed that exempting small entities would be inconsistent with the stated goals of the Proposal and the costs and burdens to these entities would be minimal.[1087] However, we are cognizant of the fact that the new rules will increase the burden on all companies and therefore the potential burden on smaller reporting companies as defined in Rule 12b-2 under the Exchange Act. To address concerns about the potential impact on smaller reporting companies, the final rule delays the compliance date for Rule 14a-11 for smaller reporting companies for a period of three years from the effective date of the rule for other companies so that smaller reporting companies can observe how the rule operates and allow them to better prepare for the implementation of the rules. We also believe that delayed implementation for these companies will allow us to evaluate the implementation of Rule 14a-11 by larger companies and provide us with the additional opportunity to consider whether adjustments to the rule would be appropriate for smaller reporting companies before the rule becomes applicable to them. In addition, in an effort to limit the cost and burden on all companies subject to the rule, including smaller reporting companies, we have limited use of Rule 14a-11 to nominations by shareholders who have maintained significant continuous holdings in the company, and we have extended the required holding period to at least three years at the time the notice of nomination is filed with the Commission and transmitted to the company. We expect that these eligibility requirements will help achieve the stated objective without unduly burdening any particular group of companies.

C. Small Entities Subject to the Rules

The final rules will affect some companies that are small entities. The Regulatory Flexibility Act defines "small entity" to mean "small business," "small organization," or "small governmental jurisdiction."[1088] The Commission's rules define "small business" and "small organization" for purposes of the Regulatory Flexibility Act for each of the types of entities regulated by the Commission. Securities Act Rule 157[1089] and Exchange Act Rule 0-10(a)[1090] define a company, other than an investment company, to be a "small business" or "small organization" if it had total assets of $5 million or less on the last day of its most recent fiscal year. We estimate that there are approximately 1,209 issuers that may be considered small entities.[1091]

For purposes of the Regulatory Flexibility Act, an investment company is a small entity if it, together with other investment companies in the same group of related investment companies, has net assets of $50 million or less as of the end of its most recent fiscal year.[1092] We estimate that approximately 168 registered investment companies and 33 business development companies meet this definition. The new rules may affect each of the approximately 201 issuers that may be considered small entities, to the extent companies and shareholders take advantage of the rules.

[1084] *See* letter from USPE.

[1085] *See* letter from CII.

[1086] *See* letters from AFSCME; D. Nappier.

[1087] *See* letter from CII.

[1088] 5 U.S.C. 601(6).

[1089] 17 CFR 230.157.

[1090] 17 CFR 240.0-10(a).

[1091] The estimated number of reporting small entities is based on 2009 data, including the Commission's EDGAR database and Standard & Poor's.

[1092] 17 CFR 270.0-10(a).

D. Reporting, Recordkeeping and Other Compliance Requirements

The final rules are designed to require, under certain circumstances, Exchange Act reporting companies (other than debt-only companies and companies whose applicable state or foreign law provisions or governing documents prohibit shareholder nominations) subject to the federal proxy rules, including small entities, to include shareholder nominees for director in the company's proxy materials. Nominating shareholders or groups, including nominating shareholders that are small entities, will be required to meet certain eligibility requirements and to provide disclosure in Schedule 14N about the nominating shareholders and the nominee, and companies will be required to include the disclosure provided by the nominating shareholder or group in the company's proxy materials.

The final rules also will enable shareholders to include proposals in the company's proxy materials that seek to establish a procedure under a company's governing documents for the inclusion of one or more shareholder director nominees in the company's proxy materials. A nominating shareholder or group, including a nominating shareholder or group that is a small entity, using an applicable state or foreign law provision or a provision in the company's governing documents to submit a nomination for director to be included in a company's proxy materials will be required to provide disclosure in new Schedule 14N about the nominating shareholder or group and the nominee. Companies also will be required to include disclosure about the nominating shareholder or group and the nominee in the company's proxy materials when a shareholder submits a nomination for director for inclusion in the company's proxy materials pursuant to an applicable state or foreign law provision or a company's governing documents.

We have no reason to expect that the amendment to Rule 14a-8(i)(8) will substantially increase the number of shareholder proposals to smaller companies and likely will have little impact on small entities. With respect to Rule 14a-11, there is some data indicating that smaller companies are subject to more proxy contests as a group than larger companies,[1093] but the data do not demonstrate that the frequency is disproportionately larger at smaller companies relative to other companies. In addition, we did not receive data substantiating a disproportionate impact on smaller companies.

With respect to investment companies, we assume that small investment companies, which may operate with thin profit margins, would be particularly affected by the rules and the attendant costs, including the loss of the benefits of a cluster or unitary board.[1094] However, the costs resulting from the loss of the benefits of a cluster or unitary board are costs associated with the traditional state law rights to nominate and elect directors, and are not costs incurred for including shareholder nominees in the company's proxy materials. We also note that any increased costs and decreased efficiency of an investment company's board as a result of the fund complex no longer having a unitary or cluster board would occur, if at all, only in the event that investment company shareholders elect the shareholder nominee. Investment companies may include information in the proxy materials making investors aware of the company's views on the perceived benefits of a unitary or cluster board and the potential for increased costs and decreased efficiency if the shareholder nominees are elected.

E. Agency Action to Minimize Effect on Small Entities

The Regulatory Flexibility Act directs us to consider significant alternatives that would accomplish the stated objective, while minimizing any significant adverse impact on small entities. In connection with the new rules, we considered the following alternatives:

- the establishment of differing compliance or reporting requirements or timetables that take into account the resources available to small entities;

[1093] *See, e.g.*, Bebchuk (2007).   [1094] *See* letter from ICI.

- the clarification, consolidation or simplification of the rule's compliance and reporting requirements for small entities;

- the use of performance rather than design standards; and

- an exemption for small entities from coverage under the proposals.

As noted in the Proposing Release, the Commission has considered a variety of reforms to achieve its regulatory objectives while minimizing the impact on small entities. As one possible approach, we considered in 2003 requiring companies to include shareholder nominees for director in a company's proxy materials only upon the occurrence of certain events so that the rule would apply only in situations where there was a demonstrated failure in the proxy process related to director nominations and elections. We sought comment in the Proposing Release on this approach, with commenters arguing both for[1095] and against[1096] the approach. We have not taken this approach in the final rules because we do not believe it is appropriate to limit the rule to companies where specified events have occurred. Moreover, we are not aware of data suggesting that such specified events are less likely to occur at smaller companies than at larger companies.

We considered changes to Rule 14a-8(i)(8) in 2007 that would enable shareholders to have their proposals for bylaw amendments regarding the procedures for nominating directors included in the company's proxy materials provided the shareholder submitting the proposal made certain disclosures and beneficially owned more than 5% of the company's shares. Although this approach could potentially reduce the number of shareholder proposals submitted to smaller entities by establishing a minimum threshold for having such proposals included in the company's proxy statement, we have not taken this approach because, as noted above, we do not expect the final rule to substantially increase the number of shareholder proposals to smaller companies. In addition, we have not relied exclusively on an amendment to Rule 14a-8(i)(8) to achieve our regulatory goals because we seek to provide shareholders with a more immediate and direct means of effecting change in the boards of directors of the companies in which they invest. For these reasons, as well as the reasons discussed throughout the release, we believe that these final rules may better achieve the Commission's objectives.

We also sought comment on whether the proposed tiered approach—under which shareholders or shareholder groups at larger companies would have to satisfy a lower ownership threshold than shareholders or shareholder groups at smaller companies in order to rely on Rule 14a-11—is appropriate and workable. We considered whether the effect of the tiered approach may make it less likely that shareholders at smaller companies will nominate directors under Rule 14a-11, but determined not to adopt this approach because the data available to us did not indicate a meaningful difference between small entities and entities generally in regard to concentration of long-term share ownership.[1097]

We considered whether a delayed compliance date for Rule 14a-11 for smaller reporting companies, which would include most small entities, would reduce the burden on these entities. After considering the comments discussed above, we have determined to

---

[1095] *See* letters from ADP; Alaska Air; Allstate; American Electric Power; Anadarko; AT&T; Avis Budget; Barclays; Biogen; Boeing; BRT; Burlington Northern; R. Burt; Callaway; Chevron; CIGNA; CNH Global; Comcast; Cummins; Deere; Eaton; Exxon-Mobil; FedEx; FMC Corp.; FPL Group; Frontier; General Mills; C. Holliday; IBM; ITT; J. Kilts; E.J. Kullman; N. Lautenbach; McDonald's; J. Miller; Motorola; Office Depot; O'Melveny & Myers; P&G; PepsiCo; Pfizer; Protective; Ryder; Sara Lee; Sherwin

Williams; Theragenics; TI; TW Telecom; G. Tooker; UnitedHealth; Xerox.

[1096] *See* letters from ABA; AFSCME; CalSTRS; CFA Institute; CII; COPERA; T. DiNapoli; Florida State Board of Administration; ICGN; N. Lautenbach; LIUNA; D. Nappier; Nathan Cummings Foundation; OPERS; Pax World; Relational; Sodali; SWIB; TIAA-CREF; G. Tooker; USPE; ValueAct Capital.

[1097] For further discussion, *see* Section II.B.4. above.

delay the compliance date of Rule 14a-11 for smaller reporting companies for a period of three years from the effective date for other companies. We believe that a delayed compliance date for smaller reporting companies will allow those companies to observe how Rule 14a-11 operates for other companies and may allow them to better prepare for the implementation of the rules and, as noted, will give us a further opportunity to consider adjustments for smaller reporting companies. In addition, in an effort to limit the cost and burden on all companies subject to the rule, including smaller reporting companies, we have limited use of Rule 14a-11 to nominations by shareholders who have maintained significant continuous holdings in the company, and we have extended the required holding period to at least three years at the time the notice of nomination is filed with the Commission and transmitted to the company. We expect that these eligibility requirements will help achieve the stated objective without unduly burdening any particular group of companies.

We are not adopting different disclosure standards based on the size of the issuer. We believe uniform disclosure will be helpful to voting decisions on shareholder-nominated directors at companies of all sizes. Because we are delaying the compliance date of Rule 14a-11 for smaller reporting companies, we believe this will allow them additional time to prepare to comply with the new rule and observe the rule's impact on larger companies, which should allow smaller reporting companies to be able to comply with the same disclosure standards when the rule becomes applicable to them.

We considered the use of performance standards rather than design standards in the final rules. The final rule contains both performance standards and design standards. We proposed design standards to the extent that we believe compliance with particular requirements are necessary. However, to the extent possible, our rules impose performance standards. For example, under Rule 14a-11, a nominating shareholder or group can provide a 500-word statement of support concerning each of its nominee or nominees for director, but we do not specify the content. Similarly, shareholders can submit a proposal that seeks to establish a procedure under a company's governing documents for the inclusion of one or more shareholder director nominees in the company's proxy materials. By allowing shareholders to submit such proposals, we seek to provide shareholders and companies with a measure of flexibility to tailor the means through which they can comply with the standards. Even though Rule 14a-11 provides a procedure from which companies may not opt out, companies and shareholders are not prohibited from adopting nominating procedures that could further facilitate shareholders' ability to include their own director nominees in company proxy materials. Amended Rule 14a-8(i)(8) facilitates this process. In that respect, the rules provide both design and performance standards, as appropriate.

Lastly, as discussed above, we believe that the final rules should apply regardless of company size, as was proposed.[1098] The purpose of the rules is to facilitate the exercise of shareholders' traditional state law rights to nominate and elect directors to company boards of directors and thereby enable shareholders to participate more meaningfully in the nomination and election of directors at the companies in which they invest. We believe that shareholders of smaller reporting companies should be able to exercise these rights to the same extent as shareholders of larger reporting companies. Therefore, we are not persuaded that exempting smaller reporting companies from the final rules would be consistent with this goal.

Nonetheless, as discussed above, we recognize that smaller reporting companies may have had less experience with existing forms of shareholder involvement in the proxy process and may have less-developed infrastructures for managing these matters. The final rules therefore include a phase-in period that delays the compliance date of Rule 14a-11 for smaller reporting companies for three years from the effective date of the rule.

[1098] *See* Section II.B.3.f. above.

VII. STATUTORY AUTHORITY AND TEXT OF THE AMENDMENTS

The amendments are made pursuant to Sections 3(b), 13, 14, 15, 23(a) and 36 of the Securities Exchange Act of 1934, as amended, Sections 10, 20(a) and 38 of the Investment Company Act of 1940, as amended, and Sections 971 (a) and (b) of the Dodd-Frank Act.

List of Subjects

17 CFR Parts 200

Freedom of information, Reporting and recordkeeping requirements, Securities.

17 CFR Parts 232, 240, and 249

Reporting and recordkeeping requirements, Securities.

In accordance with the foregoing, the Securities and Exchange Commission is amending Title 17, chapter II of the Code of Federal Regulations as follows:

PART 200—ORGANIZATION; CONDUCT AND ETHICS; AND INFORMATION AND REQUESTS

Subpart D—Information and Requests

1. The authority citation for Part 200, Subpart D, continues to read, in part, as follows:

Authority: 5 U.S.C. 552, as amended, 15 U.S.C. 77f(d), 77s, 77ggg(a), 77sss, 78m(F)(3), 78w, 80a-37, 80a-44(a), 80a-44(b), 80b-10(a), and 80b-11.

* * * * *

2. Add § 200.82a to read as follows:

§ 200.82a Public availability of materials filed pursuant to § 240.14a-11(g) and related materials.

Materials filed with the Commission pursuant to Rule 14a-11(g) under the Securities Exchange Act of 1934 (17 CFR 240.14a-11(g)), written communications related thereto received from interested persons, and each related no-action letter or other written communication issued by the staff of the Commission, shall be made available to any person upon request for inspection or copying.

PART 232—REGULATION S-T—GENERAL RULES AND REGULATIONS FOR ELECTRONIC FILINGS

3. The authority citation for Part 232 continues to read, in part, as follows:

Authority: 15 U.S.C. 77f, 77g, 77h, 77j, 77s(a), 77z-3, 77sss(a), 78c(b), 78*l*, 78m, 78n, 78o(d), 78w(a), 78*ll*, 80a-6(c), 80a-8, 80a-29, 80a-30, 80a-37, and 7201 *et seq.*; and 18 U.S.C. 1350.

* * * * *

4. Amend § 232.13 by revising paragraph (a)(4) (the note remains unchanged) to read as follows:

§ 232.13 Date of filing; adjustment of filing date.

(a) * * *

(4) Notwithstanding paragraph (a)(2) of this section, a Form 3, 4 or 5 (§§ 249.103, 249.104, and 249.105 of this chapter) or a Schedule 14N (§ 240.14n-101 of this chapter) submitted by direct transmission on or before 10 p.m. Eastern Standard Time or Eastern

Daylight Saving Time, whichever is currently in effect, shall be deemed filed on the same business day.

* * * * *

PART 240—GENERAL RULES AND REGULATIONS, SECURITIES EX-CHANGE ACT OF 1934

5. The authority citation for Part 240 continues to read, in part, as follows:

Authority: 15 U.S.C. 77c, 77d, 77g, 77j, 77s, 77z-2, 77z-3, 77eee, 77ggg, 77nnn, 77sss, 77ttt, 78c, 78d, 78e, 78f, 78g, 78i, 78j, 78j-1, 78k, 78k-1, 78*l*, 78m, 78n, 78o, 78p, 78q, 78s, 78u-5, 78w, 78x, 78*ll*, 78mm, 80a-20, 80a-23, 80a-29, 80a-37, 80b-3, 80b-4, 80b-11, and 7201, *et seq.*; and 18 U.S.C. 1350 and 12 U.S.C. 5221(e)(3), unless otherwise noted.

* * * * *

6. Amend § 240.13a-11 by revising paragraph (b) to read as follows:

§ 240.13a-11 Current reports on Form 8-K (§ 249.308 of this chapter).

* * * * *

(b) This section shall not apply to foreign governments, foreign private issuers required to make reports on Form 6-K (17 CFR 249.306) pursuant to § 240.13a-16, issuers of American Depositary Receipts for securities of any foreign issuer, or investment companies required to file reports pursuant to § 270.30b1-1 of this chapter under the Investment Company Act of 1940, except where such an investment company is required to file:

(1) Notice of a blackout period pursuant to § 245.104 of this chapter;

(2) Disclosure pursuant to Instruction 2 to § 240.14a-11(b)(1) of information concerning outstanding shares and voting; or

(3) Disclosure pursuant to Instruction 2 to § 240.14a-11(b)(10) of the date by which a nominating shareholder or nominating shareholder group must submit the notice required pursuant to § 240.14a-11(b)(10).

* * * * *

7. Amend § 240.13d-1 by revising paragraphs (b)(1)(i) and (c)(1) and adding Instruction 1 to paragraph (b)(1) to read as follows:

§ 240.13d-1 Filing of Schedules 13D and 13G.

* * * * *

(b)(1) * * *

(i) Such person has acquired such securities in the ordinary course of his business and not with the purpose nor with the effect of changing or influencing the control of the issuer, nor in connection with or as a participant in any transaction having such purpose or effect, including any transaction subject to § 240.13d-3(b), other than activities solely in connection with a nomination under § 240.14a-11; and

* * * * *

Instruction 1 to paragraph (b)(1). For purposes of paragraph (b)(1)(i) of this section, the exception for activities solely in connection with a nomination under § 240.14a-11 will not be available after the election of directors.

* * * * *

(c) * * *

(1) Has not acquired the securities with any purpose, or with the effect, of changing or influencing the control of the issuer, or in connection with or as a participant in any transaction having that purpose or effect, including any transaction subject to § 240.13d-3(b), other than activities solely in connection with a nomination under § 240.14a-11;

* * * * *

Instruction 1 to paragraph (c)(1). For purposes of paragraph (c)(1) of this section, the exception for activities solely in connection with a nomination under § 240.14a-11 will not be available after the election of directors.

* * * * *

8. Amend § 240.13d-102 by revising the sentences following the introductory text in Items 10(a) and (c) as follows:

§ 240.13d-102 Schedule 13G—Information to be included in statements filed pursuant to § 240.13d-1(b), (c), and (d) and amendments thereto filed pursuant to § 240.13d-2.

* * * * *

Item 10. Certifications

(a) * * *

By signing below I certify that, to the best of my knowledge and belief, the securities referred to above were acquired and are held in the ordinary course of business and were not acquired and are not held for the purpose of or with the effect of changing or influencing the control of the issuer of the securities and were not acquired and are not held in connection with or as a participant in any transaction having that purpose or effect, other than activities solely in connection with a nomination under § 240.14a-11.

* * * * *

(c) * * *

By signing below I certify that, to the best of my knowledge and belief, the securities referred to above were not acquired and are not held for the purpose of or with the effect of changing or influencing the control of the issuer of the securities and were not acquired and are not held in connection with or as a participant in any transaction having that purpose or effect, other than activities solely in connection with a nomination under § 240.14a-11.

* * * * *

9. Amend § 240.14a-2 by:

a. Revising paragraph (b) introductory text; and

b. Adding paragraphs (b)(7) and (b)(8).

The revision and additions read as follows:

§ 240.14a-2 Solicitations to which § 240.14a-3 to § 240.14a-15 apply.

* * * * *

(b) Sections 240.14a-3 to 240.14a-6 (other than paragraphs 14a-6(g) and 14a-6(p)), § 240.14a-8, § 240.14a-10, and §§ 240.14a-12 to 240.14a-15 do not apply to the following:

* * * * *

(7) Any solicitation by or on behalf of any shareholder in connection with the formation of a nominating shareholder group pursuant to § 240.14a-11, provided that:

(i) The soliciting shareholder is not holding the registrant's securities with the purpose, or with the effect, of changing control of the registrant or to gain a number of seats on the board of directors that exceeds the maximum number of nominees that the registrant could be required to include under § 240.14a-11(d);

(ii) Each written communication includes no more than:

(A) A statement of each soliciting shareholder's intent to form a nominating shareholder group in order to nominate one or more directors under § 240.14a-11;

(B) Identification of, and a brief statement regarding, the potential nominee or nominees or, where no nominee or nominees have been identified, the characteristics of the nominee or nominees that the shareholder intends to nominate, if any;

(C) The percentage of voting power of the registrant's securities that are entitled to be voted on the election of directors that each soliciting shareholder holds or the aggregate percentage held by any group to which the shareholder belongs; and

(D) The means by which shareholders may contact the soliciting party.

(iii) Any written soliciting material published, sent or given to shareholders in accordance with this paragraph must be filed by the shareholder with the Commission, under the registrant's Exchange Act file number, or, in the case of a registrant that is an investment company registered under the Investment Company Act of 1940 (15 U.S.C. 80a-1 *et seq.*), under the registrant's Investment Company Act file number, no later than the date the material is first published, sent or given to shareholders. Three copies of the material must at the same time be filed with, or mailed for filing to, each national securities exchange upon which any class of securities of the registrant is listed and registered. The soliciting material must include a cover page in the form set forth in Schedule 14N (§ 240.14n-101) and the appropriate box on the cover page must be marked.

(iv) In the case of an oral solicitation made in accordance with the terms of this section, the nominating shareholder must file a cover page in the form set forth in Schedule 14N (§ 240.14n-101), with the appropriate box on the cover page marked, under the registrant's Exchange Act file number (or in the case of an investment company registered under the Investment Company Act of 1940 (15 U.S.C. 80a-1 *et seq.*), under the registrant's Investment Company Act file number), no later than the date of the first such communication.

Instruction to paragraph (b)(7). The exemption provided in paragraph (b)(7) of this section shall not apply to a shareholder that subsequently engages in soliciting or other nominating activities outside the scope of § 240.14a-2(b)(8) and § 240.14a-11 in connection with the subject election of directors or is or becomes a member of any other group, as determined under section 13(d)(3) of the Act (15 U.S.C. 78m(d)(3) and § 240.13d-5(b)), or otherwise, with persons engaged in soliciting or other nominating activities in connection with the subject election of directors.

(8) Any solicitation by or on behalf of a nominating shareholder or nominating shareholder group in support of its nominee that is included or that will be included on the registrant's form of proxy in accordance with § 240.14a-11 or for or against the registrant's nominee or nominees, provided that:

(i) The soliciting party does not, at any time during such solicitation, seek directly or indirectly, either on its own or another's behalf, the power to act as proxy for a shareholder and does not furnish or otherwise request, or act on behalf of a person who furnishes or requests, a form of revocation, abstention, consent or authorization;

(ii) Any written communication includes:

(A) The identity of each nominating shareholder and a description of his or her direct or indirect interests, by security holdings or otherwise;

(B) A prominent legend in clear, plain language advising shareholders that a shareholder nominee is or will be included in the registrant's proxy statement and that they should read the registrant's proxy statement when available because it includes important information (or, if the registrant's proxy statement is publicly available, advising shareholders of that fact and encouraging shareholders to read the registrant's proxy statement because it includes important information). The legend also must explain to shareholders that they can find the registrant's proxy statement, other soliciting material, and any other relevant documents at no charge on the Commission's Web site; and

(iii) Any written soliciting material published, sent or given to shareholders in accordance with this paragraph must be filed by the nominating shareholder or nominating shareholder group with the Commission, under the registrant's Exchange Act file number, or, in the case of a registrant that is an investment company registered under the Investment Company Act of 1940 (15 U.S.C. 80a-1 *et seq.*), under the registrant's Investment Company Act file number, no later than the date the material is first published, sent or given to shareholders. Three copies of the material must at the same time be filed with, or mailed for filing to, each national securities exchange upon which any class of securities of the registrant is listed and registered. The soliciting material must include a cover page in the form set forth in Schedule 14N (§ 240.14n-101) and the appropriate box on the cover page must be marked.

Instruction 1 to paragraph (b)(8). A nominating shareholder or nominating shareholder group may rely on the exemption provided in paragraph (b)(8) of this section only after receiving notice from the registrant in accordance with § 240.14a-11(g)(1) or § 240.14a-11(g)(3)(iv) that the registrant will include the nominating shareholder's or nominating shareholder group's nominee or nominees in its form of proxy.

Instruction 2 to paragraph (b)(8). Any solicitation by or on behalf of a nominating shareholder or nominating shareholder group in support of its nominee included or to be included on the registrant's form of proxy in accordance with § 240.14a-11 or for or against the registrant's nominee or nominees must be made in reliance on the exemption provided in paragraph (b)(8) of this section and not on any other exemption.

Instruction 3 to paragraph (b)(8). The exemption provided in paragraph (b)(8) of this section shall not apply to a person that subsequently engages in soliciting or other nominating activities outside the scope of § 240.14a-11 in connection with the subject election of directors or is or becomes a member of any other group, as determined under section 13(d)(3) of the Act (15 U.S.C. 78m(d)(3) and § 240.13d-5(b)), or otherwise, with persons engaged in soliciting or other nominating activities in connection with the subject election of directors.

* * * * *

10. Amend § 240.14a-4 by:

a. Revising the first sentence of paragraph (b)(2) introductory text; and

b. Adding a sentence to the end of paragraph (b)(2) concluding text.

The revision and addition read as follows:

§ 240.14a-4 Requirements as to proxy.

* * * * *

(b) * * *

(2) A form of proxy that provides for the election of directors shall set forth the names of persons nominated for election as directors, including any person whose nomination

by a shareholder or shareholder group satisfies the requirements of § 240.14a-11, an applicable state or foreign law provision, or a registrant's governing documents as they relate to the inclusion of shareholder director nominees in the registrant's proxy materials. * * *

* * * Means to grant authority to vote for any nominees as a group or to withhold authority for any nominees as a group may not be provided if the form of proxy includes one or more shareholder nominees in accordance with § 240.14a-11, an applicable state or foreign law provision, or a registrant's governing documents as they relate to the inclusion of shareholder director nominees in the registrant's proxy materials.

* * * * *

11. Amend § 240.14a-5 by:

a. Revising paragraph (e)(1) to remove "and" at the end of the paragraph;

b. Revising paragraph (e)(2) to remove the period at the end of the paragraph and add in its place "; and"; and

c. Adding paragraph (e)(3) to read as follows:

§ 240.14a-5 Presentation of information in proxy statement.

* * * * *

(e) * * *

(3) The deadline for submitting nominees for inclusion in the registrant's proxy statement and form of proxy pursuant to § 240.14a-11, an applicable state or foreign law provision, or a registrant's governing documents as they relate to the inclusion of shareholder director nominees in the registrant's proxy materials for the registrant's next annual meeting of shareholders.

* * * * *

12. Amend § 240.14a-6 by:

a. Redesignating paragraphs (a)(4), (a)(5), (a)(6), and (a)(7) as paragraphs (a)(5), (a)(6), (a)(7), and (a)(8) respectively;

b. Adding new paragraph (a)(4);

c. Adding a sentence at the end of Note 3 to paragraph (a); and

d. Adding paragraph (p).

The revisions and additions read as follows:

§ 240.14a-6 Filing requirements.

(a) * * *

(4) A shareholder nominee for director included pursuant to § 240.14a-11, an applicable state or foreign law provision, or a registrant's governing documents as they relate to the inclusion of shareholder director nominees in the registrant's proxy materials.

* * * * *

Note 3. * * * The inclusion of a shareholder nominee in the registrant's proxy materials pursuant to § 240.14a-11, an applicable state or foreign law provision, or a registrant's governing documents as they relate to the inclusion of shareholder director nominees in the registrant's proxy materials does not constitute a "solicitation in opposition" for purposes of Rule 14a-6(a) (§ 240.14a-6(a)), even if the registrant opposes the shareholder nominee and solicits against the shareholder nominee and in favor of a registrant nominee.

* * * * *

(p) *Solicitations subject to § 240.14a-11.* Any soliciting material that is published, sent or given to shareholders in connection with § 240.14a-2(b)(7) or (b)(8) must be filed with the Commission as specified in that section.

13. Amend § 240.14a-8 by revising paragraph (i)(8) as follows:

§ 240.14a-8 Shareholder proposals.

* * * * *

(i) * * *

(8) *Director elections*: If the proposal:

(i) Would disqualify a nominee who is standing for election;

(ii) Would remove a director from office before his or her term expired;

(iii) Questions the competence, business judgment, or character of one or more nominees or directors;

(iv) Seeks to include a specific individual in the company's proxy materials for election to the board of directors; or

(v) Otherwise could affect the outcome of the upcoming election of directors.

* * * * *

14. Amend § 240.14a-9 by adding a paragraph (c), removing the authority citation following the section, and redesignating notes (a), (b), (c), and (d) as a., b., c., and d.

The addition reads as follows:

§ 240.14a-9 False or misleading statements.

* * * * *

(c) No nominee, nominating shareholder or nominating shareholder group, or any member thereof, shall cause to be included in a registrant's proxy materials, either pursuant to the federal proxy rules, an applicable state or foreign law provision, or a registrant's governing documents as they relate to including shareholder nominees for director in a registrant's proxy materials, include in a notice on Schedule 14N (§ 240.14n-101), or include in any other related communication, any statement which, at the time and in the light of the circumstances under which it is made, is false or misleading with respect to any material fact, or which omits to state any material fact necessary in order to make the statements therein not false or misleading or necessary to correct any statement in any earlier communication with respect to a solicitation for the same meeting or subject matter which has become false or misleading.

* * * * *

15. Add § 240.14a-11 to read as follows:

§ 240.14a-11 Shareholder nominations.

(a) *Applicability.* In connection with an annual (or a special meeting in lieu of an annual) meeting of shareholders, or a written consent in lieu of such meeting, at which directors are elected, a registrant will be required to include in its proxy statement and form of proxy the name of a person or persons nominated by a shareholder or group of shareholders for election to the board of directors and include in its proxy statement the disclosure about such nominee or nominees and the nominating shareholder or members of the nominating shareholder group as specified in Item 5 of Schedule 14N (§ 240.14n-101), provided that the conditions set forth in paragraph (b) of this section are satisfied. This rule will not apply to a registrant if:

(1) The registrant is subject to the proxy rules solely because it has a class of debt securities registered under section 12 of the Exchange Act (15 U.S.C. 78*l*); or

(2) Applicable state or foreign law or a registrant's governing documents prohibit the registrant's shareholders from nominating a candidate or candidates for election as director.

(b) *Eligibility.* A shareholder nominee or nominees shall be included in a registrant's proxy statement and form of proxy if the following requirements are satisfied:

(1) The nominating shareholder individually, or the nominating shareholder group in the aggregate, holds at least 3% of the total voting power of the registrant's securities that are entitled to be voted on the election of directors at the annual (or a special meeting in lieu of the annual) meeting of shareholders or on a written consent in lieu of such meeting, on the date the nominating shareholder or nominating shareholder group files the notice on Schedule 14N (§ 240.14n-101) with the Commission and transmits the notice to the registrant;

Instruction 1 to paragraph (b)(1). In the case of a registrant other than an investment company registered under the Investment Company Act of 1940 (15 U.S.C. 80a-1 *et seq.*), for purposes of (b)(1) of this section, in determining the total voting power of the registrant's securities that are entitled to be voted on the election of directors, the nominating shareholder or nominating shareholder group may rely on information set forth in the registrant's most recent quarterly or annual report, and any current report subsequent thereto, filed with the Commission pursuant to this Act, unless the nominating shareholder or nominating shareholder group knows or has reason to know that the information contained therein is inaccurate. In the case of a registrant that is an investment company registered under the Investment Company Act of 1940, for purposes of (b)(1) of this section, in determining the total voting power of the registrant's securities that are entitled to be voted on the election of directors, the nominating shareholder or nominating shareholder group may rely on information set forth in the following documents, unless the nominating shareholder or nominating shareholder group knows or has reason to know that the information contained therein is inaccurate:

a. In the case of a registrant that is a series company as defined in Rule 18f-2(a) under the Investment Company Act of 1940 (§ 270.18f-2(a) of this chapter), the Form 8-K (§ 249.308 of this chapter) described in Instruction 2 to paragraph (b)(1) of this section; or

b. In the case of other investment companies, the registrant's most recent annual or semi-annual report filed with the Commission on Form N-CSR (§ 249.331 and § 274.128 of this chapter).

Instruction 2 to paragraph (b)(1). If the registrant is an investment company that is a series company (as defined in § 270.18f-2(a) of this chapter), the registrant must disclose pursuant to Item 5.08 of Form 8-K (§ 249.308 of this chapter) the total number of shares of the registrant outstanding and entitled to be voted (or if the votes are to be cast on a basis other than one vote per share, then the total number of votes entitled to be voted and the basis for allocating such votes) on the election of directors as of the end of the most recent calendar quarter.

Instruction 3 to paragraph (b)(1). a. When determining the total voting power of the registrant's securities, which is the denominator in the calculation of the percentage of voting power held by the nominating shareholder individually or the nominating shareholder group in the aggregate, calculate the aggregate number of votes derived from all classes of securities of the registrant that are entitled to vote on the election of directors regardless of whether solicitation of a proxy with respect to those securities would require compliance with Exchange Act Regulation 14A (§ 240.14a-1 *et seq.*).

b. When determining the total voting power of the registrant's securities held by the nominating shareholder or any member of the nominating shareholder group, which is the numerator in the calculation of the percentage:

1. Calculate the number of votes derived only from securities with respect to which solicitation of a proxy would require compliance with Exchange Act Regulation 14A (§ 240.14a-1 *et seq.*) and over which the nominating shareholder or any the member of the nominating shareholder group, as the case may be, has voting power and investment power, either directly or through any person acting on their behalf;

2. Notwithstanding the voting power calculation specified in paragraph b.1. of this instruction, add to the result of the calculation specified in paragraph b.1. of this instruction any votes attributable to securities with respect to which solicitation of a proxy would require compliance with Exchange Act Regulation 14A (§ 240.14a-1 *et seq.*) that have been loaned by or on behalf of the nominating shareholder or any member of the nominating shareholder group to another person, if the nominating shareholder or member of the nominating shareholder group, as the case may be, or any person acting on their behalf, has the right to recall the loaned securities, and will recall the loaned securities upon being notified that any of the nominating shareholder's or group's nominees will be included in the registrant's proxy statement and proxy card; and

3. Subtract from the result of the calculation specified in paragraphs b.1. and b.2. of this instruction the number of votes attributable to securities of the registrant entitled to vote on the election of directors, regardless of whether solicitation of a proxy with respect to those securities would require compliance Exchange Act Regulation 14A (§ 240.14a-1 *et seq.*), that the nominating shareholder or any member of the nominating shareholder group, as the case may be, or any person acting on their behalf, has sold in a short sale, as defined in 17 CFR 242.200(a), that is not closed out, or has borrowed for purposes other than a short sale.

c. For purposes of the voting power calculation in paragraph b.1. of this instruction:

1. A shareholder has voting power directly only when the shareholder has the power to vote or direct the voting, and investment power directly only when the shareholder has the power to dispose or direct the disposition, of the securities; and

2. A securities intermediary (as defined in § 240.17Ad-20(b)) shall not have voting power or investment power over securities for purposes of paragraph b.1. of this instruction solely because such intermediary holds such securities by or on behalf of another person, notwithstanding that pursuant to the rules of a national securities exchange such intermediary may vote or direct the voting of such securities without instruction.

Instruction 4 to paragraph (b)(1). If a registrant has more than one class of outstanding securities entitled to vote on the election of directors and those classes do not vote together in the election of all directors, then the voting power of the registrant's securities for purposes of the calculation of both the numerator and denominator specified in Instruction 3 to paragraph (b)(1) should be determined only on the basis of the voting power of the class or classes of securities that would be voting together on the election of the person or persons sought to be nominated by the nominating shareholder or the nominating shareholder group.

(2) The nominating shareholder or each member of the nominating shareholder group has held the amount of securities that are used for purposes of satisfying the minimum ownership requirement of paragraph (b)(1) of this section continuously for at least three years as of the date the notice on Schedule 14N (§ 240.14n-101) is filed with the

Commission and transmitted to the registrant and must continue to hold that amount of securities through the date of the subject election of directors;

Instruction to paragraph (b)(2). To determine whether the amount of securities that are used for purposes of satisfying the minimum ownership requirement of paragraph (b)(1) has been held continuously during the three year period prior to the date the Schedule 14N (§ 240.14n-101) is filed and during the period after the Schedule 14N is filed through the date of the subject election of directors, and with respect to all points in time during those periods:

a. Include only the amount of securities with respect to which a solicitation of a proxy would require compliance with Exchange Act Regulation 14A (§ 240.14a-1 *et seq.*) and over which the nominating shareholder or the member of the nominating shareholder group, as the case may be, has voting power and investment power, either directly or through any person acting on their behalf;

b. Notwithstanding the voting power determination specified in paragraph a. of this instruction, include the amount of securities that have been loaned by or on behalf of the nominating shareholder or any member of the nominating shareholder group to another person, if the nominating shareholder or member of the nominating shareholder group, as the case may be, or any person acting on their behalf:

1. Has the right to recall the loaned securities; and

2. With respect to the period from the date the Schedule 14N (§ 240.14n-101) is filed through the date of the subject election of directors, will recall the loaned securities upon being notified that any of the person's nominees will be included in the registrant's proxy statement and proxy card;

c. Reduce the amount of securities held by the amount of securities, on a class basis, that the nominating shareholder or any member of the nominating shareholder group, as the case may be, or any person acting on their behalf, sold in a short sale, as defined in 17 CFR 242.200(a), during the periods, or borrowed for purposes other than a short sale; and

d. Adjust the amount of securities held to give effect to any changes in the amount of securities during the periods resulting from stock splits, reclassifications or other similar adjustments by the registrant.

(3) The nominating shareholder or each member of the nominating shareholder group provides proof of ownership of the amount of securities that are used for purposes of satisfying the ownership and holding period requirements of paragraphs (b)(1) and (b)(2) of this section. If the nominating shareholder or each member of the nominating shareholder group is not the registered holder of the securities, the nominating shareholder or each member of the nominating shareholder group must provide proof of ownership in the form of one or more written statements from the registered holder of the nominating shareholder's securities (or the brokers or banks through which those securities are held) verifying that, as of a date within seven calendar days prior to filing the notice on Schedule 14N (§ 240.14n-101) with the Commission and transmitting the notice to the registrant, the nominating shareholder or each member of the nominating shareholder group, continuously held the amount of securities being used to satisfy the ownership threshold for a period of at least three years. The written statement or statements proving ownership must be attached as an appendix to Schedule 14N on the date the notice is filed with the Commission and transmitted to the registrant, and provide the information specified in Item 4 of Schedule 14N. In the alternative, if the nominating shareholder or member of the nominating shareholder group has filed a Schedule 13D (§ 240.13d-101), Schedule 13G (§ 240.13d-102), Form 3 (§ 249.103 of this chapter), Form 4 (§ 249.104 of this chapter), and/or Form 5 (§ 249.105 of this chapter), or amendments to those documents, reflecting ownership of the securities as of or before the date on which the three-year eligibility period begins, the nominating shareholder or member of the nominating shareholder group may attach the filing as an appendix to the Schedule 14N or incorporate the filing by reference into the Schedule 14N;

Instruction to paragraph (b)(3). If the nominating shareholder or member of the nominating shareholder group must provide proof of ownership in the form of a written statement with respect to securities held through a broker or bank that is a participant in the Depository Trust Company or other clearing agency acting as a securities depository, then a statement from such broker or bank will satisfy the requirements of paragraph (b)(3) of this section. If the securities are held through a broker or bank (*e.g.*, in an omnibus account) that is not a participant in a clearing agency acting as a securities depository, the nominating shareholder or member of the nominating shareholder group must also obtain and submit a separate written statement specified in the Instruction to Item 4 of Schedule 14N (§ 240.14n-101).

(4) The nominating shareholder or each member of the nominating shareholder group provides a statement, as specified in Item 4(b) of Schedule 14N (§ 240.14n-101), on the date the notice on Schedule 14N is filed with the Commission and transmitted to the registrant, that the nominating shareholder or each member of the nominating shareholder group intends to continue to hold the amount of securities that are used for purposes of satisfying the minimum ownership requirement of paragraph (b)(1) of this section through the date of the meeting;

(5) The nominating shareholder or each member of the nominating shareholder group provides a statement, as specified in Item 4(b) of Schedule 14N (§ 240.14n-101), on the date the notice on Schedule 14N is filed with the Commission and transmitted to the registrant, regarding the nominating shareholder's or group's intent with respect to continued ownership of the registrant's securities after the election;

(6) The nominating shareholder (or where there is a nominating shareholder group, each member of the nominating shareholder group) is not holding any of the registrant's securities with the purpose, or with the effect, of changing control of the registrant or to gain a number of seats on the board of directors that exceeds the maximum number of nominees that the registrant could be required to include under paragraph (d) of this section;

(7) Neither the nominee nor the nominating shareholder (or where there is a nominating shareholder group, any member of the nominating shareholder group) has an agreement with the registrant regarding the nomination of the nominee;

Instruction to paragraph (b)(7). Negotiations between the nominee, the nominating shareholder or nominating shareholder group and the nominating committee or board of the registrant to have the nominee included in the registrant's proxy statement and form of proxy as a registrant nominee, where those negotiations are unsuccessful, or negotiations that are limited to whether the registrant is required to include the shareholder nominee in the registrant's proxy statement and form of proxy in accordance with this section, will not represent a direct or indirect agreement with the registrant.

(8) The nominee's candidacy or, if elected, board membership would not violate controlling federal law, state law, foreign law, or rules of a national securities exchange or national securities association (other than rules regarding director independence) or, in the case that the nominee's candidacy or, if elected, board membership would violate such laws or rules, such violation could not be cured by the time provided in paragraph (g)(2) of this section;

(9) In the case of a registrant other than an investment company, the nominee meets the objective criteria for "independence" of the national securities exchange or national securities association rules applicable to the registrant, if any, or, in the case of a registrant that is an investment company, the nominee is not an "interested person" of the registrant as defined in section 2(a)(19) of the Investment Company Act of 1940 (15 U.S.C. 80a-2(a)(19));

Instruction to paragraph (b)(9). For purposes of this provision, the nominee would be required to meet the definition of "independence" that is generally applicable to directors of the registrant and not any particular definition of independence applicable to members of the audit committee of the registrant's board of directors. To the extent a national securities exchange or national securities association rule imposes a standard regarding independence that requires a subjective determination by the board or a group or committee of the board (for example, requiring that the board of directors or any group or committee of the board of directors make a determination regarding the existence of factors material to a determination of a nominee's independence), the nominee would not be required to meet the subjective determination of independence as part of the shareholder nomination process.

(10) The nominating shareholder or nominating shareholder group provides notice to the registrant on Schedule 14N (§ 240.14n-101), as specified by § 240.14n-1, of its intent to require that the registrant include that shareholder's or group's nominee in the registrant's proxy statement and form of proxy. This notice must be transmitted to the registrant on the date it is filed with the Commission. The notice must be filed with the Commission and transmitted to the registrant no earlier than 150 calendar days, and no later than 120 calendar days, before the anniversary of the date that the registrant mailed its proxy materials for the prior year's annual meeting, except that, if the registrant did not hold an annual meeting during the prior year, or if the date of the meeting has changed by more than 30 calendar days from the prior year, or if the registrant is holding a special meeting or conducting an election of directors by written consent, then the nominating shareholder or nominating shareholder group must transmit the notice to the registrant and file its notice with the Commission a reasonable time before the registrant mails its proxy materials, as specified by the registrant in a Form 8-K (§ 249.308 of this chapter) filed pursuant to Item 5.08 of Form 8-K; and

Instruction 1 to paragraph (b)(10). If the registrant held a meeting the previous year and the date of the current year's annual meeting has not changed by more than 30 calendar days from the date of the previous year's annual meeting, the window period for filing a notice on Schedule 14N (§ 240.14n-101) with the Commission and transmitting that notice to the registrant should be calculated by determining the release date disclosed in the registrant's previous year's proxy statement, increasing the year by one, and counting back 150 calendar days and 120 calendar days for the beginning and end of the window period, respectively. Where the 120 calendar day deadline falls on a Saturday, Sunday or holiday, the deadline will be treated as the first business day following the Saturday, Sunday or holiday.

Instruction 2 to paragraph (b)(10). If the registrant did not hold an annual meeting the previous year, or if the date of the current year's annual meeting has been changed by more than 30 calendar days from the date of the previous year's annual meeting, or if the registrant is holding a special meeting or conducting the election of directors by written consent, the registrant must disclose pursuant to Item 5.08 of Form 8-K (§ 249.308 of this chapter) the date by which a shareholder or group must submit the notice required pursuant to paragraph (b)(10) of this section, which date shall be a reasonable time prior to the date the registrant mails its proxy materials for the meeting.

(11) The nominating shareholder or nominating shareholder group provides the certifications required by Schedule 14N (§ 240.14n-101) on the date the notice on Schedule 14N is filed with the Commission and transmitted to the registrant.

Instruction to paragraph (b). A registrant will not be required to include a nominee or nominees submitted by a nominating shareholder or nominating shareholder group pursuant to this section if the nominating shareholder or any member of the nominating shareholder group also submits any other nomination to that registrant and/or is participating in more than one nominating shareholder group for that registrant. In addition, a registrant will not be required to include a nominee or nominees if a nominating shareholder or member of a nominating shareholder group:

a. Is or becomes a member of any other group, as determined under section 13(d)(3) of the Act (15 U.S.C. 78m(d)(3) and § 240.13d-5(b)), or otherwise, with persons engaged in soliciting or other nominating activities in connection with the subject election of directors;

b. Is separately conducting a solicitation in connection with the subject election of directors other than a solicitation subject to § 240.14a-2(b)(8) in relation to those nominees it has nominated pursuant to this section or for or against the registrant's nominees; or

c. Is acting as a participant in another person's solicitation in connection with the subject election of directors.

(c) *Statement of support.* A registrant will be required to include a statement of support submitted by a nominating shareholder or nominating shareholder group in Item 5(i) of the notice on Schedule 14N (§ 240.14n-101), provided that the statement of support does not exceed 500 words per nominee. If a statement of support submitted by a nominating shareholder or nominating shareholder group exceeds 500 words per nominee, the registrant will be required to include the nominee or nominees, provided that the eligibility requirements and other conditions of the rule are satisfied, but the registrant may exclude the supporting statement(s).

(d) *Maximum number of shareholder nominees.* (1) A registrant will be required to include in its proxy statement and form of proxy one shareholder nominee or the number of nominees that represents 25% of the total number of the registrant's board of directors, whichever is greater, submitted by a nominating shareholder or nominating shareholder group pursuant to this section, subject to the limitations in paragraphs (d)(2), (d)(3), (d)(4), and (d)(5) of this section. A registrant may exclude a nominee or nominees if including the nominee or nominees would result in the registrant exceeding the maximum number of nominees it is required to include in its proxy statement and form of proxy pursuant to this provision.

Instruction to paragraph (d)(1). Depending on board size, 25% of the board may not result in a whole number. In those instances, the registrant will round down to the closest whole number below 25% to determine the maximum number of shareholder nominees for director that the registrant is required to include in its proxy statement and form of proxy.

(2) Where the registrant has one or more directors currently serving on its board of directors who were elected as a shareholder nominee pursuant to this section, and the term of that director or directors extends past the election of directors for which it is soliciting proxies, the registrant will not be required to include in the proxy statement and form of proxy more shareholder nominees than could result in the total number of directors who were elected as shareholder nominees pursuant to this section and serving on the board being more than one shareholder nominee or 25% of the total number of the registrant's board of directors, whichever is greater.

(3) Where the registrant has multiple classes of securities and each class is entitled to elect a specified number of directors, the registrant will be required to include the lesser of the number of nominees that the nominating shareholder's or group's class is entitled to elect or 25% of the registrant's board of directors, but in no case less than one nominee.

(4) Where the registrant agrees to include in its proxy statement and form of proxy, as an unopposed registrant nominee, the nominee or nominees of the nominating shareholder or nominating shareholder group that otherwise would be eligible under this section to have its nominees included in the registrant's proxy materials, the nominee will be considered a shareholder nominee for purposes of calculating the maximum number of shareholder nominees that must be included in the registrant's proxy statement and form of proxy, provided that the nominating shareholder or nominating shareholder group filed its notice on Schedule 14N (§ 240.14n-101) before beginning communications with the registrant about the nomination.

(5) A nominee included in a registrant's proxy statement and form of proxy as a result of an agreement between the nominee or nominating shareholder (or where there is a nominating shareholder group, any member of the nominating shareholder group) and

the registrant, other than as specified in paragraph (d)(4) of this section, will not be counted as a shareholder nominee for purposes of calculating the maximum number of shareholder nominees that the registrant is required to include in its proxy statement and form of proxy.

Instruction to paragraph (d)(5). Negotiations between the nominee, the nominating shareholder or nominating shareholder group and the nominating committee or board of the registrant to have the nominee included in the registrant's proxy statement and form of proxy as a registrant nominee, where those negotiations are unsuccessful, or negotiations that are limited to whether the registrant is required to include the shareholder nominee in the registrant's proxy statement and form of proxy in accordance with this section, will not represent a direct or indirect agreement with the registrant.

(e) *Order of priority for shareholder nominees.* (1) In the event that more than one eligible shareholder or group of shareholders submits a nominee or nominees for inclusion in the registrant's proxy materials pursuant to this section, the registrant shall include in the proxy statement and form of proxy the nominee or nominees of the nominating shareholder or nominating shareholder group with the highest qualifying voting power percentage disclosed as of the date of filing the Schedule 14N (§ 240.14n-101) (as determined in calculating ownership to satisfy the requirement as specified in paragraph (b)(1) of this section) from which the registrant received a notice filed and transmitted as specified in paragraph (b)(10) of this section, up to and including the total number of nominees required to be included by the registrant pursuant to this section. Where the nominating shareholder or nominating shareholder group with the highest qualifying voting power percentage that is otherwise eligible to rely on this section and that filed and transmitted the notice as specified in paragraph (b)(10) of this section does not nominate the maximum number of individuals required to be included by the registrant, the nominee or nominees of the nominating shareholder or nominating shareholder group with the next highest qualifying voting power percentage from which the registrant received the notice filed and transmitted as specified in paragraph (b)(10) of this section would be included in the registrant's proxy statement and form of proxy, if any, up to and including the total number required to be included by the registrant. This process would continue until the registrant has included the maximum number of nominees it is required to include in its proxy statement and form of proxy pursuant to paragraph (d) of this section or the registrant exhausts the list of eligible nominees.

(2) Prior to the time a registrant has commenced printing its proxy statement and form of proxy, if a nominating shareholder or nominating shareholder group withdraws or is disqualified, a registrant will be required to include in its proxy statement and form of proxy the nominee or nominees of the nominating shareholder or nominating shareholder group with the next highest qualifying voting power percentage, disclosed as of the date of filing the Schedule 14N (§ 240.14n-101) (as determined in calculating ownership to satisfy the requirement as specified in paragraph (b)(1) of this section), from which the registrant received a notice filed and transmitted as specified in paragraph (b)(10) of this section, if any, up to and including the total number required to be included by the registrant. This process would continue until the registrant included the maximum number of nominees it is required to include in its proxy statement and form of proxy pursuant to paragraph (d) of this section or the registrant exhausts the list of eligible nominees. If the registrant has commenced printing its proxy statement and form of proxy, the registrant will not be required to include a nominee or nominees in its proxy statement and form of proxy in place of a nominee or nominees that has withdrawn or has been disqualified.

(3) If a nominee or nominees withdraws or is disqualified after the registrant provides notice to the nominating shareholder or nominating shareholder group of the registrant's intent to include the nominee or nominees in its proxy statement and form of proxy, the registrant will be required to include in its proxy statement and form of proxy any other eligible nominee submitted by that nominating shareholder or nominating shareholder group. If that nominating shareholder or nominating shareholder group did not include

any other eligible nominees in its notice filed on Schedule 14N (§ 240.14n-101), then the registrant will be required to include the nominee or nominees of the nominating shareholder or nominating shareholder group with the next highest voting power percentage, disclosed as of the date of filing the Schedule 14N (§ 240.14n-101) (as determined in calculating ownership to satisfy the requirement as specified in paragraph (b)(1) of this section), from which the registrant received a notice filed and transmitted as specified in paragraph (b)(10) of this section, if any, up to and including the total number required to be included by the registrant. This process would continue until the registrant included the maximum number of nominees it is required to include in its proxy statement and form of proxy pursuant to paragraph (d) of this section or the registrant exhausts the list of eligible nominees. If the registrant has commenced printing its proxy statement and form of proxy, the registrant will not be required to include a nominee or nominees in its proxy statement and form of proxy in place of a nominee or nominees that has withdrawn or has been disqualified.

(4) Notwithstanding the other provisions of this paragraph, if a registrant has multiple classes of securities and each class is entitled to elect a specified number of directors, and nominating shareholders or groups of nominating shareholders of more than one of those classes submit a number of eligible nominees for inclusion in the registrant's proxy materials pursuant to this section that is greater than 25% of the total number of the registrant's board of directors, the registrant shall include in the proxy statement and form of proxy the nominee or nominees of the nominating shareholders or groups on the basis of the proportion of total voting power in the election of directors attributable to each class, rounding to the closest whole number, if necessary, and otherwise in accordance with paragraph (e) of this section.

Instruction 1 to paragraph (e). In determining the priority of the nominee or nominees to be included in the registrant's proxy materials, the registrant will be required to consider only the nominee or nominees that would otherwise be required to be included under the provisions of this section.

Instruction 2 to paragraph (e). If the registrant is including shareholder director nominees from more than one nominating shareholder or nominating shareholder group, as described in this paragraph, and including all of the shareholder director nominees of the nominating shareholder or nominating shareholder group that is last in priority would result in exceeding the maximum number required under paragraph (d) of this section, the nominating shareholder or nominating shareholder group that is last in priority may specify which of its nominees are to be included in the registrant's proxy materials.

(f) *False or misleading statements.* The registrant is not responsible for any information in the notice from the nominating shareholder or nominating shareholder group submitted as required by paragraph (b)(10) of this section or otherwise provided by the nominating shareholder or nominating shareholder group that is included in the registrant's proxy materials.

(g) *Determinations regarding eligibility.* (1) If the registrant determines that it will include a shareholder nominee, it must notify the nominating shareholder or nominating shareholder group (or their authorized representative) upon making this determination. In no event should the notification be postmarked or transmitted electronically later than 30 calendar days before it files its definitive proxy statement and form of proxy with the Commission.

(2) If the registrant determines that it may exclude a shareholder nominee pursuant to a provision in paragraph (a), (b), (d), or (e) of this section, or exclude a statement of support pursuant to paragraph (c) of this section, the registrant must notify in writing the nominating shareholder or nominating shareholder group (or their authorized representative) of this determination. This notice must be postmarked or transmitted electronically to the nominating shareholder or nominating shareholder group (or their authorized representative) no later than 14 calendar days after the close of the period for submission specified in paragraph (b)(10) of this section.

(i) The registrant's notice to the nominating shareholder or nominating shareholder group (or their authorized representative) that it has determined that it may exclude a shareholder nominee or statement of support must include an explanation of the registrant's basis for determining that it may exclude the nominee or statement of support.

(ii) The nominating shareholder or nominating shareholder group shall have 14 calendar days after receipt of the registrant's notice pursuant to paragraph (g)(2)(i) of this section to respond to the registrant's notice and correct any eligibility or procedural deficiencies identified in that notice. The nominating shareholder's or nominating shareholder group's response must be postmarked or transmitted electronically to the registrant no later than 14 calendar days after receipt of the registrant's notice.

(3) If the registrant intends to exclude a shareholder nominee or statement of support, after providing the requisite notice of and time for the nominating shareholder or nominating shareholder group to remedy any eligibility or procedural deficiencies in the nomination or statement, the registrant must provide notice of the basis for its determination to the Commission no later than 80 calendar days before it files its definitive proxy statement and form of proxy with the Commission. The Commission staff may permit the registrant to make its submission later than 80 calendar days before the registrant files its definitive proxy statement and form of proxy if the registrant demonstrates good cause for missing the deadline.

(i) The registrant's notice to the Commission shall include:

(A) Identification of the nominating shareholder or each member of the nominating shareholder group, as applicable;

(B) The name of the nominee or nominees;

(C) An explanation of the registrant's basis for determining that the registrant may exclude the nominee or nominees or a statement of support; and

(D) A supporting opinion of counsel when the registrant's basis for excluding a nominee or nominees relies on a matter of state or foreign law.

(ii) The registrant must file its notice to the Commission and simultaneously provide a copy to the nominating shareholder or each member of the nominating shareholder group (or their authorized representative). At the time the registrant files its notice, the registrant also may seek an informal statement of the Commission staff's views with regard to its determination to exclude from its proxy materials a nominee or nominees or a statement of support. The Commission staff may provide an informal statement of its views to the registrant along with a copy to the nominating shareholder or nominating shareholder group (or their authorized representative);

(iii) The nominating shareholder or nominating shareholder group may submit a response to the registrant's notice to the Commission. This response must be postmarked or transmitted electronically to the Commission no later than 14 calendar days after the nominating shareholder's or nominating shareholder group's receipt of the registrant's notice to the Commission. The nominating shareholder or nominating shareholder group must simultaneously provide to the registrant a copy of its response to the Commission.

(iv) If the registrant seeks an informal statement of the Commission staff's views with regard to its determination to exclude a shareholder nominee or nominees, the registrant shall provide the nominating shareholder or nominating shareholder group (or their authorized representative) with notice, either postmarked or transmitted electronically, promptly following receipt of the staff's response, of whether it will include or exclude the shareholder nominee; and

(v) The exclusion of a shareholder nominee or a statement of support by a registrant where that exclusion is not permissible under paragraph (a), (b), (c), (d), or (e) of this section shall be a violation of this section.

Instruction 1 to paragraph (g). When a registrant must provide a notice to a nominating shareholder, member of a nominating shareholder group, or authorized representative of a nominating shareholder group, the registrant is responsible for providing the notice in a manner that evidences timely transmission. Where a nominating shareholder, member of a nominating shareholder group, or authorized representative of a nominating shareholder group responds to a notice, the nominating shareholder, member of a nominating shareholder group, or authorized representative of a nominating shareholder group is responsible for providing the response in a manner that evidences timely transmission.

Instruction 2 to paragraph (g). Neither the composition of the nominating shareholder group nor the shareholder nominee may be changed as a means to correct a deficiency identified in the registrant's notice to the nominating shareholder or nominating shareholder group under paragraph (g)(2) of this section; however, where a nominating shareholder or nominating shareholder group submits a number of nominees that exceeds the maximum number required to be included by the registrant under the circumstances set forth in paragraph (d) of this section, the nominating shareholder or nominating shareholder group may specify which nominee or nominees are not to be included in the registrant's proxy materials.

Instruction 3 to paragraph (g). Unless otherwise indicated in this section, the burden is on the registrant to demonstrate that it may exclude a nominee or statement of support.

16. Amend § 240.14a-12 by removing the heading following paragraph (c)(2)(iii) "Instructions to § 240.14a-12"; by removing the numbers 1. and 2. of instructions 1 and 2 to § 240.14a-12 and adding in their places the phrases "*Instruction 1 to § 240.14a-12.*" and "*Instruction 2 to § 240.14a-12.*", respectively; and adding Instruction 3 to § 240.14a-12 to read as follows:

§ 240.14a-12 Solicitation before furnishing a proxy statement.

* * * * *

Instruction 3 to § 240.14a-12. Inclusion of a nominee pursuant to § 240.14a-11, an applicable state or foreign law provision, or a registrant's governing documents as they relate to the inclusion of shareholder director nominees in the registrant's proxy materials, or solicitations by a nominating shareholder or nominating shareholder group that are made in connection with that nomination constitute solicitations in opposition subject to § 240.14a-12(c), except for purposes of § 240.14a-6(a).

17. Add § 240.14a-18 to read as follows:

§ 240.14a-18 Disclosure regarding nominating shareholders and nominees submitted for inclusion in a registrant's proxy materials pursuant to applicable state or foreign law, or a registrant's governing documents.

To have a nominee included in a registrant's proxy materials pursuant to a procedure set forth under applicable state or foreign law, or the registrant's governing documents addressing the inclusion of shareholder director nominees in the registrant's proxy materials, the nominating shareholder or nominating shareholder group must provide notice to the registrant of its intent to do so on a Schedule 14N (§ 240.14n-101) and file that notice, including the required disclosure, with the Commission on the date first transmitted to the registrant. This notice shall be postmarked or transmitted electronically to the registrant by the date specified by the registrant's advance notice provision or, where no such provision is in place, no later than 120 calendar days before the anniversary of the date that the registrant mailed its proxy materials for the prior year's annual meeting, except that, if the registrant did not hold an annual meeting during the prior year, or if the date of the meeting has changed by more than 30 calendar days from the prior year, then the nominating shareholder or nominating shareholder group must provide notice a reasonable time before the registrant mails its proxy materials, as specified by the registrant in a Form 8-K (§ 249.308 of this chapter) filed pursuant to Item 5.08 of Form 8-K.

Instruction to § 240.14a-18. The registrant is not responsible for any information provided in the Schedule 14N (§ 240.14n-101) by the nominating shareholder or nominating shareholder group, which is submitted as required by this section or otherwise provided by the nominating shareholder or nominating shareholder group that is included in the registrant's proxy materials.

18. Amend § 240.14a-101 by:

a. Revising Item 7 as follows:

   i.   Redesignating paragraph (e) as paragraph (g); and

   ii.   Adding new paragraph (e) and paragraph (f); and

b. Adding paragraphs (18) and (19) to Item 22(b).

The additions read as follows:

§ 240.14a-101—Schedule 14A. Information required in proxy statement.

SCHEDULE 14A INFORMATION

* * * * *

Item 7. * * *

* * * * *

(e) If a shareholder nominee or nominees are submitted to the registrant for inclusion in the registrant's proxy materials pursuant to § 240.14a-11 and the registrant is not permitted to exclude the nominee or nominees pursuant to the provisions of § 240.14a-11, the registrant must include in its proxy statement the disclosure required from the nominating shareholder or nominating shareholder group under Item 5 of § 240.14n-101 with regard to the nominee or nominees and the nominating shareholder or nominating shareholder group.

Instruction to Item 7(e). The information disclosed pursuant to paragraph (e) of this Item will not be deemed incorporated by reference into any filing under the Securities Act of 1933 (15 U.S.C. 77a *et seq.*), the Securities Exchange Act of 1934 (15 U.S.C. 78a *et seq.*), or the Investment Company Act of 1940 (15 U.S.C. 80a-1 *et seq.*), except to the extent that the registrant specifically incorporates that information by reference.

(f) If a registrant is required to include a shareholder nominee or nominees submitted to the registrant for inclusion in the registrant's proxy materials pursuant to a procedure set forth under applicable state or foreign law, or the registrant's governing documents providing for the inclusion of shareholder director nominees in the registrant's proxy materials, the registrant must include in its proxy statement the disclosure required from the nominating shareholder or nominating shareholder group under Item 6 of § 240.14n-101 with regard to the nominee or nominees and the nominating shareholder or nominating shareholder group.

Instruction to Item 7(f). The information disclosed pursuant to paragraph (f) of this Item will not be deemed incorporated by reference into any filing under the Securities Act of 1933 (15 U.S.C. 77a *et seq.*), the Securities Exchange Act of 1934 (15 U.S.C. 78a *et seq.*), or the Investment Company Act of 1940 (15 U.S.C. 80a-1 *et seq.*), except to the extent that the registrant specifically incorporates that information by reference.

* * * * *

Item 22. Information required in investment company proxy statement.

* * * * *

(b) * * *

(18) If a shareholder nominee or nominees are submitted to the Fund for inclusion in the Fund's proxy materials pursuant to § 240.14a-11 and the Fund is not permitted to exclude the nominee or nominees pursuant to the provisions of § 240.14a-11, the Fund must include in its proxy statement the disclosure required from the nominating shareholder or nominating shareholder group under Item 5 of § 240.14n-101 with regard to the nominee or nominees and the nominating shareholder or nominating shareholder group.

Instruction to paragraph (b)(18). The information disclosed pursuant to paragraph (b)(18) of this Item will not be deemed incorporated by reference into any filing under the Securities Act of 1933 (15 U.S.C. 77a *et seq.*), the Securities Exchange Act of 1934 (15 U.S.C. 78a *et seq.*), or the Investment Company Act of 1940 (15 U.S.C. 80a-1 *et seq.*), except to the extent that the Fund specifically incorporates that information by reference.

(19) If a Fund is required to include a shareholder nominee or nominees submitted to the Fund for inclusion in the Fund's proxy materials pursuant to a procedure set forth under applicable state or foreign law or the Fund's governing documents providing for the inclusion of shareholder director nominees in the Fund's proxy materials, the Fund must include in its proxy statement the disclosure required from the nominating shareholder or nominating shareholder group under Item 6 of § 240.14n-101 with regard to the nominee or nominees and the nominating shareholder or nominating shareholder group.

Instruction to paragraph (b)(19). The information disclosed pursuant to paragraph (b)(19) of this Item will not be deemed incorporated by reference into any filing under the Securities Act of 1933 (15 U.S.C. 77a *et seq.*), the Securities Exchange Act of 1934 (15 U.S.C. 78a *et seq.*), or the Investment Company Act of 1940 (15 U.S.C. 80a-1 *et seq.*), except to the extent that the Fund specifically incorporates that information by reference.

* * * * *

19. Amend Part 240 by adding an undesignated center heading and §§ 240.14n-1 through 240.14n-3 and § 240.14n-101 to read as follows:

REGULATION 14N: FILINGS REQUIRED BY CERTAIN
NOMINATING SHAREHOLDERS

§ 240.14n-1 Filing of Schedule 14N.

(a) A shareholder or group of shareholders that submits a nominee or nominees in accordance with § 240.14a-11 or a procedure set forth under applicable state or foreign law, or a registrant's governing documents providing for the inclusion of shareholder director nominees in the registrant's proxy materials shall file with the Commission a statement containing the information required by Schedule 14N (§ 240.14n-101) and simultaneously provide the notice on Schedule 14N to the registrant.

(b)(1) Whenever two or more persons are required to file a statement containing the information required by Schedule 14N (§ 240.14n-101), only one statement need be filed. The statement must identify all such persons, contain the required information with regard to each such person, indicate that the statement is filed on behalf of all such persons, and include, as an appendix, their agreement in writing that the statement is filed on behalf of each of them. Each person on whose behalf the statement is filed is responsible for the timely filing of that statement and any amendments thereto, and for the completeness and accuracy of the information concerning such person contained therein; such person is not responsible for the completeness or accuracy of the information concerning the other persons making the filing.

(2) If the group's members elect to make their own filings, each filing should identify all members of the group but the information provided concerning the other persons making the filing need only reflect information which the filing person knows or has reason to know.

§ 240.14n-2 Filing of amendments to Schedule 14N.

(a) If any material change occurs with respect to the nomination, or in the disclosure or certifications set forth in the Schedule 14N (§ 240.14n-101) required by § 240.14n-1(a), the person or persons who were required to file the statement shall promptly file or cause to be filed with the Commission an amendment disclosing that change.

(b) An amendment shall be filed within 10 calendar days of the final results of the election being announced by the registrant stating the nominating shareholder's or the nominating shareholder group's intention with regard to continued ownership of their shares.

§ 240.14n-3 Dissemination.

One copy of Schedule 14N (§ 240.14n-101) filed pursuant to §§ 240.14n-1 and 240.14n-2 shall be mailed by registered or certified mail or electronically transmitted to the registrant at its principal executive office. Three copies of the material must at the same time be filed with, or mailed for filing to, each national securities exchange upon which any class of securities of the registrant is listed and registered.

§ 240.14n-101 Schedule 14N—Information to be included in statements filed pursuant to § 240.14n-1 and amendments thereto filed pursuant to § 240.14n-2.

Securities and Exchange Commission, Washington, D.C. 20549

Schedule 14N

Under the Securities Exchange Act of 1934

(Amendment No._)*

_____

(Name of Issuer)

_____

(Title of Class of Securities)

_____

(CUSIP Number)

_____

[ ] Solicitation pursuant to § 240.14a-2(b)(7)

[ ] Solicitation pursuant to § 240.14a-2(b)(8)

[ ] Notice of Submission of a Nominee or Nominees in Accordance with § 240.14a-11

[ ] Notice of Submission of a Nominee or Nominees in Accordance with Procedures Set Forth Under Applicable State or Foreign Law, or the Registrant's Governing Documents

*The remainder of this cover page shall be filled out for a reporting person's initial filing on this form, and for any subsequent amendment containing information which would alter the disclosures provided in a prior cover page.

The information required in the remainder of this cover page shall not be deemed to be "filed" for the purpose of Section 18 of the Securities Exchange Act of 1934 ("Act") or otherwise subject to the liabilities of that section of the Act but shall be subject to all other provisions of the Act.

(1) Names of reporting persons: _____

(2) Mailing address and phone number of each reporting person (or, where applicable, the authorized representative): _____

(3) Amount of securities held that are entitled to be voted on the election of directors held by each reporting person (and, where applicable, amount of securities held in the aggregate by the nominating shareholder group), but including loaned securities and net of securities sold short or borrowed for purposes other than a short sale: _____

(4) Number of votes attributable to the securities entitled to be voted on the election of directors represented by amount in Row (3) (and, where applicable, aggregate number of votes attributable to the securities entitled to be voted on the election of directors held by group): _____

Instructions for Cover Page:

(1) *Names of Reporting Persons*—Furnish the full legal name of each person for whom the report is filed—*i.e.*, each person required to sign the schedule itself—including each member of a group. Do not include the name of a person required to be identified in the report but who is not a reporting person.

(3) and (4) *Amount Held by Each Reporting Person*—Rows (3) and (4) are to be completed in accordance with the provisions of Item 3 of Schedule 14N.

Notes: Attach as many copies of parts one through three of the cover page as are needed, one reporting person per copy.

Filing persons may, in order to avoid unnecessary duplication, answer items on Schedule 14N by appropriate cross references to an item or items on the cover page(s). This approach may only be used where the cover page item or items provide all the disclosure required by the schedule item. Moreover, such a use of a cover page item will result in the item becoming a part of the schedule and accordingly being considered as "filed" for purposes of Section 18 of the Act or otherwise subject to the liabilities of that section of the Act.

SPECIAL INSTRUCTIONS FOR COMPLYING WITH SCHEDULE 14N

Under Sections 14 and 23 of the Securities Exchange Act of 1934 and the rules and regulations thereunder, the Commission is authorized to solicit the information required to be supplied by this Schedule. The information will be used for the primary purpose of determining and disclosing the holdings and interests of a nominating shareholder or nominating shareholder group. This statement will be made a matter of public record. Therefore, any information given will be available for inspection by any member of the public.

Because of the public nature of the information, the Commission can use it for a variety of purposes, including referral to other governmental authorities or securities self-regulatory organizations for investigatory purposes or in connection with litigation involving the Federal securities laws or other civil, criminal or regulatory statutes or provisions. Failure to disclose the information requested by this schedule may result in civil or criminal action against the persons involved for violation of the Federal securities laws and rules promulgated thereunder, or in some cases, exclusion of the nominee from the registrant's proxy materials.

General instructions to item requirements

The item numbers and captions of the items shall be included but the text of the items is to be omitted. The answers to the items shall be prepared so as to indicate clearly the coverage of the items without referring to the text of the items. Answer every item. If an item is inapplicable or the answer is in the negative, so state.

Item 1(a). Name of registrant

Item 1(b). Address of registrant's principal executive offices

Item 2(a). Name of person filing

Item 2(b). Address or principal business office or, if none, residence

Item 2(c). Title of class of securities

Item 2(d). CUSIP No.

Item 3. Ownership

Provide the following information, in accordance with Instruction 3 to § 240.14a-11(b)(1):

(a) Amount of securities held and entitled to be voted on the election of directors (and, where applicable, amount of securities held in the aggregate by the nominating shareholder group): _____.

(b) The number of votes attributable to the securities referred to in paragraph (a) of this Item: _____.

(c) The number of votes attributable to securities that have been loaned but which the reporting person:

(i) has the right to recall; and

(ii) will recall upon being notified that any of the nominees will be included in the registrant's proxy statement and proxy card: _____.

(d) The number of votes attributable to securities that have been sold in a short sale that is not closed out, or that have been borrowed for purposes other than a short sale: _____.

(e) The sum of paragraphs (b) and (c), minus paragraph (d) of this Item, divided by the aggregate number of votes derived from all classes of securities of the registrant that are entitled to vote on the election of directors, and expressed as a percentage: _____.

Item 4. Statement of Ownership from a Nominating Shareholder or Each Member of a Nominating Shareholder Group Submitting this Notice Pursuant to § 240.14a-11

(a) If the nominating shareholder, or each member of the nominating shareholder group, is the registered holder of the shares, please so state. Otherwise, attach to the Schedule 14N one or more written statements from the persons (usually brokers or banks) through which the nominating shareholder's securities are held, verifying that, within seven calendar days prior to filing the shareholder notice on Schedule 14N with the Commission and transmitting the notice to the registrant, the nominating shareholder continuously held the amount of securities being used to satisfy the ownership threshold for a period of at least three years. In the alternative, if the nominating shareholder has filed a Schedule 13D (§ 240.13d-101), Schedule 13G (§ 240.13d-102), Form 3 (§ 249.103 of this chapter), Form 4 (§ 249.104 of this chapter), and/or Form 5 (§ 249.105 of this chapter), or amendments to those documents, reflecting ownership of the securities as of or before the date on which the three-year eligibility period begins, so state and incorporate that filing or amendment by reference.

(b) Provide a written statement that the nominating shareholder, or each member of the nominating shareholder group, intends to continue to hold the amount of securities that are used for purposes of satisfying the minimum ownership requirement of § 240.14a-11(b)(1) through the date of the meeting of shareholders, as required by § 240.14a-11(b)(4). Additionally, provide a written statement from the nominating shareholder or each member of the nominating shareholder group regarding the nominating shareholder's or nominating shareholder group member's intent with respect to continued ownership after the election of directors, as required by § 240.14a-11(b)(5).

Instruction to Item 4. If the nominating shareholder or any member of the nominating shareholder group is not the registered holder of the securities and is not proving ownership for purposes of § 240.14a-11(b)(3) by providing previously filed Schedules 13D or 13G or Forms 3, 4, or 5, and the securities are held in an account with a broker or bank that is a participant in the Depository Trust Company ("DTC") or other clearing agency acting as a securities depository, a written statement or statements from that participant or participants in the following form will satisfy § 240.14a-11(b)(3):

As of [date of this statement], [name of nominating shareholder or member of the nominating shareholder group] held at least [number of securities owned continuously for at least three years] of the [registrant's] [class of securities], and has held at least this amount of such securities continuously for [at least three years]. [Name of clearing agency participant] is a participant in [name of clearing agency] whose nominee name is [nominee name].

[name of clearing agency participant]

By: [name and title of representative]

Date:

If the securities are held through a broker or bank (*e.g.* in an omnibus account) that is not a participant in a clearing agency acting as a securities depository, the nominating shareholder or member of the nominating shareholder group must (a) obtain and submit a written statement or statements (the "initial broker statement") from the broker or bank with which the nominating shareholder or member of the nominating shareholder group maintains an account that provides the information about securities ownership set forth above and (b) obtain and submit a separate written statement from the clearing agency participant through which the securities of the nominating shareholder or member of the nominating shareholder group are held, that (i) identifies the broker or bank for whom the clearing agency participant holds the securities, and (ii) states that the account of such broker or bank has held, as of the date of the separate written statement, at least the number of securities specified in the initial broker statement, and (iii) states that this account has held at least that amount of securities continuously for at least three years.

If the securities have been held for less than three years at the relevant entity, provide written statements covering a continuous period of three years and modify the language set forth above as appropriate.

For purposes of complying with § 240.14a-11(b)(3), loaned securities may be included in the amount of securities set forth in the written statements.

Item 5. Disclosure Required for Shareholder Nominations Submitted Pursuant to § 240.14a-11

If a nominating shareholder or nominating shareholder group is submitting this notice in connection with the inclusion of a shareholder nominee or nominees for director in the registrant's proxy materials pursuant to § 240.14a-11, provide the following information:

(a) A statement that the nominee consents to be named in the registrant's proxy statement and form of proxy and, if elected, to serve on the registrant's board of directors;

(b) Disclosure about the nominee as would be provided in response to the disclosure requirements of Items 4(b), 5(b), 7(a), (b) and (c) and, for investment companies, Item 22(b) of Schedule 14A (§ 240.14a-101), as applicable;

(c) Disclosure about the nominating shareholder or each member of a nominating shareholder group as would be required of a participant in response to the disclosure requirements of Items 4(b) and 5(b) of Schedule 14A (§ 240.14a-101), as applicable;

(d) Disclosure about whether the nominating shareholder or any member of a nominating shareholder group has been involved in any legal proceeding during the past ten years, as specified in Item 401(f) of Regulation S-K (§ 229.10 of this chapter). Disclosure pursuant to this paragraph need not be provided if provided in response to Item 5(c) of this section;

Instruction 1 to Item 5(c) and (d). Where the nominating shareholder is a general or limited partnership, syndicate or other group, the information called for in paragraphs (c) and (d) of this Item must be given with respect to:

a. Each partner of the general partnership;

b. Each partner who is, or functions as, a general partner of the limited partnership;

c. Each member of the syndicate or group; and

d. Each person controlling the partner or member.

Instruction 2 to Item 5(c) and (d). If the nominating shareholder is a corporation or if a person referred to in a., b., c. or d. of Instruction 1 to paragraphs (c) and (d) of this Item is a corporation, the information called for in paragraphs (c) and (d) of this Item must be given with respect to:

a. Each executive officer and director of the corporation;

b. Each person controlling the corporation; and

c. Each executive officer and director of any corporation or other person ultimately in control of the corporation.

(e) Disclosure about whether, to the best of the nominating shareholder's or group's knowledge, the nominee meets the director qualifications, if any, set forth in the registrant's governing documents;

(f) A statement that, to the best of the nominating shareholder's or group's knowledge, in the case of a registrant other than an investment company, the nominee meets the objective criteria for "independence" of the national securities exchange or national securities association rules applicable to the registrant, if any, or, in the case of a registrant that is an investment company, the nominee is not an "interested person" of the registrant as defined in section 2(a)(19) of the Investment Company Act of 1940 (15 U.S.C. 80a-2(a)(19)).

Instruction to Item 5(f). For this purpose, the nominee would be required to meet the definition of "independence" that is generally applicable to directors of the registrant and not any particular definition of independence applicable to members of the audit committee of the registrant's board of directors. To the extent a national securities exchange or national securities association rule imposes a standard regarding independence that requires a subjective determination by the board or a group or committee of the board (for example, requiring that the board of directors or any group or committee of the board of directors make a determination regarding the existence of factors material to a determination of a nominee's independence), the nominee would not be required to meet the subjective determination of independence as part of the shareholder nomination process.

(g) The following information regarding the nature and extent of the relationships between the nominating shareholder or nominating shareholder group, the nominee, and/or the registrant or any affiliate of the registrant:

(1) Any direct or indirect material interest in any contract or agreement between the nominating shareholder or any member of the nominating shareholder group, the nominee, and/or the registrant or any affiliate of the registrant (including any employment agreement, collective bargaining agreement, or consulting agreement);

(2) Any material pending or threatened legal proceeding in which the nominating shareholder or any member of the nominating shareholder group and/or the nominee is a party or a material participant, and that involves the registrant, any of its executive officers or directors, or any affiliate of the registrant; and

(3) Any other material relationship between the nominating shareholder or any member of the nominating shareholder group, the nominee, and/or the registrant or any affiliate of the registrant not otherwise disclosed;

Note to Item 5(g)(3). Any other material relationship of the nominating shareholder or any member of the nominating shareholder group or nominee with the registrant or any affiliate of the registrant may include, but is not limited to, whether the nominating shareholder or any member of the nominating shareholder group currently has, or has had in the past, an employment relationship with the registrant or any affiliate of the registrant (including consulting arrangements).

(h) The Web site address on which the nominating shareholder or nominating shareholder group may publish soliciting materials, if any; and

(i) Any statement in support of the shareholder nominee or nominees, which may not exceed 500 words for each nominee, if the nominating shareholder or nominating shareholder group elects to have such statement included in the registrant's proxy materials.

Item 6. Disclosure Required by § 240.14a-18

If a nominating shareholder or nominating shareholder group is submitting this notice in connection with the inclusion of a shareholder nominee or nominees for director in the registrant's proxy materials pursuant to a procedure set forth under applicable state or foreign law, or the registrant's governing documents provide the following disclosure:

(a) A statement that the nominee consents to be named in the registrant's proxy statement and form of proxy and, if elected, to serve on the registrant's board of directors;

(b) Disclosure about the nominee as would be provided in response to the disclosure requirements of Items 4(b), 5(b), 7(a), (b) and (c) and, for investment companies, Item 22(b) of Schedule 14A (§ 240.14a-101), as applicable;

(c) Disclosure about the nominating shareholder or each member of a nominating shareholder group as would be required in response to the disclosure requirements of Items 4(b) and 5(b) of Schedule 14A (§ 240.14a-101), as applicable;

(d) Disclosure about whether the nominating shareholder or any member of a nominating shareholder group has been involved in any legal proceeding during the past ten years, as specified in Item 401(f) of Regulation S-K (§ 229.10 of this chapter). Disclosure pursuant to this paragraph need not be provided if provided in response to Item 6(c) of this section;

Instruction 1 to Item 6(c) and (d). Where the nominating shareholder is a general or limited partnership, syndicate or other group, the information called for in paragraphs (c) and (d) of this Item must be given with respect to:

a. Each partner of the general partnership;

b. Each partner who is, or functions as, a general partner of the limited partnership;

c. Each member of the syndicate or group; and

d. Each person controlling the partner or member.

Instruction 2 to Item 6(c) and (d). If the nominating shareholder is a corporation or if a person referred to in a., b., c. or d. of Instruction 1 to paragraphs (c) and (d) of this Item is a corporation, the information called for in paragraphs (c) and (d) of this Item must be given with respect to:

a. Each executive officer and director of the corporation;

b. Each person controlling the corporation; and

c. Each executive officer and director of any corporation or other person ultimately in control of the corporation.

(e) The following information regarding the nature and extent of the relationships between the nominating shareholder or nominating shareholder group, the nominee, and/or the registrant or any affiliate of the registrant:

(1) Any direct or indirect material interest in any contract or agreement between the nominating shareholder or any member of the nominating shareholder group, the nominee, and/or the registrant or any affiliate of the registrant (including any employment agreement, collective bargaining agreement, or consulting agreement);

(2) Any material pending or threatened legal proceeding in which the nominating shareholder or any member of the nominating shareholder group and/or nominee is a party or a material participant, involving the registrant, any of its executive officers or directors, or any affiliate of the registrant; and

(3) Any other material relationship between the nominating shareholder or any member of the nominating shareholder group, the nominee, and/or the registrant or any affiliate of the registrant not otherwise disclosed; and

Instruction to Item 6(e)(3). Any other material relationship of the nominating shareholder or any member of the nominating shareholder group with the registrant or any affiliate of the registrant may include, but is not limited to, whether the nominating shareholder or any member of the nominating shareholder group currently has, or has had in the past, an employment relationship with the registrant or any affiliate of the registrant (including consulting arrangements).

(f) The Web site address on which the nominating shareholder or nominating shareholder group may publish soliciting materials, if any.

Item 7. Notice of Dissolution of Group or Termination of Shareholder Nomination

Notice of dissolution of a nominating shareholder group or the termination of a shareholder nomination shall state the date of the dissolution or termination.

Item 8. Signatures

(a) The following certifications shall be provided by the filing person submitting this notice pursuant to § 240.14a-11, or in the case of a group, each filing person whose securities are being aggregated for purposes of meeting the ownership threshold set out in § 240.14a-11(b)(1) exactly as set forth below:

I, [identify the certifying individual], after reasonable inquiry and to the best of my knowledge and belief, certify that:

(1) I [or if signed by an authorized representative, the name of the nominating shareholder or each member of the nominating shareholder group, as appropriate] am [is] not holding any of the registrant's securities with the purpose, or with the effect, of changing control of the registrant or to gain a number of seats on the board of directors that exceeds the maximum number of nominees that the registrant could be required to include under § 240.14a-11(d);

(2) I [or if signed by an authorized representative, the name of the nominating shareholder or each member of the nominating shareholder group, as appropriate] otherwise satisfy [satisfies] the requirements of § 240.14a-11(b), as applicable;

(3) The nominee or nominees satisfies the requirements of § 240.14a-11(b), as applicable; and

(4) The information set forth in this notice on Schedule 14N is true, complete and correct.

(b) The following certification shall be provided by the filing person or persons submitting this notice in connection with the submission of a nominee or nominees in accordance with procedures set forth under applicable state or foreign law or the registrant's governing documents:

I, [identify the certifying individual], after reasonable inquiry and to the best of my knowledge and belief, certify that the information set forth in this notice on Schedule 14N is true, complete and correct.

Dated:_____

Signature: _____

Name/Title: _____

The original statement shall be signed by each person on whose behalf the statement is filed or his authorized representative. If the statement is signed on behalf of a person by his authorized representative other than an executive officer or general partner of the filing person, evidence of the representative's authority to sign on behalf of such person shall be filed with the statement, *provided, however*, that a power of attorney for this purpose which is already on file with the Commission may be incorporated by reference. The name and any title of each person who signs the statement shall be typed or printed beneath his signature.

Attention: Intentional misstatements or omissions of fact constitute Federal criminal violations (see 18 U.S.C. 1001).

20. Amend § 240.15d-11 by revising paragraph (b) to read as follows:

§ 240.15d-11 Current reports on Form 8-K (§ 249.308 of this chapter).

* * * * *

(b) This section shall not apply to foreign governments, foreign private issuers required to make reports on Form 6-K (17 CFR 249.306) pursuant to § 240.15d-16, issuers of American Depositary Receipts for securities of any foreign issuer, or investment companies required to file reports pursuant to § 270.30b1-1 of this chapter under the Investment Company Act of 1940, except where such an investment company is required to file:

(1) Notice of a blackout period pursuant to § 245.104 of this chapter;

(2) Disclosure pursuant to Instruction 2 to § 240.14a-11(b)(1) of information concerning outstanding shares and voting; or

(3) Disclosure pursuant to Instruction 2 to § 240.14a-11(b)(10) of the date by which a nominating shareholder or nominating shareholder group must submit the notice required pursuant to § 240.14a-11(b)(10).

* * * * *

PART 249—FORMS, SECURITIES EXCHANGE ACT OF 1934

21. The authority citation for Part 249 continues to read, in part, as follows:

Authority: 15 U.S.C. 78a *et seq.* and 7201 *et seq.*; and 18 U.S.C. 1350, unless otherwise noted.

* * * * *

22. Amend Form 8-K (referenced in § 249.308) by:

a. Adding a sentence at the end of General Instruction B.1;

b. Removing the phrase "Section 5.06" in the heading and adding in its place "Item 5.06"; and

c. Adding Item 5.08.

The additions read as follows:

Note: The text of Form 8-K does not, and this amendment will not, appear in the Code of Federal Regulations.

Form 8-K

* * * * *

GENERAL INSTRUCTIONS

* * * * *

B. Events to be Reported and Time for Filing Reports

1. * * * A report pursuant to Item 5.08 is to be filed within four business days after the registrant determines the anticipated meeting date.

* * * * *

Item 5.08 Shareholder Director Nominations

(a) If the registrant did not hold an annual meeting the previous year, or if the date of this year's annual meeting has been changed by more than 30 calendar days from the date of the previous year's meeting, then the registrant is required to disclose the date by which a nominating shareholder or nominating shareholder group must submit the notice on Schedule 14N (§ 240.14n-101) required pursuant to § 240.14a-11(b)(10), which date shall be a reasonable time before the registrant mails its proxy materials for the meeting. Where a registrant is required to include shareholder director nominees in the registrant's proxy materials pursuant to either an applicable state or foreign law provision, or a provision in the registrant's governing documents, then the registrant is required to disclose the date by which a nominating shareholder or nominating shareholder group must submit the notice on Schedule 14N required pursuant to § 240.14a-18.

(b) If the registrant is a series company as defined in Rule 18f-2(a) under the Investment Company Act of 1940 (§ 270.18f-2 of this chapter), then the registrant is required to disclose in connection with the election of directors at an annual meeting of shareholders (or, in lieu of such an annual meeting, a special meeting of shareholders) the total number of shares of the registrant outstanding and entitled to be voted (or if the votes are to be cast on a basis other than one vote per share, then the total number of votes entitled to be voted and the basis for allocating such votes) on the election of directors at such meeting of shareholders as of the end of the most recent calendar quarter.

* * * * *

By the Commission.

Elizabeth M. Murphy
Secretary

Date: August 25, 2010

APPENDIX 3
Short-Term Borrowings Disclosure

SECURITIES AND EXCHANGE COMMISSION

17 CFR Parts 229 and 249

Release Nos. 33-9143; 34-62932; File No. S7-22-10

RIN 3235-AK72

SHORT-TERM BORROWINGS DISCLOSURE

AGENCY: Securities and Exchange Commission.

ACTION: Proposed rule.

SUMMARY: We are proposing amendments to enhance the disclosure that registrants provide about short-term borrowings. Specifically, the proposals would require a registrant to provide, in a separately captioned subsection of Management's Discussion and Analysis of Financial Condition and Results of Operations, a comprehensive explanation of its short-term borrowings, including both quantitative and qualitative information. The proposed amendments would be applicable to annual and quarterly reports, proxy or information statements that include financial statements, registration statements under the Securities Exchange Act of 1934, and registration statements under the Securities Act of 1933. We are also proposing conforming amendments to Form 8-K so that the Form would use the terminology contained in the proposed short-term borrowings disclosure requirement.

In a companion release, we are providing interpretive guidance that is intended to improve overall discussion of liquidity and capital resources in Management's Discussion and Analysis of Financial Condition and Results of Operations in order to facilitate understanding by investors of the liquidity and funding risks facing the registrant.

DATES: Comments should be received on or before November 29, 2010.

ADDRESSES: Comments may be submitted by any of the following methods:

Electronic Comments:

- Use the Commission's Internet comment form *(http://www.sec.gov/rules/proposed.shtml);*
- Send an e-mail to *rule-comments@sec.gov.* Please include File Number S7-22-10 on the subject line; or
- Use the Federal Rulemaking ePortal *(http://www.regulations.gov).* Follow the instructions for submitting comments.

Paper Comments:

- Send paper comments in triplicate to Elizabeth M. Murphy, Secretary, Securities and Exchange Commission, 100 F Street, NE, Washington, DC 20549-1090.

All submissions should refer to File Number S7-22-10. This file number should be included on the subject line if e-mail is used. To help us process and review your comments more efficiently, please use only one method. The Commission will post all comments on the Commission's Internet website *(http://www.sec.gov/rules/proposed.shtml).* Comments are also available for website viewing and printing in the Commission's Public Reference Room, 100 F Street, NE, Washington, DC 20549, on official business days between the hours of 10:00 a.m. and 3:00 p.m. All comments received will be posted without change; we do not edit personal identifying information from submissions. You should submit only information that you wish to make available publicly.

FOR FURTHER INFORMATION CONTACT: Christina L. Padden, Attorney Fellow in the Office of Rulemaking, at (202) 551-3430, or Stephanie L. Hunsaker, Associate Chief Accountant, at (202) 551-3400, in the Division of Corporation Finance; or Wesley R. Bricker, Professional Accounting Fellow, Office of the Chief Accountant at (202) 551-5300; U.S. Securities and Exchange Commission, 100 F Street, NE, Washington, DC 20549.

SUPPLEMENTARY INFORMATION: We are proposing amendments to Item 303[1] of Regulation S-K[2] and amendments to Forms 8-K[3] and 20-F[4] under the Securities Exchange Act of 1934 ("Exchange Act").[5]

The proposed amendments include:

- a new disclosure requirement in Management's Discussion and Analysis of Financial Condition and Results of Operations ("MD&A") relating to short-term borrowings that would be designated as Item 303(a)(6) of Regulation S-K;

- amendments to Item 303(b) of Regulation S-K that would require interim period disclosure of short-term borrowings with the same level of detail as is proposed for annual presentation;

- conforming amendments to Item 5 of Form 20-F to add short-term borrowings disclosure requirements;

- conforming amendments to the definition of "direct financial obligations" in Items 2.03 and 2.04 of Form 8-K; and

- revisions to Item 303 of Regulation S-K and Item 5 of Form 20-F to update the references to United States generally accepted accounting principles ("U.S. GAAP") to reflect the release by the Financial Accounting Standards Board ("FASB") of its FASB Accounting Standards Codification ("FASB Codification").

Table of Contents
I.   **BACKGROUND AND SUMMARY**
II. **DISCUSSION OF THE PROPOSED AMENDMENTS**
    A.   **Short-Term Borrowings Disclosure**
    B.   **Treatment of Foreign Private Issuers and Smaller Reporting Companies**
    C.   **Leverage Ratio Disclosure Issues**
    D.   **Technical Amendments Reflecting FASB Codification**
    E.   **Conforming Amendments to Definition of "Direct Financial Obligation" in Form 8-K**
    F.   **Transition**
III. **GENERAL REQUEST FOR COMMENT**
IV. **PAPERWORK REDUCTION ACT**
    A.   **Background**
    B.   **Burden and Cost Estimates Related to the Proposed Amendments**
    C.   **Request for Comment**
V.   **COST-BENEFIT ANALYSIS**
    A.   **Introduction and Objectives of Proposals**
    B.   **Benefits**
    C.   **Costs**
    D.   **Request for Comment**

---

[1] 17 CFR 229.303.
[2] 17 CFR 229.10 *et al.*
[3] 17 CFR 249.308.

[4] 17 CFR 249.220f.
[5] 15 U.S.C. 78a *et seq.*

I. BACKGROUND AND SUMMARY

Over the past several years, we have provided guidance and have engaged in rulemaking initiatives to improve the presentation of information about funding and liquidity risk.[6] As we have emphasized in past guidance, MD&A disclosure relating to liquidity and capital resources is critical to an assessment of a company's prospects for the future and even the likelihood of its survival.[7] We believe that leverage and liquidity continue to be significant areas of focus for investors,[8] particularly as many failures in the financial crisis arose due to liquidity constraints.[9]

A critical component of a company's liquidity and capital resources is often its access to short-term borrowings for working capital and to fund its operations.[10] Traditional sources of funding, such as trade credit, bank loans, and long-term or medium-term debt instruments, remain important for many types of businesses.[11] However, other short-term financing techniques, including commercial paper, repurchase transactions and securitizations, have become increasingly common among financial institutions and industrial companies alike.[12]

---

[6] See, e.g., Disclosure in Management's Discussion and Analysis About Off-Balance Sheet Arrangements, Contractual Obligations and Contingent Liabilities and Commitments, Release No. 33-8144 (Nov. 4, 2002) [67 FR 68054] (the "OBS Proposing Release"); Disclosure in Management's Discussion and Analysis About Off-Balance Sheet Arrangements, Contractual Obligations and Contingent Liabilities and Commitments, Release No. 33-8182 (Jan. 28, 2003) [68 FR 5982] (the "OBS Adopting Release") (adopting rules for disclosure in MD&A of off-balance sheet arrangements and aggregate contractual obligations); and Commission Guidance Regarding Management's Discussion and Analysis of Financial Condition and Results of Operations, Release No. 33-8350 (Dec. 19, 2003) [68 FR 75056] (the "2003 Interpretive Release") (providing interpretive guidance on disclosure in MD&A, including liquidity and capital resources).

[7] See 2003 Interpretive Release, supra note 6, at 75062. See also Commission Statement About Management's Discussion and Analysis of Financial Condition and Results of Operations, Release No. 33-8056 (Jan. 22, 2002) [67 FR 3746] (the "2002 Interpretive Release") and the OBS Adopting Release, supra note 6.

[8] See L. H. Pedersen, When Everyone Runs for the Exit, 5 INT'L J. CENT. BANKING 177 (2009) ("[t]he global crisis that started in 2007 provides ample evidence of the importance of liquidity risk. . . . [t]he crisis spilled over to other credit markets, money markets, convertible bonds, stocks and over-the-counter derivatives."); M. Brunnermeier, Deciphering the Liquidity and Credit Crunch 2007-2008, 23 J. ECON. PERSP. 77 (2009); M. Brunnermeier & L. Pedersen, Market Liquidity and Funding Liquidity, 22 REV. FIN. STUD. 2201 (2009); R. Huang, How Committed Are Bank Lines of Credit? Evidence from the Subprime Mortgage Crisis, (working paper) (Aug. 2010), available at http://www.phil.frb.org/research-and-data/publications/working-papers/2010/wp10-25.pdf; P. Strahan et al., Liquidity Risk Management and Credit Supply in the Financial Crisis, (working paper) (May 2010), available at http://papers.ssrn.com/sol3/papers.cfm?abstract_id=1601992.

[9] See, e.g., K. Ayotte & D. Steele, Bankruptcy or Bailouts?, 35 J. CORP. L. 469 (2010) (discussing illiquidity and insolvency for financial institutions in the context of the recent financial crisis); When the River Runs Dry, ECONOMIST, Feb. 11, 2010 ("Many of those clobbered in the crisis were struck down by a sudden lack of cash or funding sources, not because they ran out of capital.").

[10] See D. Booth & J. Renier, Fed Policy in the Financial Crisis: Arresting the Adverse Feedback Loop, FRBD Economic Letter (Sept. 2009), available at http://www.dallasfed.org/research/eclett/2009/el0907.html ("Many businesses were hampered by the squeeze on short-term financing, a key source of working capital needed to prevent deeper reductions in inventories, jobs and wages.").

[11] See, generally, B. Becker & V. Ivashina, Cyclicality of Credit Supply: Firm Level Evidence (May 2010) (Harvard Working Paper); C. M. James, Market Conditions and the Use of Bank Lines of Credit, FRBSF Economic Letter 2009-27 (Aug. 2009), available at http://www.frbsf.org/publications/economics/letter/2009/el2009-27; M. Campello et al., Liquidity Management and Corporate Investment During a Financial Crisis (July 2010) (working paper) (examining how non-financial companies choose among various sources of liquidity), available at http://faculty.fuqua.duke.edu/~charvey/Research/Working_Papers/W99_Liquidity_management_and.pdf; V. Ivashina & D. Scharfstein, Bank Lending During the Financial Crisis of 2008, J. FIN. ECON. (forthcoming), available at http://ssrn.com/abstract=1297337 (examining the increase in draw-downs or threats of drawdowns of existing credit lines by commercial and industrial firms and the related impact on bank lending).

[12] See S. Sood, Is the Ride Coming to an End?, GLOBAL INVESTOR, May 1, 2009 ("Treasurers need to look harder at a broader range of funding alternatives, e.g., debt factoring, invoice factoring and trade finance which are essentially forms of collateralized financing"); M. Lemmon et al., The Use of Asset-backed Securitization and Capital Structure in Industrial Firms: An Empirical Investigation (May 2010), available at http://www.fma.org.

Recent events have shown that these types of arrangements can be impacted, sometimes severely and rapidly, by illiquidity in the markets as a whole.[13] When market liquidity is low, short-term borrowings present increased risks: that financing rates will increase or terms will become unfavorable, that it will be more costly or impossible to roll over short-term borrowings, or for financial institutions, that demand depositors will withdraw funds.[14]

Moreover, short-term financing arrangements can present complex accounting and disclosure issues, even when market conditions are stable.[15] Due to their short-term nature, a company's use of such arrangements can fluctuate materially during a reporting period, which means that presentation of period-end amounts of short-term borrowings alone may not be indicative of that company's funding needs or activities during the period. For example, a bank that routinely enters into repurchase transactions during the quarter might curtail that activity at quarter-end,[16] resulting in a period-end amount of outstanding borrowings that does not necessarily reflect its business operations or related risks. Likewise, a retailer may have significant short-term borrowings during the year to finance inventory that is sold by year-end (and where those short-term borrowings are repaid by year-end). In that case, where the need to finance inventory purchases fluctuates, impacted by the timing and volume of inventory sales, the ability to have access to short-term borrowings may be very important to the company. Therefore, although the financial services sector has been in the spotlight, the issues arising from short-term borrowings are not limited to that sector.[17]

Recent events have suggested that investors could benefit from additional transparency about companies' short-term borrowings, including particularly whether these borrowings vary materially during reporting periods compared to amounts reported at period-end without investor appreciation of those variations.[18] Although current MD&A rules generally require disclosure of a registrant's use of short-term borrowing arrangements and the registrant's exposure to related risks and uncertainties,[19] without a

---

[13] *See* J. Tirole, *Illiquidity and All Its Friends* (Bank for International Settlements, Working Paper No. 303, 2010), *available at* http://www.bis.org ("[t]he recent crisis, we all know, was characterized by massive illiquidity." In addition, "Overall there has been a tremendous increase in the proportion of short-term liabilities in the financial sector"). *See also, e.g.,* P. Eavis, *Lehman's Racy Repo*, WALL ST. J., Mar. 12, 2010 (suggesting that repo financing "is highly vulnerable in times of panic, as the credit crisis showed"); A. Martin et al., *Repo Runs*, FRBNY Staff Report No. 444 (Apr. 2010) (demonstrating that institutions funded by short-term collateralized borrowings are subject to the threat of runs similar to those faced by commercial banks).

[14] *See, e.g.,* Brunnermeier, *supra* note 8, at 79-80; *see also* C. Borio, *Market Distress and Vanishing Liquidity: Anatomy and Policy Options* (Bank for International Settlements, Working Paper No. 158, 2004), *available at* http://www.bis.org ("Under stress, risk management practices, funding liquidity constraints, and in the most severe cases, concerns with counter-party risk become critical.").

[15] *See, e.g.,* the Division of Corporation Finance, Sample Letter Sent to Public Companies Asking for Information Related to Repurchase Agreements, Securities Lending Transactions, or Other Transactions Involving the Transfer of Financial Assets (Mar. 2010) (the "2010 Dear CFO Letter"), *available at* http://www.sec.gov/divisions/corpfin/guidance/cfore purchase0310.htm.

[16] *See* V. Kotomin & D. Winters, *Quarter-End Effects in Banks: Preferred Habitat or Window Dressing?*, 29 J. FIN. RES. 1 (2006); M. Rappaport & T. McGinty, *Banks Trim Debt, Obscuring Risks*, WALL ST. J., May 25, 2010.

[17] *See, e.g.,* W. Dudley, President & CEO, FRBNY, Remarks at the Center for Economic Policy Studies Symposium: More Lessons From the Crisis, (Nov. 13, 2009), *available at* http://newyorkfed.org/newsevents/ speeches/2009/dud091113.html (noting "[a] key vulnerability turned out to be the misplaced assumption that securities dealers and others would be able to obtain very large amounts of short-term funding even in times of stress"); J. Lahart, *U.S. Firms Build Up Record Cash Piles*, WALL ST. J., June 10, 2010 ("In the darkest days of late 2008, even large companies faced the threat that they wouldn't be able to do the everyday, short-term borrowing needed to make payrolls and purchase inventory.").

[18] *See, e.g.,* Financial Crisis Inquiry Commission, Hearing on "The Shadow Banking System" (May 5, 2010) (transcript *available at* http://www.fcic.gov/ hearings/pdfs/2010-0505-Transcript.pdf).

[19] *See* Item 303(a)(1) and (2) of Regulation S-K and Instruction 5 to paragraph 303(a) [17 CFR 229.303] (noting that liquidity generally shall be discussed on both a long-term and short-term basis); *see also* 2002 Interpretive Release, *supra* note 7 (providing interpretive guidance on MD&A, noting "registrants should consider describing the sources of short-term funding and the circumstances that are reasonably likely to affect those sources of liquidity").

specific requirement to disclose information about intra-period short-term borrowings, investors may not have access to sufficient information to understand companies' actual funding needs and financing activities or to evaluate the liquidity risks faced by companies during the reporting period. To address these issues, we are proposing to amend the MD&A requirements to enhance disclosure that registrants provide regarding the use and impact of short-term financing arrangements during each reporting period. The principal aspects of the proposals are outlined below.

First, the proposed amendments would add new disclosure requirements relating to short-term borrowings, similar to the provisions for annual disclosure of short-term borrowings that are currently applicable to bank holding companies in accordance with the disclosure guidance set forth in Industry Guide 3, Statistical Disclosure by Bank Holding Companies ("Guide 3").[20] The proposed amendments would codify the Guide 3 provisions for disclosure of short-term borrowings in Regulation S-K, would require disclosure on an annual and quarterly basis, and would be expanded to apply to all companies that provide MD&A disclosure, not only to financial institutions. If the proposals are adopted, we expect to authorize the Commission's staff to eliminate the corresponding provisions of Guide 3 to avoid redundant disclosure requirements.[21]

Second, we are proposing amendments to the requirements applicable to "foreign private issuers" in the "Operating and Financial Review and Prospects" item in Form 20-F to add short-term borrowings disclosure requirements, which would be substantially similar to the proposed amendments to MD&A, but without the requirement for quarterly reporting since foreign private issuers are not subject to quarterly reporting requirements.

Third, we are proposing conforming amendments to the definition of "direct financial obligations" in Items 2.03 and 2.04 of Form 8-K.

Finally, the proposed amendments would update the references to U.S. GAAP in Item 303 of Regulation S-K and Item 5 of Form 20-F to reflect the FASB Codification.

Over time, to enhance the information provided to investors through MD&A we have supplemented the principles-based disclosure requirements governing MD&A with more detailed and specific MD&A disclosure requirements, such as the contractual obligations table and the off-balance sheet arrangements disclosure requirements.[22] Our proposal to require quantitative and qualitative information about short-term borrowings is similarly designed to enhance investor understanding of a company's financial position and liquidity. We emphasize, however, that the addition of these specific disclosure requirements to MD&A supplements, and is not a substitute for, the required discussion and analysis that enables investors to understand the company's business as seen through the eyes of management.[23]

In a companion release, we are providing interpretive guidance that is intended to improve the overall discussion of liquidity and funding in MD&A in order to facilitate understanding by investors of the liquidity and funding risks facing registrants.

---

[20] *See* 17 CFR 229.801, Item VII.

[21] Guide 3, as originally promulgated in 1968 under the designations Guide 61 and Guide 3, served as an expression of the policies and practices of the Commission's Division of Corporation Finance in order to assist issuers in the preparation of their registration statements and reports. *See* Guides for Preparation and Filing of Registration Statements, Release No. 33-4936 (Dec. 9, 1968) [33 FR 18617]. In 1982, these guides were redesignated as Securities Act Industry Guide 3 and Exchange Act Industry Guide 3, and were included in the list of industry guides in Items 801 and 802 of Regulation S-K, but were not codified as rules. *See* Rescission of Guides and Redesignation of Industry Guides, Release No. 33-6384 [47 FR 11476], at 11476

("The list of industry guides has been moved to into Regulation S-K, which serves as the central repository of disclosure requirements under the Securities Act and Exchange Act, in order to more effectively put registrants on notice of their existence. These guides remain as an expression of the policies and practices of the Division of Corporation Finance and their status is unaffected by this change.") If the proposed amendments are adopted, the Commission would authorize its staff to amend Guide 3 to eliminate Item VII in its entirety.

[22] *See* Items 303(a)(4) and (5) of Regulation S-K [17 CFR 229.303(a)(4) and (5)].

[23] *See* 2003 Interpretive Release, *supra* note 6, at 75056.

II. DISCUSSION OF THE PROPOSED AMENDMENTS

A. Short-Term Borrowings Disclosure

1. Existing Requirements for Disclosure of Short-Term Borrowings

Existing MD&A requirements call for discussion and analysis of a registrant's liquidity and capital resources. With respect to liquidity, registrants must identify any known trends or any known demands, commitments, events or uncertainties that will result in or that are reasonably likely to result in the registrant's liquidity increasing or decreasing in any material way.[24] Registrants are also required to identify and separately describe internal and external sources of liquidity.[25] With respect to capital resources, a registrant is required to describe any known material trends, favorable or unfavorable, in its capital resources, indicating any expected material changes in the mix and relative cost of such resources.[26] In its discussion of capital resources, a registrant is also required to consider changes between equity, debt and any off-balance sheet financing arrangements.[27] However, other than in connection with this discussion of liquidity and capital resources under Item 303(a)(1) and (2) of Regulation S-K, companies that do not provide Guide 3 disclosure are not subject to any line item requirements for the reporting of specific data regarding short-term borrowing amounts or information about intra-period borrowing levels.

Registrants that are bank holding companies provide statistical disclosures in accordance with the industry guidance set forth in Guide 3.[28] Guide 3 is primarily intended to provide supplemental data to facilitate analysis and to allow for comparisons of sources of income and evaluations of exposures to risk.[29] One of the important provisions of Guide 3 is annual disclosure of average, maximum month-end, and period-end amounts of short-term borrowings.[30] Registrants that follow the provisions of Guide 3 provide three years of annual data, broken out into three categories of short-term borrowings, namely: federal funds purchased and securities sold under agreements to repurchase, commercial paper, and other short-term borrowings.[31] We believe that this data is useful to show the types of short-term financings constituting a portion of the bank holding company's liquidity profile, as well as to highlight differences between period-end and intra-period short-term financing activity and the overall liquidity risks it faces during the period. Given the utility of this data in analyzing liquidity and funding risks, we are proposing to require all registrants to provide disclosure in their MD&A similar to the short-term borrowings information called for by Guide 3.[32] Further, since liquidity and funding risks can change rapidly over the course of a year, we are proposing to require the information for both annual and interim periods.

---

[24] See Item 303(a)(1) of Regulation S-K [17 CFR 229.303(a)(1)].

[25] Id.

[26] See Item 303(a)(2)(ii) of Regulation S-K [17 CFR 229.303(a)(2)].

[27] Id.

[28] See 17 CFR 229.801. Bank holding companies typically include this disclosure in the MD&A section of their filings.

[29] See Proposed Revision of Financial Statement Requirements and Industry Guide Disclosures for Bank Holding Companies, Release No. 33-6417 (July 9, 1982) [47 FR 32158] at 32159.

[30] See Item VII of Guide 3.

[31] Id. Item VII of Guide 3 calls for the presentation of information for each category of short-term borrowings that is reported in the financial statements pursuant Article 9 of Regulation S-X. Rule 9-03.13(3) of Regulation S-X [17 CFR 210.9-03.13(3)] requires separate balance sheet disclosure of "amounts payable for (1) federal funds purchased and securities sold under agreements to repurchase, (2) commercial paper, and (3) other short-term borrowings."

[32] As described below in codifying the Guide 3 short-term borrowings provisions in Regulation S-K, we are proposing several changes from the existing provisions of Item VII of Guide 3. The changes include: expanding the categories of short-term borrowings that require disclosure; expanding the applicability to all registrants that are required to provide MD&A disclosure; requiring financial companies to provide disclosure of the daily maximum amount during the period, as well as averages on a daily average basis; requiring a discussion and analysis of short-term borrowings arrangements; and requiring quarterly reporting of short-term borrowings. See "Proposed New Short-Term Borrowings Disclosure in MD&A."

We note that, in 1994, in connection with the elimination of various financial statement disclosure schedules, the Commission eliminated a short-term borrowings disclosure requirement for registrants that were not bank holding companies, which was similar to the existing Guide 3 short-term borrowings disclosure guidance.[33] Former Rule 12-10 of Regulation S-X[34] required those registrants to include with their financial statements a schedule of short-term borrowings that disclosed the maximum amount outstanding during the year, the average amount outstanding during the year, and the weighted-average interest rate during the period, with amounts broken out into specified categories of short-term borrowings.[35]

While former Rule 12-10 of Regulation S-X was similar to the short-term borrowing requirements proposed in this release, we believe there are important differences. In proposing to eliminate the schedule, the Commission noted that "the disclosures concerning the registrant's liquidity and capital resources that are required in MD&A would appear to be sufficiently informational to permit elimination of the short-term borrowing schedule."[36] Although we believe that a thorough discussion of liquidity and capital resources under existing MD&A requirements often would provide qualitative information comparable to that elicited by the proposed requirements, we expect that the proposed requirements would serve as a useful framework for the provision of both quantitative and qualitative information about short-term borrowings that would supplement the registrant's discussion of liquidity and capital resources. We also believe that, in contrast to the presentation required in the financial statement schedule that was eliminated in 1994, the information would be more useful to investors if it is provided in MD&A, in tabular form, coupled with a discussion and analysis to provide context for the quantitative data.

Among the primary reasons cited for the repeal of Rule 12-10 were the practical difficulties involved in gathering the data and preparing meaningful disclosure.[37] We note that some of those practical difficulties may be less relevant today because of technological advancements in accounting systems that have become more widely used by companies since 1994. In addition, the requirements proposed today contain a number of features designed to address some of the practical difficulties cited by prior commentators in connection with former Rule 12-10. More importantly, however, recent events suggest that more detailed information about average short-term borrowings would facilitate a better understanding of whether a registrant's period-end figures are indicative of levels during the period. In light of these changes, we believe the balance of factors may have shifted, such that the utility of the disclosure justifies the burden of preparing it.

2. Proposed New Short-Term Borrowings Disclosure in MD&A

Summary of Proposed Requirements

We are proposing to amend our MD&A requirements to include a new section that would provide tabular information about a company's short-term borrowings, as well as a discussion and analysis of those short-term borrowings. We note that the current Guide 3 disclosure of short-term borrowings does not call for a qualitative discussion of the reasons for use by a registrant of the particular types of financing techniques, or of the drivers of differences between average amounts and period-end amounts outstanding for the period. We believe that including a requirement for a narrative explanation together with tabular data would provide important information so that investors can better

---

[33] *See* Financial Statements of Significant Foreign Equity Investees and Acquired Foreign Businesses of Domestic Issuers and Financial Schedules, Release No. 33-7118 (Dec. 13, 1994) [59 FR 65632].

[34] 17 CFR 210.12-10.

[35] The categories in former Rule 12-10 were amounts payable to: banks for borrowings; factors or other

financial institutions for borrowings; and holders of commercial paper.

[36] *See* Financial Statements of Significant Foreign Equity Investees and Acquired Foreign Businesses of Domestic Issuers and Financial Schedules, Release No. 33-7055 (Apr. 19, 1994) [59 FR 21814], at 21818.

[37] *See* Release No. 33-7118, *supra* note 30, at 65635.

understand the role of short-term financing and its related risks to the registrant as viewed through the eyes of management.

The proposed amendments would codify in Regulation S-K the Guide 3 provisions for disclosure of short-term borrowings applicable to bank holding companies and would apply to all companies that provide MD&A disclosure, not only to bank holding companies and other financial institutions. If the proposals are adopted, we expect to authorize the Commission's staff to eliminate the corresponding provisions of Guide 3 in their entirety to avoid redundant disclosure requirements for bank holding companies. As proposed, registrants would be required to provide disclosure in MD&A of:

- the amount in each specified category of short-term borrowings at the end of the reporting period and the weighted average interest rate on those borrowings;

- the average amount in each specified category of short-term borrowings for the reporting period and the weighted average interest rate on those borrowings;

- for registrants meeting the proposed definition of "financial company," the maximum daily amount of each specified category of short-term borrowings during the reporting period; and

- for all other registrants, the maximum month-end amount of each specified category short-term borrowings during the reporting period.

We believe that the largest amount of short-term borrowings outstanding during the period is an important data point for assessing the intra-period fluctuation of short-term borrowings and, thus, of liquidity risk. Given the critical nature of liquidity and funding matters to a financial company's business activities, we believe it may be important for an investor to know the maximum amount that a financial company has borrowed in any given period as an indication of its short-term financing needs. We are proposing that financial companies be required to disclose the maximum daily amount of short-term borrowings outstanding. Both Guide 3 and former Rule 12-10 called for disclosure of the maximum month-end amounts, which is the standard we are proposing to require for registrants that are not "financial companies." As explained below, we are proposing monthly, rather than daily, maximum amounts for non-financial companies in view of the costs that non-financial companies may encounter in recording daily amounts and the information needs of investors.

Definition of Short-Term Borrowings

Under the proposed rule, "short-term borrowings" would be defined by reference to the various categories of arrangements that comprise the short-term obligations reflected in a registrant's financial statements, and all registrants would be required to present information for each category of short-term borrowings.[38] Specifically, as proposed, "short-term borrowings" would mean amounts payable for short-term obligations that are:

- federal funds purchased and securities sold under agreements to repurchase;

- commercial paper;

- borrowings from banks;

---

[38] Consistent with the approach taken in Guide 3 and in former Rule 12-10 of Regulation S-X, we propose to define "short-term borrowings" by reference to the amounts payable for various categories of short-term obligations that are typically stated separately on the balance sheet in accordance with Regulation S-X. Under U.S. GAAP, short-term obligations are those that are scheduled to mature within one year after the date of an entity's balance sheet or, for those entities that use the operating cycle concept of working capital, within an entity's operating cycle that is longer than one year. *See* FASB ASC 210-10-20. As such, the proposed definition of short-term borrowings is intended to be a subset of short-term obligations under U.S. GAAP.

- borrowings from factors or other financial institutions; and

- any other short-term borrowings reflected on the registrant's balance sheet.[39]

These categories are derived from the categories of short-term borrowings specified in Guide 3 and Rule 9-03 of Regulation S-X,[40] as well as certain categories of current liabilities set forth in Rule 5-02 of Regulation S-X.[41] Registrants that are bank holding companies and other companies that follow Guide 3 prepare their financial statements in accordance with Article 9 of Regulation S-X and present separate line items for categories of short-term borrowings on the face of their balance sheets under Rule 9-03 of Regulation S-X. Registrants that are commercial or industrial companies prepare their financial statements in accordance with Article 5 of Regulation S-X and present separate categories of current liabilities on the face of their balance sheets under Rule 5-02 of Regulation S-X.[42]

Categories and Disaggregation

Rather than creating different disclosure categories for registrants based solely on existing financial reporting rules applicable to certain types of entities, the proposed requirement draws on the categories from both Rule 9-03 and Rule 5-02 so that a registrant must present each of the categories that is relevant to the types of short-term financing activities it conducts, even if that category is not required to be reported as a separate line item on its balance sheet under Regulation S-X.[43] As a result, for example, registrants currently subject to Guide 3 would need to provide disclosure for the same categories as all other registrants. We believe this approach will result in more meaningful disclosure, since it will elicit more specific information regarding the borrowing methods actually used by the registrant. Foreign private issuers that do not prepare financial statements under U.S. GAAP would be permitted to provide disclosure of categories that correspond to the classifications used for such types of short-term borrowings under the comprehensive set of accounting principles that the company uses to prepare its primary financial statements, so long as the disclosure is provided at a level of detail that satisfies the objective of the disclosure requirement.[44]

The proposed requirements do not include a quantitative threshold for purposes of disaggregating amounts into categories of short-term borrowings. For bank holding companies, this would be a change from existing Guide 3 instructions, which allow categories to be aggregated where they do not exceed 30% of the company's stockholders' equity at the end of the period.[45] On the one hand, including such a threshold

---

[39] This last category is derived from the balance sheet line item in Rule 9-03.13(3) of Regulation S-X [17 CFR 210.9-03.13(3)] for "other short-term borrowings." Amounts that a registrant includes on its balance sheet under a line item for "other short-term borrowings" that do not fall into one of the other proposed categories would be disclosed under this category.

[40] 17 CFR 210.9-03.

[41] Rule 5-02.19(a) of Regulation S-X [17 CFR 210.5-02.19(a)] also requires separate disclosure in the balance sheet of amounts payable to trade creditors, related parties, and underwriters, promoters and employees (other than related parties). Consistent with the approach taken in former Rule 12-10 of Regulation S-X and in existing Guide 3 provisions, we are proposing to define short-term borrowings more narrowly than "current liabilities" or "short-term obligations."

[42] Registrants that are insurance companies follow Article 7 of Regulation S-X, which also incorporates certain standards of Article 5. For example, under Rule 7-03.16(b), insurance companies must include disclosure required by Rule 5-02.19(b), if the aggregate

short-term borrowings from banks, factors and other financial institutions and commercial paper issued exceeds five percent of total liabilities. *See* 17 CFR 210.5-02.19(b) and 17 CFR 210.7-03.16(b).

[43] In such circumstances, a registrant should consider whether additional information should be provided to identify the financial statement line items where the period-end short-term borrowings amounts are reported.

[44] *See* proposed Instruction 1 to Item 5.H of Form 20-F. This approach is consistent with the existing Instruction 5 to Item 5 of Form 20-F for issuers that file financial statements that comply with International Financial Reporting Standards ("IFRS") as issued by the International Accounting Standards Board ("IASB"). It is also consistent with the approach taken for tabular disclosure of contractual obligations in Form 20-F for filers that do not use U.S. GAAP.

[45] *See* Instruction to Item VII of Guide 3. If the proposals are adopted, we expect to authorize our staff to eliminate Item VII of Guide 3 in its entirety. In that case, a registrant that provides Guide 3 information

could ease the compliance burden for a company where the distinction among categories of short-term borrowings is not material. On the other hand, including such a quantitative threshold could diminish the comparability of information across companies and, more fundamentally, could defeat the objective of specifically highlighting the types of short-term borrowing arrangements that expose registrants to liquidity risks. Accordingly, the allocation of amounts into the various categories is intended to achieve this purpose so that investors can assess the proportionate exposure to the funding risk and market risk inherent in the borrowing arrangements.

In circumstances where aggregate amounts within a category of short-term borrowings are subject to a wide range of interest rates and exchange rates, we note that disclosure of those aggregate amounts may not be comparable or meaningful. For example, a company with operations outside of the United States may have, for a variety of reasons (such as the need to finance its subsidiaries in local currency or as a hedge against an asset denominated in that currency), foreign currency-denominated borrowings that have a significantly higher interest rate than the rate on its dollar-denominated borrowings. Under those circumstances, combining those dollar-denominated borrowings with the foreign currency-denominated borrowings could distort the presentation of the interest rates for the company, causing the combined weighted average interest rate on the borrowings to be much higher than the company would incur to borrow in U.S. dollars alone. This would be particularly true if the borrowings are denominated in the currency of an economy that has experienced high rates of inflation. To address this issue, the proposal would include a requirement to further disaggregate amounts by currency or interest rate to the extent necessary to promote understanding or to prevent aggregate amounts from being misleading. Additional footnote disclosure describing the method for disaggregation is proposed to be required where necessary to an understanding of the data, stating, for example, the timing and exchange rates used for currency translations and any other pertinent data relating to the calculation of the amounts provided.

Requirements for "Financial Companies" and Other Companies

As noted above, the proposed rule would distinguish between registrants that engage in financial activities as their business and all other registrants for purposes of calculating and reporting maximum amounts outstanding and average amounts outstanding during the reporting period. Registrants that are "financial companies" would be required to compile and report data for the maximum daily amounts outstanding (meaning the largest amount outstanding at the end of any day in the reporting period) and the average amounts outstanding during the reporting period computed on a daily average basis (meaning the amount outstanding at the end of each day, averaged over the reporting period). Registrants that are not "financial companies" would be required to report the maximum month-end amounts outstanding (meaning the largest amount outstanding at the end of the last day of any month in the reporting period) and would be required to disclose the basis used for calculating the average amounts reported. These registrants would not be required to present average outstanding amounts computed on a daily average basis, but, under the proposal, the averaging period used must not exceed a month.

For purposes of the proposed requirement, a "financial company" would mean a registrant that, during the relevant reported period, is engaged to a significant extent[46] in the business of lending, deposit-taking, insurance underwriting or providing investment advice, or is a broker or dealer as defined in Section 3 of the Exchange Act,[47] and includes, without limitation, an entity that is, or is the holding company of, a bank, a

---

(Footnote Continued)

would need to follow the proposed Item 303(a)(6) for its short-term borrowings disclosure in MD&A.

[46] We are not proposing a specific threshold or definition of "significant" for this purpose. As described below, we are proposing an instruction that allows a registrant to present the short-term borrowings attributable to any non-financial operations separately using the reporting rules for non-financial companies.

[47] 15 U.S.C. 78c. *See also* proposed Item 303(a)(6)(iv) of Regulation S-K and Item 5.H.4 of Form 20-F.

savings association, an insurance company, a broker, a dealer, a business development company,[48] an investment adviser, a futures commission merchant, a commodity trading advisor, a commodity pool operator, or a mortgage real estate investment trust.[49] Although this non-exclusive list[50] would be provided in the rule as guidance to registrants, the proposed definition itself is intentionally flexible, so that disclosure of maximum daily amount outstanding and the average amount outstanding during the reporting period computed on a daily average basis would be required to be provided by registrants that are engaged to a significant extent in the business of lending, deposit-taking, insurance underwriting, providing investment advice, or are brokers or dealers or any of the other enumerated types of entities, regardless of their nominal industry affiliation, organizational structure or primary regulator.

Some registrants that are engaged in both financial and non-financial businesses may meet the definition of "financial company," such as manufacturing companies that have a subsidiary that provides financing to its customers to purchase its products. For those registrants, the costs involved in providing averages computed on a daily average basis and maximum daily amounts of short-term borrowings may not be justified by the benefit to investors, where only a portion of their activities are financial in nature. To address this, the proposal would provide an instruction that would permit a company to provide separate short-term borrowings disclosure for its financial and non-financial business operations. A company relying on the instruction would be required to provide averages computed on a daily average basis and maximum daily amounts for the short-term borrowings arrangements of its financial operations, and would be permitted to follow the requirements and instructions applicable to non-financial companies for purposes of the short-term borrowings arrangements of its non-financial operations. The instruction would also require the company to provide an explanatory footnote to the

---

[48] Business development companies are a category of closed-end investment companies that are not registered under the Investment Company Act of 1940, but are subject to certain provisions of that Act. *See* Section 2(a)(48) and Sections 54-65 of the Investment Company Act of 1940 [15 U.S.C. 80a-2(a)(48) and 80a-53-64].

[49] A mortgage real estate investment trust, or mortgage REIT, is a type of real estate investment trust that invests in mortgages and interests in mortgages. Mortgage REITs typically rely on the exemption from registration under the Investment Company Act of 1940 provided by Section 3(c)(5)(C) of that Act. [15 U.S.C. 80a-3(c)(5)(C)].

[50] We note that the Dodd-Frank Wall Street Reform and Consumer Protection Act of 2010 (Pub. L. No. 111-203) ("Dodd-Frank Act") includes defined terms for "financial institution," "financial company," and "non-bank financial company" which are used in various contexts in that legislation. Our proposed definition of "financial company" is informed by the terms used in the legislation, but is not exactly the same. Because each of those terms has a definition specific to the regulatory purpose of the section of the legislation in which it is used, none is perfectly aligned with the disclosure aim of our proposed requirement. Therefore, in keeping with the over-arching principles-based approach to MD&A requirements, we are proposing a definition of "financial company" based on the types of business activities that expose a company to similar liquidity risks that banks face.

The enumerated examples of entities that would be considered "financial companies" for purposes of

the proposed rule are similar to the entities covered by the definition of "financial institution" contained in Sec. 803 of the Dodd-Frank Act, which includes: a depository institution, as defined in Section 3 of the Federal Deposit Insurance Act (12 U.S.C. 1813); a branch or agency of a foreign bank, as defined in Section 1(b) of the International Banking Act of 1978 (12 U.S.C. 3101); an organization operating under Section 25 or 25A of the Federal Reserve Act (12 U.S.C. 601–604a and 611 through 631); a credit union, as defined in Section 101 of the Federal Credit Union Act (12 U.S.C. 1752); a broker or dealer, as defined in Section 3 of the Securities Exchange Act of 1934 (15 U.S.C. 78c); an investment company, as defined in Section 3 of the Investment Company Act of 1940 (15 U.S.C. 80a–3); an insurance company, as defined in Section 2 of the Investment Company Act of 1940 (15 U.S.C. 80a–2); an investment adviser, as defined in Section 202 of the Investment Advisers Act of 1940 (15 U.S.C. 80b–2); a futures commission merchant, commodity trading advisor, or commodity pool operator, as defined in Section 1a of the Commodity Exchange Act (7 U.S.C. 1a); and any company engaged in activities that are financial in nature or incidental to a financial activity, as described in Section 4 of the Bank Holding Company Act of 1956 (12 U.S.C. 1843(k)).

In addition, we expect that registrants that meet the existing definition of "bank holding company" in Rule 102 of Regulation S-X [17 CFR 210.1-02] would be "financial companies" under the proposed definition.

table with information to enable readers to understand how the operations were grouped for purposes of the disclosure.

Although investors could benefit from having all registrants provide data for maximum daily amounts and average amounts computed on a daily average basis, we preliminarily believe that it is appropriate to limit these daily requirements to entities that are engaged in activities that are financial in nature. Because of the nature of their business activities, we believe it may be important for an investor to have information about the daily amounts of borrowings of financial companies, particularly where borrowed funds are invested in assets that contribute to their earnings activities. We believe that most banks would be able to track daily short-term borrowings without unreasonable effort or expense, and some companies that engage in financial businesses may already track this type of information for their own risk management purposes.

We expect that many other non-bank companies that engage in these types of activities do not currently track this information on a daily basis, so this proposed requirement could impose significant costs on these entities. On balance, however, we preliminarily believe that the importance of the information in the financial company setting justifies the increased costs. By contrast, for companies that are not financial companies, we are not proposing to require maximum daily amounts or averages calculated on a daily average basis because we preliminarily believe that the information with respect to those issuers is less important to investors than in the context of financial companies, and that the combination of our existing and proposed requirements should provide sufficient information about their use of short-term borrowings. However, we request comment on this issue below.

Narrative Discussion of Short-Term Borrowings

In order to provide context for the short-term borrowings data, we are also proposing to require a narrative discussion of short-term borrowings arrangements.[51] This narrative discussion is not currently included in Guide 3. The topics proposed to be included would be:

- a general description of the short-term borrowings arrangements included in each category (including any key metrics or other factors that could reduce or impair the registrant's ability to borrow under the arrangements and whether there are any collateral posting arrangements) and the business purpose of those arrangements;[52]

- the importance to the registrant of its short-term borrowings arrangements to its liquidity, capital resources, market-risk support, credit-risk support or other benefits;[53]

- the reasons for the maximum amount for the reporting period, including any non-recurring transactions or events, use of proceeds or other information that provides context for the maximum amount; and

- the reasons for any material differences between average short-term borrowings for the reporting period and period-end short-term borrowings.

This proposed short-term borrowings discussion and analysis is intended to highlight short-term financing activities and to complement the other MD&A requirements relating to liquidity and capital resources, but it is not intended to be repetitive of other disclosures relating to liquidity and capital resources. In preparing the short-term borrowings disclosure, we anticipate that a registrant would need to consider its disclosures of cash requirements presented in the contractual obligations table, its disclosures of off-balance sheet arrangements, as well as its other liquidity and capital resources

---

[51] See proposed Item 303(a)(6)(ii) of Regulation S-K.

[52] A discussion of the business purpose of the arrangements might encompass topics such as the use of proceeds of the borrowings and the reasons for the particular structure of the arrangements.

[53] Similar to the existing requirement in Item 303(a)(4)(i)(B) of Regulation S-K, this proposed requirement is intended to provide investors with an understanding of the importance to the registrant of its short-term borrowings as a financial matter and as they relate to the funding of its operations and to its risk management activities.

disclosures.[54] For example, the company may have significant payments under operating leases or may have entered into a significant repurchase agreement that is accounted for as a sale that will be settled shortly after the balance sheet date and that are disclosed in the contractual obligations table. To be able to settle these amounts, the company may plan to use existing short-term financing arrangements that will limit its ability to borrow for other purposes, such as making loans or financing inventory, which in turn can impact operations. In this example, the company should discuss these items together and explain the implications. A registrant would need to consider ways to integrate the proposed disclosures, together with disclosures made under existing MD&A requirements, into a clear, comprehensive description of its liquidity profile. For example, a registrant could consider organizing its discussion to address overall liquidity, and then short-term and long-term borrowings and liquidity needs.

As discussed above, we believe investors would benefit from an expanded discussion and analysis about a company's use of short-term borrowings. We believe that disclosure of a company's short-term borrowings data, with a comprehensive discussion of its overall approach to short-term financings and the role of short-term borrowings in the company's funding of its operations and business plan, can provide investors with additional information necessary to better evaluate a registrant's current short-term liquidity profile and potential future trends in its liquidity and funding risks.

Request for Comment

1. Is information about short-term borrowings and intra-period variations in the level of short-term borrowings useful to investors? If so, should we require specific line item disclosure of this information in MD&A, as proposed, or would existing MD&A requirements for disclosure of liquidity and capital resources provide sufficient disclosure about these issues? If a specific MD&A requirement would be appropriate, does the proposed requirement capture the type of information about short-term borrowings that is important to investors? If not, how should we change the proposed requirement? For example, should we require disclosure of the weighted average interest rate on the short-term borrowings, as proposed?

2. Consistent with the approach taken in Guide 3 and in former Rule 12-10 of Regulation S-X, we propose to define "short-term borrowings" by reference to the amounts payable for various categories of short-term obligations that are typically reflected as short-term obligations on the balance sheet and stated as separate line items in accordance with Regulation S-X. Is the proposed definition sufficiently clear? If not, what changes should be made to the proposed definition? For example, should the definition refer to "short-term obligations" as defined in U.S. GAAP?[55] In connection with any response, please provide information as to the costs associated with the implementation of any changes to the proposed definition.

3. Are the proposed categories of short-term borrowings appropriate? If not, why not, and how should we change the proposed requirement? For example, should we apply different categories to Guide 3 companies as compared to other companies, as was the case when former Rule 12-10 of Regulation S-X was in effect? Are the proposed categories appropriately tailored so that companies can monitor and provide the proposed disclosure? In particular, is the category for "any other short-term borrowings reflected on the registrant's balance sheet" too broad? If so, how should it be narrowed? Are there other categories of short-term borrowings that should be broken out? For example, should amounts relating to repurchase arrangements be disaggregated into those that are collateralized by

---

[54] *See* Item 303(a)(1) and (a)(2) of Regulation S-K.

[55] *See, e.g.,* FASB ASC 210-10-20 ("Short-term obligations are those that are scheduled to mature within one year after the date of an entity's balance sheet or, for those entities that use the operating cycle concept of working capital described in paragraphs 210-10-45-3 and 210-10-45-7, within an entity's operating cycle that is longer than one year.").

U.S. Treasury securities and those that are collateralized by other assets? If so, please include in your discussion the reasons such information would be meaningful to investors and provide an indication of the costs and burdens associated with providing that level of detail.

4. Is disaggregation by currency or other grouping useful to the understanding of aggregate short-term borrowing amounts? Would the proposed requirement for disaggregation provide an appropriate level of detail? Is it sufficiently clear? Instead, should we prescribe a specified method or threshold for disaggregation? If so, describe it. For example, should we require information to be presented separately by currency where there is a significant amount of borrowings that are not denominated in the company's reporting currency? If so, should we specify a threshold amount (e.g., 5, 15 or 20% of borrowings) and what should that threshold be? Or should the amounts instead be disaggregated into more generalized categories, such as "domestic" and "foreign" borrowings? Please provide details about the costs and benefits of any alternatives to the proposed disaggregation provision, and discuss whether requiring companies to follow a specific disaggregation method would impose practical difficulties on companies (or particular types of companies) when they are gathering and compiling the proposed short-term borrowings disclosure.

5. We note that Guide 3 currently provides a quantitative threshold for separate disclosure of short-term borrowings by category. The proposed short-term borrowings provision does not contain a specific quantitative disclosure threshold for separate disclosure of amounts in the different categories of short-term borrowings. Should we establish a quantitative disclosure threshold for the separate categories of short-term borrowings, such as above a specified percentage of liabilities or stockholders' equity (e.g., 5, 10, 20, 30 or 40%)? If so, how should the threshold be computed? Should this quantitative disclosure threshold apply to all companies?

6. As proposed, "financial companies" would be required to provide the largest daily amount of short-term borrowings. We understand that banks and bank holding companies track this information on a daily basis in connection with the preparation of reports to banking regulators. We also expect that other non-bank companies engaged in financial businesses that would fall within the scope of the proposed requirement do not currently track this type of information on a daily basis. Is this information useful to investors? What are the burdens and costs of requiring registrants that meet the definition of "financial company" but are not banks to meet that requirement?

7. Is the activities-based definition of "financial company" sufficiently clear? Are the activities identified (lending, deposit taking, insurance underwriting, providing investment advice, broker or dealer activities) as part of the definition appropriate, or are they overly-inclusive (or under-inclusive)? Should we provide a definition of the term "significant" as used in the proposed definition? If so, should we provide a numerical, threshold-based definition (e.g., 10% of total assets)? If so, what should the threshold be? Should it relate to assets or should it relate to revenues and income? Should we specify certain types of entities in the definition, as proposed? Should other entities be added to or excluded from the definition? If so, please provide details. Are there any circumstances that would cause an entity to come under the proposed definition that should be excluded, and if so, why?

8. Should all registrants that are financial companies be required to provide the maximum daily amount of short-term borrowings, as proposed? Should registrants that are not financial companies be required to provide the maximum daily amount of short-term borrowings, rather than permitting them to provide the maximum month-end amount as is proposed? Do registrants that are not financial companies have systems to track and calculate this information on a daily basis? What are the burdens and costs of requiring companies engaged in non-financial businesses to meet that requirement? Should registrants that are

not financial companies be required to disclose each month-end amount rather than the maximum, as proposed? Should registrants also be required to provide the minimum month-end (or daily for financial companies) amount outstanding? What are the burdens and costs of requiring companies to meet those requirements?

9. Is the proposed accommodation for reporting that would allow financial companies to present information about their non-financial businesses on the same basis as other non-financial companies appropriate? Would this address cost concerns for these companies? Is the proposed instruction to implement this accommodation sufficiently clear?

10. Should registrants be required to provide the largest amount of short-term borrowings outstanding *at any time* during the reporting period (meaning intra-day as opposed to close of business)? Would this amount be difficult for registrants to track?

11. As proposed, registrants that are financial companies would be required to provide average amounts outstanding computed on a daily average basis. Should averages computed on a daily average basis be required only for certain companies (for example, bank holding companies, banks, savings associations, broker-dealers)? If so, why and which companies? In this connection, please describe whether financial companies that are not banks typically close their books on a daily basis and whether they have the systems to track and calculate this daily balance information used to compute averages on a daily average basis. What are the burdens and costs for a registrant (that is not a bank) to meet the proposed requirement? Are some types of businesses, such as multinationals, disproportionately affected by such costs? If so, please explain why. Is there an alternative requirement for such a business that would still meet the disclosure objective?

12. As proposed, registrants that are not financial companies would be permitted to use a different averaging period, such as weekly or monthly, so long as the period used is not longer than a month. Is it appropriate to allow this type of flexibility given the possibility that longer averaging periods could mask fluctuations? Are certain borrowing practices more likely to be impacted than others, such as overdrafts used as financing? Is there an alternative requirement or instruction that could eliminate this issue while not imposing undue costs and burdens and still meeting the disclosure objective?

13. Should we require a narrative discussion of short-term borrowing arrangements, as proposed? Are the narrative discussion topics useful to investors? Are there other discussion topics that would be useful to investors? If so, what other topics should we require to be discussed? Should we tailor the disclosure to omit information that may be unimportant to investors? If so, what information, and why, and which registrants would be affected?

14. Do the proposed discussion topics provide enough flexibility to companies to fully and clearly describe their short-term borrowings arrangements?

15. If the proposals are adopted, we expect to authorize our staff to amend Guide 3 to eliminate Item VII in its entirety. Are there any other technical amendments that would be appropriate, such as the elimination of cross-references in other Commission rules or forms, if the staff removes Item VII from Guide 3?

3. Reporting Periods

As proposed, the requirements would be applicable to annual and quarterly reports and registration statements. For annual reports, information would be presented for the three most recent fiscal years and for the fourth quarter. In addition, registrants preparing registration statements with audited full-year financial statements would be required to include short-term borrowings disclosure for the three most recent full fiscal year periods and interim information for any subsequent interim periods, consistent in each case with general MD&A requirements and instructions applicable to the relevant registration statement form requirements. For quarterly reports, information would be presented for the relevant quarter, without a requirement for comparative data. For registrants that are not subject to Guide 3, we are proposing a yearly phase-in of the requirements for comparative annual data until all three years are included in the annual presentation. This is described under the heading "Transition" in this release. Notwithstanding this transitional accommodation, all registrants would be permitted to provide three full years during the transition period.

A principal objective of the proposed disclosure is to provide transparency about intra-period borrowings activity, as a supplement to disclosure of period-end amounts. To achieve this purpose in each reporting period, we are proposing that disclosure in quarterly reports and interim period disclosure in registration statements include short-term borrowings information presented with the same level of detail as would be provided for annual periods.[56] Companies would need to include the full presentation of quantitative and qualitative information for short-term borrowings during the interim period, rather than *only* disclosing material changes that have occurred since the previous balance sheet date. In addition, registrants would be required to identify material changes from previously reported disclosures in the discussion and analysis, so that any material changes would be highlighted. This layered approach is intended to enhance transparency of short-term borrowing activities during the specific quarterly period, while still emphasizing material changes so that investors can more easily understand how the exposures have evolved from past reporting periods.

In addition, registrants would be required to provide quarterly short-term borrowings information for the fourth fiscal quarter in their annual report. Because the disclosure is intended to provide additional transparency about a registrant's short-term borrowing practices, including the ability of the registrant to obtain financing to conduct its business, and the costs of that financing, during the year, we believe that short-term borrowings data for the fourth quarter would be useful to investors. As this type of reporting requirement would be a departure from our long-standing approach to the presentation of fourth quarter financial information in MD&A contained in annual reports, we specifically request comment below on this issue, and particularly whether material information as to short-term borrowing activities prior to year-end would be lost without separate quarterly disclosure for the fourth quarter.

As proposed, interim period disclosures would be presented without comparative period data.[57] We believe that this data is most meaningful to show changes from annual borrowing amounts and any intra-period variations from period-end amounts. In addition, because any seasonal trends in the information should generally already be disclosed under existing MD&A requirements, we preliminarily do not believe it is necessary to specifically require prior period comparisons to identify seasonality in borrowing levels. Moreover, other than the presentation of short-term borrowings information for the fourth fiscal quarter, registrants would not be required to include a quarterly breakdown of short-term borrowings information in their annual report. Because quarterly information would be available in Forms 10-Q for all quarters other than the fourth quarter, we do not believe that repeating that quarterly information in the annual report would be useful to investors.

These interim period requirements would not apply to registrants that are foreign private issuers or smaller reporting companies. In addition, smaller reporting companies would be permitted to disclose two fiscal years rather than three, in accordance with

---

[56] We are proposing to revise the "Instructions to Paragraph 303(b)" in Item 303 of Regulation S-K to accomplish this change to interim period reporting requirements. The proposed instructions would only apply to disclosure pursuant to Item 303(a)(6). *See* 17 CFR 229.303(b).

[57] Proposed Instruction 8 to Paragraph 303(b) would require the registrant to include narrative discussion that highlights any material changes from prior periods. In doing so, registrants should consider whether including comparative period data would make the presentation of those material changes more clear.

existing disclosure accommodations for small entities. For a discussion of the treatment of these types of entities, see the discussion under "Treatment of Foreign Private Issuers and Smaller Reporting Companies" in this release.

Request for Comment

16. Are the proposed reporting periods appropriate? Should we require annual short-term borrowings information in annual reports, as proposed? Should annual reports instead include a quarterly breakdown of short-term borrowings information? Should annual reports include quarterly information for the fourth fiscal quarter in addition to annual information, as proposed? For example, would disclosure of information for the fourth fiscal quarter be necessary to highlight any efforts to reduce borrowings at year-end, below the levels prevailing throughout the fourth fiscal quarter? Is the presentation of this information for the fourth fiscal quarter, in isolation without corresponding quarterly financial statements and MD&A for that period, potentially misleading? If so, what additional information should be required? Should quarterly reports be required to include quarterly information, as proposed? Should registration statements be required to include annual and interim information, as proposed? In each case, explain the reasons for requiring the applicable reporting periods and provide information as to whether investors would find the information useful. Please also include details about additional costs involved.

17. Should we require quarterly disclosure at the same level of detail as annual period disclosure, as proposed? Does the proposed presentation provide information that is useful to investors? Describe in detail the costs and benefits of providing full (rather than material changes) interim period disclosures of the proposed short-term borrowings information. Instead, should we require quarterly reports to include disclosure of material changes only? If so, why? How would disclosure of material changes address the issue of transparency of intra-period borrowings?

18. For annual periods, should we require, as proposed, three years of comparative data? Or would data for the current year, without historical comparison periods, provide investors with adequate information? Describe in detail the costs and benefits of providing comparative period disclosures in this context.

19. Is the proposed disclosure for the current interim period sufficient, or should we also require comparative period data? If so, which comparative periods would be most useful? Explain how prior period comparisons would be useful to investors; for example, would prior period comparisons be needed to identify seasonality in borrowing levels? If so, instead of requiring comparative data, should we specifically require companies to qualitatively describe trends or seasonality in borrowing levels? Describe in detail the costs and benefits of providing comparative period disclosures in this context.

20. Should we require year-to-date information in addition to quarterly information for interim periods? Would year-to-date information be useful to investors? Describe in detail the costs and benefits of providing year-to-date information in this context.

4. Application of Safe Harbors for Forward-Looking Statements

In some instances, the disclosure provided in response to the proposed short-term borrowings narrative discussion requirements could include disclosure of forward-looking information.[58] We are not, however, proposing to extend the safe harbor in Item 303(c) of Regulation S-K to include disclosures of forward-looking information made pursuant to proposed Item 303(a)(6). This safe harbor was adopted in connection with

---

[58] *See generally* proposed Item 303(a)(6)(ii)(B), (C) and (D) of Regulation S-K.

the adoption of Items 303(a)(4) and (a)(5) and explicitly applies the statutory safe harbors of Sections 27A[59] of the Securities Act and 21E[60] of the Exchange Act to those Items in order to remove possible ambiguity about whether the statutory safe harbors would be available for that information.[61] The disclosure required by Items 303(a)(4) and (a)(5) consists primarily of forward-looking information, and as such, issuers and market participants expressed particular concerns about the application of existing safe harbors to that disclosure.[62] In the proposing release for Item 303(c), we requested comment as to whether the safe harbor in Item 303(c) should be expanded to cover all forward-looking information in MD&A.[63] We declined to adopt such an expansion. We preliminarily believe that the proposed short-term borrowings disclosure requirements, which primarily concern disclosure of historical amounts together with qualitative information about the registrant's use of short-term borrowings, would not present any distinctive issues under the application of the statutory safe harbor, and, accordingly, we are not proposing to provide any specific provision or guidance as to its application to this information. Companies would need to treat forward-looking information disclosed pursuant to proposed Item 303(a)(6) in the same manner as other MD&A disclosure for purposes of the statutory safe harbor. We further note that nothing in the proposed requirements would limit (or expand) the scope of the statutory safe harbor, the safe harbor rules under Securities Act Rule 175 or Exchange Act Rule 3b-6, or Item 303(c) of Regulation S-K.

Request for Comment:

21. Is there any need for further guidance from the Commission with respect to the application of either the statutory or the rule-based safe harbors to the information called for by the proposed short-term borrowings disclosure requirement? If so, please provide details as to the potential ambiguity in the application of existing safe harbors. In particular, what information called for by the proposed requirements raises doubt as to the applicability of the statutory safe harbor or the safe harbor rules under Securities Act Rule 175 or Exchange Act Rule 3b-6?

22. Should Item 303(c) of Regulation S-K be revised to also cover forward-looking information disclosed pursuant to the proposed short-term borrowings disclosure requirement?

B. Treatment of Foreign Private Issuers and Smaller Reporting Companies

1. Foreign Private Issuers (other than MJDS filers)

The proposed amendments would apply to foreign private issuers that are not MJDS filers.[64] The existing MD&A-equivalent disclosure requirements in

---

[59] 15 U.S.C. 77z-2.

[60] 15 U.S.C. 78u-5.

[61] *See* OBS Adopting Release, *supra* note 6, at 5993.

[62] *See, e.g.*, Letter of Committee on Federal Regulation of Securities of the American Bar Association's Section of Business Law in Response to the OBS Proposing Release, *available at* http://www.sec.gov/rules/proposed/s74202.shtml ("[B]ecause of the inherent predictive nature of disclosures of contingent liabilities and commitments . . . . [W]e are concerned that the failure to include that provision would lead to a negative inference that such disclosure is not covered by the safe harbor.").

In the OBS Adopting Release, the Commission emphasized that notwithstanding the safe harbor provided in Item 303(c) of Regulation S-K, the statutory safe harbor, by its terms, as well as the safe harbor rules under Securities Act Rule 175 [17 CFR 230.175] and

Exchange Act Rule 3b-6 [17 CFR 240.3b-6] may be available for the forward-looking disclosure required by Items 303(a)(4) and (5) of Regulation S-K.

[63] *See* OBS Proposing Release, *supra* note 6, at 68065-68066.

[64] The term "MJDS filers" refers to registrants that file reports and registration statements with the Commission in accordance with the requirements of the U.S.-Canadian Multijurisdictional Disclosure System (the "MJDS"). The definition for "foreign private issuer" is contained in Exchange Act Rule 3b-4(c) [17 CFR 240.3b-4(c)]. A foreign private issuer is any foreign issuer other than a foreign government, except for an issuer that has more than 50% of its outstanding voting securities held of record by U.S. residents and any of the following: a majority of its officers and directors are citizens or residents of the United States, more than 50% of its assets are located in the United

Form 20-F[65] currently mirror the substantive MD&A requirements for U.S. companies, and we believe that our proposed changes to the MD&A requirements for U.S. companies would provide important disclosure to investors that should also be provided by foreign private issuers. Accordingly, we are proposing a new paragraph H under Item 5 (Operational and Financial Review and Prospects) in Form 20-F covering short-term borrowings.

Because foreign private issuers using a comprehensive set of accounting principles other than U.S. GAAP might capture data and prepare their financial statements using different categories of short-term borrowings, we propose to include an instruction to paragraph H that would permit a foreign private issuer to base the categories of short-term borrowings used in the rule on the classifications for such types of short-term borrowings under the comprehensive set of accounting principles which the company uses to prepare its primary financial statements, so long as the disclosure is provided in a level of detail that satisfies the objective of the Item 5.H disclosure requirement.[66] This approach is consistent with the approach to contractual obligations disclosure in Item 5.F, for which foreign private issuers are instructed to base their tabular disclosure on the classifications of obligations used in the generally accepted accounting principles under which the company prepares its primary financial statements.[67] Similarly, in connection with references to FASB pronouncements used in Item 5 of Form 20-F, issuers that file financial statements that comply with IFRS as issued by the IASB are instructed to "provide disclosure that satisfies the objective of Item 5 disclosure requirements."[68] Other than this instruction regarding the categorization of short-term borrowings, the short-term borrowings disclosure requirement proposed for Form 20-F is substantially similar to the proposed provision applicable to U.S. issuers.

The reporting periods applicable to U.S. issuers are proposed to also apply to foreign private issuers, except with respect to quarterly reporting. For annual reports on Form 20-F, foreign private issuers would present three years of annual short-term borrowings data, subject to the proposed transition accommodation applicable to all registrants that are not bank holding companies. Foreign private issuers preparing registration statements with audited full-year financial statements would be required to include short-term borrowings disclosure for the three most recent full fiscal year periods and quarterly information for any subsequent interim periods included in the registration statement in accordance with the requirements of the relevant registration statement form. The proposed amendments for U.S. issuers would require quarterly disclosure of short-term borrowings in quarterly reports on Form 10-Q.[69] Foreign private issuers,however, are not required to file quarterly reports with the Commission, and therefore the proposed

---

(Footnote Continued)

States, or its business is principally administered in the United States.

[65] Form 20-F is the combined registration statement and annual report form for foreign private issuers under the Exchange Act.

It also sets forth disclosure requirements for registration statements filed by foreign private issuers under the Securities Act. In designing the integrated disclosure regime for foreign private issuers the Commission endeavored to "design a system that parallels the system for domestic issuers but also takes into account the different circumstances of foreign registrants." Integrated Disclosure System for Foreign Private Issuers, Release No. 33-6360 (Nov. 20, 1981) [46 FR 58511]. As such, the requirements of Item 5 of Form 20-F are analogous to those in Item 303 of Regulation S-K. Although the wording is not identical, we interpret Item 5 as requiring the same disclosure as Item 303 of Regulation S-K. *See* Rules, Registration and Annual Report for Foreign Private Issuers, Release

No. 34-16371 (Nov. 29, 1979) [44 FR 70132] (adopting Form 20-F and stating that the Commission would consider revisions when MD&A requirements in Regulation S-K were adopted); Integrated Disclosure System for Foreign Private Issuers, Release No. 33-6360 (revising Form 20-F to add requirements consistent with the MD&A requirements in Regulation S-K); International Disclosure Standards, Release No. 33-7745 (Sept. 28, 1999)[64 FR 53900] (adopting revisions to Form 20-F to conform to international disclosure standards endorsed by the International Organization of Securities Commissions in 1998); *see also* OBS Adopting Release, *supra* note 6, at 5992 n. 135.

[66] *See* proposed Instruction 1 to Item 5.H of Form 20-F.

[67] *See* Instruction 2 to Item 5.F of Form 20-F.

[68] *See* Instruction 5 to Item 5 of Form 20-F.

[69] 17 CFR 249.308a. *See* proposed Instruction 8 to Item 303(b) of Regulation S-K [17 CFR 229.303(b)].

amendments would not apply to Form 6-K[70] reports submitted by foreign private issuers.[71] Thus, unless a foreign private issuer (other than an MJDS filer) files a Securities Act registration statement that must include interim period financial statements and related MD&A-equivalent disclosure,[72] it would not be required to update its disclosure under proposed Item 5.H of Form 20-F more than annually.

Request for Comment

23. Should we apply the proposed amendments to foreign private issuers' annual reports on Form 20-F, as proposed? Or should we exclude these annual reports from the scope of the amendments? If so, why?

24. Should we apply the proposed amendments to foreign private issuers' registration statements, as proposed? Or should these registration statements be excluded from the scope of the proposed rules? In particular, should we not require the interim period short-term borrowings information to be included in the registration statements of foreign private issuers? If not, why?

25. Should we limit the application of the new disclosure requirements to foreign private issuers that are banks or bank holding companies, or that are financial companies? If so, why?

26. Is the instruction to proposed Item 5.H regarding the categories of short-term borrowings appropriate? Is the instruction clear? If not, how can it be clarified?

2. MJDS Filers

The proposed amendments would not affect MJDS filers. The disclosure provided by Canadian issuers is generally that which is required under Canadian law, and we do not propose to depart from our approach with respect to financial disclosure provided by MJDS filers. Accordingly, we are not proposing to further amend Form 40-F at this time.

Request for Comment

27. Should we amend Form 40-F to include the new short-term borrowings disclosure requirements? If so, why?

3. Smaller Reporting Companies

Smaller reporting companies currently provide disclosure pursuant to Item 303, subject to the special accommodation provided in Item 303(d) that, among other things, permits the exclusion of tabular disclosure of contractual obligations under Item 303(a)(5). The proposed short-term borrowings disclosure requirements would apply to smaller reporting companies, except that quarterly disclosures would not be required unless material changes have occurred during that interim period (as is the case under existing requirements for interim period disclosure) and information for the fourth fiscal quarter would not be required in annual reports. To this end, we propose to amend Item 303(d) to clarify that smaller reporting companies need only provide the proposed Item 303(a)(6) information on an annual basis and, in interim periods, if any material changes have

---

[70] 17 CFR 249.306. A foreign private issuer must furnish under cover of Form 6-K material information that it: makes public or is required to make public under its home country laws, files or is required to file with a stock exchange on which its securities are traded and which was made public by that exchange under the rules of the stock exchange or distributes or is required to distribute to security holders. In instances where a foreign private issuer is furnishing interim information on short-term borrowings under those circumstances, we would encourage the foreign private issuer to consider providing an update to its annual short-term

borrowings disclosure, although it would not be required to do so.

[71] This treatment is consistent with the approach we took when adopting off-balance sheet arrangements and contractual obligations disclosure. *See* OBS Adopting Release, *supra* note 6, at 5992 n. 139.

[72] The proposed amendments would apply to Securities Act registration statements on Forms F-1 [17 CFR 239.31], F-3 [17 CFR 239.33] and F-4 [17 CFR 239.34]. Each of these registration statements references the disclosure requirements in Form 20-F.

occurred.[73] In addition, for smaller reporting companies providing financial information on net sales and revenues and on income from continuing operations for only two years, only two years of short-term borrowings information would be required, consistent with the scaled MD&A disclosure requirement for smaller reporting companies under existing Item 303(d).

This accommodation for interim period disclosure is intended to balance the practical impact of the disclosure requirement with the need to enhance disclosure of liquidity risks facing smaller reporting companies. While liquidity risks, particularly those arising from short-term borrowings, are equally important for smaller reporting companies, we also believe that smaller reporting companies are likely to have fewer complex financing alternatives available. Accordingly, we believe that smaller reporting companies would not likely have as many significant changes to the liquidity profile presented in periodic reports as other reporting companies. Thus, we do not believe that the burden of preparing expanded interim period reporting is justified by the incremental information that would be provided compared to that provided under the existing interim updating model applicable to smaller reporting companies.

Request for Comment

28. Does the proposal strike the proper balance between imposing proportional costs and burdens on smaller reporting companies while providing adequate information to investors? Would the proposed new short-term borrowings disclosure be useful to investors in smaller reporting companies? Are there any features of the proposed requirements that would impose unique difficulties or significant costs for smaller reporting companies? If so, how should we change the requirements to reduce those difficulties or costs while still achieving the disclosure objective?

29. Should we provide the proposed exemption for interim period updating to smaller reporting companies? If not, please discuss whether the expanded level of interim period disclosure by smaller reporting companies would be useful to investors and why.

30. Would the gathering of data and preparation of expanded interim period disclosure be burdensome to smaller reporting companies? Could the proposed requirement be structured a different way for smaller reporting entities so as to enable interim period reporting without imposing a significant cost? If so, please provide details of such an alternative.

31. Are the nature of the short-term borrowings and the related risks different for smaller reporting companies such that additional or alternate disclosure would be appropriate? In particular, would the proposed annual requirement for disclosing short-term borrowings information cause a smaller reporting company to collect the same data it would need to collect for interim reporting, such that the expanded level of interim period disclosure proposed for registrants that are not smaller reporting companies would not be unduly burdensome?

C. Leverage Ratio Disclosure Issues

Many observers believe that high leverage at financial institutions, in the U.S. and globally, was a contributing factor to the financial crisis.[74] As a result, investors and

---

[73] Proposed "Instruction 8 to Paragraph 303(b)" would exclude smaller reporting companies from the requirement to provide all the information specified in paragraph (a)(6) in interim periods. As proposed, Item 303(d) would state that smaller reporting companies are only required to provide material changes to the information specified in proposed Item 303(a)(6) in interim periods. The proposed revisions to Item 303(d) would not affect the existing accommodation for disclosure of Item 303(a)(5) information.

[74] See, e.g., Financial Stability Board, *Report of the Financial Stability Forum on Addressing Pro-cyclicality in the Financial System* (2009) *available at* http://www.financialstabilityboard.org/publications/r_0904a.pdf; S. Deng, *SIVs, Bank Leverage and Subprime Mortgage Crisis,* (Dec. 2009), *available at* http://ssrn.com/abstract=1319431.

market participants are increasingly focused on leverage ratio disclosures, particularly for banks and for non-bank financial institutions.[75] Similarly, we believe that investors may benefit from additional transparency about the capitalization and leverage profile of non-financial companies, particularly for those companies that rely heavily on external financing and credit markets to fund their businesses and future growth.

Under U.S. GAAP, bank holding companies are currently required to disclose certain capital and leverage ratios (calculated in accordance with the requirements of their primary banking regulator) in the financial statements that are included in filings with the Commission.[76] The Commission's staff has observed that some bank holding companies also include disclosure of these ratios in their MD&A presented in annual and quarterly reports. The financial statement disclosure by bank holding companies of their capital and leverage ratios provides to investors some of the same information that banking regulators use to assess a bank's capital adequacy and leverage levels.[77] For U.S. banks and thrifts, the standards applied by the various banking agencies are substantially uniform,[78] which means that the ratios that bank holding companies are required to include in their financial statements filed with the Commission should be calculated using consistent methodology. Consistent with existing disclosure rules, where disclosed ratios are likely to be materially impacted by known events such as short-term borrowings, contractual obligations or off-balance sheet arrangements, or are not otherwise indicative of the registrant's leverage profile, additional disclosure would be required in order to provide an understanding of the registrant's financial condition and prospects.[79]

We are considering whether to extend a leverage ratio disclosure requirement to companies that are not bank holding companies. We understand that, outside the banking industry, a variety of metrics are used to evaluate a company's debt levels and capital adequacy. There does not appear to be a "one-size-fits all" leverage ratio that is used by companies or investors. For example, we understand that financial analysts, credit analysts and other sophisticated users of financial statements tend to apply their own models and calculate their own ratios for use in their analyses of a registrant's financial health, using their own proprietary calculation methods.[80] We also understand that there is not a consensus on how to measure and treat "off-balance sheet" leverage for purposes of calculating leverage or capital ratios. We are requesting comment today as to the scope of a potential disclosure requirement, and importantly, how such a requirement would take into account the differences among metrics and industries while still providing comparability.

---

[75] See, e.g., K. D'Hulster, The Leverage Ratio, WORLD BANK PUB. POL'Y J. (2009); J. Gabilondo, Financial Moral Panic! Sarbanes-Oxley, Financier Folk Devils, and Off-Balance Sheet Arrangements, 36 SETON HALL L. REV. 781 (2006) (proposing that a financial transparency ratio would reduce the public information gap arising from off-balance sheet arrangements); P. M. Hildebrand, Vice-Chairman of the Governing Board of the Swiss National Bank, Is Basel II Enough? The Benefits of a Leverage Ratio, London School of Economics Financial Markets Group Lecture, Dec. 15, 2008, available at http://www.bis.org/review/r081216d.pdf; Standard & Poor's, The Basel III Leverage Ratio is a Raw Measure but Could Supplement Risk Based Capital Measures, April 15, 2010, available at http://www.bis.org/publ/bcbs165/splr.pdf.

[76] See FASB ASC 942-505-50, Regulatory Capital Disclosures. Specifically, bank holding companies must present their required and actual ratios and

amounts of Tier 1 leverage, Tier 1 risk based capital, and total risk based capital, (for savings institutions) tangible capital, and (for certain banks and bank holding companies) Tier 3 capital for market risk. Under U.S. GAAP, bank holding companies are required to include this information in the footnotes to their financial statements.

[77] See Regulation Y, Appendices A (Risk-Based Capital), B (Leverage Measure) and D (Tier I Leverage Measure) [12 CFR 225].

[78] See The Federal Reserve Board et al., Joint Report: Differences in Capital and Accounting Standards among the Federal Banking and Thrift Agencies (Feb. 5, 2003) [68 FR 5976].

[79] See, e.g., Item 303(a)(1) of Regulation S-K, and Instructions 1, 2 and 3 to Paragraph 303(a).

[80] See, e.g., P. Kraft, Rating Agency Adjustment to GAAP Financial Statements and Their Effect on Ratings and Bond Yields (Nov. 1, 2009) at http://ssrn.com/abstract=1266381.

Request for Comment

32. Should all types of registrants be required to provide leverage ratio disclosure and discussion? Are there differences among industries or types of businesses that would need to be addressed in such a requirement so that it is meaningful to investors? If so, how should "leverage ratio" be defined in this context? Is comparability across companies and industries important, or is the disclosure more meaningful if it is presented in the context of the particular registrant's business?

33. Rather than extending the leverage ratio disclosure requirement to include all registrants, should we extend it only to other financial institutions or financial services companies? If so, how should the scope of included companies be defined? Would the proposed definition of "financial company" used in proposed Item 303(a)(6) work for this purpose? How should "leverage ratio" be defined in this context? Is there a different metric that would be more useful to investors? Should the ratio include "off-balance sheet" leverage or off-balance sheet equity adjustments? If so, describe how such a ratio would be calculated. What are the costs and benefits of defining a leverage ratio that would be applicable to all registrants? Where relevant, discuss the usefulness of a standardized ratio requirement given that many users of financial statements make their own calculations.

34. Should bank holding companies be required to include the same level of disclosure of leverage and capital ratios for quarterly financial statements as they do for annual financial statements, rather than quarterly reporting of material changes? Should additional disclosures be required to accompany existing ratio disclosure that would make it more meaningful?

D. Technical Amendments Reflecting FASB Codification

On June 30, 2009, the FASB issued FASB Statement of Financial Accounting Standards No. 168, The *FASB Accounting Standards Codification and the Hierarchy of Generally Accepted Accounting Principles—a replacement of FASB Statement No. 162*, to establish the FASB Codification as the source of authoritative non-Commission accounting principles recognized by the FASB to be applied by nongovernmental entities in the preparation of financial statements in conformity with U.S. GAAP. In August 2009, we issued guidance regarding the interpretation of references in the Commission's rules and staff guidance to specific standards under U.S. GAAP in light of the FASB Codification.[81] As noted in that interpretive release, the Commission and its staff intend to embark on a longer term rulemaking and updating initiative to revise comprehensively specific references to specific standards under U.S. GAAP in the Commission's rules and staff guidance. Although we plan to make those comprehensive changes at a later date, we believe it is appropriate, at the same time that we propose to make other amendments to Item 303 of Regulation S-K and Item 5 of Form 20-F, to propose technical amendments to these provisions to reflect the FASB Codification. These proposed technical amendments include:

- updating the U.S. GAAP references in the definition of "off-balance sheet arrangement" in Item 303(a)(4)(ii) of Regulation S-K and Item 5.E.2 of Form 20-F;

---

[81] *See* Commission Guidance Regarding the Financial Accounting Standards Board's Accounting Standards Codification, Release No. 33-9062A (Aug. 19, 2009)[74 FR 42772] (stating that, concurrent with the effective date of the FASB Codification, references in the Commission's rules and staff guidance to specific standards under U.S. GAAP should be understood to mean the corresponding reference in the FASB Codification).

- updating U.S. GAAP references in the existing definitions of "Long-Term Debt Obligation," "Capital Lease Obligation" and "Operating Lease Obligation" in Item 303(a)(5)(ii) of Regulation S-K;[82] and

- updating U.S. GAAP references in instructions 8 and 9 of the Instructions to Paragraph 303(a) of Regulation S-K.

As part of our continuing initiative to update the references in the Commission's rules and staff guidance, we believe that these proposed technical amendments would assist registrants in applying the relevant definitions and instructions, without needing to spend time and resources to identify the corresponding FASB provision as contemplated by the interpretive guidance.

Request for Comment

35. Are there any additional revisions to the provisions of Regulation S-K or Form 20-F affected by the proposal that would be necessary or appropriate to reflect the release by the FASB of its FASB codification?

E. Conforming Amendments to Definition of "Direct Financial Obligation" in Form 8-K

We are proposing revisions to the definition of "direct financial obligation" used in Items 2.03 and 2.04 of Form 8-K to conform to the definition of short-term borrowings used in proposed Item 303(a)(6). Specifically, the proposed amendment would revise paragraph (4) of the definition of "direct financial obligation" contained in Item 2.03(c) of Form 8-K.[83]

The current definition of "direct financial obligation" was adopted as part of the 2004 adoption of Items 2.03 and 2.04 of Form 8-K, in connection with updates to Form 8-K to require real-time disclosure of material information regarding changes in a company's financial condition or operations as mandated by Section 409 of the Sarbanes-Oxley Act of 2002.[84] Items 2.03 and 2.04 of Form 8-K are intended to provide real-time disclosure when a company becomes obligated under a direct financial obligation or off-balance sheet arrangement that is material to the company, and upon the triggering of an increase or acceleration of any of those types of transactions where the impact would be material to the company. This real-time disclosure was intended to supplement and align with the requirements for annual and quarterly disclosure of off-balance sheet arrangements and contractual obligations under Items 303(a)(4) and (a)(5) of Regulation S-K. Acknowledging the importance of short-term financing disclosure to an understanding of a company's financial condition and risk profile, we included certain short-term debt obligations in the definition of "direct financial obligations," along with the long-term debt, leases and purchase obligations identified by reference to Item 303(a)(5) of Regulation S-K.

---

[82] The instructions to Item 5.F (Tabular Disclosure of Contractual Obligations) of Form 20-F direct registrants to provide disclosure of contractual obligations (other than purchase obligations, for which a definition is provided) based on the classifications used in the generally accepted accounting principles under which the registrant prepares its primary financial statements. Accordingly, no update for FASB codification is necessary for Item 5.F of Form 20-F.

[83] Item 2.03(c) defines a "direct financial obligation" as any of the following: (1) a long-term debt obligation, as defined in Item 303(a)(5)(ii)(A) of Regulation S-K [17 CFR 229.303(a)(5)(ii)(A)]; (2) a capital lease obligation, as defined in Item 303(a)(5)(ii)(B) of

Regulation S-K [17 CFR 229.303(a)(5)(ii)(B)];(3) an operating lease obligation, as defined in Item 303(a)(5)(ii)(C) of Regulation S-K [17 CFR 229. 303(a)(5)(ii)(C)]; or (4) a short-term debt obligation that arises other than in the ordinary course of business. The item defines "short-term debt obligation" as a payment obligation under a borrowing arrangement that is scheduled to mature within one year, or, for those companies that use the operating cycle concept of working capital, within a company's operating cycle that is longer than one year.

[84] Pub. L. No. 107-204, 116 Stat. 745 (2002). *See* Additional Form 8-K Disclosure Requirements and Acceleration of Filing Date, Release No. 33-8400 (Mar. 16, 2004) [69 FR 15594].

We believe it is appropriate to align the existing reporting requirements for short-term debt obligations under Items 2.03 and 2.04 of Form 8-K with the new proposed definition of short-term borrowings in Item 303(a)(6), in order to continue to provide consistency of disclosure. Accordingly, we are proposing to amend clause (4) of the definition of direct financial obligation to refer to "a short-term borrowing, as defined in Item 303(a)(6)(iii) of Regulation S-K (17 CFR 229.303(a)(6)(iii) that arises other than in the ordinary course of business."[85] In doing so, however, we propose to retain the existing carve-out in the definition of direct financial obligation for obligations that arise in the ordinary course of business, in order to maintain the focus of Items 2.03 and 2.04 on real-time disclosure of individual transactions that are not routine or "ordinary course" financing transactions. If we were to eliminate the ordinary course of business carve-out in the definition, we do not believe that the level of material information provided would justify the burden on registrants to prepare, and the burden on investors to review and understand, potentially voluminous disclosure about routine transactions. In addition, we believe that the proposed short-term borrowings disclosures in MD&A would provide investors with timely information about fluctuations in short-term borrowings levels and about short-term borrowings practices, such that current reporting on Form 8-K of particular instances of significant fluctuations that arise due to ordinary course transactions would not necessarily provide additional insight to investors. Moreover, a registrant that experiences a material increase in short-term borrowings during a reporting period that is not consistent with past practices would likely need to consider carefully whether the underlying transactions causing the fluctuations fall within the meaning of "ordinary course of business" for purposes of Items 2.03 and 2.04.

Request for Comment

36. Instead of amending the definition of "direct financial obligation" to refer to proposed Item 303(a)(6), should the category of short-term financings included in the definition of "direct financial obligation" for purposes of Items 2.03 and 2.04 of Form 8-K differ from the standard used in proposed Item 303(a)(6)? Describe how the standards should differ and explain why. For example, should we retain the existing reference to "short-term debt obligation" instead?

37. Is the proposed definition of short-term borrowings sufficiently tailored so as to exclude borrowing obligations that arise in the ordinary course of business, so that the carve-out in the definition of direct financial obligation is unnecessary? Should the carve-out for obligations that arise in the ordinary course of business be retained, as proposed? Describe the costs and burdens for companies if the carve-out were eliminated, particularly the burden on management to make an assessment of materiality of each short-term borrowing transaction within the filing timeframe. Is current reporting of routine short-term borrowing transactions that are material to the registrant sufficient? Would the new reporting requirements regarding short-term borrowing practices and average borrowings sufficiently improve reporting on this topic, so that Form 8-K reporting of ordinary course short-term borrowings would be unnecessary? Explain why or why not.

F. Transition

In connection with the proposed short-term borrowings disclosure, we are proposing a transition accommodation for registrants that are not bank holding companies or subject to Guide 3 that would, for purposes of the annual reporting requirement, permit those companies to phase in compliance with the comparable annual period disclosure under proposed Item 303(a)(6). In the initial year of the transition period, these companies would be required to include short-term borrowings information for the most recent fiscal year and permitted to omit information for the two preceding fiscal years. In the

---

[85] *See* proposed revisions to Item 2.03(c)(4) of Form 8-K.

second year of the transition period, these companies would be required to include the two most recent fiscal years, and permitted to omit the third preceding fiscal year. In the third year of the transition period, and thereafter, these companies would be required to include disclosure for the each of the three most recent fiscal years as prescribed in proposed Item 303(a)(6)(v). This transition accommodation would not apply to bank holding companies or other companies subject to Guide 3, since those companies already provide this disclosure for the three most recent fiscal years (or two fiscal years for certain smaller bank holding companies).[86]

Request for Comment

38. Is the proposed transition accommodation appropriate? Should we require all companies to present all required periods at the outset?

39. Would the proposed transition accommodation be useful for registrants? Is it sufficiently clear? Should we extend it to cover bank holding companies? If so, why?

40. Are any other transition accommodations necessary for any aspects of the proposed requirements? Would any of the proposed requirements present any particular difficulty or expense that should be addressed by a transition accommodation? If so, please explain what would be needed and why. For example, should we provide a transition period to allow smaller reporting companies and/or non-bank companies time to set up systems to gather the data for the proposed disclosure? If so, what should that period be?

III. GENERAL REQUEST FOR COMMENT

We request and encourage any interested person to submit comments on any aspect of our proposals, other matters that might have an impact on the amendments, and any suggestions for additional changes. With respect to any comments, we note that they are of greatest assistance to our rulemaking initiative if accompanied by supporting data and analysis of the issues addressed in those comments and by alternatives to our proposals where appropriate.

IV. PAPERWORK REDUCTION ACT

A. Background

Certain provisions of the proposed amendments contain "collection of information" requirements within the meaning of the Paperwork Reduction Act of 1995 (PRA).[87] We are submitting the proposed amendments to the Office of Management and Budget (OMB) for review in accordance with the PRA.[88] The titles for the collection of information are:

(A) "Regulation S-K" (OMB Control No. 3235-0071);[89]

(B) "Form 10-K" (OMB Control No. 3235-0063);

(C) "Form 10-Q" (OMB Control No. 3235-0070);

(D) "Form 8-K" (OMB Control No. 3235-0060);

(E) "Form 20-F" (OMB Control No. 3235-0288);

(F) "Form 10" (OMB Control No. 3235-0064);

(G) "Form S-1" (OMB Control No. 3235-0065);

---

[86] *See* General Instruction 3 of Guide 3.
[87] 44 U.S.C. 3501 *et seq.*
[88] 44 U.S.C. 3507(d) and 5 CFR 1320.11.
[89] The paperwork burden from Regulation S-K and the Industry Guides is imposed through the forms that are subject to the disclosures in Regulation S-K and the

Industry Guides and is reflected in the analysis of those forms. To avoid a Paperwork Reduction Act inventory reflecting duplicative burdens, for administrative convenience, we estimate the burdens imposed by each of Regulation S-K and the Industry Guides to be a total of one hour.

(H) "Form F-1" (OMB Control No. 3235-0258);

(I) " Form S-4" (OMB Control No. 3235-0324);

(J) "Form F-4" (OMB Control No. 3235-0325);

(K) "Proxy Statements—Regulation 14A (Commission Rules 14a-1 through 14a-15) and Schedule 14A" (OMB Control No. 3235-0059);

(L) "Information Statements—Regulation 14C (Commission Rules 14c-1 through 14c-7) and Schedule 14C" (OMB Control No. 3235-0057); and

(M) "Form N-2" (OMB Control No. 3235-0026).

These regulations, schedules and forms were adopted under the Securities Act and the Exchange Act, and in the case of Form N-2, the Investment Company Act of 1940.[90] They set forth the disclosure requirements for periodic and current reports, registration statements, and proxy and information statements filed by companies to help investors make informed investment and voting decisions. The hours and costs associated with preparing, filing and sending each form or schedule constitute reporting and cost burdens imposed by each collection of information. An agency may not conduct or sponsor, and a person is not required to respond to, a collection of information unless it displays a currently valid OMB control number.

We anticipate that the proposed amendments to Item 303 of Regulation S-K and to Item 5 of Form 20-F would increase existing disclosure burdens for annual reports on Form 10-K and Form 20-F, quarterly reports on Form 10-Q, current reports on Form 8-K, proxy and information statements, and registration statements on Forms 10, S-1, F-1, S-4, F-4 and N-2 by requiring new disclosure and discussion of short-term borrowings to be provided on an annual and interim basis.

At the same time, the proposed technical amendments to Item 303 of Regulation S-K and Item 5.E of Form 20-F that update references to U.S. GAAP to reflect the FASB Codification would not increase existing disclosure burdens for annual reports on Form 10-K and Form 20-F, quarterly reports on Form 10-Q, current reports on Form 8-K, proxy and information statements, and registration statements on Forms 10, S-1, F-1, S-4, F-4 and N-2.

We also estimate that the amendments to the definition of "direct financial obligation" for purposes of disclosure requirements in Items 2.03 and 2.04 of Form 8-K would not increase existing disclosure burdens for filings of Form 8-K. Although we propose to amend the existing definition to conform to the terminology used in the proposed MD&A requirements, we propose to retain the existing carve-out for ordinary course obligations. Thus, we assume that the proposed change in the definition would not substantially change the existing scope of the disclosure requirement, and, therefore, the proposed amendments would not increase the number of Form 8-K filings nor add incremental costs and burdens to the existing disclosure burden under Form 8-K. We solicit comment on whether our assumption is correct, and if not, how to estimate the additional number of Forms 8-K that would be filed pursuant to the proposed amendments to the definition of "direct financial obligation." We note that, based on the number of filings made under Items 2.03 and 2.04 of Form 8-K in 2009, only approximately 4% of all Form 8-K filings would be made in connection with those Items.

Compliance with the proposed amendments would be mandatory. Responses to the information collections would not be kept confidential, and there would be no mandatory retention period for the information disclosed.

B. Burden and Cost Estimates Related to the Proposed Amendments

As discussed below, we have estimated the average number of hours a company would spend preparing and reviewing the proposed disclosure requirements and the average

---

[90] 15 U.S.C. 80a-1 *et seq.*

hourly rate for outside professionals. In deriving our estimates, we recognize that some companies would experience costs in excess of those averages in the first year of compliance with the proposed amendments, and some companies may experience less than the average costs. The estimates of reporting and cost burdens provided in this PRA analysis address the time, effort and financial resources necessary to provide the proposed collections of information and are not intended to represent the full economic cost of complying with the proposal.

For purposes of the PRA, we estimate that over a three year period, the average annual incremental paperwork burden for all companies to prepare the disclosure that would be required under the proposals to be approximately 872,458 hours of company personnel time and a cost of approximately $144,061,000 for the services of outside professionals.[91] These estimates include the time and the cost of implementing data gathering systems and disclosure controls and procedures, the time and cost of in-house preparers, review by executive officers, in-house counsel, outside counsel, in-house accounting staff, independent auditors and members of the audit committee, and the time and cost of filing documents and retaining records.

Our methodologies for deriving the burden hour and cost estimates presented in the tables below represent the average burdens for all registrants who are required to provide the disclosure, both large and small. As discussed elsewhere in this release, the time required to prepare the proposed disclosures could vary significantly depending on, among other factors, the nature of the registrant's business, its capital structure, its internal controls and disclosure controls systems, its risk management systems and other applicable regulatory requirements. In addition, the estimates do not distinguish between registrants that are bank holding companies and other registrants. Although bank holding companies and other companies that currently provide Guide 3 disclosure would already collect and disclose on an annual basis some of the information covered by the new requirements, the new requirements are not identical to the provisions of Guide 3. Accordingly, for purposes of these estimates, we assume that bank holding companies would have the same burden as other registrants, although they might not actually incur additional expenses for those portions of the new requirements that are the same as the existing provisions of Guide 3.

Because our estimates assume that 100% of public companies engage in short-term borrowings from time to time, we estimate that the same percentage of companies would be impacted by the proposed disclosure requirements for short-term borrowings.[92] Therefore, for those companies that do not engage in short-term borrowing activities during a reporting period, the incremental burdens and costs may be lower than our estimate. However, because these companies may still need to implement systems and controls to capture short-term borrowings data that is not currently collected, we have assumed that they would share the same average burden and cost estimate. In addition, we assume that the burden hours of the proposed amendments would be comparable to the burden hours related to similar disclosure requirements, such as off-balance sheet arrangements disclosure requirements,[93] contractual obligations disclosure requirements,[94] and requirements for the qualitative and quantitative disclosure of market

---

[91] We calculated an annual average over a three-year period because OMB approval of PRA submissions covers a three-year period. For administrative convenience, the presentation of totals related to the paperwork burden hours have been rounded to the nearest whole number. The estimates reflect the burden of collecting and disclosing information under the PRA. Other costs associated with the proposed amendments are discussed in below under "Cost-Benefit Analysis."

[92] We further assume that the proposed amendments would not affect the number of filings.

[93] OBS Adopting Release, *supra* note 6, at 5994 (which we estimated to be 14.5 hours for annual reports and proxy statements, 16 hours for registration statements and 10 hours for quarterly reports).

[94] OBS Adopting Release, *supra* note 6, at 5994 (which we estimated to be 7.5 hours for annual reports and proxy statements, 8.5 hours for registration statements and 3 hours for quarterly reports).

risk,[95] which call for quantitative and/or qualitative discussion and analysis of financial data.

We derived the estimates by estimating the total amount of time it would take a company to implement systems to capture the data, implement related disclosure controls and procedures, prepare and review the disclosure pursuant to the proposed short-term borrowings requirements. We first estimated the total amount of time it would take a company to prepare and review the proposed disclosure for each form, using the estimates for the comparable disclosure requirements identified above as a starting point. Because we believe that the proposed rules would impose an increased burden on companies in connection with the implementation of data gathering systems and the implementation of related disclosure controls and procedures as compared to those comparable disclosure requirements, we added hours to those estimates, to reflect our best estimate of the additional time needed to implement the new systems.

The tables below illustrate the total incremental annual compliance burden of the collection of information in hours and in cost under the proposed amendments for annual reports, proxy and information statements, quarterly reports and current reports on Form 8-K under the Exchange Act (Table 1) and for registration statements under the Securities Act and Exchange Act (Table 2). There is no change to the estimated burden of the collection of information under Regulation S-K because the burdens that Regulation S-K imposes are reflected in our revised estimates for the forms. The burden estimates were calculated by multiplying the estimated number of annual responses by the estimated average number of hours it would take a company to prepare and review the proposed disclosure requirements. We recognize that some registrants may need to include MD&A disclosure in more than one filing covering the same period, accordingly actual numbers may be lower than our estimates.

We have based our estimated number of annual responses on the actual number of filings during the 2009 fiscal year, with three exceptions. First, we reduced the number of annual responses for Schedules 14A and 14C, based on our belief that only a minimal number of companies that file these schedules would need to prepare MD&A disclosure for the filing, rather than incorporating by reference from a periodic report. Second, we reduced the number of annual responses for Form N-2, based on our estimate of the number of Form N-2 filings made by business development companies in 2009 because only business development companies are required to include MD&A disclosure in a Form N-2.[96] In addition, we recognize that smaller reporting companies would be exempted from "full" interim period reporting in their quarterly reports rather than only reporting material changes on a quarterly basis. To reflect this, we reduced the number of annual responses of Forms 10-Q by our estimate of the number of Forms 10-Q filed by smaller reporting companies.[97]

For Exchange Act reports and proxy and information statements, we estimate that 75% of the burden of preparation is carried by the company internally and that 25% of the burden of preparation is carried by outside professionals retained by the company at an average cost of $400 per hour.[98] For registration statements, we estimate that 25% of the burden of preparation is carried by the company internally and that 75% of the burden of

---

[95] Disclosure of Accounting Policies for Derivative Financial Instruments and Derivative Commodity Instruments and Disclosure of Qualitative and Quantitative Information About Market Risk Inherent in Derivative Financial Instruments, Other Financial Instruments and Derivative Commodity Instruments, Release No. 33-7386 (Jan. 31, 1997) [62 FR 6044] (which we estimated to be 80 hours total per registrant).

[96] The current estimate of annual responses for Form N-2 is 205. Our best estimate of the total number of Forms N-2 filed in 2009 by business development companies is 29. Accordingly, for purposes of Table 2, we reduced the current estimate of annual responses for Form N-2 (205 Form N-2 filings) to 29 Form N-2 filings.

[97] This adjustment is based on our best estimate of the number of Forms 10-Q filed by smaller reporting companies in 2009.

[98] For Form 20-F, we estimate that 25% of the burden is carried by the company and 75% by outside professionals because we assume that foreign private issuers rely more heavily on outside counsel for preparation of the Form.

preparation is carried by outside professionals retained by the company at an average cost of $400 per hour. The portion of the burden carried by outside professionals is reflected as a cost, while the portion of the burden carried by the company is reflected in hours.

Table 1. Incremental Paperwork Burden under the proposed amendments for annual reports, quarterly reports, Forms 8-K and proxy and information statements:

	Annual Responses[99]	Incremental Burden Hours/Form	Total Incremental Burden Hours	75% Company	25% Professional	Professional Costs
	(A)	(B)	(C)=(A)*(B)	(D)=(C)*0.75	(E)=(C)*0.25	(F)=(E)*$400
10-K	13,545	40	541,800	406,350	135,450	$54,180,000
20-F	942	30	28,260	7,065	21,195	$8,478,000
10-Q	28,841	20	574,840	431,130	143,710	$57,484,000
8-K	115,795	0	0	0	0	0
SCH 14A	365	30	10,950	8,212.5	2,737.5	$1,095,000
SCH 14C	34	30	1,020	765	255	$102,000
Total	159,522	150	1,156,860	853,522.5	303,347.5	$121,339,000

Table 2. Incremental Paperwork Burden under the proposed amendments for registration statements:

	Annual Responses[100]	Incremental Burden Hours/Form	Total Incremental Burden Hours	75% Company	25% Professional	Professional Costs
	(A)	(B)	(C)=(A)*(B)	(D)=(C)*0.25	(E)=(C)*0.75	(F)=(E)*$400
S-1	1,168	35	40,880	10,220	30,660	$12,264,000
F-1	42	35	1,470	367.5	1,102.5	$441,000
S-4	619	35	21,665	5416.25	16,248.75	$6,499,500
F-4	68	35	2,380	595	1,785	$714,000
10	238	35	8,330	2,082.5	6,247.5	$2,499,000
N-2	29	35	1,015	253.75	761.25	$304,500
Total	2,164	210	75,740	18,935	56,805	$22,722,000

1. Annual Reports and Proxy/Information Statements

We estimate that the preparation of annual reports currently results in a total annual compliance burden of 21,986,455 hours and an annual cost of outside professionals of $3,591,562,980. We estimate that the preparation of proxy and information statements currently result in a total annual compliance burden of 735,122 hours and an annual cost of outside professionals of $86,608,526.

---

[99] Except as described above, the number of responses reflected in the table equals the actual number of forms and schedules filed with the Commission during the 2009 fiscal year.

[100] Except as described above, the number of responses reflected in the table equals the actual number of forms filed with the Commission during the 2009 fiscal year.

As set forth in Table 1 above, if the proposals were adopted, we estimate that the incremental cost of outside professionals for annual reports would be approximately $62,658,000 per year and the incremental company burden would be approximately 413,415 hours per year; and, for proxy and information statements, the total incremental cost of outside professionals would be approximately $1,197,000 per year and the incremental company burden would be approximately 8,978 hours per year. For purposes of our submission to the OMB under the PRA, if the proposals were adopted, the total cost of outside professionals for annual reports would be approximately $3,654,220,980 per year and the total company burden would be approximately 22,399,870 hours per year; and the total cost of outside professionals for proxy and information statements would be approximately $87,805,526 per year and the total company burden would be approximately 744,100 hours per year.

2. Quarterly Reports

We estimate that Form 10-Q preparation currently results in a total annual compliance burden of 4,559,793 hours and an annual cost of outside professionals of $607,972,400. As set forth in Table 1 above, if the proposals were adopted, we estimate that the incremental cost of outside professionals for quarterly reports would be approximately $57,484,000 per year and the incremental company burden would be approximately 431,130 hours per year. For purposes of our submission to the OMB under the PRA, if the proposals were adopted, the total cost of outside professionals for quarterly reports would be approximately $665,456,400 per year and the total annual company burden for quarterly reports would be approximately 4,990,923 hours per year.

3. Current Reports on Form 8-K

Form 8-K prescribes information about significant events that a registrant must disclose on a current basis. We are proposing amendments to the definitions used in Items 2.03 and 2.04 of Form 8-K that revise the terminology used, but which we assume would not significantly impact the scope of information required to be disclosed under those items. Accordingly, we estimate that the proposed amendments would not increase the number of current reports filed on Form 8-K nor add incremental costs and burdens to the existing disclosure burden under Form 8-K. If the proposed revisions to Items 2.03 and 2.04 of Form 8-K were adopted, we estimate that, on average, completing and filing a Form 8-K would require the same amount of time currently spent by entities completing the form—approximately 4 hours.

We estimate that Form 8-K preparation currently results in a total annual compliance burden of 493,436 hours and an annual cost of outside professionals of $65,791,500.

4. Registration Statements

We estimate that the preparation of registration statements that would be affected by the proposed amendments currently has a total annual compliance burden of 1,023,273 hours and an annual cost of outside professionals of $1,127,687,401. As set forth in Table 2 above, if the proposals were adopted, we estimate that the incremental cost of outside professionals for registration statements would be approximately $22,722,000 per year and the incremental company burden would be approximately 18,935 hours per year. For purposes of our submission to the OMB under the PRA, if the proposals were adopted, the total cost of outside professionals for registration statements would be approximately $1,150,409,401 per year and the total company burden would be approximately 1,042,208 hours per year.

C. Request for Comment

Pursuant to 44 U.S.C. 3506(c)(2)(B), we request comment in order to:

- Evaluate whether the proposed collections of information are necessary for the proper performance of the functions of the Commission, including whether the information would have practical utility;

- Evaluate the accuracy of our estimates of the burden of the proposed collections of information;

- Determine whether there are ways to enhance the quality, utility, and clarity of the information to be collected;
- Evaluate whether there are ways to minimize the burden of the collections of information on those who respond, including through the use of automated collection techniques or other forms of information technology; and
- Evaluate whether the proposed amendments would have any effects on any other collections of information not previously identified in this section.

Any member of the public may direct to us any comments concerning the accuracy of these burden estimates and any suggestions for reducing the burdens. Persons who desire to submit comments on the collection of information requirements should direct their comments to the OMB, Attention: Desk Officer for the Securities and Exchange Commission, Office of Information and Regulatory Affairs, Washington, DC 20503, and send a copy of the comments to Elizabeth M. Murphy, Secretary, Securities and Exchange Commission, 100 F Street, NE, Washington, DC 20549-1090, with reference to File No. S7-22-10. Requests for materials submitted to the OMB by us with regard to these collections of information should be in writing, refer to File No. S7-22-10 and be submitted to the Securities and Exchange Commission, Office of Investor Education and Advocacy, 100 F Street NE, Washington DC 20549-0213. Because the OMB is required to make a decision concerning the collections of information between 30 and 60 days after publication, your comments are best assured of having their full effect if the OMB receives them within 30 days of publication.

V. COST-BENEFIT ANALYSIS

A. Introduction and Objectives of Proposals

We are proposing amendments to enhance the disclosure that companies provide about short-term borrowings in order to provide more useful disclosure to investors about liquidity and short-term financings and to enhance investor understanding of issuers' liquidity. The proposed amendments are intended to improve disclosure by expanding and supplementing existing requirements.

First, the proposals would require a registrant to provide a comprehensive explanation of its short-term borrowings, including both quantitative and qualitative information. In addition, we are proposing conforming amendments to Form 8-K so that the Form uses the terminology contained in the proposed short-term borrowings disclosure requirement. Finally, we are making technical amendments to Item 303 of Regulation S-K to revise references to U.S. GAAP to reflect the FASB Codification.

The proposals seek to improve transparency of a company's short-term borrowings in order to provide investors with comprehensive information about a company's liquidity profile and demands on capital resources in each reporting period. The proposals also aim to clarify existing MD&A requirements in these areas to assist registrants in preparing disclosure that is meaningful, useful and clear. Ultimately, the proposals are expected to enhance the ability of investors to make informed investment decisions and to allocate capital on a more efficient basis.

We considered alternative regulatory approaches for achieving these objectives, including providing further interpretive guidance on existing MD&A disclosure requirements and encouraging companies to voluntarily provide quantitative and qualitative information on short-term borrowings where material to their financial condition. Although some public companies are voluntarily providing more detailed information as to short-term financings in their MD&A, we have observed that some companies generally do not provided investors with the desired level of detail in their disclosure absent a specific disclosure requirement or guidance, such as Guide 3. To elicit more detailed and comparable disclosures regarding a company's short-term borrowings activities in each reporting period as part of its overall liquidity profile, we are proposing mandated disclosure of short-term borrowings to complement existing MD&A disclosures.

B. Benefits

The proposed disclosures would benefit investors by informing them about the fluctuations in short-term borrowings during the reporting period. Information about the variability of borrowing levels and variations in types of borrowing activities over the course of the reporting period should enable investors to better understand the ability of a registrant to obtain the financing it needs to conduct its business operations and the costs of that financing, and how those may vary during the reporting period. The transparency of the financial statements should increase because investors would be able to learn more about the amount of financial risk taken by the company, its liquidity and capital resources, and the amount of capital deployed in earning activities by the company on an on-going basis during the year, including at quarter-ends. The proposed narrative discussion of the short-term borrowings arrangements, including the importance of those arrangements to the registrant in terms of its liquidity and capital resources, should provide investors with insight into the magnitude of the registrant's short-term borrowing activities, the specific material impact of the short-term borrowing arrangements on the registrant, and the factors that could affect its ability to continue to use those short-term borrowing arrangements.

The proposed disclosures would inform investors about the amount of financial risk taken by the company.[101] For some businesses, short-term borrowings may decrease or increase at quarter- and year-ends due to innate fluctuations in cash flow obligations. In other cases, management may be deliberately reducing short-term debt at period ends.[102] Regardless of the cause, period-end financial statements could be less informative regarding the financial risks taken by companies *during* the period. The proposed disclosures should add transparency to the ongoing risks taken by companies. These disclosures should also help facilitate a more accurate understanding of a company's liquidity and capital resources.

The proposed disclosures should also inform investors about the amount of capital deployed in earning activities by a company and thus help evaluate its overall source of profitability. Investors should benefit from knowing whether the period-end balance sheet fully reflects all intra-period activities and assets. The disclosure should also enable more accurate comparisons between companies that engage in a pattern of borrowing and those that do not.

Thus, the new disclosures should enhance transparency and competition especially in industries where short-term borrowing practices are common. Similar disclosure requirements exist in a more limited fashion for banks and bank holding companies under applicable banking regulations.[103] Therefore, bank regulators find this information to be useful in monitoring the risk of these institutions.[104]

---

[101] K. Kelly et al., *Big Banks Move to Mask Risk Levels—Quarter-End Loan Figures Sit 42% Below Peak, Then Rise as New Period Progresses*, WALL ST. J., Apr. 9, 2010; and M. Rappaport & T. McGinty, *supra* note 16 (reporting that "the practice, known as end-of-quarter 'window dressing' on Wall Street, suggests that the banks are carrying more risk most of the time than their investors or customers can easily see. This activity has accelerated since 2008 . . .").

[102] M. Griffiths & D. Winters, *The Turn of the Year in Money Markets: Tests of the Risk-Shifting Window Dressing and Preferred Habitat Hypotheses*, J. BUS, 2005, vol. 78, no. 4.; M. Griffiths & D. Winters, *On a Preferred Habitat for Liquidity at the Turn-of-the-Year: Evidence from the Term-Repo Market*, 12 J. FIN. SERV. RES. 1, 1997; V. Kotomin & D. Winters, *Quarter-End Effects in Banks: Preferred Habitat or Window Dressing?*, 29 J. FIN. SERV. RES. 1, 2006.

[103] Banks and bank holding companies report the quarterly average for federal funds sold and securities purchased under agreements to resell (FFIEC 031 and 041 Schedule RC-K, and FR Y-9C Schedule HC-K).

[104] *See e.g.*, Board of Governors of the Federal Reserve System, Announcement of Board Approval Under Delegated Authority and Submission to OMB, (March. 18, 2006) [71 FR 11194]. ("The FR Y-9 family of reports historically has been, and continues to be, the primary source of financial information on [bank holding companies] between on-site inspections. Financial information from these reports is used to detect emerging financial problems, to review performance and conduct pre-inspection analysis, to monitor and evaluate capital adequacy, to evaluate [bank holding company] mergers and acquisitions, and to analyze a [bank holding company's] overall financial condition to ensure safe and sound operations.").

The proposed amendments are likely to increase transparency. Therefore, information asymmetry and information risk would be lower and investors should demand a lower risk premium and rate of return.[105] Thus, the proposed disclosures would help reduce cost of capital and improve capital allocation and formation in the overall economy.

C. Costs

The proposals to require short-term borrowings disclosure on an annual and quarterly basis are new. In connection with the new disclosure requirements, registrants would be required to incur additional direct costs to which they were previously not subject, and could incur indirect costs as well. Because the proposed requirements require additional disclosures that are not currently provided in connection with Guide 3 compliance, bank holding companies would also incur additional direct and indirect costs to which they were previously not subject. Furthermore, as noted in our PRA analysis, we estimate that registrants would incur higher costs in the initial reporting periods than would be incurred in ongoing reporting periods.

We estimate that the proposals would impose new disclosure requirements on approximately 10,380 public companies.[106] We estimate that the collection of information and the preparation of the disclosure would involve multiple parties, including in-house preparers, senior management, in-house accounting staff, in-house counsel, information technology personnel, outside counsel, outside auditors and audit committee members. For purposes of our PRA analysis, we estimated that company personnel would spend approximately 872,204 hours per year (84 hours per company) to prepare, review and file the proposed disclosure. We also estimated that companies would spend approximately $143,756,500 ($13,849 per company) on outside professionals to comply with the proposed requirements.

We believe that the proposed amendments could increase the costs for some companies to collect the information necessary to prepare the disclosure. We also believe that the proposed amendments will impose different costs for companies, depending on whether they are bank-holding companies that currently provide Guide 3 information, financial companies as defined in the proposed rule, non-financial companies, or smaller reporting companies, as described below. Although management must already consider short-term borrowing information as it prepares its financial statements and MD&A under existing requirements, the proposed amendments could impose significant incremental costs for the collection and calculation of data, particularly in connection with the registrant's initial compliance.

In particular, this disclosure requires the production of new data for companies that are not already reporting this type of data voluntarily or to their primary regulators. In some industries, companies may readily have access to this information in their systems while others may not be producing it on a daily basis as would be required for financial companies under the proposals. For example, insurance companies may find it difficult to produce daily balances for each day that is necessary for the average and maximum short-term borrowing disclosures applicable to them. In addition, companies that are not financial companies under the proposed definition, particularly those with multi-national operations, may not currently be producing the data necessary for the monthly average and maximum short-term borrowings disclosures, and they may be faced with complex calculation issues when gathering the data from multiple jurisdictions. For many companies, the costs of data production may be high.

---

[105] *See* D. Easley & M. O'Hara, *Information and the Cost of Capital*, 59 J. FIN. 1553 (2004) (arguing that the information composition between public and non-public information affects the cost of capital because investors demand a higher return from their investments when they face asymmetric information); R. Lambert et al., *Accounting Information, Disclosure,* *and the Cost of Capital*, 45 J. ACCT. RES. 385 (2007) (deriving conditions under which an increase in information quality leads to an unambiguous decline in the cost of capital).

[106] We estimate that all registrants who filed annual reports in 2009 would be required to provide the proposed disclosures.

For bank holding companies currently subject to Guide 3, costs will likely arise primarily from the preparation of incremental disclosure in MD&A (*i.e.*, the proposed requirements for maximum daily amounts instead of maximum monthly amounts and the proposed narrative discussion of short-term borrowings arrangements) as well as quarterly reporting of this information (rather than on an annual basis alone). These bank holding companies already report to the Commission average short-term borrowings data computed based on daily averages on an annual basis, pursuant to Item VII of Guide 3. Of the approximately 10,380 public companies, we estimate that approximately 800 are bank holding companies.

For registrants that meet the proposed definition of "financial company" but that are not bank holding companies, such as insurance companies, broker-dealers, business development companies, and financing companies, the costs imposed could be substantial because, as requirements that are newly applicable to these entities, costs would likely include implementing or adjusting data gathering systems to capture daily balance information, implementing new disclosure controls and procedures, time spent by internal accounting staff to compile the data, as well as the preparation of narrative disclosure. As a portion of these costs would arise from data collection, the costs of compliance in the initial reporting period would likely be higher because systems may need to be implemented or adjusted. We estimate that, in addition to the approximately 800 bank holding companies, approximately 700 registrants would meet the proposed definition of "financial company."

Registrants that do not meet the definition of "financial companies" could have lower costs than those registrants that are financial companies, because they would not be required to compile data based on daily balances. Again, the requirements would be newly applicable, and could require these registrants to incur costs to implement or adjust data gathering systems to capture month-end balance information, the implementation of new disclosure controls and procedures, time spent by internal accounting staff to compile the data, as well as preparation of narrative disclosure. For companies that do not currently close their books on a monthly basis, the costs of gather the data would likely be higher than those that do, because monthly balances would not be readily available from existing books and records systems. The implementation or adjustment of data gathering systems would likely cause costs to be higher for these companies in the initial compliance period. We estimate that the number of registrants that are not financial companies and that are not smaller reporting companies, is approximately 7,640.

For smaller reporting companies, the proposed requirements would also be newly applicable, and costs incurred would be similar to those applicable to large reporting companies, except that, as proposed, smaller reporting companies would only be required to provide two years of annual short-term borrowings information, rather than three years, and would not be required to provide quarterly disclosure on the same level of detail as annual disclosure. Accordingly, in addition to the costs to prepare and review the disclosure, smaller reporting companies that do not currently track the data needed to compile the short-term borrowings disclosure or that do not currently close their books on a monthly basis, would incur costs to implement or adjust data collection systems and disclosure controls and procedures. On the other hand, small entities without such systems would be more likely to engage in financing activities that are less complex, where the compilation and calculation of such data would not raise significant burdens. In addition, the cost estimates set forth in our PRA analysis may be lower for a small entity to the extent its costs for personnel and outside professionals are lower than our assumed amounts. As discussed elsewhere in this release, we estimate that there are approximately 1,240 smaller reporting companies.

In addition, registrants that are not smaller reporting companies could incur increased costs in connection with the preparation of their quarterly reports, as the amendments call for disclosure in quarterly reports at the same level of detail as in annual reports. To provide this increased level of detail, registrants may need to alter their existing disclosure controls and procedures for quarterly reporting. For purposes of our PRA analysis, we estimated that company personnel would spend approximately 18 additional hours per year to prepare, review and file the proposed disclosure in Form 10-Q. We estimate that approximately 8,200 registrants (based on our estimated number of annual report filers, less smaller reporting companies and foreign private issuers) would be subject to the requirement to provide quarterly disclosure at the same level of detail as in annual reports.

Companies may also be faced with indirect costs arising from the amendments. For example, companies may need to consider the impact of the amendments on their financing plans, to the extent the gathering of data and preparation of disclosure imposes significant time burdens. Specifically, companies could decide to delay registered offerings or conduct unregistered offerings if they are unable to gather data and prepare the new disclosures without significant time and expense. This indirect cost should decrease over time, as companies implement disclosure controls and procedures to comply with the new disclosures. In other cases, companies may alter their short-term borrowings activities in response to the proposed disclosure, in order to avoid incurring the cost of compliance, and in doing so could incur transaction costs or opportunity costs that they would not face without a mandatory disclosure requirement.

In certain cases, mandatory required disclosure requirements can have adverse effects for companies and their shareholders if the disclosures reveal confidential information and trade secrets of a company. In the case of the proposed short-term borrowings, however, such indirect costs should be minimal due to the non-proprietary nature of short-term borrowings. There is some possibility that a company's competitors could be able to *infer* proprietary or sensitive information about a company's business operations or strategy from disclosure about short-term borrowings arrangements. If this were the case, it could disproportionately impact companies that meet the proposed definition of "financial company," to the extent that amounts calculated based on daily balance information provide a more accurate basis for such inferences. We preliminarily believe that the likelihood of this impact is low.

D. Request for Comment

We request data to quantify the costs and the value of the benefits described above. We seek estimates of these costs and benefits, as well as any costs and benefits not already defined, that may result from the adoption of these proposed amendments. We also request qualitative feedback on the nature of the benefits and costs described above and any benefits and costs we may have overlooked.

VI. CONSIDERATION OF IMPACT ON THE ECONOMY, BURDEN ON COMPETITION AND PROMOTION OF EFFICIENCY, COMPETITION AND CAPITAL FORMATION

Section 23(a)(2) of the Exchange Act requires us,[107] when adopting rules under the Exchange Act, to consider the impact that any new rule would have on competition. In addition, Section 23(a)(2) prohibits us from adopting any rule that would impose a burden on competition not necessary or appropriate in furtherance of the purposes of the Exchange Act.

Section 2(b) of the Securities Act[108] and Section 3(f) of the Exchange Act[109] require us, when engaging in rulemaking where we are required to consider or determine whether an action is necessary or appropriate in the public interest, to consider, in addition to the protection of investors, whether the action will promote efficiency, competition, and capital formation.

The proposed amendments are intended to enhance disclosure in MD&A relating to registrants' liquidity profile in each reporting period by highlighting and expanding

---

[107] 15 U.S.C. 78w(a)(2).
[108] 15 U.S.C. 77b(b).

[109] 15 U.S.C. 78c(f).

disclosure requirements for short-term borrowings. The proposed amendments to Form 8-K, which would conform the disclosure requirements in the Form to the proposed amendments to Regulation S-K, are intended to continue to provide real-time disclosure in connection with these topics.

The proposed amendments may increase the usefulness of MD&A. The ability of users of financial information to understand registrants' financial statements and to determine the existence of trends in borrowing and funding activity is expected to improve as a result of the disclosure of average and maximum short-term borrowings during each reporting period.

The proposed amendments also should increase the efficiency of U.S. capital markets by providing investors with additional and more timely information about registrants' borrowing and funding activities, including borrowing activities that are not apparent on the face of period-end financial statements and exposures to market and funding liquidity risks. This information could be used by investors in allocating capital across companies, and toward companies where the risk incentives appear better aligned with an investor's appetite for risk. Furthermore, these reductions in the asymmetry of information between registrants and investors could reduce registrants' cost of capital as investors may demand a lower risk premium when they have access to more information.[110]

In certain cases, mandatory required disclosure requirements can have adverse effects for companies and their shareholders if the disclosures reveal confidential information and trade secrets of a company. In the case of the proposed short-term borrowings, however, such indirect costs should be minimal due to the non-proprietary nature of short-term borrowings. There is some possibility that a company's competitors could be able to *infer* proprietary or sensitive information about a company's business operations or strategy from disclosure about short-term borrowings arrangements. If this were the case, it could disproportionately impact companies that meet the proposed definition of "financial company," to the extent that amounts calculated based on daily balance information provide a more accurate basis for such inferences. We preliminarily believe that the likelihood of this impact is low.

We request comment on whether the proposed amendments would promote efficiency, competition, and capital formation or have an impact or burden on competition. Commentators are requested to provide empirical data and other factual support for their view to the extent possible.

VII. SMALL BUSINESS REGULATORY ENFORCEMENT FAIRNESS ACT

For purposes of the Small Business Regulatory Enforcement Fairness Act of 1996 (SBREFA)[111] we solicit data to determine whether the proposed rule amendments constitute a "major" rule. Under SBREFA, a rule is considered "major" where, if adopted, it results or is likely to result in:

- An annual effect on the economy of $100 million or more (either in the form of an increase or a decrease);

- A major increase in costs or prices for consumers or individual industries; or

- Significant adverse effects on competition, investment or innovation.

Commentators should provide empirical data on (a) the potential annual effect on the economy; (b) any increase in costs or prices for consumers or individual industries; and (c) any potential effect on competition, investment or innovation.

---

[110] *See* D. Easley & M. O'Hara, *supra* note 98, and R. Lambert et al., *supra* note 98.

[111] Pub. L. No. 104-121, tit. II, 110 Stat. 857 (1996).

VIII. INITIAL REGULATORY FLEXIBILITY ACT ANALYSIS

This Initial Regulatory Flexibility Analysis (IRFA) has been prepared in accordance with the Regulatory Flexibility Act.[112] It relates to proposed revisions to the rules and forms under the Securities Act and Exchange Act to enhance disclosure that registrants provide in MD&A regarding short-term borrowings.

A. Reasons for, and Objectives of, the Proposed Action

The proposed amendments are intended to enhance disclosure in MD&A relating to registrants' liquidity profile by highlighting and expanding disclosure requirements for short-term borrowings. The proposed amendments to Form 8-K, which would conform the disclosure requirements in the Form to the proposed amendments to Regulation S-K, are intended to continue to provide real-time disclosure in connection with these topics. These amendments are being proposed to increase transparency in the presentation of registrants' borrowing and funding activities and exposure to liquidity risks in connection with that activity. This increased transparency in areas of increasing importance to investors is intended to maintain investor confidence in the full and fair disclosure required of all registrants.

B. Legal Basis

We are proposing the amendments pursuant to Sections 6, 7, 10, 19(a) and 28 of the Securities Act and Sections 12, 13, 14, 15(d), 23(a) and 36 of the Exchange Act.

C. Small Entities Subject to the Proposed Action

The proposed amendments would affect some companies that are small entities. The Regulatory Flexibility Act defines "small entity" to mean "small business," "small organization," or "small governmental jurisdiction."[113] The Commission's rules define "small business" and "small organization" for purposes of the Regulatory Flexibility Act for each of the types of entities regulated by the Commission. Securities Act Rule 157[114] and Exchange Act Rule 0-10(a)[115] define a company, other than an investment company, to be a "small business" or "small organization" if it had total assets of $5 million or less on the last day of its most recent fiscal year. We estimate that there are approximately 1,240 companies that may be considered small entities.[116] The proposed amendments would affect small entities that (i) have a class of securities that are registered under Section 12 of the Exchange Act, or are required to file reports under Section 15(d) of the Exchange Act and (ii) are required to provide MD&A disclosure under applicable rules and forms or disclosure under Items 2.03 and 2.04 of Form 8-K. In addition, the proposals also would affect small entities that file, or have filed, a registration statement (that is required to include MD&A disclosure under the applicable rules and forms) that has not yet become effective under the Securities Act and that has not been withdrawn.

The data underlying the proposed short-term borrowing disclosures should be available from a company's books and records, although it may not currently be collected on month-end basis or daily basis, as proposed in the rule. As discussed in our PRA analysis, we believe that the collection and calculation of short-term borrowing data in the form proposed may have a cost impact on registrants, including small entities, that do not currently maintain information technology systems for the collection of the required data. On the other hand, small entities without such systems would be more likely to engage in financing activities that are less complex, where the compilation and calculation of such data would not raise significant burdens. In addition, the cost

---

[112] 5 U.S.C. 603.

[113] 5 U.S.C. 601(6).

[114] 17 CFR 230.157.

[115] 17 CFR 240.0-10(a).

[116] This includes approximately 30 business development companies that are small entities. For purposes of the Regulatory Flexibility Act, an investment company (including a business development company) is a small entity if it, together with other investment companies in the same group of related investment companies, has net assets of $50 million or less as of the end of its most recent fiscal year. 17 CFR 270.0-10(a).

estimates set forth in our PRA analysis may be lower for a small entity to the extent its costs for personnel and outside professionals are lower than our assumed amounts.

We are proposing an accommodation for smaller reporting companies, such that expanded disclosures of short-term borrowings would not be required for interim periods and annual period data would only be required for two years rather than three years.

D. Reporting, Recordkeeping, and Other Compliance Requirements

The proposed amendments are intended to enhance disclosure about short-term borrowings. These proposals would require a small entity to:

- provide, in a separately captioned subsection of MD&A, a comprehensive explanation of its short-term borrowings, including both quantitative and qualitative information; and

- use a revised definition of "direct financial obligation" for purposes of disclosure requirements in Items 2.03 and 2.04 of Form 8-K.

These proposed amendments largely would apply to both large and small entities equally, except that smaller reporting companies would benefit from the proposed exclusion from expanded interim reporting of short-term borrowings and would provide two years of annual data rather than three. As noted above, the proposed short-term borrowings disclosure should be available from a company's books and records and tracked with existing internal controls without a significant incremental burden imposed on small entities, except to the extent that it doesn't track the data on a monthly basis.

E. Duplicative, Overlapping, or Conflicting Federal Rules

We believe the proposed amendments would not duplicate, overlap, or conflict with other federal rules. The proposed new requirements for short-term borrowings disclosures provide specific, additional information that would be complementary to existing MD&A requirements.

F. Significant Alternatives

The Regulatory Flexibility Act directs us to consider alternatives that would accomplish our stated objectives, while minimizing any significant adverse impact on small entities. In connection with the proposed disclosure amendments, we considered the following alternatives:

- Establishing different compliance or reporting requirements or timetables that take into account the resources available to small entities;

- Clarifying, consolidating or simplifying compliance and reporting requirements under the rules for small entities;

- Using performance rather than design standards; and

- Exempting small entities from all or part of the requirements.

Currently, small entities are subject to the same MD&A requirements as larger registrants under Item 303 of Regulation S-K, except that smaller reporting companies are permitted to exclude information as to their contractual obligations.[117] The proposed amendments would not alter the exclusions applicable to smaller reporting companies, except, as discussed above, an additional exclusion would be provided for smaller reporting companies so that they would not need to provide the proposed expanded interim period disclosures of short-term borrowings and would be permitted to provide two years of annual data instead of three years. The remaining proposed disclosure

---

[117] Item 303(d) of Regulation S-K provides an exclusion for smaller reporting companies from the requirements of Item 303(a)(5), and permits smaller reporting companies to provide, if they meet specified conditions, only two fiscal years of information on the impact of inflation and changing prices pursuant to Item 303(a)(3)(iv).

requirements would apply to small entities to the same extent as larger registrants, and would require clear, straightforward disclosure about short-term borrowings.

Except for the exclusions noted above, we are not proposing to change existing alternative reporting requirements under Item 303 of Regulation S-K, or establish additional different compliance requirements or an exemption from coverage of the proposed amendments for small entities. The proposed amendments would provide investors with greater transparency into the liquidity profile of registrants, by highlighting short-term borrowings. With potentially fewer financing options available to small entities, information about critical funding risks and future commitments is important to investors in the context of small entities as it is in the context of larger entities. Therefore, we do not believe it is appropriate to develop separate requirements for small entities that would involve clarification, consolidation, or simplification of the proposed disclosure requirements, other than the proposed exclusions discussed above. We do not believe that these proposed disclosures would create a significant new burden for small entities, and, we believe that uniform, comparable disclosures across all companies would be beneficial for investors and the markets.

We have used design standards and performance standards in connection with the proposed amendments. We rely on design standards for two reasons. First, based on our past experience, we believe that the proposed requirements would result in disclosure that is more useful to investors than if there were specific, enumerated informational requirements. The proposed requirements are intended to elicit more comprehensive and clear disclosure, while still affording registrants the ability to tailor the disclosure to reflect their specific activities and to provide the information that is most important in the context of their specific business. Second, the proposed amendments would promote consistent disclosure among all companies, providing information that is increasingly important to investors. Our existing MD&A requirements are largely performance standards, designed to elicit disclosure unique to the particular company.

Finally, we believe that requiring additional short-term borrowings information in MD&A is the most effective way to elicit the disclosure both for small entities. MD&A's existing emphasis on liquidity and capital resources, as well as identification of significant uncertainties and events, makes the placement of the disclosure as part of MD&A an appropriate choice. Because the proposed disclosure of short-term borrowings is intended to supplement the discussions of liquidity and capital resources already required to be provided by smaller reporting companies under existing rules, we believe the inclusion of the proposed requirements in MD&A would reduce redundant disclosure requirements and promote investors' understanding of this important and, at times highly complex, information.

We seek comment on whether we should exempt small entities from any of the proposed amendments or scale the proposed disclosure requirements to reflect the characteristics of small entities and the needs of their investors.

G. Solicitation of Comments

We encourage the submission of comments with respect to any aspect of this Initial Regulatory Flexibility Analysis. In particular, we request comments regarding:

- How the proposed amendments can achieve their objective while lowering the burden on small entities;

- The number of small entities that may be affected by the proposed amendments;

- The existence or nature of the potential impact of the proposed amendments on small entities discussed in the analysis; and

- How to quantify the impact of the proposed amendments.

Respondents are asked to describe the nature of any impact and provide empirical data supporting the extent of the impact. Such comments will be considered in the preparation of the Final Regulatory Flexibility Analysis, if the proposed rule amendments are adopted, and will be placed in the same public file as comments on the proposed amendments themselves.

IX. STATUTORY AUTHORITY AND TEXT OF THE PROPOSED AMENDMENTS

The amendments contained in this release are being proposed under the authority set forth in Sections 6, 7, 10, 19(a) and 28 of the Securities Act and Sections 12, 13, 14, 15(d), 23(a) and 36 of the Exchange Act.

List of Subjects

17 CFR Parts 229 and 249

Reporting and recordkeeping requirements, Securities.

TEXT OF THE PROPOSED AMENDMENTS

For the reasons set out in the preamble, the Commission proposes to amend Title 17, Chapter II, of the Code of Federal Regulations as follows:

PART 229—STANDARD INSTRUCTIONS FOR FILING FORMS UNDER SECURITIES ACT OF 1933, SECURITIES EXCHANGE ACT OF 1934 AND ENERGY POLICY AND CONSERVATION ACT OF 1975—REGULATION S-K

1. The authority citation for Part 229 continues to read in part as follows:

Authority: 15 U.S.C. 77e, 77f, 77g, 77h, 77j, 77k, 77s, 77z-2, 77z-3, 77aa(25), 77aa(26), 77ddd, 77eee, 77ggg, 77hhh, 77iii, 77jjj, 77nnn, 77sss, 78c, 78i, 78j, 78l, 78m, 78n, 78o, 78u-5, 78w, 78*ll*, 78mm, 80a-8, 80a-9, 80a-20, 80a-29, 80a-30, 80a-31(c), 80a-37, 80a-38(a), 80a-39, 80b-11, and 7201 *et seq.*; and 18 U.S.C. 1350, unless otherwise noted.

* * * * *

2. Amend Section 229.303 by:

a. Removing the phrase "paragraphs (a)(1) through (5) of this Item" and adding in its place "paragraphs (a)(1) through (a)(6) of this Item" in the second sentence of the introductory text of paragraph (a);

b. Revising paragraphs (a)(4)(ii)(A), (a)(4)(ii)(C) and (a)(4)(ii)(D), and (a)(5)(ii)(A), (a)(5)(ii)(B) and (a)(5)(ii)(C);

c. Redesignating the "Instructions to paragraph 303(a) (4)" to directly follow paragraph (a)(4)(ii)(D);

d. Adding a new paragraph (a)(6) directly above the "Instructions to paragraph 303(a)";

e. Revising the fourth sentence of Instruction 8 to paragraph 303(a);

f. Revising Instruction 9 to paragraph 303(a);

g. Adding the phrase "except as provided in Instruction 8 to paragraph 303(b)" at the end of the first sentence of Instruction 3 of the Instructions to paragraph (b) of Item 303;

h. Adding Instruction 8 to the Instructions to paragraph (b) of Item 303; and

i. Revising paragraph (d).

The revisions and additions read as follows:

§ 229.303 (Item 303) Management's Discussion and Analysis of Financial Condition and Results of Operations.

* * * * *

(a) * * *

(4) * * *

(ii) * * * *

(A) Any obligation under a guarantee contract that has any of the characteristics identified in FASB ASC Topic 460, *Guarantees*, paragraph 460-10-15-4, as may be modified or supplemented, and that is not excluded from the initial recognition and measurement provisions of FASB ASC paragraphs 460-10-15-7, 460-10-25-1, and 460-10-30-1;

(B) * * *

(C) Any obligation, including a contingent obligation, under a contract that would be accounted for as a derivative instrument, except that it is both indexed to the registrant's own stock and classified in stockholders' equity in the registrant's statement of financial position, and therefore excluded from the scope of FASB ASC Topic 815, *Derivatives and Hedging*, pursuant to FASB ASC subparagraph 815-15-74(a), as may be modified or supplemented;

(D) Any obligation, including a contingent obligation, arising out of a variable interest (as defined in the FASB ASC Master Glossary, as may be modified or supplemented) in an unconsolidated entity that is held by, and material to, the registrant, where such entity provides financing, liquidity, market risk or credit risk support to, or engages in leasing, hedging or research and development services with, the registrant.

(5) * * *

(ii) * * *

(A) *Long-Term Debt Obligation* means a payment obligation under long-term borrowings referenced in FASB ASC Topic 470, *Debt*, paragraph 470-10-50-1, as may be modified or supplemented.

(B) *Capital Lease Obligation* means a payment obligation under a lease classified as a capital lease pursuant to FASB ASC Topic 840, *Leases*, as may be modified or supplemented.

(C) *Operating Lease Obligation* means a payment obligation under a lease classified as an operating lease and disclosed pursuant to FASB ASC Topic 840, as may be modified or supplemented.

* * * * *

(6) *Short-term Borrowings.* (i) In tabular format, provide for each category of short-term borrowings specified in paragraph (a)(6)(iii) of this Item and for the periods specified in paragraph (a)(6)(v) of this Item:

(A) The average amount outstanding during each reported period and the weighted average interest rate thereon;

(B) The amount outstanding at the end of each reported period and the weighted average interest rate thereon;

(C)(*1*) For registrants that are financial companies, the maximum daily amount outstanding during each reported period or

(*2*) For registrants that are not financial companies, the maximum month-end amount outstanding during each reported period; and

(D) For any of the amounts referred to in paragraphs (a)(6)(i)(A), (B) or (C) of this Item, disaggregate the amounts in the table by currency, interest rate or other meaningful category, to the extent presentation of separate amounts is necessary to promote understanding or to prevent aggregate amounts from being misleading, and include a footnote to the table indicating the method of disaggregation and any other pertinent data relating to the calculation of the amounts presented, including, without limitation, the timing and exchange rates used for currency translations.

(ii) Discuss the registrant's short-term borrowings, including the items specified in paragraphs (a)(6)(ii)(A) through (D) of this Item to the extent necessary to an understanding of such borrowings and the current or future effect on the registrant's financial condition, changes in financial condition, revenues or expenses, results of operations, liquidity, capital expenditures or capital resources:

(A) A general description of the short-term borrowings arrangements included in each category (including any key metrics or other factors that could reduce or impair the company's ability to borrow under any of such arrangements and whether there are any collateral posting arrangements) and the business purpose to the registrant of such short-term borrowings;

(B) The importance to the registrant of such short-term borrowings in respect of its liquidity, capital resources, market-risk support, credit-risk support or other benefits;

(C) The reasons for any material differences between average short-term borrowings and period-end borrowings; and

(D) The reasons for the maximum outstanding amounts in each reported period, including any non-recurring transactions or events, use of proceeds or other information that provides context for the maximum amount.

(iii) As used in this paragraph (a)(6), the term "*short-term borrowings*" includes amounts payable for short-term obligations that are:

(A) Federal funds purchased and securities sold under agreements to repurchase;

(B) Commercial paper;

(C) Borrowings from banks;

(D) Borrowings from factors or other financial institutions; and

(E) Any other short-term borrowings reflected on the registrant's balance sheet.

(iv) As used in this paragraph (a)(6), the term "*financial company*" means a registrant that, during the reported period, is engaged to a significant extent in the business of lending, deposit-taking, insurance underwriting or providing investment advice, or is a broker or dealer as defined in Section 3 of the Exchange Act (15 U.S.C. 78c), and includes, without limitation, an entity that is, or is the holding company of, a bank, a savings association, an insurance company, a broker, a dealer, a business development company as defined in Section 2(a)(48) of the Investment Company Act of 1940 (15 U.S.C. 80a-2(a)(48)), an investment adviser, a futures commission merchant, a commodity trading advisor, a commodity pool operator, or a mortgage real estate investment trust.

(v) Information required by this paragraph (a)(6) shall be presented for each of the three most recent fiscal years, and, in the case of annual reports filed on Form 10-K (referenced in § 249.310), information for the registrant's fourth fiscal quarter presented in accordance with the requirements for interim periods set forth in Instruction 8 to paragraph (b) of this Item 303; *provided* that a registrant that is a smaller reporting company may provide the information required for each of the two most recent fiscal years in accordance with paragraph (d) of this Item 303 and, in the case of annual reports filed on Form 10-K (referenced in § 249.310), is not required to include information for the fourth fiscal quarter.

Instruction 1 to Paragraph 303(a)(6): Where a registrant meets the definition of financial company, but also has operations that do not involve lending, deposit-taking, insurance underwriting, providing investment advice, or broker or dealer activities, it may present the information specified in Item 303(a)(6)(i) separately for such operations. In doing so, the registrant may disclose averages and maximum amounts for such operations using the rules and instructions applicable to registrants that are not financial companies, provided that it must disclose averages computed on a daily average basis and maximum daily amounts for its operations that fall within the definition of financial company. For purposes of making this segregation, the registrant should make the distinction assuming the business in question were itself a registrant. Additional information should be presented by footnote to enable readers to understand how the registrant's operations have been grouped for purposes of the disclosure.

Instruction 2 to Paragraph 303(a)(6): For registrants that are financial companies, averages called for by paragraph (a)(6) of this Item are averages computed on a daily average basis (which means the amount outstanding at the end of each day, averaged over the reporting period). For all other registrants, the basis used for calculating the averages must be identified, and the averaging period used must not exceed a month.

Instruction 3 to Paragraph 303(a)(6): As used in this Item 303(a)(6), the maximum daily amount outstanding during a reported period means the largest amount outstanding at the end of any day in the reported period, and the maximum month-end amount outstanding during a reported period means the largest amount outstanding at the end of the last day of any month in the reported period.

Instructions to Paragraph 303(a):

* * * * *

8. * * * However, registrants may elect to voluntarily disclose supplemental information on the effects of changing prices as provided for in FASB ASC Topic 255, *Changing Prices*, or through other supplemental disclosures. * * *

9. Registrants that elect to disclose supplementary information on the effects of changing prices as specified by FASB ASC Topic 255 may combine such explanations with the discussion and analysis required pursuant to this Item or may supply such information separately with appropriate cross-reference.

* * * * *

(b) * * *

Instructions to Paragraph 303(b):

* * * * *

8. Notwithstanding anything to the contrary in this Item 303, a registrant that is not a smaller reporting company must include the disclosure required pursuant to (a)(6) of this Item for each interim period for which financial statements are included or required to be included by Article 3 of Regulation S-X (17 CFR 210.3-01 to 3.18), and for the registrant's fourth fiscal quarter in the case of an annual report filed on Form 10-K (referenced in § 249.310), and must provide an updated discussion and analysis of the information presented. The discussion and analysis should also highlight any material changes from prior periods. For purposes of interim period disclosures of short-term borrowings required by paragraph (a)(6) of this Item, the term "*reported period*" used in paragraph (a)(6) of this Item means the most recent interim period presented or, in the case of an annual report filed on Form 10-K (referenced in § 249.310), the registrant's fourth fiscal quarter.

* * * * *

(d) *Smaller reporting companies.* A smaller reporting company, as defined in § 229.10(f)(1) of this Chapter, may provide the information required in paragraphs (a)(3)(iv) and (a)(6) of this Item for the last two most recent fiscal years of the registrant if it provides financial information on net sales and revenues and on income from continuing operations for only two years. For interim periods, a smaller reporting company is not required to follow Instruction 8 to paragraph 303(b) and, instead, must discuss material changes to the information specified in paragraphs (a)(4) and (a)(6) of this Item from the end of the preceding fiscal year (and, if included, from the corresponding interim balance sheet date of the preceding fiscal year) to the date of the most recent interim balance sheet provided. In the case of an annual report filed on Form 10-K (referenced in § 249.310), a smaller reporting company is not required to provide information for the fourth quarter of the most recent fiscal year.

* * * * *

PART 249—FORMS, SECURITIES EXCHANGE ACT OF 1934

3. The authority citation for part 249 continues to read in part as follows:

Authority: 15 U.S.C. 78a et seq. and 7201 et seq.; and 18 U.S.C. 1350, unless otherwise noted.

* * * * *

4. Form 8-K (referenced in § 249.308) is amended by:

a. Revising paragraph (c)(4) of Item 2.03; and

b. Removing paragraph (e) of Item 2.03.

The revisions read as follows:

Note: The text of Form 8-K does not, and this amendment will not, appear in the Code of Federal Regulations.

Form 8-K

* * * * *

Item 2.03 Creation of a Direct Financial Obligation or an Obligation under an Off-Balance Sheet Arrangement of a Registrant.

* * * * *

(c) * * *

(4) a short-term borrowing, as defined in Item 303(a)(6)(iii) of Regulation S-K (17 CFR 229.303(a)(6)(iii)), that arises other than in the ordinary course of business.

* * * * *

5. Form 20-F (referenced in § 249.220f) Item 5 is amended by:

a. Revising paragraphs (a) and (d) of Item 5.E.2;

b. Adding Item 5.H; and

c. Adding Instructions to Item 5.H after the "Instructions to Item 5.F".

The revisions and additions read as follows:

Note: The text of Form 20-F does not, and this amendment will not, appear in the Code of Federal Regulations.

Form 20-F

* * * * *

Item 5. Operating and Financial Review and Prospects

* * * * *

E. Off-balance sheet arrangements.

* * * * *

2. * * *

(a) Any obligation under a guarantee contract that has any of the characteristics identified in FASB ASC Topic 460, Guarantees, paragraph 460-10-15-4, as may be modified or supplemented, excluding the types of guarantee contracts described in FASB ASC paragraphs 46010-15-7, 460-10-25-1, and 460-10-30-1;

(b) * * *

(c) * * *

(d) Any obligation, including a contingent obligation, arising out of a variable interest (as defined in the FASB ASC Master Glossary, as may be modified or supplemented) in an unconsolidated entity that is held by, and material to, the company, where such entity provides financing, liquidity, market risk or credit risk support to, or engages in leasing, hedging or research and development services with, the company.

* * * * *

H. Short-Term Borrowings

1. In tabular format, provide for each category of short-term borrowings specified in Item 5.H.3 of this Form and for the periods specified in Item 5.H.5 of this Form:

(a) The average amount outstanding during each reported period and the weighted average interest rate thereon;

(b) The amount outstanding at the end of each reported period and the weighted average interest rate thereon;

(c)(*i*) For companies that are financial companies, the maximum daily amount outstanding during each reported period; or

(*ii*) For companies that are not financial companies, the maximum month-end amount outstanding during each reported period; and

(d) For any of the amounts referred to in (a), (b) or (c) of this Item 5.H.1, disaggregate the amounts in the table by currency, interest rate or other meaningful category, to the extent presentation of separate amounts is necessary to promote understanding or to prevent aggregate amounts from being misleading, and include a footnote to the table indicating the method of disaggregation and any other pertinent data relating to the calculation of the amounts presented, including, without limitation, the timing and exchange rates used for currency translations.

2. Provide a discussion of the company's short-term borrowings, including the items specified in paragraphs (a) through (d) of this Item 5.H.2 to the extent necessary to an understanding of such borrowings and the current or future effect on the company's financial condition, changes in financial condition, revenues or expenses, results of operations, liquidity, capital expenditures or capital resources:

(a) A general description of the short-term borrowings included in each category (including any key metrics or other factors that could reduce or impair the company's ability to borrow under any of such arrangements and whether there are any collateral posting arrangements) and the business purpose to the company of such short-term borrowings;

(b) The importance to the company of such short-term borrowings in respect of its liquidity, capital resources, market-risk support, credit-risk support or other benefits;

(c) The reasons for any material differences between average short-term borrowings and period-end borrowings; and

(d) The reasons for the maximum outstanding amounts in each reported period, including any non-recurring transactions or events, use of proceeds or other information that provides context for the maximum amount.

3. As used in this Item 5.H, the term *"short-term borrowings"* means amounts payable for short-term obligations that are:

(a) Federal funds purchased and securities sold under agreements to repurchase;

(b) Commercial paper;

(c) Borrowings from banks;

(d) Borrowings from factors or other financial institutions; and

(e) Any other short-term borrowings reflected in the company's balance sheet.

4. As used in this Item 5.H, the term *"financial company"* means a company that, during the reported period, is engaged to a significant extent in the business of lending, deposit-taking, insurance underwriting or providing investment advice, or is a broker or dealer as defined in Section 3 of the Exchange Act (15 U.S.C. 78c), and includes, without limitation, an entity that is or is the holding company of, a bank, a savings association, an insurance company, a broker, a dealer, a business development company as defined in Section 2(a)(48) of the Investment Company Act of 1940 (15 U.S.C. 80a-2(a)(48)), an investment adviser, a futures commission merchant, a commodity trading advisor, a commodity pool operator, or a mortgage real estate investment trust.

5. Information required by this Item 5.H shall be presented for each of the three most recent fiscal years.

* * * * *

Instructions to Item 5.H:

1. Notwithstanding Item 5.H.3, the categories of short-term borrowings disclosed pursuant to Item 5.H of this Form may be based on the classifications for such types of short-term borrowings used under the comprehensive set of accounting principles that the company uses to prepare its primary financial statements, so long as the disclosure is provided at a level of detail that satisfies the objective of this Item 5.H disclosure requirement.

2. Where a company meets the definition of financial company, but also has operations that do not involve lending, deposit-taking, insurance underwriting, providing investment advice, or broker or dealer activities, it may present the information specified in Item 5.H.1 of this Form separately for such operations. In doing so, the company may disclose averages and maximum amounts for such operations using the rules and instructions applicable to companies that are not financial companies, provided that it must disclose averages computed on a daily average basis and maximum daily amounts for its operations that fall within the definition of financial company. For purposes of making this segregation, the company should make the distinction assuming the business in question were itself a registrant. Additional information should be presented by footnote to enable readers to understand how the company's operations have been grouped for purposes of the disclosure.

3. For companies that are financial companies, averages called for by this Item 5.H are averages computed on a daily average basis (which means the amount outstanding at the end of each day, averaged over the reporting period). For all other companies, the basis used for calculating the averages must be identified, and the averaging period used must not exceed a month.

4. As used in this Item 5.H, the maximum daily amount outstanding during a reported period means the largest amount outstanding at the end of any day in the reported period,

and the maximum month-end amount outstanding during a reported period means the largest amount outstanding at the end of the last day of any month in the reported period.

* * * * *

By the Commission.

Elizabeth M. Murphy

Secretary

September 17, 2010

APPENDIX 4
Concept Release on the U.S. Proxy System

SECURITIES AND EXCHANGE COMMISSION

17 CFR Parts 240, 270, 274, and 275

[Release Nos. 34-62495; IA-3052; IC-29340; File No. S7-14-10]

RIN 3235-AK43

CONCEPT RELEASE ON THE U.S. PROXY SYSTEM

AGENCY: Securities and Exchange Commission.

ACTION: Concept release; request for comments.

SUMMARY: The Commission is publishing this concept release to solicit comment on various aspects of the U.S. proxy system. It has been many years since we conducted a broad review of the system, and we are aware of industry and investor interest in the Commission's consideration of an update to its rules to promote greater efficiency and transparency in the system and enhance the accuracy and integrity of the shareholder vote. Therefore, we seek comment on the proxy system in general, including the various issues raised in this release involving the U.S. proxy system and certain related matters.

DATES: Comments should be received on or before October 20, 2010.

ADDRESSES: Comments may be submitted by any of the following methods:

Electronic comments:

- Use the Commission's Internet comment form (http://www.sec.gov/rules/concept. shtml);
- Send an e-mail to rule-comments@sec.gov. Please include File Number S7-14-10 on the subject line; or
- Use the Federal eRulemaking Portal (http://www.regulations.gov). Follow the instructions for submitting comments.

Paper comments:

- Send paper comments in triplicate to Elizabeth M. Murphy, Secretary, Securities and Exchange Commission, 100 F Street, NE, Washington, DC 20549-1090.

All submissions should refer to File Number S7-14-10. This file number should be included on the subject line if e-mail is used. To help us process and review your comments more efficiently, please use only one method. The Commission will post all comments on the Commission's Internet Web site (*http://www.sec.gov/rules/concept.shtml*). Comments are also available for Web site viewing and copying in the Commission's Public Reference Room, 100 F Street, NE, Washington, DC 20549, on official business days between the hours of 10:00 a.m. and 3:00 p.m. All comments received will be posted without change; we do not edit personal identifying information from submissions. You should submit only information that you wish to make available publicly.

FOR FURTHER INFORMATION CONTACT: Raymond A. Be or Lawrence A. Hamermesh, Division of Corporation Finance, at (202) 551-3500, Susan M. Petersen or Andrew Madar, Division of Trading & Markets, at (202) 551-5777, Holly L. Hunter-Ceci or Brian P. Murphy, Division of Investment Management, at (202) 551-6825, or Joshua White, Division of Risk, Strategy, and Financial Innovation, at (202) 551-6655, 100 F Street, NE, Washington, DC 20549.

SUPPLEMENTARY INFORMATION:

I.   Introduction

II.   The Current Proxy Distribution and Voting Process
- A.   Types of Share Ownership and Voting Rights
  1. Registered Owners
  2. Beneficial Owners
- B.   The Process of Soliciting Proxies
  1. Distributing Proxy Materials to Registered Owners
  2. Distributing Proxy Materials to Beneficial Owners
     a. The Depository Trust Company
     b. Securities Intermediaries: Broker-Dealers and Banks
- C.   Proxy Voting Process
- D.   The Roles of Third Parties in the Proxy Process
  1. Transfer Agents
  2. Proxy Service Providers
  3. Proxy Solicitors
  4. Vote Tabulators
  5. Proxy Advisory Firms

III.   Accuracy, Transparency, and Efficiency of the Voting Process
- A.   Over-Voting and Under-Voting
  1. Imbalances in Broker Votes
     a. Securities Lending
     b. Fails to Deliver
  2. Current Reconciliation and Allocation Methodologies Used by Broker-Dealers to Address Imbalances
     a. Pre-Reconciliation Method
     b. Post-Reconciliation Method
     c. Hybrid Reconciliation Methods
  3. Potential Regulatory Responses
  4. Request for Comment
- B.   Vote Confirmation
  1. Background
  2. Potential Regulatory Responses
  3. Request for Comment
- C.   Proxy Voting by Institutional Securities Lenders
  1. Background
  2. Lack of Advance Notice of Meeting Agenda
     a. Background
     b. Potential Regulatory Responses
     c. Request for Comment
  3. Disclosure of Voting by Funds
     a. Background
     b. Potential Regulatory Responses
     c. Request for Comment
- D.   Proxy Distribution Fees
  1. Background
     a. Current Fee Schedules
     b. Notice and Access Model
     c. Current Practice Regarding Fees Charged
  2. Potential Regulatory Responses
  3. Request for Comment

IV.   Communications and Shareholder Participation
- A.   Issuer Communications with Shareholders
  1. Background
  2. Potential Regulatory Responses
  3. Request for Comment
- B.   Means to Facilitate Retail Investor Participation
  1. Background

* * * * *

I. Introduction

Regulation of the proxy solicitation process is one of the original responsibilities that Congress assigned to the Commission in 1934. The Commission has actively monitored the proxy process since receiving this authority and has considered changes when it appeared that the process was not functioning in a manner that adequately protected the interests of investors.[1] In recent years, a number of our proxy-related rulemakings have been spurred by the Internet and other technological advances that enable more efficient communications. For example, we have adopted the "notice and access" model for the delivery of proxy materials,[2] as well as rules to facilitate the use of electronic shareholder forums.[3] Perceived deficiencies in the proxy distribution process have prompted other proxy-related rulemakings, such as rules to reinforce the obligation of issuers to distribute proxy materials to banks and brokers on a timely basis[4] and to permit the "householding" of proxy materials.[5] We have also periodically revised our rules requiring certain types of disclosures in the proxy statement, such as information on executive compensation and corporate governance matters.[6] We also have pending a proposal to adopt rules that would require, under certain circumstances, a company to include in its proxy materials a shareholder's, or group of shareholders', nominees for director.[7]

During many of these previous proxy-related rulemakings, commentators raised concerns about the proxy system as a whole.[8] In addition, the Commission's staff often receives complaints from individual investors about the administration of the proxy system.[9] We believe that these concerns and complaints merit attention because they address a subject of considerable importance—the corporate proxy–which, given the wide dispersion of shareholders, is the principal means by which shareholders can exercise their voting rights.

Accordingly, in this release, we are reviewing and seeking public comment as to whether the U.S. proxy system as a whole operates with the accuracy, reliability, transparency, accountability, and integrity that shareholders and issuers should rightfully expect. With over 600 billion shares voted every year at more than 13,000 shareholder

---

[1] For a history of the Commission's efforts to regulate the proxy process since 1934, see Jill E. Fisch, *From Legitimacy to Logic: Reconstructing Proxy Regulation*, 46 Vand. L. Rev. 1129 (Oct. 1993).

[2] 17 CFR 240.14a-16; Shareholder Choice Regarding Proxy Materials, Release No. 34-56135 (July 26, 2007) [72 FR 42222] ("Notice and Access Release"); Amendments to Rules Requiring Internet Availability of Proxy Materials, Release No. 33-9108 (Feb. 22, 2010) [75 FR 9074].

[3] 17 CFR 240.14a-17; Electronic Shareholder Forums, Release No. 34-57172 (Jan. 18, 2008) [73 FR 4450]. These amendments clarified that participation in an electronic shareholder forum that could potentially constitute a solicitation subject to the proxy rules is exempt from most of the proxy rules if all of the conditions to the exemption are satisfied. In addition, the amendments state that a shareholder, issuer, or third party acting on behalf of a shareholder or issuer that establishes, maintains or operates an electronic shareholder forum will not be liable under the federal securities laws for any statement or information provided by another person participating in the forum. The amendments did not provide an exemption from Rule 14a-9 [17 CFR 240.14a-9], which prohibits fraud in connection with the solicitation of proxies.

[4] *See* 17 CFR 14b-1 and 14b-2; Timely Distribution of Proxy and Other Soliciting Material, Release No. 34-33768 (Mar. 16, 1994) [59 FR 13517].

[5] Delivery of Proxy Statements and Information Statements to Households, Release No. 33-7912 (Oct. 27, 2000) [65 FR 65736]. "Householding" permits a securities intermediary to send only one copy of proxy materials to multiple accounts within the same household under specified conditions. *Id.*

[6] *See, e.g.*, Proxy Disclosure Enhancements, Release No. 33-9089 (Dec. 16, 2009) [74 FR 68334] and Executive Compensation and Related Person Disclosure, Release No. 33-8732A (Aug. 9, 2006) [71 FR 53158].

[7] *See* Facilitating Shareholder Director Nominations, Release Nos. 33-9046, 34-60089, IC-287665 (June 10, 2009) [74 FR 29024].

[8] *See, e.g.*, Request for Rulemaking Concerning Shareholder Communications, April 12, 2004–Business Roundtable Petition 4-493 ("BRT Petition"); comment letter to Release No. 33-9046, note 7, above, from Altman Group; comment letters to Security Holder Director Nominations, Release No. 34-48626 (Oct. 14, 2003) [68 FR 60784] from Intel and Georgeson Shareholder Communications.

[9] Most commonly submitted to the Commission's Office of Investor Education and Advocacy, these complaints raise issues such as, for example, technical problems with electronic voting platforms offered by proxy service providers and failures by issuers to respond to shareholder complaints about proxy-related matters.

meetings,[10] shareholders should be served by a well-functioning proxy system that promotes efficient and accurate voting. Moreover, recent developments, such as the revisions to Rule 452 of the New York Stock Exchange ("NYSE") limiting the ability of brokers to vote uninstructed shares in uncontested director elections[11] and other corporate governance trends such as increased adoption of a majority voting standard for the election of directors[12] have highlighted the importance of accuracy and accountability in the voting process.

The manner in which proxy materials are distributed and votes are processed and recorded involves a level of complexity not generally understood by those not involved in the process. This complexity stems, in large part, from the nature of share ownership in the United States, in which the vast majority of shares are held through securities intermediaries such as broker-dealers or banks; this structure supports prompt and accurate clearance and settlement of securities transactions, yet adds significant complexity to the proxy voting process.[13] As a result, the proxy system involves a wide array of third-party participants in addition to companies and their shareholders, including brokers, banks, custodians, securities depositories, transfer agents, proxy solicitors, proxy service providers, proxy advisory firms, and vote tabulators.[14] The use of some of these third parties improves efficiencies in processing and distributing proxy materials to shareholders, while at the same time the increased reliance on these third parties—some of which are not directly regulated by federal or state securities regulators—adds complexity to the proxy system and makes it less transparent to shareholders and to issuers. Studies of the proxy systems in other jurisdictions, including the United Kingdom and the European Union, have made similar observations.[15]

---

[10] See Broadridge 2009 Key Statistics and Performance Ratings, *available at* http://www.broadridge.com/investor-communications/us/2009ProxyStats.pdf.

[11] Order Approving Proposed Rule Change, as modified by Amendment No. 4, to Amend NYSE Rule 452 and Corresponding Listed Company Manual Section 402.08 to Eliminate Broker Discretionary Voting for the Election of Directors, Except for Companies Registered under the Investment Company Act of 1940, and to Codify Two Previously Published Interpretations that Do Not Permit Broker Discretionary Voting for Material Amendments to Investment Advisory Contracts with an Investment Company, Release No. 34-60215 (July 1, 2009) [74 FR 33293] (Commission approval of amendments to NYSE Rule 452).

[12] Historically, many corporate directors were elected under a plurality standard, which required only that a candidate receive more votes than other candidates, but not a majority of the votes. Since there ordinarily are not more candidates than seats, the election threshold has historically been low and shareholder participation was less important to electing directors. See American Bar Association Section of Business Law, Report of the Committee on Corporate Laws on Voting by Shareholders for the Election of Directors (Mar. 13, 2006), *available at* http://www.abanet.org/buslaw/committees/CL270000pub/directorvoting/20060313000001.pdf. From 2005 to 2007, however, a majority of companies in the S&P 500 index adopted a voting policy, through bylaw amendments or changes in corporate governance principles, that requires directors who do not receive a majority of votes cast at the meeting in favor of their election to tender their resignation to the board, which resignation the board may or may not accept. See Claudia H. Allen, Study of Majority Voting in Director Elections (Nov. 12,

2007), *available at* http://www.ngelaw.com/files/upload/majoritystudy111207.pdf.

[13] See Final Report of the Securities and Exchange Commission on the Practice of Recording the Ownership of Securities in the Records of the Issuer in Other than the Name of the Beneficial Owner of such Securities Pursuant to Section 12(m) of the Securities Exchange Act of 1934, Dec. 3, 1976 (the "Street Name Study").

[14] The focus of this release is the U.S. proxy system. We recognize, however, that many U.S. persons hold shares in non-U.S. issuers. While this release does not address the processes and procedures followed by participants when non-U.S. issuers distribute proxy-related materials to U.S. persons, we are interested in information about those processes and procedures. We also seek comment about whether we should consider regulatory responses to issues that may arise in that area.

[15] A report from the United Kingdom has characterized its voting process as one in which the chain of accountability is complex, where there is a lack of transparency and where there are a large number of different participants, each of whom may give a different priority to voting. See Review of the impediments to voting UK shares: Report by Paul Myners to the Shareholder Voting Working Group (Jan. 2004) ("Myners Report"). The European Union also has considered issues related to proxy voting and has enacted rules and legislation in response. As a result, the European Union passed a directive on the exercise of certain rights of shareholders in listed companies in July 2007, which covers many of the matters discussed in this release. See Directive 2007/36/EC of the European Parliament and of the Council (July 11, 2007) ("Shareholder Rights Directive"). The Shareholder Rights Directive addresses the issues of record dates,

We begin this concept release with an overview of the U.S. proxy system. We then outline some of the concerns that have been raised regarding the accuracy, reliability, transparency, accountability, and integrity of this system, as well as possible regulatory responses to these concerns. These concerns generally relate to three principal questions:

- Whether we should take steps to enhance the accuracy, transparency, and efficiency of the voting process;

- Whether our rules should be revised to improve shareholder communications and encourage greater shareholder participation; and

- Whether voting power is aligned with economic interest and whether our disclosure requirements provide investors with sufficient information about this issue.

In reviewing the performance of the proxy system, the Commission's staff has recently had numerous discussions with a variety of participants in the proxy voting process, and we appreciate the insights these participants have provided.[16] While we set forth a number of general and specific questions, we welcome comments on any other concerns related to the proxy process that commentators may have, and we specifically invite comment on any costs, burdens or benefits that may result from possible regulatory responses identified in this release. We recognize that the various aspects of the proxy system that we address in this release are interconnected, and that changes to one aspect may affect other aspects, as well as complement or frustrate other potential changes.[17] We encourage the public to consider these relationships when formulating comments. Interested persons are also invited to comment on whether alternative approaches, or a combination of approaches, would better address the concerns raised by the current process.

We are mindful that, while we have recently amended—and are considering amending—a number of our rules that relate to the proxy process, further amendments to those rules or additional guidance about our views on their application may be appropriate to address concerns raised by the application of those rules. Although the discussion in this release generally focuses on the broader proxy system, we remain interested in ways to improve our proxy disclosure, solicitation, and distribution rules. We seek public comment on the concerns about those rules.

II. The Current Proxy Distribution and Voting Process

A fundamental tenet of state corporation law is that shareholders have the right to vote their shares to elect directors and to approve or reject major corporate transactions at shareholder meetings.[18] Under state law, shareholders can appoint a proxy to vote their

---

(Footnote Continued)

transparency, electronic communications, conflicts of interest, financial intermediaries and other parties involved in the proxy voting process.

[16] Beginning in September of 2009, the Commission's staff has met with representatives of the following groups and individuals to discuss issues about the U.S. proxy system: The Altman Group; Broadridge Financial Solutions, Inc.; Broadridge Steering Committee; Council of Institutional Investors ("CII"); Edwards, Angell, Palmer & Dodge; Glass, Lewis & Co.; the Hong Kong Securities & Futures Commission; International Corporate Governance Network ("ICGN"); InvestShare; McKenzie Partners; Mediant Communications; Moxy Vote; National Investor Relations Institute ("NIRI"); Proxy Governance, Inc.; RiskMetrics Group; Professor Edward Rock; Shareholder Communications Coalition; Securities Industry and Financial Markets Association ("SIFMA"); Society of Corporate Secretaries and Governance

Professionals; Sodali; Target Corp.; TIAA-CREF; the U.K. Financial Reporting Council; and Weil, Gotshal & Manges, LLP. The staff has also been in communication with other regulators, including the Federal Reserve, FDIC, Office of the Comptroller of Currency, and Office of Thrift Supervision. Several of the above-listed parties provided written materials to the staff, which we are including in the public comment file for this release. The SEC Investor Advisory Committee has also recommended an inquiry into data-tagging proxy information, as described in Section IV.C below.

[17] For example, the feasibility of establishing a means of vote confirmation may depend on whether and to what extent we continue to allow beneficial owners to object to the disclosure of their identities to issuers. *See* Sections III.B and IV.A, below.

[18] *See, e.g.*, Del. Code Ann. tit. 8, §§ 211 and 212; Model Bus. Corp. Act §§7.01 and 7.21. While voting in the election of directors is largely the exclusive right of

shares on their behalf at shareholder meetings,[19] and the major national securities exchanges generally require their listed companies to solicit proxies for all meetings of shareholders.[20] Because most shareholders do not attend public company shareholder meetings in person, voting occurs almost entirely by the use of proxies that are solicited before the shareholder meeting,[21] thereby resulting in the corporate proxy becoming "the forum for shareholder suffrage."[22] Issuers with a class of securities registered under Section 12 of the Securities Exchange Act of 1934 ("Exchange Act") and issuers that are registered under the Investment Company Act of 1940 ("Investment Company Act") are required to comply with the federal proxy rules in Regulation 14A when soliciting proxies from shareholders.[23]

A. Types of Share Ownership and Voting Rights

The proxy solicitation process starts with the determination of who has the right to receive proxy materials and vote on matters presented to shareholders for a vote at shareholder meetings. The method for making this determination depends on the way the shares are owned. There are two types of security holders in the U.S.—registered owners and beneficial owners.

1. Registered Owners

Registered owners (also known as "record holders") have a direct relationship with the issuer because their ownership of shares is listed on records maintained by the issuer or its transfer agent.[24] State corporation law generally vests the right to vote and the other rights of share ownership in registered owners.[25] Because registered owners have the right to vote, they also have the authority to appoint a proxy to act on their behalf at shareholder meetings.[26]

(Footnote Continued)

stockholders, state law may permit the corporation to grant voting rights to holders of other securities, such as debt. *See, e.g.,* Del. Code Ann. tit. 8, § 221. For a brief review of the rationale for voting by shareholders, see Frank H. Easterbrook and Daniel R. Fischel, The Economic Structure of Corporate Law (1991). We refer to Delaware law frequently because of the large percentage of public companies incorporated under that law. The Delaware Division of Corporations reports that over 50% of U.S. public companies are incorporated in Delaware. We refer to the Model Business Corporation Act as well because the corporate statutes of many states adopt or closely track its provisions.

[19] *See, e.g.,* Del Code Ann. tit. 8, § 212(b); Model Bus. Corp. Act §7.22(b).

[20] *See, e.g.,* NYSE Listed Company Manual § 402.04(a); Nasdaq Listing Rule 5620(b).

[21] Although voting rights in public companies are exercised only at the meeting of shareholders, the votes cast at the meeting are almost entirely by proxy and the voting decisions have been made during the proxy solicitation process.

[22] *Roosevelt v. E.I duPont de Nemours & Co.,* 958 F.2d 416, 422 (D.C. Cir. 1992).

[23] 17 CFR 240.14a-1 *et seq.*; 17 CFR 270.20a-1. However, securities of foreign private issuers are exempt from the proxy rules. *See* 17 CFR 240.3a12-3.

[24] The Uniform Commercial Code ("UCC") defines the term "registered form," as applied to a certificated

security, as a form in which the security certificate specifies a person entitled to the security, and a transfer of the security may be registered on books maintained for that purpose by or on behalf of the issuer, or the security certificate so states. UCC 8-102(a)(13) (1994). Rule 14a-1 under the Exchange Act [17 CFR 240.14a-1] defines the term "record holder" for purposes of Rules 14a-13, 14b-1 and 14b-2 [17 CFR 240.14a-13, 14b-1, 14b-2] to mean any broker, dealer, voting trustee, bank, association or other entity that exercises fiduciary powers which holds securities on behalf of beneficial owners and deposits such securities for safekeeping with another bank. Additionally, the Commission's transfer agent rules refer to registered owners as security holders, which means owners of securities registered on the master security holder file of the issuer. Rule 17Ad-9 under the Exchange Act [17 CFR 240.17Ad-9] defines master security holder file as the official list of individual security holder accounts.

[25] *See, e.g.,* Del. Code Ann. tit. 8, § 219(c); Model Bus. Corp. Act §1.40(21); *but see* Model Bus. Corp. Act §7.23 (permitting corporations to establish procedures by which beneficial owners become entitled to exercise rights, including voting rights, otherwise exercisable by shareholders of record).

[26] *See, e.g.,* Del. Code Ann. tit. 8, § 212(b); Model Bus. Corp. Act §7.22(b).

Registered owners can hold their securities either in certificated form[27] or in electronic (or "book-entry") form through a direct registration system ("DRS"),[28] which enables an investor to have his or her ownership of securities recorded on the books of the issuer without having a physical securities certificate issued.[29] Under DRS, an investor can electronically transfer his or her securities to a broker-dealer to effect a transaction without the risk, expense, or delay associated with the use of securities certificates. Investors holding their securities in DRS retain the rights of registered owners, without having the responsibility of holding and safeguarding securities certificates.

2. Beneficial Owners

The vast majority of investors in shares issued by U.S. companies today are beneficial owners, which means that they hold their securities in book-entry form through a securities intermediary, such as a broker-dealer or bank.[30] This is often referred to as owning in "street name." A beneficial owner does not own the securities directly. Instead, as a customer of the securities intermediary, the beneficial owner has an entitlement to the rights associated with ownership of the securities.[31]

B. The Process of Soliciting Proxies

The following diagram illustrates the flow of proxy materials that typically occurs during a solicitation. The steps illustrated in the diagram and descriptions of the relevant parties are discussed below.

---

[27] A securities certificate evidences that the owner is registered on the books of the issuer as a shareholder. State commercial laws specify rules concerning the transfer of the rights that constitute securities and the establishment of those rights against the issuer and other parties. *See* Official comment to Article 8-101, The American Law Institute and National Conference of Commissioners of Uniform State Laws, Uniform Commercial Code, 1990 Official Text with Comments (West 1991).

[28] For more information about DRS generally, see Securities Transactions Settlement, Release No. 33-8398 (Mar. 11, 2004) [69 FR 12922]. For a detailed description of DRS and the DRS facilities administered by DTC, see Order Granting Accelerated Approval of a Proposed Rule Change Relating to the Procedures to Establish a Direct Registration System, Release No. 34-37931 (Nov. 7, 1996) [61 FR 58600] (order granting approval to establish DRS) and Notice of Filing of Amendment and Order Granting Accelerated Approval of a Proposed Rule Change Relating to Implementation of the Profile Modification System Feature of the Direct Registration System, Release No. 34-41862 (Sept. 10, 1999) [64 FR 51162] (order approving implementation of the Profile Modification System).

[29] DRS is an industry initiative aimed at dematerializing equities in the U.S. market. Dematerialization of securities occurs where there are no paper certificates available, and all transfers of ownership are made through book-entry movements. Immobilization of securities occurs where the underlying certificate is kept in a securities depository (or held in custody for the depository by the issuer's transfer agent) and transfers of ownership are recorded through electronic book-entry movements between the depository's participants' accounts. Securities are partially immobilized (as is the case with most U.S. equity securities traded on an exchange or securities association) when the street name positions are immobilized at the securities depository but certificates are still available to investors directly registered on the issuer's books. Although most options, municipal, government and many debt securities trading in the U.S. markets are currently dematerialized, many equity and some debt securities remain immobilized or partially immobilized at the Depository Trust Company ("DTC"). For more information about DTC, see Section II.B.2.a, below. Most if not all equity securities not on deposit at DTC but trading publicly in the U.S. markets remain fully certificated.

[30] For purposes of Commission rules pertaining to the transfer of certain securities, a "securities intermediary" is defined under Exchange Act Rule 17Ad-20 [17 CFR 240.17Ad-20] as a clearing agency registered under Exchange Act Section 17A [15 USC 78q-1] or a person, including a bank, broker, or dealer, that in the ordinary course of its business maintains securities accounts for others in its capacity as such. The UCC defines the term slightly differently, but for purposes of this release, this distinction is irrelevant. *See* UCC 8-102(a)(14) (1994).

[31] The rights and interests that a customer has against a securities intermediary's property are created by the agreements between the customer and the securities intermediary, as well as by the UCC, as adopted in the relevant jurisdiction. Under the UCC, beneficial owners have a "securities entitlement" to the fungible bulk of securities held by the broker-dealer or bank. An "entitlement holder" is defined as a person identified in the records of a securities intermediary as the person having a security entitlement against the securities intermediary. UCC 8-503 (1994). A securities intermediary is obligated to provide the entitlement holder with all of the economic and governance rights that comprise the financial asset and that the entitlement holder can look only to that intermediary for performance of the obligations. *See generally* UCC 8-501 *et seq.* (1994).

Diagram 1: The Flow of Proxy Materials

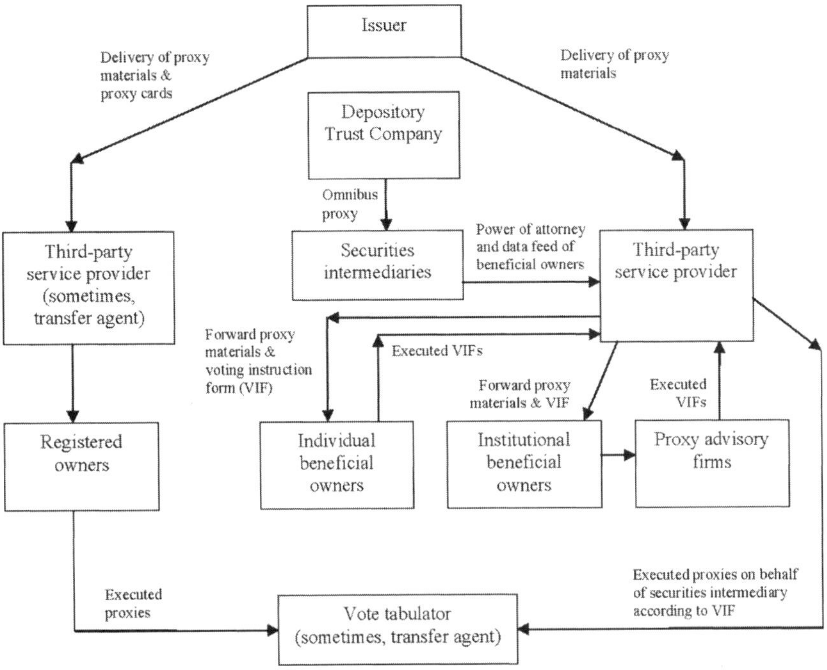

1. Distributing Proxy Materials to Registered Owners

It is a relatively simple process for an issuer to send proxy materials to registered owners because their names and addresses are listed in the issuer's records, which are usually maintained by a transfer agent. As the left side of Diagram 1 illustrates, proxy materials are sent directly from the issuer through its transfer agent or third-party proxy service provider to all registered owners in paper or electronic form.[32] Registered owners execute the proxy card and return it to the issuer's transfer agent or vote tabulator for tabulation.

2. Distributing Proxy Materials to Beneficial Owners

As the right side of Diagram 1 illustrates, the process of distributing proxy materials to beneficial owners is more complicated than it is for registered owners. The indirect system of ownership in the U.S. permits securities intermediaries to hold securities for their customers, and there can be multiple layers of securities intermediaries leading to

---

[32] Commission rules provide, generally, that proxy materials can be provided electronically to shareholders who have affirmatively consented to electronic delivery. *See* Use of Electronic Media for Delivery Purposes, Release No. 33-7233 (Oct. 6, 1995) [60 FR 53458]. In addition, the Commission has adopted the notice and access model that permits issuers to send shareholders a Notice of Internet Availability of Proxy Materials in lieu of the traditional paper packages including the proxy statement, annual report and proxy card. *See* Notice and Access Release, note 2, above. These two concepts work in tandem. Although an issuer electing to send a Notice in lieu of a full package generally would be required to send a paper copy of that Notice, it may send that Notice electronically to a shareholder who has provided an affirmative consent to electronic delivery.

one beneficial owner. This potential for multiple tiers of securities intermediaries presents a number of challenges in the distribution of proxy materials.

a. The Depository Trust Company

In most cases, the chain of ownership for beneficially owned securities of U.S. companies begins with the Depository Trust Company ("DTC"), a registered clearing agency acting as a securities depository.[33] Most large U.S. broker-dealers and banks are DTC participants, meaning that they deposit securities with, and hold those securities through, DTC.[34] DTC's nominee, Cede & Co., appears in an issuer's stock records as the sole registered owner of securities deposited at DTC. DTC holds the deposited securities in "fungible bulk," meaning that there are no specifically identifiable shares directly owned by DTC participants.[35] Rather, each participant owns a pro rata interest in the aggregate number of shares of a particular issuer held at DTC. Correspondingly, each customer of a DTC participant—such as an individual investor—owns a pro rata interest in the shares in which the DTC participant has an interest.

Once an issuer establishes a date for the shareholder meeting and a record date for shareholders entitled to vote on matters presented at the meeting, it sends a formal announcement of these dates to DTC, which DTC forwards to all of its participants.[36] The issuer then requests from DTC a "securities position listing"[37] as of the record date, which identifies the participants having a position in the issuer's securities and the number of securities held by each participant.[38] DTC must promptly respond by providing the issuer with a list of the number of shares in each DTC participant's account as of the record date.[39] The record date securities position listing establishes the number of shares that a participant is entitled to vote through its DTC proxy.[40]

For each shareholder meeting, DTC executes an "omnibus proxy"[41] transferring its right to vote the shares held on deposit to its participants.[42] In this manner, broker-dealer

---

[33] DTC provides custody and book-entry transfer services of securities transactions in the U.S. market involving equities, corporate and municipal debt, money market instruments, American depositary receipts, and exchange-traded funds. In accordance with its rules, DTC accepts deposits of securities from its participants (*i.e.*, broker-dealers and banks), credits those securities to the depositing participants' accounts, and effects book-entry movements of those securities. For more information about DTC, *see http://www.dtcc.com/about/subs/dtc.php.*

[34] Participants in DTC are usually broker-dealers or banks. Currently, there are approximately 400 DTC participants. *See http://www.dtcc.com/customer/directories/dtc/dtc.php.* Other jurisdictions have entities similar to the DTC. For example, Canada has the Clearing and Depository Services Inc., which is its national securities depository and clearing and settlement entity.

[35] *See* UCC 8-503(b) (1994) (a beneficial owner's property interest with respect to shares "is a pro rata property interest in all interests in that financial asset held by the securities intermediary").

[36] NYSE-listed issuers are also required to provide the NYSE with notification of the record and meeting dates. *See* NYSE Listed Company Manual § 401.02.

[37] Exchange Act Rule 17Ad-8 defines a "securities position listing" as a list of those participants in the clearing agency on whose behalf the clearing agency holds the issuer's securities and of the participant's respective positions in such securities as of a specified date. 17 CFR 240.17Ad-8(a).

[38] Pursuant to Exchange Act Rule 17Ad-8, DTC may charge issuers requesting securities position listings a fee designed to recover the reasonable costs of providing the list. 17 CFR 240.17Ad-8(b). An issuer or its agent, generally a transfer agent or authorized third-party service provider, can subscribe to DTC's service that allows the subscriber to obtain the securities position listing once or on a weekly, monthly, or more frequent basis.

[39] Upon request, a registered clearing agency must furnish a securities position listing promptly to each issuer whose securities are held in the name of the clearing agency or its nominee. 17 CFR 140.17Ad-8(b).

[40] In addition to the shares held in its DTC account, some participants may also own additional securities at other securities depositories, through custodians, or in registered form.

[41] Rather than issue each participant a separate proxy to vote its shares, DTC drafts a single proxy (the "omnibus proxy") granting to each of the multiple participants listed in the proxy the right to vote the number of shares attributed to it in the omnibus proxy.

[42] As noted in recent litigation, the execution by DTC of an omnibus proxy is neither automatic nor legally required, but occurs as a matter of common practice. *Kurz v. Holbrook*, 989 A.2d 140, 170 (Del. Ch. 2010), *rev'd on other grounds, Crown EMAK Partners, LLC v. Kurz*, 992 A.2d 377 Del. 2010) ("There does not appear to be any authority governing *when* a DTC omnibus proxy is issued, who should ask for it, or what event triggers it. The parties tell me that

and bank participants in DTC obtain the right to vote directly the shares that they hold through DTC.

b. Securities Intermediaries: Broker-Dealers and Banks

Once the issuer identifies the DTC participants holding positions in its securities, it is required to send a search card[43] to each of those participants, as well as other securities intermediaries that are registered owners, to determine whether they are holding shares for beneficial owners and, if so, the number of sets of proxy packages needed to be forwarded to those beneficial owners. This process may involve multiple tiers of securities intermediaries holding securities on behalf of other securities intermediaries, with search cards distributed to each securities intermediary in the chain of ownership.

Commission rules require broker-dealers to respond to the issuer within seven business days with the approximate number of customers of the broker-dealer who are beneficial owners of the issuer's securities.[44] The Commission's rules also require banks to follow a similar process except that banks must respond to the issuer within one business day with the names and addresses of all respondent banks[45] and must respond within seven business days with the approximate number of customers of the bank who are beneficial owners of shares.[46]

Once the search card process is complete, the issuer should know the approximate number of beneficial owners owning shares through each securities intermediary. The issuer must then provide the securities intermediary, or its third-party proxy service provider, with copies of its proxy materials (including, if applicable, a Notice of Internet Availability of Proxy Materials) for forwarding to those beneficial owners. The securities intermediary must forward these proxy materials to beneficial owners no later than five business days after receiving such materials.[47] Securities intermediaries are entitled to reasonable reimbursement for their costs in forwarding these materials.[48]

Instead of receiving and executing a proxy card (as registered owners receive and do), the beneficial owner receives a "voting instruction form" or "VIF" from the securities intermediary, which permits the beneficial owner to instruct the securities intermediary how to vote the beneficially owned shares. Although the VIF does not give the beneficial owner the right to attend the meeting, a beneficial owner typically can attend the meeting by requesting the appropriate documentation from the securities intermediary.

(Footnote Continued)

DTC has no written policies or procedures on the matter.").

[43] The search card must request: (1) the number of beneficial owners; (2) the number of proxy soliciting materials and annual reports needed for forwarding by the intermediaries to their beneficial owner customers; and (3) the name and address of any agent appointed by the bank or broker-dealer to process a request for a list of beneficial owners. The search card must be sent out at least 20 business days prior to the record date unless impracticable, in which case it must be sent as many days before the record date as practicable. 17 CFR 240.14a-13(a).

[44] 17 CFR 240.14b-1(b)(1).

[45] A respondent bank is a bank that holds securities through another bank that is the record holder of those securities. See Facilitating Shareholder Communications, Release No. 34-23276 (May 29, 1986) [51 FR 20504].

[46] 17 CFR 240.14b-2(b)(1) and 17 CFR 240.14b-2(b)(2). Banks are required to execute omnibus proxies in favor of respondent banks. 17 CFR 240.14b-2(b)(2).

[47] 17 CFR 240.14b-1(b)(2) and 17 CFR 240.14b-2(b)(3). The exchanges have rules that regulate the process and procedures by which member firms must transmit proxy materials to beneficial owners, collect voting instructions from beneficial owners, and vote shares held in the member firm's name. See, e.g., NYSE Rules 450 through 460 and FINRA Rule 2251.

[48] 17 CFR 240.14a-13(a)(5). In addition, most of the exchanges have rules specifying the maximum rates that member firms may charge listed issuers as reasonable reimbursement. For example, the NYSE rule includes a schedule of "fair and reasonable rates of reimbursement" of member broker-dealers for their out-of-pocket expenses, including reasonable clerical expenses, incurred in connection with issuers' proxy solicitations of beneficial owners. NYSE Rule 465 Supplemental Material. The other exchanges have similar rules. See the discussion on proxy distribution fees in Section III.D below.

C. Proxy Voting Process

Once the proxy materials have been distributed to the registered owners and beneficial owners of the securities, the means by which shareholders vote their shares differs. As Diagram 1 illustrates, registered owners execute the proxy card and return it to the vote tabulator, either by mail, by phone, or through the Internet. Beneficial owners, on the other hand, indicate their voting instructions on the VIF and return it to the securities intermediary or its proxy service provider, either by mail, by phone, or through the Internet.[49] The securities intermediary, or its proxy service provider, tallies the voting instructions that it receives from its customers. As discussed in further detail in Section IV.A of this release, the securities intermediary, or its proxy service provider, then executes and submits to the vote tabulator a proxy card for all securities held by the securities intermediary's customers.[50]

In certain situations, a broker-dealer may use its discretion to vote shares if it does not receive instructions from the beneficial owner of the shares. Historically, broker-dealers were generally permitted to vote shares on uncontested matters, including uncontested director elections, without instructions from the beneficial owner.[51] The NYSE recently revised this rule to prohibit broker-dealers from voting uninstructed shares with regard to any election of directors.[52]

D. The Roles of Third Parties in the Proxy Process

Issuers, securities intermediaries, and shareholders often retain third parties to perform a number of proxy-related functions, including forwarding proxy materials, collecting voting instructions, voting shares, soliciting proxies, tabulating proxies, and analyzing proxy issues.

1. Transfer Agents

Issuers are required to maintain a record of security holders for state law purposes[53] and often hire a transfer agent[54] to maintain that record.[55] Transfer agents, as agents of

---

[49] Beneficial owners' voting instructions submitted by telephone account for a very small percentage of votes received by proxy service providers; for the shares of most beneficial owners who do not vote through a proprietary service for institutional investors, voting instructions are conveyed by paper or via the Internet, in approximately the same proportion. See Broadridge 2009 Key Statistics and Performance Ratings, note 10, above.

[50] As noted above, the securities intermediary receives the right to execute a proxy through the omnibus proxy executed in its favor by DTC and the other securities intermediaries in the chain of ownership through which it holds the securities. Although Rule 14b-2(b)(3) [17 CFR 240.14b-2(b)(3)] explicitly permits a bank to execute a proxy in favor of its beneficial owners, and nothing in our rules prohibits a broker-dealer from doing so, it is our understanding that these intermediaries usually solicit voting instructions from their beneficial owner and execute proxies on behalf of their beneficial owners rather than executing proxies that delegate their voting authority to those beneficial owners. Beneficial owners may, however, request a proxy and attend the shareholder meeting. It is our understanding that both banks and broker-dealers will issue a proxy that the beneficial owner may use to attend a meeting if requested to do so.

[51] See NYSE Rule 452.

[52] NYSE Rule 452 and NYSE Listed Issuer Manual § 402.08(B). This prohibition does not apply to issuers registered under the Investment Company Act.

[53] E.g., Del. Code Ann. tit. 8, § 219(a); Model Bus. Corp. Act §16.01(c).

[54] Section 3(a)(25) of the Exchange Act defines a "transfer agent" as any person who engages on behalf of an issuer of securities or on behalf of itself as an issuer of securities in (1) countersigning such securities upon issuance, (2) monitoring the issuance of such securities with a view to preventing unauthorized issuance, (3) registering the transfer of securities, (4) exchanging or converting such securities, or (5) transferring record ownership of securities by bookkeeping entry without the physical issuance of securities certificates. For more information about the role of transfer agents, see www.stai.org.

[55] Exchange Act Rules 17Ad-6, 17Ad-7, 17Ad-9, 17Ad-10, and 17Ad-11 govern how transfer agents acting for issuers of securities registered under Section 12 of the Exchange Act (or that would have to be registered but for the exemption under Section 12(g)(2)(b)(i) and (ii) of the Exchange Act) must maintain certain records of the issuer, including, but not limited to, the official record of ownership (i.e., the "masterfile") and the official record of the number of securities issued and outstanding (i.e., the "control book" or the "registrar"). These rules do not address the distribution of issuer communications, including proxy materials, or the remittance of proxies or voting

the issuer, are obliged to confirm to a vote tabulator (if the transfer agent does not itself perform the tabulation function) matters such as the amount of shares outstanding, as well as the identity and holdings of registered owners entitled to vote. Transfer agents are required to register with the Commission, which inspects and currently regulates some of their functions.[56]

2. Proxy Service Providers

To facilitate the proxy material distribution and voting process for beneficial owners, securities intermediaries typically retain a proxy service provider to perform a number of processing functions, including forwarding the proxy materials by mail or electronically and collecting voting instructions.[57] To enable the proxy service provider to perform these functions, the securities intermediary gives the service provider an electronic data feed of a list of beneficial owners and the number of shares held by each beneficial owner on the record date. The proxy service provider, on behalf of the intermediary, then requests the appropriate number of proxy material sets from the issuer for delivery to the beneficial owners. Upon receipt of the packages, the proxy service provider, on behalf of the intermediary, mails either the proxy materials with a VIF, or a Notice of Internet Availability of Proxy Materials,[58] to beneficial owners. Although we do not directly regulate such proxy service providers, our regulations governing the proxy process-related obligations of securities intermediaries apply to the way in which proxy service providers perform their services because they act as agents for, and on behalf of, those intermediaries and typically vote proxies on behalf of those intermediaries pursuant to a power of attorney.

3. Proxy Solicitors

Issuers sometimes hire third-party proxy solicitors to identify beneficial owners holding large amounts of the issuers' securities and to telephone shareholders to encourage them to vote their proxies consistent with the recommendations of management. This often occurs when there is a contested election of directors, and issuer's management and other persons are competing for proxy authority to vote securities in the election (commonly referred to as a "proxy contest"). In addition, an issuer may hire a proxy solicitor in uncontested situations when voting returns are expected to be insufficient to meet state quorum requirements or when an important matter is being considered. Issuers and other soliciting persons are required to disclose the use of such services and estimated costs for such services in their proxy statements.[59]

4. Vote Tabulators

Under many state statutes, an issuer must appoint a vote tabulator (sometimes called "inspectors of elections" or "proxy tabulators") to collect and tabulate the proxy votes

---

(Footnote Continued)

instructions. To a lesser extent, the UCC, as adopted by states, also governs certain aspects of transfer agent activity relating to rights of issuers, shareholders, securities intermediaries, and those holding through securities intermediaries, some of which relate to the right to vote. The application of the UCC in this context is beyond the scope of this release.

[56] Persons acting as transfer agents for any security registered under Section 12 of the Exchange Act or which would be required to be registered except for the exemption from registration provided by subsection (g) (2)(B) or (g)(2)(G) of Section 12 must register with the Commission (or, for transfer agents that are banks, with their appropriate regulatory agency) and pursuant to Section 17A of the Exchange Act must comply with

Commission rules and regulations. 15 U.S.C. 78q-1(c)(1) and (d)(1).

[57] A single proxy service provider, Broadridge Financial Services, Inc. ("Broadridge"), states that it currently handles over 98% of the U.S. market for such proxy vote processing services. *See http://www .broadridge.com/investor-communications/us/institutions/ proxy-disclosure.asp.*

[58] A Notice is sent pursuant to provisions in Rule 14a-16. 17 CFR 240.14a-16.

[59] Item 4 of 17 CFR 240.14a-101. If similar services are performed by employees of the issuer, however, the estimated costs of such services need to be disclosed only if the employees are specially engaged for the solicitation.

as well as votes submitted by shareholders in person at a meeting.[60] We understand that often the issuer's transfer agent will act as the vote tabulator because most major transfer agents have the infrastructure to communicate with registered holders, proxy service providers, and securities intermediaries, while also being able to reconcile the identity of voters that are registered owners and the number of votes to the issuer's records. However, sometimes the issuer will hire an independent third party to perform this function, often to certify important votes. The vote tabulator is ultimately responsible for determining that the correct number of votes has been submitted by each registered owner.[61] In addition, proxies submitted by securities intermediaries that are not registered owners, but have been granted direct voting rights through DTC's omnibus proxy, are reconciled with DTC's securities position listing. Although the Commission does regulate transfer agents (which often serve as vote tabulators) in their roles as transfer agents, the Commission does not currently regulate vote tabulators or the function of tabulating proxies by transfer agents.

5. Proxy Advisory Firms

Institutional investors typically own securities positions in a large number of issuers. Therefore, they are presented annually with the opportunity to vote on many matters and often must exercise fiduciary responsibility in voting.[62] Some institutional investors may retain an investment adviser to manage their investments, and may also delegate proxy voting authority to that adviser. To assist them in their voting decisions, investment advisers (or institutional investors if they retain voting authority) frequently hire proxy advisory firms to provide analysis and voting recommendations on matters appearing on the proxy. In some cases, proxy advisory firms are given authority to execute proxies or voting instructions on behalf of their client. Some proxy advisory firms also provide consulting services to issuers on corporate governance or executive compensation matters, such as helping to develop an executive compensation proposal to be submitted for shareholder approval. Some proxy advisory firms may also qualitatively rate or score issuers, based on judgments about the issuer's governance structure, policies, and practices. As discussed in more detail elsewhere in this release, some of the activities of a proxy advisory firm can constitute a solicitation, which is governed by our proxy rules.[63] Some, but not all, proxy advisory firms operating in our markets are currently registered with us as investment advisers.[64]

III. Accuracy, Transparency, and Efficiency of the Voting Process

Investor and issuer interests may be undermined when perceived defects in the proxy system—or uncertainties about whether there are any such defects—are believed to impair its accuracy, transparency, and cost-efficiency. Because even the perception of such defects can lead to lack of confidence in the proxy process, we seek to explore concerns that have been expressed about the accuracy, transparency, and efficiency of that process and ways in which those concerns might be addressed.

A. Over-Voting and Under-Voting

On occasion, vote tabulators (including transfer agents acting in that capacity) receive votes from a securities intermediary that exceed the number of shares that the securities intermediary is entitled to vote. The extent to which such votes are accepted depends on instructions from the issuer, state law, and the vote tabulator's internal policies. For example, it is our understanding that some vote tabulators accept votes from a DTC participant on a "first-in" basis up to the aggregate amount indicated in DTC's records

---

[60] *See, e.g.,* Del. Code Ann. tit. 8, §231; Model Bus. Corp. Act §7.29.

[61] *Id.* As noted above, transfer agents, who already possess the list of record owners, often tabulate the vote, so they possess the necessary information to make this determination. It is our understanding that, when the vote tabulator is an entity other than the transfer

agent, the issuer or its transfer agent typically will provide the vote tabulator with the list of record owners to enable the vote tabulator to make this determination.

[62] *See* Section V.A.1, below.

[63] *Id.*

[64] *Id.*

—that is, once the votes cast by the participant exceed the number of positions indicated on the securities position listing, the vote tabulator will refuse to accept any votes subsequently remitted. Conversely, other vote tabulators, we understand, refuse to accept any votes from a securities intermediary if the aggregate number of votes submitted exceeds the vote tabulator's records for that intermediary.

In an attempt to address issuers' concerns about the potential for over-voting, securities intermediaries and their service providers have implemented systems that compare the number of votes submitted by a securities intermediary to its ownership positions as reflected in DTC's records and notify that securities intermediary when it has submitted votes in excess of its ownership positions. The securities intermediary may then adjust its vote to reflect the correct number of votes before the service provider submits that vote to the vote tabulator.[65] The corrected information is then sent to the vote tabulator. The means by which securities intermediaries reconcile these differences has raised some concern regarding the accuracy of the vote, including whether the votes are being allocated to the beneficial owners in the correct amounts.

1. Imbalances in Broker Votes

For securities held at DTC, a DTC participant may vote only the number of securities held by that participant in its DTC account on the record date for a shareholder meeting. Sometimes the number of securities of a particular issuer held in the DTC participant's account will be less than the number of securities that the DTC participant has credited in its own books and records to its customers' accounts. Although there may be many reasons why the number of securities held by a broker-dealer at DTC does not match the total number of securities credited to the broker-dealer's customers' accounts, as discussed in more detail below, this situation principally arises in connection with lending transactions and "fails to deliver"[66] in the clearance and settlement system.

Because of the way broker-dealers track securities lending transactions,[67] if all of a broker-dealer's customers owning a particular issuer's securities actually voted, the broker-dealer may receive voting instructions for more securities than it is entitled to vote. Moreover, the existing clearance and settlement system was not designed to assign particular shares of a security to a particular investor, due to netting and holding securities in fungible bulk.[68] Thus, it is not currently possible to match a particular investor's vote to a specific securities position held at a securities depository. When a broker-dealer has fewer positions or shares reflected on the securities position listing[69] than it has reflected on its books and records, the broker-dealer must determine if and how it should allocate the votes it has among its customer and proprietary accounts and then reconcile the actual voting instructions it receives with the number of securities the broker-dealer is permitted to vote with the issuer. Depending on a variety of factors, this process can lead to over-voting or under-voting by beneficial owners.

a. Securities Lending

When a customer purchases shares on margin, a portion of the securities in the customer's account may be used to collateralize the margin loan.[70] As part of the customer's margin agreement, the customer typically agrees to allow the broker-dealer to use those securities to raise money to fund the margin loan. Consequently, broker-dealers may lend out customers' margin securities. In addition, broker-dealers may enter

---

[65] SIFMA and individual broker-dealers have suggested several different methodologies as to how this may be accomplished, but we do not believe there is consensus among the industry participants or a standard operating procedure currently in place.

[66] See Section III.A.1.b, below.

[67] We understand that because securities are held in fungible bulk, broker-dealers typically do not allocate loaned securities to a particular account.

[68] See Section IV.A.1, below.

[69] See Section I.B.2.a, above, for a discussion of securities position listings.

[70] A broker-dealer must maintain possession and control of all fully-paid and excess margin securities. 17 CFR 240.15c3-3(b)(1).

into stock loan arrangements with investors (typically institutional investors or other broker-dealers) whereby the broker-dealer borrows the investors' fully-paid securities.[71]

Stock loan agreements typically transfer to the borrower the right to vote the borrowed securities.[72] Thus, for example, when an institutional investor, such as a fund, lends its portfolio securities to a borrower, the right to vote those securities also transfers to the borrower.[73] As a result, the institutional investor that lends its portfolio securities generally loses its ability to vote those securities, unless and until the loan is terminated and the securities are returned before the record date in question.[74]

Even though a broker-dealer has the ability to lend its customers' margin securities pursuant to a stock loan agreement, because shares are held in fungible bulk, it may not be practical to inform a customer when an actual loan has been made and it may be unclear which lending investor has lost the right to vote. Therefore, a customer may expect to vote all of its securities because it does not necessarily know whether its securities have in fact been loaned. If the lending broker-dealer does not allocate a certain number of shares to a lending investor as having been borrowed, but instead sends a VIF indicating that the lending investor has the right to vote all of the securities credited to its account, including the loaned margin securities, both the lending and borrowing broker-dealers may submit voting instructions from two customers for a single share, which may give rise to an over-voting situation.

b. Fails to Deliver

An imbalance between a securities intermediary's position reflected on the securities position listing and the position reflected in its own books and records may also occur because of fails to deliver in the clearance and settlement system.[75] Every day the NSCC, a registered clearing agency, nets each of its members' trades to a single buy or sell obligation for each issue traded.[76] Because NSCC acts as a central counterparty for its members' trades, its members are obligated to deliver securities to, and entitled to receive securities from, NSCC at settlement, and not to or from other broker-dealers. Although the delivery of securities usually occurs as expected on the settlement date, there are occasions when broker-dealers fail to make timely delivery, often for reasons outside of their control.[77]

---

[71] When borrowing fully-paid securities, Exchange Act Rule 15c3-3(b)(3) requires, among other things, that a broker-dealer enter into a separate written agreement with the customer and provide the customer with a schedule of the securities actually borrowed as well as the collateral provided to the customer. 17 CFR 240.15c3-3(b)(3).

[72] See Master Securities Lending Agreement at 6, available at www.sifma.org/services/stdforms/pdf/master_sec_loan.pdf.

[73] If an institutional lender lends out portfolio securities after the record date for a particular shareholder vote, the lender would normally retain the right to vote the proxies for that particular shareholder vote.

[74] If the lending broker-dealer attempts to recall the loan, the borrowing broker-dealer may not be able to return the securities in a timely manner because, among other things, it may have reloaned or sold the security to another party and is unable to obtain shares to return to the lending broker-dealer.

[75] Fails to deliver in all equity securities have declined significantly since the adoption of Interim Final Temporary Rule 204T in October 2008. See Amendments to Regulation SHO, Release No. 34-58773 (Oct. 14, 2008) [73 FR 61706]. See also Memorandum from the Staff Re: Impact of Recent SHO Rule Changes on Fails to Deliver, Nov. 4, 2009,

available at http://www.sec.gov/spotlight/shortsales/oeamemo110409.pdf (stating, among other things, that the average daily number of aggregate fails to deliver for all securities decreased from 2.21 billion to 0.25 billion for a total decline of 88.5% when comparing a pre-Rule to post-Rule period); Memorandum from the Staff Re: Impact of Recent SHO Rule Changes on Fails to Deliver, Nov. 26, 2008, available at http://www.sec.gov/comments/s7-30-08/s73008-37.pdf; Memorandum from the Staff Re: Impact of Recent SHO Rule Changes on Fails to Deliver, Mar. 20, 2009, available at http://www.sec.gov/comments/s7-30-08/s73008-107.pdf.

[76] NSCC nets securities in its "Continuous Net Settlement" system pursuant to rules and procedures approved by the Commission. For more information on NSCC's rules and procedures, see www.dtcc.com/legal/rules_proc/nscc_rules.pdf. See Section IV.A.1, below, for additional information about the role of NSCC.

[77] For example, broker-dealers may fail to deliver securities because of: (1) delays by customers delivering to the broker-dealer the shares being sold; (2) a broker-dealer's inability to purchase or borrow shares needed for settlement; or (3) a broker-dealer's inability to obtain transfer of title of securities in time for settlement. For more information on fails to deliver in the U.S. clearance and settlement system, see Short Sales,

Pursuant to NSCC rules, if an NSCC broker-dealer member "fails to deliver" the securities it owes to NSCC on the settlement date, NSCC will allocate this fail to one of many contra-side broker-dealers due to receive securities without trying to attribute the fail to the specific broker-dealer that originally traded with the broker-dealer that failed to deliver.[78] The broker-dealer to which the fail is allocated will not receive the securities and will not be credited with this position at DTC until delivery is actually made.

Even though the broker-dealer has not actually received the securities, the broker-dealer usually will credit its customers' accounts with the purchased securities on settlement date. If the broker-dealer's fail-to-receive position continues through the record date for a corporate election, DTC may not yet recognize the broker-dealer's entitlement to vote this position. As with loaned securities, the broker-dealer may still try to allocate votes to all of its customers that its records reflect as owning those securities, even though DTC has not credited the broker's account with those securities or with the corresponding right to vote those securities through DTC.

2. Current Reconciliation and Allocation Methodologies Used by Broker-Dealers to Address Imbalances

Because the ownership of individual shares held beneficially is not tracked in the U.S. clearance and settlement system, when imbalances occur, broker-dealers must decide which of their customers will be permitted to vote and how many shares each customer will be permitted to vote. Neither our rules nor SRO rules currently mandate that a reconciliation be performed, or the use of a particular reconciliation or allocation methodology. Broker-dealers have developed a number of different approaches as to how votes are "allocated" among customer accounts.[79] We understand that these approaches are often influenced by whether the broker-dealers' customers are primarily retail or institutional investors.

Most broker-dealers have adopted a reconciliation method to balance the aggregate number of shares they are entitled to vote with the aggregate number of shares credited to customer and proprietary accounts.[80] The primary reconciliation methods are: (1) pre-mailing reconciliation ("pre-reconciliation"); (2) post-mailing reconciliation ("post-reconciliation"); and (3) a hybrid form of the pre-reconciliation and post-reconciliation methods.[81] These methods are described in more detail below. If the broker-dealer finds that it is holding fewer shares at DTC than it has credited to customer and proprietary accounts, it may choose to give up its own votes, as represented by shares credited to its proprietary accounts, by allocating some or all of those votes to its customers, or it may choose to allocate to its customers only the voting rights attributable to customer accounts.

a. Pre-Reconciliation Method

A broker-dealer using the pre-reconciliation method compares the number of shares it holds in aggregate at DTC and elsewhere with its aggregate customer account position

---

(Footnote Continued)

Release No. 34-50103 (July 28, 2004) [69 FR 48008] and Amendments to Regulation SHO, Release No. 34-60388 (July 27, 2009) [74 FR 38266].

[78] If a broker-dealer fails to deliver securities to NSCC, NSCC allocates this fail to a broker-dealer member that is due to receive the securities.

[79] For more information on proxy processing and broker-dealer's reconciliation and allocation processes, see "Briefing Paper: Roundtable on Proxy Voting Mechanics," (May 24, 2007), *available at* http://www.sec.gov/spotlight/proxyprocess/proxyvotingbrief.htm ("Roundtable Briefing Paper"), or "Unofficial Transcript of the Roundtable Discussion on Proxy Voting Mechanics," (May 24, 2007), *available at* http://www.sec.gov/news/openmeetings/2007/openmtg_trans052407.pdf ("Roundtable Transcript"). The term "allocation" refers to the process by which a broker-dealer determines which of its customers will be allowed to vote and how many shares will be allotted to each of those customers.

[80] Not all broker-dealers have developed policies and procedures to address the reconciliation and allocation of votes among their customers because historically broker-dealers have usually had enough shares on deposit at DTC to provide a vote to all customers wanting to vote.

[81] Roundtable Transcript, note 79, above.

before it sends VIFs to its customers.[82] If the aggregate number of shares it holds is less than the number of shares the broker-dealer has credited to its customer accounts, then the broker-dealer will determine which of its customers will be permitted to vote and how many votes will be allocated to each of those customers. Broker-dealers using the pre-reconciliation method request voting instructions from their customers with respect to only those customer positions to which votes have been allocated. We understand that most broker-dealers give customers with fully-paid securities and excess margin securities first priority in the distribution of votes. It is also our understanding that broker-dealers using the pre-reconciliation method tend to have more institutional customers than retail customers.[83]

Broker-dealers using the pre-reconciliation method have indicated that this method ensures that the votes customers cast will be counted.[84] On the other hand, given that some broker-dealers have estimated that only 20% to 30% of their retail customers usually vote, some believe that pre-reconciliation may result in an "under-vote" because investors allocated the ability to vote may not do so, and other investors who do vote may be allocated a number of votes fewer than the number of shares they beneficially own. In addition, some broker-dealers have indicated that the pre-reconciliation method is more expensive than the post-reconciliation method because post-reconciliation only needs to be performed when a broker-dealer receives voting instructions in excess of the number of shares that it holds.

b. Post-Reconciliation Method

A broker-dealer using the post-reconciliation method compares its aggregate position at DTC and elsewhere[85] with its actual aggregate customer account position only after receiving VIFs from its customers. Broker-dealers using the post-reconciliation method request voting instructions from their customers with respect to all shares credited to their customer accounts, including for those shares that may have been purchased on margin, loaned to another entity, or not received because of a fail to deliver. We understand that broker-dealers using the post-reconciliation method tend to have primarily retail customers rather than institutional customers.[86]

In the event that a broker-dealer receives voting instructions from its customers in excess of its aggregate securities position, the broker-dealer adjusts its vote count prior to casting its vote with the issuer. The manner in which the adjustment is made varies among broker-dealers. Some firms simply reduce the number of proprietary position votes cast. Others allocate fewer votes to customers with securities purchased on margin or on loan.

Because of the low level of participation by retail voters, some of the brokerdealers using the post-reconciliation method have indicated to the Commission that the number of over-vote situations is not a significant problem and can be addressed in a number of ways, including, but not limited to, the broker-dealer using its proprietary positions to redress any imbalance. The costs associated with the post-reconciliation method are generally considered to be less than those associated with the pre-reconciliation method because the broker-dealer does not have to go through the costly process of allocating votes among customers unless its customers remit VIFs for more shares than the broker-dealer is entitled to vote in the aggregate.

c. Hybrid Reconciliation Methods

Some broker-dealers have developed hybrid reconciliation methods that use aspects of both pre- and post-reconciliation methods. For example, in one hybrid reconciliation

---

[82] *Id.*
[83] *Id.*
[84] *Id.*
[85] The aggregate number of shares the broker-dealer is entitled to vote may constitute more than just its

position on deposit at DTC. For example, the broker-dealer may have additional securities on deposit at a foreign depository or in certificated form.
[86] Roundtable Transcript, note 79, above.

method, a broker-dealer will allocate votes to all of its customers with fully-paid securities but will also allow each margin account customer to instruct the broker-dealer that it would like to vote its shares. The broker-dealer will allocate any shares not needed to cover fully-paid account holders to those margin customers who indicated they wanted to vote, thereby giving these margin customers priority over other margin customers.[87]

3. Potential Regulatory Responses

Broker-dealers have indicated to the Commission staff that most broker-dealers select an allocation and reconciliation method that best accommodates their particular customer base and best advances the firm's particular business strategy. For example, those firms focusing on retail customers generally will have more customer accounts owning smaller amounts of securities and casting relatively few votes and, as a result, may prefer the post-reconciliation method over the pre-reconciliation method.

The customers of a broker-dealer may not be aware of the allocation and reconciliation method used by the firm. We are interested in receiving views on whether it would be helpful to investors if broker-dealers publicly disclosed the allocation and reconciliation method used by the firm during each proxy season, as well as the likely effect of that method on whether the customers' voting instructions would actually be reflected in the broker-dealer's proxy sent to the vote tabulator. Such disclosure could be in writing and provided to customers upon opening an account and on an annual basis, and made available to the general public on the broker-dealer's Web site. This disclosure could help investors to decide if a particular broker-dealer's method suits their investment goals. Alternatively, we are interested in receiving views on whether it would be beneficial to investors if broker-dealers were required to use a particular reconciliation method.

Given the lack of empirical data on whether over-voting or under-voting is occurring and if so, to what extent, we also would like to receive views on whether investors, issuers, and the proxy system overall would benefit from having additional data from proxy participants regarding over-voting and under-voting to determine whether further regulatory action should be considered. This data would allow us to determine the scope of the problem, if any, and give us detailed information that would further assist us in determining whether current regulations are effective or additional regulation is appropriate. Such information may also indicate if one particular method is working better for investors and the market than other methods.

4. Request for Comment

- What are the advantages or disadvantages of the various methods of allocation or reconciliation currently used by securities intermediaries and the effectiveness of such methods?

- Is there any evidence, statistical, anecdotal or otherwise, of material over-voting or under-voting, and if so, what is the size and impact of over-voting or under-voting? For example, is there any evidence that over-voting or under-voting has determined the outcome of a vote or materially changed the voting results?

- Are there any concerns caused by over-voting or under-voting that are not described above? Are there particular concerns regarding the impact of either over-voting or under-voting with respect to specific types of voting decisions, such as merger transactions, the election of directors where a majority vote is required, or shareholder advisory votes regarding executive compensation? What, if any, alternatives should we consider to the current system, and what would be the costs and benefits of any alternative process?

---

[87] *Id.*

- Would requiring broker-dealers to disclose their allocation and reconciliation process adequately address the concerns related to over-voting and under-voting by beneficial owners?

- Would information about vote allocation and reconciliation methods be helpful to investors or adequately address any concerns related to those processes?

- Would a particular type of vote allocation and reconciliation method better protect investors' interests?

- Do the varying methods of vote allocation affect the potential to audit votes cast by beneficial holders?

- Should investors who have fully paid for their securities be allocated voting rights over those who purchased the securities on margin? Should beneficial holders be allocated voting rights over broker-dealer proprietary accounts?

- Should brokers be required to disclose the effect of share lending programs on the ability of retail investors to cast votes?

- Does the current system of settlement and clearance of securities transactions in the U.S. create any problems or inefficiencies in the proxy process in regard to matters other than over-voting or under-voting? If so, what are they, and what steps should we consider in order to address them?

B. Vote Confirmation

1. Background

A number of market participants, including both individual and institutional investors, have raised concerns regarding the inability to confirm whether an investor's shares have been voted in accordance with the investor's instructions. As discussed more fully in Section II, beneficial owners cast their votes through a securities intermediary, which, in turn, uses a proxy service provider to collect and send the votes to the vote tabulator.[88] Beneficial owners, particularly institutional investors, often want or need to confirm that their votes have been timely received by the vote tabulator and accurately recorded. Similarly, securities intermediaries want to be able to confirm to their customers that their votes have been timely received and accurately recorded. Issuers also want to be able to confirm that the votes that they receive from securities intermediaries on behalf of beneficial owners properly reflect the votes of those beneficial owners. We understand that, on occasion, errors have been made when a third party fails to timely submit votes on behalf of its clients.[89]

The inability to confirm voting information is caused in part because no one individual participant in the voting process—neither issuers, transfer agents, vote tabulators, securities intermediaries, nor third party proxy service providers—possesses all of the information necessary to confirm whether a particular beneficial owner's vote has been timely received and accurately recorded. A number of market participants contend that some proxy service providers, transfer agents, or vote tabulators are unwilling or unable to share voting information with each other or with investors and securities intermediaries. There are currently no legal or regulatory requirements that compel these entities to share information with each other in order to allow for vote confirmations.

---

[88] Some securities intermediaries may not have sufficient shares on deposit at DTC to allocate a vote to every share position credited to every customer's account. In those cases, the securities intermediary may have to allocate a specific number of votes to some customers that is fewer than the number of shares credited to those customers' accounts. See Section III.A, above, for a more in-depth discussion of why and how securities intermediaries reconcile and allocate votes to their customers.

[89] *See, e.g.*, Adam Jones, "Riddle of the Missing Unilever Votes Solved," Financial Times, Aug. 15, 2003; "Mum on a Recount," Pensions & Investments, Aug. 10, 2009, *available at* http://www.pionline.com/article/20090810/PRINTSUB/308109996; Meagan Thompson-Mann, Policy Briefing No. 3—Voting Integrity: Practices for Investors and the Global Proxy Advisory Industry, The Millstein Center for Corporate Governance and Performance, Mar. 2, 2009, at 10-11 ("Thompson-Mann Policy Briefing").

The inability to confirm that votes have been timely received and accurately recorded creates uncertainty regarding the accuracy and integrity of votes cast at shareholder meetings. At a time when votes on matters presented to shareholders are increasingly meaningful and consequential to all shareholders, this lack of transparency could potentially impair confidence in the proxy system.[90] Because of the inability to ascertain the integrity of the votes cast by beneficial owners, concerns have been raised by investors that it may be difficult to assess the accuracy of the current proxy system as a whole.

2. Potential Regulatory Responses

In the Commission's view, both record owners and beneficial owners should be able to confirm that the votes they cast have been timely received and accurately recorded and included in the tabulation of votes, and issuers should be able to confirm that the votes that they receive from securities intermediaries/proxy advisory firms/proxy service providers on behalf of beneficial owners properly reflect the votes of those beneficial owners. We understand that there may be a number of operational and legal complexities with any proposed solution and that the costs and benefits associated with any options should be carefully weighed.

One possible solution may be for all participants in the voting chain to grant to issuers, or their transfer agents or vote tabulators, access to certain information relating to voting records, for the limited purpose of enabling a shareholder or securities intermediary to confirm how a particular shareholder's shares were voted. To protect the identities of objecting beneficial owners from issuers, a system could assign each beneficial owner a unique identifying code, which could then be used to create an audit trail from beneficial owner to proxy service provider to transfer agent/vote tabulator. Issuers (or their agents, such as transfer agents or vote tabulators) would, in turn, confirm to record owners, beneficial owners, and securities intermediaries upon request that any particular votes cast by them or on their behalf have been received and voted as instructed. This process could be fully automated such that a vote confirmation could be provided by the issuer (or its agent) to the record owner or, in the case of beneficial owners, to the securities intermediary or proxy service provider and sent by email to the beneficial owner.

Confirmation of the vote information may also facilitate the ability of market participants and state and federal regulatory authorities or courts to ascertain the accuracy of a particular election or the overall proxy system. Moreover, transparency of the process should promote investor confidence as well.

3. Request for Comment

- To what extent have shareholders had difficulty in confirming whether their submitted votes have been tabulated? To what extent have issuers had difficulty in determining whether the votes submitted by securities intermediaries/proxy advisory firms/proxy service providers accurately reflect the voting instructions submitted by beneficial owners?

- To what extent do investors believe that their votes have not been accurately transmitted or tabulated, and what is the basis for such belief? Is there sufficient information about the ways that investors actually place their votes, for example, by telephone, on paper, or via the Internet?[91] Do investors have concerns about whether the method they use to place their votes affects the likelihood that their vote will be accurately recorded?

---

[90] The Organisation of Economic Co-operation and Development ("OECD"), consisting primarily of jurisdictions with high income and developed markets, has voiced similar concerns about this lack of transparency in several jurisdictions and recommends addressing it through legal and regulatory changes. *Corporate Governance: A Survey of OECD Countries* (2004) ("OECD Survey").

[91] *See* note 49, above.

- Should all participants in the voting chain grant access to their share voting records to issuers and their transfer agents/vote tabulators, for the limited purpose of enabling confirmation of a shareholder's vote? What are the benefits and costs associated with sharing such information?

- What is the best way to preserve any continuing anonymity of those investors who choose not to have their identities disclosed to the issuer?

- Would the creation of a unique identifier for each beneficial owner be feasible? Would such a system achieve the objective of allowing record owners and beneficial owners to confirm that their vote was cast in accordance with their instructions and confirm the number of shares cast on their behalf? What are the costs and benefits associated with such a system?

- Should issuers (and their agents) confirm to registered owners, beneficial owners, or securities intermediaries that the issuer has received and properly tabulated their votes? Should this confirmation be limited to an informal confirmation that votes have been counted, or should shareholders be able to obtain some form of proof that their votes have been counted? What type of documentation would constitute sufficient proof? What are the benefits and costs of such alternatives? Are there other steps that would enable beneficial owners to verify that their votes have been counted?

- Should investors also be able to obtain access to share voting records for the limited purpose of enabling an audit of the shareholder vote?

- Should issuers and securities intermediaries (and their agents) be required to reconcile and verify voting at the beneficial owner level? Would this be consistent with state law, which vests voting rights in the registered owner? Would other reconciliation and verification requirements be consistent with the purposes underlying state law?

- Should proxy participants periodically evaluate and test the effectiveness of their voting controls and procedures? If so, to whom should the results of these tests or the participants' conclusions on effectiveness be disclosed? Should disclosure be to the Commission, to clients, or also to the public?

C. Proxy Voting by Institutional Securities Lenders

Institutional securities lenders play a significant role in the proxy voting process, and we believe that it is important to evaluate the impact of their share lending on that process, and to consider ways in which the efficacy and transparency of share voting on the part of such institutions could potentially be improved. In particular, and as discussed below, we seek to examine whether decisions to recall loaned securities in connection with shareholder votes might be more timely and better informed. We also seek to examine whether increased disclosure of the votes cast by institutional securities lenders might improve the transparency of the voting process.

1. Background

Many institutions with investment portfolios of securities—such as insurance companies, pension funds, mutual funds, and college endowments—engage in securities lending to earn additional income on securities that would otherwise be sitting idle in their portfolios. When an institution lends out its portfolio securities, all incidents of ownership relating to the loaned securities, including voting rights, generally transfer to the borrower for the duration of the loan.[92] Accordingly, if the lender wants, or is obligated,

---

[92] *See, e.g.,* Thomas P. Lemke *et al., Regulation of Investment Companies* at 8.02[1][2][vi][A] (2006) ("legal title to the [loaned] securities (along with voting rights and rights to dividends and distributions) passes to the borrower for the term of the loan; when the securities are returned, the fund regains title"). *See also* Master Securities Loan Agreement, note 72, above, at 7.1 (generally the borrower receives all the incidents of ownership of the borrowed securities while loan is open).

to vote the loaned securities, the lender must terminate the loan and recall the loaned securities prior to the record date.[93]

2. Lack of Advance Notice of Meeting Agenda

a. Background

Some institutional securities lenders have proxy voting policies that require the lender, in the event of a material vote, to get back the loaned securities in order to vote the proxies.[94] While issuers are required to provide information in the proxy statement about the matters to be voted on at a shareholder meeting, the proxy statement typically is not mailed out until after the record date. Therefore, those institutional lenders that desire, or are obligated, to vote proxies with respect to securities on loan in the event of a material vote face the challenge of learning what matters will be voted on at shareholder meetings sufficiently in advance of the record date so that the lenders can determine whether they want to get the loaned securities back before the record date.

We understand that some institutional securities lenders may try to obtain timely information about meeting agendas through a variety of informal means, including media reports. We are also told, however, that this informal process is not an effective substitute for a formal process that would alert securities lenders to the matters to be voted on at shareholder meetings in time to terminate the loan and receive the loaned securities. We understand that, in some instances, securities lenders learn of material votes too late to recall the loans to vote the proxies.[95]

b. Potential Regulatory Responses

In considering possible solutions, we note that, under Section 401.02 of the NYSE Listed Company Manual, NYSE-listed issuers must provide the exchange with notice of the record and meeting dates for shareholder meetings at least ten days prior to the record date for the meeting, unless it is not possible to do so. That notice must describe the matters to be voted upon at the meeting, unless it is accompanied by printed material being sent to shareholders which describes those matters. We understand, however, that this formal notice is not disseminated to the public and may not contain specific descriptions of all matters to be voted on at the meeting.

Consequently, one possible regulatory response is to ask the NYSE to revise its rules to require public dissemination of a notice, in advance of the record date, that contains information about the record and meeting dates as well as specific descriptions of all matters to be voted upon. Other SROs could also be asked to adopt similar rules. An alternative possibility is a requirement for all issuers subject to our proxy rules to disclose the agenda by public means, such as by filing a report on Form 8-K (or as an alternative to such a filing requirement, permitting the issuance of a press release or a posting on a corporate Web site).

In identifying these alternatives, we are mindful that it can be difficult for issuers to disclose complete meeting agendas in advance of the record date because the agenda may not be established at that time for a variety of reasons, including board consideration of initiatives proposed by management and Commission staff review of no-action requests regarding Rule 14a-8 shareholder proposals.

---

[93] It is not typically feasible for the lender to retain proxy voting rights while the loan is open because the borrower typically transfers the loaned securities (for example, in a short sale), and the eventual transferee needs full right and title to the acquired securities.

[94] For example, the Commission staff has agreed not to object if voting rights pass with the lending of securities provided that if the management of the lending fund has knowledge that a material event will occur with respect to a security on loan, the fund directors would be obligated to recall such loan in time to vote the proxies. *See, e.g.*, State Street Bank & Trust Company, SEC Staff No-Action Letter (Sept. 29, 1972).

[95] *See* Roundtable Transcript, note 79, above.

c. Request for Comment

- Should the Commission propose a rule to require issuers to disclose publicly the meeting agenda sufficiently in advance of the record date to permit securities lenders to determine whether any of the matters warrant a termination of the loan so that they may vote the proxies? If so, how many days would constitute sufficient notice to the public?

- What are the advantages and disadvantages, practical and as a matter of policy, to requiring issuers to provide this advance notice to the public? For instance, would the issuer know, sufficiently in advance, all of the items to be on the agenda, particularly shareholder proposals which may be the subject of a request for no-action relief being considered by the Commission's staff?[96] How could such a requirement provide notice of contested matters and other non-management proposals to be considered at the meeting? Could we address concerns by allowing issuers to publish an agenda that is "subject to change"? If so, should we limit such changes to shareholder proposals for which the issuer is seeking no-action relief? How often does uncertainty about a meeting agenda preclude issuers from disclosing the agenda in sufficient time for shareholders to recall loans before the record date?

- Would a mechanism that alerts lending shareholders to meeting agendas well in advance of record dates have positive and desirable effects on the proxy solicitation system such that the Commission should encourage and facilitate this? Would such a mechanism increase the number of lenders recalling loans, and result in greater loan instability, with adverse effects on the capital markets? If there are competing interests, which should prevail, and why?

- How could an advance notice requirement be effected? Should the Commission propose rules applicable to all issuers subject to the proxy rules? Or, should the SROs amend or adopt listing standards requiring their listed issuers to provide advance notice to the public of record and meeting dates and specific descriptions of all matters to be voted on at the shareholder meeting?

- If we required advance notice, through what medium should such notice to shareholders be made? Should issuers be required to issue a press release or make a company Web site posting in addition to filing a notice with the Commission? Would such notice be sufficient for shareholders?

- We also request data regarding the recall of loaned securities by institutional shareholder lenders in order to vote the shares. Please include information regarding the circumstances in which the recalls did and did not occur, and whether the shares were ultimately voted.

3. Disclosure of Voting by Funds

a. Background

Management investment companies registered under the Investment Company Act (collectively, "funds") are required to disclose on Form N-PX how they vote proxies relating to portfolio securities.[97] In adopting this requirement in 2003, the Commission stated that "[i]nvestors in mutual funds have a fundamental right to know how the fund casts proxy votes on shareholders' behalf."[98] Indeed, the Commission required funds to disclose whether they cast their vote for or against management, in an effort to benefit

---

[96] When an issuer seeks to exclude a shareholder proposal submitted pursuant to Rule 14a-8, it must file its reasons with the Commission. 17 CFR 240.14a-8(j).

[97] *See* Disclosure of Proxy Voting Policies and Proxy Voting Records by Registered Management Investment Companies, Release No. IC-25932 (Jan. 31, 2003) [68 FR 6564].

[98] *Id.* at 6566.

fund shareholders by improving transparency and enabling them to monitor whether their funds approved or disapproved of the governance of portfolio companies.[99]

As noted above, when a fund lends its portfolio securities, all incidents of ownership relating to the loaned securities, including proxy voting rights, generally transfer to the borrower for the duration of the loan.[100] Accordingly, the fund generally loses its ability to vote the proxies of such securities, unless and until the loan is terminated and the securities are returned to the lender prior to the record date in question.

Currently, Form N-PX requires disclosure of proxy voting information "for each matter relating to a portfolio security considered at any shareholder meeting held during the period covered by the report and with respect to which the registrant was entitled to vote."[101] However, Form N-PX does not require disclosure of the number of shares for which proxies were voted, nor does the Form require disclosure with respect to portfolio securities on loan when, as is generally the case, the fund is not entitled to vote proxies relating to those securities. Thus, for example, if a fund lends out 99% of its portfolio holdings of XYZ Corporation and therefore votes only 1% of its holdings of XYZ, Form N-PX would disclose that the fund voted proxies with respect to shares of XYZ, but would not also disclose that the fund did not vote 99% of its holdings of XYZ because they were on loan.

b. Potential Regulatory Responses

We seek to examine whether Form N-PX should be amended to require disclosure of the actual number of votes cast by funds.

c. Request for Comment

- Should Form N-PX require disclosure of the actual number of shares voted? Should Form N-PX require disclosure of the number of portfolio securities for which a fund did not vote proxies because the securities were on loan or for other reasons?

- What would be the costs to funds of disclosing the actual number of proxy votes? What would be the costs to funds of disclosing the number of portfolio securities for which a fund did not vote proxies?

D. Proxy Distribution Fees

1. Background

One of the most persistent concerns that has been expressed to the Commission's staff, particularly by issuers, involves the structure and size of fees charged for the distribution of proxy materials to beneficial owners.

a. Current Fee Schedules

Pursuant to Exchange Act Rules 14b-1 and 14b-2, respectively, broker-dealers and banks must distribute certain materials received from an issuer or other soliciting party to their customers who are beneficial owners of securities of that issuer. These materials include proxy statements, information statements, annual reports, proxy cards, and other proxy soliciting materials.[102] A broker-dealer or bank does not need to satisfy this obligation, however, unless the issuer provides "assurance of reimbursement of the

---

[99] *Id.* at 6565.

[100] *See* note 92, above.

[101] *See* Item 1 to Form N-PX. Form N-PX requires disclosure of the following: the name of the issuer of the portfolio security; the exchange ticker symbol of the portfolio security; the Council on Uniform Securities Identification Procedures (CUSIP) number for the portfolio security; the shareholder meeting date; a brief identification of the matter voted on; whether the matter was proposed by the issuer or by a security holder; whether the fund cast its vote on the matter; how the fund cast its vote (*e.g.*, for or against proposal, or abstain; for or withhold regarding election of directors); and whether the fund cast its vote for or against management.

[102] 17 CFR 240.14b-1(b); 17 CFR 240.14b-2(b).

broker's or dealer's reasonable expenses, both direct and indirect," that the broker-dealer will incur in distributing the materials to its customers.[103]

In adopting these rules, we did not determine what constituted "reasonable expenses" that were eligible for reimbursement. Rather, the SROs submitted rule filings with us pursuant to Section 19(b) of the Exchange Act to establish these amounts.[104] Because SROs represent both issuers and broker-dealers, we believed that SROs would be best positioned to "make a fair evaluation and allocation" of the costs associated with the distribution of shareholder materials.[105] Accordingly, SRO-adopted rules, approved by the Commission, establish the maximum amount that an SRO member may receive for soliciting proxies from, and distributing other issuer materials to, beneficial owners on behalf of issuers.[106]

Since 1937, the New York Stock Exchange has required issuers, as a matter of policy, to reimburse its members for out of pocket costs of forwarding proxy materials.[107] Reimbursement rates were formally established by rule in 1952, and have been revised periodically since then.[108] Today, NYSE Rules 451 and 465 establish the fee structure for which a NYSE member organization may be reimbursed[109] for expenses incurred in connection with the forwarding of proxy materials, annual reports, and other materials to beneficial owners.[110] The NYSE initially proposed this fee structure as part of a one-year pilot program, which elicited a number of comments before the Commission approved the pilot program in 1997.[111] The pilot program was extended several times, during which time the NYSE participated in the Proxy Voting Review Committee, which was established to review the pilot fee structure.[112] In 2002, the NYSE proposed to implement the fee structure on a permanent basis, with some changes, in light of the recommendations of the Proxy Voting Review Committee.[113] Some commentators raised concerns about the amount of the fees and the absence of competition that might help determine the appropriate level for those fees.[114] In approving the fee

---

[103] 17 CFR 240.14b-1(c)(2); 17 CFR 240.14b-2(c)(2).

[104] 15 U.S.C. 78s(b). *See, e.g.*, Order Granting Approval to Proposed Rule Change and Notice of Filing and Order Granting Accelerated Approval to Amendment No. 1 to Proposed Rule Change Relating to a One-Year Pilot Program for Transmission of Proxy and Other Shareholder Communication Material, Release No. 34-38406 (Mar. 14, 1997) [62 FR 13922]. We note that, inapproving a rule filing, we must find that such filing is consistent with the Exchange Act. For example, Section 6(b)(4) of the Exchange Act requires that the rules of an exchange "provide for the equitable allocation of reasonable dues, fees, and other charges among its members and issuers and other persons using its facilities." 15 U.S.C. 78f(b)(4).

[105] *See* Release No. 34-38406, note 104, above.

[106] *See* text accompanying notes 116 to 120, below.

[107] *See* Report and Recommendations of the Proxy Working Group to the New York Stock Exchange ("Proxy Working Group Report"), June 5, 2006, *available at* http://www.nyse.com/pdfs/REVISED_NYSE_Report_6_5_06.pdf, at 23.

[108] *Id.*

[109] It should be noted that the NYSE fee schedule under Rule 451 for expenses incurred in connection with proxy solicitations is the same as the fee schedule for expenses incurred in mailing interim reports or other material pursuant to Rule 465. For purposes of this release, references to fees will cite to NYSE Rule 465. Pursuant to Rule 465, member organizations are entitled to receive reimbursement for all out of pocket

expenses, including clerical expenses as well as actual costs, including postage costs, the cost of envelopes, and communication expenses incurred in receiving voting returns either electronically or telephonically. *See* NYSE Rule 465(2) and Supplementary Material to Rule 465.20.

[110] The vast majority of firms that distribute issuer material to beneficial owners are reimbursed at the NYSE fee schedule rates because most of the brokerage firms are NYSE members or members of other exchanges that have rules similar to the NYSE's rules.

[111] *See* Release No. 34-38406, note 104, above.

[112] *See* Order Approving Proposed Rule Change and Amendment No. 1 Thereto by the New York Stock Exchange, Inc. Amending Its Rules Regarding the Transmission of Proxy and Other Shareholder Communication Material and the Proxy Reimbursement Guidelines Set Forth In Those Rules, and Requesting Permanent Approval of the Amended Proxy Reimbursement Guidelines, Release No. 34-45644 (Mar. 25, 2002) [67 FR 15440] ("NYSE Fee Structure Order").

[113] *Id.*

[114] *Id. See also* Order Approving Proposed Rule Change and Notice of Filing and Order Granting Accelerated Approval to Amendment No. 1 to Proposed Rule Change Relating to the Reimbursement of Member Organizations for Costs Incurred in the Transmission of Proxy and Other Shareholder Communication Material, Release No. 34-41177 (Mar. 16, 1999) [64 FR 14294].

structure on a permanent basis, we stated that we expected the NYSE to monitor the fees to confirm that they continued to relate to "reasonable expenses."[115]

Currently, the rates set by the NYSE for the forwarding of an issuer's proxy materials include:[116]

- A "Base Mailing Fee" of $0.40 for each beneficial owner account when there is not an opposing proxy (the "Base Mailing Fee"). This fee applies for each set of proxy materials, regardless of whether the materials have been mailed or the mailing has been suppressed or eliminated.

- An "Incentive Fee" of $0.25 per beneficial owner account for issuers whose securities are held by many beneficial owners and $0.50 per account for issuers with few beneficial owners.[117] This fee, which is in addition to the Base Mailing Fee, applies when the need to mail materials in paper format has been eliminated, for instance, by eliminating duplicative mailings to multiple accounts at the same address.[118]

- A "Nominee Coordination Fee" of $20 per "nominee"—*i.e.*, securities intermediaries that are either registered holders or identified on the DTC securities position listing—which is paid to a proxy service provider that coordinates the mailings for multiple securities intermediaries.

- An additional "Nominee Coordination Fee" of $0.05 per beneficial owner account for issuers whose securities are held by many beneficial owners[119] and $0.10 per account for issuers with few beneficial owners.[120]

While a member organization, such as a securities intermediary, may seek reimbursement for less than the approved rates, it may not seek reimbursement for an amount higher than the approved rates listed in Rule 465, or for items or services not enumerated in Rule 465, "without the prior notification to and consent of the person soliciting proxies or the issuer."[121]

When the fees were approved in 2002, we expected the NYSE "to continue its ongoing review of the proxy fee process, including considering alternatives to SRO standards that would provide a more efficient, competitive, and fair process."[122] We

---

[115] *See* NYSE Fee Structure Order, note 112, above.

[116] *See* NYSE Supplementary Material to Rule 465.20.

[117] The Incentive Fee is $0.25 for each account for issuers whose shares are held in at least 200,000 nominee accounts, and $.50 for each account for issuers whose shares are held in fewer than 200,000 accounts. According to the NYSE, the cost to service large issuers, *i.e.*, issuers whose shares are held in at least 200,000 nominee accounts, is less than the cost to service small issuers because of economies of scale, which justifies a smaller Incentive Fee for large issuers. *See* NYSE Fee Structure Order, note 112, above.

[118] NYSE Rule 465 includes the following examples as being eligible for the Incentive Fee: "multiple proxy ballots or forms in one envelope with one set of material mailed to the same household, by distributing multiple proxy ballots or forms electronically thereby reducing the sets of material mailed, or by distributing some or all material electronically."

[119] The per-account Nominee Coordination Fee is $0.05 for each account for each issuer's securities for issuers whose shares are held in at least 200,000 beneficial owner accounts held by nominees, and $.10 for each account for each issuer's securities for issuers whose shares are held in fewer than 200,000 beneficial owner accounts held by nominees. *See* NYSE Fee

Structure Order, note 112, above. According to the NYSE, as with Incentive Fees, the cost to service large issuers is less than the cost to service small issuers because of economies of scale, which justifies a smaller Nominee Coordination Fee per account for large issuers. *Id.*

[120] For example, if an issuer's securities are held in 10,000 beneficial owner accounts holding in street name, and those accounts are divided among ten securities intermediaries, the fees discussed above would be assessed as follows:

- Base Mailing Fee of 10,000 accounts x $0.40 per account, or $4,000; Incentive Fee of 5,000 accounts suppressed x $0.50 per account, or $2,500 (assuming 50% of the accounts are eligible for the incentive fee);

- Nominee Coordination Fee of 10 securities intermediaries x $20 per intermediary, or $200; and

- Additional Nominee Coordination Fee of 10,000 accounts x $0.10 per account, or $1,000.

[121] *See* NYSE Supplementary Material to Rule 465.23.

[122] *See* NYSE Fee Structure Order, note 112, above. In the NYSE Order, we also stated that we expected NYSE to "periodically review these fees to ensure they are related to 'reasonable expenses . . . in accordance with the [Exchange] Act, and propose changes where appropriate." *Id.*

also indicated that market participants should consider ways in which market forces could determine reasonable rates of reimbursement, rather than have these rates be set by the NYSE under its rules.[123]

In 2006, the Proxy Working Group considered the NYSE's current fee structure and indicated that Rule 465's fees "may be expensive to issuers but generally result[ ] in shareholders receiving and being able to vote proxies in a timely manner. This is an important benefit of the current system."[124] The Proxy Working Group also noted, however, that "issuers and shareholders deserve periodic confirmation that the system is performing as cost-effectively, efficiently and accurately as possible, with the proper level of responsibility and accountability in the system."[125] The Proxy Working Group also recommended that the NYSE should "continue to explore alternative systems . . . such that a competitive system, with fees set by the free market, could eventually succeed the current system."[126] The Proxy Working Group recommended that the NYSE engage an independent third party to analyze and make recommendations regarding the structure and amount of fees paid under Rule 465 and to study the performance of the proxy service provider that currently has the largest market share and the business process by which the distribution of proxies occurs. To date, this review has not been done. Subsequently, the Proxy Working Group's Cost and Pricing Subcommittee considered the changes brought about through the notice and access model and decided that the notice and access fees were not covered under current NYSE fee rules and concluded that they should allow participants to negotiate their own fees.[127]

After the NYSE fee structure for proxy distribution was established on a permanent basis in 2002, other SROs adopted similar rules. For example, the NYSE Amex LLC ("Amex") and the Financial Industry Regulatory Authority, Inc. ("FINRA") revised their rules (Amex Rule 576, Amex Section 722 of the Amex Company Guide, and NASD IM-2260, respectively) to adopt similar provisions.[128]

b. Notice and Access Model

Neither the NYSE nor any other SRO has established maximum fees that member firms may charge issuers for deliveries of proxy materials using the notice and access method. The majority of broker-dealers have contracts with one proxy service provider to distribute proxies to beneficial owners.[129] If an issuer elects the "notice-only" delivery option for any or all accounts, that proxy service provider currently charges an "Incremental Fee," ranging from $0.05 to $0.25 per account for positions in excess of 6,000,[130] in addition to the other fees permitted to be charged under NYSE Rule 465. This Incremental Fee is charged to all accounts, even if the issuer has elected to continue

---

[123] *Id.*

[124] Proxy Working Group Report, note 107, above, at 5.

[125] *Id.*, at 26.

[126] *Id.*, at 29.

[127] *See* August 27, 2007 Addendum to the Report and Recommendations of the Proxy Working Group to the New York Stock Exchange dated June 5, 2006 ("Proxy Working Group Addendum"), *available at* http://www.nyse.com/pdfs/PWGAddendumfinal.pdf.

[128] *See* Notice of Filing and Immediate Effectiveness of Proposed Rule Change by the American Stock Exchange LLC Amending Exchange Rules 576 and 585, and Sections 722 and 725 of the Amex Company Guide, Release No. 34-46146 (June 28, 2002) [67 FR 44902] and Notice of Filing and Immediate Effectiveness of Proposed Rule Change by the National Association of Securities Dealers, Inc. Relating to an Amendment to NASD Interpretive Material 2260, Release No. 34-47392 (Feb. 21, 2003) [68 FR 9730]. NASD Rule 2260 and NASD IM-2260 were recently

renumbered as FINRA Rule 2251 in the Consolidated FINRA Rulebook. *See* Order Granting Approval of Proposed Rule Change to Adopt FINRA Rule 2251 (Forwarding of Proxy and Other Issuer-Related Materials) in the Consolidated FINRA Rulebook, Release No. 34-61052 (Nov. 23, 2009) [74 FR 62857].

[129] Broadridge, as the service provider for most U.S. broker-dealers holding customer accounts, distributes the vast majority of proxy mailings to beneficial owners. *See* Proxy Working Group Report, note 107, above, at 24 ("ADP [(now Broadridge) is] the agent for almost all banks and brokerage houses.").

[130] The Incremental Fee for 1 to 6,000 positions is $1,500. Above 6,000 positions, the fee is charged on a per-account basis, and varies according to the number of positions. As such, the Incremental Fee ranges from $.25 per account for 6,001 to 10,000 positions to $.05 per account for greater than 500,000 positions. *See* Broadridge Fee Schedule, at *http://www.broadridge.com/notice-and-access/pdfs/Reference_Rev1_31.pdf.*

"full set" delivery to some accounts. Several issuers have expressed concerns about these fees associated with the notice and access model.

c. Current Practice Regarding Fees Charged

As noted above, broker-dealers generally outsource their delivery obligations to proxy service providers.[131] The proxy service provider enters into a contract with the broker-dealer and acts as a billing and collection agent for that broker-dealer. As such, the proxy service provider bills issuers on behalf of the broker-dealer with which it has contracted, collects the fees from the issuer to which the broker-dealer is entitled pursuant to SRO rules, and pays to the broker-dealer any difference between the fee that the broker-dealer is entitled to collect and the amount that the broker-dealer has agreed to pay the proxy service provider for its services.[132]

It is our understanding that Broadridge currently bills issuers, on behalf of its broker-dealer clients, the maximum fees allowed by NYSE Rule 465.[133] However, we understand that the fees that Broadridge charges its large broker-dealer clients for its services sometimes are less than the maximum NYSE fees charged to issuers on the broker-dealers' behalf, resulting in funds being remitted from Broadridge to a subset of its broker-dealer clients. This practice raises the question as to whether the fees in the NYSE schedule currently reflect "reasonable reimbursement." While the issuer pays the proxy distribution fees, the issuer has little or no control over the process by which the proxy service provider is selected, the terms of the contract between the broker-dealer and the proxy service provider, or the fees that are incurred through the proxy distribution process.

Several other issues concerning the appropriateness of fees have also been raised in recent years. For example, it is our understanding that, once a paper mailing is suppressed, the securities intermediary, or its agent, collects the Incentive Fee, not only for the year in which the shareholder makes that election, but also for every subsequent year, even though the continuing role of the securities intermediary, or its agent, in eliminating these paper mailings is limited to keeping track of the shareholder's election.[134] Further, it is our understanding that, with respect to certain managed accounts, where hundreds or thousands of beneficial owners may delegate their voting decisions to a single investment manager, the Base Mailing Fee and the Incentive Fee are assessed for all accounts, even though only one set of proxy materials is transmitted to the investment manager.[135]

In summary, many issues have been raised about fees, focusing mostly on whether the current fee structure for delivering proxy materials to beneficial owners reflects reasonable rates of reimbursement.

2. Potential Regulatory Responses

We have previously recognized the potential benefits of allowing the marketplace, rather than SRO rules and guidelines, to determine reasonable rates of reimbursement for

---

[131] See NYSE Fee Structure Order, note 112, above. According to the NYSE, this shift was attributable to the fact that member firms believed that proxy distribution "was not a core broker-dealer business and that capital could be better used elsewhere." Id.

[132] See Release No. 34-38406, note 104, above. See also Broadridge Form 10-K for the fiscal year ended June 30, 2009, at 4.

[133] See Broadridge Fee Schedule, note 130, above.

[134] This Incentive Fee is intended to encourage securities intermediaries to reduce proxy distribution costs on behalf of issuers because intermediaries otherwise may have no motivation to reduce an issuer's forwarding costs. See SIFMA, Report on the Shareholder Communications Process with Street Name

Holders, and the NOBO-OBO Mechanism (June 10, 2010) ("SIFMA Report"), at 14 (describing categories of ongoing costs of maintaining current e-mail addresses and related databases and systems), available in the public comment file to this release.

[135] See Letter from Thomas L. Montrone of The Securities Transfer Association to Chairman Mary Schapiro, dated June 2, 2010 (stating that "We believe that many issuers are being assessed unreasonable fees under Rule 465 related to share ownership in separate managed accounts ("SMAs") in which the investor has delegated responsibility for management of the account and is not being provided with any proxy materials"), available in the public comment file to this release.

the distribution of proxy materials. As noted above, at the time of adoption of the current fee structure, we did not expect that the discussion of reasonable rates of reimbursement would end. Rather, we noted that market forces should ultimately determine competitive and reasonable rates of reimbursement, and urged the NYSE to identify ways to achieve this goal, consistent with the continued protection of shareholder voting rights in a competitive marketplace for proxy distribution.[136] While the Proxy Working Group did suggest ways to re-evaluate the NYSE's current fee structure, such as conducting "cost studies, commission audits and surveys of various constituencies involved,"[137] to date those suggestions have not been implemented. A proxy distribution process that fosters competition could give issuers, which are responsible for reimbursing only reasonable proxy distribution costs, more control over that process and remove the Commission and SROs from the business of setting rates. However, we understand that, without a competitive market, there may be a continued need for regulated fees.

In addition, we recognize the importance of maintaining a proxy distribution system that is efficient, reliable, and accurate. We note that various groups have previously attested to the efficiency, reliability, and accuracy of the current proxy distribution system.[138] However, given developments in the securities market overall and proxy solicitation rules, such as the notice and access model, it appears to be an appropriate time for SROs to review their existing fee schedules to determine whether they continue to be reasonably related to the actual costs of proxy solicitation.

One alternative that has been suggested by a commentator is the creation of a central data aggregator that is given the right to collect beneficial owner information from securities intermediaries, but is required to provide that information to any agent designated by the issuer.[139] The aggregator would be entitled to structured compensation for its activities. This could create competition among service providers for the distribution of the proxy materials by making the beneficial owner information available to all service providers, allowing them to compete in providing services to forward proxy materials. This would also place the choice of proxy service provider in the hands of the entity that must pay for the distribution—the issuer—rather than the securities intermediary, which has no incentive to reduce costs.

Some of the other potential regulatory responses discussed in this release also would affect the current system of distributing proxy materials and, therefore, the process of setting proxy distribution fees. For instance, adopting a system under which securities intermediaries grant proxies to underlying beneficial owners (as discussed in Section III.A) would permit issuers to negotiate fees and services with proxy service providers because the issuers would be directly soliciting proxies from those beneficial owners.

3. Request for Comment

- Does the current fee/rebate structure reflect reasonable expenses? Why or why not? If not, how should these rates be revised?

- Should the fee structure allow for reimbursement of the Incentive Fee on an ongoing basis once the paper mailings have already been eliminated?

- How are proxy distribution fees billed with respect to separately managed accounts? Should certain kinds of accounts, such as separately managed accounts,

---

[136] *See* NYSE Fee Structure Order, note 112, above.

[137] *See* Proxy Working Group Report, note 107, above, at 26-27.

[138] *See, e.g.,* letter from Donald D. Kittell, Securities Industry Association, to Nancy M. Morris, Secretary, Commission, dated Feb. 13, 2006 ("The current system for delivering proxies to 80 percent of shareholders–those holding in 'street name'—has proven to be very efficient and cost-effective.") available in the public comment file to this release. *See also* Proxy Working Group Report, note 107, above, at 25 (citing to letter from Richard H. Koppes, Facilitator, Proxy Voting Review Committee, to Sharon Lawson, Senior Special Counsel, Commission, dated Feb. 28, 2002).

[139] *See* Shareholder Communications Coalition, *Public Issuer Proxy Voting: Empowering Individual Investors and Encouraging Open Shareholder Communications* (Aug. 4, 2009) ("SCC Discussion Draft"), at 6, available in the public comment file to this release.

where multiple beneficial owners may delegate their voting decisions to a single investment manager, be eligible for different treatment under the current fee structure?

- Are separately managed accounts different from "wrap" accounts for which issuers may not be charged suppression fees for providing proxy communication services to holders of WRAP accounts?[140]

- Does the current fee structure discourage issuers from communicating with beneficial owners beyond delivery of the required proxy materials?

- Should there be an independent third-party audit of the current fee structure, as recommended by the Proxy Working Group?

- Do broker-dealers using a proxy service provider incur costs that justify rebates from the proxy service provider? If so, what are the costs, can they be quantified, and are they commensurate with the payments received from the proxy service provider? Do these costs exist only for larger broker-dealers or for broker-dealers of all sizes? Should the current rebates between Broadridge and larger broker-dealers be permitted under the current fee structure? Should current contractual arrangements between proxy service providers and their clients affect the determination of whether fees are fair and reasonable?

- Currently, SRO rules do not set rates for reimbursement of expenses associated with the notice and access model. In the absence of SRO rules, on what basis do market participants currently determine whether the reimbursement of expenses associated with the notice and access model is, in fact, reasonable?

- Should the current fee structure that is set forth in SRO rules be revised to include fees for notice and access delivery? If so, what fees for the notice and access model might constitute "reasonable reimbursement?"

- Does the current proxy distribution system—in which the proxy service provider is selected by a broker-dealer but paid by the issuer—create a lack of incentives to reduce costs for issuers? Should the issuer have more control over the selection and payment of the proxy service provider, and if so, what alternatives to the current system would facilitate this? What are the potential benefits and drawbacks of such alternatives?

- What factors are currently affecting the level of competition in the market for proxy service providers and their fees? What principles should guide the Commission's current consideration of competition among proxy service providers? Would multiple competing service providers affect the quality of service?

- What steps would be necessary to enable prices to be based on competitive market forces? What are the potential benefits and drawbacks of moving to a system where prices are determined by competitive market forces? What effect, if any, would this have in terms of accuracy, accountability, reliability, cost, and efficiency of the proxy distribution system? Would a market-based model increase or decrease costs for issuers? Would cost increases or decreases be more likely for small to midsize issuers?

- If issuers were able to solicit proxies directly from beneficial owners, what effect would that likely have on proxy distribution costs? Would costs be reduced through the introduction of competition and better alignment of economic incentives? Or, could the loss of economies of scale increase costs? Would each issuer likely negotiate fees on its own with a proxy service provider? Would the impact be different for large, medium, or small issuers?

---

[140] It is our understanding that a wrap account is a certain type of account that is managed by an outside investment manager.

- What are the practical and legal implications of deregulating fees in light of the existing contracts between proxy service providers and broker-dealers? For example, would these contracts need to be re-negotiated?

- What are the potential merits and drawbacks of having a central data aggregator collect beneficial owner information from securities intermediaries? How would reimbursement to the aggregator, as the distributor of information, be determined?

- Would changes to the OBO/NOBO mechanism, or the creation of a central data aggregator, encourage competition in the proxy distribution sector? Would competition increase or lower costs? Would competition increase or decrease accountability?

- A number of investors have complained about the services of proxy service providers (and transfer agents performing similar functions). How are investors' interests addressed, if at all, in the selection of proxy service providers? Are the interests of investors in this process given adequate weight?

IV. Communications and Shareholder Participation

We first examine a number of concerns relating to the ability of issuers to communicate with shareholders, the level of shareholder participation in the proxy voting process, and the ability of investors to obtain and evaluate information pertinent to voting decisions. Because of the importance of shareholder voting, as discussed above, we seek additional information about ways in which issuer communications with shareholders, shareholder participation and shareholder use of information might be improved.

A. Issuer Communications with Shareholders

1. Background

The first area of concern that we address arises out of the practice of holding securities in street name—that is, interposing securities intermediaries between issuers and the beneficial owners of their securities. This practice developed in order to facilitate the prompt and accurate processing of an increasingly large volume of securities transactions.[141] The efficiency of the clearance and settlement system in the U.S. is due in large part to the ability to "net" transactions, whereby contracts to buy or sell securities between broker-dealers are replaced with net obligations to a registered clearing agency, the National Securities Clearing Corporation ("NSCC"). To make netting possible, securities must be held in fungible bulk at DTC.

There is broad consensus[142] that the enormous volume of transactions cleared and settled in the U.S., which currently involve transactions valued at over $1.48 quadrillion annually,[143] requires a centralized netting facility (*i.e.*, NSCC) and a depository (*i.e.*, DTC) that facilitates book-entry settlement of securities transactions. It is our understanding that this approach to clearance and settlement has produced significant efficiencies, lower costs, and risk management advantages. At the same time, however, the practice of holding securities in fungible bulk has made it more difficult for issuers to identify their beneficial owners and to communicate directly with them.

---

[141] For a history of the U.S. shareholder system, see Alan L. Beller & Janet L. Fisher, The OBO/NOBO Distinction in Beneficial Ownership: Implications for Shareowner Communications and Voting (February 2010), *available at* http://www.cii.org/UserFiles/file/CII%20White%20Paper%20-%20The%20OBO-NOBO%20Distinction%20in%20Beneficial%20Ownership%20February%202010.pdf, at 8-10. This report

(the "CII OBO/NOBO Report") was published by the Council of Institutional Investors.

[142] *See* "Recommendations for Securities Settlement Systems," CFSS/IOSCO Task Force (Nov. 2001) and "Global Clearing and Settlement, A Plan of Action," published by the Group of Thirty ("G-30") (Jan. 30, 2003).

[143] *See* http://www.dtcc.com/about/business/statistics.php.

In light of recent developments in corporate governance, including the elimination of the broker discretionary vote on uncontested elections of directors, commentators have claimed a greater need for issuers to be able to communicate with their shareholders.[144] These commentators have argued that the number of contested issues in shareholder meetings has increased, that voting outcomes are under more pressure, and that, as a result, certain changes should be made to our rules in order to facilitate communications by issuers with their beneficial owners.[145] More broadly, commentators have questioned whether the current system of share ownership and the Commission's communications and proxy rules adequately serve the needs of investors and issuers.[146]

The history of our efforts to address the impediments to communication associated with our securities ownership system goes back more than three decades. In 1976, we reported to Congress on the effects of the practice of holding securities in street name.[147] While we concluded that the practice of registering securities in nominee (that is, DTC or a securities intermediary) and street name was consistent with the purposes of the Exchange Act, we recognized that issuers were experiencing difficulties in communicating with their shareholders who hold securities in nominee and street name. In an effort to enhance communication, we revised the proxy rules to require issuers, as more fully described above, to do the following:

- Inquire of securities intermediaries whether other persons beneficially owned the securities they held of record; and

- Supply securities intermediaries with a sufficient number of sets of proxy materials to forward to beneficial owners.[148]

To promote direct communication between issuers and their beneficial owners, we adopted rules in 1983, effective in 1985, to require broker-dealers and banks to provide issuers, at their request, with lists of the names and addresses of beneficial owners who did not object to having such information provided to issuers.[149] These owners are often

---

[144] *See* Proxy Working Group Report, note 107, above, at 22 (discussing comments received with respect to a then-proposed amendment, which was recently adopted, to Rule 452 eliminating broker-dealer voting in the election of directors).

[145] *See, e.g.,* CII OBO/NOBO Report, note 141, above, at 11 ("Recent developments in corporate governance will place more pressure on voting outcomes and increase the need for both companies and shareowners to have an effective and reliable framework for communications."); letter from Shareholder Communications Coalition to Chairman Mary Schapiro (Aug. 4, 2009), *available at* http://www.shareholdercoalition.com/SCCLettertoSECChairmanMarySchapiroAug2009.pdf.

[146] In 2004, the BRT Petition urged the Commission "to conduct a thorough review of the current shareholder communications system." BRT Petition, note 8, above. The petition recommended that "the Commission require brokers and banks to provide issuers with contact information for all beneficial owners and permit the direct mailing of all communications (including proxy materials) to beneficial owners." *Id. See also* Marcel Kahan & Edward B. Rock, *The Hanging Chads of Corporate Voting,* 96 Georgetown Law Journal 1227 (2008); J. Robert Brown Jr., *The Shareholder Communication Rules and the Securities and Exchange Commission: An Exercise in Regulatory Utility or Futility,* 13 Journal of Corporation Law 683 (1988); David C. Donald, *The Rise and Effects of the Indirect Holding System: How Corporate America Ceded Its Shareholders to Intermediaries* (Sept. 26, 2007),

available at http://papers.ssrn.com/sol3/papers.cfm?abstract_id=1017206.

[147] Street Name Study, note 13, above.

[148] Notice of Adoption of Amendments to Rules 14a-3, 14c-3 and 14c-7 under the Exchange Act to Improve the Disclosure in, and the Dissemination of, Annual Reports to Security Holders and to Improve the Dissemination of Annual Reports on Form 10-K or 12-K Filed with the Commission Under the Exchange Act, Release No. 34-11079 (Oct. 31, 1974) [39 FR 40766]. These requirements, which were originally included in Rule 14a-3(d), are currently set forth in Rule 14a-13 [17 CFR 240.14a-13]. Facilitating Shareholder Communications, Release No. 34-22533 (Oct. 15, 1985) [51 FR 44276]. Based in part on the recommendation of the Street Name Study, we adopted additional rules in 1977 facilitating the transmission of proxy materials from issuers to beneficial owners. Requirements for Dissemination of Proxy Information to Beneficial Owners by Issuers and Intermediary Broker-Dealers, Release No. 34-13719 (July 5, 1977) [42 FR 35953].

[149] *See* Facilitating Shareholder Communications Provisions, Release No. 34-20021 (July 28, 1983) [48 FR 35082]. Exchange Act Rule 14a-13(b)(5) enables an issuer to obtain a list of its NOBOs only, which means that broker-dealers and banks must classify their beneficial owners as either objecting or non-objecting beneficial owners, based on the investor's election. A requesting issuer must reimburse the intermediaries for their reasonable expenses in preparing the NOBO list. 17 CFR 240.14a-13(b)(5). The NYSE and other exchanges establish a per-holder fee that member

referred to as "non-objecting beneficial owners" or "NOBOs." When a beneficial owner objects to disclosure of its name and address to the issuer—often referred to as "objecting beneficial owners" or "OBOs"—the beneficial owner may be contacted only by the securities intermediary (or the intermediary's agent) with the customer relationship with the beneficial owner.[150] According to one estimate, 70% to 80% of all public issuers' shares are held in street name, and 75% of those shares, or 52% to 60% of all shares, are held by OBOs.[151] It is our understanding that some types of large institutional investors, such as mutual funds[152] and retirement plans, often choose OBO status.[153]

We understand that there are concerns about the cost and efficiency of the current system of communications between issuers and investors, including the following:[154]

- Issuers have indicated to the staff that the majority of their street name securities are held by OBOs through securities intermediaries, making it very difficult to determine the identity and holdings of their investors. Issuers believe that the recent changes in corporate governance, including the move to majority voting of directors, the elimination of broker discretionary voting in uncontested director elections, and a possible drop in retail voting percentages,[155] call for more direct communication between issuers and their shareholders. These communications may include using a proxy solicitor to contact shareholders by telephone. However, an issuer cannot make these direct appeals for shareholders to participate in the issuer's corporate governance if it does not know the identity of those shareholders.

- Issuers also have indicated to the staff that they face considerable expense in communicating with beneficial owners, either OBOs or NOBOs, indirectly through securities intermediaries or their agents. Issuers are required to reimburse securities intermediaries for expenses incurred in forwarding communications to beneficial owners. These expenses include reimbursement for postage, envelopes and communication expenses as well as fees to proxy service providers.[156]

- Some issuers have claimed that the expense of obtaining the list of NOBOs from the securities intermediary or its proxy service provider deters some issuers,

---

(Footnote Continued)

brokers can charge for preparation of the NOBO list. *E.g.*, NYSE Rule 465. Notwithstanding these limitations on the fees, issuers, particularly those with large shareholder bases, have indicated that the cost to obtain such lists can be prohibitive.

[150] *See* 17 CFR 240.14b-1(b)(3)(i). Several commentators have indicated that, in a number of foreign jurisdictions, public issuers have the right to learn the identity of individuals and institutions with voting rights or beneficial owner interests in their shares. *See, e.g.*, BRT Petition, note 8, above; Kahan, note 146, above; Donald, note 146, above.

[151] Proxy Working Group Report at 10-11, note 107, above.

[152] Although mutual funds disclose their securities holdings on Forms N-Q and N-CSR, those disclosures are made as of the end of the quarter, which may not coincide with the record date used to determine shareholders entitled to vote at a meeting.

[153] One recent report states that while "73% of retail shareholders are NOBOs, . . . [m]ost institutional shareholders—about 71%—are OBOs, accounting for about 91% of all institutionally held shares." SIFMA Report, note 134, above, at 7.

[154] Concerns about whether or not to disclose shareholder identities are shared by regulators in several jurisdictions. For example, in Canada, companies

are under no obligation to send proxy materials to shareholders who do not disclose their underlying identity. *See* OECD Survey, note 90, above. In the United Kingdom, companies have the right to ask any person whom the company knows or has reasonable cause to believe has an interest in its shares to declare that interest. UK Companies Act 2006—Section 793: Notice by company requiring information about interests in its shares, *available at* (http://www.opsi.gov.uk/acts/acts2006/ukpga_20060046_en_45). The failure to do so may enable the company to apply for a court order directing that the shares in question be subject to certain restrictions involving voting rights, transfers and other limitations. UK Companies Act 2006—Sections 794 and 797. Given that shareholders have the right to dismiss the board at any time in the United Kingdom, companies generally believe it is important that the board know who its shareholders are and pay attention to what they want. Thus, the company should be entitled to know who owns its shares in order to ensure accountability in both directions.

[155] It is unclear whether such a drop has occurred. *See* note 196 and accompanying text, below.

[156] *See* Section III.D, above. *See also* Supplementary Material to NYSE Rules 451 and 465; NYSE Listed Issuer Manual § 402.10(A).

particularly widely-held issuers, from using the NOBO list to communicate with beneficial owners.[157] We have also received expressions of concern from broker-dealers about the difficulty of maintaining an accurate NOBO list when a class of securities is actively traded.

- We also have heard that issuers may desire more flexibility to design the proxy materials (*e.g.*, forms of VIFs, packaging of materials, etc.) that are sent to beneficial owners. Some issuers believe that the current uniform appearance of proxy materials used by some of the proxy service providers may lead to reduced interest in the materials by beneficial owners. Other commentators have suggested that VIFs do not sufficiently inform shareholders as to how their shares will be voted if they do not provide instructions on all the matters included on the VIFs.[158]

- Some issuers also have expressed concerns regarding potential quality control problems that have arisen, from time to time, with the services provided by proxy service providers. Similarly, retail investors have complained to our Office of Investor Education and Advocacy, from time to time, that proxy materials have been delivered late. To the extent that delivery of proxy materials is delayed, the utility of issuer-investor communication through the proxy process is impaired.

2. Potential Regulatory Responses

Many issuers, securities intermediaries and commentators believe that there can be more efficient and cost-effective ways for issuers to communicate directly with their shareholders. Some commentators have advocated for significant changes. The 2004 Business Roundtable rulemaking petition ("BRT Petition")[159] recommended that the Commission enable issuers to communicate directly with their beneficial owners by requiring broker-dealers and banks to execute an omnibus proxy in favor of their underlying beneficial owners and by eliminating the ability of beneficial owners to object to the disclosure of their identities to issuers. The BRT Petition argued that eliminating objecting beneficial owner status would create a more efficient proxy system by allowing issuers to bypass securities intermediaries and their agents in forwarding proxy materials and by simplifying the voting and tabulation process.

In 2009, the Shareholder Communications Coalition[160] filed a letter supporting the BRT Petition and providing more specific recommendations on how to implement a system that eliminates objecting beneficial owner status and grants the right to vote directly to the beneficial owners through an omnibus proxy.[161] This proposed system would separate the functions of beneficial owner data aggregation and proxy communications distribution, thereby making beneficial owner data available to the issuer's (and not the securities intermediary's) agent. The system would identify all beneficial owners except those that elect to remain anonymous by registering shares in a nominee account.[162]

---

[157] Under current NYSE rules, the issuer is required to pay $0.065 per NOBO name, plus reasonable expenses of the broker-dealer's agent in providing the information. NYSE Rule 465 Supplementary Material, *available at* http://nyserules.nyse.com/NYSETools/PlatformViewer.asp?searched=1&selectednode=chp%5F1%5F5%5F13%5F1&CiRestriction=465&manual=%2Fnyse%2Frules%2Fnyse%2Drules%2F; FINRA Rule 2251 Supplementary Material.

[158] *See* James McRitchie, Request for rulemaking to amend Rule 14a-4(b)(1) under the Securities Exchange Act of 1934 to prohibit conferring discretionary authority to issuers with respect to non-votes on the voter information form or proxy. No. 4-583 (May 15, 2009).

[159] *See* BRT Petition, note 8, above.

[160] The Shareholder Communications Coalition is an umbrella group that represents the views of The Business Roundtable, the Society of Corporate Secretaries and Governance Professionals, the National Investor Relations Institute, and the Securities Transfer Association.

[161] *See* SCC Discussion Draft, note 139, above.

[162] A beneficial owner could continue to remain anonymous by hiring a third party to hold the securities for the beneficial owner. In this circumstance, however, the cost of this agency arrangement would be borne by the beneficial owner.

Others advocate less comprehensive change and encourage adoption of an approach in which an issuer would be entitled to a list of all beneficial owners, but only as of the record date for a particular meeting.[163] In such a system (an "annual NOBO" system), objecting beneficial owners would not be able to shield their identity for purposes of a shareholder meeting. At any other time during the year, objecting beneficial owner information would not be available to the issuer or any other party. An annual NOBO system would enable issuers to communicate directly with all of their shareholders, both registered and beneficial owners, for purposes of a shareholder meeting, while minimizing the possibility that the investor information will be used for purposes other than proxy solicitation, such as determining an investor's trading strategies.

Others have suggested more gradual change.[164] In order to encourage holding in NOBO rather than OBO status, some have suggested various steps to promote selection of NOBO status, such as educating investors about OBO and NOBO status when they open their accounts or periodically. Other steps may involve the elections made by investors when they open their accounts. While our rules contemplate that investors must object to disclosure of their identities to issuers,[165] neither our rules nor self-regulatory organization ("SRO") rules currently require disclosure of the consequences of choosing OBO or NOBO status, or specify broker-dealer policies or procedures with regard to their clients' choice of OBO or NOBO status. In particular, if a securities intermediary's standard customer agreement includes a default election of OBO status, it could promote a less than fully considered election of OBO status. While several broker-dealers have informed us that they currently default beneficial owners to NOBO status, it has been recommended that the default agreement used by all broker-dealers be NOBO status, or that broker-dealers provide informational materials to their customers prior to allowing the customers to elect OBO status and contact customers who elect OBO status periodically to re-elect their OBO/NOBO status.

In addition, there remains the issue of whether beneficial owners have a privacy right with respect to the disclosure of their ownership positions. We have been informed of a variety of privacy considerations: some investors, particularly institutional investors, select OBO status for competitive reasons, in order to mask their investment strategies; other investors may prefer OBO status in order to minimize the communications (particularly telephone calls) they receive regarding their investments.[166] In either case, however, according to a study by the NYSE, investor preference for OBO status may be cost-sensitive and perhaps even overstated.[167]

3. Request for Comment

As discussed above, we are considering whether regulatory action is needed to make it easier for issuers to communicate with their investors. In particular, we seek comment on whether we should eliminate the OBO/NOBO distinction, thereby making all beneficial

---

[163] The Altman Group, "Practical Solutions to Improve the Proxy Voting System" (Oct. 2009), *available at* http://altmangroup.com/pdf/Practical SolutionTAG.pdf (identifying this approach as the "ABO" or "all beneficial owners" system). We use the term "annual NOBO" because we believe it better reflects the fact that, under the system, an OBO would be treated as if it were a NOBO, but only annually or for specific proxy solicitations.

[164] *See, e.g.*, CII OBO/NOBO Report, note 141, above.

[165] *See* Exchange Act Rule 14b-1(b)(3)(i) [17 CFR 240.14b-1(b)(3)(i)] (requiring broker-dealers to provide names, addresses, and securities positions of customers who have not objected to disclosure of such information); Exchange Act Rule 14b-2(b)(4) [17 CFR 240.14b-1(b)(3)(i)] (requiring banks to provide names, addresses, and securities positions of customers that

have not objected to disclosure of such information for customer accounts established after December 28, 1986, but requiring affirmative consent to disclosure of such information for customer accounts opened before that date).

[166] *See* SIFMA Report, note 134, above, at 10, 12, 20-22.

[167] Investor Attitudes Study Conducted for NYSE Group—April 7, 2006, *available at* http://www .nyse.com/pdfs/Final_ORC_Survey.pdf. In that study, 71% of respondents indicated that they would provide contact information to the issuers in which they invest if asked. In addition, the study notes that investor preference for NOBO status increases if fees are imposed on continuing to maintain OBO status: with the imposition of a $50 annual fee, preference for OBO status declines from 36% to 5%. *Id.* at 3.

owner information available to the issuer, or require broker-dealers to disclose the consequences of choosing OBO or NOBO status, or whether OBO or NOBO status should be the default choice. We also are exploring ways in which issuers can communicate directly with beneficial owners, such as requiring securities intermediaries to transfer proxy voting authority to some or all beneficial owners, so that issuers can solicit proxies directly from such holders. In this regard, we seek comment on the following questions:

- Do our existing rules inappropriately inhibit issuers from effectively communicating with investors? If so, what changes should we make to our rules to improve investor communication? Even if our rules do not inappropriately inhibit issuers from effectively communicating with investors, do the rules significantly raise the cost of communicating? Do any non-Commission rules inappropriately inhibit issuers from effectively communicating with investors? What are the benefits and costs of the various changes proposed by commentators?

- Do investors consider the degree and manner of communication with issuers to be adequate?

- To what extent are proxy materials not being delivered in a timely fashion? Are any changes in our rules or other rules required to improve timeliness of delivery, either with respect to registered or beneficial owners?

- What impact does the uniform appearance of proxy materials such as the VIF have on shareholder participation in proxy voting? Would investors, especially retail investors, be more likely to vote if there was less uniformity in the appearance of proxy materials?

- Is the format and layout of proxy cards and VIFs clear and easy to use from the perspective of investors? Could the layout be improved to enhance investor participation? Do the formats of proxy cards and VIFs appropriately set out the consequences of not voting or giving voting instructions on one or more specific matters?

- To what extent has the loss of broker discretionary votes in uncontested elections of directors increased the likelihood that issuers will not meet quorum requirements? Would the availability of less-costly means of communication with shareholders improve issuers' ability to meet quorum requirements?

- Do investors have legitimate privacy interests with respect to the disclosure of their share ownership? In what ways would an investor be harmed if his or her identity and the size of his or her holdings are disclosed to issuers? Should an investor be able to indicate that he or she does not wish to be contacted by an issuer? Do broker-dealers or banks have legitimate commercial interests in keeping the identities of their customers confidential? How should these interests be balanced against an issuer's interest in identifying and communicating with its investors? Is this balance different for individual and institutional investors, and if so, would different treatment in regard to OBO status be appropriate? Are there technological solutions that would facilitate communication while protecting the identities of shareholders?

- Issuers have expressed interest in not only communicating with shareholders, but also in identifying them. While these interests can be complementary, is one more important than the other? Should any regulatory changes that may be considered by the Commission emphasize one over the other?

- Are there merits to, or concerns about, establishing a central beneficial owner data aggregator for use by issuers, as suggested by the Shareholder Communications Coalition and as described above?

- Is competition in the proxy distribution service market needed, and if so, what changes to facilitate issuers' communications with investors would also encourage competition in the proxy distribution service market?

- Should we consider rules that would shift the cost of distributing proxy materials to broker-dealers for customers who choose to be objecting beneficial owners?

- Do our rules adequately address how beneficial owners elect objecting or non-objecting beneficial owner status when they open their accounts? Should there be a requirement that beneficial owners' account agreements adopt any specific election as the default choice? If so, would it matter whether the Commission, FINRA, or the stock exchanges imposed that requirement? Should the required default choice be for objecting or non-objecting beneficial owner status? Are there other ways in which default positions can be established for customers of securities intermediaries? Should there be a standardized form for customers to elect either NOBO or OBO status?

- Should we or SROs instead, or in addition, consider requiring securities intermediaries to provide informational materials to their customers prior to allowing the customer to elect OBO or NOBO status? What should be included in such informational materials, and how frequently should investors be provided with such materials? Should we consider requiring securities intermediaries to inform customers of the reasons for and against choosing to disclose or shield their identities?

- Should a broker-dealer periodically request that customers reaffirm their OBO/NOBO status selection? If so, how should the cost of this periodic evaluation be allocated?

- Should we consider revising our rules to require that securities intermediaries provide an omnibus proxy to their underlying beneficial owners and identify them to the issuer? If we were to propose such a rule, should we limit it to granting proxies to NOBOs since their identities are already available to issuers? How would such a system address the way securities transactions are cleared and settled?

- What are the costs and benefits of the annual NOBO system suggested by commentators? Would disclosure of all beneficial owners, limited to information as of the record date of a shareholder meeting, harm those investors (for example, would it reveal trading strategies of those investors)? Would implementing the annual NOBO system adversely affect any privacy interests of OBOs? As a practical matter, would issuers be able to contact OBOs using this information for subsequent shareholder meetings?

- What problems might arise if issuers or their transfer agents have greater access to or control of shareholder lists? How could we provide for fair and efficient access to those lists by other soliciting parties?

B. Means to Facilitate Retail Investor Participation

1. Background

As we seek to promote and facilitate shareholder voting in general, we understand that the level of voting by retail investors is a particular area of concern. Retail investor participation rates in the proxy voting process historically have been low.[168] Given the importance of proxy voting, we view significant lack of participation by retail investors in proxy voting as a source of concern, even in companies in which retail share ownership represents a relatively small portion of total voting power. We understand that this situation is not limited to the U.S., as the level of voting by shareholders in other jurisdictions has also caused concern.[169]

---

[168] *See* Roundtable Briefing Paper, note 79, above.   [169] *See, e.g.,* Myners Report, note 15, above.

2. Potential Regulatory Responses

a. Investor Education

Commentators have indicated that there is confusion among investors regarding the proxy voting process and the importance of voting. [170] Investors accustomed to brokers voting their shares on their behalf may be unaware that, as a result of the recent revisions to NYSE Rule 452, brokers can no longer vote investors' shares in uncontested elections of corporate directors without instructions from the investors. In addition, many investors may be confused by the distinction between record and beneficial ownership and how that may affect their voting rights. These commentators have recommended the development of a significant investor education campaign to inform investors about the proxy voting process and the importance of voting as one way in which communication and proxy voting could be improved.

We believe that improved investor education may help dispel some of these potential misunderstandings and create interest in the voting process. There are several ways in which we can enhance the educational opportunities for investors. We recently created a new section on our investor site, *www.investor.gov*, to provide educational materials about proxy mechanics generally and the notice and access model for the delivery of proxy materials. The new proxy matters section can be found at *www.investor.gov/proxy-matters*.[171] We understand that a number of issuers and shareholder organizations have provided links from their Web sites to these educational materials. In addition, NYSE recently revised examples of letters containing the information and instructions required to be given by NYSE members to beneficial owners to inform beneficial owners that brokers are no longer allowed to vote shares held by beneficial owners on uncontested elections of directors, unless the beneficial owner has provided voting instructions.[172]

Another possible venue for investor education is issuers' Web sites and brokers' Web sites. Many investors go to issuer Web sites to obtain information about the issuers in which they invest, and an increasing number of investors review their holdings and effect securities transactions through their brokers' Web sites. More proxy-related educational materials located on an issuer's or broker's Web site may be helpful to investors. In addition, although some explanation of how the proxy process works is often included on the back of the proxy card (or on the VIF), that information can be difficult to read and is often presented in small print. We are interested in whether improving the presentation of information on the proxy card or VIF would have an effect on voting participation.

Finally, we are interested in whether we should also consider the scope, format, and content of the communications between brokers and their customers that occur in connection with opening customers' accounts. The account-opening process may be a good opportunity to communicate important information about the shareholder voting process.

---

[170] *See* Proxy Working Group Report, note 107, above, at 15.

[171] The staff of the Commission initiated an educational program on proxy voting matters for retail investors with the goal of increasing investor awareness about the importance of participating in director elections and other issues brought before shareholders at annual and special meetings. A plain-language "Spotlight on Proxy Matters page" in question and answer format was developed on the SEC Web site to explain proxy voting procedures. In addition, the staff of our Office of Investor Education and Advocacy has spoken before investor and issuer organizations to promote the Web site material and to urge their involvement in proxy voting educational programming.

To date, this ongoing effort has yielded more than 25,000 unique visits to the Proxy Matters website and 1,430 references on Google. The staff plans to continue and expand the education and outreach to retail investors in preparation for the 2011 proxy season. As part of this outreach program, we are exploring potential opportunities to link proxy educational materials directly to online brokerage accounts and other locations that may be visited frequently by retail shareholders.

[172] *See* Notice of Filing and Immediate Effectiveness of Proposed Rule Change to Modify the Sample Broker Letters Set Forth In Rule 451, Release No. 34-61046 (Nov. 20, 2009) [74 FR 62849].

b. Enhanced Brokers' Internet Platforms

As noted above, many investors use their brokers' Web sites as "one-stop shopping" for their investment needs. It is our understanding, however, that many of these Web sites do not provide information about upcoming corporate actions or enable retail investors to use the same platform for proxy voting. Rather, many brokers hire a third-party proxy service provider to handle the collection of voting instructions. Therefore, those investors must go to a different Web site, not run by the broker, in order to submit voting instructions to their broker. We are interested in receiving views on whether receiving notices of upcoming corporate votes and having the ability to access proxy materials and a VIF through the investor's account page on the broker's Web site would be helpful to investors. We also wish to explore whether other communications from broker to customer could encourage more active and better informed participation in the proxy voting process.

c. Advance Voting Instructions

Some commentators have recommended that we adopt rules to facilitate what has been called "client-directed voting" as a means to increase investor participation in the voting process.[173] In general, this concept contemplates that brokers or other parties[174] would solicit voting instructions from retail investors on particular topics (*e.g.*, election of directors, ratification of auditors, approval of equity compensation plans, action on shareholder proposals) in advance of their receiving the proxy materials from companies.[175] The advance voting instructions would then be applied to proxy cards or VIFs related to the investors' securities holdings, unless the investors changed those instructions. Investors would be able (but not required) to instruct their securities intermediaries or other parties to vote their shares in any number of ways, including the following:

- Vote shares in accordance with the board of directors' recommendations;

- Vote shares against the board of directors' recommendations;

- Vote shares related to particular types of proposals (for example, shareholder proposals related to environmental or social issues) consistent with recommendations issued by specified interest groups, proxy advisory firms, investors, or voting policies;

- Abstain from voting shares; or

- Vote shares proportionally with the brokerage firm's customers' instructed votes, or the instructed votes of its institutional or retail customers only.[176]

The advance voting instructions would generally be given by the investors at the time they sign their brokerage agreements or sign up for the proxy voting service, or periodically thereafter, and would always be revocable. Investors would also be able to change the advance voting instructions at any time.

In connection with each proxy solicitation, investors who had given advance voting instructions would receive a proxy card or VIF pre-marked in accordance with those voting instructions, along with the proxy materials required by the federal securities laws. Investors could override any of the advanced voting instructions applicable to that proxy solicitation by checking or clicking on an appropriate election box before the vote is submitted. Absent instructions to the contrary, the securities intermediary or

---

[173] *See* Proxy Working Group Addendum, note 127, above. We use the term "advance voting instructions" rather than "client-directed voting" because we believe it more precisely identifies the salient feature of this approach to shareholder voting.

[174] Such parties could include proxy advisory firms or other third parties offering voting platforms to facilitate voting by retail investors.

[175] As noted above, proxy advisory services sometimes submit votes on behalf of their institutional investor clients pursuant to the clients' proxy voting policies.

[176] *See* Proxy Working Group Addendum, note 127, above; *see also* John Wilcox, Fixing the Problems with Client-Directed Voting, March 5, 2010, *available at* http://blogs.law.harvard.edu/corpgov/2010/03/05/fixing-the-problems-with-client-directed-voting/.

other party would vote the investor's shares in accordance with the advance voting instructions as pre-marked on the proxy card or VIF.

In connection with the proposal to amend NYSE Rule 452,[177] we received several comment letters that discussed advance voting instructions as an alternative to the NYSE Rule 452 amendment[178] or advocated that such voting instructions should be considered in conjunction with the NYSE Rule 452 amendment.[179] In the order approving the NYSE Rule 452 amendment, we noted that advance voting instructions raise a variety of questions and concerns, such as requiring investors to make a voting decision in advance of receiving a proxy statement containing the disclosures mandated under the federal securities laws and possibly without consideration of the specific issues to be voted upon.[180] The Proxy Working Group also expressed concern that advance voting instructions could act as a disincentive for retail investors to vote after reviewing proxy materials if they had already given such instructions.[181] On the other hand, supporters of advance voting instructions stated that the implementation of voting based on such instructions could help issuers solve quorum problems, encourage greater retail shareholder participation in the voting process by making it easier for investors to vote, better permit shareholders to exercise their franchise, and result in more discussion and involvement between investors and their brokers on proxy issues.[182]

While we will continue to consider the advisability of allowing third parties, such as broker-dealers, to solicit instructions regarding the voting of shares by retail investors without the benefit of information that is contained in disclosures that our rules require in connection with shareholder votes, we recognize that facilitating the use of advance voting instructions can be viewed as providing retail investors with a component of the services now made available to institutional investors by proxy advisory firms. However, retail investors are not necessarily in the same position as institutional investors. Some institutional investors rely upon pre-developed voting policies and procedures to ensure consistency across portfolios, to aid in post-vote monitoring and reporting, and otherwise to comply with applicable fiduciary duties. Some retail shareholders may not be as likely to monitor, or hire others to monitor, the application of their advance voting instructions.

There is currently no applicable exemption for securities intermediaries to solicit advance voting instructions from their customers. Exchange Act Rule 14a-2(a)(1) provides an exemption from the proxy solicitation rules to securities intermediaries when they forward proxy materials on behalf of issuers and request voting instructions.[183] This exemption, however, requires securities intermediaries to "promptly furnish" proxy materials to the person solicited. By definition, brokers seeking to obtain advance voting

---

[177] On July 1, 2009, the Commission approved an amendment to NYSE Rule 452 and Section 402.08 of the NYSE Listed Issuer Manual that eliminated discretionary voting by brokers in uncontested director elections. See Release No. 34-60215, note 11, above.

[178] See comment letters from American Bar Association ("ABA Letter"); American Business Conference; Agilent Technologies, Inc.; Business Roundtable; United States Chamber of Commerce; Connecticut Water; DTE Energy; First Financial Holdings, Inc.; Furniture Brands International; General Electric; Intel Corporation; Jacksonville Bancorp Inc.; McKesson Corporation; Monster Worldwide, Inc.; Nucor Corporation; Provident Bank; Provident Financial Services, Inc.; Quest Diagnostics Inc.; Synalloy Corporation; and Veeco Instruments Inc to Notice of Filing of Proposed Rule Change, as modified by Amendment No. 4, to Amend NYSE Rule 452 and Listed Company Manual Section 402.08 to Eliminate Broker Discretionary Voting for the Election of Directors and Codify Two Previously Published

Interpretations That Do Not Permit Broker Discretionary Votes for Material Amendments to Investment Advisory Contracts, Release No. 34-59464 (Feb. 26, 2009), available at http://www.sec.gov/comments/sr-nyse-2006-92/nyse200692.shtml.

[179] See comment letters from American Express; Society of Corporate Secretaries and Governance Professionals ("Governance Professionals Letter"); Honeywell; JPMorgan Chase & Co.; and Shareholder Communications Coalition to Release No. 34-59464, note 178, above, available at http://www.sec.gov/comments/sr-nyse-2006-92/nyse200692.shtml.

[180] See Release No. 34-60215, note 11, above, at 34.

[181] See Proxy Working Group Addendum, note 127, above, at 5.

[182] Id. at 5-6. See also Governance Professionals Letter, note 179, above; ABA Letter, note 177, above; and Frank G. Zarb, Jr. and John Endean, "The Case for 'Client Directed Voting,'" Law 360 (Jan. 4, 2010).

[183] 17 CFR 240.14a-2(a)(1).

instructions from customers would not be able to satisfy this requirement. In the absence of an applicable exemption for the solicitation of advance voting instructions, Rule 14a-4(d) states that no proxy shall confer authority to vote at any annual meeting other than the next annual meeting after the date on which the form of proxy is first sent.[184] In addition, that rule prohibits a proxy from granting authority to vote with respect to more than one meeting.[185]

To pursue this alternative further, there are a number of issues that would need to be considered. Advance voting instructions could be solicited to varying levels of detail. For instance, such an instruction could be very broad, such as "vote consistent with management's recommendations" or "vote consistent with the recommendations of XYZ Environmental Group." The grant of such broad authority could raise concerns about the extent to which the investor's vote is an informed one. Greater specificity in a request for instructions, however, could provide an investor with greater certainty regarding what his or her instruction relates to. For example, an instruction to "vote consistent with [management's or other party's] recommendations regarding corporate governance issues" would provide more certainty.

In addition, if we were to permit advance voting instructions, we would need to address other issues including whether such instructions should be re-affirmed on a periodic basis; whether they should apply to the voting of shares of issuers that the investor did not own when the original instructions were submitted; whether they should be re-affirmed each time an investor purchases additional shares of an issuer's stock for which that investor has already submitted voting instructions; and whether brokers can seek from investors advance voting instructions that vary by company.

We are interested in receiving views on whether permitting advance voting instructions would increase retail investor participation in the voting process, and on whether such instructions would be appropriate as a general matter. If such instructions would increase retail investor participation and would be appropriate, we are interested in receiving views on any conditions or requirements that we should consider applying to the solicitation of such instructions.

d. Investor-to-Investor Communications

We are interested in receiving views on whether investor interest in matters presented to shareholders is affected by the extent to which investors are able to communicate with other investors about their opinions regarding matters up for a vote. It is our understanding that there tends to be higher voting participation in situations that involve increased communications and high investor interest, such as well-publicized proxy contests. We have, in the past, adopted several provisions designed to enhance shareholder communications between investors and the issuer, as well as among investors, including:

- Exempting communications with investors from the proxy statement delivery and disclosure requirements where the soliciting person is not seeking proxy authority and does not have, among other things, a substantial interest in the matter (other than as an investor in the issuer);[186]

- Permitting an investor to publicly announce how it intends to vote and provide the reasons for that decision without having to comply with the proxy rules;[187] and

---

[184] 17 CFR 240.14a-4(d)(2).
[185] 17 CFR 240.14a-4(d)(3).
[186] 17 CFR 240.14a-2(b)(1). The rule specifies certain individuals and entities, such as affiliates of the registrant, that are not entitled to rely on the exemption.

Also, if the shareholder owns more than $5 million of the registrant's securities, it must furnish a Notice of Exempt Solicitation to the Commission. 17 CFR 240.14a-6(g).
[187] 17 CFR 240.14a-1(*l*)(2)(iv).

- Broadening the types of communications that are permissible prior to the distribution of a definitive proxy statement.[188]

In addition, in 2007, we adopted rules promoting the use of electronic shareholder forums on the Internet for investor communications.[189] It is our understanding that such forums have not been used extensively. We are interested in receiving views on whether, if further steps are taken to facilitate informed discussion among investors, the level of investor voting participation and informed proxy voting would be likely to increase. In addition, we are interested in receiving views on whether any additional forums for shareholder-to-shareholder communications would be helpful.

e. Improving the Use of the Internet for Distribution of Proxy Materials

In 2007, we amended the proxy rules to adopt a "notice and access model."[190] This model provides issuers with two options for making their proxy materials available: the "notice-only option"[191] and the "full set delivery option." Under the notice-only option, the issuer must post its proxy materials on a publicly-accessible Web site and send a notice to shareholders at least 40 days before the shareholder meeting date to inform them of the electronic availability of the proxy materials, and explain how to access those materials.[192] Under this option, an issuer must also provide paper or e-mail copies of proxy materials at no charge to shareholders who request such copies.[193]

Issuers may also select the "full set delivery" option, where the issuer delivers a full set of proxy materials to shareholders, along with the Notice of Internet Availability of Proxy Materials on a Web site, and posts the proxy materials to a publicly-accessible Web site.[194] An issuer may use the notice-only option to provide proxy materials to some shareholders, and the full set delivery option to provide proxy materials to other shareholders.[195]

It has been suggested that our adoption of rules permitting the dissemination of proxy materials through a "notice and access" model has contributed to a decline in retail investor participation in voting. We believe that it is difficult to conclude, based on existing data, that notice and access has caused changes in voter participation. To be sure, the number of retail accounts submitting voting instructions when issuers use the notice-only option is lower than the number of retail accounts submitting voting instructions when issuers use the full-set delivery option. The number of retail shares being voted, however, does not appear to differ substantially.[196] More importantly, because issuers can elect whether to use the notice-only model, it is difficult to discern whether patterns in voting behavior are due to notice and access or to other factors. Issuers who

---

[188] 17 CFR 240.14a-12; Regulation of Takeovers and Security Holder Communications, Release No. 33-7760 (Oct. 22, 1999) [64 FR 61408].

[189] *See* Release No. 34-57172, note 3, above.

[190] *See* Notice and Access Release, note 2, above.

[191] The notice and access model is a concept separate from, but complementary to, electronic delivery. The notice and access model permits an issuer (or a securities intermediary at the direction of the issuer) to deliver a notice (typically in paper) informing shareholders that proxy materials are available on the Internet in lieu of sending a full paper set of proxy materials. Electronic delivery, on the other hand, arises from our guidance in Release No. 33-7233, note 32, above. In that release, we explained that delivery of materials (including proxy materials) may be made electronically under certain circumstances, including if a shareholder has provided affirmative consent to electronic delivery. An issuer or securities intermediary may send this notice electronically to a shareholder if that shareholder has affirmatively consented to electronic delivery.

[192] *See* 17 CFR 240.14a-16; Notice and Access Release, note 2, above.

[193] 17 CFR 240.14a-16.

[194] *Id.* The issuer may elect to include all of the information required to appear in the Notice in the proxy statement and proxy card. *Id.*

[195] *Id.*

[196] *See* Broadridge, Notice and Access: 2010 Statistical Overview of Use with Beneficial Shareholders, *available at* http://www.broadridge.com/notice-and-access/FY10_full_year.pdf ("2010 Broadridge Statistical Overview"). This report indicates that, during the 2009 and 2010 proxy seasons, 31.95% and 27.29%, respectively, of retail shares were voted at issuers not using notice and access, while 28.70% and 31.01%, respectively of retail shares were voted at issuers using notice and access. On the other hand, 19.39% and 19.21%, respectively, of retail accounts were voted at issuers not using notice and access, while 12.72% and 13.85%, respectively, of retail accounts were voted at issuers using notice and access.

choose the notice-only model may differ from other issuers in ways that may also correlate with voter participation, such as size or other characteristics. Some issuers have chosen a hybrid model, continuing to distribute full packages of proxy solicitation materials to selected shareholders based on the size of their holdings or their voting histories,[197] suggesting that these issuers may believe that full-set delivery affects voter participation in some cases.

Another possible option to encourage shareholder participation, while still allowing issuers to use the notice-only option, would be to permit the inclusion of a proxy card or VIF with the Notice of Internet Availability of Proxy Materials when an issuer or other soliciting shareholder elects to use the notice-only option under the notice and access model for the delivery of proxy materials. Currently, Exchange Act Rule 14a-16 explicitly prohibits the soliciting party from including a proxy card or VIF with the Notice in the same mailing.[198] Although we initially proposed a model that would have allowed soliciting parties to include a proxy card or VIF with the Notice, we ultimately adopted a rule that prohibited the inclusion of the proxy card or VIF and noted commentators' concerns that "physically separating the card from the proxy statement, as originally proposed, may lead to the type of uninformed voting that the proxy rules are intended to prevent."[199]

3. Request for Comment

With respect to investor education, we ask the following questions:

- To what extent should we take additional steps to encourage retail investor participation in the proxy process?

- To what extent would greater use of plain English, some form of summary of proxy materials, or layered formats in Web-based disclosure make proxy materials more accessible to retail investors?

- To what extent are retail voter participation levels affected by process-related impediments to participation? If affected by impediments, what are they and should we seek to remove them? What costs and benefits are associated with efforts to increase participation?

- Would additional investor education improve retail investor participation in the proxy process? How could such a program best reach both registered owners and beneficial owners? What would be the benefits and costs of such a program? What should be in the educational materials and who should decide what goes in them?

- Should brokers more clearly highlight and disclose key policies, including a shareholder's voting rights and default positions, such as OBO/NOBO, when a customer enters into a brokerage agreement? Should brokers provide counseling to potential customers to enhance understanding of such provisions in the brokerage agreement? When a customer enters into a brokerage agreement, should brokers be required to obtain the preferences of the client regarding whether to receive proxy materials electronically, and inform issuers of that election automatically when securities of that issuer are purchased?

- What role should the Commission play in promoting or developing the education campaign? How can the SEC's investor education Web sites be made more useful? For example, should the Web site provide interactive instruction?

With respect to enhanced issuers' and brokers' Internet platforms, we ask the following questions:

---

[197] *Id.*
[198] 17 CFR 240.14a-16(e). A proxy card or VIF may be included with a Notice if at least 10 days have passed since the date a Notice was first sent to shareholders. 17 CFR 240.14a-16(h)(1).
[199] Internet Availability of Proxy Materials, Release No. 34-55146 (Jan. 22, 2007) [72 FR 4148] at 4153.

- Would an issuer's Web site or a broker's Web site be a useful location for investor educational information? Are there other methods to effectively educate investors? What would be the costs and benefits of requiring issuers or securities intermediaries to include such information on their Web sites?

- Should issuers or brokers enhance their Web sites, if they have one, to provide the issuers' shareholders or the brokers' customers, respectively, with the ability to receive notices of upcoming corporate votes, to access proxy materials and to vote shares through their personal account pages? What would be the costs of such a system? Would adding this service for investors make them more likely to vote? To what extent do issuers and brokers currently provide such functionality on their Web sites?

- Should we encourage the creation of inexpensive or free proxy voting platforms that would provide retail investors with access to proxy research, vote recommendations, and vote execution? If so, how?

With respect to advance voting instructions, we ask the following questions:

- Should we consider allowing securities intermediaries to solicit voting instructions in advance of distribution of proxy materials pursuant to an exemption from the proxy solicitation rules? Should there be any conditions on any such exemption, and if so, what should they be?

- To what extent would voting instructions made without the benefit of proxy materials result in less informed voting decisions? Are there countervailing benefits to permitting the solicitation of such instructions? To what extent does the revocability of advance voting instructions mitigate concerns over less informed voting decisions?

- With regard to the use of advance voting instructions, are retail investors at a disadvantage as compared to institutional investors that use the services of a proxy advisory firm? If so, how? Are there aspects of the services and relationship between proxy advisory firms and their clients that would not exist between securities intermediaries soliciting advance voting instructions and their customers? If so, how should these differences be addressed, if at all?

- If such solicitation of advance voting instructions were permitted, what level of specificity should the solicitation of advanced voting instructions be required (or permitted) to have? Is it appropriate to permit the solicitation of a broad scope of voting authority?

- Should we allow the solicitation by securities intermediaries of advance voting instructions for all types of proxy proposals, or should it be limited to certain types of proposals? For example, should we permit solicitation of advance voting instructions with respect to shareholder proposals, proxy contests, or proposals subject to "vote no" campaigns?

- If solicitation of advance voting instructions were permitted, should the investor be permitted to instruct the securities intermediary to vote in accordance with the recommendations of management, a proxy advisory firm, or other specified persons? How neutral or balanced should the solicitation of advance voting instructions be?

- If we were to allow the solicitation of advance voting instructions, should we require an investor to reaffirm its voting instructions periodically? If so, how often? Should we require an investor to reaffirm its voting instructions every time it purchases additional shares of a stock for which that investor has already submitted a voting instruction, or when it purchases shares of a new issuer?

- If we were to allow advance voting instructions, what would be an appropriate range of options available to an investor? Should advance voting instructions only be permitted when the investor has meaningful options from which to choose?

- How difficult would it be to obtain advance voting instructions from existing brokerage customers? What would be the costs of obtaining advance voting instructions for existing accounts? Who should bear the costs of soliciting such instructions?

- If we were to allow the solicitation of advance voting instructions, would it undermine or promote the purpose of the recent amendment to NYSE Rule 452 to prohibit brokers from voting uninstructed shares in uncontested elections of directors?

With respect to investor-to-investor communications, we ask the following questions:

- To what extent are investor interest in matters presented to shareholders and investor voting participation affected by the lack of investor-to-investor communications regarding those matters?

- Have electronic shareholder forums been used extensively? Are there any revisions to Rule 14a-2(b)(6), which currently provides an exemption for electronic shareholder forums, that would make it easier to establish such forums? For example, is there a way for an entity establishing an electronic shareholder forum to confirm the shareholder status of participants on the forum? If a securities intermediary provides information, such as a control number, to enable such confirmation, should precautions be taken to ensure that personal information about those investors is not disclosed?

- Should we consider revising the electronic shareholder forum rules to shorten the 60-day period to promote more shareholder-to-shareholder communication closer to the meeting date? If so, what would be an appropriate time period?

- Are there any other new rules or revisions to existing rules that would facilitate communications among investors? If so, what would those revisions be?

- Would any additional guidance regarding the scope of our rules and definitions, such as the definition of the term "solicitation," improve the extent and quality of investor participation in the proxy voting process?

With respect to possible revisions to the notice and access model, we ask the following questions:

- Should we consider requiring that companies using a "notice and access" model for distributing proxy materials use that model on a stratified basis to encourage retail voting participation? For example, should we require that issuers send full sets of proxy materials to shareholders who have voted on paper in the past two years?

- Should we consider amending our rules to permit inclusion of a proxy card or VIF with a Notice of Internet Availability of Proxy Materials?

- Are there other changes that we can make to the notice and access model to improve voting participation? For example, should we require affirmative consent from a shareholder before an issuer is allowed to send that customer only a Notice of Internet Availability of Proxy Materials?

- Should we eliminate the notice and access model altogether?

C. Data-Tagging Proxy-Related Materials

1. Background

Issuers soliciting proxies are required to distribute a proxy statement[200] and to disclose the results of shareholder votes within four business days after the end of the meeting at

---

[200] The proxy statement must include the information required by Schedule 14A of the Exchange Act. [17 CFR 240.14a-101] The Commission's rules also generally require issuers not soliciting proxies from

which the vote was held.[201] Funds are generally required to disclose annually on Form N–PX[202] how they vote proxies relating to portfolio securities.[203] In the discussion below, we address whether this information could be organized and made available to investors in ways that might enhance the level and quality of shareholder participation in the proxy voting process.

In 2004, as part of our longstanding efforts to increase transparency in general and the usefulness of information in particular, we began an initiative to assess the benefits of interactive data[204] and its potential for improving the timeliness, accuracy, and analysis of financial and other filed information.[205] Data becomes interactive when it is labeled, or "tagged," using a computer markup language that can be processed by software for analysis. Such computer markup languages use standard sets of definitions, or "taxonomies," that translate text-based information in Commission filings into interactive data that can be retrieved, searched, and analyzed through automated means.

Our efforts regarding interactive data thus far have resulted in our adoption of rules that, in general, currently or ultimately will require:

- Public issuers, including foreign private issuers, to provide their financial statements to the Commission and on their corporate Web sites, if any, in interactive data format using eXtensible Business Reporting Language ("XBRL");[206]

- Mutual funds[207] to provide the risk/return summary section of their prospectuses to the Commission and on their Web sites, if any, in XBRL format;[208]

- Rating agencies to provide certain ratings information on their Web sites in XBRL format;[209]

(Footnote Continued)

shareholders entitled to vote on a matter to distribute an information statement that must include the similar information required by Schedule 14C of the Exchange Act [17 CFR 240.14c-101]. Accordingly, the data-tagging discussion in this Section IV.C relates to the information required by Schedule 14C in the same manner it relates to corresponding information required by Schedule 14A.

[201] Item 5.07 of Form 8-K [referenced in 17 CFR 249.308].

[202] 17 CFR 274.129. See Section III.C, above, for a further discussion of Form N-PX.

[203] In this Section IV.C, we use the term "proxy statement and voting information" to refer collectively to the information required by Schedule 14A, Schedule 14C, Item 5.07 of Form 8-K and Form N-PX.

[204] In this Section IV.C, we generally refer to "tagged data" as "interactive data" because users are able to interact with the data by processing it.

[205] See Press Release No. 2004-97 (July 22, 2004), available at http://www.sec.gov/news/press/2004-97.htm.

[206] Interactive Data to Improve Financial Reporting, Release No. 33-9002 (Jan. 30, 2009) [74 FR 6776] as corrected by Interactive Data to Improve Financial Reporting, Release No. 33-9002A (Apr. 1, 2009) [74 FR 15666]. Issuers that are or will be required to provide their financial statements in interactive data format using XBRL are permitted to provide such interactive data before they are required to do so. Funds are permitted to provide financial information in interactive data format using XBRL as an exhibit to

certain filings in our electronic filing system under a voluntary filer program that initially was implemented in 2005.

[207] In this Section IV.C, we use the term "mutual fund" to mean an open-end management investment company. An open-end management investment company is an investment company, other than a unit investment trust or face-amount certificate company, which offers for sale or has outstanding any redeemable security of which it is the issuer. See Sections 4 and 5(a)(1) of the Investment Company Act [15 U.S.C. 80a-4 and 80a-5(a)(1)].

[208] Interactive Data for Mutual Fund Risk/Return Summary, Release No. 33-9006 (Feb. 11, 2009) [74 FR 7748] as corrected by Interactive Data for Mutual Fund Risk/Return Summary; Correction, Release No. 33-9006A (May 1, 2009) [74 FR 21255]. Mutual funds are permitted to provide their risk/return summary information in interactive data format (using XBRL) before they are required to do so. The public companies, foreign private issuers and mutual funds permitted or required to provide financial statement or risk/return summary information in interactive data format are required to continue to provide the information in traditional format as well.

[209] Amendments to Rules for Nationally Recognized Statistical Rating Organizations, Release No. 34-61050 (Nov. 23, 2009) [74 FR 63832] and Amendments to Rules for Nationally Recognized Statistical Rating Organizations, Release No. 34-59342 (Feb. 2, 2009) [74 FR 6456].

- Money market funds to provide portfolio holdings information to the Commission in interactive data format using eXtensible Markup Language ("XML");[210]

- Transfer agents to provide registration, activity and withdrawal information to the Commission in XML format;[211]

- Issuers to provide notice of Regulation D[212] exempt offering information to the Commission in XML format[213] or through the Commission's online forms Web site that tags the information in XML;[214] and

- Officers, directors, and principal owners to provide beneficial ownership information under Section 16(a) of the Exchange Act[215] to the Commission in XML format[216] or through the Commission's online forms Web site that tags the information in XML.[217]

Currently, proxy statement and voting information is neither required nor permitted to be provided to the Commission in interactive data format. As a result, shareholders cannot retrieve, search, and use this information through automated means in the form in which it is provided to the Commission.

2. Potential Regulatory Responses

We are interested in receiving views on whether it would be beneficial to investors to permit or require issuers, including funds, to provide proxy statement and voting information in interactive data format in addition to the traditional format. We are also interested in understanding the costs of providing additional tagged information. A significant amount of the textual data in the proxy statement is well-structured and may be suitable for data tagging. If issuers provided reportable items in interactive data format, shareholders may be able to more easily obtain specific information about issuers, compare information across different issuers, and observe how issuer-specific information changes over time as the same issuer continues to file in an interactive data format. This could both facilitate more informed voting and investment decisions and assist in automating regulatory filings and business information processing.[218]

Under our current rules, issuers are permitted or required to provide specified information in interactive data format only as described above. We have, however, previously considered, and sought comment on, permitting or requiring interactive data for other

---

[210] Money Market Fund Reform, Release No. IC-29132 (Feb. 23, 2010) [75 FR 10060]. The XBRL format is compatible with and derives from the XML format.

[211] Electronic Filing of Transfer Agent Forms, Release No. 34-54864 (Dec. 4, 2006) [71 FR 74698].

[212] 17 CFR 230.501–508.

[213] *See* EDGAR Form D XML Technical Specification (Version 7.4.0), *available at* http://www.sec.gov/info/edgar/formdxmltechspec.htm.

[214] Electronic Filing and Revision of Form D, Release No. 33-8891 (Feb. 6, 2008) [73 FR 10592].

[215] 15 U.S.C. 78p(a).

[216] *See* EDGAR Ownership XML Technical Specification (Version 3), *available at* http://www.sec.gov/info/edgar/ownershipxmltechspec.htm.

[217] Mandated Electronic Filing and Web Site Posting for Forms 3, 4 and 5, Release No. 33-8230 (May 7, 2003) [68 FR 25788].

[218] We anticipate that any interactive data format version of the information permitted or required would not replace the traditional format version, at least not initially. In general, interactive data currently is machine-readable only. Without the use of software, interactive data is illegible to the human eye. As a result, we expect that any interactive data would be provided in a separate schedule or exhibit. It is possible, however, that at some point in the future technology will evolve in a manner that would permit human-readable text and interactive data to appear in the same document.

types of information in XBRL or another format.[219] Most recently, in the 2008 release proposing the required filing of financial statements in XBRL format,[220] we expanded upon our 2006 request for comment on making executive compensation information available in interactive data format.[221] In the 2008 release, we did not propose permitting or requiring interactive data for executive compensation, but asked a series of questions related to whether we should. As noted in the 2009 release adopting the financial statement XBRL requirements, some commentators supported the idea of eventually tagging non-financial statement information such as executive compensation because of its usefulness to investors,[222] while others expressed concern that variations among issuers in executive compensation practices may not lend themselves to the development of standard tags and suggested that any tagging be voluntary rather than required.[223]

In connection with our efforts to improve communication in the proxy context, we are interested in receiving views on whether we should reconsider whether to permit or require proxy statement and voting information to be provided in interactive data format.[224]

3. Request for Comment

- Should we permit issuers, including funds, to provide proxy statement and voting information to the Commission and on their corporate Web sites, if any, in an interactive data format? If so, are there benefits to one tagging language (*e.g.*, XBRL) over another? [225] Should we require issuers to provide such information to the Commission and on their corporate Web sites, if any, in an interactive data format? Should we also permit or require the tagging of executive compensation information even if it is not in the proxy statement, but rather, in the annual report on Form 10-K?[226]

- Are there any other types of information for which we should permit or require tagging in order to improve the efficiency and quality of proxy voting? For example, should we permit or require tagging of information contained in proxy statements filed by non-management parties?

---

[219] With regard to format, we solicited comment in our 2004 interactive data concept release regarding the ability of interactive data to add value to Commission filings, whether in XBRL or another interactive data format. Enhancing Commission Filings Through the Use of Tagged Data, Release No. 33-8497 (Sept. 27, 2004) [69 FR 59111].

[220] Interactive Data to Improve Financial Reporting, Release No. 33-8924 (May 30, 2008) [73 FR 32794].

[221] Executive Compensation and Related Party Disclosure, Release No. 33-8655 (Jan. 27, 2006) [71 FR 6542]. In 2007, as further discussed below, our staff used XBRL to tag Summary Compensation Table data provided by large filers and created rendering software that enabled investors to not only view compensation information but also manually calculate compensation and compare compensation across companies. The software was called the Executive Compensation Reader. We made these efforts to show how interactive data might provide investors with easier and faster analysis. SEC Press Release 2007-268 (Dec. 21, 2007).

[222] *See, e.g.*, comment letter to Release No. 33-9002, note 206, above, from California Public Employees' Retirement System.

[223] *See, e.g.*, comment letters to Release 33-9002, note 206, above, from American Bar Association, Johnson & Johnson, Pfizer, General Mills, and Society of Corporate Secretaries and Governance Professionals.

[224] Our solicitation of comment regarding providing proxy statement and voting information in interactive data format is consistent with the Resolution on Tag Data for Proxy and Vote Filings adopted by the Securities and Exchange Commission Investor Advisory Committee. *See http://www.sec.gov/spotlight/ invadvcomm/iacproposedresproxyvotingtrans.pdf.*

[225] Currently, there apparently is no standard set of XBRL definitions, or "taxonomy," available to enable an issuer to provide proxy statement and voting information or any subset of such information in XBRL format. XBRL US, however, is developing a taxonomy for at least some information a proxy statement requires. *See http://xbrl.us/Learn/Pages/Initiatives. aspx* ("Broadridge Financial Solutions contributed a proxy taxonomy to XBRL US in Q4 2008. XBRL US will incorporate the taxonomy into a master digital dictionary of terms.").

[226] 17 CFR 249.310.

- If we permit or require interactive data for the information contained in a proxy statement, should we permit or require it for only a subset of that information, such as executive compensation,[227] director experience[228] and other directorships,[229] transactions with related persons,[230] or corporate governance?[231] Should we permit or require it for only a subset of executive compensation information, such as the Summary Compensation Table,[232] Director Compensation Table,[233] Outstanding Equity Awards at Fiscal Year-End Table,[234] or Compensation Discussion and Analysis?[235]

- Would it be useful to investors for issuers to provide their proxy statement and voting information, or some subset of that information, in interactive data format? If so, would it be useful for issuers to provide the information both to the Commission and on their corporate Web sites, if any? Would data-tagging enable investors to access proxy information more easily or to compare information regarding different issuers and/or changes in information over time with respect to a specific issuer or a set of issuers? Would this ability result in better informed voting decisions? For instance, should officer and director identities be tagged and linked to their unique Commission Central Index Key (CIK) identifier, which would enable investors to more easily determine whether they have relationships with other Commission filers? Would investors benefit if governance attributes, such as board leadership structure[236] and director independence, were tagged?[237]

- Would requiring issuers to provide proxy statements and voting information in interactive data format assist issuers in automating their business information processing?

- Approximately how much would it cost issuers to provide each of the following in interactive data format:

  ○ All information contained in a proxy statement;

  ○ Executive compensation information only; and

  ○ Voting information disclosed pursuant to Item 5.07 of Form 8-K or Form N-PX?

- With respect to cost, would it be preferable to defer any requirement to tag proxy-related materials until the issuer has been fully phased-in to the financial statement interactive data requirements, or would it be relatively easy to accomplish the tagging of proxy-related materials before, or at the same time as, becoming subject to the financial statement requirements?

- Is it feasible for funds to tag Form N-PX in a manner that provides for uniform identification of each matter voted (*e.g.*, for every fund to assign the same tag to

---

[227] As we noted in Release No. 33-8924, note 220, above, there was substantial interest in financial Web pages that linked to the Executive Compensation Reader that temporarily was posted on our Web site beginning in late 2007. The Executive Compensation Reader displayed the Summary Compensation Table disclosure of 500 large companies that followed the executive compensation rules adopted in 2006 in reporting 2006 compensation information in their proxy statements filed with the Commission. By using the reader, an investor could view amounts included in the Summary Compensation Table Stock Awards and Option Awards columns based on either the full grant date fair value of the awards granted during the fiscal year, or the compensation cost of awards recognized for financial statement reporting purposes with respect to the fiscal year, and recalculate the Total Compensation column accordingly.

[228] Item 401(e)(1) of Regulation S-K [17 CFR 229.401(e)(1)].

[229] Item 401(e)(2) of Regulation S-K [17 CFR 229.401(e)(2)].

[230] Item 404(a) of Regulation S-K [17 CFR 229.404 (a)].

[231] Item 407 of Regulation S-K [17 CFR 229.407].

[232] Items 402(c) and 402(n) of Regulation S-K [17 CFR 229.402(c) and 402(n)].

[233] Items 402(k) and 402(r) of Regulation S-K [17 CFR 229.402(k) and 402(r)].

[234] Items 402(f) and 402(p) of Regulation S-K [17 CFR 229.402(f) and 402(p)].

[235] Item 402(b) of Regulation S-K [17 CFR 229.402 (b)].

[236] Item 407(h) of Regulation S-K [17 CFR 229.407 (h)].

[237] Item 407(a) of Regulation S-K [17 CFR 229.407 (a)].

the election of directors at XYZ Corporation) if issuers of portfolio securities do not themselves create these tags by tagging their proxy statements? What alternatives exist, other than having issuers of portfolio securities tag their proxy statements and assign tags to each matter on their proxy statements, that could result in uniform tags being assigned by all funds on Form N-PX to each corporate matter? What would be the costs associated with those alternatives?

- Whether or not we permit or require interactive data tagging, should Form N-PX require standardized reporting formats so that comparisons between funds are easier?

- Should persons other than the issuer be required to file proxy materials in interactive data format?

- How will retail investors have access to interactive data/XBRL software that will enable them to take advantage of interactive data formats?

V. Relationship between Voting Power and Economic Interest

As discussed below, investor and issuer confidence in the legitimacy of shareholder voting may be based on the belief that, except as expressly agreed otherwise, shareholders entitled to vote in the election of directors and other matters have a residual economic (or equity) interest in the company that is commensurate with their voting rights. To the extent that votes are cast by persons lacking such an economic interest in the company, confidence in the proxy system could be undermined. This section examines the possibility of misalignment of voting power in general and three areas in which concerns have been expressed about whether our regulations play a role in the misalignment of voting power from economic interest: the increasingly important role of proxy advisory firms; the impediments in our rules to allowing issuers to set voting record dates that more closely match the date on which voting actually occurs; and hedging and other strategies that allow the voting rights of equity securities to be held or controlled by persons without an equivalent economic interest in the company.

A. Proxy Advisory Firms

1. The Role and Legal Status of Proxy Advisory Firms

Over the last twenty-five years, institutional investors, including investment advisers, pension plans, employee benefit plans, bank trust departments and funds, have substantially increased their use of proxy advisory firms, reflecting the tremendous growth in institutional investment as well as the fact that, in many cases, institutional investors have fiduciary obligations to vote the shares they hold on behalf of their beneficiaries.[238] Institutional investors typically own securities positions in a large number of issuers.

Every year, at shareholders' meetings, these investors face decisions on how to vote their shares on a significant number of matters, ranging from the election of directors and the approval of stock option plans to shareholder proposals submitted under Exchange Act Rule 14a-8,[239] which often raise significant policy questions and corporate governance issues. At special meetings of shareholders, investors also face voting decisions when a merger or acquisition or a sale of all or substantially all of the assets of the company is presented to them for approval.

---

[238] *See, e.g.*, GAO Report to Congress, Corporate Shareholder Meetings—Issues Relating to Firms That Advise Institutional Investors on Proxy Voting (June 2007) ("GAO Report") at 6-7 (attributing the growth in the use of proxy voting advisers, in part, to the Commission's recognition of fiduciary obligations associated with voting proxies by registered investment advisers and its adoption of the proxy voting Advisers Act Rule 206(4)-6(17 CFR 275.206(4)-6), requiring registered investment advisers to "adopt and implement written policies and procedures that are reasonably designed to ensure that you vote client securities in the best interest of clients, which procedures must include how you address material conflicts that may arise between your interests and those of your clients").

[239] 17 CFR 240.14a-8.

In order to assist them in exercising their voting rights on matters presented to shareholders, institutional investors may retain proxy advisory firms to perform a variety of functions, including the following:

- Analyzing and making voting recommendations on the matters presented for shareholder vote and included in the issuers' proxy statements;

- Executing votes on the institutional investors' proxies or VIFs in accordance with the investors' instructions, which may include voting the shares in accordance with a customized proxy voting policy resulting from consultation between the institutional investor and the proxy advisory firm, the proxy advisory firm's proxy voting policies, or the institution's own voting policy;

- Assisting with the administrative tasks associated with voting and keeping track of the large number of voting decisions;

- Providing research and identifying potential risk factors related to corporate governance; and

- Helping mitigate conflict of interest concerns raised when the institutional investor is casting votes in a matter in which its interest may differ from the interest of its clients.[240]

Firms that are in the business of supplying these services to clients for compensation—in particular, analysis of and recommendations for voting on matters presented for a shareholder vote—are widely known as proxy advisory firms.[241] Institutional clients compensate proxy advisory firms on a fee basis for providing such services, and proxy advisory firms typically represent that their analysis and recommendations are prepared with a view toward maximizing long-term share value or the investment goals of the institutional client.

Issuers may also be consumers of the services provided by some proxy advisory firms. Some proxy advisory firms provide consulting services to issuers on corporate governance or executive compensation matters, such as assistance in developing proposals to be submitted for shareholder approval. Some proxy advisory firms also qualitatively rate or score issuers' corporate governance structures, policies, and practices,[242] and provide consulting services to corporate clients seeking to improve their corporate governance ratings. As a result, some proxy advisory firms provide vote recommendations to institutional investors on matters for which they also provided consulting services to the issuer. Some proxy advisory firms disclose these dual client relationships; others also have opted to attempt to address the conflict through the creation of "fire walls" between the investor and corporate lines of business.

Depending on their activities, proxy advisory firms may be subject to the federal securities laws in at least two notable respects. First, because of the breadth of the definition of "solicitation,"[243] proxy advisory firms may be subject to our proxy rules because they provide recommendations that are reasonably calculated to result in the procurement, withholding, or revocation of a proxy. As a general matter, the furnishing of proxy voting advice constitutes a "solicitation" subject to the information and filing requirements in the proxy rules.[244] In 1979, however, we adopted Exchange Act Rule

---

[240] *See* Proxy Voting by Investment Advisers, Release No. IA-2106 (Jan. 31, 2003) at text accompanying note 25 (stating that an adviser could demonstrate that the vote was not a product of a conflict of interest if it voted client securities, in accordance with a pre-determined policy, based upon the recommendations of an independent third party).

[241] *E.g.*, GAO Report, note 238, above, at 1.

[242] For example, The RiskMetrics Group ("RiskMetrics") publishes "governance risk indicators." Information on these ratings is *available at* http://www.

riskmetrics.com/GRId-info. Proxy advisory firms are not the only types of businesses that offer corporate governance ratings or scores.

[243] Exchange Act Rule 14a-1(*l*)(iii) [17 CFR 240.14a-1(*l*)(iii)] defines the solicitation of proxies to include "[t]he furnishing of a form of proxy or other communication to security holders under circumstances reasonably calculated to result in the procurement, withholding or revocation of a proxy."

[244] *See* Shareholder Communications, Shareholder Participation in the Corporate Electoral Process and

14a-2(b)(3)[245] to exempt the furnishing of proxy voting advice by any advisor to any other person with whom the advisor has a business relationship from the informational and filing requirements of the federal proxy rules, provided certain conditions are met.[246] Specifically, the advisor:

- Must render financial advice in the ordinary course of its business;

- Must disclose to the person any significant relationship it has with the issuer or any of its affiliates, or with a shareholder proponent of the matter on which advice is given, in addition to any material interest of the advisor in the matter to which the advice relates;

- May not receive any special commission or remuneration for furnishing the proxy voting advice from anyone other than the recipients of the advice; and

- May not furnish proxy voting advice on behalf of any person soliciting proxies.

Even if exempt from the informational and filing requirements of the federal proxy rules, the furnishing of proxy voting advice remains subject to the prohibition on false and misleading statements in Rule 14a-9.[247]

Second, when proxy advisory firms provide certain services, they meet the definition of investment adviser under the Advisers Act and thus are subject to regulation under that Act. A person is an "investment adviser" if the person, for compensation, engages in the business of providing advice to others as to the value of securities, whether to invest in, purchase, or sell securities, or issues reports or analyses concerning securities.[248] As described above, proxy advisory firms receive compensation for providing voting recommendations and analysis on matters submitted for a vote at shareholder meetings. These matters may include shareholder proposals, elections for boards of directors, or corporate actions such as mergers. We understand that typically proxy advisory firms represent that they provide their clients with advice designed to enable institutional clients to maximize the value of their investments. In other words, proxy advisory firms provide analyses of shareholder proposals, director candidacies or corporate actions and provide advice concerning particular votes in a manner that is intended to assist their institutional clients in achieving their investment goals with respect to the voting securities they hold. In that way, proxy advisory firms meet the definition of investment adviser because they, for compensation, engage in the business of issuing reports or analyses concerning securities and providing advice to others as to the value of securities.

The Supreme Court has construed Section 206 of the Advisers Act as establishing a federal fiduciary standard governing the conduct of investment advisers.[249] The Court stated that "[t]he Advisers Act of 1940 reflects a congressional recognition of the delicate fiduciary nature of an investment advisory relationship as well as a congressional intent to eliminate, or at least to expose, all conflicts of interest which might incline an investment adviser—consciously or unconsciously—to render advice which

---

(Footnote Continued)

Corporate Governance Generally, Release No. 34-16104 (Aug. 13, 1979) at note 25. Of course, the issue of whether or not a particular communication constitutes a solicitation depends both upon the specific nature and content of the communication and the circumstances under which it is transmitted. *See* Broker-Dealer Participation in Proxy Solicitations, Release No. 34-7208 (Jan. 7, 1964).

[245] 17 CFR 240.14a-2(b)(3).

[246] *See* Shareholder Communications and Shareholder Participation in the Corporate Electoral Process and Corporate Governance Generally, Release No. 34-16356 (Nov. 21, 1979) [44 FR 68769]. In 1992, the Commission confirmed that the Rule 14a-2(b)(3)

exemption is available to proxy advisory firms that render only proxy voting advice. *See* Regulation of Communications Among Shareholders, Release No. 34-31326 (Oct. 16, 1992) [57 FR 48276], at note 41.

[247] 17 CFR 240.14a-9.

[248] Advisers Act Section 202(a)(11) [15 USC 80b-2 (a)(11)]. Sections 202(a)(11)(A) through (G) of the Advisers Act address exclusions to the definition of the term "investment adviser." [15 USC 80b-2(a)(11)(A)-(G)].

[249] Transamerica Mortgage Advisors, Inc. v. Lewis, 444 U.S. 11, 17 (1979); SEC v. Capital Gains Research Bureau, Inc., 375 U.S. 180, 191-192 (1963)

was not disinterested."[250] As investment advisers, proxy advisory firms owe fiduciary duties to their advisory clients.

In addition, Section 206 of the Advisers Act, [251] the antifraud provision, applies to any person that meets the definition of investment adviser, regardless of whether that person is registered with the Commission. Section 206(1) of the Advisers Act prohibits an investment adviser from "employ[ing] any device, scheme, or artifice to defraud any client or prospective client."[252] Section 206(2) prohibits an investment adviser from engaging in "any transaction, practice or course of business which operates as a fraud or deceit on any client or prospective client."[253] As we stated recently, the Commission has authority under Section 206(4) of the Advisers Act to adopt rules "reasonably designed to prevent, such acts, practices, and courses of business as are fraudulent, deceptive or manipulative."[254] Congress gave the Commission this authority to, among other things, address the "question as to the scope of the fraudulent and deceptive activities which are prohibited [by Section 206],"[255] and thereby permit the Commission to adopt prophylactic[256] rules that may prohibit acts that are not themselves fraudulent.[257]

Proxy advisory firms also may have to register with the Commission as investment advisers. Whether a particular investment adviser is required to register with the Commission depends on several factors. Investment advisers are generally prohibited from registering with the Commission if they have less than $25 million in assets under management.[258] Congress established this threshold in 1996 to bifurcate regulatory responsibility between the Commission and the states.[259] The Commission retains authority to exempt advisers from the prohibition on registration if the prohibition

---

[250] Capital Gains, 375 U.S. at 191-192.

[251] 15 U.S.C. 80b-6.

[252] 15 U.S.C. 80b-6(1).

[253] 15 U.S.C. 80b-6(2).

[254] Political Contributions by Certain Investment Advisers, Advisers Act Release No. 3043 (July 1, 2010) at 16, *citing* 15 U.S.C. 80b-6(4). Section 206(4) was added to the Advisers Act in Pub. L. No. 86-750, 74 Stat. 885, at sec. 9 (1960).

[255] *See* H.R. REP. NO. 2197, 86th Cong., 2d Sess., at 7-8 (1960) (stating that "[b]ecause of the general language of section 206 and the absence of express rule-making power in that section, there has always been a question as to the scope of the fraudulent and deceptive activities which are prohibited and the extent to which the Commission is limited in this area by common law concepts of fraud and deceit . . . [Section 206(4)] would empower the Commission, by rules and regulations to define, and prescribe means reasonably designed to prevent, acts, practices, and courses of business which are fraudulent, deceptive, or manipulative. This is comparable to Section 15(c)(2) of the Securities Exchange Act [15 U.S.C. 78o(c)(2)] which applies to brokers and dealers."). *See also* S. REP. NO. 1760, 86th Cong., 2d Sess., at 8 (1960) ("This [section 206(4) language] is almost the identical wording of section 15(c)(2) of the Securities Exchange Act of 1934 in regard to brokers and dealers."). The Supreme Court, in *United States v. O'Hagan*, interpreted nearly identical language in section 14(e) of the Securities Exchange Act [15 U.S.C. 78n(e)] as providing the Commission with authority to adopt rules that are "definitional and prophylactic" and that may prohibit acts that are "not themselves fraudulent . . . if the prohibition is 'reasonably designed to prevent . . . acts and practices [that] are fraudulent.'" *United States v.*

O'Hagan, 521 U.S. 642, 667, 673 (1997). The wording of the rulemaking authority in section 206(4) remains substantially similar to that of section 14(e) and section 15(c)(2) of the Securities Exchange Act. *See also* Prohibition of Fraud by Advisers to Certain Pooled Investment Vehicles, Advisers Act Release No. 2628 (Aug. 3, 2007) [72 FR 44756] (stating, in connection with the suggestion by commenters that section 206(4) provides us authority only to adopt prophylactic rules that explicitly identify conduct that would be fraudulent under a particular rule, "We believe our authority is broader. We do not believe that the commenters' suggested approach would be consistent with the purposes of the Advisers Act or the protection of investors.").

[256] S. REP. NO. 1760, note 255, above, at 4, 8. The Commission has used this authority to adopt eight rules that address abusive advertising practices, custodial arrangements, the use of solicitors, required disclosures regarding advisers' financial conditions and disciplinary histories, prohibition against political contributions by certain investment advisers ("pay to play"), proxy voting, compliance procedures and practices, and deterring fraud with respect to pooled investment vehicles. 17 CFR 275.206(4)-1; 275.206 (4)-2; 275.206(4)-3; 275.206(4)-4; 275.206(4)-5; 275.206(4)-6; 275.206(4)-7; and 275.206(4)-8.

[257] *See* HR. REP. NO. 2197, note 255, above.

[258] Advisers Act Section 203A [15 USC 80b-3(a)]. If such an adviser is an adviser to an investment company registered under the Investment Company Act, however, it must register with the Commission. *See id.*

[259] National Securities Markets Improvement Act of 1996, Pub. L. No. 104-290, 110 Stat. 3416 (codified as amended in scattered sections of the United States Code).

would be "unfair, a burden on interstate commerce, or otherwise inconsistent with the purposes" of the prohibition.[260]

Proxy advisory firms are unlikely to have sufficient assets under management to register with the Commission because they typically do not manage client assets.[261] Proxy advisory firms may nonetheless be eligible to register because they qualify for one of the exemptions from the registration prohibition under Rule 203A-2 under the Advisers Act. In particular, some proxy advisory firms may be able to rely on the exemption for "pension consultants"[262] if they have pension plan clients with an aggregate minimum value of $50 million.[263]

Proxy advisory firms that are registered as investment advisers with the Commission are subject to a number of additional regulatory requirements that provide important protections to the firm's clients. For example, registered investment advisers have to make certain disclosures on their Form ADV.[264] Among other things, these disclosures include information about arrangements that the adviser has that involve certain conflicts of interest with its advisory client.[265] In addition, proxy advisory firms that are registered investment advisers are required to adopt, implement, and annually review an internal compliance program consisting of written policies and procedures that are reasonably designed to prevent the adviser or its supervised persons from violating the Advisers Act.[266] Every registered proxy advisory firm that is registered as an investment adviser also must designate a chief compliance officer to oversee its compliance program. This compliance officer must be knowledgeable about the Advisers Act and have authority to develop and enforce appropriate compliance policies and procedures for the adviser.[267] A proxy advisory firm that is registered as an investment adviser also is required to establish, maintain, and enforce policies and procedures reasonably designed to prevent the misuse of material non-public information.[268] Proxy advisory firms that are registered as investment advisers also are required to create and preserve certain records that our examiners review when performing an inspection of an adviser.[269]

2. Concerns About the Role of Proxy Advisory Firms

The use of proxy advisory firms by institutional investors raises a number of potential issues. For example, to the extent that conflicts of interest on the part of proxy advisory firms are insufficiently disclosed and managed, shareholders could be misled and

---

[260] Advisers Act Section 203A(c) [15 USC 80b-3(c)].

[261] For the purpose of calculating assets under management, an adviser must look to those securities portfolios for which it provides "continuous and regular supervisory or management services." *See* Instruction 5 to Item 5F of Form ADV [17 CFR 279.1].

[262] Advisers Act Rule 203A-2(b) [17 CFR 275.203A-2(b)] provides that "[a]n investment adviser is a pension consultant . . . if the investment adviser provides investment advice to: Any employee benefit plan described in Section 3(3) of the Employee Retirement Income Security Act of 1974 ("ERISA") [29 U.S.C. 1002(3)]; Any governmental plan described in Section 3(32) of ERISA (29 U.S.C. 1002(32); or Any church plan described in Section 3(33) of ERISA (29 U.S.C. 1002(33)."

[263] *See id.* A number of proxy advisory firms are currently registered with the Commission under the pension consultant exemption.

[264] *See* Advisers Act Rule 203-1 [17 CFR 275.203-1]. Form ADV consists of two parts. The information provided by advisers in Part I of that form provides the Commission with census-like information on investment adviser registrants and is critical to the examination program in assessing risk and planning

examinations. It also requires investment advisers to report disciplinary events of the adviser and its employees. *See* Advisers Act Rule 204-1 [17 CFR 275.204-1].

[265] Part II of Form ADV, or a brochure containing the information in the Form, is required to be delivered to advisory clients or prospective clients by Rule 204-3 under the Advisers Act [17 CFR 275.204-3]. In addition to the disclosure of certain conflicts of interest, Part II contains information including the adviser's fee schedule and the educational and business background of management and key advisory personnel of the adviser. Part II is currently not submitted to the SEC but must be kept by advisers in their files and made available to the SEC upon request and is "considered filed." *See* Advisers Act Rule 204-1(c) [17 CFR 275.204-1(c)]. Form ADV must be updated at least annually or when there are material changes. *See* Advisers Act Rule 204-1 [17 CFR 275.204-1].

[266] Advisers Act Rule 206(4)-7 [17 CFR 275.206(4)-7].

[267] Advisers Act Rule 206(4)-7(c) [17 CFR 275.206 (4)-7(c)].

[268] Section 204 A of the Advisers Act [15 USC 80b-4a].

[269] Advisers Act Rule 204-2 [17 CFR 275.204-2].

informed shareholder voting could be impaired. To the extent that proxy advisory firms develop, disseminate, and implement their voting recommendations without adequate accountability for informational accuracy in the development and application of voting standards, informed shareholder voting may be likewise impaired. Furthermore, some have argued that proxy advisory firms are controlling or significantly influencing shareholder voting without appropriate oversight, and without having an actual economic stake in the issuer.[270] In evaluating any potential regulatory response to such issues, we are interested in learning commentators' views regarding appropriate means of addressing these issues, including the application of the proxy solicitation rules and Advisers Act registration provisions to proxy advisory firms. We are also interested in learning commentators' views as to whether these issues are affected—and if so, how— by the fact that there is one dominant proxy advisory firm in the marketplace, Institutional Shareholder Services ("ISS"),[271] whose long-standing position, according to the Government Accountability Office, "has been cited by industry analysts as a barrier to competition."[272]

In order to address these issues, which we describe in additional detail below, we would like to receive views about the role that proxy advisory firms play in the proxy voting process, which could, for instance, assist in determining whether additional regulatory requirements might be appropriate, such as the extent to which oversight of proxy advisory firms registered as investment advisers might be improved. Below we outline the two principal areas of concern about the proxy advisory industry that have come to our attention.

a. Conflicts of Interest

Perhaps the most frequently raised concern about the proxy advisory industry relates to conflicts of interest.[273] The Government Accountability Office has issued two reports since 2004 examining conflicts of interest in proxy voting by institutional investors.[274] The GAO Report issued in 2007 addressed, among other things, conflicts of interest that may exist for proxy advisory firms, institutional investors' use of the firms' services and the firms' potential influence on proxy vote outcomes, as well as the steps that the Commission has taken to oversee these firms.[275] The GAO Report noted that the most commonly cited conflict of interest for proxy advisory firms is when they provide both proxy voting recommendations to investment advisers and other institutional investors and consulting services to corporations seeking assistance with proposals to be presented to shareholders or with improving their corporate governance ratings.[276]

---

[270] See comment letters to Release No. 33-9046, note 7, above, from The Business Roundtable and IBM. It has been suggested, for example, that some issuers have adopted corporate governance practices simply to meet a proxy advisory firm's standards, even though they may not see the value of doing so. See GAO Report, note 238, above, at 10.

[271] See GAO Report, note 238, above, at 13 (stating that, "[a]s the dominant proxy advisory firm, ISS has gained a reputation with institutional investors for providing reliable, comprehensive proxy research and recommendations, making it difficult for competitors to attract clients and compete in the market"). As of June 2007, ISS's client base included an estimate of 1,700 institutional investors, more than the other four major firms combined. Id. ISS was acquired by Risk-Metrics in January 2007, which in turn was acquired on June 1, 2010 by MSCI, Inc. See "MSCI Completes Acquisition of RiskMetrics," (June 1, 2010), available at http://www.riskmetrics.com/news_releases/20100601_msci.

[272] GAO Report, note 238, above, at 2.

[273] See generally Thompson-Mann Policy Briefing, note 89, above, at 8; GAO Report, note 238, above.

[274] GAO Report, note 238, above. The GAO issued an earlier report in 2004 that described, among other things, conflicts of interest in the proxy voting system with respect to pension plans and actions taken to manage them by plan fiduciaries. See GAO, Pension Plans: Additional Transparency and Other Actions Needed in Connection with Proxy Voting (Aug. 10, 2004), available at http://www.gao.gov/new.items/d04749.pdf.

[275] GAO Report, note 238, above. That report noted that the Commission had not identified any major violations in its examinations of such firms that were registered as investment advisers.

[276] In its report, GAO described the business model of ISS as containing this particular conflict and noted that the proxy advisory firm took steps to manage the conflict by disclosing the relationships it had with corporate governance clients and implementing policies and procedures to separate its consulting services from proxy voting services. See GAO Report, note 238, above, at 10-11. These potential conflicts of interest of

In particular, this conflict of interest arises if a proxy advisory firm provides voting recommendations on matters put to a shareholder vote while also offering consulting services to the issuer or a proponent of a shareholder proposal on the very same matter.[277] The issuer in this situation may purchase consulting services from the proxy advisory firm in an effort to garner the firm's support for the issuer when the voting recommendations are made.[278] Similarly, a proponent may engage the proxy advisory firm for advice on voting recommendations in an effort to garner the firm's support for its shareholder proposals. The GAO Report also noted that the firm might recommend a vote in favor of a client's shareholder proposal in order to keep the client's business.

A conflict also arises when a proxy advisory firm provides corporate governance ratings on issuers to institutional clients, while also offering consulting services to corporate clients so that those issuers can improve their corporate governance ranking.[279] The GAO Report also described the potential for conflicts of interest when owners or executives of the proxy advisory firm have significant ownership interests in, or serve on the board of directors of, issuers with matters being put to a shareholder vote on which the proxy advisory firm is offering vote recommendations. In such cases, institutional investors told the GAO that some proxy advisory firms would not offer vote recommendations to avoid the appearance of a conflict of interest.

It is our understanding that at least one proxy advisory firm provides a generic disclosure of such conflicts of interest by stating that the proxy advisory firm "may" have a consulting relationship with the issuer, without affirmatively stating whether the proxy advisory firm has or had a relationship with a specific issuer or the nature of any such relationship. Some have argued that this type of general disclosure is insufficient, even if the proxy advisory firm has confidentiality walls between its corporate consulting and proxy research departments.[280]

b. Lack of Accuracy and Transparency in Formulating Voting Recommendations

Some commentators have expressed the concern that voting recommendations by proxy advisory firms may be made based on materially inaccurate or incomplete data, or that the analysis provided to an institutional client may be materially inaccurate or incomplete.[281] To the extent that a voting recommendation is based on flawed data or analysis, issuers have expressed a desire for a process to correct the mistake. We understand, however, that proxy advisory firms may be unwilling, as a matter of policy, to accept any attempted communication from the issuer or to reconsider recommendations in light of such communications. Even if a proxy advisory firm entertains comment from the issuer and amends its recommendation, votes may have already been cast based on the prior recommendation. Accordingly, some issuers have expressed a desire to be involved in reviewing a draft of the proxy advisory firm's report, if only for the limited purpose of ensuring that the voting recommendations are based on accurate issuer data.

(Footnote Continued)

proxy advisory firms are not limited to the United States. *See* OECD Survey, note 90, above (expressing concern about the integrity of financial intermediaries and the need for more concrete rules).

[277] *See* GAO Report, note 238, above. Not all proxy advisory firms provide both types of services; some proxy advisory firms differentiate their services by not providing consulting services to corporations. *See* http://www.ejproxy.com/about.aspx; http://www.glasslewis.com/solutions/proxypaper.php; and www.marcoconsulting.com/2.3.html.

[278] *See* Thompson-Mann Policy Briefing, note 89, above, at 9. *See also* comment letter to Proxy Disclosure and Solicitation Enhancements, Release No.

33-9052 (July 10, 2009) [74 FR 35076], from Pearl Meyer and Partners, at 12.

[279] *See* Paul Rose, *The Corporate Governance Industry*, 32 Iowa J. Corp. L. 887, 903 (2007).

[280] *See generally* comment letter to Release No. 33-9052, note 278, above, from Oppenheimer Funds.

[281] *See, e.g.*, White Paper on RiskMetrics Report on Target Corporation, *available at* http://tgtfiles.target.com/empl/pdfs/RMG_Analysis.pdf (identifying asserted inaccurate or misleading statements or assessments in RiskMetrics' report on the 2009 proxy contest involving Target Corporation); Matthew Greco, "New, New Ranking of the Shareholder Friendly, Unfriendly," Securities Data Publishing, May 13, 1996.

Some proxy advisory firms have claimed that they are willing to discuss matters with issuers, but that some issuers are unwilling to enter into such discussions.

There also is a concern that proxy advisory firms may base their recommendation on one-size-fits-all governance approach.[282] As a result, a policy that would benefit some issuers, but that is less suitable for other issuers, might not receive a positive recommendation, making it less likely to be approved by shareholders.

Rule 14a-2(b)(3)'s exemption of proxy advisory firms does not mandate that a firm relying on the exemption have specific procedures in place to ensure that its research or analysis is materially accurate or complete prior to recommending a vote.[283] While voting advice by firms relying on the Rule 14a-2(b)(3) exemption remains subject to the antifraud provisions of the proxy rules contained in Rule 14a-9[284]—and those antifraud provisions should deter the rendering of voting advice that is misleading or inaccurate—it is our understanding that certain participants in the proxy process believe that additional oversight mechanisms could improve the likelihood that voting recommendations are based on materially accurate and complete information. In addition, as a fiduciary, the proxy advisory firm has a duty of care requiring it to make a reasonable investigation to determine that it is not basing its recommendations on materially inaccurate or incomplete information.

3. Potential Regulatory Responses

a. Potential Solutions Addressing Conflicts of Interest

Revising or providing interpretive guidance on the proxy rule exemption in Exchange Act Rule 14a-2(b)(3)[285] could be one potential solution to the concerns regarding a proxy advisory firm's disclosures about conflicts of interest. Exchange Act Rule 14a-2(b)(3)(ii) requires that a person furnishing proxy voting advice to another person must disclose to its client "any significant relationship" it has with the issuer, its affiliates, or a shareholder proponent of the matter on which advice is given. It appears that some proxy advisory firms currently provide disclosure limited to the fact that the firm "may" provide consulting or other advisory services to issuers. However, we believe that such disclosure should be examined further to determine whether it adequately indicates to shareholders the existence of a potential conflict with respect to any particular proposal. Therefore, we are interested in receiving views on whether this rule should be revised or whether we should provide additional guidance regarding the requirements of this rule. Specifically, we could revise the rule to require more specific disclosure regarding the presence of a potential conflict.

Alternatively, or in addition, we seek comment on whether proxy advisory firms operate the kind of national business or have an impact on the securities markets that Advisers Act Section 203A(c)[286] was designed to address, and whether, as a result, we should establish an additional exemption from the prohibition on federal registration for proxy advisory firms to register with the Commission as investment advisers. We could also provide additional guidance, if necessary, on the fiduciary duty of proxy advisors who are investment advisers to deal fairly with clients and prospective clients, and to disclose fully any material conflict of interest. We also could provide guidance or propose a rule requiring specific disclosure by proxy advisory firms that are registered as investment advisers regarding their conflicts of interest, including, for example, on Form ADV.

---

[282] The concern regarding a potential one-size-fits-all approach to proxy advice is not limited to U.S. proxy participants. The OECD also has expressed concern that there is a danger of one-size-fits-all voting advice (*e.g.*, applicable to compensation and a box-ticking approach by shareholders minimizing analysis and responsibilities of shareholders) so that a competitive market for advice needs to be encouraged. *See* OECD, Corporate Governance and the Financial Crisis: Key Findings and Main Messages (June 2009), *available at* http://www.oecd.org/dataoecd/3/10/43056196.pdf.

[283] 17 CFR 240.14a-2(b)(3).

[284] 17 CFR 240.14a-9.

[285] 17 CFR 240.14a-2(b)(3).

[286] 15 USC 80b-3a(c).

Finally, in light of the similarity between the proxy advisory relationship and the "subscriber-paid" model for credit ratings, we could consider whether additional regulations similar to those addressing conflicts of interest on the part of Nationally Recognized Statistical Rating Organizations ("NRSROs")[287] would be useful responses to stated concerns about conflicts of interest on the part of proxy advisory firms. For example, such regulations could prohibit certain conflicts of interest and require proxy advisory firms to file periodic disclosures, akin to Form NRSRO, describing any conflicts of interest and procedures to manage them.

b. Potential Solutions Addressing Accuracy and Transparency in Formulating Voting Recommendations

We have identified a number of potential approaches that might address concerns about accuracy or transparency in the formulation of voting recommendations by proxy advisory firms. For example, proxy advisory firms could provide increased disclosure regarding the extent of research involved with a particular recommendation and the extent and/or effectiveness of its controls and procedures in ensuring the accuracy of issuer data. Proxy advisory firms could also disclose policies and procedures for interacting with issuers, informing issuers of recommendations, and handling appeals of recommendations.[288] We could also consider requiring proxy advisory firms to file their voting recommendations with us as soliciting material, at least on a delayed basis, to facilitate independent evaluation by market participants of the quality of those recommendations.

3. Request for Comment

As discussed above, we are considering the extent to which the voting recommendations of proxy advisory firms serve the interests of investors in informed proxy voting, and whether, and if so, how, we should take steps to improve the utility of such recommendations to investors. In particular, we seek comment on whether we should clarify existing regulations or propose additional regulations to address concerns about the existence and disclosure of conflicts of interest on the part of proxy advisory firms, and about the accuracy and transparency of the formulation of their voting recommendations. Accordingly, we seek commentators' views generally on proxy advisory firms and invite comment on the following questions:

---

[287] NRSROs are credit rating agencies that assess the creditworthiness of obligors as entities or with respect to specific securities or money market instruments and that have elected to be registered with the Commission under Section 15E of the Exchange Act. 15 USC 78o-7. Sections 15E and 17 of the Exchange Act provide the Commission with exclusive authority to implement registration, recordkeeping, financial reporting, and oversight rules with respect to NRSROs. 15 USC 78o-7 and 78q.

One commentator has suggested that the Commission's rules that govern NRSROs may be useful templates for developing a regulatory program addressing conflicts of interest and other issues with respect to the accuracy and transparency of voting recommendations provided by proxy advisory firms. Such rules include provisions that: (i) require rating actions to be made publicly available on the NRSRO's Internet Web site [17 CFR 240.17g-2(d)(3)]; (ii) prohibit certain conflicts of interest [17 CFR 240.17g-5(c); Form NRSRO Exhibits 6-7]; (iii) require the disclosure and management of certain other conflicts of interest that arise in the normal course of engaging in the business of issuing credit ratings [17 CFR 240.17g-5

(b)]; and (iv) require disclosure of, among other things, performance measurement statistics, sources of information, models and metrics used, qualifications and compensation of analysts, and procedures and methodologies used to determine credit ratings, including procedures for (A) interacting with management of rated issuers, (B) informing issuers of rating decisions, and (C) appealing final or pending rating decisions. [Form NRSRO, Exhibits 1, 2, 8 and 13]. We recognize that the role of NRSROs and proxy advisory firms differ and that following a similar regulatory approach might not be appropriate. We also recognize that the costs and benefits of the NRSRO regulation differ from the costs and benefits of potential additional regulation of proxy advisory firms.

[288] See, e.g., Thompson-Mann Policy Briefing, note 89, above, at 25 (advocating that a proxy advisory firm should, where feasible and appropriate, prior to issuing or revising a recommendation, advise the issuer of the critical information and principal considerations upon which a recommendation will be based and afford the issuer an opportunity to clarify any likely factual misperceptions).

- Do proxy advisory firms perform services for their clients in addition to or different from those noted above?

- Is additional regulation of proxy advisory firms necessary or appropriate for the protection of investors? Why or why not? If so, what are the implications of regulation through the Advisers Act or the proxy solicitation rules under the Exchange Act? Are any other regulatory approaches equally or better suited to provide appropriate additional regulation? Are there regulatory approaches used in connection with NRSROs that may be appropriate to consider applying to proxy advisory firms?

- Are there conflicts of interest (other than those described above) when a proxy advisory firm provides services to both investors, including shareholder proponents, and issuers? If so, are those conflicts appropriately addressed by current laws, regulations, and industry practices?

- Are there conflicts of interest where a proxy advisory firm is itself a publicly held company? If so, what are they and how should they be addressed?

- What policies and procedures, if any, do proxy advisory firms use to ensure that their voting recommendations are independent and not influenced by the fees they receive for services to corporate clients or shareholder proponent clients?

- Is the disclosure that proxy advisory firms currently provide to investor clients regarding conflicts of interest adequate? Would specific disclosure of potential conflicts and conflict of interest policies be sufficient, or is some other form of regulation necessary (*e.g.*, prohibiting such conflicts)?

- Do issuers modify or change their proposals to increase the likelihood of favorable recommendations by a proxy advisory firm?

- Do issuers adopt particular governance standards solely to meet the standards of a proxy advisory firm? If so, why do issuers behave in this manner?

- Should proxy advisory firms be required to disclose publicly their decision models for approval of executive compensation plans? Would this alleviate concerns regarding potential conflicts of interest when issuers pay consulting fees for access to such models?

- What is the competitive structure of the market for proxy advisory firms, and what are the reasons for it? Does competition vary across the types of services provided by the proxy advisory firms or the subset of issuers that they cover? Does the industry's competitive structure affect the quality of the recommendations? If there is, as we understand it, one proxy advisory firm that has a significantly larger market share than other firms,[289] does that affect the quality of the recommendations made by that proxy advisory firm or by other proxy advisory firms? Are there any other effects caused by the fact that there is one dominant proxy advisory firm?

- How do institutional investors use the voting recommendations provided by proxy advisory firms? What empirical data exists regarding how, and to what extent, institutional investors vote consistently, or inconsistently, with such recommendations?

- What criteria and processes do proxy advisory firms use to formulate their recommendations and corporate governance ratings? Does the lack of a direct pecuniary interest in the effects of their recommendations on shareholder value affect how they formulate recommendations and corporate governance ratings? Would greater disclosure about how recommendations and corporate governance ratings are generated and how voting recommendations are made affect the quality of the ratings and the recommendations?

---

[289] GAO Report, note 238, above, at 13 (describing ISS as "the dominant proxy advisory firm").

- Are existing procedures followed by proxy advisory firms sufficient to ensure that proxy research reports provided to investor clients are materially accurate and complete? If not, how should proxy advisory firms be encouraged to provide investors with the information they need to make informed voting decisions?

- If additional oversight is needed, should it be in the form of regulatory oversight or issuer involvement? Would requiring delayed public disclosure of voting recommendations be an appropriate means to promote accurate voting recommendations?

- Do proxy advisory firms control or significantly influence shareholder voting without appropriate oversight? If so, is there empirical evidence that demonstrates this control or significant influence? If such proxy advisory firms do control or significantly influence shareholder voting, is that inappropriate, and if so, should the Commission take action to address it? If so, what specific action should the Commission take?

- Are there any proxy advisory firms that cannot rely on an exemption to the prohibition on Advisers Act registration? If so, why do the exemptions not apply to those proxy advisory firms?

- Do proxy advisory firms operate the kind of national business that the Advisers Act Section 203A(c) was designed to address? Should we create an additional exemption from the prohibition on federal registration for proxy advisory firms to register as investment advisers? If so, what standard should we use?

- Do the current regulatory requirements for registered investment advisers adequately address advisers whose business is primarily providing proxy voting services? If we consider new rulemaking in this area, what should the rules address? Should we amend Form ADV to require specific disclosures by registered investment advisers that are proxy advisory firms?

- Do proxy advisory firms maintain an audit trail for votes cast on behalf of clients? Do proxy advisory firms monitor whether votes cast are appropriately counted, and if so, how?

B. Dual Record Dates

1. Background

Under state corporation law, issuers set a record date in advance of a shareholder meeting, and holders of record on the record date are entitled to notice of the meeting and to vote at the meeting. State corporation law also governs how far in advance of the meeting a record date can be—typically, no more than 60 days before the date of the meeting.[290] The record date that an issuer selects has implications under the federal securities laws. Our rules require issuers that have a class of securities registered under Section 12 of the Exchange Act and certain investment companies to provide either proxy materials or an information statement to every investor of the class entitled to vote.[291] Additionally, Rule 14a-13 requires that if an issuer intends to solicit proxies for an upcoming meeting and knows that its securities are held by securities intermediaries, it generally must make an inquiry of each such securities intermediary at least 20 business days prior to the record date to ascertain the number of copies of sets of proxy materials needed to supply the materials to the beneficial owners.[292]

---

[290] *See, e.g.*, Del. Code Ann. tit. 8, § 213(a) ; Model Bus. Corp. Act § 7.05.

[291] Additionally, Section 402.04 of the NYSE Listed Issuer Manual provides that "[a]ctively operating issuers are required to solicit proxies for all meetings of shareholders," and NASDAQ Listing Rule 5620(b) provides that "[e]ach Issuer that is not a limited partnership shall solicit proxies and provide proxy statements for all meetings of Shareholders."

[292] 17 CFR 240.14a-13. Rule 14c-7 contains a parallel requirement for issuers intending to distribute information statements. 17 CFR 240.14c-7.

Historically, the same record date has been used for determining both which share-holders are entitled to notice of an upcoming meeting and which shareholders are entitled to vote. However, some states are enacting changes to this procedure. For example, effective August 1, 2009, the Delaware General Corporation Law permits, but does not require, Delaware corporations to use separate record dates for making these two determinations.[293] One important result of this change is that it potentially allows an issuer, by establishing a voting record date close to the meeting date, to decrease the likelihood that as of the meeting date persons entitled to vote at the meeting (*i.e.*, the holders on the voting record date) will no longer have an economic interest in the issuer.[294]

2. Difficulties in Setting a Voting Record Date Close to a Meeting Date

Although Delaware's amended statute permits a voting record date[295] to be as late as the date of the meeting itself,[296] certain logistical and legal matters currently prevent issuers from setting such a voting record date.[297] For example, Rule 14c-2(b) requires that if information statements are being distributed, they must be sent or given to holders of the class of securities entitled to vote at least 20 calendar days prior to the meeting date. Because the investors entitled to receive the information statements, by definition, cannot be identified until the voting record date,[298] issuers intending to distribute information statements currently would be unable to set a voting record date that is fewer than 20 calendar days prior to the corresponding meeting.

We have not adopted a 20 calendar day requirement with respect to proxy materials,[299] but we have stated that "the materials must be mailed sufficiently in advance of the meeting date to allow five business days for processing by the banks and broker-dealers and an additional period to provide ample time for delivery of the material, consideration of the material by the beneficial owners, return of their voting instructions,

---

[293] Del. Code Ann. tit. 8, § 213(a). Section 213 provides that the record date for determining which shareholders are entitled to notice of a meeting "shall not be more than 60 nor less than 10 days before the date of such meeting," and that Unless the board determines otherwise, "such date shall also be the record date for determining the stockholders entitled to vote at such meeting." The August 1, 2009 amendment provides that as an alternative, the board may determine "that a later date on or before the date of the meeting shall be the date for making such determination." Recently proposed amendments to the Model Business Corporation Act, especially §7.07(e) of that Act, adopt a similar approach in permitting dual record dates. *See* Changes in the Model Business Corporation Act—Proposed Amendments to Shareholder Voting Provisions Authorizing Remote Participation in Shareholder Meetings and Bifurcated Record Dates, 65 Bus. Law. 153, 156-160 (Nov. 2009).

[294] *See* James L. Holzman and Paul A. Fioravanti, Jr., "Review of Developments in Delaware Corporation Law," Apr. 2009, at 2, *available at* http://www.prickett.com/PrinterFriendly/Articles/2009_Review_of_Developments.pdf (explaining that the ability to move the voting record date closer to meeting date should promote voting only by those who continue to have an economic interest).

[295] For purposes of this release, the term "voting record date" refers to the date used in determining the stockholders entitled to vote at the meeting, and the term "notice record date" refers to the date used for determining the stockholders entitled to notice of the meeting. "Voting-record-date shareholders" and

"notice-record-date shareholders" refer to share-holders who hold their shares as of the record date that is specified.

[296] *See* Charles M. Nathan, "'Empty Voting' and Other Fault Lines Undermining Shareholder Democracy: The New Hunting Ground for Hedge Funds," *available at* http://lw.com/upload/pubContent/_pdf/pub1878_1.Commentary.Empty.Voting.pdf (explaining that, "[w]ith modern technology, there is no apparent need to retain an advance record date concept to manage shareholder voting. Rather, the record date could be as late as the close of business on the night preceding the meeting, with a voting period (*i.e.*, the time for which the polls remain open) at or in conjunction with the meeting lasting several hours or perhaps a full working day.").

[297] Conversely, the record date for traded companies in the United Kingdom must be set at a time that is not more than 48 hours before the time for the holding of the meeting. The Companies (Shareholders' Rights) Regulations 2009 No. 1632 (Regulation 20, section 360B), *available at* http://www.opsi.gov.uk/si/si2009/uksi_20091632_en_3#pt3-l1g9.

[298] Rules 14a-1(h) and 14c-1(h) define "record date" as "the date as of which the record holders of securities entitled to *vote* at a meeting or by written consent or authorization shall be determined" (emphasis added).

[299] We note, however, that Section 401.03 of the NYSE Listed Issuer Manual "recommends that a minimum of 30 days be allowed between the record and meeting dates so as to give ample time for the solicitation of proxies."

and transmittal of the vote from the bank or broker-dealer to the tabulator."[300] Additionally,

- Instructions to Schedule 14A, Form S-4, and Form F-4 prescribe certain situations in which, if the materials being sent to shareholders incorporate information by reference, the issuer must send its proxy statement or prospectus to investors at least 20 business days before the meeting;[301]

- Rule 14a-16(a)(1) requires issuers not relying on the full set delivery option to provide a Notice of Internet Availability of Proxy Materials at least 40 calendar days before the meeting date;[302] and

- Certain of our rules and forms require that if a limited partnership roll-up transaction is being proposed, the disclosure document must be distributed no later than the lesser of 60 calendar days prior to the meeting date or the maximum number of days permitted for giving notice under applicable state law.[303]

Because these provisions require a period of time between the mailing of materials and the meeting date and because, under a dual record date system, the investors to whom the materials must be mailed (that is, those investors entitled to vote at the meeting) would not be identified until the voting record date, [304] issuers are limited in how close to the meeting date their voting record date can be.

Issuers also need to consider logistical matters in deciding the timing of their voting record date and their mailing. They need to find out how many copies of their materials to print, print the materials, and distribute the materials to transfer agents and to proxy service providers so that they can be delivered to registered and beneficial owners. Exchange Act Rules 14a-13, 14b-1, 14b-2, and 14c-7 govern this process, but we understand that in practice those rules reflect only a subset of the time-consuming logistical hurdles issuers need to go through. In this release, we are inviting submission of additional information on this process and suggestions for streamlining it.

3. Potential Regulatory Responses

In light of the changes to state law, we seek to explore whether to propose action to accommodate issuers that wish to use separate record dates where permitted by state law, and if so, what action we should take. In analyzing this situation, we are faced with competing considerations. On one hand, the closer to a meeting date a voting record date is, the more likely it is that investors who are entitled to vote will still have an economic interest in the issuer at the time of the shareholder meeting. Thus, setting the voting record date close to the meeting date avoids disenfranchising the shareholders who purchase their shares after the record date for notice of the meeting. Moreover, facilitating the use of a notice record date that significantly precedes a voting record date may assist shareholders in recalling loaned securities in order to vote them. On the other hand, investors who are entitled to vote need adequate time to receive the proxy materials and consider the matters presented to them for approval. Inadequate time can lead to uninformed voting decisions or, in some cases, a decision by the investor not to vote at all, a problem that was highlighted in 2007 as we considered adopting the notice and access rules.[305]

---

[300] Release No. 34-33768, note 4, above.

[301] *See* Note D.3 to Schedule 14A, General Instruction A.2 to Form S-4, and General Instruction A.2 to Form F-4.

[302] 17 CFR 240.14a-16(a)(1).

[303] Section 14(h)(1)(J) of the Exchange Act, Rule 14a-6(*l*), Rule 14c-2(c), General Instruction I.2 to Form S-4, and General Instruction G.2 to Form F-4.

[304] Under our rules, the issuer must send an information statement to all shareholders entitled to vote at a meeting, but from whom no proxy is being solicited. 17 CFR 240.14c-2. Thus, the issuer effectively must send either a proxy statement or an information statement to any shareholder entitled to vote at a meeting, including those that acquire the securities after the notice record date, but before the voting record date.

[305] *See* Release 34-55146, note 199, above, at note 25.

If we choose to facilitate issuers' use of separate record dates, we could choose between two general models, one focusing principally on the notice record date and the other focusing principally on the voting record date. The first model would be to require issuers to provide proxy materials or an information statement, as applicable, to those who are investors as of the notice record date. This model parallels the Delaware provision in that it focuses the information-delivery obligation on persons who are investors as of the notice record date. One open question under this first model is whether issuers should subsequently be obligated to send the disclosure document to those who were not investors as of the notice record date but who become investors by the voting record date.[306]

The second model would be to require issuers to provide the disclosure document to those who are investors as of the voting record date. An open issue under this model is whether and how issuers should be obligated to make the disclosure document public at some point before the voting record date.

Under either model, it is possible that some investors will obtain a proxy card or VIF, fill it out and submit it, and then buy additional shares or sell some shares, all prior to the voting record date. Thus, the number of shares held at the time of submission of the proxy or VIF may differ from the number of shares that are ultimately voted on behalf of the investor. In such a situation, we would need to consider how the proxy or VIF already submitted by the investor would be affected, as well as the legal and operational implications that this situation may impose on broker-dealers and their customers and the costs associated with developing a process to address it, in light of the complex beneficial ownership structure described earlier in this release.

Investors may benefit from receiving information about the effect that trades subsequent to the submission of their proxy or VIF will have on their voting rights. Therefore, additional disclosure may be necessary in proxy and information statements. One possible disclosure would be to establish that if an investor submits a proxy or VIF prior to the voting record date, all of the shares held by the investor as of the voting record date would be voted in accordance with the proxy or VIF, in the absence of specific contrary instructions from the investor.[307] Another alternative would be to clarify that a proxy or VIF would not be used to vote more shares than the investor held at the time he or she submitted the proxy or VIF, so that shares acquired after the notice record date would not be voted unless that investor submits a separate proxy or voting instruction for those shares. However, it appears that each of these approaches may risk undermining the purpose of facilitating a voting record date that is closer to the meeting date.

4. Request for Comment

- Do issuers wish to use dual record dates? If so, why?

- The Delaware amendment became effective on August 1, 2009. Should we first see how popular the dual-record-date provision is before providing a regulatory response? Or, are our rules an impediment to using dual record dates, so that it is difficult to assess whether this new approach would be viewed favorably by issuers or investors unless we change our rules?

- In view of the competing policy considerations described above, if we respond, should we respond in a way that generally facilitates issuers' ability to use the dual-record-date approach or in a way that discourages it? Which direction would be better for investors? Is there a more neutral approach that would better serve the interests of investors?

---

[306] The theory for not imposing this requirement would be that voting-record-date shareholders will have the information available to them if they desire to see it. The information will be available on the Internet pursuant to Rule 14a-16(b)(1) and (d), and in many cases press releases and media reports would publicize the availability of the information.

[307] The investor would, of course, continue to be able to revise his or her previous votes prior to the meeting.

- Even if it is too early for us to take action that either facilitates or discourages issuers' use of dual record dates, does the mere existence of a two-record-date regime create confusion or uncertainty in the interpretation of any of our existing rules? If so, which rules need to be clarified or revised? For example, should we consider proposing to clarify or to revise:

  o Rules 14a-1(h) and 14c-1(h), which define "record date" as, essentially, the voting record date;

  o Item 6(b) of Schedule 14A, which requires issuers to "[s]tate the record date, if any, with respect to this solicitation"; or

  o Rules 14a-13(a)(3) and 14c-7(a)(3), which require issuers to send an inquiry at least 20 business days prior to the record date?

- Would any SRO rules or recommendations need to be revised or clarified in order to facilitate the use of dual record dates?

- Under the first model described above, after an issuer distributes its disclosure document to investors as of the notice record date, the issuer might need to send the disclosure document, or at least a notice of the availability of the disclosure document, to those who become investors after the notice record date but before the voting record date.

  o Would this obligation be appropriate?

  o If not, how would new investors obtain the means to vote, such as a proxy card, a VIF, or a control number to vote electronically or telephonically? Would they be limited to attending the meeting in person? Would new beneficial owners be able to vote or attend at all?

  o Given that the investors who are entitled to vote are the investors as of the voting record date, would the first model (in which some investors who ultimately would not be entitled to vote would receive proxy materials) serve any useful interest if such an obligation were not imposed?

  o If we do not impose such an obligation on issuers, should they be able to choose which new investors to send the disclosure document to, or should an "all or none" requirement apply? If they should have a choice, on what basis should they be able to choose?

  o Finally, what impact would the first model have on the costs of distributing proxy materials?

- Under the second model described above, because the voting record date might be close to, or on, the meeting date, would it be necessary to require issuers to make public their disclosure document at some point before the voting record date? What would be the most appropriate way for them to do so, and how far in advance of the voting record date or the meeting date should they be required to do so? Should we consider different requirements for different sizes of issuers (for example, permit more reliance on media outlets and less reliance on physical mailings for larger issuers)?

- Which of the two general approaches outlined above is more appropriate? What other general approaches should we consider?

- Would broker-dealers be able, or have sufficient time, to track accurately which beneficial owners would have the right to vote on the voting record date if it is close to the shareholder meeting? If so, what would be the cost to broker-dealers to establish such tracking systems?

- As discussed above, some of our rules specify a minimum number of days before a meeting by which an issuer must distribute its disclosure document. Should we consider shortening or eliminating any of these time periods? If we shorten any of them, what is an appropriate amount of time to replace it with?

- Should we propose to specify a minimum number of days that must elapse between the mailing of a proxy statement and a meeting, as Rule 14c-2(b) does with information statements? If we were to do so, what would be an appropriate number of days, and should the number be flexible to account for such possibilities as overnight or electronic delivery, or electronic or telephonic voting?[308] In what ways can or should we rely on technology to reduce these time periods?

- Should we propose that federal proxy rules prescribe a form of proxy that permits the shareholder to specify the extent to which an executed proxy should be applied to shares that are bought after the proxy is submitted and before the voting record date?

- Would voting all of the shares in accordance with the instructions on the proxy or VIF present issues under Rule 14a-10(b), which prohibits the solicitation of "any proxy which provides that it shall be deemed to be dated as of any date subsequent to the date on which it is signed by the security holder"? If so, should that rule be amended, and how?

C. "Empty Voting" and Related "Decoupling" Issues

1. Background and Reasons for Concern

As noted in the Introduction, this release primarily focuses on whether the U.S. proxy system operates with the accuracy, reliability, transparency, accountability, and integrity that shareholders and issuers should rightfully expect. These expectations are shaped in part by the Commission's proxy solicitation, disclosure and other rules, the rules of the national securities exchanges, as well as by the substantive rights granted under state corporate law and the charter and bylaw provisions of individual corporations. At their core, these expectations are based on the foundational understanding that, absent contractual or legal provisions to the contrary, a "shareholder" possesses both voting rights and an economic interest in the company.

The ability to separate a share's voting rights from the economic stake through, for instance, what has been dubbed "empty voting" and "decoupling" challenges this foundational understanding.[309] The term "empty voting" has been defined to refer to the circumstance in which a shareholder's voting rights substantially exceed the shareholder's economic interest in the company.[310] In this circumstance, the exercise of the right to vote is viewed as "empty" because the votes have been emptied of a commensurate economic interest in the shares (and, at the extreme, may even be associated with a negative economic interest in the sense of benefiting from a decline in the share price). Here, the bundle of rights and obligations customarily associated with share ownership

---

[308] The OECD recommends that measures should be taken, both by regulators and by all the institutions involved in the voting chain (issuers, custodians, *etc.*) to remove obstacles and to encourage the use of flexible voting mechanisms such as electronic voting. Corporate Governance and the Financial Crisis—Key Findings and Main Messages, note 282, above.

[309] *See,* e.g., Henry T. C. Hu & Bernard Black, *Equity and Debt Decoupling and Empty Voting II: Importance and Extensions,* 156 University of Pennsylvania Law Review 625-739 (2008) [hereinafter, *Hu & Black, Empty Voting II*]; Henry T. C. Hu & Bernard Black, *Debt, Equity, and Hybrid Decoupling: Governance and Systemic Risk Implications,* 14 European Financial Management 663-709 (2008) [hereinafter *Hu and Black, Debt and Hybrid Decoupling*]. Henry Hu currently serves as the Director of the Division of Risk, Strategy, and Financial Innovation at the Commission.

[310] For the purposes of this release, empty voting does not include dual class or similar share structures in which the corporate charter prescribes disproportionate allocation of voting and economic rights, albeit in a fully disclosed fashion. Likewise, for purposes of this release empty voting does not encompass the situation in which the individuals within an institutional investor who determine that investor's voting decisions act independently of the person or persons making economic investment decisions in regard to the security being voted. *See,* e.g., Charles M. Nathan & Parul Mehta, The Parallel Universes of Institutional Investing and Institutional Voting (Mar. 6, 2010), *available at* http://www.lw.com/upload/pubContent/_pdf/pub3463_1 .pdf; *cf.* James McRitchie, Parallel Universes Undercuts Its Own Arguments (Apr. 16, 2010), *available at* http:// corpgov.net/wordpress/?tag=nathan. Unlike the dual class situation, this latter situation could involve undisclosed decoupling of voting decisions from economic considerations.

has been "decoupled." Empty voting is an example of decoupling and can occur in a variety of ways, some of which we describe briefly below.

Such decoupling raises potential practical and theoretical considerations for voting of shares. For example, an empty voter with a negative economic interest in the company may prefer that the company's share price fall rather than increase. Such a person's voting motivation contradicts the widely-held assumption that equity securities are voted based on an interest in increasing shareholder value and in a way to protect shareholders' interests or enhance the value of the investment in the securities. That assumption—a core premise of state statutes requiring shareholder votes to elect directors and approve certain corporate decisions—may be undermined by the possibility that persons with voting power may have little or no economic interest or, even worse, have a negative economic interest in the shares they vote. It is a source of some concern that elections of directors and other important corporate actions, such as business combinations, might be decided by persons who could have the incentive to elect unqualified directors or block actions that are in the interests of the shareholders as a whole. Significant decoupling of voting rights from economic interest could potentially undermine investor confidence in the public capital markets.[311]

On the other hand, empty voting may not always be contrary to the interests of shareholders. One article argues, for instance, that informed investors[312] could potentially improve electoral outcomes through empty voting by taking long economic positions, acquiring disproportionate voting power from less informed shareholders,[313] and casting votes that are more informed and thus more likely to contribute to shareholder value.[314]

As discussed below, regardless of whether empty voting is deemed to be "good" or "bad," there is a strong argument for ensuring that there is transparency about the use of empty voting. If a voter acquires shares with a view to influencing or controlling the outcome of a vote but takes steps to reduce the risk of economic loss or even achieve a negative economic interest, disclosure of the empty voter's status and intentions could be important information to other shareholders.[315]

The Commission needs to further evaluate empty voting and related techniques in order to properly review the reliability, accuracy, transparency, accountability, and integrity of the current proxy system and the challenges that may be posed by empty voting and related techniques. Therefore, we are seeking information on the myriad ways in which decoupling can occur, and its nature, extent, and effects on shareholder voting and the proxy process.[316] We understand that responses explicitly intended to address

---

[311] For an academic analysis of many of the efficiency-related effects of equity decoupling, positive as well as negative, *see* Hu & Black, *Debt and Hybrid Decoupling*, note 309, above, at 667-672. For a discussion of how outsiders as well as incumbent management (e.g., managers, controlling shareholders, and corporations themselves) may try engaging in equity decoupling strategies, *see* Hu & Black, *Empty Voting II*, note 309, above, at 628-654 and 661-681.

[312] We do not express an opinion as to whether any particular class of investor will always make a shareholder-maximizing vote. For purposes of this discussion, it is sufficient to assume that, generally speaking, a highly informed investor is more likely to vote in a manner that will add to shareholder value than a less informed investor.

[313] Notably, the nature of the decoupling in these circumstances is qualitatively different than that in which a person holding the right to vote has no economic interest, or a negative economic interest, in the issuer. Rather, such an investor has a positive economic interest, and while there is decoupling insofar as that investor holds voting rights that derive from shares

owned by a different investor, that investor has voting interests that are aligned with the economic interest of investors generally.

[314] *See* Susan E. K. Christoffersen, Christopher C. Geczy, David K. Musto, and Adam V. Reed, *Vote Trading and Information Aggregation*, Journal of Finance, Vol. 62, 2007, pp. 2897–2929.

[315] Item 6 of Schedule 13D requires disclosure of contracts, arrangements, understandings, or relationships with respect to the securities covered by the Schedule, but the filing of Schedule 13D is triggered only when a person owns greater than 5% of a Section 12-registered equity security, as such ownership is calculated according to the pertinent rules.

[316] Separately, as described in Section V.C.2.b, below, the staff has initiated a project to review longstanding requirements as to disclosure of holdings of securities. The information gathered in connection with both projects, as well as any rule changes that may flow from such projects, could be helpful to the Commission, as well as to shareholders, issuers and state legislatures.

aspects of empty voting have already started to occur at the state corporate law and individual corporation level.[317]

2. Empty Voting Techniques and Potential Downsides

a. Empty Voting Using Hedging-Based Strategies

A variety of techniques can be used to accomplish empty voting. One technique is to hold shares but to hedge the economic interest in those shares. A shareholder could hedge that economic interest in a wide variety of ways, including by buying either exchange-traded or OTC put options. In a recent Commission enforcement action, a registered investment adviser agreed to settle charges that it had violated Section 13(d) of the Exchange Act in furtherance of a strategy of "essentially buying votes."[318] The investment adviser purchased shares of a prospective acquirer "for the exclusive purpose of voting the shares in a merger and influencing the outcome of the vote" on a proposed acquisition of a company in which the investment adviser owned a large block of stock.[319] At the same time, the investment adviser entered into swap transactions with the banks from which it purchased the acquirer's shares, so that it "was able to acquire the voting rights to nearly ten percent of [the acquirer]'s stock without having any economic risk and no real economic stake in the company, [and] was able to do this without making a significant financial outlay."[320]

While the practice of empty voting was not asserted as a substantive violation in the enforcement action, the matter illustrates how hedging techniques can be used to obtain voting power without having economic exposure on the securities being voted. The use of hedging by insiders also can result in empty voting. Executives entering into "collars" transactions, for instance, retain full voting rights despite having hedged a portion of their economic interest.[321]

Empty voting can also be accomplished by the use of credit derivatives (rather than through the use of put options and other equity derivatives), a process dubbed "hybrid decoupling."[322] For example, instead of using put options to hedge its economic interest in shares, a shareholder may enter into credit default swap transactions with a derivatives dealer. If a company experiences poor economic performance, the likelihood of the company defaulting on its debt increases, and so the shareholder's credit default swap holdings will likely rise in value.[323]

---

[317] For example, Delaware has amended its General Corporation Law to allow corporations to adopt measures to respond to certain record date capture strategies. *See* Bryn Vaaler, United States: DGCL Amendments Authorize Proxy Access And Expense Reimbursement Bylaws, Reverse Schoon v. Troy Corp., Mondaq Business Briefing, May 12, 2009, *available at* http://www.mondaq.com/unitedstates/article.asp?articleid=79322. Some corporations have adopted bylaws that, under certain circumstances, require shareholders submitting a proposal to disclose how they have hedged the economic interests associated with their share positions. *See* Matt Andrejczak, "Sara Lee, Coach set rules to deter devious shareholders," MarketWatch, Apr. 2, 2008.

[318] *See* In the Matter of Perry Corp., Release No. 34-60351, July 21, 2009 at ¶19, *available at* http://www.sec.gov/litigation/admin/2009/34-60351.pdf.

[319] *Id.* at ¶33.

[320] *Id.* at ¶18.

[321] In a "collar" transaction, the investor sells a call option at one strike price and purchases a put option at a lower strike price. For little or no cost, the investor thereby limits the potential for appreciation or depreciation to the range – the "collar" – defined by the two strike prices. Academic research indicates that CEOs, directors, and senior executives have used this strategy to hedge their economic interest in the firm's stock. *See* Carr Bettis, John Bizjak, and Michael Lemmon, *Managerial Ownership, Incentive Contracting, and the Use of Zero-Cost Collars and Equity Swaps by Corporate Insiders*, Journal of Financial and Quantitative Analysis, 2001, at 3.

[322] *See* Hu & Black, *Debt and Hybrid Decoupling*, note 309, above, at 688-690.

[323] And just as "equity decoupling" and "hybrid decoupling" could sometimes incentivize some shareholders to use their voting rights against the best interests of the company and other shareholders, some believe that a pattern that has been termed "debt decoupling"—the unbundling of the economic rights, contractual control rights, and other rights normally associated with debt—may sometimes raise incentive issues as to some debtholders. These debtholders, dubbed "empty creditors," may sometimes even have the incentive to use the control rights the debtholders have in their loan agreements or bond indentures to try to cause a company to go into bankruptcy. *See* Hu & Black, *Debt and Hybrid Decoupling*, note 309 above, at

Finally, hedging-based strategies need not even involve holding either the debt or equity of the company in which the shareholder is voting, or derivatives linked to such debt or equity. A shareholder may, for instance, be able to hedge its exposure to a company's shares through purchasing assets correlated in some fashion to the company's share price. In the case of an acquisition, for example, a shareholder in the potential acquirer which also holds a larger equity interest in the target company, may arguably be characterized as being an empty voter with a negative economic interest in the acquirer. That is, the more the acquirer overpays for the target, the more net profit the investor would achieve. Other correlated assets that may be used in empty voting strategies may include, for example, shares of a competitor or a supplier.

b. Empty Voting Using Non-Hedging Based Strategies

There are a variety of situations in which empty voting may arise without any hedging at all. For example, active trading between a voting record date and the actual voting date may result in many voters having voting rights different from their economic stakes. An investor who sells shares after the voting record date retains the right to vote the shares without having any economic interest in them. Another example of empty voting without hedging is the voting of employees' unallocated shares in an employee stock ownership plan ("ESOP"). In an ESOP, while employees only have a contingent economic interest in the unallocated shares, the shares have full voting rights and are voted by a trustee, who either exercises discretion in voting or votes in proportion to vested ESOP shares. Effectively, either the trustee or the employees may become empty voters.[324]

One important non-hedging based technique that appears to have been used outside the United States is borrowing shares in the stock lending market. Under standard stock lending arrangements, the borrower of the shares has the voting rights associated with the shares borrowed, but relatively little or no economic interest in the shares.[325] Thus, simply by paying a fee to borrow the shares, the borrower can "buy" votes associated with the shares without having any corresponding economic interest. And the size of the fee could be reduced by borrowing the shares immediately before the record date, and returning the shares immediately afterwards.[326] Within the U.S. this sort of practice appears to be limited by Regulation T, under which securities loans by institutional investors through their broker-dealers are restricted to distinct "permitted purposes" under the Federal Reserve Board's Regulation T, such as execution of a short sale.[327] Borrowing securities to obtain the right to vote, however, may occur outside the purview of Regulation T in certain circumstances.

(Footnote Continued)

665-66 and 679-688; "CDSs and bankruptcy—No empty threat," The Economist, June 18, 2009.

[324] *See* Hu & Black, *Empty Voting II*, note 309 above, at 648-651 (as to restricted stock voting rights and certain ESOPs).

[325] *See, e.g.*, Master Securities Lending Agreement at 7.1-7.5, note 72, above.

[326] Some observers believe that this stock lending-based strategy has occurred in Hong Kong and the United Kingdom. *See* Kara Scannell, "Outside Influence: How Borrowed Shares Swing Company Votes – SEC and Others Fear Hedge-Fund Strategy May Subvert Elections," Wall Street Journal, Jan. 26, 2007, at page A1.

[327] *See* Federal Reserve Board Regulation T, 12 C.F.R. §220.2. This regulation limits the purposes for which broker-dealers who do not transact with customers from the general public may lend shares. Regulation T's "purpose test" generally provides that borrowers may only borrow securities for short selling, covering delivery fails, and similar purposes. For a fuller description of Regulation T, see Charles E. Dropkin, "Developing Effective Guidelines for Managing Legal Risks-U.S. Guidelines," Securities Lending and Repurchase Agreements 167, 172-176 (Frank J. Fabozzi and Steven V. Mann, eds., 2005). Essentially, Regulation T requires broker-dealers to make a good faith effort to ascertain the borrower's purpose and cannot lend shares for voting purposes because that is not a permitted purpose under Regulation T. 17 CFR 220.10(a). The standard securities lending agreement in the U.S. generally will contain a representation and warranty that the borrower, and any person to whom the borrower relends the borrowed securities, are only borrowing consistent with the "purpose test" (unless the borrowed securities are "exempted securities"). See, e.g., Master Securities Lending Agreement, note 72, above, at 9.5 (at www.sifma.org/services/stdforms/pdf/master_sec_loan.pdf).

3. Potential Regulatory Responses

As one possible response to empty voting and related phenomena, the Commission could consider requiring disclosure that creates transparency.[328] The proxy rules, the periodic reporting system, and rules adopted pursuant to statutory provisions such as Sections 13(d), 13(f), and 13(g) of the Exchange Act might be modified or a new disclosure system could be developed to elicit fuller disclosure of empty voting. More robust disclosure may be helpful to all of the participants in the proxy process as well as for regulators. For instance, if an investor acquires substantial voting rights that are not disclosed, then the other shareholders may not be aware of the potentially heightened importance of their vote. Without such information, shareholders may have insufficient information as to the need to vote and to take coordinated or other actions to protect their interests. By improving transparency, investors would have the option to choose to respond to such information and make a better informed investment or voting decision. Issuers also may be in a position to take responsible and appropriate action in response to disclosure of empty voting strategies, such as increasing their solicitation efforts.

Beyond gathering information and enhancing transparency, the following are some of the possible responses to empty voting and other types of decoupling that could be considered by the Commission, Congress, state legislatures, and individual issuers.

- Require voters to certify on the form of proxy or VIF that they held the full economic interest in the shares being voted at the time the proxy was executed, or, if not, disclose the extent to which their economic interest in the shares was shorted or hedged.

- Require disclosure of the shareholder meeting agenda sufficiently ahead of the record date to enable investors who have loaned their securities to recall those loans to retain voting control of those securities.[329]

- Permit only persons who possess pure long positions (*i.e.*, economic interests not shorted or hedged) in the underlying shares to vote by proxy, or allow proxy voting only commensurate with their net long positions (*e.g.*, economic interests after adjusting for equity or credit derivative-based hedging or short positions), or require a cooling-off period for those who have no or negative economic interests (after public disclosure) before voting.

- Prohibit empty voting, especially in situations where there is a negative economic interest.

4. Request for Comment

- What is the potential for, and actual prevalence of, all forms of equity, debt, and hybrid decoupling (including empty voting)? Are these techniques employed differently by "outside" investors, company insiders, and the company itself? Does decoupling raise public policy concerns, for example in relation to the disclosure requirements of Section 13(d)? Are existing disclosure requirements under Section 13(d) and other provisions of federal securities laws sufficient to address the entire range of concerns raised by equity, debt, and hybrid decoupling?

- Can the potentially beneficial and potentially detrimental aspects of debt, equity, or hybrid decoupling be meaningfully distinguished? Are there adverse consequences if there are empty voters, or even empty voters with negative economic interests, especially if their votes are outcome determinative? Are there examples of situations in which empty voting was outcome determinative?

---

[328] The staff is also working on the separate but related project of reviewing current disclosure requirements relating to holdings of financial instruments, including short sale positions and derivatives positions.

[329] *See* Section III.C.2, above.

- What are the mechanisms that result in debt, equity, and hybrid decoupling giving rise to public policy concerns? How important are these different mechanisms? To what extent can credit derivatives, correlated assets (such as, for example, shares of other participants in a takeover battle), or other financial instruments be used, and to what extent are they being used, to accomplish empty voting? To what extent does debt decoupling raise issues similar to those raised by equity decoupling or hybrid decoupling and how might regulatory or other responses to debt decoupling differ?

- At what economic threshold or percentage of voting power threshold is decoupling —by any one individual, by group, or by shareholders in the aggregate—material to the company and its security holders?

- Are certain companies (for instance, due to their ownership or capital structure) particularly vulnerable to potential adverse effects of debt, equity, or hybrid decoupling?

- Do concerns about decoupling economic interests and voting rights extend to the decoupling of voting and investment management functions within institutional investors?[330] If so, would one or more regulatory responses, involving disclosure or otherwise, be appropriate?

- Under what circumstances should disclosure of a shareholder's net economic interest be required, along with any associated decoupling? If such net economic interest is required to be disclosed, how should "net economic interest" be defined, given the myriad ways in which such decoupling can occur? Should our rules require disclosure regarding, and/or certification of, beneficial and economic ownership as part of the form of proxy or VIF? Or should this matter be left to state law or bylaws adopted by individual companies?

- If companies and company executives themselves engage in decoupling, do existing disclosure requirements result in sufficient transparency for investors to observe this behavior? If not, what level of disclosure would provide sufficient transparency? What changes to Schedules 13D or 13G, periodic disclosure requirements, Securities Act disclosure rules, the proxy rules, or other aspects of securities law are advisable?

- Are there circumstances (such as empty voting while holding a negative economic interest) where debt, equity, and hybrid decoupling appear to be fundamentally detrimental to the shareholders, debtholders, or the issuer itself? Are existing disclosure requirements, or changes to existing disclosure requirements, sufficient to address any such concerns? Should the Commission consider additional remedial actions? What role should federal law, state law and individual corporate actions play in addressing any such concerns?

- Should we propose rule changes to provide more disclosure and transparency as to equity, debt, or hybrid decoupling? If so, should this disclosure be in proxy solicitation materials, periodic reports, or disclosures pursuant to Sections 13(d), 13(g), and/or 13(f)? Should we develop a specific new form or report relating to short sales, short sale positions, and debt, equity, or other derivatives that could be used to identify instances of potential or actual empty voting or other kinds of equity, debt, or hybrid decoupling? Should any requirements related to decoupling disclosure also require disclosure of credit derivatives positions, as would occur with hybrid decoupling? Should debt decoupling be subject to disclosure requirements and, if so, what disclosure requirements would be appropriate? To what extent would new legislation be necessary in order to impose any of these requirements?

- If we were to propose any enhanced or new disclosure requirements, what should the filing deadlines be under various circumstances in order to inform the

---

[330] *See* Nathan & Mehta, note 310, above.

marketplace on a timely basis, while providing adequate time for those responsible for complying with the requirement to collect the information and prepare the filing?

- What should be the triggers for such disclosure requirements? For instance, in establishing such a trigger, is the more than 5% equity ownership threshold of Exchange Act Section 13(d) analogous in any way? Are the current "beneficial owner" concepts contemplated by Regulation 13D-G, some variation of such concepts, or some altogether different concept of ownership appropriate for determining whether a disclosure requirement is triggered? Or should decoupling-related disclosures not be based on conceptions of ownership, but instead be based on the nature of the investor and presence of investment discretion, as with Form 13F? Are there alternatives to "ownership," the nature of the investor, and presence of investment discretion that should be considered?

- What level of detail should be required for decoupling-related disclosures, recognizing the complexity of, for example, many OTC derivatives?

- If, pursuant to state law or a company's articles or bylaws, there are substantive limitations on empty voting or other forms of decoupling, should the Commission accommodate the implementation of such limitations by, for instance, requiring disclosure or ownership certifications on the form of proxy or VIF?

- To what extent is Regulation T, by its terms, effective in limiting the borrowing of shares for voting purposes? Should the Commission or another regulator propose a new rule that would prohibit or restrict borrowing securities for purposes of obtaining the right to vote those securities?

VI. Conclusion

The U.S. proxy system is the fundamental infrastructure of shareholder suffrage since the corporate proxy is the principal means by which shareholders exercise their voting rights. The development of issuer, securities intermediary, and shareholder practices over the years, spurred in part by technological advances, has made the system complex and, as a result, less transparent to shareholders and to issuers. It is our intention that this system operate with the reliability, accuracy, transparency, and integrity that shareholders and issuers should rightfully expect.

We are interested in the public's opinions regarding the matters discussed in this concept release. We encourage all interested parties to submit comment on these topics. In addition, we solicit comment on any other aspect of the mechanics of proxy distribution and collection that commentators believe may be improved upon.

By the Commission,

Elizabeth M. Murphy
Secretary

Dated: July 14, 2010

APPENDIX 5

Listing Standards for Compensation Committees

SECURITIES AND EXCHANGE COMMISSION

17 CFR PARTS 229 and 240

[RELEASE NOS. 33-9199; 34-64149; File No. S7-13-11]

RIN 3235-AK95

LISTING STANDARDS FOR COMPENSATION COMMITTEES

AGENCY: Securities and Exchange Commission.

ACTION: Proposed rule.

SUMMARY: We are proposing a new rule and rule amendments to implement the provisions of Section 952 of the Dodd-Frank Wall Street Reform and Consumer Protection Act of 2010, which adds Section 10C to the Securities Exchange Act of 1934 (the "Exchange Act"). Section 10C requires the Commission to adopt rules directing the national securities exchanges (the "exchanges") and national securities associations to prohibit the listing of any equity security of an issuer that is not in compliance with Section 10C's compensation committee and compensation adviser requirements. In accordance with the statute, the proposed rule would direct the exchanges to establish listing standards that, among other things, require each member of a listed issuer's compensation committee to be a member of the board of directors and to be "independent," as defined in the listing standards of the exchanges adopted in accordance with the proposed rule. In addition, Section 10C(c)(2) of the Exchange Act requires the Commission to adopt new disclosure rules concerning the use of compensation consultants and conflicts of interest.

DATES: Comments should be received on or before April 29, 2011.

ADDRESSES: Comments may be submitted by any of the following methods:

Electronic Comments:

- Use the Commission's Internet comment form (*http://www.sec.gov/rules/proposed.shtml*);
- Send an e-mail to *rule-comments@sec.gov*; or
- Use the Federal Rulemaking ePortal (*http://www.regulations.gov*). Follow the instructions for submitting comments.

Paper Comments:

- Send paper comments in triplicate to Elizabeth M. Murphy, Secretary, U.S. Securities and Exchange Commission, 100 F Street, NE, Washington, DC 20549-1090.

All submissions should refer to File Number S7-13-11. This file number should be included on the subject line if e-mail is used. To help us process and review your comments more efficiently, please use only one method. The Commission will post all comments on the Commission's Internet website (*http://www.sec.gov/rules/proposed.shtml*). Comments are also available for website viewing and printing in the Commission's Public Reference Room, 100 F Street, NE, Washington, DC 20549, on official business days between the hours of 10:00 a.m. and 3:00 p.m. All comments received will be posted without change; we do not edit personal identifying information from submissions. You should submit only information that you wish to make available publicly.

FOR FURTHER INFORMATION CONTACT: Nandini A. Acharya, Attorney-Adviser, or N. Sean Harrison, Special Counsel, at (202) 551-3430, in the Office of Rulemaking, Division of Corporation Finance, U.S. Securities and Exchange Commission, 100 F Street, NE, Washington, DC 20549-3628.

SUPPLEMENTARY INFORMATION: We are proposing to add new Rule 10C-1 under the Securities Exchange Act of 1934.[1] We are also proposing amendments to Item 407[2] of Regulation S-K.[3]

TABLE OF CONTENTS

---

[1] 15 U.S.C. 78a *et seq.*
[2] 17 CFR 229.407.

[3] 17 CFR 229.10 *et seq.*

I. BACKGROUND AND SUMMARY

We are proposing a new rule and rule amendments to implement the provisions of Section 952 of the Dodd-Frank Wall Street Reform and Consumer Protection Act of 2010 (the "Act"),[4] which adds Section 10C to the Securities Exchange Act of 1934 (the "Exchange Act"). Section 10C requires the Commission to direct the national securities exchanges[5] (the "exchanges") and national securities associations[6] to prohibit the listing of any equity[7] security of an issuer, with certain exemptions, that does not comply with Section 10C's compensation committee and compensation adviser requirements.[8]

Specifically, Section 10C(a)(1) of the Exchange Act requires the Commission to adopt rules directing the exchanges to prohibit the listing of any equity security of an issuer, with certain exemptions, that is not in compliance with the independence requirements for members of the compensation committee of the board of directors of an issuer. In accordance with the statute, the rules, once adopted, would require the exchanges to establish listing standards that require each member of a listed issuer's compensation committee to be a member of the board of directors and to be "independent." The term "independent" is not defined in Section 10C(a)(1). Instead, the section provides that "independent" is to be defined by the exchanges after taking into consideration "relevant factors." As provided in Section 10C(a)(1), the "relevant factors" are required to include (1) the source of compensation of a member of the board of directors of an issuer, including any consulting, advisory, or other compensatory fee paid by the issuer to such member of the board of directors, and (2) whether a member of the board of directors of an issuer is affiliated with the issuer, a subsidiary of the issuer, or an affiliate of a subsidiary of the issuer. Section 10C(a)(4) of the Exchange Act requires our rules to permit the exchanges to exempt particular relationships from the independence requirements, as each exchange determines is appropriate, taking into consideration the size of an issuer and any other relevant factors.

In addition to the independence requirements set forth in Section 10C(a), Section 10C(f) of the Exchange Act requires the Commission to adopt rules directing the exchanges to prohibit the listing of any security of an issuer that is not in compliance with the following requirements relating to compensation committees and compensation advisers, as set forth in paragraphs (b)-(e) of Section 10C:

---

[4] Pub. L. No. 111-203, 124 Stat. 1900 (2010).

[5] A "national securities exchange" is an exchange registered as such under Section 6 of the Exchange Act [15 U.S.C. 78f]. There are currently fifteen national securities exchanges registered under Section 6(a) of the Exchange Act: NYSE Amex (formerly the American Stock Exchange), BATS Exchange, BATS Y-Exchange, NASDAQ OMX BX (formerly the Boston Stock Exchange), C2 Options Exchange, Chicago Board Options Exchange, Chicago Stock Exchange, EDGA Exchange, EDGX Exchange, International Securities Exchange, The NASDAQ Stock Market, National Stock Exchange, New York Stock Exchange, NYSE Arca and NASDAQ OMX PHLX (formerly Philadelphia Stock Exchange). Certain exchanges are registered with the Commission through a notice filing under Section 6(g) of the Exchange Act for the purpose of trading security futures. See Section II.B.1, below, for a discussion of these types of exchanges.

[6] A "national securities association" is an association of brokers and dealers registered as such under Section 15A of the Exchange Act [15 U.S.C. 78o-3]. The Financial Industry Regulatory Authority ("FINRA") is the only national securities association registered with the Commission under Section 15A(a) of the Exchange Act. Because FINRA does not list equity securities, we refer only to the exchanges in this release.

In addition, Section 15A(k) of the Exchange Act [15 U.S.C. 78o-3(k)] provides that a futures association registered under Section 17 of the Commodity Exchange Act [7 U.S.C. 21] shall be registered as a national securities association for the limited purpose of regulating the activities of members who are registered as broker-dealers in security futures products pursuant to Section 15(b)(11) of the Exchange Act [15 U.S.C. 78o(b)(11)]. See Section II.B.2, below, for a discussion regarding security futures products.

[7] See Section II.B.2, below, for a discussion of the scope of Section 10C, including our conclusion that it does not apply to issuers with only listed debt securities. That section also proposes an exemption for securities futures products and standardized options, and clarifies that national securities and futures associations that do not list securities do not have to adopt specific rules in accordance with this rulemaking and Section 10C of the Exchange Act.

[8] See Exchange Act Sections 10C(a) and (f).

- Each compensation committee must have the authority, in its sole discretion, to retain or obtain the advice of compensation consultants, independent legal counsel and other advisers (collectively, "compensation advisers");[9]

- Before selecting any compensation adviser, the compensation committee must take into consideration specific factors identified by the Commission that affect the independence of compensation advisers;[10]

- The compensation committee must be directly responsible for the appointment, compensation and oversight of the work of any compensation adviser;[11] and

- Each listed issuer must provide appropriate funding for the payment of reasonable compensation, as determined by the compensation committee, to compensation advisers.[12]

Finally, Section 10C(c)(2) requires each issuer to disclose in any proxy or consent solicitation material for an annual meeting of shareholders (or a special meeting in lieu of the annual meeting), in accordance with Commission regulations, whether the issuer's compensation committee retained or obtained the advice of a compensation consultant; whether the work of the compensation consultant has raised any conflict of interest; and, if so, the nature of the conflict and how the conflict is being addressed.

We are proposing new Exchange Act Rule 10C-1 to implement the compensation committee listing requirements of Sections 10C(a)-(g)[13] of the Exchange Act. To implement Section 10C(c)(2) of the Exchange Act, we are proposing rule amendments to Regulation S-K to require disclosure, in any proxy or information statement relating to an annual meeting of shareholders at which directors are to be elected (or special meeting in lieu of the annual meeting), of whether the issuer's compensation committee retained or obtained the advice of a compensation consultant; whether the work of the compensation consultant has raised any conflict of interest; and, if so, the nature of the conflict and how the conflict is being addressed. In connection with these amendments, we also propose to revise the current disclosure requirements with respect to the retention of compensation consultants.[14]

II. DISCUSSION OF THE PROPOSALS

A. Proposed Listing Requirements

1. Applicability of Listing Requirements

In enacting Section 10C of the Exchange Act, Congress intended to require that "board committees that set compensation policy will consist only of directors who are independent."[15] In addition, Congress sought to provide "shareholders in a public company" with "additional disclosures involving compensation practices."[16] Although Section 10C includes numerous provisions applicable to the "compensation committees" of listed issuers, it does not require a listed issuer to have a compensation committee or a committee that performs functions typically assigned to a compensation committee. Nor does Section 10C include provisions that have the effect of requiring a compensation committee as a practical matter. For example, it does not require that the compensation of executives be approved by a compensation committee.

---

[9] Exchange Act Sections 10C(c)(1)(A) and 10C(d)(1).
[10] Exchange Act Section 10C(b).
[11] Exchange Act Sections 10C(c)(1)(B) and 10C(d)(2).
[12] Exchange Act Section 10C(e).
[13] Section 10C(g) of the Exchange Act exempts controlled companies from the requirements of Section 10C.

[14] See Item 407(e) of Regulation S-K; Proxy Disclosure Enhancements, Release No. 33-9089 (Dec. 16, 2009) [74 FR 68334].
[15] See H.R. Rep. No. 111-517, Joint Explanatory Statement of the Committee of Conference, Title IX, Subtitle E "Accountability and Executive Compensation," at 872-873 (Conf. Rep.) (June 29, 2010).
[16] Id.

Neither the Act nor the Exchange Act defines the term "compensation committee."[17] Our rules do not currently require, and our proposed rules would not mandate, that an issuer establish a compensation committee. However, current exchange listing standards generally require listed issuers either to have a compensation committee or to have independent directors determine, recommend or oversee specified executive compensation matters.[18] For example, the New York Stock Exchange ("NYSE") requires a listed issuer to have a compensation committee composed solely of independent directors and to assign various executive compensation-related tasks to that committee.[19] On the other hand, the NASDAQ Stock Market ("Nasdaq") does not mandate that a listed issuer have a compensation committee, but requires that executive compensation be determined or recommended to the board for determination either by a compensation committee composed solely of independent directors or by a majority of the board's independent directors in a vote in which only independent directors participate.[20] Some of the other exchanges have standards comparable to the NYSE's and require their listed issuers to have independent compensation committees.[21] Other exchanges have standards comparable to Nasdaq's and, in the absence of an independent compensation committee, permit executive compensation determinations to be made or recommended by a majority of independent directors on the listed issuer's board.[22]

Proposed Rule 10C-1(b) would direct the exchanges to adopt listing standards that would be applicable to any committee of the board that oversees executive compensation, whether or not the committee performs multiple functions and/or is formally designated as a "compensation committee." We believe this is appropriate in order to capture board committees that perform these functions and to avoid the possibility that a listed issuer might avoid the proposed requirements merely by assigning a different name to a committee that is functionally equivalent to a compensation committee. For example, if a listed issuer has a designated "corporate governance committee" whose responsibilities include, among other matters, oversight of executive compensation, such committee

---

[17] By contrast, Section 3(a)(58) of the Exchange Act defines an "audit committee" as a committee (or equivalent body) established by and amongst the board of directors of an issuer for the purpose of overseeing the accounting and financial reporting processes of the issuer and audits of the financial statements of the issuer; and if no such committee exists with respect to an issuer, the entire board of directors of the issuer. Our proposed rules would not preclude the exchanges from defining "compensation committee."

[18] There are some exchanges registered under Section 6(a) of the Exchange Act that have not adopted listing standards that require executive compensation determinations for listed issuers to be made or recommended by an independent compensation committee or independent directors. However, these exchanges, which include the International Securities Exchange, LLC, EDGA Exchange, Inc., EDGX Exchange, Inc., BATS Exchange, Inc., BATS Y-Exchange, Inc. and C2 Options Exchange, Inc., currently either trade securities only pursuant to unlisted trading privileges or trade only standardized options. In addition, the listing standards of certain exchanges that are registered with the Commission for the purpose of trading security futures do not address executive compensation matters. See Section II.B.1, below, for a discussion of these types of exchanges.

[19] See NYSE Listed Company Manual Section 303A.05. Section 303A.05 permits a listed issuer's board to allocate the responsibilities of the compensation committee to another committee, provided that the committee is composed entirely of independent directors and has a committee charter. The NYSE exempts certain issuers from this requirement, including controlled companies, limited partnerships, companies in bankruptcy, and closed-end and open-end management investment companies registered under the Investment Company Act of 1940 ("Investment Company Act"). See NYSE Listed Company Manual Section 303A.00.

[20] See Nasdaq Rule 5605(d). We understand that less than 2% of Nasdaq listed issuers utilize the alternative of having independent board members, and not a committee, oversee compensation. See also Nasdaq IM 5605-6, stating that the Nasdaq structure is intended to provide flexibility for a company to choose an appropriate board structure and to reduce resource burdens, while ensuring independent director control of compensation decisions. Nasdaq exempts certain issuers from this requirement, including asset-backed issuers and other passive issuers, cooperatives, limited partnerships, and management investment companies registered under the Investment Company Act. See Nasdaq Rule 5615(a).

[21] NYSE Arca, Inc., National Stock Exchange, Inc., and NASDAQ OMX PHLX, Inc. See NYSE Arca Rule 5.3(k)(4); National Stock Exchange Rule 15.5(d)(5); and NASDAQ OMX PHLX Rule 867.05.

[22] NASDAQ OMX BX, Inc., NYSE Amex LLC, Chicago Board Options Exchange, Incorporated, and Chicago Stock Exchange, Inc. See NASDAQ OMX BX Rule 4350(c)(3); NYSE Amex Company Guide Section 805; Chicago Board Options Exchange Rule 31.10; and Chicago Stock Exchange Article 22, Rules 19(d) and 21.

would be subject to the compensation committee listing standards to be adopted pursuant to our new rules, as would a committee designated as a "human resources committee" whose responsibilities include oversight of executive compensation. However, proposed Rule 10C-1(b) would not require the listing standards to apply to those independent directors who oversee executive compensation in lieu of a board committee, since Section 10C refers only to compensation committees.[23]

Request for Comment

- Should the exchanges be required to only list issuers with compensation committees?

- Our proposed rules would apply to a listed issuer's compensation committee, or in the absence of such a committee, any other board committee that performs functions typically performed by a compensation committee, including oversight of executive compensation. Is this proposed functional approach appropriate and workable? If not, why not?

- As noted above, the listing standards of some exchanges permit a listed issuer to have its executive compensation matters be determined, or recommended to the board for determination, either by a compensation committee composed solely of independent directors or, in the absence of such a committee, by a majority of independent directors in a vote in which only independent directors participate. Should our rules implementing Section 10C require the exchanges to mandate that independent directors performing this function in the absence of a formal committee structure also be subject to our new rules? Would so doing be consistent with the mandate of Section 10C of the Exchange Act?

2. Independence Requirements

Most exchanges that list equity securities require that the board of directors of a listed issuer be composed of a majority of directors that qualify as "independent" under their listing standards.[24] As noted above, most exchanges that list equity securities require directors on compensation committees or directors determining or recommending executive compensation matters to be "independent" under their general independence standards. Although independence requirements and standards for determining independence vary somewhat among the different exchanges, listing standards prescribe certain bright-line independence tests (including restrictions on compensation, employment and familial or other relationships with the listed issuer that could interfere with the exercise of independent judgment) that directors must meet in order to be considered independent. For example, both NYSE and Nasdaq rules preclude a finding of independence if the director is or recently was employed by the listed issuer,[25] the director's immediate family member is or recently was employed as an executive officer of the listed issuer,[26] or the director or director's family member received compensation from the listed issuer in excess of specified limits.[27] In addition, under both NYSE and Nasdaq rules, directors may be disqualified based on their or their family members' relationships with a listed issuer's auditor,[28] affiliation with entities that have material business relationships with

---

[23] To the extent no board committee is authorized to oversee executive compensation, board determinations with respect to executive compensation matters may be made by the full board with only independent directors participating. In such cases, under state corporate law, we understand that action by the independent directors would generally be considered action by the full board, not action by a committee.

[24] *See* NYSE Listed Company Manual Section 303A.01; Nasdaq Rule 5605(b)(1); NYSE AMEX LLC Company Guide Section 802(a); Chicago Board Options Exchange Rule 31.10(a); Chicago Stock Exchange Article 22, Rules 19(a) and 21(a); NASDAQ OMX BX Rule 4350(c)(1); NASDAQ OMX PHLX

Rule 867.01; National Stock Exchange Rule 15.5(d)(1). NYSE Amex and the Chicago Stock Exchange permit smaller issuers to have a 50% independent board. *See* NYSE Amex Company Guide Section 801(h); Chicago Stock Exchange Article 22, Rules 19(a), 19(b)(1)(C)(iii), and 21(a).

[25] *See* NYSE Listed Company Manual Section 303A.02(b)(i); Nasdaq Rule 5605(a)(2)(A).

[26] *See* NYSE Listed Company Manual Section 303A.02(b)(i); Nasdaq Rule 5605(a)(2)(C).

[27] *See* NYSE Listed Company Manual Section 303A.02(b)(ii); Nasdaq Rule 5605(a)(2)(B).

[28] *See* NYSE Listed Company Manual Section 303A.02(b)(iii); Nasdaq Rule 5605(a)(2)(F).

the listed issuer,[29] or employment at a company whose compensation committee includes any of the listed issuer's executive officers.[30] We note, however, that with the exception of audit committee membership requirements, stock ownership alone will not automatically preclude a director from being considered independent under either NYSE or Nasdaq listing standards.[31]

In addition to requiring directors to meet objective criteria of independence, the NYSE and Nasdaq also require their listed issuers' boards to affirmatively determine that each independent director either, in NYSE's case, has no material relationship with the company[32] or, in Nasdaq's case, has no relationship which, in the opinion of the issuer's board of directors, would interfere with the director's exercise of independent judgment in carrying out his or her responsibilities.[33] The other exchanges have similar requirements.[34]

Under current Commission rules, listed issuers are required to identify each director who is independent, using the same definition of independence used for determining whether a majority of the board of directors is independent.[35] If an exchange has independence requirements for members of the compensation committee, then listed issuers are required to identify each member of the compensation committee who is not independent under those requirements.[36] If a listed issuer does not have a separately designated compensation committee or committee performing similar functions, then the issuer must identify all members of the board who do not meet the independence requirements for compensation committee members.[37]

In addition to meeting exchange listing standards, there are other reasons for members of the compensation committee to be independent. For example, in order for a securities transaction between an issuer and one of its officers or directors to be exempt from short-swing profit liability under Section 16(b) of the Exchange Act, the transaction must be approved by the full board of directors or by a committee of the board that is composed solely of two or more "Non-Employee Directors," as defined in Exchange Act Rule 16b-3(b)(3).[38] We understand that many issuers use their independent compensation committees to avail themselves of this exemption.[39] Similarly, if an issuer wishes to preserve the tax deductibility of the amounts of certain awards paid to executive officers, among other things, the performance goals of such awards must be determined by a compensation committee composed of two or more "outside directors," as defined in

---

[29] *See* NYSE Listed Company Manual Section 303A.02(b)(v); Nasdaq Rule 5605(a)(2)(D).

[30] *See* NYSE Listed Company Manual Section 303A.02(b)(iv); Nasdaq Rule 5605(a)(2)(E).

[31] *See* Commentary to NYSE Listed Company Manual Section 303A.02(a); Nasdaq Rule 5605; Nasdaq IM-5605.

[32] *See* NYSE Rule 303A.02.a

[33] *See* Nasdaq Rule 4200(a)(15).

[34] *See, e.g.,* NYSE Arca Rule 5.3(k)(1) or NYSE AMEX LLC Company Guide Section 803.A.02.

[35] Item 407(a) of Regulation S-K.

[36] *Id.*

[37] *Id.*

[38] As defined in Exchange Act Rule 16b-3(b)(3)(i) [17 CFR 240.16b-3(b)(3)(i)], a "Non-Employee Director" is a director who is not currently an officer (as defined in Rule 16a-1(f)) of the issuer or a parent or subsidiary of the issuer, or otherwise currently employed by the issuer or a parent or subsidiary of the issuer; does not receive compensation, either directly or indirectly, from the issuer or a parent or subsidiary of the issuer, for services rendered as a consultant or in any capacity other than as a director, except for an amount that does not exceed the dollar amount for which disclosure would be required pursuant to Item 404(a) of Regulation S-K; and does not possess an interest in any other transaction for which disclosure would be required pursuant to Item 404(a) of Regulation S-K. In addition, Rule 16b-3(b)(3)(ii) provides that a Non-Employee Director of a closed-end investment company is a director who is not an "interested person" of the issuer, as that term is defined in Section 2(a)(19) of the Investment Company Act [15 U.S.C. 80a-2(a)(19)].

[39] *See* letter from Sullivan and Cromwell LLP to Facilitating Shareholder Director Nominations, Release No. 34-60089, available at http://www.sec.gov/comments/s7-10-09/s71009-430.pdf ("In our experience, many compensation committee charters require their members to meet the requirements of Rule 16b-3 and Section 162(m)."); Ira G. Bogner & Michael Krasnovsky, *Exchange Rules Impact Compensation Committee Composition,* METROPOLITAN CORP. COUNS., April 2004, at 17 ("Most compensation committees of public companies include at least two directors that are 'outside directors' under Section 162(m) of the Internal Revenue Code . . . and 'non-employee directors' under Rule 16b-3 of the Securities Exchange Act. . . .").

Section 162(m) of the Internal Revenue Code.[40] The definitions of "Non-Employee Director" and "outside director" are similar to the exchanges' definitions of director independence.

In order to implement the requirements of Section 10C(a)(1) of the Exchange Act, proposed Rule 10C-1(b)(1)(i) would require each member of a listed issuer's compensation committee to be a member of the issuer's board of directors and to be independent. As required by Section 10C(a)(1), proposed Rule 10C-1(b)(1)(ii) would direct the exchanges to develop a definition of independence applicable to compensation committee members after considering relevant factors, including, but not limited to, the source of compensation of a director, including any consulting, advisory or other compensatory fee paid by the issuer to such director, and whether the director is affiliated with the issuer, a subsidiary of the issuer, or an affiliate of a subsidiary of the issuer. Other than the factors set out in Section 10C(a)(1), we do not propose to specify any additional factors that the exchanges must consider in determining independence requirements for members of compensation committees, although we request comment regarding whether there are any other such factors that should be included in our rule.

In proposing Rule 10C-1(b)(1), we considered the similarities and differences between Section 952 of the Act and Section 301 of the Sarbanes-Oxley Act of 2002.[41] Section 301 of the Sarbanes-Oxley Act added Section 10A(m)(1) to the Exchange Act,[42] which required the Commission to direct the exchanges to prescribe independence requirements for audit committee members. Although the independence factors in Section 10C(a)(1) are similar to those in Section 10A(m)(1)—and indeed, Section 952 of the Act essentially provides the compensation committee counterpart to the audit committee requirements of Section 301 of the Sarbanes-Oxley Act—there is one significant difference. Section 10C(a) requires only that the exchanges "*consider* relevant factors" (emphasis added), which include the source of compensation and any affiliate relationship, in developing independence standards for compensation committee members, whereas Section 10A(m) expressly states that certain relationships preclude independence: an audit committee member "*may not*, other than in his or her capacity as a member of the audit committee . . . [a]ccept any consulting, advisory, or other compensatory fee from the issuer; or [b]e an affiliated person of the issuer or any subsidiary thereof" (emphasis added).[43]

As a result, the exchanges have more discretion to determine the standards of independence that audit and compensation committee members are required to meet. Section 10A(m) prescribes minimum criteria for the independence of audit committee members and permits the exchanges to adopt more stringent independence criteria as they deem appropriate, subject to approval pursuant to Section 19(b) of the Exchange Act. In contrast, Section 10C gives the exchanges the flexibility to establish their own minimum independence criteria for compensation committee members after considering the relevant factors enumerated in Section 10C(a)(3)(A)-(B). The exchanges may add other factors, as each such exchange deems appropriate, subject to approval pursuant to Section 19(b) of the Exchange Act.

---

[40] A director is an "outside director" if the director (A) is not a current employee of the publicly held corporation; (B) is not a former employee of the publicly held corporation who receives compensation for prior services (other than benefits under a tax-qualified retirement plan) during the taxable year; (C) has not been an officer of the publicly held corporation; and (D) does not receive remuneration from the publicly held corporation, either directly or indirectly, in any capacity other than as a director. For this purpose, remuneration includes any payment in exchange for goods or services. Section 162(m) of the Internal Revenue Code of 1986, as amended. Treas. Reg. Section 1.162-27(e)(3).

[41] Pub. L. 107-204, 116 Stat. 745 (2002).

[42] 15 U.S.C. 78j-1(m)(1).

[43] *See* Section 10A(m) of the Exchange Act. Exchange Act Rule 10A-3 states that in order to be considered "independent," an audit committee member cannot accept any consulting, advisory or other compensatory fee (other than receipt of fixed amounts under a retirement plan for prior service with the listed issuer) and, for non-investment company issuers, cannot be an affiliated person of the issuer or its subsidiaries. For investment company issuers, the audit committee member cannot be an "interested person" of the issuer as defined in Section 2(a)(19) of the Investment Company Act.

To comply with proposed Rule 10C-1, the exchanges' definitions of independence for compensation committee members would be implemented through proposed rule changes that the exchanges would file pursuant to Section 19(b) of the Exchange Act, which are subject to the Commission's approval.[44] Proposed Rule 10C-1(a)(4) would require that each proposed rule change submission include, in addition to any information required under Section 19(b) of the Exchange Act and the rules thereunder: a review of whether and how existing or proposed listing standards satisfy the requirements of this rule; a discussion of the exchange's consideration of factors relevant to compensation committee member independence; and the definition of independence applicable to compensation committee members that the exchange proposes to adopt in light of such review.[45] The Commission would then consider, prior to final approval, whether the exchanges considered the relevant factors outlined in Section 10C(a) and whether the exchanges' proposed rule changes are consistent with the requirements of Section 6(b) of the Exchange Act.

Because these relevant factors cover the same matters as the prohibitions in Section 10A(m)'s definition of audit committee independence, we believe the exchanges would likely consider whether those prohibitions should also be applicable to compensation committee members. The exchanges would not be required to adopt those prohibitions in their definitions and will have flexibility to consider other factors in developing their definitions. For example, we understand that there are concerns, as expressed by several commentators,[46] about a prohibition against allowing directors affiliated with significant investors (such as private equity funds or venture capital firms) to serve on compensation committees.[47] Some commentators have noted that such directors are highly motivated to rigorously oversee compensation and are well-positioned to exercise independent judgment regarding compensation.[48] In addition, some commentators have noted that, although there is a need for audit committee members to be able to exercise objective oversight of an issuer's financial reporting, with respect to the oversight of executive compensation, the interests of representatives of major shareholders are generally aligned with those of other shareholders.[49]

---

[44] The standard of review for approving proposed exchange listing standards is found in Section 19(b)(2)(C) of the Exchange Act, which provides that "[t]he Commission shall approve a proposed rule change of a self-regulatory organization if it finds that such proposed rule change is consistent with the requirements of this title and the rules and regulations issued under this title that are applicable to such organization." Under Section 6(b) of the Exchange Act, the rules of an exchange must be "designed to prevent fraudulent and manipulative acts and practices, to promote just and equitable principles of trade, to foster cooperation and coordination with persons engaged in regulating, clearing, settling, processing information with respect to, and facilitating transactions in securities, to remove impediments to and perfect the mechanism of a free and open market and a national market system, and, in general, to protect investors and the public interest."

[45] A filing would be required even if an exchange finds that its existing rules satisfy the requirements of proposed Rule 10C-1.

[46] To facilitate public input on the Act, the Commission has provided a series of e-mail links, organized by topic, on its website at *http://www.sec.gov/spotlight/ regreformcomments.shtml*. The public comments we received are available on our website at *http://www.sec .gov/comments/df-title-xv/specialized-disclosures/spec ializeddisclosures-8.pdf*. The public comments we have received on Section 952 of the Act are available on our website at *http://www.sec.gov/comments/df-title-*

ix/executive-compensation/executive-compensation .shtml.

Several commentators have suggested that stock ownership alone should not automatically disqualify a board member from serving as an independent director on the compensation committee. *See, e.g.*, letters from American Bar Association, Brian Foley & Company, Inc, Compensia, Davis Polk & Wardwell, LLP and Frederick W. Cook & Co., Inc.

[47] One of these commentators noted that one or more venture capital firms sometimes hold significant equity positions and also have one of their partners serving as a director and member of the board's compensation committee. In this commentator's experience, these individuals, by virtue of their ongoing history with the listed company as well as their familiarity and experience with executive compensation practices in their industry sector, are valuable members of the compensation committee who can offer perspective and expertise which are largely in line with that of that of the company's shareholders. *See* letter from Compensia.

[48] *See* letter from Frederic W. Cook & Co., Inc. (stating that venture capital and private equity firms "will often have a more demanding pay-for-performance orientation than any other category of investor").

[49] *See, e.g.*, letters from Davis Polk & Wardwell LLP, American Bar Association, Compensia and Frederic W. Cook & Co., Inc.

The exchanges may determine that, even though affiliated directors are not allowed to serve on audit committees, such a blanket prohibition would be inappropriate for compensation committees, and certain affiliates, such as representatives of significant shareholders, should be permitted to serve. The exchanges might also conclude that other relationships or factors linked more closely to executive compensation matters, such as relationships between the members of the compensation committee and the listed issuer's executive management, should be addressed in the definition of independence.

Because the compensation committee independence requirements of Section 10C, unlike the audit committee independence requirements of Section 10A(m), do not require that the exchanges prohibit all affiliates from serving on a compensation committee, we do not believe it is necessary to separately define the term "affiliate" for purposes of proposed Rule 10C-1. As our proposed rule does not establish required independence standards, we also believe it is unnecessary to create any safe harbors for particular relationships, as we did when we adopted our audit committee independence requirements.[50] Although each exchange must consider the affiliate relationships specified in the rule in establishing compensation committee independence standards, there is no requirement to adopt listing standards precluding compensation committee membership based on all such relationships. Accordingly, we do not propose a separate definition of "affiliate" for use in connection with proposed Rule 10C-1.

Request for Comment

- Rather than establishing minimum independence standards that the exchanges must apply to compensation committee members, our proposed rule would permit each exchange to establish its own independence criteria, provided the exchange considers the relevant factors specified in Section 10C relating to affiliate relationships and sources of compensation. Is this approach appropriate? Is there a better approach that would be consistent with the requirements of Section 10C?

- The proposed independence factors that must be considered relate to current relationships between the issuer and the compensation committee member, which is consistent with the approach in Rule 10A-3(b)(1) for audit committee members. Should the required factors also extend to a "look back" period before the appointment of the member to the compensation committee? (We note that the exchanges currently have look-back periods for their definitions of independence for purposes of determining whether a majority of the board of directors is independent.) For members already serving on compensation committees when the new listing standards take effect, should the required factors also extend to a "look back" period before the effective date of the new listing standards? If so, what period (*e.g.*, three years or five years) would be appropriate? Should there be different look-back periods for different relationships or different parties? If so, what should they be, and why?

- Should there be additional factors apart from the two proposed factors required to be considered? For example, should the exchanges be required to include business or personal relationships between a compensation committee member and an executive officer of the issuer as mandatory factors for consideration? Should the exchanges be required to include board interlocks or employment of a director at a company included in the listed issuer's compensation peer group as mandatory factors for consideration? Would any such requirements unduly restrain a company in setting the composition of its board of directors?

- Large shareholders may be deemed affiliates by virtue of the percentage of their shareholdings. As noted above, some commentators have expressed the view that directors affiliated with large shareholders should continue to be permitted to serve

---

[50] *See* Exchange Act Rule 10A-3(e)(1)(ii) [17 CFR 240.10A-3(e)(1)(ii)] (providing that a person will be deemed not to be in control of a specified person for purposes of this section if the person "is not the ben- eficial owner, directly or indirectly, of more than 10% of any class of voting equity securities of the specified person; and is not an executive officer of the specified person").

on compensation committees because their interests are aligned with other shareholders with respect to compensation matters. Would a director affiliated with a shareholder with a significant ownership interest who is otherwise independent be sufficiently independent for the purpose of serving on the compensation committee? Would the interests of all shareholders be aligned with the interests of large shareholders with respect to oversight of executive compensation? Should our rules implementing Section 10C provide additional or different guidance or standards for the consideration of the affiliated person factor?

3. Authority to Engage Compensation Advisers; Responsibilities; and Funding

Section 10C(c)(1) of the Exchange Act provides that the compensation committee of a listed issuer may, in its sole discretion, retain or obtain the advice of a "compensation consultant,"[51] and Section 10C(d)(1) extends this authority to "independent legal counsel and other advisers"[52] (collectively, "compensation advisers"). Both sections also provide that the compensation committee shall be directly responsible for the appointment, compensation, and oversight of the work of compensation advisers. Sections 10C(c)(1)(C) and 10C(d)(3) provide that the compensation committee's authority to retain, and responsibility for overseeing the work of, compensation advisers may not be construed to require the compensation committee to implement or act consistently with the advice or recommendations of a compensation adviser or to affect the ability or obligation of the compensation committee to exercise its own judgment in fulfillment of its duties. To ensure that the listed issuer's compensation committee has the necessary funds to pay for such advisers, Section 10C(e) provides that a listed issuer shall provide "appropriate funding," as determined by the compensation committee, for payment of "reasonable compensation" to compensation consultants, independent legal counsel and other advisers to the compensation committee.[53]

Proposed Rule 10C-1(b)(2) implements Sections 10C(c)(1) and (d)(1) by repeating the provisions set forth in those sections regarding the compensation committee's authority to retain or obtain a compensation adviser, its direct responsibility for the appointment, compensation and oversight of the work of any compensation adviser, and the related rules of construction. In addition, proposed Rule 10C-1(b)(3) implements Section 10C(e) by repeating the provisions set forth in that section regarding the requirement that listed issuers provide for appropriate funding for payment of reasonable compensation to compensation advisers.

We note that while the statute provides that compensation committees of listed issuers shall have the express authority to hire "independent legal counsel," the statute does not require that they do so. Similar to our interpretation[54] of Section 10A(m) of the Exchange Act, which gave the audit committee authority to engage "independent legal counsel,"[55] we do not construe the requirements related to independent legal counsel and other advisers as set forth in Section 10C(d)(1) of the Exchange Act as requiring a compensation committee to retain independent legal counsel or as precluding a compensation committee from retaining non-independent legal counsel or obtaining advice from in-house counsel or outside counsel retained by the issuer or management.

---

[51] *See* Exchange Act Section 10C(c)(1).

[52] *See* Exchange Act Section 10C(d)(1).

[53] *See* Exchange Act Section 10C(e).

[54] *See* Standards Relating to Listed Company Audit Committees, Release No. 33-8220 (Apr. 9, 2003) [68 FR 18788], at fn. 114 ("As proposed, the requirement does not preclude access to or advice from the company's internal counsel or regular outside counsel. It also does not require an audit committee to retain independent counsel.").

[55] *See* Exchange Act Section 10A(m)(5) ("Each audit committee shall have the authority to engage independent counsel and other advisers, as it determines necessary to carry out its duties.").

Request for Comment

- Is additional specificity in the proposed rule needed to provide clearer guidance to listed issuers? For example, should we define what constitutes an "independent legal counsel"? If so, how?

- Should we clarify more explicitly in the implementing rule that this provision is not intended to preclude the compensation committee from conferring with in-house legal counsel or the company's outside counsel or from retaining non-independent counsel?

- Our audit committee rules implementing Section 10A(m) provide that each listed issuer must provide funding for ordinary administrative expenses of the audit committee that are necessary or appropriate in carrying out its duties.[56] Would such a provision be helpful with respect to the compensation committee? Do compensation committees have administrative expenses? If so, are they significant?

4. Compensation Adviser Independence Factors

Section 10C(b) of the Exchange Act provides that the compensation committee may select a compensation adviser only after taking into consideration the factors identified by the Commission. In accordance with Section 10C(b), these factors would apply not only to the selection of compensation consultants, but also to the selection of legal counsel and other advisers to the committee. The statute does not require a compensation adviser to be independent, only that the compensation committee consider the enumerated independence factors before selecting a compensation adviser. Section 10C(b) specifies that the independence factors identified by the Commission must be competitively neutral[57] and include, at minimum:

- The provision of other services to the issuer by the person that employs the compensation consultant, legal counsel or other adviser;

- The amount of fees received from the issuer by the person that employs the compensation consultant, legal counsel or other adviser, as a percentage of the total revenue of the person that employs the compensation consultant, legal counsel, or other adviser;

- The policies and procedures of the person that employs the compensation consultant, legal counsel or other adviser that are designed to prevent conflicts of interest;

- Any business or personal relationship of the compensation consultant, legal counsel, or other adviser with a member of the compensation committee; and

- Any stock of the issuer owned by the compensation consultant, legal counsel or other adviser.

Because Exchange Act Section 10C does not require compensation advisers to be independent—only that the compensation committee consider factors that may bear upon independence—we do not believe that this provision contemplates that the Commission would necessarily establish materiality or bright-line numerical thresholds that would determine whether or when the factors listed in Section 10C of the Exchange Act, or any

---

[56] *See* Exchange Act Rule 10A-3(b)(5)(iii).

[57] Although there is no relevant legislative history, we assume this is intended to address the concern expressed by the multi-service compensation consulting firms that the disclosure requirements the Commission adopted last year are not competitively neutral because they do not address potential conflicts of interest presented by boutique consulting firms that are dependent on the revenues of a small number of clients.

See letter from Towers Perrin, commenting on Proxy Disclosure and Solicitation Enhancements, Release No. 33-9052 (July 10, 2009), available at *http://www.sec .gov/comments/s7-13-09/s71309-90.pdf.* The list in Section 10C, which covers both multi-service firm "other services" conflicts and boutique firm "revenue concentration" conflicts, is consistent with this assumption.

other factors added by the Commission or by the exchanges, must be considered germane by a compensation committee. For example, we do not believe that our rules should provide that a committee must consider stock owned by an adviser only if ownership exceeds a specified minimum percentage of the issuer's stock, or that a committee must consider the amount of revenues that the issuer's business represents for an adviser only if the percentage exceeds a certain percentage of the adviser's revenues. Therefore, proposed Rule 10C-1(b)(4) would require the listing standards developed by the exchanges to include the independence factors set forth in the statute and incorporated into the rule without any materiality or bright-line thresholds or cut-offs. Under the proposed rules, the exchanges may add other independence factors that must be considered by compensation committees of listed issuers.

We believe the factors set forth in Section 10C(b) are generally comprehensive. We are not proposing any additional compensation adviser independence factors at this time, although we are soliciting comment as to whether there are any additional independence factors that should be taken into consideration by a listed issuer's compensation committee when selecting a compensation adviser. We are also soliciting comment as to whether the factors set forth in Section 10C(b) and proposed Rule 10C-1(b)(4) are competitively neutral.

We have already received several comment letters with respect to the compensation adviser independence factors.[58] Commentators are generally supportive of the five factors listed in Section 10C(b), but believe that the factors should be used only in guiding the compensation committee in its selection process, not as an outright bar or prohibition against any one category of compensation adviser.[59] One commentator stated that in requiring the factors to be "competitively neutral," Congress sought to ensure that companies "have the flexibility to select the types of adviser[s] that best meet their particular needs."[60] Several commentators suggested that the stock ownership independence factor should relate only to shares of the listed issuer owned directly by the consulting firm or by advisers immediately engaged by the compensation committee.[61] Other commentators sought clarification on what constitutes a "business" or "personal" relationship between the compensation adviser and a member of the compensation committee.[62] In light of our overall approach to implementing the independence factors as provided in Section 10C(b), we are not proposing to address these points, but solicit comment below on whether we should.

Request for Comment

- Section 10C(b) specifies that the independence factors identified by the Commission must be competitively neutral, but does not state how we should determine whether a factor is competitively neutral. Are there any issues that should be considered to determine or assess whether a factor is competitively neutral?

- Are the five factors identified in Section 10C(b) of the Exchange Act competitively neutral among different types of compensation advisers? If not, what modifications or adjustments should be made in order to make these factors competitively neutral? Are there specific categories of compensation advisers that would be adversely affected by the compensation committee's use of these factors to assess independence?

- Are there any factors affecting independence that we should add to the list of factors identified in proposed Rule 10C-1(b)(4)? If so, what are they and why should they be included?

---

[58] *See, e.g.*, letters from Mercer, Meridian Compensation Partners, LLC, Pay Governance LLC and Frederick W. Cook & Co., Inc.

[59] *See, e.g.*, letter from Pay Governance LLC.

[60] *See* letter from Towers Watson.

[61] *See, e.g.*, letters from Frederick W. Cook & Co., Inc and Mercer.

[62] *See, e.g.*, letters from Mercer and Pay Governance LLC.

- Would the existence of a business or personal relationship between a compensation adviser and an executive officer of the issuer be relevant in considering whether to engage the compensation adviser? If so, why? Should we add this to the required list of factors that must be considered?

- Based on the language in Section 10C(b)(2), which distinguishes between the adviser and the person that employs the adviser, a personal or business relationship between the person employing the adviser and a member of the compensation committee would not be covered by the proposed rule (which, like Section 10C(b)(2)(D), only refers to relationships between the adviser and the compensation committee). Should the required list of factors also include a business or personal relationship between the person employing the compensation adviser and a member of the compensation committee? Along those lines, should it also cover a business or personal relationship between the person employing the adviser and an executive officer of the issuer?

- Should we provide materiality, numerical or other thresholds that would apply to whether or when the independence factors must be considered by a compensation committee? If so, what should they be? For example, should we require consideration of stock ownership only if the amount of stock owned constitutes a significant portion of an adviser's net worth, such as 10%?

- Would law firms be affected by the requirement to consider independence factors in a way that would be materially different than how compensation consultants would be affected?

- Should we clarify what is covered by "provision of other services" in proposed Rule 10C-1(b)(4)(i)?

- We interpret "any stock of the issuer owned by the compensation consultant, independent legal counsel or other adviser" in proposed Rule 10C-1(b)(4)(v) to include shares owned by the individuals providing services to the compensation committee and their immediate family members. We do not believe this factor is intended to extend to the person that employs the adviser since Section 10C(b) is specific when factors extend to the employer and that language is not included for stock ownership. Is this an appropriate interpretation of this factor? If not, why and how should this phrase be interpreted? Should it also cover the person that employs the adviser?

- Should we define or clarify the meaning of the phrase "business or personal relationship," as used in proposed Rule 10C-1(b)(4)(iv), and if so, how?

- Would the proposed requirements have any unintended effects on the compensation committee or its process to select a compensation adviser? If so, please explain.

- Should we adopt rule amendments to Regulation S-K to require listed issuers to describe the compensation committee's process for selecting compensation advisers pursuant to the new listing standards? Would information about the compensation committee's selection process – how it works, what it requires, who is involved, when it takes place, whether it is followed – provide transparency to the compensation adviser selection process and provide investors with information that may be useful to them as they consider the effectiveness of the selection process? Or, would such a requirement result in too much detail about this process in the context of disclosure regarding executive compensation?

5. Opportunity to Cure Defects

Section 10C(f)(2) of the Exchange Act specifies that our rules must provide for appropriate procedures for an issuer to have a reasonable opportunity to cure any defects that would be the basis for a prohibition of the listing of an issuer's securities as a result of its failure to meet the requirements set forth in Section 10C, before imposition of such a prohibition.[63] To implement this requirement, proposed Rule 10C-1(a)(3) would require the exchanges to establish such procedures (if their existing procedures are not adequate) before they prohibit the listing of, or delist, any security of an issuer.

As a preliminary matter, we believe that existing continued listing or maintenance standards and delisting procedures of most of the exchanges would satisfy the requirement for there to be reasonable procedures for an issuer to have an opportunity to cure any defects on an ongoing basis. Most exchanges have already adopted procedures to provide issuers with notice and opportunity for a hearing, an opportunity for an appeal and an opportunity to cure defects before their securities are delisted.[64] Nonetheless, we expect that the rules of each exchange would provide for definite procedures and time periods for compliance with the proposed requirements to the extent they do not already do so.

When we adopted Exchange Act Rule 10A-3(a)(3), which requires that issuers be given an opportunity to cure violations of the audit committee listing requirements, we noted that several commentators to the proposing release for those rules expressed concern regarding rare situations that may occur where an audit committee member ceases to be independent for reasons outside the member's reasonable control.[65] For example, a listed issuer's audit committee member could be a partner in a law firm that provides no services to the listed issuer, but the listed issuer could acquire another company that is one of the law firm's clients. Without an opportunity to cure such a defect, the audit committee member would cease to be independent. Additional time may be necessary to cure such defects, such as ceasing the issuer's relationship with the audit committee member's firm or replacing the audit committee member. Accordingly, in our final rule, we provided that the exchanges' rules may provide that if a member of an audit committee ceases to be independent for reasons outside the member's reasonable control, that person, with notice by the issuer to the applicable national securities exchange or national securities association, may remain an audit committee member of the listed issuer until the earlier of the next annual meeting of the listed issuer or one year from the occurrence of the event that caused the member to be no longer independent.[66]

We are proposing that there should be the same opportunity to cure violations of the independence requirements for compensation committee members, for the same reasons we adopted such provisions for curing violations of the independence requirements for audit committee members. Accordingly, consistent with Rule 10A-3(a)(3), proposed Rule 10C-1(a)(3) provides that the exchanges' rules may provide that if a member of a compensation committee ceases to be independent for reasons outside the member's reasonable control, that person, with notice by the issuer to the applicable exchange, may remain a compensation committee member of the listed issuer until the earlier of the next annual meeting of the listed issuer or one year from the occurrence of the event that caused the member to be no longer independent.

Request for Comment

- Should the exchanges be required to establish specific procedures for curing defects regarding compliance with compensation committee listing requirements

---

[63] *See* Exchange Act Section 10C(f)(2).

[64] *See, e.g.,* NYSE Listed Company Manual Section 801-805; Nasdaq Equity Rules 5800 Series; NYSE AMEX LLC Company Guide Section 1009 and Part 12; Chicago Board Options Exchange Rule 31.94; Chicago Stock Exchange Article 22, Rules 4, 17A, and 22; Nasdaq OMX BX Rule 4800 series; Nasdaq OMX PHLX Rule 811. Neither NYSE Arca nor the National Stock Exchange has a rule that specifically requires listed companies to be given an opportunity to submit a plan to regain compliance with corporate governance

listing standards other than audit committee requirements; issuers listed on these exchanges, however, are provided notice, an opportunity for a hearing, and an opportunity for an appeal prior to delisting. *See* NYSE Arca Rule 5.5(m); National Stock Exchange Rule 15.7 and Chapter X.

[65] *See* Standards Relating to Listed Company Audit Committees, Release No. 33-8220 (Apr. 9, 2003).

[66] *See* Exchange Act Rule 10A-3(a)(3) [17 CFR 240.10A-3(a)(3)].

apart from those proposed? If so, what should these procedures be? Should there be a specific course for redress other than the delisting process?

- Should our rule, as proposed, allow exchange rules that would permit the continued service of a compensation committee member who ceases to be independent for reasons outside the member's reasonable control? If so, should our rule impose a maximum time limit for such continued service? Should our rule require that the issuer use reasonable efforts to replace the member who is no longer independent as promptly as practicable?

- Should our rule include specific provisions that set time limits for an opportunity to cure defects other than for instances where a compensation committee member ceases to be independent for reasons outside the member's reasonable control? If so, what time limits would be appropriate?

- Should companies that have just completed initial public offerings be given additional time to comply with the requirements, as is permitted by Exchange Act Rule 10A-3(b)(1)(iv)(A) with respect to audit committee independence requirements?

B. Implementation of Listing Requirements

1. Exchanges Affected

Section 10C of the Exchange Act by its terms applies to all national securities exchanges and national securities associations.[67] These entities, to the extent that their listing standards do not already comply with the rules we adopt under Section 10C, will be required to issue or modify their rules, subject to Commission review, to conform their listing standards to our new rules. An exchange that lists or trades security futures products (as defined in Exchange Act Section 3(a)(56))[68] may register as a national securities exchange under Section 6(g) of the Exchange Act solely for the purpose of trading security futures products.[69] Because the Exchange Act definition of "equity security" includes security futures on equity securities,[70] we believe it is necessary to clarify the application of proposed Rule 10C-1 to those national securities exchanges registered solely pursuant to Section 6(g).

Given that Section 10C(f) of the Act makes no distinction between exchanges registered pursuant to Section 6(a) and those registered pursuant to Section 6(g), we have not proposed a wholesale exemption from the requirements of Rule 10C-1 for those

---

[67] The OTC Bulletin Board (OTCBB) and the OTC Markets Group (previously known as the Pink Sheets and Pink OTC Markets) would not be affected by the proposed requirements, and therefore issuers whose securities are quoted on these interdealer quotation systems similarly would not be affected, unless their securities also are listed on an exchange. The OTCBB is an interdealer quotation system for the over-the-counter securities market operated by FINRA that collects and distributes market maker quotes to subscribers. It does not, however, have a listing agreement or arrangement with the issuers whose securities are quoted on the system. Although market makers may be required to review and maintain specified information about the issuer and to furnish that information to the OTCBB, the issuers whose securities are quoted on it are not required to file any information with the system. The OTC Markets Group is not a registered national securities exchange or association, nor is it operated by a registered national securities exchange or association, and thus is not covered by the terms of the proposed rule.

[68] Exchange Act Section 3(a)(56) defines the term "security futures product" to mean "a security future or any put, call, straddle, option, or privilege on any security future." 15 U.S.C. 78c(a)(56).

[69] Exchanges currently registered solely pursuant to Section 6(g) of the Exchange Act include the Board of Trade of the City of Chicago, Inc.; the CBOE Futures Exchange, LLC; the Chicago Mercantile Exchange, Inc.; One Chicago, LLC; the Island Futures Exchange, LLC; and NQLX LLC.

[70] Under Section 3(a)(11) of the Exchange Act, the term "equity security" is defined as any stock or similar security; or any security future on any such security; or any security convertible, with or without consideration, into such a security, or carrying any warrant or right to subscribe to or purchase such a security; or any such warrant or right; or any other security which the Commission shall deem to be of similar nature and consider necessary or appropriate, by such rules and regulations as it may prescribe in the public interest or for the protection of investors, to treat as an equity security.

exchanges registered solely pursuant to Section 6(g). However, as discussed below, we are proposing to exempt security futures products from the scope of proposed Rule 10C-1. Accordingly, to the extent our final rule exempts the listing of security futures products from the scope of Rule 10C-1, any national securities exchange registered as such solely pursuant to Section 6(g) of the Exchange Act and that lists and trades only security futures products would not be required to file a rule change in order to comply with Rule 10C-1.

Currently, the only registered national securities association under Section 15A(a) of the Exchange Act is FINRA.[71] However, FINRA does not list securities.[72] While we recognize that Section 10C of the Act specifically requires national securities associations to prohibit the listing of any equity security of an issuer that does not comply with the requirements of Section 10C, as FINRA does not list any securities and does not have listing standards under its rules, we do not expect FINRA to have to develop listing standards regarding compensation committees in compliance with proposed Rule 10C-1.[73] Nevertheless, as Section 10C specifically references national securities associations, proposed Rule 10C-1 would apply to any registered national securities association that lists equity securities in the future.

Request for Comment

- Should we exempt certain exchanges or associations from Section 10C of the Exchange Act? If so, why, and which exchanges or associations should we exempt and why?
- Would we need to exempt an exchange from Section 10C if we also exempt the class of securities listed on such exchange?

2. Securities Affected

a. Listed Equity Securities

Section 10C of the Exchange Act specifies in one subsection that the compensation committee listing requirements are intended to apply to issuers with listed equity securities, but another subsection may suggest that it applies to issuers with any listed securities. Section 10C(a) provides that the Commission shall direct the exchanges to prohibit the listing of any "equity security" of an issuer (other than several types of exempted issuers) that does not comply with the compensation committee member independence requirements. Section 10C(f)(1), which states generally the scope of the compensation committee and compensation adviser listing requirements, provides that, "[n]ot later than 360 days after the date of enactment of this section, the Commission shall, by rule, direct the national securities exchanges and national securities associations to prohibit the listing of *any security* of an issuer that is not in compliance with the requirements of this section" (emphasis added).

The Senate-passed version of the bill did not distinguish between equity and non-equity securities, referencing only the prohibition against the listing of "any security" of an issuer not in compliance with the independence requirements. The House-passed version would have required the Commission to adopt rules to direct the exchanges to prohibit the listing of "any class of equity security" of an issuer that is not in compliance with the compensation committee independence standards, as well as with any of the other provisions of that section, including the provisions relating to compensation advisers. According to a press release from the House Financial Services Committee, this language was added during final House deliberations to clarify that the compensation

---

[71] Regarding the National Futures Association (NFA), see note 6, above, and note 73, below.
[72] See note 6, above.
[73] Similarly, we do not expect the NFA, which is registered under Section 15A(k) for the limited purpose of regulating the activities of members who are registered as broker-dealers in security futures products, see note 6, above, to develop listing standards regarding compensation committees in compliance with proposed Rule 10C-1.

committee independence standards would apply only to "public companies, not to companies that have only an issue of publicly-registered debt."[74]

Because the Senate-passed version of the bill (which did not specify "equity" securities) was used as the base for the conference draft, it appears that addition of "equity" securities in Section 10C(a) of the conference draft is deliberate. Unlike the House-passed bill, however, the final bill specifically references equity securities only in connection with compensation committee independence requirements.

Based on this legislative history, we believe that the compensation committee and other requirements in Section 10C are intended to apply only to issuers with listed equity securities.[75] As noted above, the provision governing compensation committee independence is specifically limited to issuers of equity securities. Against this backdrop, in our view, it is unlikely that Congress intended the remaining compensation committee provisions (compensation adviser independence factors, authority to retain compensation advisers, and responsibility for the appointment, compensation and oversight of the work of the compensation advisers) to apply to issuers with only listed debt securities. We note that the NYSE currently exempts debt-only listed issuers from the compensation committee listing requirements that apply to issuers listing equity securities.[76] In addition, Exchange Act Rule 3a12-11 exempts listed debt securities from most of the requirements in our proxy and information statement rules.[77] Finally, most, if not all, issuers with only listed debt securities, other than foreign private issuers, are privately held.[78] Thus, subjecting issuers of such securities to the requirements of proposed Rule 10C-1 would not serve the general intent of the Act's executive compensation provisions of protecting "shareholders in a public company."[79] In light of the legislative history and our and the exchanges' historical approach to issuers with only listed debt securities, we believe the new listing standards required by Section 10C are intended to apply only to issuers with listed equity securities.

Request for Comment

- We read Section 10C as applying only to issuers with listed equity securities, and our proposed rules are consistent with that view. Should we instead mandate that the requirements of Sections 10C(b) through (e) be applied to a broader range of issuers, including issuers with only listed debt securities or issuers with other types of listed securities? Why or why not?

---

[74] See http://www.house.gov/apps/list/press/financialsvcs_dem/press_072809.shtml.

[75] Although Section 10C is, in many respects, similar to Section 10A(m), there are differences in some of the statutory language. In this regard, we note that the audit committee independence requirements included in Section 10A(m) of the Exchange Act, as set forth in Section 301 of the Sarbanes-Oxley Act, are applicable generally to "listed securities," and no reference is made to equity securities. Therefore, although Section 10A(m) applies to issuers whether they have listed debt or equity, we do not believe this should necessarily prescribe the scope of Section 10C.

[76] See NYSE Listed Company Manual Section 303A.00.

[77] In adopting this rule, the Commission determined that debt holders would receive sufficient protection from the indenture contract, the Trust Indenture Act, the proxy rules' antifraud proscriptions, and the Exchange Act rules that facilitate the transmission of materials to beneficial owners. See Exemptive Relief and Simplification of Filing Requirements for Debt Securities To Be Listed on a National Securities Exchange, Release No. 34-34922 (Nov. 1, 1994) [59 FR 55342].

[78] Based on information reported in the most recent annual reports on Forms 10-K, 20-F and 40-F that are available on EDGAR, and current public quotation and trade data on issuers whose debt securities are listed on an exchange, such as the *NYSE Listed and Traded Bonds* and *NYSE Amex Listed Bonds*, we estimate that there are approximately 76 issuers that list only debt securities on an exchange. Of these 76 issuers, approximately 21 are wholly-owned subsidiaries that would be exempt from proposed Exchange Act Rule 10C-1 pursuant to Section 10C(g) of the Act. None of these 76 issuers has a class of equity securities registered under Section 12 of the Exchange Act.

[79] See H.R. Rep. No. 111-517, Joint Explanatory Statement of the Committee of Conference, Title IX, Subtitle E "Accountability and Executive Compensation," at 872 (Conf. Rep.) (June 29, 2010) ("In this subtitle, Congress provides shareholders in a public company with a vote on executive compensation and additional disclosures regarding compensation practices.").

b. Securities Futures Products and Standardized Options

The Exchange Act's definition of "equity security" includes any security future on any stock or similar security.[80] The Commodity Futures Modernization Act of 2000 (the "CFMA")[81] permits national securities exchanges registered under Section 6 of the Exchange Act[82] and national securities associations registered under Section 15A(a) of the Exchange Act[83] to trade futures on individual securities and on narrow-based security indices ("security futures")[84] without such securities being subject to the registration requirements of the Securities Act of 1933 (the "Securities Act") and Exchange Act so long as they are cleared by a clearing agency that is registered under Section 17A of the Exchange Act[85] or that is exempt from registration under Section 17A(b)(7)(A) of the Exchange Act. In December 2002, we adopted rules to provide comparable regulatory treatment for standardized options.[86]

The clearing agency for security futures products and standardized options is the issuer of these securities,[87] but its role as issuer is fundamentally different from an issuer of common stock of an operating company. The purchaser of these securities does not, except in the most formal sense, make an investment decision regarding the clearing agency. As a result, information about the clearing agency's business, its officers and directors and its financial statements is less relevant to investors in these securities than information about the issuer of the underlying security. Similarly, the investment risk in these securities is determined by the market performance of the underlying security rather than the performance of the clearing agency, which is a self-regulatory organization subject to regulatory oversight. Furthermore, unlike a conventional issuer, the clearing agency does not receive the proceeds from sales of security futures products or standardized options.[88]

In recognition of these fundamental differences, the Commission provided exemptions for security futures products and standardized options when it adopted the audit committee listing requirements in Exchange Act Rule 10A-3.[89] Specifically, Rule 10A-3(c) exempts the listing of a security futures product cleared by a clearing agency that is registered pursuant to Section 17A of the Exchange Act or that is exempt from registration pursuant to Section 17A(b)(7)(A) and the listing of a standardized option issued by a clearing agency that is registered pursuant to Section 17A of the Exchange Act. For the same reasons that we exempted these securities from Rule 10A-3, we propose to exempt these securities from Rule 10C-1, as we believe that there would be no benefit to investors or to the public interest in subjecting the issuers of these securities to the requirements of proposed Rule 10C-1.

---

[80] Exchange Act Section 3(a)(11).

[81] Pub. L. No. 106-554, 114 Stat. 2763 (2000).

[82] 15 U.S.C. 78f.

[83] 15 U.S.C. 78o-3(a).

[84] Exchange Act Section 3(a)(56) [15 U.S.C. 78c(a)(56)], and Commodities Exchange Act Section 1a(32) [7 U.S.C. 1a(32)] define "security futures product" as a security future or any put, call, straddle, option, or privilege on any security future.

[85] 15 U.S.C. 78q-1.

[86] See Release No. 33-8171 (Dec. 23, 2002) [68 FR 188]. In that release, we exempted standardized options issued by registered clearing agencies and traded on a registered national securities exchange or on a registered national securities association from all provisions of the Securities Act, other than the antifraud provision of Section 17, as well as the Exchange Act registration requirements. Standardized options are defined in Exchange Act Rule 9b-1(a)(4) [17 CFR 240.9b-1(a)(4)] as option contracts trading on a national securities exchange, an automated quotation system of a registered securities association, or a foreign securities

exchange which relate to option classes the terms of which are limited to specific expiration dates and exercise prices, or such other securities as the Commission may, by order, designate.

[87] See Fair Administration and Governance of Self-Regulatory Organizations; Disclosure and Regulatory Reporting by Self-Regulatory Organizations; Recordkeeping Requirements for Self-Regulatory Organizations; Ownership and Voting Limitations for Members of Self-Regulatory Organizations; Ownership Reporting Requirements for Members of Self-Regulatory Organizations; Listing and Trading of Affiliated Securities by a Self-Regulatory Organization, Release No. 34-50699 (Nov. 18, 2004) [69 FR 71126], at n. 260 ("Standardized options and security futures products are issued and guaranteed by a clearing agency. Currently, all standardized options and security futures products are issued by the Options Clearing Corporation ('OCC').").

[88] However, the clearing agency may receive a clearing fee from its members.

[89] See Exchange Act Rules 10A-3(c)(4) and (5).

Request for Comment

- Is our proposed exemption for securities futures products and standardized options necessary or appropriate in the public interest and consistent with the protection of investors?

- Alternatively, would it further the goal of investor protection to adopt Rule 10C-1 without the proposed exemption for securities futures products and standardized options?

3. Exemptions

a. General Approach to Exemptions

Section 10C of the Exchange Act has four different provisions relating to exemptions from some or all of the requirements of Section 10C:

- Section 10C(a)(1) provides that our rules shall direct the exchanges to prohibit the listing of any equity security of an issuer, other than an issuer that is in one of five specified categories, that is not in compliance with the compensation committee member independence requirements of Section 10C(a)(2);

- Section 10C(a)(4) provides that our rules shall authorize the exchanges to exempt a particular relationship from the independence requirements applicable to compensation committee members, as each exchange determines is appropriate, taking into consideration the size of the issuer and other relevant factors;

- Section 10C(f)(3) provides that our rules shall authorize the exchanges to exempt any category of issuer from the requirements of Section 10C, taking into account the potential impact of the requirements on smaller reporting companies;[90] and

- Section 10C(g) specifically exempts controlled companies, as defined in Section 10C(g), from all of the requirements of Section 10C.

We can exempt any person, security or transaction, or any class or classes of person, securities or transactions, from any of the requirements of the Exchange Act, to the extent that such exemption is necessary or appropriate in the public interest, and is consistent with the protection of investors.[91] In addition, as noted above, Section 10C(f)(3) provides that our rules shall authorize the exchanges to exempt any category of issuers from the requirements of Section 10C.[92] As with any listing standards, listing

---

[90] Exchange Act Rule 12b-2 defines "smaller reporting company" as "an issuer that is not an investment company, an asset-backed issuer . . . , or a majority-owned subsidiary of a parent that is not a smaller reporting company and that: (1) Had a public float of less than $75 million as of the last business day of its most recently completed second fiscal quarter, computed by multiplying the aggregate worldwide number of shares of its voting and non-voting common equity held by non-affiliates by the price at which the common equity was last sold, or the average of the bid and asked prices of common equity, in the principal market for the common equity; or (2) In the case of an initial registration statement under the Securities Act or Exchange Act for shares of its common equity, had a public float of less than $75 million as of a date within 30 days of the date of the filing of the registration statement, computed by multiplying the aggregate worldwide number of such shares held by non-affiliates before the registration plus, in the case of a Securities Act registration statement, the number of such shares included in the registration statement by the estimated

public offering price of the shares; or (3) In the case of an issuer whose public float as calculated under paragraph (1) or (2) of this definition was zero, had annual revenues of less than $50 million during the most recently completed fiscal year for which audited financial statements are available." Whether or not an issuer is a smaller reporting company is determined on an annual basis.

[91] *See* Exchange Act Section 36.

[92] We are proposing to implement Section 10C(c)(2)'s compensation consultant disclosure requirements by amending Item 407(e)(3) of Regulation S-K. See Section II.C., below, for a discussion of these proposed amendments. Because Item 407 of Regulation S-K is not part of Section 10C, Section 10C(f)(3) would not permit exchanges to exempt any category of issuers from our proposed revisions to Item 407, if adopted. We request comment below on whether smaller reporting companies should be exempt from our proposed disclosure requirements in the event the exchanges exempt such companies from the listing standards required by Section 10C.

standards implementing this provision would be subject to Commission review pursuant to Section 19(b) of the Exchange Act. In view of this statutory approach, we are preliminarily of the view that it should be up to the exchanges to propose the categories of issuers to be exempted from Section 10C's requirements, subject to our review in the rule filing process. Because issuers frequently consult the exchanges regarding independence determinations and committee responsibilities, the exchanges may be in the best position to identify the types of common relationships that are likely to compromise the ability of an issuer's compensation committee to make impartial determinations on executive compensation and the types of issuers that should be exempted from the other compensation committee listing requirements. Accordingly, relying on the exchanges to exercise their exemptive authority under our rules may result in more efficient and effective determinations as to the types of relationships and the types of issuers that merit an exemption, whether in whole or in part, from the requirements of Section 10C.

We note that Section 10C of the Exchange Act makes no distinction between domestic and foreign issuers, other than to exempt from the independence requirements foreign private issuers that disclose in their annual reports the reasons why they do not have independent compensation committees. Many listed foreign private issuers maintain compensation committees, and other than the committee member independence requirements in proposed Rule 10C-1(b)(1), the proposed rule and rule amendments, therefore, would apply to foreign private issuers as well as domestic issuers.

Because the exchanges will be permitted to propose exemptions to the listing standards required by Section 10C and our rules, we do not propose to exempt any category of issuer or any relationship from rules implementing Section 10C, other than the five categories of issuers not subject to the compensation committee independence requirements, as directed by Section 10C(a)(1), securities futures products and standardized options, as discussed above in Section II.B.2.b, and the equity securities of controlled companies, as directed by Section 10C(g).

Instead of providing exemptions in our rules, consistent with Section 10C(f)(3), proposed Rule 10C-1(b)(5)(i) permits the exchanges to exempt a category of issuers from the requirements of Section 10C, as each exchange determines is appropriate. In determining appropriate exemptions, the exchanges are required by the statute to take into account the potential impact of the requirements of Section 10C on smaller reporting issuers.[93]

Request for Comment

- Should the Commission exempt any types of issuers, such as registered management investment companies, foreign private issuers or smaller reporting companies, from some or all of the requirements of Section 10C? If so, why? Instead, should the Commission, as proposed, defer to the exchanges for exemptions from Section 10C's requirements, rather than propose and adopt exemptions in our rules?

- Should the Commission issue additional guidance to the exchanges as to the factors that should weigh in favor of granting exemptions? What concerns, if any,

---

[93] *See* Exchange Act Section 10C(f)(3)(B). Section 10C of the Exchange Act includes no express exemptions for smaller reporting companies. We note that neither NYSE nor Nasdaq currently exempts smaller reporting companies from their corporate governance requirements. Other than limited exemptions from requirements to have a majority independent board or three-member audit committee—for example, NYSE Amex and the Chicago Stock Exchange permit smaller issuers to have a 50% independent board and a minimum of two members on the issuer's audit committee—we are unaware of any corporate governance listing standards or related exemptions that are tailored to smaller reporting companies. *See* NYSE Amex Company Guide Section 801(h); Chicago Stock Exchange Article 22, Rules 19(a), 19(b)(1)(C)(iii), and 21(a). Section 10C(f)(3) requires the exchanges to take into account the potential impact of the listing requirements on smaller reporting issuers when exercising the exemptive authority permitted by our rules. Any such exemptions, rule changes and any other new listing requirements would be subject to Commission approval through the rule submission process under Section 19(b) of the Exchange Act.

should the Commission be aware of in reviewing exemptions proposed by the exchanges?

- Rather than exempt any category of issuers, should the Commission require the exchanges to give additional time to certain types of issuers to comply with the requirements of Section 10C, such as companies that have just completed initial public offerings? Or, should we defer to the exchanges to provide temporary exemptions, as proposed?

b. Issuers Not Subject to Independence Requirements

As noted above, Exchange Act Section 10C(a)(1) provides that our rules shall direct the exchanges to prohibit the listing of any equity security of an issuer, other than an issuer that is in one of five specified categories, that is not in compliance with the compensation committee member independence requirements of Section 10C(a)(2). These five categories include controlled companies, limited partnerships, companies in bankruptcy proceedings, open-end management investment companies registered under the Investment Company Act[94] and foreign private issuers that provide annual disclosures to shareholders of the reasons why the foreign private issuer does not have an independent compensation committee. Accordingly, proposed Rule 10C-1(b)(1)(iii) provides that these five categories of issuers are not subject to an exchange's compensation committee independence requirements and, therefore, an issuer that is in one of these categories cannot be delisted for not complying with such requirements.

Controlled Companies

Section 10C(g)(2) of the Exchange Act defines "controlled company" as an issuer that is listed on an exchange and holds an election for the board of directors of the issuer in which more than 50 percent of the voting power is held by an individual, a group or another issuer. Proposed Rule 10C-1(c)(2) would incorporate this definition of "controlled company."

Limited Partnerships

Section 10C does not define the term "limited partnerships." In general, a limited partnership is a form of business ownership and association consisting of one or more general partners who are fully liable for the debts and obligations of the partnership and one or more limited partners whose liability is limited to the amount invested.[95] We do not propose to define this term in proposed Rule 10C-1(c), although we solicit comment on whether we should do so.

Companies in Bankruptcy Proceedings

Section 10C does not define the scope of "companies in bankruptcy proceedings." This term is used in Commission rules without definition.[96] We do not propose to define the scope of "companies in bankruptcy proceedings," although we solicit comment on whether we should do so.

Open-End Management Investment Companies

Section 10C does not define the term "open-end management investment company." Under the Investment Company Act, an open-end management investment company is an investment company, other than a unit investment trust or face-amount certificate company, that offers for sale or has outstanding any redeemable security of which it is

---

[94] 15 U.S.C. 80a-1 *et seq.*
[95] *See* Unif. Ltd. P'ship Act §§ 102, 303 and 404 (2001).

[96] *See, e.g.,* Section 55(a)(3)(A) of the Investment Company Act [15 U.S.C. 80a-54(a)(3)(A)]; Item 1107(k) of Regulation AB [17 CFR 229.1107(k)]; and Rule 457 under the Securities Act [17 CFR 230.457].

the issuer.[97] We propose to define this term by referencing Section 5(a)(1) of the Investment Company Act.

Foreign Private Issuers

Under Section 10C(a), a foreign private issuer that provides annual disclosure to shareholders of the reasons why the foreign private issuer does not have an independent compensation committee would be exempt from the compensation committee independence requirements. Exchange Act Rule 3b-4 defines "foreign private issuer" as "any foreign issuer other than a foreign government, except for an issuer that has more than 50% of its outstanding voting securities held of record by U.S. residents and any of the following: a majority of its officers and directors are citizens or residents of the United States, more than 50% of its assets are located in the United States, or its business is principally administered in the United States."[98] Since this definition applies to all Exchange Act rules, we do not believe it is necessary to provide a cross-reference to Rule 3b-4 in our proposed rules.

We note that certain foreign private issuers have a two-tier board, with one tier designated as the management board and the other tier designated as the supervisory or non-management board. In this circumstance, we believe that the supervisory or non-management board would be the body within the company best equipped to comply with the proposed requirements. Consistent with our approach to Rule 10A-3, we propose to clarify that in the case of foreign private issuers with two-tier boards of directors, the term "board of directors" means the supervisory or non-management board. As such, to the extent the supervisory or non-management board forms a separate compensation committee, proposed Rule 10C-1 would apply to that committee, with the exception of the committee member independence requirements, assuming the foreign private issuer discloses why it does not have an independent compensation committee in its annual report.

Request for Comment

- Should we provide a definition of "limited partnership" in our proposed rules? If so, what should it be?

- Should we define the scope of "companies in bankruptcy proceedings"? If so, what should that scope be?

- Do we need to clarify, as proposed, that in the case of foreign private issuers with two-tier boards of directors, the term "board of directors" means the supervisory or non-management board?

c. Relationships Exempt from Independence Requirements

As noted above, Section 10C(a)(4) of the Exchange Act provides that the Commission's rules shall permit an exchange to exempt a particular relationship from the compensation committee independence requirements, as such exchange deems appropriate, taking into consideration the size of the issuer and any other relevant factors.[99] To implement this provision, proposed Rule 10C-1(b)(1)(iii)(B) would authorize the exchanges to establish listing standards under the Section 19(b) process that exempt particular relationships between members of the compensation committee and listed issuers that might otherwise impair the member's independence, taking into consideration the size of an issuer and any other relevant factors.

---

[97] *See* Sections 4 and 5(a)(1) of the Investment Company Act [15 U.S.C. 80a-4 and 80a-5(a)(1)]. Open-end and closed-end management investment companies registered under the Investment Company Act are generally exempt from current exchange listing standards that require listed issuers to either have a compensation committee or to have independent directors determine, recommend, or oversee specified executive compensation matters. *See, e.g.,* NYSE Listed Company Manual Section 303A.00; Nasdaq Rule 5615(a)(5); NYSE Arca Rule 5.3; NYSE AMEX LLC Company Guide Section 801.

[98] 17 CFR 240.3b-4(c).

[99] *See* Exchange Act Section 10C(a)(4).

We do not propose to exempt any particular relationships from the independence requirements at this time. As with the authority to exempt particular categories of issuers, we are preliminarily of the view that it should be up to the exchanges to identify and propose the types of particular relationships that should be exempted from the independence requirements.

Request for Comment

- Should the Commission, as proposed, defer to the exchanges to identify and propose the types of particular relationships to be exempted from the independence requirements? If not, why not?

- Should we give guidance to the exchanges on how they should analyze relationships to determine whether an exemption is warranted or not?

- Some of the exchanges, in their existing compensation committee listing standards, permit a listed issuer with a compensation committee comprised of at least three members to include one director who is not independent and is not a current officer or employee, or immediate family member of a current officer or employee, on the compensation committee for no more than two years if the issuer's board, under exceptional and limited circumstances, determines that such individual's membership on the committee is required in the best interests of the company and its shareholders.[100] Should our proposed rule expressly permit the exchanges to continue this practice by exempting certain relationships from the independence requirements, based on the conditions outlined above? Should our proposed rule expressly prohibit the exchanges from continuing this practice?

- What issues should an exchange consider in proposing an exemption?

- Exchange Act Rule 10A-3 requires listed issuers that avail themselves of an exemption from the audit committee independence requirements to disclose such reliance on an exemption in the listed issuer's proxy statement and Form 10-K or, in the case of a registered management investment company, Form N-CSR. Should we similarly require any issuer availing itself of any of the exemptions set forth directly in Section 10C(a)(1) of the Exchange Act or any exemption granted by the relevant exchange to disclose that fact in its proxy statement and Form 10-K or, in the case of a registered management investment company, Form N-CSR or another form? Under current rules, an issuer is required to identify any compensation committee members who are not independent. In light of this requirement, is a specific requirement to note reliance on an exemption unnecessary?

- If a listed issuer's board of directors determines, in accordance with applicable listing standards, to appoint a director to the compensation committee who is not independent, including as a result of exceptional or limited or similar circumstances, should we require the issuer to disclose the nature of the relationship that makes that individual not independent and the reasons for the board of directors' determination.

C. Compensation Consultant Disclosure and Conflicts of Interest

Section 10C(c)(2) of the Exchange Act requires that, in any proxy or consent solicitation material for an annual meeting (or a special meeting in lieu of the annual meeting), each issuer must disclose, in accordance with regulations of the Commission, whether:

- the compensation committee has retained or obtained the advice of a compensation consultant; and

---

[100] *See* NYSE Amex LLC Company Guide, Section 805(b); NYSE Arca Rule 5.3(k)(4); Nasdaq Rule 5605(d)(3); NASDAQ OMX BX Rule 4350(c)(3)(C); Chicago Board Options Exchange Rule 31.10(c)(3); and Chicago Stock Exchange Article 22, Rule 19(d)(3).

- the work of the compensation consultant has raised any conflict of interest and, if so, the nature of the conflict and how the conflict is being addressed.

Item 407 of Regulation S-K currently requires Exchange Act registrants that are subject to the proxy rules to provide certain disclosures concerning their compensation committees and the use of compensation consultants.[101] Item 407(e)(3)(iii) generally requires registrants to disclose "any role of compensation consultants in determining or recommending the amount or form of executive and director compensation," including:

- identifying the consultants;

- stating whether such consultants were engaged directly by the compensation committee or any other person;

- describing the nature and scope of the consultants' assignment, and the material elements of any instructions given to the consultants under the engagement; and

- disclosing the aggregate fees paid to a consultant for advice or recommendations on the amount or form of executive and director compensation and the aggregate fees for additional services if the consultant provided both and the fees for the additional services exceeded $120,000 during the fiscal year.[102]

The current item excludes from the disclosure requirement any role of compensation consultants limited to consulting on any broad-based plan that does not discriminate in scope, terms or operation in favor of executive officers or directors of the registrant and that is available generally to all salaried employees, or limited to providing information that either is not customized for a particular registrant or is customized based on parameters that are not developed by the compensation consultant, and about which the compensation consultant does not provide advice.[103]

Given the similarities between the disclosure required by Section 10C(c)(2) and the disclosure required by Item 407 of Regulation S-K for registrants subject to our proxy rules, we propose to integrate Section 10C(c)(2)'s disclosure requirements with the existing disclosure rule, rather than simply "tacking on" the new requirements to the existing ones. Section 10C(c)(2) specifies that these disclosures are to be required "in any proxy or consent solicitation material for an annual meeting of the shareholders (or a special meeting in lieu of the annual meeting)." By contrast, our proxy rules currently require issuers to provide disclosure relating to the retention of a compensation consultant and fees paid to consultants only in proxy or information statements for annual meetings at which directors are to be elected, and not for all annual meetings. However, Section 10C(c)(2) also provides that the compensation consultant disclosures be made "in accordance with regulations of the Commission." Because we view this disclosure as being most relevant in the context of a meeting at which directors will be elected, consistent with our current rules, we propose to require Section 10C(c)(2)'s compensation consultant and conflict of interest disclosure only for proxy and information statements for annual meetings (or a special meeting in lieu of an annual meeting) at which directors are to be elected.

---

[101] Registered investment companies are subject to separate proxy disclosure requirements set forth in Item 22 of Schedule 14A, which do not include the compensation committee disclosure described in Item 407(e) of Regulation S-K. See Item 7(g) of Schedule 14A. Consistent with our current regulations, registered investment companies would continue to provide disclosure under Item 22 and would not be subject to the amendments to Item 407(e) proposed in this release.

[102] See current Items 407(e)(3)(iii)(A) and (B) [17 CFR 229.407(e)(3)(iii)(A) and 229.407(e)(3)(iii)(B)]. Fee disclosure, however, is not required for compensation consultants that work with management if the

compensation committee has retained a separate consultant. In promulgating these requirements, we recognized that in this situation the compensation committee may not be relying on the compensation consultant used by management, and, therefore, potential conflicts of interest are less of a concern.

[103] See Proxy Disclosure Enhancements, Release No. 33-9089 (Dec. 16, 2009) [74 FR 68334]. The Commission determined (based on comments it received on the rule proposal) that the provision of such work by a compensation consultant does not raise conflict of interest concerns that warrant disclosure of the consultant's selection, terms of engagement or fees.

Section 10C(f) of the Exchange Act requires us to adopt rules directing the exchanges to prohibit the listing of any security of an issuer that is not in compliance with the requirements of Section 10C, which include Section 10C(c)(2)'s disclosure requirements. Consequently, we are required to extend these disclosure requirements to listed issuers other than controlled companies,[104] but we are not required to extend them to all Exchange Act registrants subject to our proxy rules. However, given the similar nature of the disclosure required by current Item 407(e) and Section 10C(c)(2) and the apparent common purpose of these disclosure requirements, and to avoid any potential confusion that could arise from having different disclosure requirements on the same topic for listed issuers on one hand and for unlisted issuers and controlled companies on the other, we propose to combine the current Item 407(e) and Section 10C(c)(2) into one disclosure requirement that would apply to Exchange Act registrants subject to our proxy rules, whether listed or not, whether they are controlled companies or not.

We note that the trigger for disclosure about compensation consultants under Section 10C(c)(2) of the Exchange Act is worded differently from the trigger for disclosure under the amendments to Item 407 that we adopted in 2009.[105] Specifically, Section 10C(c)(2) states that the issuer must disclose whether the "compensation committee retained or obtained the advice of a compensation consultant." By contrast, as noted above, our current rule refers to whether compensation consultants played "any role" in the registrant's process for determining or recommending the amount or form of executive or director compensation. Once disclosure is required, the specifics of what must be disclosed are also different. With regard to conflicts of interest, our current rule requires detailed disclosure about fees in certain circumstances in which there may be a conflict of interest, whereas Section 10C(c)(2) is more open-ended and requires disclosure of any conflict of interest, the nature of the conflict and how the conflict is being addressed, which our existing rules do not require.

As proposed, revised Item 407(e)(3)(iii) would have a disclosure trigger that is consistent with the statutory language and would, therefore, require the registrant to disclose whether the compensation committee has "retained or obtained" the advice of a compensation consultant during the registrant's last completed fiscal year. We anticipate that the practical effect of the proposed change would be minimal, as we believe it would be unusual for a consultant to play a role in determining or recommending the amount of executive compensation without the compensation committee also retaining or obtaining the consultant's advice. And, we believe having a consistent trigger for disclosure would benefit issuers and investors by reducing potential confusion about the disclosure requirements.

Consistent with Section 10C(c)(2), disclosure of whether the compensation committee obtained or retained the advice of a compensation consultant during the registrant's last completed fiscal year and whether the consultant's work raised any conflict of interest and, if so, the nature of the conflict and how it is being addressed, would be required without regard to the existing exceptions in Item 407(e)(3). For example, disclosure about the compensation consultant would be required even if the consultant provides only advice on broad-based plans or provides only non-customized benchmark data. In this regard, we would be broadening the scope of disclosure currently required by Item 407(e)(3)(iii). We believe this is consistent with the purposes of Section 10C(c)(2), which is to require disclosure about compensation consultants and any conflicts of interest they have in a competitively neutral fashion. We solicit comment, however, on whether any of the current exclusions should extend to this new disclosure requirement or, conversely, whether we should eliminate the exclusions with respect to the existing disclosure requirements. We also solicit comment on whether it would be preferable to retain the existing requirements without modification and add the new requirements without integrating them into the existing ones.

---

[104] Section 10C(g) specifically exempts controlled companies, as defined in Section 10C(g), from all of the requirements of Section 10C. Controlled companies are subject to our existing Item 407(e)(3) disclosure requirements.

[105] *Id.*

The other existing disclosure requirements of Item 407(e)(3) would remain the same, aside from amending the fee disclosure requirements to link the disclosure of fees to the compensation committee "retaining or obtaining the advice of a compensation consultant" and to management "retaining or obtaining the advice of a compensation consultant."[106] The disclosure of the aggregate fees paid to a compensation consultant is intended to enable security holders to assess the potential for conflicts of interest resulting from the compensation consultant's financial incentive to provide services to the issuer in addition to executive compensation consulting services. We believe that this disclosure benefits investors and complements the required Section 10C(c)(2) disclosures, and therefore propose to retain this existing disclosure requirement, modified as noted above.

To provide guidance to issuers as to whether the compensation committee or management has "obtained the advice" of a compensation consultant,[107] we are proposing an instruction to clarify this statutory language. This instruction would provide that the phrase "obtained the advice" relates to whether a compensation committee or management has requested or received advice from a compensation consultant, regardless of whether there is a formal engagement of the consultant or a client relationship between the compensation consultant and the compensation committee or management or any payment of fees to the consultant for its advice.

Currently, Item 407(e)(3) focuses on the conflicts of interest that may arise from a compensation consultant also providing other non-executive compensation consulting services to an issuer, which may lead the consultant to provide executive compensation advice favored by management in order to obtain or retain such other assignments. Section 10C(c)(2) is more open-ended about conflicts of interest in that it requires issuers to disclose whether the work of a compensation consultant raised "any conflict of interest" and, if so, the nature of the conflict and how the conflict is being addressed. The term "conflict of interest" is not defined in Section 10C(c)(2), and our proposed rule would not supply a definition.

As discussed above, Sections 10C(f) and 10C(b) of the Exchange Act require the Commission to adopt rules directing the exchanges to prohibit the listing of the securities of an issuer whose compensation committee does not consider the independence factors identified by the Commission when retaining compensation advisers. Section 10C(b)(2) identifies specific factors that must be included in these listing standards and, as described above, we are proposing to include them in proposed Rule 10C-1(b)(4)(i) through (v).[108]

In light of the link between the requirement that the compensation committees of listed issuers consider independence factors before retaining compensation advisers and the disclosure requirements about compensation consultants and their conflicts of interest, we believe it would be appropriate to provide some guidance to issuers as to the factors that should be considered in determining whether there is a conflict of interest that would trigger disclosure under the proposed amendments. Therefore, we propose to include an instruction that identifies the factors set forth in proposed Rule 10C-1(b)(4)(i) through (v) as among the factors that issuers should consider in determining whether there is a conflict of interest that may need to be disclosed in response to our proposed amendments to Item 407(e)(3)(iii). Although only listed issuers will be required to consider the five independence factors before selecting a compensation consultant, we believe that these five factors will be helpful to all Exchange Act registrants subject to the proxy rules in assessing potential conflicts of interest.

---

[106] *See* proposed Items 407(e)(3)(iii)(A) and (B). The fee disclosure requirements would continue to include the existing exclusions for consulting on any non-discriminatory, broad-based plan or providing non-customized information.

[107] *See* letter from Compensia.

[108] See Section II.A.4, above, for a description of proposed Rule 10C-1(b)(4)(i) through (v).

We have not concluded that the presence or absence of any of these individual factors indicates that a compensation consultant has a conflict of interest that would require disclosure under the proposed amendments, nor have we concluded that there are no other circumstances or factors that might present a conflict of interest for a compensation consultant retained by a compensation committee. Moreover, if, under our rules, disclosure of fees paid to a compensation consultant is required, this does not reflect a conclusion that a conflict of interest is present.[109] In addition to considering the factors enumerated above and any other factors that the exchanges may highlight in applicable listing standards, the issuer would need to consider the specific facts and circumstances relating to a consultant's engagement to determine whether there may be a conflict of interest that would be required to be disclosed under our new rules.

If a compensation committee determines that there is a conflict of interest with the compensation consultant based on the relevant facts and circumstances, the issuer would be required to provide a clear, concise and understandable description of the specific conflict and how the issuer has addressed it. A general description of an issuer's policies and procedures to address conflicts of interest or the appearance of conflicts of interest would not suffice.

Request for Comment

- We request comment on our proposed implementation of the requirements of Section 10C(c)(2). Is it appropriate to limit Section 10C(c)(2)'s disclosure requirement to proxy and information statements for meetings at which directors are to be elected? If not, why not? Is it appropriate to extend Section 10C(c)(2)'s disclosure requirement to controlled companies and those Exchange Act registrants that are not listed issuers, as proposed? If not, why not?

- Should we amend Forms 20-F and 40-F to require foreign private issuers that are not subject to our proxy rules to provide annual disclosure of the type required by Section 10C(c)(2)? Why or why not?

- Is it preferable to integrate the Section 10C(c)(2) disclosure requirements with the existing requirements of Item 407(e)(3), as proposed, or, instead, should we add the new requirements without modifying the existing requirements of the item?

- Should we extend any of the current exclusions under Item 407(e)(3) to the new Section 10C(c)(2) disclosures? Conversely, should we eliminate altogether the exclusions under Item 407(e)(3)?

- Are there any additional disclosures concerning conflicts of interest involving the activities of compensation consultants that would be beneficial to investors?

- Is additional clarification necessary regarding the phrase "obtained the advice"? Does our proposed instruction provide adequate guidance to issuers on how to interpret that phrase?

- Do the five factors in proposed Rule 10C-1(b)(4)(i) through (v) help issuers determine whether there is a "conflict of interest"? Should we define the term "conflict of interest"? If so, how? Are there other factors that should be considered in determining whether there is a conflict of interest? If so, should these factors also be identified in the proposed instruction?

- Because a compensation committee may be reluctant or unable to definitively conclude whether a conflict of interest exists, should we also include the

---

[109] See Proxy Disclosure Enhancements, Release No. 33-9089 (Dec. 16, 2009) [74 FR 68334] ("Our amendments as adopted are intended to facilitate investors' consideration of whether, in providing advice, a compensation consultant may have been influenced by a desire to retain other engagements from the company. This does not reflect a conclusion that we believe that a conflict of interest is present when disclosure is required under our new rule, or that a compensation committee or a company could not reasonably conclude that it is appropriate to engage a consultant that provides other services to the company requiring disclosure under our new rule.").

appearance of a conflict of interest in our interpretation of what constitutes a "conflict of interest" that must be disclosed under our proposed rules? Why or why not? Should we include potential conflicts of interest in our interpretation? Why or why not? We note that our 2009 amendments to Item 407(e) did not conclude that there was a conflict of interest posed by a consultant providing additional services to the issuer, only that there was a potential conflict of interest.

- Should we should require fee disclosure for other types of potential conflicts of interest, such as revenue concentration, in light of Section 10C(c)(2)'s requirement that the factors considered by the compensation committee before engaging compensation advisers be "competitively neutral"? For example, to address revenue concentration, we could require disclosure of an adviser's fees received from the issuer (in percentage terms) if such fees comprise more than 10% of the adviser's annual revenues. Would this be appropriate?

- Although a listed issuer's compensation committee is required to consider independence factors before selecting any compensation adviser, Section 10C(c)(2) requires conflict of interest disclosure only as to compensation *consultants*. Should we also extend this disclosure requirement to other types of advisers to the compensation committee, such as legal counsel? Why or why not?

- As proposed, and consistent with current rules, Item 407(e)(3) would apply to smaller reporting companies. Should we exempt such companies from these disclosure requirements? Do many smaller reporting companies' compensation committees retain or obtain the advice of compensation consultants? Should an exemption be provided if the exchanges exempt such companies from the listing standards required by Section 10C?

D. Transition and Timing

The Act requires us to issue rules directing the exchanges to prohibit the listing of issuers not in compliance with Section 10C "not later than 360 days after" the enactment of Section 10C, or by July 16, 2011.[110] The Act did not establish a specific deadline by which the listing standards promulgated by the exchanges must be in effect. To facilitate timely implementation of the proposals, we propose that each exchange must provide to the Commission, no later than 90 days after publication of our final rule in the Federal Register, proposed rules or rule amendments that comply with our final rule. Further, each exchange would need to have final rule or rule amendments that comply with our final rule approved by the Commission no later than one year after publication of our final rule in the Federal Register. We request comment below on the appropriateness of these periods.

Section 10C(c)(2) requires that each issuer disclose in any proxy or consent solicitation material for an annual meeting of shareholders (or a special meeting in lieu of the annual meeting) whether the issuer's compensation committee retained or obtained the advice of a compensation consultant; whether the work of the compensation consultant has raised any conflict of interest; and, if so, the nature of the conflict and how the conflict is being addressed. Although the statute specifies that this disclosure would be required with respect to meetings occurring on or after the date that is one year after the enactment of Section 10C, which would be July 21, 2011, the statute also requires these disclosures to be "in accordance with regulations of the Commission," and our regulations do not currently require such disclosures to be made. Consequently, Section 10C(c)(2)'s compensation consultant and conflict of interest disclosures would not be required for proxy or information statements filed in definitive form before the effective date of our rules implementing Section 10C(c)(2).

---

[110] *See* Section 10C(f)(1) of the Exchange Act [15 U.S.C. 78j-3(f)(1)]. The Act was enacted on July 21, 2010. The 360th day following enactment would be July 16, 2011.

Request for Comment

- Do the proposed implementation dates provide sufficient time for exchanges to propose and obtain Commission approval for new or amended rules to meet the requirements of our proposed rules? If not, what other dates would be appropriate, and why?

- What factors should the Commission consider in determining these dates?

- Should our rules also specify the dates by which listed issuers must comply with an exchange's new or amended rules meeting the requirements of our proposed rules? If so, what dates would be appropriate? Should there be uniformity among the exchanges with respect to the dates by which their listed issuers must comply with the exchanges' new or amended rules?

- Would a period beyond the proposed date be necessary or appropriate for compliance by smaller reporting companies? Are there special considerations that we should take into account for foreign private issuers?

General Request for Comment

We request and encourage any interested person to submit comments on any aspect of our proposals, other matters that might have an impact on the amendments, and any suggestions for additional changes. With respect to any comments, we note that they are of greatest assistance to our rulemaking initiative if accompanied by supporting data and analysis of the issues addressed in those comments and by alternatives to our proposals where appropriate.

III. PAPERWORK REDUCTION ACT

A. Background

Certain provisions of the proposed rule and rule amendments contain "collection of information" requirements within the meaning of the Paperwork Reduction Act of 1995 (PRA).[111] We are submitting the proposed rule and rule amendments to the Office of Management and Budget (OMB) for review in accordance with the PRA.[112] The titles for the collection of information are:

(1) "Regulation 14A and Schedule 14A" (OMB Control No. 3235-0059);

(2) "Regulation 14C and Schedule 14C" (OMB Control No. 3235-0057); and

(3) "Regulation S-K" (OMB Control No. 3235-0071).[113]

Regulation S-K was adopted under the Securities Act and Exchange Act; Regulations 14A and 14C and the related schedules were adopted under the Exchange Act. The regulations and schedules set forth the disclosure requirements for proxy and information statements filed by companies to help investors make informed investment and voting decisions. The hours and costs associated with preparing, filing and sending the schedules constitute reporting and cost burdens imposed by each collection of information. An agency may not conduct or sponsor, and a person is not required to respond to, a collection of information unless it displays a currently valid OMB control number. Compliance with the proposed rule and rule amendments would be mandatory. Responses to the information collections would not be kept confidential and there would be no mandatory retention period for the information disclosed.

---

[111] 44 U.S.C. 3501 *et seq.*

[112] 44 U.S.C. 3507(d) and 5 CFR 1320.11.

[113] The paperwork burden from Regulation S-K is imposed through the forms that are subject to the disclosure requirements in Regulation S-K and is reflected in the analysis of these forms. To avoid a Paperwork Reduction Act inventory reflecting duplicative burdens, for administrative convenience we estimate the burden imposed by Regulation S-K to be a total of one hour.

B. Summary of Proposed Rule and Rule Amendments

As discussed in more detail above, we are proposing new Rule 10C-1 under the Exchange Act and amendments to Item 407(e) of Regulation S-K. Proposed Rule 10C-1 would implement the requirements of Section 10C of the Exchange Act, as added by Section 952 of the Act. Specifically, proposed Rule 10C-1 would direct the exchanges to prohibit the listing of any equity security of an issuer, with certain exemptions, that is not in compliance with Section 10C's compensation committee and compensation adviser requirements. We are proposing to adopt several limited exemptions from the requirements of proposed Rule 10C-1 and to authorize the exchanges to include other exemptions in their listing standards, pursuant to the rule filing process under Section 19(b) of the Exchange Act, as each exchange determines is appropriate, taking into consideration the size of the issuer and any other relevant factors.

To implement Section 10C(c)(2), we are proposing to amend Item 407(e)(3) of Regulation S-K to require disclosure, in any proxy or information statement relating to an annual meeting of shareholders (or a special meeting in lieu of an annual meeting) at which directors are to be elected, of whether the issuer's compensation committee (or another board committee performing similar functions) retained or obtained the advice of a compensation consultant; whether the work of the compensation consultant has raised any conflict of interest; and, if so, the nature of the conflict and how the conflict is being addressed.[114] We also propose to combine and streamline these disclosure requirements with the existing disclosure requirements of Item 407(e)(3).

C. Burden and Cost Estimates Related to the Proposed Amendments

The proposed amendments to Item 407(e)(3) of Regulation S-K would require, if adopted, additional disclosure in proxy or information statements filed on Schedule 14A or Schedule 14C relating to an annual meeting of shareholders (or a special meeting in lieu of an annual meeting) at which directors are to be elected and would increase the burden hour and cost estimates for each of those forms. For purposes of the PRA, we estimate the total annual increase in the paperwork burden for all affected issuers to comply with our proposed collection of information requirements to be approximately 23,940 hours of in-house personnel time and approximately $3,192,000 for the services of outside professionals.[115] These estimates include the time and the cost of collecting the information, preparing and reviewing disclosure, filing documents, and retaining records. In deriving our estimates, we assumed that the burden hours of the proposed disclosure requirements would be comparable to the burden hours related to similar disclosure requirements under our current rules regarding compensation consultants.[116] Based on our assumptions, we estimated that the proposed amendments to Item 407(e)(3)(iii) of Regulation S-K would impose on average four incremental burden hours.[117]

The table below shows the total annual compliance burden, in hours and in costs, of the collection of information pursuant to the proposed amendments to proxy and information statements and to Regulation S-K.[118] The burden estimates were calculated by multiplying the estimated number of responses by the estimated average amount of time it would take an issuer to prepare and review the proposed disclosure requirements. The portion of the burden carried by outside professionals is reflected as a cost, while the

---

[114] Section 10C(c)(2) requires listed issuers to provide this disclosure; we propose to extend this disclosure requirement to non-listed issuers as well. We have not, however, proposed to require comparable disclosure from foreign private issuers, as foreign private issuers are not subject to Exchange Act Sections 14(a) and 14(c). *See* Exchange Act Rule 3a12-3.

[115] Our estimates represent the average burden for all issuers, both large and small.

[116] *See* Proxy Disclosure Enhancements, Release No. 33-9089 (Dec. 16, 2009) [74 FR 68334] (in which the Commission estimated the average incremental disclosure burden for the rule amendments to Item 407(e)(3) relating to compensation consultants to be three hours).

[117] These four incremental burden hours would be in addition to the three incremental burden hours relating to our current compensation consultant disclosure rules. *Id.*

[118] For convenience, the estimated hour and cost burdens in the table have been rounded to the nearest whole number.

portion of the burden carried by the issuer internally is reflected in hours. For purposes of the PRA, we estimate that 75% of the burden of preparation of Schedules 14A and 14C is carried by the issuer internally and that 25% of the burden of preparation is carried by outside professionals retained by the issuer at an average cost of $400 per hour. There is no change to the estimated burden of the collections of information under Regulation S-K because the burdens that this regulation imposes are reflected in our burden estimates for Schedules 14A and 14C.

Table 1. Incremental Paperwork Burden under the proposed amendments for Schedules 14A and 14C.

	Number of responses (A)[119]	Incremental burden hours/form (B)	Total incremental burden hours (C)=(A)*(B)	Internal company time (D)	External professional time (E)	Professional costs (F)=(E)*$400
Sch. 14A	7,300	4	29,200	21,900	7,300	$2,920,000
Sch. 14C	680	4	2,720	2,040	680	$272,000
Total	7,980		31,920	23,940	7,980	$3,192,000

D. Request for Comment

Pursuant to 44 U.S.C. 3506(c)(2)(B), we request comment in order to:

- Evaluate whether the proposed collections of information are necessary for the proper performance of the functions of the Commission, including whether the information will have practical utility;

- Evaluate the accuracy of our assumptions and estimates of the burden of the proposed collections of information;

- Determine whether there are ways to enhance the quality, utility and clarity of the information to be collected;

- Evaluate whether there are ways to minimize the burden of the collections of information on those who respond, including through the use of automated collection techniques or other forms of information technology; and

- Evaluate whether the proposed amendments will have any effects on any other collections of information not previously identified in this section.

Any member of the public may direct to us any comments concerning the accuracy of these burden estimates and any suggestions for reducing these burdens. Persons submitting comments on the collection of information requirements should direct their comments to the Office of Management and Budget, Attention: Desk Officer for the U.S. Securities and Exchange Commission, Office of Information and Regulatory Affairs, Washington, DC 20503, and send a copy to Elizabeth M. Murphy, Secretary, U.S. Securities and Exchange Commission, 100 F Street, NE, Washington, DC 20549-1090, with reference to File No. S7-13-11. Requests for materials submitted to OMB by the Commission with regard to these collections of information should be in writing, refer to File No. S7-13-11 and be submitted to the U.S. Securities and Exchange Commission, Office of Investor Education and Advocacy, 100 F Street NE, Washington DC 20549-0213. Because the OMB is required to make a decision concerning the collections of information between 30 and 60 days after publication of this release, your comments are best assured of having their full effect if the OMB receives them within 30 days of publication.

---

[119] The number of responses reflected in the table equals the actual number of schedules filed with the Commission during the 2010 fiscal year.

IV. COST-BENEFIT ANALYSIS

A. Introduction and Objectives of Proposals

We are proposing rulemaking to implement and supplement the provisions of the Act relating to compensation committees and compensation advisers. Section 952 of the Act amends the Exchange Act by adding new Section 10C. Section 10C(a)(1) requires the Commission to adopt rules directing the exchanges to prohibit the listing of any equity security of an issuer, with certain exemptions, that is not in compliance with the independence requirements for members of the compensation committee. In accordance with the statute, the rules, once adopted, would require the exchanges to establish listing standards that require each member of a listed issuer's compensation committee to be a member of the board of directors and to be "independent." The term "independent" is not defined in Section 10C(a)(1). Instead, the section provides that "independent" is to be defined by the exchanges after taking into consideration relevant factors, including, but not limited to, the source of compensation of a director, including any consulting, advisory or other compensatory fee paid by the issuer to the director, and whether the director is affiliated with the issuer, a subsidiary of the issuer, or an affiliate of a subsidiary of the issuer.

In addition to the independence requirements set forth in Section 10C(a), Section 10C(f) requires the Commission to adopt rules directing the exchanges to prohibit the listing of any security of an issuer that is not in compliance with the following requirements relating to compensation committees and compensation advisers, as set forth in paragraphs (b) through (e) of Section 10C:

- Each compensation committee must have the authority, in its sole discretion, to retain or obtain the advice of compensation consultants, independent legal counsel and other advisers (collectively, "compensation advisers");[120]

- Before selecting any compensation adviser, the compensation committee must take into consideration specific factors identified by the Commission that affect the independence of compensation advisers;[121]

- The compensation committee must be directly responsible for the appointment, compensation and oversight of the work of any compensation adviser;[122] and

- Each listed issuer must provide appropriate funding for the payment of reasonable compensation, as determined by the compensation committee, to compensation advisers.[123]

Finally, Section 10C(c)(2) requires each listed issuer to disclose in any proxy or consent solicitation material for an annual meeting of shareholders (or a special meeting in lieu of the annual meeting), in accordance with Commission regulations, whether the issuer's compensation committee retained or obtained the advice of a compensation consultant; whether the work of the compensation consultant has raised any conflict of interest; and, if so, the nature of the conflict and how the conflict is being addressed.

Under Section 10C, our rules must permit the exchanges to exempt particular categories of issuers from the requirements of Section 10C and particular relationships from the compensation committee independence requirements of Section 10C(a). Our rules must also provide for appropriate procedures for an issuer to have a reasonable opportunity to cure any defects that might otherwise result in the delisting of the issuer's securities.

We are proposing new Exchange Act Rule 10C-1 to implement the compensation committee listing requirements of Sections 10C(a)-(g) of the Exchange Act. Proposed Rule 10C-1 closely tracks the statutory requirements of Section 10C. To implement

---

[120] Exchange Act Sections 10C(c)(1)(A) and 10C(d)(1) [15 U.S.C. 78j-3(c)(1)(A) and (d)(1)].

[121] Exchange Act Section 10C(b) [15 U.S.C. 78j-3(b)].

[122] Exchange Act Sections 10C(c)(1)(B) and 10C(d)(2) [15 U.S.C. 78j-3(c)(1)(B) and (d)(2)].

[123] Exchange Act Section 10C(e) [15 U.S.C. 78j-3(e)].

Section 10C(c)(2) of the Exchange Act, we are proposing rule amendments to Regulation S-K to require disclosure, in any proxy or information statement relating to an annual meeting of shareholders at which directors are to be elected (or special meeting in lieu of the annual meeting), of whether the issuer's compensation committee retained or obtained the advice of a compensation consultant; whether the work of the compensation consultant has raised any conflict of interest; and, if so, the nature of the conflict and how the conflict is being addressed. In connection with these amendments, we also propose to revise the current disclosure requirements relating to the retention of compensation consultants by providing a uniform trigger for when compensation consultant disclosures will be required. In addition, our proposed amendments would eliminate the existing exception from the requirement to identify compensation consultants and describe their engagements for those cases in which a consultant's role is limited to consulting on a broad-based plan or providing information that either is not customized for a particular registrant or that is customized based on parameters that are not developed by the compensation consultant, and about which the compensation consultant does not provide advice.

The Commission is sensitive to the costs and benefits imposed by the proposed rule and rule amendments. The discussion below focuses on the costs and benefits of the proposals made by the Commission to implement the Act within its permitted discretion, rather than the costs and benefits of the Act itself.

B. Benefits

The proposed rulemaking is intended to implement and supplement the requirements of Section 10C of the Exchange Act as set forth in Section 952 of the Act.

Required Listing Standards

Under proposed Rule 10C-1, the exchanges would be directed to adopt listing standards that would apply to any committee of the board that oversees executive compensation, whether or not such committee performs other functions or is formally designated as a "compensation committee." We believe this aspect of the rule proposal may help achieve the objectives of the Act by providing clarity and reducing any uncertainty about the application of Section 10C. Moreover, this may benefit investors because it would limit the ability of listed issuers to circumvent the compensation committee independence requirements under Section 10C by delegating oversight of executive compensation to a board committee that is not formally designated as the "compensation committee," but performs that function.

As directed by Section 10C, proposed Rule 10C-1 directs the exchanges to develop a definition of independence applicable to compensation committee members after considering the relevant factors set forth in Exchange Act Section 10C(a)(3). We do not propose to specify any additional factors that the exchanges must consider in determining independence requirements for compensation committee members. We believe that permitting exchanges greater latitude in crafting the required independence standards, subject to Commission review pursuant to Section 19(b) of the Exchange Act, may result in more efficient and effective determinations as to what types of relationships should preclude a finding of independence with respect to membership on a board committee that oversees executive compensation. Because issuers frequently consult the exchanges regarding independence determinations, the exchanges may be in the best position to identify the types of common relationships that are likely to compromise the ability of an issuer's compensation committee to make impartial determinations on executive compensation.

Disclosure Amendments

Our proposed amendments to Item 407(e)(3) of Regulation S-K would require the specific disclosures mandated by Section 10C(c)(2). While no other disclosures are proposed to be required, our proposed amendments would extend the disclosure requirement of Section 10C(c)(2) to issuers, whether listed or not, that file proxy or information statements relating to an election of directors. Although controlled companies are exempt from the requirements of Section 10C, we propose to extend the disclosure requirements of Section 10C(c)(2) to controlled companies in order to have uniform compensation consultant disclosure requirements for all issuers subject to our proxy rules. Under the proposed amendments, in addition to the disclosure currently required by Item 407(e)(3), issuers would be required to disclose whether the compensation committee has retained or obtained the advice of a compensation consultant, whether the work of the compensation consultant has raised any conflict of interest, and, if so, the nature of the conflict and how the conflict is being addressed.

We believe that requiring these disclosures of issuers subject to the proxy rules will benefit investors by providing them with easily understandable and uniform disclosure regarding compensation consultant conflicts of interest. Under our existing disclosure rules, these issuers must already discuss the selection of compensation consultants and disclose the nature and scope of their assignment, including any material instructions or directions governing their performance under the engagement. We believe the proposed amendment would complement these existing disclosure requirements by increasing the transparency of issuers' policies regarding compensation consultant conflicts of interest. To the extent that the relationships between an issuer and a compensation consultant are more transparent under the proposed amendments, investors should benefit through their ability to better monitor the process of recommending and determining executive and director pay. The increased disclosure should improve the ability of investors to monitor performance of directors responsible for overseeing compensation consultants, thus enabling them to make more informed voting and investment decisions.

We also propose to harmonize current Item 407(e)(3)(iii)'s disclosure triggers with the requirements of Section 10C(c)(2). Our goal in proposing uniform disclosure triggers is to prevent the adoption of potentially duplicative or overlapping disclosure requirements; we also believe that providing a uniform standard for when these disclosures will be required will benefit issuers by allowing them to streamline their procedures for ensuring proper disclosure compliance.

The proposed amendments also include an instruction that provides guidance to issuers as to whether the compensation committee has "obtained the advice" of a compensation consultant. This instruction should benefit issuers by providing clarity and reducing any uncertainty about whether disclosure under the new rules is required. In addition, we propose to include an instruction that identifies the factors set forth in proposed Rule 10C-1(b)(4)(i) through (v) as among the factors to be considered in determining whether there is a conflict of interest that may need to be disclosed in response to our proposed amendments to Item 407(e)(3)(iii). Although only listed issuers will be required to consider the five independence factors before selecting a compensation consultant, we believe that identifying these five factors as factors that should be considered in determining whether conflict of interest disclosure is required will aid all Exchange Act registrants subject to the proxy rules in complying with their proxy disclosure obligations.

C. Costs

Required Listing Standards

Under our proposed rules, exchanges would be required to adopt independence requirements that apply to members of listed issuer compensation committees or committees performing equivalent functions, but not to directors who oversee executive compensation matters in the absence of such committees. Some exchange listing standards currently require issuers to form compensation or equivalent committees; others require independent directors to oversee specified compensation matters but do not require the formation of a compensation or equivalent committee. Exchanges that do not require the formation of a compensation or equivalent committee could, on their own initiative, determine to apply the same independence standards to directors who oversee compensation matters in the absence of a compensation committee as they do to formally organized compensation committees. In the event they do not, however, issuers could seek to list on such exchanges in order to avoid having to comply with the compensation committee independence standards that would apply at the exchanges that require the formation of a compensation or equivalent committee. Further, to the extent exchanges compete for listings, they may have an incentive to propose standards that issuers may find less onerous. This could result in costs to exchanges to the extent they lose issuer listings, as well as costs to issuers to the extent they choose to alter their existing committee structure to avoid having to comply with the new standards.

Our decision not to exempt additional categories of issuers, beyond those specified in Section 10C(a)(1), from the independence requirements of our proposed rule and instead to rely on the various exchanges to propose additional exemptions for appropriate categories of issuers, may also result in certain direct or indirect costs. For example, the exchanges will bear the direct cost of evaluating whether additional exemptions would be appropriate and including such exemptions in the rule filings that they are required to make in order to comply with our proposed rule.

Disclosure Amendments

As noted above, our proposal implements the requirements of Section 10C(c)(2). In addition, although not required by Section 10C(c)(2), we propose to require all issuers subject to our proxy rules, rather than only listed issuers, to provide the disclosures called for by Section 10C(c)(2). We also propose to combine and streamline the new disclosure requirements with the existing compensation consultant disclosure requirements. Specifically, we propose to provide a uniform trigger for when compensation consultant disclosures will be required and eliminate the existing exception from the requirement to identify compensation consultants and describe their engagements for those cases in which a consultant's role is limited to consulting on a broad-based plan or providing non-customized benchmark compensation information.

As a result, controlled companies and non-listed issuers will incur costs in disclosing all compensation consultant engagements and in determining and disclosing whether the work of any compensation consultant has raised any conflict of interest, the nature of the conflict, and how the conflict is being addressed. These costs, which would not be required to be incurred by Section 10C(c)(2), may be mitigated to an extent because our existing rules already require issuers subject to our proxy rules to disclose, with limited exceptions, any role of compensation consultants in determining or recommending the amount or form of executive and director compensation. As a result, these issuers will already have developed procedures for collecting and analyzing information about the use of compensation consultants.

For purposes of the PRA, we estimate the aggregate annual cost of the proposed compensation consultant and related conflicts of interest disclosure to be approximately 23,940 hours of company personnel time and approximately $3,192,000 for the services of outside professionals. However, this amount includes the costs associated with the disclosure requirements of Section 10C(c)(2) of the Exchange Act, as well as our proposed extension of the disclosure requirement to controlled companies and non-listed issuers and the revisions proposed for the purpose of integrating the new disclosure requirements with existing Item 407(e)(3). As a result, a portion of the reporting costs are attributable to the requirements of the Act rather than to our proposed amendments to Item 407.

We have not proposed that compensation committees of non-listed issuers be required to consider the independence of compensation consultants or other compensation advisers before they are selected; nonetheless, in light of our proposal that issuers subject to our proxy rules will be required to identify and disclose how they manage any conflicts of interest raised by the work of compensation consultants that serve as advisers to the compensation committee, non-listed issuers may incur additional costs to develop more formalized selection processes than they otherwise would have absent such a disclosure requirement. For example, to prepare for the disclosure requirement, at the time any compensation consultant is selected, compensation committees of non-listed issuers may devote additional time and resources to analyzing and assessing the independence of the compensation consultant and addressing and resolving potential conflicts of interest. Although our proposed disclosure requirement will not preclude compensation committees from selecting the compensation consultant of their choosing, such committees may elect to engage new, alternative or additional compensation advisers after considering what disclosure might be required under our proposed rules. Such decisions could result in additional costs to issuers, including costs related to termination of existing services and search and engagement costs to retain new advisers. In addition, costs may increase if an issuer decides to engage multiple compensation consultants for services that had previously been provided by a single consultant.

As a mitigating factor, our proposed rules would require issuers to provide narrative disclosure regarding the management of conflicts of interest. To the extent a non-listed issuer's compensation committee determines to retain a compensation consultant, despite potential conflicts of interest, this provision provides the issuer a means to communicate to investors both the reasons why the committee believes that retaining the consultant and managing the potential conflict of interest is the best approach and the methods employed by the issuer to manage or address the potential conflict.

D. Request for Comment

We request data to quantify the costs and the value of the benefits described above. We seek estimates of these costs and benefits, as well as any costs and benefits not already defined, that may result from the adoption of these proposed amendments. We also request qualitative feedback on the nature of the benefits and costs described above and any benefits and costs we may have overlooked.

V. CONSIDERATION OF IMPACT ON THE ECONOMY, BURDEN ON COMPETITION AND PROMOTION OF EFFICIENCY, COMPETITION AND CAPITAL FORMATION

Section 23(a)(2) of the Exchange Act requires us, when adopting rules under the Exchange Act, to consider the impact that any new rule would have on competition.[124] In addition, Section 23(a)(2) prohibits us from adopting any rule that would impose a burden on competition not necessary or appropriate in furtherance of the purposes of the Exchange Act.

Section 2(b) of the Securities Act[125] and Section 3(f) of the Exchange Act[126] require us, when engaging in rulemaking where we are required to consider or determine whether an action is necessary or appropriate in the public interest, to consider, in addition to the protection of investors, whether the action will promote efficiency, competition, and capital formation.

Our proposed rule and rule amendments would implement the requirements of Section 952 of the Act, which added Section 10C to the Exchange Act. Among other provisions, Section 10C requires us to direct the exchanges to prohibit the listing of any equity security of an issuer that is not in compliance with Section 10C's compensation committee and compensation adviser requirements. It is possible that some listed issuers might find the proposed requirements too onerous and seek to list on foreign exchanges or other markets to avoid compliance. This could cause U.S. exchanges to lose trading volume. We do not believe our proposed rules are likely to have this effect, as issuers listed on U.S. exchanges must, for the most part, already provide for executive compensation oversight by independent directors.[127] It is also possible that, in competing for listings, the exchanges could adopt different definitions of independence for compensation committee members, which could affect an issuer's decision about where to list its securities.

---

[124] 15 U.S.C. 78w(a)(2).
[125] 15 U.S.C. 77b(b).
[126] 15 U.S.C. 78c(f).

[127] *See, e.g.,* NYSE Listed Company Manual Section 303A.05(a) and Nasdaq Rule 5605(d).

Section 10C also requires disclosure from listed issuers, other than controlled companies, as to their use and oversight of compensation consultants. We propose to require companies subject to our proxy rules, including controlled companies, to provide this disclosure, whether listed or not. We believe this expansion of the statutory disclosure requirement will promote uniform disclosure on these topics among reporting companies and may allow investors to better understand the process by which compensation committees select compensation consultants and manage conflicts of interest.

Our proposals may promote efficiency and competitiveness of the U.S. capital markets by increasing the transparency of executive compensation decision-making processes and by improving the ability of investors to make informed voting and investment decisions, which may encourage more efficient capital formation. The proposals also may affect competition among compensation consultants. By requiring disclosure of the existence and management of potential compensation consultant conflicts of interest, our proposed rules may lead compensation committees to engage in more thorough and deliberative analyses of adviser independence. If this results in the selection of compensation advisers that are more independent or impartial than might otherwise be chosen, this could in turn promote more efficient executive compensation determinations. The proposed disclosure also could incent consultants to compete on the basis of their policies that serve to minimize any potential conflicts of interest or, to the extent other consultants are available, lead compensation committees to avoid hiring consultants perceived as having a conflict of interest.

We request comment on whether the proposed amendments, if adopted, would promote efficiency, competition and capital formation or have an impact or burden on competition. Commentators are requested to provide empirical data and other factual support for their views, to the extent possible.

VI. SMALL BUSINESS REGULATORY ENFORCEMENT FAIRNESS ACT

For purposes of the Small Business Regulatory Enforcement Fairness Act of 1996 (SBREFA),[128] we solicit data to determine whether the proposed rule amendments constitute a "major" rule. Under SBREFA, a rule is considered "major" where, if adopted, it results or is likely to result in:

- An annual effect on the economy of $100 million or more (either in the form of an increase or a decrease);

- A major increase in costs or prices for consumers or individual industries; or

- Significant adverse effects on competition, investment or innovation.

Commentators should provide empirical data on (1) the potential annual effect on the economy; (2) any increase in costs or prices for consumers or individual industries; and (3) any potential effect on competition, investment or innovation.

VII. INITIAL REGULATORY FLEXIBILITY ACT ANALYSIS

This Initial Regulatory Flexibility Analysis (IRFA) has been prepared in accordance with the Regulatory Flexibility Act.[129] This IRFA involves proposals to direct the national securities exchanges and national securities associations to prohibit the listing of an equity security of an issuer that is not in compliance with several requirements relating to the issuer's compensation committee, and to revise the disclosure requirements of Regulation S-K Item 407 related to compensation consultants.

A. Reasons for, and Objectives of, the Proposed Action

We are proposing amendments to implement Section 10C of the Exchange Act as added by Section 952 of the Act. The proposals would direct the exchanges to prohibit the listing of equity securities of any issuer that does not comply with Section 10C's

---

[128] 5 U.S.C. 801 et seq.   [129] 5 U.S.C. 603.

compensation committee and compensation adviser requirements. Our proposed amendments would also require issuers to provide certain disclosures regarding their use of compensation consultants and management of compensation consultant conflicts of interest.

B. Legal Basis

We are proposing the amendments pursuant to Sections 6, 7, 10, and 19(a) of the Securities Act; and Sections 10C, 12, 13, 14, 15(d), 23(a) and 36 of the Exchange Act.

C. Small Entities Subject to the Proposed Action

The proposals would affect exchanges that list equity securities and issuers subject to our proxy rules. The Regulatory Flexibility Act defines "small entity" to mean "small business," "small organization," or "small governmental jurisdiction."[130] The Commission's rules define "small business" and "small organization" for purposes of the Regulatory Flexibility Act for each of the types of entities regulated by the Commission. Exchange Act Rule 0-10(e) provides that the term "small business" or "small organization," when referring to an exchange, means any exchange that: (1) has been exempted from the reporting requirements of Exchange Act Rule 601;[131] and (2) is not affiliated with any person (other than a natural person) that is not a small business or small organization, as defined under Exchange Act Rule 0-10. No exchanges are small entities because none meet these criteria. Securities Act Rule 157[132] and Exchange Act Rule 0-10(a)[133] define a company, other than an investment company, to be a "small business" or "small organization" if it had total assets of $5 million or less on the last day of its most recent fiscal year. We estimate that there are approximately 1,207 registrants, other than registered investment companies, that may be considered small entities. The proposed amendments would affect small entities that have a class of securities that are registered under Section 12 of the Exchange Act. An investment company, including a business development company, is considered to be a "small business" if it, together with other investment companies in the same group of related investment companies, has net assets of $50 million or less as of the end of its most recent fiscal year.[134] We believe that the amendments to Item 407(e) of Regulation S-K would affect small entities that are business development companies that have a class of securities registered under Section 12 of the Exchange Act. We estimate that there are approximately 31 business development companies that may be considered small entities.

D. Reporting, Recordkeeping and other Compliance Requirements

Under the proposals, the exchanges will be directed to prohibit the listing of an equity security of an issuer that does not comply with Section 10C's compensation committee and compensation adviser requirements. These requirements relate to: the independence of compensation committee members; the authority of the compensation committee to engage compensation advisers; the compensation committee's responsibility for considering factors that affect the independence of compensation advisers prior to their selection; the compensation committee's responsibility for the appointment, compensation, and oversight of the work of compensation advisers; funding for advisers engaged by the compensation committee; and the opportunity to cure defects.

The proposals would also require additional disclosure about the use of compensation consultants and conflicts of interest. Large and small entities would be subject to the same disclosure requirements. The proposals would require small entities subject to the proxy rules to provide disclosure of whether:

- the compensation committee has retained or obtained the advice of a compensation consultant; and

---

[130] 5 U.S.C. 601(6).
[131] 17 CFR 242.601.
[132] 17 CFR 230.157.

[133] 17 CFR 240.0-10(a).
[134] 17 CFR 270.0-10(a).

- the work of a compensation consultant has raised any conflict of interest and, if so, the nature of the conflict and how the conflict is being addressed.

The proposals will impose additional costs on small entities in order to comply with the new listing standards and to collect, record and report the disclosures that we propose to require. Our existing disclosure rules require small entities to disclose information regarding any compensation consultant that plays a role in determining or recommending the amount and form of executive and director compensation in proxy and information statements. The additional information concerning compensation consultants that would be required under the proposals should be readily available to these small entities. Also, we believe that many small entities do not use the services of a compensation consultant, which would significantly minimize the impact of the reporting and recordkeeping requirements under the proposals on small entities. In addition, we believe that the impact of the proposals on small entities will be lessened because most aspects of the proposals apply only to listed issuers, and the quantitative listing standards applicable to issuers listing securities on an exchange, such as market capitalization, minimum revenue, and shareholder equity requirements, will serve to limit the number of small entities that would be affected.

E. Duplicative, Overlapping or Conflicting Federal Rules

We believe the proposed amendments would not duplicate, overlap, or conflict with other federal rules.

F. Significant Alternatives

The Regulatory Flexibility Act directs us to consider alternatives that would accomplish our stated objectives, while minimizing any significant adverse impact on small entities. In connection with the proposed disclosure amendments, we considered the following alternatives:

- Clarifying, consolidating or simplifying compliance and reporting requirements under the rules for small entities;

- Using performance rather than design standards;

- Exempting small entities from all or part of the requirements; and

- Establishing different compliance or reporting requirements or timetables that take into account the resources available to small entities.

We believe that our proposed amendments would require clear and straightforward disclosure of the use of compensation consultants and the management of compensation consultant conflicts of interest. We believe that our proposed rules will promote consistent disclosure among all companies without creating a significant new burden for small entities.

The proposals attempt to clarify, consolidate and simplify the compliance and reporting requirements for all entities, including small entities, by including instructions to the amendments to clarify the circumstances under which disclosure is required. We have used a mix of design and performance standards in developing the proposed disclosure requirements. Based on our past experience, we believe the amendments will be more useful to investors if there are specific disclosure requirements; however, we have not proposed specific procedures or arrangements that an issuer must develop to comply with the proposed amendments. The additional disclosure requirements are intended to result in more comprehensive and clear disclosure.

Although we preliminarily believe that an exemption for small entities from coverage of the proposals would not be appropriate at this time, we seek comment on whether we should exempt small entities from any of the proposed disclosure requirements or scale the proposed amendments to reflect the characteristics of small entities and the needs of their investors. Further, as directed by Exchange Act Section 10C, our proposed rules would permit the exchanges to exempt particular categories of issuers from the requirements of Section 10C and particular relationships from the compensation committee membership requirements of Section 10C(a), taking into account the potential impact of the requirements on smaller reporting companies. To the extent exchanges adopt such exemptions for small entities, the compliance burden would be reduced.

At this time, we do not believe that different compliance methods or timetables for small entities would be appropriate. The proposals are intended to improve the accountability for and transparency of executive compensation determinations. The specific disclosure requirements in the proposals will promote consistent disclosure among all issuers, including small entities. Separate compliance requirements or timetables for small entities could interfere with achieving the goals of the statute and our proposals. Nevertheless, we solicit comment on whether different compliance requirements or timetables for small entities would be appropriate, and consistent with the purposes of Section 952 of the Dodd-Frank Act.

G. Solicitation of Comments

We encourage the submission of comments with respect to any aspect of this Initial Regulatory Flexibility Analysis. In particular, we request comments regarding:

- How the proposed amendments can achieve their objective while lowering the burden on small entities;

- The number of small entities that may be affected by the proposed amendments;

- Whether small entities should be exempt from the rules;

- The existence or nature of the potential impact of the proposed amendments on small entities discussed in the analysis; and

- How to quantify the impact of the proposed amendments.

Respondents are asked to describe the nature of any impact and provide empirical data supporting the extent of the impact. Such comments will be considered in the preparation of the Final Regulatory Flexibility Analysis, if the proposed rule amendments are adopted, and will be placed in the same public file as comments on the proposed amendments themselves.

VIII. STATUTORY AUTHORITY AND TEXT OF THE PROPOSED AMENDMENTS

The amendments contained in this release are being proposed under the authority set forth in Sections 6, 7, 10, and 19(a) of the Securities Act and Sections 10C, 12, 13, 14, 15(d), 23(a), and 36 of the Exchange Act.

List of Subjects in 17 CFR Parts 229 and 240

Reporting and recordkeeping requirements, Securities.

TEXT OF THE PROPOSED AMENDMENTS

For the reasons set out in the preamble, the Commission proposes to amend title 17, chapter II, of the Code of Federal Regulations as follows:

PART 229—STANDARD INSTRUCTIONS FOR FILING FORMS UNDER SECURITIES ACT OF 1933, SECURITIES EXCHANGE ACT OF 1934 AND ENERGY POLICY AND CONSERVATION ACT OF 1975 - REGULATION S-K

1. The general authority citation for part 229 is revised and the sub-authorities are removed to read as follows:

Authority: 15 U.S.C. 77e, 77f, 77g, 77h, 77j, 77k, 77s, 77z-2, 77z-3, 77aa(25), 77aa(26), 77ddd, 77eee, 77ggg, 77hhh, 77iii, 77jjj, 77nnn, 77sss, 78c, 78i, 78j, 78j-3, 78*l*, 78m, 78n, 78n-1, 78o, 78u-5, 78w, 78*ll*, 78mm, 80a-8, 80a-9, 80a-20, 80a-29, 80a-30, 80a-31(c),

80a-37, 80a-38(a), 80a-39, 80b-11, and 7201 *et seq.*; and 18 U.S.C. 1350, unless otherwise noted.

* * * * *

2. Revise § 229.407(e)(3)(iii) to read as follows:

§ 229.407 (Item 407) Corporate governance.

* * * * *

(e) * * *

(3) * * *

(iii) Whether the compensation committee (or another board committee performing equivalent functions) retained or obtained the advice of a compensation consultant during the registrant's last completed fiscal year, identifying such consultants, stating whether such consultants were engaged directly by the compensation committee (or another board committee performing equivalent functions), describing the nature and scope of the consultant's assignment and the material elements of the instructions or directions given to the consultant with respect to the performance of the consultant's duties under the engagement, and discussing whether the work of the consultant has raised any conflict of interest and, if so, the nature of the conflict and how the conflict is being addressed:

(A) If the compensation committee (or another board committee performing equivalent functions) retained or obtained the advice of a compensation consultant and the consultant's services were not limited to consulting on any broad-based plan that does not discriminate in scope, terms, or operation, in favor of executive officers or directors of the registrant, and that is available generally to all salaried employees, or providing information that either is not customized for a particular registrant or that is customized based on parameters that are not developed by the compensation consultant, and about which the compensation consultant does not provide advice, and the compensation consultant or its affiliates also provided additional services to the registrant or its affiliates in an amount in excess of $120,000 during the registrant's last completed fiscal year, then disclose the aggregate fees for determining or recommending the amount or form of executive and director compensation and the aggregate fees for such additional services. Disclose whether the decision to engage the compensation consultant or its affiliates for these other services was made, or recommended, by management, and whether the compensation committee (or another board committee performing equivalent functions) or the board approved such other services of the compensation consultant or its affiliates.

(B) If the compensation committee (or another board committee performing equivalent functions) has not retained or obtained the advice of a compensation consultant, but management has retained or obtained the advice of a compensation consultant and the consultant's services were not limited to consulting on any broad-based plan that does not discriminate in scope, terms, or operation, in favor of executive officers or directors of the registrant, and that is available generally to all salaried employees, or providing information that either is not customized for a particular registrant or that is customized based on parameters that are not developed by the compensation consultant, and about which the compensation consultant does not provide advice, and such compensation consultant or its affiliates has provided additional services to the registrant in an amount in excess of $120,000 during the registrant's last completed fiscal year, then disclose the aggregate fees for determining or recommending the amount or form of executive and director compensation and the aggregate fees for any additional services provided by the compensation consultant or its affiliates.

Instruction 1 to Item 407(e)(3). For purposes of this paragraph, a compensation committee (or another board committee performing equivalent functions) or management has "obtained the advice" of a compensation consultant if such committee or management has requested or received advice from a compensation consultant, regardless of whether there is a formal engagement of the consultant or a client relationship between the compensation consultant and the compensation committee or management or any payment of fees to the consultant for its advice.

Instruction 2 to Item 407(e)(3). For purposes of this paragraph, the factors outlined in § 240.10C-1(b)(4)(i) through (v) of this chapter are among the factors that should be considered in determining whether a conflict of interest exists.

* * * * *

PART 240 – GENERAL RULES AND REGULATIONS, SECURITIES EXCHANGE ACT OF 1934

3. The general authority citation for Part 240 is revised to read as follows:

Authority: 15 U.S.C. 77c, 77d, 77g, 77j, 77s, 77z-2, 77z-3, 77eee, 77ggg, 77nnn, 77sss, 77ttt, 78c, 78d, 78e, 78f, 78g, 78i, 78j, 78j-1, 78j-3, 78k, 78k-1, 78*l*, 78m, 78n, 78n-1, 78o, 78o-4, 78p, 78q, 78s, 78u-5, 78w, 78x, 78*ll*, 78mm, 80a-20, 80a-23, 80a-29, 80a-37, 80b-3, 80b-4, 80b-11, and 7201 *et seq.*; and 18 U.S.C. 1350, and 12 U.S.C. 5221(e)(3), unless otherwise noted.

4. Add an undesignated center heading following § 240.10A-3 to read as follows:

Requirements Under Section 10C

5. Add § 240.10C-1 to read as follows:

§ 240.10C-1 Listing standards relating to compensation committees.

(a) Pursuant to section 10C(a) of the Act (15 U.S.C. 78j-3(a)) and section 952 of the Dodd-Frank Wall Street Reform and Consumer Protection Act of 2010 (Pub. L. 111-203, 124 Stat. 1900):

(1) *National Securities Exchanges.* The rules of each national securities exchange registered pursuant to section 6 of the Act (15 U.S.C. 78f), to the extent such national securities exchange lists equity securities, must, in accordance with the provisions of this section, prohibit the initial or continued listing of any equity security of an issuer that is not in compliance with the requirements of any portion of paragraph (b) or (c) of this section.

(2) *National Securities Associations.* The rules of each national securities association registered pursuant to section 15A of the Act (15 U.S.C. 78o-3), to the extent such national securities association lists equity securities in an automated inter-dealer quotation system, must, in accordance with the provisions of this section, prohibit the initial or continued listing in an automated inter-dealer quotation system of any equity security of an issuer that is not in compliance with the requirements of any portion of paragraph (b) or (c) of this section.

(3) *Opportunity to Cure Defects.* The rules required by paragraphs (a)(1) and (a)(2) of this section must provide for appropriate procedures for a listed issuer to have a reasonable opportunity to cure any defects that would be the basis for a prohibition under paragraph (a) of this section, before the imposition of such prohibition. Such rules may provide that if a member of a compensation committee ceases to be independent in accordance with the requirements of this section for reasons outside the member's reasonable control, that person, with notice by the issuer to the applicable national securities exchange or national securities association, may remain a compensation committee member of the listed issuer until the earlier of the next annual shareholders meeting of the listed issuer or one year from the occurrence of the event that caused the member to be no longer independent.

(4) *Implementation.* (i) Each national securities exchange and national securities association that lists equity securities must provide to the Commission, no later than 90 days after publication of this section in the Federal Register, proposed rules or rule amendments that comply with this section. Each submission must include, in addition to any

other information required under section 19(b) of the Act (15 U.S.C. 78s(b)) and the rules thereunder, a review of whether and how existing listing standards satisfy the requirements of this rule, a discussion of the consideration of factors relevant to compensation committee independence conducted by the national securities exchange or national securities association, and the definition of independence applicable to compensation committee members that the national securities exchange or national securities association proposes to adopt in light of such review.

(ii) Each national securities exchange and national securities association that lists equity securities must have rules or rule amendments that comply with this section approved by the Commission no later than one year after publication of this section in the Federal Register.

(b) *Required Standards.* The requirements of this section apply to the compensation committees of listed issuers. If a listed issuer has a committee of the board performing functions typically performed by a compensation committee, including oversight of executive compensation, then such committee, even if it is not designated as a compensation committee or performs other functions, shall be fully subject to the requirements of this section.

(1) *Independence.* (i) Each member of the compensation committee must be a member of the board of directors of the listed issuer, and must otherwise be independent.

(ii) *Independence Requirements.* In determining independence requirements for members of compensation committees, the national securities exchanges and national securities associations shall consider relevant factors, including, but not limited to:

(A) The source of compensation of a member of the board of directors of an issuer, including any consulting, advisory or other compensatory fee paid by the issuer to such member of the board of directors; and

(B) Whether a member of the board of directors of an issuer is affiliated with the issuer, a subsidiary of the issuer or an affiliate of a subsidiary of the issuer.

(iii) *Exemptions from the Independence Requirements.* (A) The listing of equity securities of the following categories of listed issuers are not subject to the requirements of paragraph (b)(1) of this section:

(*1*) Controlled companies;

(*2*) Limited partnerships;

(*3*) Companies in bankruptcy proceedings;

(*4*) Open-end management investment companies registered under the Investment Company Act of 1940; and

(*5*) Any foreign private issuer that discloses in its annual report the reasons that the foreign private issuer does not have an independent compensation committee.

(B) In addition to the issuer exemptions set forth in paragraph (b)(1)(iii)(A) of this section, a national securities exchange or a national securities association, pursuant to section 19(b) of the Act (15 U.S.C. 78s(b)) and the rules thereunder, may exempt from the requirements of paragraph (b)(1) of this section a particular relationship with respect to members of the compensation committee, as each national securities exchange or national securities association determines is appropriate, taking into consideration the size of an issuer and any other relevant factors.

(2) *Authority to Engage Compensation Consultants, Independent Legal Counsel and Other Compensation Advisers.* The compensation committee of a listed issuer, in its capacity as a committee of the board of directors, may, in its sole discretion, retain or obtain the advice of a compensation consultant, independent legal counsel or other adviser. The compensation committee shall be directly responsible for the appointment, compensation and oversight of the work of any compensation consultant, independent

legal counsel and other adviser to the compensation committee. Nothing in this paragraph shall be construed:

(i) To require the compensation committee to implement or act consistently with the advice or recommendations of the compensation consultant, independent legal counsel or other adviser to the compensation committee; or

(ii) To affect the ability or obligation of a compensation committee to exercise its own judgment in fulfillment of the duties of the compensation committee.

(3) *Funding.* Each listed issuer must provide for appropriate funding, as determined by the compensation committee, in its capacity as a committee of the board of directors, for payment of reasonable compensation to a compensation consultant, independent legal counsel or any other adviser to the compensation committee.

(4) *Independence of Compensation Consultants and Other Advisers.* The compensation committee of a listed issuer may select a compensation consultant, legal counsel, or other adviser to the compensation committee only after taking into consideration the following factors, as well as any other factors identified by the relevant national securities exchange or national securities association in its listing standards:

(i) The provision of other services to the issuer by the person that employs the compensation consultant, legal counsel or other adviser;

(ii) The amount of fees received from the issuer by the person that employs the compensation consultant, legal counsel or other adviser, as a percentage of the total revenue of the person that employs the compensation consultant, legal counsel, or other adviser;

(iii) The policies and procedures of the person that employs the compensation consultant, legal counsel or other adviser that are designed to prevent conflicts of interest;

(iv) Any business or personal relationship of the compensation consultant, legal counsel, or other adviser with a member of the compensation committee; and

(v) Any stock of the issuer owned by the compensation consultant, legal counsel or other adviser.

(5) *General Exemptions.* (i) The national securities exchanges and national securities associations, pursuant to section 19(b) of the Act (15 U.S.C. 78s(b)) and the rules thereunder, may exempt from the requirements of this section certain categories of issuers, as the national securities exchange or national securities association determines is appropriate, taking into consideration the potential impact of such requirements on smaller reporting issuers.

(ii) The requirements of this section shall not apply to any controlled company.

(iii) The listing of a security futures product cleared by a clearing agency that is registered pursuant to section 17A of the Act (15 U.S.C. 78q-1) or that is exempt from the registration requirements of section 17A(b)(7)(A) (15 U.S.C. 78q-1(b)(7)(A)) is not subject to the requirements of this section.

(iv) The listing of a standardized option, as defined in § 240.9b-1(a)(4), issued by a clearing agency that is registered pursuant to section 17A of the Act (15 U.S.C. 78q-1) is not subject to the requirements of this section.

(c) *Definitions.* Unless the context otherwise requires, all terms used in this section have the same meaning as in the Act. In addition, unless the context otherwise requires, the following definitions apply for purposes of this section:

(1) In the case of foreign private issuers with a two-tier board system, the term *board of directors* means the supervisory or non-management board.

(2) The term *controlled company* means an issuer:

(i) That is listed on a national securities exchange or by a national securities association; and

(ii) That holds an election for the board of directors of the issuer in which more than 50 percent of the voting power is held by an individual, a group or another issuer.

(3) The terms *listed* and *listing* refer to equity securities listed on a national securities exchange or listed in an automated inter-dealer quotation system of a national securities association or to issuers of such securities.

(4) The term *open-end management investment company* means an open-end company, as defined by Section 5(a)(1) of the Investment Company Act of 1940 (15 U.S.C. 80a-5(a)(1)), that is registered under that Act.

By the Commission.

Elizabeth M. Murphy
Secretary

March 30, 2011

APPENDIX 6
XYZ Corporation
Questionnaire for Directors and Executive Officers

This questionnaire is being furnished to all directors and officers of XYZ Corporation (the "Company"). The purpose of the questionnaire is to obtain information required to be disclosed in the Company's (i) Annual Report on Form 10-K for the year ended December 31, 2011, and (ii) Proxy Statement in connection with its 2012 Annual Stockholders Meeting. These disclosure documents are required to be prepared in accordance with the Securities Exchange Act of 1934, as amended (the "Exchange Act").

Before completing this questionnaire, please read carefully the definitions that are included in the Glossary attached as Annex A. Unless otherwise directed, answer every question and state your answers as of the date this questionnaire is completed. If you have any doubt as to whether any matter should be reported, please give the relevant facts so that those responsible for preparing the appropriate disclosure documents can make the decision whether such information should be included in such documents. If additional space is required for you to fully answer any of the questions, please complete your answer on a separate sheet and attach it to the questionnaire.

The term "Company" means XYZ Corporation and, unless the question expressly states otherwise, includes subsidiaries of XYZ Corporation.

Biographical Information

1. Name and Date of Birth. Please state your full name, address and date of birth.

Name:

Address:

Date of Birth:

2. Position with Company. Please indicate all positions (including as a director) and offices with the Company which you currently hold or have held, together with the term or length of time you have held any such position or office. Please also list any other material relationship you have or have had with the Company.

List of Positions/Relationships:

Company:

Term/Dates:

3. Arrangements for Selection of Directors or Executive Officers. Were you selected to serve as a director, nominated to become a director, or selected to serve as an executive officer of the Company pursuant to any arrangement or understanding between yourself and any other person (except the directors and executive officers of the Company acting in such capacity)?

☐ I was not selected to serve in my present capacity pursuant to an arrangement.

☐ I was selected to serve in my present capacity according to the following arrangement (Describe the arrangement or understanding and name the person whom it was with):

4. Family Relationships. Are you related by blood, marriage or adoption to any director, executive officer or nominee to become a director of the Company? If so, state the identity of the director, executive officer or nominee and the nature of the relationship. Relationships more remote than first cousin need not be mentioned.

☐ I am not related to a director, executive officer or nominee.

☐ I am related to a director, executive officer or nominee as follows:

Identity of Officer, Director or Nominee:

Nature of Relationship:

5. Business Experience. Please give a brief account of your business experience since December 31, 2006 (together with applicable dates); include your principal occupations and employment during that period and the name and principal business of any corporation or other organization in which such occupations and employment were carried on and state whether such corporation or organization is a parent, subsidiary or other affiliate of the Company. If you are an executive officer of the Company and have been employed by the Company for less than five years, include a brief explanation of the nature of your responsibilities in prior positions. What is required is information relating to the level of your professional competence, which may include, depending upon the circumstances, such specific information as the size of the operation supervised. You may also provide any other biographical information you would like considered for inclusion in the Form 10-K and/or Proxy Statement. For convenience, your biography from the Company's Proxy Statement for 2010 is attached; please mark any corrections on the biography or note any additions below. If you make no mark and add no new information below, it will be assumed the attached biography is correct and requires no changes.

Dates:

Position/Responsibilities:

Corporation Name and Address:

Parent, Subsidiary or Affiliate of the Company:

Business Relationships

6.1 Directorships. Please list all directorships you have held since January 1, 2007 in publicly-held companies or companies registered under the Investment Company Act of 1940, as amended (the "Investment Company Act").

☐ I have not held any such directorships.

☐ I have held the following directorships:

Company's Name:

Term:

6.2 Other Positions. Since December 31, 2010, were you (i) a member of the compensation committee of another entity or other committee performing equivalent functions or (ii) a member of the board of directors of another entity? Do not include any tax exempt entity under Section 501(c)(3) of the Internal Revenue Code. Please circle the name of any entity for which the entire board of directors performed compensation committee functions.

☐ I have not held any of such positions.

☐ I have held the following positions:

Entity's Name:

Position:

Term:

6.2.1 If you have held any such position, have any of the executive officers of that entity served on the compensation committee (or other board committee performing equivalent functions or, in the absence of any such committee, the entire Board of Directors) of the Company or as a director of the Company since December 31, 2010?

☐ No executive officer of that entity has served in such capacity with the Company.

☐ One or more executive officers of that entity have served in such capacity with the Company.

Describe:

Legal Proceedings

7. Legal Proceedings. Have any of the following events occurred since December 31, 2001, including any events that occurred before December 31, 2001, if any developments relating to such events occurred after December 31, 2001? If so, please describe.

7.1 Bankruptcy Petition. Was a petition under the federal bankruptcy laws or any state insolvency law filed by or against, or a receiver, fiscal agent or similar officer appointed by a court for the business or property of, (i) you, (ii) any partnership in which you were a general partner at or within two years before such event, or (iii) any corporation or business association of which you were an executive officer at or within two years before such event?

☐ No such petition has been filed.

☐ A petition has been filed.

Describe:

7.2 Criminal Proceedings. Were you convicted in a criminal proceeding or are you the named subject of a pending criminal proceeding? Omit traffic violations and other minor offenses.

☐ I have not been convicted in a, or named in a pending, criminal proceeding.

☐ I have been convicted in a, or named in a pending, criminal proceeding. Describe:

7.3 Injunctions. Were you the subject of any order, judgment or decree, not subsequently reversed, suspended or vacated, of any court of competent jurisdiction, permanently or temporarily enjoining or otherwise limiting you from any of the following activities:

7.3.1 Acting as a futures commission merchant, introducing broker, commodity trading advisor, commodity pool operator, floor broker, leverage transaction merchant, any other person regulated by the Commodity Futures Trading Commission, or an associated person of any of the foregoing, or as an investment advisor, underwriter, broker or dealer in securities, or as an affiliated person, director or employee of any investment company, bank, savings and loan association or insurance company, or engaging in or continuing any conduct or practice in connection with such activity?

☐ I have not been the subject of any such court order, judgment or decree.

☐ I have been the subject of such a court order, judgment or decree. Describe:

7.3.2 Engaging in any type of business practice?

☐ I have not been the subject of any such court order, judgment or decree.

☐ I have been the subject of such a court order, judgment or decree. Describe:

7.3.3 Engaging in any activity in connection with the purchase or sale of any security or commodity or in connection with any violation of federal or state securities laws or federal commodities laws?

☐ I have not been the subject of any such court order, judgment or decree.

☐ I have been the subject of such a court order, judgment or decree. Describe:

7.4 Suspensions. Were you the subject of any order, judgment or decree, not subsequently reversed, suspended or vacated, of any federal or state authority barring, suspending, or otherwise limiting for more than 60 days your right to engage in any of the activities described in question 7.3.1 above or your right to be associated with persons engaged in any such activity?

☐ I have not been the subject of any such judgment, order or decree.

☐ I have been the subject of such a judgment, order or decree. Describe:

7.5 Securities and Commodities Law Violations, etc. Were you found by a court of competent jurisdiction in a civil action or by the SEC or the Commodities Futures Trading Commission to have violated any federal or state securities or commodities law where such judgment or finding has not subsequently been reversed, suspended or vacated?

☐ I have not been found in violation of any federal or state securities or commodities law.

☐ I have been found in violation of a federal or state securities or commodities law. Describe:

7.5.1 Are you presently the subject of any investigation by the SEC or the Commodities Futures Trading Commission that could result in the finding of a violation of any federal or state securities or commodities laws?

☐ I am not the subject of any investigation regarding violations of any federal or state securities or commodities laws.

☐ I am the subject of an investigation regarding violations of any federal or state securities or commodities laws. Describe:

7.5.2 Have you been a party to any settlement in connection with an alleged violation of any federal or state securities or commodities law?

☐ I have not been a party to any settlement in connection with an alleged violation of any federal or state securities law.

☐ I have been a party to a settlement in connection with an alleged violation of a federal or state securities law. Describe:

7.5.3 Were you the subject of, or a party to, any Federal or State judicial or administrative order, judgment, decree, or finding, not subsequently reversed, suspended or vacated, relating to an alleged violation of:

Note: If the matter in (a)–(c) below involved the settlement of a civil proceeding among private litigants, it need not be described.

(a) Any Federal or State securities or commodities law or regulation?

☐ I have not been the subject of, or a party to, any such matters.

☐ I have been the subject of, or a party to, such matters. Describe:

(b) Any law or regulation respecting financial institutions or insurance companies including, but not limited to, a temporary or permanent injunction, order of disgorgement or restitution, civil money penalty or temporary or permanent cease-and-desist order, or removal or prohibition order?

☐ I have not been the subject of, or a party to, any such matters.

☐ I have been the subject of, or a party to, such matters. Describe:

(c) Any law or regulation prohibiting mail or wire fraud or fraud in connection with any business entity?

☐ I have not been the subject of, or a party to, any such matters.

☐ I have been the subject of, or a party to, such matters. Describe:

7.5.4 Were you the subject of, or a party to, any sanction or order, not subsequently reversed, suspended or vacated, of any self-regulatory organization (as defined in Section 3(a)(26) of the Exchange Act (15 U.S.C. 78c(a)(26))), any registered entity (as defined in Section 1(a)(29) of the Commodity Exchange Act (7 U.S.C. 1(a)(29))), or any equivalent exchange, association, entity or organization that has disciplinary authority over its members or persons associated with a member.

☐ I have not been the subject of, or a party to, any such sanction or order.

☐ I have been the subject of, or a party to, such sanction or order. Describe:

Legal Proceedings Adverse to the Company

8.1 General. Describe briefly any material pending or contemplated legal proceeding known to you to which the Company is a party or of which any of the Company's property is the subject. If the business ordinarily results in actions for negligence or other claims, no such action or claim need be described unless it departs from the normal kind of such actions.

☐ I know of no pending legal proceedings to which the Company is a party.

☐ I know of such legal proceedings.

Describe, including the name of the court or agency in which the proceedings are pending, the date initiated, the principal parties thereto, a description of the factual basis alleged to underlie the proceeding and the relief sought:

8.2 Personal. Do you know of any pending or contemplated legal proceedings (including administrative proceedings and investigations by governmental authorities) in which either you or any associate of yours is a party adverse to the Company, or in which either you or any associate has an interest adverse to the Company?

☐ I know of no pending or contemplated legal proceedings where either I or an associate is a party, or has an interest, adverse to the Company.

☐ I know of legal proceedings where either I or an associate is a party, or has an interest, adverse to the Company.

Describe, including the name of the court or agency in which the proceedings are pending, the date initiated, the principal parties thereto, a description of the factual basis alleged to underlie the proceeding and the relief sought:

8.3 Other Directors, Officers, Security Holders and Affiliates. Do you know of any pending or threatened legal proceeding in which any other director or officer or any affiliate of the Company, or any security holder who owns of record or is the beneficial owner of more than 5% of any class of voting securities of the Company, or any associate of any such director, officer, affiliate or security holder, is a party adverse to the Company or in which such director, officer, affiliate, security holder or associate has any interest adverse to the Company?

☐ I know of no such pending or threatened legal proceeding involving such parties.

☐ I know of legal proceedings where such parties have an interest adverse to the Company.

Describe, including the name of the court or agency in which the proceedings are pending, the date initiated, the principal parties thereto, a description of the factual basis alleged to underlie the proceeding and the relief sought:

8.4 Governmental Proceeding. Do you know of any legal, regulatory or administrative proceeding brought or contemplated by any governmental authority (including, but not limited to, antitrust, price-fixing, tax, environmental, copyright or patent litigation) to which the Company is or may be a party or of which the property of the Company or its subsidiaries is the subject?

☐ I know of no such pending or threatened governmental proceeding.

☐ I know of a governmental proceeding to which the Company or its property is subject.

Describe, including the name of the court or agency in which the proceedings are pending, the date initiated, the principal parties thereto, a description of the factual basis alleged to underlie the proceeding and the relief sought:

8.5 Have you ever been involved in any material lawsuit, investigation, inquiry or action that has affected or involved, or has the potential to affect or involve, the Company?

☐ I have not been involved in any such lawsuit, investigation, inquiry or action.

☐ I have been involved in such a lawsuit, investigation, inquiry or action.

Describe, including the name of the court or agency in which the proceedings are pending, the date initiated, the principal parties thereto, a description of the factual basis alleged to underlie the proceeding and the relief sought:

Director and Executive Officer Compensation

9. Compensation. The Company is required to disclose *all* compensation awarded to, earned by, or paid to you during the fiscal year ended December 31, 2011. Information concerning salary, bonus, director fees, securities paid or awarded to you by the Company, earnings on non-equity incentive plan awards, changes in pension values, above-market earnings on nonqualified deferred compensation and contributions by the Company to a 401(k) plan for the fiscal year ended December 31, 2011, will be obtained directly from the Company. Please describe any payment or other personal compensation or benefit, other than salary, bonus, securities, director fees, earnings on non-equity incentive plan awards, changes in pension values, above-market earnings on nonqualified deferred compensation and contributions by the Company to a 401(k) plan, received by you or any member of your family from any party for services rendered to the Company during the fiscal year ended December 31, 2011. Perquisites and other personal benefits should be valued on the basis of the aggregate incremental cost to the provider of providing such benefits. Among the benefits which should be reported are the following:

(1) payments for home repairs and improvements (including security systems);

(2) payments for housing and other living expenses (including mortgage and rental payments or the cost of domestic service);

(3) the personal use of Company property, such as Company-furnished automobiles, airplanes, boats or yachts or use of a stadium skybox or season tickets;

(4) the personal use of a Company-furnished apartment, hotel room or vacation accommodations;

(5) payment of personal entertainment and related expenses;

(6) payments for membership in a country club or other social or recreational clubs (excluding civic or service clubs);

(7) payment of personal vacation or travel expenses;

(8) payment of legal, financial planning, tax or other professional fees for matters unrelated to the business of the Company;

(9) personal use of the Company's staff;

(10) benefits that you have obtained from third parties, such as cash payments, favorable bank loans and benefits from suppliers, if the Company directly or indirectly compensates the third party for providing the benefits to you;

(11) commuting expenses;

(12) discounts on the Company's products or services not generally available to employees on a non-discriminatory basis;

(13) consulting fees earned from, or paid or payable by, or on behalf of the Company and/or the subsidiaries (including joint ventures);

(14) annual costs of payments and promises pursuant to director legacy programs and similar charitable awards; and

(15) payment of life or other insurance premiums for coverage of persons or property unrelated to the Company's business.

Please note that the examples given above are not meant to be exhaustive. Also note that the personal benefits to be described should not be limited to those items that you have reported, or plan to report, on your income tax return. You need not describe personal benefits that are integrally and directly related to your job performance, such as parking spaces that are closer to business facilities but not otherwise preferential office space and furnishings at Company maintained offices.

☐ I have received no such payments.

☐ I have received the following payments:

Fiscal Year:

Description:

Value:

10. Third-Party Payments. Did anyone other than the Company or its subsidiaries make any payment to you during the fiscal year ended December 31, 2011, for services you performed for the Company or its subsidiaries? If so, please describe.

11. Termination of Employment and Change-in-Control Arrangements. Please describe any compensatory plan or arrangement, including payments to be received from the Company, if such plan or arrangement results or will result from the resignation, retirement or any other termination of your employment with the Company, or from a change-in-control of the Company or a change in your responsibilities following a change-in-control.

☐ No such compensatory plans or arrangements exist.

☐ Yes such following compensatory plan or arrangement exists. Describe:

Security Ownership of Certain Beneficial Owners and Management

12. Please state below the name of any individual, corporation, group or other entity personally known by you to be the beneficial owner of more than 5% any class of voting or equity securities of the Company. A "group" for this purpose is any general partnership, limited partnership, syndicate or other group formed for the purpose of acquiring voting or equity securities of the Company. Please describe any relationship you have with such securities holder.

☐ I know of no such securities holder.

☐ I know of such securities holder. Describe:

13. Please state in the table below the amount of voting or equity securities of the Company of which you are the beneficial owner on the date hereof. Please review at this time the definition for "beneficial owner" in the attached Glossary.

Even though you may not actually have or share voting or investment power with respect to securities owned by persons in your family or living in your home, you should include such shares in your beneficial ownership disclosure in the table on the next page and if you wish you may then disclaim such beneficial ownership below and in your answer to Question 14. If any of the securities listed have been pledged, have been otherwise deposited as collateral, are the subject matter of any voting trust or other similar agreement or are the subject of any contract providing for the sale or other disposition of securities, please describe the details on a separate sheet and attach it to this questionnaire.

☐ I hold no voting or equity securities of the Company.

☐ I hold voting or equity securities of the Company as listed below:

Number of Shares of Common Stock Beneficially Owned

Shares owned beneficially by you: _____

Of such shares:

Shares as to which you have sole voting power _____

Shares as to which you have shared voting power _____

Shares as to which you have sole investment power _____

Shares as to which you have shared investment power _____

Shares that you have a right to acquire within 60 days after the date hereof (e.g., pursuant to the exercise of an option, warrant or other right that is or will be exercisable within 60 days) _____

Shares the beneficial ownership of which you disclaim (see Question 14) _____

Shares pledged, deposited as collateral, or subject to a voting trust or contract for sale or other disposition _____

With respect to all securities of the Company you beneficially own, please describe in the space provided below or on an attached sheet, the nature of your beneficial ownership (e.g., direct, indirect by your spouse or other family member, a partnership or trust jointly with another person, or underlying an option, warrant or other right that is or will be exercisable within 60 days) and the nature of any pledge (e.g., shares directly pledged in connection with a loan, placed in a margin account or subject to a hedging arrangement):

14. If you wish to disclaim beneficial ownership of any of shares reported above, please furnish the following information with respect to the person or persons who are the beneficial owners of the shares in question:

Name of Beneficial Owner:

Relationship of Such Person to You:

Number of Shares Beneficially Owned:

15. Do you hold more than 5% of any class of voting securities of the Company pursuant to any voting trust or similar agreement?

☐ I do not hold more than 5% of any class of voting securities of the Company pursuant to a voting trust agreement.

☐ I hold more than 5% of any class of voting securities of the Company pursuant to a voting trust agreement.

Describe, including the amount held or to be held pursuant to the trust or agreement, the duration of the agreement and, if you are a voting trustee, an outline of your voting rights and other powers under the trust or agreement:

16. Please describe any arrangements, including the pledge of voting securities, the operation of which may at a subsequent date result in a change of control of the Company.

☐ I know of no such arrangements.

☐ I know of such an arrangement or arrangements. Describe:

Certain Relationships and Related Transactions

17. Describe briefly if you, any associate of yours or any member of your immediate family had or will have any direct or indirect material interest in any transaction, or series of similar transactions, which took place since December 31, 2010, or any

currently proposed transaction, or series of similar transactions, to which the Company or any of its subsidiaries was or is to be a party, in which the amount involved exceeds $120,000. Describe the nature of your or your family member's interest in the transaction(s), the amount involved in such transaction(s) and, if possible, the amount of interest in dollars that you or your family member had or will have in the transaction(s).

☐ There is not nor will there be any such material interest in any such transaction.

☐ There is or will be a material interest in the following transaction(s). Describe:

18. Did you or your associates have any transactions at any time since December 31, 2010, or do you or your associates have any presently proposed transactions, to which a pension, retirement, savings or similar plan provided by the Company or any subsidiary was or is proposed to be a party? If so, please describe.

☐ I know of no such transaction.

☐ I know of such a transaction. Describe:

19. Are you now, or have you since December 31, 2010, been, an executive officer of, or do you now own, or have you owned, of record or beneficially, since December 31, 2010, in excess of a 10% equity interest in, any firm, corporation or other business or professional entity:

19.1 that has made at any time during the Company's fiscal year ended December 31, 2011, or has made or proposes to make during the Company's current fiscal year, payments to the Company for property or services in any single fiscal year of the last three fiscal years in excess of the greater of (i) $200,000 or (ii) 5% of (x) the Company's consolidated gross revenues for the applicable fiscal year or (y) the other entity's consolidated gross revenues for the applicable fiscal year;

☐ I have no such interest.

☐ I have such an interest. See Question 24.

19.2 to which the Company has made at any time during the Company's fiscal year ended December 31, 2011, or has made or proposes to make during the Company's current fiscal year, payments for property or services in any single fiscal year of the last three fiscal years in excess of the greater of 5% of (x) the Company's consolidated gross revenues for the applicable fiscal year or (y) the other entity's consolidated gross revenues for the applicable fiscal year; or

☐ I have no such interest.

☐ I have such an interest. See Question 23.

19.3 to which the Company was indebted at December 31, 2011, or has been indebted at any time since December 31, 2010, in an aggregate amount in excess of the greater of (i) $200,000 or (ii) 5% of the Company's total consolidated assets at December 31, 2011, which totaled _____.

☐ I have no such interest.

☐ I have such an interest. See Question 23.

20. Are you, or is a member of your immediate family now or have you or a member of your immediate family during the Company's fiscal year ended December 31, 2011, been a partner or a member of, or of counsel to, a law firm that the Company has retained during the Company's fiscal year ended December 31, 2011, or has retained or proposes to retain during the current fiscal year? If so, state the fees paid to such firm by the Company if the amount exceeds the greater of (i) $200,000 or (ii) 5% of the firm's gross revenues for the applicable fiscal year.

☐ I have no such relationship.

☐ I have such a relationship. See Question 23.

21. Are you or is a member of your immediate family now, or have you or a member of your immediate family during the Company's fiscal year ended December 31, 2011, been a partner or executive officer of any investment banking firm that has performed services for the Company, other than as a participating underwriter in a syndicate, during the fiscal year ended December 31, 2011, or that the Company has or proposes to have perform services during the current year? If so, state the compensation received by such firm if the amount exceeds the greater of (i) $200,000 or (ii) 5% of the investment banking firm's consolidated gross revenues for the fiscal year.

☐ I have no such relationship.

☐ I have such a relationship. See Question 23.

22. Do you or any member of your immediate family have, or have you or a member of your immediate family had, any other relationship substantially similar in nature and scope to those relationships listed in questions 19–21 above, or derived a special benefit from any such relationship, whether or not it exceeded the thresholds set forth in questions 19-21 above?

☐ No such other relationship exists.

☐ Another relationship exists. See Question 23.

23. If you answered yes to any of questions 19–22 above, describe each such relationship, including in your description the identity of each entity, the amount of business done with the Company during the past three fiscal years of the Company and the amount of business proposed to be done during the current fiscal year.

Name of Entity:

Nature of My Affiliation with Entity:

Relationship of Company and Entity:

Amount of Business Done with Company:

Amount of Payments Proposed:

24. If you or any of your associates, or any corporation or organization of which any of the persons specified herein is an executive officer or partner or is, directly or indirectly, the beneficial owner of 10% or more of any class of equity security or any trust or any other estate in which any of the persons specified herein has a substantial interest or as to which such person serves as the trustee or in a similar capacity, was indebted to the Company at any time since December 31, 2010, in an amount in excess of $120,000, state (i) the largest aggregate amount of indebtedness outstanding at any time during such period, (ii) the nature of the indebtedness and of the transaction(s) in which it was incurred (if such indebtedness arose under Section 16(b) of the Exchange Act and has not been discharged by payment, state the amount of any profit realized and describe the transaction), (iii) the amount of indebtedness outstanding as of the date hereof, (iv) the amount of interest paid during such period and (v) the rate or amount of interest paid or charged. If indebtedness of an associate or immediate family member is described, name the associate or immediate family member and explain your relationship with the associate.

☐ I know of no such indebtedness.

☐ Such indebtedness exists or has existed. Describe:

25. Please list the full name, form (e.g., partnership, corporation, etc.), nature of business done by, and principal place of business of each of your associates (See the

definition of associate in the attached Glossary) referred to in the answers to this questionnaire and your relationship with such associates as follows, if applicable:

Name:

Form:

Nature of Business Done:

Principal Place of Business:

Relationship:

Disbursements of Company Assets

26. Have you been involved in any manner in any of the following: any political contributions by the Company or from its assets, whether legal or illegal; the disbursement or receipt of Company funds outside the normal system of accountability; payments, whether direct or indirect, to or from (i) foreign or domestic governments, officials, employees or agents or (ii) political parties, their officials or candidates or (iii) candidates for political office for purposes other than the satisfaction of lawful obligations, or any transaction which has as its intended effect the transfer of Company assets for the purpose of effecting such a payment; the improper or inaccurate recording of payments and receipts on the books of the Company or any of its subsidiaries; or any other matters of a similar nature involving disbursements of Company assets?

☐ I have not been involved with any of the named activities, persons, or books.

☐ I have been involved with any of the named activities, persons or books. Describe:

27. Change in Control. Do you know of any arrangement, including any pledge of securities of the Company, which resulted in the fiscal year ended December 31, 2011, or may result in the future, in a change of control of the Company? If so, please describe.

28. Indemnification. Describe below any contract or arrangement (other than the law of the state of the Company's incorporation, the Company's articles of incorporation and by-laws or directors and officers' liability insurance) under which you, as a director or officer of the Company, are insured or indemnified in any manner against any liability that you may incur in such capacity.

I understand that the information that I am furnishing herein will be used by the Company in connection with the preparation of the Form 10-K and the Proxy Statement. I will advise the Company as soon as possible if any events occur between now and the date of the 2012 annual meeting of shareholders that would change my answer to any question asked above.

Dated: _____, 2012

Signature: _____

Print Name: _____

ANNEX A

GLOSSARY

Affiliate

The term "affiliate" means any person (including a partnership, corporation, limited liability company or other legal entity, such as a trust or estate) that directly, or indirectly through one or more intermediaries, controls, or is controlled by, or is under common control with the Company.

Arrangement

The term "arrangement" means any agreement, plan, contract, authorization or understanding, whether or not set forth in a formal document.

Associate

The term "associate" means:

(a) any corporation or organization, other than the Company, of which you are an officer or partner or are, directly or indirectly, the "beneficial owner" of 10% or more of any class of equity securities;

(b) any trust or other estate in which you have a beneficial interest or as to which you serve as trustee or in a similar fiduciary capacity; or

(c) your spouse, or any relative of yours, or relative of your spouse living in your home or who is a director or officer of the Company.

Beneficial Owner

You are the "beneficial owner" of a security if you, directly or indirectly, through any contract, arrangement, understanding, relationship or otherwise have or share:

(a) the power to vote, or to direct the voting of, such security, or

(b) the power to dispose, or to direct the disposition, of such security.

You are also the "beneficial owner" of a security if you, directly or indirectly, create or use a trust, proxy, power of attorney, pooling arrangement or any other contract, arrangement, or device with the purpose or effect of divesting yourself of "beneficial ownership" of a security or preventing the vesting of such "beneficial ownership." Therefore, whether or not you are the record holder of securities, you may be the "beneficial owner" of securities held by you for your own benefit (regardless of how registered) and securities held by others for your benefit (regardless of how registered), such as by custodians, brokers, nominees, pledgees, etc., and including securities held by an estate or trust in which you have an interest as legatee or beneficiary, securities owned by a partnership of which you are a partner, securities held by a personal holding company of which you are a stockholder, etc., and securities held in the name of your spouse, minor children and any other relative sharing the same home.

Finally, you are deemed to be the "beneficial owner" of a security if you have the right to acquire "beneficial ownership" of such security at any time within sixty (60) days, including, but not limited to, (a) through the exercise of any option, warrant or right or (b) through the conversion of a security or (c) pursuant to the power to revoke a trust, discretionary account or similar arrangement or (d) pursuant to the automatic termination of a trust, discretionary account or similar arrangement.

Note that the same security may be beneficially owned by more than one person. For example, several co-trustees may share the power to vote or dispose of shares.

Control

The term "control" means the possession, directly or indirectly, of the power to direct or cause the direction of the management and policies of any person, whether through the ownership of voting securities, by contract or otherwise.

Executive Officer

The term "executive officer" means the president, principal executive officer, principal financial officer, principal accounting officer, any vice president in charge of a principal business unit, division or function (such as sales, administration or finance), any other officer who performs a policy-making function and any other person who performs similar policy-making functions.

Immediate Family

The term "immediate family" includes your spouse, parents, children, siblings, mothers and fathers-in-law, sons and daughters-in-law, and brothers and sisters-in-law, whether by blood, marriage or adoption, any person to whom you directly or indirectly contribute financial support and anyone (other than a tenant or domestic employee) who shares your home.

Material Relationship

The term "material relationship" has not been defined by the SEC. However, the SEC has indicated that it will probably construe as a "material relationship" any relationship which tends to prevent arm's-length bargaining in dealings with a company or its subsidiary companies, whether arising from a close business connection or family relationship, a relationship of control or otherwise. It seems prudent, therefore, to consider that you would have such a relationship, for example, with any organization of which you are an officer, director, trustee or partner or in which you own, directly or indirectly, 10% or more of the outstanding voting stock, or in which you have some other substantial interest, and with any person or organization with whom you have, or with whom any relative or spouse (or any person or organization as to which you have any of the other foregoing relationships) has, a contractual or other business relationship (e.g., commercial, individual, banking, consulting, legal, accounting or other).

Plan

The term "plan" includes, but is not limited to, any plan, contract, authorization or "arrangement," whether or not set forth in any formal documents, pursuant to which the following may be received: cash, stock, restricted stock, phantom stock, stock options, stock appreciation rights, stock options in tandem with stock appreciation rights, warrants, convertible securities, performance units and performance shares. A plan may be applicable to one person.

Transaction

The term "transaction" is to be understood in its broadest sense and includes the direct or indirect receipt of anything of value.

Please note that your answers in this questionnaire should disclose indirect as well as direct interests in material transactions. Transactions in which you would have a direct interest would include your purchasing or leasing anything of value (e.g., stock in a business acquired by the Company, office space, plants, Company apartments, computers, raw materials, finished goods, etc.) from, or selling or leasing anything of value to, or borrowing or lending cash or other property from or to, the Company. Transactions in which you would have an indirect interest are similar transactions with the Company by any corporation or organization described in clause (a) of the definition for "associate."

Please note that the examples given above are not meant to be exhaustive.

APPENDIX 7

XYZ Corporation

Supplement to Directors' and Officers' Questionnaire

This questionnaire is being furnished to all non-employee members of the Board of Directors of XYZCorporation (the "Company"). This questionnaire supplement is intended to obtain information to enable the Company (1) to comply with the rules and regulations of the Securities and Exchange Commission (the "SEC"), applicable provisions of the Sarbanes-Oxley Act of 2002 and the regulations adopted thereunder and the Nasdaq Corporate Governance Requirements and (2) to make required disclosure in the Company's filings with the SEC. Please take the time to completely and accurately answer the questions. Most of the questions are intended to elicit information regarding members' independence from the Company's management. **Only members of the Audit Committee need to answer the questions in Section II—Financial Expertise.**

Before completing this questionnaire supplement please read carefully the definitions which are included in the glossary. Unless otherwise directed, answer every question and state your answers as of the date this questionnaire supplement is completed. If you have any doubt as to whether any matter should be reported, please give the relevant facts so that those responsible for preparing the Company's proxy statement for its 2012 annual meeting of stockholders (the "Proxy Statement") can make the decision whether such information affects the disclosure in such documents. If additional space is required for you to fully answer any of the questions, please complete your answer on a separate sheet and attach it to this questionnaire supplement.

Please bear in mind that the Proxy Statement will be understood to be accurate as of the date of such document. Therefore, it is necessary to update your answers if you learn of additional material information after you complete this questionnaire.

QUESTIONS

THE TERM "COMPANY" INCLUDES SUBSIDIARIES OF THE COMPANY, UNLESS THE QUESTION EXPRESSLY STATES OTHERWISE

I. INDEPENDENCE

1. *Compensation.* Please list any payments (including, without limitation, consulting, advisory or compensatory fees or political contributions) that you, your spouse, parents, children and siblings, whether by blood, marriage or adoption, or any person who shares a home with you ("Family Member"), or any entity in which you are a partner, member or officer, or in which you occupy a similar position, and that provided accounting, consulting, legal, investment banking, financial or other advisory or similar services to the Company, received during any of fiscal years 2009, 2010 and 2011, or are receiving during the current fiscal year, from the Company or any of its affiliates, other than compensation for service as a member of the Board, Audit Committee or other committee of the Board or pension or other forms of deferred compensation for prior service (provided such compensation is not contingent in any way on continued service).

☐ I have received no such payments.

☐ I or persons or entities listed above have received the following payments:

Recipient/Nature of Recipient's Relationship To You:[1]

Value:

Description:

---

[1] If recipient is your child or stepchild, please include his or her age.

2. *Affiliated Person.* Are you or a Family Member an affiliate of the Company or any of its subsidiaries (apart from your capacity as a member of the Board and any committee of the Board)? In answering this question, please refer to the definition of "affiliate" included in the glossary.

☐ No ☐ Yes

If "Yes," please describe such affiliation:

_____

_____

_____

3. Since January 1, 2009, have you been employed by the Company?

☐ No ☐ Yes

If "Yes," please describe:

_____

_____

_____

4. *Preparation of Financial Statements.* Have you, at any time since January 1, 2009, participated in the preparation of the financial statements of the Company?

☐ No ☐ Yes

If "Yes," please describe:

_____

_____

_____

5. *Family Relationships.* Please indicate whether any Family Member currently is employed, or, since January 1, 2009, has been employed, by the Company.

☐ No ☐ Yes

If "Yes," please describe such relationship:

_____

_____

_____

6. *Business Relationships.* Are you or a Family Member now, or have you or a Family Member been since January 1, 2009, an executive officer of or partner in, or do you or a Family Member now own, or have you or a Family Member since January 1, 2009, owned, of record or as the beneficial owner of an equity interest in (other than a less than 5% interest in a publicly-held entity), any organization, including a charitable or not-for-profit entity, to which the Company made, or from which the Company received, payments (other than those arising solely from investments in the Company's securities) in the current fiscal year or any of the fiscal years 2009, 2010 or 2011?

☐ No ☐ Yes

If "Yes," please provide the information below.

Organization:

Year:

Relationship:

Revenue Amount ($):

% of Gross Revenue of Recipient:

7. *Outside Auditor.* Are you or any Family Member now a current partner or employee of the Company's outside auditor, or since January 1, 2009, were you or any Family Member a partner or employee of such firm who worked on the Company's audit, assurance or tax compliance (but not tax planning)?

☐ No ☐ Yes

If "Yes," please describe:

_____

_____

_____

8. *Compensation Committee Interlocks.* Are you or any Family Member now, or since January 1, 2009, were you or any Family Member, employed as an executive officer of any entity where at any time since January 1, 2009, a Company executive officer served on that entity's Board of Directors or compensation committee?

☐ No ☐ Yes

If "Yes," please describe:

_____

_____

_____

9. *Affiliation with Charitable, Educational and Not-for-Profit Entities.* Are you now, or since January 1, 2009, were you, a partner, director, trustee, executive officer or other controlling person of any charitable, educational or not-for-profit entities?

☐ No ☐ Yes

If "Yes," please list the positions you held:

Entity:

Position:

10. *Other Relationships.* Do you have any other relationships, however slight or remote, with the Company, its senior management or other directors that could possibly be considered to interfere, or appear to interfere, with your exercising independent judgment in carrying out your responsibilities as a director?

☐ No ☐ Yes

If "Yes," please describe such affiliation:

_____

_____

_____

II. FINANCIAL EXPERTISE

1. Can you read and understand financial statements, including balance sheets, income statements and cash flow statements?

☐ No ☐ Yes

2. Do you have an understanding of generally accepted accounting principles?

☐ No ☐ Yes

3. Do you have the ability to assess the general application of generally accepted accounting principles in connection with accounting for estimates, accruals and reserves?

☐ No ☐ Yes

4. Do you have an understanding of Audit Committee functions?

☐ No ☐ Yes

5. Do you have an understanding of internal control over financial reporting?

☐ No ☐ Yes

6. *Business Experience.* Describe below any business experience you have had that:

(a) required you to be able to read and understand financial statements, including balance sheets, income statements and cash flow statements;

(b) involved (1) preparing, auditing, analyzing or evaluating financial statements, actively supervising one or more persons engaged in those activities or overseeing or assessing the performance of companies or public accountants with respect to those activities and/or (2) the application of generally accepted accounting principles in connection with accounting for estimates, accruals and reserves;

(c) entailed public accounting or auditing;

(d) involved experience with internal accounting controls and procedures for financial reporting;

(e) entailed financial management or oversight (e.g., as principal executive officer, principal financial officer, principal accounting officer, controller, public accountant or auditor) or involved actively supervising a person or persons in such position; and/or

(f) involved preparation or review of annual reports on Form 10-K and/or quarterly reports on Form 10-Q.

Dates:

Organization:

Public or Private?

Industry:

Position:

Job Duties:

7. *Academic Background.* Do you hold any finance and/or accounting degrees?

☐ No ☐ Yes

If "Yes," please describe these degrees:

Institution:

Degree:

Major and/or Minor:

If your degrees are not in a finance or accounting field, please indicate whether your formal education (undergraduate, graduate and postgraduate) included advanced-level courses in finance and/or accounting.

☐ No ☐ Yes

If "Yes," please generally describe these courses, including the years these courses were taken.

Course Title/Description:

Year(s):

8. *Professional Certifications and Licenses.* Do you hold any financial or accounting related professional certifications or licenses, including as a certified public accountant, from a recognized private body?

☐ No ☐ Yes

If "Yes," please list these certifications and licenses along with the dates on which they were achieved, whether you are in good standing with such private bodies and the length of time you have been actively certified (and, if you are a certified public accountant, the length of time you have actively practiced as such).

Name/Description:

Date Achieved:

Are you required, as a condition of maintaining these certifications or licenses, to obtain continuing professional education (CPE)?

☐ No ☐ Yes

If "Yes," please describe these requirements and how you have met them since January 1, 2008.

License/Certification:

CPE Requirements:

Achieved Through:

9. Have you ever served on any Audit Committee of any company other than the Company that, at the time you served, was required to file annual reports on Form 10-K and quarterly reports on Form 10-Q?

☐ No ☐ Yes

If "Yes," please describe:

_____

_____

_____

10. *Other Information.* Please describe any other qualifications or experience relevant to an evaluation of your financial literacy and your accounting and financial expertise.

I understand that the information that I am furnishing herein will be used by the Company in connection with the preparation of its Proxy Statement and Annual Report on Form 10-K, verifying the audit committee's compliance with NASDAQ's requirements and in determining whether I am an "independent director" as defined by the applicable rules of the Nasdaq Stock Market. I will advise the Company as soon as reasonably practical if any events occur after the date hereof that would change my answer to any question asked above.

Dated: _____, 2012

Signature _____

Print Name _____

GLOSSARY

Affiliate

The term "affiliate" of an entity means any person that directly, or indirectly through one or more intermediaries, controls, or is controlled by, or is under common control with, such entity. The term "control" means the possession, direct or indirect, of the power to direct or cause the direction of the management and policies of an entity, whether through the ownership of voting securities, by contract or otherwise.

Beneficial Owner

You are the "beneficial owner" of a security if you, directly or indirectly, through any contract, arrangement, understanding, relationship or otherwise have or share:

(a) the power to vote, or to direct the voting of, such security, or

(b) the power to dispose, or to direct the disposition, of such security.

You are also the "beneficial owner" of a security if you, directly or indirectly, create or use a trust, proxy, power of attorney, pooling arrangement or any other contract, arrangement, or device with the purpose or effect of divesting yourself of "beneficial ownership" of a security or preventing the vesting of such "beneficial ownership." Therefore, whether or not you are the record holder of securities, you may be the "beneficial owner" of securities held by you for your own benefit (regardless of how registered) and securities held by others for your benefit (regardless of how registered), such as by custodians, brokers, nominees, pledgees, etc., and including securities held by an estate or trust in which you have an interest as legatee or beneficiary, securities owned by a partnership of which you are a partner, securities held by a personal holding company of which you are a stockholder, etc., and securities held in the name of your spouse, minor children and any relative sharing the same home.

Finally, you are deemed to be the "beneficial owner" of a security if you have the right to acquire "beneficial ownership" of such security at any time within sixty (60) days, including but not limited to, (a) through the exercise of any option, warrant or right or (b) through the conversion of a security or (c) pursuant to the power to revoke a trust, discretionary account or similar arrangement or (d) pursuant to the automatic termination of a trust, discretionary account or similar arrangement.

Note that the same security may be beneficially owned by more than one person. For example, several co-trustees may share the power to vote or dispose of shares.

Executive Officer

The term "executive officer" means the president, principal executive officer, principal financial officer, principal accounting officer, any vice president in charge of a principal business unit, division or function (such as sales, administration or finance), any other officer who performs policy-making functions and any other person who performs similar policy-making functions for a company.

APPENDIX 8

XYZ Corporation

Form 5 Questionnaire for Directors and Executive Officers

As you know, as a director or executive officer of XYZ Corporation (the "Company"), (1) a Form 3 was filed on your behalf with the SEC either when the Company became a public company or when you were later designated an executive officer or appointed a director of the Company to reflect your beneficial ownership of the Company's common stock at such time and (2) Form 4s have been filed on your behalf with the SEC as required from time to time in order to report your transactions, if any, in securities of the Company. In addition to Form 4, the SEC has a year-end "clean-up" Form 5 that you are required to file if any one or more of the following events have occurred:

(a) You have had any transactions in the Company's securities during calendar year 2011 that were exempt from current Form 4 reporting (e.g., gifts and inheritances) and were not previously reported on Form 4 voluntarily; or

(b) You have had any transactions in the Company's securities during calendar year 2011 that should have been reported on a Form 4 (e.g., open market or private sales and purchases and stock option exercises), but were not reported.

For your convenience, copies of your Form 4 filings for 2011, if any, are attached. If there were any transactions in the Company's securities during 2011 that were not reported on the attached Forms (whether or not such transactions are required to be reported), please list those transactions below. Please focus in particular on gifts (especially year-end gifts) to charities or family members, stock option, stock appreciation rights, or restricted stock grants that you may have received and stock options you may have exercised. In addition, please include any transactions by which your form of ownership changed (e.g., transfers to family members or trusts). If the amount of securities shown as beneficially owned by you on your most recent Form does not agree with your current records (e.g., because of purchases under the Company's employee stock purchase plan), please provide any information needed to reconcile the Form and your records.

Owner (Direct, or name of indirect owner)[1]: _____

Transaction Date[2]: _____

Transaction Code[3]: _____

Amount of Securities Acquired (A) or Disposed of (D): _____

Amount of Securities Beneficially Owned at End of 2011: _____

---

[1] Indirect ownership may include, for example, securities held in the name of your spouse or other immediate family member who shares your residence or securities attributable to your interest in a trust or partnership.

[2] Transaction Date:
(1) Brokerage transactions—trade date
(2) Other purchases and sales—date firm commitment is made
(3) Option/SARs exercises—date of exercise
(4) Gifts—date on which gift is made
(5) Securities grants—date on which Company made grant

[3] Transaction Code:
(P) Open Market or Private Purchase

(S) Open Market or Private Sale
(G) Gift
(A) Grant of Derivative Security
(M) Exercise of Exempted Derivative Security
(W) Acquisition or Disposition by Will or Inheritance
(X) Exercise of Derivative Security (specify if in-the-money or out-of-the-money)
(C) Conversion of Derivative Security
(E) Expiration of Derivative Positions
(H) Expiration (or Cancellation) of Derivative Position with Value Received
(J) Other Acquisition or Disposition (describe transaction on another page).

Amount of Purchase, Sale or Exercise or Conversion Price (per share): _____

Vesting Date/ Expiration Date[4]: _____

If any of the transactions or holdings for 2011 described above require that you file a Form 5, we will prepare the form on your behalf for your review and signature and will file it with the SEC. Please note that Form 5s must be received by the SEC no later than February 15, 2012, and that your responses to this questionnaire will be used in connection with providing required disclosure regarding delinquent Section 16 filings in the Company's proxy statement for its 2012 annual meeting of stockholders. As such, please return this completed and executed questionnaire to _____ as soon as possible, but no later than January _____, 2012.

I have reviewed the requirements for filing a Form 5 as set forth in (a) and (b) above and:

☐ I am not required to file a Form 5 for 2011.

☐ I may be required to report the transactions or holdings for 2011 described above.

Date:_____, 2012

_____ Signature

_____ Print Name

---

[4] Provide this information for all derivative securities disclosed (e.g., options and warrants).

APPENDIX 9

Interpretation: Commission Guidance Regarding Management's
Discussion and Analysis of Financial Condition
and Results of Operations

17 CFR Parts 211, 231 and 241

[Release Nos. 33-8350; 34-48960; FR-72]

Agency: Securities and Exchange Commission.

Action: Interpretation.

Summary: The Commission is publishing interpretive guidance regarding the disclosure commonly known as Management's Discussion and Analysis of Financial Condition and Results of Operations, or MD&A, which is required by Item 303 of Regulation S-K, Items 303(b) and (c) of Regulation S-B, Item 5 of Form 20-F and Paragraph 11 of General Instruction B of Form 40-F. This guidance is intended to elicit more meaningful disclosure in MD&A in a number of areas, including the overall presentation and focus of MD&A, with general emphasis on the discussion and analysis of known trends, demands, commitments, events and uncertainties, and specific guidance on disclosures about liquidity, capital resources and critical accounting estimates.

Effective Date: December 29, 2003.

For Further Information Contact: Questions about specific filings should be directed to staff members responsible for reviewing the documents the registrant files with the Commission. General questions about this release should be referred to Todd Hardiman, Karl Hiller, Nina Mojiri-Azad, Mara Ransom, or Sondra Stokes, Division of Corporation Finance, at (202) 824-5300, Securities and Exchange Commission, 450 5th Street N.W., Washington, D.C. 20549-0401.

Supplementary Information:

I. Overview

A. Purpose

This release interprets requirements for Management's Discussion and Analysis of Financial Condition and Results of Operations ("MD&A").[1] It provides guidance to assist companies:

---

[1] The requirements are set forth in Item 303 of Regulation S-K (Management's Discussion & Analysis of Financial Condition and Results of Operations) [17 CFR 229.303], Items 303(b) and (c) of Regulation S-B (Management's Discussion & Analysis of Financial Condition and Results of Operations, and Off-balance sheet arrangements) [17 CFR 228.303(b) and (c)], Item 5 of Form 20-F (Operating and Financial Review and Prospects) [17 CFR 249.220f], and General Instruction B.(11) of Form 40-F (Off-balance sheet arrangements) [17 CFR 249.240f].

Although the wording of the MD&A requirement in Form 20-F was revised in 1999, the Commission's adopting release noted that we interpret that Item as calling for the same disclosure as Item 303 of Regulation S-K. See Release No. 33-7745 (Sept. 28, 1999) [64 FR 53900 at 59304]. In addition, Instruction 1 to Item 5 in Form 20-F provides that issuers should refer to the Commission's 1989 interpretive release on MD&A

disclosure under Item 303 of Regulation S-K (Interpretive Release: Management's Discussion and Analysis of Financial Condition and Results of Operations; Certain Investment Company Disclosures, Release No. 33-6835 (May 18, 1989) [54 FR 22427] (the "1989 Release")) for guidance in preparing the discussion and analysis by management of the company's financial condition and results of operations required in Form 20-F. Therefore, although this release refers primarily to Item 303 of Regulation S-K, it also is intended to apply to MD&A drafted pursuant to Item 5 of Form 20-F.

In addition, the guidance in this release applies to small business issuers that are subject to the disclosure requirements of Items 303(b) and (c) of Regulation S-B. Small business issuers, like all other companies subject to SEC reporting obligations, should consider the interpretive guidance based on their own particular facts and circumstances.

- in preparing MD&A disclosure that is easier to follow and understand; and
- in providing information that more completely satisfies our previously enunciated principal objectives of MD&A.

We believe that management's most important responsibilities include communicating with investors in a clear and straightforward manner. MD&A is a critical component of that communication. The Commission has long sought through its rules, enforcement actions and interpretive processes to elicit MD&A that not only meets technical disclosure requirements but generally is informative and transparent. We believe and expect that when companies follow the guidance in this release, the overall quality of their MD&A will improve. The Division of Corporation Finance will continue to review MD&A submitted after this guidance is released and take action as appropriate. In addition, we have instructed the Division to keep us apprised of whether this guidance has produced improved disclosure, and to suggest additional Commission action related to MD&A as appropriate.

B. Approach to MD&A

The purpose of MD&A is not complicated. It is to provide readers information "necessary to an understanding of [a company's] financial condition, changes in financial condition and results of operations."[2] The MD&A requirements are intended to satisfy three principal objectives:

- to provide a narrative explanation of a company's financial statements that enables investors to see the company through the eyes of management;
- to enhance the overall financial disclosure and provide the context within which financial information should be analyzed; and
- to provide information about the quality of, and potential variability of, a company's earnings and cash flow, so that investors can ascertain the likelihood that past performance is indicative of future performance.[3]

MD&A should be a discussion and analysis of a company's business as seen through the eyes of those who manage that business. Management has a unique perspective on its business that only it can present. As such, MD&A should not be a recitation of financial statements in narrative form or an otherwise uninformative series of technical responses to MD&A requirements, neither of which provides this important management perspective. Through this release we encourage each company and its management to take a fresh look at MD&A with a view to enhancing its quality. We also encourage early top-level involvement by a company's management in identifying the key disclosure themes and items that should be included in a company's MD&A.

Based on our experience with many companies' current disclosures in MD&A, we believe there are a number of general ways for companies to enhance their MD&A consistent with its purpose. The recent review experiences of the staff of the Division of Corporation Finance, including its Fortune 500 review,[4] have led us to conclude that additional guidance would be especially useful in the following areas:

- the overall presentation of MD&A;
- the focus and content of MD&A (including materiality, analysis, key performance measures and known material trends and uncertainties);
- disclosure regarding liquidity and capital resources; and

---

[2] Item 303(a) of Regulation S-K [17 CFR 229.303(a)].

[3] See Commission Statement About Management's Discussion and Analysis of Financial Condition and Results of Operations, Release No. 33-8056 (Jan. 22, 2002) [67 FR 3746] ("January 2002 Release").

[4] See Summary by the Division of Corporation Finance of Significant Issues Addressed in the Review of the Periodic Reports of the Fortune 500 Companies (Feb. 27, 2003) ("Fortune 500 Summary") available at www.sec.gov/divisions/corpfin/fortune500rep.htm.

- disclosure regarding critical accounting estimates.

Therefore, in this release, we emphasize the following points regarding overall presentation:

- within the universe of material information, companies should present their disclosure so that the most important information is most prominent;
- companies should avoid unnecessary duplicative disclosure that can tend to overwhelm readers and act as an obstacle to identifying and understanding material matters; and
- many companies would benefit from starting their MD&A with a section that provides an executive-level overview that provides context for the remainder of the discussion.

We also emphasize the following points regarding focus and content:

- in deciding on the content of MD&A, companies should focus on material information and eliminate immaterial information that does not promote understanding of companies' financial condition, liquidity and capital resources, changes in financial condition and results of operations (both in the context of profit and loss and cash flows);[5]
- companies should identify and discuss key performance indicators, including nonfinancial performance indicators, that their management uses to manage the business and that would be material to investors;
- companies must identify and disclose known trends, events, demands, commitments and uncertainties that are reasonably likely to have a material effect on financial condition or operating performance;[6] and
- companies should provide not only disclosure of information responsive to MD&A's requirements, but also an analysis that is responsive to those requirements that explains management's view of the implications and significance of that information and that satisfies the objectives of MD&A.

C. Impact of Increased Amounts of Information Available to Companies

Companies have access to and use substantially more detailed and timely information about their financial condition and operating performance than they did when our MD&A requirements initially were introduced or when we last provided general interpretive guidance.[7] Some of this information is itself non-financial in nature, but bears on companies' financial condition and operating performance. The increased availability of information is relevant to companies in preparing MD&A for the following reasons:

- First, companies must evaluate an increased amount of information to determine which information they must disclose. In doing so, companies should avoid the unnecessary information overload for investors that can result from disclosure of information that is not required, is immaterial, and does not promote understanding.

---

[5] In this release we sometimes use the term "financial condition and operating performance" to refer to the required subjects of MD&A of financial condition, liquidity and capital resources, changes in financial condition and results of operations (both in the context of profit and loss and cash flows).

[6] Note 27 to the 1989 Release states, "MD&A mandates disclosure of specified forward-looking information, and specifies its own standards for disclosure—i.e., reasonably likely to have a material effect. The specific standard governs the circumstances

in which Item 303 requires disclosure. The probability/magnitude test for materiality approved by the Supreme Court in *Basic v. Levinson*, 108 S. Ct. 978 (1988), is inapposite to Item 303 disclosure."

[7] *See, e.g., Improving Business Reporting—A CustomerFocus; Meeting the Information Needs of Investors and Creditors*, Comprehensive Report of the Special Committee on Financial Reporting, American Institute of Certified Public Accountants (AICPA) (1994) ("Jenkins Report").

- Second, in identifying, discussing and analyzing known material trends and uncertainties, companies are expected to consider all relevant information, even if that information is not required to be disclosed.

D. Liquidity and Capital Resources

We devote a separate section of this release to disclosure in MD&A regarding liquidity and capital resources. In that section, we emphasize the need for attention to disclosure of cash requirements and sources of cash. We believe that:

- companies should consider enhanced analysis and explanation of the sources and uses of cash and material changes in particular items underlying the major captions reported in their financial statements, rather than recitation of the items in the cash flow statements;

- companies using the indirect method[8] in preparing their cash flow statements should pay particular attention to disclosure and analysis of matters that are not readily apparent from their cash flow statements; and

- companies also should consider whether their MD&A should include enhanced disclosure regarding debt instruments, guarantees and related covenants.

E. Critical Accounting Estimates

Finally, we have included a separate section in this release regarding accounting estimates and assumptions that may be material due to the levels of subjectivity and judgment necessary to account for highly uncertain matters or the susceptibility of such matters to change, and that have a material impact on financial condition or operating performance. Companies should consider enhanced discussion and analysis of these critical accounting estimates and assumptions that:

- supplements, but does not duplicate, the description of accounting policies in the notes to the financial statements; and

- provides greater insight into the quality and variability of information regarding financial condition and operating performance.

F. Effect on Prior Commission Statements

This release does not modify existing legal requirements or create new legal requirements. Rather, we intend this release to assist companies in preparing MD&A by providing interpretive guidance and, in some cases, providing additional guidance in areas that the Commission has addressed previously. We do not believe that the guidance in this release conflicts with prior Commission guidance, nor is it our intention to alter any prior Commission guidance.

---

[8] In Financial Accounting Standards Board (FASB) Statement of Financial Accounting Standards (SFAS) No. 95, *Statement of Cash Flows* (Nov. 1987), the FASB allowed the indirect method of reporting net cash flow from operating activities by adjusting net income to reconcile it to net cash flow from operating activities. Under that method, the major classes of operating cash receipts and payments are determined indirectly by determining the change in asset and liability accounts that relate to operating income. However, in SFAS 95, the FASB encouraged companies to use the direct method of reporting net cash flow from operating activities rather than the indirect method. The direct method reports net cash flow from operations by summing major classes of gross cash receipts, such as customer payments, and gross cash payments, such as cash paid to employees. The direct method also requires a reconciliation of net income to net cash flow from operating activities. The FASB gave its opinion that the direct method is "the more comprehensive and presumably more useful approach."

While this release refers primarily to U.S. GAAP, the underlying events and circumstances described in the release ordinarily will be applicable to foreign private issuers and should be discussed to the extent material. Consistent with the Instructions to Form 20-F, however, companies using that form should focus on the primary financial statements in their discussion and analysis in Item 5 (Operative and Financial Review Prospects). Also, companies are required to discuss in Item 5 of Form 20-F any aspects of the differences between foreign and U.S. GAAP that they believe are necessary for an understanding of the financial statements as a whole. *See* Instruction 2 to Item 5 of Form 20-F [17 CFR 249.220f].

II. Background

The following is a chronology of certain prior Commission action regarding MD&A:

1980—We adopted the present form of the disclosure requirements for MD&A.[9]

1981—We published the staff's interpretive guidance for MD&A after its review of disclosures that were prepared in accordance with the then-recently adopted disclosure requirements.[10]

1987—We sought public comment on the adequacy of MD&A and on proposed revisions submitted by members of the professional accounting community.[11]

1989—We published an interpretive release that addressed a number of disclosure matters that should be considered by companies in preparing MD&A.[12] The 1989 Release provided guidance in various areas, including required prospective information, analysis of long and short-term liquidity and capital resources, material changes in financial statement line items, required interim period disclosure, segment analysis, participation in high-yield financings, highly leveraged transactions or non-investment grade loans and investments, the effects of federal financial assistance upon the operations of financial institutions and the disclosure of preliminary merger negotiations.

December 2001—As part of its process of reviewing financial and non-financial disclosures made by public companies, the Division of Corporation Finance announced that it would preliminarily review the annual reports filed in 2002 by the Fortune 500 companies, and undertake further review as appropriate, consistent with its selective review program. The focus of the project was to identify "disclosure that appeared to be critical to an understanding of each company's financial position and results, but which, at least on its face, seemed to conflict significantly with generally accepted accounting principles [GAAP] or SEC rules, or to be materially deficient in explanation or clarity."[13] As a result of this review, comment letters, many of which commented on companies' MD&A, were sent to more than 350 of the Fortune 500 companies. Earlier this year, the Division published a summary of the most frequent general areas of comment resulting from this review.[14]

December 2001—The Commission issued cautionary advice to companies regarding the need for greater investor awareness of the sensitivity of financial statements to the methods, assumptions, and estimates underlying their preparation. This cautionary advice encouraged public companies to include in their MD&A full explanations of their "critical accounting policies," the judgments and uncertainties affecting the application of those policies, and the likelihood that materially different amounts would be reported under different conditions or using different assumptions.[15]

January 2002—After receiving a petition requesting additional MD&A interpretive guidance,[16] we issued a statement "to suggest steps that issuers should consider in meeting their current disclosure obligations with respect to the topics described."[17] The statement provided explicit interpretive guidance on certain MD&A topics considered material to an understanding of companies' operations. The topics addressed by the release were liquidity and capital resources (including off-balance sheet arrangements),

---

[9] Final Rule: Amendments to Annual Report Form, Related Forms, Rules, Regulations, and Guides; Integration of Securities Acts Disclosure Systems, Release No. 33-6231 (Sept. 2, 1980) [45 FR 63630].

[10] Management's Discussion and Analysis of Financial Condition and Results of Operations, Release No. 33-6349 (Sept. 28, 1981) 23 SEC Docket 962 [Release not published in the Federal Register].

[11] Concept Release on Management's Discussion and Analysis of Financial Condition and Operations, Release No. 33-6711 (April 24, 1987) [52 FR 13715].

[12] 1989 Release.

[13] Fortune 500 Summary.

[14] Id.

[15] Cautionary Advice Regarding Disclosure About Critical Accounting Policies, Release No. 33-8040 (Dec. 12, 2001) [66 FR 65013] ("December 2001 Release").

[16] On December 31, 2001 the Commission received a petition from Arthur Andersen LLP, Deloitte and Touche, LLP, Ernst & Young LLP, KPMG LLP and Price-waterhouseCoopers LLP. The American Institute of Certified Public Accountants endorsed the petition. A copy of the petition is available at www.sec.gov/rules/petitions/petndiscl_12312001.htm.

[17] See January 2002 Release.

trading activities involving non-exchange traded contracts accounted for at fair value, and relationships and transactions with persons or entities that derive benefits from their non-independent relationships with the company or the company's related parties.[18]

May 2002—We proposed additional MD&A disclosure requirements, which remain under consideration, regarding the application of companies' critical accounting estimates.[19]

January 2003—We adopted additional disclosure requirements regarding off-balance sheet arrangements and aggregate contractual obligations.[20] The new rules require the disclosure of off-balance sheet arrangements in a designated section of MD&A and an overview of certain known contractual obligations in a tabular format.[21]

We also have brought numerous enforcement actions based on alleged violations of MD&A requirements and will continue to bring such actions under appropriate circumstances.[22]

Based on recent experiences, we have determined that additional interpretive guidance regarding the requirements of MD&A will be useful to companies in enhancing overall disclosure under MD&A requirements.

III. Overall Approach to MD&A

A. The Presentation of MD&A

Since the introduction of our MD&A requirements, many companies have become larger, more global and more complex. At the same time, the combination of our rules and investors' demands have led to an increase in the number of subjects and matters addressed in MD&A. For these and other reasons, many companies' MD&A have become necessarily lengthy and complex. Unfortunately, the presentation of the MD&A of too many companies also may have become unnecessarily lengthy, difficult to understand and confusing.

MD&A, like other disclosure, should be presented in clear and understandable language. We understand that complex companies and situations require disclosure of complex matters and we are not in any way seeking over-simplification or "dumbing down" of MD&A. However, we believe that companies can improve the clarity and understandability

---

[18] *Id.*

[19] Proposed Rule: Disclosure in Management's Discussion and Analysis about the Application of Critical Accounting Policies, Release No. 33-8098 (May 10, 2002) [67 FR 35620] ("2002 Critical Accounting Policies Proposal").

[20] Final Rule: Disclosure in Management's Discussion and Analysis About Off-Balance Sheet Arrangements and Aggregate Contractual Obligations, Release No. 33-8182 (Jan. 28, 2003) [68 FR 5982] ("2003 Off-Balance Sheet Release").

The overall guidance in this Interpretive Release is applicable to all MD&A discussions, including those related to off-balance sheet arrangements. As such, it should be applied to General Instruction B.(11) of Form 40-F and Item 303(c) of Regulation S-B, in addition to the other sections set out in note 1, above. We are not addressing specifically disclosures of off-balance sheet arrangements in this release, however, because we have little experience with companies' application of the new rules, which are effective for companies' registration statements, annual reports and proxy or information statements that are required to include financial statements for their fiscal years ending on or after June 15, 2003. Companies (other than small business issuers) must include the table of con-

tractual obligations in registration statements, annual reports, and proxy or information statements that are required to include financial statements for the fiscal years ending on or after December 15, 2003. In addition, Section 401(c) of the Sarbanes-Oxley Act requires us to complete a study and report to the President and Congress next year on these types of disclosures.

[21] The tabular disclosure is not required for small business issuers by Item 303 of Regulation S-B.

[22] *See, e.g., In the Matter of Edison Schools, Inc.,* Release No. 34-45925 (May 14, 2002); *In the Matter of Sony Corporation and Sumio Sano,* Release No. 34-40305 (Aug. 5, 1998); *In the Matter of Bank of Boston Corp.,* Initial Decision Release No. 81 (Dec. 22, 1995); *In the Matter of Gibson Greetings, Inc., Ward A. Cavanaugh, and James H. Johnsen,* Release No. 34-36357 (Oct. 11, 1995); *In the Matter of America West Airlines, Inc.,* Release No. 34-34047 (May 12, 1994); *In the Matter of Salant Corporation and Martin F. Tynan,* Release No. 34-34046 (May 12, 1994); *In the Matter of Shared Medical Systems Corporation,* Release No. 34-33632 (Feb. 17, 1994); *In the Matter of Caterpillar Inc.,* Release No. 34-30532 (Mar. 31, 1992); *In the Matter of American Express Company,* Release No. 34-23332 (June 17, 1986).

of their MD&A by using language that is clearer and less convoluted. We believe that efforts by companies to provide clearer and better organized presentations of MD&A can result in more understandable disclosure that does not sacrifice the appropriate level of complexity or nuance. In order to engender better understanding, companies should prepare MD&A with a strong focus on the most important information, provided in a manner intended to address the objectives of MD&A. In particular:

- Companies should consider whether a tabular presentation of relevant financial or other information may help a reader's understanding of MD&A. For example, a company's MD&A might be clearer and more concise if it provides a tabular comparison of its results in different periods, which could include line items and percentage changes as well as other information determined by a company to be useful, followed by a narrative discussion and analysis of known changes, events, trends, uncertainties and other matters. A reader's understanding of a company's fair value calculations or discounted cash flow figures also could, in some situations, be enhanced by providing a tabular summary of the company's various material interest and discount rate assumptions in one location.

- Companies should consider whether the headings they use assist readers in following the flow of, or otherwise assist in understanding, MD&A, and whether additional headings would be helpful in this regard.

- Many companies' MD&A could benefit from adding an introductory section or overview that would facilitate a reader's understanding. As with all disclosure, what companies would appropriately include in an introduction or overview will depend on the circumstances of the particular company. As a general matter, an introduction or overview should include the most important matters on which a company's executives focus in evaluating financial condition and operating performance and provide the context for the discussion and analysis of the financial statements. Therefore, an introduction or overview should not be a duplicative layer of disclosure that merely repeats the more detailed discussion and analysis that follows.

- While all required information must of course be disclosed, companies should consider using a "layered" approach. Such an approach would present information in a manner that emphasizes, within the universe of material information that is disclosed, the information and analysis that is most important. This presentation would assist readers in identifying more readily the most important information. Using an overview or introduction is one example of a layered approach. Another is to begin a section containing detailed analysis, such as an analysis of period-toperiod information, with a statement of the principal factors, trends or other matters that are the principal subjects covered in more detail in the section.

We would expect a good introduction or overview to provide a balanced, executive-level discussion that identifies the most important themes or other significant matters with which management is concerned primarily in evaluating the company's financial condition and operating results. A good introduction or overview would:

- include economic or industry-wide factors relevant to the company;

- serve to inform the reader about how the company earns revenues and income and generates cash;

- to the extent necessary or useful to convey this information, discuss the company's lines of business, location or locations of operations, and principal products and services (but an introduction should not merely duplicate disclosure in the Description of Business section); and

- provide insight into material opportunities, challenges and risks, such as those presented by known material trends and uncertainties, on which the company's executives are most focused for both the short and long term, as well as the actions they are taking to address these opportunities, challenges and risks.

Because these matters do not generally remain static from period to period, we would expect the introduction to change over time to remain current. As is true with all sections of MD&A, boilerplate disclaimers and other generic language generally are not helpful in providing useful information or achieving balance, and would detract from the purpose of the introduction or overview.

An introduction or overview, by its very nature, cannot disclose everything and should not be considered by itself in determining whether a company has made full disclosure. Further, the failure to include disclosure of every material item in an introduction or overview should not trigger automatically the application of the "buried facts" doctrine, in which a court would consider disclosure to be false and misleading if its overall significance is obscured because material is "buried," such as in a footnote or an appendix.[23]

Throughout MD&A, including in an introduction or overview, discussion and analysis of financial condition and operating performance includes both past and prospective matters. In addressing prospective financial condition and operating performance, there are circumstances, particularly regarding known material trends and uncertainties, where forward-looking information is required to be disclosed. We also encourage companies to discuss prospective matters and include forward-looking information in circumstances where that information may not be required, but will provide useful material information for investors that promotes understanding.

B. The Content and Focus of MD&A

In addition to enhancing MD&A through the use of clearer language and presentation, many companies could improve their MD&A by focusing on the most important information disclosed in MD&A. Disclosure should emphasize material information that is required or promotes understanding and de-emphasize (or, if appropriate, delete) immaterial information that is not required and does not promote understanding.

Our MD&A requirements call for companies to provide investors and other users with material information that is necessary to an understanding of the company's financial condition and operating performance, as well as its prospects for the future.[24] While the desired focus of MD&A for a particular company will depend on the facts and circumstances of the company, some guidance about the content and focus of MD&A is generally applicable.

1. Focus on Key Indicators of Financial Condition and Operating Performance

As discussed, one of the principal objectives of MD&A is to give readers a view of the company through the eyes of management by providing both a short and long-term analysis of the business.[25] To do this, companies should "identify and address those key variables and other qualitative and quantitative factors which are peculiar to and necessary for an understanding and evaluation of the individual company."[26]

Financial measures generally are the starting point in ascertaining these key variables and other factors. However, financial measures often tell only part of how a company manages its business. Therefore, when preparing MD&A, companies should consider whether disclosure of all key variables and other factors that management uses to manage the business would be material to investors, and therefore required.[27] These key variables

---

[23] See, e.g., Final Rule: Plain English Disclosure, Release No. 33-7497 (Jan. 28, 1998) [63 FR 6370 at 6375] (citing Gould v. American Hawaiian Steamship Company, 331 F. Supp. 981 (D. Del. 1971); Kohn v. American Metal Climax, Inc., 322 F. Supp. 1331 (E.D. Pa. 1970), modified, 458 F.2d 255 (3d Cir. 1972).)

[24] See 1989 Release, Part III.A.

[25] See, e.g., Release No. 33-6711 (Apr. 24, 1987) [52 FR 13715 at 13717] ("an opportunity to look at the company through the eyes of management by providing both a short and long-term analysis of the business of the company.").

[26] 1989 Release, Part III.A (citing Release No. 33-6349 (Sept. 28, 1981) 23 SEC Docket 962 at 964 [Release not published in the Federal Register]).

[27] Examples of such other factors, depending on the circumstances of a particular company, can include

manufacturing plant capacity and utilization, backlog, trends in bookings and employee turnover rates. See, e.g., Quality, Transparency, Accountability, Lynn E. Turner, Chief Accountant, Securities and Exchange Commission, Remarks Before Financial Executives Institute (Apr. 26, 2001), available at www.sec.gov/news/speech/spch485.htm.

Companies should also consider disclosing information that may be peripheral to the accounting function, but is integral to the business or operating activity. Examples of such measures, depending on the circumstances of a particular company, can include those based on units or volume, customer satisfaction, time-to-market, interest rates, product development, service offerings, throughput capacity, affiliations/joint undertakings, market demand, customer/vendor relations, employee retention, business strategy, changes in the managerial approach or structure, and other factors may be non-financial, and companies should consider whether that nonfinancial information should be disclosed.

Many companies currently disclose non-financial business and operational data.[28] Academics, authors, and consultants also have researched the types of information, outside of financial statement measures, that would be helpful to investors and other users.[29] Such information may relate to external or macro-economic matters as well as those specific to a company or industry. For example, interest rates or economic growth rates and their anticipated trends can be important variables for many companies. Industry-specific measures can also be important for analysis, although common standards for the measures also are important. Some industries commonly use non-financial data, such as industry metrics and value drivers.[30] Where a company discloses such information, and there is no commonly accepted method of calculating a particular non-financial metric, it should provide an explanation of its calculation to promote comparability across companies within the industry. Finally, companies may use non-financial performance measures that are company-specific.

In addition, if companies disclose material information (historical or forward-looking) other than in their filed documents (such as in earnings releases or publicly accessible analysts' calls or companion website postings) they also should evaluate that material information to determine whether it is required to be included in MD&A, either because it falls within a specific disclosure requirement or because its omission would render misleading the filed document in which the MD&A appears. We are not seeking to sweep into MD&A all the information that a company communicates. Rather, companies should consider their communications and determine what information is material and is required in, or would promote understanding of, MD&A.

Since we adopted the MD&A requirements, and even since the last comprehensive guidance on MD&A we released in 1989, there have been significant advancements in the ability to develop and access information quickly and effectively. Changes in business enterprise systems, communications and other aspects of information technology have significantly increased the amount of information available to management, as well as the speed with which they receive and are able to use information.[31] There is therefore a larger and more up-to-date universe of information, financial and non-financial alike, that companies have and should evaluate in determining whether disclosure is required. This situation presents companies with the challenge of identifying information that is required to be disclosed or that promotes understanding, while avoiding unnecessary information overload for readers by not disclosing a greater body of information, just because it is available, where disclosure is not required and does not promote understanding. Further, with advances in technology contributing to increasing amounts and currency of information, the factors relied upon by companies to operate and analyze the business may change. As this occurs, the discussion in MD&A should change over time to maintain an appropriate focus on material factors.

The focus on key performance indicators can be enhanced not only through the language and content of the discussion, but also through a format that will enhance the understanding of the discussion and analysis. The order of the information need not follow the order presented in Item 303 of Regulation S-K if another order of presentation would better facilitate readers' understanding. MD&A should provide a frame of reference that allows readers to understand the effects of material changes and events and known material trends

---

(Footnote Continued)

regulatory actions or regulatory environment, and any other pertinent macroeconomic measures. Because these measures are generally non-financial in nature, we do not believe that their disclosure generally will raise issues under Item 10(e) of Regulation S-K [17 CFR 229.10(e)] or Item 10(h) of Regulation S-B [17 CFR 228.10(h)].

[28] *See Improving Business Reporting: Insights into Enhancing Voluntary Disclosures*, Steering Committee Report of the Business Reporting Research Project of

the FASB (2001) available at www.fasb.org; the Jenkins Report; Financial Accounting Series Special Report, *Business and Financial Reporting, Challenges from the New Economy* (FASB) (2001) ("Special Report on Improving Business Reporting").

[29] *See* Special Report on Improving Business Reporting.

[30] *See, e.g.*, the Jenkins Report; the Special Report on Improving Business Reporting.

[31] *See* the Jenkins Report.

and uncertainties arising during the periods being discussed, as well as their relative importance. To satisfy the objectives of MD&A, companies also should provide a balanced view of the underlying dynamics of the business, including not only a description of a company's successes, but also of instances when it failed to realize goals, if material. Good MD&A will focus readers' attention on these key matters.

2. Focus on Materiality

Companies must provide specified material information in their MD&A,[32] and they also must provide other material information that is necessary to make the required statements, in light of the circumstances in which they are made, not misleading.[33] MD&A must specifically focus on known material events and uncertainties that would cause reported financial information not to be necessarily indicative of future operating performance or of future financial condition.[34] Companies must determine, based on their own particular facts and circumstances, whether disclosure of a particular matter is required in MD&A. However, the effectiveness of MD&A decreases with the accumulation of unnecessary detail or duplicative or uninformative disclosure that obscures material information.[35] Companies should view this guidance as an opportunity to evaluate whether there is information in their MD&A that is no longer material or useful, and therefore should be deleted, for example where there has been a change in their business or the information has become stale.

As the complexity of business structures and financial transactions increase, and as the activities undertaken by companies become more diverse, it is increasingly important for companies to focus their MD&A on material information. In preparing MD&A, companies should evaluate issues presented in previous periods and consider reducing or omitting discussion of those that may no longer be material or helpful, or revise discussions where a revision would make the continuing relevance of an issue more apparent.

Companies also should focus on an analysis of the consolidated financial condition and operating performance, with segment data provided where material to an understanding of consolidated information. Segment discussion and analysis should be designed to avoid unnecessary duplication and immaterial detail that is not required and does not promote understanding of a company's overall financial condition and operating performance.

Both Instruction 4 to Item 303 of Regulation S-K and the 1989 Release address the requirement of discussion and analysis of changes in line items. A review of current MD&A provided by some companies, however, reveals that this is a portion of MD&A

---

[32] *See, e.g.,* Item 303(a)(1) of Regulation S-K [17 CFR 229.303(a)(1)] (requiring the identification of "known trends or known demands, commitments, events or uncertainties that will result in or that are reasonably likely to result in the registrant's liquidity increasing or decreasing in any material way"). *See also* Item 303(a)(2)(i) of Regulation S-K [17 CFR 229.303(a)(2)(i)] (requiring a description of registrant's material commitments for capital expenditures).

[33] *See* Securities Act Rule 408 [17 CFR 230.408], Securities Exchange Act of 1934 Section 10(b) [15 U.S.C. § 78j(b)], Exchange Act Rule 10b-5 [17 CFR 240.10b-5], and Exchange Act Rule 12b-20 [17 CFR 240.12b-20]. *See also, In the Matter of Edison Schools, Inc.,* Release No. 34-45925 (May 14, 2002) (finding, among other things, that the company failed to provide accurate and complete disclosure about its reported revenues); *In the Matter of Sony Corporation and Sumio Sano,* Release No. 34-40305 (Aug. 5, 1998) (finding that the company violated Section 13(a) of the Exchange Act by making inadequate disclosures about the nature and the extent of Sony Pictures' net losses and their impact on the consolidated results Sony was reporting); *In the Matter of Caterpillar Inc.,* Release

No. 34-30532 (Mar. 31, 1992) (finding failure to disclose the impact of a subsidiary's foreign operations on the company's results of operations violated Section 13(a) of the Exchange Act).

[34] Instruction 3 to Item 303(a) of Regulation S-K [17 CFR 229.303(a)].

[35] *See, e.g.,* Instruction 4 to Item 303(a) of Regulation SK (indicating that repetition and line-by-line analysis is not required nor is it appropriate when the causes for a change in one line item also relate to other line items and indicating that, to the extent the changes from year to year are readily computable from the financial statements, the changes need not be recited in the discussion). The 1989 Release also addressed these points directly. *See* 1989 Release, Part III.D.

Where companies believe that information from the face of financial statements is helpful to readers in MD&A, they should consider using a tabular presentation that shows the decimal percentages of components or year-over-year percentage changes of the financial statement line items. An appropriate analysis of this data, to the extent that it is material, should accompany the tabular presentation consistent with the guidance in Section III.B.3 of this Release.

that can include an excessive amount of duplicative disclosure, as well as disclosure of immaterial items that do not promote understanding. The 1989 Release explicitly provides for the grouping of line items for purposes of discussion and analysis in a manner that avoids duplicative disclosure. In addition, Instruction 4 and the guidance in the 1989 Release do not require a discussion of every line item and its changes without regard to materiality. Discussion of a line item and its changes should be avoided where the information that would be disclosed is not material and would not promote understanding of MD&A.

Companies also must assess the materiality of items in preparing disclosure in their quarterly reports. There may be different quantitative and qualitative factors to consider when deciding whether to include certain information in a specific quarterly or annual report. The 1989 Release addresses some aspects of MD&A disclosure in the context of quarterly filings. That release clarifies that material changes to items disclosed in MD&A in annual reports should be discussed in the quarter in which they occur.[36] There also may be circumstances where an item may not be material in the context of a discussion of annual results of operations but is material in the context of interim results.

Disclosure in MD&A in quarterly reports is complementary to that made in the most recent annual report and in any intervening quarterly reports. Therefore, there may be cases, particularly where adequate disclosure is included in the MD&A in those earlier reports, where further disclosure in a quarterly report is not necessary. If, however, disclosure in those earlier reports does not adequately foreshadow subsequent events, or if new information that impacts known trends and uncertainties becomes apparent in a quarterly period, additional disclosure should be considered and may be required.

3. Focus on Material Trends and Uncertainties

One of the most important elements necessary to an understanding of a company's performance, and the extent to which reported financial information is indicative of future results, is the discussion and analysis of known trends, demands, commitments, events and uncertainties. Disclosure decisions concerning trends, demands, commitments, events, and uncertainties generally should involve the:

- consideration of financial, operational and other information known to the company;
- identification, based on this information, of known trends and uncertainties; and
- assessment of whether these trends and uncertainties will have, or are reasonably likely to have, a material impact on the company's liquidity, capital resources or results of operations.

As we have explained in prior guidance, disclosure of a trend, demand, commitment, event or uncertainty is required unless a company is able to conclude either that it is not reasonably likely that the trend, uncertainty or other event will occur or come to fruition, or that a material effect on the company's liquidity, capital resources or results of operations is not reasonably likely to occur.[37] (In this release we sometimes use the term "known material trends and uncertainties" to describe trends, demands, commitments, events or uncertainties as to which disclosure is required.)

In identifying known material trends and uncertainties, companies should consider the substantial amount of financial and non-financial information available to them, and whether or not the available information itself is required to be disclosed. This information, over time, may reveal a trend or general pattern in activity, a departure or isolated variance

---

[36] *See* 1989 Release, Part III.E.

[37] *See* January 2002 Release at 3748 ("two assessments management must make where a trend, demand, commitment, event or uncertainty is known: 1. Is the known trend, demand, commitment, event or uncertainty likely to come to fruition? If management determines that it is not reasonably likely to occur, no disclosure is required. 2. If management cannot make that determination, it must evaluate objectively the consequences of the known trend, demand, commitment, event or uncertainty, on the assumption that it will come to fruition. Disclosure is then required unless management determines that a material effect on the registrant's financial condition or results of operations is not reasonably likely to occur" (*citing* the 1989 Release)).

from an established trend, an uncertainty, or a reasonable likelihood of the occurrence of such an event that should be disclosed.

One of the principal objectives of MD&A is to provide information about the quality and potential variability of a company's earnings and cash flow, so that readers can ascertain the likelihood that past performance is indicative of future performance. Ascertaining this indicative value depends to a significant degree on the quality of disclosure about the facts and circumstances surrounding known material trends and uncertainties in MD&A. Quantification of the material effects of known material trends and uncertainties can promote understanding. Quantitative disclosure should be considered and may be required to the extent material if quantitative information is reasonably available.

As discussed in the 1989 Release, the disclosures required to address known material trends and uncertainties in the discussion and analysis should not be confused with optional forward-looking information. Not all forward-looking information falls within the realm of optional disclosure. In particular, material forward-looking information regarding known material trends and uncertainties is required to be disclosed as part of the required discussion of those matters and the analysis of their effects.[38] In addition, forward-looking information is required in connection with the disclosure in MD&A regarding off-balance sheet arrangements.[39]

4. Focus on Analysis

MD&A requires not only a "discussion" but also an "analysis" of known material trends, events, demands, commitments and uncertainties. MD&A should not be merely a restatement of financial statement information in a narrative form. When a description of known material trends, events, demands, commitments and uncertainties is set forth, companies should consider including, and may be required to include, an analysis explaining the underlying reasons or implications, interrelationships between constituent elements, or the relative significance of those matters.

Identifying the intermediate effects of trends, events, demands, commitments and uncertainties alone, without describing the reasons underlying these effects, may not provide sufficient insight for a reader to see the business through the eyes of management. A thorough analysis often will involve discussing both the intermediate effects of those matters and the reasons underlying those intermediate effects. For example, if a company's financial statements reflect materially lower revenues resulting from a decline in the volume of products sold when compared to a prior period, MD&A should not only identify the decline in sales volume, but also should analyze the reasons underlying the decline in sales when the reasons are also material and determinable. The analysis should reveal underlying material causes of the matters described, including for example, if applicable, difficulties in the manufacturing process, a decline in the quality of a product, loss in competitive position and market share, or a combination of conditions.

Similarly, where a company's financial statements reflect material restructuring or impairment charges, or a decline in the profitability of a plant or other business activity, MD&A should also, where material, analyze the reasons underlying these matters, such as an inability to realize previously projected economies of scale, a failure to renew or secure key customer contracts, or a failure to keep downtime at acceptable levels due to aging equipment. Whether favorable or unfavorable conditions constitute or give rise to the material trends, demands, commitments, events or uncertainties being discussed, the analysis should consist of material substantive information and present a balanced view of the underlying dynamics of the business.

---

[38] *See* 1989 Release, Part III.B.

[39] In connection with our adoption of the off-balance sheet arrangements disclosure requirements, we eliminated a portion of the instructions in Item 303 of Regulation S-K that stated that registrants were not required to provide forward-looking information. Deleting that portion of the instructions did not affect requirements to provide forward-looking information in other circumstances where required or reduce the availability of any safe harbor for forward-looking information. *See also* 2003 Off-Balance Sheet Release. *See* Securities Act Section 27A [15 U.S.C. § 77z-2], Securities Act Rule 175 [17 CFR 230.175], Exchange Act Section 21E [17 U.S.C. § 78u-5], and Exchange Act Rule 3b-6 [17 CFR 240.3b-6].

If there is a reasonable likelihood that reported financial information is not indicative of a company's future financial condition or future operating performance due, for example, to the levels of subjectivity and judgment necessary to account for highly uncertain matters and the susceptibility of such matters to change, appropriate disclosure in MD&A should be considered and may be required. For example, if a change in an estimate has a material favorable impact on earnings, the change and the underlying reasons should be disclosed so that readers do not incorrectly attribute the effect to operational improvements. In addition, if events and transactions reported in the financial statements reflect material unusual or non-recurring items, aberrations, or other significant fluctuations, companies should consider the extent of variability in earnings and cash flow, and provide disclosure where necessary for investors to ascertain the likelihood that past performance is indicative of future performance. Companies also should consider whether the economic characteristics of any of their business arrangements, or the methods used to account for them, materially impact their results of operations or liquidity in a structured or unusual fashion, where disclosure would be necessary to understand the amounts depicted in their financial statements.

IV. Liquidity and Capital Resources

Our rules require companies to provide disclosure in the related categories of liquidity and capital resources.[40] This information is critical to an assessment of a company's prospects for the future and even the likelihood of its survival.[41] A company is required to include in MD&A the following information, to the extent material:

- historical information regarding sources of cash and capital expenditures;
- an evaluation of the amounts and certainty of cash flows;
- the existence and timing of commitments for capital expenditures and other known and reasonably likely cash requirements;
- discussion and analysis of known trends and uncertainties;
- a description of expected changes in the mix and relative cost of capital resources;
- indications of which balance sheet or income or cash flow items should be considered in assessing liquidity; and
- a discussion of prospective information regarding companies' sources of and needs for capital, except where otherwise clear from the discussion.[42]

Discussion and analysis of this information should be considered and may be required to provide a clear picture of the company's ability to generate cash and to meet existing and known or reasonably likely future cash requirements.

In determining required or appropriate disclosure, companies should evaluate separately their ability to meet upcoming cash requirements over both the short and long term.[43] Merely stating that a company has adequate resources to meet its short-term and/or long-term cash requirements is insufficient unless no additional more detailed or nuanced information is material. In particular, such a statement would be insufficient if there are any known material trends or uncertainties related to cash flow, capital resources, capital requirements, or liquidity.

A. Cash Requirements

In order to identify known material cash requirements, companies should consider whether the following information would have a material impact on liquidity (discussion of immaterial matters, and especially generic disclosure or boilerplate, should be avoided):

---

[40] *See* Item 303(a)(1) and (2) of Regulation S-K [17 CFR 229.303(a)(1) and (2)].

[41] *See* January 2002 Release; 2003 Off-Balance Sheet Release.

[42] *See* 1989 Release, Part III.C. *See also* Item 303(a)(1) and (2) of Regulation S-K [17 CFR 229.303(a)(1) and (2)], and Instructions 2 and 5 thereto.

[43] Short-term liquidity is defined as a period of twelve months or less and long-term is defined as a period in excess of twelve months. *See* 1989 Release, Part III.C. Note that the period of time over which a long-term discussion of liquidity is relevant is dependent upon the timing of the cash requirements of a company, as well as the period of time over which cash flows are managed. A vague reference to periods in excess of twelve months may not be sufficient.

- funds necessary to maintain current operations, complete projects underway and achieve stated objectives or plans;
- commitments for capital or other expenditures[44]; and
- the reasonably likely exposure to future cash requirements associated with known trends or uncertainties, and an indication of the time periods in which resolution of the uncertainties is anticipated.

One starting point for a company's discussion and analysis of cash requirements is the tabular disclosure of contractual obligations,[45] supplemented with additional information that is material to an understanding of the company's cash requirements.[46]

For example, if a company has incurred debt in material amounts, it should explain the reasons for incurring that debt and the use of the proceeds, and analyze how the incurrence of that debt fits into the overall business plan, in each case to the extent material.[47] Where debt has been incurred for general working capital purposes, the anticipated amount and timing of working capital needs should be discussed, to the extent material.[48]

Companies should address, where material, the difficulties involved in assessing the effect of the amount and timing of uncertain events, such as loss contingencies, on cash requirements and liquidity. Any such discussion should be specific to the circumstances and informative, and companies should avoid generic or boilerplate disclosure. In addition, because of these difficulties and uncertainties, companies should consider whether they need to make or change disclosure in connection with quarterly as well as annual reports.

B. Sources and Uses of Cash

As with the discussion and analysis of the results of operations, a company's discussion and analysis of cash flows should not be a mere recitation of changes and other information evident to readers from the financial statements. Rather, MD&A should focus on the primary drivers of and other material factors necessary to an understanding of the company's cash flows and the indicative value of historical cash flows.

In addition to explaining how the cash requirements identified in MD&A fit into a company's overall business plan, the company should focus on the resources available to satisfy those cash requirements. Where there has been material variability in historical cash flows, MD&A should focus on the underlying reasons for the changes, as well as on their reasonably likely impact on future cash flows and cash management decisions. Even where reported amounts of cash provided and used by operations, investing activities or financing have been consistent, if the underlying sources of those cash flows have materially varied, analysis of that variability should be provided. The discussion and analysis of liquidity should focus on material changes in operating, investing and financing cash flows, as depicted in the statement of cash flows, and the reasons underlying those changes.

1. Operations

The discussion and analysis of operating cash flows should not be limited by the manner of presentation in the statement of cash flows.[49] Alternate accounting methods of deriving and presenting cash flows exist, and while they generally yield the same numeric result

---

[44] *See* Item 303(a)(2)(i) of Regulation S-K [17 CFR 229.303(a)(2)(i)].

[45] *See* Item 303(a)(5) of Regulation S-K [17 CFR 229.303(a)(5)].

[46] For example, the cash requirements for items such as interest, taxes or amounts to be funded to cover post-employment (including retirement) benefits may not be included in the tabular disclosure, but should be discussed if material.

[47] For example, debt may have been issued to fund the construction of a new plant, which will allow the company to expand its operations into a specific geo-

graphic area. Understanding that relationship and the expected commencement date of plant operations puts the cash requirement for the debt into an appropriate context to understand liquidity.

[48] Companies are reminded of their related disclosure obligations under Item 504 (Use of Proceeds) of Regulation S-K [17 CFR 229.504] and the requirement to update this disclosure in Item 701(f) (Use of Proceeds) of Regulation SK [17 CFR 229.701(f)].

[49] *See* Instruction 4 to Item 303(a) of Regulation S-K [17 CFR 229.303(a)].

in the major captions, they involve the disclosure of different types of information. When preparing the discussion and analysis of operating cash flows, companies should address material changes in the underlying drivers (*e.g.* cash receipts from the sale of goods and services and cash payments to acquire materials for manufacture or goods for resale), rather than merely describe items identified on the face of the statement of cash flows, such as the reconciling items used in the indirect method of presenting cash flows.[50]

For example, consider a company that reports an overall increase in the components of its working capital other than cash[51] with the effect of having a material decrease in net cash provided by operations in the current period. If the increase in working capital was driven principally by an increase in accounts receivable that is attributable not to an increase in sales, but rather to a revised credit policy resulting in an extended payment period for customers, these facts would need to be addressed in MD&A to the extent material, along with the resulting decrease in cash provided by operations, if not otherwise apparent. In addition, if there is a material trend or uncertainty, the impact of the new credit policy on cash flows from operations should be disclosed.[52] While a cash flow statement prepared using the indirect method would report that various individual components of working capital increased or decreased during the period by a specified amount, it would not provide a sufficient basis for a reader to analyze the change. If the company reports negative cash flows from operations, the disclosure provided in MD&A should identify clearly this condition, discuss the operational reasons for the condition if material, and explain how the company intends to meet its cash requirements and maintain operations. If the company relies on external financing in these situations, disclosure of that fact and the company's assessment of whether this financing will continue to be available, and on what terms, should be considered and may be required.

A company should consider whether, in order to make required disclosures, it is necessary to expand MD&A to address the cash requirements of and the cash provided by its reportable segments or other subdivisions of the business, including issues related to foreign subsidiaries, as well as the indicative nature of those results.[53] A company also should discuss the effect of an inability to access the cash flow and financial assets of any consolidated entities. For example, an entity may be consolidated but, because the company lacks sufficient voting interests or the assets are legally isolated, the company may be unable to utilize the entity's cash flow, cash on hand, or other assets to satisfy its own liquidity needs.

2. Financing

To the extent material, a company must provide disclosure regarding its historical financing arrangements and their importance to cash flows, including, to the extent material, information that is not included in the financial statements. A company should discuss and analyze, to the extent material:

- its external debt financing;

- its use of off-balance sheet financing arrangements;

- its issuance or purchase of derivative instruments linked to its stock;

- its use of stock as a form of liquidity; and

- the potential impact of known or reasonably likely changes in credit ratings or ratings outlook (or inability to achieve changes).

In addition to these historical items, discussion and analysis of the types of financing that are, or that are reasonably likely to be, available (or of the types of financing that a

---

[50] *See* SFAS No. 95.
[51] Working capital is defined as current assets less current liabilities. *See* Chapter 3, AICPA Accounting Research Bulletin (ARB) No. 43, *Restatement and Revision of Accounting Research Bulletins* (June 1953).
[52] To the extent that this change also materially impacts results of operations, discussion and analysis

would also be required in that section, but companies should attempt to avoid unnecessary or confusing duplication.
[53] *See* Item 303(a) of Regulation S-K [17 CFR 229.303(a)].

company would want to use but that are, or are reasonably likely to be, unavailable) and the impact on the company's cash position and liquidity, should be considered and may be required. For example, where a company has decided to raise or seeks to raise material external equity or debt financing, or if it is reasonably likely to do so in the future, discussion and analysis of the amounts or ranges involved, the nature and the terms of the financing, other features of the financing and plans, and the impact on the company's cash position and liquidity (as well as results of operations in the case of matters such as interest payments) should be considered and may be required.[54]

C. Debt Instruments, Guarantees and Related Covenants

There are at least two scenarios in which companies should consider whether discussion and analysis of material covenants related to their outstanding debt (or covenants applicable to the companies or third parties in respect of guarantees or other contingent obligations)[55] may be required.[56]

First, companies that are, or are reasonably likely to be, in breach of such covenants[57] must disclose material information about that breach and analyze the impact on the company if material. That analysis should include, as applicable and to the extent material:

- the steps that the company is taking to avoid the breach;

- the steps that the company intends to take to cure, obtain a waiver of or otherwise address the breach;

- the impact or reasonably likely impact of the breach (including the effects of any cross-default or cross-acceleration or similar provisions) on financial condition or operating performance; and

- alternate sources of funding to pay off resulting obligations or replace funding.

Second, companies should consider the impact of debt covenants on their ability to undertake additional debt or equity financing. Examples of these covenants include, but are not limited to, debt incurrence restrictions, limitations on interest payments, restrictions on dividend payments and various debt ratio limits. If these covenants limit, or are reasonably likely to limit, a company's ability to undertake financing to a material extent, the company is required to discuss the covenants in question and the consequences of the limitation to the company's financial condition and operating performance. Disclosure of alternate sources of funding and, to the extent material, the consequences (including but not limited to the cost) of accessing them should also be considered and may be required.

D. Cash Management

Companies generally have some degree of flexibility in determining when and how to use their cash resources to satisfy obligations and make other capital expenditures. MD&A should describe known material trends or uncertainties relating to such determinations. For example, a decision by a company in a highly capital-intensive business to spend significantly less on plant and equipment than it has historically may result in long-term effects that should be disclosed if material. Material effects could include more cash, less interest expense and lower depreciation, but higher future repair and maintenance expenses or a higher cost base than the company would otherwise have.

---

[54] We believe that disclosure satisfying the requirements of MD&A can be made consistently with the restrictions of Section 5 of the Securities Act. *See, e.g.,* Securities Act Rules 135c [17 CFR 230.135c].

[55] *See* FASB Interpretation No. (FIN) 45, *Guarantor's Accounting and Disclosure Requirements for Guarantees, Including Indirect Guarantees of Indebtedness of Others* (Nov. 2002); 2003 Off-Balance Sheet Release; and the discussion *infra,* regarding off-balance sheet arrangements.

[56] *See In the Matter of America West Airlines, Inc.,* Release No. 34-34047 (May 12, 1994) (finding that the company failed to discuss uncertainties regarding its ability to comply with covenants).

[57] Companies also must take a similar approach to discussion and analysis with respect to mandatory prepayment provisions, "put" rights and other similar provisions.

V. Critical Accounting Estimates

Many estimates and assumptions involved in the application of GAAP have a material impact on reported financial condition and operating performance and on the comparability of such reported information over different reporting periods. Our December 2001 Release reminded companies that, under the existing MD&A disclosure requirements, a company should address material implications of uncertainties associated with the methods, assumptions and estimates underlying the company's critical accounting measurements.[58] In May 2002 we proposed rules, which remain under consideration, that would broaden the scope of disclosures beyond those currently required.[59]

When preparing disclosure under the current requirements, companies should consider whether they have made accounting estimates or assumptions where:

- the nature of the estimates or assumptions is material due to the levels of subjectivity and judgment necessary to account for highly uncertain matters or the susceptibility of such matters to change; and

- the impact of the estimates and assumptions on financial condition or operating performance is material.

If so, companies should provide disclosure about those critical accounting estimates or assumptions in their MD&A.

Such disclosure should supplement, not duplicate, the description of accounting policies that are already disclosed in the notes to the financial statements. The disclosure should provide greater insight into the quality and variability of information regarding financial condition and operating performance. While accounting policy notes in the financial statements generally describe the method used to apply an accounting principle, the discussion in MD&A should present a company's analysis of the uncertainties involved in applying a principle at a given time or the variability that is reasonably likely to result from its application over time.

A company should address specifically why its accounting estimates or assumptions bear the risk of change. The reason may be that there is an uncertainty attached to the estimate or assumption, or it just may be difficult to measure or value. Equally important, companies should address the questions that arise once the critical accounting estimate or assumption has been identified, by analyzing, to the extent material, such factors as how they arrived at the estimate, how accurate the estimate/assumption has been in the past, how much the estimate/assumption has changed in the past, and whether the estimate/assumption is reasonably likely to change in the future. Since critical accounting estimates and assumptions are based on matters that are highly uncertain, a company should analyze their specific sensitivity to change, based on other outcomes that are reasonably likely to occur and would have a material effect. Companies should provide quantitative as well as qualitative disclosure when quantitative information is reasonably available and will provide material information for investors.

For example, if reasonably likely changes in the long-term rate of return used in accounting for a company's pension plan would have a material effect on the financial condition or operating performance of the company, the impact that could result given the range of reasonably likely outcomes should be disclosed and, because of the nature of estimates of long-term rates of return, quantified.

Amendments to the Codification of Financial Reporting Policies

The "Codification of Financial Reporting Policies" announced in Financial Reporting Release 1 (April 15, 1982) [47 FR 21028] is updated:

1. By adding to the following new sections to the Financial Reporting Codification from the release:

---

[58] December 2001 Release.   [59] *See* 2002 Critical Accounting Policies Proposal.

(III)   Overall Approach to MD&A

(IV)   Liquidity and Capital Resources

(V)   Critical Accounting Estimates

2.   By revising the footnotes from those sections of the release which contain a short form citation to include the complete citation form rather than the short form.

3.   By renumbering the footnotes from those sections of the release to run in the Financial Reporting Codification consecutively from number 1 through number 37.

The Codification is a separate publication of the Commission. It will not be published in the Code of Federal Regulations System.

List of Subjects

17. CFR Parts 211, 231 and 241

Securities.

Amendments to the Code of Federal Regulations.

For the reasons set forth above, the Commission is amending title 17, chapter II of the Code of Federal Regulations as set forth below:

PART 211—INTERPRETATIONS RELATING TO FINANCIAL REPORTING MATTERS

1. Part 211, Subpart A, is amended by adding Release No. FR-72 and the release date of December 19, 2003 to the list of interpretive releases.

PART 231—INTERPRETATIVE RELEASES RELATING TO THE SECURITIES ACT OF 1933 AND GENERAL RULES AND REGULATIONS THEREUNDER

2. Part 231 is amended by adding Release No. 33-8350 and the release date of December 19, 2003 to the list of interpretive releases.

PART 241—INTERPRETATIVE RELEASES RELATING TO THE SECURITIES EXCHANGE ACT OF 1934 AND GENERAL RULES AND REGULATIONS THEREUNDER

3. Part 241 is amended by adding Release No. 34-48960 and the release date of December 19, 2003 to the list of interpretive releases.

By the Commission.

Margaret H. McFarland

Deputy Secretary

Dated: December 19, 2003

APPENDIX 10

Proposed Rule: Disclosure in Management's Discussion and Analysis About the Application of Critical Accounting Policies

AGENCY: Securities and Exchange Commission.

ACTION: Notice of Proposed Rulemaking 17 CFR Parts 228, 229 and 249; Release Nos. 33-8098; 34-45907; International Series Release No. 1258; File No. S7-16-02; RIN 3235-AI44

SUMMARY: As an initial step in improving the transparency of companies' financial disclosure, the Commission is proposing disclosure requirements that would enhance investors' understanding of the application of companies' critical accounting policies. The proposals would encompass disclosure in two areas: accounting estimates a company makes in applying its accounting policies and the initial adoption by a company of an accounting policy that has a material impact on its financial presentation. Under the first part of the proposals, a company would have to identify the accounting estimates reflected in its financial statements that required it to make assumptions about matters that were highly uncertain at the time of estimation. Disclosure about those estimates would then be required if different estimates that the company reasonably could have used in the current period, or changes in the accounting estimate that are reasonably likely to occur from period to period, would have a material impact on the presentation of the company's financial condition, changes in financial condition or results of operations. A company's disclosure about these critical accounting estimates would include a discussion of: the methodology and assumptions underlying them; the effect the accounting estimates have on the company's financial presentation; and the effect of changes in the estimates. Under the second part of the proposals, a company that has initially adopted an accounting policy with a material impact would have to disclose information that includes: what gave rise to the initial adoption; the impact of the adoption; the accounting principle adopted and method of applying it; and the choices it had among accounting principles. Companies would place all of the new disclosure in the "Management's Discussion and Analysis of Financial Condition and Results of Operations" section (commonly referred to as "MD&A") of their annual reports, registration statements and proxy and information statements. In addition, in the MD&A section of their quarterly reports, U.S. companies would have to update the information regarding their critical accounting estimates to disclose material changes.

DATES: Comments should be received on or before July 19, 2002.

Addresses: You should send three copies of your comments to Jonathan G. Katz, Secretary, U.S. Securities and Exchange Commission, 450 Fifth Street, NW, Washington, DC, 20549-0609. You also may submit your comments electronically to the following address: rule-com-ments@sec.gov. All comment letters should refer to File No. S7-16-02; this file number should be included in the subject line if you use electronic mail. Comment letters will be available for public inspection and copying at the Commission's Public Reference Room, 450 Fifth Street, NW, Washington, DC 20549-0102. We will post electronically-submitted comment letters on the Commission's Internet Web site (http://www.sec.gov). We do not edit personal identifying information, such as names or electronic mail addresses, from electronic submissions. Submit only information you wish to make publicly available.

FOR FURTHER INFORMATION CONTACT: Questions about this release should be referred to Anita Klein or Andrew Thorpe, Division of Corporation Finance (202-942-2980) or Jackson Day or Jenifer Minke-Girard, Office of the Chief Accountant (202-942-4400), Securities and Exchange Commission, 450 Fifth Street, NW, Washington, DC 20549.

SUPPLEMENTARY INFORMATION: We are proposing amendments to Item 303[1] of Regulation S-K,[2] Item 303[3] of Regulation S-B[4] and Item 5 of Form 20-F[5] under the Securities Exchange Act of 1934[6] ("Exchange Act").

Table of Contents

---

[1] 17 CFR 229.303.
[2] 17 CFR 229.10 *et seq.*
[3] 17 CFR 228.303.

[4] 17 CFR 228.10 *et seq.*
[5] 17 CFR 249.308b.
[6] 15 U.S.C. § 78a *et seq.*

VI.   Cost-Benefit Analysis

VII.   Effects On Efficiency, Competition and Capital Formation

VIII.   Initial Regulatory Flexibility Analysis

IX.   Small Business Regulatory Enforcement Fairness Act

X.   Codification Update

Statutory Bases and Text of Proposed Amendments

I. Executive Summary

One important challenge facing our capital markets today is the need to improve the quality and transparency of corporate disclosure. Our capital markets could reach a higher level of efficiency and investor confidence if companies were to provide higher-quality, more insightful financial information. To serve that purpose, we issued cautionary advice in December 2001 regarding MD&A disclosure.[7] In that release, we recognized the need for disclosure that allows investors to understand more completely the manner in which, and degree to which, a company's reported operating results, financial condition and changes in financial condition depend on estimates involved in applying accounting policies that entail uncertainties and subjectivity. We also asked companies to begin better addressing investors' need for this disclosure.

As contemplated in that release, we are now proposing to amend the MD&A requirements[8] to mandate improved disclosure in a new "Application of Critical Accounting Policies" section in companies' filed annual reports, annual reports to shareholders, registration statements and proxy and information statements.[9] The new section would encompass disclosure both about accounting estimates resulting from the application of critical accounting policies and the initial adoption of accounting policies that have a material impact on a company's financial presentation. The proposed disclosure requirements would apply to all companies except small business issuers that have not had revenues from operations during the last two fiscal years. The proposed MD&A disclosure requirements would cover the most recent fiscal year and any subsequent interim period for which financial statements are required to be presented.

To determine whether an accounting estimate[10] involved in applying the company's accounting policies would entail disclosure under the proposals, a company would have to answer two questions:

---

[7] *See* Securities Act Release No. 8040, FR-60 (Dec. 12, 2001) [66 FR 65013]. *See also* Securities Act Release No. 8056, FR-61 (Jan. 22, 2002) [67 FR 3746]. In addition, we recently announced our intention to propose other changes in disclosure rules to improve the financial reporting and disclosure system. *See* SEC Press Release No. 2002-22 (Feb. 13, 2002).

[8] We propose to amend Item 303 of Regulation S-K, and the parallel provisions in Regulation S-B (which applies to small business issuers) and Form 20-F (which applies to foreign private issuers).

[9] The proposals would not alter which documents require presentation of an MD&A. MD&A disclosure is only required in proxy and information statements themselves if action is to be taken with respect to: (1) the modification of any class of securities of the registrant; (2) the issuance or authorization for issuance of securities of the registrant; or (3) mergers, consolidations, acquisitions and similar matters. *See* Items 11, 12 and 14 of Schedule 14A, 17 CFR 240.14a-101. Investors otherwise receive the MD&A disclosure in the annual report to shareholders that must accompany

or precede any proxy or information statement relating to an annual meeting at which directors are to be elected. *See* 17 CFR 240.14a-3.

[10] An accounting estimate is an approximation made by management of a financial statement element, item or account in the financial statements. Accounting estimates in historical financial statements measure the effects of past business transactions or events, or the present status of an asset or liability. *See Codification of Statements on Auditing Standards* (including related Auditing Interpretations) ("AU") § 342, *Auditing Accounting Estimates* ("AU § 342"), paragraphs 1-3. For purposes of the proposals, an accounting estimate would include one for which a change in the estimate is inseparable from the effect of a change in accounting principle. *See* Accounting Principles Board ("APB") Opinion No. 20, *Accounting Changes* (July 1971) ("APB No. 20"), paragraph 11. See also proposed Item 303(b)(3)(ii)(A) of Regulation S-B, 17 CFR 228.303(b)(3)(ii)(A); proposed Item 303(c)(2)(i) of Regulation S-K, 17 CFR 229.303(c)(2)(i); and proposed Item 5.E.2.(a) of Form 20-F, 17 CFR 249.220f.

(1) Did the accounting estimate require us to make assumptions about matters that were highly uncertain at the time the accounting estimate was made?

(2) Would different estimates that we reasonably could have used in the current period, or changes in the accounting estimate that are reasonably likely to occur from period to period, have a material impact on the presentation of our financial condition, changes in financial condition or results of operations?

If the answers to both questions are "yes," the accounting estimate would be a "critical accounting estimate," and disclosure would be required in the new "Application of Critical Accounting Policies" section.

The proposed disclosure about these accounting estimates would involve three basic elements.[11] The first element would be the basic disclosures needed to understand the accounting estimates. A company would have to describe them, identify where and how they affect the company's reported financial results, financial condition and changes in financial condition, and, where material, identify the affected line items. It would have to describe the methodology underlying each critical accounting estimate, the assumptions that are about highly uncertain matters and other assumptions that are material. If applicable, a company would have to discuss why it could have chosen in the current period estimates that would have had a materially different impact on the company's financial presentation. Similarly, a company would have to discuss, if applicable, why the accounting estimate is reasonably likely to change in future periods with a material impact on the company's financial presentation.[12]

A company would have to identify the segments[13] of its business that a critical accounting estimate affects. A company also would have to provide appropriate parts of the proposed disclosure for affected segments where a failure to present that information would result in an omission that renders the disclosure materially misleading.

The second element of the proposed disclosure about critical accounting estimates would give investors a better understanding of the sensitivity of the reported operating results and financial condition to changes in those estimates or their underlying assumption(s). For each critical accounting estimate, a company would discuss changes that would result either from: (i) making reasonably possible, near-term changes in the most material assumption(s) underlying the estimate; or (ii) using in place of the recorded estimate the ends of the range of reasonably possible amounts which the company likely determined when formulating its recorded estimate. The company would describe the impact of those changes on the company's overall financial performance and, to the extent material, on the line items in the company's financial statements. In addition, the proposals would require a quantitative and qualitative discussion of management's history of changing its critical accounting estimates in recent years.

The third element of the proposed disclosure about critical accounting estimates would require a company to state whether or not senior management discussed the development, selection and disclosure of those estimates with the company's audit committee. This part of the proposals is designed to inform investors about whether there is oversight of critical accounting estimates by audit committee members and may incidentally encourage such oversight and increase reliability of the proposed MD&A disclosure about critical accounting estimates.

Our proposals also address MD&A disclosure regarding initial adoption of an accounting policy. If an accounting policy initially adopted by a company had a material impact on

---

[11] In the MD&A section of quarterly reports, U.S. companies would have to update their critical accounting estimates disclosure to reflect material changes.

[12] The statutory and Commission rule safe harbors for forward-looking statements would be available to companies satisfying their terms and conditions in making forward-looking statements in connection with the proposed critical accounting estimates discussion. *See* Securities Act Section 27A, 15 U.S.C. § 77z-2, Securities Act Rule 175, 17 CFR 230.175, Exchange Act Section 21E, 15 U.S.C. § 78u-5, and Exchange Act Rule 3b-6, 17 CFR 240.3b-6.

[13] A segment for financial reporting purposes is defined by Financial Accounting Standards Board ("FASB") Statement of Financial Accounting Standards ("SFAS") No. 131, *Disclosures about Segments of an Enterprise and Related Information* (June 1997) ("SFAS No. 131").

the company's financial presentation, the company would provide certain disclosures about that initial adoption unless it resulted solely from new accounting literature issued by a recognized accounting standard setter. The initial adoption of an accounting policy may occur in situations such as when events or transactions affecting the company occur for the first time, or were previously immaterial in their effect but become material, or events or transactions occur that are clearly different in substance from previous ones.

The proposed MD&A disclosure about the initial adoption of accounting policies seeks more qualitative information from companies about those types of situations. The disclosures we are proposing would include a description of:

- The events or transactions that gave rise to the initial adoption;

- The accounting principle adopted and the method of applying that principle; and

- The impact, discussed qualitatively, on the company's financial presentation.

In addition, if upon initial adoption the company had a choice between acceptable accounting principles under generally accepted accounting principles (GAAP), the company would disclose that it made a choice, explain the alternatives and state why it made the choice that it did.

Further, if no accounting literature governed the accounting upon initial adoption, the company would have to explain which accounting principle and method of application it decided to use and how it made its decision.

All of the proposed MD&A disclosure regarding the application of critical accounting policies would have to be presented in language and a format that is clear, concise and understandable to the average investor. Boilerplate disclosures, or disclosures written in overly technical accounting terminology, would not satisfy the proposed requirements.

Our proposals do not attempt to address all circumstances where a company may exercise discretion in its accounting under GAAP. We focus our proposals on two areas involving the application of critical accounting policies in which there is a clear need for improved disclosure—critical accounting estimates and the initial adoption of accounting policies that have a material impact. As discussed below, disclosure in many other areas of accounting judgment is provided by existing MD&A requirements, materiality standards and financial statement disclosure requirements.

II. Background

A. Current MD&A Disclosure

For decades, the regulations governing disclosure in registration statements under the Securities Act of 1933 ("Securities Act") and the Exchange Act, as well as annual and quarterly reports and proxy and information statements by public companies under the Exchange Act, have mandated MD&A disclosure.[14] MD&A disclosure should satisfy three related objectives:

(1) to provide a narrative explanation of companies' financial statements that enables investors to see the company through the eyes of management;

(2) to improve overall financial disclosure and provide the context within which financial statements should be analyzed; and

(3) to provide information about the quality of, and potential variability of, a company's earnings and cash flow, so that investors can ascertain the likelihood that past performance is indicative of future performance.[15]

---

[14] See Item 303 of Regulation S-K, 17 CFR 229.303, Item 303 of Regulation S-B, 17 CFR 228.303 and Item 5 of Form 20-F, referenced in 17 CFR 249.220f. Although the current MD&A disclosure requirements were adopted starting in 1980, earlier versions date back to 1968. See Securities Act Release Nos. 6231 (Sept. 2, 1980) [45 FR 63630] and 4936 (Dec. 9, 1968) [33 FR 18617]. See also Securities Act Release No. 5520 (Aug. 14, 1974) [39 FR 31894].

[15] See Securities Act Release No. 6711 (Apr. 23, 1987) [52 FR 13715], Section II.

In MD&A, a company must discuss its results of operations, liquidity and capital resources and other information necessary to an understanding of the company's financial condition or changes in financial condition. A well-prepared MD&A discussion focuses on explaining a company's financial results and condition by identifying key elements of the business model and the drivers and dynamics of the business, and also addressing key variables. A company currently must disclose known trends, demands, commitments, events and uncertainties that are reasonably likely to occur and have material effects.[16]

In addition to these general subjects, a company must include in MD&A historical and prospective analysis of its financial statements, and identify the cause of material changes from prior periods in the line items of the financial statements where those changes are reflected. A company must analyze significant components of revenues or expenses needed to understand the results of operations. It also must discuss significant or unusual economic events or transactions that materially affected results of operations. Finally, a company also must discuss its ability to generate adequate amounts of cash to meet its short-term and long-term needs for capital and identify the anticipated sources of funds necessary to fulfill its commitments.

These requirements do not call for, and indeed we have discouraged and continue to discourage companies from providing, rote calculations of percentage changes in figures in the financial statements combined with boilerplate recitations of a surfeit of inadequately differentiated material and immaterial factors related to such changes. Rather, companies should emphasize material factors and their underlying reasons and preferably omit, or at least differentiate, immaterial information.

Recognizing the paramount importance of MD&A information to investors, in addition to today's proposal, we intend to continue to focus on improving disclosure in this area. In particular, we are considering MD&A proposals that will focus discussion on the three key objectives of MD&A noted above. We are considering a more explicit requirement for a summary of the MD&A section that would, in relatively short form, identify what management considers the most important factors in determining its financial results and condition, including the principal factors driving them, the principal trends on which management focuses and the principal risks to the business. We also are considering how to adjust the relative attention devoted in MD&A towards a more general discussion of material matters and away from a detailed description of business results that too often recites information that is otherwise available or is not material to investors.

In addition, we are continuing our consideration of subjects as to which we believe MD&A disclosure is particularly important, including the topics discussed in our January 22, 2002 release regarding MD&A.[17] For example, investors have become increasingly concerned about the sufficiency of disclosure regarding structured finance transactions, including those consummated using special purpose entities. A company's relationships with those types of entities may facilitate its transfer of, or access to, assets. Investors need to know more about the liquidity risk, market price risks and effects of "off-balance sheet" transaction structures and obligations. Another item of concern is a lack of transparent disclosure about transactions where that information appeared necessary to understand how significant aspects of the business were conducted. Investors would better understand financial statements in many circumstances if MD&A included descriptions of all material transactions involving related persons or entities, with a clear discussion of terms that differ from those which would likely be negotiated with clearly independent

---

[16] In assessing whether disclosure of a trend, event, etc. is required, management must consider both whether it is reasonably likely to occur and whether a material effect is reasonably likely to occur. As the Commission noted when it adopted the requirement, the "reasonably likely to occur" test is to be used rather than the *Basic v. Levinson* probability and magnitude test for materiality of contingent events. *See* Securities Act Release No. 6835 (May 18, 1989) [54 FR 22427] at fns. 27-28 and accompanying text.

[17] Securities Act Release No. 8056; FR-61 (Jan. 22, 2002) [67 FR 3746].

parties. Investors should understand these transactions' business purpose and economic substance, their effects on the financial statements, and any special risks or contingencies arising from them.

Finally, we are considering improvements to MD&A disclosures relating to trend information. We believe that investors may be better able to see the company through management's eyes if MD&A includes information about the trends that a company's management follows and evaluates in making decisions about how to guide the company's business. As with today's proposal, that disclosure would naturally entail a certain degree of forward-looking information.

B. Current Disclosure in Financial Statements about Accounting Estimates

Currently, GAAP and generally accepted auditing standards acknowledge that there are numerous circumstances in which companies, in applying accounting policies, exercise judgment and make estimates for purposes of the financial statements. For example, they call for companies to communicate in a number of circumstances about the use of estimates in the preparation of financial information. The use of estimates results in the presentation of many amounts that are in fact approximate rather than exact.[18] For example, APB No. 20 notes that "changes in estimates used in accounting are necessary consequences of periodic presentation of financial statements" because preparing financial statements requires estimating the effects of future events, and future events and their effects cannot be perceived with certainty.[19] Estimating the impact of those events therefore requires the exercise of judgment. Because the preparation of financial statements requires estimates that are likely to change over time, APB No. 20 requires disclosure about changes in estimates that are expected to affect several future reporting periods and that are not made each period in the ordinary course of accounting. It recommends disclosure if the effects of other changes in the estimate are material.[20]

In addition, AICPA Statement of Position No. 94-6[21] requires general disclosure in notes to financial statements that the preparation of financial statements requires the use of estimates in the determination of the carrying amounts of assets or liabilities, including gain or loss contingencies.[22] That Statement also requires note disclosure regarding those specific estimates when known information indicates that it is at least reasonably possible[23] that the estimate will change in the near term and the effect would be material to the financial statements.[24] A company must disclose the nature of the uncertainty, in addition to stating that a change in the estimate in the near term is at least reasonably possible. SOP 94-6, encourages, but does not require, disclosure of the factors that cause an estimate to be susceptible to change from period to period.[25]

SOP 94-6 references SFAS No. 5, which itself requires certain disclosures about accounting estimates—specifically, estimated losses that arise from loss contingencies. A company

---

[18] *See* American Institute of Certified Public Accountants ("AICPA") Statement of Position ("SOP") No. 94-6, *Disclosure of Certain Significant Risks and Uncertainties* (Dec. 1994), ("SOP 94-6"), paragraph B-20; *See also* AU § 380, *Communication with Audit Committees* ("AU § 380") and AU § 508, *Reports on Audited Financial Statements* (Apr. 1998).

[19] *See* APB No. 20, paragraph 10.

[20] *See* APB No. 20, paragraph 33.

[21] *See* SOP 94-6, particularly paragraphs 11-19.

[22] *See* FASB SFAS No. 5, Accounting for Contingencies (Mar. 1975) ("SFAS No. 5"), paragraph 1, which defines a contingency as "an existing condition, situation, or set of circumstances involving uncertainty as to possible gain . . . or loss . . . to an enterprise that will ultimately be resolved when one or more future events occur or fail to occur. Resolution of the uncertainty may confirm the acquisition of an asset or the

reduction of a liability or the loss or impairment of an asset or the incurrence of a liability."

[23] The term "reasonably possible" as used in SOP 94-6 is consistent with its use in SFAS No. 5. *See* SOP 94-6, fn. 7. SFAS No. 5 states that "reasonably possible" means the chance of a future transaction or event occurring is more than remote but less than likely. Reasonably possible events are less likely to occur than probable events.

[24] SOP 94-6, paragraph 17, notes: "Whether the estimate meets the criteria for disclosure under this SOP does not depend on the amount that has been reported in the financial statements, but rather on the materiality of the effect that using a different estimate would have had on the financial statements. Simply because an estimate resulted in the recognition of a small financial statement amount, or no amount, does not mean that disclosure is not required under this SOP."

[25] *See* SOP 94-6, paragraph 14.

is required to accrue (by a charge to income) an estimated loss from a loss contingency if certain criteria are met.[26] If an estimated loss does not meet the criteria for accrual, but there is at least a reasonable possibility that a loss may have been incurred, the company is required to disclose the nature of the contingency and an estimate of the possible loss or range of loss, or state that an estimate of the loss cannot be made. Although SFAS No. 5 elicits useful disclosure about certain accounting estimates, not all uncertainties inherent in the accounting process give rise to loss contingencies as that term is used in SFAS No. 5, and therefore that Statement does not apply to all estimates in the financial statements.[27]

Further, while not specifically requiring disclosure about estimates, APB Opinion No. 22 requires disclosure about the application of accounting policies which may entail generalized disclosure about estimation techniques.[28] APB No. 22 notes that a company's accounting principles, and their method of application, can affect significantly the presentation of its financial position, results of operations and cash flows,[29] and accordingly, requires disclosure that describes those accounting principles and the company's methods of applying them.[30] In particular, APB No. 22 indicates that a company should provide disclosure when:

- unusual or innovative applications of accounting principles materially affect the determination of financial position, results of operations or cash flows (such as the recognition of revenue);
- a selection is made among alternative permissible policies; or
- policies are unique to the industry of the reporting company.[31]

Under APB No. 22, a company's disclosure also should encompass important judgments as to appropriateness of principles relating to revenue recognition and allocation of asset costs to current and future periods. Although the particular format or location of these APB No. 22 disclosures in financial statements is not prescribed by GAAP, a summary of these significant accounting policies is customarily the first note to the financial statements.

Finally, some accounting standards currently prescribe specific disclosures about accounting estimates or the underlying methodologies and assumptions.[32] For example, Statement of Financial Accounting Standards No. 132 requires specific disclosures of the assumptions used in accounting for pensions and other post-retirement benefits.[33] Statement of Financial Accounting Standards No. 140 requires disclosure regarding the measurement of retained interests in securitized financial assets, including the methodology, assumptions and sensitivity of the assumptions used in determining their fair value.[34]

---

[26] See SFAS No. 5, paragraph 8. An estimated loss should be accrued when both it is probable that an asset has been impaired or a liability has been incurred and the amount of the loss can be reasonably estimated. Also, when it is probable that an asset has been impaired or a liability has been incurred and the reasonable estimate of the loss is a range, the company is required to accrue an amount for the loss. See FASB Interpretation No. 14, *Reasonable Estimation of the Amount of a Loss* (Sept. 1976), paragraph 3.

[27] See SFAS No.5, paragraph 2.

[28] See APB Opinion No. 22, *Disclosure of Accounting Policies* (Apr. 1972) ("APB No. 22").

[29] See APB No. 22, paragraphs 6-7. APB No. 22 defines accounting policies of a reporting entity as "the specific accounting principles and the methods of applying those principles that are judged by the management of the entity to be the most appropriate in the circumstances to present fairly financial position, results of operations, and cash flows in accordance with generally accepted accounting principles. . . ." APB No. 22, paragraph 6, as amended.

[30] See APB No. 22, paragraph 12.

[31] Id.

[32] In addition to the examples cited in the paragraph, see the disclosure requirements in FASB SFAS No. 107, *Disclosures about Fair Value of Financial Instruments* (Dec. 1991); FASB SFAS No. 123, *Accounting for Stock-Based Compensation* (Oct. 1995) ("SFAS No. 123"); and FASB SFAS No. 144, *Accounting for the Impairment or Disposal of Long-Lived Assets* (Aug. 2001) ("SFAS No. 144").

[33] See FASB SFAS No. 132, *Employers' Disclosures about Pensions and Other Postretirement Benefits* (Feb. 1998).

[34] See FASB SFAS No. 140, *Accounting for Transfers and Servicing of Financial Assets and Extinguishments of Liabilities* (a replacement of FASB Statement No. 125) (Sept. 2000).

C. Current Disclosure in Financial Statements about Initial Adoption of Accounting Policies

Certain general requirements under GAAP may elicit information about the initial adoption of an accounting policy by a company. When companies present comparative financial statements, any exceptions to comparability between the most recent period and prior periods must be clearly presented.[35] In addition, if a company initially adopts an accounting policy and considers that policy to be a significant accounting policy, the company would provide certain disclosures about that policy as required by APB No. 22.[36]

APB No. 20 provides financial statement disclosure requirements for accounting changes, which include changes in an accounting principle, an accounting estimate and the reporting entity.[37] Neither "(a) the initial adoption of an accounting principle in recognition of events or transactions occurring for the first time or that previously were immaterial in their effect nor (b) adoption or modification of an accounting principle necessitated by transactions or events that are clearly different in substance from those previously occurring" are considered, however, to be "accounting changes" under GAAP.[38] As discussed below, our proposals about initial adoption of accounting policies address these circumstances that are not accounting changes under GAAP if they have a material impact on a company's financial presentation.

III. PROPOSED RULES

A. Objectives of the Current Proposals

Our proposals would promote greater investor understanding of a company's important accounting estimates that reflect significant management judgment and uncertainty, and of a company's initial adoption of accounting policies that may reflect such judgment and uncertainty. Our primary objectives are:

- to enhance investors' understanding of the existence of, and necessity for, estimation in a company's financial statements;

- to focus investors on the important estimates that are particularly difficult for management to determine and where management therefore exercises significant judgment;

- to give investors an understanding of the impact those estimates have on the presentation of a company's financial condition, changes in financial condition or results of operations;

- to give investors an appreciation for how sensitive those estimates are; and

- to give investors an understanding of new material accounting policies as they arise and affect a company's financial results.

Our aim is to increase the transparency of the application of those accounting policies where management is the most prone to use judgment, generally because objective data and methodologies do not exist for the estimates or management is given initial policy choices under GAAP. We believe that it is these accounting policies that are least understood by investors and that mandated disclosure regarding areas of the application of them would provide meaningful insight into the importance of estimates and adoption of policies to a company's financial presentation. With a greater understanding of the application of critical accounting policies, we believe that investors would be in a better position to assess the quality of, and potential variability of, a company's earnings.

We propose to mandate enhanced disclosure of critical accounting estimates and initial adoption of material policies by specifically linking them to the objectives of MD&A,

---

[35] *See* Accounting Research Bulletin (ARB) No. 43, *Restatement and Revision of Accounting Research Bulletins* (June 1953), Chapter 2, "Form of Statements," Section A, "Comparative Financial Statements," paragraph 3, and paragraph 2 ("the well recognized principle that any change in practice which affects comparability should be disclosed").

[36] *See* APB No. 22, paragraph 12.

[37] *See* APB No. 20, paragraph 6.

[38] *See* APB No. 20, paragraph 8.

and the type of disclosure presented in MD&A. A focused discussion of these areas is well-suited to MD&A because it would further explain to investors the company's financial condition "through management's eyes." Moreover, MD&A's emphasis on disclosure of significant uncertainties and favorable or unfavorable trends naturally dovetails with disclosure of the more subjective aspects used in arriving at critical accounting estimates or selecting which accounting policies to adopt initially. Finally, as we have noted previously, the less technical language customarily used outside the financial statements may be conducive to a clearer explanation to investors of the effects of estimates, assumptions, methodologies and initial accounting policy adoption on a company's financial reporting.[39]

B. Scope of the Proposals

Our proposals address estimates that a company makes in preparing financial statements using accounting policies under GAAP and the initial adoption by a company of an accounting policy under GAAP that has a material impact on its financial presentation.[40] We believe the proposals address directly and clearly two areas where there is a need for improved disclosure. While certain elements of our proposed critical accounting estimates disclosure are subsumed in existing general MD&A requirements, we believe more direct and complete requirements in our rules would lead to improved disclosure. In addition, while there are financial statement disclosure requirements that would elicit certain information about initially adopted accounting policies in some cases, our proposals are designed to provide additional MD&A disclosure that would assist investors to understand better a company's new accounting policies.

We are leaving disclosure about other circumstances where a company may exercise discretion over its accounting under GAAP to existing MD&A disclosure requirements, materiality standards and existing financial statement disclosure requirements. Our proposals do not, for example, alter disclosure requirements regarding a company's change from an accounting policy it has been using to another policy acceptable under GAAP.[41] The proposals also do not require disclosure of a company's adoption of a new accounting pronouncement where the company must make its best judgment as to how to apply the new accounting pronouncement in the absence of interpretive guidance.

Discipline surrounding a company's changes in accounting policies is provided under GAAP and the federal securities laws. When a company changes an accounting policy, the company must determine that the alternative principle is preferable under the circumstances.[42] We require that the company file a letter from its independent public accountant confirming its opinion to that effect.[43] In addition, a company is required to make certain disclosures in the financial statements about the accounting change, including the nature and justification for the change and its effect on income when the change is made.[44] In its justification for the change, the company is required to explain clearly why the newly adopted accounting principle is preferable.[45]

---

[39] *See* Securities Act Release No. 7793 (Jan. 21, 2000) [65 FR 4585] (suggesting that additions to financial disclosure outside the financial statements could help address concerns relating to lack of transparency in some aspects of financial reporting within the financial statements).

[40] These could include estimates made on a one-time basis, on a few occasions, or on a recurring basis.

[41] When a company has selected an accounting policy from acceptable alternatives, it is required under GAAP to make certain disclosures about that accounting policy. See APB No. 22, paragraph 12. *See supra* fns. 28-31 and accompanying text.

U.S. GAAP provides only a limited number of situations in which more than one method of accounting would be considered acceptable. Over the years, the combined efforts of accounting standard setters, the accounting profession, public and non-public companies, and regulatory agencies have significantly reduced the number of acceptable alternatives in U.S. GAAP.

See APB No. 22, paragraph 5. Areas remaining in U.S. GAAP in which there are acceptable alternatives include inventory pricing and depreciation methods. *See* APB No. 20, paragraph 9. *See also* SFAS No. 123 (providing a choice of accounting methods for an employee stock option or similar equity instrument).

[42] *See* APB No. 20, paragraph 16.

[43] *See* Accounting Series Release No. 177 (Sept. 10, 1975) [40 FR 46107], as codified in the Codification of Financial Reporting Policies § 304.02, *Preferability Letters*, Fed. Sec. L. Rep. (CCH) 73,096. *See also* Item 601(b)(18) of Regulations S-K and S-B, 17 CFR 229.601(b)(18) and 17 CFR 228.601(b)(18). A preferability letter generally is not required when a company adopts a new accounting policy as a result of implementing a new accounting pronouncement or rule issued by the FASB, AICPA or SEC.

[44] *See* APB No. 20, paragraphs 17-30.

[45] *Id.*

In addition to the existing disclosure requirements in the financial statements, scrutiny over management's discretion and judgment in applying accounting policies occurs on a number of different levels. Auditors are required to inform audit committees about management's "initial selection of and changes in significant accounting policies or their application" and about management's judgments and estimates.[46] We have encouraged companies, management, audit committees and auditors to consult with our accounting staff if they are uncertain about the application of GAAP.[47] We also have committed to provide assistance to companies in a timely fashion to address problems before they happen.

We recognize that the circumstances where a company may exercise discretion over its accounting policies under GAAP could yield significantly different financial results. Given the existing disclosure regime, we are not currently proposing additional MD&A disclosure to address all of these cases. Companies should provide complete, transparent disclosure under the applicable requirements. While we believe the proposed disclosure may be sufficient to achieve our currently stated objective, we may revisit the other circumstances where a company may exercise discretion over its accounting policies under GAAP at a later date.

We solicit comment with regard to broadening the scope of our proposals to achieve a more expansive objective.

- Should we require additional MD&A disclosure specifically regarding the effects of a change by a company from one accounting policy to another acceptable (and preferable) accounting policy under GAAP?

- Should we require in MD&A a discussion of the impact that alternative accounting policies acceptable under GAAP would have had on a company's financial statements even when a company did not choose to apply the alternatives?

- What costs would companies incur if they had to prepare disclosure about the effects of alternative accounting policies that could have been chosen but were not?

- Beyond a company's initial adoption of those policies, should we require disclosure in MD&A regarding a company's reasons for choosing, and the effects of applying, accounting policies used for unusual or innovative transactions or in emerging areas? Similarly, should we require companies to disclose in MD&A the effects of accounting policies that a company could have adopted, but did not adopt, for unusual or innovative transactions or in emerging areas?

- Should we require more disclosure by companies about their process of making estimates, or in other areas of discretion relating to recognition and measurement in financial statements? If so, please describe in detail.

- Should we require in MD&A a discussion of the impact of a company's choice among accounting methods under GAAP that are used in the company's industry (for example, the completed contract and the percentage of completion methods of accounting for construction-type contracts[48])? Should we require that type of disclosure only where a company uses a method under GAAP that is not generally used by other companies in the industry?

C. Proposed Disclosure about Critical Accounting Estimates

To inform investors of each critical accounting estimate and to place it in the context of the company's financial presentation, we would require the following information in the MD&A section:[49]

---

[46] *See* AU § 380, paragraphs 7 and 8.

[47] *See, e.g.,* Securities Act Release No. 8040, FR-60 (Dec. 12, 2001).

[48] *See* SOP No. 81-1, *Accounting for Performance of Construction-Type and Certain Production-Type Contracts* (July 1981).

[49] In addition to the information specifically required, a company would be required to provide any other information necessary to keep its disclosure from being materially misleading. *See* Securities Act Rule 408, 17 CFR 230.408, and Exchange Act Rule 12b-20, 17 CFR 240.12b-20.

- A discussion that identifies and describes:
  - ○ the critical accounting estimate;
  - ○ the methodology used in determining the critical accounting estimate;
  - ○ any underlying assumption that is about highly uncertain matters and any other underlying assumption that is material;
  - ○ any known trends, demands, commitments, events or uncertainties that are reasonably likely to occur and materially affect the methodology or the assumptions described;
  - ○ if applicable, why different estimates that would have had a material impact on the company's financial presentation could have been used in the current period; and
  - ○ if applicable, why the accounting estimate is reasonably likely to change from period to period with a material impact on the financial presentation;

- An explanation of the significance of the accounting estimate to the company's financial condition, changes in financial condition and results of operations and, where material, an identification of the line items in the company's financial statements affected by the accounting estimate;

- A quantitative discussion of changes in overall financial performance and, to the extent material, line items in the financial statements if the company were to assume that the accounting estimate were changed, either by using reasonably possible near-term changes in the most material assumption(s) underlying the accounting estimate or by using the reasonably possible range of the accounting estimate[50];

- A quantitative and qualitative discussion of any material changes made to the accounting estimate in the past three years, the reasons for the changes, and the effect on line items in the financial statements and overall financial performance[51];

- A statement of whether or not the company's senior management has discussed the development and selection of the accounting estimate, and the MD&A disclosure regarding it, with the audit committee of the company's board of directors;

- If the company operates in more than one segment, an identification of the segments of the company's business the accounting estimate affects; and

- A discussion of the accounting estimate on a segment basis, to the extent that a failure to present that information would result in an omission that renders the disclosure materially misleading.

Unless otherwise stated, the discussion would cover the financial statements for the most recent fiscal year and any subsequent period for which interim period financial statements are required to be included.[52]

1. Accounting estimates covered under the proposals

A number of circumstances can require a company to make accounting estimates. For example, a company typically will estimate the net realizable value of its accounts receivable and of its inventory.[53] Not all accounting estimates in a company's financial statements,

---

[50] If those changes could have a material effect on the company's liquidity or capital resources, then the company also would have to explain that effect.

[51] As described below, we would phase in the three-year period and use two years for small business issuers.

[52] The proposed rules would apply equally to business development companies. Business development companies are defined in Section 2(a)(48) of the Investment Company Act of 1940. *See* 15 USC § 80a-2(a)(48). Business development companies are a category of closed-end investment companies that are not required to register under the Investment Company

Act, but file Forms 10-K and 10-Q, and also include MD&A in their annual reports to shareholders.

[53] Other examples of accounting estimates include: property and casualty insurance loss reserves, current obligations that will be fulfilled over several years, future returns of products sold, the amount of cash flows expected to be generated by a specific group of assets, revenues from contracts accounted for by the percentage of completion method and pension and warranty expenses. *See* AU § 342, paragraph 2. For a more detailed list, *see* the Appendix to AU § 342.

however, will necessarily be critical accounting estimates to which the proposed disclosure relates. An accounting estimate would be a critical accounting estimate for purposes of the proposed disclosure only if it meets two criteria. First, the accounting estimate must require a company to make assumptions about matters that are highly uncertain at the time the accounting estimate is made. Second, it must be the case that different estimates that the company reasonably could have used for the accounting estimate in the current period, or changes in the accounting estimate that are reasonably likely to occur from period to period, would have a material impact on the presentation of the company's financial condition, changes in financial condition or results of operations.[54]

For purposes of the first criterion, a matter involves a high degree of uncertainty if it is dependent on events remote in time that may or may not occur, or it is not capable of being readily calculated from generally accepted methodologies or derived with some degree of precision from available data. Accordingly, a matter that is highly uncertain requires management to use significant judgment in making assumptions about that matter. The application of management's judgment in those circumstances typically results in management developing a range within which it believes the accounting estimate should fall.

The second criterion focuses the proposals further on two types of accounting estimates involved in the application of accounting policies. First, it includes accounting estimates for which a company in the current period could reasonably have recorded in the financial statements an amount sufficiently different such that it would have had a material impact on the company's financial presentation. Second, it includes any accounting estimate that is reasonably likely to change from period to period to the extent that the change would have a material impact on the company's financial presentation. Thus, whether management's judgment has an impact primarily in the current period or on an ongoing basis (or both), the estimate would qualify.

Under the proposals, a company would discuss any accounting estimate that it determines to be critical. We believe that few of a company's accounting estimates generally would meet those thresholds. We do not currently propose an outside limit to the number of accounting estimates that a company must discuss under the proposals. As the term "critical accounting estimate" implies, however, the disclosure should not encompass a long list of accounting estimates resulting from the application of accounting policies which cover a substantial number of line items in the company's financial statements.[55] While the number of critical accounting estimates will vary by company, we would expect a very few companies to have none at all and the vast majority of companies to have somewhere in the range of three to five critical accounting estimates. The number could be at the high end of the range, or be slightly higher, for companies that conclude that one or more critical accounting estimates must be identified and discussed primarily because of particular segments. Investors, however, will not benefit from a lengthy discussion of a multitude of accounting estimates in which the truly critical ones are obscured. If we adopt the proposals without a maximum number, we may monitor disclosure to determine whether disclosure would be improved if a maximum number were set.

We seek comment on the proposed definition of critical accounting estimates.

- Is the definition appropriately tailored?

- Does the definition capture the appropriate type and scope of accounting estimates?

- Is the definition appropriately designed to identify the accounting estimates that require management to use significant judgment or that are the most uncertain? If not, what other aspects descriptive of that type of estimate should be included?

---

[54] "Critical accounting estimate" is defined in proposed Item 303(b)(3)(ii)(B) of Regulation S-B, 17 CFR 228.303(b)(3)(ii)(B); proposed Item 303(c)(2)(ii) of Regulation S-K, 17 CFR 229.303(c)(2)(ii); and proposed Item 5.E.2.(b) of Form 20-F, 17 CFR 249.220f.

[55] *See* proposed Instruction 3 to paragraph (b)(3) of Item 303 of Regulation S-B, 17 CFR 228.303(b)(3); proposed Instruction 4 to paragraph (c) of Item 303 of Regulation S-K, 17 CFR 229.303(c); and proposed Instruction 3 to Item 5.E of Form 20-F, 17 CFR 249.220f.

- Is the definition appropriately designed to identify the accounting estimates involving a high potential to result in a material impact on the company's financial presentation?

- Would it be difficult for a company to discern which of its accounting estimates require assumptions about highly uncertain matters? If so, how could the proposal better target them?

- Should we consider setting a minimum percentage impact on results of operations in the second criterion of the definition, or would that be unnecessary because the proposed definition would not capture changes that have an insignificant impact?

- How many accounting estimates would a company typically identify as critical accounting estimates under the proposed definition?

- Would a company with multiple segments have a greater number of critical accounting estimates than a company without multiple segments? If so, please provide an explanation.

- Should we establish a maximum number of accounting estimates that may be discussed as critical accounting estimates (e.g., seven)? If so, what should the maximum number be and what criteria should be applied to set the number so as to strike the appropriate balance between information truly useful to investors and overly extensive disclosure of marginal use? If a maximum were set, should the number of segments a company has be considered?

- Should we expand the definition to include MD&A disclosure of volatile accounting estimates that use complex methodologies but do not involve significant management judgment? Should we do so only when the underlying assumptions or methodologies of those estimates are not commonly used and therefore not understood by investors?

2. Identification and description of the accounting estimate, the methodology used, certain assumptions and reasonably likely changes

A company first would have to identify and describe each critical accounting estimate in such a way that it gives the appropriate context for investors reading that section and reflects management's view of the importance of the critical accounting estimate.[56] A company would have to disclose the methodology it used in determining the estimate. It also would have to disclose the assumptions underlying the accounting estimate that reflect matters highly uncertain at the time the estimate was made as well as other assumptions underlying the estimate that are material. We recognize that a critical accounting estimate may involve multiple assumptions. The proposed disclosure would focus in the first instance on those that are about highly uncertain matters because they have the greatest potential to make the accounting estimate highly susceptible to change.

If applicable, the company would have to describe why different estimates could have been used in the current period and why the accounting estimate is reasonably likely to change from period to period in the financial statements. For example, a critical accounting estimate related to a significant portfolio of over-the-counter derivative contracts may require that a company estimate the fair value of such contracts using a model or other valuation method. In that case, the company would disclose the methods it employs to estimate fair value, *e.g.*, the types of valuation models used such as the present value of estimated future cash flows, and assumptions such as an estimated price in the absence of a quoted market price.[57]

A company also would have to explain known trends, demands, commitments, events or uncertainties that are reasonably likely to occur and materially affect the assumptions made or the methodology used. Like the requirements elsewhere in MD&A, disclosure

---

[56] *See* proposed Item 303(b)(3)(iii)(A) of Regulation S-B, 17 CFR 228.303(b)(3)(iii)(A); proposed Item 303(c)(3)(i) of Regulation S-K, 17 CFR 229.303(c)(3)(i); and proposed Item 5.E.3.(a) of Form 20-F, 17 CFR 249.220f.

[57] *See also* Securities Act Release No. 8056, FR-61 (Jan. 22, 2002) [67 FR 3746], Section II.B. (providing an example of a critical accounting estimate related to non-exchange traded contracts accounted for at fair value).

would be required if the trend, demand, commitment, event or uncertainty is currently known, it is reasonably likely to occur and it is reasonably likely to have a material impact. Disclosure would not be required if management could affirmatively conclude that the trend, demand, commitment, event or uncertainty is not reasonably likely to come to fruition or that a material effect is not reasonably likely to occur.[58]

3. Impact of the estimate on financial condition, changes in financial condition and results of operations

For each critical accounting estimate, a company would have to explain its significance to the company's financial condition, changes in financial condition and results of operations and, where material, identify its effect on the line items in the company's financial statements.[59] Because not all estimates themselves are line items in the financial statements,[60] their existence and their effect may not be readily apparent. Thus, this disclosure would provide additional information and clarity for investors.

4. Quantitative disclosures

There are two areas of the proposed MD&A disclosure relating to critical accounting estimates in which we explicitly would require a presentation of quantitative information.[61] First, the proposals would require disclosure that demonstrates the sensitivity of financial results to changes made in connection with each critical accounting estimate. Second, the proposals would require quantitative disclosure relating to historical changes in a company's critical accounting estimates in the past three years.

a. Quantitative disclosures to demonstrate sensitivity

We propose to require that a company present quantitative information about changes in its overall financial performance and, to the extent material, line items in the financial statements that would result if certain changes relating to a critical accounting estimate were assumed to occur. The company would identify the change being assumed and discuss quantitatively its impact on the company. Because the point of the disclosure is to demonstrate the degree of sensitivity, the impact on overall financial performance would be discussed regardless of how large that is.

As proposed, a company would have two possible choices of changes it would assume for purposes of the sensitivity analysis. First, the company could choose to assume that it changed the most material assumption or assumptions underlying the critical accounting estimate and discuss the results of those changes. Second, the company could choose to assume that the critical accounting estimate itself changes. In addition to providing two choices of methods to demonstrate sensitivity, we allow a company to determine the amount of the change that it assumes for this analysis rather than attempting to standardize those amounts. Under the first choice, a company could select the alternative material assumption or assumptions to use as long as the alternative represents a change that is reasonably possible in the near term. "Reasonably possible" means the chance of a future transaction or event occurring is more than remote but less than likely.[62] "Near-term" means a period of time going forward up to one year from the date of the financial statements.[63] Under the second choice, the company would use the upper and the lower

---

[58] *See supra* fn. 16.

[59] *See* proposed Item 303(b)(3)(iii)(B) of Regulation S-B, 17 CFR 228.303(b)(3)(iii)(B); proposed Item 303(c)(3)(ii) of Regulation S-K, 17 CFR 229.303(c)(3)(ii); and proposed Item 5.E.3.(b) of Form 20-F, 17 CFR 249.220f.

[60] For example, an estimate of fair value used to measure an impairment loss on a long-lived asset may not itself appear as a line item in the financial statements.

[61] *See* proposed Item 303(b)(3)(iii)(C) of Regulation S-B, 17 CFR 228.303(b)(3)(iii)(C); proposed Item 303(c)(3)(iii) of Regulation S-K, 17 CFR 229.303(c)(3)(iii); and proposed Item 5.E.3.(c) of Form 20-F, 17 CFR 249.220f.

[62] "Reasonably possible" would have the same meaning as defined in SFAS No. 5. *See supra* fn. 23. *See also* proposed Item 303(b)(3)(ii)(D) of Regulation S-B, 17 CFR 228.303(b)(3)(ii)(D); proposed Item 303(c)(2)(iv) of Regulation S-K, 17 CFR 229.303(c)(2)(iv); and proposed Item 5.E.2.(d) of Form 20-F, 17 CFR 249.220f.

[63] "Near-term" would have the same meaning as defined in SOP 94-6 at paragraph 7. *See* proposed Item 303(b)(3)(ii)(C) of Regulation S-B, 17 CFR 228.303(b)(3)(ii)(C); proposed Item 303(c)(2)(iii) of Regulation S-K, 17 CFR 229.303(c)(2)(iii); and proposed Item 5.E.2.(c) of Form 20-F, 17 CFR 249.220f.

ends of the range of reasonably possible estimates which it likely determined in formulating its recorded critical accounting estimate. It would substitute the upper end of the range for the recorded estimate and discuss the results. It would do the same for the lower end of the range.

We believe the most informative disclosure about sensitivity would result if we allow companies significant flexibility to customize these analyses. Our approach would accommodate different types of companies, different critical accounting estimates and different types of underlying assumptions. The parameters selected for the sensitivity analysis must, however, be realistic and meaningful measures of change.[64] For purposes of the sensitivity analysis, a company should disclose, if known or available, the likelihood of occurrence of the changes it selects, such as estimated probabilities of occurrence or standard deviations where applicable.

Under the first choice for demonstrating sensitivity, we would provide that a company choose its most material assumption underlying the critical accounting estimate and alter it at least twice[65] to reflect reasonably possible, near-term changes.[66] A company would have to complete the analysis assuming a positive change in the assumption. It would also have to complete the analysis assuming a negative change. In some cases, a company may not be able to select a single most material assumption to use for purposes of these analyses, or it may believe that using a single assumption would not provide meaningful sensitivity information for investors. If that were to occur, a company either could select the second choice for analyzing sensitivity (*i.e.*, using the ends of the range) or it could demonstrate the effects of near-term reasonably possible changes in more than one material assumption underlying the critical accounting estimate. If the company chooses the latter course of action, it also would have to disclose clearly the separate effect of each changed assumption.

In general, we believe the impact of a positive change and the impact of a negative change would both have to be disclosed where a company is assuming changes in its most material assumption (or assumptions). There may be cases, however, where both types of changes would not be applicable. In some instances, an increase in an assumption, but not a decrease in an assumption, or vice versa, would have no effect on the line items or the overall financial performance and therefore would not have to be discussed other than noting that fact.[67] It is conceivable that in other cases either a decrease or an increase would not be reasonably possible and therefore would not have to be discussed other than noting that fact.

With the proposed analysis, a company would demonstrate sensitivity of reported results to changes that affect its critical accounting estimates. Investors would have a better understanding of the extent to which there is a correlation between management's key assumptions and the company's overall financial performance. Investors also would understand better which particular line items in reported results would be materially affected and how much. In addition, a company would be required to state whether those assumed changes could have a material effect on the company's liquidity or capital resources. If they could have such an effect, the company would have to explain how, as a company

---

[64] For example, companies would be required to select meaningful changes in material assumptions and not ones so minute as to avoid, or materially understate, any demonstration for investors of sensitivity. *See* proposed Instruction 1 to paragraph (b)(3) of Item 303 of Regulation S-B, 17 CFR 228.303(b)(3); proposed Instruction 1 to paragraph (c) of Item 303 of Regulation S-K, 17 CFR 229.303(c); and proposed Instruction 1 to Item 5.E of Form 20-F, 17 CFR 249.220f.

[65] Where use of only one positive change, or use of only one negative change, would render the analysis materially misleading, companies would have to include more than one assumed positive change, or more than one assumed negative change, to avoid that result.

[66] In completing the analysis, companies would have to consider whether assumed events that alter the most material assumption also could have some impact on other assumptions made in formulating the critical accounting estimate. For example, if a company were to assume a reasonably possible near-term change in fuel prices occurred, that change may impact multiple assumptions underlying a critical accounting estimate that each take fuel prices into account. Companies would have to determine whether and how their other assumptions would change and disclose the aggregate effect of all of those changes.

[67] For an example of when this could take place, *see* *infra* Example 3 in Section III.D.

currently is required to explain in MD&A when factors affecting liquidity or capital resources are present.[68]

From the proposed disclosure, the average investor should be able to ascertain the general degree to which the company's results of operations, liquidity and capital resources are susceptible to changes in management's views relating to critical accounting estimates. Along with the other provisions in the proposal, this quantitative and qualitative disclosure conveys information about the impact of management's subjective assumptions on current and future financial results.

We request comment on the proposed identification and analysis of changes.

- Are there some types of critical accounting estimates or some circumstances where the proposed disclosure relating to sensitivity would not be meaningful or otherwise helpful to investors? If so, which estimates or what circumstances?

- In addition to the two choices we propose for assuming changes relating to the critical accounting estimates to analyze sensitivity, are there others that we should permit? Should we require instead that all companies use the same method? If so, which one?

- Should we require a company to use whichever of the two proposed choices demonstrates the greatest impact on the company's financial presentation?

- Are there circumstances under which a company should be required to demonstrate sensitivity using both of the proposed choices?

- Are there any critical accounting estimates for which neither of the two choices for selecting the assumed changes would be appropriate?

- Will companies be able to select appropriate changes in their most material assumption or assumptions, or should we provide further guidance?

- To enhance an investors' ability to compare the sensitivity of various companies' financial statements to changes relating to a particular type of accounting estimate, should we standardize the changes that companies must assume for various types of estimates? If so, what should they be and why? For example, should we set a specified percentage increase and decrease to assume (*e.g.*, a 10% increase and decrease), or a presumptive increase and decrease, provided that degree of change is reasonably possible in the near term?

- Conversely, would any changes we standardize not be equally meaningful to measure sensitivity, or equally probable, for various accounting estimates, industries and companies, and thus reduce the value of any disclosure about sensitivity?

b. Quantitative and qualitative disclosures concerning past changes in the estimate

We recognize that a company will change its accounting estimates over time as new events occur or as management acquires more experience or additional information. Existing MD&A disclosure rules would call for discussion of the effects of changes in accounting estimates where those changes are material to an investor's understanding of financial position or results of operations. For example, MD&A currently requires companies to disclose:

- information necessary for an understanding of financial condition, changes in financial condition and results of operations[69];

- significant components of revenues or expenses that should, in the company's judgment, be described in order to understand results of operations[70];

---

[68] *See, e.g.*, Item 303(a)(1)-(2) of Regulation S-K, 17 CFR 229.303(a)(1)-(2).

[69] *See, e.g.*, Item 303(a) of Regulation S-K, 17 CFR 229.303(a).

[70] *See, e.g.*, Item 303(a)(3)(i) of Regulation S-K, 17 CFR 229.303(a)(3)(i).

- a material change in the relationship between costs and revenues resulting from a known event[71];

- matters that will have an impact on future operations and have not had an impact in the past[72]; and

- matters that have had an impact on reported operations and are not expected to have an impact upon future operations.[73]

Notwithstanding the existing MD&A disclosure requirements, we believe it would be appropriate to require specific disclosure regarding past changes in critical accounting estimates. This type of information required under the proposal would give investors a clear understanding of a company's recent history of those changes. A company other than a small business issuer would have to include the proposed quantitative and qualitative discussion of any material changes in those accounting estimates under the proposals during the past three fiscal years.[74] A small business issuer would discuss material changes in its critical accounting estimates during the past two years.[75] Companies would have to identify how the material changes affected measurements in the financial statements and their overall financial performance.[76] This would enable investors to evaluate management's formulation of critical accounting estimates over time.

Companies also would be required to describe the reasons for those changes. If no material changes in the critical accounting estimates were made in the prescribed time period, or if a company did not make that estimate during any part of that period, a company would only be required to disclose that fact.

Although the period covered for the proposed disclosure of past changes in critical accounting estimates would be two years for small business issuers and three years for other companies, our proposed requirement relating to past changes would be put into effect in stages. Thus, when a small business issuer or other company files its first covered report, registration statement or proxy or information statement following adoption of the proposed rules, the rules would require it to provide the proposed specific past changes disclosure only for the past one or two years respectively. For example, if the first report were an annual report on Form 10-K for the fiscal year ended December 31, 2002, the company would include that information in the "Application of Critical Accounting Policies" section of MD&A about changes in 2001 and 2002 (and a small business issuer would include it only for 2002). In the first annual report, registration statement or proxy or information statement filed by a company more than one year following the effective date of the rules, it would have to provide that information for the past three years (two years for a small business issuer).[77]

We solicit comment on the proposed disclosure of past material changes in critical accounting estimates.

---

[71] *See, e.g.,* Item 303(a)(3)(ii) of Regulation S-K, 17 CFR 229.303(a)(3)(ii).

[72] *See, e.g.,* Instruction 3(A) to Item 303(a) of Regulation S-K, 17 CFR 229.303(a).

[73] *See, e.g.,* Instruction 3(B) to Item 303(a) of Regulation S-K, 17 CFR 229.303(a).

[74] *See* proposed Item 303(c)(3)(iv) of Regulation S-K, 17 CFR 229.303(c)(3)(iv), and proposed Item 5.E.3.(d) of Form 20-F, 17 CFR 249.220f. As part of its disclosure, a company would have to include discussion of assumptions that changed materially from a prior period but did not cause the estimate itself to change by a material amount. For example, a company could change two or more material assumptions underlying an accounting estimate, but the changes in the assumptions could have an offsetting impact, resulting in no material change to the amount of the accounting estimate recorded in the financial statements.

[75] *See* proposed Item 303(b)(3)(iii)(D) of Regulation S-B, 17 CFR 228.303(b)(3)(iii)(D). These periods correspond to the time frame currently encompassed by the MD&A requirements applicable to each of those types of companies.

[76] *Compare* APB No. 20, paragraph 33, which requires financial statement disclosure of the effect on income before extraordinary items, net income, and related per share amounts of the current period for a change in an estimate not made in the ordinary course of accounting that materially affects several future periods.

[77] Of course, the phase-in of the specific MD&A disclosure about changes in estimates would not delay the effect of the rest of the proposed changes or affect the requirements for disclosure under current MD&A rules.

- Is sufficient disclosure of these changes already required under current MD&A requirements?

- Is a three-year period the most appropriate period of time over which investors should consider changes? If not, why would a shorter or longer period be more appropriate?

- Would requiring disclosure over a longer period, such as five years, make it easier for investors to identify trends? If so, over how many years should we phase in a longer period requirement?

- Should we mandate a standardized format for quantitative disclosure about past changes in critical accounting estimates (*e.g.*, a chart illustrating the dollar value of the change from the prior year for each year showing the impacted line items and other effects in each year)?

5. Senior management's discussions with the audit committee

Independent auditors discuss accounting estimates with management in order to conduct an audit, and the auditors may discuss them with the audit committee. In 1999, following the recommendations in the Report of the Blue Ribbon Committee on Improving the Effectiveness of Corporate Audit Committees, we adopted a rule that would require an audit committee report in proxy or information statements connected to board of director elections.[78] Among other items, the audit committee report must state whether the audit committee has discussed with the independent auditors the matters required to be discussed by Statement on Auditing Standards ("SAS") No. 61 (codified in AU § 380), as may be modified or supplemented.[79] SAS 61 requires independent auditors to communicate certain matters related to the conduct of an audit to those who have responsibility for oversight of the financial reporting process, specifically the audit committee. With respect to accounting estimates, SAS 61 states, "[t]he auditor should determine that the audit committee is informed about the process used by management in formulating particularly sensitive accounting estimates and about the basis for the auditor's conclusions regarding the reasonableness of those estimates."[80] In addition, in connection with each SEC engagement, the auditor should discuss with the audit committee the auditor's judgments about the quality of the entity's accounting principles as applied in its financial reporting. The discussion should include items that have a significant impact on the financial statements (for example, estimates, judgments and uncertainties, among other items).[81]

In addition to the disclosure relating to SAS 61 (as amended), the audit committee report must state whether the audit committee has reviewed and discussed the audited financial statements with management.[82] Because that item relates to the financial statements generally, a focused discussion on critical accounting estimates may or may not result from it. Moreover, the newly required disclosure in MD&A would not be a part of the financial statements, and therefore would not necessarily be covered by that proxy statement disclosure requirement.

The existing audit committee report also requires audit committees to state whether, based on discussions with management and the auditors, the committee recommended to the board of directors that the audited financial statements be included in the company's Form 10-K or 10-KSB for the last fiscal year.[83] This disclosure requirement conveys whether the audit committee review of the financial statements and discussions with management and the auditors have provided a basis for recommending to the board that the audited financial statements be filed with the Commission. This item too does not

---

[78] *See* Exchange Act Release No. 42266 (Dec. 22, 1999) [64 FR 73389] and Item 306 of Regulation S-K, 17 CFR 229.306.

[79] *See* Item 306(a)(2) of Regulation S-K, 17 CFR 229.306(a)(2), SAS No. 61, *Communication with Audit Committees* (Apr. 1988) ("SAS 61") and SAS No. 90, *Audit Committee Communications* (Dec. 1999) ("SAS 90") (amending SAS 61 and AU § 380).

[80] SAS 61, paragraph 8.

[81] *See* AU § 380, paragraph 11 (added by SAS 90).

[82] *See* Item 306(a)(1) of Regulation S-K, 17 CFR 229.306(a)(1).

[83] *See* Item 306(a)(4) of Regulation S-K, 17 CFR 229.306(a)(4).

require any specific discourse between management and the audit committee about critical accounting estimates.

We believe that senior management should discuss the company's critical accounting estimates with the audit committee of its board of directors.[84] If specific discussions between senior management and audit committees regarding the development, selection and disclosure of the critical accounting estimates were to take place, the audit committee may seek to understand the company's critical accounting estimates, the underlying assumptions and methodologies, the appropriateness of management's procedures and conclusions, and the disclosure about those accounting estimates. This type of oversight would have the potential to improve the quality and the transparency of disclosure.

Requiring a company to disclose in MD&A whether or not senior management has engaged in discussions with the audit committee about the critical accounting estimates would give investors a better understanding of whether such oversight by those responsible for the general oversight of the financial reporting process was applied to those accounting estimates and the disclosure about those accounting estimates. We therefore are proposing to require such disclosure.[85] When senior management and the audit committee have not had those discussions, we would require disclosure that they have not, and an explanation of the reasons why they have not.[86] If the company does not have an audit committee, then the proposed disclosure would address discussions with the board committee that performs equivalent functions to those of an audit committee or, if no such committee exists, the entire board of directors.[87] Unlike the audit committee report, our proposed disclosure of discussions between the audit committee and senior management would not be limited to proxy and information statements that involve the election of directors.[88]

We do not propose to require disclosure of the substance of the discussions between senior management and the audit committee. We believe that such a requirement could deter the type of open discourse that we expect to take place in those discussions.

We request comment on the proposed disclosure about discussions between senior management and the audit committee regarding the development, selection and disclosure of critical accounting estimates.

- To what extent does senior management currently discuss critical accounting estimates with the audit committee of the board of directors and the company's auditors?

- Would the proposed requirement provide useful information to investors?

- Would the proposed disclosure be a catalyst for discussion between audit committees and senior management? Could it chill discussions?

- Is there other related disclosure that should be required for the benefit of investors?

---

[84] *See* Securities Act Release No. 8040, FR-60 (Dec. 12, 2001) [66 FR 65013].

[85] *See* proposed Item 303(b)(3)(iii)(E) of Regulation S-B, 17 CFR 228.303(b)(3)(iii)(E); proposed Item 303(c)(3)(v) of Regulation S-K, 17 CFR 229.303(c)(3)(v); and proposed Item 5.E.3.(e) of Form 20-F, 17 CFR 249.220f.

[86] The proposed MD&A disclosure is distinguishable from the audit committee report in annual proxy or information statements. Under the proxy requirements, the audit committee must prepare a report and state whether it recommended, based on its review and discussions with management and the auditors, that the financial statements be included in the Form 10-K. In our proposals, we would not require an audit committee report or recommendation, but only that the company state whether or not discussions between the audit committee and senior management occurred and, if they did not, why not. We therefore are not convinced that a liability exemption like that applicable to the

audit committee report is necessary for disclosure in MD&A of whether or not a company's senior management has discussed the development and selection of critical accounting estimates, and the disclosure in MD&A regarding them.

[87] If the registrant is not a corporation, the disclosure would address senior management's discussions with the equivalent group responsible for the oversight of the financial reporting process.

[88] This disclosure would be required in annual reports filed with the Commission, annual reports to shareholders, registration statements and proxy and information statements. When a new critical accounting estimate is identified in a quarterly report, there also would be disclosure in the Form 10-Q or Form 10-QSB regarding whether the development, selection and disclosure regarding the estimate was discussed by management with the audit committee of the board of directors.

- Should we require that companies disclose any unresolved concerns of the audit committee about the critical accounting estimates or the related MD&A disclosure?

- Should we require disclosure of any specific procedures employed by the audit committee to ensure that the company's response to the proposed disclosure requirements is complete and fair?

- Should we consider requiring disclosure of whether the audit committee recommends the disclosure be included in the MD&A, which is akin to the disclosure required in the Item 306 audit committee report?

- Instead of the proposed disclosure, should we amend Item 306 of Regulation S-K and Regulation S-B to require that the audit committee report disclose whether the audit committee has reviewed and discussed with senior management the development, selection and disclosure regarding critical accounting estimates?

- If we were to amend Items 306 in this manner, should we also expand them to include the discussions about critical accounting estimates between senior management and the audit committee as one of the bases for the audit committee's recommendation to include the financial statements in the annual report?

- Should we expand Items 306 to require disclosure of whether, based on an audit committee's review of and discussions about the MD&A, the audit committee recommended to the board of directors that the MD&A be included in the company's annual report?

- Should we expand Items 306 to require disclosure of whether the audit committee has reviewed and discussed the entire MD&A disclosure (current and proposed) with management and/or the auditors?

- If any of a company's accounting policies diverge, to its knowledge, from the policies predominately applied by other companies in the same industry, should we require that the company disclose, possibly in connection with the audit committee report, whether the audit committee has had discussions with senior management about the appropriateness of the accounting policies being used? When such discussions have taken place, should we require that the company disclose the audit committee's unresolved concerns about the divergent accounting policies being applied? Prior to the adoption of our proposals, to what extent would a company know that its accounting policies diverge from those of other companies in its industry?

6. Disclosure relating to segments

Current MD&A disclosure requirements provide companies with the discretion to include a discussion of segment information where, in the company's judgment, such a discussion would be appropriate to an understanding of the company.[89] In 1989, we stated in an interpretive release, "[t]o the extent any segment contributes in a materially disproportionate way to [revenues, profitability, and cash needs], or where discussion on a consolidated basis would present an incomplete and misleading picture of the enterprise, segment disclosure should be included."[90] In accordance with this interpretation, we are proposing disclosure regarding the impact of critical accounting estimates on segments of a company's business.[91] Where applicable, we believe that this disclosure would be important for investors because it would enable them to determine which reported segments' results are dependent on management's subjective estimates, and material information would be provided on a segment basis.

Under the proposals, if a company operates in more than one segment[92] and a critical accounting estimate affects fewer than all of the segments, the company would have to

---

[89] *See* Item 303(a) of Regulation S-K, 17 CFR 229.303(a).

[90] *See* Securities Act Release No. 6835 (May 18, 1989) [54 FR 22427].

[91] *See* proposed Item 303(b)(3)(iii)(F) of Regulation S-B, 17 CFR 228.303(b)(3)(iii)(F); proposed Item

303(c)(3)(vi) of Regulation S-K, 17 CFR 229.303(c)(3)(vi); and proposed Item 5.E.3.(f) of Form 20-F, 17 CFR 249.220f.

[92] *See* SFAS No. 131 for requirements as to presentation of segment disclosure in the financial statements.

identify the segments it affects. A company also would have to determine whether it must include, in addition to the disclosure on a company-wide basis, a separate discussion of the critical accounting estimates for each identified segment about which disclosure is otherwise required.[93] That determination would follow an analysis similar to that in the 1989 guidance. A company would have to provide a discussion on a segment basis to the extent that discussion only on a company-wide basis would result in an omission that renders the disclosure materially misleading.[94] We would not mandate repetition on a segment basis of all matters discussed on a company-wide basis. Rather, a company would have to disclose only that information necessary to avoid an incomplete or misleading picture.

We request comment regarding identification of the segments affected and the proposed additional disclosure of the critical accounting estimates on a segment basis.

- Should we provide more guidance for determining the circumstances that warrant segment disclosure?

- Should we require the additional segment discussion only when more than one segment is affected?

D. Examples of Proposed Disclosure about Critical Accounting Estimates

To assist in understanding the scope of the MD&A disclosure that is proposed, we have developed three examples. Each example examines how a fictional public company that has identified a critical accounting estimate could draft MD&A disclosure to satisfy the proposal. The examples are illustrative only. In addition, our January 22, 2002 release provides an example of disclosure that companies should consider when discussing in MD&A trading activities involving contracts that are accounted for at fair value where a lack of market price quotations necessitates the use of fair value estimation techniques.[95]

Example 1

Background

Alphabetical Company manufactures and distributes electrical equipment used in largescale commercial pumping and water treatment facilities. The company operates in four business segments. The company's equipment carries standard product warranties extending over a period of 6 to 10 years. If equipment covered under the standard warranty requires repair, the company provides labor and replacement parts to the customer at no cost. Historically, the costs of fulfilling warranty obligations have principally related to providing replacement parts, with labor costs representing the remainder. Over the past 3 years, the cost of copper included in replacement parts constituted approximately 35% to 40% of the total cost of warranty obligations.

Aliability for the expected cost of warranty-related claims is established when equipment is sold. The amount of the warranty liability accrued reflects the company's estimate of the expected future costs of honoring its obligations under the warranty plan. Because of the long-term nature of the company's equipment warranties, estimating the expected cost of such warranties requires significant judgment. Based on management's evaluation of analysts' forecasts for copper prices, management believes a 30% decrease in copper prices or a 50% increase in copper prices is reasonably possible in the near term. In each of the last three years, warranty expense represented approximately 19% to 22% of cost of sales.

---

[93] Certain foreign private issuers providing disclosure under Item 17 of Form 20-F are not required to provide segment disclosure in their filed financial statements and therefore would not be required to provide a quantitative discussion of the identified segments.

[94] Any discussion on a segment basis would appear in the section of MD&A devoted to critical accounting estimates, and not in the separate discussion of segment results in MD&A.

[95] *See* Securities Act Release No. 8056, FR-61 (Jan. 22, 2002) [67 FR 3746], Section II.B.

Possible MD&A disclosure under the proposal

Application of Critical Accounting Policies

Alphabetical's products are covered by standard product warranty plans that extend 6 to 10 years. A liability for the expected cost of warranty-related claims is established when equipment is sold. The amount of the warranty liability accrued reflects our estimate of the expected future costs of honoring our obligations under the warranty plan. We believe the accounting estimate related to warranty costs is a "critical accounting estimate" because: changes in it can materially affect net income, it requires us to forecast copper prices in the distant future which are highly uncertain and require a large degree of judgment, and copper is a significant raw material in the replacement parts used in warranty repairs. The estimate for warranty obligations is a critical accounting estimate for all of our four segments.

Historically, the costs of fulfilling our warranty obligations have principally related to replacement parts, with labor costs representing the remainder. Over the past 3 years, the cost of copper included in our parts constituted approximately 35% to 40% of the total cost of warranty repairs. Over that same period, warranty expense represented approximately 19% to 22% of cost of sales.

Over the past 10 years, the price of copper has exhibited significant volatility. For example, during 1994, the price of copper rose by approximately 72%, while in 2001 the price decreased by approximately 19%. Our hedging programs provide adequate protection against short-term volatility in copper prices, as described in "Risk Management," but our hedging does not extend beyond 5 years. Accordingly, our management must make assumptions about the cost of that raw material in periods 6 to 10 years in the future. Management forecasts the price of copper for the portion of our estimated copper requirements not covered by hedging. Our forecasts are based principally on long-range price forecasts for copper which are published by private research companies specializing in the copper markets.

Each quarter, we reevaluate our estimate of warranty obligations, including our assumptions about the cost of copper. During 2001, we decreased our estimated cost of unhedged copper purchases over the next 10 years by 15%, reflecting a growing excess of supply over forecasted demand, which reduced our accrued warranty costs and our cost of sales (and, accordingly, increased operating income) by $15 million. In contrast, during 2000, long-term price forecasts were essentially unchanged, so we made no adjustments to our estimated cost of unhedged copper purchases over the next 10 years. During 1999, copper prices increased by approximately 28% over the prior year. Long-term prices also reflected increases in prices over those projected in 1998. Thus, in 1999, we increased our estimated cost of unhedged copper purchases over the next 10 years (through 2009) by 15%. That increase in our estimate resulted in an $18 million addition to our accrued warranty cost and our cost of sales, and an equal reduction in our operating income.

If, for the unhedged portion of our estimated copper requirements, we were to decrease our estimate of copper prices as of December 31, 2001 by 30%, our accrued warranty costs and cost of sales would have been reduced by approximately $27 million or 6% and 4%, respectively, while operating income would have increased by 9%. If we were to increase our estimate as of December 31, 2001 by 50%, our accrued warranty costs and cost of sales would have been increased by approximately $45 million or 10% and 7%, respectively, while our operating income would have been reduced by 23%.

A very significant increase in our estimated warranty obligation, such as one reflecting the increase in copper prices that occurred in 1994, could lower our earnings and increase our leverage ratio (leverage refers to the degree to which a company utilizes borrowed funds). That, in turn, could limit our ability to borrow money through our revolving credit facilities described in "Liquidity and Capital Resources."

Our management has discussed the development and selection of this critical accounting estimate with the audit committee of our board of directors and the audit committee has reviewed the company's disclosure relating to it in this MD&A.

Example 2

Background

MQB Corp. is a developer and publisher of desktop publishing software that operates in two segments. MQB distributes its products primarily through third-party distributors, resellers, and retailers (customers). Like many companies in the software industry, MQB has a product return policy and has historically accepted significant product returns. MQB permits its customers to return software titles published and distributed by the company within 120 days of purchase.

MQB recognizes revenues under SOP 97-2, "Software Revenue Recognition." The company ships its products FOB (Free on Board) shipping point. Therefore, legal title to the products passes to the customers upon shipment, and the company has no legal obligation for product damage in transit. Accordingly, MQB recognizes revenue upon shipment of its software products, provided that collection of payment is determined to be probable and no significant obligations on MQB's part remain. Payment is due from customers 30 days after shipment. At the time revenue is recorded, MQB accounts for estimated future returns by reducing sales by its estimate of future returns and by reducing accounts receivable by the same amount. For example, MQB reduced its gross sales and accounts receivable by 12% for its fiscal year ended December 31, 2001 to reflect estimated product returns. In the last three years, the range in which the company has reduced its gross sales and accounts receivable to reflect product returns has been between 11% and 13%.

MQB receives weekly reports from distributors and retailers regarding the amount of MQB products in their inventory. A historical correlation exists between levels of inventory held by distributors and retailers (together, the distribution channel) and the amount of returns that actually occur. The weekly reports from distributors and retailers provide the company with visibility into the distribution channel such that MQB has the ability to estimate future returns. In each of the past few years, actual returns have varied from period to period, although they have not exceeded the estimated amounts by more than 5%. The company's products are, however, subject to intense marketplace competition, including several recently introduced competing products. If actual returns significantly exceed the previously estimated amounts, it would result in materially lower sales and net income before taxes in one or more future periods.

Possible MD&A disclosure under the proposal

Application of Critical Accounting Policies

Our recognition of revenue from sales to distributors and retailers (the "distribution channel") is impacted by agreements we have giving them rights to return our software titles within 120 days after purchase. At the time we recognize revenue, upon shipment of our software products, we reduce our measurements of those sales by our estimate of future returns and we also reduce our measurements of accounts receivable by the same amount.

For our products, a historical correlation exists between the amount of distribution channel inventory and the amount of returns that actually occur. The greater the distribution channel inventory, the more product returns we expect. For each of our products, we monitor levels of product sales and inventory at our distributors' warehouses and at retailers as part of our effort to reach an appropriate accounting estimate for returns. In estimating returns, we analyze historical returns, current inventory in the distribution channel, current economic trends, changes in consumer demand, introduction of new competing software and acceptance of our products.

In recent years, as a result of a combination of the factors described above, we have materially reduced our gross sales to reflect our estimated amount of returns. It is also possible that returns could increase rapidly and significantly in the future. Accordingly, estimating product returns requires significant management judgment. In addition, different return estimates that we reasonably could have used would have had a material impact on our reported sales and thus have had a material impact on the presentation of the results of operations. For those reasons, we believe that the accounting estimate related to product returns is a "critical accounting estimate." Our estimate of product returns is a critical accounting estimate for both of our segments. Management of the company has discussed the development and selection of this critical accounting estimate with the audit committee of our board of directors and the audit committee has reviewed the company's disclosure relating to it in this MD&A.

We are aware of several recently introduced products that compete with several of our significant products. These new competitive factors have not, to date, materially impacted returns; therefore, we have made no adjustment as a result of these factors in our estimated returns for 2001. In our highly competitive marketplace, these factors have some potential to increase our estimates of returns in the future. The introduction of new competing products has impacted our estimate of returns in the past. In 1999, we increased our estimate of returns over the previous year by 1%, as a percentage of gross sales, because of increased inventory in the distribution channel due to new products introduced by two of our competitors.

In preparing our financial statements for the year ended December 31, 2001, we estimated future product returns for all of our products to be $145 million, and we reduced our gross sales by that amount. Our 2001 estimate for returns was $20 million greater than our estimate in 2000 and $15 million greater than our estimate in 1999. From 1999 to 2000, products introduced by two of our competitors in 1998 lost market share to our products and our sales increased. Due to our increased sales in 2000, the distribution channel inventory declined over levels in 1999, which also resulted in a 2% decline in the estimated amount of returns, as a percentage of gross sales. In 2001, with the slow down in consumer spending over the prior period, distribution channel inventory grew faster than sales, necessitating an increase in the estimated returns equal to 1% of gross sales. The estimates for returns represented approximately 12%, 11% and 13% of our gross sales for 2001, 2000 and 1999, respectively.

If we were to assume that our estimate of future product returns for all of our products was changed to the upper end or lower end of the range we developed in the course of formulating our estimate, the estimate for future returns as of December 31, 2001 would range from $130 million to $160 million. Accordingly, the amounts by which we would reduce gross sales and operating income also would range from $130 million to $160 million as compared to the recorded amount of $145 million. In each of the years in the three-year period ended 2001, our actual returns have not deviated from our estimates by more than 5%. Our actual returns for 2000 and 1999 were $129 million and $134 million, respectively. If we were to change our estimate of future product returns to the high end of the range, there would be no material impact on our liquidity or capital resources.

Example 3

Background

Betascott Company manufactures and sells data storage devices including computer hard drives. The hard drive industry is subject to intense competition and significant shifts in market share amongst the competitors. In the last three years, Betascott has reported falling sales and market share, which has contributed to a fiscal year 2001 loss from operations in the hard drive segment. (This trend is separately discussed in MD&A.)

As of December 31, 2001, the company had $200 million in property, plant and equipment ("PP&E") used in producing hard drives. The company's accounting policies require that it test long-lived assets for impairment whenever indicators of impairment exist. The 2001 fiscal year loss from operations in that segment, coupled with the company's falling sales and market share, are indicators of a potential impairment of the hard drive-related PP&E.

The company follows the provisions of FASB SFAS No. 121, *Accounting for the Impairment of Long-Lived Assets and for Long-Lived Assets to Be Disposed Of.*[96] That accounting standard requires that if the sum of the future cash flows expected to result from the assets, undiscounted and without interest charges, is less than a company's reported value of the assets, then the asset is not recoverable and the company must recognize an impairment. The amount of impairment to be recognized is the excess of the reported value of the assets over the fair value of those assets.

The hard drive-related PP&E accounts for approximately 67% of Betascott's PP&E. The sum of Betascott's current estimate of expected future cash flows from its hard drive-related PP&E, undiscounted and without interest charges, is near the reported value of that PP&E. In the year ended December 31, 2001, Betascott would have been required to recognize an impairment loss of approximately $30 million if its estimate of those future cash flows had been 10% lower.

Possible MD&A disclosure under the proposal

Application of Critical Accounting Policies

We evaluate our property, plant and equipment ("PP&E") for impairment whenever indicators of impairment exist. Accounting standards require that if the sum of the future cash flows expected to result from a company's asset, undiscounted and without interest charges, is less than the reported value of the asset, an asset impairment must be recognized in the financial statements. The amount of impairment to recognize is calculated by subtracting the fair value of the asset from the reported value of the asset.

As we discuss in the notes to the financial statements, we operate in four segments, one of which is the hard drive segment. In our hard drive segment, we reviewed our hard drive-related PP&E for impairment as of December 31, 2001, due to a trend of declining sales and market share. We determined that the undiscounted sum of the expected future cash flows from the assets related to the hard drive segment exceeded the recorded value of those assets, so we did not recognize an impairment in accordance with GAAP. The PP&E in our hard-drive segment represents approximately two-thirds of our total PP&E.

We believe that the accounting estimate related to asset impairment is a "critical accounting estimate" because: (1) it is highly susceptible to change from period to period because it requires company management to make assumptions about future sales and cost of sales over the life of the hard drive-related PP&E (generally seven years); and (2) the impact that recognizing an impairment would have on the assets reported on our balance sheet as well as our net loss would be material. Management's assumptions about future sales prices and future sales volumes require significant judgment because actual sales prices and volumes have fluctuated in the past and are expected to continue to do so. Management has discussed the development and selection of this critical accounting estimate with the audit committee of our board of directors and the audit committee has reviewed the company's disclosure relating to it in this MD&A.

In estimating future sales, we use our internal budgets. We develop our budgets based on recent sales data for existing products, planned timing of new product launches, customer commitments related to existing and newly developed products, and current unsold inventory held by distributors.

Our estimates of future cash flows assume that our sales of hard drive inventory will remain consistent with current year sales. While actual sales have declined by an average of approximately 2% per year during the last three years, our introduction of the Stored line of hard drives in August 2001 has resulted in a 0.5% increase in market share over the last five months of 2001, and a corresponding increase in sales of 5% over the comparable 5-month period last year. We therefore have assumed that sales will not

---

[96] SFAS No. 144 superseded SFAS No. 121 and is effective for financial statements issued for fiscal years beginning after December 15, 2001.

continue to decline in the future. We have also assumed that our costs will have annual growth of approximately 2%. This level of costs is comparable to actual costs incurred over the last two years, following the 1999 restructuring of the hard drive division (which is described in the note 2 to the financial statements).

In each of the last two years, we have tested the hard drive-related PP&E for impairment and in each year we determined that, based on our assumptions, the sum of the expected future cash flows, undiscounted and without interest charges, exceeded the reported value and therefore we did not recognize an impairment. Because 2001 sales were lower than those in 2000 and 1999, despite the improvement in the latter part of the year, and because our estimates of future cash flows are assumed to be consistent with current year sales, the current year impairment analysis includes estimated sales that are 2% and 5% less than those assumed in the 2000 and 1999 impairment tests, respectively.

As of December 31, 2001, we estimate that our future cash flows, on an undiscounted basis, are greater than our $200 million investment in hard drive-related PP&E. Any increases in estimated future cash flows would have no impact on the reported value of the hard drive-related PP&E. In contrast, if our current estimate of future cash flows from hard drive sales had been 10% lower, those cash flows would have been less than the reported amount of the hard drive-related PP&E. In that case, we would have been required to recognize an impairment loss of approximately $30 million, equal to the difference between the fair value of the equipment (which we would have determined by calculating the discounted value of the estimated future cash flows) and the reported amount of the hard drive-related PP&E. A $30 million impairment loss would have reduced PP&E and Total Assets as of December 31, 2001 by 10% and 3%, respectively. That impairment loss also would have increased Net Loss Before Taxes, for the year ended December 31, 2001, by 100%.

If we had been required to recognize an impairment loss on our hard-drive related PP&E, it would likely not have affected our liquidity and capital resources because, even with the impairment loss, we would have been within the terms of the tangible net-worth covenant in our long-term debt agreement discussed in note 5 to the financial statements.

E. Auditor Examination of MD&A Disclosure Relating to Critical Accounting Estimates

A company's management bears primary responsibility for its accounting estimates. Auditors also have important responsibilities regarding a company's accounting estimates. A company's auditor currently is responsible for evaluating the reasonableness of the accounting estimates made by management in the context of the financial statements taken as a whole.[97] When a company's audited financial statements are included in an annual report filed with the Commission, the independent auditor is required to read the information in the entire filed document, including the MD&A, and consider whether such information, or the manner of its presentation, is materially inconsistent with information, or the manner of its presentation, appearing in the financial statements.[98]

Despite the current auditing standards, and the auditor's consideration of the proposed MD&A disclosure that may take place by virtue of them, we are considering whether to take additional steps with a view to ensuring the accuracy and reliability of the proposed disclosure. Subjecting the MD&A disclosure to the auditing process itself would require

---

[97] *See* AU § 342, paragraph 4. In evaluating the reasonableness, the auditor's objective is "to obtain sufficient competent evidential matter to provide a reasonable assurance that

All accounting estimates that could be material to the financial statements have been developed.

Those accounting estimates are reasonable in the circumstances.

The accounting estimates are presented in conformity with applicable accounting principles and are properly disclosed."

AU § 342, paragraph 7. The auditor normally focuses on key factors and assumptions that are significant to the accounting estimate, that are sensitive to variations, that are deviations from historical patterns or that are subjective and susceptible to misstatement and bias. *See* AU § 342, paragraph 9.

[98] *See* AU § 550, *Other Information in Documents Containing Audited Financial Statements* ("AU § 550").

the imposition of auditing standards, including examination of the disclosure itself, application of auditing processes regarding internal controls, coverage in management representations of material relevant to the disclosure and other procedures. One possible approach would be to adopt a requirement that an independent auditor must examine, in accordance with Attestation Standards,[99] the new MD&A disclosure relating to critical accounting estimates.

The American Institute of Certified Public Accountants has established standards and procedures when an auditor is engaged by a company to examine and render an opinion that the disclosure in a company's MD&A satisfies applicable Commission requirements.[100] An auditor's objective in an examination is to express an opinion on:

- whether the MD&A presentation includes in all material respects the required elements of the disclosure mandated by the Commission;

- whether the historical financial amounts have been accurately derived, in all material respects, from the company's financial statements; and

- whether the underlying information, determinations, estimates and assumptions of the company provide a reasonable basis for the disclosures contained in the MD&A.[101]

To complete an examination, an auditor must examine documents and records and accumulate sufficient evidence in support of the disclosures and assumptions and take other steps to get reasonable assurance of detecting both intentional and unintentional misstatements that are material to the MD&A presentation.[102] To accept an examination engagement, an auditor must have sufficient knowledge about the company and its operations. AT § 701 therefore requires that an auditor must have at least audited the company's financial statements for the most recent period covered by the MD&A, and the other periods covered by the MD&A must have been audited by it or another auditor.[103]

Auditor examinations of MD&A disclosure are, we believe, undertaken on few occasions. Some companies have engaged independent auditors to conduct an examination of their MD&A disclosures either in connection with their initial public offering or after a major restructuring or acquisition when the company disclosure is being presented on a pro forma basis.[104] In one case, an auditor examination of MD&A was undertaken pursuant to a settlement with the Commission of an enforcement action alleging material deficiencies in the company's past MD&A disclosure.[105]

---

[99] See Codification of Statements on Standards for Attestation Engagements ("AT") § 101, *Attest Engagements* and AT § 701, *Management's Discussion and Analysis.*

[100] AT § 701 contemplates two levels of service by an auditor with respect to MD&A: an "examination" of an MD&A presentation and a more limited "review" of an MD&A presentation. Unlike an examination, a review culminates with the auditor giving negative assurance. The auditor's review report states whether any information came to the auditor's attention to cause him or her to believe that: the MD&A presentation taken as a whole does not include in all material respects the required elements of the disclosure; the historical financial amounts have not been accurately derived, in all material respects, from the company's financial statements; or the underlying information, determinations, estimates and assumptions of the company do not provide a reasonable basis for the disclosures contained in the MD&A. In undertaking a review, an auditor is expected to apply analytical procedures and make inquiries of people at the company who are responsible for financial, accounting and operational matters, but is not expected to test

accounting records through inspection or observation, obtain corroborating evidence in response to inquiries, or take other steps required during an MD&A examination. An auditor's review report is not intended to be filed with the Commission. See AT § 701, paragraph 2.

[101] See AT § 701, paragraph 5.

[102] See AT § 701, paragraphs 28-29.

[103] See AT § 701, paragraph 6.

[104] Goldman Sachs engaged an auditor to review its MD&A disclosure in connection with its initial public offering. See Form S-1, Commission File No. 333-74449. In addition, in the course of reading agreements between issuers and their underwriters created in connection with registered offerings, the staff has noted that approximately 50 companies have agreed to engage an auditor to conduct an examination of the company's MD&A disclosure as a condition to closing.

[105] In 1998, we issued a cease-and-desist order in a settlement with Sony Corporation that required Sony to engage an independent auditor to examine its MD&A disclosure for the fiscal year ending March 31, 1999. See *SEC v. Sony Corporation*, Litigation Release No. 15832 (Aug. 5, 1998).

We solicit comment with respect to independent auditor examinations of the proposed MD&A disclosure regarding critical accounting estimates.

- Should we require that the critical accounting estimates disclosure in the MD&A undergo an auditor examination comparable to that enumerated in AT § 701?

- Would these engagements significantly improve the disclosure provided in MD&A?

- In practice, when companies engage auditors to examine the MD&A pursuant to AT § 701, does it elicit a higher quality of disclosure than when auditors consider only, as currently required, whether an MD&A is materially inconsistent with the financial statements?

- If we were to require examinations by auditors of part or all of MD&A disclosures, should we also require that a company file, or disclose the results of, the auditor's reports?

- If we do not require auditors' examinations of MD&A disclosure but an auditor nonetheless examines MD&A disclosure on critical accounting estimates, should we require that the auditor's report be filed or the results be disclosed?

- What would be the relative benefits and costs of a requirement for an auditor examination with respect to the critical accounting estimates portion of the MD&A?

- Should we require an auditor "review" under standards comparable to AT § 701,[106] as opposed to an auditor "examination" of the critical accounting estimates MD&A disclosure?

- Do current requirements relating to what an auditor must consider make an examination or review of the proposed MD&A disclosure under standards comparable to AT § 701 unnecessary?

- If we do not require auditor examination or review, are there other steps we should take to help ensure the quality of disclosure in this proposed section of MD&A?

F. Quarterly Updates

Material changes relating to critical accounting estimates may occur from fiscal period to fiscal period. For example, management could materially change an accounting estimate previously disclosed as a critical accounting estimate because it changes the methodology for computing it. A company could determine that an additional accounting estimate met the standards and is a critical accounting estimate for the period subsequent to its most recent annual or quarterly report. A company also could materially change one of the important assumptions underlying an existing critical accounting estimate (which may or may not result in a change to the critical accounting estimate depending on what changes in other assumptions underlying the estimate are made). Any of these changes could have a material effect on the company's financial condition, changes in financial condition or results of operations. We expect that U.S. companies would be evaluating accounting estimates and the underlying assumptions and methodologies on at least a quarterly basis[107] and therefore we believe that quarterly updates to reflect material developments would be appropriate. Disclosure of material developments made only at the end of each fiscal year also may not identify changes quickly enough to inform investors adequately.

In quarterly reports on Form 10-Q or Form 10-QSB, companies would be required to provide an update to the MD&A information related to critical accounting estimates

---

[106] See supra fn. 100.

[107] The procedures performed by an independent accountant to issue a review report on the financial statements filed in a Form 10-Q generally would include reading information such as that found in the MD&A section of the Form 10-Q. Further, the independent accountant's association with those financial statements would require the independent accountant to read the MD&A. See AU § 722, *Interim Financial Information*, paragraph 35 and AU § 550, paragraph 4.

discussed in the company's last filed annual or quarterly report under the Exchange Act.[108] Newly identified critical accounting estimates would be disclosed in the same manner as in an annual report. If other material changes have occurred that would render the critical accounting estimates disclosure in the company's latest report materially out of date or otherwise materially misleading, we propose that those changes and their effect be described in the quarterly report. The proposed rules would not, however, require quarterly updates with regard to the proposed quantitative and qualitative discussion concerning past material changes in critical accounting estimates in annual reports, registration statements and proxy and information statements.

We solicit comment on the quarterly updating requirement for U.S. companies.

- Are there some accounting estimates or material assumptions or methodologies that would normally be considered by companies only on a less frequent basis than quarterly? If so, which ones? Should they be omitted from the quarterly updating requirement on that basis?

- Is the scope of the disclosure required in a quarterly update appropriate? If not, what should be added or omitted?

G. Proposed Disclosure about Initial Adoption of Accounting Policies

A company initially adopts an accounting policy when events or transactions that affect the company occur for the first time, when events or transactions that were previously immaterial in their effect become material, or when events or transactions occur that are clearly different in substance from previous events or transactions. For example, a company may for the first time enter into transactions involving derivative instruments, such as interest rate swaps, or may begin selling a new type of product that has delivery terms and conditions that are different from those associated with the products the company has previously been selling.

If an initially adopted accounting policy has a material impact on the company's financial condition, changes in financial condition or results of operations, that impact will likely be of interest to investors, to financial analysts and others. If a company considers an accounting policy that it has initially adopted to be a significant accounting policy, the company would provide certain disclosures about that accounting policy as required by APB No. 22. Those disclosures are typically in the first note to the financial statements.[109] The disclosure provided in the notes to the financial statements, however, may not adequately describe, in a qualitative manner, the impact of the initially adopted accounting policy or policies on the company's financial presentation. We are therefore proposing additional MD&A disclosure to further describe, where a material impact exists, the initial adoption of accounting policies.[110] The proposed MD&A disclosure would be provided in companies' filed annual reports, annual reports to shareholders, registration statements and proxy and information statements and would include description of:

- The events or transactions that gave rise to the initial adoption of an accounting policy;

- The accounting principle that has been adopted and the method of applying that principle; and

---

[108] *See* proposed Item 303(b)(3)(v) of Regulation S-B, 17 CFR 228.303(b)(3)(v), and proposed Item 303(c)(5) of Regulation S-K, 17 CFR 229.303(c)(5). To assist companies in preparing quarterly updates, we would allow them to presume that investors have read, or have access to, the discussion of critical accounting estimates in their previously filed Exchange Act annual reports and any quarterly reports filed subsequent to the most recent annual report.

[109] *See* APB No. 22, paragraphs 12 and 15.

[110] *See* proposed Item 303(b)(3)(iv) of Regulation S-B, 17 CFR 228.303(b)(3)(iv); proposed Item 303(c)(4) of Regulation S-K, 17 CFR 229.303(c)(4); and proposed Item 5.E.4. of Form 20-F, 17 CFR 249.220f. These proposed disclosures would not be required if the initial adoption of an accounting policy solely results from adoption of new accounting literature issued by a recognized accounting standard setter (including, in the U.S., new accounting pronouncements or rules issued by the FASB, AICPA or SEC or a new consensus of the Emerging Issues Task Force (EITF)).

- The impact (discussed qualitatively) resulting from the initial adoption of the accounting policy on the company's financial condition, changes in financial condition and results of operations.

If, upon initial adoption of one of those accounting policies, a company is permitted a choice among acceptable accounting principles,[111] the company also would be required to explain in MD&A that it had made a choice among acceptable alternatives, identify the alternatives, and describe why it made the choice that it did. In addition, where material, the company would have to provide a qualitative discussion of the impact on the company's financial condition, changes in financial condition and results of operations that the alternatives would have had. Finally, if no accounting literature exists that governs the accounting for the events or transactions giving rise to the initial adoption of a material accounting policy (*e.g.*, the events or transactions are unusual or novel or otherwise have not been contemplated in past standard-setting projects), the company would be required to explain its decision regarding which accounting principle to use and which method of applying that principle to use.

We seek comment on the proposed disclosures related to initial adoption of accounting policies.

- Would the proposed disclosures about initial adoption of accounting policies provide useful information to investors and other readers of financial reports?

- Are there particular situations involving the initial adoption of a material accounting policy for which we should require additional disclosure? If so, what are those situations and what additional disclosure should we require?

- Should we require companies to disclose, in MD&A or in the financial statements, the estimated effect of adopting accounting policies that they could have adopted, but did not adopt, upon initial accounting for unusual or novel transactions?

- What would be the costs for companies to prepare disclosure about the effects of alternative accounting policies that could have been chosen but were not?

- Would investors be confused if companies presented disclosure of the effects of acceptable alternative policies that were not chosen?

- Should we require in MD&A a discussion of whether the accounting policies followed by a company upon initial adoption differ from the accounting policies applied, in similar circumstances, by other companies in its industry, and the reasons for those differences? Please explain. If such a discussion should be required, please identify the specific disclosures companies should make.

- Would a company know the policies applied in similar circumstances by other companies in its industry? If not, would auditing firms or other financial advisors be able to assist companies in determining whether their accounting policies generally diverge from industry practices?

H. Disclosure Presentation

The proposals would require that a company present the required information in a separate section of MD&A. While the proposed disclosure may relate to other aspects of the discussion in MD&A, such as the results of operations or liquidity and capital resources, we have chosen to separate it both to highlight the discussion and because we believe the proposed discussion would present information that is better communicated separately to promote understanding.

The proposed MD&A discussion must be presented in language, and a format, that is clear, concise and understandable to the average investor.[112] The disclosure should not be

---

[111] *See supra* fn. 31 and accompanying text.
[112] *See* proposed Instruction 3 to paragraph (b)(3) of Item 303 of Regulation S-B, 17 CFR 228.303(b)(3); proposed Instruction 4 to paragraph (c) of Item 303 of Regulation S-K, 17 CFR 229.303(c); and proposed Instruction 3 to Item 5.E. of Form 20-F, 17 CFR 249.220f.

presented in such a way that only an investor who is also an accountant or an expert on a particular industry would be able to understand it fully. To reinforce the importance of the disclosure being presented in a manner that investors will understand, we also would specify that the proposed disclosure must not be presented, for example, solely as a single discussion of the aggregate consequences of multiple critical accounting estimates or the aggregate consequences of the initial application of multiple new accounting policies.[113] Because a company may identify and discuss more than one critical accounting estimate or more than one newly adopted accounting policy, and those estimates or those policies could materially affect a company's financial presentation in differing ways, a separate discussion of the application of each estimate and each new accounting policy will facilitate investors' understanding of the implications of each one.

Boilerplate disclosures that do not specifically address the company's particular circumstances and operations also would not satisfy the proposed requirements.[114] Disclosure that could easily be transferred from year to year, or from company to company, with no change would neither inform investors adequately nor reflect the independent thinking that must accompany the periodic assessment by management that is intended under the proposal. Finally, the purpose of the proposed disclosure would be hindered if a company were to include disclosures that consisted principally of blanket disclaimers of legal responsibility for its application of a new accounting policy or its development of its critical accounting estimates in light of the uncertainties associated with them.

While the Commission fully expects companies to craft the proposed disclosure responsibly to take advantage of any available safe harbors, simple disclaimers of legal liability would be contrary to the disclosure goals underlying the proposal and would not be permitted.[115]

We solicit comment on the disclosure presentation aspects of the proposals.

- Should the proposed disclosure be presented in a separate section of MD&A or should we require that it be integrated into the other discussions of financial condition, changes in financial condition, results of operations and liquidity and capital resources when the proposed disclosure is closely related to an aspect discussed in those separate sections of MD&A?

- Should other requirements relating to the language and format be added to the requirement for clear, concise and understandable disclosure? If so, what requirements?

I. Application to Foreign Private Issuers

In annual reports and registration statements filed with the Commission by foreign private issuers,[116] we propose to apply the same MD&A disclosure requirements regarding the application of accounting policies that would apply to U.S. companies.[117] Foreign private issuers, however, may present their financial statements either in accordance with U.S. GAAP, in accordance with GAAP of a foreign country, or in accordance with International Accounting Standards and International Financial Reporting Standards issued by the International Accounting Standards Committee and the International Accounting Standards Board. If financial statements are presented in accordance with non-U.S. GAAP, a reconciliation to U.S. GAAP accompanies them. The MD&A disclosure that foreign private issuers currently make in documents filed with the Commission[118] must focus on

---

[113] *Id.*
[114] *Id.*
[115] *Id.*
[116] Foreign private issuers are non-governmental foreign issuers that primarily are owned by non-U.S. investors or are primarily located, doing business and managed outside the U.S. *See* 17 CFR 240.3b-4. Foreign governments, and Canadian issuers filing reports and registration statements with the Commission pursuant to Canadian disclosure requirements under the Multijurisdictional Disclosure System with Canada, would be unaffected by the proposals.

[117] Under the proposals, the MD&A disclosure would apply to foreign private issuers regardless of whether they reconcile in accordance with Item 17 or Item 18 of Form 20-F.

[118] Item 5 in Form 20-F, the provision parallel to disclosure entitled "MD&A" for domestic issuers, is entitled "Operating and Financial Review and Prospects."

the primary financial statements, whether those are prepared in accordance with non-U.S. GAAP or U.S. GAAP, although the reconciliation also must be taken into account.[119]

The proposed MD&A disclosure regarding critical accounting estimates would do the same. If the primary financial statements were in non-U.S. GAAP, the company would have to consider critical accounting estimates in connection with both its primary financial statements and its reconciliation to U.S. GAAP. The reasons are essentially two. First, a company could make an accounting estimate under non-U.S. GAAP that would not constitute a critical accounting estimate or could use a method under non-U.S. GAAP that would not involve an estimate, but in applying U.S. GAAP in the reconciliation could be required to make different assumptions that involve highly uncertain matters therefore causing it to be highly susceptible to change where change would have a material impact. For example, non-U.S. GAAP may permit or require derivative instruments held as investments to be reported at cost (or not recognized), while U.S. GAAP would require the same instruments to be reported at fair value. If the instruments are not traded and therefore no quoted market prices are available, assumptions about highly uncertain matters would be required to estimate fair value for purposes of the reconciliation.

Second, a foreign private issuer could apply different accounting methods under U.S. GAAP than under non-U.S. GAAP, and while both may involve critical accounting estimates, they may do so for different reasons that investors would need to understand. For example, both non-U.S. GAAP and U.S. GAAP may require recognition of liabilities for environmental or mass tort claims. However, the methodologies, assumptions and judgments necessary to estimate the amount to recognize may be significantly different under the two different GAAPs. Thus, a foreign private issuer would be required also to include the proposed disclosure for any critical accounting estimate that is related to the application of U.S. GAAP.[120]

Similarly, the proposed MD&A disclosures about the initial adoption of accounting policies would focus on the primary financial statements but also take into account the reconciliation to U.S. GAAP. When a foreign private issuer initially adopts an accounting policy under non-U.S. GAAP, it may have different acceptable alternative principles available to it than it would if it were initially adopting an accounting policy under U.S. GAAP. Those alternatives may be unfamiliar to investors. Accordingly, we would require that the foreign private issuer provide the proposed disclosure about initial adoption in relation to its primary financial statements. Foreign private issuers also would be required to consider the reconciliation to U.S. GAAP. The reconciliation would not necessarily present an initial adoption of an accounting policy simply because the company is initially adopting a policy under non-U.S. GAAP. In the event that it does, however, and it has the requisite material impact on the foreign private issuer's financial presentation, we believe disclosure would be appropriate.

The Commission has fundamentally conformed the non-financial statement disclosure requirements for foreign private issuers to the non-financial statement disclosure requirements adopted by the International Organization of Securities Commissions (IOSCO).[121] The MD&A-equivalent provision is intended to mirror in substance the MD&A requirements for U.S. companies in Regulation S-K.[122] Our application of the proposed critical

---

[119] Instruction 2 to Item 5 states that the "discussion should focus on the primary financial statements presented in the document. You should refer to the reconciliation to U.S. GAAP, if any, and discuss any aspects of the differences between foreign and U.S. GAAP, not otherwise discussed in the reconciliation, that you believe are necessary for an understanding of the financial statements as a whole."

[120] See proposed Instruction 2 to Item 5 of Form 20-F, 17 CFR 249.220f.

[121] See Securities Act Release No. 7745 (Sept. 28, 1999) [64 FR 53900].

[122] Although the wording of the MD&A requirement in Form 20-F was revised in 1999, the Commission's adopting release noted that we interpret that Item as calling for the same disclosure as Item 303 of Regulation S-K. See Securities Act Release No. 7745 (Sept. 28, 1999) [64 FR 53900 at 59304]. In addition, Instruction 1 to Item 5 in Form 20-F provides that issuers should refer to the Commission's 1989 interpretive release on MD&A disclosure under Item 303 of Regulation S-K (Securities Act Release No. 6835 (May 18, 1989) [54 FR 22427]) for guidance in preparing the discussion and analysis by management of the company's financial condition and results of operations required in Form 20-F.

accounting estimates disclosure and the disclosure regarding initial adoption of an accounting policy to foreign private issuers is consistent with the current approach to MD&A. MD&A disclosure is narrative financial disclosure and the proposed MD&A disclosure can be viewed particularly as an important new aspect of financial disclosure.

Foreign private issuers are not required to submit quarterly reports on Form 10-Q or Form 10-QSB to the Commission. Instead, foreign private issuers submit information on Form 6-K, which encompasses only information that the issuer makes public under its home country requirements.[123] In addition, foreign private issuers are exempt from U.S. proxy and information statement disclosure requirements.[124] Thus, unless a foreign private issuer files a registration statement that must include interim period financial statements and related MD&A disclosure, it would not be required to update the proposed MD&A disclosure more frequently than annually. Foreign private issuers could, however, voluntarily disclose newly identified critical accounting estimates and any other material changes to the most recent MD&A disclosure on Form 6-K, and we encourage them to do so.

We request comment regarding the proposed MD&A disclosure of the application of critical accounting policies as it relates to foreign private issuers.

- Should we apply different standards for foreign private issuers with respect to the proposed MD&A disclosure?

- Are there specific items of the proposed disclosure that would be less appropriate for foreign private issuers? If so, what should substitute for that disclosure?

- Should we consider applying an updating requirement to the proposed critical accounting estimates disclosure for foreign private issuers that do not file quarterly reports? If so, what should trigger that updating requirement?

- Are there reasons to distinguish this aspect of MD&A disclosure when foreign private issuers otherwise may not prepare MD&A-equivalent disclosure on a quarterly basis?

J. Application to Small Business Issuers

Small business issuers[125] are permitted to register and report under somewhat different disclosure requirements than those applicable to larger companies. With respect to MD&A disclosure, the requirements for small business issuers and larger companies are substantially similar.[126] One exception, however, is that small business issuers that have not had revenues from operations in each of the last two fiscal years (or the last fiscal year and any interim period presented in the furnished financial statements) must provide business plan disclosure rather than MD&A disclosure.[127] Those small business issuers must discuss in the business plan disclosure matters such as: how they will satisfy their requirements for cash and raise additional funds in the next 12 months; planned product research and development in that period; expected acquisitions or dispositions of plant and significant equipment; and anticipated significant changes in the number of employees.

Under our proposals, we would not apply the new requirements for MD&A disclosure to the small business issuers disclosing their business plans instead of providing MD&A disclosure. We believe a modified approach is consistent with the objectives underlying the small business issuer disclosure system's alteration of the MD&A disclosure requirements for these companies. Thus, we would not add to the compliance burdens for these

---

[123] Many foreign country disclosure systems do not require quarterly reporting. Nonetheless, some registered foreign private issuers do report financial information on a quarterly basis. If a foreign regulatory authority were to adopt the proposed MD&A requirements, foreign private issuers subject to it would provide the information on Form 6-K.

[124] *See* 17 CFR 240.3a12-3(b).

[125] "Small business issuer" is defined to mean any entity that (1) has revenues of less than $25,000,000, (2) is a United States or Canadian issuer, (3) is not an investment company, and (4) if a majority-owned subsidiary, has a parent corporation that also is a small business issuer. An entity is not a small business issuer, however, if it has a public float (the aggregate market value of the outstanding equity securities held by nonaffiliates) of $25,000,000 or more. *See* 17 CFR 228.10.

[126] *Compare* Item 303 of Regulation S-B, 17 CFR 228.303, to Item 303 of Regulation S-K, 17 CFR 229.303.

[127] *See* Item 303(a) of Regulation S-B, 17 CFR 228.303(a).

small companies. Small business issuers with a recent history of revenues would be required to provide the proposed MD&A disclosure.

We request comment regarding the application to small business issuers of the proposed MD&A disclosure.

- Should we require the proposed MD&A disclosure for small business issuers with no recent revenues even though MD&A disclosure by them is otherwise not required? If so, why?

- Are there modifications or simplifications to the proposed disclosure requirements that we could make, consistent with our ongoing simplification and reduction of burden for small business issuers, that still would achieve the goal of providing investors with an adequate understanding of the implications of management's critical accounting estimates and its initial adoption of accounting policies with a material impact?

- Should we create an exemption from the quarterly updating, or simplify it, for small business issuers?

K. Application of Safe Harbors for Forward-looking Information

As we note in the proposed MD&A requirements, companies preparing disclosure under the proposal that would constitute a forward-looking statement should consider the conditions under which several existing safe harbors apply.[128] As defined in the relevant statutory provisions, a "forward-looking statement" generally is

- statement containing a projection of revenues, income (or loss), earnings (or loss) per share, capital expenditures, dividends, capital structure, or other financial items;

- a statement of the plans and objectives of management for future operations, including plans or objectives relating to the products or services of the issuer;

- a statement of future economic performance, including any such statement contained in MD&A;

- any statement of assumptions underlying or relating to any statement described in the three bullet points above; or

- any report issued by an outside reviewer retained by an issuer, to the extent that the report assesses a forward-looking statement made by the issuer.[129]

The Exchange Act and the Securities Act contain parallel safe harbor protection for forward-looking statements against private legal actions that are based on allegations of a material misstatement or omission.[130] In addition, two Commission rules under those Acts that predate the adoption of the statutory safe harbors also provide protection for forward-looking statements.

The statutory safe harbors provide three separate bases for a company to claim the protection against liability for forward-looking statements made in the company's MD&A. First, a forward-looking statement would fall within that safe harbor if it is identified as forward-looking and it is accompanied by meaningful cautionary statements that identify important factors that could cause actual results to differ materially from those in the forward-looking statement. Second, the safe harbor protects from private

---

[128] *See* proposed Instruction 2 to Item 303 of Regulation S-B, 17 CFR 228.303; proposed Instruction 2 to Item 303(c) of Regulation S-K, 17 CFR 229.303(c); and proposed Instruction 2 to Item 5.E of Form 20-F, 17 CFR 249.220f.

[129] *See* 15 U.S.C. §§ 77z-2 and 78u-5.

[130] While the statutory safe harbors by their terms do not apply to forward-looking statements included in financial statements prepared in accordance with U.S. GAAP, they do cover MD&A disclosures. The statu-

tory safe harbors would not apply, however, if the MD&A forward-looking statement were made in connection with: an initial public offering, a tender offer, an offering by a partnership or a limited liability company, a roll-up transaction, a going private transaction, an offering by a blank check company or a penny stock issuer, or an offering by an issuer convicted of specified securities violations or subject to certain injunctive or cease and desist actions. *See* 15 U.S.C. § 77z-2(b) and § 78u-5(b).

liability any forward-looking statement that is not material. Finally, the safe harbor precludes private liability if a plaintiff fails to prove that the forward-looking statement was made by or with the approval of an executive officer of the company who had actual knowledge that it was false or misleading. The statutory safe harbors cover statements by reporting companies, persons acting on their behalf, outside reviewers retained by them, and their underwriters (when using information from, or derived from, the companies).

The Commission safe harbor rules that apply to forward-looking statements are Rule 175 under the Securities Act and Rule 3b-6 under the Exchange Act.[131] Under those rules, a forward-looking statement made by or on behalf of a company is deemed not to be a fraudulent statement if it is made in good faith and made or reaffirmed with a reasonable basis. The rule-based safe harbors apply to a company if it is a reporting company at the time it makes the forward-looking statement or if it is not a reporting company but it is making the statement in a Securities Act registration statement[132] or an Exchange Act registration statement. The safe harbors cover forward-looking statements in filed documents, in annual reports to shareholders and in Part 1 of Forms 10-Q and 10-QSB.[133]

Some of the proposed MD&A disclosure, but not all of it, would require a company to make forward-looking statements. For example, a company's disclosure of the reasonably possible, near-term changes in its most material assumption(s) underlying accounting estimates would qualify as forward-looking statements, but its quantitative disclosure of the changes it made to its accounting estimates during the past three years would not. Other examples of forward-looking statements that could be made in response to the proposed mandates are: a discussion of the assumptions underlying an estimate that involve, for example, projections of future sales; and a discussion of the expected effect if a known uncertainty were to come to fruition and result in a change in management's assumptions.

In light of the forward-looking statements that would be required, we propose to delete the statements in the existing MD&A rules that indicate that companies are not required to make forward-looking statements under those rules.[134] New Instructions would note that forward-looking statements are required, provide some examples of required forward-looking statements and alert companies preparing the proposed MD&A disclosure to consider the terms, conditions and scope of the safe harbors in drafting their disclosure.

---

[131] *See* 17 CFR 230.175 and 17 CFR 240.3b-6. Forward-looking statements covered by the safe harbors under Rules 175 and 3b-6 are:

● projection of revenues, income (loss), earnings (loss) per share, capital expenditures, dividends, capital structure, other financial items;

● management's plans and objectives for future operations;

● statements of future economic performance in MD&A; and

● statements of assumptions underlying or relating to any of the above.

[132] Thus, unlike the statutory safe harbors, the Rule 175 safe harbor would protect MD&A forward-looking statements made in a registration statement or prospectus for an initial public offering.

[133] The rule safe harbors also cover statements that reaffirm forward-looking statements made in those documents and forward-looking statements made prior to filing or submission of those documents that are reaffirmed in those documents.

' In addition to the statutory and rule safe harbors directed at forward-looking statements, companies preparing the proposed MD&A disclosure also could be protected by the "bespeaks caution" legal doctrine that has developed through case law and is recognized by most circuit courts of appeal. *See, e.g., Lilley v. Charren,* 2001 U.S. App. LEXIS 19430 (9th Cir. 2001); *EP Medsystems, Inc. v. Echocath Inc.,* 235 F.3d 865; (3d Cir. 2000); *Parnes v. Gateway 2000,* 122 F.3d 539 (8th Cir. 1997). The bespeaks caution doctrine recognizes that forecasts, projections and expectations must be read in context and that accompanying cautionary language can render a misstatement or omission immaterial or render a plaintiff's reliance on it unreasonable. For a forward-looking statement to be covered by the bespeaks caution doctrine, there must be adequate cautionary language that warns investors of the potential risks related to the forward-looking statement.

[134] *See* Instruction 2 to Item 303 of Regulation S-B, 17 CFR 228.303; Instruction 7 to Item 303(a) of Regulation S-K, 17 CFR 229.303(a); Instruction 6 to Item 303(b) of Regulation S-K, 17 CFR 229.303(b); and Instruction 3 to Item 5 of Form 20-F, 17 CFR 249.220f.

We request comment regarding the application of safe harbors for forward-looking information to the proposed MD&A disclosure.

- Is there any need for further guidance from the Commission with respect to the application of either the statutory or rule safe harbors?

IV. General Request for Comment

The Commission is proposing these amendments to the MD&A requirements to improve the quality and relevance of explanatory disclosure about a company's financial condition, changes in financial condition, results of operations and reasonably likely trends, demands, commitments, events and uncertainties affecting a company. We welcome your comments. We solicit comment, both specific and general, upon each component of the proposals.

If you would like to submit written comments on the proposals, to suggest additional changes or to submit comments on other matters that might affect the proposals, we encourage you to do so.

We also solicit comment on the following general aspects of the proposals:

- Is the additional information elicited by the proposals useful to investors, other users of company disclosure and readers of a company's financial statements? If not, how can it be improved to achieve that goal?

- In addition to the requirements we propose, are there particular aspects of critical accounting estimates or their development or impact that the proposals should specifically require companies to address? If so, what are they?

- In addition to the requirements we propose, are there particular aspects concerning a company's initial adoption of an accounting policy that the proposals should specifically require companies to address? If so, what are they?

- Is disclosure necessary concerning the procedures that management follows in selecting its critical accounting estimates? If so, what additional disclosure should be provided?

- Is additional disclosure or regulation necessary or appropriate concerning the role of the audit committee in discussing the critical accounting estimates and the disclosure about them that management drafts?

- In addition to the proposed disclosure, should we adopt a specific requirement that a company must provide any other information that is needed to make the proposed disclosure reflective of management's view of the critical accounting estimates and the initially adopted policies being discussed?

- For critical accounting estimates of fair value, should we mandate the example in FR-61[135] as part of these rules? If yes, do other areas exist for which that type of detailed disclosure would be appropriate?

- If the proposed disclosure would involve competitive or other sensitive information, are there any mechanisms that would ensure full and accurate disclosure while reducing a company's risk of competitive harm?

- Are there some aspects of the proposed disclosure that should be retained while eliminating other parts of the proposed disclosure? We solicit comment on the desirability of adopting some sections of the proposed rules, but not all sections.

Any interested person wishing to submit written comments on any aspect of the proposals, as well as on other matters that might have an impact on the proposals, is requested to do so. In addition, we request comment on whether any further changes to our rules and forms are necessary or appropriate to implement the objectives of the proposals. Please submit three copies of your comment letter to Jonathan G. Katz, Secretary, U.S.

---

[135] *See* Securities Act Release No. 8056, FR-61 (Jan. 22, 2002) [67 FR 3746], Section II.B. (providing an example of a critical accounting estimate related to non-exchange-traded contracts accounted for at fair value).

Securities and Exchange Commission, 450 Fifth Street, NW, Washington, DC 20549-0609. You may also submit comments electronically to the following e-mail address: rule-comments@sec.gov.[136] All comments should refer to file number S7-16-02. If you are commenting by e-mail, include this file number in the subject line. We will make comments available for public inspection and copying in the Commission's public reference room at 450 Fifth Street, NW, Washington, DC 20549-0102. In addition, we will post electronically submitted comments on our Internet website (www.sec.gov).

V. Paperwork Reduction Act

A. Background

The proposed amendments to Regulations S-B, S-K[137] and Form 20-F "contain collection of information" requirements within the meaning of the Paperwork Reduction Act of 1995 ("PRA").[138] We are submitting the proposal to the Office of Management and Budget ("OMB") for review in accordance with the PRA.[139] The titles for the collections of information are:

(1)   "Form S-1" (OMB Control No. 3235-0065);

(2)   "Form F-1" (OMB Control No. 3235-0258);

(3)   "Form SB-2" (OMB Control No. 3235-0418);

(4)   "Form S-4" (OMB Control No. 3235-0324);

(5)   "Form F-4" (OMB Control No. 3235-0325);

(6)   "Form 10" (OMB Control No. 3235-0064);

(7)   "Form 10-SB" (OMB Control No. 3235-0419);

(8)   "Form 20-F" (OMB Control No. 3235-0288);

(9)   "Form 10-K" (OMB Control No. 3235-0063);

(10)   "Form 10-KSB" (OMB Control No. 3235-0420);

(11)   "Proxy Statements—Regulation 14A (Commission Rules 14a-1 through 14a-15) and Schedule 14A" (OMB Control No. 3235-0059);

(11)   "Information Statements—Regulation 14C (Commission Rules 14c-1 through 14c-7 and Schedule 14C)" (OMB Control No. 3235-0057);

(13)   "Form 10-Q" (OMB Control No. 3235-0070);

(14)   "Form 10-QSB" (OMB Control No. 3235-0416);

(15)   "Regulation S-K" (OMB Control No. 3235-0071); and

(16)   "Regulation S-B" (OMB Control No. 3235-0417).

---

[136] For more information on how to submit comments electronically, *see* www.sec.gov/rules/submit-comments.htm.

[137] While we are proposing amendments to Regulations S-B and S-K, the burden is imposed through the forms that refer to the disclosure regulations. To avoid a Paperwork Reduction Act inventory with duplicative burdens, we estimate the burdens imposed by Regulations S-B and S-K to be one hour.

[138] 44 U.S.C. § 3501 *et seq.*

[139] 44 U.S.C. § 3507(d) and 5 CFR 1320.11.

These regulations and forms were adopted pursuant to the Securities Act and the Exchange Act and set forth the disclosure requirements for annual and quarterly reports, registration statements and proxy and information statements filed by companies to ensure that investors are informed. The hours and costs associated with preparing, filing, and sending these forms constitute reporting and cost burdens imposed by each collection of information. An agency may not conduct or sponsor, and a person is not required to respond to, a collection of information unless it displays a currently valid control number.

Under the proposals, we would require companies to include a discussion of the application of critical accounting policies in the MD&A section of annual reports, registration statements and proxy and information statements and make updates to some of that disclosure quarterly. We believe that the proposed MD&A disclosure would provide investors with a better understanding of management's application of accounting policies and how those accounting policies affect the financial statements. We believe this disclosure would increase transparency regarding financial disclosure. Compliance with the revised disclosure requirements would be mandatory. There would be no mandatory retention period for the information disclosed, and responses to the disclosure requirements would not be kept confidential.

We estimate the annual incremental paperwork burden for all companies to prepare the disclosure that would be required under our proposals to be approximately 781,911 hours and a cost of approximately $98,467,000.[140] We estimated the average number of hours each entity spends completing the form and the average hourly rate for outside professionals from discussions with persons regularly involved in completing the forms.[141]

B. Registration Statements

Table 1 below illustrates the total annual compliance burden of the proposed collection of information in hours and in cost for registration statements under the Securities Act and the Exchange Act. The burden was calculated by multiplying the estimated number of responses by the estimated average number of hours each entity spends completing the form. We have based our estimated number of annual responses on the actual number of filers during the 2001 fiscal year. We have estimated that, based on a three-year sample period, the average amount of time it would take to prepare the application of critical accounting policies disclosure for registration statements would be approximately 34 hours.

To determine the average total number of hours each entity spends completing each form, we added the estimated hour increment discussed below to the current burden hour estimate for each form reported to OMB. For registration statements, we estimate that 25% of the burden of preparation is carried by the company internally and that 75% of the burden of preparation is carried by outside professionals retained by the company at an average cost of $300 per hour. The portion of the burden carried by outside professionals is reflected as a cost, while the portion of the burden carried by the company internally is reflected in hours. The incremental cost of outside professionals for registration statements would be approximately $22,811,000 per year and the incremental company burden would be approximately 25,345 hours per year. For purposes of our submission to OMB under the PRA, the total cost of outside professionals for registration statements would be approximately $3,740,773,000 per year and the company burden would be approximately 4,156,415 hours per year.

To determine a new PRA burden per form that would accurately reflect the amount of respondents required to prepare the new disclosure, we adjusted the 34-hour incremental burden for some of the forms of registration statements. For the other registration statements

---

[140] For convenience, the estimated PRA hour burdens have been rounded to the nearest whole number, and the estimated PRA cost burdens have been rounded to the nearest $1,000.

[141] In connection with this rulemaking, we have contacted a few companies to obtain cost estimates for preparing the proposed disclosure. Also, in connection with other recent rulemakings, we have had discussions with several private law firms to estimate an hourly rate of $300 as the cost of outside professionals that assist companies in preparing these disclosures.

in Table 1, we used the 34-hour burden estimate. We adjusted the incremental burden to account for the fact that some registration statements allow incorporation by reference, and other forms would not require the company to substantially change a previously prepared MD&A.[142] We have adjusted the incremental burden for Forms S-1, F-1, S-4 and F-4 in recognition of the fact that many repeat issuers complete these forms.[143] A repeat issuer (who is already a reporting company) would not have to prepare an entirely new MD&A for each new registration statement because it would have already prepared MD&A for its periodic reports.

To account for this, we estimate that 40% of the Forms S-1, 65% of Forms F-1, 38% of Forms S-4 and 34% of Forms F-4 would be required to carry the full burden of preparing entirely new MD&A disclosure about the application of critical accounting policies.[144] To reflect the fact that the proposed disclosure would only be prepared anew for a subset of the total forms filed, yet the collection burden is calculated and submitted to OMB for 100% of the forms filed, we reduced the incremental burden hours for the above forms by the percentage of respondents who would not be required to carry the full burden of preparing new disclosure about the application of critical accounting policies. Therefore, we estimate that the average annual incremental burden for all Forms S-1 would be 14 hours per form, which is approximately 40% of the 34-hour burden estimate for preparing the disclosure. We estimate that the average annual incremental burden for all Forms F-1 would be 22 hours per form, which is approximately 65% of the 34-hour burden estimate for preparing the disclosure. We estimate that the average annual incremental burden for all Forms S-4 would be 13 hours per form, which is approximately 38% of the 34-hour burden estimate for preparing the disclosure. Finally, we estimate that the average annual incremental burden for all Forms F-4 would be 12 hours per form, which is 34% of the 34-hour burden estimate for preparing the disclosure.

Table 1: Registration Statements (Columns in bold are the PRA burdens submitted to OMB)

	Annual Responses	Total Hours/Form	Total Burden	25% Company	75% Professional	$300 Prof. Cost
	(A)	(B)	(C)=(A)*(B)	(D)=(C)*0.25	(E)=(C)*0.75	(F)=(E)*$300
S-1	452	1,742	787,384	**196,846**	590,538	$ 177,161,000
F-1	48	1,905	91,440	**22,860**	68,580	$ 20,574,000
SB-2	698	582	406,236	**101,559**	304,677	$ 91,403,000
S-4	3,774	3,973	14,994,102	**3,748,526**	11,245,577	$ 3,373,673,000
F-4	211	1,323	279,153	**69,788**	209,365	$ 62,810,000
Form 10	91	126	11,466	**2,867**	8,600	$ 2,580,000
10-SB	458	122	55,876	**13,969**	41,907	$ 12,572,000
Total			16,625,657	**4,156,415**		$ 3,740,773,000

C. Annual Reports and Proxy/Information Statements

Table 2 below illustrates the total annual compliance burden of the collection of information in hours and in cost for annual reports and proxy and information statements under

---

[142] We have not included registration statements where a registrant fulfills its MD&A disclosure obligation entirely through incorporation by reference (such as Forms S-3 and S-2).

[143] In addition, Forms S-4 and F-4 allow for incorporation by reference when the issuer would be eligible.

[144] We derived these percentages from the proportion of new issuers to total issuers derived from our internal database.

the Exchange Act. The burden was calculated by multiplying the estimated number of responses by the estimated average number of hours each entity spends completing the form.

We have based our estimated number of annual responses on the actual number of filers during the 2001 fiscal year. We have estimated that, based on a three-year sample period, the average amount of time it would take to prepare disclosure about the application of critical accounting policies for annual reports and proxy and information statements would be approximately 29 hours. To determine the average total number of hours each entity spends completing each form, we added the 29-hour increment to the current burden hours estimated for each form. For Exchange Act reports and proxy and information statements, we estimate that 75% of the burden of preparation is carried by the company internally and that 25% of the burden of preparation is carried by outside professionals retained by the company at an average cost of $300 per hour.[145] The portion of the burden carried by outside professionals is reflected as a cost, while the portion of the burden carried by the company internally is reflected in hours. The incremental cost of outside professionals for annual reports and proxy/information statements would be approximately $32,508,000 per year and the incremental company burden would be approximately 325,083 hours per year. For purposes of our submission to OMB under the PRA the total cost of outside professionals for annual reports and proxy/information statements would be approximately $1,738,387,000 per year and the company burden would be approximately 17,383,796 hours per year.

To determine the average total number of hours each entity spends completing each form, we added the estimated hour increment discussed above to the current burden hour estimate for each form reported to OMB. We made one exception, however, with respect to Schedules 14A and 14C. Those schedules only require MD&A in three situations: (1) the modification of any class of securities of the company; (2) the issuance or authorization for issuance of securities of the company; or (3) mergers, consolidations, acquisitions and similar matters.[146] In addition, many of these Schedules are filed by reporting companies. Because in many instances reporting companies would have previously prepared MD&A for their periodic reports, we estimate that 5% of Schedules 14A and 14C would require a company to prepare an entirely new MD&A.[147] To reflect the fact that only the above percentage would require new disclosure, yet the collection burden is calculated and submitted to OMB for 100% of the Schedules filed, we reduced the incremental burden hours for Schedules 14A and 14C by the percentage of respondents who would not be required to carry the full burden of preparing new disclosure about the application of critical accounting policies. Therefore, we estimate that the average annual incremental burden for these forms would be approximately 2 hours, which is approximately 5% of the 34-hour burden estimate for registration statements.

---

[145] This allocation of the burden is a departure from our past PRA submissions for Exchange Act periodic reports and proxy and information statements, for which we estimated that the company carried 25% of the burden internally and 75% of the burden of preparation was carried by outside professionals retained by the company. We believe that this new allocation more accurately reflects current practice for annual and quarterly reports and proxy and information statements.

[146] *See* Items 11, 12 and 14 of Schedule 14A, 17 CFR 240.14a-101.

[147] That percentage is our best estimate based on our belief that the percentage of companies that file Schedules 14A and 14C that would actually be required to carry the full burden of preparing the proposed disclosure would be minimal.

**Table 2: Annual Reports and Proxy/Information Statements
(Columns in bold are the PRA burdens submitted to OMB)**

	Annual Responses	Total Hours/Form	Total Burden	75% Professional	25% Company	$300 Prof. Cost
	(A)	(B)	(C)=(A)* (B)	(E)=(C) *0.75	(D)=(C) *0.25	(F)=(E)* $300
20-F	1,177	1,752	2,062,104	**1,546,578**	515,526	$ 154,658,000
10-K	9,384	1,749	16,412,616	**12,309,462**	4,103,154	$ 1,230,946,000
10-KSB	3,789	1,205	4,565,745	**3,424,309**	1,141,436	$ 342,431,000
SCH 14A	8,239	16	131,824	**98,868**	32,956	$ 9,887,000
SCH 14C	407	15	6,105	**4,579**	1,526	$ 458,000
Total			23,178,394	**17,383,796**		$ 1,738,380,000

D. Quarterly Reports

Table 3 below illustrates the total annual compliance burden of the collection of information in hours and in cost for quarterly reports under the Exchange Act. The burden was calculated by multiplying the estimated number of responses by the esti-mated average number of hours each entity spends completing the form. We have based our estimated number of annual responses on the actual number of filers during the 2001 fiscal year. We have estimated that, based on a three-year sample period, the average amount of time it would take each year to add the new disclosures would be 15 hours per form for each company.[148]

To determine the average total number of hours each entity spends completing each form, we added the 15-hour increment to the current burden hours for each form. For quarterly reports, we estimate that 75% of the burden of preparation is carried by the company internally and that 25% of the burden of preparation is carried by outside professionals retained by the company at an average cost of $300 per hour. The portion of the burden carried by outside professionals is reflected as a cost, while the portion of the burden carried by the company internally is reflected in hours. Additionally, there would be no change to the estimated burden of the collection of information entitled "Regulation S-B" and "Regulation S-K" because the burdens are already reflected in our estimates for the forms. The incremental cost of outside professionals for quarterly reports would be approximately $43,148,000 per year and the incremental company burden would be approximately 431,483 hours per year. For purposes of our submission to OMB under the PRA, the total cost of outside professionals for quarterly reports and Regulation S-K and S-B would be approximately $427,395,000 per year and the com-pany burden would be 4,273,945 hours per year.

---

[148] That estimate assumes that all U.S. reporting companies would have material updates to disclosure about critical accounting estimates in each quarter.

Table 3: Quarterly Reports and Regulations S-K and S-B
(Columns in bold are the PRA burdens submitted to OMB)

	Annual Responses	Total Hours/Form	Total Burden	75% Company	25% Professional	$300 Prof. Cost
	(A)	(B)	(C)=(A)* (B)	(E)=(C) *0.75	(D)=(C) *0.25	(F)=(E)* $300
10-Q	26,746	151	4,038,646	**3,028,985**	1,009,662	$ 302,899,000
10-QSB	11,608	143	1,659,944	**1,244,958**	414,986	$124,496,000
Regulation S-K	0	1	1	**1**	0	$ 0
Regulation S-B	0	1	1	**1**	0	$0
Total				**4,273,945**		$ 427,395,000

E. Solicitation of Comment

Pursuant to 44 U.S.C. § 3506(c)(2)(B), we solicit comments to: (i) evaluate whether the proposed collection of information is necessary for the proper performance of the functions of the agency, including whether the information will have practical utility; (ii) evaluate the accuracy of our estimate of the burden of the proposed collection of information; (iii) determine whether there are ways to enhance the quality, utility and clarity of the information to be collected; and (iv) evaluate whether there are ways to minimize the burden of the collection of information on those who are to respond, including through the use of automated collection techniques or other forms of information technology.

Persons submitting comments on the collection of information requirements should direct the comments to the Office of Management and Budget, Attention: Desk Officer for the Securities and Exchange Commission, Office of Information and Regulatory Affairs, Washington, DC 20503, and should send a copy to Jonathan G. Katz, Secretary, Securities and Exchange Commission, 450 Fifth Street, NW, Washington, DC 20549-0609, with reference to File No. S7-16-02. Requests for materials submitted to OMB by the Commission with regard to these collections of information should be in writing, refer to File No. S7-16-02, and be submitted to the Securities and Exchange Commission, Records Management, Office of Filings and Information Services. OMB is required to make a decision concerning the collection of information between 30 and 60 days after publication of this release. Consequently, a comment to OMB is assured of having its full effect if OMB receives it within 30 days of publication.

VI. Cost-Benefit Analysis

A. Background

The Commission is proposing disclosure rules to address investors' increasing demand for greater transparency with respect to the application of companies' accounting policies and their effects. The proposed disclosure about the application of critical accounting policies encompasses a company's critical accounting estimates and its initial adoption of accounting policies that have a material impact. While the existing disclosure requirements in GAAP result in some basic disclosure of a company's material changes in accounting estimates, initial adoption of accounting policies and risks and uncertainties that may materially affect the financial statements, the proposals would require companies to provide more comprehensive information and analysis about a company's application of critical accounting policies. Because of the potential impact of a company's critical accounting policies and the subjectivity and complexity involved, they are important for investors' understanding of a company's overall financial condition, changes in financial condition and results of operations. The proposals would require companies that are reporting, raising capital in the registered public markets or asking shareholders for their votes to identify their critical accounting estimates and their initial adoption of material accounting policies. For those applications, a company would provide a meaningful analysis of their impact in the "Management's Discussion and Analysis" section of the disclosure documents.

B. Objectives of Proposed Disclosure of Critical Accounting Estimates

Beyond the disclosure of the application of accounting policies provided for in the accounting literature, our proposals would provide additional key information in MD&A that enhances understanding of a company's financial statements, and provides information about the quality of, and potential variability of, a company's earnings. Our proposals would give management the impetus to discuss candidly, and provide insight into, the company's critical accounting estimates and its initial adoption of accounting policies that have a material impact. Our proposals are expected to increase investor understanding, to enhance the ability of investors to make informed investment decisions and to allocate capital on a more efficient basis.

C. Alternative Regulatory Approaches

We considered alternative regulatory actions for achieving the proposed disclosure and greater transparency of a company's application of critical accounting policies. We considered encouraging companies to provide disclosure regarding the application of critical accounting policies.[149] Although some public companies are voluntarily providing more detailed information in their financial statements, it has been noted that some companies generally have not been providing investors with the desired level of detail in their disclosure. To stimulate higher quality disclosures regarding the application of critical accounting policies, we are proposing mandated disclosures.

The proposed mandated disclosures are likely to result in a more focused and descriptive discussion of the company's critical accounting estimates and initial adoption of accounting policies that have a material impact. In addition, mandated disclosures regarding the application of critical accounting policies should benefit investors because the enumerated disclosure under the proposed rule would likely be more comparable across all firms and consistent over time.[150]

In addition to voluntary disclosure, we considered various methods of mandating this disclosure to the public. We are proposing what we believe to be the least onerous method that retains the primary benefit of increased transparency. One alternative approach we considered was to change accounting rules regarding the presentation of financial statements to require more disclosure in the financial statements with respect to the application of critical accounting policies. Another approach we considered was to require companies to file schedules of all accounting estimates as exhibits to their quarterly and annual filings. These schedules would contain a demonstration of how a company calculated each estimate.

Unlike these alternative approaches, we believe that the placement of the proposed disclosure in the MD&A would encourage management to provide more insightful disclosure in a manner more understandable to the average investor than these other disclosure alternatives.

We solicit comment with respect to alternative regulatory approaches.

- Is there evidence that market forces would elicit the disclosures we are proposing?[151]

---

[149] *See* Securities Act Release No. 8040, FR-60 (Dec. 12, 2001) [66 FR 65013]. *See also* Securities Act Release No. 8056, FR-61 (Jan. 22, 2002) [67 FR 3746].

[150] *See generally*, Kothari, S., *Capital Markets Research In Accounting*, 31 Journal of Accounting and Economics 105 (2001). This author suggests that mandated disclosures provide useful information to markets reducing information processing costs for investors by providing for consistent, comparable disclosures.

[151] *See generally*, Healy, P. and K. Palepu, *Information Asymmetry, Corporate Disclosure and Capital Markets: a Review of the Empirical Disclosure Literature*, 31 Journal of Accounting and Economics 405 (2001).

The authors argue that one reason why firms are reluctant to disclose voluntarily is that they face significant proprietary and litigation costs.

- What are the relative costs and benefits of pursuing these or other alternative regulatory solutions to elicit disclosure of the application of critical accounting policies?

D. Potential Benefits of the Proposed Rules

The primary anticipated benefit of the proposed rules is to increase transparency of the financial condition, changes in financial condition and operating results of companies and to reduce the information asymmetry between management and investors. Current market events have evidenced a need to provide investors with a clearer understanding of where a company's accounting policies, estimates, assumptions and methodologies materially affect the financial statements when they are prepared.[152] The proposed disclosure is intended to enhance the quality of the disclosure in the MD&A section by providing more information about management's insight into the company. By making information about the application of critical accounting policies and their implications on the presentation of the company's financial position available and more understandable, the proposals would benefit investors both directly and indirectly through the financial analysts and the credit rating agencies whose analyses investors consider. Greater transparency would thus enable investors to make more informed investment decisions and to allocate capital on a more efficient basis.

As a secondary benefit to investors, a possible by-product of the proposed MD&A disclosure may be to deter improper accounting practices by some companies. For example, the proposed disclosure of critical accounting estimates could make inappropriate earnings management more difficult because it could be easier to detect. The proposed disclosure could also assist investors in evaluating management's performance. With the proposed disclosure, an investor may be better able to judge whether management applies the company's accounting policies either aggressively or conservatively.

Another possible beneficial by-product of the proposed MD&A disclosure could be to increase the discipline and oversight of management in their application of a company's critical accounting policies. In order to prepare the disclosure, management would be required to review and explain the company's application of accounting policies, and the reasonably likely impact. The proposed disclosure could increase management's motivation to exercise greater discipline in applying the company's accounting policies because the material assumptions and methodologies would be more transparent and subject to greater investor scrutiny. In light of this possibility, both auditors and audit committees may also improve their oversight of the application of critical accounting policies.

We solicit comment with respect to the potential benefits of the proposed MD&A disclosure.

- We solicit quantitative data to assist our assessment of the benefits of identifying critical accounting estimates and analyzing their effects on the financial statements and explaining the initial adoption of material accounting policies and their impacts in the manner proposed.

- Would the proposed disclosure serve as a deterrent for improper accounting practices?

E. Potential Costs of Proposed Rules

1. Costs of Preparing Disclosure

We estimate that proposed rules would impose a new disclosure requirement on approximately 14,000 public companies.[153] We anticipate that the average company's application of critical accounting policies disclosure would consist of about six pages of additional text when the company is required to prepare the proposed disclosure in its entirety. We

---

[152] *See generally*, Marcia Vickers, Mike McNamee et al., The Betrayed Investor, *BusinessWeek*, Feb. 25, 2002 at 105.
[153] We derived this estimate by assessing the number of registrants who filed annual reports last year, and subtracting an estimated number of small business issuers who we expect would not be required to provide the disclosure.

estimate that the disclosure would involve multiple parties, including in-house preparers, senior management, in-house counsel, outside counsel, outside auditors, and audit committee members. For purposes of the Paperwork Reduction Act,[154] we estimated that company personnel would spend approximately 780,000 hours per year (56 hours per company) to prepare, review and file the proposed disclosure. Based on our estimated cost of in-house staff time, we estimated the PRA hour-burden would translate into an approximate cost of $98,000,000 ($7,000 per company).[155] We also estimated that companies would spend approximately $98,000,000 ($7000 per company) on outside professionals to comply with the disclosure.[156] We also estimate that companies will incur some additional printing and dissemination costs.[157] We are unable to estimate the potential printing and dissemination costs because there is a wide possible range of paper and ink available and different companies will print a different number of reports depending on their shareholder base.

While companies may face increased costs associated with the preparation, review, filing, printing and dissemination of these disclosures, we believe our proposals would not substantially increase the costs to collect the information necessary to prepare the proposed disclosure. This information should largely be readily available from each company's books and records. Since management must calculate accounting estimates and apply initially adopted accounting policies to prepare the required financial statements, the proposed disclosure may not impose significant incremental costs for the collection and calculation of data. In addition, management is likely to already conduct analysis of the application of the company's accounting policies in the course of managing the business activities of the company. We recognize that management does not currently describe its analysis and is likely to confer with legal counsel in drafting the disclosure. Because of the wide variance among public companies, it is difficult to estimate the average cost. We did contact a few companies that voluntarily had provided information about critical accounting policies in their 2001 Form 10-Ks. They indicated that preparation of the proposed disclosure would cost from approximately $5,000 to $500,000 per year.

We solicit comment regarding the potential cost of compliance with the proposals.

- What types of expenses would companies incur in order to comply with the proposed disclosure requirements?

- What would the average printing and dissemination costs be for each firm?

- We solicit quantitative data to assist our assessment of the compliance costs of identifying critical accounting estimates and the initial adoption of accounting policies that have a material impact and analyzing their effects on the financial statements in the manner proposed.

2. Competitive Harm

There is some possibility that a company's competitors could be able to infer proprietary or sensitive information from disclosure about management's application of critical accounting policies under our proposals. To the extent that all companies make the proposed disclosure, that impact may diminish.

We solicit comment regarding possible competitive harm.

- To what degree would our proposed disclosure requirements create competitively harmful effects upon public companies?

- How could we minimize those effects?

---

[154] 44 U.S.C. § 3501 et seq.

[155] This cost estimate is based on data obtained from *The SIA Report on Management and Professional Earnings in the Securities Industry* (Oct. 2001).

[156] To derive our estimates for the Paperwork Reduction Act, we multiplied the number of filers for each form by the incremental hours per form. The portion of the product carried by the company is reflected in hours and the portion carried by outside professionals is reflected as a cost.

[157] See generally, Del Jones, Companies Beef Up Their Annual Reports, *USA Today*, Mar. 12, 2002 at 1B.

3. Perception of Increased Liability

With any new disclosure mandate, there may be an increased chance that a company could include a materially misleading statement or a material omission in its disclosure document. A company may be concerned that it could be subjected to increased liability due to the disclosure required by the proposed rules. For example, one aspect of our proposed rules would require a quantitative and qualitative analysis to depict the effects of changing a critical accounting estimate. Companies may believe that this disclosure would subject them to potential liability if actual changes to the critical accounting estimates affect line items and overall financial performance to a greater or lesser degree than disclosed. Companies may particularly be concerned with the potential liability when required disclosure is forward-looking in nature.

In part to help alleviate this perception, we are proposing the new disclosure be included in the MD&A section—a section not excluded from the coverage of the safe harbor for forward-looking statements provided by the Private Securities Litigation Reform Act of 1995.[158] Those safe harbors were designed to help companies reduce the costs of litigation relating to those types of statements. The PSLRA safe harbors, as well as those provided by existing Commission Rules 175 and 3b-6 and the "bespeaks caution" legal doctrine created by the courts, should reduce potential litigation costs of companies that craft the disclosure under the proposed rules to meet the conditions of those safe harbors and that doctrine.

We are soliciting comment with regard to the perception of increased liability.

- What are the potential litigation and liability costs that would be associated with the proposed disclosure requirements?

F. Small Business Issuers

We have proposed to require that those small business issuers that must currently make MD&A disclosure also must provide disclosure about the application of critical accounting policies. Small business issuers that are not currently required to prepare MD&A would not be subject to the proposed MD&A disclosure. Thus, only small business issuers that have generated revenues in the past two years would be required to disclose the proposed information about their application of critical accounting policies. The proposals would not impose additional costs for start-up and early stage businesses at a time when they need their resources for growth. We believe the burden on small firms may be less significant overall because these firms would be likely to have fewer critical accounting estimates. We do not have specific data, however, with respect to that assumption.

We ask commenters to provide us with data to estimate the costs of the proposed regulations for small business issuers.

- Would small business issuers on average have fewer critical accounting estimates to discuss?
- Who would prepare the disclosure for small business issuers?
- What types of expenses would be incurred to prepare this disclosure?

G. Foreign Private Issuers

We propose to apply to foreign private issuers the same MD&A disclosure requirements regarding the application of critical accounting policies that would apply to U.S. companies. Foreign private issuers, however, may present their financial statements either in accordance with U.S. GAAP, in accordance with GAAP of a foreign country, or in accordance with International Accounting Standards and International Financial Reporting Standards issued by the International Accounting Standards Committee and the International Accounting Standards Board. If financial statements are presented in accordance with non-U.S. GAAP, a reconciliation to U.S. GAAP accompanies them. If the primary financial

---

[158] Pub. L. No. 104-67, 109 Stat. 737 (1995).

statements were in non-U.S. GAAP, the company would have to consider the application of critical accounting policies in connection with both its primary financial statements and its reconciliation to U.S. GAAP. Therefore, foreign private issuers may incur additional costs with regard to the proposed disclosure because of possible additional disclosure regarding the reconciliation to U.S. GAAP.

Offsetting this additional cost, however, is the fact that foreign private issuers would not be required to submit quarterly reports on Form 10-Q or Form 10-QSB to the Commission. In addition, foreign private issuers are exempt from U.S. proxy and information statement disclosure requirements.[159] Thus, unless a foreign private issuer files a registration statement that must include interim period financial statements and related MD&A disclosure, it generally would not be required to update the proposed MD&A disclosure more frequently than annually. Therefore, the overall cost of compliance could be lower for foreign private issuers than for U.S. companies.

We ask commenters to provide us with data to estimate the costs of the proposed regulations for foreign private issuers.

- On average, would the U.S. GAAP reconciliation cause foreign private issuers to have more critical accounting estimates and more initial adoptions of accounting policies to discuss than a U.S. company? If so, how many more?

H. Request for Comments

To assist the Commission in its evaluation of the costs and benefits of the proposed disclosure discussed in this release, we request that commenters provide views and data relating to any costs and benefits associated with the proposed rules.

VII. Effects on Efficiency, Competition and Capital Formation

Section 23(a)(2) of the Exchange Act[160] requires us, when adopting rules under the Exchange Act, to consider the anti-competitive effects. The proposed rules are intended to make information about the application of critical accounting policies and their implications for the presentation of a company's financial condition, changes in financial condition and operating results more understandable to investors. We have identified one possible area where the proposed rules could potentially place a burden on competition. In our cost-benefit analysis above, we note that there is some possibility that a company's competitors could be able to infer proprietary or sensitive information from disclosure about management's application of critical accounting policies under our proposals. To the extent that all companies make the proposed disclosure, that impact may diminish. In our cost-benefit analysis above, we request comment regarding the degree to which our proposed disclosure requirements would create competitively harmful effects upon public companies, and how to minimize those effects. We request comment on any disproportionate cross-sectional burdens among the firms affected by our proposals that could have anti-competitive effects.

Section 2(b) of the Securities Act[161] and Section 3(f) of the Exchange Act[162] require us, when engaging in rulemaking that requires us to consider or determine whether an action is necessary or appropriate in the public interest, to consider, in addition to the protection of investors, whether the action will promote efficiency, competition and capital formation. We believe the proposed disclosure may promote market efficiency by making information about the application of critical accounting policies, and their impact on the presentation of the company's financial position, more understandable. As a result, we believe that investors may be able to make more informed investment decisions and capital may be allocated on a more efficient basis. In addition, we believe this disclosure would assist investors in evaluating management. The possibility of these effects, their magnitude if they were to occur and the extent to which they would be offset by the costs of the proposals are difficult to quantify. We request comment on these matters and how the proposed amendments, if adopted, would affect efficiency and capital formation.

---

[159] *See* 17 CFR 240.3a12-3(b).
[160] 15 U.S.C. § 78w(a)(2).

[161] 15 U.S.C. § 77b(b).
[162] 15 U.S.C. § 78c(f).

Commenters are requested to provide empirical data and other factual support to the extent possible.

VIII. Initial Regulatory Flexibility Analysis

This Initial Regulatory Flexibility Analysis has been prepared in accordance with 5 U.S.C. 603. It relates to proposed revisions to Item 303 of Regulation S-K,[163] Item 303 of Regulation S-B[164] and Item 5 of Form 20-F.[165] The proposals require a company to discuss the application of critical accounting policies. The new disclosure would be included in the MD&A section of a company's annual reports, registration statements and proxy and information statements. Companies would be required to update the portion of the proposed MD&A information about critical accounting estimates by disclosing material changes quarterly on Form 10-Q or Form 10-QSB.

A. Reasons for the Proposed Action

The requirements of GAAP for disclosure in financial statements and the current requirements in MD&A have not resulted in the type of discussion of the application of critical accounting policies that our proposals would require. The potential consequences of not taking this action to require disclosure regarding the application of critical accounting policies are: (a) less transparency in the presentation of companies' financial statements and, correspondingly, a lesser understanding of companies' financial condition, changes in financial condition and results of operations when making investment decisions; and (b) a potential decrease in investor confidence in the full and fair disclosure system that is the hallmark of the U.S. capital markets.

B. Objectives

Beyond the disclosure of the application of accounting policies provided for in the accounting literature, our proposals would provide additional key information in MD&A that enhances understanding of a company's financial statements, and provides information about the quality of, and potential variability of, a company's earnings. Our proposals would give management the impetus to discuss candidly, and provide insight into, the company's application of critical accounting policies. We believe that our proposals may increase investor understanding, enhance the ability of investors to make informed investment decisions and allocate capital on a more efficient basis.

C. Legal Basis

We are proposing the amendments under the authority set forth in Sections 7, 10 and 19 of Securities Act of 1933 and Sections 12, 13, 14 and 23 of the Securities Exchange Act of 1934.

D. Small Entities Subject to the Proposed Regulation and Rules

The proposals would affect companies that are small entities. Exchange Act Rule 0-10(a)[166] and Securities Act Rule 157[167] define a company, other than an investment company, to be a "small business" or "small organization" if it had total assets of $5 million or less on the last day of its most recent fiscal year. As of February 20, 2002, we estimated that there were approximately 2,500 companies, other than investment companies, that may be considered small entities. The proposed disclosure requirements would apply to any small entity that fulfills its disclosure obligations by either complying with our standard disclosure requirements[168] or providing the "Management's Discussion and Analysis" disclosure item contained in our optional disclosure system available only to small businesses.[169] If a small entity elects to fulfill its disclosure obligations pursuant to our optional disclosure system for small businesses, it would be required to comply with our proposed rule only if it had revenues during the past two fiscal years. While we

---

[163] 17 CFR 229.303.
[164] 17 CFR 228.303.
[165] 17 CFR 249.220f.
[166] 17 CFR 270.0-10(a).

[167] 17 CFR 230.157.
[168] Regulation S-K, 17 CFR 229.10-229.1016.
[169] Regulation S-B, 17 CFR 228.10-228.701.

believe that there are a number of small entities that therefore would not be required to comply with our proposals, we are unable to quantify that number. We request comment on the number of small entities that would not be required to comply with our proposals.

E. Reporting, Recordkeeping and Other Compliance Requirements

Small entities would either utilize existing personnel or hire an outside professional to provide the proposed disclosure. This would impose incremental costs on small entities in connection with drafting, reviewing, filing, printing and disseminating additional disclosure in annual reports, registration statements, proxy and information statements and quarterly reports. The data underlying the proposed disclosure should be readily available from a company's books and records. Thus, the proposed rules involve relatively low incremental costs for the collection and calculation of data. This belief is based on the fact that management already must calculate the critical accounting estimates and apply initially adopted accounting policies to prepare the required financial statements. In addition, the burden on small entities of disclosing the effects of those estimates and changes in them may be less because it is possible that these firms may have fewer critical accounting estimates that would be covered by the proposals.

The proposed rule was designed to reduce costs for small entities by requiring the proposed disclosure only in the event that a small business issuer has generated revenue in the past two years. Our proposals thus would avoid applying the new requirements for MD&A disclosure relating to the application of critical accounting policies to start-up or developing companies that need not provide MD&A disclosure otherwise. Those companies describe a business plan rather than the traditional MD&A. In addition, small business issuers that provide the critical accounting estimates disclosure would only be required to provide a quantitative discussion of past material changes in estimates for the last two fiscal years. This corresponds to the income statements required to be included in our small business forms. Other companies would be required to discuss this information for the past three years.

F. Duplicative, Overlapping or Conflicting Federal Rules

We believe that there are no rules that conflict with or completely duplicate the proposed rules. There is a possible partial overlap with financial statement requirements requiring disclosure about material changes in critical accounting estimates and risks and uncertainties that could materially affect the financial statements and with MD&A requirements that may require some discussion of the application of critical accounting policies if that is essential to an understanding of a company's financial condition, changes in financial condition or results of operations. However, those requirements do not include much of the information specifically targeted for inclusion in the proposed rules.

G. Significant Alternatives

The Regulatory Flexibility Act directs the Commission to consider significant alternatives that would accomplish the stated objective, while minimizing any significant adverse impact on small entities. In connection with the proposals, we considered the following alternatives:

(a) The establishment of differing compliance or reporting requirements or timetables that take into account the resources available to small entities;

(b) The clarification, consolidation, or simplification of disclosure related to critical accounting estimates for small entities;

(c) The use of performance rather than design standards; and

(d) An exemption for small entities from coverage under the proposals.

We have drafted the proposed disclosure rules to require clear and straightforward disclosure in MD&A. Separate disclosure requirements for small entities would not yield the disclosure that we believe to be necessary to achieve our objectives. In addition, the informational needs of investors in small entities are typically as great as the needs of investors in larger companies. Therefore, it does not seem appropriate to develop separate requirements for small entities involving clarification, consolidation or simplification of the proposed disclosure.

We have used design rather than performance standards in connection with the proposals for three reasons. First, we believe the proposed disclosure would be more useful to investors if there were enumerated informational requirements. The proposed mandated disclosures may be likely to result in a more focused and comprehensive discussion of the company's application of its critical accounting policies. Second, mandated disclosures regarding the application of critical accounting policies may benefit investors in small entities because the enumerated disclosure under the proposed rule would likely be more comparable across all firms and consistent over time. Third, a mandated discussion of a company's application of critical accounting policies is uniquely suited to the MD&A disclosure in light of MD&A's emphasis on the identification of significant uncertainties and events and favorable or unfavorable trends. Therefore, adding a disclosure requirement to the existing MD&A appears to be the most effective method of eliciting the disclosure.

As noted above, we have proposed not to cover small business issuers that have not generated revenue during the last two years. We have made this accommodation in recognition of the fact that a limited modified approach is consistent with the objectives underlying the small business issuer disclosure system's alteration of the MD&A requirements for these companies and reduction of compliance burdens for these small companies. We believe that exempting small entities further from coverage of the proposals would not be appropriate. Investors in smaller companies may want and benefit from the disclosures about the application of critical accounting policies just as much as investors in larger companies. We note that a study commissioned by the Committee of Sponsoring Organizations of the Treadway Commission found that the incidence of financial fraud was greater at small companies.[170] Accordingly, a possible secondary benefit to investors in small entities may be to deter improper accounting practices. For example, the proposed disclosure could make inappropriate earnings management more difficult because it could be easier to detect.

H. Solicitation of Comments

We encourage the submission of comments with respect to any aspect of this Initial Regulatory Flexibility Analysis. In particular, we request comments regarding: (i) the number of small entities that may be affected by the proposals; (ii) the existence or nature of the potential impact of the proposals on small entities discussed in the analysis; and (iii) how to quantify the impact of the proposed revisions. Commenters are asked to describe the nature of any impact and provide empirical data supporting the extent of the impact. Such comments will be considered in the preparation of the Final Regulatory Flexibility Analysis, if the proposals are adopted, and will be placed in the same public file as comments on the proposed amendments themselves.

IX. Small Business Regulatory Enforcement Fairness Act

For purposes of the Small Business Regulatory Enforcement Fairness Act of 1996 ("SBREFA"),[171] a rule is "major" if it has resulted, or is likely to result in:

- An annual effect on the economy of $100 million or more;

- A major increase in costs or prices for consumers or individual industries; or

- Significant adverse effects on competition, investment or innovation.

We preliminarily believe that our proposals could constitute a "major rule" under SBREFA. We request comment on whether our proposals would be a "major rule" for purposes of SBREFA. We solicit comment and empirical data on: (a) the potential effect

---

[170] *See* Beasley, Carcello and Hermanson, Fraudulent Financial Reporting: 1987-1997, and Analysis of U.S. Public Companies (Mar. 1999).

[171] Pub. L. No. 104-121, Title II, 110 Stat. 857 (1996).

on the U.S. economy on an annual basis; (b) any potential increase in costs or prices for consumers or individual industries; and (c) any potential effect on competition, investment or innovation.

X. Codification Update

The Commission proposes to amend the "Codification of Financial Reporting Policies" announced in Financial Reporting Release No. 1 (April 15, 1982):

By adding Section 501.12, captioned "The Application of Critical Accounting Policies," to include the text in the adopting release that discusses the final rules, which, if the proposed rules are adopted, would be substantially similar to Section III of this release.

The Codification is a separate publication of the Commission. It will not be published in the Code of Federal Regulations.

STATUTORY BASES AND TEXT OF PROPOSED AMENDMENTS

We are proposing amendments to Commission's existing rules under the authority set forth in Sections 7, 10 and 19 of the Securities Act and Sections 12, 13, 14 and 23 of the Exchange Act.

List of Subjects

17 CFR Parts 228, 229 and 249

Reporting and recordkeeping requirements, Securities.

Text of Proposed Amendments

In accordance with the foregoing, the Securities and Exchange Commission proposes to amend Title 17, chapter II of the Code of Federal Regulations as follows:

PART 228—INTEGRATED DISCLOSURE SYSTEM FOR SMALL BUSINESS ISSUERS

1. The authority citation for Part 228 continues to read as follows:

Authority: 15 U.S.C. 77e, 77f, 77g, 77h, 77j, 77k, 77s, 77z-2, 77z-3, 77aa(25), 77aa(26), 77ddd, 77eee, 77ggg, 77hhh, 77jjj, 77nnn, 77sss, 78*l*, 78m, 78n, 78*o*, 78u-5, 78w, 78*ll*, 78mm, 80a-8, 80a-29, 80a-30, 80a-37 and 80b-11.

2. Section 228.303 is amended by adding paragraph (b)(3) and Instructions to paragraph (b)(3) and revising Instruction 2 of Instructions to Item 303 to read as follows:

§ 228.303 (Item 303) Management's Discussion and Analysis or Plan of Operation.

* * * * *

(b) * * *

(3) *The application of critical accounting policies.*

(i) Annual reports, registration statements and proxy and information statements. In an annual report filed under the Exchange Act, an annual report to shareholders prepared under § 240.14a-3 or § 240.14c-3 of this chapter, a registration statement filed under the Securities Act or the Exchange Act, or a proxy or information statement filed under the Exchange Act, include a separately-captioned section in "Management's Discussion and Analysis" setting forth the disclosure regarding the small business issuer's application of critical accounting policies required by paragraphs (b)(3)(iii) and (b)(3)(iv) of this section. Except as otherwise stated, the discussion must cover the financial statements for the most recent fiscal year and any subsequent period for which interim period financial statements are required to be included.

(ii) *Definitions.*

(A) *Accounting estimate.* As used in Item 5.E., the term *accounting estimate* means an approximation made by management of a financial statement element, item or account in the financial statements.

(B) *Critical accounting estimate.* An accounting estimate recognized in the financial statements presented is a *critical accounting estimate* for purposes of this section if:

(1) The accounting estimate requires the small business issuer to make assumptions about matters that are highly uncertain at the time the accounting estimate is made; and

(2) Different estimates that the small business issuer reasonably could have used in the current period, or changes in the accounting estimate that are reasonably likely to occur from period to period, would have a material impact on the presentation of the small business issuer's financial condition, changes in financial condition or results of operations.

(C) *Near-term.* As used in Item 5.E.3., the term *near-term* means a period of time going forward up to one year from the date of the financial statements.

(D) *Reasonably possible.* As used in Item 5.E.3., the term *reasonably possible* means the chance of a future transaction or event occurring is more than remote but less than likely.

(iii) *Disclosure regarding critical accounting estimates.* For each critical accounting estimate:

(a) Identify and describe the accounting estimate. Describe the methodology underlying the accounting estimate. Describe the assumptions underlying the accounting estimate that relate to matters highly uncertain at the time the estimate was made. Describe any other underlying assumptions that are material. Discuss any known trends, demands, commitments, events or uncertainties that are reasonably likely to occur and materially affect the methodology or assumptions described. Disclose, if applicable, why different estimates that would have had a material impact on the small business issuer's financial presentation could have been used in the current period. Describe, if applicable, why the accounting estimate is reasonably likely to change from period to period with a material impact on the financial presentation;

(b) Explain the significance of the accounting estimate to the small business issuer's financial condition, changes in financial condition and results of operations and, where material, identify the line items in the financial statements affected by the accounting estimate;

(c) (1) Present either:

(i) A quantitative discussion of changes in overall financial performance, and to the extent material the line items in the financial statements, assuming that reasonably possible near-term changes occur, both negative and positive (where applicable), in the most material assumption or assumptions underlying the accounting estimate; or

(ii) A quantitative discussion of changes in overall financial performance, and to the extent material the line items in the financial statements, assuming that the accounting estimate was changed to the upper end and the lower end of the range of reasonable possibilities determined by the small business issuer in the course of formulating its recorded estimate; and

(2) Discuss the impact, if material, on the company's liquidity or capital resources if any of the changes being assumed for purposes of satisfying paragraph 5.E.3.(iii)(C)(1)(i) or paragraph 5.E.3.(iii)(C)(1)(ii) of this Item were in effect.

(d) Present a quantitative and qualitative discussion of any material changes made to the accounting estimate in the past three years (or in the past two years for any filing made before [one year after the effective date of the final rule]), describe the reasons for the changes and discuss the effect on line items in the financial statements and overall financial performance;

(e) Disclose whether or not your senior management has discussed the development and selection of the critical accounting estimates, and the MD&A disclosure regarding them, with the audit committee of your board of directors (or the equivalent oversight group). If your senior management has not had these discussions, disclose the reasons why not; and

(f) If the company operates in more than one segment, identify the disclosed segments that the accounting estimate affects. To the extent that the disclosure under the requirements this Item 5.E. made only on a company-wide basis would result in an omission that renders the disclosure materially misleading, include a separate discussion on a segment basis for the identified segments of the small business issuer business about which disclosure is otherwise required.

4. Disclosure regarding initial adoption of an accounting policy. If an accounting policy initially adopted by the company (other than those solely resulting from the adoption of new accounting literature issued by a recognized accounting standard setter) had a material impact on its financial condition, changes in financial condition or results of operations, disclose:

(a)   The events or transactions that gave rise to the initial adoption;

(b)   The accounting principle that has been adopted and the method of applying that principle;

(c)   The impact, qualitatively, on the financial condition, changes in financial condition and results of operations of the company;

(d)   If the company is permitted a choice between acceptable accounting principles, an explanation it made such a choice, what the alternatives were, and why it made the choice that it did (including, where material, qualitative disclosure of the impact on financial condition, changes in financial condition and results of operations that alternatives would have had); and

(e)   If no accounting literature exists that governs the accounting for the events or transactions giving rise to the initial adoption, an explanation of the company's decision regarding which accounting principle to use and which method of applying that principle to use.

Instructions to Item 5: * * *

2. * * * With respect to the disclosure under Item 5.E., although the discussion would focus on the primary financial statements, you also must consider any reconciliation to U.S. GAAP and include disclosure required under Item 5.E. for any critical accounting estimate that is related to the application of U.S. GAAP and for any initial adoption of an accounting policy that is related to the application of U.S. GAAP.

Instruction to Item 5.A:

* * * * *

Instructions to Item 5.E:

1. The changes being assumed in connection with Item 5.E.3.(c)(1) must be meaningful and therefore may not be so minute as to avoid, or materially understate, any demonstration of sensitivity.

2. Item 5 requires you to make certain forward-looking statements. Examples of forward-looking statements include, but are not limited to: a company's disclosure of the reasonably possible, near-term changes in its assumptions underlying accounting estimates; a discussion of the assumptions underlying an estimate that involve, for example, projections of

future sales; and a discussion of the expected effect if a known uncertainty were to come to fruition and result in a change in management's assumptions. If the terms and conditions of Section 27A of the Securities Act (15 U.S.C. 77z-2), Section 21E of the Exchange Act (15 U.S.C. 78u-5), § 230.175 of this chapter or § 249.3b-6 of this chapter are satisfied, forward-looking statements would be entitled to the safe harbor protection. Companies are encouraged to consider the terms, conditions and scope of those safe harbors when drafting disclosure, particularly when preparing disclosure under the provisions of Item 5.E.

3. All information provided under Item 5.E. must be presented in clear, concise format and language that is understandable to the average investor. The information provided in Item 5.E. must not be presented, for example: only as a general discussion of multiple critical accounting estimates in the aggregate or of multiple new accounting policies in the aggregate; as boilerplate disclosures that do not specifically address the company's particular circumstances and operations; as lists of accounting estimates relating to each material line item in the company's financial statements; or as disclosures that consist principally of disclaimers of legal liability for the company's preparation of critical accounting estimates or initial application of an accounting policy.

4. Refer to the Commission's release number 33-_____ dated _____, 200_ (adopting Item 5.E.) for guidance in preparing the disclosure relating to critical accounting estimates in this discussion and analysis by management of the company's financial condition, changes in financial condition and results of operations.

* * * * *

By the Commission.

Margaret H. McFarland

Deputy Secretary

Dated: May 10, 2002

APPENDIX 11

SEC Division of Corporation Finance Staff Legal Bulletins 14, 14A, 14B, 14C, 14D, 14E, and 14F—Shareholder Proposals

Division of Corporation Finance Staff Legal Bulletin No. 14

Shareholder Proposals

Date: July 13, 2001

Action: Publication of CF Staff Legal Bulletin

Summary: This staff legal bulletin provides information for companies and shareholders on rule 14a-8 of the Securities Exchange Act of 1934.

Supplementary Information: The statements in this legal bulletin represent the views of the Division of Corporation Finance. This bulletin is not a rule, regulation or statement of the Securities and Exchange Commission. Further, the Commission has neither approved nor disapproved its content.

Contact Person: For further information, please contact Jonathan Ingram, Michael Coco, Lillian Cummins or Keir Gumbs at (202) 942-2900.

A. What is the purpose of this bulletin?

The Division of Corporation Finance processes hundreds of rule 14a-8 no-action requests each year. We believe that companies and shareholders may benefit from information that we can provide based on our experience in processing these requests. Therefore, we prepared this bulletin in order to

- explain the rule 14a-8 no-action process, as well as our role in this process;

- provide guidance to companies and shareholders by expressing our views on some issues and questions that commonly arise under rule 14a-8; and

- suggest ways in which both companies and shareholders can facilitate our review of no-action requests.

Because the substance of each proposal and no-action request differs, this bulletin primarily addresses procedural matters that are common to companies and shareholders. However, we also discuss some substantive matters that are of interest to companies and shareholders alike.

We structured this bulletin in a question and answer format so that it is easier to understand and we can more easily respond to inquiries regarding its contents. The references to "we," "our" and "us" are to the Division of Corporation Finance. You can find a copy of rule 14a-8 in Release No. 34-40018, dated May 21, 1998, which is located on the Commission's website at www.sec.gov/rules/final/34-40018.htm.

B. Rule 14a-8 and the no-action process

1. What is rule 14a-8?

Rule 14a-8 provides an opportunity for a shareholder owning a relatively small amount of a company's securities to have his or her proposal placed alongside management's proposals in that company's proxy materials for presentation to a vote at an annual or special meeting of shareholders. It has become increasingly popular because it provides an avenue for communication between shareholders and companies, as well as among shareholders themselves. The rule generally requires the company to include the proposal unless the shareholder has not complied with the rule's procedural requirements or the proposal falls within one of the 13 substantive bases for exclusion described in the table below.

Substantive Basis	Description
Rule 14a-8(i)(1)	The proposal is not a proper subject for action by shareholders under the laws of the jurisdiction of the company's organization.
Rule 14a-8(i)(2)	The proposal would, if implemented, cause the company to violate any state, federal or foreign law to which it is subject.
Rule 14a-8(i)(3)	The proposal or supporting statement is contrary to any of the Commission's proxy rules, including rule 14a-9, which prohibits materially false or misleading statements in proxy soliciting materials.
Rule 14a-8(i)(4)	The proposal relates to the redress of a personal claim or grievance against the company or any other person, or is designed to result in a benefit to the shareholder, or to further a personal interest, which is not shared by the other shareholders at large.
Rule 14a-8(i)(5)	The proposal relates to operations that account for less than 5% of the company's total assets at the end of its most recent fiscal year, and for less than 5% of its net earnings and gross sales for its most recent fiscal year, and is not otherwise significantly related to the company's business.
Rule 14a-8(i)(6)	The company would lack the power or authority to implement the proposal.
Rule 14a-8(i)(7)	The proposal deals with a matter relating to the company's ordinary business operations.
Rule 14a-8(i)(8)	The proposal relates to an election for membership on the company's board of directors or analogous governing body.
Rule 14a-8(i)(9)	The proposal directly conflicts with one of the company's own proposals to be submitted to shareholders at the same meeting.
Rule 14a-8(i)(10)	The company has already substantially implemented the proposal.
Rule 14a-8(i)(11)	The proposal substantially duplicates another proposal previously submitted to the company by another shareholder that will be included in the company's proxy materials for the same meeting.
Rule 14a-8(i)(12)	The proposal deals with substantially the same subject matter as another proposal or proposals that previously has or have been included in the company's proxy materials within a specified time frame and did not receive a specified percentage of the vote. Please refer to questions and answers F.2, F.3 and F.4 for more complete descriptions of this basis.
Rule 14a-8(i)(13)	The proposal relates to specific amounts of cash or stock dividends.

2. How does rule 14a-8 operate? The rule operates as follows:

- the shareholder must provide a copy of his or her proposal to the company by the deadline imposed by the rule;

- if the company intends to exclude the proposal from its proxy materials, it must submit its reason(s) for doing so to the Commission and simultaneously provide the shareholder with a copy of that submission. This submission to the Commission of reasons for excluding the proposal is commonly referred to as a no-action request;

- the shareholder may, but is not required to, submit a reply to us with a copy to the company; and

- we issue a no-action response that either concurs or does not concur in the company's view regarding exclusion of the proposal.

3. What are the deadlines contained in rule 14a-8?

Rule 14a-8 establishes specific deadlines for the shareholder proposal process. The following table briefly describes those deadlines.

120 days before the release date disclosed in the previous year's proxy statement	Proposals for a regularly scheduled annual meeting must be received at the company's principal executive offices not less than 120 calendar days before the release date of the previous year's annual meeting proxy statement. Both the release date and the deadline for receiving rule 14a-8 proposals for the next annual meeting should be identified in that proxy statement.
14-day notice of defect(s)/response to notice of defect(s)	If a company seeks to exclude a proposal because the shareholder has not complied with an eligibility or procedural requirement of rule 14a-8, generally, it must notify the shareholder of the alleged defect(s) within 14 calendar days of receiving the proposal. The shareholder then has 14 calendar days after receiving the notification to respond. Failure to cure the defect(s) or respond in a timely manner may result in exclusion of the proposal.
80 days before the company files its definitive proxy statement and form of proxy	If a company intends to exclude a proposal from its proxy materials, it must submit its no-action request to the Commission no later than 80 calendar days before it files its definitive proxy statement and form of proxy with the Commission unless it demonstrates "good cause" for missing the deadline. In addition, a company must simultaneously provide the shareholder with a copy of its no-action request.
30 days before the company files its definitive proxy statement and form of proxy	If a proposal appears in a company's proxy materials, the company may elect to include its reasons as to why shareholders should vote against the proposal. This statement of reasons for voting against the proposal is commonly referred to as a statement in opposition. Except as explained in the box immediately below, the company is required to provide the shareholder with a copy of its statement in opposition no later than 30 calendar days before it files its definitive proxy statement and form of proxy.
Five days after the company has received a revised proposal	If our no-action response provides for shareholder revision to the proposal or supporting statement as a condition to requiring the company to include it in its proxy materials, the company must provide the shareholder with a copy of its statement in opposition no later than five calendar days after it receives a copy of the revised proposal.

In addition to the specific deadlines in rule 14a-8, our informal procedures often rely on timely action. For example, if our no-action response requires that the shareholder revise the proposal or supporting statement, our response will afford the shareholder seven calendar days from the date of receiving our response to provide the company with the revisions. In this regard, please refer to questions and answers B.12.a and B.12.b.

4. What is our role in the no-action process?

Our role begins when we receive a no-action request from a company. In these no-action requests, companies often assert that a proposal is excludable under one or more parts of rule 14a-8. We analyze each of the bases for exclusion that a company asserts, as well as any arguments that the shareholder chooses to set forth, and determine whether we concur in the company's view.

The Division of Investment Management processes rule 14a-8 no-action requests submitted by registered investment companies and business development companies.

Rule 14a-8 no-action requests submitted by registered investment companies and business development companies, as well as shareholder responses to those requests, should be sent to

U.S. Securities and Exchange Commission
Division of Investment Management
Office of Chief Counsel
450 Fifth Street, N.W.
Washington, D.C. 20549

All other rule 14a-8 no-action requests and shareholder responses to those requests should be sent to

U.S. Securities and Exchange Commission
Division of Corporation Finance
Office of Chief Counsel
450 Fifth Street, N.W.
Washington, D.C. 20549

5. What factors do we consider in determining whether to concur in a company's view regarding exclusion of a proposal from the proxy statement?

The company has the burden of demonstrating that it is entitled to exclude a proposal, and we will not consider any basis for exclusion that is not advanced by the company. We analyze the prior no-action letters that a company and a shareholder cite in support of their arguments and, where appropriate, any applicable case law. We also may conduct our own research to determine whether we have issued additional letters that support or do not support the company's and shareholder's positions. Unless a company has demonstrated that it is entitled to exclude a proposal, we will not concur in its view that it may exclude that proposal from its proxy materials.

6. Do we base our determinations solely on the subject matter of the proposal?

No. We consider the specific arguments asserted by the company and the shareholder, the way in which the proposal is drafted and how the arguments and our prior no-action responses apply to the specific proposal and company at issue. Based on these considerations, we may determine that company X may exclude a proposal but company Y cannot exclude a proposal that addresses the same or similar subject matter. The following chart illustrates this point by showing that variations in the language of a proposal, or different bases cited by a company, may result in different responses.

As shown below, the first and second examples deal with virtually identical proposals, but the different company arguments resulted in different responses. In the second and third examples, the companies made similar arguments, but differing language in the proposals resulted in different responses.

Company	Proposal	Bases for exclusion that the company cited	Date of our response	Our response
PG&E Corp.	Adopt a policy that independent directors are appointed to the audit, compensation and nomination committees.	Rule 14a-8(b) only	Feb. 21, 2000	We did not concur in PG&E's view that it could exclude the proposal. PG&E did not demonstrate that the shareholder failed to satisfy the rule's

				minimum ownership requirements. PG&E included the proposal in its proxy materials.
PG&E Corp.	Adopt a bylaw that independent directors are appointed for all future openings on the audit, compensation and nomination committees.	Rule 14a-8(i)(6) only	Jan. 22, 2001	We concurred in PG&E's view that it could exclude the proposal. PG&E demonstrated that it lacked the power or authority to implement the proposal. PG&E did not include the proposal in its proxy materials.
General Motors Corp.	Adopt a bylaw requiring a transition to independent directors for each seat on the audit, compensation and nominating committees as openings occur (emphasis added).	Rules 14a-8(i)(6) and 14a-8(i)(10)	Mar. 22, 2001	We did not concur in GM's view that it could exclude the proposal. GM did not demonstrate that it lacked the power or authority to implement the proposal or that it had substantially implemented the proposal. GM included the proposal in its proxy materials.

7. Do we judge the merits of proposals?

No. We have no interest in the merits of a particular proposal. Our concern is that shareholders receive full and accurate information about all proposals that are, or should be, submitted to them under rule 14a-8.

8. Are we required to respond to no-action requests?

No. Although we are not required to respond, we have, as a convenience to both companies and shareholders, engaged in the informal practice of expressing our enforcement position on these submissions through the issuance of no-action responses. We do this to assist both companies and shareholders in complying with the proxy rules.

9. Will we comment on the subject matter of pending litigation?

No. Where the arguments raised in the company's no-action request are before a court of law, our policy is not to comment on those arguments. Accordingly, our no-action response will express no view with respect to the company's intention to exclude the proposal from its proxy materials.

10. How do we respond to no-action requests?

We indicate either that there appears to be some basis for the company's view that it may exclude the proposal or that we are unable to concur in the company's view that it may exclude the proposal. Because the company submits the no-action request, our response is addressed to the company. However, at the time we respond to a no-action request, we provide all related correspondence to both the company and the shareholder. These materials are available in the Commission's Public Reference Room and on commercially available, external databases.

11. What is the effect of our no-action response?

Our no-action responses only reflect our informal views regarding the application of rule 14a-8. We do not claim to issue "rulings" or "decisions" on proposals that companies indicate they intend to exclude, and our determinations do not and cannot adjudicate the merits of a company's position with respect to a proposal. For example, our decision not to recommend enforcement action does not prohibit a shareholder from pursuing rights that he or she may have against the company in court should management exclude a proposal from the company's proxy materials.

12. What is our role after we issue our no-action response?

Under rule 14a-8, we have a limited role after we issue our no-action response. In addition, due to the large number of no-action requests that we receive between the months of December and February, the no-action process must be efficient. As described in answer B.2, above, rule 14a-8 envisions a structured process under which the company submits the request, the shareholder may reply and we issue our response. When shareholders and companies deviate from this structure or are unable to resolve differences, our time and resources are diverted and the process breaks down. Based on our experience, this most often occurs as a result of friction between companies and shareholders and their inability to compromise. While we are always available to facilitate the fair and efficient application of the rule, the operation of the rule, as well as the no-action process, suffers when our role changes from an issuer of responses to an arbiter of disputes. The following questions and answers are examples of how we view our limited role after issuance of our no-action response.

a. If our no-action response affords the shareholder additional time to provide documentation of ownership or revise the proposal, but the company does not believe that the documentation or revisions comply with our no-action response, should the company submit a new no-action request?

No. For example, our no-action response may afford the shareholder seven days to provide documentation demonstrating that he or she satisfies the minimum ownership requirements contained in rule 14a-8(b). If the shareholder provides the required documentation eight days after receiving our no-action response, the company should not submit a new no-action request in order to exclude the proposal. Similarly, if we indicate in our response that the shareholder must provide factual support for a sentence in the supporting statement, the company and the shareholder should work together to determine whether the revised sentence contains appropriate factual support.

b. If our no-action response affords the shareholder an additional seven days to provide documentation of ownership or revise the proposal, who should keep track of when the seven-day period begins to run?

When our no-action response gives a shareholder time, it is measured from the date the shareholder receives our response. As previously noted in answer B.10, we send our response to both the company and the shareholder. However, the company is responsible for determining when the seven-day period begins to run. In order to avoid controversy, the company should forward a copy of our response to the shareholder by a means that permits the company to prove the date of receipt.

13. Does rule 14a-8 contemplate any other involvement by us after we issue a no-action response?

Yes. If a shareholder believes that a company's statement in opposition is materially false or misleading, the shareholder may promptly send a letter to us and the company explaining the reasons for his or her view, as well as a copy of the proposal and statement in opposition. Just as a company has the burden of demonstrating that it is entitled to exclude a proposal, a shareholder should, to the extent possible, provide us with specific factual information that demonstrates the inaccuracy of the company's statement in opposition. We encourage shareholders and companies to work out these differences before contacting us.

14. What must a company do if, before we have issued a no-action response, the shareholder withdraws the proposal or the company decides to include the proposal in its proxy materials?

If the company no longer wishes to pursue its no-action request, the company should provide us with a letter as soon as possible withdrawing its no-action request. This allows us to allocate our resources to other pending requests. The company should also provide the shareholder with a copy of the withdrawal letter.

15. If a company wishes to withdraw a no-action request, what information should its withdrawal letter contain?

In order for us to process withdrawals efficiently, the company's letter should contain

- a statement that either the shareholder has withdrawn the proposal or the company has decided to include the proposal in its proxy materials;

- if the shareholder has withdrawn the proposal, a copy of the shareholder's signed letter of withdrawal, or some other indication that the shareholder has withdrawn the proposal;

- if there is more than one eligible shareholder, the company must provide documentation that all of the eligible shareholders have agreed to withdraw the proposal;

- if the company has agreed to include a revised version of the proposal in its proxy materials, a statement from the shareholder that he or she accepts the revisions; and

- an affirmative statement that the company is withdrawing its no-action request.

C. Questions regarding the eligibility and procedural requirements of the rule

Rule 14a-8 contains eligibility and procedural requirements for shareholders who wish to include a proposal in a company's proxy materials. Below, we address some of the common questions that arise regarding these requirements.

1. To be eligible to submit a proposal, rule 14a-8(b) requires the shareholder to have continuously held at least $2,000 in market value, or 1%, of the company's securities entitled to be voted on the proposal at the meeting for at least one year by the date of submitting the proposal. Also, the shareholder must continue to hold those securities through the date of the meeting. The following questions and answers address issues regarding shareholder eligibility.

a. How do you calculate the market value of the shareholder's securities?

Due to market fluctuations, the value of a shareholder's investment in the company may vary throughout the year before he or she submits the proposal. In order to determine whether the shareholder satisfies the $2,000 threshold, we look at whether, on any date within the 60 calendar days before the date the shareholder submits the proposal, the shareholder's investment is valued at $2,000 or greater, based on the average of the bid and ask prices. Depending on where the company is listed, bid and ask prices may not always be available. For example, bid and ask prices are not provided for companies listed on the New York Stock Exchange. Under these circumstances, companies and shareholders should determine the market value by multiplying the number of securities the shareholder held for the one-year period by the highest selling price during the 60 calendar days before the shareholder submitted the proposal. For purposes of this calculation, it is important to note that a security's highest selling price is not necessarily the same as its highest closing price.

b. What type of security must a shareholder own to be eligible to submit a proposal?

A shareholder must own company securities entitled to be voted on the proposal at the meeting.

Example

A company receives a proposal relating to executive compensation from a shareholder who owns only shares of the company's class B common stock. The company's class B common stock is entitled to vote only on the election of directors. Does the shareholder's ownership of only class B stock provide a basis for the company to exclude the proposal?

Yes. This would provide a basis for the company to exclude the proposal because the shareholder does not own securities entitled to be voted on the proposal at the meeting.

c. How should a shareholder's ownership be substantiated?

Under rule 14a-8(b), there are several ways to determine whether a shareholder has owned the minimum amount of company securities entitled to be voted on the proposal at the meeting for the required time period. If the shareholder appears in the company's records as a registered holder, the company can verify the shareholder's eligibility independently. However, many shareholders hold their securities indirectly through a broker or bank. In the event that the shareholder is not the registered holder, the shareholder is responsible for proving his or her eligibility to submit a proposal to the company. To do so, the shareholder must do one of two things. He or she can submit a written statement from the record holder of the securities verifying that the shareholder has owned the securities continuously for one year as of the time the shareholder submits the proposal. Alternatively, a shareholder who has filed a Schedule 13D, Schedule 13G, Form 4 or Form 5 reflecting ownership of the securities as of or before the date on which the oneyear eligibility period begins may submit copies of these forms and any subsequent amendments reporting a change in ownership level, along with a written statement that he or she has owned the required number of securities continuously for one year as of the time the shareholder submits the proposal.

(1) Does a written statement from the shareholder's investment adviser verifying that the shareholder held the securities continuously for at least one year before submitting the proposal demonstrate sufficiently continuous ownership of the securities?

The written statement must be from the record holder of the shareholder's securities, which is usually a broker or bank. Therefore, unless the investment adviser is also the record holder, the statement would be insufficient under the rule.

(2) Do a shareholder's monthly, quarterly or other periodic investment statements demonstrate sufficiently continuous ownership of the securities?

No. A shareholder must submit an affirmative written statement from the record holder of his or her securities that specifically verifies that the shareholder owned the securities continuously for a period of one year as of the time of submitting the proposal.

(3) If a shareholder submits his or her proposal to the company on June 1, does a statement from the record holder verifying that the shareholder owned the securities continuously for one year as of May 30 of the same year demonstrate sufficiently continuous ownership of the securities as of the time he or she submitted the proposal?

No. A shareholder must submit proof from the record holder that the shareholder continuously owned the securities for a period of one year as of the time the shareholder submits the proposal.

d. Should a shareholder provide the company with a written statement that he or she intends to continue holding the securities through the date of the shareholder meeting?

Yes. The shareholder must provide this written statement regardless of the method the shareholder uses to prove that he or she continuously owned the securities for a period of one year as of the time the shareholder submits the proposal.

2. In order for a proposal to be eligible for inclusion in a company's proxy materials, rule 14a-8(d) requires that the proposal, including any accompanying supporting statement, not exceed 500 words. The following questions and answers address issues regarding the 500-word limitation.

a. May a company count the words in a proposal's "title" or "heading" in determining whether the proposal exceeds the 500-word limitation?

Any statements that are, in effect, arguments in support of the proposal constitute part of the supporting statement. Therefore, any "title" or "heading" that meets this test may be counted toward the 500-word limitation.

b. Does referencing a website address in the proposal or supporting statement violate the 500-word limitation of rule 14a-8(d)?

No. Because we count a website address as one word for purposes of the 500-word limitation, we do not believe that a website address raises the concern that rule 14a-8(d) is intended to address. However, a website address could be subject to exclusion if it refers readers to information that may be materially false or misleading, irrelevant to the subject matter of the proposal or otherwise in contravention of the proxy rules. In this regard, please refer to question and answer F.1.

3. Rule 14a-8(e)(2) requires that proposals for a regularly scheduled annual meeting be received at the company's principal executive offices by a date not less than 120 calendar days before the date of the company's proxy statement released to shareholders in connection with the previous year's annual meeting. The following questions and answers address a number of issues that come up in applying this provision.

a. How do we interpret the phrase "before the date of the company's proxy statement released to shareholders?"

We interpret this phrase as meaning the approximate date on which the proxy statement and form of proxy were first sent or given to shareholders. For example, if a company having a regularly scheduled annual meeting files its definitive proxy statement and form of proxy with the Commission dated April 1, 2001, but first sends or gives the proxy statement to shareholders on April 15, 2001, as disclosed in its proxy statement, we will refer to the April 15, 2001 date as the release date. The company and shareholders should use April 15, 2001 for purposes of calculating the 120-day deadline in rule 14a-8(e)(2).

b. How should a company that is planning to have a regularly scheduled annual meeting calculate the deadline for submitting proposals?

The company should calculate the deadline for submitting proposals as follows:

• start with the release date disclosed in the previous year's proxy statement;

• increase the year by one; and

• count back 120 calendar days.

Examples

If a company is planning to have a regularly scheduled annual meeting in May of 2003 and the company disclosed that the release date for its 2002 proxy statement was April 14, 2002, how should the company calculate the deadline for submitting rule 14a-8 proposals for the company's 2003 annual meeting?

• The release date disclosed in the company's 2002 proxy statement was April 14, 2002.

• Increasing the year by one, the day to begin the calculation is April 14, 2003.

• "Day one" for purposes of the calculation is April 13, 2003.

• "Day 120" is December 15, 2002.

• The 120-day deadline for the 2003 annual meeting is December 15, 2002.

• A rule 14a-8 proposal received after December 15, 2002 would be untimely.

If the 120th calendar day before the release date disclosed in the previous year's proxy statement is a Saturday, Sunday or federal holiday, does this change the deadline for receiving rule 14a-8 proposals?

No. The deadline for receiving rule 14a-8 proposals is always the 120th calendar day before the release date disclosed in the previous year's proxy statement. Therefore, if the deadline falls on a Saturday, Sunday or federal holiday, the company must disclose this date in its proxy statement, and rule 14a-8 proposals received after business reopens would be untimely.

c. How does a shareholder know where to send his or her proposal?

The proposal must be received at the company's principal executive offices. Shareholders can find this address in the company's proxy statement. If a shareholder sends a proposal to any other location, even if it is to an agent of the company or to another company location, this would not satisfy the requirement.

d. How does a shareholder know if his or her proposal has been received by the deadline?

A shareholder should submit a proposal by a means that allows him or her to determine when the proposal was received at the company's principal executive offices.

4. Rule 14a-8(h)(1) requires that the shareholder or his or her qualified representative attend the shareholders' meeting to present the proposal. Rule 14a-8(h)(3) provides that a company may exclude a shareholder's proposals for two calendar years if the company included one of the shareholder's proposals in its proxy materials for a shareholder meeting, neither the shareholder nor the shareholder's qualified representative appeared and presented the proposal and the shareholder did not demonstrate "good cause" for failing to attend the meeting or present the proposal. The following questions and answers address issues regarding these provisions.

a. Does rule 14a-8 require a shareholder to represent in writing before the meeting that he or she, or a qualified representative, will attend the shareholders' meeting to present the proposal?

No. The Commission stated in Release No. 34-20091 that shareholders are no longer required to provide the company with a written statement of intent to appear and present a shareholder proposal. The Commission eliminated this requirement because it "serve[d] little purpose" and only encumbered shareholders. We, therefore, view it as inappropriate for companies to solicit this type of written statement from shareholders for purposes of rule 14a-8. In particular, we note that shareholders who are unfamiliar with the proxy rules may be misled, even unintentionally, into believing that a written statement of intent is required.

b. What if a shareholder provides an unsolicited, written statement that neither the shareholder nor his or her qualified representative will attend the meeting to present the proposal? May the company exclude the proposal under this circumstance?

Yes. Rule 14a-8(i)(3) allows companies to exclude proposals that are contrary to the proxy rules, including rule 14a-8(h)(1). If a shareholder voluntarily provides a written statement evidencing his or her intent to act contrary to rule 14a-8(h)(1), rule 14a-8(i)(3) may serve as a basis for the company to exclude the proposal.

c. If a company demonstrates that it is entitled to exclude a proposal under rule 14a-8(h)(3), can the company request that we issue a no-action response that covers both calendar years?

Yes. For example, assume that, without "good cause," neither the shareholder nor the shareholder's representative attended the company's 2001 annual meeting to present the shareholder's proposal, and the shareholder then submits a proposal for inclusion in the company's 2002 proxy materials. If the company seeks to exclude the 2002 proposal under rule 14a-8(h)(3), it may concurrently request forward-looking relief for any proposal(s) that the shareholder may submit for inclusion in the company's 2003 proxy materials. If we grant the company's request and the company receives a proposal from the shareholder in connection with the 2003 annual meeting, the company still has an obligation under rule 14a-8(j) to notify us and the shareholder of its intention to exclude the shareholder's proposal from its proxy materials for that meeting. Although we will retain that notice in our records, we will not issue a no-action response.

5. In addition to rule 14a-8(h)(3), are there any other circumstances in which we will grant forward-looking relief to a company under rule 14a-8?

Yes. Rule 14a-8(i)(4) allows companies to exclude a proposal if it relates to the redress of a personal claim or grievance against the company or any other person or is designed to result in a benefit to the shareholder, or to further a personal interest, that is not shared by the other shareholders at large. In rare circumstances, we may grant forward-looking relief if a company satisfies its burden of demonstrating that the shareholder is abusing rule 14a-8 by continually submitting similar proposals that relate to a particular personal claim or grievance. As in answer C.4.c, above, if we grant this relief, the company still has an obligation under rule 14a-8(j) to notify us and the shareholder of its intention to exclude the shareholder's proposal(s) from its proxy materials. Although will retain that notice in our records, we will not issue a no-action response.

6. What must a company do in order to exclude a proposal that fails to comply with the eligibility or procedural requirements of the rule?

If a shareholder fails to follow the eligibility or procedural requirements of rule 14a-8, the rule provides procedures for the company to follow if it wishes to exclude the proposal. For example, rule 14a-8(f) provides that a company may exclude a proposal from its proxy materials due to eligibility or procedural defects if

- within 14 calendar days of receiving the proposal, it provides the shareholder with written notice of the defect(s), including the time frame for responding; and
- the shareholder fails to respond to this notice within 14 calendar days of receiving the notice of the defect(s) or the shareholder timely responds but does not cure the eligibility or procedural defect(s).

Section G.3—Eligibility and Procedural Issues, below, contains information that companies may want to consider in drafting these notices. If the shareholder does not timely respond or remedy the defect(s) and the company intends to exclude the proposal, the company still must submit, to us and to the shareholder, a copy of the proposal and its reasons for excluding the proposal.

a. Should a company's notices of defect(s) give different levels of information to different shareholders depending on the company's perception of the shareholder's sophistication in rule 14a-8?

No. Companies should not assume that any shareholder is familiar with the proxy rules or give different levels of information to different shareholders based on the fact that the shareholder may or may not be a frequent or "experienced" shareholder proponent.

b. Should companies instruct shareholders to respond to the notice of defect(s) by a specified date rather than indicating that shareholders have 14 calendar days after receiving the notice to respond?

No. Rule 14a-8(f) provides that shareholders must respond within 14 calendar days of receiving notice of the alleged eligibility or procedural defect(s). If the company provides a specific date by which the shareholder must submit his or her response, it is possible that the deadline set by the company will be shorter than the 14-day period required by rule 14a-8(f). For example, events could delay the shareholder's receipt of the notice. As such, if a company sets a specific date for the shareholder to respond and that date does not result in the shareholder having 14 calendar days after receiving the notice to respond, we do not believe that the company may rely on rule 14a-8(f) to exclude the proposal.

c. Are there any circumstances under which a company does not have to provide the shareholder with a notice of defect(s)? For example, what should the company do if the shareholder indicates that he or she does not own at least $2,000 in market value, or 1%, of the company's securities?

The company does not need to provide the shareholder with a notice of defect(s) if the defect(s) cannot be remedied. In the example provided in the question, because the shareholder cannot remedy this defect after the fact, no notice of the defect would be required. The same would apply, for example, if

- the shareholder indicated that he or she had owned securities entitled to be voted on the proposal for a period of less than one year before submitting the proposal;

- the shareholder indicated that he or she did not own securities entitled to be voted on the proposal at the meeting;

- the shareholder failed to submit a proposal by the company's properly determined deadline; or

- the shareholder, or his or her qualified representative, failed to attend the meeting or present one of the shareholder's proposals that was included in the company's proxy materials during the past two calendar years.

In all of these circumstances, the company must still submit its reasons regarding exclusion of the proposal to us and the shareholder. The shareholder may, but is not required to, submit a reply to us with a copy to the company.

D. Questions regarding the inclusion of shareholder names in proxy statements

1. If the shareholder's proposal will appear in the company's proxy statement, is the company required to disclose the shareholder's name?

No. A company is not required to disclose the identity of a shareholder proponent in its proxy statement. Rather, a company can indicate that it will provide the information to shareholders promptly upon receiving an oral or written request.

2. May a shareholder request that the company not disclose his or her name in the proxy statement?

Yes. However, the company has the discretion not to honor the request. In this regard, if the company chooses to include the shareholder proponent's name in the proxy statement, rule 14a-8(l)(1) requires that the company also include that shareholder proponent's address and the number of the company's voting securities that the shareholder proponent holds.

3. If a shareholder includes his or her e-mail address in the proposal or supporting statement, may the company exclude the e-mail address?

Yes. We view an e-mail address as equivalent to the shareholder proponent's name and address and, under rule 14a-8(l)(1), a company may exclude the shareholder's name and address from the proxy statement.

E. Questions regarding revisions to proposals and supporting statements

In this section, we first discuss the purpose for allowing shareholders to revise portions of a proposal and supporting statement. Second, we express our views with regard to revisions that a shareholder makes to his or her proposal before we receive a company's no-action request, as well as during the course of our review of a no-action request. Finally, we address the circumstances under which our responses may allow shareholders to make revisions to their proposals and supporting statements.

1. Why do our no-action responses sometimes permit shareholders to make revisions to their proposals and supporting statements?

There is no provision in rule 14a-8 that allows a shareholder to revise his or her proposal and supporting statement. However, we have a longstanding practice of issuing no-action responses that permit shareholders to make revisions that are minor in nature and do not alter the substance of the proposal. We adopted this practice to deal with proposals that generally comply with the substantive requirements of the rule, but contain some relatively minor defects that are easily corrected. In these circumstances, we believe that the concepts underlying Exchange Act section 14(a) are best served by affording an opportunity to correct these kinds of defects.

Despite the intentions underlying our revisions practice, we spend an increasingly large portion of our time and resources each proxy season responding to no-action requests regarding proposals or supporting statements that have obvious deficiencies in terms of accuracy, clarity or relevance. This is not beneficial to all participants in the process and diverts resources away from analyzing core issues arising under rule 14a-8 that are matters of interest to companies and shareholders alike. Therefore, when a proposal and supporting statement will require detailed and extensive editing in order to bring them into compliance with the proxy rules, we may find it appropriate for companies to exclude the entire proposal, supporting statement, or both, as materially false or misleading.

2. If a company has received a timely proposal and the shareholder makes revisions to the proposal before the company submits its no-action request, must the company accept those revisions?

No, but it may accept the shareholder's revisions. If the changes are such that the revised proposal is actually a different proposal from the original, the revised proposal could be subject to exclusion under

- rule 14a-8(c), which provides that a shareholder may submit no more than one proposal to a company for a particular shareholders' meeting; and

- rule 14a-8(e), which imposes a deadline for submitting shareholder proposals.

3. If the shareholder decides to make revisions to his or her proposal after the company has submitted its no-action request, must the company address those revisions?

No, but it may address the shareholder's revisions. We base our no-action response on the proposal included in the company's no-action request. Therefore, if the company indicates in a letter to us and the shareholder that it acknowledges and accepts the shareholder's changes, we will base our response on the revised proposal. Otherwise, we will base our response on the proposal contained in the company's original no-action request. Again, it is important for shareholders to note that, depending on the nature and timing of the changes, a revised proposal could be subject to exclusion under rule 14a-8(c), rule 14a-8(e), or both.

4. If the shareholder decides to make revisions to his or her proposal after the company has submitted its no-action request, should the shareholder provide a copy of the revisions to us?

Yes. All shareholder correspondence relating to the no-action request should be sent to us and the company. However, under rule 14a-8, no-action requests and shareholder responses to those requests are submitted to us. The proposals themselves are not submitted to us. Because proposals are submitted to companies for inclusion in their proxy materials, we will not address revised proposals unless the company chooses to acknowledge the changes.

5. When do our responses afford shareholders an opportunity to revise their proposals and supporting statements?

We may, under limited circumstances, permit shareholders to revise their proposals and supporting statements. The following table provides examples of the rule 14a-8 bases under which we typically allow revisions, as well as the types of permissible changes:

Basis	Type of revision that we may permit
Rule 14a-8(i)(1)	When a proposal would be binding on the company if approved by shareholders, we may permit the shareholder to revise the proposal to a recommendation or request that the board of directors take the action specified in the proposal.
Rule 14a-8(i)(2)	If implementing the proposal would require the company to breach existing contractual obligations, we may permit the shareholder to

revise the proposal so that it applies only to the company's future contractual obligations.

Rule 14a-8(i)(3)	If the proposal contains specific statements that may be materially false or misleading or irrelevant to the subject matter of the proposal, we may permit the shareholder to revise or delete these statements. Also, if the proposal or supporting statement contains vague terms, we may, in rare circumstances, permit the shareholder to clarify these terms.
Rule 14a-8(i)(6)	Same as rule 14a-8(i)(2), above.
Rule 14a-8(i)(7)	If it is unclear whether the proposal focuses on senior executive compensation or director compensation, as opposed to general employee compensation, we may permit the shareholder to make this clarification.
Rule 14a-8(i)(8)	If implementing the proposal would disqualify directors previously elected from completing their terms on the board or disqualify nominees for directors at the upcoming shareholder meeting, we may permit the shareholder to revise the proposal so that it will not affect the unexpired terms of directors elected to the board at or prior to the upcoming shareholder meeting.
Rule 14a-8(i)(9)	Same as rule 14a-8(i)(8), above.

F. Other questions that arise under rule 14a-8

1. May a reference to a website address in the proposal or supporting statement be subject to exclusion under the rule?

Yes. In some circumstances, we may concur in a company's view that it may exclude a website address under rule 14a-8(i)(3) because information contained on the website may be materially false or misleading, irrelevant to the subject matter of the proposal or otherwise in contravention of the proxy rules. Companies seeking to exclude a website address under rule 14a-8(i)(3) should specifically indicate why they believe information contained on the particular website is materially false or misleading, irrelevant to the subject matter of the proposal or otherwise in contravention of the proxy rules.

2. Rule 14a-8(i)(12) provides a basis for a company to exclude a proposal dealing with substantially the same subject matter as another proposal or proposals that previously has or have been included in the company's proxy materials. How does rule 14a-8(i)(12) operate?

Rule 14a-8(i)(12) operates as follows:

a. First, the company should look back three calendar years to see if it previously included a proposal or proposals dealing with substantially the same subject matter. If it has not, rule 14a-8(i)(12) is not available as a basis to exclude a proposal from this year's proxy materials.

b. If it has, the company should then count the number of times that a proposal or proposals dealing with substantially the same subject matter was or were included over the preceding five calendar years.

c. Finally, the company should look at the percentage of the shareholder vote that a proposal dealing with substantially the same subject matter received the last time it was included.

- If the company included a proposal dealing with substantially the same subject matter only once in the preceding five calendar years, the company may exclude a proposal from this year's proxy materials under rule 14a-8(i)(12)(i) if it received less than 3% of the vote the last time that it was voted on.

- If the company included a proposal or proposals dealing with substantially the same subject matter twice in the preceding five calendar years, the company may exclude a proposal from this year's proxy materials under rule 14a-8(i)(12)(ii) if it received less than 6% of the vote the last time that it was voted on.

- If the company included a proposal or proposals dealing with substantially the same subject matter three or more times in the preceding five calendar years, the company may exclude a proposal from this year's proxy materials under rule 14a-8 (i)(12)(iii) if it received less than 10% of the vote the last time that it was voted on.

3. Rule 14a-8(i)(12) refers to calendar years. How do we interpret calendar years for this purpose?

Because a calendar year runs from January 1 through December 31, we do not look at the specific dates of company meetings. Instead, we look at the calendar year in which a meeting was held. For example, a company scheduled a meeting for April 25, 2002. In looking back three calendar years to determine if it previously had included a proposal or proposals dealing with substantially the same subject matter, any meeting held in calendar years 1999, 2000 or 2001—which would include any meetings held between January 1, 1999 and December 31, 2001—would be relevant under rule 14a-8(i)(12).

Examples

A company receives a proposal for inclusion in its 2002 proxy materials dealing with substantially the same subject matter as proposals that were voted on at the following shareholder meetings:

Calendar Year	1997	1998	1999	2000	2001	2002	2003
Voted on?	Yes	No	No	Yes	No	—	—
Percentage	4%	N/A	N/A	4%	N/A	—	—

May the company exclude the proposal from its 2002 proxy materials in reliance on rule 14a-8(i)(12)?

Yes. The company would be entitled to exclude the proposal under rule 14a-8(i)(12)(ii). First, calendar year 2000, the last time the company included a proposal dealing with substantially the same subject matter, is within the prescribed three calendar years. Second, the company included proposals dealing with substantially the same subject matter twice within the preceding five calendar years, specifically, in 1997 and 2000. Finally, the proposal received less than 6% of the vote on its last submission to shareholders in 2000. Therefore, rule 14a-8(i)(12)(ii), which permits exclusion when a company has included a proposal or proposals dealing with substantially the same subject matter twice in the preceding five calendar years and that proposal received less than 6% of the shareholder vote the last time it was voted on, would serve as a basis for excluding the proposal.

If the company excluded the proposal from its 2002 proxy materials and then received an identical proposal for inclusion in its 2003 proxy materials, may the company exclude the proposal from its 2003 proxy materials in reliance on rule 14a-8(i)(12)?

No. Calendar year 2000, the last time the company included a proposal dealing with substantially the same subject matter, is still within the prescribed three calendar years. However, 2000 was the only time within the preceding five calendar years that the company included a proposal dealing with substantially the same subject matter, and it received more than 3% of the vote at the 2000 meeting. Therefore, the company would not be entitled to exclude the proposal under rule 14a-8(i)(12)(i).

4. How do we count votes under rule 14a-8(i)(12)?

Only votes for and against a proposal are included in the calculation of the shareholder vote of that proposal. Abstentions and broker non-votes are not included in this calculation.

Example

A proposal received the following votes at the company's last annual meeting:

- 5,000 votes for the proposal;
- 3,000 votes against the proposal;
- 1,000 broker non-votes; and
- 1,000 abstentions.

How is the shareholder vote of this proposal calculated for purposes of rule 14a-8(i)(12)?

This percentage is calculated as follows:

formula: votes for proposal divided by the sum of votes against the proposal and votes for the proposal equals voting percentage

Applying this formula to the facts above, the proposal received 62.5% of the vote.

example using previous formula: five thousand divided by the sum of three

G. How can companies and shareholders facilitate our processing of no-action requests or take steps to avoid the submission of no-action requests?

Eligibility and procedural issues

1. Before submitting a proposal to a company, a shareholder should look in the company's most recent proxy statement to find the deadline for submitting rule 14a-8 proposals. To avoid exclusion on the basis of untimeliness, a shareholder should submit his or her proposal well in advance of the deadline and by a means that allows the shareholder to demonstrate the date the proposal was received at the company's principal executive offices.

2. A shareholder who intends to submit a written statement from the record holder of the shareholder's securities to verify continuous ownership of the securities should contact the record holder before submitting a proposal to ensure that the record holder will provide the written statement and knows how to provide a written statement that will satisfy the requirements of rule 14a-8(b).

3. Companies should consider the following guidelines when drafting a letter to notify a shareholder of perceived eligibility or procedural defects:

- provide adequate detail about what the shareholder must do to remedy all eligibility or procedural defects;
- although not required, consider including a copy of rule 14a-8 with the notice of defect(s);
- explicitly state that the shareholder must respond to the company's notice within 14 calendar days of receiving the notice of defect(s); and
- send the notification by a means that allows the company to determine when the shareholder received the letter.

4. Rule 14a-8(f) provides that a shareholder's response to a company's notice of defect(s) must be postmarked, or transmitted electronically, no later than 14 days from the date the shareholder received the notice of defect(s). Therefore, a shareholder should respond to the company's notice of defect(s) by a means that allows the shareholder to demonstrate when he or she responded to the notice.

5. Rather than waiting until the deadline for submitting a no-action request, a company should submit a no-action request as soon as possible after it receives a proposal and determines that it will seek a no-action response.

6. Companies that will be submitting multiple no-action requests should submit their requests individually or in small groups rather than waiting and sending them all at once.

We receive the heaviest volume of no-action requests between December and February of each year. Therefore, we are not able to process no-action requests as quickly during this period. Our experience shows that we often receive 70 to 80 no-action requests a week during our peak period and, at most, we can respond to 30 to 40 requests in any given week. Therefore, companies that wait until December through February to submit all of their requests will have to wait longer for a response.

7. Companies should provide us with all relevant correspondence when submitting the no-action request, including the shareholder proposal, any cover letter that the shareholder provided with the proposal, the shareholder's address and any other correspondence the company has exchanged with the shareholder relating to the proposal. If the company provided the shareholder with notice of a perceived eligibility or procedural defect, the company should include a copy of the notice, documentation demonstrating when the company notified the shareholder, documentation demonstrating when the shareholder received the notice and any shareholder response to the notice.

8. If a shareholder intends to reply to the company's no-action request, he or she should try to send the reply as soon as possible after the company submits its no-action request.

9. Both companies and shareholders should promptly forward to each other copies of all correspondence that is provided to us in connection with no-action requests.

10. Due to the significant volume of no-action requests and phone calls we receive during the proxy season, companies should limit their calls to us regarding the status of their no-action request.

11. Shareholders who write to us to object to a company's statement in opposition to the shareholder's proposal also should provide us with copies of the proposal as it will be printed in the company's proxy statement and the company's proposed statement in opposition.

Substantive issues

1. When drafting a proposal, shareholders should consider whether the proposal, if approved by shareholders, would be binding on the company. In our experience, we have found that proposals that are binding on the company face a much greater likelihood of being improper under state law and, therefore, excludable under rule 14a-8(i)(1).

2. When drafting a proposal, shareholders should consider what actions are within a company's power or authority. Proposals often request or require action by the company that would violate law or would not be within the power or authority of the company to implement.

3. When drafting a proposal, shareholders should consider whether the proposal would require the company to breach existing contracts. In our experience, we have found that proposals that would result in the company breaching existing contractual obligations face a much greater likelihood of being excludable under rule 14a-8(i)(2), rule 14a-8(i)(6), or both. This is because implementing the proposals may require the company to violate law or may not be within the power or authority of the company to implement.

4. In drafting a proposal and supporting statement, shareholders should avoid making unsupported assertions of fact. To this end, shareholders should provide factual support for statements in the proposal and supporting statement or phrase statements as their opinion where appropriate.

5. Companies should provide a supporting opinion of counsel when the reasons for exclusion are based on matters of state or foreign law. In determining how much weight to afford these opinions, one factor we consider is whether counsel is licensed to practice law in the jurisdiction where the law is at issue. Shareholders who wish to contest a company's reliance on a legal opinion as to matters of state or foreign law should, but are not required to, submit an opinion of counsel supporting their position.

H. Conclusion

Whether or not you are familiar with rule 14a-8, we hope that this bulletin helps you gain a better understanding of the rule, the no-action request process and our views on some issues and questions that commonly arise during our review of no-action requests. While not exhaustive, we believe that the bulletin contains information that will assist both companies and shareholders in ensuring that the rule operates more effectively. Please contact us with any questions that you may have regarding information contained in the bulletin.

* * * * *

Division of Corporation Finance: Staff Legal Bulletin No. 14A

Date: July 12, 2002

Action: Publication of CF Staff Legal Bulletin

Summary: This staff legal bulletin provides information for companies and shareholders regarding rule 14a-8 of the Securities Exchange Act of 1934. Supplementary Information: The statements in this staff legal bulletin represent the views of the Division of Corporation Finance. This bulletin is not a rule, regulation or statement of the Securities and Exchange Commission. Further, the Commission has neither approved nor disapproved its content.

Contact Person: For further information, please contact Keir D. Gumbs at (202) 942-2900.

Rule 14a-8 provides an opportunity for a shareholder owning a relatively small amount of a company's securities to have his or her proposal placed alongside management's proposals in that company's proxy materials for presentation to a vote at an annual or special meeting of shareholders. The rule generally requires the company to include the proposal unless the shareholder has not complied with the rule's procedural requirements or the proposal falls within one of the rule's 13 substantive bases for exclusion.

Rule 14a-8(i)(7) is one of the substantive bases for exclusion in rule 14a-8. It provides a basis for excluding a proposal that deals with a matter relating to the company's ordinary business operations. The fact that a proposal relates to ordinary business matters does not conclusively establish that a company may exclude the proposal from its proxy materials. As the Commission stated in Exchange Act Release No. 40018, proposals that relate to ordinary business matters but that focus on "sufficiently significant social policy issues . . . would not be considered to be excludable because the proposals would transcend the day-to-day business matters."[1]

In the 2001-2002 proxy season, shareholders submitted proposals to several companies relating to equity compensation plans. Some of these proposals requested that the companies submit for shareholder approval all equity compensation plans that potentially would result in material dilution to existing shareholders. We received four no-action requests from companies seeking to exclude these proposals from their proxy materials in reliance on rule 14a-8(i)(7). In each instance, we took the view that the proposal could be excluded in reliance on rule 14a-8(i)(7) because the proposal related to general employee compensation, an ordinary business matter.[2]

The Commission has stated that proposals involving "the management of the workforce, such as the hiring, promotion, and termination of employees," relate to ordinary business matters.[3] Our position to date with respect to equity compensation proposals is consistent with this guidance and the Division's historical approach to compensation

---

[1] *See* Amendments to Rules on Shareholder Proposals, Exchange Act Release No. 40018 (May 21, 1998).

[2] *See* Adobe Systems (February 1, 2002) (proposal requesting that Adobe's Board of Directors "submit all equity compensation plans (other than those that would not result in material potential dilution) to shareholders

for approval"); *see also* Cadence Design Systems (March 20, 2002); AutoDesk, Inc. (April 1, 2002); Synopsys, Inc. (April 1, 2002).

[3] *See* Exchange Act Release No. 40018 (May 21, 1998).

proposals. Since 1992, we have applied a bright-line analysis to proposals concerning equity or cash compensation:

- We agree with the view of companies that they may exclude proposals that relate to general employee compensation matters in reliance on rule 14a-8(i)(7)[4]; and

- We do not agree with the view of companies that they may exclude proposals that concern only senior executive and director compensation in reliance on rule 14a-8(i)(7).[5]

The Commission has previously taken the position that proposals relating to ordinary business matters "but focusing on sufficiently significant social policy issues . . . generally would not be considered to be excludable, because the proposals would transcend the day-to-day business matters and raise policy issues so significant that it would be appropriate for a shareholder vote."[6] The Division has noted many times that the presence of widespread public debate regarding an issue is among the factors to be considered in determining whether proposals concerning that issue "transcend the day-to-day business matters."[7]

We believe that the public debate regarding shareholder approval of equity compensation plans has become significant in recent months. Consequently, in view of the widespread public debate regarding shareholder approval of equity compensation plans and consistent with our historical analysis of the "ordinary business" exclusion, we are modifying our treatment of proposals relating to this topic.[8] Going forward, we will take the following approach to rule 14a-8(i)(7) submissions concerning proposals that relate to shareholder approval of equity compensation plans:[9]

- *Proposals that focus on equity compensation plans that may be used to compensate only senior executive officers and directors.* As has been our position since 1992, companies may not rely on rule 14a-8(i)(7) to omit these proposals from their proxy materials.

- *Proposals that focus on equity compensation plans that may be used to compensate senior executive officers, directors and the general workforce.* If the proposal seeks to obtain shareholder approval of all such equity compensation plans, without regard to their potential dilutive effect, a company may rely on rule 14a-8(i)(7) to omit the proposal from its proxy materials. If the proposal seeks to obtain shareholder approval of all such equity compensation plans that potentially would result in material dilution to existing shareholders, a company may not rely on rule 14a-8(i)(7) to omit the proposal from its proxy materials.

- *Proposals that focus on equity compensation plans that may be used to compensate the general workforce only, with no senior executive officer or director participation.* If the proposal seeks to obtain shareholder approval of all such equity compensation plans, without regard to their potential dilutive effect, a company may rely on rule 14a-8(i)(7) to omit the proposal from its proxy materials. If the proposal seeks to obtain shareholder approval of all such equity compensation plans that potentially would result in material dilution to existing shareholders, a company may not rely on rule 14a-8(i)(7) to omit the proposal from its proxy materials.

Companies and shareholders with questions about this bulletin are encouraged to call Keir D. Gumbs, Office of Chief Counsel of the Division of Corporation Finance, at (202) 942-2900.

---

[4] *See e.g.,* Bio-Technology General Corporation (April 28, 2000).

[5] *See e.g.,* Battle Mountain Gold Company (February 13, 1992).

[6] *See* Exchange Act Release No. 40018 (May 21, 1998).

[7] *See e.g.,* Transamerica Corporation (January 10, 1990) and Aetna Life and Casualty Company (February 13, 1992).

[8] This bulletin addresses only the specific matter of shareholder proposals relating to shareholder approval of equity compensation plans. We are not addressing or commenting on any other positions concerning shareholder proposals relating to equity compensation or cash compensation.

[9] We recognize that the New York Stock Exchange and the Nasdaq Stock Market have, or are in the process of adopting, rules to require companies listed or quoted by them to provide for shareholder approval of some equity compensation plans. This bulletin does not address those rules.

* * * * *

Shareholder Proposals: Staff Legal Bulletin No. 14B

Action: Publication of CF Staff Legal Bulletin

Date: September 15, 2004

Summary: This staff legal bulletin provides information for companies and shareholders regarding rule 14a-8 of the Securities Exchange Act of 1934.

Supplementary Information: The statements in this legal bulletin represent the views of the Division of Corporation Finance. This bulletin is not a rule, regulation, or statement of the Securities and Exchange Commission. Further, the Commission has neither approved nor disapproved its content.

Contacts: For further information, please contact the Office of Chief Counsel in the Division of Corporation Finance at (202) 942-2900.

A. What is the purpose of this bulletin?

On July 13, 2001, the Division of Corporation Finance published SLB No. 14 in order to:

explain the rule 14a-8 no-action process, as well as our role in this process;

provide guidance to companies and shareholders by expressing our views on some issues and questions that arise commonly under rule 14a-8; and

suggest ways in which both companies and shareholder proponents can facilitate our review of no-action requests.

SLB No. 14 addressed primarily those procedural matters that are common to companies and shareholder proponents and discussed some substantive matters that are of interest to companies and shareholder proponents alike.

On July 12, 2002, the Division of Corporation Finance published SLB No. 14A. SLB No. 14A clarified our position on shareholder proposals related to equity compensation plans.

The purpose of this bulletin is to clarify and update some of the guidance that is included in SLB No. 14 and to provide additional guidance on issues that arise commonly under rule 14a-8. Specifically, this bulletin containsour views regarding:

the application of rule 14a-8(i)(3);

common issues regarding a company's notice of defect(s) to a shareholder proponent under rule 14a-8(f);

the application of the 80-day requirement in rule 14a-8(j);

opinions of counsel under rule 14a-8(j)(2)(iii); and

processing matters relating to the availability of submitted materials and the mailing and public availability of our responses.

This bulletin includes a discussion of rule 14a-9 and its interaction with the operation of rule 14a-8. This discussion applies to our review of rule 14a-8 no-action requests only; it does not apply to other contexts, such as our review of disclosure contained in proxy statement filings and additional soliciting materials that may be considered materially false or misleading under rule 14a-9.

The references to "we," "our," and "us" are to the Division of Corporation Finance. You can find a copy of rule 14a-8 in Exchange Act Release No. 34-40018 (May 21, 1998), which is located on the Commission's website at www.sec.gov/rules/final/34-40018.htm. You can find a copy of SLB No. 14 on the Commission's website at www.sec.gov/interps/

legal/cfslb14.htm. You can find a copy of SLB No. 14A on the Commission's website at www.sec.gov/interps/legal/cfslb14a.htm.

B.   Under rule 14a-8(i)(3), when will the staff grant requests to exclude either all or part of a proposal or supporting statement based on false or misleading statements?

1.   Rule 14a-8(i)(3)

Question 9 in rule 14a-8 reads, "If I have complied with the procedural requirements, on what other bases may a company rely to exclude my proposal?" Thirteen bases are then listed as answers to Question 9. The third basis, which is cited as rule 14a-8(i)(3), provides:

Violation of proxy rules: If the proposal or supporting statement is contrary to any of the Commission's proxy rules, including § 240.14a-9, which prohibits materially false or misleading statements in proxy materials.

It is important to note that rule 14a-8(i)(3), unlike the other bases for exclusion under rule 14a-8, refers explicitly to the supporting statement as well as the proposal as a whole. Accordingly, companies have relied on rule 14a-8(i)(3) to exclude portions of the supporting statement, even if the balance of the proposal and the supporting statement may not be excluded. Companies have requested that the staff concur in the appropriateness of excluding statements in reliance on rule 14a-8(i)(3) for a number of reasons, including the following:

Vagueness—Companies have argued that the proposal may be excluded in its entirety if the language of the proposal or the supporting statement render the proposal so vague and indefinite that neither the stockholders voting on the proposal, nor the company in implementing the proposal (if adopted), would be able to determine with any reasonable certainty exactly what actions or measures the proposal requires.

Impugning Statements—Companies have argued that they may exclude statements in a supporting statement because they fall within Note (b) to rule 14a-9, which states that "[m]aterial which directly or indirectly impugns character, integrity or personal reputation or directly or indirectly makes charges concerning improper, illegal or immoral conduct or associations, without factual foundation" is an example of "what, depending upon particular facts and circumstances, may be misleading within the meaning of [rule 14a-9]."

Irrelevant Statements—Companies have argued that they may exclude statements in a supporting statement because they are irrelevant to the subject matter of the proposal being presented. It is argued that it is appropriate to exclude these statements because they mislead shareholders by making unclear the nature of the matter on which they are being asked to vote.

Opinions Presented as Fact—Companies have argued that they may exclude statements in a supporting statement because they are presented as fact when they are the opinion of the shareholder proponent. It is argued that it is appropriate to exclude these statements because they are contrary to rule 14a-9 in that they may mislead shareholders into believing that the statements are fact and not opinion.

Statements Without Factual Support—Companies have argued that they may exclude statements in a supporting statement because they are presented as fact, but do not cite to a source that proves that statement. It is argued that it is appropriate to exclude these statements because they are contrary to rule 14a-9 in that they may be false and misleading and should be accompanied by a citation to permit shareholders to assess the context in which the source presented the information. As we noted in SLB No. 14, we spend an increasingly large portion of our time and resources each proxy season responding to no-action requests regarding asserted deficiencies in terms of clarity, relevance, or accuracy in proposals and supporting statements.

2. Our approach to rule 14a-8(i)(3) no-action requests

As we noted in SLB No. 14, there is no provision in rule 14a-8 that allows a shareholder to revise his or her proposal and supporting statement. We have had, however, a long-standing practice of issuing no-action responses that permit shareholders to make revisions that are minor in nature and do not alter the substance of the proposal. We adopted this practice to deal with proposals that comply generally with the substantive requirements of rule 14a-8, but contain some minor defects that could be corrected easily. Our intent to limit this practice to minor defects was evidenced by our statement in SLB No. 14 that we may find it appropriate for companies to exclude the entire proposal, supporting statement, or both as materially false or misleading if a proposal or supporting statement would require detailed and extensive editing in order to bring it into compliance with the proxy rules.

3. The need to clarify our views under rule 14a-8(i)(3)

Unfortunately, our discussion of rule 14a-8(i)(3) in SLB No. 14 has caused the process for company objections and the staff's consideration of those objections to evolve well beyond its original intent. The discussion in SLB No. 14 has resulted in an unintended and unwarranted extension of rule 14a-8(i)(3), as many companies have begun to assert deficiencies in virtually every line of a proposal's supporting statement as a means to justify exclusion of the proposal in its entirety. Our consideration of those requests requires the staff to devote significant resources to editing the specific wording of proposals and, especially, supporting statements. During the last proxy season, nearly half the no-action requests we received asserted that the proposal or supporting statement was wholly or partially excludable under rule 14a-8(i)(3).

We believe that the staff's process of becoming involved in evaluating wording changes to proposals and/or supporting statements has evolved well beyond its original intent and resulted in an inappropriate extension of rule 14a-8(i)(3). In addition, we believe the process is neither appropriate under nor consistent with rule 14a-8(l)(2), which reads, "The company is not responsible for the contents of [the shareholder proponent's] proposal or supporting statement." Finally, we believe that current practice is not beneficial to participants in the process and diverts resources away from analyzing core issues arising under rule 14a-8.

4. Clarification of our views regarding the application of rule 14a-8(i)(3)

Accordingly, we are clarifying our views with regard to the application of rule 14a-8(i)(3). Specifically, because the shareholder proponent, and not the company, is responsible for the content of a proposal and its supporting statement, we do not believe that exclusion or modification under rule 14a-8(i)(3) is appropriate for much of the language in supporting statements to which companies have objected. Accordingly, going forward, we believe that it would not be appropriate for companies to exclude supporting statement language and/or an entire proposal in reliance on rule 14a-8(i)(3) in the following circumstances:

the company objects to factual assertions because they are not supported;

the company objects to factual assertions that, while not materially false or misleading, may be disputed or countered;

the company objects to factual assertions because those assertions may be interpreted by shareholders in a manner that is unfavorable to the company, its directors, or its officers; and/or

the company objects to statements because they represent the opinion of the shareholder proponent or a referenced source, but the statements are not identified specifically as such.

We believe that it is appropriate under rule 14a-8 for companies to address these objections in their statements of opposition.

There continue to be certain situations where we believe modification or exclusion may be consistent with our intended application of rule 14a-8(i)(3). In those situations, it may be appropriate for a company to determine to exclude a statement in reliance on rule 14a-8(i)(3) and seek our concurrence with that determination. Specifically, reliance on rule 14a-8(i)(3) to exclude or modify a statement may be appropriate where:

> statements directly or indirectly impugn character, integrity, or personal reputation, or directly or indirectly make charges concerning improper, illegal, or immoral conduct or association, without factual foundation;

> the company demonstrates objectively that a factual statement is materially false or misleading;

> the resolution contained in the proposal is so inherently vague or indefinite that neither the stockholders voting on the proposal, nor the company in implementing the proposal (if adopted), would be able to determine with any reasonable certainty exactly what actions or measures the proposal requires—this objection also may be appropriate where the proposal and the supporting statement, when read together, have the same result; and

> substantial portions of the supporting statement are irrelevant to a consideration of the subject matter of the proposal, such that there is a strong likelihood that a reasonable shareholder would be uncertain as to the matter on which she is being asked to vote.

In this regard, rule 14a-8(i)(3) permits the company to exclude a proposal or a statement that is contrary to any of the proxy rules, including rule 14a-9, which prohibits *materially* false or misleading statements. Further, rule 14a-8(g) makes clear that the company bears the burden of demonstrating that a proposal or statement may be excluded. As such, the staff will concur in the company's reliance on rule 14a-8(i)(3) to exclude or modify a proposal or statement only where that company has demonstrated objectively that the proposal or statement is *materially* false or misleading.

C. What are common issues regarding companies' notices of defect(s)?

1. How should companies draft notices of defect(s)?

We put forth the following guidance in SLB No. 14 for companies to consider when drafting letters to notify shareholder proponents of eligibility or procedural defects:

> provide adequate detail about what the shareholder proponent must do to remedy the eligibility or procedural defect(s);

> although not required, consider including a copy of rule 14a-8 with the notice of defect(s);

> explicitly state that the shareholder proponent must transmit his or her response to the company's notice within 14 calendar days of receiving the notice of defect(s); and

> send the notification by a means that allows the company to determine when the shareholder proponent received the letter.

We believe that this guidance continues to be of significant benefit to companies, and we urge all companies to consider it when drafting notices of defect(s) under rule 14a-8.

2. Is there any further guidance to companies with regard to what their notices of defect(s) should state about demonstrating proof of the shareholder proponent's ownership?

Yes. If the company cannot determine whether the shareholder satisfies the rule 14a-8 minimum ownership requirements, the company should request that the shareholder provide proof of ownership that satisfies the requirements of rule 14a-8. The company should use language that tracks rule 14a-8(b), which states that the shareholder proponent "must" prove its eligibility by submitting:

the shareholder proponent's written statement that he or she intends to continue holding the shares through the date of the company's annual or special meeting; and either:

a written statement from the "record" holder of the securities (usually a broker or bank) verifying that, at the time the shareholder proponent submitted the proposal, the shareholder proponent continuously held the securities for at least one year; or

a copy of a filed Schedule 13D, Schedule 13G, Form 3, Form 4, Form 5, or amendments to those documents or updated forms, reflecting the shareholder proponent's ownership of shares as of or before the date on which the one-year eligibility period begins and the shareholder proponent's written statement that he or she continuously held the required number of shares for the one-year period as of the date of the statement.

We have expressed the view consistently that a company does not meet its obligation to provide appropriate notice of defects in a shareholder proponent's proof of ownership where the company refers the shareholder proponent to rule 14a-8(b) but does not either:

address the specific requirements of that rule in the notice; or

attach a copy of rule 14a-8(b) to the notice.

D. What are the consequences if the staff denies a company's request for a waiver of rule 14a-8(j)'s 80-day requirement? Will the company have to wait 80 days to file its definitive proxy materials?

No, the company is not required to wait 80 days to file its definitive proxy materials. Rule 14a-8(j) provides that if the company intends to exclude a proposal from its proxy materials, it must file its reasons with the Commission no later than 80 calendar days before it files its definitive proxy statement and form of proxy with the Commission. Rule 14a-8(j) also requires the company to simultaneously provide the shareholder proponent with a copy of its submission. The staff may permit the company to make its submission later than 80 days before the company files its definitive proxy statement and form of proxy if the company demonstrates "good cause" for missing the deadline. In that instance, the failure to comply with rule 14a-8(j) would not require the company to delay its filing date until the expiration of 80 days from the date that it submits its no-action request. The most common basis for the company's showing of good cause is that the proposal was not submitted timely and the company did not receive the proposal until after the 80-day deadline had passed.

There are instances in which the staff will not agree that a company has demonstrated good cause for failing to make its rule 14a-8 submission at least 80 days before the intended filing of its definitive proxy materials. In those instances, we generally will consider the bases upon which the company intends to exclude a proposal, as we believe that is an appropriate exercise of our responsibilities under rule 14a-8. When we advise such a company and the shareholder proponent of our views regarding the application of rule 14a-8 to the proposal, we also will advise them of our view that the company has not followed the appropriate procedure under rule 14a-8. As noted above, our response in that situation would not require the company to wait to file its proxy materials until 80 days after its rule 14a-8 submission. Companies that have not demonstrated good cause for failing to make a timely rule 14a-8 submission should be aware that, despite our expression of a view with regard to the application of the eligibility or substantive requirements of rule 14a-8 to a proposal, the filing of their definitive proxy materials before the expiration of the 80-day time period in that situation may not be in accordance with the procedural requirements of rule 14a-8. Further, companies should note that, in issuing such a response, we are making no determination as to the appropriateness of filing definitive proxy materials less than 80 days after the date of the rule 14a-8(j) submission.

We will consider the timeliness of a rule 14a-8 no-action request in determining whether to respond. We reserve the right to decline to respond to rule 14a-8 no-action requests if the company does not comply with the time frame in rule 14a-8(j).

E. When should companies and shareholder proponents provide a supporting opinion of counsel and what should counsel to companies and shareholder proponents consider in drafting such an opinion?

Rule 14a-8(i)(1) and rule 14a-8(i)(2) permit the company to exclude a proposal if it meets its burden of demonstrating that the proposal is improper under state law or that the proposal, if implemented, would cause the company to violate any state, federal, or foreign law to which it is subject. Rule 14a-8(i)(6) permits the company to exclude a proposal if it meets its burden of demonstrating that the company would lack the power or authority to implement the proposal. Rule 14a-8(j)(2)(iii) requires the company to provide the Commission with a supporting opinion of counsel when the asserted reasons for exclusion are based on matters of state or foreign law. In submitting such an opinion of counsel, the company and its counsel should consider whether the law underlying the opinion of counsel is unsettled or unresolved and, whenever possible, the opinion of counsel should cite relevant legislative authority or judicial precedents regarding the opinion of counsel. Proposals that would result in the company breaching existing contractual obligations may be excludable under rule 14a-8(i)(2), rule 14a-8(i)(6), or both, because implementing the proposal would require the company to violate applicable law or would not be within the power or authority of the company to implement. If a company asserts either of these bases for exclusion in its rule 14a-8 submission, it expedites the staff's review and often assists the company in meeting its burden of demonstrating that it may exclude the proposal when the company provides a copy of the relevant contract, cites specific provisions of the contract that would be violated, and explains how implementation of the proposal would cause the company to breach its obligations under that contract. The submission also should provide a supporting opinion of counsel or indicate that the arguments advanced under state or foreign law constitute the opinion of counsel.

In analyzing an opinion of counsel that is submitted under rule 14a-8(j)(2)(iii), we consider whether counsel is licensed to practice law in the jurisdiction where the law is at issue. We also consider the extent to which the opinion makes assumptions about the operation of the proposal that are not called for by the language of the proposal. Shareholder proponents who wish to contest a company's reliance on an opinion of counsel as to matters of state or foreign law may, but are not required to, submit an opinion of counsel supporting their position.

F. What should companies and shareholder proponents know about how we process no-action requests?

1. Availability of materials provided to us

Commission rule 82, which can be found at 17 CFR § 200.82, reads as follows (citations are omitted):

Materials filed with the Commission pursuant to rule 14a-8(d) under the Securities Exchange Act of 1934 [the predecessor of current rule 14a-8(j)], written communications related thereto received from any person, and each related no-action letter or other written communication issued by the staff of the Commission, shall be made available to any person upon request for inspection or copying.

In adopting rule 82, the Commission stated, "all materials required to be filed with the Commission pursuant to proxy rule 14a-8[j] will be considered public records of the Commission. [Rule 82] also provides for the public availability of written communications related to the materials filed pursuant to rule 14a-8[(j)] which may be voluntarily submitted by shareholder-proponents or other persons." See Exchange Act Release No. 9785 (September 22, 1972). As such, when a company submits a no-action request, we forward a copy of the request to the Commission's Public Reference Room immediately.

In order to ensure that the staff's process is fair to all parties, we base our determinations on the written materials provided to us. While we will respond to telephone questions from the company or the shareholder proponent regarding the status of a request, we do not discuss the substantive nature of any specific no-action request with either the company or the shareholder proponent. Therefore, we request that any additional information that the company or the shareholder proponent would like to provide be submitted to us and the other party in writing.

2. Availability of responses

After we have completed our review of a no-action request, we generally send our response to the request by mail to both the shareholder proponent who submitted the proposal and the company that submitted the request. In addition, we forward a copy of our response, along with the relevant correspondence, to the Commission's Public Reference Room at the time that we issue the response. Commercial databases that check the Public Reference Room routinely for new no-action responses issued by the Division often upload the responses to their systems. As a result, the company or the shareholder proponent often may find our response in the Public Reference Room or on a commercial database prior to their receipt of that response.

3. Facilitating prompt, consistent delivery of responses to companies and shareholder proponents

During the highest volume periods of the rule 14a-8 season, the mailing of our no-action responses may be delayed and the company and the shareholder proponent may not receive the copies that are sent by mail immediately after the issuance of our no-action response. As such, we may fax copies of our responses in order to ensure that shareholder proponents and companies are given timely responses and to avoid prejudicing either party unnecessarily in resolving disputes that may arise in connection with the rule 14a-8 no-action requests. When we have a fax number for both the company and the shareholder proponent, we will fax our response to each if we are unable to mail the response promptly; when we have a fax number for the company but not for the shareholder proponent, we will fax the response to the company where the company agrees to forward promptly our response to the shareholder proponent. It is important to note that the practice of faxing copies of our no-action responses is a courtesy and is not required by Commission rules.

In order to facilitate the prompt delivery of our responses by providing us as much contact information regarding the shareholder proponent as possible, companies should provide us with all relevant correspondence when submitting a no-action request. In this regard, our review is facilitated best when a company's correspondence with us includes the shareholder proposal, any cover letter that the shareholder proponent provided with the proposal, the shareholder's address and fax number, and any other correspondence the company has exchanged with the shareholder relating to the proposal.

G. Conclusion

We hope that this bulletin, along with SLB No. 14 and SLB No. 14A, helps you gain a better understanding of rule 14a-8, the no-action request process, and our views on some significant issues and questions that arise commonly during our review of rule 14a-8 no-action requests. We believe that these bulletins contain information that will assist in the efficient operation of the rule 14a-8 process for both companies and shareholders.

Division of Corporation Finance
Securities and Exchange Commission

Shareholder Proposals

Staff Legal Bulletin No. 14C (CF)

Action: Publication of CF Staff Legal Bulletin

Date: June 28, 2005

Summary: This staff legal bulletin provides information for companies and shareholders regarding rule 14a-8 under the Securities Exchange Act of 1934.

Supplementary Information: The statements in this legal bulletin represent the views of the Division of Corporation Finance. This bulletin is not a rule, regulation, or statement of the Securities and Exchange Commission. Further, the Commission has neither approved nor disapproved its content. The references to "we," "our," and "us" are to the Division of Corporation Finance.

Contacts: For further information, please contact the Office of Chief Counsel in the Division of Corporation Finance at (202) 551-3500.

A. What is the purpose of this bulletin?

This bulletin is part of a continuing effort by the Division of Corporation Finance to identify and provide guidance on issues that arise commonly under rule 14a-8. Specifically, this bulletin contains information regarding:

- the addresses for submitting no-action requests and shareholder responses to those requests;
- the application of rule 14a-8(i)(6) to proposals calling for director independence;
- the application of rule 14a-8(i)(7) to proposals referencing environmental or public health issues;
- the application of rule 14a-8(l);
- the company facsimile number shareholder proponents should rely on when transmitting proposals and responses to notices of defects;
- the written materials that should accompany a no-action request;
- the withdrawal of a proposal submitted by multiple shareholder proponents; and
- the circumstances under which we will transmit our no-action responses by facsimile.

The following additional guidance regarding rule 14a-8 is available on the Commission's website:

- the text of rule 14a-8, which is in Exchange Act Release No. 40018 (May 21, 1998), at *www.sec.gov/rules/final/34-40018.htm*;
- SLB No. 14, which explains the rule 14a-8 no-action process and addresses matters of interest to companies and shareholder proponents, at *www.sec.gov/interps/legal/cfslb14.htm*;
- SLB No. 14A, which clarifies our position on shareholder proposals related to equity compensation plans, at *www.sec.gov/interps/legal/cfslb14a.htm*; and
- SLB No. 14B, which clarifies and updates some of the guidance contained in SLB No. 14, at *www.sec.gov/interps/legal/cfslb14b.htm*.

B. Have the addresses for submitting no-action requests and shareholder responses to those requests changed from those published in SLB No. 14?

Yes. The Commission has moved its headquarters. As a result, you should use the following addresses:

- rule 14a-8 no-action requests submitted by registered investment companies and business development companies, as well as shareholder responses to those requests, should be sent to:

    U.S. Securities and Exchange Commission
    Division of Investment Management
    Office of Legal and Disclosure
    901 E Street, N.W.
    Washington, D.C. 20549

- all other rule 14a-8 no-action requests and shareholder responses to those requests should be sent to:

    U.S. Securities and Exchange Commission
    Division of Corporation Finance
    Office of Chief Counsel
    100 F Street, N.E.
    Washington, D.C. 20549

C. Under rule 14a-8(i)(6), when do we concur with a company's view that there is a basis for excluding a proposal calling for director independence?

1. Rule 14a-8(i)(6)

Rule 14a-8(i)(6) is one of the substantive bases for exclusion in rule 14a-8. It permits a company to exclude a proposal that the company would lack the power or authority to implement.

2. Our analysis of no-action requests from companies that intend to rely on rule 14a-8(i)(6) to exclude proposals calling for director independence

Our analysis of whether a proposal that seeks to impose independence qualifications on directors is beyond the power or authority of the company to implement focuses primarily on whether the proposal requires continued independence at all times. In this regard, although we would not agree with a company's argument that it is unable to ensure the election of independent directors, we would agree with the argument that a board of directors lacks the power to ensure that its chairman or any other director will retain his or her independence at all times. As such, when a proposal is drafted in a manner that would require a director to maintain his or her independence at all times, we permit the company to exclude the proposal under rule 14a-8(i)(6) on the basis that the proposal does not provide the board with an opportunity or mechanism to cure a violation of the standard requested in the proposal. In contrast, if the proposal does not require a director to maintain independence at all times or contains language permitting the company to cure a director's loss of independence, any such loss of independence would not result in an automatic violation of the standard in the proposal and we, therefore, do not permit the company to exclude the proposal under rule 14a-8(i)(6).

We believe that our approach is consistent with Commission rules relating to director independence. Specifically, Exchange Act rule 10A-3, adopted pursuant to Exchange Act Section 10A(m), mandates various audit committee requirements for most exchange-listed issuers, including a requirement that audit committees consist entirely of independent directors. Although rule 10A-3 requires entirely independent audit committees for most listed issuers, the rule also contemplates that a director may cease to be independent. In addition, both Section 10A(m) and rule 10A-3 require that an issuer have an opportunity to cure any non-compliance with the applicable audit committee independence requirements before such non-compliance may serve as a basis for prohibiting the listing of the issuer's securities. Therefore, we believe that our view that a board lacks the power to ensure that a director maintains his or her independence at all times is consistent with Section 10A(m) and rule 10A-3, which not only contemplate that a board member may lose independence, but require that mechanisms exist to allow an issuer to cure such a loss.

The following chart illustrates our analysis of the aplication of rule 14a-8(i)(6) to proposals calling for director independence, and demonstrates that, as we indicated in question and answer B.6 of SLB No 14, differing language in proposals may result in different no-action responses.

Company	Proposal	Date of our response	Our response
Allied Waste Industries, Inc.	"The shareholders . . . urge the Board of Directors . . . to amend the by-laws to require that an independent director who has not served as the chief executive of the Company serve as Board Chair."	Mar. 21, 2005	We concurred in Allied Waste's view that it could exclude the proposal under rule 14a-8(i)(6). In doing so, our response noted that the proposal did not provide the board with an opportunity or mechanism to cure a violation of the independence standard requested in the proposal.
Merck & Co., Inc.	"The shareholders . . . request that the Board of Directors establish a policy of separating the roles of Board Chair and Chief Executive Officer (CEO) whenever possible, so that an independent director who has not served as an executive officer of the Company serves as Chair of the Board of Directors."	Dec. 29, 2004	We did not concur in Merck's view that it could exclude the proposal under rule 14a-8(i)(6). The proposal provided the board with an opportunity or mechanism to cure a violation of the independence standard requested in the proposal.
The Walt Disney Co.	"[T]he shareholders . . . urge the Board of Directors to amend the Corporate Governance Guidelines, and take whatever other actions are necessary to set as a company policy that the Chairman of the Board of Directors will always be an independent member of the Board of Directors, except in rare and explicitly spelled out, extraordinary circumstances."	Nov. 24, 2004	We did not concur in Disney's view that it could exclude the proposal under rule 14a-8(i)(6). The proposal provided the board with an opportunity or mechanism to cure a violation of the independence standard requested in the proposal.

D. Under rule 14a-8(i)(7), when do we concur with a company's view that there is a basis for excluding a proposal referencing environmental or public health issues as relating to the ordinary business matter of evaluating risk?

1. Rule 14a-8(i)(7)

Rule 14a-8(i)(7) is another of the substantive bases for exclusion in rule 14a-8. It permits a company to exclude a proposal that deals with a matter relating to the company's ordinary business operations. The fact that a proposal relates to ordinary business matters does not conclusively establish that a company may exclude the proposal from its proxy materials. As the Commission stated in Exchange Act Release No. 40018, proposals that relate to ordinary business matters but that focus on "sufficiently significant social policy issues . . . would not be considered to be excludable, because the proposals would transcend the day-to-day business matters. . . ."

2. Our analysis of no-action requests from companies that intend to rely on rule 14a-8(i)(7) to exclude proposals as relating to an evaluation of risk

Each year, we are asked to analyze numerous proposals that make reference to environmental or public health issues. In determining whether the focus of these proposals is a significant social policy issue, we consider both the proposal and the supporting statement as a whole. To the extent that a proposal and supporting statement focus on the company engaging in an internal assessment of the risks or liabilities that the company faces as a result of its operations that may adversely affect the environment or the public's health, we concur with the company's view that there is a basis for it to exclude the proposal under rule 14a-8(i)(7) as relating to an evaluation of risk. To the extent that a proposal and supporting statement focus on the company minimizing or eliminating operations that may adversely affect the environment or the public's health, we do not concur with the company's view that there is a basis for it to exclude the proposal under rule 14a-8(i)(7). The following chart illustrates this distinction.

Company	Proposal	Date of our response	Our response
Xcel Energy Inc.	"That the Board of Directors report . . . on (a) the economic risks associated with the Company's past, present, and future emissions of carbon dioxide, sulphur dioxide, nitrogen oxide and mercury emissions, and the public stance of the company regarding efforts to reduce these emissions and (b) the economic benefits of committing to a substantial reduction of those emissions related to its current business activities (i.e. potential improvement in competitiveness and profitability)."	Apr. 1, 2003	We concurred in Xcel's view that it could exclude the proposal under rule 14a-8(i)(7), as relating to an evaluation of risks and benefits.
Exxon Mobil Corp.	"[S]hareholders request . . . a report . . . on the potential environmental damage that would result from the company drilling for oil and gas in protected areas. . . ."	Mar. 18, 2005	We did not concur in ExxonMobil's view that it could exclude the proposal under rule 14a-8(i)(7).

E. Must a company submit a no-action request to exclude a shareholder proponent's name or address from its proxy statement under rule 14a-8(l)?

No. Rule 14a-8(l) is a self-executing provision of the rule that permits a company to exclude from its proxy statement a shareholder proponent's name, address, and number of voting securities held, as long as the company includes a statement that it will provide this information to shareholders promptly upon receiving an oral or written request.

F. What company facsimile number should a shareholder proponent rely on when transmitting a proposal or transmitting a response to a notice of defects?

A shareholder proponent is encouraged to submit a proposal or a response to a notice of defects by a means that allows him or her to determine when the proposal or response was received by the company, such as by facsimile. However, if the shareholder proponent transmits these materials by facsimile, the shareholder proponent should ensure that he or she has obtained the correct facsimile number for making such submissions. For example, if the shareholder proponent obtains the company's facsimile number from a third-party website, and the facsimile number is incorrect, the shareholder proponent's proposal may be subject to exclusion on the basis that the shareholder proponent failed to submit the proposal or response in a timely manner. As such, shareholder proponents should use the facsimile number for submitting proposals that the company disclosed in its most recent proxy statement. In those instances where the company does not disclose in its proxy statement a facsimile number for submitting proposals, we encourage shareholder proponents to contact the company to obtain the correct facsimile number for submitting proposals and responses to notices of defects.

G. When submitting a no-action request, should a company provide us with all relevant correspondence exchanged with the shareholder proponent(s)?

Yes. As we indicated in question and answer G.7 of SLB No. 14 and question and answer F.3 of SLB No. 14B, a company should provide us with all relevant correspondence when submitting a no-action request. In this regard, we wish to reiterate that our process may be delayed unless the company provides with its no-action request:

- a copy of the shareholder proposal;
- copies of any cover letters that the shareholder proponent(s) provided with the proposal;
- any addresses and facsimile numbers of the shareholder proponent(s); and
- any other correspondence the company has exchanged with the shareholder proponent(s) relating to the proposal, such as any notices of defects and any shareholder responses to the notices.

H. When a company submits a letter withdrawing a no-action request for a proposal submitted by multiple proponents, should the company include documentation demonstrating that each shareholder proponent has agreed to withdraw the proposal?

Yes. As we indicated in question and answer B.15 of SLB No. 14, when a proposal is submitted by multiple shareholder proponents and the proposal is withdrawn, the company should include with its withdrawal letter documentation demonstrating that each shareholder proponent has agreed to withdraw the proposal. In this regard, if each shareholder proponent has designated a lead individual to act on its behalf, and the company is able to demonstrate that the individual is authorized to act on behalf of all of the shareholder proponents, the company need only provide a letter from that lead individual indicating that it is withdrawing the proposal on behalf of all of the shareholder proponents. You can find additional guidance regarding withdrawals of no-action requests in questions and answers B.14 and B.15 of SLB No. 14.

I. Will we transmit our no-action responses by facsimile to companies and shareholder proponents?

Yes. As we indicated in question and answer F.3 of SLB No. 14B, we may transmit our responses by facsimile during the highest volume periods of the rule 14a-8 season to ensure that companies and shareholder proponents are given timely responses. If we are unable to mail our response promptly, we will transmit our response by facsimile if the company requests such a transmission and provides facsimile numbers for both the company and the shareholder proponent. We will not transmit the response to the company by facsimile when we have a facsimile number for the company but not for the shareholder proponent.

We wish to reiterate that the practice of transmitting copies of our no-action responses by facsimile is a courtesy and is not required by Commission rules. In addition, we remind companies and shareholder proponents that commercial databases check the Commission's Public Reference Room routinely for new no-action responses issued by the Division and upload the responses to their systems. As a result, the company or the shareholder proponent often may find our response in the Public Reference Room or on a commercial database prior to their receipt of that response.

J. Conclusion

We hope that this bulletin, along with SLB No. 14, SLB No. 14A, and SLB No. 14B, helps you gain a better understanding of rule 14a-8, the no-action request process, and our views on some significant issues that arise commonly during our review of rule 14a-8 no-action requests. We believe that these bulletins contain information that will assist in the efficient operation of the rule 14a-8 process for both companies and shareholders.

Division of Corporation Finance
Securities and Exchange Commission

Shareholder Proposals

Staff Legal Bulletin No. 14D (CF)

Action: Publication of CF Staff Legal Bulletin

Date: November 7, 2008

Summary: This staff legal bulletin provides information for companies and shareholders regarding rule 14a-8 under the Securities Exchange Act of 1934.

Supplementary Information: The statements in this legal bulletin represent the views of the Division of Corporation Finance. This bulletin is not a rule, regulation, or statement of the Securities and Exchange Commission. Further, the Commission has neither approved nor disapproved its content. The references to "we," "our," and "us" are to the Division of Corporation Finance.

Contacts: For further information, please contact the Office of Chief Counsel in the Division of Corporation Finance at (202) 551-3500.

A. What is the purpose of this bulletin?

This bulletin is part of a continuing effort by the Division of Corporation Finance to identify and provide guidance on issues that commonly arise under rule 14a-8. Specifically, this bulletin contains information regarding:

- shareholder proposals that recommend, request, or require a board of directors to unilaterally amend the company's articles or certificate of incorporation;

- a new e-mail address established for the receipt of rule 14a-8 no-action requests and related correspondence;

- whether a company must send a notice of defect if the company's records indicate that the proponent has not owned the minimum amount of securities for the required period of time as set forth in rule 14a-8(b); and

- the requirement that a proponent send copies of correspondence to the company and the manner in which the company and a proponent should provide additional correspondence to us and to each other.

The following additional guidance regarding rule 14a-8 is available on the Commission's web site:

- *SLB No. 14*, which explains the rule 14a-8 no-action process and addresses matters of interest to companies and proponents;

- *SLB No. 14A*, which clarifies our position on shareholder proposals related to equity compensation plans;

- *SLB No. 14B*, which clarifies and updates some of the guidance contained in SLB No. 14; and

- *SLB No. 14C*, which addresses additional matters of interest to companies and proponents, and clarifies and updates some of the guidance contained in SLB No. 14 and SLB No. 14B.

B. A shareholder proposal recommends, requests, or requires that the board of directors amend the company's charter. If, under applicable state law, the charter can be amended only if the amendment is initiated by the board and subsequently approved by the shareholders, may a company exclude a proposal under rule 14a-8(i)(1), rule 14a-8(i)(2), or rule 14a-8(i)(6) based solely on the argument that the board does not have the unilateral authority or power under state law to amend the charter?

If a proposal recommends, requests, or requires the board of directors to amend the company's charter, we may concur that there is some basis for the company to omit the proposal in reliance on rule 14a-8(i)(1), rule 14a-8(i)(2), or rule 14a-8(i)(6) if the company meets its burden of establishing that applicable state law requires any such amendment to be initiated by the board and then approved by shareholders in order for the charter to be amended as a matter of law. In accordance with longstanding staff practice, however, our response may permit the proponent to revise the proposal to provide that the board of directors "take the steps necessary" to amend the company's charter. If the proponent revises the proposal in this manner within the time frame specified in our response letter, we do not believe there would be a basis for the company to exclude the proposal under rule 14a-8(i)(1), rule 14a-8(i)(2), or rule 14a-8(i)(6). The chart below includes examples of revisions that we have previously permitted in response to no-action requests similar to those discussed in this question and answer.

Company	Proposal	Date of our response	Our response
SBC Communications Inc.	Resolved that as of December 31, 2005 the number of SBC Board of Director seats will be reduced from twenty one (21) to fourteen (14).	Jan. 11, 2004	We concurred in the company's view that the proposal could be excluded under rules 14a-8(i)(2) and 14a-8(i)(6), unless the proponent revised the proposal as a recommendation or request that the board of directors take the steps necessary to implement the proposal.
Gyrodyne Co. of America, Inc.	It is proposed that the classified board be abolished and all Directors, effective after the election of Directors in 1999, be elected annually.	Aug. 18, 1999	We concurred in the company's view that the proposal could be excluded under rule 14a-8(i)(1), unless the proponent revised the proposal as a recommendation or request that the board of directors take the steps necessary to implement the proposal.
Sears, Roebuck and Co.	Resolved: That the stockholders . . . urge the Board of Directors to amend the Company's Restated Certificate of Incorporation to declassify the Board of Directors for the purpose of Director elections.	Feb. 17, 1989	We concurred in the company's view that the proposal could be excluded under rules 14a-8(c)(2) and 14a-8(c)(6) [now rules 14a-8(i)(2) and 14a-8(i)(6)], unless the proponent revised the proposal to urge that the board of directors take the steps necessary to effect the proposed amendment to the certificate of incorporation.

C. May companies and shareholders e-mail us rule 14a-8 no-action requests and related correspondence?

Yes. We have established a new e-mail address for the receipt of no-action requests and correspondence related to rule 14a-8. Companies and proponents may submit requests for no-action relief under rule 14a-8 and related correspondence to us at *shareholderproposals@sec.gov*. This mailbox should not be used to submit other types of no-action requests or correspondence. Please include your name and telephone number in any submission directed to this mailbox. Remember that your e-mail is not confidential, and others may intercept and read your e-mail. We will process no-action requests and related correspondence received through this mailbox in the same manner as requests and correspondence submitted in paper.

D. If a proponent is listed in a company's records as a registered holder, and the records indicate that the proponent has not owned the minimum amount of securities for the required period of time as set forth in rule 14a-8(b), must the company send the proponent a notice of defect if it wishes to exclude the proposal on eligibility grounds?

Yes. If a proponent is listed in a company's records as a registered holder, the company can confirm that the proponent's holdings satisfy the ownership eligibility requirements of rule 14a-8(b). Because the proponent can also hold the company's securities by other means, however, such as through a broker or bank, the company's records do not prove conclusively that the proponent fails to meet the ownership eligibility requirement. As a result, in situations in which a company's records indicate that the proponent does not satisfy the ownership eligibility requirement in rule 14a-8(b), the company must inform the proponent that the proponent must provide proof of ownership that satisfies the requirements of rule 14a-8(b) if the company intends to exclude the proposal based upon the proponent's failure to satisfy the requirements of rule 14a-8(b).

E. Does rule 14a-8 require proponents to provide companies with any correspondence they send to us? If so, how should the correspondence be transmitted?

Yes. Rule 14a-8(k) requires a proponent to provide the company with a copy of any correspondence submitted in response to the company's no-action request. In addition, as stated in section G.9 of SLB No. 14, both the company and the proponent should promptly forward to each other copies of all correspondence provided to us in connection with rule 14a-8 no-action requests. We encourage companies and proponents to use the same means of transmitting correspondence to each other as they use to transmit materials to us. For example, if a company transmits correspondence to us via overnight mail, the company should transmit a copy to the proponent via overnight mail as well.

F. Conclusion

We hope that this bulletin, along with SLB No. 14, SLB No. 14A, SLB No. 14B, and SLB No. 14C, helps you gain a better understanding of rule 14a-8, the no-action request process, and our views on some significant issues that commonly arise during our review of rule 14a-8 no-action requests. We believe that these bulletins contain information that will assist in the efficient operation of the rule 14a-8 process for both companies and shareholders.

http://www.sec.gov/interps/legal/cfslb14d.htm

Division of Corporation Finance
Securities and Exchange Commission

Shareholder Proposals

Staff Legal Bulletin No. 14E (CF)

Action: Publication of CF Staff Legal Bulletin

Date: October 27, 2009

Summary: This staff legal bulletin provides information for companies and shareholders regarding Rule 14a-8 under the Securities Exchange Act of 1934.

Supplementary Information: The statements in this legal bulletin represent the views of the Division of Corporation Finance. This bulletin is not a rule, regulation or statement of the Securities and Exchange Commission. Further, the Commission has neither approved nor disapproved its content. The references to "we," "our" and "us" are to the Division of Corporation Finance.

Contacts: For further information, please contact the Office of Chief Counsel in the Division of Corporation Finance at (202) 551-3500.

A. What is the purpose of this bulletin?

This bulletin is part of a continuing effort by the Division of Corporation Finance to provide guidance on important issues arising under Rule 14a-8. Specifically, this bulletin contains information regarding:

- the application of Rule 14a-8(i)(7) to proposals relating to risk;

- the application of Rule 14a-8(i)(7) to proposals focusing on succession planning for a company's chief executive officer (CEO); and

- the manner in which shareholder proponents and companies can notify us that they will be submitting correspondence in connection with a no-action request.

You can find additional guidance regarding Rule 14a-8 in the following bulletins that are available on the Commission's web site: *SLB No. 14, SLB No. 14A, SLB No. 14B, SLB No. 14C* and *SLB No. 14D*.

B. What analytical framework will we apply in determining whether a company may exclude a proposal related to risk under Rule 14a-8(i)(7)?

Over the past decade, we have received numerous no-action requests from companies seeking to exclude proposals relating to environmental, financial or health risks under Rule 14a-8(i)(7). As we explained in SLB No. 14C, in analyzing such requests, we have sought to determine whether the proposal and supporting statement as a whole relate to the company engaging in an evaluation of risk, which is a matter we have viewed as relating to a company's ordinary business operations. To the extent that a proposal and supporting statement have focused on a company engaging in an internal assessment of the risks and liabilities that the company faces as a result of its operations, we have permitted companies to exclude these proposals under Rule 14a-8(i)(7) as relating to an evaluation of risk. To the extent that a proposal and supporting statement have focused on a company minimizing or eliminating operations that may adversely affect the environment or the public's health, we have not permitted companies to exclude these proposals under Rule 14a-8(i)(7).

We have recently witnessed a marked increase in the number of no-action requests in which companies seek to exclude proposals as relating to an evaluation of risk. In these requests, companies have frequently argued that proposals that do not explicitly request an evaluation of risk are nonetheless excludable under Rule 14a-8(i)(7) because they would require the company to engage in risk assessment.

Based on our experience in reviewing these requests, we are concerned that our application of the analytical framework discussed in SLB No. 14C may have resulted in the unwarranted exclusion of proposals that relate to the evaluation of risk but that focus on significant policy issues. Indeed, as most corporate decisions involve some evaluation of risk, the evaluation of risk should not be viewed as an end in itself, but rather, as a means to an end. In addition, we have become increasingly cognizant that the adequacy of risk management and oversight can have major consequences for a company and its shareholders. Accordingly, we have reexamined the analysis that we have used for risk proposals, and upon reexamination, we believe that there is a more appropriate framework to apply for analyzing these proposals.

On a going-forward basis, rather than focusing on whether a proposal and supporting statement relate to the company engaging in an evaluation of risk, *we* will *instead focus on the subject matter to which the risk pertains* or that gives rise to the risk. The fact that a proposal would require an evaluation of risk will not be dispositive of whether the proposal may be excluded under Rule 14a-8(i)(7). Instead, similar to the way in which we analyze proposals asking for the preparation of a report,[1] the formation of a committee[2] or the inclusion of disclosure in a Commission-prescribed document[3]—where we look to the underlying subject matter of the report, committee or disclosure to determine whether the proposal relates to ordinary business—we will consider whether the underlying subject matter of the risk evaluation involves a matter of ordinary business to the company. In those cases in which a proposal's underlying subject matter transcends the day-to-day business matters of the company and raises policy issues so significant that it would be appropriate for a shareholder vote, the proposal generally will not be excludable under Rule 14a-8(i)(7) as long as a sufficient nexus exists between the nature of the proposal and the company.[4] Conversely, in those cases in which a proposal's underlying subject matter involves an ordinary business matter to the company, the proposal generally will be excludable under Rule 14a-8(i)(7). In determining whether the subject matter raises significant policy issues and has a sufficient nexus to the company, as described above, we will apply the same standards that we apply to other types of proposals under Rule 14a-8(i)(7).[5]

In addition, we note that there is widespread recognition that the board's role in the oversight of a company's management of risk is a significant policy matter regarding the governance of the corporation. In light of this recognition, a proposal that focuses on the board's role in the oversight of a company's management of risk may transcend the day-to-day business matters of a company and raise policy issues so significant that it would be appropriate for a shareholder vote.

---

[1] See Exchange Act Release No. 20091 (Aug. 16, 1983) [48 FR 38218] ("In the past, the staff has taken the position that proposals requesting issuers to prepare reports on specific aspects of their business or to form special committees to study a segment of their business would not be excludable under Rule 14a-8(c)(7). Because this interpretation raises form over substance and renders the provisions of paragraph (c)(7) largely a nullity, the Commission has determined to adopt the interpretive change set forth in the Proposing Release. Henceforth, the staff will consider whether the subject matter of the special report or the committee involves a matter of ordinary business; where it does, the proposal will be excludable under Rule 14a-8(c)(7).").

[2] See Id.

[3] See Johnson Controls, Inc. (Oct. 26, 1999) ("Similar to our previous change in position regarding the excludability of proposals requesting preparation and dissemination of special reports to shareholders on specific aspects of a registrant's business (see Release 34-20091 (Aug. 16, 1983)), we have determined that

proposals requesting additional disclosures in Commission-prescribed documents should not be omitted under the 'ordinary business' exclusion solely because they relate to the preparation and content of documents filed with or submitted to the Commission. We now believe that our prior interpretation elevated form over substance. Beginning today, we therefore will consider whether the subject matter of the additional disclosure sought in a particular proposal involves a matter of ordinary business; where it does, we believe it may be excluded under rule 14a-8(i)(7).").

[4] The determination as to whether a proposal deals with a matter relating to a company's ordinary business operations is made on a case-by-case basis, taking into account factors such as the nature of the proposal and the circumstances of the company to which it is directed. See Exchange Act Release No. 40018 (May 21, 1998) [63 FR 29106].

[5] See id.; see, e.g., Lowe's Companies, Inc. (Feb. 1, 2008).

C. May a company rely on Rule 14a-8(i)(7) to exclude a proposal that focuses on CEO succession planning?

During the past two proxy seasons, we received a number of no-action requests from companies seeking to exclude proposals relating to CEO succession planning in reliance on Rule 14a-8(i)(7). These proposals generally requested that the companies adopt and disclose written and detailed CEO succession planning policies with specified features, including that the board develop criteria for the CEO position, identify and develop internal candidates, and use a formal assessment process to evaluate candidates. We expressed the view that these proposals could be excluded in reliance on Rule 14a-8(i)(7) because the proposals related to the termination, hiring or promotion of employees.[6]

The Commission stated in Exchange Act Release No. 40018 (May 21, 1998) that proposals involving "the management of the workforce, such as the hiring, promotion, and termination of employees" relate to ordinary business matters. Our position to date with respect to CEO succession planning proposals was based on this guidance and the Division's historical approach to proposals relating to employee hiring and promotion. In the same release, however, the Commission recognized that a proposal relating to ordinary business matters may transcend the company's day-to-day business matters and raise policy issues so significant that it would be appropriate for a shareholder vote.[7]

One of the board's key functions is to provide for succession planning so that the company is not adversely affected due to a vacancy in leadership. Recent events have underscored the importance of this board function to the governance of the corporation. We now recognize that CEO succession planning raises a significant policy issue regarding the governance of the corporation that transcends the day-to-day business matter of managing the workforce. As such, we have reviewed our position on CEO succession planning proposals and have determined to modify our treatment of such proposals. Going forward, we will take the view that a company generally may not rely on Rule 14a-8(i)(7) to exclude a proposal that focuses on CEO succession planning.[8]

D. May companies and shareholder proponents alert us that they intend to submit correspondence related to a no-action request?

Yes. If a company or a shareholder proponent intends to submit correspondence in connection with a no-action request, we encourage them to contact us so that, if possible, we can review the correspondence prior to issuing our no-action response. We also encourage companies and shareholder proponents to provide us with the date by which they intend to submit their correspondence. Companies and shareholder proponents can either call us at (202) 551-3500 or e-mail us at *shareholderproposals@sec.gov* to notify us of the pending submission. As we stated in SLB No. 14, if a shareholder proponent intends to reply to the company's no-action request, he or she should try to send the reply as soon as possible after the company submits its no-action request.

E. Conclusion

We hope that this bulletin, along with our other bulletins, helps you gain a better understanding of Rule 14a-8, the no-action request process, and our views on some significant issues that commonly arise during our review of Rule 14a-8 no-action requests. We believe that these bulletins contain information that will assist in the efficient operation of the Rule 14a-8 process for both companies and shareholders.

http://www.sec.gov/interps/legal/cfslb14e.htm

---

[6] *See, e.g., National Instruments Corp.* (Mar. 5, 2009).

[7] The Commission also noted that, "[f]rom time to time, in light of experience dealing with proposals in specific subject areas, and reflecting changing societal views, the Division adjusts its view with respect to 'social policy' proposals involving ordinary business." Exchange Act Release No. 40018.

[8] *Such a* proposal could *be* excluded *under* Rule *14a-8(i)(7)*, however, *if it* seeks to micro-manage the company by probing too deeply into matters of a complex nature upon which shareholders, as a group, would not be in a position to make an informed judgment. *See* Exchange Act Release No. 40018.

Division of Corporation Finance
Securities and Exchange Commission

Shareholder Proposals

Staff Legal Bulletin No. 14F (CF)

Action: Publication of CF Staff Legal Bulletin

Date: October 18, 2011

Summary: This staff legal bulletin provides information for companies and shareholders regarding Rule 14a-8 under the Securities Exchange Act of 1934.

Supplementary Information: The statements in this bulletin represent the views of the Division of Corporation Finance (the "Division"). This bulletin is not a rule, regulation or statement of the Securities and Exchange Commission (the "Commission"). Further, the Commission has neither approved nor disapproved its content.

Contacts: For further information, please contact the Division's Office of Chief Counsel by calling (202) 551-3500 or by submitting a web-based request form at https://tts.sec.gov/cgi-bin/corp_fin_interpretive.

A. The purpose of this bulletin

This bulletin is part of a continuing effort by the Division to provide guidance on important issues arising under Exchange Act Rule 14a-8. Specifically, this bulletin contains information regarding:

- Brokers and banks that constitute "record" holders under Rule 14a-8(b)(2)(i) for purposes of verifying whether a beneficial owner is eligible to submit a proposal under Rule 14a-8;

- Common errors shareholders can avoid when submitting proof of ownership to companies;

- The submission of revised proposals;

- Procedures for withdrawing no-action requests regarding proposals submitted by multiple proponents; and

- The Division's new process for transmitting Rule 14a-8 no-action responses by email.

You can find additional guidance regarding Rule 14a-8 in the following bulletins that are available on the Commission's website: SLB No. 14, SLB No. 14A, SLB No. 14B, SLB No. 14C, SLB No. 14D and SLB No. 14E.

B. The types of brokers and banks that constitute "record" holders under Rule 14a-8(b)(2)(i) for purposes of verifying whether a beneficial owner is eligible to submit a proposal under Rule 14a-8

1. Eligibility to submit a proposal under Rule 14a-8

To be eligible to submit a shareholder proposal, a shareholder must have continuously held at least $2,000 in market value, or 1%, of the company's securities entitled to be voted on the proposal at the shareholder meeting for at least one year as of the date the shareholder submits the proposal. The shareholder must also continue to hold the required amount of securities through the date of the meeting and must provide the company with a written statement of intent to do so.[1]

---

[1] *See* Rule 14a-8(b).

The steps that a shareholder must take to verify his or her eligibility to submit a proposal depend on how the shareholder owns the securities. There are two types of security holders in the U.S.: registered owners and beneficial owners.[2] Registered owners have a direct relationship with the issuer because their ownership of shares is listed on the records maintained by the issuer or its transfer agent. If a shareholder is a registered owner, the company can independently confirm that the shareholder's holdings satisfy Rule 14a-8(b)'s eligibility requirement.

The vast majority of investors in shares issued by U.S. companies, however, are beneficial owners, which means that they hold their securities in book-entry form through a securities intermediary, such as a broker or a bank. Beneficial owners are sometimes referred to as "street name" holders. Rule 14a-8(b)(2)(i) provides that a beneficial owner can provide proof of ownership to support his or her eligibility to submit a proposal by submitting a written statement "from the 'record' holder of [the] securities (usually a broker or bank)," verifying that, at the time the proposal was submitted, the shareholder held the required amount of securities continuously for at least one year.[3]

2. The role of the Depository Trust Company

Most large U.S. brokers and banks deposit their customers' securities with, and hold those securities through, the Depository Trust Company ("DTC"), a registered clearing agency acting as a securities depository. Such brokers and banks are often referred to as "participants" in DTC.[4] The names of these DTC participants, however, do not appear as the registered owners of the securities deposited with DTC on the list of shareholders maintained by the company or, more typically, by its transfer agent. Rather, DTC's nominee, Cede & Co., appears on the shareholder list as the sole registered owner of securities deposited with DTC by the DTC participants. A company can request from DTC a "securities position listing" as of a specified date, which identifies the DTC participants having a position in the company's securities and the number of securities held by each DTC participant on that date.[5]

3. Brokers and banks that constitute "record" holders under Rule 14a-8(b)(2)(i) for purposes of verifying whether a beneficial owner is eligible to submit a proposal under Rule 14a-8

In *The Hain Celestial Group, Inc.* (Oct. 1, 2008), we took the position that an introducing broker could be considered a "record" holder for purposes of Rule 14a-8(b)(2)(i). An introducing broker is a broker that engages in sales and other activities involving customer contact, such as opening customer accounts and accepting customer orders, but is not permitted to maintain custody of customer funds and securities.[6] Instead, an introducing broker engages another broker, known as a "clearing broker," to hold custody of

---

[2] For an explanation of the types of share ownership in the U.S., *see* Concept Release on U.S. Proxy System, Release No. 34-62495 (July 14, 2010) [75 FR 42982] ("Proxy Mechanics Concept Release"), at Section II.A. The term "beneficial owner" does not have a uniform meaning under the federal securities laws. It has a different meaning in this bulletin as compared to "beneficial owner" and "beneficial ownership" in Sections 13 and 16 of the Exchange Act. Our use of the term in this bulletin is not intended to suggest that registered owners are not beneficial owners for purposes of those Exchange Act provisions. *See* Proposed Amendments to Rule 14a-8 under the Securities Exchange Act of 1934 Relating to Proposals by Security Holders, Release No. 34-12598 (July 7, 1976) [41 FR 29982], at n.2 ("The term 'beneficial owner' when used in the context of the proxy rules, and in light of the purposes of those rules, may be interpreted to have a broader meaning than it would for certain other purpose[s] under the federal securities laws, such as reporting pursuant to the Williams Act.").

[3] If a shareholder has filed a Schedule 13D, Schedule 13G, Form 3, Form 4 or Form 5 reflecting ownership of the required amount of shares, the shareholder may instead prove ownership by submitting a copy of such filings and providing the additional information that is described in Rule 14a-8(b)(2)(ii).

[4] DTC holds the deposited securities in "fungible bulk," meaning that there are no specifically identifiable shares directly owned by the DTC participants. Rather, each DTC participant holds a pro rata interest or position in the aggregate number of shares of a particular issuer held at DTC. Correspondingly, each customer of a DTC participant – such as an individual investor – owns a pro rata interest in the shares in which the DTC participant has a pro rata interest. *See* Proxy Mechanics Concept Release, at Section II.B.2.a.

[5] *See* Exchange Act Rule 17Ad-8.

[6] *See* Net Capital Rule, Release No. 34-31511 (Nov. 24, 1992) [57 FR 56973] ("Net Capital Rule Release"), at Section II.C.

client funds and securities, to clear and execute customer trades, and to handle other functions such as issuing confirmations of customer trades and customer account statements. Clearing brokers generally are DTC participants; introducing brokers generally are not. As introducing brokers generally are not DTC participants, and therefore typically do not appear on DTC's securities position listing, *Hain Celestial* has required companies to accept proof of ownership letters from brokers in cases where, unlike the positions of registered owners and brokers and banks that are DTC participants, the company is unable to verify the positions against its own or its transfer agent's records or against DTC's securities position listing.

In light of questions we have received following two recent court cases relating to proof of ownership under Rule 14a-8[7] and in light of the Commission's discussion of registered and beneficial owners in the Proxy Mechanics Concept Release, we have reconsidered our views as to what types of brokers and banks should be considered "record" holders under Rule 14a-8(b)(2)(i). Because of the transparency of DTC participants' positions in a company's securities, we will take the view going forward that, for Rule 14a-8(b)(2)(i) purposes, only DTC participants should be viewed as "record" holders of securities that are deposited at DTC. As a result, we will no longer follow *Hain Celestial*.

We believe that taking this approach as to who constitutes a "record" holder for purposes of Rule 14a-8(b)(2)(i) will provide greater certainty to beneficial owners and companies. We also note that this approach is consistent with Exchange Act Rule 12g5-1 and a 1988 staff no-action letter addressing that rule,[8] under which brokers and banks that are DTC participants are considered to be the record holders of securities on deposit with DTC when calculating the number of record holders for purposes of Sections 12(g) and 15(d) of the Exchange Act.

Companies have occasionally expressed the view that, because DTC's nominee, Cede & Co., appears on the shareholder list as the sole registered owner of securities deposited with DTC by the DTC participants, only DTC or Cede & Co. should be viewed as the "record" holder of the securities held on deposit at DTC for purposes of Rule 14a-8(b)(2)(i). We have never interpreted the rule to require a shareholder to obtain a proof of ownership letter from DTC or Cede & Co., and nothing in this guidance should be construed as changing that view.

How can a shareholder determine whether his or her broker or bank is a DTC participant?

Shareholders and companies can confirm whether a particular broker or bank is a DTC participant by checking DTC's participant list, which is currently available on the Internet at http://www.dtcc.com/downloads/membership/directories/dtc/alpha.pdf.

What if a shareholder's broker or bank is not on DTC's participant list?

The shareholder will need to obtain proof of ownership from the DTC participant through which the securities are held. The shareholder should be able to find out who this DTC participant is by asking the shareholder's broker or bank.[9]

---

[7] *See KBR Inc. v. Chevedden*, Civil Action No. H-11-0196, 2011 U.S. Dist. LEXIS 36431, 2011 WL 1463611 (S.D. Tex. Apr. 4, 2011); *Apache Corp. v. Chevedden*, 696 F. Supp. 2d 723 (S.D. Tex. 2010). In both cases, the court concluded that a securities intermediary was not a record holder for purposes of Rule 14a-8(b) because it did not appear on a list of the company's non-objecting beneficial owners or on any DTC securities position listing, nor was the intermediary a DTC participant.

[8] *Techne Corp.* (Sept. 20, 1988).

[9] In addition, if the shareholder's broker is an introducing broker, the shareholder's account statements should include the clearing broker's identity and telephone number. *See* Net Capital Rule Release, at Section II.C.(iii). The clearing broker will generally be a DTC participant.

If the DTC participant knows the shareholder's broker or bank's holdings, but does not know the shareholder's holdings, a shareholder could satisfy Rule 14a-8(b)(2)(i) by obtaining and submitting two proof of ownership statements verifying that, at the time the proposal was submitted, the required amount of securities were continuously held for at least one year – one from the shareholder's broker or bank confirming the shareholder's ownership, and the other from the DTC participant confirming the broker or bank's ownership.

How will the staff process no-action requests that argue for exclusion on the basis that the shareholder's proof of ownership is not from a DTC participant?

The staff will grant no-action relief to a company on the basis that the shareholder's proof of ownership is not from a DTC participant only if the company's notice of defect describes the required proof of ownership in a manner that is consistent with the guidance contained in this bulletin. Under Rule 14a-8(f)(1), the shareholder will have an opportunity to obtain the requisite proof of ownership after receiving the notice of defect.

C. Common errors shareholders can avoid when submitting proof of ownership to companies

In this section, we describe two common errors shareholders make when submitting proof of ownership for purposes of Rule 14a-8(b)(2), and we provide guidance on how to avoid these errors.

First, Rule 14a-8(b) requires a shareholder to provide proof of ownership that he or she has "continuously held at least $2,000 in market value, or 1%, of the company's securities entitled to be voted on the proposal at the meeting for at least one year by the date you submit the proposal" (emphasis added).[10] We note that many proof of ownership letters do not satisfy this requirement because they do not verify the shareholder's beneficial ownership for the entire one-year period preceding and including the date the proposal is submitted. In some cases, the letter speaks as of a date *before* the date the proposal is submitted, thereby leaving a gap between the date of the verification and the date the proposal is submitted. In other cases, the letter speaks as of a date *after* the date the proposal was submitted but covers a period of only one year, thus failing to verify the shareholder's beneficial ownership over the required full one-year period preceding the date of the proposal's submission.

Second, many letters fail to confirm continuous ownership of the securities. This can occur when a broker or bank submits a letter that confirms the shareholder's beneficial ownership only as of a specified date but omits any reference to continuous ownership for a one-year period.

We recognize that the requirements of Rule 14a-8(b) are highly prescriptive and can cause inconvenience for shareholders when submitting proposals. Although our administration of Rule 14a-8(b) is constrained by the terms of the rule, we believe that shareholders can avoid the two errors highlighted above by arranging to have their broker or bank provide the required verification of ownership as of the date they plan to submit the proposal using the following format:

"As of [date the proposal is submitted], [name of shareholder] held, and has held continuously for at least one year, [number of securities] shares of [company name] [class of securities]."[11]

---

[10] For purposes of Rule 14a-8(b), the submission date of a proposal will generally precede the company's receipt date of the proposal, absent the use of electronic or other means of same-day delivery.

[11] This format is acceptable for purposes of Rule 14a-8(b), but it is not mandatory or exclusive.

As discussed above, a shareholder may also need to provide a separate written statement from the DTC participant through which the shareholder's securities are held if the shareholder's broker or bank is not a DTC participant.

D. The submission of revised proposals

On occasion, a shareholder will revise a proposal after submitting it to a company. This section addresses questions we have received regarding revisions to a proposal or supporting statement.

1. A shareholder submits a timely proposal. The shareholder then submits a revised proposal before the company's deadline for receiving proposals. Must the company accept the revisions?

Yes. In this situation, we believe the revised proposal serves as a replacement of the initial proposal. By submitting a revised proposal, the shareholder has effectively withdrawn the initial proposal. Therefore, the shareholder is not in violation of the one-proposal limitation in Rule 14a-8(c).[12] If the company intends to submit a no-action request, it must do so with respect to the revised proposal.

We recognize that in Question and Answer E.2 of SLB No. 14, we indicated that if a shareholder makes revisions to a proposal before the company submits its no-action request, the company can choose whether to accept the revisions. However, this guidance has led some companies to believe that, in cases where shareholders attempt to make changes to an initial proposal, the company is free to ignore such revisions even if the revised proposal is submitted before the company's deadline for receiving shareholder proposals. We are revising our guidance on this issue to make clear that a company may not ignore a revised proposal in this situation.[13]

2. A shareholder submits a timely proposal. After the deadline for receiving proposals, the shareholder submits a revised proposal. Must the company accept the revisions?

No. If a shareholder submits revisions to a proposal after the deadline for receiving proposals under Rule 14a-8(e), the company is not required to accept the revisions. However, if the company does not accept the revisions, it must treat the revised proposal as a second proposal and submit a notice stating its intention to exclude the revised proposal, as required by Rule 14a-8(j). The company's notice may cite Rule 14a-8(e) as the reason for excluding the revised proposal. If the company does not accept the revisions and intends to exclude the initial proposal, it would also need to submit its reasons for excluding the initial proposal.

3. If a shareholder submits a revised proposal, as of which date must the shareholder prove his or her share ownership?

A shareholder must prove ownership as of the date the original proposal is submitted. When the Commission has discussed revisions to proposals,[14] it has not suggested that a

---

[12] As such, it is not appropriate for a company to send a notice of defect for multiple proposals under Rule 14a-8(c) upon receiving a revised proposal.

[13] This position will apply to all proposals submitted after an initial proposal but before the company's deadline for receiving proposals, regardless of whether they are explicitly labeled as "revisions" to an initial proposal, unless the shareholder affirmatively indicates an intent to submit a second, *additional* proposal for inclusion in the company's proxy materials. In that case, the company must send the shareholder a notice of defect pursuant to Rule 14a-8(f)(1) if it intends to exclude either proposal from its proxy materials in reliance on Rule 14a-8(c). In light of this guidance,

with respect to proposals or revisions received before a company's deadline for submission, we will no longer follow *Layne Christensen Co.* (Mar. 21, 2011) and other prior staff no-action letters in which we took the view that a proposal would violate the Rule 14a-8(c) one-proposal limitation if such proposal is submitted to a company after the company has either submitted a Rule 14a-8 no-action request to exclude an earlier proposal submitted by the same proponent or notified the proponent that the earlier proposal was excludable under the rule.

[14] *See, e.g.*, Adoption of Amendments Relating to Proposals by Security Holders, Release No. 34-12999 (Nov. 22, 1976) [41 FR 52994].

revision triggers a requirement to provide proof of ownership a second time. As outlined in Rule 14a-8(b), proving ownership includes providing a written statement that the shareholder intends to continue to hold the securities through the date of the shareholder meeting. Rule 14a-8(f)(2) provides that if the shareholder "fails in [his or her] promise to hold the required number of securities through the date of the meeting of shareholders, then the company will be permitted to exclude all of [the same shareholder's] proposals from its proxy materials for any meeting held in the following two calendar years." With these provisions in mind, we do not interpret Rule 14a-8 as requiring additional proof of ownership when a shareholder submits a revised proposal.[15]

E. Procedures for withdrawing no-action requests for proposals submitted by multiple proponents

We have previously addressed the requirements for withdrawing a Rule 14a-8 no-action request in SLB Nos. 14 and 14C. SLB No. 14 notes that a company should include with a withdrawal letter documentation demonstrating that a shareholder has withdrawn the proposal. In cases where a proposal submitted by multiple shareholders is withdrawn, SLB No. 14C states that, if each shareholder has designated a lead individual to act on its behalf and the company is able to demonstrate that the individual is authorized to act on behalf of all of the proponents, the company need only provide a letter from that lead individual indicating that the lead individual is withdrawing the proposal on behalf of all of the proponents.

Because there is no relief granted by the staff in cases where a no-action request is withdrawn following the withdrawal of the related proposal, we recognize that the threshold for withdrawing a no-action request need not be overly burdensome. Going forward, we will process a withdrawal request if the company provides a letter from the lead filer that includes a representation that the lead filer is authorized to withdraw the proposal on behalf of each proponent identified in the company's no-action request.[16]

F. Use of email to transmit our Rule 14a-8 no-action responses to companies and proponents

To date, the Division has transmitted copies of our Rule 14a-8 no-action responses, including copies of the correspondence we have received in connection with such requests, by U.S. mail to companies and proponents. We also post our response and the related correspondence to the Commission's website shortly after issuance of our response.

In order to accelerate delivery of staff responses to companies and proponents, and to reduce our copying and postage costs, going forward, we intend to transmit our Rule 14a-8 no-action responses by email to companies and proponents. We therefore encourage both companies and proponents to include email contact information in any correspondence to each other and to us. We will use U.S. mail to transmit our no-action response to any company or proponent for which we do not have email contact information.

Given the availability of our responses and the related correspondence on the Commission's website and the requirement under Rule 14a-8 for companies and proponents to copy each other on correspondence submitted to the Commission, we believe it is unnecessary to transmit copies of the related correspondence along with our no-action response. Therefore, we intend to transmit only our staff response and not the correspondence we receive from the parties. We will continue to post to the Commission's website copies of this correspondence at the same time that we post our staff no-action response.

http://www.sec.gov/interps/legal/cfslb14f.htm

---

[15] Because the relevant date for proving ownership under Rule 14a-8(b) is the date the proposal is submitted, a proponent who does not adequately prove ownership in connection with a proposal is not permitted to submit another proposal for the same meeting on a later date.

[16] Nothing in this staff position has any effect on the status of any shareholder proposal that is not withdrawn by the proponent or its authorized representative.

APPENDIX 12
Internet Availability of Proxy Materials

SECURITIES AND EXCHANGE COMMISSION

17 CFR PARTS 240, 249 and 274

[RELEASE NOS. 34-55146; IC-27671; File No. S7-10-05]

RIN 3235-AJ47

INTERNET AVAILABILITY OF PROXY MATERIALS

AGENCY: Securities and Exchange Commission.

ACTION: Final rule; request for comment on Paperwork Reduction Act burden estimates.

SUMMARY: We are adopting amendments to the proxy rules under the Securities Exchange Act of 1934 that provide an alternative method for issuers and other persons to furnish proxy materials to shareholders by posting them on an Internet Web site and providing shareholders with notice of the availability of the proxy materials. Issuers must make copies of the proxy materials available to shareholders on request, at no charge to shareholders. The amendments put into place processes that will provide shareholders with notice of, and access to, proxy materials while taking advantage of technological developments and the growth of the Internet and electronic communications. Issuers that rely on the amendments may be able to significantly lower the costs of their proxy solicitations that ultimately are borne by shareholders. The amendments also might reduce the costs of engaging in a proxy contest for soliciting persons other than the issuer. The amendments do not apply to business combination transactions. The amendments also do not affect the availability of any existing method of furnishing proxy materials.

DATES: *Effective Date*: March 30, 2007.

Compliance Date: Persons may not send a Notice of Internet Availability of Proxy Materials to shareholders prior to July 1, 2007.

Comment Due Date: Comments on the Paperwork Reduction Act burden estimate should be received on or before March 30, 2007.

ADDRESSES: Comments may be submitted by any of the following methods:

Electronic comments:

- Use the Commission's Internet comment form (http://www.sec.gov/rules/proposed.shtml); or

- Send an e-mail to rule-comments@sec.gov. Please include File Number S7-10-05 on the subject line; or

- Use the Federal eRulemaking Portal (http://www.regulations.gov). Follow the instructions for submitting comments.

Paper comments:

- Send paper comments in triplicate to Nancy M. Morris, Secretary, U.S. Securities and Exchange Commission, 100 F Street, NE, Washington, DC 20549-1090.

All submissions should refer to File Number S7-10-05. To help us process and review your comments more efficiently, please use only one method. The Commission will post all comments on its Internet Web site (http://www.sec.gov/rules/final.shtml). Comments also are available for public inspection and copying in the Commission's Public Reference

Room, 100 F Street, NE, Washington, DC 20549. All comments received will be posted without change; we do not edit personal identifying information from submissions. You should submit only information that you wish to make publicly available.

FOR FURTHER INFORMATION CONTACT: Raymond A. Be, Special Counsel, Office of Rulemaking, Division of Corporation Finance, at (202) 551-3430, Securities and Exchange Commission, 100 F Street, NE, Washington, DC 20549-3628.

SUPPLEMENTARY INFORMATION: We are amending Rules 14a-2,[1] 14a-3,[2] 14a-4,[3] 14a-7,[4] 14a-8,[5] 14a-12,[6] 14a-13,[7] 14b-1,[8] 14b-2,[9] 14c-2,[10] 14c-3,[11] 14c-5,[12] 14c-7,[13] Schedule 14A,[14] Schedule 14C,[15] Form 10-K,[16] Form 10-KSB,[17] Form 10-Q,[18] and Form 10-QSB,[19] under the Securities Exchange Act of 1934[20] and Form N-SAR[21] under the Exchange Act and the Investment Company Act of 1940.[22] We also are adding new Rule 14a-16 under the Exchange Act.

Table of Contents

---

[1] 17 CFR 240.14a-2.
[2] 17 CFR 240.14a-3.
[3] 17 CFR 240.14a-4.
[4] 17 CFR 240.14a-7.
[5] 17 CFR 240.14a-8.
[6] 17 CFR 240.14a-12.
[7] 17 CFR 240.14a-13.
[8] 17 CFR 240.14b-1.
[9] 17 CFR 240.14b-2.
[10] 17 CFR 240.14c-2.
[11] 17 CFR 240.14c-3.

[12] 17 CFR 240.14c-5.
[13] 17 CFR 240.14c-7.
[14] 17 CFR 240.14a-101.
[15] 17 CFR 240.14c-101.
[16] 17 CFR 249.310.
[17] 17 CFR 249.310a.
[18] 17 CFR 249.308a.
[19] 17 CFR 249.308b.
[20] 15 U.S.C. 78a *et seq.*
[21] 17 CFR 249.330 and 274.101.
[22] 15 U.S.C. 80a-1 *et seq.*

I. Introduction

On December 8, 2005, we proposed amendments to update the proxy rules to take greater advantage of communications technology by supplementing the existing regulatory framework with an alternative "notice and access" proxy model that could reduce significantly the printing and mailing costs associated with furnishing proxy materials to shareholders.[23] Under the notice and access model that we proposed, an issuer would be able to satisfy its obligations under the Commission's proxy rules by posting its proxy materials on a publicly-accessible Internet Web site (other than the Commission's EDGAR Web site) and providing shareholders with a notice informing them that the materials are available and explaining how to access those materials. Under the proposal, an issuer relying on the model would be required to provide a requesting shareholder with a copy of the proxy materials in paper or by e-mail, at no charge to the shareholder. We proposed that soliciting persons other than the issuer also would be able to rely on the notice and access model.

We received approximately 140 comment letters on the proposed notice and access model from a variety of interested parties, including issuers and their agents, shareholders, intermediaries and their agents, financial printers, manufacturers of mailing products, and academics. There was significant disagreement among the commenters regarding these key issues raised by the proposed model:

- The sufficiency of current Internet access among the U.S. population such that the proposed model would be desirable[24];

- The effect that the proposed notice and access model might have on levels of proxy voting by shareholders[25];

---

[23] Release No. 34-52926 (Dec. 8, 2005) [70 FR 74597]. For purposes of this release only, the term "proxy materials" includes proxy statements on Schedule 14A, proxy cards, information statements on Schedule 14C, annual reports to security holders required by Rules 14a-3 and 14c-3 of the Exchange Act, notices of shareholder meetings, additional soliciting materials, and any amendments to such materials. For purposes of this release, the term does not include materials filed under Rule 14a-12.

[24] See, for example, letters suggesting that current rates of Internet access are sufficient from American Bar Association (ABA), America's Community Bankers (ACB), Association of Ameritech SBC Retirees (SBC Retirees), Business Roundtable (BRT),

Computershare Ltd. (Computershare), Proxinvest, Gary Tannahill, Hermes, Investment Company Institute (ICI), Securities Transfer Association (STA), and Sullivan & Cromwell. But also see, for example, letters from Association of BellTel Retirees (BellTel Retirees), Todd Collier, Joel Brown, James Davis, Donna Garal, Clark Green, Heather Harper, Frank Inman, William Lafollette, James Phipps, Beth Spletter, Megan Stroinski, and the United States Postal Service (USPS) suggesting that those rates are not sufficient.

[25] Some commenters believed that the proposed model might result in a decline in voting by shareholders. See, for example, letters from Automatic Data Processing, Inc. (ADP), James Angel, Timothy Buchman, State Board of Administration of Florida (Florida

- The level of security and privacy on the Internet[26];

- The extent of potential savings to issuers and those conducting proxy contests that choose to rely on the proposed model[27]; and

- Whether the proposed model may make the proxy delivery system, particularly as it relates to beneficial owners holding in street name through their brokers or other intermediaries, too complex.[28]

Several commenters suggested revisions related to the proposed notice and access model, including the following:

- The proposed rules should allow a shareholder to make an election to receive paper copies of the proxy materials with respect to any future solicitations that would remain in place until subsequently revoked by the shareholder[29];

- An issuer should have to make the proxy card available to shareholders through the same medium it uses to make the proxy statement available to them[30];

- The Commission should review and simplify the proxy delivery system as a whole rather than addressing the issue of electronic delivery of proxy materials in isolation[31]; and

- The New York Stock Exchange ("NYSE") should review its current schedule of maximum fees that its member firms may charge issuers to forward issuers' proxy materials to beneficial owners.[32]

Although there was a mixed reaction to the proposal,[33] we believe that current levels of access to the Internet merit adoption of the notice and access model as an alternative to the existing proxy distribution system. In this regard, we note that more than 10.7 million beneficial shareholders already have given their affirmative consent to electronic delivery of proxy materials and approximately 87.8% of shares voted were voted electronically or telephonically during the 2006 proxy season.[34] Moreover, research submitted to us during the comment period indicates that approximately 80% of investors in the United States have access to the Internet in their homes, a greater percentage than we estimated at the proposing stage.[35] Several commenters expressed the view that the current level of Internet usage is sufficiently high to warrant adoption of the proposed

---

(Footnote Continued)

State Board), Fund of Stockowners Rights (Stockowners Rights), IR Web Report, and Securities Industry Association (SIA). However, other commenters believed the rules may increase shareholder voting by facilitating the voting process. See, for example, letters from AFL-CIO, Robert Atkinson, Institutional Shareholder Services (ISS), Proxinvest, and Society of Corporate Secretaries and Governance Professionals (SCSGP).

[26] See, for example, letters from James Angel, Todd Collier, James Davis, William LaFollette, Matthew McGuire, and USPS.

[27] See, for example, letters from ADP and Computershare.

[28] See letter from ABA.

[29] See letters from American Business Council (ABC), AFL-CIO, James Angel, CALSTRS, Florida State Board, Ohio Public Employees Retirement System (OPERS), San Diego City Employees' Retirement System (San Diego Retirement), SIA, William Sjostrom, Stocklein Law Group, Swingvote, and Paul Uhlenhop.

[30] See letters from ACB, AFL-CIO, Amalgamated Bank of LongView Funds (Amalgamated Bank), Bell-

Tel Retirees, Council of Institutional Investors (CII), Florida State Board, Carl Hagberg, International Brotherhood of Teamsters (Teamsters), National Retiree Legislative Network (NRLN), San Diego Retirement, and Swingvote.

[31] See, for example, letters from BRT, Committee of Concerned Shareholders (Concerned Shareholders), Computershare, Carl Hagberg, Mellon, and STA.

[32] See letters from BRT, Computershare, and SCSGP.

[33] It appeared that many commenters opposing adoption mistakenly believed that they would lose the ability to receive paper copies. Others objected to having to request paper copies under the notice and access model. See, for example, letters from Arthur Comings, Dave Few, George Liddell, Robert Link, and Chloris Wolski.

[34] According to data available on the Web site of ADP. See www.ics.adp.com/release11/public_site/about/stats.html.

[35] See letter from ADP. At the proposing stage, we estimated that 75% of people in the United States had Internet access, but we did not have an estimate for the percentage of investors with Internet access.

notice and access model.[36] Although some commenters did not think that Internet access is sufficiently widespread, particularly among seniors,[37] to warrant implementation of the proposed model at this time,[38] the requirement that any shareholder lacking Internet access, or preferring delivery of a copy of the proxy materials, can make a permanent request to receive a copy of the proxy materials (and all future proxy materials) at no charge should substantially mitigate the concern about Internet access.

Therefore, we are adopting the proposal substantially as proposed. The final rules are intended to allow issuers and other soliciting persons to establish procedures that will promote use of the Internet as a reliable and cost-efficient means of making proxy materials available to shareholders. Among those shareholders who access the proxy materials electronically, the rules also may increase the use of the Internet for voting proxies. An issuer's or other soliciting person's election to follow the notice and access model will be voluntary.[39]

Under the final rules, as discussed in more detail below, an issuer may satisfy its obligation under the Commission's proxy rules to furnish proxy materials to shareholders in connection with a proxy solicitation by posting its proxy materials on a publicly-accessible Internet Web site (other than the Commission's EDGAR Web site) and sending a Notice of Internet Availability of Proxy Materials ("Notice") to shareholders at least 40 calendar days before the shareholder meeting date indicating that the proxy materials are available and explaining how to access those materials.[40] Shareholders must have a means to execute a proxy as of the time on which the Notice is sent.[41] The Notice also must explain how a shareholder can request a copy of the proxy materials and how a shareholder can indicate a preference to receive a paper or e-mail copy of any proxy materials distributed under the notice and access model in the future. An issuer may not send a proxy card along with the Notice; however, 10 calendar days or more after sending the Notice, the issuer may send a proxy card to shareholders.[42] If an issuer chooses to send a proxy card without a copy of the proxy statement under this provision, a copy of the Notice must accompany the proxy card so that recipients will be notified again about the Web site on which the proxy statement is accessible. Finally, the notice and access model may not be used in conjunction with a proxy solicitation related to a business combination transaction.

Shareholders and other persons conducting their own proxy solicitations may rely on the notice and access model under requirements substantially similar to the requirements that would apply to issuers. As a result, these rules may have the effect of reducing the cost of engaging in a proxy contest. However, unlike the requirements for an issuer, a

---

[36] See, for example, letters from ABA, ACB, BRT, Computershare, Hermes, ICI, Proxinvest, SBC Retirees, STA, Sullivan & Cromwell, and Gary Tannahill,.

[37] See, for example, letters from American Association of Retired Persons (AARP), BellTel Retirees, Timothy Buchman, Todd Collier, NRLN, Printing Industries of America (PIA), Stockowners Rights, and Telephone Pioneers of America.

[38] See, for example, letters from BellTel Retirees, Joel Brown, Todd Collier, James Davis, Donna Garal, Clark Green, Heather Harper, Frank Inman, William Lafollette, James Phipps, Beth Spletter, Megan Stroinski, and USPS.

[39] In a companion release, the Commission is proposing to require issuers and other soliciting persons to follow a substantially similar model. See Release No. 34-55147.

[40] An issuer or other soliciting person also must continue to comply with Exchange Act Rules 14a-6 [17 CFR 240.14a-6] and 14c-5 [17 CFR 240.14c-5], which require the issuer or other soliciting person to file its proxy statement (or information statement) and additional soliciting material with the Commission. An

issuer also must continue to comply with Exchange Act Rules 14a-3(c) [17 CFR 240.14a-3(c)] and 14c-3(b) [17 CFR 240.14c-3(b)], which require an issuer to submit copies of its annual report to security holders to the Commission. The rules that we are adopting in this release do not affect any current Commission filing requirement, except that an issuer or other soliciting person following the notice and access model would be required to file the Notice as additional soliciting material under Exchange Act Rule 14a-6(b) [17 CFR 240.14a-6(b)].

[41] As discussed in more detail in Section II.A.2 of this release, an issuer or any other soliciting person must provide a means for executing proxies available at the time the Notice is sent. It may not wait until it sends a paper or e-mail copy of the proxy card 10 calendar days or more after sending the Notice to provide shareholders with a means to execute a proxy.

[42] An issuer may send a proxy card to shareholders before the conclusion of the 10-day period if the proxy card is accompanied or preceded by a copy, via the same medium, of the proxy statement and annual report to security holders if required by Rule 14a-3(b).

soliciting person other than the issuer may selectively choose the shareholders from whom it desires to solicit proxies without the need to send an information statement to all other shareholders.

The new rules do not affect the availability of other means of providing proxy materials to shareholders, such as obtaining affirmative consents for electronic delivery pursuant to existing Commission guidance.[43] Thus, an issuer may rely on affirmative consents to furnish proxy materials to some shareholders, and rely on the notice and access model to furnish the materials to others.

We are making several significant revisions to the proposed notice and access model in response to commenters' concerns. First, the final rules do not permit a proxy card to accompany the Notice as we originally proposed, although the rules do permit an issuer or other soliciting person to send a proxy card 10 calendar days or more after it sends the Notice, provided that a copy of the Notice or accompanies the proxy card.[44] Second, we are adopting a requirement that issuers and other soliciting persons send the Notice to shareholders at least 40 calendar days before the shareholder meeting date, rather than 30 calendar days before the meeting, as proposed. We are making this change so that issuers and other soliciting persons will still have at least a 30-day period in which they can send a proxy card to shareholders if they choose to do so.

Third, in addition to the proposed requirement that a shareholder be able to request a paper or e-mail copy of the proxy materials for a particular meeting, the final rules require an issuer to allow shareholders to elect to receive paper or e-mail copies of proxy materials that the issuer will distribute in the future in reliance on the notice and access model. Similarly, intermediaries must allow beneficial owners to elect to receive paper or e-mail copies of any proxy materials that will be distributed in the future in reliance on the notice and access model with respect to all securities held in the beneficial owner's account. Fourth, under the new rules, an intermediary must prepare its own Notice for distribution to beneficial owners.

Fifth, the intermediary's Notice sent to a beneficial owner will direct the owner to request paper or e-mail copies from his or her intermediary, rather than from the issuer. Finally, the final rules do not permit soliciting persons other than the issuer to engage in a conditional solicitation as proposed and, therefore, the rules require such persons to send a copy of the proxy materials upon request from a shareholder to whom they have sent a Notice.

II. Description of the Amendments

A. The Notice and Access Model for Issuers

The notice and access model that we are adopting provides an alternative means for an issuer to furnish proxy materials to its shareholders. These proxy materials include:

- notices of shareholder meetings;
- Schedule 14A proxy statements and consent solicitation statements;
- forms of proxy (*i.e.*, proxy cards);

---

[43] Release No. 33-7233 (Oct. 6, 1995) [60 FR 53458] (the "1995 Interpretive Release") provided guidance on electronic delivery of prospectuses, annual reports to security holders and proxy solicitation materials under the Securities Act of 1933 [15 U.S.C. 77a *et seq.*], the Securities Exchange Act of 1934, and the Investment Company Act of 1940. Release No. 33-7288 (May 9, 1996) [61 FR 24644] (the "1996 Interpretive Release") provided guidance on electronic delivery of required information by broker-dealers and transfer agents under the Securities Act, the Exchange Act, and the Investment Company Act. Release No. 33-7856 (Apr. 28, 2000) [65 FR 25843] (the "2000 Interpretive Release") provided guidance on the use of electronic media to deliver documents under the federal securities laws, an issuer's liability for Web site content, and basic legal principles that issuers and market intermediaries should consider in conducting online offerings.

[44] An issuer or other soliciting person may, in the course of a solicitation, send several proxy cards to a shareholder. Under the notice and access model, the Notice must accompany each proxy card sent to a shareholder unless the issuer or other soliciting person sends a proxy statement with, or before, the proxy card and by the same medium as the proxy card is sent.

- Schedule 14C information statements;
- annual reports to security holders[45];
- additional soliciting materials[46]; and
- any amendments to such materials that are required to be furnished to shareholders.

In the proposing release, we sought comment on whether reliance on the notice and access model should be limited to particular types of issuers, shareholders, or transactions. The only restriction that we proposed was that the rules should not apply to business combination transactions. Commenters in favor of the notice and access model generally supported broad availability of the notice and access model.[47] Therefore, the new rules permit any issuer to use the notice and access model to disseminate its proxy materials to all types of shareholders, whether registered or beneficial owners, and with respect to any solicitation except those related to business combination transactions.

1. Notice of Internet Availability of Proxy Materials

To notify shareholders of the availability of the proxy materials on an Internet Web site, an issuer relying on the notice and access model must send a Notice to shareholders 40 calendar days[48] or more in advance of the shareholder meeting date or, if no meeting is to be held, 40 calendar days or more in advance of the date that consents or authorizations may be used to effect the corporate actions.[49] We believe that it is important for the Notice to be furnished in a way that brings it to each shareholder's attention. Therefore, no other materials may accompany the Notice except for the notice of a shareholder meeting required under state corporation law.[50] An issuer also may combine the Notice with the state law notice unless state law prohibits such combination.

We have extended the proposed 30-day deadline for delivery of the Notice to a 40-day deadline to provide issuers with time to encourage shareholders who have not executed a proxy to participate in the voting process and to provide shareholders with sufficient time to receive the Notice, request copies of the materials, if desired, and review the proxy materials prior to executing a proxy. Under the new rules, an issuer may send a proxy card 10 calendar days or more after sending the Notice. If an issuer chooses to send a proxy card under this provision, a proxy statement and annual report need not accompany the proxy card.[51] However, if a copy of the proxy statement and annual report do not accompany or precede the proxy card, a copy of the Notice must accompany the proxy card so that shareholders can access the specified Web site without referring to the earlier Notice. This 10-day waiting period is designed to provide shareholders with sufficient time to access the proxy materials, or request a copy of the proxy materials, before the issuer sends a proxy card without an accompanying proxy statement and annual report.

If an issuer chooses to follow the notice and access model, the Notice of Internet Availability of Proxy Materials must include the following information in clear and understandable terms:[52]

---

[45] The requirement in Exchange Act Rules 14a-3(b) and 14c-3(a) to furnish annual reports to security holders does not apply to registered investment companies [17 CFR 240.14a-3(b) and 240.14c-3(a)]. The rules that we are adopting do not apply to the requirement in Section 30(e) of the Investment Company Act of 1940 [15 U.S.C. 80a-29(e)] and the rules thereunder that every registered investment company transmit reports to shareholders at least semi-annually.

[46] Our rules permit, but do not require, delivery of additional soliciting materials. See Rule 14a-6(b).

[47] See, for example, letters from ABC, ACB, Association of Corporate Counsel (ACC), Proxinvest, SCSGP, STA, and Sullivan & Cromwell.

[48] For purposes of determining this 40-day period under the new rules, the first day of this period would be the day on which the issuer sends the Notice. The 40th day would be the day prior to the meeting date or date of the corporate action.

[49] The Notice could be sent electronically to shareholders who have previously provided affirmative consent, or other evidence to show delivery, pursuant to our earlier guidance on electronic delivery. See the 1995 Interpretive Release and the 2000 Interpretive Release.

[50] The rules also permit a reply card for requesting a paper or e-mail copy of the proxy materials to accompany the Notice.

[51] Of course, an issuer still would be obligated to send a copy of the proxy statement and annual report if a shareholder requests a copy. An issuer also may send a proxy card before the end of the 10-day period if it is accompanied by the proxy statement and annual report.

[52] Appropriate changes must be made to the Notice if the issuer is providing an information statement pursuant to Regulation 14C or seeking to effect a corporate action by written consent.

- A prominent legend in bold-face type that states:

  "Important Notice Regarding the Availability of Proxy Materials for the Shareholder Meeting to Be Held on [insert meeting date].

    o **This communication presents only an overview of the more complete proxy materials that are available to you on the Internet. We encourage you to access and review all of the important information contained in the proxy materials before voting.**

    o **The [proxy statement] [information statement] [annual report to security holders] [is/are] available at [Insert Web site address].**

    o **If you want to receive a paper or e-mail copy of these documents, you must request one. There is no charge to you for requesting a copy. Please make your request for a copy as instructed below on or before [Insert a date] to facilitate timely delivery."**

- The date, time, and location of the meeting or, if corporate action is to be taken by written consent, the earliest date on which the corporate action may be effected;

- A clear and impartial identification of each separate matter intended to be acted on and the issuer's recommendations regarding those matters, but no supporting statements;

- A list of the materials being made available at the specified Web site;

- (1) A toll-free telephone number; (2) an e-mail address; and (3) an Internet Web site address where the shareholder can request a copy of the proxy materials, for all meetings and for the particular meeting to which the Notice relates;

- Any control/identification numbers that the shareholder needs to access his or her proxy card;

- Instructions on how to access the proxy card, provided that such instructions do not enable a shareholder to execute a proxy without having access to the proxy statement and annual report; and

- Information on how to obtain directions to be able to attend the meeting and vote in person.

In response to commenters, we have added certain items to this list of permissible Notice information. First, we are clarifying that the Notice must contain instructions on how to access the proxy card. Such information should include any control or identification numbers necessary for the shareholder to execute a proxy, but may not include a means to execute a proxy, such as a telephone number, which would enable the shareholder to execute a proxy without having access to the proxy statement and annual report.

A shareholder's execution of a proxy via an Internet voting platform indicates that the shareholder has access to the Internet and, as such, is able to access the proxy materials electronically under the new rules. Similarly, if a shareholder executes a proxy via a telephone number placed on the Internet Web site which provides electronic access to the proxy materials, that indicates the shareholder has access to the Internet. However, if a telephone number for executing a proxy is placed on the Notice, there can be no assurance that a shareholder executing a proxy by means of that telephone number has access to the Internet Web site. Accordingly, placing such a telephone number on the Notice is not permitted. A telephone number for executing a proxy may, however, be provided on a proxy card sent to shareholders 10 calendar days or more after the Notice was sent because, by that time, a shareholder is likely to have had sufficient time to access the materials on the Internet or request copies.

Also, in response to comments, we have revised the rules to require an issuer or other soliciting person to include instructions in the Notice about: (1) how a shareholder can request delivery of copies of proxy materials in paper or by e-mail in the future[53]; and

---

[53] See letters from ABA, Mellon Investor Services (Mellon), and SCSGP.

(2) how to attend the shareholder meeting and vote in person. The new rules also require the Notice to include an Internet Web site on which a shareholder can request a copy of the proxy materials, in addition to a toll-free telephone number and an e-mail address for that purpose.

The Notice may include only the information specified above, unless it is being combined with the state law meeting notice, in which case any information required by state law also may be included in the Notice. While not required, to reduce the chance of parties creating false Notices to extract confidential information from shareholders, the Notice also may contain a statement advising shareholders that they are not required to provide any personal information, other than the identification or control number provided in the Notice (if such a number is used), to execute a proxy.

To ensure that the Notice is clear and understandable, it must meet substantially the same plain English principles as apply to key sections of Securities Act prospectuses pursuant to Securities Act Rule 421(d).[54] Both commenters remarking on the plain English aspect of the proposal supported such a requirement.[55]

Several commenters recommended that issuers should be able to include more information in the Notice than we proposed. They suggested that the rules should allow the Notice to incorporate information from the proxy statement and annual report that those commenters believe is the most important information contained in those documents. They believed that presenting this information on the Notice would enable shareholders to make an informed decision based on the Notice alone.[56] We believe that the proxy statement and annual report to security holders represent the information necessary to make an informed voting decision. The Notice is intended merely to make shareholders aware that these proxy materials are available on an Internet Web site; it is not intended to serve as a stand-alone basis for making a voting decision. Because the disclosures in the proxy statement and annual report represent the information necessary for a voting decision, we do not believe it is appropriate to permit issuers and other soliciting persons to present only selected information from the proxy statement or annual report to security holders in the Notice.

The form of the Notice will constitute other soliciting material that the issuer or other soliciting person must file with the Commission pursuant to Rule 14a-6(b)[57] no later than the date on which it is first sent or given to shareholders.[58]

a. Householding

Consistent with the proposal, the final rules permit an issuer to "household" the Notice pursuant to Rule 14a-3(e).[59] Accordingly, an issuer could send a single copy of the Notice to one or more shareholders residing at the same address if the issuer satisfies all of the Rule 14a-3(e) conditions.[60] An issuer is not required to re-solicit specific consent regarding the householding of the Notice from shareholders if it has obtained their consent to householding of proxy materials in the past. However, an issuer following the notice and access model must allow each householded account to execute separate proxies. Therefore, the issuer must provide separate identification or control numbers, if it uses such numbers, to each account at the shared address, as required by the current householding rule.[61] Alternately, an issuer also may send

---

[54] 17 CFR 230.421(d).

[55] See letters from Florida State Board and Proxinvest.

[56] See letters from Carl Hagberg, Hermes, and James Reed. For example, one commenter suggested that each proposal be accompanied by the "pros and cons" associated with that proposal. See letter from James Reed. Another commenter recommended that the president's letter, Management's Discussion and Analysis and selected financial information be included. See letter from Carl Hagberg.

[57] 17 CFR 240.14a-6(b).

[58] See Rule 14a-16(i) [17 CFR 240.14a-16(i)].

[59] 17 CFR 240.14a-3(e).

[60] If the Notice is sent via e-mail, the householding rules do not permit the sending of only one copy of the Notice to all shareholders in the household. Instead the Notice must be separately e-mailed to each shareholder. See Rule 14a-3(e)(1)(ii)(B)(*4*) [17 CFR 240.14a-3(e)(1)(ii)(B)(*4*)].

[61] Issuers also are required to share a listing of the shareholders that have consented to householding with soliciting shareholders, or afford the benefit of such consents to a soliciting shareholder if the issuer is mailing proxy materials on the shareholder's behalf. See Rule 14a-7(a)(2) [17 CFR 240.14a-7(a)(2)].

separate Notices for each householded account in a single envelope. Commenters generally supported this aspect of the proposal.[62]

b. Security and Privacy on the Internet

Several commenters were concerned about security and confidentiality of shareholder information that may be transmitted over the Internet.[63] We believe that the final rules ameliorate many of these concerns. We address those concerns below.

i. Theft of Identification or Control Numbers

Some commenters were concerned that computer hackers may use any identifying information sent to shareholders to access their accounts.[64] The Notice may contain identification or control numbers for executing proxies or providing voting instructions, if an issuer or intermediary uses such numbers. We understand that these numbers, which are in common use today, usually provide the user only with access to execute proxies or provide voting instructions; they do not enable the user to buy or sell securities in a shareholder's account or transfer funds from that account. Thus, more sensitive activities, such as trading securities or transferring funds, could not be performed by someone who has stolen this identifying information. Finally, we note that 85% of shares voted already are voted electronically using such identification or control numbers.

ii. "Phishing"

One commenter expressed concern that, if Notices are sent electronically, shareholders may be tricked into disclosing personal information to persons fraudulently purporting to be issuers or intermediaries by fake "phishing" e-mails purporting to be official Notices, but designed to extract personal information from a shareholder.[65] We do not believe that the rules would provide significant opportunity for abuse through phishing for the following reasons.

First, an issuer may send a Notice by e-mail only if the shareholder has affirmatively consented to such delivery. Second, the Notice is not permitted to request any confidential information from the shareholder. Rather, the only confidential information that a shareholder must provide to access the proxy card would be a confidential identification or control number used by many issuers and intermediaries to track votes. As noted above, this number does not provide access to a shareholder's brokerage or bank account or permit the transfer of funds from a shareholder's account. Therefore, the shareholder's account number and other personal financial information would not be in jeopardy of being stolen. The rules do permit an issuer or other soliciting person to include on the Notice a protective warning to shareholders, advising them that no personal information other than the identification or control number is necessary to execute a proxy.[66]

iii. Misuse of Information by Issuers and Other Soliciting Persons

Other commenters were concerned that issuers themselves, or other soliciting persons, may use shareholder information inappropriately. For example, they were concerned that an issuer may use shareholders' e-mail addresses for purposes other than proxy communications, such as advertising, or sell the e-mail addresses to third parties.[67] As a protective measure, one commenter suggested that the Internet Web site on which the proxy statement is posted should not require installation of cookies on the shareholder's computer as a prerequisite for access to the Web site.[68]

We agree that shareholder information gathered under the amended rules should be used only for the purposes of furnishing proxy materials to shareholders. Thus, we have

---

[62] See letters from BRT, Computershare, Proxinvest, and SCSGP.

[63] See, for example, letters from James Angel, Todd Collier, James Davis, William LaFollette, Matthew McGuire, and USPS.

[64] Record holders could not be subject to such manipulation because they do not hold their securities in a trading account with the company in the same sense as beneficial owners hold their securities in a brokerage account.

[65] See letter from William LaFollette.

[66] See Rule 14a-16(f)(3) [17 CFR 240.14a-16(f)(3)].

[67] See letter from Thomas Richardson.

[68] See letter from Bowne & Co.

revised the final rules to clarify that an issuer or its agent must maintain the Internet Web site on which the proxy materials are posted in a manner that does not infringe on the anonymity of a shareholder accessing that Web site.[69] For example, it may not track the identity of persons accessing that Web site to view the proxy statement.[70] In addition, the Web site cannot require the installation of any "cookies" or other software that might collect information about the accessing person. Further, the issuer and its agents may not use any e-mail address obtained from a shareholder for the purpose of requesting a copy of proxy materials for any purpose other than to send a copy of those materials to that shareholder. Finally, an issuer may not transfer a shareholder's e-mail address to other persons without the shareholder's express consent, except in connection with the distribution of proxy materials, such as an agent handling the proxy distribution on the issuer's behalf.[71]

2. Proxy Card

Under the notice and access model that we are adopting, an issuer is not permitted to furnish the proxy card together with the initial Notice for a particular solicitation. An issuer following the notice and access model must post the proxy card on the Web site with the proxy statement and any annual report no later than the time at which the Notice is sent to shareholders so that the documents are electronically available at the time shareholders receive the Notice.[72] In addition, on that Web site, the issuer must concurrently provide shareholders with at least one method of executing a proxy vote.[73] We believe that a shareholder who accesses proxy materials on the Internet Web site should be able to execute a proxy as soon as the shareholder is able to electronically access the proxy statement. An issuer may provide a means to execute a proxy through a variety of methods, including by providing an electronic voting platform linked to the Web site where the proxy materials are posted or a telephone number for executing a proxy. Merely providing a shareholder with a means to request a paper proxy card would not be sufficient because a shareholder would not be able to execute a proxy at the time it accesses the proxy materials.

We received a significant number of comments on the aspect of our proposal that would have permitted the proxy card to accompany the Notice. Numerous commenters were concerned that physically separating the card from the proxy statement, as originally proposed, may lead to the type of uninformed voting that the proxy rules are intended to prevent.[74] Some commenters were concerned that issuers may attempt to structure their solicitations in a manner that discourages access to the proxy statement, particularly with respect to shareholder proposals.[75] Others, however, believed that separating the card from the proxy statement would not lead to such problems.[76]

We note these concerns and have revised the rules to require the proxy card to be accessible on the Internet along with the proxy statement and any annual report when the Notice is sent. The issuer may not send a proxy card with its initial Notice. However, we recognize that an issuer may wish to undertake subsequent soliciting activities to encourage shareholders who have not executed a proxy to do so. Currently, issuers often send replacement proxy cards accompanied by additional soliciting materials to shareholders who have not yet voted. To facilitate this re-solicitation process, the rules permit an issuer that is following the notice and access model to send a proxy card 10 calendar days or more after sending the Notice. This 10-day waiting period still provides a 30-day period during which an issuer can encourage shareholders to execute a proxy. Any such

---

[69] See Rule 14a-16(k)(1) [17 CFR 240.14a-16(k)(1)].

[70] Of course, the issuer would be permitted to track the identity, by means of the shareholder entering an issuer-provided control/identification number, of persons voting on an electronic platform in order to validate the election results.

[71] See Rule 14a-16(k)(2) [17 CFR 240.14a-16(k)(2)]. Rule 14a-16(k) is not designed to create new duties in private rights of action under the federal securities laws.

[72] See Rule 14a-16(b)(1) [17 CFR 240.14a-16(b)(1)].

[73] See Rule 14a-16(b)(4) [17 CFR 240.14a-16(b)(4)].

[74] See, for example, letters from ACB, AFL-CIO, Amalgamated Bank, BellTel Retirees, CII, Florida State Board, Carl Hagberg, NRLN, San Diego Retirement, Swingvote, and Teamsters.

[75] See, for example, letters from AFL-CIO, Florida State Board, and Teamsters.

[76] See, for example, letters from ABA, ACC, BRT, Computershare, ISS, New York State Bar Association (NY State Bar), and Proxinvest.

subsequent solicitation efforts may, but need not, include a copy of the proxy statement and any annual report to security holders. However, if the subsequent communication includes a proxy card, it also must include either a copy of the proxy statement and any annual report or a copy of the Notice.[77]

3. Internet Web Site Posting of Proxy Materials

All proxy materials to be furnished through the notice and access model, other than additional soliciting materials, must be posted on a specified Internet Web site by the time the issuer sends the Notice to shareholders.[78] These materials must remain on that Web site and be accessible to shareholders through the conclusion of the related shareholder meeting, at no charge to the shareholder. As discussed above, the Notice must identify clearly the Internet Web site address at which the proxy materials are available. The Internet Web site address must be specific enough to lead shareholders directly to the proxy materials,[79] rather than to the home page or other section of the Web Site on which the proxy materials are posted, so that shareholders do not have to browse the Web site to find the materials. The Internet Web site that an issuer uses to electronically furnish its proxy materials to shareholders must be a publicly accessible Internet Web site other than the Commission's EDGAR Web site.[80] Commenters agreed that simply providing a link to the proxy materials on EDGAR was insufficient.[81]

Commenters were divided with respect to the type of document format that issuers or other soliciting persons should be required to use to post proxy materials on the Web site. This disagreement centered on whether most shareholders would prefer to be able to print out the document and read the hard copy version or read the document online. The final rules require the electronically posted proxy materials to be presented on the Internet Web site in a format, or formats, convenient for both printing and viewing online.[82] Under technology commonly in use today, this may require posting the materials in two different formats. First, the materials should be posted in a format that provides a version of those materials, including all charts, tables, graphics, and similarly formatted information, that is substantially identical to the paper version of the materials.

In addition, to take better advantage of the capabilities of the Internet, the materials also must be presented in a readily searchable format, such as HTML. This type of format would make the proxy materials easier to read on a computer screen. In addition, such a version may incorporate additional user-friendly features such as hyperlinks from a table of contents to enable shareholders to quickly and easily navigate through the document. Many Internet Web sites today provide documents in dual formats such as this. We believe this requirement will impose minimal burden on issuers. We also believe that, as technology progresses, new formats may be developed that will improve shareholders' ability to print copies and read copies on their screens. Finally, to the extent a shareholder may need additional software to view the document, the Web site must contain a link to enable the shareholder to obtain the software free of charge.[83]

4. Period of Reliance

The decision by an issuer or other soliciting person to follow the notice and access model is effective only with respect to a particular meeting. An issuer's choice to rely on

---

[77] See Rule 14a-16(h) [17 CFR 240.14a-16(h)].

[78] Additional soliciting materials used after the Notice is sent must be posted on the specified Web site no later than the day on which those materials are first sent or given to shareholders.

[79] This Web site could be a central site with prominent links to each of the proxy-related disclosure documents listed in the Notice, as well as proxy materials posted on the Web site after the Notice is sent.

[80] An issuer must continue to comply with Rules 14a-6 and 14c-5, which require the soliciting person to file its proxy statement (or information statement) and additional soliciting material with the Commission. An issuer also must continue to comply with Rules

14a-3(c) and 14c-3(b), which require an issuer to submit copies of its annual report to security holders to the Commission. The issuer must comply with these requirements by the time it posts the materials on the Web site.

[81] See letters from James Angel, SCSGP, and Swingvote.

[82] See Rule 14a-16(c) [17 CFR 240.14a-16(c)].

[83] See the 1995 Interpretive Release No. 33-7233, at n. 24 and the accompanying text; Release No. 33-8128 (Sep. 16, 2002) [67 FR 58480]; Release No. 33-8230 (May 7, 2003) [68 FR 25788]; and Release No. 33-8518 (Dec. 22, 2004) [70 FR 1505].

the notice and access model for one meeting therefore does not affect its determination of whether to rely on the model for subsequent meetings.[84] Similarly, a shareholder that does not request a paper or e-mail copy of the proxy materials for one meeting is not bound by that decision with respect to any other shareholder meeting. Each time an issuer chooses to rely on the notice and access model for a shareholder meeting, it must comply anew with all of the requirements under that model, including delivery of the Notice and the 40-day notice period.

We are adopting one important exception to this general principle. Numerous commenters were concerned that a shareholder desiring a paper or e-mail copy would have to request such a copy every year from each issuer in which he or she owns securities.[85] We agree with commenters that this could be unduly burdensome for a shareholder who owns numerous securities. The commenters recommended that a provision be made that permits a shareholder to make a single election to receive a paper or e-mail copy of the proxy materials on a continuing basis in the future. We agree with those commenters and have revised the rules to enable shareholders to make a permanent election to receive paper or e-mail copies from each issuer.[86]

5. State Law Notices

State business and corporation laws typically set forth shareholder meeting requirements, including meeting notice and voting requirements. The new rules are not intended to affect any applicable state law requirement concerning the delivery of any document related to a shareholder meeting or proxy solicitation. Thus, to the extent that state law requires a notice of shareholder meeting and proxy materials to be delivered by a particular means, the rules do not alter those requirements.[87] For example, if the state in which an issuer is incorporated requires notices of shareholder meetings and proxy materials to be transmitted directly to shareholders in paper, the notice and access model does not provide an issuer with an option to satisfy its state law obligations by posting those materials on an Internet Web site.

6. Additional Soliciting Materials

New Rule 14a-16 and revised Rules 14c-2 and 14c-3 require an issuer to post any additional soliciting materials required to be filed under Rule 14a-6(b) on the same Internet Web site on which the proxy materials are posted no later than the day on which the additional soliciting materials are first sent to shareholders or made public.[88] Beyond the posting of the additional soliciting materials on the Internet Web site, issuers may decide which additional means, if any, are most effective for disseminating these materials (*e.g.*, direct mail, e-mail, newspaper publication, etc.).

7. Requests for Copies of Proxy Materials

An issuer that satisfies its requirement to furnish proxy materials through the notice and access model has a separate requirement under Rule 14a-16(j)[89] to deliver a copy of the proxy statement, annual report to security holders (if applicable) and proxy card to a requesting

---

[84] To the extent the Commission adopts the universal Internet availability model in companion Release 34-55147, this option will no longer be available to issuers.

[85] See, for example, letters from ABC, AFL-CIO, James Angel, CALSTRS, Florida State Board, OPERS, San Diego Retirement, SIA, William Sjostrom, Stocklein Law Group, Swingvote, and Paul Uhlenhop.

[86] A shareholder that elects to receive paper or e-mail copies may, in the future, revoke that election. However, an issuer may continue to request that shareholder to accept electronic delivery or the notice and access model or seek that shareholder's affirmative consent to electronic delivery. Nothing in the proxy rules prohibits an issuer from structuring incentives to encourage shareholders to accept electronic delivery or the notice and access model.

[87] See Rule 14a-16(e) [17 CFR 240.14a-16(e)]. Issuers typically include the meeting notices required by state law at the beginning of their proxy statements. As discussed previously, the new rules would permit any information necessary to meet a state law requirement to accompany or be combined with the Notice.

[88] Exchange Act Rule 14a-6(b) requires an issuer or other soliciting person choosing to deliver additional soliciting materials to file them with the Commission, in the same form that they are sent to shareholders, no later than the date that they are first sent or given to shareholders.

[89] 17 CFR 240.14a-16(j).

shareholder. Upon receipt of a request from a shareholder for a copy of the proxy statement, annual report, or proxy card, the issuer must send a copy (in paper or by e-mail, as requested) of those proxy materials to the shareholder within three business days after receiving the request, even if the request is made after the date of the shareholder meeting or corporate action to which the proxy materials relate. However, under the final rules, an issuer would be obligated to provide copies of the proxy materials only up until one year after the conclusion of the meeting or corporate action to which the materials relate. When the issuer provides a paper copy of the proxy materials in response to a shareholder request, the issuer must use first class mail or other reasonably prompt means of delivery.

A few commenters believed that a requirement to send copies of the proxy statement after the shareholder meeting has been held would be an unnecessary burden.[90] However, the proxy statement contains a portion of the total package of annual disclosure for public companies; in fact, many public companies satisfy their obligation to include information in Part III of the Form 10-K by including the information in their proxy statements and incorporating that information by reference into the Form 10-K.[91] Just as the proxy rules require issuers to undertake in their proxy statements or annual reports to shareholders to provide copies of annual reports on Form 10-K for the most recent fiscal year to requesting shareholders,[92] we believe it is appropriate to require issuers to provide copies of the proxy materials to requesting shareholders even after the shareholder meeting date. However, because the proxy statement (like the Form 10-K) is filed on EDGAR, we believe there should be a limit on the length of the period during which a shareholder may request a copy of the proxy materials from the issuer. Therefore, the final rules require issuers to provide the proxy statement and annual report to security holders only for one year after the conclusion of the meeting to which those materials relate.[93]

We agree with the views of commenters that the proposed two-business-day time-frame may be too short for issuers to respond efficiently to paper requests of the proxy materials.[94] Further, it is likely that a longer response period that enables an issuer to better cumulate batches of copies would reduce the cost of complying with the rules. However, these concerns must be balanced against our view that requests for copies be handled promptly. Thus, we have extended the response time to three business days.[95]

The requirements that an issuer deliver the Notice at least 40 calendar days before the shareholder meeting date and respond to a request for a copy of the proxy materials within three business days are designed to provide a shareholder with sufficient time to request a copy, receive it, review the proxy materials and make an informed voting decision. Several commenters believed that placing a deadline on shareholders to request copies would be appropriate.[96] We do not believe such a deadline would be appropriate, particularly because the proxy statement is part of the "package" of disclosures we have deemed important for investors, as discussed above. However, under the rules, it is incumbent on the shareholder to request a copy in sufficient time to receive the copy of the proxy materials, review that copy, and execute a proxy. The rules require the issuer to insert a date in the Notice by which a shareholder should request a copy to ensure timely delivery.[97]

Finally, we recognize that some issuers may be hesitant to adopt the notice and access model because of the potential dangers of significantly underestimating, or overestimating, the number of paper copies of the proxy materials that will be needed. If an issuer underestimates that number, the cost of printing additional copies may be great. Similarly, overestimating that number would lead to unnecessary cost. We note that there is nothing in the rules that would prevent an issuer from sending a shareholder a communication

---

[90] See letters from BRT and SCSGP.

[91] See Instruction G(3) to Form 10-K, referenced in 17 CFR 249.310.

[92] See Rule 14a-3(b)(10) [17 CFR 240.14a-3(b)(10)].

[93] See Rule 14a-16(j)(3) [17 CFR 240.14a-16(j)(3)].

[94] See, for example, letters from BRT, Computershare, ICI, NY State Bar, SCSGP, SIA, and Sullivan & Cromwell.

[95] See letters from Computershare, ICI, and STA.

[96] See letters from Computershare, SCSGP, and Sullivan & Cromwell.

[97] See Rule 14a-16(d)(1) [17 CFR 240.14a-16(d)(1)]. This date is intended to be a recommendation to shareholders to facilitate timely delivery, but does not restrict a shareholder's ability to request copies after that date.

well in advance of a proxy solicitation to determine the shareholder's interest in receiving paper copies.[98] Indeed, such a communication may be used to start creating a list of shareholders that wish to receive paper copies in the future. This may help issuers to estimate the number of paper copies that it needs to print for the solicitation.

B. The Role of Intermediaries

1. Background

The process of distributing proxy materials to beneficial owners is considerably more complicated than direct delivery of the materials by an issuer to its record holders.[99] The proxy rules include four rules, Exchange Act Rule 14a-13, Rule 14b-1, Rule 14b-2, and Rule 14c-7 referred to collectively as the "shareholder communications rules," that impose obligations on issuers and intermediaries to ensure that beneficial owners receive proxy materials and are given the opportunity to participate in the shareholder voting process. Basically, these rules require issuers to send their proxy materials to intermediaries for forwarding to the beneficial owners.

Exchange Act Rule 14b-1 sets forth the obligations of registered brokers and dealers in connection with the prompt forwarding of certain issuer communications to beneficial owners. Rule 14b-2 sets forth similar obligations of banks, associations, and other entities that exercise fiduciary powers. Under these rules, upon request by the issuer, these intermediaries are required to indicate to the issuer within seven business days of receiving the request:

- the approximate number of customers of the intermediary that are beneficial owners of the issuer that are held of record by the intermediary;

- if the issuer has indicated pursuant to Rule 14a-13(a)[100] or 14c-7(a)[101] that it will distribute the annual report to security holders to beneficial owners who have not objected to disclosure to the issuer of their names, addresses, and securities positions, the number of beneficial owners who have objected to such disclosure[102]; and

- the identity of any agents of the intermediary acting on the intermediary's behalf to fulfill its obligations under the rule.

Pursuant to Rules 14b-1 and 14b-2, within five business days of receiving proxy materials from the issuer, the intermediary must forward the materials to beneficial owners who will not receive those materials directly from the issuer pursuant to Rule 14a-13(c)[103] or Rule 14c-7(c).[104] Beneficial owners typically do not execute proxy cards because, under most state laws, only the record owner (*i.e.*, the intermediary) has the authority to vote on matters presented to shareholders. As a result, intermediaries forward the proxy materials, other than the proxy card, along with a request for voting instructions. The request for voting instructions is similar to the proxy card, but is prepared by the intermediary instead of the issuer and the beneficial owner returns his or her voting instructions to the intermediary rather than to the issuer or independent vote tabulator. The intermediary is required to vote the beneficial owner's shares in accordance with the owner's voting instructions when formally executing the proxy card.[105] The intermediary then returns the proxy card to the issuer or its vote tabulator.

---

[98] A communication to shareholders that is limited to explaining the notice and access model generally and determining whether shareholders wish to receive future proxy materials in paper or by e-mail would not be associated with a particular solicitation and therefore would not be considered a Notice under the new rules.

[99] The discussion in this section of "beneficial owners" refers to beneficial owners whose names and addresses do not appear directly in issuers' stock registers because they hold their securities through a broker, bank, trustee, or similar intermediary.

[100] 17 CFR 240.14a-13(a).

[101] 17 CFR 240.14c-7(a).

[102] In the case of bank intermediaries, Rule 14b-2 requires a bank to disclose the number of customers with accounts opened on or before December 28, 1986, who gave affirmative consent to disclosure to the issuer and the number of customers with accounts opened after December 28, 1986, who did not object to such disclosure.

[103] 17 CFR 240.14a-13(c).

[104] 17 CFR 240.14c-7(c).

[105] See Rule 14b-2(b)(3) [17 CFR 240.14b-2(b)(3)].

2. Discussion of the Amendments

Under the amendments, an intermediary may follow the notice and access model only if the issuer requests it to do so and, in such cases, must follow that model. The amendments revise Rules 14b-1 and 14b-2 to require brokers, banks, and similar intermediaries, at the request of an issuer, to furnish proxy materials, including a Notice of Internet Availability of Proxy Materials, to beneficial owners of the issuer's securities based on the notice and access model.[106] If an issuer does not request intermediaries to follow the notice and access model, an intermediary could, on its own initiative, continue to rely on any other permitted method of furnishing proxy materials to beneficial owners, including the electronic delivery of proxy materials by affirmative consents, but could not follow the notice and access model on its own initiative. Comments varied on whether an intermediary should be allowed to follow the notice and access model on its own initiative.[107] We believe that the issuer should be allowed to determine the best means for distributing its proxy materials, because the issuer ultimately pays the costs of that distribution.

With respect to beneficial owners, an issuer or other soliciting person relying on the notice and access model must provide the intermediary with all information necessary for the intermediary to prepare its own Notice of Internet Availability of Proxy Materials in sufficient time for the intermediary to prepare and send its Notice to beneficial owners at least 40 days before the meeting date.[108] We understand that issuers, intermediaries and their agents currently coordinate a similar exchange of information to enable intermediaries to prepare and print requests for voting instructions ahead of their receipt of the proxy statement and annual report to security holders for forwarding to beneficial owners.[109] We expect such coordination to continue to facilitate timely preparation of the intermediary's Notice. Therefore, we have not included a specific timeframe in the rules for delivery of this information.[110] Upon receipt of that information, the intermediary or its agent must prepare its own Notice, tailored for the intermediary's beneficial owner customers.[111] The intermediary must send this Notice to beneficial owners at least 40 calendar days before the date of the shareholder meeting.[112]

The intermediary's Notice will generally contain the same information as an issuer's Notice,[113] with certain revisions to reflect the differences between registered holders and beneficial owners. Specifically, the intermediary's Notice must contain the following information:

- A prominent legend in bold-face type that states:

  "Important Notice Regarding the Availability of Proxy Materials for the Shareholder Meeting to Be Held on [insert meeting date].[114]

  o **This communication presents only an overview of the more complete proxy materials that are available to you on the Internet. We encourage you to access and review all of the important information contained in the proxy materials before voting.**

---

[106] See Rules 14b-1(d) and 14b-2(d) [17 CFR 240.14b-1(d) and 240.14b-2(d)].

[107] See, for example, letters from ABA, ACC, Computershare, and SCSGP, supporting issuer control, as opposed to the letters from SIA, Swingvote, and University Bancorp, urging more control by intermediaries.

[108] See Rule 14a-16(a)(2) [17 CFR 240.14a-16(a)(2)].

[109] Our rules set forth a series of timeframes regarding distribution of proxy materials to beneficial owners to facilitate timely delivery of those materials.

[110] Rule 14a-16(a)(2) requires an issuer to provide the information to an intermediary "in sufficient time" for the intermediary to prepare its own Notice. Other soliciting persons would be expected to provide their information to intermediaries in sufficient time to meet their applicable deadlines.

[111] An intermediary's Notice prepared in accordance with this rule would be impartial for purposes of Rule 14a-2(a)(1) [17 CFR 240.14a-2(a)(1)] and need not be filed pursuant to Rule 14a-6(b) [17 CFR 240.14a-6(b)] unless an intermediary solicits proxies on its own behalf.

[112] In the case of a Notice of a soliciting person other than the issuer, the intermediary must send the Notice to beneficial owners by the later of: (1) 40 calendar days prior to the meeting; or (2) 10 calendar days after the issuer first sends its proxy materials to investors. See Section II.C of this release.

[113] See Rule 14a-16(d) [17 CFR 240.14a-16(d)].

[114] Appropriate changes must be made to the Notice if the issuer is providing an information statement pursuant to Regulation 14C or if the issuer or other soliciting person is seeking to effect a corporate action by written consent.

    ○   The [proxy statement] [information statement] [annual report to security holders] [is/are] available at [Insert Web site address].

    ○   If you want to receive a paper or e-mail copy of these documents, you must request one. There is no charge to you for requesting a copy. Please make your request for a copy as instructed below on or before [Insert a date] to facilitate timely delivery."

- The date, time, and location of the meeting or, if corporate action is to be taken by written consent, the earliest date on which the corporate action may be effected;

- A clear and impartial identification of each separate matter intended to be acted on and the issuer's or other soliciting person's recommendations regarding those matters, but no supporting statements; and

- A list of the materials being made available at the specified Web site.

The intermediary may choose whether to direct beneficial owners to the issuer's Web site or to its own Web site to access the proxy disclosure materials. If it directs beneficial owners to its own Web site, access to that website must be free of charge and may not compromise a beneficial owners' anonymity. If it directs beneficial owners to the issuer's Web site, the intermediary must inform beneficial owners that they can submit voting instructions to the intermediary, but cannot execute a proxy directly in favor of the issuer unless the intermediary has executed a proxy in favor of the beneficial owner. In addition, the intermediary must provide the following information in its Notice, which is similar to the information in the issuer's Notice, but applicable only to beneficial owners:

- (1) A toll-free telephone number of the intermediary or its agent, (2) an e-mail address of the intermediary or its agent, and (3) an Internet Web site of the intermediary or its agent where the shareholder can request a copy of the proxy materials, for all meetings and for the particular meeting to which the Notice relates;

- Any control/identification numbers that the beneficial owner needs to access his or her request for voting instructions;

- Instructions on how to access the request for voting instructions on the Web site of the intermediary or its agent, provided that such instructions do not enable a beneficial owner to provide voting instructions without having access to the proxy statement and annual report;

- Information on how to obtain directions to be able attend the meeting and vote in person[115]; and

- A brief description, if applicable, of the rules that permit the intermediary to vote the securities if the beneficial owner does not return his or her voting instructions.[116]

The intermediary's Notice must contain instructions on how to access the request for voting instructions on the Web site of the intermediary or its agent. Such information should include any control or identification numbers necessary for the beneficial owner to provide voting instructions. However, the intermediary's Notice cannot include a means, such as a telephone number, which would enable the beneficial owner to provide voting instructions without having access to the proxy statement and annual report. A telephone number that a beneficial owner can use to provide voting instructions may be provided on the Internet Web site on which the request for voting instructions is posted (as well as on a paper request for voting instructions sent to shareholders 10 days or more after the intermediary's Notice was sent). Like an issuer, the intermediary cannot include a request for voting instructions with its Notice. However, at the issuer's request, the intermediary will be required to send a copy of the request for voting instructions to beneficial owners, provided that 10 days have passed since the intermediary's Notice

---

[115] A beneficial owner wishing to attend the meeting and vote in person must obtain proxy voting authority from the intermediary through which he or she owns the security.

[116] See NYSE Rule 452.

was first sent. A copy of the intermediary's Notice, or a copy of the proxy statement, must accompany that request for voting instructions.

3. Request for Copies by Beneficial Owners

The intermediary's Notice must provide instructions on how a beneficial owner can request a copy of the proxy materials from the intermediary, rather than from the issuer. Under the new rules, a beneficial owner may not request a paper or e-mail copy directly from the issuer as originally proposed. We are making this revision to the proposal for several reasons. First, an issuer has no means to track the identity and preferences of beneficial owners for future solicitations because these owners are not registered in an issuer's records as shareholders of the company. This tracking can be performed most efficiently by the intermediary because only it maintains records of the beneficial owner's security holdings. Second, the intermediary is able to apply a beneficial owner's request for paper or e-mail copies across all of a beneficial owner's security holdings on an account-wide basis, making it easier for beneficial owners to elect to receive such copies with respect to all of the securities held by the beneficial owner.

If a beneficial owner requests a copy of the materials from the intermediary, the intermediary must in turn request such a copy from the issuer or other soliciting person within three business days of receiving the request from the beneficial owner. The intermediary also would have to forward the materials to the beneficial owners within three business days after receipt from the issuer or other soliciting person.[117] As originally proposed, the intermediary will be allowed to charge the issuer or other soliciting person for the cost it incurs in forwarding the copy of the proxy materials to the requesting beneficial owner.[118]

We also note that intermediaries typically keep records of whether a beneficial owner has affirmatively consented to electronic delivery of proxy materials on an account-wide basis. That is, a beneficial owner's election for electronic delivery applies to all securities in the beneficial owner's account, rather than to specific issuers. To make it clear to beneficial owners electing to receive copies of the proxy materials on an ongoing basis, the intermediary's Notice must clarify that a permanent election to receive copies of the proxy materials in paper or e-mail will apply to all securities in the beneficial owner's account.[119]

One commenter was concerned that the notice and access model only complicates an already complicated process for transmitting proxy materials to beneficial owners and may confuse shareholders.[120] Other commenters recommended that the Commission review the proxy delivery process as a whole, rather than layer this model over the existing distribution regime.[121] Although the Commission is sensitive to these concerns, a complete review of the proxy system at this time would only delay the potential benefits to issuers and shareholders offered by the notice and access model. As we gain additional experience with these rules, we will consider whether more extensive revisions to the proxy rules are warranted.

---

[117] Thus, the intermediary must request the copy from the issuer within three business days of receiving the shareholder's request. Then the issuer must send the copy to the intermediary, which is a record holder or respondent bank under the final rules, within three business days of receiving the intermediary's request. Finally, the intermediary is required to forward the copy to the requesting shareholder within three business days of receiving the copy from the issuer.

[118] See NYSE Rule 465. We note that a Proxy Working Group established by the NYSE is reviewing the NYSE's current schedule of the specific maximum fees that NYSE member firms can charge an issuer under our rules requiring issuers to reimburse intermediaries for their reasonable direct and indirect expenses for forwarding proxy materials. We intend to work closely with the NYSE to evaluate the types of revisions that may be appropriate in light of our adoption of the notice and access model, including revision of existing fees as well as the creation of any new fees that may be reasonable under the notice and access model. Although NYSE Rule 465 applies only to NYSE member firms, other national securities exchanges have a similar rule and fee schedule. Non-broker intermediaries, such as banks, also rely on the fee schedule as an industry standard.

[119] See Rules 14b-1(d)(4)(iii) and 14b-2(d)(4)(iii) [17 CFR 240.14b-1(d)(4)(iii) and 240.14b-2(d)(4)(iii)].

[120] See letter from ABA.

[121] See, for example, letters from BRT, Concerned Shareholders, Computershare, Carl Hagberg, Mellon, and STA.

In summary, the amendments would impose the following responsibilities on intermediaries that are requested by an issuer to follow the notice and access model:

- The intermediary must prepare its own Notice and deliver this Notice to its beneficial owners after receiving the meeting information from the issuer or other soliciting person;

- The intermediary must send its Notice to beneficial owners at least 40 days prior to the meeting;

- The intermediary must post its request for voting instructions on an Internet Web site;

- The intermediary must maintain records of beneficial owners who make a permanent election to receive paper or e-mail copies of the proxy materials for all securities held in the beneficial owner's account; and

- The intermediary must request a copy of the proxy materials from the issuer or other soliciting person within three business days after receiving a request from its beneficial owner customer and must forward that copy to the beneficial owner customer within three business days after receiving the copy from the issuer or other soliciting person.

C. Soliciting Persons Other Than the Issuer

Under the amendments, a person other than the issuer who undertakes his or her own proxy solicitation also can rely on the notice and access model. This situation typically would occur in the context of a proxy contest between a shareholder and management. We anticipate that the notice and access model will provide an alternative that may decrease significantly the printing and mailing costs associated with a proxy solicitation. We also believe that the same arguments that support modifying the existing framework to facilitate an alternative dissemination option for issuers apply equally to soliciting persons other than issuers.

Several commenters supported extending the notice and access model to such parties.[122] However, some commenters were concerned about the possibility of abuse of the model by shareholders conducting nuisance contests.[123] These commenters recommended that the availability of the model be limited for soliciting persons other than the issuer.[124] The proposed limitations included requiring the solicitation of all shareholders,[125] requiring soliciting persons other than the issuer to provide copies of their proxy materials upon request,[126] and imposing a minimum shareholding requirement in order for a soliciting person to take advantage of the model.[127] Although the amendments would reduce the cost of a proxy contest, they do not eliminate all costs, such as costs of preparing the soliciting materials, legal fees, proxy solicitor fees, and other significant soliciting expenses. We believe these surviving costs should discourage frivolous contests.

Although the mechanics of a solicitation under the notice and access model for a person other than the issuer are similar to those incurred by an issuer, we describe below several important differences in the way the amendments affect soliciting persons other than the issuer.

1. Mechanics of Proxy Solicitations by Persons Other Than the Issuer

The proxy rules currently treat persons other than the issuer differently from the issuer in a significant respect regarding the provision of information to shareholders regarding intended corporate actions. Specifically, an issuer must furnish to each shareholder either a proxy statement, if the issuer is soliciting proxies or consents from shareholders, or an

---

[122] See, for example, letters from CALSTRS, Computershare, and Swingvote.

[123] See, for example, letters from Glen Buchbaum.

[124] See, for example, letters from ABA, ACC, BRT, ICI, ISS, Sullivan & Cromwell, and Swingvote.

[125] See letters from BRT and Swingvote.

[126] See letter from ABA.

[127] See letters from ABA, ICI and Sullivan & Cromwell.

information statement pursuant to Section 14(c) of the Exchange Act[128] regarding shareholder meetings where corporate action is to be taken but no proxy authority or consent is sought.

Soliciting persons other than the issuer are not subject to the requirements of Section 14(c). Thus, unlike the issuer, they have no obligation to furnish an information statement to shareholders from whom no proxy authority is sought. As a result, soliciting persons can limit the cost of a solicitation by soliciting proxies only from a select group of shareholders, such as those with large holdings, without furnishing other shareholders with any information. This enables a person other than the issuer to conduct a proxy contest in a variety of ways, some of which are not available to an issuer. The amendments that we are adopting relate only to the means of furnishing information to shareholders, and thus do not affect a soliciting person's ability to effect such targeted solicitations.

Under the new rules, a soliciting person other than the issuer may follow the same procedures as the issuer.[129] In particular, it may furnish a Notice and post the proxy statement on an Internet Web site. As with an issuer, such a soliciting person may not include a proxy card with the Notice. It may, however, send a proxy card to the shareholders it is soliciting without a proxy statement 10 calendar days or more after initially sending the Notice to them, if the proxy card is accompanied either by a copy of the proxy statement or by another copy of the Notice.

A soliciting person other than the issuer may selectively solicit shareholders under the notice and access model, just as it could under the current proxy rules (e.g., the soliciting person could choose to send the Notice only to certain shareholders, such as those owning more than a specified number of shares). As we discuss in more detail below, we have made revisions to Rule 14a-7 that will enable a soliciting person to distinguish between shareholders who have requested paper copies of the proxy materials and those who have not.[130] Under the notice and access model, a soliciting person other than the issuer may choose to send a Notice only to those shareholders who have not requested paper copies of the proxy materials.

In the proposing release, we proposed a provision that would have permitted a soliciting person other than the issuer to send a Notice that would condition the solicitation on a shareholder's willingness to access the proxy materials on an Internet Web site. One commenter suggested that a soliciting person should not be permitted to condition its solicitation in this manner and should have to provide a copy of its proxy statement to a requesting shareholder.[131] We are persuaded that a shareholder receiving a Notice reasonably may conclude that he or she is entitled to receive a copy of the materials. Therefore, the final rules require a soliciting person other than an issuer to send a paper or e-mail copy of the proxy statement to any requesting shareholder to whom it has sent a Notice.[132]

2. Timeframe for Sending Notice of Internet Availability of Proxy Materials

A solicitation in opposition to the issuer's proposals to be voted on at a shareholder meeting often is not initiated until after the issuer has filed its proxy statement. As we noted in the proposing release, we therefore believe that it may be unfair to apply the same timeframe for distributing the Notice to soliciting persons as the timeframe that applies to issuers. Therefore, the amendments require a soliciting person other than the issuer that is following the notice and access model to send out its Notice by the later of: (1) 40 calendar days prior to the meeting; or (2) 10 calendar days after the issuer first sends out its proxy statement or Notice to shareholders. This is substantially the same

---

[128] 15 U.S.C. 78n(c).

[129] As with the case of an issuer, the soliciting person also may solicit shareholders concurrently by any other means, for example, by sending a proxy statement and proxy card to certain shareholders.

[130] 17 CFR 240.14a-7.

[131] See letter from ABA.

[132] The proposing release also discussed the possibility of an electronic-only solicitation in which the

soliciting person publishes a communication pursuant to Rule 14a-12 [17 CFR 240.14a-12], but does not send any Notices to shareholders. We are not adopting the electronic-only option that we discussed in the proposing release as part of the notice and access model. However, as noted in the final rules, the amendments do not affect the availability of any existing means by which an issuer or other person may furnish proxy materials under the proxy rules.

requirement we proposed, except that we have changed the proposed 30-day deadline to 40 days to conform it to our revision of the deadline for issuers.

3. Content of the Notice of Internet Availability of Proxy Materials of a Soliciting Person Other Than the Issuer

The content of the Notice sent by a soliciting person other than the issuer could be different from the content of the issuer's Notice. For example, if a solicitation in opposition is launched before the issuer has sent its own proxy statement or Notice, the full shareholder meeting agenda may not be known to the soliciting person at the time it sends its Notice to shareholders. In such a case, the soliciting person must include the agenda items in its Notice only to the extent known.[133]

Also, there may be circumstances in which a person soliciting proxies in opposition to the issuer may provide a partial proxy card, that is, a proxy card soliciting proxy authority only for the agenda items in which the soliciting person is interested rather than for all of the items, or presenting only a partial slate of directors. Typically, such a proxy would revoke any previously-executed proxy and the shareholder may lose his or her ability to vote on matters or directors other than those presented on the soliciting person's card. To prevent a shareholder from unknowingly invalidating his or her vote on those other matters, a person soliciting in opposition that is presenting such a card to shareholders must indicate clearly on its Notice whether execution of that card will invalidate the shareholder's earlier vote on the other matters or directors reflected on the issuer's proxy card.

4. Shareholder Lists and the Furnishing of Proxy Materials by the Issuer

Exchange Act Rule 14a-7 sets forth the obligation of issuers either to provide a shareholder list to a requesting shareholder or to send the shareholder's proxy materials on the shareholder's behalf. That rule provides that the issuer has the option to provide the list or send the shareholder's materials, except when the issuer is soliciting proxies in connection with a going-private transaction or a roll-up transaction.[134] Under the amendments, if the issuer is providing its shareholder list to a soliciting person, the issuer would be required to indicate which of those shareholders have permanently requested paper copies of proxy materials.[135] The proposed rules would have required an issuer to share all information about its shareholders regarding electronic delivery. We have decided to limit this requirement.

One commenter was concerned that a requirement to share information on affirmative consents may violate the issuer's privacy policies and the terms of the consent agreement between the issuer and shareholder.[136] The commenter also was concerned about divulging employees' internal company e-mail addresses. We agree with this comment and are not adopting that aspect of the proposal. However, the new rules do require an issuer to share information regarding whether a shareholder has made a permanent election to receive paper copies of the proxy materials. Such disclosure would not necessitate disclosure of a shareholder's e-mail address. In addition, a shareholder who has made a permanent election to receive paper copies of the issuer's proxy materials might reasonably expect to receive paper copies of proxy materials from other soliciting persons. Once that shareholder has made a permanent election, he or she should not be required to ask again for a paper copy of proxy materials.[137]

Similarly, if, under Rule 14a-7, the issuer elects to send the soliciting person's proxy materials, the amendments require the issuer to refrain from forwarding the other soliciting person's Notice to any shareholder who has made a permanent election to receive paper

---

[133] See Rule 14a-16(l)(3)(i) [17 CFR 240.14a-16(l)(3)(i)].

[134] See Exchange Act Rule 14a-7(b) [17 CFR 240.14a-7(b)]. If the issuer is soliciting proxies in connection with a going-private transaction or a roll-up transaction, the shareholder has the option to request the shareholder list or have the issuer send its materials.

[135] See proposed Note 3 to Exchange Act Rule 14a-7.

[136] See letter from SCSGP.

[137] As noted above, this election would be effective until a shareholder revokes that election.

copies.[138] If the soliciting person requests that the issuer follow the notice and access model, the soliciting person would be responsible for providing the issuer with copies of its Notice for all shareholders to whom it intends to provide a Notice. In that case, the issuer would have to send the soliciting person's Notice with reasonable promptness after receipt from the soliciting person. An issuer could not decide on its own whether to send a soliciting person's materials in paper or electronically. If the other soliciting person wishes to send a proxy card to shareholders 10 or more days after it first sends the Notice, the issuer would be required to forward those proxy cards in a similar fashion.[139]

5. The Role of Intermediaries With Respect to Solicitations by Persons Other Than the Issuer

Intermediaries generally furnish proxy materials to beneficial owners on behalf of soliciting persons other than the issuer under the conditions set forth in Exchange Act Rules 14b-1 and 14b-2.[140] Although intermediaries historically have transmitted a soliciting person's proxy materials in reliance on the procedures set forth in Rules 14b-1 and 14b-2, these two rules do not explicitly address an intermediary's obligations with respect to the forwarding of a soliciting person's proxy materials. As proposed, the amendments clarify that intermediaries are obligated to send proxy materials on behalf of soliciting persons other than the issuer.

D. Business Combination Transactions

As adopted, the notice and access model is not available with regard to proxy materials related to a business combination transaction, which includes transactions covered by Rule 165 under the Securities Act,[141] as well as transactions for cash consideration requiring disclosure under Item 14 of Schedule 14A. Several commenters[142] agreed that business combination transactions constitute highly extraordinary events for some issuers and frequently involve an offering of securities that must be registered under the Securities Act and require delivery of the prospectus.[143] They also typically involve proxy statements of considerable length and complexity. Other commenters nonetheless believed that the model should be extended to such transactions.[144] They noted that even more savings may be realized by extending the model to such larger documents. The Commission desires to gain more experience with the notice and access model before extending it to business combination transactions. Based on our experience with the model once it is being used for more straightforward corporate actions, we will consider at a later date whether it is appropriate to extend the model to business combination transactions.

E. Compliance Date and Monitoring

No issuer may send a Notice to shareholders before July 1, 2007. Issuers and intermediaries typically hire third parties to handle the logistics of proxy distribution. These companies will require time to adjust their systems to accommodate the notice and access model. Therefore, an issuer may not use the new model for meetings before August 10, 2007, because of the 40-day deadline. Similarly, if an issuer's meeting will be on or after August 10, 2007, it may only send the Notice on or after July 1, 2007, even if the issuer wishes to send the Notice more than 40 days prior to the meeting date.

---

[138] The other soliciting person could, of course, provide paper copies of the proxy statement and proxy card to the issuer for forwarding to those shareholders who have elected to receive paper copies.

[139] As noted above, the issuer may alternatively provide the other soliciting person with a list of shareholders pursuant to Rule 14a-7.

[140] See Randall S. Thomas & Catherine T. Dixon, Aranow & Einhorn on Proxy Contests for Corporate Control, at § 8.03(C) (3d ed. 2001).

[141] 17 CFR 230.165. This prohibition would extend to persons who solicit proxies that are not parties to the transaction and any proxy materials in opposition to the transaction.

[142] See, for example, letters from ABA, Hermes, and Sullivan & Cromwell.

[143] The prospectus delivery requirements applicable to business combination transactions were not impacted by our securities offering reform initiative because such transactions were excluded. See Release No. 33-8591 (July 19, 2005) [70 FR 44271].

[144] See, for example, letters from BRT, CALSTRS, Computershare, ICI, ISS, McData Corp, NY State Bar, Swingvote, SCSGP, William Sjostrom, and University Bancorp.

We desire to track the industry's experience with the notice and access model to determine whether the rules are achieving their intended purposes. However, we do not currently intend to impose a requirement for issuers and other parties to provide us with data and experiences with the model. We welcome information from issuers and all other parties involved in the proxy distribution process about their experience with the notice and access model on a voluntary basis. Such information would include itemized costs of proxy solicitation before and after adoption of the model, shareholder voting data before and after adoption, the number of copies requested, and any problems encountered with implementing the program. Although such information may be aggregated with the data and experiences of others and presented to the public, we do not intend to divulge the identity of responding parties.

[III. omitted in original]

IV. Conforming and Correcting Revisions to the Proxy Rules

The adopted rules reflect numerous amendments to terms used in the current proxy rules to explicitly accommodate the notice and access model. The changes are as follows:

- We substitute the term "send" and other tenses of the verb for the term "mail" and its other tenses to avoid any misunderstanding that "mail" means only paper delivery through the U.S. mail system.[145]
- We clarify that the term "address" includes an electronic mail address.[146]

Furthermore, we clarify the use of the term "annual report(s)" in the proxy rules by changing all references to either "annual report(s) to security holders" or "annual report(s) on Form 10-K and/or Form 10-KSB," as appropriate.[147] Finally, we are updating Rule 14a-2 and Forms 10-Q, 10-QSB, 10-K, 10-KSB, and N-SAR to revise outdated references to Exchange Act Rule 14a-11, which the Commission rescinded in 1999.[148]

V. Paperwork Reduction Act

A. Background

The amendments contain "collection of information" requirements within the meaning of the Paperwork Reduction Act of 1995 (PRA).[149] We published a notice requesting comment on the collection of information requirements in the proposing release, and submitted requests to the Office of Management and Budget (OMB) for approval in accordance with the PRA.[150] These requests were approved by OMB. Some of the revisions that we are making to the original proposal affect these collections of information. We will submit requests for approval of the revisions to OMB. We are requesting comment in this release with respect to these revisions.

---

[145] Rules 14a-4(c)(1), 14a-8(e)(2), 14a-8(e)(3), 14a-8(m)(3), 14a-13(a)(5), 14a-13(c), 14b-1(c)(2)(ii), 14b-2(c)(2)(ii), 14c-5(a) and 14c-7(a)(5). Also Note 2 to Rule 14a-13(a), Instruction 2 to paragraph (d)(2)(ii)(L) of Item 7 of Rule 14a-101, Note 2 to Rule 14c-7(a) and Instruction 1 to Item 4 of Rule 14c-101.

[146] Rules 14a-7(f), 14a-13(e), 14b-1(a)(2) and 14b-2(a)(4).

[147] Rules 14a-3(b)(1), 14a-3(b)(10), 14a-3(b)(13), 14a-3(e)(1)(i), 14a-3(e)(1)(i)(A), 14a-3(e)(1)(i)(B), 14a-3(e)(1)(i)(C), 14a-3(e)(1)(i)(E), 14a-3(e)(1)(ii)(A), 14a-3(e)(1)(ii)(B)(2), 14a-3(e)(1)(ii)(B)(2)(*ii*), 14a-3(e)(1)(ii)(B)(2)(*iii*), 14a-3(e)(1)(ii)(B)(*3*), 14a-3(e)(1)(iii), 14a-3(e)(2), 14a-3(e)(2)(i), 14a-3(e)(2)(ii), 14a-12(c)(1), 14b-1(b)(2), 14b-1(c)(2)(ii), 14b-1(c)(3), 14b-

2(b)(3), 14b-2(c)(2)(ii), 14b-2(c)(4), 14c-2(a)(2), 14c-3(a)(1) and 14c-3(c). Also Note to paragraph (e)(1)(i)(B) of Rule 14a-3, Note D(3) to Rule 14a-101, Note G(1) to Rule 14a-101, Instruction 1 to paragraph (d)(2)(ii)(L) of Item 7 of Rule 14a-101, paragraph (e)(2) of Item 14 of Rule 14a-101, Item 23 of Rule 14a-101, paragraph (a), (b), (c) and (d) of Item 23 to Rule 14a-101, Note 1 to paragraph (b)(2) of Rule 14b-1, Note 1 to paragraph (b) (3) of Rule 14b-2, section heading to Rule 14c-3, Item 5 of Rule 14c-101 and paragraph (a), (b), (c) and (d) of Item 5 of Rule 14c-101.

[148] See Release No. 33-7760 (Oct. 22, 1999) [64 FR 61408].

[149] 44 U.S.C. 3501 *et seq.*

[150] 44 U.S.C. 3507(d) and 5 CFR 1320.11.

The titles for the collections of information are:[151]

Regulation 14A (OMB Control No. 3235-0059)

Regulation 14C (OMB Control No. 3235-0057)

An agency may not conduct or sponsor, and a person is not required to respond to, a collection of information unless it displays a currently valid OMB control number.

B. Summary of Amendments

The amendments will apply to a particular issuer or other soliciting person only if the issuer or soliciting person voluntarily chooses to rely on the notice and access model. However, if the issuer or soliciting person opts to rely on the new alternative model, compliance with the components of the model is mandatory. The Notices, the proxy materials posted on the Web site, and copies of the proxy materials sent in response to shareholder requests will not be kept confidential.

The Notice must include the following prominent legend in bold-face type and other information described below:

"Important Notice Regarding the Availability of Proxy Materials for the Shareholder Meeting to Be Held on [insert meeting date].[152]

- o **This communication presents only an overview of the more complete proxy materials that are available to you on the Internet. We encourage you to access and review all of the important information contained in the proxy materials before voting.**

- o **The [proxy statement] [information statement] [annual report to security holders] [is/are] available at [Insert Web site address].**

- o **If you want to receive a paper or e-mail copy of these documents, you must request one. There is no charge to you for requesting a copy. Please make your request for a copy as instructed below on or before [Insert a date] to facilitate timely delivery."**

- The date, time, and location of the meeting or, if corporate action is to be taken by written consent, the earliest date on which the corporate action may be effected;

- A clear and impartial identification of each separate matter intended to be acted upon and the issuer's or other soliciting person's recommendations regarding those matters, but no supporting statements;

- A list of the materials being made available at the specified Web site;

- (1) A toll-free telephone number; (2) an e-mail address; and (3) an Internet Web site address where the shareholder can request a copy of the proxy materials, for all meetings and for the particular meeting to which the Notice relates;

- Any control/identification number that the shareholder needs to access his or her proxy card;

- Instructions on how to access the proxy card, provided that such instructions do not enable a shareholder to execute a proxy without having access to the proxy statement and annual report; and

---

[151] In the proposing release, we described the proposed Notice of Internet Availability of Proxy Materials as a new collection of information, rather than a part of our existing collections of information related to Regulations 14A and 14C. However, we subsequently submitted to OMB a PRA analysis based on revisions to the Regulation 14A and Regulation 14C collections. Based on our burden estimates associated with the Notice, the collection of information approved by OMB related to revisions to existing collections of information (Regulations 14A and 14C) and therefore we refer to those collections of information in this PRA discussion.

[152] Appropriate changes must be made to the Notice if the issuer is providing an information statement pursuant to Regulation 14C or seeking to effect a corporate action by written consent.

- Information on how to obtain directions to be able to attend the meeting and vote in person.

Intermediaries must provide a similar notice to beneficial owners. We expect that all of the factual information required to appear in the Notice will become available as part of the ordinary preparations for a shareholder meeting.

C. Comments on PRA Estimates

We requested comment on the PRA analysis contained in the proposing release. In the proposing release, we estimated the annual burden for an issuer or other soliciting person to prepare a Notice to be approximately 1.5 hours. We estimated that 75% of the burden would be prepared by the issuer and that 25% of the burden would be prepared by outside counsel retained by the issuer at an average cost of approximately $300 per hour.[153] Based on our receipt of 7,301 filings on Schedule 14A and 681 filings on Schedule 14C during our 2005 fiscal year, we estimated that 7,982 Notices would be filed annually, assuming that all issuers and other soliciting persons elected to follow the proposed notice and access model.[154] We further estimated that the total annual reporting burden would be approximately 8,980 hours.[155] Using the revised $400 average cost for retaining outside counsel, we are adjusting our annual cost estimate to approximately $1,197,300,[156] which reflects the outside counsel cost.

Although the notice and access model is an alternative to the existing model for the distribution of proxy materials to shareholders, and reliance upon it will be optional, we based our reporting burden and cost estimates on the assumption that all issuers or other soliciting persons in fiscal year 2005 would have relied on the notice and access model even though we realized that this would result in an overestimation of hour and cost burdens. The new alternative is voluntary, so the percentage of issuers and soliciting persons that will choose to rely on the new model is uncertain.

In response to commenters' remarks, we revised the proposal to require issuers to permit shareholders to make permanent elections to receive proxy materials in paper or by e-mail. An issuer must maintain records as to which of its shareholders have made such an election. Many issuers already maintain similar records to keep track of their shareholders who have affirmatively consented to electronic delivery consistent with past Commission guidance,[157] as well as their shareholders who have consented to householding of proxy materials pursuant to Rule 14a-3(e).[158] For purposes of the PRA, we estimate that a typical issuer will spend an additional five hours per year, or a total of 39,910 hours for all issuers subject to the proxy rules, to maintain these records.[159] Because this is an internal recordkeeping requirement, we do not expect a cost for hiring outside counsel.

The final rules also require an intermediary to prepare its own Notice. This Notice would be substantially the same as an issuer's Notice, but will be modified by the intermediaries to provide information that is relevant to beneficial owners rather than registered holders. According to ADP, it processes more than 95% of proxy materials that are sent to beneficial owners on behalf of intermediaries, reducing the need to create multiple intermediary Notices. In addition, the issuer or other soliciting person will provide the majority of information required in the intermediary's Notice. Therefore,

---

[153] For convenience, the estimated PRA hour burdens have been rounded to the nearest whole number, and the estimated PRA cost burdens have been rounded to the nearest $100. At the proposing stage, we used an estimated hourly rate of $300.00 to determine the estimated cost to public companies of executive compensation and related disclosure prepared or reviewed by outside counsel. We recently have increased this hourly rate estimate to $400.00 per hour after consulting with several private law firms. The cost estimates in this release are based on the $400.00 hourly rate. We request comment on this estimated hourly rate.

[154] 7,301 notices for 14A filers + 681 notices for 14C filers = 7,982 total notices.

[155] 7,982 notices × 1.5 hours per notice × .75 = 8,980 hours.

[156] 7982 notices × $400/hour × 1.5 hours/notice × .25 = $1,197,300.

[157] See the 1995 Interpretive Release.

[158] 17 CFR 240.14a-3(e).

[159] 7,982 filings with an estimated one filing per issuer or soliciting person × 5 hours = 39,910 hours.

we estimate that the burden to prepare an intermediary's Notice will be approximately one hour, or a total annual burden of 7,982 hours for all proxy solicitations.[160]

Intermediaries must also maintain records to keep track of which beneficial owners have made a permanent election to receive proxy materials in paper or by e-mail. Like issuers, intermediaries already maintain records of shareholders' affirmative consents to electronic delivery and householding of proxy materials. In addition, intermediaries maintain records as to whether their beneficial owner customers have objected, or not objected, to disclosure of their identities to the issuer. Like issuers, we believe this will result in an annual burden of 39,910 hours for intermediaries.

We did not receive any comments on the percentage of issuers and persons likely to rely on the notice and access model, nor did we receive any comments on our burden and cost estimates associated with preparing the Notice. However, several corporate commenters indicated that some issuers might be reluctant to rely on the notice and access model due to a concern that the costs of fulfillment of requests for paper copies under the model might offset some of the potential savings that they could realize from the model. We have revised the proposed model to address some of these concerns about fulfillment of requests for paper copies, but it is still difficult to predict the number of issuers and soliciting persons that will rely on the model. Therefore, we are not revising the original estimates that assume that all issuers and soliciting persons will rely on the notice and access model. As a result, these burden estimates likely are overstated. We will adjust them after we have actual experience with the notice and access model. We request comment on all of our hourly and cost burden estimates.

Any member of the public may direct to us any comments concerning these burden and cost estimates and any suggestions for reducing the burdens and costs. Persons who desire to submit comments on the collections of information requirements should direct their comments to the OMB, Attention: Desk Officer for the Securities and Exchange Commission, Office of Information and Regulatory Affairs, Washington, DC 20503, and send a copy of the comments to Nancy M. Morris, Secretary, Securities and Exchange Commission, 100 F Street, NE, Washington, DC 20549-9303, with reference to File No. S7-10-05. Requests for materials submitted to the OMB by us with regard to these collections of information should be in writing, refer to File No. S7-10-05, and be submitted to the Securities and Exchange Commission, Records Management, Office of Filings and Information Services, 100 F Street, NE, Washington, DC 20549. Because the OMB is required to make a decision concerning the collections of information between 30 and 60 days after publication, your comments are best assured of having their full effect if the OMB receives them within 30 days of publication.

VI. Cost-Benefit Analysis

A. Background

The amendments to the proxy rules enable issuers to take advantage of technological advances that have occurred in recent years to more efficiently furnish proxy materials to shareholders. We expect that these amendments will lead to significant cost reduction for proxy solicitations. The costs of solicitations ultimately are borne by shareholders. We are sensitive to the costs and benefits that result from our rules. In this section, we examine those costs and benefits.

Issuers and other persons soliciting proxies must comply with the rule amendments only if they elect to furnish proxy materials pursuant to the notice and access model. No issuer or person conducting a proxy solicitation will be required to follow the notice and access model. We expect that an issuer or other soliciting person will follow the model only if it believes that it will experience cost savings as a result. We expect that having a

---

[160] 7,982 notices × 1 hour per notice = 7,982 hours. We do not include a cost to intermediaries for hiring outside counsel because we expect that the substantive contents of an intermediary's Notice would be provided by the issuer or other soliciting person. The estimates assume that ADP will continue to process over 95% of the proxy solicitations on behalf of intermediaries, thereby eliminating the need for each intermediary to prepare a separate Notice.

choice among alternative models for furnishing proxy materials will limit the costs of the amendments by enabling issuers and other soliciting persons to choose one that is most efficient and cost effective under the issuer's or other soliciting person's particular circumstances.

B. Summary of Amendments

The amendments provide an alternative notice and access model that permits an issuer to furnish its proxy materials to shareholders by posting them on a publicly-accessible Internet Web site (other than the Commission's EDGAR Web site) and providing shareholders with a notice informing them that the materials are available and explaining how to access them. Under this alternative model, shareholders may request paper or e-mail copies of the proxy materials at no charge from the issuer.

Under the amendments, an issuer can require intermediaries to follow similar procedures when forwarding the issuer's proxy materials to beneficial owners. In addition, shareholders and other persons conducting their own proxy solicitations may follow the alternative model, under the same general requirements that apply to issuers. However, such persons will be able to limit their solicitations to shareholders who have not requested paper copies of the proxy materials from an issuer in connection with the issuer's solicitation.

C. Benefits

The benefits to investors of the amendments include the following: (1) more rapid dissemination of proxy information to shareholders using the Internet; and (2) reduced printing and mailing costs for issuers, as well as other soliciting persons engaging in proxy contests. We expect that the reductions in printing and mailing costs and the potential decrease in the costs of proxy contests to be the most significant sources of economic benefit to investors of the amendments.

In terms of paper processing alone, the benefits of the rule amendments are limited by the volume of paper processing that would occur otherwise. As we noted in the proposing release, Automatic Data Processing, Inc. (ADP) handles the vast majority of proxy mailings to beneficial owners.[161] ADP publishes statistics that provide useful background for evaluating the likely consequences of the rule amendments. ADP estimates that, during the 2006 proxy season,[162] over 69.7 million proxy material mailings were eliminated through a variety of means, including householding and existing electronic delivery methods. During that season, ADP mailed 85.3 million paper proxy items to beneficial owners. ADP estimates that the average cost of printing and mailing a paper copy of a set of proxy materials during the 2006 proxy season was $5.64. We estimate that issuers and other soliciting persons spent, in the aggregate, $481.2 million in postage and printing fees alone to distribute paper proxy materials to beneficial owners.[163] Approximately 50% of all proxy pieces mailed by ADP in 2005 were mailed during the proxy season.[164] Therefore, we estimate that issuers and other persons soliciting proxies from beneficial owners spent approximately $962.4 million in 2006 in printing and mailing costs.[165]

Based on the assumption that 19% of shareholders will choose to have paper copies sent to them when an issuer relies on the notice and access model, we estimate that the amendments could produce annual paper-related savings ranging from $48.3 million (if issuers who are responsible for 10% of all proxy mailings choose to rely on the notice and access model) to $241.4 million (if issuers who are responsible for 50% of all proxy

---

[161] We expect savings per mailing to record holders to roughly correspond to savings per mailing to beneficial owners.

[162] According to ADP data, the 2006 proxy season extended from February 15, 2006 to May 1, 2006.

[163] 85.3 million mailings × $5.64/mailing = $481.2 million.

[164] According to ADP, in 2005, 90,013,175 of 179,833,774, or 50%, of proxy pieces were mailed during the 2005 proxy season.

[165] $481.2 million / 50% = $962.4 million.

mailings choose to rely on the notice and access model).[166] This estimate excludes the effect of the provision of the amendments that will allow shareholders to make a permanent request for paper copies. That provision will enable issuers and other soliciting persons to take advantage of bulk printing and mailing rates for those requesting shareholders, and therefore should reduce the on-demand costs reflected in these calculations.[167]

We estimate that approximately 19% of shareholders will request paper copies. Commenters provided alternate estimates. For example, Computershare, a large transfer agent, estimated that less than 10% of shareholders would request paper copies.[168] According to a survey conducted by Forrester Research for ADP, 12% of shareholders report that they would always take extra steps to get their proxy materials, and as many as 68% of shareholders report that they would take extra steps to get their proxy materials in paper at least some of the time. The same survey also finds that 82% of shareholders report that they look at their proxy materials at least some of the time. These survey results suggest that shareholders may review proxy materials even if they do not vote. During the 2005 proxy season, only 44% of accounts were voted by beneficial owners. Put differently, 56%, or 84.8 million accounts, did not return requests for voting instructions. Our estimate that 19% of shareholders will request paper copies reflects the diverse estimates suggested by the available data.

Although we expect the savings to be significant, the actual paper-related benefits will be influenced by several factors that we estimate will become less important over time. First, some issuers and other soliciting persons will likely not elect to follow the alternative model. We estimate that issuers who are responsible for between 10% and 50% of all current proxy mailings will adopt the notice and access model during the first year of implementation of the amendments. Several commenters noted that some issuers may not be willing to try the model the first year, but rather will opt to wait and monitor the experience of other issuers that do try the model. Second, to the extent that some shareholders request paper copies of the proxy materials, the benefits of the amendments in terms of savings in printing and mailing costs will be reduced. Issuers are concerned that the cost per paper copy would be significantly greater if they have to mail copies of paper proxy materials to shareholders on an on-demand basis, rather than mailing the paper copies in bulk. Thus, if a significant number of shareholders request paper, the savings will be substantially reduced. Third, after adopting the notice and access model, issuers may face a high degree of uncertainty about the number of requests that they may get for paper proxy materials and may maintain unnecessarily large inventories of paper copies as a precaution. As issuers gain familiarity with the continued use of paper materials and as shareholders become more comfortable with receiving disclosures via the Internet, the number of paper copies are likely to decline, as will issuers' tendency to print many more copies than ultimately are requested. This will lead to growth in paper-related savings from the rule amendments over time.

Additional benefits will accrue from reductions in the costs of proxy solicitations by persons other than the issuer. Under the amendments, persons other than the issuer also

---

[166] This range of potential cost savings depends on data on proxy material production, home printing costs, and first-class postage rates provided by Lexecon and ADP, and supplemented with modest 2006 USPS postage rate discounts. The fixed costs of notice and proxy material production are estimated to be $2.36 per shareholder. The variable costs of fulfilling a paper requests, including handling, paper, printing and postage, are estimated to be $6.11 per copy requested. Assumptions about percentages of shareholders requesting paper copies are derived from Forrester survey data furnished by ADP and adjusted for the reported likelihood that an investor will take extra steps to get proxy materials. Our estimate of the total number of shareholders is based on data provided by ADP and SIA. According to SIA's comment letter, 78.49% of shareholders held their shares in street name. We estimate that the total number of proxy pieces mailed equals the number of pieces mailed to beneficial shareholders by ADP in 2005 divided by 78.49%, which equals 179,833,774 / 78.49%, or 229,116,797.

[167] ADP commissioned a study by Lexecon to provide estimates for the total net cost/savings of the amendments to issuers. Lexecon's study relied on 2005 postage rates with no first-class mail discounts and a higher share of color printing at home than we assume above. It estimated that if all issuers adopt the notice and access model, if 9% of shareholders choose to print the materials at home, and 19% choose to have paper copies sent to them, then the amendments would produce a net savings of $205 million for issuers in the aggregate. However, if 20% of shareholders chose to print and 39% chose to request paper copies, the amendments would produce a net cost of $181 million. See Lexecon comment letter for more details.

[168] See letter from Computershare.

can rely on the notice and access model, but will be able to limit the scope of their proxy solicitations to shareholders who have not requested paper copies of the proxy materials. We expect that the flexibility afforded to persons other than the issuer under the amendments will reduce the cost of engaging in proxy contests, thereby increasing the effectiveness and efficiency of proxy contests as a source of discipline in the corporate governance process.

The effect of the amendments of lessening the costs associated with a proxy contest will be limited by the persistence of other costs, even under the notice and access model. One commenter noted that a large percentage of the costs of effecting a proxy contest go to legal, document preparation, and solicitation fees, while a much smaller percentage of the costs is associated with printing and distribution of materials.[169] However, other commenters suggested that the paper-related cost savings that can be realized from the rule amendments are substantial enough to change the way many contests are conducted.[170]

Finally, some benefits from the amendments may arise from a reduction in what may be regarded as the environmental costs of the proxy solicitation process.[171] Specifically, proxy solicitation involves the use of a significant amount of paper and printing ink. Paper production and distribution can adversely affect the environment, due to the use of trees, fossil fuels, chemicals such as bleaching agents, printing ink (which contains toxic metals), and cleanup washes. To the extent that paper producers internalize these costs and the costs are reflected in the price of paper and other materials consumed during the proxy solicitation process, our dollar estimates of the paper-related benefits reflect the elimination of these adverse environmental consequences under the amendments.

D. Costs

An issuer's decision to use the notice and access model will introduce several new costs into the process of proxy distribution, including the following: (1) the cost of preparing, producing, and sending the Notice to shareholders; (2) the cost of processing shareholders' requests for copies of the proxy materials and maintaining their permanent election preferences; and (3) the cost to shareholders of printing proxy materials at home that would otherwise be printed by issuers.

The paper-related savings to issuers and other soliciting persons discussed under the benefits section above are adjusted for the cost of printing and sending Notices. If Notices are sent by mail, then the mailing costs may vary widely among parties. Postage rates likely would vary from $0.14 to $0.39 per Notice mailed, depending on numerous factors. In our estimates of the paper-related benefits above, we assume that each Notice costs a total of $0.42 to print and mail. Based on data from ADP and SIA, we estimate that issuers and other soliciting persons process a total of 229,116,797 accounts per year.[172] The alternative model also requires minimal added disclosures in the form of a Notice to shareholders, informing them that the proxy materials are available at a specified Internet Web site. For purposes of the PRA, we have presented the extremely conservative estimate that the preparation and filing costs of the amendments, assuming that all issuers and other soliciting persons elect to follow the procedures, will be approximately $2,020,475.[173] Under the alternate scenario presented above, these costs could range between $202,048 if 10% of issuers adopt the model and $1,010,238 if 50% of issuers adopt. The amendments also require issuers and intermediaries to maintain records of shareholders who have requested paper and e-mail copies for future proxy solicitations. We estimate that this cost to issuers and intermediaries will be approximately $9,977,500 if all issuers adopt the

---

[169] See letter from ADP.

[170] See letters from CALSTRS, Computershare, ISS, and Swingvote.

[171] See letter from American Forests.

[172] See www.ics.adp.com/release11/public_site/about/stats.html stating that ADP handled 179,833,774 in fiscal year 2005 and letter from SIA stating that beneficial accounts represent 78.49% of total accounts.

[173] For PRA purposes, we estimate that issuers would spend a total of $897,975 on outside professionals to prepare this disclosure. We also estimate that issuers would spend a total of 8,980 hours of issuer personnel time preparing this disclosure. We estimate the average hourly cost of issuer personnel time to be $125, resulting in a total cost of $1,122,500 for issuer personnel time. This results in a total cost of $2,020,475 for all issuers. We expect that costs for posting the materials on a Web site will be minimal and are included in this calculation.

notice and access model,[174] $997,500 if 10% of issuers adopt the model, and $4,988,750 if 50% of issuers adopt the model.

Issuers who adopt the notice and access model and their intermediaries will incur additional processing costs. The amendments will require an intermediary such as a bank, broker-dealer, or other association to follow the notice and access model if an issuer so requests. An intermediary that follows the notice and access model will be required to prepare its own Notice to beneficial owners, along with instructions on when and how to request paper copies and the website where the beneficial owner can access his or her request for voting instructions. Since issuers reimburse intermediaries for their reasonable expenses of forwarding proxy materials and intermediaries and their agents already have systems to prepare and deliver requests for voting instructions, we do not expect the intermediaries' role in sending their Notices to beneficial owners to significantly affect the costs associated with the rule.

Under the notice and access model, a beneficial owner must request a copy of proxy materials from its intermediary rather than from the issuer. The costs of collecting and processing requests from beneficial owners may be significant, particularly if the intermediary receives the requests of beneficial owners associated with many different issuers that specify different methods of furnishing the proxy. We expect that these processing costs will be highest in the first year after adoption but will subsequently decline as intermediaries develop the necessary systems and procedures and as beneficial owners increasingly become comfortable with accessing proxy materials online. In addition, the final rules permit a beneficial owner to specify its preference on an account-wide basis, which should reduce the cost of processing requests for copies. These costs are ultimately paid by the issuer and therefore would be included in an issuer's assessment of whether to adopt the alternative model.

Shareholders obtaining proxy materials online would incur any necessary costs associated with gaining access to the Internet. In addition, some shareholders may choose to print out the posted materials, which will entail paper and printing costs. We estimate that approximately 10% of all shareholders will print out the posted materials at home at an estimated cost of $7.05 per proxy package. Based on these assumptions, the amendments are estimated to produce annual home printing costs ranging from $16 million (if issuers who are responsible for 10% of all current proxy mailings choose to rely on the notice and access model) to $80 million (if issuers who are responsible for 50% of all current proxy mailings choose to rely on the notice and access model).[175] Investors have the option to incur no additional cost by either accessing the proxy materials online or requesting paper copies of the materials from the issuer.

VII. Consideration of Burden on Competition and Promotion of Efficiency, Competition and Capital Formation

Section 23(a)(2) of the Exchange Act[176] requires us, when adopting rules under the Exchange Act, to consider the impact that any new rule would have on competition. In addition, Section 23(a)(2) prohibits us from adopting any rule that would impose a burden on competition not necessary or appropriate in furtherance of the purposes of the Exchange Act. Section 3(f) of the Exchange Act[177] and Section 2(c) of the Investment Company Act of 1940[178] require us, when engaging in rulemaking that requires us

---

[174] For PRA purposes, we estimate that issuers and intermediaries would spend a total of 79,820 hours of issuer and intermediary personnel time maintaining these records. We estimate the average hourly cost of issuer and intermediary personnel time to be $125, resulting in a total cost of $9,977,500 for issuer and intermediary personnel time.

[175] This range of potential home printing costs depends on data provided by Lexecon and ADP. See letter from ADP. The Lexecon data was included in the ADP comment letter. To calculate home printing cost, we assume that 50% of annual report pages are printed

in color and 100% of proxy statement pages are printed in black and white. The estimated percentage of shareholders printing at home is derived from Forrester survey data furnished by ADP and adjusted for the reported likelihood that an investor will take extra steps to get proxy materials. Total number of shareholders estimated as above based on data provided by ADP and SIA. See letters from ADP and SIA.

[176] 15 U.S.C. 78w(a)(2).

[177] 15 U.S.C. 78c(f).

[178] 15 U.S.C. 80a-2(c).

to consider or determine whether an action is necessary or appropriate in the public interest, to consider, in addition to the protection of investors, whether the action will promote efficiency, competition, and capital formation. We have also discussed other impacts of the amendments in our Cost-Benefit, Paperwork Reduction Act and Final Regulatory Flexibility Act Analyses.

The amendments to the proxy rules are intended to improve efficiency by providing an alternative for issuers and other soliciting persons that could reduce the cost of soliciting proxies and sending information statements regarding shareholder meetings. Currently, many issuers must devote a significant amount of time and resources to proxy mailings. Similarly, undertaking a proxy contest is often a very costly endeavor. We expect that the amendments will reduce the time and resources related to such distributions. These costs include reimbursing intermediaries for their part in the process.

As noted elsewhere in this release, commenters expressed concern that the amendments might reduce shareholder participation in the proxy voting process, making issuers more dependent on broker discretionary voting. Such a result would affect the efficiency of the current proxy voting process. We have made revisions to the amendments to minimize such effect, by making it easier for shareholders to continue to receive paper copies of the proxy materials. Similarly, there was concern that the amendments would increase the risk of shareholders conducting frivolous proxy contests. We have also revised the final rules to minimize this possibility, by eliminating the proposed conditional solicitation.[179]

Some commenters were concerned that the added procedures would complicate the proxy distribution process, reducing the efficiency of the process. The final rules are voluntary. No issuer or other soliciting person is required to rely on the notice and access model. Those that choose to rely on the model presumably have determined that the additional procedures that they must follow would reduce their cost of soliciting proxies, thereby increasing the efficiency of the process.

We considered the effects that the amendments would have on capital formation. The final rules do not directly affect the ability of issuers to raise capital. However, they are intended to reduce the cost of soliciting proxies. In addition, they facilitate proxy disclosure via the Internet, which may improve the manner in which investors receive those disclosures, thereby improving shareholder relations.

We considered the possible effects of the amendments on competition. As noted elsewhere in this release, companies in, and related to, the financial printing industry were concerned about the negative effects that the rules may have on that industry. Conversely, these rules may create alternative industries that promote more user-friendly, computerbased systems for interaction with shareholders, thus creating new jobs and industries in this field.

VIII. Final Regulatory Flexibility Analysis

This Final Regulatory Flexibility Analysis has been prepared in accordance with 5 U.S.C. 603. It relates to amendments to the proxy rules under the Exchange Act that will provide an alternative model for issuers and other persons soliciting proxies to satisfy certain of their obligations under the Commission's proxy rules. An Initial Regulatory Flexibility Analysis (IRFA) was prepared in accordance with the Regulatory Flexibility Act in conjunction with the proposing release. The proposing release included, and solicited comment on, the IRFA.

A. Need for the Amendments

On December 8, 2005, we proposed amendments to the rules regarding provision of proxy materials to shareholders.[180] We are adopting those amendments, substantially as proposed, but with a few modifications in response to public comment. Specifically, the amendments create an alternative notice and access model by which issuers and other

---

[179] See Section III.C.1 of Release No. 34-52926 (Dec. 8, 2005) [70 FR 74597].

[180] Release No. 34-52926 (Dec. 8, 2005) [70 FR 74597].

soliciting persons can electronically furnish their proxy materials to shareholders. The amendments are intended to put into place processes that will provide shareholders with notice of, and access to, proxy materials while taking advantage of technological devel opments and the growth of the Internet and electronic communications. Issuers that rely on the amendments may be able to significantly lower the costs of their proxy solicitations that ultimately are borne by shareholders. The fact that the amendments also apply to a soliciting person other than the issuer might help to reduce the costs of engaging in a proxy contest.

The amendments also have the potential to improve the ability of shareholders to participate meaningfully in the proxy process by reducing the cost of undertaking a proxy contest and may increase management's accountability and responsiveness to shareholders due to heightened concern about the possibility of a proxy contest. This, in turn, may enhance the value of shareholders' investments.

B. Significant Issues Raised by Public Comment

In the proposing release, we requested comment on any aspect of the Initial Regulatory Flexibility Act Analysis, including the number of small entities that would be affected by the proposals, and both the qualitative and quantitative nature of the impact. We did not receive comment on the number of small entities that would be affected by the proposals. Also, no commenters noted any difference in the potential effect of the amendments on small entities as opposed to other entities.

One commenter remarked that smaller companies depend more heavily on broker discretionary voting than larger companies in order to meet state law quorum requirements.[181] Although the new rules do not affect the NYSE's broker discretionary voting rule, that commenter noted that if the final rules reduce shareholder voting, such smaller companies would become even more dependent on broker discretionary voting. As noted elsewhere in this release, we have made revisions to the amendments to minimize such effect, by making it easier for shareholders to continue to receive paper copies of the proxy materials.

C. Small Entities Subject to the Amendments

Exchange Act Rule 0-10(a)[182] defines an issuer to be a "small business" or "small organization" for purposes of the Regulatory Flexibility Act if it had total assets of $5 million or less on the last day of its most recent fiscal year. We estimate that there are approximately 2,500 public companies, other than investment companies, that may be considered small entities.

For purposes of the Regulatory Flexibility Act, an investment company is a small entity if it, together with other investment companies in the same group of related investment companies, has net assets of $50 million or less as of the end of its most recent fiscal year.[183] Approximately 157 registered investment companies meet this definition. Moreover, approximately 53 business development companies may be considered small entities.

Paragraph (c)(1) of Rule 0-10 under the Exchange Act[184] states that the term "small business" or "small organization," when referring to a broker-dealer, means a broker or dealer that had total capital (net worth plus subordinated liabilities) of less than $500,000 on the date in the prior fiscal year as of which its audited financial statements were prepared pursuant to § 240.17a-5(d); and is not affiliated with any person (other than a natural person) that is not a small business or small organization. As of 2005, the Commission estimates that there were approximately 910 broker-dealers that qualified as small entities as defined above.[185] Small Business Administration regulations define

---

[181] See letter from ABC.

[182] 17 CFR 240.0-10(a).

[183] See Rule 0-10 under the Investment Company Act of 1940 [17 CFR 270.0-10].

[184] 17 CFR 240.0-10(c)(1).

[185] These numbers are based on a review by the Commission's Office of Economic Analysis of 2005 Financial and Operational Combined Uniform Single (FOCUS) Report filings reflecting registered broker-dealers. This number does not include broker-dealers that are delinquent in their FOCUS Report filings.

"small entities" to include banks and savings associations with total assets of $165 million or less.[186] The Commission estimates that the rules will apply to approximately 9,475 banks, approximately 5,816 of which could be considered small banks with assets of $165 million or less.

No issuer is required to follow the notice and access model. However, we expect that many issuers will choose to follow the alternative model because of the substantial cost savings that they may realize. These issuers likely will include many small entities. Broker-dealer and bank intermediaries are required to comply with the notice and access model if an issuer or other soliciting person requests such intermediaries to follow the alternative model.

D. Reporting, Recordkeeping and Other Compliance Requirements

If an issuer chooses to follow the model, it will be required to prepare, file, and furnish a Notice to shareholders. Similarly, upon request from an issuer or other soliciting person, a broker-dealer or bank intermediary will be required to prepare and furnish its own Notice to beneficial owners. These Notices must include factual information that is readily available to the issuer and intermediary. An issuer relying on the notice and access model also will be required to provide copies of the proxy materials to requesting shareholders and to maintain a Web site on which to post the proxy materials. Intermediaries will be required to forward copies of the proxy materials to requesting beneficial owners and to maintain a Web site on which to post its request for voting instructions. Those Web sites must be maintained in a manner to ensure that the anonymity of persons accessing the Web sites is preserved. Finally, issuers and intermediaries must maintain records regarding which shareholders have indicated a preference to receive paper or e-mail copies of the proxy materials in the future.

E. Agency Action to Minimize Effect on Small Entities

Compliance with the alternative notice and access model is voluntary for issuers. An issuer that is a small entity, like other types of entities subject to the proxy rules, need not elect to follow the alternative model. This flexibility to comply with traditional methods of distributing proxy materials to shareholders or to comply with the notice and access model will allow a small entity to choose the compliance means that will be most cost effective for its particular situation. It is likely that only the issuers that believe they will realize cost savings or other benefits as a result of following the notice and access model will choose to do so.

Broker-dealer and bank intermediaries that are small entities must comply with the requirements of the voluntary model upon request from an issuer or other soliciting person. However, an intermediary is not required to forward proxy materials to beneficial owners unless the issuer or other soliciting person provides assurance of reimbursement of the intermediary's reasonable expenses incurred in connection with forwarding those materials. Therefore, any costs imposed on intermediaries by the rules will be borne by the issuer or other soliciting person, and ultimately shareholders. Exempting broker-dealers and banks that are small entities would lead to inconsistent means by which beneficial owners receive their proxy materials, which we believe would not be appropriate.

We considered alternatives, such as permitting an intermediary to merely forward an issuer's Notice rather than preparing its own Notice and permitting beneficial owners to request copies directly from the issuer. However, we believe that those alternatives create a high likelihood of confusion with respect to whether a beneficial owner would be entitled to execute a proxy card rather than provide voting instructions to his or her intermediary. To prevent such confusion, we have decided that such alternatives would not be appropriate.

IX. Statutory Basis and Text of Amendments

We are adopting the amendments pursuant to Sections 3(b), 10, 13, 14, 15, 23(a), and 36 of the Securities Exchange Act of 1934, as amended, and Sections 20(a), 30, and 38 of the Investment Company Act of 1940, as amended.

---

[186] 13 CFR 121.201.

List of Subjects

17 CFR Parts 240 and 249

Reporting and recordkeeping requirements, Securities.

17 CFR Part 274

Investment companies, Reporting and recordkeeping requirements, Securities.

PART 240—GENERAL RULES AND REGULATIONS, SECURITIES EXCHANGE ACT OF 1934

1. The general authority citation for Part 240 is revised to read as follows:

Authority: 15 U.S.C. 77c, 77d, 77g, 77j, 77s, 77z-2, 77z-3, 77eee, 77ggg, 77nnn, 77sss, 77ttt, 78c, 78d, 78e, 78f, 78g, 78i, 78j, 78j-1, 78k, 78k-1, 78*l*, 78m, 78n, 78*o*, 78p, 78q, 78s, 78u-5, 78w, 78x, 78*ll*, 78mm, 80a-20, 80a-23, 80a-29, 80a-37, 80b-3, 80b-4, 80b-11, and 7201 *et seq.*; and 18 U.S.C. 1350, unless otherwise noted.

* * * * *

2. Amend § 240.14a-2 by:

a. Removing the period and adding a semicolon at the end of paragraph (b)(3)(ii); and

b. Revising paragraph (b)(3)(iv).

The revision reads as follows:

§ 240.14a-2 Solicitations to which § 240.14a-3 to § 240.14a-15 apply.

* * * * *

(b) * * *

(3) * * *

(iv) The proxy voting advice is not furnished on behalf of any person soliciting proxies or on behalf of a participant in an election subject to the provisions of § 240.14a-12(c); and

* * * * *

3. Amend § 240.14a-3 by:

a. Revising paragraphs (a), (e)(1)(i), the introductory text of paragraphs (e)(1)(ii)(A) and (e)(1)(ii)(B)(2), paragraphs (e)(1)(ii)(B)(2)(*ii*), (e)(1)(ii)(B)(2)(*iii*), (e)(1)(ii)(B)(3), (e)(1)(iii), and (e)(2); and

b. Revising the term "annual report" to read "annual report to security holders" in paragraph (b)(13).

The revisions read as follows:

§ 240.14a-3 Information to be furnished to security holders.

(a) No solicitation subject to this regulation shall be made unless each person solicited is concurrently furnished or has previously been furnished with:

(1) A publicly-filed preliminary or definitive written proxy statement containing the information specified in Schedule 14A (§ 240.14a-101);

(2) A publicly-filed preliminary or definitive proxy statement, in the form and manner described in § 240.14a-16, containing the information specified in Schedule 14A (§ 240.14a-101); or

(3) A preliminary or definitive written proxy statement included in a registration statement filed under the Securities Act of 1933 on Form S-4 or F-4 (§ 239.25 or

§ 239.34 of this chapter) or Form N-14 (§ 239.23 of this chapter) and containing the information specified in such Form.

* * * * *

(e)(1)(i) A registrant will be considered to have delivered an annual report to security holders, proxy statement or Notice of Internet Availability of Proxy Materials, as described in § 240.14a-16, to all security holders of record who share an address if:

(A) The registrant delivers one annual report to security holders, proxy statement or Notice of Internet Availability of Proxy Materials, as applicable, to the shared address;

(B) The registrant addresses the annual report to security holders, proxy statement or Notice of Internet Availability of Proxy Materials, as applicable, to the security holders as a group (for example, "ABC Fund [or Corporation] Security Holders," "Jane Doe and Household," "The Smith Family"), to each of the security holders individually (for example, "John Doe and Richard Jones") or to the security holders in a form to which each of the security holders has consented in writing;

Note to paragraph (e)(1)(i)(B): Unless the registrant addresses the annual report to security holders, proxy statement or Notice of Internet Availability of Proxy Materials to the security holders as a group or to each of the security holders individually, it must obtain, from each security holder to be included in the householded group, a separate affirmative written consent to the specific form of address the registrant will use.

(C) The security holders consent, in accordance with paragraph (e)(1)(ii) of this section, to delivery of one annual report to security holders or proxy statement, as applicable;

(D) With respect to delivery of the proxy statement or Notice of Internet Availability of Proxy Materials, the registrant delivers, together with or subsequent to delivery of the proxy statement, a separate proxy card for each security holder at the shared address; and

(E) The registrant includes an undertaking in the proxy statement to deliver promptly upon written or oral request a separate copy of the annual report to security holders, proxy statement or Notice of Internet Availability of Proxy Materials, as applicable, to a security holder at a shared address to which a single copy of the document was delivered.

(ii) *Consent.* (A) *Affirmative written consent.* Each security holder must affirmatively consent, in writing, to delivery of one annual report to security holders or proxy statement, as applicable. A security holder's affirmative written consent will be considered valid only if the security holder has been informed of:

* * * * *

(B) * * *

(2) The registrant has sent the security holder a notice at least 60 days before the registrant begins to rely on this section concerning delivery of annual reports to security holders, proxy statements or Notices of Internet Availability of Proxy Materials to that security holder. The notice must:

* * * * *

(*ii*) State that only one annual report to security holders, proxy statement or Notice of Internet Availability of Proxy Materials, as applicable, will be delivered to the shared address unless the registrant receives contrary instructions;

(*iii*) Include a toll-free telephone number, or be accompanied by a reply form that is pre-addressed with postage provided, that the security holder can use to notify the registrant that the security holder wishes to receive a separate annual report to security holders, proxy statement or Notice of Internet Availability of Proxy Materials;

* * * * *

(*3*) The registrant has not received the reply form or other notification indicating that the security holder wishes to continue to receive an individual copy of the annual report to security holders, proxy statement or Notice of Internet Availability of Proxy Materials, as applicable, within 60 days after the registrant sent the notice required by paragraph (e)(1)(ii)(B)(2) of this section; and

* * * * *

(iii) *Revocation of consent.* If a security holder, orally or in writing, revokes consent to delivery of one annual report to security holders, proxy statement or Notice of Internet Availability of Proxy Materials to a shared address, the registrant must begin sending individual copies to that security holder within 30 days after the registrant receives revocation of the security holder's consent.

* * * * *

(2) Notwithstanding paragraphs (a) and (b) of this section, unless state law requires otherwise, a registrant is not required to send an annual report to security holders, proxy statement or Notice of Internet Availability of Proxy Materials to a security holder if:

(i) An annual report to security holders and a proxy statement, or a Notice of Internet of Availability of Proxy Materials, for two consecutive annual meetings; or

(ii) All, and at least two, payments (if sent by first class mail) of dividends or interest on securities, or dividend reinvestment confirmations, during a twelve month period, have been mailed to such security holder's address and have been returned as undeliverable. If any such security holder delivers or causes to be delivered to the registrant written notice setting forth his then current address for security holder communications purposes, the registrant's obligation to deliver an annual report to security holders, a proxy statement or a Notice of Internet Availability of Proxy Materials under this section is reinstated.

* * * * *

4. Amend § 240.14a-4 by:

a. Removing the authority citation following the section;

b. Revising the word "mailed" to read "sent" in the first sentence of paragraph (c)(1); and

c. Revising the word "mails" to read "sends" in the last sentence of paragraph (c)(1).

5. Amend § 240.14a-7 by:

a. Revising paragraphs (a)(2)(i) and (a)(2)(ii);

b. Adding paragraph (a)(2)(iii); and

c. In the "Notes to § 240.14a-7", revising the numerical designation "1." to read "Note 1 to § 240.14a-8", revising the numerical designation "2." to read "Note 2 to § 240.14a-7" and adding "Note 3 to § 240.14a-7".

The revisions and additions read as follows:

§ 240.14a-7 Obligations of registrants to provide a list of, or mail soliciting material to, security holders.

* * * * *

(a) * * *

(2) * * *

(i) Send copies of any proxy statement, form of proxy, or other soliciting material, including a Notice of Internet Availability of Proxy Materials (as described in § 240.14a-16), furnished by the security holder to the record holders, including banks, brokers, and similar entities, designated by the security holder. A sufficient number of copies must be sent to the banks, brokers, and similar entities for distribution to all beneficial owners designated by the security holder. The security holder may designate only record holders and/or beneficial owners who have not requested paper and/or e-mail copies of the proxy statement. If the registrant has received affirmative written or implied consent to deliver a single proxy statement to security holders at a shared address in accordance with the procedures in § 240.14a-3(e)(1), a single copy of the proxy statement or Notice of Internet Availability of Proxy Materials furnished by the security holder shall be sent to that address, provided that if multiple copies of the Notice of Internet Availability of Proxy Materials are furnished by the security holder for that address, the registrant shall deliver those copies in a single envelope to that address. The registrant shall send the security holder material with reasonable promptness after tender of the material to be sent, envelopes or other containers therefore, postage or payment for postage and other reasonable expenses of effecting such distribution. The registrant shall not be responsible for the content of the material; or

(ii) Deliver the following information to the requesting security holder within five business days of receipt of the request:

(A) A reasonably current list of the names, addresses and security positions of the record holders, including banks, brokers and similar entities holding securities in the same class or classes as holders which have been or are to be solicited on management's behalf, or any more limited group of such holders designated by the security holder if available or retrievable under the registrant's or its transfer agent's security holder data systems;

(B) The most recent list of names, addresses and security positions of beneficial owners as specified in § 240.14a-13(b), in the possession, or which subsequently comes into the possession, of the registrant;

(C) The names of security holders at a shared address that have consented to delivery of a single copy of proxy materials to a shared address, if the registrant has received written or implied consent in accordance with § 240.14a-3(e)(1); and

(D) If the registrant has relied on § 240.14a-16, the names of security holders who have requested paper copies of the proxy materials for all meetings and the names of security holders who, as of the date that the registrant receives the request, have requested paper copies of the proxy materials only for the meeting to which the solicitation relates.

(iii) All security holder list information shall be in the form requested by the security holder to the extent that such form is available to the registrant without undue burden or expense. The registrant shall furnish the security holder with updated record holder information on a daily basis or, if not available on a daily basis, at the shortest reasonable intervals; provided, however, the registrant need not provide beneficial or record holder information more current than the record date for the meeting or action.

* * * * *

Notes to § 240.14a-7.

* * * * *

Note 3 to § 240.14a-7. If the registrant is sending the requesting security holder's materials under § 240.14a-7 and receives a request from the security holder to furnish the materials in the form and manner described in § 240.14a-16, the registrant must accommodate that request.

6. Amend § 240.14a-8 by revising the word "mail" to read "send" in the last sentence of paragraph (e)(2) and in paragraph (e)(3) and the word "mails" to read "sends" in the introductory text of paragraph (m)(3).

7. Amend § 240.14a-12 by revising the term "annual report" to read "annual report to security holders" in the heading of paragraph (c)(1) and the first sentence of paragraph (c)(1).

8. Amend § 240.14a-13 by revising the word "mailing" to read "sending" in paragraph (a)(5) and the word "mail" to read "send" in Note 2 following paragraph (a) and in paragraph (c), each time it appears.

9. Add § 240.14a-16 to read as follows:

§ 240.14a-16 Internet availability of proxy materials.

(a)(1) A registrant may furnish a proxy statement pursuant to § 240.14a-3(a), or an annual report to security holders pursuant to § 240.14a-3(b), to a security holder by sending the security holder a Notice of Internet Availability of Proxy Materials, as described in this section, 40 calendar days or more prior to the security holder meeting date, or if no meeting is to be held, 40 calendar days or more prior to the date the votes, consents or authorizations may be used to effect the corporate action, and complying with all other requirements of this section.

(2) If the registrant chooses to provide the proxy statement or annual report to security holders to beneficial owners pursuant to this section, it must provide the record holder or respondent bank with all information listed in paragraph (d) of this section in sufficient time for the record holder or respondent bank to prepare, print and send a Notice of Internet Availability of Proxy Materials to beneficial owners at least 40 calendar days before the meeting date.

(b)(1) All materials identified in the Notice of Internet Availability of Proxy Materials must be publicly accessible, free of charge, at the Web site address specified in the notice on or before the time that the notice is sent to the security holder and such materials must remain available on that Web site through the conclusion of the meeting of security holders.

(2) All additional soliciting materials sent to security holders or made public after the Notice of Internet Availability of Proxy Materials has been sent must be made publicly accessible at the specified Web site address no later than the day on which such materials are first sent to security holders or made public.

(3) The Web site address relied upon for compliance under this section may not be the address of the Commission's electronic filing system.

(4) The registrant must provide security holders with a means to execute a proxy as of the time the Notice of Internet Availability of Proxy Materials is first sent to security holders.

(c) The materials must be presented on the Web site in a format, or formats, convenient for both reading online and printing on paper.

(d) The Notice of Internet Availability of Proxy Materials must contain the following:

(1) A prominent legend in bold-face type that states:

"Important Notice Regarding the Availability of Proxy Materials for the Shareholder Meeting to Be Held on [insert meeting date].

1. This communication presents only an overview of the more complete proxy materials that are available to you on the Internet. We encourage you to access and review all of the important information contained in the proxy materials before voting.

2. The [proxy statement] [information statement] [annual report to security holders] [is/are] available at [Insert Web site address].

3. If you want to receive a paper or e-mail copy of these documents, you must request one. There is no charge to you for requesting a copy. Please make your request for a copy as instructed below on or before [Insert a date] to facilitate timely delivery.";

(2) The date, time, and location of the meeting, or if corporate action is to be taken by written consent, the earliest date on which the corporate action may be effected;

(3) A clear and impartial identification of each separate matter intended to be acted on and the soliciting person's recommendations regarding those matters, but no supporting statements;

(4) A list of the materials being made available at the specified Web site;

(5) A toll-free telephone number, an e-mail address, and an Internet Web site where the security holder can request a copy of the proxy statement, annual report to security holders, and form of proxy, relating to all of the registrant's future security holder meetings and for the particular meeting to which the proxy materials being furnished relate;

(6) Any control/identification numbers that the security holder needs to access his or her form of proxy;

(7) Instructions on how to access the form of proxy, provided that such instructions do not enable a security holder to execute a proxy without having access to the proxy statement and, if required by § 240.14a-3(b), the annual report to security holders; and

(8) Information on how to obtain directions to be able to attend the meeting and vote in person.

(e)(1) The Notice of Internet Availability of Proxy Materials may not be incorporated into, or combined with, another document, except that it may be incorporated into, or combined with, a notice of security holder meeting required under state law, unless state law prohibits such incorporation or combination.

(2) The Notice of Internet Availability of Proxy Materials may contain only the information required by paragraph (d) of this section and any additional information required to be included in a notice of security holders meeting under state law; provided that:

(i) The registrant must revise the information on the Notice of Internet Availability of Proxy Materials, including any title to the document, to reflect the fact that:

(A) The registrant is conducting a consent solicitation rather than a proxy solicitation; or

(B) The registrant is not soliciting proxy or consent authority, but is furnishing an information statement pursuant to § 240.14c-2; and

(ii) The registrant may include a statement on the Notice to educate security holders that no personal information other than the identification or control number is necessary to execute a proxy.

(f)(1) Except as provided in paragraph (h) of this section, the Notice of Internet Availability of Proxy Materials must be sent separately from other types of security holder communications and may not accompany any other document or materials, including the form of proxy.

(2) Notwithstanding paragraph (f)(1) of this section, the registrant may accompany the Notice of Internet Availability of Proxy Materials with:

(i) A pre-addressed, postage-paid reply card for requesting a copy of the proxy materials; and

(ii) A copy of any notice of security holder meeting required under state law if that notice is not combined with the Notice of Internet Availability of Proxy Materials.

(g) *Plain English.*

(1) To enhance the readability of the Notice of Internet Availability of Proxy Materials, the registrant must use plain English principles in the organization, language, and design of the notice.

(2) The registrant must draft the language in the Notice of Internet Availability of Proxy Materials so that, at a minimum, it substantially complies with each of the following plain English writing principles:

(i) Short sentences;

(ii) Definite, concrete, everyday words;

(iii) Active voice;

(iv) Tabular presentation or bullet lists for complex material, whenever possible;

(v) No legal jargon or highly technical business terms; and

(vi) No multiple negatives.

(3) In designing the Notice of Internet Availability of Proxy Materials, the registrant may include pictures, logos, or similar design elements so long as the design is not misleading and the required information is clear.

(h) The registrant may, at its discretion, choose to furnish some proxy materials pursuant to § 240.14a-3(a)(1) and other proxy materials pursuant to this section, provided that the registrant may not send a form of proxy to security holders until 10 calendar days or more after the date it sent the Notice of Internet Availability of Proxy Materials to security holders, unless the form of proxy is accompanied or has been preceded by a copy of the proxy statement and any annual report to security holders that is required by § 240.14a-3(b) through the same delivery medium. If the registrant sends a form of proxy after the expiration of such 10-day period and the form of proxy is not accompanied or preceded by a copy, via the same medium, of the proxy statement and any annual report to security holders that is required by § 240.14a-3(b), then the registrant shall accompany the form of proxy with a Notice of Internet Availability of Proxy Materials.

(i) The registrant must file a form of the Notice of Internet Availability of Proxy Materials with the Commission pursuant to § 240.14a-6(b) no later than the date that the registrant first sends the notice to security holders.

(j) *Obligation to provide copies.*

(1) The registrant must send, at no cost to the record holder or respondent bank and by U.S. first class mail or other reasonably prompt means, a paper copy of the proxy statement, information statement, annual report to security holders, and form of proxy (to the extent each of those documents is applicable) to any record holder or respondent bank requesting such a copy within three business days after receiving a request for a paper copy.

(2) The registrant must send, at no cost to the record holder or respondent bank and via e-mail, an electronic copy of the proxy statement, information statement, annual report to security holders, and form of proxy (to the extent each of those documents is applicable) to any record holder or respondent bank requesting such a copy within three business days after receiving a request for an electronic copy via e-mail.

(3) The registrant is required to provide copies of the proxy materials pursuant to paragraphs (j)(1) and (j)(2) for one year after the conclusion of the meeting or corporate action to which the proxy materials relate.

(4) The registrant must maintain records of security holder requests to receive materials in paper or via e-mail for future solicitations and must continue to provide copies of the materials to a security holder who has made such a request until the security holder revokes such request.

(k) *Security holder information.*

(1) A registrant or its agent shall maintain the Internet Web site on which it posts its proxy materials in a manner that does not infringe on the anonymity of a person accessing such Web site.

(2) The registrant and its agents shall not use any e-mail address obtained from a security holder solely for the purpose of requesting a copy of proxy materials pursuant to paragraph (j) for any purpose other than to send a copy of those materials to that security holder. The registrant shall not disclose such information to any person other than an employee or agent to the extent necessary to send a copy of the proxy materials pursuant to paragraph (j).

(l) A person other than the registrant may solicit proxies pursuant to the conditions imposed on registrants by this section, provided that:

(1) A soliciting person other than the registrant is required to provide copies of its proxy materials only to security holders to whom it has sent a Notice of Internet Availability of Proxy Materials; and

(2)A soliciting person other than the registrant must send its Notice of Internet Availability of Proxy Materials by the later of:

(i) 40 calendar days prior to the security holder meeting date or, if no meeting is to be held, 40 calendar days prior to the date the votes, consents, or authorizations may be used to effect the corporate action; or

(ii) 10 calendar days after the date that the registrant first send its proxy statement or Notice of Internet Availability of Proxy Materials to security holders.

(3) *Content of the soliciting person's Notice of Internet Availability of Proxy Materials.*

(i) If, at the time a soliciting person other than the registrant sends its Notice of Internet Availability of Proxy Materials, the soliciting person is not aware of all matters on the registrant's agenda for the meeting of security holders, the soliciting person's Notice on Internet Availability of Proxy Materials must provide a clear and impartial identification of each separate matter on the agenda to the extent known by the soliciting person at that time. The soliciting person's notice also must include a clear statement indicating that there may be additional agenda items of which the soliciting person is not aware and that the security holder cannot direct a vote for those items on the soliciting person's proxy card provided at that time.

(ii) If a soliciting person other than the registrant sends a form of proxy not containing all matters intended to be acted upon, the Notice of Internet Availability of Proxy Materials must clearly state whether execution of the form of proxy will invalidate a security holder's prior vote on matters not presented on the form of proxy.

(m) This section shall not apply to a proxy solicitation in connection with a business combination transaction, as defined in § 230.165 of this chapter.

(n) This section provides a non-exclusive alternative by which an issuer or other person may furnish a proxy statement pursuant to § 240.14a-3(a) or an annual report to security holders pursuant to § 240.14a-3(b) to a security holder. This section does not affect the availability of any other means by which an issuer or other person may furnish a proxy statement pursuant to § 240.14a-3(a), or an annual report to security holders pursuant to § 240.14a-3(b), to a security holder.

10. Amend § 240.14a-101 by:

a. Revising the term "annual report" to read "annual report on Form 10-K or Form 10-KSB" in Instruction 1 to paragraph (d)(2)(ii)(L) of Item 7;

b. Revising the word "mail" to read "send" in Instruction 2 to paragraph (d)(2)(ii)(L) of Item 7; and

c. Revising Item 23.

The revision reads as follows.

§ 240.14a-101 Schedule 14A. Information required in proxy statement.

* * * * *

Item 23. Delivery of documents to security holders sharing an address. If one annual report to security holders, proxy statement, or Notice of Internet Availability of Proxy Materials is being delivered to two or more security holders who share an address in accordance with § 240.14a-3(e)(1), furnish the following information:

(a) State that only one annual report to security holders, proxy statement, or Notice of Internet Availability of Proxy Materials, as applicable, is being delivered to multiple security holders sharing an address unless the registrant has received contrary instructions from one or more of the security holders;

(b) Undertake to deliver promptly upon written or oral request a separate copy of the annual report to security holders, proxy statement, or Notice of Internet Availability of Proxy Materials, as applicable, to a security holder at a shared address to which a single copy of the documents was delivered and provide instructions as to how a security holder can notify the registrant that the security holder wishes to receive a separate copy of an annual report to security holders, proxy statement, or Notice of Internet Availability of Proxy Materials, as applicable;

(c) Provide the phone number and mailing address to which a security holder can direct a notification to the registrant that the security holder wishes to receive a separate annual report to security holders, proxy statement, or Notice of Internet Availability of Proxy Materials, as applicable, in the future; and

(d) Provide instructions how security holders sharing an address can request delivery of a single copy of annual reports to security holders, proxy statements, or Notices of Internet Availability of Proxy Materials if they are receiving multiple copies of annual reports to security holders, proxy statements, or Notices of Internet Availability of Proxy Materials.

11. Amend § 240.14b-1 by:

a. Revising paragraphs (b)(2) including the Note and (c)(2)(i);

b. Revising the term "annual reports" to read "annual reports to security holders" in paragraphs (c)(2)(ii) and (c)(3);

c. Revising the term "annual report" to read "annual report to security holders" in paragraph (c)(2)(ii);

d. Revising the word "mail" to read "send" in paragraph (c)(2)(ii); and

e. Adding paragraphs (d) and (e).

The revisions and additions read as follows:

§ 240.14b-1 Obligation of registered brokers and dealers in connection with the prompt forwarding of certain communications to beneficial owners.

(b) * * *

(2) The broker or dealer shall, upon receipt of the proxy, other proxy soliciting material, information statement, and/or annual report to security holders from the registrant or other soliciting person, forward such materials to its customers who are beneficial owners of the registrant's securities no later than five business days after receipt of the proxy material, information statement or annual report to security holders.

Note to Paragraph (b)(2): At the request of a registrant, or on its own initiative so long as the registrant does not object, a broker or dealer may, but is not required to, deliver one annual report to security holders, proxy statement, information statement, or Notice of Internet Availability of Proxy Materials to more than one beneficial owner sharing an address if the requirements set forth in § 240.14a-3(e)(1) (with respect to annual reports to security holders, proxy statements, and Notices of Internet Availability of Proxy Materials) and § 240.14c-3(c) (with respect to annual reports to security holders, information statements, and Notices of Internet Availability of Proxy Materials) applicable to registrants, with the exception of § 240.14a-3(e)(1)(i)(E), are satisfied instead by the broker or dealer.

(c) * * *

(2) * * *

(i) Its obligations under paragraphs (b)(2), (b)(3) and (d) of this section if the registrant or other soliciting person, as applicable, does not provide assurance of reimbursement of the broker's or dealer's reasonable expenses, both direct and indirect, incurred in connection with performing the obligations imposed by paragraphs (b)(2), (b)(3) and (d) of this section; or

* * * * *

(d) *Compliance with § 240.14a-16.* If a registrant or other soliciting person informs the broker or dealer that it intends to rely on § 240.14a-16 to furnish proxy materials to beneficial owners and provides all of the relevant information listed in § 240.14a-16(d) to the broker or dealer, the broker or dealer shall:

(1) Prepare and send a Notice of Internet Availability of Proxy Materials containing the information required in paragraph (e) of this section to beneficial owners no later than:

(i) With respect to a registrant, 40 calendar days prior to the security holder meeting date or, if no meeting is to be held, 40 calendar days prior to the date the votes, consents, or authorizations may be used to effect the corporate action; and

(ii) With respect to a soliciting person other than the registrant, the later of:

(A) 40 calendar days prior to the security holder meeting date or, if no meeting is to be held, 40 calendar days prior to the date the votes, consents, or authorizations may be used to effect the corporate action; or

(B) 10 calendar days after the date that the registrant first sends its proxy statement or Notice of Internet Availability of Proxy Materials to security holders.

(2) Establish a Web site at which beneficial owners are able to access the broker or dealer's request for voting instructions and, at the broker or dealer's option, establish a Web site at which beneficial owners are able to access the proxy statement and other soliciting materials, provided that such Web sites are maintained in a manner consistent with paragraphs (b), (c), and (k) of § 240.14a-16;

(3) Upon receipt of a request from the registrant or other soliciting person, send to security holders specified by the registrant or other soliciting person a copy of the request for voting instructions accompanied by a copy of the intermediary's Notice of Internet Availability of Proxy Materials 10 calendar days or more after the broker or dealer sends its Notice of Internet Availability of Proxy Materials pursuant to paragraph (d)(1); and

(4) Upon receipt of a request for a copy of the materials from a beneficial owner:

(i) Request a copy of the soliciting materials from the registrant or other soliciting person, in the form requested by the beneficial owner, within three business days after receiving the beneficial owner's request;

(ii) Forward a copy of the soliciting materials to the beneficial owner, in the form requested by the beneficial owner, within three business days after receiving the materials from the registrant or other soliciting person; and

(iii) Maintain records of security holder requests to receive a paper or e-mail copy of the proxy materials in connection with future proxy solicitations and provide copies of the proxy materials to a security holder who has made such a request for all securities held in the account of that security holder until the security holder revokes such request.

(e) *Content of Notice of Internet Availability of Proxy Materials.* The broker or dealer's Notice of Internet Availability of Proxy Materials shall:

(1) Include all information, as it relates to beneficial owners, required in a registrant's Notice of Internet Availability of Proxy Materials under § 240.14a-16(d), provided that

the broker or dealer shall provide its own, or its agent's, toll-free telephone number, an e-mail address, and an Internet Web site to service requests for copies from beneficial owners;

(2) Include a brief description, if applicable, of the rules that permit the broker or dealer to vote the securities if the beneficial owner does not return his or her voting instructions; and

(3) Otherwise be prepared and sent in a manner consistent with paragraphs (e), (f), and (g) of § 240.14a-16.

12. Amend § 240.14b-2 by:

a. Revising the introductory text of paragraph (b)(3), the Note to paragraph (b)(3), and paragraph (c)(2)(i);

b. Revising the term "annual reports" to read "annual reports to security holders" in paragraph (c)(2)(ii) and (c)(4);

c. Revising the term "annual report" to read "annual report to security holders" in paragraph (c)(2)(ii);

d. Revising the word "mail" to read "send" in paragraph (c)(2)(ii); and

e. Adding paragraphs (d) and (e).

The additions and revisions read as follows:

§ 240.14b-2 Obligation of banks, associations and other entities that exercise fiduciary powers in connection with the prompt forwarding of certain communications to beneficial owners.

* * * * *

(b) * * *

(3) Upon receipt of the proxy, other proxy soliciting material, information statement, and/or annual report to security holders from the registrant or other soliciting person, the bank shall forward such materials to each beneficial owner on whose behalf it holds securities, no later than five business days after the date it receives such material and, where a proxy is solicited, the bank shall forward, with the other proxy soliciting material and/or the annual report to security holders, either:

* * * * *

Note to Paragraph (b)(3): At the request of a registrant, or on its own initiative so long as the registrant does not object, a bank may, but is not required to, deliver one annual report to security holders, proxy statement, information statement, or Notice of Internet Availability of Proxy Materials to more than one beneficial owner sharing an address if the requirements set forth in § 240.14a-3(e)(1) (with respect to annual reports to security holders, proxy statements, and Notices of Internet Availability of Proxy Materials) and § 240.14c-3(c) (with respect to annual reports to security holders, information statements, and Notices of Internet Availability of Proxy Materials) applicable to registrants, with the exception of § 240.14a-3(e)(1)(i)(E), are satisfied instead by the bank.

* * * * *

(c) * * *

(2) * * *

(i) Its obligations under paragraphs (b)(2), (b)(3), (b)(4) and (d) of this section if the registrant or other soliciting person, as applicable, does not provide assurance of reimbursement of its reasonable expenses, both direct and indirect, incurred in connection with performing the obligations imposed by paragraphs (b)(2), (b)(3), (b)(4) and (d) of this section; or

* * * * *

(d) *Compliance with § 240.14a-16.* If a registrant or other soliciting person informs the bank that it intends to rely on § 240.14a-16 to furnish proxy materials to beneficial owners and provides all of the relevant information listed in § 240.14a-16(d) to the bank, the bank shall:

(1) Prepare and send a Notice of Internet Availability of Proxy Materials containing the information required in paragraph (e) of this section to beneficial owners no later than:

(i) With respect to a registrant, 40 calendar days prior to the security holder meeting date or, if no meeting is to be held, 40 calendar days prior to the date the votes, consents, or authorizations may be used to effect the corporate action; and

(ii) With respect to a soliciting person other than the registrant, the later of:

(A) 40 calendar days prior to the security holder meeting date or, if no meeting is to be held, 40 calendar days prior to the date the votes, consents, or authorizations may be used to effect the corporate action; or

(B) 10 calendar days after the date that the registrant first sends its proxy statement or Notice of Internet Availability of Proxy Materials to security holders.

(2) Establish a Web site at which beneficial owners are able to access the bank's request for voting instructions and, at the bank's option, establish a Web site at which beneficial owners are able to access the proxy statement and other soliciting materials, provided that such Web sites are maintained in a manner consistent with paragraphs (b), (c), and (k) of § 240.14a-16;

(3) Upon receipt of a request from the registrant or other soliciting person, send to security holders specified by the registrant or other soliciting person a copy of the request for voting instructions accompanied by a copy of the intermediary's Notice of Internet Availability of Proxy Materials 10 days or more after the bank sends its Notice of Internet Availability of Proxy Materials pursuant to paragraph (d)(1); and

(4) Upon receipt of a request for a copy of the materials from a beneficial owner:

(i) Request a copy of the soliciting materials from the registrant or other soliciting person, in the form requested by the beneficial owner, within three business days after receiving the beneficial owner's request;

(ii) Forward a copy of the soliciting materials to the beneficial owner, in the form requested by the beneficial owner, within three business days after receiving the materials from the registrant or other soliciting person; and

(iii) Maintain records of security holder requests to receive a paper or e-mail copy of the proxy materials in connection with future proxy solicitations and provide copies of the proxy materials to a security holder who has made such a request for all securities held in the account of that security holder until the security holder revokes such request.

(e) *Content of Notice of Internet Availability of Proxy Materials.* The bank's Notice of Internet Availability of Proxy Materials shall:

(1) Include all information, as it relates to beneficial owners, required in a registrant's Notice of Internet Availability of Proxy Materials under § 240.14a-16(d), provided that the bank shall provide its own, or its agent's, toll-free telephone number, e-mail address, and Internet Web site to service requests for copies from beneficial owners; and

(2) Otherwise be prepared and sent in a manner consistent with paragraphs (e), (f), and (g) of § 240.14a-16.

13. Amend § 240.14c-2 by:

a. Revising paragraph (a); and

b. Adding paragraph (d).

The revision and addition read as follows:

§ 240.14c-2 Distribution of information statement.

(a)(1) In connection with every annual or other meeting of the holders of the class of securities registered pursuant to section 12 of the Act or of a class of securities issued by an investment company registered under the Investment Company Act of 1940 that has made a public offering of securities, including the taking of corporate action by the written authorization or consent of security holders, the registrant shall transmit to every security holder of the class that is entitled to vote or give an authorization or consent in regard to any matter to be acted upon and from whom proxy authorization or consent is not solicited on behalf of the registrant pursuant to section 14(a) of the Act:

(i) A written information statement containing the information specified in Schedule 14C (§ 240.14c-101);

(ii) A publicly-filed information statement, in the form and manner described in § 240.14c-3(d), containing the information specified in Schedule 14C (§ 240.14c-101); or

(iii) A written information statement included in a registration statement filed under the Securities Act of 1933 on Form S-4 or F-4 (§ 239.25 or § 239.34 of this chapter) or Form N-14 (§ 239.23 of this chapter) and containing the information specified in such Form.

(2) Notwithstanding paragraph (a)(1) of this section:

(i) In the case of a class of securities in unregistered or bearer form, such statements need to be transmitted only to those security holders whose names are known to the registrant; and

(ii) No such statements need to be transmitted to a security holder if a registrant would be excused from delivery of an annual report to security holders or a proxy statement under § 240.14a-3(e)(2) if such section were applicable.

* * * * *

(d) A registrant may transmit an information statement to security holders pursuant to paragraph (a) of this section by satisfying the requirements set forth in § 240.14a-16; provided, however, that the registrant may revise the information required in the Notice of Internet Availability of Proxy Materials to reflect the fact that the registrant is not soliciting proxies for the meeting. This paragraph (d) provides a non-exclusive alternative by which a registrant may transmit an information statement pursuant to paragraph (a) of this section to a security holder. This paragraph (d) does not affect the availability of any other means by which a registrant may transmit an information statement pursuant to paragraph (a) of this section to a security holder.

14. Amend § 240.14c-3 by:

a. Removing the authority citation following this section;

b. Revising paragraphs (a)(1) and (c); and

c. Adding paragraph (d).

The revisions and addition read as follows:

§ 240.14c-3 Annual report to be furnished security holders.

(a) * * *

(1) The annual report to security holders shall contain the information specified in paragraphs (b)(1) through (b)(11) of § 240.14a-3.

* * * * *

(c) A registrant will be considered to have delivered a Notice of Internet Availability of Proxy Materials, annual report to security holders or information statement to security holders of record who share an address if the requirements set forth in § 240.14a-3(e)(1) are satisfied with respect to the Notice of Internet Availability of Proxy Materials, annual report to security holders or information statement, as applicable.

(d) A registrant may furnish an annual report to security holders pursuant to paragraph (a) of this section by satisfying the requirements set forth in § 240.14a-16. This paragraph (d) provides a non-exclusive alternative by which a registrant may furnish an annual report pursuant to paragraph (a) of this section to a security holder. This paragraph (d) does not affect the availability of any other means by which a registrant may furnish an annual report pursuant to paragraph (a) of this section to a security holder.

15. Amend § 240.14c-5 by revising the word "mailed" to read "sent" in the second sentence of the introductory text of paragraph (a).

16. Amend § 240.14c-7 by revising paragraph (a)(5) before the Note and the word "mail" to read "send" in Note 2 following paragraph (a).

The revision reads as follows:

§ 240.14c-7 Providing copies of material for certain beneficial owners.

(a) * * *

(5) Upon the request of any record holder or respondent bank that is supplied with Notices of Internet Availability of Proxy Materials, information statements and/or annual reports to security holders pursuant to paragraph (a)(3) of this section, pay its reasonable expenses for completing the sending of such material to beneficial owners.

* * * * *

17. Amend § 240.14c-101 by:

a. Revising the word "mailing" to read "sending" in Item 4, Instruction 1; and

b. Revising Item 5.

The revision reads as follows.

§ 240.14c-101 Schedule 14C. Information required in information statement.

* * * * *

Item 5. Delivery of documents to security holders sharing an address. If one annual report to security holders, information statement, or Notice of Internet Availability of Proxy Materials is being delivered to two or more security holders who share an address, furnish the following information in accordance with § 240.14a-3(e)(1):

(a) State that only one annual report to security holders, information statement, or Notice of Internet Availability of Proxy Materials, as applicable, is being delivered to multiple security holders sharing an address unless the registrant has received contrary instructions from one or more of the security holders;

(b) Undertake to deliver promptly upon written or oral request a separate copy of the annual report to security holders, information statement, or Notice of Internet Availability of Proxy Materials, as applicable, to a security holder at a shared address to which a single copy of the documents was delivered and provide instructions as to how a security holder can notify the registrant that the security holder wishes to receive a separate copy of an annual report to security holders, information statement, or Notice of Internet Availability of Proxy Materials, as applicable;

(c) Provide the phone number and mailing address to which a security holder can direct a notification to the registrant that the security holder wishes to receive a separate annual report to security holders, information statement, or Notice of Internet Availability of Proxy Materials, as applicable, in the future; and

(d) Provide instructions how security holders sharing an address can request delivery of a single copy of annual reports to security holders, information statements, or Notices of Internet Availability of Proxy Materials if they are receiving multiple copies of annual reports to security holders, information statements, or Notices of Internet Availability of Proxy Materials.

PART 249—FORMS, SECURITIES EXCHANGE ACT OF 1934

18. The general authority citation for Part 249 is revised to read as follows:

Authority: 15 U.S.C. 78a *et seq.*, 7202, 7233, 7241, 7262, 7264, and 7265; and 18 U.S.C. 1350, unless otherwise noted.

* * * * *

19. Amend Item 4 to "Part II—Other Information" of Form 10-Q (referenced in § 249.308a) by revising paragraph (d) to read as follows:

Note: The text of Form 10-Q does not, and this amendment will not, appear in the Code of Federal Regulations.

Form 10-Q

* * * * *

Part II—Other Information

* * * * *

Item 4. Submission of Matters to a Vote of Security Holders.

* * * * *

(d) A description of the terms of any settlement between the registrant and any other participant (as defined in Instruction 3 to Item 4 of Schedule 14A (§ 240.14a-101)) terminating any solicitation subject to § 240.14a-12(c), including the cost or anticipated cost to the registrant.

* * * * *

20. Amend Item 4 to "Part II—Other Information" of Form 10-QSB (referenced in § 249.308b) by revising paragraph (d) to read as follows:

Note: The text of Form 10-QSB does not, and this amendment will not, appear in the Code of Federal Regulations.

Form 10-QSB

* * * * *

Part II—Other Information

* * * * *

Item 4. Submission of Matters to a Vote of Security Holders.

* * * * *

(d) A description of the terms of any settlement between the registrant and any other participant (as defined in Instruction 3 to Item 4 of Schedule 14A (§ 240.14a-101)) terminating any solicitation subject to § 240.14a-12(c), including the cost or anticipated cost to the registrant.

* * * * *

21. Amend Item 4 to Part I of Form 10-K (referenced in § 249.310) by revising paragraph (d) to read as follows:

Note: The text of Form 10-K does not, and this amendment will not, appear in the Code of Federal Regulations.

Form 10-K

* * * * *

Part I

* * * * *

Item 4. Submission of Matters to a Vote of Security Holders.

* * * * *

(d) A description of the terms of any settlement between the registrant and any other participant (as defined in Instruction 3 to Item 4 of Schedule 14A (§ 240.14a-101)) terminating any solicitation subject to § 240.14a-12(c), including the cost or anticipated cost to the registrant.

* * * * *

22. Amend Item 4 to Part I of Form 10-KSB (referenced in § 249.310b) by revise paragraph (d) to read as follows:

Note: The text of Form 10-KSB does not, and this amendment will not, appear in the Code of Federal Regulations.

Form 10-KSB

* * * * *

Part I

* * * * *

Item 4. Submission of Matters to a Vote of Security Holders.

* * * * *

(d) A description of the terms of any settlement between the registrant and any other participant (as defined in Instruction 3 to Item 4 of Schedule 14A (§ 240.14a-101)) terminating any solicitation subject to § 240.14a-12(c), including the cost or anticipated cost to the registrant.

* * * * *

PART 274—FORMS PRESCRIBED UNDER THE INVESTMENT COMPANY ACT OF 1940

23. The authority citation for Part 274 continues to read, in part, as follows:

Authority: 15 U.S.C. 77f, 77g, 77h, 77j, 77s, 78c(b), 78*l*, 78m, 78n, 78*o*(d), 80a-8, 80a-24, 80a-26, and 80a-29, unless otherwise noted.

* * * * *

24. Amend Sub-Item 77C to "Instructions to Specific Items" of Form N-SAR (referenced in §§ 249.330 and 274.101) by revising paragraph (d) to read as follows:

Note: The text of Form N-SAR does not, and this amendment will not, appear in the Code of Federal Regulations.

Form N-SAR

* * * * *

Instructions to Specific Items

* * * * *

SUB-ITEM 77C: Submission of matters to a vote of security holders

(d) Describe the terms of any settlement between the registrant and any other participant (as defined in Instruction 3 to Item 4 of Schedule 14A (§ 240.14a-101)) terminating any solicitation subject to § 240.14a-12(c), including the cost or anticipated cost to the registrant.

* * * * *

SECURITIES AND EXCHANGE COMMISSION

17 CFR PARTS 200, 239 and 240

[RELEASE NOS. 34-55146A; IC-27671A; 34-56135A; IC-27911A; 33-7759A; 33-7760A; 34-42054A; 34-42055A; 39-2378A; IC-24107A; IS-1208A; FILE NOS. S7-10-05; S7-03-07; S7-28-98 and S7-29-98]

RIN 3235-AJ47; 3235-AG84 and 3235-AD97

INTERNET AVAILABILITY OF PROXY MATERIALS; REGULATION OF TAKEOVERS AND SECURITY HOLDER COMMUNICATIONS; CROSS-BORDER TENDER AND EXCHANGE OFFERS, BUSINESS COMBINATIONS AND RIGHTS OFFERINGS; CERTAIN OTHER RELATED RULE CORRECTIONS

AGENCY: Securities and Exchange Commission.

ACTION: Final rule; technical amendments.

SUMMARY: This release contains technical amendments to Rule 14a-3(a)(3)(i), which was published in the Federal Register of Wednesday, August 1, 2007 (72 FR 42221), and Rule 14a-16(m), which was published in the Federal Register of Monday, January 29, 2007 (72 FR 4147). The rules do not permit, or require, the use of the notice and access model regarding internet availability of proxy materials with respect to business combination transactions. We are also making technical amendments to Rules 14b-1 and 14b-2, which were published in the Federal Register of Wednesday, August 1, 2007 (72 FR 42221), to correct references in those rules. Further, we are making technical corrections to rules that were modified in Release Nos. 33-7759 and 33-7760, which were published in the Federal Register on November 10, 1999 (64 FR 61382 and 64 FR 61408, respectively). The amended rules revised the rules and regulations applicable to takeover transactions, including tender offers, mergers, acquisitions and similar extraordinary transactions, and, in order to facilitate U.S. investor participation, modified the rules relating to crossborder tender and exchange offers, business combinations and rights offerings relating to the securities of foreign private issuers. This document corrects certain cross-references in the regulatory text of the adopting releases, removes a reference to an inapplicable statute, otherwise corrects certain typographical errors, updates the contact information for the agency and amends the delegated authority of the Divisions of Corporation Finance and Market Regulation relating to issuer tender offers.

EFFECTIVE DATE: April 1, 2008.

FOR FURTHER INFORMATION CONTACT: Celeste M. Murphy, Special Counsel, Office of Mergers and Acquisitions at (202) 551-3440 or Ray Be, Special Counsel, Office of Rulemaking at (202) 551-3430, in the Division of Corporation Finance, U.S. Securities and Exchange Commission, 100 F Street, NE, Washington DC 20549.

SUPPLEMENTARY INFORMATION: We are amending Forms F-4, F-8, F-9, F-10, F-80 and CB under the Securities Act of 1933[187]; Rules 0-11,[188] 13e-3,[189] 13e-4,[190] 14a-2,[191] 14a3,[192] 14a-14,[193] 14a-16,[194] 14b-1,[195] 14b-2,[196] 14d-1,[197] 14d-3,[198] 14d-9,[199] and 14e-1,[200] the title to Regulation 13D,[201] and Schedules 13D,[202] 13G,[203] 13E-4F,[204] TO,[205]

---

[187] See 17 CFR 239.34, 17 CFR 239.38, 17 CFR 239.39, 17 CFR 239.40, 17 CFR 239.41, 17 CFR 239.800.
[188] 17 CFR 240.0-11.
[189] 17 CFR 240.13e-3.
[190] 17 CFR 240.13e-4.
[191] 17 CFR 240.14a-2.
[192] 17 CFR 240.14a-3.
[193] 17 CFR 240.14a-14.
[194] 17 CFR 240.14a-16.
[195] 17 CFR 240.14b-1.

[196] 17 CFR 240.14b-2
[197] 17 CFR 240.14d-1.
[198] 17 CFR 240.14d-3.
[199] 17 CFR 240.14d-9.
[200] 17 CFR 240.14e-1.
[201] 17 CFR 240.13d-1–240.13f-1.
[202] 17 CFR 240.13d-101.
[203] 17 CFR 240.13d-102.
[204] 17 CFR 240.13e-102.
[205] 17 CFR 240.14d-100.

14D-9,[206] 14D-1F[207] and 14D-9-F[208] under the Securities Exchange Act of 1934[209]; and Rules 30-1[210] and 30-3[211] of the Rules of Organization and Program Management.[212]

I. Background to Internet Availability of Proxy Materials; Correction

A. Rules 14a-3(a)(3)(i) and 14a-16(m)

On January 22, 2007, the Commission adopted,[213] among other things, new Rule 14a-16(m)[214] under the Securities Exchange Act of 1934. On July 26, 2007,[215] the Commission adopted amendments to Rule 14a-3(a)(3).[216] These rules do not permit, or require, the use of the notice and access model regarding Internet availability of proxy materials with respect to business combination transactions.

After the adoption of the rules, questions arose regarding whether the business combination transaction exclusion applied to all such certain transactions, including cash mergers. Although the discussion of this provision in the adopting release makes it clear that such transactions are covered by the exclusion, the regulatory text does not state that such transactions are excluded by virtue of its failure to reference applicable rule provisions. The proposing release had an identical discrepancy.[217] Specifically, the discussion in the adopting release stated:

> As adopted, the notice and access model is not available with regard to proxy materials related to a business combination transaction, which includes transactions covered by Rule 165 under the Securities Act, *as well as transactions for cash consideration requiring disclosure under Item 14 of Schedule 14A.* (emphasis added)

However, the regulatory text as adopted describes the business combination transactions excluded from the notice and access model as those defined in Rule 165.[218]

Accordingly, the amendments set forth in this release clarify that Rules 14a3(a)(3)(i) and 14a-16(m) do not permit, or require, the use of the notice and access model with respect to business combination transactions as defined in Rule 165 under the Securities Act, as well as transactions for cash consideration requiring disclosure under Item 14 of Schedule 14A.[219] This change is a technical correction to clarify the rule as described in the original adopting release.

B. Rules 14b-1 and 14b-2

On June 20, 2007, the Commission adopted, among other things, amendments to Rules 14b-1 and 14b-2 under the Exchange Act.[220] The amendatory language in that release erroneously contained references to "Legends 1 and 2" in paragraph (d)(5)(iii)(A) of each of those rules. These references should have been to "Legends 1 and 3," consistent with the corresponding Rule 14a-16(n)(4)(i). All of these references address the legends not required in the Notice of Internet Availability of Proxy Materials. As we stated in the adopting release, the intent of this provision is to indicate that the issuer need not include the part of the prescribed legend relating to security holder requests for copies of the documents and instructions on how to request a copy of the proxy materials. The relevant

---

[206] 17 CFR 240.14d-101.

[207] 17 CFR 240.14d-102.

[208] 17 CFR 240.14d-103.

[209] 15 U.S.C. 78a *et seq.*

[210] 17 CFR 200.30-1.

[211] 17 CFR 200.30-3.

[212] This authority relates to determining the applicability of the rules relating to issuer tender offers, which used to be interpreted by the Division of Market Regulation (now the Division of Trading and Markets). For several years, issuer tender offers have been handled only by the Division of Corporation Finance.

[213] See Release No. 34-55416 (Jan. 22, 2007) [72 FR 4147].

[214] 17 CFR 240.14a-16(m).

[215] See Release No. 34-56135 (July 26, 2007) [72 FR 42221].

[216] 17 CFR 240.14a-3(a)(3).

[217] See Release No. 34-52926 (Dec. 8, 2005) [70 FR 74598].

[218] 17 CFR 230.165.

[219] 17 CFR 240.14a-101.

[220] See Release No. 34-56135 (July 26, 2007) [72 FR 42221].

legends are Legends 1 and 3, rather than Legends 1 and 2. Therefore, we are correcting those references.

II. Discussion of Corrections to Regulation of Takeovers and Security Holder Communications; Cross-Border Tender and Exchange Offers, Business Combinations and Rights Offerings; and Certain Other Related Rule Corrections

A. Cross-references to old Schedules 14D-1 and 13E-4 and related disclosure items

The amendments to Forms F-8, F-9, F-10 and F-80 under the Securities Act, Rules 0-11, 13e-4, and 14e-1 and Schedules 13D, 13G, 3E-4F and 14D-1F under the Exchange Act and Rule 30-1 under the Rules of Organization and Program Management are necessary to correct inaccurate cross-references to a disclosure schedule that is no longer in use. We adopted changes to integrate the disclosure schedules for issuer and third-party tender offers so that one disclosure schedule is applicable to both types of tender offers.[221] Those changes combined prior Schedules 13E-4 and 14D-1, the prior disclosure schedules for issuer and third-party tender offers, respectively, into a new Schedule TO. Forms F-8, F-9, F-10 and F-80 under the Securities Act, Rule 14e-1(e) and Schedules 13D, 13G and 14D-1F under the Exchange Act and Rule 30-1 under the Rules of Organization and Program Management continue to refer to former Schedule 14D-1; Rule 13e-4 and Schedule 13E-4F under the Exchange Act continue to refer to former Schedule 13E-4. We are correcting these errors by changing the references to refer to Schedule TO. Rule 0-11 continues to refer to filings made pursuant to former Schedule 14D-1. We are correcting that error by referring to filings made under Section 14(d)(1) of the Exchange Act, consistent with similar references in Rule 0-11.

For similar reasons, the amendments to Form F-4 under the Securities Act and to Rule 14e-1 under the Exchange Act are necessary to correct inaccurate cross-references to disclosure requirements that were relocated and redesignated in the Regulation M-A Adopting Rule Release. As part of our effort to integrate the disclosure regimes applicable to issuer tender offers, third-party tender offers and going-private transactions, we adopted changes to combine all of the disclosure requirements in one central location in a subpart of Regulation S-K, referred to as Regulation M-A.[222] This eliminated the need for the disclosure schedules themselves to contain disclosure requirements, as the schedules could simply refer to the comprehensive disclosure requirements located in Regulation M-A. Form F-4 under the Securities Act continues to refer to Item 9(b)(1)-(6) of Schedule 13E-3 when it should refer to Item 1015(b) of Regulation M-A. Rule 14e-1(e) under the Exchange Act continues to refer to Item 11 of former Schedule 14D-1 when it should refer to Item 12 of Schedule TO and Item 1016(a) of Regulation M-A. We are correcting these erroneous cross-references by inserting the redesignated disclosure items.

B. Repeal of the Public Utility Holding Company Act of 1935

The amendments to Rules 13e-3, 14a-2 and 14a-14 under the Exchange Act are necessary to remove references to a statute that has been repealed. Rules 13e-3 and 14a-2 contain exceptions to the applicability of the going private and proxy solicitation rules, respectively, under specified circumstances involving holding companies registered under the Public Utility Holding Company Act of 1935.[223] Rule 14a-14 refers to several statutes, including the Public Utility Holding Company Act, to direct readers of the rule to certain defined terms.[224] The Public Utility Holding Company Act of 1935

---

[221] See Regulation of Takeovers and Security Holder Communications, Release No. 33-7760 (Oct. 22, 1999) [64 FR 61408] (the "Regulation M-A Adopting Rule Release") at II.F.1.

[222] *Id.*

[223] 17 CFR 240.13e-3(g)(3) and 17 CFR 240.14a-2(a)(5).

[224] 17 CFR 240.14a-14(b).

was repealed effective February 8, 2006.[225] We are removing these references to the Public Utility Holding Company Act in these rules.

C. Typographical errors

The amendments to Rules 13e-4, 14d-1 and 14d-3 and Schedules TO and 14D-9 under the Exchange Act are necessary to correct certain typographical errors. In one instance, the rule contains a duplicate reference to "15 U.S.C." in the citation to Section 10(a) of the Securities Act.[226] In two instances, where the rule provides a definition, the term being defined "United States" is stated twice, unlike the rest of the definitions provided in the same subsection of the rules.[227] Further, in one instance, a rule contains a cross-reference to Rule 14d-6(e)(2)(i) and (ii) when the cross-reference should be to Rule 14d-6(d)(2)(i) and (ii), because subparagraph (e) does not exist and the context in which the cross-reference is being made—giving telephonic notice of the tender offer to national securities exchanges and the National Association of Securities Dealers, Inc. ("NASD")[228]—indicates that the reference should be to subparagraph (d), which discusses the information required for summary publication.[229] In two more instances, the rules similarly contain erroneous cross-references to Rule 14d-1(f) when the cross-reference should be to Rule 14d-1(h).[230] Subparagraph (h) of Rule 14d-1 discusses the requirements for signatures and was previously located under subparagraph (f) but was redesignated when we added provisions to the tender offer rules to include exemptions from Regulation 14D in certain instances in order to facilitate the participation of U.S. holders.[231] We are correcting these typographical errors by removing the duplicative references or changing the cross-reference to the correct rule, as applicable.

D. Cross-references to former Rule 10b-13

The amendments to Schedules 13E-4F and 14D-1F under the Exchange Act are necessary to correct inaccurate cross-references to a rule that was amended and redesignated. Rule 10b-13 was redesignated as Rule 14e-5.[232] Schedules 13E-4F and 14D-1F continue to refer to Rule 10b-13. We are correcting these errors by changing the references to refer to Rule 14e-5.

E. Title to Rules 13d-1 through 13d-7

The amendment to the title of Rules 13d-1 through 13d-7, which set forth the disclosure requirements for reporting beneficial ownership, is necessary to change the reference from Regulation 13D to Regulation 13D-G. We adopted changes to those rules to, among other things, add a new schedule—Schedule 13G—that sets forth the disclosure requirements for reporting beneficial ownership and related information of certain equity securities that are held by specific investors, such as institutional investors.[233] At that time, we integrated the filing requirements for all beneficial owners under Rule 13d-1, and described this as the "initial step in the adoption of an integrated ownership reporting system to be denominated as Regulation 13D-G."[234] We are amending the title to these rules to reflect our prior intentions.

F. Reduction of paper submissions of Form CB

The amendment to the instructions for submitting Form CB reduces the number of copies of paper submissions currently required under the rule from five to two. This

---

[225] 42 U.S.C. 16451 *et seq.*

[226] See Rule 13e-4(e)(2) (17 CFR 240.13e-4(e)(2)).

[227] See Instruction 3 to Rule 13e-4(h)(8) and (i) (17 CFR 240.13e-4) and Instruction 4 to Rule 14d-1(c) and (d) (17 CFR 240.14d-1).

[228] The name of NASD has been changed to the Financial Industry Regulatory Authority, Inc. ("FINRA").

[229] See Rule 14d-3(a)(3) (17 CFR 240.14d-3(a)(3)).

[230] See Instruction to Signature for Schedules TO and 14D-9.

[231] See Cross-Border Tender and Exchange Offers, Business Combinations and Rights Offerings, Release

No. 33-7759 (Oct. 22, 1999) [64 FR 61382] ("Cross-Border Release").

[232] See the Regulation M-A Adopting Rule Release at II.G.5.a.

[233] See Filing and Disclosure Requirements Relating to Beneficial Ownership, Release No. 33-5925 (April 21, 1978) [43 FR 18484].

[234] *Id.* See also Filing and Disclosure Requirements Relating to Beneficial Ownership, Release No. 34-15348 (Nov. 22, 1978) [43 FR 55751], where we also stated that "'Regulation 13D' is recaptioned Regulation 13D-G' . . . ".

change is necessary to alleviate the cost of providing a number of copies of paper submissions that we have found to be unnecessary.

G. Elimination of paper submission of amendments on Schedule 14D-9

The amendment to Rule 14d-9(c)(1) under the Exchange Act is necessary to eliminate references to paper submissions because Schedule 14D-9 and amendments thereto are now filed electronically. This is consistent with the other rules relating to tender offer filings.

H. Relocation of agency

The amendments to Forms F-8, F-9, F-10, F-80 and CB and Schedules 13E-4F, 14D1-F and 14D-9F are necessary to update the contact information for the headquarters of the agency in light of its relocation. These changes will remove and update contact information so as to facilitate communications with the agency.

I. Delegation of Authority to the Director of the Division of Corporation Finance

Finally, we are amending the Rules of Organization and Program Management governing Delegations of Authority by removing certain delegated authority from the Division of Market Regulation and transferring part of it to the Division of Corporation Finance. Specifically, the Director of the Division of Market Regulation had the authority to grant exemptions from the issuer tender offer rules and determine the applicability of the issuer tender offer rules pursuant to Exchange Act Rule 13e-4(g) to any exchange or tender offer for which an exemptive order has been granted by a Canadian federal, provincial or territorial regulatory authority. Currently, the Division of Corporation Finance administers the application of the issuer tender offer rules, so it is not necessary for the Director of the Division of Market Regulation to have this delegated authority. We are removing the authority to grant exemptions from the issuer tender offer rules from the Director of the Division of Market Regulation and transferring the authority to determine the applicability of the issuer tender offer rules to tender and exchange offers made by issuers pursuant to Exchange Act Rule 13e-4(g) from the Director of the Division of Market Regulation to the Director of the Division of Corporation Finance.[235] The staff may submit matters to the Commission for consideration as it deems appropriate.

III. Certain Findings

Under the Administrative Procedure Act, a notice of proposed rulemaking is not required "(A) [for] interpretive rules, general statements of policy, or rules of agency organization, procedure, or practice; or (B) when the agency for good cause finds (and incorporates the finding and a brief statement of reasons therefore [*sic*] in the rules issued) that notice and public procedure thereon are impracticable, unnecessary, or contrary to the public interest."[236] The correcting amendments to Forms F-4, F-8, F-9, F-10, F-80 and CB under the Securities Act and Rules 0-11, 13e-3, 13e-4, 14a-2, 14a-3, 14a-14, 14a-16, 14b-1, 14b-2, 14d-1, 14d-3, 14d-9, and 14e-1, the title to Regulation 13D, and Schedules TO, 13E-4F, 13D, 13G, 14D-9, 14D-1F and 14D-9F under the Exchange Act are technical changes that conform the regulatory text to the intent of the Commission and correct certain cross-references and typographical errors. For these reasons, the Commission finds that there is no need to publish notice of these amendments. The amendments to the instructions for submitting Form CB, the amendment to Rule 14d-9(c)(1) under the Exchange Act, and the amendments to Rules 30-1 and 30-3 under the Rules of Organization and Program Management relate to agency organization, procedure, or practice. As such, notice of proposed rulemaking is not required.

---

[235] This transfer of authority is consistent with the broader authority that was granted to the Director of the Division of Corporation Finance in Rule 30-1(e)(16)(i) to grant or deny exemptions from the tender offer provisions of Rule 13e-4 of the Exchange Act. See Cross-Border Release. Because the broader authority contained in Rule 30-1(e)(16)(i), which covers issuer and third-party tender offers, was granted after the authority in Rule 30-1(e)(13) was granted, which covered only third-party tender offers, it is appropriate to include issuer tender offers in the authority in Rule 30-1(e)(13).

[236] 5 U.S.C. 553(b).

For similar reasons, the amendments do not require an analysis under the Regulatory Flexibility Act or analysis of major status under the Small Business Regulatory Enforcement Fairness Act.[237]

The Administrative Procedures Act also requires publication of a rule at least 30 days before its effective date unless the agency finds otherwise for good cause.[238] For the same reasons described with respect to opportunity for notice and comment, the Commission finds there is good cause for the amendments to take effect on [*insert date of publication in the Federal Register*].

IV. Need for Correction

As published, certain regulations referenced in this release contain errors that may prove to be misleading and are in need of clarification.

TEXT OF AMENDMENTS

List of Subjects

17 CFR Part 200

Administrative practice and procedure; Authority delegations (Government Agencies).

17 CFR Parts 239 and 240

Reporting and recordkeeping requirements, Securities.

Text of the Adopted Rules

Accordingly, Title 17 Chapter II of the Code of Federal Regulation is corrected by making the following amendments:

PART 200—ORGANIZATION; CONDUCT AND ETHICS; AND INFORMATION AND REQUESTS

1. The authority citation for part 200, subpart A continues to read, in part, as follows:

Authority: 15 U.S.C. 77*o*, 77s, 77sss, 78d, 78d-1, 78d-2, 78w, 78*ll*(d), 78mm, 80a-37, 80b-11, and 7202, unless otherwise noted.

* * * * *

2. Amend § 200.30-1 by revising paragraph (e)(13) to read as follows:

§ 200.30-1 Delegation of authority to Director of Division of Corporation Finance.

* * * * *

(e) * * *

(13) To determine with respect to a tender or exchange offer otherwise eligible to be made pursuant to rule 13e-4(g) (§ 240.13e-4(g) of this chapter) or rule 14d-1(b) (§ 240.14d-1(b) of this chapter) whether, in light of any exemptive order granted by a Canadian federal, provincial or territorial regulatory authority, application of certain or all of the provisions of section 13(e)(1) and sections 14(d)(1) through 14(d)(7) of the Exchange Act, rule 13e-4, Regulation 14D (§§ 240.14d-1–240.14d-103 of this chapter) and Schedules TO and 14D-9 thereunder (§§ 240.14d-100 and 240.14d-101 of this chapter), and rule 14e-1 of Regulation 14E (§§ 240.14e-1–240.14f-1 of this chapter), to such offer is necessary or appropriate in the public interest.

* * * * *

---

[237] See 5 U.S.C. 601(2) (for purposes of Regulatory Flexibility Act analysis, the term "rule" means any rule for which the agency publishes a general notice of proposed rulemaking) and 5 U.S.C. 804(3)(C) (for purposes of congressional review of agency rulemaking, the term "rule" does not include any rule of agency organization, procedure, or practice that does not substantially affect the rights or obligations of non-agency parties).

[238] See 5 U.S.C. 553(d)(3).

3. Amend § 200.30-3 by removing and reserving paragraph (a)(35).

PART 239—FORMS PRESCRIBED UNDER THE SECURITIES ACT OF 1933

4. The authority citation for Part 239 continues to read, in part, as follows:

Authority: 15 U.S.C. 77f, 77g, 77h, 77j, 77s, 77z-2, 77z-3, 77sss, 78c, 78*l*, 78m, 78n, 78*o*(d), 78u-5, 78w(a), 78*ll*, 78mm, 80a-2(a), 80a-3, 80a-8, 80a-9, 80a-10, 80a-13, 80a-24, 80a-26, 80a-29, 80a-30, and 80a-37, unless otherwise noted.

* * * * *

5. Amend Form F-4 (referenced in § 239.34) paragraph (b) of Item 4 in Part I, revise the phrase "Item 9(b)(1) through (6) of Schedule 13E-3 (§ 240.13e-100 of this chapter)" to read "Item 1015(b) of Regulation M-A (§ 229.1015(b) of this chapter)".

Note: The text of Form F-4 does not, and this amendment will not, appear in the Code of Federal Regulations.

6. Amend Form F-8 (referenced in § 239.38) by:

a. In paragraph C. of General Instruction IV., second and third sentences, revise the phrase "(202) 942-8900." to read "(202) 551-8900." and revise the phrase "(202) 942-2940." to read "(202) 551-3610."; and

b. In paragraph D. of General Instruction V., first sentence, revise the phrase "Schedule 14D-1" to read "Schedule TO".

Note: The text of Form F-8 does not, and this amendment will not, appear in the Code of Federal Regulations.

7. Amend Form F-9 (referenced in § 239.39) by:

a. In paragraph D. of General Instruction II., second and third sentences, revise the phrase "(202) 942-8900." to read "(202) 551-8900." and the phrase "(202) 942-2940." to read "(202) 551-3610."; and

b. In paragraph D. of General Instruction III., first sentence, revise the phrase "Schedule 14D-1" to read "Schedule TO".

Note: The text of Form F-9 does not, and this amendment will not, appear in the Code of Federal Regulations.

8. Amend Form F-10 (referenced in § 239.40) by:

a. In paragraph D. of General Instruction II., second and third sentences, revise the phrase "(202) 942-8900." to read "(202) 551-8900." and the phrase "(202) 942-2940." to read "(202) 551-3610."; and

b. In paragraph D. of General Instruction III., first sentence, revise the phrase "Schedule 14D-1" to read "Schedule TO".

Note: The text of Form F-10 does not, and this amendment will not, appear in the Code of Federal Regulations.

9. Amend Form F-80 (referenced in § 239.41) by:

a. In paragraph C. of General Instruction IV., second and third sentences, revise the phrase "(202) 942-8900." to read "(202) 551-8900." and the phrase "(202) 942-2940." to read "(202) 551-3610."; and

b. In paragraph D. of General Instruction V., first sentence, revise the phrase "Schedule 14D-1" to read "Schedule TO".

Note: The text of Form F-80 does not, and this amendment will not, appear in the Code of Federal Regulations.

10. Amend Form CB (referenced in § 239.800) by:

a. In paragraph A.(1), General Instruction II., second and third sentences, revise the phrase "(202) 942-8900." to read "(202) 551-8900." and the phrase "(202) 942-2940." to read "(202) 551-3610.";

b. In paragraph A.(4), first sentence, revise the phrase "you must furnish five copies" to read "you must furnish two copies"; and

c. In paragraph B., second sentence, "Instructions for Submitting Form," remove the phrase "and at least one copy".

Note: The text of Form CB does not, and this amendment will not, appear in the Code of Federal Regulations.

PART 240—GENERAL RULES AND REGULATIONS; SECURITIES EXCHANGE ACT OF 1934

11. The authority citation for Part 240 continues to read, in part, as follows:

Authority: 15 U.S.C. 77c, 77d, 77g, 77j, 77s, 77z-2, 77z-3, 77eee, 77ggg, 77nnn, 77sss, 77ttt, 78c, 78d, 78e, 78f, 78g, 78i, 78j, 78j-1, 78k, 78k-1, 78*l*, 78m, 78n, 78*o*, 78p, 78q, 78s, 78u-5, 78w, 78x, 78*ll*, 78mm, 80a-20, 80a-23, 80a-29, 80a-37, 80b-3, 80b-4, 80b-11, and 7201 *et seq.*; and 18 U.S.C. 1350, unless otherwise noted.

* * * * *

12. Amend § 240.0-11 by revising:

a. The heading to paragraph (d) "*Schedule 14D-1 filings.*" to read "*Section 14(d)(1) filings.*"; and

b. In paragraph (d), first sentence, the phrase "At the time of filing a Schedule 14D-1," to read "At the time of filing such statement as the Commission may require pursuant to section 14(d)(1) of the Act,".

13. Revise the undesignated center heading "Regulation 13D" preceding § 240.13d-1 to read "Regulation 13D-G".

14. Amend § 240.13d-101, Schedule 13D, second paragraph, first sentence of the Notes that follow the *Instructions for Cover Page* by revising the cite "(Schedule 13D, 13G, or 14D-1)" in the [*sic*] to read "(Schedule 13D, 13G, or TO)" and remove the authority citations following the section.

15. Amend § 240.13d-102, Schedule 13G, second paragraph, first sentence, of the Notes that follow the *Instructions for Cover Page* by revising the phrase "(Schedule 13D, 13G or 14D-1)" to read "(Schedule 13D, 13G or TO)" and removing the authority citations following the section.

16. Amend § 240.13e-3 by removing and reserving paragraph (g)(3) and removing the authority citations following the section.

17. Amend § 240.13e-4 by:

a. In paragraph (a)(3), second sentence, revise the cite "Schedule 13E-4" to read "Schedule TO";

b. In paragraph (e)(2), first sentence, revise the cite "(15 U.S.C. (15 U.S.C. 77j(a))" to read "(15 U.S.C. 77j(a))"; and

c. Revise Instruction 3 to *Instructions to paragraph (h)(8) and (i)*.

The revision reads as follows:

§ 240.13e-4 Tender offers by issuers.

* * * * *

Instructions to paragraphs (h)(8) and (i) of this section:

* * * * *

3. *United States* means the United States of America, its territories and possessions, any State of the United States, and the District of Columbia.

* * * * *

18. Amend § 240.13e-102, Schedule 13E-4F, by:

a. Revising the phrase "(202) 942-8900." to read "(202) 551-8900." and the phrase "(202) 942-2940." to read "(202) 551-3610." in General Instruction II.A(1), second and third sentences;

b. Revising the phrase "Schedule 13E-4" to read "Schedule TO" in General Instruction III.A. each time it appears;

c. Revising the phrase "provisions of section 13(e)(1)" to read "provisions of section 13(e)(1) of the Exchange Act" in General Instruction III.A.;

d. Revising the phrase "Rule 10b-13 under the Exchange Act (§ 240.10b-13)" to read "Rule 14e-5 under the Exchange Act (§ 240.14e-5)" in General Instruction III.C., first sentence; and

e. Revising the phrase "Rule 10b-13" to read "Rule 10b-13, the predecessor to Rule 14e-5" in General Instruction III.C., second sentence.

19. Amend § 240.14a-2 by removing and reserving paragraph (a)(5).

20. Revise paragraph (a)(3)(i) of § 240.14a-3 to read as follows:

§ 240.14a-3 Information to be furnished to security holders.

(a) * * *

(3) * * *

(i) The solicitation relates to a business combination transaction as defined in § 230.165 of this chapter, as well as transactions for cash consideration requiring disclosure under Item 14 of § 240.14a-101.

* * * * *

21. Amend § 240.14a-14, paragraph (b), last sentence, by removing the phrase "the Public Utility Holding Company Act of 1935,".

22. Revise paragraph (m) of § 240.14a-16 to read as follows:

§ 240.14a-16 Internet availability of proxy materials.

* * * * *

(m) This section shall not apply to a proxy solicitation in connection with a business combination transaction, as defined in § 230.165 of this chapter, as well as transactions for cash consideration requiring disclosure under Item 14 of § 240.14a-101.

* * * * *

23. Revise paragraph (d)(5)(iii)(A) of § 240.14b-1 to read as follows:

§ 240.14b-1 Obligation of registered brokers and dealers in connection with the prompt forwarding of certain communications to beneficial owners.

* * * * *

(d) * * *

(5) * * *

(iii) * * *

(A) Legends 1 and 3 in § 240.14a-16(d)(1); and

* * * * *

24. Revise paragraph (d)(5)(iii)(A) of § 240.14b-2 to read as follows:

§ 240.14b-2 Obligation of banks, associations and other entities that exercise fiduciary powers in connection with the prompt forwarding of certain communications to beneficial owners.

* * * * *

(d) * * *

(5) * * *

(iii) * * *

(A) Legends 1 and 3 in § 240.14a-16(d)(1); and

* * * * *

25. Amend § 240.14d-1 by revising paragraph 4. of the *Instructions to paragraphs (c) and (d)* to read as follows:

§ 240.14d-1 Scope of and definitions applicable to Regulations 14D and 14E.

* * * * *

Instructions to paragraphs (c) and (d):

* * * * *

4. *United States* means the United States of America, its territories and possessions, any State of the United States, and the District of Columbia.

* * * * *

26. Amend § 240.14d-3 by revising the introductory text of paragraph (a)(3) to read as follows:

§ 240.14d-3 Filing and transmission of tender offer statement.

(a) * * *

(3) Gives telephonic notice of the information required by Rule 14d-6(d)(2)(i) and (ii) (§ 240.14d-6(d)(2)(i) and (ii)) and mails by means of first-class mail a copy of such Schedule TO, including all exhibits thereto:

* * * * *

27. Amend § 240.14d-9, paragraph (c)(1), by removing the phrase "eight copies of" and removing the citations following the section.

28. Amend § 240.14d-100, last sentence, in the *Instruction to Signature* by revising the phrase "240.14d-1(f)" to read "240.14d-1(h)".

29. Amend § 240.14d-101, last sentence in the *Instruction to Signature*, revise the phrase "See § 240.14d-1(f)" to read "See § 240.14d-1(h)".

30. Amend § 240.14d-102 Schedule 14D1-F, by:

a. Revising the phrase "(202) 942-8900." to read "(202) 551-8900." and the phrase "(202) 942-2940." to read "(202) 551-3610." in the second and third sentences of General Instruction II.A.(1);

b. Revising each phrase "Schedule 14D-1" to read "Schedule TO" in General Instruction III.A.;

c. Revising the phrase "with the provisions of sections 14(d)(1) through 14(d)(7)" to read "with the provisions of sections 14(d)(1) through 14(d)(7) of the Exchange Act," in General Instruction III.A.;

d. Revising the phrase "Rule 10b-13" to read "Rule 14e-5" in General Instruction III.C., first sentence;

e. Revising the phrase "§ 240.10b-13" to read "§ 240.14e-5" in General Instruction III.C. first sentence; and

f. Revising the phrase "Rule 10b-13" to read "Rule 10b-13, the predecessor to Rule 14e-5" in General Instruction III.C., second sentence.

* * * * *

31. Amend § 240.14d-103, second and third sentences of General Instruction II.A.(1), revise the phrase "(202) 942-8900." to read "(202) 551-8900." and the phrase "(202) 942-2940." to read "(202) 551-3610.".

32. Amend § 240.14e-1 to revise paragraph (e) to read as follows:

§ 240.14e-1 Unlawful tender offer practices.

* * * * *

(e) The periods of time required by paragraphs (a) and (b) of this section shall be tolled for any period during which the bidder has failed to file in electronic format, absent a hardship exemption (§§ 232.201 and 232.202 of this chapter), the Schedule TO Tender Offer Statement (§ 240.14d-100), any tender offer material required to be filed by Item 12 of that Schedule pursuant to paragraph (a) of Item 1016 of Regulation M-A (§ 229.1016(a) of this chapter), and any amendments thereto. If such documents were filed in paper pursuant to a hardship exemption (*see* § 232.201 and § 232.202(d)), the minimum offering periods shall be tolled for any period during which a required confirming electronic copy of such Schedule and tender offer material is delinquent.

By the Commission.

Florence E. Harmon
Deputy Secretary

Date: March 17, 2008

SECURITIES AND EXCHANGE COMMISSION

17 CFR Parts 230 and 240

[Release Nos. 33-9108; 34-61560; IC-29131; File No. S7-22-09]

RIN 3235-AK25

AMENDMENTS TO RULES REQUIRING INTERNET AVAILABILITY OF PROXY MATERIALS

AGENCY: Securities and Exchange Commission.

ACTION: Final rule.

SUMMARY: We are amending rules under the Securities Exchange Act of 1934 and the Securities Act of 1933 to clarify and provide additional flexibility regarding the format of the Notice of Internet Availability of Proxy Materials that is sent to shareholders and to permit issuers and other soliciting persons to better communicate with shareholders by including explanatory materials regarding the reasons for the use of the notice and access proxy rules and the process of receiving and reviewing proxy materials and voting pursuant to the notice and access proxy rules. The amendments also revise the timeframe for delivering a Notice to shareholders when a soliciting person other than the issuer relies on the notice and access proxy rules and permit mutual funds to accompany the Notice with a summary prospectus.

EFFECTIVE DATE: March 29, 2010.

FOR FURTHER INFORMATION CONTACT: Steven G. Hearne, Special Counsel in the Office of Rulemaking, Division of Corporation Finance, at (202) 551-3430, or with respect to registered investment companies, Sanjay Lamba, Senior Counsel, in the Office of Disclosure Regulation, Division of Investment Management, at (202) 551-6784, 100 F Street, NE, Washington, DC 20549.

SUPPLEMENTARY INFORMATION: The Commission is amending Rule 14a-16[239] under the Securities Exchange Act of 1934[240] and Rule 498[241] under the Securities Act of 1933.[242]

TABLE OF CONTENTS

---

[239] 17 CFR 240.14a-16.
[240] 15 U.S.C. 78a *et seq.*

[241] 17 CFR 230.498.
[242] 15 U.S.C. 77a *et seq.*

III.   **Paperwork Reduction Act**
IV.   **Cost-Benefit Analysis**
V.   **Consideration of Burden on Competition and Promotion of Efficiency, Competition and Capital Formation**
VI.   **Final Regulatory Flexibility Analysis**
VII. **Statutory Authority and Text of the Amendments**

I. BACKGROUND AND OVERVIEW OF THE AMENDMENTS

On October 14, 2009, we proposed amendments to the notice and access proxy rules to remove regulatory impediments that may be reducing shareholder response rates to proxy solicitations by permitting issuers and other soliciting persons to more effectively use the notice and access model.[243] These amendments were proposed based on our continuing review of the disclosures shareholders receive when they are asked to make a voting decision and the process followed when those votes are solicited.[244] As discussed in detail below, we are adopting the proposed amendments with certain modifications based on the comments received on the proposal.

We received 25 comment letters in response to the proposed amendments.[245] These letters came from corporations, professional associations, institutional investors, law firms, transfer agents, proxy service providers and other interested parties. We have reviewed and considered all of the comments that we received on the proposed amendments. Most commenters supported the use of the notice and access model and the Commission's proposed modifications to improve its implementation.[246] The adopted rules reflect changes made in response to some of these comments. We explain our revisions with respect to each proposed rule amendment in more detail throughout this release.

In 2007, the Commission established procedures that promote the use of the Internet as a reliable and cost-efficient means of making proxy materials available to shareholders.[247] The notice and access proxy rules require all issuers and other soliciting persons to post their proxy materials on an Internet Web site and provide a Notice of Internet Availability of Proxy Materials ("Notice") to shareholders. These rules also

---

[243] Amendments to Rules Requiring Internet Availability of Proxy Materials, Release No. 33-9073 (Oct. 14, 2009) [74 FR 53954] (the "Proposing Release").

[244] See, e.g., Facilitating Shareholder Director Nominations, Release No. 33-9046 (June 10, 2009) [74 FR 29024], Proxy Disclosure Enhancements, Release No. 33-9089 (Dec. 16, 2009) [74 FR 68443], and Order Approving Proposed Rule Change, as modified by Amendment No. 4, to Amend NYSE Rule 452 and Corresponding Listed Company Manual Section 402.08 to Eliminate Broker Discretionary Voting for the Election of Directors, Except for Companies Registered under the Investment Company Act of 1940, and to Codify Two Previously Published Interpretations that Do Not Permit Broker Discretionary Voting for Material Amendments to Investment Advisory Contracts with an Investment Company, Release No. 34-60215 (July 1, 2009) [74 FR 33293].

[245] See letters from American Bar Association ("ABA"), American Business Conference ("ABC"), Ameriprise Financial, Inc. ("Ameriprise"), Association of Corporate Counsel ("ACC"), The Altman Group ("Altman"), BNY Mellon Shareowner Services ("BNY"), Broadridge Financial Solutions, Inc. ("Broadridge"), Independent Steering Committee of Broadridge Investor Communications Solutions

("Broadridge Steering Committee"), California State Teachers Retirement System ("CalSTRS"), Calvert Group Limited ("Calvert"), U.S. Chamber of Commerce ("Chamber"), Computershare Limited ("Computershare"), Corporate Governance, Diversified Global Graphics Group ("DG3"), Edison International ("Edison"), Investment Company Institute ("ICI"), Intel Corporation ("Intel"), IR WebReport.com, Moxy Vote ("Moxy"), National Investor Relations Institute ("NIRI"), Otter Tail Corporation ("Otter Tail"), Registrar and Transfer Company ("R&T"), Sullivan & Cromwell ("S&C"), Society of Corporate Secretaries and Governance Professionals ("SCSGP"), and Securities Transfer Association, Inc. ("STA").

[246] See, e.g., letters from ABA, ABC, ACC, Altman, BNY, Broadridge, Broadridge Steering Committee, CalSTRS, Calvert, Chamber, Computershare, Edison, ICI, Intel, NIRI, Otter Tail, R&T, S&C, SCSGP, and STA.

[247] See Internet Availability of Proxy Material, Release No. 34-55146 (Jan. 22, 2007) [72 FR 4148] ("Internet Availability of Proxy Material Adopting Release") and Shareholder Choice Regarding Proxy Materials, Release No. 34-56135 (July 26, 2007) [72 FR 42221].

provide issuers and other soliciting persons an option as to whether to send a full set of proxy materials to all shareholders or to send shareholders only the Notice. According to Broadridge Financial Solutions, Inc. ("Broadridge"), over 1,300 corporate issuers used the notice-only option for distribution of the Notice to some portion of their beneficial owners under the notice and access model in the 2009 proxy season.[248] Commenters, including Broadridge and transfer agents who conduct the distribution to registered owners, indicated that issuers have experienced significant cost savings in printing, postage and processing fees.[249]

As we noted in the Proposing Release, while many issuers have experienced significant cost savings using the notice-only option, statistics indicate lower shareholder response rates to proxy solicitations when the notice-only option is used.[250] We are concerned that some investors may be confused when issuers and other soliciting persons distribute proxy materials using the notice-only option and we believe our rules should be amended to provide additional flexibility for issuers and other soliciting persons to better communicate with shareholders to reduce that confusion.

We are adopting amendments today to provide issuers and other soliciting persons with additional flexibility to provide to shareholders a more effective explanation of the importance and effect of the Notice and the reasons for its use, which should better facilitate use of our rules and improve investor understanding. Specifically, the amendments provide additional flexibility regarding the format and content of the Notice, permit issuers and other soliciting persons to better communicate with shareholders by including explanatory materials regarding the reasons for the use of the notice and access rules and the process of receiving and reviewing proxy materials and voting, and revise the timeframe for delivering a Notice to shareholders when a soliciting person other than the issuer relies on the notice-only option.

II. DISCUSSION OF THE AMENDMENTS

A. Revisions to the Notice Requirements and Inclusion of Explanatory Materials

We proposed amendments to Exchange Act Rule 14a-16 to provide issuers and other soliciting persons with additional flexibility to develop a more effective Notice and to provide shareholders with guidance as to how to access the proxy materials online, request a paper copy of the proxy materials, and vote their shares. We are adopting the amendments generally as proposed with some changes as recommended by commenters.

1. Proposed Amendments

Under the amendments we proposed, issuers and other soliciting persons would have additional flexibility in formatting and selecting the language to be used in the Notice. Rather than requiring the soliciting person to include a detailed legend that may seem like boilerplate language to shareholders, we proposed to require that the information appearing on the Notice address certain topics, without specifying the exact language to

---

[248] *See* Broadridge Notice & Access, Statistical Overview of Use with Beneficial Shareholders (as of June 30, 2009) attached to the letter from Broadridge ("Broadridge Statistical Overview"). Broadridge is the largest provider of brokerage processing services with respect to beneficial owners holding through a broker or similar intermediary and has provided detailed statistical information on the use of the notice and access model. The Broadridge Statistical Overview is generally limited to comparisons between issuers that have used the notice-only option for distribution to *some portion* of their beneficial owners and issuers that *exclusively* used the full set delivery option and com-

parisons between the first and second years of use of the notice-only option. The data does not provide a comparison to an issuer's experience in the year prior to using the notice-only option for distribution.

[249] *See, e.g.,* letters from Broadridge, BNY, and R&T. Some commenters noted that processing fees were reduced on distributions to registered owners, but expressed concern about the processing fees charged by service providers for distributions to beneficial owners. *See, e.g.,* letters from Altman, BNY, ICI, NIRI, Otter Tail, R&T, and STA.

[250] *See* notes 18–20 of the Proposing Release.

be used.[251] Further, in order to mitigate confusion about the Notice and to allow issuers and other soliciting persons to better engage shareholders, we proposed to revise Exchange Act Rule 14a-16(f)(2)[252] to permit issuers and other soliciting persons to accompany the Notice with an explanation of the notice and access model, which would be limited to an explanation of the process of receiving and reviewing the proxy materials and voting. Materials designed to persuade shareholders to vote in a particular manner, change the method of delivery of proxy materials, or explain why the person was sending only a Notice to shareholders would not be permitted under the proposed amendments.

2. Comments on the Proposed Amendments

Most commenters supported the additional flexibility provided by the proposed amendments to design and prepare the Notice and provide explanatory materials, and many of these commenters offered additional suggestions for improving the proposals.[253] Several commenters recommended that the design and wording of the Notice should be required to clearly indicate that the Notice is not a proxy card and may not be voted.[254] Other commenters supported a uniform and easily recognizable design for the Notice,[255] requiring intermediaries to forward the Notice in issuer provided envelopes,[256] or requiring that the Notice identify proxy items by topic rather than specific proposals.[257]

Several commenters supported more flexibility than we had proposed for the explanatory materials, such as permitting an issuer to explain the reasons for its use of the notice-only option.[258] Commenters suggested that an issuer's rationale for using the notice-only option would enhance shareholders' understanding of the reasons for receiving the Notice, inform investors of the benefits of using the notice-only option and help to distinguish the Notice from the proxy card, without influencing a shareholder's voting decision.[259] One commenter supported additionally requiring that intermediaries be required to pass explanatory materials on to beneficial owners.[260]

Finally, one commenter noted that if the Commission approved the proposed amendments to the Notice requirements, a technical change is necessary to Exchange Act Rule 14a-16(n).[261] Rule 14a-16(n) addresses the notice and access requirements when an issuer or other soliciting person sends a full set of proxy materials to security holders. The suggested technical change related to references in Rule 14a-16(n)(4) to the disclosure requirements of the Notice in Exchange Act Rule 14a-16(d). Since the proposed amendments revise the disclosure requirements of Rule 14a-16(d), conforming changes should also be made to 14a-16(n)(4).

3. Final Rule

After considering the comments, we are adopting the amendments to our requirements regarding the Notice and the rules about what materials may accompany the initial

---

[251] As proposed, Exchange Act Rule 14a-16(d) would limit the required legend to the line "Important Notice Regarding the Availability of Proxy Materials for the Shareholder Meeting To Be Held on [insert meeting date]" and would require the other information currently required in the legend to be included in the Notice, but not as part of a specified legend.

[252] 17 CFR 240.14a-16(f)(2).

[253] See, e.g., letters from ABA, ACC, BNY, Broadridge, Broadridge Steering Committee, Calvert, Chamber, Computershare, Edison, ICI, Intel, Otter Tail, R&T, S&C, SCSGP, and STA.

[254] See, e.g., letters from ABA, Altman, Otter Tail, and Intel. Letters from ABA, Altman and Intel suggested the inclusion of a mandatory legend indicating

that a separate proxy card should be used for voting.

[255] See letter from Otter Tail.

[256] See letter from Edison.

[257] See letter from Intel suggesting that the mandated format of the Notice be changed so that matters to be addressed at the annual meeting be identified by topic rather than identifying the specific proposals in order to avoid confusion between the Notice and the proxy card.

[258] See, e.g., letters from ABA, ACC, S&C, and STA.

[259] See, e.g., letters from ABA and ACC.

[260] See letter from ABA.

[261] See letter from S&C.

distribution of the Notice as proposed with some changes as recommended by commenters. The final rule provides issuers and other soliciting persons with additional flexibility in formatting and selecting the language to be used in the Notice, as proposed. The information appearing on the Notice is required to address certain topics, without specifying the exact language to be used. In response to comments requesting that the rules specifically state that the Notice is not a form of proxy and may not be voted, we are adopting final rules that require an issuer or other soliciting person to indicate that the Notice is not a form for voting. We are not, however, adopting suggested changes to the Notice requirements that would require a prescribed legend that the Notice is not a proxy card. We are also not adopting changes to the Notice that would require a uniform design for the Notice or would require that the Notice identify proxy items by topic rather than specific identification. We believe that the requirement that the Notice indicate that it is not a form for voting and the additional flexibility provided by the revised rules, as well as the guidance regarding the requirements of redesignated Exchange Act Rule 14a-16(d)(6),[262] address the concerns raised by commenters. These changes also provide issuers and other soliciting persons the flexibility to draft the Notice more effectively. We believe that the flexibility should discourage the development of boilerplate disclosure, which is one of the problems our amendments are designed to address.

As noted above, several commenters supported additional flexibility to allow the materials to address the reasons for the use of the notice-only option.[263] Consistent with the proposal, the final rule permits issuers and other soliciting persons to accompany the Notice with an explanation of the notice and access model.[264] As proposed, new Exchange Act Rule 14a-16(f)(2)(iv)[265] allows issuers and other soliciting persons to provide an explanation of the process of receiving and reviewing the proxy materials and voting under the notice and access proxy rules. In a change from the proposal, new Exchange Act Rule 14a-16(f)(2)(iv) also permits an explanation of the reasons for the use of the notice and access rules, as some commenters suggested.

We concur that additional flexibility to explain the reasons for the use of the notice and access rules and the notice-only option may enhance shareholders' understanding of the notice and access model and, therefore, we have expanded the exception to include those topics. Materials designed to persuade shareholders to vote in a particular manner or change the method of the delivery of proxy materials are still not permitted under the revised exception.[266] As also noted above, one commenter suggested that we specifically require that intermediaries and their agents be required to distribute explanatory materials prepared in reliance on the amended rules. Since issuers and other soliciting persons are generally required to reimburse intermediaries for the reasonable expenses incurred in connection with forwarding materials to shareholders, we are not at this time specifically requiring intermediaries and their agents to forward explanatory materials. Of course, to the extent that materials that accompany the Notice are "other soliciting materials" then our current rules[267] would specifically require distribution of the materials.

---

[262] We are redesignating 17 CFR 240.14a-16(d)(2) through 17 CFR 240.14a-16(d)(8) as 17 CFR 240.14a-16(d)(5) through 17 CFR 240.14a-16(d)(11). Prior to this redesignation, the referenced paragraph was 17 CFR 240.14a-16(d)(3) as indicated in the Proposing Release. After adoption, as noted here, the referenced paragraph is 17 CFR 240.14a-16(d)(6).

[263] See note 20 above.

[264] We emphasize that under revised Rule 14a-16(f)(2) only registrants and other soliciting persons, and not other parties, may accompany a Notice with explanatory materials.

[265] This new provision is an additional exception to the general rule in Exchange Act Rule 14a-16(f) that the Notice be sent separately from other types of security holder communications.

[266] While the Notice continues to permit the soliciting person to include their recommendations as provided in redesignated Exchange Act Rule 14a-16(d)(6), as we explained in the Internet Availability of Proxy Material Adopting Release, "The Notice is intended merely to make shareholders aware that these proxy materials are available on an Internet Web site; it is not intended to serve as a stand-alone basis for making a voting decision."

[267] See 17 CFR 240.14b-1(b)(2) and 17 CFR 240.14b-2(b)(3).

In response to comments, we are also making a technical change to Exchange Act Rule 14a-16(n). Rule 14a-16(n)(4) details the notice and access disclosures that registrants and other soliciting persons are not required to include in proxy materials when they choose to send a full set of proxy materials to security holders. Since we are amending the notice and access disclosure requirements in Rule 14a-16(d), we are making conforming changes to Rule 14a-16(n)(4). Specifically, we are revising Rule 14a-16(n)(4)(i) to delete the reference to legend requirements that are no longer part of Rule 14a-16(d)(1) and to make reference to new paragraph 14a-16(d)(2) and changing the reference to "(d)(7)" in Rule 14a-16(n)(4)(iii) to "(d)(10)" to track the new numbering in Rule 14a-16(d).

Finally, we are confirming the guidance provided in the Proposing Release that it is not necessary that the Notice directly mirror the proxy card. Rather, Exchange Act Rule 14a-16(d)(6) provides that the Notice must clearly and impartially identify each separate matter intended to be acted on that will be considered at the meeting. We do not believe the Notice has to conform to the specific Exchange Act Rule 14a-4[268] formatting and content requirements for disclosure of matters on the proxy card.

B. Amendment to Notice Deadlines for Soliciting Persons Other Than the Issuer

We proposed to amend Exchange Act Rule 14a-16(*l*)(2)(ii)[269] to improve the workability of the notice and access rules that apply to soliciting persons, other than the issuer, that choose to use the notice-only option.

1. Proposed Amendment

As we noted in the Proposing Release, the current requirement in Exchange Act Rule 14a-16(*l*)(2) that requires soliciting persons to send the Notice to shareholders 10 calendar days after the date that the issuer first sends its proxy materials to shareholders can create potential compliance issues for soliciting persons. The staff review of filings may result in outstanding comments on a soliciting person's preliminary proxy statement more than 10 calendar days after the soliciting person has initially filed. The practical effect of this requirement was to limit that soliciting person's ability to use the notice-only option if the soliciting person was unable to file its definitive proxy statement with the Commission by that time. To improve implementation of the notice and access model, we proposed to amend Exchange Act Rule 14a-16(*l*)(2)(ii) to require soliciting persons relying on this alternative[270] to file a preliminary proxy statement within 10 calendar days after the issuer files its definitive proxy statement and to send its Notice to shareholders no later than the date on which it files its definitive proxy statement with the Commission.

2. Comments on the Proposed Amendment

Comments on the proposal were limited and mixed. One commenter supported the Commission's proposal for a soliciting person to file a preliminary proxy statement within 10 calendar days after the issuer files its definitive proxy statement and send its Notice no later than the date on which it files its definitive proxy statement.[271] Other commenters expressed concern that without a specific time requirement for sending the Notice prior to the shareholder meeting, shareholders may not have sufficient time to access and consider the materials provided or obtain paper copies prior to casting their vote.[272]

3. Final Rule

After considering the comments, we are adopting the revisions as proposed to amend Exchange Act Rule 14a-16(*l*)(2)(ii) to require soliciting persons other than the issuer to

---

[268] 17 CFR 240.14a-4.

[269] 17 CFR 240.14a-16(*l*)(2)(ii).

[270] Alternatively, a soliciting person may also send the Notice 40 calendar days before the shareholder meeting to which the proxy materials relate. 17 CFR 14a-16(*l*)(2)(i).

[271] *See* letter from ABA.

[272] *See, e.g.,* letters from Ameriprise, SCSGP, and S&C.

file a preliminary proxy statement within 10 calendar days after the issuer files its definitive proxy statement and to send its Notice to shareholders no later than the date on which it files its definitive proxy statement with the Commission. We continue to believe that the time period provides sufficient time for a soliciting person to prepare its proxy statement and respond to any staff comments, while still permitting the soliciting person to use the notice and access model. While the rule does not provide for a specific period of time before the meeting by which a soliciting person is required to mail the Notice, the soliciting person should, and generally it would be in their best interest to, make the Notice and proxy materials available to shareholders with sufficient time for shareholders to review the materials and make an informed voting decision.

C. Additional Comments on the Proposed Amendments and Actions Taken by the Commission

Some commenters indicated their belief that the proposed amendments would result in only modest improvements.[273] A number of commenters recommended revising the notice and access model to permit issuers to send a proxy card and business reply envelope, either with or without a short summary proxy statement accompanying the Notice in order to increase voting rates and facilitate shareholder participation.[274] Other commenters expressed support for reducing the amount of time required for sending the Notice prior to the meeting from 40 days to 30 days.[275] Still other commenters expressed concern regarding the notice and access processing fee structure, the lack of competition for proxy service providers and issuers' inability to negotiate the fees which results in limitations on the amount of the cost savings from switching to the notice and access model.[276] We are not addressing these issues at this time, as the Commission is still considering these and other ways to further encourage informed shareholder participation.

Many commenters suggested that the Commission should do more to improve not only the notice and access model, but also the proxy process generally.[277] While supporting the proposal, a number of commenters suggested that the Notice and lack of explanatory materials accompanying the Notice were not the primary reasons for reduced retail voting and advocated for more sweeping changes.[278] A few commenters did not directly address the proposed amendments, but made broader appeals regarding the proxy process or provided alternative insights,[279] and one commenter suggested that use of the notice and access model undermines investor protection and should be repealed. [280]

While we are not in this release addressing the broader concerns with the proxy system or the notice and access model raised by commenters that went beyond the scope of the proposals, we are continuing to consider these and other concerns relating to the proxy process that have been raised. At the direction of the Chairman, the Commission's staff is conducting a comprehensive review of the mechanics by which proxies are voted and the way in which information is conveyed to shareholders and is preparing a concept release to seek public comment on these issues.[281] In that review, the Commission's staff will continue to monitor shareholder activity under, and the effects of, the notice and access model. In addition, the Commission's staff is undertaking educational efforts to

---

[273] *See, e.g.*, letters from ABC and R&T.

[274] *See, e.g.*, letters from Altman, Chamber, Computershare, Edison, ICI, Intel, R&T, SCSGP, and STA.

[275] *See, e.g.*, letters from ABA, ACC, Altman, Broadridge Steering Committee, Calvert, Chamber, Computershare, ICI, Intel, NIRI, Otter Tail, R&T, and SCSGP.

[276] *See, e.g.*, letters from Altman, DG3, Otter Tail, NIRI, R&T, SCSGP, and STA.

[277] *See, e.g.*, letters from ABA, ABC, Altman, BNY, Broadridge, Broadridge Steering Committee, Chamber, Computershare, Edison, ICI, Intel, NIRI, Otter Tail, R&T, S&C, and SCSGP.

[278] *See, e.g.*, letters from ABC, Altman, ICI, NIRI, R&T, and STA.

[279] *See, e.g.*, letters from Corporate Governance, DG3, and Moxy.

[280] *See* letter from IRWebReport.com.

[281] *See* Speech by Chairman Mary Schapiro to the Practising Law Institute's 41st Annual Institute on Securities Regulation (Nov. 4, 2009) at *http://sec.gov/news/speech/2009/spch110409mls.htm.*

increase understanding of proxy mechanics generally and the notice and access model of delivery of proxy materials.[282]

D. Technical Amendments Relating to Registered Investment Companies

We are also adopting, as proposed, technical amendments to our rules for registered investment companies. Exchange Act Rule 14a-16(f)(2)(iii) currently permits a registered investment company to accompany the Notice with a prospectus or report to shareholders.[283] The Commission recently adopted rule amendments that permit mutual funds[284] to satisfy their prospectus delivery obligations by sending or giving investors key information in the form of a summary prospectus.[285] Consistent with permitting mutual funds to use a summary prospectus to satisfy their delivery obligations, we are revising our rules to permit mutual funds to accompany the Notice with a summary prospectus.[286] Commenters that addressed this issue supported the technical amendments.[287]

III. PAPERWORK REDUCTION ACT

A. Background

Certain provisions of the amendments contain a "collection of information" within the meaning of the Paperwork Reduction Act of 1995.[288] The Commission published a notice requesting comment on the collection of information requirements in the Proposing Release for the amendments, and we are submitting these requirements to the Office of Management and Budget for review in accordance with the PRA.[289] An agency may not conduct or sponsor, and a person is not required to comply with, a collection of information unless it displays a currently valid control number. Compliance with the rules as they are amended is mandatory; however, certain information collections under these rules are required and some are voluntary. Responses to the information collections will not be kept confidential and there is no mandatory retention period for the information disclosed.

B. Summary of the Final Rules

As discussed in more detail below, the amendments that we are adopting provide additional flexibility regarding the format of the Notice that is sent to shareholders, permit issuers and other soliciting persons to better communicate with shareholders by including explanatory materials regarding the reasons for the use of the notice and access rules and the process of receiving and reviewing proxy materials and voting, and revise the timeframe for delivering a Notice to shareholders when a soliciting person other than the issuer relies on the notice-only option.

---

[282] Information about the Commission's educational efforts can be found at: *http://www.sec.gov/spotlight/ proxymatters.shtml.*

[283] 17 CFR 240.14a-16(f)(2)(iii). Unless otherwise specified or the context otherwise requires, the term "prospectus" means a prospectus meeting the requirements of Section 10(a) of the Securities Act [15 U.S.C. 77j(a)]. *See* 17 CFR 240.0-1(d).

[284] We use the term "mutual fund" to mean a registered investment company that is an open-end management company as defined in Section 5(a)(1) of the Investment Company Act of 1940 [15 U.S.C. 80a-5(a)(1)].

[285] *See* Enhanced Disclosure and New Prospectus Delivery Option for Registered Open-End Management Investment Companies, Release No. 33-8998 (Jan. 13, 2009) [74 FR 4546]. Although the summary prospectus is not a Section 10(a) prospectus, it may be used to satisfy any prospectus delivery obligations under Section 5(b)(2) of the Securities Act [15 U.S.C. 77e(b)(2)]. 17 CFR 230.498(c).

[286] *See* amendment to Exchange Act Rule 14a-16(f)(2)(iii). We are also adopting a conforming amendment to Rule 498 under the Securities Act [17 CFR 230.498], which permits mutual funds to use a summary prospectus to satisfy their prospectus delivery obligations. Rule 498(f)(2) provides that a mutual fund's summary prospectus shall be given greater prominence than any accompanying materials. We are amending Rule 498(f)(2) to provide that a summary prospectus need not be given greater prominence than an accompanying Notice.

[287] *See, e.g.*, letters from ABA, Calvert, and ICI.

[288] 44 U.S.C. 3501 *et seq.*; 5 CFR 1320.11.

[289] 44 U.S.C. 3507(d) and 5 CFR 1320.11.

In the Proposing Release, we requested comment on the PRA analysis. We received no comments that addressed our burden estimates for the proposed amendments.

1. Regulation 14A and 14C

The titles for the collections of information for operating companies are:

- Regulation 14A (OMB Control No. 3235-0059); and
- Regulation 14C (OMB Control No. 3235-0057).

We previously revised these collections of information in the release that proposed the notice and access model as a voluntary model for disseminating proxy materials[290] and the release in which we adopted amendments requiring issuers and other soliciting persons to follow the model.[291] We submitted the revisions in those releases and are submitting the amendments to OMB for review in accordance with the PRA.

We have made some additional changes to the amendments, but we do not expect those changes to affect our estimates.[292] The following table summarizes for purposes of the PRA the burden estimates for Schedules 14A and 14C reflecting amendments that permit, but do not require, an issuer or other soliciting person to include explanatory materials with the Notice, which are the only amendments in the release affecting our burden estimates:

Table 1: Calculation of Incremental Paperwork Reduction Act Burden Estimates for Proxy and Information Statements.

Form	Annual Responses	Incremental Hours/Form	Incremental Burden	75% Issuer	25% Professional	$400 Professional Cost
	(A)	(B)	(C)=(A)*(B)	(D)=(C) *0.75	(E)=(C)*0.25	(F)=(E)* $400
Schedule 14A	7300	0.5	3650	2737.5	912.5	$365,000
Schedule 14C	680	0.5	340	255	85	$34,000
Total	7980		3990	2992.5	997.5	$399,000

2. Rule 20a-1

Certain provisions of the current notice and access model contain "collection of information" requirements within the meaning of the PRA, including preparation of Notices, maintaining Web sites, maintaining records of shareholder preferences, and responding to requests for copies. Those provisions increase the current burden for the existing collection of information entitled "Rule 20a-1 under the Investment Company Act of 1940,[293] Solicitation of Proxies, Consents and Authorizations" (OMB Control No. 3235-0158). Rule 20a-1 under the Investment Company Act[294] requires that the solicitation of a proxy, consent, or authorization with respect to a security issued by an investment company be in compliance with Regulation 14A,[295] Schedule 14A,[296] and all other rules and regulations adopted under Section 14(a) of the Exchange Act.[297] It also requires a fund's investment adviser, or a prospective adviser, to transmit to the person

---

[290] *See* Internet Availability of Proxy Materials, Release No. 34-52926 (Dec. 8, 2005) [70 FR 74597].

[291] *See* the Internet Availability of Proxy Material Adopting Release at note 9 above.

[292] While the revised amendments additionally permit an explanation of the reasons for an issuer's use of the notice and access rules, we expect the additional explanation to be part of the same drafting process and to be limited to a few lines of text. Likewise, the required clarification that the Notice is not a form for voting should not add materially to the time to prepare the disclosure. We therefore believe the changes do not affect our burden estimates.

[293] 15 U.S.C. 80a-1 *et seq.*

[294] 17 CFR 270.20a-1.

[295] 17 CFR 240.14a-1 *et seq.*

[296] 17 CFR 240.14a-101.

[297] 15 U.S.C. 78n(a).

making a proxy solicitation the information necessary to enable that person to comply with the rules and regulations applicable to the solicitation. The notice and access model requires all registered investment companies to post their proxy materials on an Internet Web site and furnish Notice of the materials' availability to shareholders.[298] The Notices, the proxy materials posted on the Web site, and copies of the proxy materials sent in response to shareholder requests are not kept confidential.

The following discussion summarizes the burden estimates for Rule 20a-1 that we provided in the Proposing Release. For purposes of the PRA, we estimate that the total annual reporting burden for Rule 20a-1 increased by approximately 1,378 hours and that the annual cost increased by approximately $735,000 for the services of outside professionals to comply with the disclosure provisions of the existing notice and access model. In addition, for purposes of the PRA, we estimate that a typical investment company issuer spends an additional five hours per year, or a total of 6,125 hours, to maintain these records as to which of its shareholders have made an election to receive proxy materials in paper or by e-mail. Further, we estimate that the additional burden to prepare an intermediary's Notice is approximately one hour, or a total annual burden of 1,225 hours for all investment company proxy solicitations. Finally, like investment company issuers, we estimate that the requirement to maintain records to keep track of which beneficial owners have made a permanent election to receive proxy materials in paper or by e-mail results in an additional annual burden of five hours, or a total of 6,125 hours, for intermediaries. We received no comments on the estimates and are making no adjustments. In total, we estimate that the annual PRA reporting burden for current Rule 20a-1 increased by 14,853 hours and $735,000 in professional costs to reflect compliance with the existing notice and access model.

With respect to the amendments in this release, we have made some additional clarifying changes, but we do not expect those changes to affect our estimates. We estimate that the amendments that permit, but do not require, an issuer or other soliciting person to include explanatory materials with the Notice, increase the PRA burden estimates under Rule 20a-1 by approximately 459 hours and $61,250 in professional costs.[299]

IV. COST-BENEFIT ANALYSIS

A. Introduction

We are adopting amendments designed to improve implementation of the notice and access model by revising the legend requirements in the rule to make them more flexible, permitting the Notice to be accompanied by explanatory materials regarding the reasons for the use of the notice and access rules and the process of receiving and reviewing the proxy materials and voting, and revising the timeframe for delivering a Notice to shareholders when a soliciting person other than the issuer relies on the notice-only option.[300] We received no comments on the costs and benefits of the amendments.

We expect the amendments to:

- Facilitate participation by shareholders who may be confused by the operation of the notice and access model;

- Provide additional flexibility in describing the notice and access model; and

- Facilitate participation by some soliciting persons who may currently be effectively precluded from using the notice-only option.

---

[298] *See* the Internet Availability of Proxy Material Adopting Release at note 9 above.

[299] *See* the Proposing Release for calculations underlying the burden estimates.

[300] We do not expect our proposed conforming amendment, which would permit mutual funds to accompany the Notice with a summary prospectus, to have a substantive impact on a mutual fund's decision otherwise permitted under Rule 498 of the Securities Act to provide a summary prospectus instead of a statutory prospectus to its shareholders. No commenters suggested it would have a substantial impact.

B. Benefits

As discussed above, by permitting some additional flexibility in designing the Notice and permitting explanatory materials regarding the reasons for the use of the notice and access rules and the process of receiving and reviewing the proxy materials and voting to accompany the Notice, the amendments are intended to reduce regulatory impediments and improve understanding of the notice and access model for participating shareholders. Improved understanding of the model through an explanation of the reasons for the use of the Notice and the process of receiving and reviewing proxy materials and voting should reduce confusion and may thereby improve the efficiency and effectiveness of the proxy voting system. The benefits may be limited if issuers send notices to shareholders that are less likely to respond. Some commenters noted lower shareholder response rates under the notice and access model.[301]

Revising one of the two alternative Notice deadlines applicable to soliciting persons other than issuers is intended to facilitate use of the notice-only option by soliciting persons who may otherwise be precluded from using the notice-only option because of their inability to meet the deadline for sending the Notice. This would help lower costs for those persons by reducing impediments for certain soliciting persons to participate in the proxy process through use of the notice-only option.

C. Costs

Eliminating the specific limitations of the legend requirement may result in some soliciting persons providing a more confusing Notice. This may increase the cost of shareholder participation in the proxy process, and to the extent that it affects participation, could distort votes and outcomes. In addition, an issuer or other soliciting person that chooses to include explanatory materials in the same mailing with the Notice will incur the cost of preparing that information.[302] For purposes of the PRA, we estimate that the amendments will cause an aggregate annual increase in the compliance burden for operating and investment company issuers and other soliciting persons preparing explanatory materials of approximately 3,450 hours of in-house personnel time and approximately $460,000 for the services of outside professionals.

V. CONSIDERATION OF BURDEN ON COMPETITION AND PROMOTION OF EFFICIENCY, COMPETITION AND CAPITAL FORMATION

Section 23(a) of the Exchange Act[303] requires the Commission, when making rules and regulations under the Exchange Act, to consider the impact a new rule would have on competition. Section 23(a)(2) prohibits the Commission from adopting any rule that would impose a burden on competition not necessary or appropriate in furtherance of the purposes of the Exchange Act. Section 2(b) of the Securities Act,[304] Section 3(f) of the Exchange Act[305] and Section 2(c) of the Investment Company Act[306] require the Commission, when engaging in rulemaking that requires it to consider whether an action is necessary or appropriate in the public interest, to also consider whether the action would promote efficiency, competition, and capital formation.

The amendments that we are adopting permit additional flexibility in designing the Notice, permit issuers and other soliciting persons to better communicate with shareholders by accompanying the Notice with explanatory materials regarding the reasons for the use of the notice and access rules and the process of receiving and reviewing the proxy materials and voting, and revise the timeframe for delivering a Notice to shareholders

---

[301] *See, e.g.*, Broadridge, BNY, Computershare, and R&T.

[302] Since intermediaries and their agents already have systems to prepare and deliver proxy materials and the nature of the proposed changes are relatively small, we do not expect the intermediaries' role in sending explanatory material to beneficial owners to affect their costs associated with the rule. In any event,

since soliciting persons reimburse intermediaries for their reasonable expenses of forwarding proxy materials, we do not expect intermediaries to incur costs associated with the rule.

[303] 15 U.S.C. 78w(a).

[304] 15 U.S.C. 77b(b).

[305] 15 U.S.C. 78c(f).

[306] 15 U.S.C. 80a-2(c).

when a soliciting person other than the issuer relies on the notice-only option. The amendments are designed to reduce regulatory impediments and thereby increase shareholder participation, improve implementation of the notice and access model, and enhance investor understanding of the operation of the notice and access model. These changes are intended to improve the efficiency and effectiveness of the proxy process.

No commenters suggested, and we do not anticipate, any effect on competition or capital formation as a result of these revisions.

VI. FINAL REGULATORY FLEXIBILITY ANALYSIS

This Final Regulatory Flexibility Analysis has been prepared in accordance with 5 U.S.C. 603. It relates to revisions to Exchange Act Rule 14a-16 and related changes that would permit some additional flexibility in designing the Notice, permit issuers and other soliciting persons to better communicate with shareholders by accompanying the Notice with explanatory materials regarding the reasons for the use of the notice and access rules and the process of receiving and reviewing the proxy materials and voting, and revise the timeframe for delivering a Notice to shareholders when a soliciting person other than the issuer relies on the notice-only option. An Initial Regulatory Flexibility Analysis (IRFA) was prepared in accordance with the Regulatory Flexibility Act in conjunction with the Proposing Release. The Proposing Release included, and solicited comment on, the IRFA.

A. Reasons for, and Objectives of, the Amendments

The amendments are designed to improve implementation of the notice and access model. Based on our monitoring of the effects of the notice and access model on the proxy solicitation process and the experiences that issuers and shareholders have had with the notice and access model to date, we believe that these revisions will improve the operation of the model without adversely affecting soliciting persons' or shareholders' abilities to participate effectively in the proxy process.

Improved notice design and shareholder education should help to mitigate the difference in shareholder participation in the proxy voting process observed in the use of the notice and access model to the extent the difference was caused by the restrictions in our regulations. The amendment to the timing requirements for soliciting persons other than the issuer to file their preliminary proxy statements is designed to better enable soliciting persons other than the issuer to use the notice-only option.

B. Significant Issues Raised by Commenters

We did not receive comments specifically addressing the impact of the proposed amendments on small entities.

C. Small Entities Subject to the Amendments

The amendments affect issuers that are small entities. Exchange Act Rule 0-10(a)[307] defines an issuer to be a "small business" or "small organization" for purposes of the Regulatory Flexibility Act if it had total assets of $5 million or less on the last day of its most recent fiscal year. We estimate that there are approximately 1,100 public companies, other than investment companies, that may be considered small entities.

For purposes of the Regulatory Flexibility Act, an investment company is a small entity if it, together with other investment companies in the same group of related investment companies, has net assets of $50 million or less as of the end of its most recent fiscal year.[308] Approximately 168 registered investment companies meet this definition. Moreover, approximately 33 business development companies may be considered small entities.

---

[307] 17 CFR 240.0-10(a). [308] 17 CFR 270.0-10.

Paragraph (c)(1) of Rule 0-10 under the Exchange Act[309] states that the term "small business" or "small organization," when referring to a broker-dealer, means a broker or dealer that had total capital (net worth plus subordinated liabilities) of less than $500,000 on the date in the prior fiscal year as of which its audited financial statements were prepared pursuant to Exchange Act Rule 17a-5(d);[310] and is not affiliated with any person (other than a natural person) that is not a small business or small organization. The Commission has estimated that there were approximately 910 broker-dealers that qualified as small entities as defined above.[311] Small Business Administration regulations define "small entities" to include banks and savings associations with total assets of $165 million or less.[312] The Commission estimates that the amendments might apply to approximately 9,475 banks, approximately 5,816 of which could be considered small banks with assets of $165 million or less.[313]

D. Reporting, Recordkeeping and Other Compliance Requirements

The amendments revise the timeframe for delivering a Notice to shareholders when a soliciting person other than the issuer relies on the notice-only option, require clarification that the Notice is not a form for voting and permit, but do not require, issuers or other soliciting persons to include additional, explanatory material in their Notice.

E. Agency Action to Minimize Effect on Small Entities

The purpose of the amendments is to improve the implementation of the notice and access model based on our experience with the model to date. The amendments are intended to improve the operation of the notice and access model by providing additional flexibility in designing the Notice, permitting issuers and other soliciting persons to better communicate with shareholders by accompanying the Notice with explanatory materials regarding the reasons for the use of the notice and access rules and the process of receiving and reviewing the proxy materials and voting, and revising the timeframe for delivering a Notice to shareholders when a soliciting person other than the issuer relies on the notice-only option.

We considered the use of performance standards rather than design standards in the amendments. The amendments contain both performance standards and design standards. We are revising existing design standards, such as the deadline applicable to soliciting persons other than the issuer. However, we are imposing performance standards to provide issuers, other soliciting persons and intermediaries with the flexibility to devise the means through which they can comply with such standards. For example, the amendments regarding explanatory materials do not dictate wording of such information, but allow flexibility in how to communicate the information.

We considered different compliance standards for the small entities that will be affected by the amendments. In the Proposing Release, we solicited comment regarding the possibility of different standards for small entities. We did not receive comment on this particular issue. We are not aware of any different standards that would be consistent with the purposes of the amendments.

---

[309] 17 CFR 240.0-10(c)(1).

[310] 17 CFR 240.17a-5(d).

[311] These numbers are based on a review by the Commission's Office of Economic Analysis of 2005 FOCUS Report filings reflecting registered broker-dealers. This number does not include broker-dealers that are delinquent in FOCUS Report filings.

[312] 13 CFR 121.201.

[313] We note that while not subject to the amendments, the amendments may affect these entities because they are intermediaries that are required under the Commission's proxy rules to forward proxy materials, including the Notice or any explanatory materials, on to shareholders who beneficially own their shares through the intermediaries. An intermediary is not required to forward proxy materials to beneficial owners unless the issuer or other soliciting person provides assurance of reimbursement of the intermediary's reasonable expenses incurred in connection with forwarding those materials. 17 CFR 240.14b-2(c)(2)(i). Therefore, any costs imposed on intermediaries by the rules will be borne by the issuer or other soliciting person.

VII. STATUTORY AUTHORITY AND TEXT OF THE AMENDMENTS

The amendments described in this release are being adopted under the authority set forth in Sections 6, 7, 10, and 19 of the Securities Act of 1933, as amended, Sections 3(b), 13, 14, 15, and 23(a) of the Securities Exchange Act of 1934, as amended, and Sections 8, 20(a), 24(a), 24(g), 30, and 38 of the Investment Company Act of 1940, as amended.

List of Subjects

17 CFR Parts 230 and 240

Reporting and recordkeeping requirements, Securities.

For the reasons set out in the preamble, the Commission amends Title 17, Chapter II of the Code of Federal Regulation as follows.

PART 230—GENERAL RULES AND REGULATIONS, SECURITIES ACT OF 1933

1. The authority citation for Part 230 continues to read in part as follows:

Authority: 15 U.S.C. 77b, 77c, 77d, 77f, 77g, 77h, 77j, 77r, 77s, 77z-3, 77sss, 78c, 78d, 78j, 78*l*, 78m, 78n, 78o, 78t, 78w, 78*ll*(d), 78mm, 80a–8, 80a–24, 80a–28, 80a–29, 80a–30, and 80a–37, unless otherwise noted.

* * * * *

2. Amend §230.498 by revising paragraph (f)(2) to read as follows:

§230.498 Summary Prospectuses for open-end management investment companies.

* * * * *

(f) * * *

(2) *Greater prominence.* If paragraph (c) or (d) of this section is relied on with respect to a Fund, the Fund's Summary Prospectus shall be given greater prominence than any materials that accompany the Fund's Summary Prospectus, with the exception of other Summary Prospectuses, Statutory Prospectuses, or a Notice of Internet Availability of Proxy Materials under §240.14a-16 of this chapter.

* * * * *

PART 240—GENERAL RULES AND REGULATIONS, SECURITIES EXCHANGE ACT OF 1934

3. The general authority citation for Part 240 is revised to read as follows:

Authority: 15 U.S.C. 77c, 77d, 77g, 77j, 77s, 77z–2, 77z–3, 77eee, 77ggg, 77nnn, 77sss, 77ttt, 78c, 78d, 78e, 78f, 78g, 78i, 78j, 78j–1, 78k, 78k–1, 78*l*, 78m, 78n, 78o, 78p, 78q, 78s, 78u–5, 78w, 78x, 78*ll*, 78mm, 80a–20, 80a–23, 80a–29, 80a–37, 80b–3, 80b–4, 80b–11, and 7201 *et seq.*; and 18 U.S.C. 1350 and 12 U.S.C. 5221(e)(3), unless otherwise noted.

* * * * *

4. Amend §240.14a-16 by:

a. Revising paragraph (d)(1).

b. Redesignating paragraphs (d)(2) through (d)(8) as paragraphs (d)(5) through (d)(11);

c. Adding new paragraphs (d)(2) through (d)(4);

d. Removing the word "and" at the end of paragraph (f)(2)(ii);

e. Revising paragraph (f)(2)(iii);

f. Adding paragraph (f)(2)(iv);

g. Revising paragraph (*l*)(2)(ii);

h. Revising paragraph (n)(4)(i); and

i. In paragraph (n)(4)(iii) removing the reference to "(d)(7)" and adding in its place "(d)(10)".

The revisions and additions read as follows:

§240.14a-16 Internet availability of proxy materials.

* * * * *

(d) * * *

(1) A prominent legend in bold-face type that states "Important Notice Regarding the Availability of Proxy Materials for the Shareholder Meeting To Be Held on [insert meeting date]";

(2) An indication that the communication is not a form for voting and presents only an overview of the more complete proxy materials, which contain important information and are available on the Internet or by mail, and encouraging a security holder to access and review the proxy materials before voting;

(3) The Internet Web site address where the proxy materials are available;

(4) Instructions regarding how a security holder may request a paper or email copy of the proxy materials at no charge, including the date by which they should make the request to facilitate timely delivery, and an indication that they will not otherwise receive a paper or email copy;

* * * * *

(f) * * *

(2) * * *

(iii) In the case of an investment company registered under the Investment Company Act of 1940, the company's prospectus, a summary prospectus that satisfies the requirements of §230.498(b) of this chapter, or a report that is required to be transmitted to stockholders by section 30(e) of the Investment Company Act (15 U.S.C. 80a-29(e)) and the rules thereunder; and

(iv) An explanation of the reasons for a registrant's use of the rules detailed in this section and the process of receiving and reviewing the proxy materials and voting as detailed in this section.

* * * * *

(1) * * *

(2) * * *

(ii) The date on which it files its definitive proxy statement with the Commission, provided its preliminary proxy statement is filed no later than 10 calendar days after the date that the registrant files its definitive proxy statement.

* * * * *

(n) * * *

(4) * * *

(i) Instructions regarding the nature of the communication pursuant to paragraph (d)(2) of this section;

* * * * *

By the Commission.

Elizabeth M. Murphy

Secretary

Dated: February 22, 2010

APPENDIX 13

Frequently Asked Questions: Management's Report on Internal Control Over Financial Reporting and Certification of Disclosure in Exchange Act Periodic Reports

Frequently Asked Questions (revised September 24, 2007[1])

The answers to these frequently asked questions represent the views of the staffs of the Office of the Chief Accountant and the Division of Corporation Finance. They are not rules, regulations or statements of the Securities and Exchange Commission. Further, the Commission has neither approved nor disapproved them.

Note: The Commission adopted Interpretive Guidance for Management on May 23, 2007 (Release No. 33-8810). The Commission has stated that an evaluation that is conducted in accordance with the Commission's Interpretive Guidance will satisfy the evaluation required by Exchange Act Rules 13a-15(c) and 15d-15(c). Additionally, the Commission had previously adopted rules on *Management's Report on Internal Control Over Financial Reporting and Certification of Disclosure in Exchange Act Periodic Reports* (Release No. 34-47986, June 5, 2003). Since the adoption of the Commission's rules in June 2003, we have received questions regarding the implementation and interpretation of the rules. The Commission staff continues to entertain these questions, and where appropriate, will continue to answer publicly the more frequently asked questions.

Questions on accounting matters related to management's report on internal control over financial reporting should be directed to Josh K. Jones, Professional Accounting Fellow, in the Office of the Chief Accountant, Mail Stop 7561, 100 F Street, NE, Washington, DC 20549; telephone: (202) 551-5300. Other disclosure and filing questions should be directed to Sean Harrison at (202) 551-3430, or Jonathan Ingram at (202) 551-3500 in the Division of Corporation Finance.

Question 1

Q: Financial Accounting Standards Board (FASB) Interpretation No. 46 (revised December 2003), *Consolidation of Variable Interest Entities—An Interpretation of ARB No. 51*, requires that registrants apply that guidance and, if applicable, consolidate entities based on characteristics other than voting control no later than the period ending March 15, 2004, or December 15, 2004 for small business issuers. In instances where the registrant lacks the ability to dictate or modify the internal controls of an entity consolidated pursuant to Interpretation No. 46, it may not have legal or contractual rights or authority to assess the internal controls of the consolidated entity even though that entity's financial information is included in the registrant's financial statements. Similarly, for entities accounted for via proportionate consolidation in accordance with Emerging Issues Task Force Issue No. 00-1 (EITF 00-1), management may not have the ability to assess the internal controls. How should management's report on internal control over financial reporting address these situations?

A: We would typically expect management's report on internal control over financial reporting to include controls at all consolidated entities, irrespective of the basis for

---

[1] On September 24, 2007, changes were made to eliminate frequently asked questions which the staff believed were no longer relevant, necessary, or were addressed by the Commission's issuance of Interpretive Guidance for Management on May 23, 2007 (Release No. 33-8810). These changes resulted in the elimination of previously existing frequently asked questions numbered 5, 7, 10 through 13, and 15 through 20. The remaining frequently asked questions are substantially the same and have been renumbered as a result of the elimination of the twelve previously referenced questions. Additionally, four new frequently asked questions have been added pertaining to foreign private issuers (see frequently asked questions numbered 12 through 15).

consolidation. However, in a situation where the entity was in existence prior to December 15, 2003 and is consolidated by virtue of Interpretation No. 46 (i.e., would not have been consolidated in the absence of application of that guidance) and where the registrant does not have the right or authority to assess the internal controls of the consolidated entity and also lacks the ability, in practice, to make that assessment, we believe management's report on internal control over financial reporting should provide disclosure in the body of its Form 10-K or 10-KSB regarding such entities. For example, a registrant could refer readers to a discussion of the scope of management's report on internal control over financial reporting in a section of the annual report entitled "Scope of Management's Report on Internal Control Over Financial Reporting." The registrant should disclose in the body of the Form 10-K or 10-KSB that it has not evaluated the internal controls of the entity and should also note that the registrant's conclusion regarding the effectiveness of its internal control over financial reporting does not extend to the internal controls of the entity. The registrant should also disclose any key sub-totals, such as total and net assets, revenues and net income that result from consolidation of entities whose internal controls have not been evaluated. The disclosure should note that the financial statements include the accounts of certain entities consolidated pursuant to FIN 46 or accounted for via proportionate consolidation in accordance with EITF 00-1 but that management has been unable to evaluate the effectiveness of internal control at those entities due to the fact that the registrant does not have the ability to dictate or modify the controls of the entities and does not have the ability, in practice, to evaluate those controls.

Question 2

Q: Is a registrant required to evaluate the internal control over financial reporting of an equity method investment?

A: The accounts of an equity method investee are not consolidated on a line-by-line basis in the financial statements of the investor, and as such, controls over the recording of transactions into the investee's accounts are not part of the registrant's internal control structure. However, the registrant must have controls over the recording of amounts related to its investment that are recorded in the consolidated financial statements. Accordingly, a registrant would have to consider, among other things, the controls over: the selection of accounting methods for its investments, the recognition of equity method earnings and losses, its investment account balance, etc. For example, a registrant might require that, at least annually, its equity method investees provide audited financial statements as a control over the recognition of equity method earnings and losses. However, nothing precludes a registrant from evaluating the control over financial reporting of an equity method investment, and there may be circumstances where it is not only appropriate but also may be the most effective form of evaluation. For purposes of applying this guidance, we make no distinction between those equity method investments for which the registrant is required to file audited financial statements pursuant to Rule 3-09 of Regulation S-X and those where no such requirement is triggered.

Question 3

Q: If a registrant consummates a material purchase business[2] combination during its fiscal year, must the internal control over financial reporting of the acquired business be included in management's report on internal control over financial reporting for that fiscal year?

A: As discussed above, we would typically expect management's report on internal control over financial reporting to include controls at all consolidated entities. However, we acknowledge that it might not always be possible to conduct an assessment of an

---

[2] The staff intends the term business to include those acquisitions that would constitute a business based upon the facts and circumstances as outlined in Article 11-01(d) of Regulation S-X. An acquisition may not meet the definition of a business in EITF 98-3, *Determining Whether a Nonmonetary Transaction Involves Receipt of Productive Assets or of a Business*, and would not be accounted for under SFAS No. 141, *Business Combinations*, but nevertheless may be a business under the definition in Article 11 used for SEC reporting purposes. This guidance applies irrespective of whether the acquisition is significant under Rule 1-02(w) of Regulation S-X.

acquired business's internal control over financial reporting in the period between the consummation date and the date of management's assessment. In such instances, we would not object to management referring in the report to a discussion in the registrant's Form 10-K or 10-KSB regarding the scope of the assessment and to such disclosure noting that management excluded the acquired business from management's report on internal control over financial reporting. If such a reference is made, however, management must identify the acquired business excluded and indicate the significance of the acquired business to the registrant's consolidated financial statements. Notwithstanding management's exclusion of an acquired business's internal controls from its annual assessment, a registrant must disclose any material change to its internal control over financial reporting due to the acquisition pursuant to Exchange Act Rule 13a-15(d) or 15d-15(d), whichever applies (also refer to the last two sentences in the answer to question 7). In addition, the period in which management may omit an assessment of an acquired business's internal control over financial reporting from its assessment of the registrant's internal control may not extend beyond one year from the date of acquisition, nor may such assessment be omitted from more than one annual management report on internal control over financial reporting.

Question 4

Q: If management, the accountant, or both conclude in a report included in a timely filed Form 10-K or 10-KSB that the registrant's internal control over financial reporting is not effective, would the registrant still be considered timely and current for purposes of Rule 144 and Forms S-2, S-3, and S-8 eligibility?

A: Yes, as long as the registrant's other reporting obligations are timely satisfied. As has previously been the case, the auditor's report on the audit of the financial statements must be unqualified.

Question 5

Q: If management's report on internal control over financial reporting does not identify a material weakness but the accountant's attestation report does, or vice versa, does this constitute a disagreement between the registrant and the auditor that must be reported pursuant to Item 304 of Regulation S-K or S-B?

A: No, unless the situation results in a change in auditor that would require disclosure under Item 304 of Regulation S-K or S-B. However, such differences in identification of material weaknesses could trigger other disclosure obligations.

Question 6

Q: Is a registrant required to provide management's report on internal control over financial reporting, and the related auditor attestation report, when filing a transition report on Form 10-K or 10-KSB?

A: Yes. Because transition reports filed on Forms 10-K or 10-KSB (whether by rule or by election) must contain audited financial statements, they must also include management's report on internal control, subject to the transition provisions specified in Release No. 34-47986. The transition provisions relating to management's report on internal control should be applied to the *transition period as if it were a fiscal year.* Transition reports on Form 10-Q or 10-QSB are not required to include a management report on internal control.

Question 7

Q: Is a registrant required to disclose changes or improvements to controls made as a result of preparing for the registrant's first management report on internal control over financial reporting?

A: Generally we expect a registrant to make periodic improvements to internal controls and would welcome disclosure of all material changes to controls, whether or not made in advance of the compliance date of the rules under Section 404 of the Sarbanes-Oxley Act. However, we would not object if a registrant did not disclose changes made in preparation for the registrant's first management report on internal control over financial reporting. However, if the registrant were to identify a material weakness, it should carefully consider whether that fact should be disclosed, as well as changes made in response to the material weakness.

After the registrant's first management report on internal control over financial reporting, pursuant to Item 308 of Regulations S-K or S-B, the registrant is required to identify and disclose any material changes in the registrant's internal control over financial reporting in each quarterly and annual report. This would encompass disclosing a change (including an improvement) to internal control over financial reporting that was not necessarily in response to an identified material weakness (i.e. the implementation of a new information system) if it materially affected the registrant's internal control over financial reporting. Materiality, as with all materiality judgments in this area, would be determined upon the basis of the impact on internal control over financial reporting and the materiality standard articulated in TSC Industries, Inc. v. Northway, Inc. 426 U.S. 438 (1976) and Basic Inc. v. Levinson, 485 U.S. 224 (1988). This would also include disclosing a change to internal control over financial reporting related to a business combination for which the acquired entity that has been or will be excluded from an annual management report on internal control over financial reporting as contemplated in Question 3 above. As an alternative to ongoing disclosure for such changes in internal control over financial reporting, a registrant may choose to disclose all such changes to internal control over financial reporting in the annual report in which its assessment that encompasses the acquired business is included.

Question 8

Q: In many situations, a registrant relies on a third party service provider to perform certain functions where the outsourced activity affects the initiation, authorization, recording, processing or reporting of transactions in the registrant's financial statements, such as payroll. In assessing internal controls over financial reporting, management may rely on a Type 2 SAS 70 report[3] performed by the auditors of the third party service providers. If the auditors of the third party service provider are the same as the auditors of the registrant, may management still rely on that report? Additionally, may management rely on a Type 2 SAS 70 report on the third party based on a different year-end?

A: In situations where management has outsourced certain functions to third party service provider(s), management maintains a responsibility to assess the controls over the outsourced operations. However, management would be able to rely on the Type 2 SAS 70 report even if the auditors for both companies were the same. On the other hand, if management were to engage the registrant's audit firm to also prepare the Type 2 SAS 70 report on the service organization, management would not be able to rely on that report for purposes of assessing internal control over financial reporting. Management would be able to rely on a Type 2 SAS 70 report on the service provider that is as of a different year-end. Note, however, that management is still responsible for maintaining and evaluating, as appropriate, controls over the flow of information to and from the service organization.

Question 9

Q: If a Form 10-K or Form 10-KSB is incorporated into a 1933 Securities Act filing, is a consent required related to the auditor's report on management's assessment of internal control over financial reporting?

A: Yes. Securities Act Rule 436 (17 CFR 230.436) requires filings under the 1933 Act to include a consent for all accountants' reports included or incorporated into that filing.

---

[3] AU sec 324 defines a report on controls placed in operation and test of operating effectiveness, commonly referred to as a "Type 2 SAS 70 report". This report is a service auditor's report on a service organization's description of the controls that may be relevant to a user organization's internal control as it relates to an audit of financial statements, on whether such controls were suitably designed to achieve specified control objectives, on whether they had been placed in operation as of a specific date, and on whether the controls that were tested were operating with sufficient effectiveness to provide reasonable, but not absolute, assurance that the related control objectives were achieved during the period specified.

This includes a consent for the auditor's report on management's assessment of internal control over financial reporting as well as the auditor's report on the financial statements. A new consent for the auditor's report on management's assessment of internal control over financial reporting is required in an amendment to the registration statement (a) whenever a change, other than typographical is made to the audited annual financial statements and (b) when facts are discovered that may impact the auditor's report on management's assessment of internal control over financial reporting.

Question 10

Q: Is an annual report to shareholders that meets the requirements of Exchange Act Rules 14a-3(b) or 14c-3(a) required to include management's report on internal control over financial reporting and the auditor's report on management's assessment of internal control over financial reporting?

A: We believe that the intent of Section 404 of the Sarbanes-Oxley Act and the Commission's rules is that a registrant's audited financial statements with an accompanying audit report that are contained in or accompany a proxy statement or consent solicitation statement also be accompanied by management's report on internal control over financial reporting and the auditor's report on management's assessment of internal control over financial reporting. We encourage issuers to include both management's report on internal control over financial reporting and the auditor's report on management's assessment of internal control over financial reporting in the annual report to shareholders when their audited financial statements are included. If management states in their report that internal control over financial reporting is ineffective or the auditor's report takes any form other than an unqualified opinion and these reports are not included in the annual report to shareholders, our view is that an issuer would have to consider whether the annual report to shareholders contained a material omission that made the disclosures in the annual report misleading.

Question 11

Q: The Commission's rules implementing Section 404, announced in Release No. 34-47986, require management to perform an assessment of internal control over financial reporting which includes the "preparation of financial statements for external purposes in accordance with generally accepted accounting principles." Does management's assessment under the Commission's rule specifically require management to assess internal control over financial reporting of required supplementary information? Supplementary information includes the financial statement schedules required by Regulation S-X as well as any supplementary disclosures required by the FASB. One of the most common examples of such supplementary information is certain disclosures required by the FASB Standard No. 69, *Disclosures about Oil and Gas Producing Activities.*

A: Adequate internal controls over the preparation of supplementary information are required and therefore should be in place and assessed regularly by management. The Commission's rules in Release No. 34-47986 did not specifically address whether the supplementary information should be included in management's assessment of internal control over financial reporting under Section 404. A question has been raised as to whether the supplementary information included in the financial statements should be encompassed in the scope of management's report on their assessment of internal control over financial reporting.

The Commission staff is considering this question for possible rulemaking. Additionally, the Commission staff is evaluating broader issues relating to oil and gas disclosures and will include in its evaluation whether rulemaking in this area may be appropriate. Should there be any proposed changes to the current requirements in this area, they will be subject to the Commission's standard rulemaking procedures, including a public notice and comment period in advance of rulemaking. As a result, internal control over the preparation of this supplementary information need not be encompassed in management's assessment of internal control over financial reporting until such time that the Commission has completed its evaluation of this area and issues new rules addressing such requirements.

Until then, registrants are reminded that they must fulfill their responsibilities under current requirements including Section 13(b)(2) of the Exchange Act and Exchange Act Rules 13a-14, 13a-15, 15d-14, and 15d-15.

Question 12

Q: Should a foreign private issuer that files financial statements prepared in accordance with home country generally accepted accounting principles (GAAP) or IFRS, with a reconciliation to U.S. GAAP, plan and conduct its evaluation process based on the primary financial statements, or the amounts disclosed in the reconciliation to U.S. GAAP?

A: Management of foreign private issuers should plan and scope their evaluations based upon the primary financial statements (i.e. home country GAAP or IFRS). However, management's evaluation should consider controls related to the preparation of the U.S. GAAP reconciliation because the reconciliation is a required element of the financial statements.

Question 13

Q: In evaluating the severity of identified deficiencies, how should a foreign private issuer apply the reference to "interim financial statements" in the definition of material weakness?

A: Since home country requirements regarding the preparation of interim financial information vary significantly and there are no uniform requirements under the Exchange Act for foreign private issuers to file periodic interim financial information with the Commission, the reference to "interim financial statements" in that definition is not applicable to foreign private issuers. However, foreign private issuers filing on domestic forms are subject to the same requirements with respect to interim information as domestic issuers.

Question 14

Q: How should a registrant that is a foreign private issuer treat an entity that is accounted for differently in the primary financial statements (prepared in accordance with home country GAAP or IFRS) than in the reconciliation to U.S. GAAP (e.g. consolidated in primary financial statements, but accounted for under the equity method in reconciliation to U.S. GAAP) for purposes of management's evaluation of the effectiveness of internal control over financial reporting?

A: As stated in Question 12 above, management should determine the scope of its evaluation based on the primary financial statements. Therefore, determinations as to how entities subject to these differences should be included in management's evaluation of the effectiveness of internal control over financial reporting should be based on how those entities are accounted for in the primary financial statements. However, as discussed in Question 12 above, management's evaluation should consider controls related to the preparation of the of the U.S. GAAP reconciliation.

Question 15

Q: Some foreign private issuers, based on their home country GAAP requirements, account for certain entities on a proportionate consolidation basis. How should those entities be treated for purposes of management's report on the effectiveness of internal control over financial reporting?

A: We would typically expect management's report on internal control over financial reporting to include all consolidated entities, even if those entities are consolidated on a proportionate basis.

However, there may be circumstances where the registrant does not have the right or authority to evaluate the internal controls of the entity consolidated on a proportionate basis, and also lacks the access necessary, in practice, to make that evaluation. In such circumstances, management should evaluate its controls over the recording of the amounts related to the proportionately consolidated entity recorded in the consolidated financial statements. Accordingly, if the foreign private issuer determines that the entity is within the scope of its assessment, the issuer would have to consider, among other things, the controls over the selection of accounting method for its investment and the recognition of the proportionate balances of the entity in the consolidated financial statements, including the proper elimination of intercompany balances and transactions. For example, a registrant might require that, at least annually, such entities provide audited financial statements as one of its controls over the recognition of proportionate balances in the consolidated financial statements.

In these circumstances, we believe management's report on internal control over financial reporting should provide disclosure that it has not evaluated the internal controls of the applicable proportionately consolidated entity and should also note that the registrant's conclusion regarding the effectiveness of its internal control over financial reporting does not extend to the internal controls of such entities. The registrant should also disclose any key sub-totals, such as total and net assets, revenues and net income that result from the proportionate consolidation of entities whose internal controls have not been evaluated.[4] Further, the disclosure should note that the financial statements include the accounts of certain entities accounted for via proportionate consolidation but that management has been unable to evaluate the effectiveness of internal control at those entities due to the fact that the registrant does not have the right or authority to evaluate the internal controls and does not have the access necessary, in practice, to evaluate those controls.

---

[4] See also the requirement to provide similar disclosure in the financial statements for entities that are accounted for using proportionate consolidation pursuant to Item 17(c)(2)(vii) and Item 18(a) of Form 20-F.

APPENDIX 14

SEC Division of Corporation Finance Staff Legal Bulletins 1 and 1A—Confidential Treatment Requests

Date: February 28, 1997 (Addendum included: July 11, 2001)

Action: Publication of CF Staff Legal Bulletin

Summary: This staff legal bulletin sets forth views of the Division of Corporation Finance ("Division") regarding the requirements a registrant must satisfy when requesting confidential treatment of information that otherwise is required to be disclosed in registration statements, periodic reports and other documents filed with the Securities and Exchange Commission ("Commission"). The procedures are contained in Rule 406 under the Securities Act of 1933 and Rule 24b-2 under the Securities Exchange Act of 1934.

Supplementary Information: The statements in this legal bulletin represent the views of the staff of the Division of Corporation Finance. This bulletin is not a rule, regulation or statement of the Securities and Exchange Commission. Further, the Commission has neither approved nor disapproved its content.

Contact Person: For further information, please contact L. Jacob Fien-Helfman, Special Counsel at (202) 942-2997; the Special Counsel of the office in the Division to which the company is assigned; or, for small business issuers, the Special Counsel in the Office of Small Business.

I. Background

In recent years, the number of confidential treatment requests ("CTRs" or "applications") processed by the Division has increased steadily from approximately 540 in fiscal year 1992 to more than 1,000 in fiscal year 1996. Applications as initially filed often lack the information andanalysis necessary for the staff to evaluate compliance with the requirements of the rules. Consequently, the staff frequently issues deficiency letters which require the applicant to amend its application. Often the applicant also must amend the filing covered by the application.

This legal bulletin provides guidance on the substantive and procedural requirements contained in Rule 406[1] under the Securities Act of 1933 ("Securities Act")[2] and Rule 24b-2[3] under the Securities Exchange Act of 1934 ("Exchange Act").[4] The bulletin also suggests procedures that, while not required, would facilitate the staff's processing of CTRs. This guidance should help issuers prepare complete confidential treatment applications and thereby reduce the time and costs incurred by issuers and the Division in processing confidential treatment applications.

Failure to comply with either the substantive or procedural aspects of the Commission's confidential treatment process may result in a denial of an application. In this regard, the Commission has delegated authority to the Division to grant and deny requests for confidential treatment.[5]

II. Substantive and Procedural Requirements

A. General Discussion

The federal securities laws generally require any company that is publicly held or that is registering its securities for public sale to disclose a broad range of financial and non-

---

[1] 17 CFR 230.406.
[2] 15 U.S.C. 77a *et seq.*
[3] 17 CFR 24b-2.

[4] 15 U.S.C. 78a *et seq.*
[5] See 17 CFR 200.30-1(a)(3) and 17 CFR 200.30-1(f)(3).

financial information in registration statements, annual reports and other filings made with the Commission. The disclosure requirements for financial and non-financial information primarily are found in Regulation S-K and, for small business issuers, Regulation S-B.[6] Regulation S-X sets forth the financial statement disclosure requirements.[7]

Sometimes disclosure of information required by the regulations can adversely affect a company's business and financial condition because of the competitive harm that could result from the disclosure. This issue frequently arises in connection with the requirement that a registrant file publicly all contracts material to its business other than those it enters into in the ordinary course of business.[8] Typical examples of the information that raises this concern include pricing terms, technical specifications and milestone payments. To address the potential disclosure hardship, the Commission has a system allowing companies to request confidential treatment of information filed under the Securities Act and the Exchange Act.

Specifically, Rules 406 and 24b-2 set forth the exclusive means for obtaining confidential treatment of information contained in a document filed under the Securities Act and under the Exchange Act, respectively,[9] that would be exempt from disclosure under the Freedom of Information Act ("FOIA").[10]

The rules incorporate the criteria for nondisclosure set forth in FOIA and the Commission's FOIA rules.[11] FOIA requires all federal agencies to make specified information available to the public, including the information required to be filed publicly by Commission rules. FOIA contains, however, nine specific exemptions.[12] The rules require that CTRs contain an analysis of the applicable FOIA exemption. Most applicants rely on the exemption that covers "trade secrets and commercial or financial information obtained from a person and privileged or confidential" which is commonly referred to as "the (b)(4) exemption."[13]

B. Substantive Requirements: General

1. Confidential treatment cannot be granted if the information is publicly disclosed.

The applicant must make every effort not to disclose any of the confidential information. For example, the applicant should safeguard carefully copies of agreements and restrict access to only those who have a need to know the information or who are under a duty to keep the information confidential. The application must include an affirmative representation as to the confidentiality of the information it covers.

---

[6] See 17 CFR 229.10 *et seq.* and 17 CFR 228.10 *et seq.* For purposes of this staff legal bulletin, references to specific item of Regulation S-K also pertain to analogous provisions of Regulation S-B.

[7] 17 CFR 210.1-01 *et seq.*

[8] See Item 601(b)(10) of Regulation S-K [17 CFR 29.601(b)(10)]. Item 601(b)(10) requires that: Every contract not made in the ordinary course of business which is material to the registrant and is to be performed in whole or in part at or after the filing of the registration statement or report or was entered into not more than two years before such filing.

While Rule 406 under the Securities Act of 1933, in particular, appears to contemplate confidential treatment for portions of filed documents, this Bulletin will address requests made with respect to exhibits to filings only. Issuers requesting confidential treatment with respect to other portions of filings should bring such requests to the attention of the staff before public filing.

[9] This staff legal bulletin is not intended to include an exhaustive discussion of all Commission rules relating to confidential treatment of information submitted to the Commission. For example, Rule 418 of

Regulation C under the Securities Act of 1933 [17 CFR 230.418] and Rule 12b-4 under the Securities Exchange Act of 1934 [17 CFR 240.12b-4] cover specific types of supplemental information requested by the staff in processing registrant filings with the Commission. Rule 171 under the Securities Act [17 CFR 230.171] and Rule 0-6 under the Exchange Act [17 CFR 240.0-6] cover the disclosure of information detrimental to the national security of the United States. Public availability of no-action and interpretive letters is governed by Rule 81 under the Rules of Practice [17 CFR 200.81]. Confidential treatment of other information not required to be filed under either Act is covered by Rule 83 under the Rules of Practice [17 CFR 200.83]. Confidential treatment of the CTR and supplemental information provided to the staff in connection with the processing of the CTR should be requested pursuant to Rule 83.

[10] 5 U.S.C. 552.

[11] 17 CFR 200.80 *et seq.*

[12] See 5 U.S.C. 552(b) for the list of information that is exempt from disclosure under FOIA.

[13] 5 U.S.C. 552(b)(4); 17 CFR 200.80(b)(4).

Based on the staff's experience, there are a few common mistakes that result in the inadvertent disclosure of the information that is the subject of the application.[14] The following points illustrate typical mistakes.

- For paper filings, the text can be read through the marking used to delete the information.

- For filings by the Commission's electronic filing system, EDGAR,[15] the applicant fails to remove all of the confidential information from the electronic version of the document.

- The applicant omits the information, such as pricing terms, from one part of the document, but not from another part of that document or another document or report. Applicants should be aware that information may appear in more than one place in a document. For example, a section heading may appear in the table of contents of an agreement as well as in the agreement itself. In addition, preparers of applications should pay particular attention to the description of the business of the company, the financial statement footnotes and the Management's Discussion and Analysis of Financial Condition and Results of Operations section of disclosure documents.

- Another party to the agreement has disclosed (or intends to disclose) the information publicly.

- The company has included the information in a press release or news article or has provided the information to one or more analysts.

- The company has disclosed the information in documents filed publicly with other regulators, such as insurance, banking, utility or environmental regulators.

The staff understands, however, that an applicant may in a general manner inform the market about, for example, a newly negotiated contract. This may occur through various methods such as the issuance of a press release. General disclosure about a contract should not prevent an applicant from requesting confidential treatment of selected terms of the contract that remain undisclosed.

2. Required and/or material information must be disclosed, even if confidential.

In some instances the Commission's specific disclosure requirements cover information that could be withheld under FOIA. Except in unusual circumstances, disclosure required by Regulation S-K or any other applicable disclosure requirement is not an appropriate subject for confidential treatment, regardless of the availability of an exemption under FOIA. This type of information includes, for example,

- the identity of a 10% customer;

- the dollar amount of firm backlog orders;

- interest expense and other similar terms in a material credit agreement;

- ". . . the duration and effect of all patents, trademarks, licenses, franchises and concessions held"[16];

- required disclosure in the Management's Discussion and Analysis of Financial Condition and Results of Operations section[17] relating for instance to loan arrangements and installment payment obligations on debt; and

- disclosure about related party transactions.[18]

---

[14] Even if the disclosure is made in error, whether by the issuer or its agent, the staff will not attempt to edit a filed document and will not grant confidential treatment for any of the disclosed information. See Release No. 33-6977 (February 23, 1993) [58 FR 14628].

[15] Regulation S-T [17 CFR 232 *et seq.*] requires most filings made with the Commission to be made via the Electronic Data Gathering, Analysis, and Retrieval ("EDGAR") system.

[16] See Item 101(c)(1)(iv) of Regulation S-K [17 CFR 229.101(c)(1)(iv)].

[17] See Item 303 of Regulation S-K [17 CFR 229.303].

[18] See Item 404 of Regulation S-K [17 CFR 229.404].

In addition, confidential treatment is generally not appropriate for information that is material to investors. Depending on the facts and circumstances, examples of material information could include the name of a key supplier, material contingency clauses, indemnification clauses, anti-assignability clauses, take-or-pay clauses, and financial covenants in material financing or credit agreements. Materiality must be analyzed in the context of the issuer's business, financial condition and financial results. Where there is any question about the materiality of the information, the application must address the issue and provide factual support for the issuer's belief that the information is not material to investors.[19]

C. Substantive Requirements: Specific

In addition to complying with the general substantive requirements discussed above, an application for confidential treatment must comply with several more specific substantive requirements. In the staff's experience, however, applications often do not.

1. The application should not be overly broad.

Applicants should be selective when identifying the information covered by their application. Frequently, applications are overly broad and attempt to cover information that is not confidential under FOIA and the Commission's confidential treatment system. The information covered by an application should include no more text than necessary to prevent competitive harm to the issuer. A CTR should cover only those words and phrases for which confidentiality is necessary and supported by FOIA and applicable Commission rules.

The staff will comment on applications that cover lengthy portions of agreements. Absent a satisfactory demonstration that such extensive omissions are appropriate under the Commission's confidential treatment rules, the CTR will be denied. For example, the omission of an entire section is not appropriate without an analysis that specifically addresses:

(i) why the disclosure of the existence of the section would be commercially harmful; and

(ii) why its disclosure is not necessary for the protection of investors.

2. Applicants must set forth their analysis of the exemption.

The rules require that the application include a "statement of the grounds of the objection referring to and analyzing the applicable exemption(s) from disclosure under . . . the Commission's rule adopted under [FOIA]."[20] Applicants should note that an agreement between the parties to keep information confidential does not itself provide adequate justification for confidential treatment. The Commission's confidential treatment system is premised on the disclosure requirements of the federal securities laws and FOIA, and does not contemplate nondisclosure based on a private contractual provision between the parties.

The application should avoid conclusory statements and must include a sufficient legal analysis, including case law references. Two seminal cases covering the definition of "confidential" information are National Parks and Conservation Association v. Morton, 498 F.2d 765 (D.C. Cir. 1974) and National Parks and Conservation Association v. Kleppe, 547 F.2d 673 (D.C. Cir. 1976).

The application also should include a factual analysis of the basis for the exemption requested (for example, commercial harm to the filing party) with respect to the specific information that is the subject of the request. Where the application relates to different

---

[19] See Rule 406(b)(2)(iii) [17 CFR 230.406(b)(2)(iii)].

[20] Rule 406(b)(2)(ii) [17 CFR 230.406(b)(2)(ii)]. Rule 24b-2(b)(2)(ii) [17 CF 240.24b-2(b)(2)(ii)] contains similar language.

types of information (for example, trade secrets and financial provisions), the application should address each type separately.

Finally, the application should describe anything about the issuer's business or the specific contract that would help the staff evaluate the sensitivity and importance of the information to the issuer.

3. Applicants must specify a particular duration.

The application must request a specific date (year, month and day) for the termination of confidential treatment of the subject information. Further, the application must include an analysis that supports the period requested.[21] This analysis must be specific to the confidential information and to the company and its business. The application should tie the term to specific provisions of, anticipated performance under, or other facts related to, the contract from which the confidential information is omitted.

Confidential treatment beyond the minimum term of an agreement usually is inappropriate, as the value of the information typically is associated with the effective period of an agreement. Where continued confidential treatment after the term of the agreement is justified, the staff will consider applications to extend the period. This bulletin addresses applications for extension in Section III below ("Other Matters").

4. Applicants must identify clearly the information that is the subject of the application.

Applicants must identify clearly the information that is the subject of a request for confidential treatment. To make sure there is a complete record as to which information has been granted confidential treatment, the application should describe each item or category of information omitted pursuant to the CTR. The staff will question any inconsistencies between the material identified in the application and the material deleted from the public file.

5. Applicants must consent to the release of the information for official purposes.

The application must include a written consent to the furnishing of the confidential portion "to other government agencies, offices or bodies and to the Congress."[22] Conditions to this consent—which have appeared most frequently when the applicant demands notification if the Commission releases the subject information to any of the institutions listed—are not consistent with the requirement of the rules. Applicants should recognize that in granting any order for confidential treatment pursuant to delegated authority, the staff of the Commission is not explicitly or implicitly agreeing to furnish notice other than as required under the applicable rules and regulations.

D. Procedural Requirements

1. Applicants must file the application with the Office of the Secretary.

Applicants must send every application for confidential treatment to the Office of the Secretary in an envelope marked "confidential" which is separate from the envelope for any materials which are to be or have been filed publicly.[23] Applicants should send to the filing desk only documents that they mean to have on public file.

2. Applicants, including EDGAR filers, must file the application in paper form.

Both rules require, in introductory notes, that applicants file CTRs in paper form, not by EDGAR, the electronic filing system.[24] This paper filing requirement applies regardless of whether the applicant files other documents electronically. Once an applicant files

---

[21] See Rule 406(b)(2)(ii) [CFR 230.406(b)(2)(ii)] and Rule 24b-2(b)(2)(ii) [240.24b-2(b)(2)(ii)].

[22] Rule 406(b)(2)(iv) [17 CFR 230.406(b)(2)(iv)] and Rule 24b-2(b)(2)(iii) [17 CFR 240.24b-2(b)(2)(iii)].

[23] Rule 406(b)(3) [17 CFR 230.406(b)(3)] and Rule 24b-2(b)(3) (17 CFR 240.24b-2(b)(3)].

[24] In a release issued on December 6, 1996 (Release No. 33-7369) [61 FR 65440], the Commission solicited comment as to whether the EDGAR system should be enhanced to allow confidential treatment requests to be filed electronically.

electronically by mistake information meant to be covered by a CTR, such information is immediately available to the public and is no longer confidential.[25]

3. Applicants should file the application at the same time they file the material from which they have omitted the confidential information.

The confidential treatment process contemplates that issuers file CTRs at the same time that they file the publicly disclosed portions.[26] The staff will not process the application unless and until the material from which information is omitted has been filed publicly. There is only one exception to that general rule with respect to domestic registrants. In the case of joint proxy statements/prospectuses filed confidentially pursuant to Rule 14a-6(e)(2) of Regulation 14A, the registrant customarily files the wrap registration statement on Form S-4 only after the staff has completed its review of the non-public proxy statement/prospectus.[27] The staff must review the CTR on a preliminary basis at the same time it is reviewing the proxy statement/prospectus to avoid delays in the acceleration of effectiveness at the time the registrant files the Form S-4.

4. Applicants must omit from the public filings all of the information that is the subject of the application.

As discussed above, the grant of confidential treatment is premised on the subject information being non-public. See Section II.B.1 of this bulletin. The release of the information by the issuer, even if inadvertent, precludes the grant of confidential treatment.

5. Applicants must adequately mark the confidential portions of publicly filed documents.

The applicant must "indicate at the appropriate place in the material filed that the confidential portion has been so omitted and filed separately with the Commission."[28] An application will be considered incomplete unless the publicly-filed document has been marked to indicate both that the material has been omitted pursuant to a request for confidential treatment and that the material has been filed separately.

A recommended method of marking is to place an asterisk or other mark in the precise places in the document where the applicant deletes information. If the registrant uses this method of marking, it should key the mark to a legend which includes the required language on the page from which material is omitted and/or on the first page of the exhibit. In the unusual case where the confidential information consists of multiple pages, the publicly-filed document also must include an indication of the number of pages omitted pursuant to the CTR.

Finally, the applicant should mark the exhibit index to indicate that portions of the exhibit or exhibits have been omitted pursuant to a request for confidential treatment.

6. Applicants should show clearly which portions of the complete documents filed with the application are the subject of the CTR.

The application must include one complete copy of the document clearly marked to show those portions of the document covered by the CTR. The applicant must submit the complete marked copy "in the same form as the remainder of the material filed."[29] The confidential segments should be underlined, highlighted, circled or otherwise clearly marked in that copy.

7. Applicants should indicate to whom correspondence, orders and notices should be sent.

---

[25] See note 14, supra.

[26] See Rule 406(b) [17 CFR 230.406(b)] and Rule 24b-2(b) [17 CFR 240.24b-2(b)]. As an accommodation to foreign private issuers, the Division developed an informal procedure whereby the staff will review and comment on draft registration statements. Typically, a foreign private issuer will formally file a CTR concurrently with its submission of its draft registration statement. This bulletin does not change the procedures applicable to foreign private issuers.

[27] 17 CFR 240.14a-6(e)(2).

[28] Rule 406(b) [17 CFR 230.406(b)] and Rule 24b-2(b) (17 CFR 240.24b-2(b)].

[29] Rule 406(b)(1) [17 CFR 230.406(b)(1)] and Rule 24b2(b)(1) [17 CFR 240.24b-2(b)(1)].

Rule 406(b)(2)(v) requires the application to include "the name, address and telephone number of the person to whom all notices and orders issued under [the] rule should be directed."[30] If an application filed pursuant to Rule 24b-2 does not specifically include this information, the service list for the order will include the person who prepared the application.

III. Other Matters

A. Requests for extension of previously granted orders for confidential treatment

An applicant requesting the extension of a previously granted order for confidential treatment should submit the application before the expiration date of the earlier order. After the expiration date of an order, the subject information is publicly available upon request under FOIA.

The request for extension (including the substantive supporting argument) must comply with the disclosure and confidential treatment rules at the time the applicant submits the extension request. The application should include a complete copy of the agreement or agreements, a copy of the original order, and copies of the original application and correspondence with the Commission, if available.

The substantive and procedural requirements discussed in this bulletin are equally applicable to any extension request. Therefore, the applicant should represent that (a) none of the confidential information has been disclosed, (b) disclosure of the information will cause substantial competitive harm to the issuer, and (c) disclosure of the confidential information is not necessary for protection of investors.

To the extent that the applicant cannot make these representations, the applicant should refile the agreement to disclose the information that no longer satisfies the requirements. The applicant should refile the agreement with the first filing it makes after the order expires. The extension application should include a request for confidential treatment of the information in the newly filed document as well as continuing confidential treatment for the document that the issuer filed earlier. The applicant should take care to cite the appropriate rule for each part of the application.

B. Timing of CTR Submission

1. Initial public offerings

The staff processes confidential treatment requests filed with initial public offerings pursuant to Rule 406 concurrently with the review of the registration statement. All issues must be resolved, and the CTR must be complete, before the acceleration of effectiveness of the registration statement. Issuers are advised to file the CTR at the time they initially file the registration statement, rather than waiting to file the agreements and the CTR with later amendments to the registration statement. See Section II.D.3. of this bulletin regarding the need to file the application and the agreements at the same time. In addition, because the issuer files the CTR and the registration statement separately, the staff may not be aware that a CTR has been filed at the time of the filing of the registration statement. The applicant should include a reference to the related application for confidential treatment in its cover letter to the registration statement.

2. Registered offerings by reporting companies

Regardless of whether the staff selects a registration statement for review, the staff must act on a confidential treatment request filed in connection with a registration statement pursuant to Rule 406 before the acceleration of effectiveness of a pending registration statement.

Please note that the same restriction applies to registration statements that incorporate by reference periodic reports. All CTRs filed pursuant to Rule 24b-2 must be completed before the effectiveness of the registration statement can be accelerated. The applicant

---

[30] 17 CFR 406(b)(2)(v) [17 CFR 230.406(b)(2)(v)].

should include in its cover letter to the registration statement a reference to the pending CTR, and issuers should allow enough time in their offering schedules for processing of the CTR by the staff.

3. Applications pursuant to Rule 24b-2 when no registration statement is pending

The goal of the Division is to complete the initial review of confidential treatment requests filed pursuant to Rule 24b-2 within 28 days from the filing date. Comments will usually be issued within this period. If the staff has no comments, an order will be issued granting the CTR. If the staff issues comments, applicants must respond to those comments within 21 days of the date of the comment letter. If the applicant does not respond within this period, the staff will consider, pursuant to its delegated authority from the Commission, what action is warranted, including whether to grant, deny, or grant and deny in part confidential treatment applications based on the record before it. The staff will base its action on the initial application and all amendments and supplemental information received.

Addendum to Staff Legal Bulletin No. 1.

Dated July 11, 2001

This addendum updates Staff Legal Bulletin No. 1, dated February 28, 1997, relating to the Division's processing of confidential treatment requests. The first matter discussed below represents a change from the original bulletin and the second represents an addition to it.

- In footnote 9 to the original bulletin, we stated that issuers should request confidential treatment for the application itself, as well as for any supplemental materials provided during the processing of the request, under Rule 83 of the Commission's Rules of Practice. Rule 83 governs applications for confidential treatment of information not required to be filed under the Securities Act or the Exchange Act. We have recently changed our position to be consistent with the practices of the Division of Investment Management. Requests for confidential treatment of the application and other supporting supplemental information should be submitted under Securities Act.

Regardless of whether the staff selects a registration statement for review, the staff must act on a confidential treatment request filed in connection with a registration statement pursuant to Rule 406 before the acceleration of effectiveness of a pending registration statement.

Please note that the same restriction applies to registration statements that incorporate by reference periodic reports. All CTRs filed pursuant to Rule 24b-2 must be completed before the effectiveness of the registration statement can be accelerated. The applicant should include in its cover letter to the registration statement a reference to the pending CTR, and issuers should allow enough time in their offering schedules for processing of the CTR by the staff.

3. Applications pursuant to Rule 24b-2 when no registration statement is pending

The goal of the Division is to complete the initial review of confidential treatment requests filed pursuant to Rule 24b-2 within 28 days from the filing date. Comments will usually be issued within this period. If the staff has no comments, an order will be issued granting the CTR. If the staff issues comments, applicants must respond to those comments within 21 days of the date of the comment letter. If the applicant does not respond within this period, the staff will consider, pursuant to its delegated authority from the Commission, what action is warranted, including whether to grant, deny, or grant and deny in part confidential treatment applications based on the record before it. The staff will base its action on the initial application and all amendments and supplemental information received.

Rule 406 or Exchange Act Rule 24b-2, whichever is appropriate for the underlying filing.

- In Section II.C.3 of the original bulletin, we stated that confidential treatment beyond the minimum term of an agreement is usually inappropriate. We stated in Section III.A that if an issuer wanted confidential treatment beyond the term originally granted, it should file an application for extension before the expiration of the earlier order to justify continued confidential treatment. However, we gave no guidance with respect to the length of time we would consider appropriate for continued confidential treatment. We believe the following guidelines will assist issuers in preparing their extension applications: •

— If the remaining term of the contract is greater than 10 years from the date of the extension application, we generally will only grant confidential treatment for 10 years;

— If the remaining term of the contract is less than 10 years from the date of the extension application, we will consider a request for the remaining term of the contract;

— If the remaining term of the contract is less than five years from the date of the application, but there is a possibility that it will be extended beyond its stated term, we will consider granting confidential treatment for a period of up to five years.

These guidelines assume that the applicant provides adequate support for any period requested.

APPENDIX 15
Shareholder Choice Regarding Proxy Materials

SECURITIES AND EXCHANGE COMMISSION

17 CFR PART 240

[RELEASE NOS. 34-56135; IC-27911; File No. S7-03-07]

RIN 3235-AJ79

SHAREHOLDER CHOICE REGARDING PROXY MATERIALS

AGENCY: Securities and Exchange Commission.

ACTION: Final rule

SUMMARY: We are adopting amendments to the proxy rules under the Securities Exchange Act of 1934 to provide shareholders with the ability to choose the means by which they access proxy materials. Under the amendments, issuers and other soliciting persons will be required to post their proxy materials on an Internet Web site and provide shareholders with a notice of the Internet availability of the materials. The issuer or other soliciting person may choose to furnish paper copies of the proxy materials along with the notice. If the issuer or other soliciting person chooses not to furnish a paper copy of the proxy materials along with the notice, a shareholder may request delivery of a copy at no charge to the shareholder.

DATES: *Effective Date*: January 1, 2008, except § 240.14a-16(d)(3) and § 240.14a-16(j)(3) are effective October 1, 2007.

Compliance Dates: "Large accelerated filers," as that term is defined in Rule 12b-2 under the Securities Exchange Act of 1934, not including registered investment companies, must comply with the amendments regarding proxy solicitations commencing on or after January 1, 2008. Registered investment companies, persons other than issuers, and issuers that are not large accelerated filers conducting proxy solicitations (1) may comply with the amendments regarding proxy solicitations commencing on or after January 1, 2008, and (2) must comply with the amendments regarding proxy solicitations commencing on or after January 1, 2009.

FOR FURTHER INFORMATION CONTACT: Raymond A. Be, Special Counsel, Office of Rulemaking, Division of Corporation Finance, at (202) 551-3430, Securities and Exchange Commission, 100 F Street, NE, Washington, DC 20549-3628.

SUPPLEMENTARY INFORMATION: The Commission is adopting amendments to Rules 14a-3,[1] 14a-7,[2] 14a-16,[3] 14a-101,[4] 14b-1,[5] 14b-2,[6] 14c-2,[7] and 14c-3[8] under the Securities Exchange Act of 1934.[9]

Table of Contents

---

[1] 17 CFR 240.14a-3.
[2] 17 CFR 240.14a-7.
[3] 17 CFR 240.14a-16.
[4] 17 CFR 240.14a-101.
[5] 17 CFR 240.14b-1.

[6] 17 CFR 240.14b-2.
[7] 17 CFR 240.14c-2.
[8] 17 CFR 240.14c-3.
[9] 15 U.S.C. 78a *et seq.*

I. Introduction

On January 22, 2007, we proposed amendments to the proxy rules that would require all issuers and other soliciting persons to furnish proxy materials to shareholders by posting them on an Internet Web site and providing shareholders with notice of the electronic availability of the proxy materials.[10] Under the proposal, issuers and other soliciting persons would be permitted to deliver paper or e-mail copies of their proxy materials to shareholders along with the notice. The proposal was intended to provide all shareholders with the ability to choose the means by which they access proxy materials, including via paper, e-mail or the Internet, while still affording issuers and other soliciting persons flexibility in determining how to furnish their proxy materials to shareholders.[11] In a companion release issued on the same date, we adopted the "notice and access" model that issuers and other soliciting persons may comply with on a voluntary basis for proxy solicitations commencing on or after July 1, 2007.[12]

We received 23 comment letters on the proposal. The vast majority of commenters generally supported our goal of increasing reliance on technology to improve proxy distribution.[13] However, many of the commenters thought that the Commission's timetable for adopting the proposed amendments was too aggressive.[14] They suggested that we postpone adoption of the proposal until we gain experience from operation of the voluntary rule.

Although we acknowledge the timing concerns raised by the commenters, we think that it is appropriate to adopt the proposal at this time because the model that we are adopting will provide shareholders with enhanced choices without changing significantly the obligations of an issuer or other soliciting person. The only new obligations that the revised notice and access model will impose on issuers and other soliciting persons compared to the voluntary rule is that an issuer or other person soliciting proxies who wishes to initially furnish a full set of proxy materials in paper to shareholders will be required to: (1) post those proxy materials on an Internet Web site; and (2) include a Notice of Internet Availability of Proxy Materials (Notice) with the full set or incorporate the Notice information into its proxy statement and proxy card.[15]

Furthermore, under the phase-in schedule that we are establishing for expanding the notice and access model to all issuers and other soliciting persons, the largest public companies will become subject to the model a year before any other companies become subject to the model. Most of these companies already appear to post their proxy materials and Exchange Act reports on an Internet Web site.[16] A large accelerated filer (not including registered investment companies) will have to comply with the notice and access model

---

[10] See Release No. 34-55147 (Jan. 22, 2007) [72 FR 4176].

[11] For purposes of this release, the term "proxy materials" includes proxy statements on Schedule 14A [17 CFR 240.14a-101], proxy cards, information statements on Schedule 14C [17 CFR 240.14c-101], annual reports to security holders required by Rules 14a-3 [17 CFR 240.14a-3] and 14c-3 [17 CFR 240.14c-3] of the Exchange Act, notices of shareholder meetings, additional soliciting materials, and any amendments to such materials. For purposes of this release, the term does not include materials filed under Rule 14a-12 [17 CFR 240.14a-12].

[12] Release No. 34-55146 (Jan. 22, 2007) [72 FR 4148].

[13] See letters from AARP, American Business Conference (ABC), Automatic Data Processing Brokerage Services Group, now known as Broadridge Financial Solutions, Inc. (ADP), Bank of New York (BONY), U.S. Chamber of Commerce (Chamber of Commerce), Council of Institutional Investors (CII), Commerce Finance Printers Corp. (Commerce Finance Printers), Computershare, Dechert LLP (Dechert), Kathryn Elmore and Michael Allen (Elmore & Allen), Investment Company Institute (ICI), Infosys Technologies Limited (Infosys), MailExpress, Reed Smith LLP (Reed Smith), Registrar and Transfer Company (Registrar and Transfer), Karl W. Reimers (Reimers), Ayal Rosenthal

(Rosenthal), Society of Corporate Secretaries and Governance Professionals (SCSGP), Securities Industry and Financial Markets Association (SIFMA), Mark Snyder (Snyder), Shareholder Services Association (SSA), and Securities Transfer Association, Inc. (STA).

[14] See letters from AARP, ABC, ADP, BONY, Chamber of Commerce, CII, Computershare, ICI, Reed Smith, Registrar and Transfer, SCSGP, SIFMA, SSA, and STA.

[15] The effective result of the rules is that an intermediary must prepare Notices (or incorporate Notice information in its request for voting instructions) and create Web sites for all issuers for which securities are held by the intermediary's customers, rather than only for issuers who elect to follow the notice and access model under the voluntary system.

[16] Based on a random sampling of 150 large accelerated filers, approximately 80% of such filers already post their proxy materials on a non-EDGAR Web site, while almost all of the rest provide a link on their Web site to the Commission's EDGAR system. Only a small handful of such filers do not post their proxy materials on their Web site at all. We note, however, that currently there is no requirement that such Web sites preserve the anonymity of persons accessing the Web site. See Section II.A.1.f of this release for a description of this requirement.

for solicitations beginning on or after January 1, 2008.[17] All other issuers (including registered investment companies) and soliciting persons other than issuers will have to comply with the model for solicitations beginning on or after January 1, 2009. This tiered system of implementation addresses the commenters' timing concerns by providing the Commission with a significant test group of large accelerated filers from which to obtain operating data and more than a full year to study the effects of the notice and access model and make any necessary revisions to the rules before they apply to other entities.

In addition, several commenters were concerned that the proposals would have required all issuers to establish Internet voting platforms[18] or to prepare their proxy materials at least 40 days prior to the shareholder meeting,[19] and therefore would impose significant costs on issuers. As discussed in detail below, the final rules do not require, and the proposals would not have required, an issuer or other soliciting person to establish an Internet voting platform. Similarly, the rules do not require an issuer or other soliciting person that sends a full set of proxy materials to shareholders to prepare its proxy materials at least 40 days prior to the meeting.

II. Description of the Amendments

Under the amendments, an issuer that is required to furnish proxy materials to shareholders under the Commission's proxy rules must post its proxy materials on a specified, publicly-accessible Internet Web site (other than the Commission's EDGAR Web site) and provide record holders with a notice informing them that the materials are available and explaining how to access those materials.[20] Intermediaries also must follow the notice and access model to furnish an issuer's proxy materials to beneficial owners. Persons other than the issuer conducting their own proxy solicitations must comply with the notice and access model as well. By requiring Internet availability of proxy materials, the amendments are designed to enhance the ability of investors to make informed voting decisions and to expand use of the Internet to ultimately lower the costs of proxy solicitations.

A. Notice and Access Model for Issuers: Two Options for Making Proxy Materials Available to Shareholders

The notice and access model allows an issuer to select either of the following two options to provide proxy materials to shareholders: (1) the "notice only option" and (2) the "full set delivery option." Under the notice only option, an issuer will comply with the same requirements that we adopted in connection with the voluntary notice and access model. Under these requirements, the issuer must post its proxy materials on an Internet Web site and send a Notice to shareholders to inform them of the electronic availability of the proxy materials at least 40 days before the shareholders meeting. If an issuer follows this option, it must respond to shareholder requests for copies, including a shareholder's permanent request for paper or e-mail copies of proxy materials for all shareholder meetings.

Under the full set delivery option, an issuer can deliver a full set of proxy materials to shareholders, along with the Notice. An issuer need not prepare and deliver a separate Notice if it incorporates all of the information required to appear in the Notice into its

---

[17] A large accelerated filer, as defined in Exchange Act Rule 12b-2 [17 CFR 240.12b-2], is an issuer that, as of the end of its fiscal year, has an aggregate worldwide market value of the voting and non-voting common equity held by its non-affiliates of $700 million or more, as measured on the last business day of the issuer's most recently completed second fiscal quarter; has been subject to the requirements of Section 13(a) or 15(d) of the Exchange Act for a period of at least twelve calendar months; has filed at least one annual report pursuant to Section 13(a) or 15(d) of the Exchange Act; and is not eligible to use Forms 10-KSB and 10-QSB for its annual and quarterly reports.

[18] See letters from ABC, BONY, and Registrar and Transfer.

[19] See, for example, letters from Chamber of Commerce, CII, Commerce Financial Printers, Elmore & Allen, ICI, and STA.

[20] See revised Rule 14a-3(a). The notice and access model does not apply to a proxy solicitation related to a business combination transaction. See Rule 14a-16(m) [17 CFR 240.14a-16(m)]. Also, as with the voluntary model, the notice and access model does not apply if the law of the issuer's state of incorporation would prohibit them from furnishing proxy materials in that manner. See Rule 14a-3(a)(3)(ii).

proxy statement and proxy card,[21] and it need not respond to requests for copies as required under the notice only option.

An issuer does not have to choose one option or the other as the exclusive means for providing proxy materials to shareholders. Rather, an issuer may use the notice only option to provide proxy materials to some shareholders and the full set delivery option to provide proxy materials to other shareholders. We describe both options in greater detail below.

1. The Notice Only Option: Sending a Notice Without a Full Set of Proxy Materials

We are adopting the notice only option substantially as proposed. Under the notice only option, an issuer will follow the same procedures that we have established under the existing notice and access model that issuers may choose to comply with on a voluntary basis for proxy solicitations commencing on or after July 1, 2007.[22] Under these procedures, the issuer must send a Notice to shareholders at least 40 calendar days before the shareholder meeting date, or if no meeting is to be held, at least 40 calendar days before the date that votes, consents, or authorizations may be used to effect a corporate action, indicating that the issuer's proxy materials are available on a specified Internet Web site and explaining how to access those proxy materials.[23] Issuers may household the Notice pursuant to Rule 14a-3(e).[24]

a. Contents of the Notice of Internet Availability of Proxy Materials

The Notice must contain the following information:[25]

- A prominent legend in bold-face type that states:

  "Important Notice Regarding the Availability of Proxy Materials for the Shareholder Meeting to Be Held on [insert meeting date].

  - **This communication presents only an overview of the more complete proxy materials that are available to you on the Internet. We encourage you to access and review all of the important information contained in the proxy materials before voting.**

  - **The [proxy statement] [information statement] [annual report to security holders] [is/are] available at [Insert Web site address].**

  - **If you want to receive a paper or e-mail copy of these documents, you must request one. There is no charge to you for requesting a copy. Please make your request for a copy as instructed below on or before [Insert a date] to facilitate timely delivery."**

- The date, time, and location of the meeting or, if corporate action is to be taken by written consent, the earliest date on which the corporate action may be effected;

- A clear and impartial identification of each separate matter intended to be acted on, and the issuer's recommendations, if any, regarding those matters, but no supporting statements;

- A list of the materials being made available at the specified Web site;

- (1) A toll-free telephone number; (2) an e-mail address; and (3) an Internet Web site address where the shareholder can request a copy of the proxy materials, for all meetings and for the particular meeting to which the Notice relates;

---

[21] If not soliciting proxies, an issuer may incorporate the Notice information into its information statement.
[22] See Rule 14a-16 [17 CFR 240.14a-16].
[23] Rule 14a-16(a)(1) [17 CFR 240.14a-16(a)(1)].
[24] 17 CFR 240.14a-3(e).

[25] Rule 14a-16(d) [17 CFR 240.14a-16(d)]. Appropriate changes must be made if the issuer is providing an information statement pursuant to Regulation 14C, seeking to effect a corporate action by written consent, or is a legal entity other than a corporation.

- Any control/identification numbers that the shareholder needs to access his or her proxy card;

- Instructions on how to access the proxy card, provided that such instructions do not enable a shareholder to execute a proxy without having access to the proxy statement; and

- Information about attending the shareholder meeting and voting in person.

The Notice must be written in plain English.[26] The Notice may contain only the information specified by the rules and any other information required by state law, if the issuer chooses to combine the Notice with any shareholder meeting notice that state law may require.[27] However, the Notice may contain a protective warning to shareholders, advising them that no personal information other than the identification or control number is necessary to execute a proxy.[28] In addition, a registered investment company may send its prospectus and/or report to shareholders together with the Notice.[29] The issuer must file its Notice with the Commission pursuant to Rule 14a-6(b)[30] no later than the date that it first sends the Notice to shareholders.[31]

b. Design of the specified publicly-accessible Web site

An issuer must make all proxy materials identified in the Notice publicly accessible, free of charge, at the Web site address specified in the Notice on or before the date that the Notice is sent to the shareholder.[32] The specified Web site may not be the Commission's EDGAR system.[33] The issuer also must post any subsequent additional soliciting materials on the Web site no later than the date on which such materials are first sent to shareholders or made public.[34] The materials must be presented on the Web site in a format, or formats, convenient for both reading online and printing on paper.[35] The proxy materials must remain available on that Web site through the conclusion of the shareholder meeting.[36]

c. Means to vote

An issuer also must provide shareholders with a method to execute proxies as of the time the Notice is first sent to shareholders.[37] Several commenters on the proposal questioned whether this provision would require all issuers to establish Internet voting platforms.[38] The final rules do not require, and the proposals would not have required, an issuer to establish an Internet voting platform. Rather, an issuer can satisfy this requirement through a variety of methods, including providing an electronic voting platform, a tollfree telephone number for voting, or a printable or downloadable proxy card on the Web site. As noted above, if a telephone number for executing a proxy is provided, such a telephone number may appear on the Web site, but not on the Notice because it would enable a shareholder to execute a proxy without having access to the proxy statement.

d. Request for paper or e-mail copies

An issuer must provide paper or e-mail copies at no charge to shareholders requesting such copies.[39] It also must allow shareholders to make a permanent election to receive paper or e-mail copies of proxy materials distributed in connection with future proxy

---

[26] Rule 14a-16(g) [17 CFR 240.14a-16(g)].
[27] Rule 14a-16(e) [17 CFR 240.14a-16(e)].
[28] Rule 14a-16(e)(2)(ii) [17 CFR 240.14a-16(e)(2)(ii)].
[29] See new Rule 14a-16(f)(2)(iii).
[30] 17 CFR 240.14a-6(b).
[31] Rule 14a-16(i) [17 CFR 240.14a-16(i)].
[32] Rule 14a-16(b)(1) [17 CFR 240.14a-16(b)(1)].
[33] Rule 14a-16(b)(3) [17 CFR 240.14a-16(b)(3)].
[34] Rule 14a-16(b)(2) [17 CFR 240.14a-16(b)(2)].
[35] Rule 14a-16(c) [17 CFR 240.14a-16(c)]. See Section II.A.3 of Release 34-55146 (Jan. 22, 2007) [72 FR 4148]. One commenter asked the Commission to consider the costs of requiring such formats. See letter from ICI. We believe that requiring readable and printable

formats is important so that shareholders have meaningful access to the proxy materials. When determining the readability and printability of formats, issuers should consider the size of the files because many shareholders do not have broadband connections. Although some types of files may be suitable for persons with high-speed Internet access, the readability and printability of a document may be affected significantly by the time that it takes to download the document.
[36] Rule 14a-16(b)(1) [17 CFR 240.14a-16(b)(1)].
[37] Rule 14a-16(b)(4) [17 CFR 240.14a-16(b)(4)].
[38] See letters from ABC, BONY, and Registrar and Transfer.
[39] Rule 14a-16(j) [17 CFR 240.14a-16(j)].

solicitations, and maintain records of those elections.[40] Further, the issuer must provide a toll-free telephone number, e-mail address, and Internet Web site address as a means by which a shareholder can request a copy of the proxy materials for the particular shareholder meeting referenced in the Notice or make a permanent election to receive copies of the proxy materials on a continuing basis with respect to all meetings.[41] The issuer also may include a pre-addressed, postage-paid reply card with the Notice that shareholders can use to request a copy of the proxy materials.[42]

e. Delivery of a proxy card

An issuer may not send a paper or e-mail proxy card to a shareholder until 10 calendar days or more after the date it sent the Notice to the shareholder, unless the proxy card is accompanied or preceded by a copy of the proxy statement and any annual report, if required, to security holders sent via the same medium.[43] This provision is intended to assist an issuer's efforts to solicit proxies if its initial efforts have not produced adequate response. This is similar to many issuers' current practice of sending reminder notices and duplicate proxy cards to shareholders who have not responded to the issuer's original request for proxy voting instructions.

One commenter remarking on this aspect of the proposals expressed concern that shareholders receiving proxy cards separately from the proxy statement and annual report may make their voting decisions without the benefit of access to those disclosure documents.[44] We appreciate this concern. However, at the point that a shareholder receives such a proxy card, the shareholder already would have received a Notice that provides information on how the shareholder can access the proxy materials and request copies of the materials, if desired. Moreover, the shareholder also would receive another copy of the Notice with the proxy card. We believe that, at this point, the shareholder will have had ample opportunity to either access the proxy materials on the Internet Web site or request a copy of those materials.

f. Web site confidentiality

An issuer must maintain the Internet Web site on which it posts its proxy materials in a manner that does not infringe on the anonymity of a person accessing that Web site.[45] An issuer also may not use any e-mail address provided by a shareholder solely to request a copy of proxy materials for any purpose other than to send a copy of those materials to that shareholder.[46] The issuer also may not disclose a shareholder's e-mail address to any person, except to its agent or an employee of the issuer. This disclosure may be made only for the purpose of facilitating delivery of a copy of the issuer's proxy materials by the agent or employee to a shareholder requesting a copy of the materials.

Three commenters were concerned about the provisions of the model that require a company to maintain the designated Web site in a manner that does not infringe on the anonymity of persons accessing the Web site.[47] One commenter was concerned that the prohibition on "cookies" will raise the costs of maintaining Internet Web sites.[48] Conversely, one commenter was concerned that there could be potential abuses of shareholder privacy through information tracking and collection of information on Internet Web sites.[49] Similar concerns regarding potential abuses of shareholder privacy also were raised with regard to the adoption of the voluntary notice and access model.

Although we recognize that the confidentiality requirements may increase the cost of maintaining an Internet Web site, we believe that the protection of shareholder information is important. A rule that permits issuers to discover the identity of a person accessing the Web site could effectively negate a beneficial owner's ability under the proxy rules to

---

[40] See Rule 14a-16(d)(5) and (j)(4) [17 CFR 240.14a-16(d)(5) and (j)(4)].

[41] Rule 14a-16(d)(5) [17 CFR 240.14a-16(d)(5)].

[42] Rule 14a-16(f)(2)(i) [17 CFR 240.14a-16(f)(2)(i)].

[43] Rule 14a-16(h) [17 CFR 240.14a-16(h)].

[44] See letter from CII.

[45] Rule 14a-16(k)(1) [17 CFR 240.14a-16(k)(1)]. See Section II.A.1.b.iii of Release No. 34-55146 (Jan. 22, 2007) [72 FR 4148].

[46] Rule 14a-16(k)(2) [17 CFR 240.14a-16(k)(2)].

[47] See letters from CII, ICI, and Reed Smith.

[48] See letter from ICI.

[49] See letter from CII.

object to an intermediary's disclosure of that beneficial owner's identity to the issuer.[50] In addition, a rule without this prohibition on the issuer may make some shareholders hesitant to access the proxy disclosures, which would not promote the purposes of this rule. Therefore we have retained this provision of the rule to help prevent potential abuses of shareholder information.

We do not believe that this requirement will impose any undue burden on companies. Under the rule, a company must refrain from installing cookies and other tracking features on the Web site on which the proxy materials are posted. This may require segregating those pages from the rest of the company's regular Web site or creating a new Web site. However, the rule does not require the company to turn off the Web site's connection log, which automatically tracks numerical IP addresses that connect to that Web site. Although in most cases, this IP address does not provide companies with sufficient information to identify the accessing shareholder, companies may not use these numbers to attempt to find out more information about persons accessing the Web site. In addition, shareholders still concerned about their anonymity can request copies from their intermediaries.

2. The Full Set Delivery Option: Sending a Notice with a Full Set of Proxy Materials

Under the "full set delivery option," an issuer will follow procedures that are substantially similar to the traditional means of providing proxy materials in paper.[51] Under this option, in addition to sending proxy materials to shareholders as under the traditional method, an issuer must:

- Send a Notice accompanied by a full set of proxy materials,[52] or incorporate all of the information required to appear in the Notice into the proxy statement and proxy card[53]; and

- Post the proxy materials on a publicly accessible Web site no later than the date the Notice was first sent to shareholders.[54]

Issuers may household the Notice and other proxy materials pursuant to Rule 14a-3(e).[55]

a. Contents of the Notice or incorporation of Notice information

Under the final rules that we are adopting, a separate Notice is not required if the issuer presents all of the information required in the Notice in its proxy statement and proxy card.[56] In the proposing release, we solicited comment on whether we should permit the issuer that is sending a full set to incorporate the information required in the Notice into the proxy statement and proxy card, rather than require that issuer to prepare a separate Notice. Although we did not receive any comment on this issue, we do not see a compelling reason to require an issuer to include a separate Notice when it already is sending a shareholder a full set of proxy materials. We believe that providing the Notice information in the proxy materials will provide shareholders with sufficient information to access the

---

[50] See Rules 14b-1(b) and 14b-2(b) [17 CFR 240.14b-1(b) and 240.14b-2(b)].

[51] Under the traditional proxy delivery scheme, issuers could send proxy materials to shareholders via e-mail provided they followed Commission guidance regarding such delivery, which typically required obtaining affirmative consent from individual shareholders. See Release No. 33-7233 (Oct. 6, 1995) [60 FR 53458]. Issuers may continue to rely on such guidance to send materials electronically to shareholders. See Section II.A. of this release.

[52] A "full set" of proxy materials would contain (1) a proxy statement or information statement, (2) an annual report if one is required by Rule 14a-3(b) or Rule 14c-3(a), and (3) a proxy card or, in the case of a beneficial owner, a request for voting instructions, if proxies are being solicited.

[53] See new Rule 14a-16(n)(2).

[54] As discussed below, this date does not have to be at least 40 days prior to the shareholder meeting date.

[55] 17 CFR 240.14a-3(e).

[56] Because issuers are obligated to provide proxy materials to beneficial owners, we recommend that issuers place only information required by the Notice that is relevant to all shareholders (record and beneficial owners) in the proxy statement, and present information that is relevant only to record holders on the proxy card so that beneficial owners are not confused by information in the proxy statement that would only be applicable to record holders. Required information disclosed on the proxy statement need not be repeated on the proxy card.

materials on the Internet, while reducing costs to issuers. However, an issuer may prepare a separate Notice if it desires.

The information required in the Notice, or proxy materials if no separate Notice is prepared, includes much, but not all, of the information that is required under the notice only option, including the following:[57]

- A prominent legend in bold-face type that states:

  "Important Notice Regarding the Availability of Proxy Materials for the Shareholder Meeting to Be Held on [insert meeting date].

  o **The [proxy statement] [information statement] [annual report to security holders] [is/are] available at [insert Web site address]."**

- The date, time, and location of the meeting or, if corporate action is to be taken by written consent, the earliest date on which the corporate action may be effected;

- A clear and impartial identification of each separate matter intended to be acted on and the issuer's recommendations, if any, regarding those matters, but no supporting statements;

- A list of the materials being made available at the specified Web site;

- Any control/identification numbers that the shareholder needs to access his or her proxy card; and

- Information about attending the shareholder meeting and voting in person.

The issuer is not required to provide paper or e-mail copies upon request to shareholders to whom it has furnished proxy materials under this option because it would already have provided those shareholders with a copy of the proxy materials as part of its initial distribution.[58] Therefore, the issuer need not provide instructions in the Notice as to how shareholders can request paper or e-mail copies of the proxy materials.[59]

If the issuer prepares a separate Notice, it must be written in plain English.[60] The Notice may contain only the information specified by the rules and any other information required by state law, if the issuer chooses to combine the Notice with any shareholder meeting notice that state law may require.[61] However, the Notice may contain a protective warning to shareholders, advising them that no personal information other than the identification or control number is necessary to execute a proxy.[62] The issuer must file any such separate Notice with the Commission pursuant to Rule 14a-6(b) no later than the date that it first sends the Notice to shareholders.[63]

b. Design of the specified publicly-accessible Web site

An issuer must post all proxy materials identified in the Notice, or proxy statement and proxy card if no separate Notice is prepared, on the publicly accessible Web site address specified in the Notice on or before the date that it sends the proxy materials to shareholders.[64] The specified Web site may not be the Commission's EDGAR system.[65] The issuer also must post any subsequent additional soliciting materials on the Web site no later than the date on which such materials are first sent to shareholders or made public.[66] The materials must be presented on the Web site in a format, or formats, convenient for both reading online and printing on paper.[67] The proxy materials must remain available on that Web site through the conclusion of the shareholder meeting.[68]

---

[57] See new Rule 14a-16(n)(4). Appropriate changes must be made if the issuer is providing an information statement pursuant to Regulation 14C, seeking to effect a corporate action by written consent, or is a legal entity other than a corporation.

[58] See new Rule 14a-16(n)(3)(ii).

[59] See new Rule 14a-16(n)(4)(ii).

[60] Rule 14a-16(g) [17 CFR 240.14a-16(g)].

[61] Rule 14a-16(e) [17 CFR 240.14a-16(e)].

[62] Rule 14a-16(e)(2)(ii) [17 CFR 240.14a-16(e)(2)(ii)].

[63] Rule 14a-16(i) [17 CFR 240.14a-16(i)]. If the issuer incorporates the contents of the Notice into the proxy materials, a separate filing is not required.

[64] Rule 14a-16(b)(1) [17 CFR 240.14a-16(b)(1)].

[65] Rule 14a-16(b)(3) [17 CFR 240.14a-16(b)(3)].

[66] Rule 14a-16(b)(2) [17 CFR 240.14a-16(b)(2)].

c. Means to vote

The notice and access model requires an issuer to provide shareholders with a method to execute proxies as of the time the Notice is first sent to shareholders.[69] If an issuer follows the full set delivery option, the proxy card or request for voting instructions included in the full set of proxy materials satisfies this requirement. Therefore, the issuer does not need to provide another means for shareholders to execute proxies or submit voting instructions for accounts receiving proxy materials through the full set delivery option.

d. Repeat Delivery of a Proxy Card

Even though a proxy card already will be included in the full set of proxy materials, an issuer relying on the full set delivery option subsequently may choose to deliver another copy of the proxy card to shareholders who have not returned the card. This is permissible under the current rules, and issuers commonly do so as a reminder for shareholders to vote. The reminder proxy card does not have to be accompanied by the Notice because the reminder card would have been preceded by the proxy statement via the same medium and may be sent at any time after the full set of proxy materials has been sent.[70]

e. Web site confidentiality

As under the notice only option, an issuer must maintain the Internet Web site on which it posts its proxy materials in a manner that does not infringe on the anonymity of a person accessing that Web site.[71] An issuer also may not use any e-mail address provided by a shareholder solely to request a copy of proxy materials for any purpose other than to send a copy of those materials to that shareholder.[72] The issuer also may not disclose a shareholder's e-mail address to any person other than the issuer's employee or agent to the extent necessary to send a copy of the proxy materials to a requesting shareholder.

3. Differences Between the Full Set Delivery Option and the Notice Only Option

The full set delivery option varies from the notice only option in the following ways:

- An issuer may accompany the Notice with a copy of the proxy statement, annual report to security holders, if required by Rule 14a-3(b),[73] and a proxy card[74];

- An issuer need not prepare a separate Notice if the issuer incorporates all of the Notice information into the proxy statement and proxy card[75];

- Because the issuer already has provided shareholders with a full set of proxy materials, the issuer need not provide the shareholder with copies of the proxy materials upon request[76];

- Because shareholders will not need extra time to request paper or e-mail copies, the issuer need not send the Notice and full set of proxy materials at least 40 days before the meeting date[77];

---

[69] Rule 14a-16(b)(4) [17 CFR 240.14a-16(b)(4)].

[70] See new Rule 14a-16(h)(2).

[71] Rule 14a-16(k)(1) [17 CFR 240.14a-16(k)(1)]. See Section II.A.1.b.iii of Release No. 34-55146 (Jan. 22, 2007) [72 FR 4148].

[72] Rule 14a-16(k)(2) [17 CFR 240.14a-16(k)(2)].

[73] The requirement in Exchange Act Rules 14a-3(b) and 14c-3(a) to furnish annual reports to security holders does not apply to registered investment companies [17 CFR 240.14a-3(b) and 240.14c-3(a)]. A

soliciting person other than the issuer also is not subject to this requirement. Finally, an issuer is required to provide such a report for shareholder meetings at which directors are to be elected.

[74] See new Rule 14a-16(n)(1).

[75] See new Rule 14a-16(n)(2)(ii). See also footnote 58, above.

[76] See new Rule 14a-16(n)(3)(ii).

[77] See new Rule 14a-16(n)(3)(i).

- Because the full set of proxy materials includes a proxy card or request for voting instructions, the issuer need not provide another means for voting at the time the Notice is provided unless it chooses to do so; and

- The issuer need not include the part of the prescribed legend relating to security holder requests for copies of the documents and instructions on how to request a copy of the proxy materials.[78]

a. Inclusion of a Full Set of Proxy Materials

The notice only option does not permit an issuer to accompany the Notice with any other documents.[79] In contrast, an issuer relying on the full set delivery option will deliver a full set of proxy materials, including a proxy statement, annual report to shareholders if required by Rule 14a-3(b), and a proxy card, along with the Notice. Under this option, when the Notice is initially sent, it must be accompanied by all of these documents, not just some of them. For example, an issuer may not send only the Notice and a proxy card to a shareholder as part of its initial distribution of proxy materials.[80]

b. Request for Copies of the Proxy Materials

As noted above, because an issuer relying on the full set delivery option will send shareholders copies of all of the proxy materials along with the Notice, there is no need for the issuer to provide these shareholders with a means to request a copy of the proxy materials. The issuer therefore may exclude information from the Notice on how a shareholder may request such copies.[81]

c. 40-Day Deadline

Under the full set delivery option, if an issuer or other soliciting person sends a full set of the proxy materials with the Notice, it need not comply with the 40-day deadline in Rule 14a-16 for sending the Notice. Thus, if an issuer is unable or unwilling to meet the 40-day deadline, it still may begin its solicitation after that deadline provided that it complies with the full set delivery option. Six commenters on the proposal questioned whether the proposal would have required all issuers to prepare their proxy materials at least 40 days prior to the meeting.[82] We have clarified that an issuer must comply with the 40-day period *only* if it intends to comply with the notice only option.[83]

B. Implications of the Notice and Access Model for Intermediaries

An issuer or other soliciting person must provide each intermediary with the information necessary to prepare the intermediary's Notice in sufficient time for the intermediary to prepare and send its Notice to beneficial owners within the timeframes of the model. An issuer that complies with the notice only option must provide the intermediary with the relevant information in sufficient time for the intermediary to prepare and send the Notice and post the proxy materials on the Web site at least 40 calendar days before the shareholder meeting date.[84]

An issuer that complies with the full set delivery option need not comply with the 40-day deadline. The issuer need only provide the Notice information to the intermediary in

---

[78] See new Rule 14a-16(n)(4).

[79] Rule 14a-16(f)(1) [17 CFR 240.14a-16(f)(1)]. We note however, that under the notice only option, an issuer may send the Notice and proxy card together 10 days or more after it initially sends the Notice. See new Rule 14a-16(h)(1).

[80] However, it may send a reminder proxy card at any time after it initially sends the Notice accompanied by the full set of proxy materials. See new Rule 14a-16(h)(2).

[81] See Rule 14a-16(n)(4).

[82] See, for example, letters from Chamber of Commerce, CII, Commerce Financial Printers, Elmore & Allen, ICI, and STA.

[83] See Rule 14a-16(n)(3)(i).

[84] If a soliciting person other than the issuer elects to follow the notice only option, the Notice must be sent to shareholders by the later of: (1) 40 calendar days prior to the security holder meeting date or, if no meeting is to be held, 40 calendar days prior to the date the votes, consents, or authorizations may be used to effect the corporate action; or (2) 10 calendar days after the date that the registrant first sends its proxy statement or Notice of Internet Availability of Proxy Materials to security holders. See Rule 14a-16(l)(2) [17 CFR 240.14a-16(l)(2)].

sufficient time for the intermediary to prepare and send the Notice along with the full set of materials provided by the issuer. Under this option, as with the traditional method of delivering proxy materials, the intermediary must forward the issuer's full set of proxy materials to beneficial owners within five business days of receipt from the issuer or the issuer's agent.[85]

The intermediary's Notice generally must contain the same types of information as an issuer's Notice, but must be tailored specifically for beneficial owners.[86] With respect to beneficial owners who receive a Notice under the notice only option, the intermediary also must forward paper or e-mail copies of the proxy materials upon request, permit the beneficial owners to make a permanent election to receive paper or e-mail copies of the proxy materials, keep records of beneficial owner preferences, provide proxy materials in accordance with those preferences, and provide a means to access a request for voting instructions for its beneficial owner customers no later than the date the Notice is first sent.

When the issuer is delivering full sets of proxy materials to beneficial owners, the intermediary must either prepare a separate Notice and forward it with the full set of proxy materials, or incorporate any information required in the Notice, but not appearing in the issuer's proxy statement, in its request for voting instructions.

C. Reliance on the Notice and Access Model by Soliciting Persons Other Than the Issuer

Under the amendments, a soliciting person other than the issuer also must comply with the notice and access model. Such a person may solicit proxies pursuant to the notice only option, the full set delivery option, or a combination of the two.[87] Consistent with the existing proxy rules and the voluntary model, the amendments treat such soliciting persons differently from the issuer in certain respects.

First, a soliciting person is not required to solicit every shareholder or to furnish an information statement to shareholders not being solicited. It may select the specific shareholders from whom it wishes to solicit proxies. For example, under the notice and access model, a soliciting person other than the issuer can choose to send Notices only to those shareholders who have not previously requested paper copies.[88]

Second, if a soliciting person other than the issuer elects to follow the notice only option, it must send a Notice to shareholders by the later of:

- 40 calendar days prior to the shareholder meeting date or, if no meeting is to be held, 40 calendar days prior to the date that votes, consents, or authorizations may be used to effect the corporate action; or

- 10 calendar days after the date that the issuer first sends its proxy materials to shareholders.[89]

This timing requirement does not apply to a solicitation pursuant to the full set delivery model.

If, at the time the Notice is sent, a soliciting person other than the issuer is not aware of all matters on the shareholder meeting agenda, the Notice must provide a clear and impartial identification of each separate matter to be acted upon at the meeting, to the

---

[85] See Rule 14b-1(b)(2) [17 CFR 240.14b-1(b)(2)].

[86] For a more complete discussion of the content of the intermediary's Notice, see Section II.B.2 of Release No. 34-55146 (Jan. 22, 2007) [72 FR 4148].

[87] That is, as in the case of an issuer, a soliciting person other than the issuer may solicit some shareholders using the notice only option, while soliciting other shareholders using the full set delivery option.

[88] Under Rule 14a-7(a)(2) [17 CFR 240.14a-7(a)(2)], an issuer is required to either mail the Notice on behalf of the soliciting person, in which case the soliciting person can request that the issuer send Notices only to shareholders who have not requested paper copies, or provide the soliciting person with a shareholder list, indicating which shareholders have requested paper copies. For a more complete discussion of the interaction of the model with Rule 14a-7, see Section II.C.4 of Release No. 34-55146 (Jan. 22, 2007) [72 FR 4148].

[89] Rule 14a-16(l)(2) [17 CFR 240.14a-16(l)(2)].

extent known by the soliciting person.[90] The soliciting person's Notice also must include a clear statement that there may be additional agenda items that the soliciting person is unaware of, and that the shareholder cannot direct a vote for those items on the soliciting person's proxy card provided at that time.[91] If a soliciting person other than the issuer sends a proxy card that does not reference all matters that shareholders will act upon at the meeting, the Notice must clearly state whether execution of the proxy card would invalidate a shareholder's prior vote using the issuer's card on matters not presented on the soliciting person's proxy card.[92]

III. Clarifying Amendments

Since adopting the notice and access model as a voluntary model, we have received several questions regarding implementation of that model. Some of these questions were received as comments on the proposing release to these amendments. To the extent such comments relate to the previously adopted voluntary model, the Commission's staff is working with those commenters to provide guidance regarding implementation of those rules. However, several comments indicated aspects of the adopted rules that we believe would benefit from clarification in the regulatory text. To help clarify our intent, we are adopting the following technical amendments.

A. No Requirement to Provide Recommendations

Rule 14a-16(d)(3),[93] as it was initially adopted under the voluntary notice and access model, required the Notice to contain "[a] clear and impartial identification of each separate matter intended to be acted on and the soliciting person's recommendation regarding those matters." Our intent with this provision was not to require an issuer or other soliciting person to have a recommendation for every matter. Therefore, we are revising this provision to clarify that an issuer or other a soliciting person must present its recommendation only if it chooses to make a recommendation on a particular matter to be acted upon by shareholders.

B. Deadline for Responding to Requests for Copies After the Meeting

We are also amending the requirements about the fulfillment of requests for paper or e-mail copies received after the conclusion of the meeting. The rules that we initially adopted as part of the voluntary notice and access model made no distinction in the fulfillment requirements based on whether the issuer received a request for a paper or e-mail copy before or after the meeting date. We did state in the adopting release for the voluntary notice and access model that the post-meeting fulfillment provision is intended to require issuers to provide a copy of the proxy statement for one year "[j]ust as the proxy rules require issuers to undertake in their proxy statements or annual reports to shareholders to provide copies of annual reports on Form 10-K for the most recent fiscal year to requesting shareholders."[94] The rule relating to providing copies of the annual report on Form 10-K does not require the use of First Class mail or that the issuer respond within three business days.[95] After the meeting is concluded, we do not believe there is such an urgent need to provide copies of the proxy materials in a timely manner to impose such requirements. Therefore, we are revising Rule 14a-16(j)(3)[96] to clarify that, with respect to requests for copies received after the conclusion of the meeting, an issuer is not required to use First Class mail and is not required to respond within three business days.

C. Item 4 of Schedule 14A

Item 4 of Schedule 14A[97] requires that an issuer or other soliciting person describe the methods used for soliciting proxies if not using the mails. Because the amendments require issuers and other soliciting persons to comply with Rule 14a-16 with respect to all proxy

---

[90] Rule 14a-16(l)(3)(i) [17 CFR 240.14a-16(l)(3)(i)].
[91] *Id.*
[92] Rule 14a-16(l)(3)(ii) [17 CFR 240.14a-16(l)(3)(ii)].
[93] 17 CFR 240.14a-16(d)(3).
[94] See Release No. 33-55146 (Jan. 22, 2007) [72 FR 4148].
[95] See Rule 14a-3(b) [17 CFR 240.14a-3(b)].
[96] 17 CFR 240.14a-16(j)(3).
[97] 17 CFR 240.14a-101.

solicitations not related to business combination transactions, we are revising this item to clarify that issuers and other soliciting persons need not describe the notice and access model when they are using it to solicit proxies.

IV. Compliance Dates

Large accelerated filers, not including registered investment companies, must comply with the amendments with respect to solicitations commencing on or after January 1, 2008. Registered investment companies, soliciting persons other than the issuer, and issuers that are not large accelerated filers conducting proxy solicitations (1) may comply with the amendments for solicitations commencing on or after January 1, 2008, and (2) must comply with the notice and access model for solicitations commencing on or after January 1, 2009. For example, a soliciting person other than the issuer that is soliciting proxies with respect to a shareholder meeting of a large accelerated filer is not required to follow the notice and access model until January 1, 2009, even though the large accelerated filer would be required to follow the model. However, such a soliciting person may voluntarily follow the model.

As stated above, the primary concern of most commenters on the proposal was the Commission's aggressive timetable for adopting the proposed rules. All 14 commenters on this topic requested that the Commission delay adoption of the proposed rules.[98] This group of commenters included trade associations representing issuers, transfer agents, intermediaries, proxy distribution service providers, institutional investors, and other shareholders.

Eight of these commenters were concerned that the short period between effectiveness of the voluntary model and adoption of the amendments in this release would not permit the Commission and the industry to properly evaluate the results of the voluntary model and prepare an adequate cost-benefit analysis.[99] Data that the commenters felt would be important to capture regarding the voluntary model included: (1) the effect on voter participation; (2) the costs of implementing the model; and (3) the extent to which predicted savings are actually realized by companies and other soliciting persons. These commenters recommended that the Commission not adopt the proposed amendments until it has had the opportunity to assess the data received regarding companies' experiences with the voluntary model.

With respect to costs, three of these commenters were concerned regarding the cost of adopting rules that would require issuers to develop, or hire outside services to develop, an Internet voting platform.[100] The rules that we are adopting do not require, and the proposals would not have required, such an Internet voting platform. Similarly, five commenters raised concerns regarding the ability of issuers to prepare their proxy materials at least 40 days before the date of the shareholder meeting, and costs associated with these efforts.[101] The rules that we are adopting do not require, and the proposal would not have required, all issuers to comply with the 40-day deadline if they are unable, or choose not, to do so.

As we have explained above, an issuer or other soliciting person may elect to comply with either: (1) the notice only option which is identical to the voluntary notice and access model; or (2) the full set delivery option. The latter option is substantially the same as the traditional system of providing proxy materials in paper, except that an issuer or other soliciting person complying with the full set delivery option also will have to:

- prepare and send a Notice, or incorporate the Notice information into its proxy statement and proxy card; and

---

[98] See letters from AARP, ABC, ADP, BONY, Chamber of Commerce, CII, Computershare, ICI, Reed Smith, Registrar and Transfer, SCSGP, SIFMA, SSA, and STA.

[99] See letters from Chamber of Commerce, BONY, ICI, Reed Smith, Registrar and Transfer, SCSGP, SIMFA, and STA.

[100] See letters from ABC, BONY and Registrar and Transfer.

[101] See letters from Chamber of Commerce, CII, Commerce Financial Printers, Elmore & Allen, ICI, and STA.

- post its proxy materials on a publicly accessible Web site.

As we discuss more fully in our cost-benefit analysis, we believe that the cost to issuers and other soliciting persons to comply with these two requirements will not be significant, and therefore are expanding Internet availability of proxy materials to all shareholders. Many of the commenters' concerns regarding costs were based on beliefs that the proposal would require an electronic voting platform, preparation of proxy materials at least 40 days before the shareholder meeting, and anonymity controls on the Web site that exceed what the proposal would actually require. As noted above, the proposals would not have required, and the final rules do not require, such provisions. Rather, an issuer or other soliciting person can substantially continue to follow the traditional method of proxy delivery with minimal changes. Because the amendments will not have a significant impact on the requirements placed on issuers and other soliciting persons, we believe it is appropriate to adopt them now.

We also note that commenters have expressed concern, particularly in relation to the voluntary model, that if the model has a negative effect on shareholder participation, issuers may use the model to disenfranchise certain shareholders. We recognize these concerns and intend to monitor shareholder participation and take any steps necessary to prevent such abuse.

Furthermore, the tiered compliance dates address commenters' concerns because they will allow the Commission to better analyze the impact of the rules on a subset of issuers constituting large accelerated filers.[102] As noted above, a review of existing Web sites of such issuers indicated that approximately 80% of them already post their filings, including proxy materials, on their Web site. Thus, most of the issuers that will be subject to the rules in the first year will be large issuers that appear to already post their proxy materials on their Web site. Therefore, we believe that this group is in the best position with respect to implementation costs in the first year while we evaluate the performance of the model. Adopting the amendments before the 2008 proxy season effectively creates a test group of issuers, enabling the Commission to study the performance of the model with a significant number of larger issuers and providing the Commission with an opportunity to make any necessary revisions to the rules before they apply to all issuers and other soliciting persons.

V. Paperwork Reduction Act

Certain provisions of the amendments contain "collection of information" requirements within the meaning of the Paperwork Reduction Act of 1995 ("PRA"), including preparation of Notices, maintaining Web sites, maintaining records of shareholder preferences, and responding to requests for copies. The titles for the collections of information are:

Regulation 14A (OMB Control No. 3235-0059)

Regulation 14C (OMB Control No. 3235-0057)

We requested public comment on these collections of information in the release proposing the notice and access model as a voluntary model for disseminating proxy materials,[103] and submitted them to the Office of Management and Budget ("OMB") for review in accordance with the PRA. We received approval for the collections of information. We submitted a revised PRA analysis to OMB in conjunction with the release adopting the notice and access model as a voluntary model.[104] In those releases, we assumed conservatively that all issuers and other persons soliciting proxies would follow the voluntary model because the proportion of issuers and other soliciting persons that would elect to follow the model was uncertain.

---

[102] One commenter specifically noted that the timeframe would not allow the Commission to analyze the effects of one full year of compliance for large accelerated filers who chose to accept the voluntary model. See letter from the Chamber of Commerce. The tiered system will allow the Commission to analyze a full year of experience under the notice and access model for all large accelerated filers.

[103] Release No. 34-52926 (Dec. 8, 2005) [70 FR 74597].

[104] Release No. 34-55146 (Jan. 22, 2007) [72 FR 4147].

The rules that we are adopting require all issuers and other soliciting persons to follow the notice and access model, including the preparation of the Notice, as we assumed for our prior PRA analysis. Therefore, we estimate that the rule amendments will not impose any new recordkeeping or information collection requirements beyond those described in the release adopting the voluntary model, or necessitate revising the burden estimates for any existing collections of information requiring OMB's approval.

VI. Cost-Benefit Analysis

A. Background

We are adopting amendments to the proxy rules under the Exchange Act substantially as proposed that require issuers and other soliciting persons (jointly referred to as "soliciting parties") to follow the notice and access model for furnishing proxy materials. The amendments are intended to provide all shareholders with the ability to choose the means by which they access proxy materials, to expand use of the Internet to ultimately lower the costs of proxy solicitations, and to improve shareholder communications.

B. Summary of the Amendments

The notice and access model that we are adopting requires soliciting parties to furnish proxy materials by posting them on a specified, publicly-accessible Internet Web site (other than the Commission's EDGAR Web site) and providing shareholders with a notice informing them that the materials are available and explaining how to access them. Under the model, soliciting parties may choose between two options with respect to how they will provide proxy materials to shareholders. Under the first option, the notice only option, a soliciting party may follow the procedures in Exchange Act Rule 14a-16 that we adopted on January 22, 2007, in connection with the voluntary model.[105] Under this option, a soliciting party would send only a Notice indicating the Internet availability of the proxy materials to a solicited shareholder at least 40 days prior to the shareholders meeting and provide that shareholder with a paper or e-mail copy of the proxy materials upon request.

Under the second option, the full set delivery option, soliciting parties may follow procedures substantially similar to the traditional method of sending paper copies of the proxy materials to a shareholder by accompanying the Notice with a full set of proxy materials. Under the full set delivery option, the soliciting party is not required to send the Notice and the full set of proxy materials at least 40 days prior to the shareholders meeting and need not provide a means for shareholders to request another set of the proxy materials. Moreover, a soliciting party need not prepare a separate Notice if it includes all of the information otherwise required in a Notice in the proxy statement or proxy card.

A soliciting party may use the notice only option to provide proxy materials to some shareholders and the full set delivery option to provide proxy materials to other shareholders. The amendments also require intermediaries to follow similar procedures to provide beneficial owners with access to the proxy materials. Soliciting parties may not use the model with respect to a business combination transaction.

C. Benefits

1. Versatility of the Internet

Historically, soliciting parties decided whether to provide shareholders with the choice to receive proxy materials by electronic means. The amendments, which build on and incorporate the voluntary model that we adopted in January, are intended to provide all shareholders with the ability to choose the means by which they access proxy materials, to expand use of the Internet potentially to lower the costs of proxy solicitations, and to improve the efficiency of the proxy process and shareholder communications. The amendments provide all shareholders with the ability to choose whether to access proxy materials in paper, by e-mail or via the Internet. As technology continues to progress,

---

[105] Release No. 34-55146 (Jan. 22, 2007) [72 FR 4147].

accessing the proxy materials on the Internet should increase the utility of our disclosure requirements to shareholders. Information in electronic documents is often more easily searchable than information in paper documents. Shareholders will be better able to go directly to any section of the document that they are particularly interested in. The amendments also will permit shareholders to more easily evaluate data and transfer data using analytical tools such as spreadsheet programs. Such tools enable users to compare relevant data about several companies more easily.

In addition, encouraging shareholders to use the Internet in the context of proxy solicitations may encourage improved shareholder communications in other ways. Current and future Internet communications innovations may enhance shareholders' ability to interact not only with management, but with each other. Such access may improve shareholder relations to the extent that shareholders feel that they have enhanced access to management. Centralizing an issuer's disclosure on a Web site may facilitate shareholder access to other important information, such as research reports and news concerning the issuer. We believe that increased reliance on the Internet for making proxy materials available to shareholders could ultimately lower the cost of soliciting proxies for all soliciting parties.

2. [Reduction in] Paper Processing Costs

One of the purposes of the voluntary model was to reduce paper processing costs related to proxy solicitations. We previously estimated savings assuming that soliciting parties responsible for 10% to 50% of all proxy mailings would follow that model. We do not assume that the amendments will cause a soliciting party to change its decision under the voluntary model whether to send only a Notice or to send a full set of proxy materials to shareholders. Therefore, we do not assume for this analysis any savings in paper processing costs as a result of these particular amendments. However, because the voluntary model just recently became effective for proxy solicitations commencing on or after July 1, 2007, and therefore has not been used by many soliciting parties and because these amendments create a single notice and access model that includes aspects of the voluntary model, we are presenting a cost-benefit analysis that addresses the notice and access model as a whole, including our assessment of the benefits and costs created by the amendments.

As we discussed in the adopting release for the voluntary model, the paper-related benefits of the notice and access model are limited by the volume of paper processing that would occur otherwise. As we noted in that release, Automatic Data Processing, Inc.[106] (ADP) handles the vast majority of proxy mailings to beneficial owners.[107] ADP publishes statistics that provide useful background for evaluating the likely consequences of the rule amendments. ADP estimates that, during the 2006 proxy season,[108] over 69.7 million proxy material mailings were eliminated through a variety of means, including householding and existing electronic delivery methods. During that season, ADP mailed 85.3 million paper proxy items to beneficial owners. ADP estimates that the average cost of printing and mailing a paper copy of a set of proxy materials during the 2006 proxy season was $5.64. We estimate that soliciting parties spent, in the aggregate, $481.2 million in postage and printing fees alone to distribute paper proxy materials to beneficial owners during the 2006 proxy season.[109] Approximately 50% of all proxy pieces mailed by ADP in 2005 were mailed during the proxy season.[110] Therefore, extrapolating this

---

[106] ADP recently spun off its brokerage services group, which is now called Broadridge Financial Solutions, Inc. However, because its comment letter was submitted when the group was part of ADP and carries the ADP letterhead, we continue to refer to the company as ADP for purposes of this release.

[107] We expect savings per mailing to record holders to roughly correspond to savings per mailing to beneficial owners.

[108] According to ADP data, the 2006 proxy season extended from February 15, 2006 to May 1, 2006.

[109] 85.3 million mailings × $5.64/mailing = $481.2 million.

[110] According to ADP, in 2005, 90,013,175 proxy pieces out of a total 179,833,774 proxy pieces were mailed during the 2005 proxy season. Thus, we estimate that 50% of proxy pieces are mailed during the proxy season (90,013,175 proxy pieces during the season / 179,833,774 total proxy pieces = 0.5 or 50%).

percentage to 2006, we estimate that soliciting parties from beneficial owners spent approximately $962.4 million in 2006 in printing and mailing costs.[111]

As was the case with the voluntary model, for soliciting parties following the notice only option, paper-related savings may be reduced by the cost of fulfilling requests for paper copies.[112] We estimate that approximately 19% of shareholders would request paper copies from such soliciting parties. Commenters on the voluntary model provided alternate estimates. For example, Computershare, a large transfer agent, estimated that less than 10% of shareholders would request paper copies.[113] According to a survey conducted by Forrester Research for ADP, 12% of shareholders report that they would always take extra steps to get their proxy materials, and as many as 68% of shareholders report that they would take extra steps to get their proxy materials in paper at least some of the time. The same survey also finds that 82% of shareholders report that they look at their proxy materials at least some of the time. These survey results suggest that shareholders may review proxy materials even if they do not vote. During the 2005 proxy season, only 44% of accounts were voted by beneficial owners. Put differently, 56%, or 84.8 million accounts, did not return requests for voting instructions. Our estimate that 19% of shareholders would request paper copies reflects the diverse estimates suggested by the available data.

Based on the assumption that 19% of shareholders would choose to have paper copies sent to them when a soliciting party initially sends them only a Notice, we estimated that the voluntary model could produce annual paper-related savings ranging from $48.3 million (if soliciting parties responsible for 10% of all proxy mailings choose to follow the notice only option) to $241.4 million (if soliciting parties responsible for 50% of all proxy mailings choose to follow the notice only option).[114] This estimate excludes the effect of the provision of the amendments that would allow shareholders to make a permanent request for paper copies. That provision enables soliciting parties to take advantage of bulk printing and mailing rates for those requesting shareholders, and therefore should reduce the on-demand costs reflected in these calculations.

Although we expect the savings to be significant from the notice and access model as a whole, the actual paper-related benefits will be influenced by several factors that we estimate should become less important over time. First, to the extent that shareholders request paper copies of the proxy materials, the benefits of the notice and access model in terms of savings in printing and mailing costs will be reduced. Soliciting parties have expressed concern that the cost per paper copy would be significantly greater if they have to mail copies of paper proxy materials to shareholders on an on-demand basis, rather than mailing the paper copies in bulk. Thus, if a significant number of shareholders request paper, the savings will be substantially reduced. Second, soliciting parties may face a high degree of uncertainty about the number of requests that they may get for paper proxy materials and may maintain unnecessarily large inventories of paper copies as a precaution.

---

[111] $481.2 million / 50% = $962.4 million.

[112] Soliciting parties that choose to follow the full set delivery option will not incur fulfillment costs. Such soliciting parties are not required to provide paper copies to shareholders upon request because they would have provided such copies at the outset.

[113] See letter commenting on Release No. 34-52926 (Dec. 8, 2005) [70 FR 74598] from Computershare.

[114] This range of potential cost savings depends on data on proxy material production, home printing costs, and first-class postage rates provided by Lexecon and ADP, and supplemented with modest 2006 USPS postage rate discounts. The fixed costs of notice and proxy material production are estimated to be $2.36 per shareholder, including $0.42 to print and mail the Notice. The variable costs of fulfilling a paper request, including handling, paper, printing and postage, are estimated to be $6.11 per copy requested. Our estimate of the total number of shareholders is based on data provided by ADP and SIFMA (at the time it submitted

these comments, the SIFMA was known as the Securities Industry Association or SIA). According to SIFMA's comment letter on Release No. 34-52926 (Dec. 8, 2005) [70 FR 74598], 78.49% of shareholders held their shares in street name. We estimate that the total number of proxy pieces mailed to both registered holders and beneficial owners is approximately 229,116,797 (179,833,774 proxy pieces to beneficial owners / 78.49% = 229,116,799 total proxy pieces). To calculate the potential cost savings, for the percentage of proxy piece mailings replaced by the Notice (10% or 50% times 229,116,799 proxy pieces), we estimate the total savings of not printing and sending full sets ($5.64) and subtract the estimated costs of printing and sending Notices and fulfilling paper requests ($2.36 + (19.2% × $6.11)). 10% × 229,116,799 proxy pieces × ($5.64 × ($2.36 + (19.2% × $6.11)) = $48.3 million. 50% × 229,116,799 proxy pieces × ($5.64 × ($2.36 + (19.2% × $6.11)) = $241.4 million.

As soliciting parties gain experience with the number of sets of paper materials that they need to supply to requesting shareholders, and as shareholders become more comfortable with receiving disclosures via the Internet, the number of paper copies are likely to decline, as would soliciting parties' tendency to print many more copies than ultimately are requested. This should lead to growth in paper-related savings from the notice and access model over time.

3. Reduction in the Cost of Proxy Contests

Benefits would accrue under the notice and access model from additional reductions in the costs of proxy solicitations by persons other than the issuer. Soliciting persons other than the issuer also must comply with the notice and access model, but can limit the scope of their proxy solicitations to shareholders who have not requested paper copies of the proxy materials. The flexibility afforded to persons other than the issuer under the model ultimately may reduce the cost of engaging in proxy contests, thereby increasing the effectiveness and efficiency of proxy contests as a source of discipline in the corporate governance process. However, because the amendments do not significantly change the options available to such soliciting person from the existing rules, we do not anticipate that the amendments will change significantly the number of soliciting persons other than issuers who select the notice only option as opposed to the number who would have chosen to follow the voluntary model.

The effect of the notice and access model of lessening the costs associated with a proxy contest will be limited by the persistence of other costs. One commenter on the proposal to create the voluntary model noted that a large percentage of the costs of effecting a proxy contest go to legal, document preparation, and solicitation fees, while a much smaller percentage of the costs is associated with printing and distribution of materials.[115] However, other commenters suggested that the paper-related cost savings that can be realized from the rule amendments are substantial enough to change the way many contests are conducted.[116]

4. Environmental Benefits

Finally, some benefits from the notice and access model, as revised, may arise from a reduction in what may be regarded as the environmental costs of the proxy solicitation process.[117] Specifically, proxy solicitation involves the use of a significant amount of paper and printing ink. Paper production and distribution can adversely affect the environment, due to the use of trees, fossil fuels, chemicals such as bleaching agents, printing ink (which contains toxic metals), and cleanup washes. Although not all of these costs may be internalized by paper producers, to the extent that such producers do internalize these costs and the costs are reflected in the price of paper and other materials consumed during the proxy solicitation process, our dollar estimates of the paper-related benefits reflect the elimination of these adverse environmental consequences under the model.

D. Costs

The amendments require all soliciting parties, including those who follow the full set delivery option, to (1) prepare and print a Notice (or incorporate Notice information into its proxy statement and proxy card) and (2) post the proxy materials on an Internet Web site. Because the notice only option is identical to the voluntary model, soliciting parties that choose that option will incur the same costs and savings as they would have under the voluntary model.

1. Costs Under the Notice Only Option

A soliciting party that chooses to follow the notice only option would incur the same costs as a soliciting party that chose to follow the voluntary model. These costs include

---

[115] See letter commenting on Release No. 34-52926 (Dec. 8, 2005) [70 FR 74598] from ADP.

[116] See letters commenting on Release No. 34-52926 (Dec. 8, 2005) [70 FR 74598] from CALSTRS, Computershare, ISS, and Swingvote.

[117] See letter commenting on Release No. 34-52926 (Dec. 8, 2005) [70 FR 74598] from American Forests.

the following: (1) the cost of preparing, producing, and sending the Notice to shareholders; (2) the cost of posting proxy materials on an Internet Web site; (3) providing a means to execute a proxy as of the date that the Notice is sent; and (4) the cost of processing shareholders' requests for copies of the proxy materials and maintaining their permanent election preferences if a soliciting party elects to follow the notice only option.

Under the amendments, soliciting parties must prepare and print the Notice to shareholders and post their proxy materials on an Internet Web site. As noted above, these costs would apply to soliciting parties irrespective of which option they choose. A soliciting party following the notice only option also must separately send the Notice to shareholders. As we stated in the release adopting the voluntary model, the paper-related savings to soliciting parties discussed under the benefits section above are adjusted for the cost of preparing, printing and sending Notices.

In the release adopting the voluntary model, we assumed, for purposes of the PRA, that all soliciting parties would elect to follow the procedures, resulting in a total estimated cost to prepare the Notice of approximately $2,020,475.[118] We are adjusting this amount to $2,469,475 to reflect a change in the basis of our cost estimate for personnel time.[119] Based on the percentage range of soliciting parties that we estimated would adopt the voluntary model, we estimated that these costs for soliciting parties who follow the notice only option could range between $246,948 (if soliciting parties responsible for 10% of all proxy mailings followed the notice only option) and $1,234,736 (if soliciting parties responsible for 50% of all proxy mailings followed the notice only option).[120]

If Notices are sent by mail, then the mailing costs may vary widely among parties. Postage rates likely would vary from $0.14 to $0.41 per Notice mailed, depending on numerous factors. In our estimates of the paper-related benefits above, we assume that each Notice costs a total of $0.13 to print and $0.29 to mail. Based on data from ADP and SIA, we estimate that soliciting parties send a total of 229,116,797 proxy pieces per year.[121] In the release adopting the voluntary model, we assumed that only those soliciting parties that choose to follow the voluntary model would incur these printing and mailing costs. We estimated that the costs to print the Notices would range from $9.6 million (if soliciting parties responsible for 10% of all current proxy mailings choose to follow the notice only option) and $48.1 million (if soliciting parties responsible for 50% of current proxy mailings choose to follow the notice only option).[122] These same costs would be incurred by soliciting parties following the notice only option under the revised model.

Soliciting parties that follow the notice only option must post their proxy materials on an Internet Web site. Although costs for establishing a Web site and posting materials on it can vary greatly, the rules do not require elaborate Web site design. The rules only require that a soliciting party obtain a Web site and post several documents on that

---

[118] In the voluntary model adopting release, we estimated that soliciting parties would spend a total of $897,975 on outside professionals to prepare this disclosure. We also estimated that soliciting parties would spend a total of 8,980 hours of personnel time preparing this disclosure. We estimated the average hourly cost of personnel time to be $125, resulting in a total cost of $1,122,500 for personnel time and a total cost of $2,020,475 ($1,122,500 + $897,975 = $2,020,475).

[119] We are adjusting this estimate of personnel time to be $175 to be consistent with our other releases. This results in an in-house cost of $1,571,500 (8,980 hours × $175/hour = $1,571,500) and a total cost of $2,469,475 ($1,571,500 + $897,975 = $2,469,475) for soliciting parties following the notice only option. For purposes of the PRA analysis, we are not adjusting the hourly burden imposed on soliciting parties and, therefore, are not revising our PRA submission.

[120] $2,469,475 * 10% = $246,948. $2,469,475 * 50% = $1,234,736.

[121] See www.ics.adp.com/release11/public_site/about/stats.html stating that ADP handled 179,833,774 in fiscal year 2005 and letter commenting on Release No. 34-52926 (Dec. 8, 2005) [70 FR 74598] from SIFMA stating that beneficial accounts represent 78.49% of total accounts.

[122] 10% × 229,116,797 × ($0.13 + $0.29) = $9.6 million. 50% × 229,116,797 × ($0.13 + $0.29) = $48.1 million. As stated above, these costs would be significantly offset by savings as a result of not being required to print and mail full sets of proxy materials, resulting in a net savings of $48.3 million (if issuers responsible for 10% of all proxy mailings choose to follow the notice only option) to $241.4 million (if issuers responsible for 50% of all proxy mailings choose to follow the notice only option) for issuers choosing to follow the notice only option.

Web site. Several companies currently provide Web hosting services for free, including significant memory to post the required documents and bandwidth to handle several thousand "hits" per month.[123] We also noted that several Web hosting services provided Web sites which would handle up to five million hits per month are available for approximately $5 to $8 per month, or $60 to $96 per year.[124] Based on a review of several Internet Web page design firms, we estimate that the cost of designing a Web site that meets the basic requirements of the notice and access model would be approximately $300. Thus, we estimate that the approximate total cost to establish a new Web site would be approximately $360 per year for a soliciting party, or a range of $0.3 million (if soliciting parties responsible for 10% of all proxy mailings would not have followed the voluntary model) to $1.4 million (if soliciting parties responsible for 50% of all proxy mailings would not have followed the voluntary model).[125] This estimate assumes that the soliciting party obtains a new Web site to post the proxy materials. We believe that the cost to soliciting parties that already maintain Web sites would be less.

The Web site on which the proxy materials are posted must maintain the anonymity of shareholders accessing the site. As discussed elsewhere in the release, this requirement requires a soliciting party to refrain from installing software on the Web site that tracks the identity of persons accessing the Web site. Thus, this requirement does not impose any added burden on soliciting party establishing new Web sites. A soliciting party that already has a Web site must segregate a portion of that Web site so that any tracking software on its general Web site does not track persons accessing the portion containing the proxy materials. Such segregation of the Web site requires minimal effort and should not impose a significant burden on such parties.

The rules also require that the proxy materials be posted in a format or formats convenient for printing on paper or viewing online. One commenter was concerned that this would impose an unnecessary burden on soliciting parties. Currently, Internet Web sites regularly present the same document in multiple formats for the convenience of readers. In particular, Internet Web sites regularly post large files for Internet users with broadband connections and smaller files for users who do not have broadband connections. In light of this common practice on the Internet, we do not believe that this requirement will impose a significant burden on soliciting parties.

Soliciting parties must provide a means to vote as of the date on which the Notice is first sent. Those following the notice only option can do so by creating an electronic voting platform, providing a telephone number or posting a printable proxy card on the Web site. Some commenters questioned whether the model would require the creation of an electronic voting platform, which they estimated would cost approximately $3,000.[126] The amendments do not require such a voting platform. A soliciting party may simply post a printable proxy card or a telephone number for executing a proxy on its Web site, which should impose little burden.

The cost of processing shareholders' requests for copies of the proxy materials if a soliciting party elects to follow the notice only option is addressed as an offset to the savings discussed in the Benefits section of this analysis.

The amendments also require issuers and intermediaries to maintain records of shareholders who have requested paper and e-mail copies for future proxy solicitations. We estimate that this total cost if all issuers followed the notice only option would be approxi-

---

[123] A review found free Web hosting services that permit the posting of up to 100M of data, with a bandwidth capacity of 10,000MB. A document's size can vary dramatically depending on its design. Typical proxy statement and annual report sizes vary from 200KB for documents with few graphics such as an annual report on Form 10-K to 5MB for elaborate "glossy" annual reports. Based on this range of sizes, we estimate that a free Web hosting service would enable between 1,000 and 25,000 "hits" per month.

[124] We found several services that permit the posting of up to 300GB of data, with a bandwidth capacity of 3000GB, and include web design programs at prices between $5 and $8 per month.

[125] Based on filings in our last fiscal year, we estimate 7,982 proxy solicitations per year. 10% × 7,982 × $360 = $0.3 million. 50% × 7,982 × $360 = $1.4 million.

[126] See letters from BONY and Registrar and Transfer.

mately $13,098,500.[127] Thus, we estimated the cost due to the voluntary model would be approximately $1.3 million (if issuers responsible for 10% of all proxy mailings followed the notice only option) and $6.5 million (if issuers responsible for 50% of all proxy mailings followed the notice only option).[128]

2. Costs Under the Full Set Delivery Option

A soliciting party following the full set delivery option must either prepare a Notice or incorporate the Notice information into its proxy statement or proxy card. We base our estimates on preparing a separate Notice because we believe this would involve a greater cost. However, we anticipate that a significant number of soliciting parties would choose to incorporate the information into their materials. Based on the range that we estimated for soliciting parties following the notice only option, we estimate that soliciting parties responsible for 50% to 90% of all proxy mailings would choose to follow the full set delivery option. Soliciting parties who follow this option would not incur mailing costs in addition to costs incurred under the traditional system because the Notice would be included in the much larger package of the full set of proxy materials.

When the Commission adopted the voluntary model, we estimated that soliciting parties responsible for 10% to 50% of all proxy mailings would rely on the voluntary model. Under the amendments, we assume that soliciting parties that we estimated would not have followed the voluntary model (i.e., soliciting parties responsible for 50% to 90% of all proxy mailings) would incur the cost of preparing and printing a Notice (or incorporating Notice information into their proxy materials)[129] and posting the proxy materials on an Internet Web site.

We estimate that the cost for soliciting parties that would not have followed the voluntary model to prepare a Notice will range between $1.2 million (if soliciting parties responsible for 50% of all proxy mailings would not have followed the voluntary model) and $2.2 million (if soliciting parties responsible for 90% of all proxy mailings would not have followed the voluntary model).[130]

Similarly, we estimate that the cost for such parties of printing the Notice will range between $14.9 million[131] (if soliciting parties responsible for 50% of all proxy mailings would not have followed the voluntary model) and $26.8 million[132] (if soliciting parties responsible for 90% of all proxy mailings would not have followed the voluntary model). Soliciting parties can significantly reduce this cost to print the Notice by incorporating the Notice information into the proxy materials instead of printing a separate Notice. Printing costs for the full set of proxy materials would be identical to such costs under the traditional method of providing proxy materials by mail and therefore do not represent an incremental cost increase as a result of these rules.

We do not expect an incremental increase in mailing cost for the Notice for soliciting parties that choose the full set delivery option because the Notice is substantially smaller than the full set of proxy materials currently sent under the traditional system and must accompany that full set (or be incorporated into the proxy statement and proxy card).

In addition, under the amendments, soliciting parties that would not have followed the voluntary model must post their proxy materials on an Internet Web site. As we noted

---

[127] In the voluntary model adopting release, we estimated, for PRA purposes, that issuers and intermediaries would spend a total of 79,820 hours of issuer and intermediary personnel time maintaining these records. We estimate the average hourly cost of issuer and intermediary personnel time to be $175, resulting in a total cost of $13,068,500 for issuer and intermediary personnel time.

[128] $13,098,500 × 10% = $1,309,850. $13,098,500 × 50% = $6,549,250.

[129] We do not expect an incremental increase in mailing cost for the Notice for soliciting parties that choose the full set delivery option because the Notice is substantially smaller than the full set of proxy materials currently sent under the traditional system and must accompany that full set (or be incorporated into those materials).

[130] As noted above, we calculated a total cost of $2,469,475 for preparing the Notice for purposes of the PRA. $2,469,475 * 50% = $1,234,736. $2,469,475 * 90% = $2,222,528.

[131] 50% × 229,116,797 × $0.13 = $14.9 million.

[132] 90% × 229,116,797 × $0.13 = $26.8 million. We assume that the additional cost of mailing the Notice together with the full set of proxy materials is negligible.

above, although costs for establishing a Web site and posting materials on it can vary greatly, the rules do not require elaborate Web site design. The rules only require that a soliciting party obtain a Web site and post several documents on that Web site. As with the notice only option, we estimate that the approximate total cost to establish a new Web site would be approximately $360 per year for a soliciting party, or a range of $1.4 million (if soliciting parties responsible for 50% of all proxy mailings would not have followed the voluntary model) to $2.6 million (if soliciting parties responsible for 90% of all proxy mailings would not have followed the voluntary model).[133]

3. Costs to Intermediaries

Soliciting parties and intermediaries will incur additional processing costs under the notice and access model. The amendments require an intermediary such as a bank, broker-dealer, or other association to follow the notice and access model with respect to all issuers. An intermediary must prepare its own Notice to beneficial owners, along with instructions on when and how to request paper copies and the Web site where the beneficial owner can access his or her request for voting instructions. Since soliciting parties reimburse intermediaries for their reasonable expenses of forwarding proxy materials and intermediaries and their agents already have systems to prepare and deliver requests for voting instructions, we do not expect the involvement of intermediaries in sending their Notices to significantly affect the costs associated with the rules.

Under the notice and access model, a beneficial owner desiring a copy of the proxy materials from a soliciting party following the notice only option must request such a copy from its intermediary. The costs of collecting and processing requests from beneficial owners may be significant, particularly if the intermediary receives the requests of beneficial owners associated with many different soliciting parties that specify different methods of furnishing the proxy. We expect that these processing costs will be highest in the first year after adoption but will subsequently decline as intermediaries develop the necessary systems and procedures and as beneficial owners increasingly become comfortable with accessing proxy materials online. In addition, the amendments permit a beneficial owner to specify its preference on an account-wide basis, which should reduce the cost of processing requests for copies. These costs ultimately are paid by the soliciting party.

4. Costs to Shareholders

Under the amendments, a shareholder can avoid any additional cost by accessing the proxy materials on the Internet if they already have Internet access or by requesting copies of the proxy materials from the soliciting parties if the shareholder is a record holder or the intermediary if the shareholder is a beneficial owner. Shareholders who do not already have Internet access and wish to access the proxy materials online would incur any necessary costs associated with gaining access to the Internet. In addition, some shareholders may choose to print out the posted materials, which would entail paper and printing costs. We estimate that approximately 10% of all shareholders receiving a Notice under the notice only option would print out the posted materials at home at an estimated cost of $7.05 per proxy package. Based on these assumptions, we estimated that the voluntary model could produce incremental annual home printing costs ranging from $16 million (if soliciting parties responsible for 10% of all current proxy mailings follow the notice only option) to $80 million (if soliciting parties responsible for 50% of all current proxy mailings follow the notice only option).[134] Shareholders of issuers that follow the full set delivery option would not incur such costs.

---

[133] 50% × 7,982 × $360 = $1.4 million. 90% × 7,982 × $360 = $2.6 million.
[134] This range of potential home printing costs depends on data provided by Lexecon and ADP. See letter from ADP. The Lexecon data was included in the ADP comment letter. To calculate home printing cost, we assume that 50% of annual report pages are printed in color and 100% of proxy statement pages are printed in black and white. The estimated percentage of shareholders printing at home is derived from Forrester survey data furnished by ADP and adjusted for the reported likelihood that an investor will take extra steps to get proxy materials. Total number of shareholders estimated as above based on data provided by ADP and SIFMA. See letters commenting on Release No. 34-52926 (Dec. 8, 2005) [70 FR 74598] from ADP and SIFMA.

5. Comments Regarding Unanticipated Costs

Several commenters expressed concern with the adoption of these amendments before the Commission has collected operating data from the voluntary model. The recommended delaying adoption until the market has had more experience with the voluntary model before requiring companies to follow the notice and access model. As we note elsewhere in the release, the amendments adopted in this release do not require soliciting parties to follow procedures substantially different from the procedures available under the voluntary model. Soliciting parties who wish to furnish their proxy materials via traditional paper delivery may continue to do so, with the only added requirements being that they must post their proxy materials on an Internet Web site and prepare a Notice (or incorporate the Notice information into their proxy statement and proxy card).

In addition, only large accelerated filers that are subject to the proxy rules will be subject to the requirements in 2008. All other filers need not, but may, follow the notice and access model before January 1, 2009. Most large accelerated filers already appear to post their proxy materials on the Internet. As noted above, a review of existing Web sites of such issuers indicated that approximately 80% of them already post their filings, including proxy materials, on their Web site. Thus, most of the issuers that will be subject to the rules in the first year will be large issuers that already post their proxy materials on their Web site. Therefore, we believe that no company will incur significant cost as a result of these amendments in the first year, while we evaluate the performance of the model. Although they may need to implement some procedures to ensure the anonymity of persons accessing those materials, we do not believe this requirement will impose a significant burden on these companies.

Furthermore, the tiered compliance dates address commenters' concerns because they will allow the Commission to better analyze the impact of the rules on a subset of issuers constituting large accelerated filers.[135] Adopting the amendments for large accelerated filers before the 2008 proxy season effectively creates a test group of issuers, enabling the Commission to study the performance of the model with a significant number of larger issuers and to make any necessary revisions to the rules before they apply to all issuers and other soliciting persons.

6. Comment on the Complexity of the Notice and Access Model

One commenter expressed concern that the proposed rule would make the proxy delivery system too complex for beneficial owners holding in street name through their brokers or other intermediaries.[136] We acknowledge that the amendments provide shareholders with more options with respect to the manner in which they are able to access their proxy materials, and thereby add complexity to the proxy distribution system. However, we believe that shareholder choice as to the means by which they access proxy materials and the expanded use of the Internet to provide such information to shareholders ultimately will provide shareholders with better access to information, which we believe can make the proxy process more efficient. In adopting the voluntary model, we created a provision that allows a shareholder to make a one-time election of the means by which they access proxy materials to simplify the model for those shareholders. In addition, by choosing to follow the full set delivery option, issuers and other soliciting persons wishing to do so can continue to furnish their proxy materials through procedures substantially similar to traditional methods of furnishing proxy materials. These provisions should significantly simplify the process for all shareholders.

---

[135] One commenter specifically noted that the timeframe would not allow the Commission to analyze the effects of one full year of compliance for large accelerated filers who chose to accept the voluntary model. See letter from the Chamber of Commerce. The tiered system will allow the Commission to analyze a full year of experience under the notice and access model for all large accelerated filers.

[136] See letter from Reed Smith. We received similar comments on our proposals to adopt the notice and access model as a voluntary means of furnishing proxy materials.

VII. Consideration of Burden on Competition and Promotion of Efficiency, Competition and Capital Formation

Section 23(a)(2) of the Exchange Act[137] requires us, when adopting rules under the Exchange Act, to consider the impact that any new rule would have on competition. In addition, Section 23(a)(2) prohibits us from adopting any rule that would impose a burden on competition not necessary or appropriate in furtherance of the purposes of the Exchange Act. Section 3(f) of the Exchange Act[138] and Section 2(c) of the Investment Company Act of 1940[139] require us, when engaging in rulemaking that requires us to consider or determine whether an action is necessary or appropriate in the public interest, to consider, in addition to the protection of investors, whether the action will promote efficiency, competition, and capital formation.

The amendments require all issuers and other soliciting persons to follow the notice and access model for all proxy solicitations, other than those associated with business combination transactions. The amendments are intended to provide all shareholders with the ability to choose the means by which they access proxy materials, to expand use of the Internet to lower the costs of proxy solicitations, and to improve shareholder communications. Historically, issuers decided whether to provide shareholders with the choice to receive proxy materials by electronic means. The amendments provide all shareholders with the ability to choose whether to access proxy materials in paper, by e-mail or via the Internet. We believe that expanded use of electronic communications to replace current modes of disclosures on paper and physical mailings will increase the efficiency of the shareholder communications process. Use of the Internet permits technology developers to enhance a shareholder's experience with respect to such communications. It permits interactive communications at real-time speeds. Improved shareholder communications may improve relationships between shareholders and management. Retail investors may have easier access to management. In turn, this may lead to increased confidence and trust in well-managed, responsive issuers.

The amendment may have the effect of initially raising costs on issuers and other soliciting persons by requiring persons who choose to follow the full set delivery option to post the proxy materials on a Web site and prepare a Notice (or incorporate Notice information into their proxy statement and proxy card). Commenters were concerned that the amendments may create other inefficiencies such as reducing shareholder voting participation and increased reliance on broker discretionary voting. The amendments do not significantly differ from the voluntary model. Issuers who are concerned about a reduction in voting participation still have the option to send a full set of proxy materials to all shareholders. Therefore, we do not believe that the amendments will have a significant impact compared to the previously-adopted voluntary model on shareholder voting participation, and hence reliance on broker discretionary voting.

We also considered the effect of the amendments on competition and capital formation, including the effect that the amendments may have on industries servicing the proxy soliciting process. We do not anticipate any significant effects on capital formation. We also anticipate that some companies whose business model is based on the dissemination of paper-based proxy materials may experience some adverse competition effects from the amendments. However, the full set delivery option permits companies to continue to send paper copies to shareholders. Thus, we do not anticipate that the amendments will have an incremental impact on this industry different from the voluntary model. The amendments may also promote competition among Internet-based information services.

VIII. Final Regulatory Flexibility Analysis

This Final Regulatory Flexibility Analysis has been prepared in accordance with 5 U.S.C. 603. It relates to amendments to the rules and forms under the Exchange Act that require issuers, other persons soliciting proxies, and intermediaries to follow the notice and access model for all proxy solicitations except for those associated with a business

---

[137] 15 U.S.C. 78w(a)(2).
[138] 15 U.S.C. 78c(f).

[139] 15 U.S.C. 80a-2(c).

combination transaction. An Initial Regulatory Flexibility Analysis (IRFA) was prepared in accordance with the Regulatory Flexibility Act in conjunction with the proposing release. The proposing release included, and solicited comment on, the IRFA.

A. Need for the Amendments

On January 22, 2007, we proposed amendments to the rules regarding provision of proxy materials to shareholders. We are adopting those amendments, substantially as proposed. Specifically, the amendments require issuers and other persons soliciting proxies to provide shareholders with Internet access to proxy materials. The amendments are intended to provide all shareholders with the ability to choose the means by which they access proxy materials, to expand use of the Internet to ultimately lower the costs of proxy solicitations, and to improve shareholder communications. We anticipate that the model will enhance the ability of investors to make informed decisions and ultimately to lower the costs of proxy solicitations.

The amendments also will provide all shareholders with the ability to choose whether to access proxy materials in paper, by e-mail or via the Internet. Developing technologies on the Internet should expand the ways in which required disclosures can be used by shareholders. Electronic documents are more easily searchable than paper documents. Users are better able to go directly to any section of the document that they believe to be the most important. They also permit users to more easily evaluate data. It enables users to more easily download data into spreadsheet or other analytical programs so that they can perform their own analyses more efficiently. A centralized Web site containing proxy-related disclosure may facilitate shareholder access to other relevant information such as research reports and news about the issuer.

In addition, encouraging shareholders to use the Internet in the context of proxy solicitations may have the side-effect of improving shareholder communications in other ways. Internet tools may enhance shareholders' ability to communicate not only with management, but with each other. Such direct access may improve shareholder relations to the extent shareholders have improved access to management.

B. Significant Issues Raised by Public Comment

Five commenters were concerned that smaller firms may not realize the savings contemplated by the mandatory model and may even incur increased costs.[140] One commenter suggested that the Commission develop "ways to 'scale' the notice and access model for smaller public companies so as to reduce the cost of compliance," but did not provide any recommendations on how to do so.[141]

Several commenters were concerned about the increased set-up costs for issuers, including small entities. One commenter estimated that, based on its "back-of-envelope" estimate, the cost of outsourcing the requirements to a third party provider could cost companies over $5,000 and may exceed $10,000, including the establishment of an Internet voting platform.[142] Three other commenters estimated that the proposal would cost companies approximately $3,000 to establish such an Internet voting plat-form.[143] However, as noted previously, the amendments do not require companies to establish such a platform.[144] One of these commenters noted that although posting the proxy materials on the Internet is not necessarily expensive or difficult, outsourcing this function to an outside firm could cost hundreds, if not thousands, of dollars to do so.[145]

One commenter was concerned that the prohibition on "cookies" raises the costs for maintaining the Web sites.[146] Although this prohibition does raise the cost to maintain the Web sites, we believe that eliminating this prohibition may have a negative effect on

---

[140] .2wSee letters from ABC, BONY, Reed Smith, Registrar and Transfer, and STA.

[141] See letter from ABC.

[142] See letter from ABC.

[143] See letters from BONY, Registrar and Transfer, and STA.

[144] See letters from BONY and Registrar and Transfer.

[145] See letter from Registrar and Transfer.

[146] See letter from ICI.

shareholders' willingness to access the proxy materials via an Internet Web site. We do not believe this requirement will create undue burden on companies. Soliciting parties must refrain from installing cookies and other tracking features on the Web site or portion of the Web site where the proxy materials are posted. This may require segregating those pages from the rest of the soliciting party's regular Web site or creating a new Web site. However, the rules do not require the company to turn off the Web site's connection log, which automatically tracks numerical IP addresses that connect to that Web site. Although in most cases, this IP address does not provide a soliciting party with sufficient information to identify the accessing shareholder, soliciting parties may not use these numbers to attempt to find out more information about persons accessing the Web site.

C. Small Entities Subject to the Amendments

The amendments affect issuers that are small entities. Exchange Act Rule 0-10(a)[147] defines an issuer to be a "small business" or "small organization" for purposes of the Regulatory Flexibility Act if it had total assets of $5 million or less on the last day of its most recent fiscal year. We estimate that there are approximately 1,100 public companies, other than investment companies, that may be considered small entities.[148]

For purposes of the Regulatory Flexibility Act, an investment company is a small entity if it, together with other investment companies in the same group of related investment companies, has net assets of $50 million or less as of the end of its most recent fiscal year.[149] Approximately 164 registered investment companies meet this definition. Moreover, approximately 51 business development companies may be considered small entities.

Paragraph (c)(1) of Rule 0-10 under the Exchange Act[150] states that the term "small business" or "small organization," when referring to a broker-dealer, means a broker or dealer that had total capital (net worth plus subordinated liabilities) of less than $500,000 on the date in the prior fiscal year as of which its audited financial statements were prepared pursuant to § 240.17a-5(d); and is not affiliated with any person (other than a natural person) that is not a small business or small organization. As of 2005, the Commission estimates that there were approximately 910 broker-dealers that qualified as small entities as defined above.[151] Small Business Administration regulations define "small entities" to include banks and savings associations with total assets of $165 million or less.[152] The Commission estimates that the rules might apply to approximately 9,475 banks, approximately 5,816 of which could be considered small banks with assets of $165 million or less.

D. Reporting, Recordkeeping and Other Compliance Requirements

The amendments require all issuers, including small entities, to follow the notice and access model. This model does not significantly change an issuer's obligations under current rules. An issuer choosing to follow the notice only option would incur costs identical to costs that it would have incurred under the voluntary model. An issuer following the full set delivery option would incur two costs in addition to the current cost of sending proxy materials under the traditional method: (1) the cost of preparing a Notice of Internet Availability of Proxy Materials and (2) the cost of posting the proxy materials on a Web site with anonymity controls.

For purposes of the Paperwork Reduction Act, we have estimated that the Notice would take approximately 1.5 hours to prepare because the information is readily available to

---

[147] 17 CFR 240.0-10(a).

[148] The estimated number of reporting small entities is based on 2007 data including the Commission's EDGAR database and Thomson Financial's Worldscope database. This represents an update from the number of reporting small entities estimated in prior rulemakings. See, for example, *Executive Compensation and Related Disclosure*, Release No. 33-8732A (Aug. 29, 2006) [71 FR 53158] (in which the Commission estimated a total of 2,500 small entities, other than investment companies).

[149] 17 CFR 270.0-10.

[150] 17 CFR 240.0-10(c)(1).

[151] These numbers are based on a review by the Commission's Office of Economic Analysis of 2005 FOCUS Report filings reflecting registered broker-dealers. This number does not include broker-dealers that are delinquent on FOCUS Report filings.

[152] 13 CFR 121.201.

the issuer. We estimated that 75% of that burden would be incurred by in-house, while 25% of the burden would reflect costs of outside counsel, at a cost of $400 per hour, or approximately $150 per Notice. With respect to printing the Notice, for purposes of the Cost-Benefit Analysis we estimated a cost of $0.13 per copy to print the Notice. However, an issuer may reduce this cost by incorporating the Notice information into its proxy materials.

As we noted in our Cost-Benefit Analysis, we anticipate the cost of posting the proxy materials on a publicly accessible Web site to be relatively low. Although an issuer may choose to pay more for an elaborate Web site, the rules do not require such a Web site. An issuer with a small shareholder base may be able to post its materials on a free Web hosting service. As we note in more detail in the Cost-Benefit Analysis, based on our estimate of the typical size of a proxy statement and annual report, we estimate such services provide sufficient bandwidth for approximately 1,000 to 25,000 hits per month.[153] We also noted that several Web hosting services provided Web sites which would handle up to five million hits per month are available for approximately $5 to $8 per month, or $60 to $96 per year. Based on a review of several Internet Web page design firms, we estimate that the design of a Web site meeting the base requirements of the rules would be approximately $300.

Intermediaries must follow substantially similar requirements with respect to beneficial owners of the issuer's securities. Issuers, including small entities, are required to reimburse intermediaries for the cost of complying with these requirements. These costs are incorporated in our estimate of costs to issuers.

E. Agency Action to Minimize Effect on Small Entities

The amendments require all issuers and intermediaries, including small entities, to follow the notice and access model. The purpose of the amendments is to provide all shareholders with the ability to choose the means by which they can access proxy materials, to expand use of the Internet to ultimately lower the costs of proxy solicitations, and to improve shareholder communications. Exempting small entities would not be consistent with this goal and we do not believe that the additional compliance requirements that we are imposing are significant.

We believe that in the long run, use of the Internet for shareholder communications not only may decrease costs for all issuers, but also may improve the quality of shareholder communications by enhancing a shareholder's ability to search and manipulate proxy disclosures. However, in the short term, we are adopting a tiered system of compliance dates to minimize the burdens on smaller issuers, including small entities. Under this tiered system, issuers that are not large accelerated filers need not comply with the requirements until January 1, 2009. This would provide smaller issuers more time to adjust to the amendments and learn from the experiences of larger filers. Furthermore, adopting the amendments for large accelerated filers before the 2008 proxy season effectively creates a test group of issuers, enabling the Commission to study the performance of the model with a significant number of larger issuers and to make any necessary revisions to the rules before they apply to all issuers, including small entities.

Intermediaries that are small entities also are subject to the amendments. We understand that the task of forwarding proxy materials to over 95% of beneficial ownership accounts currently is handled by a single entity. Because a third-party outsourcing alternative is readily available and issuers are required to reimburse such costs to the intermediary, we believe that imposing the amendments on small entities will not create a substantial burden on small entities. Thus, we have decided not to exempt intermediaries that are small entities from the amendments. Such an exemption may create disparity in the way share-

---

[153] These calculations are based on typical file sizes of proxy statements and annual reports. The lower capacity (1,000) corresponds to files that are elaborate "glossy" annual statements. We believe the higher capacity (25,000) is a more reasonable estimate for small entities because small entities tend to send annual reports on Form 10-K to meet their Rule 14a-3(b) requirements rather than spend the significant cost of producing a "glossy" annual report.

holders receive proxy materials. Shareholders owning securities through such intermediaries would not have the ability to choose the means by which they receive proxy disclosures.

We considered the use of performance standards rather than design standards in the amendments. The amendments contain both performance standards and design standards. We are adopting design standards to the extent that we believe compliance with particular requirements is necessary. For example, we are using a design standard with respect to the contents of the Notice so that investors get uniform information regarding access to important information. However, to the extent possible, we are adopting rules that impose performance standards to provide issuers, other soliciting persons and intermediaries with the flexibility to devise the means through which they can comply with such standards. For example, we are adopting a performance standard for providing for anonymity on the Web site so that issuers and other soliciting persons can determine for themselves the least costly option to meet the requirement.

IX. Statutory Basis and Text of Amendments

We are adopting the amendments pursuant to Sections 3(b), 10, 13, 14, 15, 23(a), and 36 of the Securities Exchange Act of 1934, as amended, and Sections 20(a), 30, and 38 of the Investment Company Act of 1940, as amended.

List of Subjects

17 CFR Part 240

Reporting and recordkeeping requirements, Securities.

For the reasons set out in the preamble, Title 17, Chapter II of the Code of Federal Regulations is amended as follows.

PART 240—GENERAL RULES AND REGULATIONS, SECURITIES EXCHANGE ACT OF 1934

1. The authority citation for Part 240 continues to read, in part, as follows:

Authority: 15 U.S.C. 77c, 77d, 77g, 77j, 77s, 77z-2, 77z-3, 77eee, 77ggg, 77nnn, 77sss, 77ttt, 78c, 78d, 78e, 78f, 78g, 78i, 78j, 78j-1, 78k, 78k-1, 78*l*, 78m, 78n, 78*o*, 78p, 78q, 78s, 78u-5, 78w, 78x, 78*ll*, 78mm, 80a-20, 80a-23, 80a-29, 80a-37, 80b-3, 80b-4, 80b-11, and 7201 *et seq.*; and 18 U.S.C. 1350, unless otherwise noted.

* * * * *

2. Amend § 240.14a-3 by revising paragraph (a) to read as follows:

240.14a-3 Information to be furnished to security holders.

(a) No solicitation subject to this regulation shall be made unless each person solicited is concurrently furnished or has previously been furnished with:

(1) A publicly filed preliminary or definitive proxy statement, in the form and manner described in § 240.14a-16, containing the information specified in Schedule 14A (§ 240.14a-101);

(2) A preliminary or definitive written proxy statement included in a registration statement filed under the Securities Act of 1933 on Form S-4 or F-4 (§ 239.25 or § 239.34 of this chapter) or Form N-14 (§ 239.23 of this chapter) and containing the information specified in such Form; or

(3) A publicly filed preliminary or definitive proxy statement, not in the form and manner described in § 240.14a-16, containing the information specified in Schedule 14A (§ 240.14a-101), if:

(i) The solicitation relates to a business combination transaction as that term is defined in § 230.165 of this chapter; or

(ii) The solicitation may not follow the form and manner described in § 240.14a-16 pursuant to the laws of the state of incorporation of the registrant;

* * * * *

3. Amend § 240.14a-7 by removing Note 3 to § 240.14a-7.

4. Amend § 240.14a-16 by:

a. Revising paragraphs (a), (d)(3), (f)(2)(i), (f)(2)(ii), (h), (j)(3), and (n); and

b. Adding paragraph (f)(2)(iii).

The revisions and additions to read as follows:

240.14a-16 Internet availability of proxy materials.

(a)(1) A registrant shall furnish a proxy statement pursuant to § 240.14a-3(a), or an annual report to security holders pursuant to § 240.14a-3(b), to a security holder by sending the security holder a Notice of Internet Availability of Proxy Materials, as described in this section, 40 calendar days or more prior to the security holder meeting date, or if no meeting is to be held, 40 calendar days or more prior to the date the votes, consents or authorizations may be used to effect the corporate action, and complying with all other requirements of this section.

(2) Unless the registrant chooses to follow the full set delivery option set forth in paragraph (n) of this section, it must provide the record holder or respondent bank with all information listed in paragraph (d) of this section in sufficient time for the record holder or respondent bank to prepare, print and send a Notice of Internet Availability of Proxy Materials to beneficial owners at least 40 calendar days before the meeting date.

* * * * *

(d) * * *

(3) A clear and impartial identification of each separate matter intended to be acted on and the soliciting person's recommendations, if any, regarding those matters, but no supporting statements;

* * * * *

(f) * * *

(2) * * *

(i) A pre-addressed, postage-paid reply card for requesting a copy of the proxy materials;

(ii) A copy of any notice of security holder meeting required under state law if that notice is not combined with the Notice of Internet Availability of Proxy Materials; and

(iii) In the case of an investment company registered under the Investment Company Act of 1940, the company's prospectus or a report that is required to be transmitted to stockholders by section 30(e) of the Investment Company Act (15 U.S.C. 80a-29(e)) and the rules thereunder.

* * * * *

(h) The registrant may send a form of proxy to security holders if:

(1) At least 10 calendar days or more have passed since the date it first sent the Notice of Internet Availability of Proxy Materials to security holders and the form of proxy is accompanied by a copy of the Notice of Internet Availability of Proxy Materials; or

(2) The form of proxy is accompanied or preceded by a copy, via the same medium, of the proxy statement and any annual report to security holders that is required by § 240.14a-3(b).

* * * * *

(j) * * *

(3) The registrant must provide copies of the proxy materials for one year after the conclusion of the meeting or corporate action to which the proxy materials relate, provided that, if the registrant receives the request after the conclusion of the meeting or corporate action to which the proxy materials relate, the registrant need not send copies via First Class mail and need not respond to such request within three business days.

* * * * *

(n) *Full Set Delivery Option.*

(1) For purposes of this paragraph (n), the term full set of proxy materials shall include all of the following documents:

(i) A copy of the proxy statement;

(ii) A copy of the annual report to security holders if required by § 240.14a-3(b); and

(iii) A form of proxy.

(2) Notwithstanding paragraphs (e) and (f)(2) of this section, a registrant or other soliciting person may:

(i) Accompany the Notice of Internet Availability of Proxy Materials with a full set of proxy materials; or

(ii) Send a full set of proxy materials without a Notice of Internet Availability of Proxy Materials if all of the information required in a Notice of Internet Availability of Proxy Materials pursuant to paragraphs (d) and (n)(4) is incorporated in the proxy statement and the form of proxy.

(3) A registrant or other soliciting person that sends a full set of proxy materials to a security holder pursuant to this paragraph (n) need not comply with

(i) The timing provisions of paragraphs (a) and (l)(2); and

(ii) The obligation to provide copies pursuant to paragraph (j).

(4) A registrant or other soliciting person that sends a full set of proxy materials to a security holder pursuant to this paragraph (n) need not include in its Notice of Internet Availability of Proxy Materials, proxy statement, or form of proxy the following disclosures:

(i) Paragraphs 1 and 3 of the legend required by paragraph (d)(1);

(ii) Instructions on how to request a copy of the proxy materials; and

(iii) Instructions on how to access the form of proxy pursuant to paragraph (d)(7).

5. Amend § 240.14a-101 by revising the first sentence of Item 4(a)(c) to read as follows:

§ 240.14a-101 Schedule 14A. Information required in proxy statement.

* * * * *

Item 4. Persons Making the Solicitation—(a) * * *

(3) If the solicitation is to be made otherwise than by the use of the mails or pursuant to § 240.14a-16, describe the methods to be employed. * * *

* * * * *

6. Amend § 240.14b-1 by:

a. Revising the introductory text of paragraph (d); and

b. Adding paragraph (d)(5).

The revision and addition read as follows.

§ 240.14b-1 Obligation of registered brokers and dealers in connection with the prompt forwarding of certain communications to beneficial owners.

* * * * *

(d) Upon receipt from the soliciting person of all of the information listed in § 240.14a-16(d), the broker or dealer shall:

* * * * *

(5) Notwithstanding any other provisions in this paragraph (d), if the broker or dealer receives copies of the proxy statement and annual report to security holders (if applicable) from the soliciting person with instructions to forward such materials to beneficial owners, the broker or dealer:

(i) Shall either:

(A) Prepare a Notice of Internet Availability of Proxy Materials and forward it with the proxy statement and annual report to security holders (if applicable); or

(B) Incorporate any information required in the Notice of Internet Availability of Proxy Materials that does not appear in the proxy statement into the broker or dealer's request for voting instructions to be sent with the proxy statement and annual report (if applicable);

(ii) Need not comply with the following provisions:

(A) The timing provisions of paragraph (d)(1)(ii); and

(B) Paragraph (d)(4); and

(iii) Need not include in its Notice of Internet Availability of Proxy Materials or request for voting instructions the following disclosures:

(A) Legends 1 and 2 in § 14a-16(d)(1) of this chapter; and

(B) Instructions on how to request a copy of the proxy materials.

* * * * *

7. Amend § 240.14b-2 by:

a. Revising the introductory text of paragraph (d); and

b. Adding paragraph (d)(5).

The revision and addition read as follows.

§ 240.14b-2 Obligation of banks, associations and other entities that exercise fiduciary powers in connection with the prompt forwarding of certain communications to beneficial owners.

* * * * *

(d) Upon receipt from the soliciting person of all of the information listed in § 240.14a-16(d), the bank shall:

* * * * *

(5) Notwithstanding any other provisions in this paragraph (d), if the bank receives copies of the proxy statement and annual report to security holders (if applicable) from the soliciting person with instructions to forward such materials to beneficial owners, the bank:

(i) Shall either:

(A) Prepare a Notice of Internet Availability of Proxy Materials and forward it with the proxy statement and annual report to security holders (if applicable); or

(B) Incorporate any information required in the Notice of Internet Availability of Proxy Materials that does not appear in the proxy statement into the bank's request for voting instructions to be sent with the proxy statement and annual report (if applicable);

(ii) Need not comply with the following provisions:

(A) The timing provisions of paragraph (d)(1)(ii); and

(B) Paragraph (d)(4); and

(iii) Need not include in its Notice of Internet Availability of Proxy Materials or request for voting instructions the following disclosures:

(A) Legends 1 and 2 in § 14a-16(d)(1) of this chapter; and

(B) Instructions on how to request a copy of the proxy materials.

* * * * *

8. Amend § 240.14c-2 by revising paragraph (d) to read as follows:

§ 240.14c-2 Distribution of information statement.

* * * * *

(d) A registrant shall transmit an information statement to security holders pursuant to paragraph (a) of this section by satisfying the requirements set forth in § 240.14a-16; provided, however, that the registrant shall revise the information required in the Notice of Internet Availability of Proxy Materials, including changing the title of that notice, to reflect the fact that the registrant is not soliciting proxies for the meeting.

9. Amend § 240.14c-3 by revising paragraph (d) to read as follows:

§ 240.14c-3 Annual report to be furnished security holders.

* * * * *

(d) A registrant shall furnish an annual report to security holders pursuant to paragraph (a) of this section by satisfying the requirements set forth in § 240.14a-16.

By the Commission.

Florence E. Harmon
Deputy Secretary

July 26, 2007